Encyclopedia of
THE ENLIGHTENMENT

REVISED EDITION

Peter Hanns Reill
University of California, Los Angeles
Consulting Editor

Ellen Judy Wilson
Principal Author

☑®
Facts On File, Inc.

Encyclopedia of the Enlightenment, Revised Edition

Copyright © 2004, 1996 by Book Builders Incorporated

Facts On File, Inc.
132 West 31st Street
New York NY 10001

Library of Congress Cataloging-in-Publication Data

Wilson, Ellen Judy.
Encyclopedia of the Enlightenment / Peter Hanns Reill, consulting editor;
Ellen Judy Wilson, principal author.—Rev. ed.
p. cm.
Includes bibliographical references and index.
ISBN 0-8160-5335-9
1. Enlightenment—Encyclopedias. 2. Philosophy—Encyclopedias.
I. Reill, Peter Hanns. II. Title.

B802.W48 2004
937.25'03—dc22   2003022973

Facts On File books are available at special discounts when purchased in bulk quantities for businesses, associations, institutions, or sales promotions. Please call our Special Sales Department in New York at (212) 967-8800 or (800) 322-8755.

You can find Facts On File on the World Wide Web at http://www.factsonfile.com

Text design by Joan M. Toro
Cover design by Cathy Rincon

Printed in the United States of America

VB FOF 10 9 8 7 6 5 4 3 2 1

This book is printed on acid-free paper.

CONTENTS

List of Illustrations
iv

Preface to the Revised Edition
vii

Introduction
ix

How to Use This Book
xii

Chronology
xiv

Entries A to Z
1

Selected Bibliography
643

Index
647

LIST OF ILLUSTRATIONS

Royal palace at Versailles	2
John Adams	5
Jean Le Rond d'Alembert	11
George III	13
William and Mary	17
18th-century map of the stars	25
Johann Sebastian Bach	34
Jeremy Bentham	49
William Blackstone	58
Georges-Louis Leclerc, comte de Buffon	75
Edmund Burke	78
Domestic clothmaking	92
Catherine II (the Great)	97
Marquise du Châtelet	102
Antoine and Marie-Anne Lavoisier, by David	104
Alchemical-chemical lab	105
Workers carrying and examining tea	107
Bird beaks and feet	116
Ships in front of East India Company warehouse	121
Étienne Bonnot de Condillac	123
Marie-Jean Caritat, marquis de Condorcet	125
Grand orrery, by Rowley	128
Residenztheater, Munich	137
The Death of Socrates, by David	140
"The Signing of the Declaration of Independence," by Savage	142
Madame du Deffand	145
René Descartes	152
Denis Diderot	159
Coat of arms of the East India Company	168
Engraving from *Émile*	173
Page from the *Encyclopédie*	175
Birds from the *Encyclopédie*	176

Portrait/frontispiece of Equiano's autobiography   187

A Young Girl Reading, by Fragonard   201

Benjamin Franklin   205

Freemasons   210

Louis XVI and the Paris mob   213

Parisian women march to Versailles to demand the return of
    Louis XVI to Paris   214

Mrs. Garrick, by Gainsborough   218

Engraving of Ferdinando Galiani   219

Luigi Galvani   222

"Ancient of Days" by Blake   227

Salon of Madame Geoffrin, by Debucourt   229

Edward Gibbon   231

Johann Wolfgang von Goethe   235

Henri, Abbé Gregoire   245

Broken Eggs, by Greuze   247

Drawing of the residence of governor-general of the West Indies,
    Guadeloupe Island   249

François-Dominique Toussaint Louverture   253

George Frederick Handel   260

Johann Gottfried Herder   268

Frontispiece for *Leviathan*   273

Marriage à la Mode: "The Marriage Settlement," by Hogarth   276

"Orgy at Rose Tavern," by Hogarth   277

Monument of George Washington   281

David Hume   284

Francis Hutcheson   289

Political cartoon featuring John Bull   294

Mineral technology, from the *Encyclopédie*   297

Thomas Jefferson, by Peale   307

The Hoshana Rabba festival   311

Immanuel Kant   318

Laocoon   333

Gottfried Wilhelm Leibniz   338

Mademoiselle de Lespinasse   341

Lending library, Margate, 1700s   346

Louis XIV   354

Louis XVI   357

The Death of Marat, by David   369

Maria Theresa   370

Queen Marie-Antoinette with Her Children, by Élizabeth Vigée Lebrun   372

Frère Jacques performing surgery   381

Moses Mendelssohn   384

Victor de Riqueti, marquis de Mirabeau   394

"John Law Crowned by Folly"   395

Charles-Louis de Secondat, baron de la Brède et de Montesquieu   397

Montgolfier hot-air balloon   401

Wolfgang Amadeus Mozart, at age seven, with his father and sister   406

Kassel Wilhelmshohe, by Eleazar Zeisig   409

"The Horse America, throwing his Master"   415

Formal garden, Hatfield House   417

Pantheon, Rome   421

Reflecting telescope   424

Cover art, *Gulliver's Travels*   430

Scene from *The Magic Flute*   435

Thomas Paine   442

Monticello   444

Frederick the Great   451

François Quesnay   454

Madame de Pompadour, portrait by Boucher   465

Joseph Priestley   471

18th-century public sanitation projects   474

Oxford Canal lock   475

Interior of public health facility-hospital, Middlesex   483

"Louis XVI and Malesherbes," political cartoon   484

Enslaved Africans   491

Allegorical representation of America's struggle for independence   506

Mrs. Siddons as the Tragic Muse   508

Bill of Rights   510

The Kaisersaal, Würzburg   517

The Last Words of Jean-Jacques Rousseau, by Moreau le Jeune   525

Friedrich Schiller, sketch by Professor Weitsch   535

Benjamin Thompson, count Rumford   538

La Reveuse, by Greuze   547

Adam Smith   558

British coffeehouse   560

Mathematician Karl Gauss   573

Illustration from *Gulliver's Travels*   581

"Agriculture, Ploughing," engraving from the *Encyclopédie*   585

Actor James Quin as Coriolanus, engraving   588

The Capture of Carthage, by Tiepolo   591

David Rittenhouse   597

Stalking Turkey   598

Anne-Robert-Jacques Turgot, baron de l'Aulne   601

Giovan Battista Vico   612

Voltaire (François-Marie Arouet)   619

Engraving of Captain Cook in the Sandwich Islands   621

Gilles, by Watteau   626

"Portland vase," by Wedgwood   628

Christian Wolff   635

Mary Wollstonecraft   636

PREFACE TO THE REVISED EDITION

The revised edition of the *Encyclopedia of the Enlightenment* expands upon the first in many ways. Inspired by the latest scholarship on the 18th century, it incorporates new themes and extends others. It contains 140 new, updated, or expanded articles. Among the new themes are two of major significance: the Enlightenment in a global context and what is sometimes called the "Counter-Enlightenment," that is, the interest in spiritualism and esotericism that emerged in the late 18th century. A third theme, religion and the Enlightenment, received significant attention in the first edition but has been enriched in the present one by the inclusion of several new articles. Contemporary scholarship increasingly has demonstrated that the Enlightenment was a global movement, affecting peoples across the Earth in ways positive and negative and also borrowing and transforming ideas from the cultures of lands "discovered" by Europeans. Articles such as "colonialism," "imperialism," "Haitian Revolution," "orientalism," "Noble Savage," "voyages of discovery," "picturesque," and many more chart the Enlightenment's spread and impact as well as its reception of non-European cultural impulses. Although there were many articles in the first edition that covered issues centering on spiritualism and esotericism, movements usually considered outside the pale of the Enlightenment, they are now complemented by articles on "hermeticism," "magic," and "secret societies." The first edition challenged the traditional view of the Enlightenment as a body of thought opposed to religion, and recent research has underlined the fact that it was not. There was indeed a "religious Enlightenment," a movement toward tolerance within religious establishments, a renewal of belief based on the translation and application of Enlightenment concepts into religious terms, and a modernization of religious practice that gave great weight to individual experience. New articles on "Gallicanism," the "Great Awakening," "millenarianism," and the "Abbé Henri Gregoire," among others, make this point clearer.

Through the addition of new articles, as well as the expansion of earlier ones, other central issues of the Enlightenment receive new emphasis in this edition. The topic of political thought and action, an issue as vital to us today as it was to the men and women of the Enlightenment, now includes articles on "rights," "justice," "revolution," "capital punishment," "civil society," "virtue," and "honor," which, when read with the cross-referenced articles, provide the reader with a thorough introduction to the central political questions we have inherited from the Enlightenment. We also address the Enlightenment's utilitarian side by introducing articles on "statistics," "demography," "public health," "probability," "free trade," and "capitalism," tools and concepts developed during the Enlightenment to assist in the practical goal of improving society. Guided by contemporary scholarship, which has also looked at the Enlightenment as a broad movement engaging much of Europe's and America's educated elite, we also include articles on the "Republic of Letters," "cosmopolitanism," "politeness," and the "Radical Enlightenment." Finally, we have increased our coverage of the arts and sciences as well as the already strongly represented areas of gender and race.

The new volume thus remains faithful to our original goal of presenting the Enlightenment in all its wonderful depth and complexity. Students will find that this volume can help them meet the demands of the recently formulated national standards for world history and American history. Lay readers, in turn, will find in its pages an opportunity to meet the many ways that the Enlightenment contributed to creating the world and the crucial issues of the 21st century. In all, this second edition of the *Encyclopedia of the Enlightenment* offers the most comprehensive single-volume coverage of the Enlightenment in print.

—Peter Hanns Reill

INTRODUCTION

The Enlightenment is one of the crucial periods in Western history. For both admirers and critics alike, it is considered the beginning of modernity, the time when the basic questions facing our world were posed, though not answered, at least adequately. As such, the Enlightenment can be seen from two vantage points. On the one hand, its shapers and followers undertook a far-ranging critique of the world they had inherited. All aspects of traditional life—religion, political organization, social structure, science, human relations, human nature, history, economics, and the very grounds of human understanding—were subjected to intense scrutiny and investigation. On the other hand, proponents of the Enlightenment attempted to establish adequate grounds for a clearer and surer understanding of these topics. In short, the Enlightenment was characterized by the dynamic between criticism and innovation. Both sides of this equation—the criticisms leveled and the solutions proposed—still shape much of our contemporary culture.

The traditional definitions of the Enlightenment have located the source for these activities in its supposed veneration of reason. In fact, the Enlightenment is often called the "Age of Reason." The title is misleading on two counts. It seems to imply that the proponents of the Enlightenment were abstract thinkers, more concerned with utopian proposals than with practical solutions. But more important, it suggests that reason as an activity was enshrined over everything else, that recognition of the passions, desires, and the senses was largely ignored. Both assumptions are incorrect. However one evaluates Enlightenment proposals, one basic strain runs through them all, namely a great disdain for abstract answers based upon empty logic. Perhaps the worst epithet one could hurl at an opponent was that he or she was a victim of "the spirit of systems."

One need look at only three of the problems directly addressed—legal reform, economics, and political reform—to apprehend the pragmatic bent of Enlightenment thought. Cesare Beccaria, in his epoch-making work *On Crimes and Punishments,* boldly launched an attack upon torture, the death penalty, and a judicial system that favored the wealthy and powerful over the poor and the weak; it inaugurated a widespread movement that led to the curtailment of torture, limited the death penalty, and instituted the beginnings of prison reform. Economic reorganization became the central plank in the Physiocratic program and was revolutionized by Adam Smith in *The Wealth of Nations,* which laid out an economic program that still enjoys great popularity today. Political theory found its direct application in the new constitutions established during the last third of the century, the most prominent being the American and French experiments; Jefferson's Declaration of Independence and the writings of Madison, Jay, and Hamilton supporting the new federal constitution still reverberate as does the equally, if not more influential, Declaration of the Rights of Man penned during the French Revolution. Most of the political assumptions Americans hold dear—separation of church and state, the balance of power, and protection of individual rights as embodied in the Bill of Rights—are direct, pragmatic applications of Enlightenment theory.

Not only was the Enlightenment critical of abstract reasoning and utopian solutions, it also laid the basis for the critique of reason by rediscovering the darker side of human nature—the passions, desires, and sensations. Seventeenth-century assertions of the primacy of human reason as the defining feature of human existence (embodied by Descartes's assertion "I think, therefore I am") soon came under attack. Feeling and sensation replaced reason as the grounds upon which all human understanding and activity were founded. Beginning with the formulations of Locke progressing through those of Condillac, Hume, Reid, Rousseau, and culminating in Kant's *Critique of Reason,* reason as an autonomous activity, inborn and universally distributed, was subjected to a thoroughgoing reevaluation. In the process, new areas of human experience became the subject of reflection: They included the concept of the sublime in literature, attempts to forge the discipline of "aesthetics" to understand the beautiful in art, sculpture, and literature, the appreciation of the power of self-interest in all human activities, the importance of local conditions and historical traditions in shaping human lives, and the power and sway of sexuality in human nature. All of these excursions into the nonrational led one commentator to characterize the Enlightenment as the "classical age of irrationalism," classical because it recognized the power of irrationalism in ruling everyday life but refused to surrender to its sway. Rather, it assumed that a redirection of these elemental powers could produce beneficial effects.

Rather than committing itself to abstract reason, the Enlightenment turned to critical analysis: the open-ended questioning of traditional facts guided by observation, imagination, and a thorough grounding in empirical data. This was called the critical method and drew its inspiration from Newton's formulation of the procedures for scientific explanation. That one should turn to science (then called natural philosophy) as a guide was no accident, for one of the overriding assumptions of enlightened thought was that nature served as the grand analogy for all human activity. Human society, it was believed, should be brought into harmony with nature. In more traditional interpretations of the Enlightenment, the assumption has been made that since nature served as the grand analogy and Newton as the Enlightenment's most important spokesman, the age was basically dominated by a Newtonian worldview. In one sense this was true. Not only were many of his principles quickly accepted, but Newton also became the symbol for the power of natural philosophy to transform the world. Alexander Pope summed up this view in his couplet:

> Nature and Nature's law lay hid in the Night
> God said, "Let Newton be" and all was light.

Newton's symbolic function, however, did not ensure the total dominance of his views or of those of his followers (who often modified or simplified Newton's positions). As modern research is showing, Enlightenment science was not monolithic: Various strains of natural philosophic thought, including Leibnizian, Cartesian, animist, vitalist, and, toward the end of the century, a congeries of positions now consigned to the category of "pseudoscience," all contended for dominance in the realm of natural philosophy.

What was true of science was equally true for all other areas of human interest and action. The Enlightenment, though defined by some general characteristics, varied according to person, place, and time. The Enlightenment was not a unitary movement, but rather consisted of overlapping variations, all interacting and defining themselves against the past and one another. Thus, for example, on the personal level, Voltaire and Rousseau proposed radically diametrical visions of the Enlightenment, though both are considered representatives of the French Enlightenment. Similar disputes can be seen elsewhere: in Germany between Mendelssohn and Jacobi, and in Great Britain between Hume and Reid. Beyond personal interpretation, regional and national differences played a great role. Though we should be wary of imposing our contemporary idea of nationality upon the past (the nation-state as we know it hardly existed at the time), it cannot be denied that there were a number of Enlightenments that can, for example, be called the French, English, Scottish, German, Swiss, Italian, and American Enlightenments. Finally, the Enlightenment, as any broadly based movement, did not stand still. Its expressions varied over time, responding to the situations in which they were formulated and the success and failure of earlier attempts to redefine basic spheres of human activity.

There is now a tendency to distinguish an early, high, and late Enlightenment. Exact periodization has always been the bane of historians, and this case is no exception. Generally, however, the early Enlightenment is considered to have begun around the last decade of the 17th century, the most convenient year being 1688, which marked both the Glorious Revolution in England and the publication of Newton's *Principia,* events that had an enormous impact upon later thought. The high Enlightenment is associated with the great figures of the French Enlightenment, supplemented by their non-French associates or allies. Voltaire, Montesquieu, Diderot, Rousseau, Hume, Lessing, and Beccaria define the period, usually running from about 1730 to 1780 (covering their most productive periods and including the American Revolution). The late Enlightenment concentrates upon the last third of the eighteenth century, often concluding with the French Revolution. However, there are those who, speaking of the "long eighteenth century," end the Enlightenment somewhere in the first decade or two of the nineteenth century (depending upon place and person). There even have been formulations that have tried to bridge the seeming gap between the Enlightenment and Romanticism, such as "the Romantic Enlightenment" or enlightened romanticism.

Modern scholarship has given us a picture of the Enlightenment that is much more complicated, variegated, and perhaps confusing than the interpretations organized around the stereotypes of past generations. At times, it may appear that there is nothing that really holds it all together, yet there was what one might call a generally shared "Enlightenment attitude" toward human thinking and activity. It was assumed that humans could, through introspection, the free exercise of one's abilities, and active commitment, make life better in this world; that true progress could be achieved, although that progress was never automatic (decline was a constant threat) or to be taken for granted once achieved. This image of freedom achieved through dint of hard work driven on by the will to improve one's own world was eloquently voiced by Immanuel Kant in his famous essay, "What Is Enlightenment?" *"Was ist Aufklärung?"*:

> Enlightenment is man's release from his self-incurred tutelage. Tutelage is man's inability to make use of his understanding without direction from another. Self-incurred is this tutelage when its causes lie not in lack of reason but in lack of resolution and courage to use it without direction from another.

Kant then suggested that the motto of the Enlightenment should be:

> Dare to know! Have courage to use your own reason!

It is an imperative that is as important today as it was in 1784 when Kant wrote it.

—Peter Hanns Reill

HOW TO USE THIS BOOK

As you peruse the pages of the expanded edition of this *Encyclopedia of the Enlightenment,* you are giving yourself a wonderful gift: the opportunity to discover the images, insights, and new ideas that can come from men and women of the past. Let your mind wander before you begin reading—perhaps to Paris, London, Berlin, or Vienna—places that may well seem familiar, if only because you have encountered them on television, at the movies, or in books. Next, embark on a fantasy adventure into an unfamiliar era—the 18th century—by altering your familiar mental images. Get rid of the automobiles, the Eiffel Tower in Paris, Piccadilly Circus in London, the Ringstrasse in Vienna, or the Gedächtniskirche in Berlin. Wipe out images of broad thoroughfares, paved sidewalks, large stores, high-rise buildings, and brightly lit streets. Imagine a skyline broken by cathedrals, churches, and palaces rather than by the headquarters of private corporations or high-rise condominiums. Add carriages, horses, horse-drawn carts loaded with goods for the market, open air stalls, thick mud, and an onslaught of unpleasant odors. Next, notice the people—mostly on foot and, in most cases, not opulently dressed. Listen quietly to their conversation: They are, without a doubt, grumbling about the burden of taxes, bemoaning the high price of bread, criticizing the failings of their governments, and voicing their fears about money, disease, and death. Stop a moment with them, as they settle in for an afternoon of coffee and talk at Café Procope or any of hundreds of neighborhood coffeehouses. Now, listen more closely and observe: Why there, at that table in the corner, is a man who looks for all the world like Benjamin Franklin. And could that be Thomas Jefferson chatting in French with friends? They seem to be discussing politics and religion, arguing about the best form of government, about freedom of speech, religious toleration, and the best ways to guarantee prosperity for a greater number of people. Over in another corner of your fantasy coffeehouse, you might find Voltaire engaged in a lively and sometimes acerbic discussion with Rousseau about the social value of theater and music. In the meantime, David Hume, the notorious Scottish skeptic, has dropped in only to be drawn into an intense debate with Helvétius and Condorcet about the possibility of perfecting human beings through education. By now, you must be experiencing an odd sense of déjà vu. Haven't you heard all of this before, on televised news viewed in the comfort of your 20th-century home?

And that is just the point of this introductory fantasy excursion. The Enlightenment, the historical phenomenon that you are beginning to explore, is an era at once strange and distant, yet familiar; an era in which European and American men and women began talking of problems in terms that are strikingly modern. But too often, because these ideas are so familiar, we assume that we know the Enlightenment, that it can have little new to say to us. That is precisely what this book hopes to correct by offering a picture of the rich kaleidoscope of ideas and policies—both successes and failures—that were created by 18th-century writers, journalists, artists, scientists, philosophers, and statesmen.

The *Encyclopedia of the Enlightenment* has been conceived and written as a point of departure for anyone—student or general reader—who wishes to begin encountering this world in all its complexities. In its pages, readers will find 140 new articles that enrich the breadth of the original volume and introduce readers to some of the scholarly findings of the last decade. It also contains general articles covering topics such as capitalism, political theory, justice, law, religion, science, education, aesthetics, music, art and architecture, the novel, colonialism, slavery, and the European voyages of discovery. These articles are complemented by shorter topical articles covering specific concepts, individual lives, and major publications. (When possible, readers have been provided with publication dates. Missing dates may be located with the help of bibliographic tools used by professional librarians. Some works without dates were never published but rather were circulated as manuscripts.) Pertinent background information is provided in articles treating the various independent states of Europe and the cities where the Enlightenment was created and lived.

Anyone intending to use this book should begin by reading the article on the ENLIGHTENMENT. This will provide a succinct statement of the major issues of that era and will also introduce readers to the overall plan of the book. The next step will be determined by the reader's specific research interests. Generally, it is best to proceed to the article that covers that specific interest: a biography, for example, or a discussion of a distinct concept. But readers should not stop at that point, because this book has been written with the assumption that cross-references (indicated by small capital letters) will also be read. These articles add to the material given in individual entries and also help, in most cases, to place the individual thinkers or concepts into the broader web of interrelated ideas that define the Enlightenment.

A few examples will elucidate this point. John Locke, one of the English "fathers" of the Enlightenment, is known to most students as the creator of the notion that the human mind at birth is a tabula rasa (blank slate). This idea was actually part of a broad theory of psychology, and Locke was one of the seminal figures in defining that subject. Therefore, the article PSYCHOLOGY should also be consulted. This will introduce students to the many questions with which Locke was grappling and will lead them to articles about supporters and opponents of his ideas. It will also lead into the realm of epistemology, a subject that was still part of philosophy and of great concern to natural scientists. Locke, however, was also a political theorist whose beliefs were, in some respects, intimately linked to his perspectives on human psychology. Therefore, readers will find themselves directed by the cross-references to the article POLITICAL THEORY. If readers invest the time required to read these articles, they will find that broad vistas have been opened into the Enlightenment, a world of complex relations between ideas.

The example of AESTHETICS will also help to illustrate the importance of the cross-references. Readers interested in this subject should consult the general article of that title, where they will find themselves introduced to the way in which people of different European nations treated the basic themes of the Enlightenment. They will begin learning not only of the more familiar English and French treatments of aesthetics, but also of the manner in which German-speaking thinkers developed these ideas. Readers will, in this manner, begin learning of the complexities, tensions, and downright contradictions that existed in the Enlightenment.

Suppose, as a third example, that a student decides to explore the subject of TOLERATION. After reading that article, cross-references lead to the general article RELIGION. That article, perhaps surprisingly, leads not only to POLITICAL THEORY, ABSOLUTISM, and specific individuals, but also to SCIENCE and PSYCHOLOGY. Thus, from one rather narrow concept, a whole world of thought emerges.

This world can also be glimpsed using the chronology that immediately follows. It provides an overview of the major events of the Enlightenment, with an emphasis on influential publications and works of art. The chronology can be read through for a quick tour of artistic and political highlights; its cross-references will lead back to the entries with, it is hoped, a greater sense of the order of things.

Above all, readers should approach this book in the best spirit of the Enlightenment, with an inquiring and critical mind. Ask questions of what you read and welcome paradoxes. They can lead to new insights, about the Enlightenment, about Western patterns of thinking, even about problems facing us in the 21st century. In other words, "Dare to know" And enjoy the experience!

—Ellen Judy Wilson

CHRONOLOGY

1674–78   Nicolas de MALEBRANCHE: *De la recherche de la vérité*

1677   Benedict de SPINOZA: *Ethics* (posthumous publication)

1678   Richard SIMON: *Histoire critique du Vieux Testament*

1685   LOUIS XIV revokes Edict of Nantes
Edict of Potsdam welcomes French HUGUENOTS to Brandenburg-Prussia

1685–94   QUARREL BETWEEN THE ANCIENTS AND MODERNS

1686   Bernard le Bovier de FONTENELLE: *Entretiens sur la pluralité des mondes*

1687   Isaac NEWTON: *Principia mathematica*

1688–89   GLORIOUS REVOLUTION in England
Catholic king James II forced to abandon throne of England
Protestants WILLIAM III AND MARY II seize power

1689   John LOCKE: first of the *Letters on Toleration* published

1690   Locke: *Essay On Human Understanding*
Locke: *Two Treatises on Government*

1693   Locke: *Some Thoughts Concerning Education*

1695   Locke: *The Reasonableness of Christianity*

1697   Pierre BAYLE: *Dictionnaire historique et critique*
PETER I (THE GREAT) of Russia tours Europe

1700   Gottfried Wilhelm LEIBNIZ outlines plans for the Berlin Academy
William CONGREVE: *The Way of the World*

1702–04   Revolt of the CAMISARDS

1703   Founding of the city of SAINT PETERSBURG in Russia

1704   NEWTON: *Opticks*

1705   Edmond HALLEY predicts 1785 return of comet

1707   ENGLAND and SCOTLAND join to form Great Britain

1707   Johann Friedrich BÖTTGER introduces kaolin, the secret ingredient of Chinese porcelain, and invents European hard-paste porcelain

1709   Bartolommeo Cristofori (1655–1731) builds the oldest piano (called the fortepiano) still extant in Florence

1710   George BERKELEY: *Treatise Concerning the Principle of Human Knowledge*
LEIBNIZ: *Theodicée*

1711–14   Joseph ADDISON and Richard STEELE publish *The SPECTATOR*

1711   Third earl of SHAFTESBURY: *Characteristicks of Men, Manners, Opinions*

1714   Leibniz: *Monadologie*
Bernard MANDEVILLE: *Fable of the Bees*
Daniel Gabriel FAHRENHEIT invents the mercury thermometer
Johann Lukas von HILDEBRANDT begins construction of the Belvedere Palace for Prince Eugène of Savoy

1715–23   Regency in France during the minority years of LOUIS XV

1716   Johann Bernard FISCHER VON ERLACH begins construction of the Church of Saint Charles Borromeo in Vienna

1717   George Frederick HANDEL's *Water Music* performed

1719   Daniel DEFOE: *Robinson Crusoe*
Balthasar NEUMANN begins work on the Episcopal Residence in Würzburg

1720   Eliza HAYWOOD: *Love in Excess*

1721   Baron de MONTESQUIEU: *Lettres persanes* (Persian Letters)
Performance of the Brandenburg Concertos by Johann Sebastian BACH

1721–23   Johann Jakob BODMER and Johann Jakob BREITINGER edit the journal *Die Diskurse der Mahlern*

1722   Jean-Philippe RAMEAU: *Traité de l'Harmonie*
MORAVIAN BRETHREN fleeing persecution take refuge in Saxony at the estate of German religious reformer Count von ZINZENDORF

1724–49   J. S. Bach: Mass in B Minor

1724   Peter the Great founds the SAINT PETERSBURG ACADEMY OF SCIENCES

1725   Giambattista VICO: *Principi di una Scienza Nuova*

1726   Jonathan SWIFT: *Gulliver's Travels*

1729   Albrecht von HALLER publishes the poem *Les Alpes*

1730   Marquise du DEFFAND's salon assumes prominence in Paris
Pierre MARIVAUX: *Le Jeu de l'Amour et du Hasard*

1732   William HOGARTH: *The Harlot's Progress*

1733   Giovanni Battista PERGOLESI: *La Serva Padrona*
Alexander POPE: *Essay on Man*

1734   VOLTAIRE: *Lettres anglaises ou philosophiques*
Foundation of the University of Göttingen

1734–35   Hogarth: *A Rake's Progress*

1738   Voltaire: *Éléments de la philosophie de Newton*

1738–40   David HUME: *A Treatise of Human Nature*

1739–40   Charles de BROSSES: *Lettres familières écrites d'Italie*

1740s   The ENGLISH GARDEN style becomes popular throughout Europe

1740   Samuel RICHARDSON: *Pamela*

1740   Frederick II (the Great) of Prussia: *Anti-Machiavel*

1740–86   Reign of Frederick the Great of Prussia

1740–80   Reign of MARIA THERESA in the HAPSBURG EMPIRE

1740–48   WAR OF THE AUSTRIAN SUCCESSION

1741   Handel: *Messiah*

1743   Jean Le Rond d'ALEMBERT: *Traité de dynamique*

1745   Emanuel SWEDENBORG: *De Cultu et Amore dei*
John Turberville NEEDHAM: Discoveries with the microscope

1745–64   Ascendancy of marquise de POMPADOUR

1746   Etienne-Bonnot de CONDILLAC: *Essai sur l'origines des conaissances humaines*

1748   Leonhard EULER: *Introductio in analysin infinitorum*
Montesquieu: *Esprit des lois*

1749   Denis DIDEROT: *Lettre sur les aveugles*

1749   Comte de BUFFON: Beginning of publication of *Histoire naturelle*

1750   Jean Jacques ROUSSEAU: *Discours sur les lettres et les arts*

1750–77   Marquês de POMBAL is minister in Portugal

1751   Giovanni Battista TIEPOLO: Ceiling fresco for the Kaiserssaal in the Episcopal Residence at Würzburg
d'Alembert: *Discours préliminaire* for volume I of the *Encyclopédie*

1751–54   Benjamin FRANKLIN: *Experiments and Observations on Electricity*

1751–72   Publication of the *Encyclopédie*, edited by Diderot and d'Alembert

1752   Voltaire: *Le siècle de Louis XIV*
Charlotte LENNOX: *The Female Quixote*

1753   Prince KAUNITZ becomes chancellor of Austria

1755   Euler: *Institutiones calculi differentialis*
LISBON EARTHQUAKE (November 1)
Jean-Baptiste GREUZE: *Le père de famille*
Rousseau: *Discours sur les origines et les fondements de l'inégalité*
Johann Joachim WINCKELMANN: *Gedanken über die Nachahmung der griechischen Werke*
Moses MENDELSSOHN: *Philosophischen Gespräche*
Samuel JOHNSON's letter to Lord Chesterfield refusing the latter's offer of patronage for Johnson's *Dictionary*

1755–92   Jacques-Germain SOUFFLOT: Construction of the Panthéon in Paris

1756   DIPLOMATIC REVOLUTION
Posthumous publication of marquise du CHÂTELET's French translation of Newton's *Principia mathematica*

1756–63   SEVEN YEARS' WAR

1757   Robert-François DAMIENS attempts to assassinate Louis XV
Edmund BURKE: *On the Sublime and Beautiful*

1757–66   Albrecht von HALLER: *Elementa physiologiae corporis humani*

1758   Carolus LINNAEUS: Publication of the 10th edition of the *Systema naturae*
Claude-Adrien HELVÉTIUS: *De l'esprit*
François QUESNAY: *Tableau économique*
Hume: *Enquiry Concerning Human Understanding*
Thomas GAINSBOROUGH: *The Painter's Daughters Chasing a Butterfly*

1759   Voltaire: *Candide* published
            Expulsion of the JESUITS from Portugal
            Adam SMITH: *Theory of Moral Sentiments*
1759–67   Laurence STERNE: *Tristram Shandy*
1759–88   Reign of CHARLES III OF SPAIN
1760   James MACPHERSON: Ossian poems
1760–1820   Reign of George III (1738–1820) in
            England
1761   Rousseau: LA NOUVELLE HÉLOISE
1761, 1769 Observation of the transits of Venus
1762   Rousseau: ÉMILE and *Le Contrat social*
            (Social contract)
            Execution of Jean CALAS in Toulouse
            Christoph Willibald GLUCK: ORPHEO ED
            EURIDICE
1762–96   Reign of CATHERINE II (THE GREAT) in
            Russia
1763   Kant: *Beobachtunger über das Gefül des*
            Schönen und Erhaben
            Voltaire: *Traité sur la tolérance*
            Britain gains control of French Canada
1764   Voltaire: *Dictionnaire philosophique*
            Winckelmann: *Geschichte der Kunst des*
            Altertums
            Marchese di BECCARIA: *Tratto dei delitti e*
            delle pene
            James HARGREAVES invents the spinning
            jenny, patented 1770
1765   Jean Honoré FRAGONARD: *The Bathers*
            Leibniz: Posthumous publication of
            Nouveaux essais sur l'entendement humain
1765–69   Sir William BLACKSTONE: *Commentaries on*
            the Laws of England
1765–90   Joseph II of Austria rules the Hapsburg
            Empire
1766   Baron de l'Aulne (TURGOT): *Réflexions sur la*
            formation et la distribution des richesses
            Gotthold Ephraim LESSING: *Laokoon*
            Oliver GOLDSMITH: *The Vicar of Wakefield*
1767   Expulsion of the Jesuits from Spain
            Paul-Henri-Thiry d'HOLBACH publishes *Le*
            Christianisme dévoilée under the name
            Nicolas Boulanger
            Gluck: *Alceste*
1768   Rousseau: *Dictionnaire de la musique*
            Quesnay: *Physiocratie*
            Captain James COOK begins his voyage to
            the South Pacific
1769   Diderot writes *Le Rêve d'Alembert*
1769–90   Joshua REYNOLDS: *Discourses on Art*
1770   Holbach: *Système de la nature*
            Ferdinando GALIANI: *Dialogues sur le*
            commerce des blés
            Guillaume-Thomas François de RAYNAL:
            Histoire des deux Indes

            Gainsborough: *The Blue Boy*
            James WATT patents the steam engine
1770–84   Construction of Monticello, home of
            Thomas JEFFERSON
1772   Johann Wolfgang von GOETHE: *Goetz von*
            Berlichingen
1772–75   Second world expedition of Captain Cook
1773   Jacques-Henri BERNARDIN DE SAINT-PIERRE:
            Voyage à l'Île de France
            Diderot: *Supplément au voyage de*
            Bougainville
1774   Goethe: *Die Leiden des jungen Werthers*
            Joseph PRIESTLEY isolates oxygen
1774–76   Turgot serves as controlleur général in
            France
1774–79   Friedrich Heinrich JACOBI: *Eduard Allwills*
            Papiere
1775   AMERICAN REVOLUTION begins
1775–76   Johann Friedrich BLUMENBACH: *De generis*
            humani varietate natura
1776–79   Last voyage of Captain Cook
1776   Jeremy BENTHAM: *A Fragment on*
            Government
            Smith: *An Inquiry into the Nature and*
            Causes of the WEALTH OF NATIONS
            United States's DECLARATION OF
            INDEPENDENCE
            Thomas Paine: COMMON SENSE
1776–88   Edward GIBBON: *The History of the Decline*
            and Fall of the Roman Empire
1779   Lessing: *Nathan der Weise*
            Hume: *Dialogues Concerning Natural*
            Religion
            Pennsylvania passes the first U.S. abolition
            law
1780   Jean-Antoine HOUDON: *Voltaire*
1781   Kant: *Kritik der reinen Vernunft*
            Abolition of SERFDOM in Austria
            Edicts of toleration in Austria and Sweden
            Johann Christoph Friedrich SCHILLER: *Die*
            Räuber
1782   Choderlos de LACLOS: *Les Liaisons*
            dangereuses
1783   MONTGOLFIER brothers Jacques-Etienne
            and Michel-Joseph make first balloon
            ascent
            Pierre-Augustin Caron de BEAUMARCHAIS:
            First performance of *Le Mariage de Figaro*
            Mendelssohn: *Jerusalem oder über die*
            religiöse Macht und Judentum
            Reynolds: *Portrait of Mrs. Siddons as the*
            Tragic Muse
1784   East India Act
1784–91   Johann Gottfried HERDER: *Ideen zur*
            Philosophie der Geschichte der Menschheit

1785   Mendelssohn: *Morgenstunden oder über das Dasein Gottes*

Jacobi: *Über die Lehre des Spinoza*

Jacques-Louis DAVID paints *Le Serment des Horaces*

Kant: "WAS IST AUFKLÄRUNG"

1786   Wolfgang Amadeus MOZART: *Marriage of Figaro* premiere

François-André-Adrien PLUQUET: *Le Luxe*

1787   Mozart: DON GIOVANNI

1787–88   James MADISON: *The Federalist Papers*

1788   Kant: *Kritik der praktischen Vernunft*

Joseph-Louis LAGRANGE: *Mécanique analytique*

1788–1820   Chinese plants introduced in England, including chrysanthemums, hydrangeas, peonies, magnolias, and tiger lilies

1789   Antoine LAVOISIER: *Traité élémentaire de chimie*

FRENCH REVOLUTION begins

Bentham: *An Introduction to the Principles of Morals and Legislation*

DECLARATION OF THE RIGHTS OF MAN AND CITIZEN

1790   Kant: *Kritik der Urteilskraft*

Edmund Burke: *Reflections on the Revolution in France*

1791   UNITED STATES BILL OF RIGHTS

Premiere of Mozart's THE MAGIC FLUTE

1791–92   Paine: THE RIGHTS OF MAN

1791–1804   François-Dominique-TOUISSANT LOUVERTURE leads the HAITIAN REVOLUTION

1792   Mary WOLLSTONECRAFT: VINDICATION OF THE RIGHTS OF WOMAN

1793   LOUIS XVI executed in France

William GODWIN: *Enquiry Concerning Political Justice*

1794   William BLAKE: *Songs of Experience*

1795   Marquis de CONDORCET: *Tableau historique des progrès de l'esprit humain*

Schiller begins publishing the journal *Die Horen*

1796   Edward JENNER uses cowpox as a vaccination against smallpox

Marquis de LAPLACE: *Exposition du système du monde*

1798   Joseph HAYDN: *The Creation*

Thomas Robert MALTHUS: *An Essay on the Principle of Population*

1799   Napoleon (1769–1821) overthrows the French Directory

1799–1825   Laplace: *Traité de mécanique céleste*

1800   Jean-Baptiste-Pierre-Antoine de Monet de LAMARCK: *Système des animaux sans vertèbres*

1801   Act of Union joins Ireland to Great Britain

1803   Louisiana Purchase

1804   Napoleon crowns himself emperor of the French

Creation of the Republic of Haiti

Schiller: *Wilhelm Tell*

1807   Abolition of the slave trade in Britain

1808   Ludwig van Beethoven: Fifth Symphony

1808–32   Goethe: *Faust*

1809   Lamarck: *Philosophie zoologique*

1810–14   Francisco José de GOYA y Lucientes: *Los desastres de la guerra*

Abel, Karl Friedrich (1723–1787) *German viola da gambist, composer, and impresario*

Abel was born at Cothen just after Johann Sebastian BACH departed from that city with his family. The Abels were a family of musicians, and J. S. Bach stood as godfather to Karl Friedrich's elder sister. It has been claimed that Abel studied at the St. Thomasschule in Leipzig under Bach, but no record exists of his attendance. In 1748, Abel obtained a post in the Dresden court orchestra.

In 1759, Abel moved to LONDON, where he was enthusiastically received as a virtuoso performer on the viola da gamba. After the arrival of Johann Christian BACH in 1762, the two men took lodgings together. In 1763, they opened a subscription for a weekly series of concerts where they presented their own compositions played by outstanding musicians. A highly popular series, it continued until Bach's death in 1782.

Afterward, Abel continued the concert series, but without much success. He returned to Germany in 1783, then moved back to London in 1785. At that time, he participated in the Professional Concert, a series established in 1785. Abel continued performing until 1787, when he died of alcohol-induced illness.

Charles BURNEY, the chronicler of musical life in 18th-century London, credited Johann Christian BACH and Karl Friedrich Abel with transforming English musical tastes by demonstrating the delights of the new classical style. Prior to their activities, English audiences had preferred the BAROQUE STYLE compositions of George Frederick HANDEL, Francesco Xaviero Geminiani (1687–1762), and Arcangelo CORELLI (1653–1713).

Abel was the last great virtuoso of the viola da gamba; the violoncello replaced it in both chamber music and orchestral compositions. Abel's compositions were highly regarded by his contemporaries. They included symphonies, trios, quartets, concertos, and sonatas, many of which were published during his life. The sonatas for viola da gamba are among the most interesting of his works. The painter Thomas GAINSBOROUGH, who was a friend, left two portraits of Abel.

abolition movement   *See* SLAVERY.

absolutism   A specific form of monarchy, the theory and practice of which played an especially significant role in Europe in the 17th and 18th centuries. The term *absolutism* is a product of early 19th-century thought. It refers simply to a form of government in which the monarch has unlimited power; it carries with it connotations of despotism and tyranny.

In the late 16th century and 17th century, however, when various forms of sovereignty (i.e., final authority beyond which there is no appeal) and government were being widely discussed, the term *absolute* had a different meaning, derived from Aristotelian and scholastic writings about POLITICAL THEORY. An absolute form of government was one that was pure, untainted by elements from any other form. This meaning derived from the Latin verb *absolvere,* "to loose, to free," which in its participial form, *absolutus,* signifies "pure" or "free of foreign elements." Thus, an absolute monarchy was a pure monarchy that was free of any democratic or aristocratic components. Sovereignty in such a kingdom was a unity, indivisible, a whole without constituent parts. The absolute monarch ruled as the supreme executive, legislator, and judge; no parliament, court, or other constituted body could claim a fundamental right to share in the exercise of sovereign power.

The possession of such all-encompassing power, however, did not give the monarch license to act as a tyrant, following whatever policy he or she fancied in a given instance. Rather, the monarch owed allegiance to the fundamental laws of the land, however uncertain the definition of such laws might be. He or she also owed allegiance to the divine laws of God. Arbitrary exercise of power without respect for fundamental law was not absolute rule, but rather despotism.

The 17th century produced several justifications of absolute monarchy. Bishop BOSSUET, the adviser to King LOUIS XIV OF FRANCE, for example, offered an eloquent argument based on the DIVINE RIGHT OF KINGS. God was the ultimate source of the monarch's power, and the absolute authority of God in the universe provided the model for kingship. In ENGLAND, Robert Filmer (1588–1653) argued for the legitimacy of absolute sovereignty by appealing to the alleged divine origins and superiority of the patriarchal (father-dominated) family. The absolute monarch, he believed, functioned in a manner analogous to the male head of the family. Filmer's opponent, Thomas HOBBES, used the new MECHANICAL PHILOSOPHY and the notion of the social contract to develop a powerful and highly influential statement of the practical value of absolutism.

Arguments favoring absolutism were countered by theorists who believed that royal power must be limited by other groups in order to avoid despotism. John LOCKE and Charles-Louis de Secondat, better known as Baron de MONTESQUIEU, developed widely read arguments along these lines, and their points of view remained highly influential throughout the ENLIGHTENMENT.

The Royal Palace at Versailles, France. King Louis XIV of France had the palace at Versailles designed and constructed as an architectural symbol of his absolute power. *(Courtesy New York Public Library)*

The personal reign of Louis XIV in FRANCE (1660–1715) is sometimes presented in history texts as the quintessential example of absolutism in practice; his reign even provided the model for older historical definitions of absolutism. This older historical model, however common in modern texts, unfortunately confuses the king's claims with the actual facts of his reign. Examination of the political struggles that occurred during Louis's long rule reveals that, in spite of his enormous extensions of royal power, royal freedom to act was always limited to some extent by tradition and by entrenched privilege.

The tenuousness of Louis XIV's absolute control in France became starkly apparent shortly after his death. Social and political groups whose traditional powers had been suppressed reemerged to cause unceasing political turmoil. The ARISTOCRATIC RESURGENCE of the 18th century, the interminable quarrels between 18th-century French kings and PARLEMENTS, and the failure of royal fiscal reforms all demonstrated the inability of 18th-century monarchs to exercise absolute power. Eventually, the entire political structure collapsed in the upheavals of the FRENCH REVOLUTION.

Whatever the failures of absolutism in practice, it must be stressed that the vision of Louis XIV as the ultimate representative of absolutism had its origin in the political treatises written during Louis's reign, and was continued by his critics during the Enlightenment. When VOLTAIRE, for example, wrote SIÈCLE DE LOUIS XIV, he was voicing this interpretation of the reign, albeit with a unique assessment of its effects.

During the Enlightenment, two important variations of absolutism—ENLIGHTENED ABSOLUTISM and ENLIGHTENED DESPOTISM—emerged within the community of European nations. Kings and ministers in France, PORTUGAL, MILAN, and Tuscany, for example, attempted reforms from above that showed the influence of enlightened ideals. In central and eastern Europe, FREDERICK II (THE GREAT) OF PRUSSIA, JOSEPH II OF AUSTRIA, and CATHERINE II (THE GREAT) of Russia provided examples of the strengths and weaknesses inherent in enlightened despotism.

Throughout the Enlightenment, the subject of absolutism played an important role in political theory and in practical reform efforts. The idea of absolute rule retained its appeal for some enlightened observers of 18th-century politics, but eventually most PHILOSOPHES abandoned their support of absolutism, calling instead for some form of limited monarchy or representative government.

absolutism, enlightened   General term used by historians to describe a form of European polity specific to the 18th century and guided by certain political principles of the ENLIGHTENMENT. Forms of enlightened absolutism were practiced in FRANCE under LOUIS XV; in the HAPSBURG EMPIRE during the co-regency of MARIA THERESA and her son JOSEPH II; in PRUSSIA under FREDERICK II (THE GREAT); in Russia under CATHERINE II (THE GREAT); in SPAIN under CHARLES III; and even in ROME under Pope BENEDICT XIV. enlightened absolutism is related to, but distinct from, both 17th-century ABSOLUTISM and CAMERALISM. Whether it differs from ENLIGHTENED DESPOTISM is a subject of debate.

As with other forms of absolutism, enlightened absolutism locates sovereignty in the person of the monarch rather than in the nation or the people, as is the case in constitutional monarchies and republics. The power and legitimacy of a 17th-century absolute king derived directly from God, the creator of the universe. In 18th-century enlightened absolutism, rule by divine right was replaced by rule according to NATURAL LAW, the law that supposedly governed the natural world and human beings. Natural law recognized God as the indirect source of royal power since this law was one of God's creations, but an absolute monarchy based on natural law was less intimately connected to the sacred order than was a divine rights monarchy. One of the consequences of this change was the ability to define the essence of a state in other than religious terms, thus making the establishment of religious TOLERATION possible even in the absence of a constitutional SEPARATION OF CHURCH AND STATE.

ENLIGHTENED MONARCHS also justified their rules by claiming that they stood above all sociopolitical factions, ruling not as the spokesperson for any specific group but, according to Frederick II, as "the first servant of the state." Underlying this argument was the assumption that the monarch's powers were not arbitrary but based on the common good, a theory embodied in practice by the use of leading enlightened figures instead of members of the traditional ruling elite as ministers to kings and queens. The marques de POMBAL in Portugal, Josef von SONNENFELS in the Hapsburg Empire, and Anne-Robert-Jacques TURGOT and Jacques NECKER in France were outstanding examples of this new type of minister.

Like 17th-century absolutists, enlightened absolute monarchs favored policies that strengthened their states. They tried to streamline bureaucracies, subdue unruly subjects, reform taxation structures, and build strong militaries. Traditional absolute rulers such as Louis XIV in France based their actions on theories of MERCANTILISM and reasons of state, not on universal, egalitarian principles. They saw their subjects as sources of labor and wealth and as means to the end of state glorification, not as individuals endowed with RIGHTS by the natural order of the universe.

By comparing taxation policies in the two types of absolute monarchies, it is possible to see how enlightened principles affected royal policies. European states in the 17th and 18th centuries rested on a social system of privilege that exempted the nobility and other groups from various forms of taxation. While traditional absolute monarchs and their ministers tended to work within this system of privilege, enlightened monarchs and ministers tried to establish new principles for tax policy, based on enlightened universalism and egalitarianism. One result was an increase in proposals to tax all subjects, no matter their social rank. A second was a spate of proposals designed to rationalize the tax system by reducing the number of taxes and simultaneously spreading the tax burden over the population. French tax reform efforts under Louis XV followed these enlightened principles, although they were unsuccessful.

The Hapsburg Empire provides another instructive example of the effects of enlightened absolutism in a state: the distinction between cameralism and enlightened absolutism. Maria Theresa's long reign (1717–80) saw two separate periods of reform, the first governed primarily by cameralist principles and the second guided by a combination of cameralism and Enlightenment ideas. The First Theresian Reform radically restructured the administration of the monarchy and extended tax liability to noble lands, thus allowing the Hapsburg state and its people to recover from the devastation of the WAR OF THE AUSTRIAN SUCCESSION. Conceived and implemented by Count Friedrich Wilhelm Haugwitz with Maria Theresa's blessing and support, the Austrian monarchy was strengthened, centralized, and enriched in a process that extended some prosperity even to peasants.

The Second Theresian Reform unfolded while Maria Theresa ruled Austria jointly with her son Joseph II. Guided by the reformer Wenzel KAUNITZ and inspired by Joseph's enlightened egalitarian principles, this reform introduced changes intended specifically to alleviate the suffering of peasants and commoners by limiting the privileges of the nobility. New laws reduced the number of days of obligatory labor (*robot*) that a lord could demand from his peasants; a new system of public schools expanded the availability of education; and domestic experiments by Milanese reformers made Hapsburg-ruled Lombardy an international symbol of enlightenment. Within the state government, the bureaucracy was regularized and a system of entrance exams instituted to ensure that competent, knowledgeable people rather than merely well-connected aristocrats could enter government service. Thus, reform under enlightened absolutism redefined the relationship of the monarchy to its subjects, even while continuing to strengthen the state.

See also DIVINE RIGHT OF KINGS; JUSTICE AND THE LAW.

Further reading: Alfred Cobban, *A History of Modern France, Vol. I: 1715–1799. Old Régime and Revolution*, 3rd ed. (Baltimore: Penguin Books, 1963); Charles W. Ingrao, *The Habsburg Monarchy, 1618–1815*, 2nd ed. (Cambridge: Cambridge University Press, 2000); Daniel Roche, *France in the Enlightenment*, tr. Arthur Goldhammer (Cambridge, Mass.: Harvard University Press, 1998).

Adam, Robert and James (Robert, 1728–1792 and James, 1730–1794) *Scottish architects and interior designers*

Robert and James Adam created a neoclassical style of architectural and interior decoration—the Adam style—that superseded the popularity of the PALLADIAN STYLE after 1770.

Robert and James Adam were the sons of William Adam, the leading Scottish architect of his time. Robert pursued his higher education at the University of Edinburgh and then moved to ROME (1755–57). He was admitted to the Academy of Saint Luke in Rome and studied classical architecture and archaeology with C. Clérisseau, a French antiquarian and architect. With Clérisseau, he toured throughout the Italian peninsula studying artifacts from the ancient Roman era.

Returning to Great Britain in 1758, Adam settled in London, where, in 1760, he obtained his first important commission: to design a screen for the British Admiralty. By 1761, he had received an appointment as architect of the king's works.

James Adam followed in his brother's footsteps, traveling throughout the Italian peninsula on a grand tour with Clérisseau that lasted from 1760 until 1763. James then joined Robert in London, where the two men entered into a highly successful business collaboration. They were assisted by their youngest brother, William, who served as business manager.

Together, Robert and James Adam created a neoclassical style notable for its delicate qualities. Their stucco interiors incorporated the devices of ROCOCO style but transformed that style by utilizing straight lines and symmetry inspired by ancient classical designs. The ceilings, chimney pieces, silver, and furniture created by the Adam brothers enjoyed great popularity during the 1770s.

Robert Adam remodeled several English country manors, including Syon House, Kedleston Hall, and Kenwood House. Luton Hoo and Mersham-le-Hatch were built entirely from his plans. He also designed London townhouse interiors such as the front drawing room at Home House (1772–73). His London Adelphi project (begun in 1768) consisted of an area of fine town houses located on an embankment supported by Romanized arches and vaults. Of that project, the Royal Society of Arts Building (1772–74) remains standing. The Register House in Edinburgh is one of his only extant public buildings.

Robert Adam published two books on architecture: *The Ruins of the Palace of the Emperor Diocletian at Spalatro* (1764) and, with his brother James, *The Works . . . of Robert and James Adam* (1773).

See also CHIPPENDALE; ITALY; NEOCLASSICISM.

Adams, John (1735–1826) *American statesman and political theorist who served as the first vice president and second president of the United States*
John Adams was born in Braintree, Massachusetts. His father, also John Adams, was a farmer who served in the colonial militia. His mother, Susanna Boylston Adams,

came from a family of prosperous doctors and merchants. Young Adams graduated from Harvard College in 1755, after having studied both ancient Greek and Roman literature and the works of 18th-century writers such as John LOCKE, MONTESQUIEU, and David HUME. Adams then pursued a law degree and was admitted to the Boston bar in 1758. He became one of the leading constitutional lawyers in Massachusetts.

Adams began to distinguish himself in the political struggles that led up to the AMERICAN REVOLUTION. As a leader of the American Whig Party, he opposed the Stamp Act of 1765, denouncing it in a meeting with the Massachusetts governor and council as an instance of taxation without consent.

Adams's defense of individual rights and commitment to certain constitutional principles prevented him from becoming a blind partisan of popular colonial opinion. As a result, he assumed responsibility for defending the British soldiers accused of murder in the so-called Boston Massacre (1770). This action, however counter to public sentiment, failed to eclipse Adams's political career; he was elected just one year later (1771) as a member of the Massachusetts House of Representatives.

Between 1774 and 1778 Adams was a delegate to the Continental Congress. He served with Thomas JEFFERSON and Benjamin FRANKLIN on the committee charged with drafting the DECLARATION OF INDEPENDENCE (1776) and assisted on several diplomatic missions in Europe. He served in FRANCE (1778–79 and 1782), the UNITED PROVINCES OF THE NETHERLANDS (1780), and Great Britain (1785–88).

Adams advanced the cause of American independence by securing a loan for the United States from the Dutch government. The Dutch also granted official recognition to the new nation. In PARIS with John JAY, Adams negotiated the peace treaty with Great Britain (1782) that ended the War of Independence.

In 1789 and again in 1792, Adams was elected to the vice presidency of the United States. He then served as second president (1797–1801). His association with the Federalist Party and his unpopular policies such as the Alien and Sedition Acts (1798) helped bring about his defeat by Thomas Jefferson in the elections of 1800. After that election, Adams retired to private life.

In the course of his career, Adams developed a political position that demonstrated his knowledge of the POLITICAL THEORY and practical issues central to the ENLIGHTENMENT. His *Dissertation on the Canon and Feudal Law* (1768) discussed American discontent with British policies in terms of the struggle between emerging individualism and the corporatist traditions of the ANCIEN RÉGIME.

The *Defense of the Constitutions of Government of the United States* (1787–88) surveyed all republics known to history, analyzing their strengths and weaknesses. *The Federalist Papers* (1787–88), by James MADISON, John Jay,

Portrait of John Adams. A prominent figure in the American Revolution, John Adams championed the political ideals of the Enlightenment and helped to put them into practice in the framing of the American Constitution. *(Courtesy Independence National Historical Park)*

and Alexander HAMILTON, and Adams's book together spelled out the basic theory of federalism.

Adams's book presented his belief in the importance of the SEPARATION OF POWERS as a check against despotism. It defended the federal structure of the new United States against criticisms from the philosophe and former French controller general of finances, Anne-Robert-Jacques TURGOT.

Adams believed that the division of authority between federal and state governments would prevent the abuse of power, but he wanted a strong federal government. He also supported the idea of a strong executive branch as a protection against power abuses by the legislature. Within the legislature itself, Adams believed that abuses of power could best be prevented by establishing a bicameral (two chambers) structure. Isolating the wealthy in a separate house of the legislature (the Senate) would protect the political authority of the middle classes (the House). These views were readily misinterpreted and caused Adams to be conceived by some Americans as an aristocrat. But in fact, Adams was hoping to prevent the United States from constructing a system that would allow aristocratic elements to become entrenched in power.

Adams's work, while recognizing the importance of the balance of powers in structuring a republic, departs from the classic position taken by Montesquieu in the SPIRIT OF LAWS. Where Montesquieu believed that intermediary bodies of aristocrats such as the French PARLEMENTS provided the necessary balance against despotic rule from an absolute monarch, Adams proposed that such intermediary bodies were likely sources of power abuse. As a preventive, Adams called for the creation of a strong executive branch.

Adams, then, was a major political theorist during the critical decades in which the UNITED STATES OF AMERICA was born. His works illustrate one of several models that grew logically from enlightened political ideals.

See also WASHINGTON.

Addison, Joseph (1672–1719) *English essayist, poet, and statesmen, considered one of the great masters of English prose*
Joseph Addison collaborated with his childhood friend Richard STEELE in the production of the influential literary journals *The Tatler* (1709–11) and *The SPECTATOR* (1711–12 and 1714). *The Spectator,* in particular, became an outstanding literary instrument of the ENLIGHTENMENT, and imitations appeared throughout Europe.

Addison and Steele aimed to create a more enlightened reading public by offering lively, witty, satirical, critical, and enjoyable essays whose content would educate and stimulate moral development. They intended also to popularize and to disseminate the new forms of philosophy that were being created in universities and high intellectual circles by presenting important concepts in the form of examples drawn from life.

Addison, the son of the Anglican dean of Lichfield, received his elementary education in Lichfield and at the Charterhouse school. He met Richard Steele at Charterhouse. He studied at Oxford University, remaining as a fellow of Magdalen College until 1711. In 1711, faced with the necessity of choosing between entering the Anglican clergy or pursuing a secular life, Addison chose the latter route. Consequently, he resigned his fellowship at Magdalen and moved to LONDON.

Addison had already established a reputation as a skilled poet; his poem "To Mr. Dryden" had appeared in 1693 in John DRYDEN's *Examen Poeticum*. In London, Addison met William CONGREVE and also acquired the friendship and patronage of the Whig leaders, Lord Chancellor Sir John Somers and Charles Montagu (later Earl of Halifax). With their assistance, Addison secured a royal pension of £300 per year. He also traveled on the European continent between 1699 and 1703 as tutor to Montagu's son, Edward Wortley Montagu.

Addison's subsequent employment consisted of a 1704 appointment as successor to John LOCKE in the post of commissioner of appeals in excise (tax appeals); an appointment as undersecretary of state (1705–08); ser-

vice as secretary to the lord lieutenant of Ireland (1708–10); member of Parliament (first election 1708); secretary for Ireland (1715); commissioner of trade (1716); and secretary of state (1717–18).

Addison's first literary triumph came with the poem *The Campaign* (1705), written to celebrate the English victory over the French at Blenheim. His major period of literary creativity, however, occurred during the years when he was writing for *The Tatler* and *The Spectator.* Addison contributed essays regularly to both journals. He also started the *Whig Examiner* (1710) and wrote the series of political commentaries entitled *The Freeholder, or Political Essays* (1715–16). In addition, he wrote dramas, including the successful tragedy *Cato* (1713) and *The Drummer* (1716), both of which were produced at Drury Lane Theatre.

Adelung, Johan Christoph (1732–1806) *German philologist and grammarian*
After studying theology at the UNIVERSITY OF HALLE, Johann Christoph Adelung assumed a position as librarian at Gotha. In 1787, through the patronage of the publisher Breitkopf, Adelung obtained a prestigious post as a director of the Dresden library.

Adelung devoted himself to the production of a comprehensive dictionary, *Versuch eines vollständigen grammatisch-kritischen Wörterbuches der hochdeutschen Mundart* (Attempt at a complete grammatical-critical dictionary of High German speech; 1774–86), that presented various facets of the development and structure of German language: history, grammar, word formation, stylistics, and spelling. He also contributed a pioneering piece of cultural history entitled *Versuch einer Geschichte der Cultur des menschlichen Geschlechts* (History of the culture of the human race; 1782). At the time of his death, Adelung was writing *Mithridates, oder allgemeine Sprachenkunde* (Mithridates, or universal science of language, published 1806–17). The work offered translations of the Lord's Prayer in more than 500 languages. By comparing these translations, Adelung formulated some general rules about the formation and development of human language. The work was completed by Johann Severin Vater and contained contributions on the Basque language written by Wilhelm von Humboldt.

Adelung's research and publications played a major role in the elevation of German into a literary language. A highpoint of the German Enlightenment (AUFKLÄRUNG), this development helped to create the atmosphere in which later literary romanticism flourished.

aesthetics A branch of philosophy that studies beauty and the processes by which it is created and recognized. The word is derived from the Greek *aisthetikos*, which refers to sensory perceptions. The ENLIGHTENMENT produced considerable ferment and novelty in these areas. Its legacy includes the erection of aesthetics into a separate discipline within philosophy; new emphasis on the human act of creating; a rethinking of the relations among REASON, feeling, and imagination in creative processes; and new definitions of the concepts of the SUBLIME and of GENIUS. The term *aesthetics* was actually coined during the Enlightenment by the Prussian philosopher Alexander Gottlieb BAUMGARTEN.

However new the discipline of aesthetics, its basic subject matter had been treated in ancient Greek and Roman philosophy as well as in later systems of thought. The Enlightenment inherited two different 17th-century traditions regarding aesthetic matters. One tradition stemmed from French RATIONALISM and was encapsulated in the forms of NEOCLASSICISM. The second tradition grew from British EMPIRICISM and raised aesthetic questions in the context of PSYCHOLOGY and MORAL PHILOSOPHY. Both traditions sought to develop theories of artistic form based in NATURE, although the definitions given to that term varied dramatically. Both also tended to think of beauty as something with objective existence outside the personal experience of the observer. The substance given these major themes, however, sharply distinguished the two traditions, giving rise to conflicts that enlightened thinkers later tried to resolve.

As the period of the Enlightenment opened in France, an intellectual quarrel was raging in the realm of aesthetics. Dubbed the QUARREL BETWEEN THE ANCIENTS AND THE MODERNS, this dispute dwelt on the question of whether the rigid forms of ancient Latin literary classics were preferable to modern, less highly structured forms.

The aesthetic ideals allegedly represented by ancient classics had been formulated by Nicolas Boileau (1636–1711) in his *L'Art poétique* (The Art of poetry; 1674). Inspired by the idea that objective laws order everything in the universe according to mathematical REASON, Boileau spelled out a set of rules for the production of poetic works. Since the norms of beauty were derived from ancient classical works, Boileau's system came to be known as French CLASSICISM or neoclassicism.

This style raised the Cartesian principles of clarity, order, and simplicity into standards for poetic creation. The job of the artist consisted of using his reasoning ability to produce works that imitated the splendid, serene, rational structure of nature. Beauty was thus associated with the exercise of the intellect and with orderly structures akin to mathematics. Literary classicism also raised the idea of unity—of time, of place, and of action—to a central position in composition and stressed that good writing required clear thinking. Proper subject matter was drawn from antiquity; hence the concentration on themes drawn from mythology and from other Greek and Latin classics.

The aesthetic ideals of classicism received official sanction during the reign of King LOUIS XIV. Following the theory of ABSOLUTISM, he expanded his authority to cover the arts by establishing royal academies devoted to upholding classical principles.

In the meantime, British empiricism was giving rise to aesthetic theories that concentrated on the primacy of experience in the perception of beauty. In addition, British empiricists gave imagination a role in creative processes and stressed the importance of subjective feelings in our experiences of beauty. The foundations for this approach had been laid by Francis BACON, Thomas HOBBES, and John LOCKE.

Bacon had assigned responsibility for poetry to the mental faculty of imagination; in contrast, he had assigned philosophy to the faculty of reason and history to memory. Hobbes and Locke had laid the foundations for a psychology that made sensory experience the source of all basic ideas. Since sensory experience was easily equated with feeling, the groundwork was laid for aesthetic theories that centered on the emotional causes of our ideas of beauty.

The first decades of the 18th century produced a new approach in the works of Anthony Ashley Cooper, third earl of SHAFTESBURY. This approach laid the groundwork for later treatments of aesthetics by the German writers Gotthold Ephraim LESSING, Johann Gottfried HERDER, and Immanuel KANT. For Shaftesbury, the primary issue in aesthetics lay neither in the rational analysis of objective beauty nor in the discussion of the subjective, emotional sources of our experiences of beauty. Rather, he stressed that our sense of beauty derives from the exercise of the mental faculty called intuition.

Intuition grasps reality in immediate, whole terms, thereby giving us a special type of knowledge about the world. In recognizing beauty through intuitive processes, people gain an intellectual and understanding of the inner structure of the universe, but the mental processes followed in arriving at this knowledge differ from those used in rational analysis or in sensory experience.

In addition to giving intuition a major role in creative processes, Shaftesbury introduced two additional concepts of central importance to enlightened aesthetics: He defined beauty as disinterested pleasure, and he stressed the genius involved in artistic creation.

Shaftesbury proposed that harmony underlies both beauty and virtue; thus, aesthetics and ethics were inextricably linked. People perceive harmony through the operation of a special mental faculty that he called the "moral sense." Francis HUTCHESON, the Scottish moral philosopher, incorporated Shaftesbury's ideas into his *An Inquiry Into the Origin of Our Ideas of Beauty and Virtue* (1725). This book helped spread Shaftesbury's ideas to a wide audience. Hutcheson translated Shaftesbury's "moral sense" into the "inner sense of beauty." His work provided the foundations for the Scottish school of moral philosophy and aesthetics whose major enlightened figures were Adam FERGUSON, Lord Kames, and David HUME.

During the early 18th century, French writers were developing a critical stance toward neoclassicism. *La manière de bien penser dans les ouvrages de l'esprit* (The way of thinking clearly in the works of the mind; 1687) by Dominique Bouhours suggested that aesthetic value lies not in precise, distinct creations, but in works based on a wealth of unusual mental associations. Boileau had always linked beauty to correctness or propriety, giving it a moral dimension. Bouhours insisted that a spirit of sensitivity (*délicatesse*) was more important. Such sensitivity perceives not only clarity but also contrasts between dark and light. It encourages various ways of expressing ideas, freeing art from the restrictions imposed by neoclassic rules.

Abbé Jean-Baptiste DU BOS developed Bouhours's line of thought in his *Réflections critiques sur la poésie et la peinture* (Critical reflections on poetry and painting; 1719). He made subjective experience and introspection central to creating and to perceiving beauty. He also proposed that certain subjects require special genres for artistic expression. No single form can represent the wealth of artistic insight available to humankind.

These approaches to questions of beauty helped to create the cult of SENSIBILITY, the aesthetic forms and associated values of the 18th-century ROCOCO style. Rococo style had manifestations in art (painting, sculpture, and architecture), MUSIC, and LITERATURE (the novel of sentiment). Its artistic productions aimed at delighting the senses, thereby producing feelings of pleasure. But the cult of sensibility also stimulated a second type of creation, one that sought to serve utilitarian or education purposes. In these instances, the arousal of feelings was designed to produce sympathetic responses in observers. Identification with the situation of a literary character, for example, could result in intensified awareness and insight on the part of individuals, helping them to understand some moral issue.

In the lands of German linguistic heritage, a struggle emerged in the 1720s over the dominance of French classical aesthetics. The ground was broken by Johann Jakob BODMER and Johann Jakob BREITINGER, two Swiss critics and journalists who launched an attack on the powerful German critic Johann Christoph GOTTSCHED. Bodmer and Breitinger defended the roles of imagination, emotion, and enthusiasm in the expression of creative genius against Gottsched's claims for the importance of reason.

Toward the middle of the 18th century, in a period of notable vitality, new themes and concepts began to appear in aesthetics. The theories associated with neoclassicism continued to have supporters, even during the period when such art was unpopular, and, by the last decades of the 18th century, were revitalized in the realms of art and music. But many writers were struggling to find new ways of thinking about creative processes and products.

The Prussian philosopher Alexander Gottlieb Baumgarten began systematizing the study of aesthetics, transforming it into a branch of philosophy. A disciple of the philosophers Gottfried Wilhelm LEIBNIZ and Christian WOLFF, Baumgarten sought to construct a logic of the imagination. He believed that imagination plays a central role in creative processes and wanted to explain how it operates. The *Aesthetica* (Aesthetics; 1750–58) presented his analysis in a series of precise definitions and logical propositions. Baumgarten retained the Leibnizian notion that the imagination provides a lower form of understanding than reason; but he gave the imagination a new dignity as the central factor in creative acts. The imagination yields intuitive knowledge, an immediate grasping of the whole. This whole cannot be broken down by rational analysis (reason) into parts without losing some of its essence. And, indeed, no need exists to break down intuition in this way. Art draws on intuitive, imaginative knowledge in order to convey both intellectual truths and emotional impact.

Until this period, aesthetics had dealt only with the concept of beauty. But at midcentury, aesthetic theorists separated the idea of the sublime from the idea of beauty, providing the former with a distinct theoretical formulation. The new theory of the sublime received its earliest statement in *A Philosophical Enquiry into the Origin of Our Ideas of the Sublime and Beautiful* (1757) by Edmund BURKE. Burke distinguished the beautiful from the sublime on the grounds that our experiences of these two artistic forms are different. Beauty, as originally conceived by Shaftesbury, excites feelings of pleasure untainted by desire. But the sublime excites feelings of horror and intense awareness of pain or danger. Burke believed that both beauty and the sublime exercise power by producing physiological responses in the observer. Beauty, Burke thought, relaxes the solid parts of the body, whereas the sublime produces tension.

Writers such as Denis DIDEROT, Claude-Adrien HELVÉTIUS, Johann Wolfgang von GOETHE, Friedrich SCHILLER, and Johann Gottfried Herder also began exploring the concept of genius, raising it to central importance in creative processes. They struggled to define the meaning of genius in terms both of historical example and human nature. In Helvétius's hands, genius became a product of EDUCATION and environment. Diderot defined it as a function of heredity and of the material processes of the mind. For Herder, Schiller, and Goethe, however, the possession of genius provided the guarantee of human FREEDOM, enabling individuals to rise above the confines of conventional wisdom. Geniuses acting by creating revealed the divine aspects of human nature; they resembled God, the creator of all.

Gotthold Ephraim Lessing contributed significantly toward establishing the notion of freedom in aesthetic pursuits. Lessing constructed his position from ideas that were already current. Nevertheless, he joined them in a particularly effective and novel manner, whose influence was acknowledged by Goethe and his generation. As a critic, Lessing conceived his role as a constructive one; he sought to provoke creative individuals to explore the possibilities of their art forms. His most influential work was *Laokoon, oder, über die Grenzen der Malerei und Poesie* (Laocoon, or, over the boundaries between painting and poetry; 1766), better known simply as LAOKOON. In this work, he criticized the neoclassicism espoused by the art historian Johann Joachim WINCKELMANN. Lessing maintained that Winckelmann's ideals of noble simplicity and quiet grandeur might be valid for painting, but that they would not serve the needs of poetry. The poet must concern himself with the passions and with emotion-driven action. Lessing also explored the relationship between genius and rules, examined the significance of symbols in arts CLASSIFICATION, and developed a doctrine of "mixed sensations."

Aesthetic theorists divided over the question of whether beauty and other aesthetic qualities have an objective existence outside human experience. Shaftesbury and Hutcheson, as well as the neoclassicists and empiricists, had tended to believe that objective beauty exists. David Hume, however, had suggested that our judgments of beauty and morality are subjective, dependent on individual preferences, cultural factors, and other environmental factors. Nevertheless, he had recognized that people often agree about what constitutes beauty. If the experience of beauty was subjective, then aesthetic theorists were faced with the challenge of explaining the causes of agreement. Diderot had attempted a compromise that rooted both subjectivity and objectivity in the material structures and operations of the brain.

The works of Immanuel Kant, appearing at the close of the Enlightenment, attempted to create a viable synthesis from the many conflicting strands that had appeared during the 18th century. Kant addressed aesthetics in his *Kritik der Urteilskraft* (Critique of judgment; 1790), the third of his three volumes examining the foundations of human knowledge. Kant believed that the experience of beauty is subjective, based in the pleasurable feelings a beautiful object calls forth. But, because these feelings involve a disinterested delight (he borrowed here from Shaftesbury), we think of them as universal, shared by all people. In contrast, if these pleasurable feelings are accompanied by desire for the beautiful object, then subjective self-interest is clearly involved; we cannot, therefore, assume that our experience is shared by everyone else.

In aesthetics, as with other disciplines, the Enlightenment produced a rich array of ideas. These ideas arose out of the perceived conflict between reason and feeling; out of discussions about the limits of human knowledge; and out of the variety of definitions that were given to nature and the natural. In the end, in order to resolve the tensions, the realm of discussion was shifted to new territory. In the place of reason and feeling, the concept of intuition became central. Artistic expression was claimed

as a specifically human activity, valid strictly on those terms. Thus, it no longer was necessary to speak of its relation to the universal truths and whole knowledge known only to God. Finally, as art became a specifically human form of expression, artists gained a freedom from rules and necessities that had hindered their predecessors. The Enlightenment thus imposed important questions that would be taken up in ROMANTICISM and eventually developed in different directions.

See also BAROQUE STYLE; ENGLISH GARDEN; HAMANN; INTUITION AND IMAGINATION; PALLADIAN STYLE.

Further reading: Giancarlo Carabelli, *On Hume and Eighteenth-Century Aesthetics: The Philosopher on a Swing* (New York: Peter Lang, 1995); W. J. Hipple, *The Beautiful, The Sublime and the Picturesque in Eighteenth-Century British Aesthetic Theory* (Carbondale: Southern Illinois University Press, 1957); Robert Edward Norton, *Beautiful Soul: Aesthetic Morality in the Eighteenth Century* (Ithaca, N.Y.: Cornell University Press, 1995).

affinity chemistry An influential form of 18th-century chemistry that was ultimately discredited by the developments of the CHEMICAL REVOLUTION at the end of the century. Affinity chemistry was a chemistry of elements that recognized many more than the traditional four elements—earth, air, fire, and water—of Aristotelian-based approaches. It postulated that the different elements had inherently varying degrees of attraction for one another. These attractions helped to explain why certain elements combined readily and others resisted combination. The 18th-century affinity chemists produced tables of affinity that showed these relationships. The German novelist and scientist Johann Wolfgang von GOETHE used affinity as the central organizing force in his novel *Die Wahlverwandschaften* (*Elective Affinities*; 1809).

Major affinity chemists were Torbern Olof BERGMAN, Carl Wilhelm SCHEELE, Étienne-François Geoffroy, Guillaume François Rouelle, Pierre-Joseph Macquer, Johann Georg Gmelin, and Claude Louis BERTHOLLET. Scholars debate whether Antoine LAVOISIER should be treated as an affinity chemist.

Age of Reason, The A two-part tract ("Part One," 1794; "Part Two," 1795) analyzing RELIGION; written by the English-American political philosopher and propagandist Thomas PAINE. Paine, a supporter of the moderate phase of the FRENCH REVOLUTION, was living in PARIS when he was imprisoned during the Reign of Terror. He wrote "Part One" of *The Age of Reason* from his prison cell. The American poet and writer Joel BARLOW smuggled the manuscript from the prison and oversaw its publication in FRANCE.

"Part One" advocates DEISM, a form of NATURAL RELIGION that was popular during the ENLIGHTENMENT. Using common rational arguments, Paine attacked revealed religion, especially in its Christian form. He also discredited miracles and suggested that Christian fervor had fueled many atrocities in history. Paine preferred a rational religion rooted in the REASON and law that underlie the structure of the universe. This religion recognized God as the creator of the universe, but denied that he played an active role in human history. Paine also advocated religious TOLERATION as the only reasonable policy for states.

These arguments caused little stir in France or the UNITED STATES, but met with hostility in ENGLAND. The Americans had recently protected religious freedom by creating in 1787 a constitution that separated church from state. The French had recently abolished the ties of their state with ROMAN CATHOLICISM. But the English remained officially wedded to the Anglican Church; consequently, government censors in England banned "Part One" of *The Age of Reason*, outlawing both its publication and possession.

Paine published "Part Two" of *The Age of Reason* in 1795. He continued his use of reason as a critical tool against religion. This time, the Bible received his attention. Book by book, Paine examined the Bible, pointing out difficulties with its stories and positions. "Part Two" created a firestorm of protest in the United States, and Paine was accused of ATHEISM.

See also BIBLICAL CRITICISM; SEPARATION OF CHURCH AND STATE.

alchemy   An ancient approach to medicine and chemistry, reformulated in the Renaissance, that continued to contribute to certain strands of 18th-century thought.

Theories of alchemy were numerous and varied in content, but in general, they exhibited two major interests. One type of alchemy, that which underlay the IATRO-CHEMISTRY developed by Paracelsus in the late Renaissance, stressed the search for a universal chemical medicine (panacea). The second type stressed the search for the fundamental principles of matter symbolized in the quest for the philosopher's stone and the attempts to transmute, that is, to change, base metals into gold. All forms tended to be practiced in a culture of secrecy that helped to perpetuate official loathing for and accusations against its adherents. Alchemy was often associated in reality and in popular perceptions with natural magic or with radical religious, political, and social visions of the world. As a result, its practitioners were frequently condemned as heretics by both Roman Catholic and Protestant theologians.

Throughout the ENLIGHTENMENT, alchemy inspired certain avenues of thought. In the late 17th century, as the threads of the early Enlightenment began to coalesce, it played an important role in the scientific thought of such major figures as Isaac NEWTON and perhaps Gottfried Wilhelm LEIBNIZ. The German chemist Georg Ernst

STAHL espoused alchemy as a young man but later abandoned it.

In the middle of the 18th century, when the rational forms of the Enlightenment began to yield their dominant position, inquiries into irrational traditions inspired by alchemy began to play an important role. But their influence was felt less in science than in radical political and social theories and in popular forms of entertainment. Thus, alchemical notions appear in 18th-century Rosicrucianism and certain forms of Freemasonry. They also were manipulated by adventures and charlatans such as the conte di CAGLIOSTRO, Giovanni CASANOVA, the comte de SAINT-GERMAIN, and Louis-Claude de SAINT-MARTIN. In addition, evidence suggests that the German novelist, poet, and scientist Johann Wolfgang von GOETHE, the enlightened radical Lutheran theologian Johann Salomo SEMLER, and the Pietist Friedrich Christoph OETINGER all inquired into various alchemical theories and practices. In short, the alchemical vision of the universe survived through the Enlightenment, helping to shape some of its most novel ideas.

See also FREEMASONS; HERMETICISM; ROSICRUCIANS; SECRET SOCIETIES.

Alembert, Jean Le Rond d' (1717–1783) *French philosophe, mathematician, and writer, who with Denis Diderot edited the* Encyclopédie

Jean Le Rond d'Alembert was the illegitimate son of the salon hostess Madame de Tencin and of Louis Camus, chevalier Destouches-Canon. Following the customs of the era, Madame de Tencin abandoned her unwanted infant on the steps of the baptistry of the Cathedral of Notre-Dame in PARIS. Since the baptistry was called the Church of Saint-Jean le Rond, the infant was given that name. He later assumed the name d'Alembert.

The chevalier Destouches-Canon assisted in placing his child with Madame Rousseau, the wife of a glassmaker. D'Alembert thus grew up in humble circumstances on rue Michel-le-Comte, in the artisan quarter of the Marais district. He retained lifelong ties to these social circumstances, developing a philosophy that transformed the humble life devoid of luxury into a positive social trait for an intellectual.

Madame de Tencin chose to remain aloof from her son, but the chevalier Destouches remained involved, providing for his son's education and leaving him an inheritance that provided a modest annuity.

D'Alembert studied at the prestigious Collège des Quatres-Nations operated by the JESUITS. He received a degree in law in 1738 but never practiced that profession. Instead, he devoted himself to MATHEMATICS AND MECHANICS, rapidly launching a successful career. The Academy of Sciences in Paris received him in 1741 as an adjunct in the astronomy section and, beginning in 1745, provided him with a coveted pension.

Portrait of d'Alembert. Jean Le Rond d'Alembert, a mathematician and member of the French Academy of Sciences, worked with Denis Diderot as an editor of the famed *Encyclopédie*. D'Alembert wrote the *Discours préliminaire* (Preliminary Discourse) for the project, outlining its goals and intellectual structure. *(Courtesy New York Public Library)*

D'Alembert devoted the early years of his career to calculus and to terrestrial and celestial mechanics. His *Traité de dynamique* (Treatise on dynamics; 1743), *Traité de l'équilibre et du mouvement des fluides* (Treatise on the equilibrium and movement of fluids; 1744), *Réflexions sur la cause générale des vents* (Reflections on the general causes of winds; 1747), *Recherches sur les cordes vibrantes* (Research on vibrating strings; 1747), and *Recherches sur la précession des équinoxes et sur la nutation de la terre* (Research on the precession of the equinoxes and on the nutation of the Earth; 1749) established him as an impressive presence in the Academy of Sciences. He eventually became a powerful protector of young mathematicians, helping to launch the careers of the marquis de CONDORCET, Joseph-Louis LAGRANGE, and the marquis de LAPLACE.

The *Traité de dynamique* gave mathematical expressions for three laws of motion identified by d'Alembert. The first law was the same as Newton's first law (the law of inertia). D'Alembert's second and third laws dealt respectively with the analysis of motion by means of a parallelogram and with the problem of equilibrium. This work also presented a concept of motion and momentum, and a method for their analysis, that has acquired the name "d'Alembert's principle."

The *Traité de dynamique* also addressed the famous *vis viva* controversy. In this scientific quarrel, partisans of Newton and Leibniz argued over the proper mathematical expression for the magnitude of a force. D'Alembert attempted to resolve the issue by pointing out that both expressions work but in different instances, and that, at best, the concept of force did not refer to a real thing but only to a set of observed relations between bodies.

D'Alembert began attending the salon of Madame GEOFFRIN in the middle 1740s. His comic imitations of Comédie Française actors and witty conversation made him immediately popular. He also began to frequent the gatherings held by Madame DU DEFFAND, where in 1754 he met Julie de LESPINASSE. D'Alembert and Mademoiselle de Lespinasse developed a lifelong devotion to each other and shared quarters for several years. When Madame Du Deffand and Mademoiselle de Lespinasse quarreled in 1760, d'Alembert left the Du Deffand salon with his friend and assisted in establishing a rival gathering. He nursed Mademoiselle de Lespinasse throughout her illness with smallpox, and her death in 1776 caused him much grief.

The patronage of Madame Du Deffand significantly helped d'Alembert; she, for example, secured his appointment to the prestigious Académie Française (French Academy of Sciences) in 1754. At the time, d'Alembert was already a member of the BERLIN ACADEMY (1747) and would eventually obtain an associate membership in the Swedish Academy (1756).

D'Alembert was invited by DIDEROT in 1750 to assume joint editorship of the ENCYCLOPÉDIE, a position he maintained until his fear of French censorship caused him to abandon the task. His abrupt resignation (precise date unknown) was triggered by the furor over his article "Genève" in volume seven of the *Encyclopédie* (published October 1757). Diderot noted the event in a letter of February 1758 to VOLTAIRE.

Diderot had charged d'Alembert at the beginning of the project with preparing a preface for the *Encyclopédie*. In the resulting *Discours préliminaire*, published in 1751 with volume one of the *Encyclopédie*, d'Alembert outlined the history of human thought and provided a chart derived from Francis BACON, illustrating the relationships among the various sciences and arts. D'Alembert believed that human thought had been marked by PROGRESS since the Renaissance and predicted its continual development through the discovery of new sciences.

The *Discours préliminaire* also presented the theory of sensation PSYCHOLOGY that had been developed by John LOCKE and expanded by Étienne-Bonnot de CONDILLAC. Following the principles of this psychological theory, d'Alembert claimed that both scientific knowledge and moral truth derive from physical perceptions, emotions, and feelings.

As he grew older, d'Alembert began to doubt that human knowledge could continue growing indefinitely, and he also embraced a degree of SKEPTICISM regarding the ability of the human mind to know things with certainty. He explored aspects of EPISTEMOLOGY (the philosophy of knowledge), grounding truth in REASON, but later he decided that human recognition of some truths might also require some type of inspirational experience.

D'Alembert pursued aspects of aesthetics, especially in LITERATURE and MUSIC. Again, he preferred that both art forms have thorough grounding in rules based on reason: he admired classical forms of composition because of their ordered adherence to specific compositional rules. In music, however, he yearned to see harmonic structures expand beyond the strict forms spelled out in the treatises of his friend Jean-Philippe RAMEAU. D'Alembert's position, then was ambivalent; he called for art forms that would be useful, true, and also pleasing to the senses.

In 1752, while in the middle of the *Encyclopédie* publication, D'Alembert received an invitation from the Prussian king FREDERICK II (THE GREAT) to assume the presidency of the Berlin Academy. D'Alembert declined, but nevertheless received an annual pension of 2,000 livres from Frederick. He had the first edition of his *Mélanges de littérature et de philosophie* (Miscellaneous works of literature and philosophy; 1753) published in BERLIN. He met Frederick in 1755 at Wesel and traveled to Berlin for a longer visit in 1763.

In 1762, d'Alembert refused a post in SAINT PETERSBURG as tutor to the son of the Russian empress CATHERINE II (THE GREAT). He responded to the invitation by dedicating the 1763 edition of his *Mélanges de littérature et de philosophie,* and the 1762 version of his *Eléments de musique théorique et pratique suivant les principes de M. Rameau, éclaircis, dévelopées et simplifiés* (Elements of music theory and practice, clarified, developed, and simplified; 1752, 1762, 1766, 1772, and 1779), to Catherine. With both Frederick the Great and Catherine the Great, d'Alembert maintained a steady correspondence.

In 1772, d'Alembert began his long years of service as perpetual secretary of the French Academy, writing the customary eulogies of its members. These were published in his six-volume *Histoire des membres de l'Académie* (History of the members of the academy; 1785–87).

D'Alembert left a lasting mark on the ENLIGHTENMENT through his many activities. His contributions to mathematics and mechanics extended the power of calculus as a tool for expressing physical laws, and his patronage of other mathematicians provided valuable services to the profession. The *Encyclopédie* project bore his individual imprint, especially since its general program first reached the reading public through his *Discours préliminaire.* Finally, as the perpetual secretary of the French Academy and as a frequent guest at various Parisian salons, d'Alembert participated in the important social life of the enlightened Paris, developing and spreading his ideas through conversation as well as in print.

In addition to the books and papers already cited, the following works by d'Alembert must be noted: *Essai sur la société des gens de lettres avec les grands* (Essay on the association of men of letters with great men; 1753), a discussion of the negative effects of aristocratic patronage on intellectual freedom; *Recherches sur différents points importants du système du monde* (Research on different important points in the system of the world; 1754–56), an investigation on the three-body problem (the problem of the mathematical relations among three heavenly bodies all acting with gravitational force on each other); *Essai sur les éléments de philosophie* (Essay on the elements of philosophy; 1759); *Mémoire sur la théorie mathématique de l'inoculation* (Memoir on the mathematical theory of inoculation; 1761), an inquiry into the application of probability theory in evaluating risks in INOCULATION; and *Eclaircissements sur la déstruction des jésuites* (Clarifications on the destruction of the Jesuits; 1765) published anonymously.

See also FRENCH ACADEMY OF SCIENCES.

Further reading: Jean Le Rond d'Alembert, *Preliminary Discourse to the Encyclopedia of Diderot,* tr. and ed. Richard N. Schwab (Indianapolis: Bobbs-Merrill, 1963); Thomas L. Hankins, *Jean D'Alembert: Science and the Enlightenment* (New York: Taylor & Francis, 1990); Terence M. Russell and Ann-Marie Thornton, *Gardens and Landscapes in the Encyclopedie of Diderot and D'Alembert: The Letterpress Articles and Selected Engravings* (Burlington, Vt.: Ashgate, 1999).

Algarotti, Francesco (1712–1764) *Italian writer whose career illustrates the important role played in the Enlightenment by popularizing writers who spread knowledge of contemporary philosophy and the arts to general readers*
A native of VENICE, Francesco Algarotti studied mathematics and philosophy at the University of Bologna, then pursued further studies in ROME, PARIS, LONDON, and SAINT PETERSBURG.

Algarotti supported the physics of Isaac NEWTON and contributed to the dissemination of Newtonian ideas in Europe. His popularization, *Il Newtonianismo per le dame ovvero dialoghi sopra la luce e i colori* (Newtonianism for women, or dialogues on light and on colors; 1737), attracted the attention of VOLTAIRE, who assisted Algarotti in obtaining a position with FREDERICK II (THE GREAT) OF PRUSSIA. Algarotti and Frederick became close friends and corresponded regularly with each other after Algarotti's departure from Prussia in 1742.

After five years in Saxony (1742–47), where he wrote essays for art exhibitions and opera openings, Algarotti returned to the Italian peninsula. After his death in 1764, Frederick had a tombstone for him erected in Pisa. The inscription read "Hic jacet Ovidii aemulus et Newtoni disciplus" (Here lies the emulator of Ovid and the disciple of Newton).

See also ITALY.

American Philosophical Society   A scientific society founded by Benjamin FRANKLIN in PHILADELPHIA in 1743 and incorporated as the American Philosophical Society in 1780. For Europeans, the American Philosophical Society was the recognized center of American activities in the sciences.

The organization grew out of the artisans' Junto, a debating society that Franklin had established in 1727. Junto members were artisans concerned with the implications of political issues for their businesses and social positions.

Prominent members of the American Philosophical Society included Franklin, Thomas JEFFERSON, and David RITTENHOUSE.

See also SCIENTIFIC ACADEMIES.

American Revolution   War fought from 1775 to 1783 by 13 British colonies in North America to secure their independence from Great Britain. Several European countries—FRANCE, SPAIN, and the UNITED PROVINCES OF THE NETHERLANDS—joined the American colonists in their struggle. The war concluded with British recognition of the new UNITED STATES OF AMERICA.

Colonial desires for independence grew from escalating economic, social, and political tensions over British policies in North America. Until the 1730s, the colonies functioned politically in a semi-independent fashion. Several colonies enjoyed the right of selecting their own governors and legislators. In the 1730s, however, the British government began tightening its control of the colonies. It replaced some old colonial charters with new ones that rescinded the right to select governors. Then, after the 1763 British victory in the French and Indian Wars, 10,000 British soldiers were placed in frontier garrisons, and the colonists were required to pay their bills. Furthermore, the British government turned to the colonies as a source of extra revenue to offset the large debts it had incurred during the war.

These events provided the background for the famous colonial rebellion against taxation, which began in 1765, when the British Parliament passed the Stamp Act. American colonists protested against taxation without consent and rioted. Parliament withdrew the stamp tax but passed the Declaratory Act (1766) in which it claimed far-reaching powers over the colonies. In 1767, Parliament attempted to enforce these powers by imposing the Townshend taxes on colonial imports of lead, glass, paint, paper, and tea. Colonists responded with boycotts against these goods and with continued political protests. The so-called Boston Massacre (1770), an event of great symbolic impor-

Portrait of George III, king of England. As king from 1760 until 1820, George III supported policies in the American colonies that precipitated the American Revolution. *(Courtesy New York Public Library)*

tance to the colonists, occurred during this period. Parliament yielded once again, withdrawing the Townshend Acts. In 1773, however, it authorized the EAST INDIA COMPANY to collect a new duty on colonial tea imports. Protests and riots, including such well-known events as the Boston Tea Party (1773), resulted.

The British Parliament decided to limit the freedom of unruly colonists in Massachusetts by changing the colony's charter. In the Act for Better Regulating the Government of Massachusetts Bay, the Parliament restricted the powers of the colonial representative assembly while strengthening those of the governor. The conflict between colonists and Britain thus escalated over issues of political rights and liberties.

At this point, the American colonists called the First Continental Congress (1774) into session. Its members demanded the repeal of the so-called Coercive or Intolerable Acts—the Tea Act and the Act for Better Regulating the Government of Massachusetts Bay. Tensions with Britain continued to escalate until finally, in April 1775, the first skirmishes of the American Revolution broke out at Lexington and Concord in Massachusetts.

In the years leading to this event, American colonial leaders drew on the European ENLIGHTENMENT for political theories and principles. The constitutional ideas of John LOCKE, MONTESQUIEU, Jean-Jacques ROUSSEAU, Samuel PUFENDORF, Hugo Grotius, Emmerich de VATTEL, and Jean-Jacques BURLAMAQUI joined with the tradition of civic humanism in republics, with NATURAL RIGHTS theory, with the legal interpretations of Sir William BLACKSTONE, and with ideals cherished by English DISSENTERS (the Puritans in America), to create a potent political program. The Scottish Enlightenment contributed a new vision of human nature, economic activity, and history in works by David HUME, Adam SMITH, Thomas REID, Adam FERGUSON, and Francis HUTCHESON. All these intellectual strands merged in the works of writers such as Benjamin FRANKLIN, Thomas PAINE, John ADAMS, Thomas JEFFERSON, John JAY, Samuel Adams, Richard PRICE, and Joseph PRIESTLEY to create theoretical support for practical political claims.

The Second Continental Congress (1775) met to organize the colonies for protracted war with Britain. George Washington received the command of the Continental Army. A committee consisting of Jefferson, Adams, Franklin, Robert R. Livingston, and Roger Sherman drafted the document that became the DECLARATION OF INDEPENDENCE. It was formally adopted in July 1776.

The battles of the American Revolution occurred throughout the North American colonies. Both the British and the Americans won important battles. But in 1777, the victory of American soldiers fighting under General Horatio Gates at the battle of Saratoga, New York, tipped the balance in favor of the rebels by convincing the French to enter the war openly as allies of the Americans.

The French fleet arrived in North American waters in 1778. In 1781, the combined action of this French fleet and of French and American soldiers brought victory at Yorktown, Virginia. The English commander, General Charles Cornwallis, surrendered to the Americans and French on October 19, 1781. A preliminary peace treaty was signed in November 1782. With the final Treaty of Paris (1783), Great Britain formally recognized the independence of the United States of America.

In the aftermath of the Revolution, American leaders set about incorporating the principles of the Enlightenment into the constitution of the new nation. The UNITED STATES CONSTITUTION structured the government according to principles such as the SEPARATION OF POWERS and religious TOLERATION. It formally established a SEPARATION OF CHURCH AND STATE. The DECLARATION OF INDEPENDENCE had spoken of inalienable human rights such as life, liberty, and the pursuit of HAPPINESS, all conceived within the context of enlightened theories. The American Revolution thus stood as the first successful, broad political reform in which principles of the Enlightenment provided part of the underlying inspiration.

The events of the American Revolution created great excitement and ferment in Europe. In salons, coffeehouses, reading clubs, lodges of FREEMASONS, and UNIVERSITIES, the American experiment was discussed and analyzed. The periodical PRESS published commentaries and reports by both European and American writers.

PHILOSOPHES such as Brissot, CONDORCET, Hume, Smith, and DIDEROT actively supported American actions while Thomas Paine, Joel BARLOW, and Benjamin Franklin helped also to popularize the cause. The Dutch reformers known as the Patriots drew actively on the American example in designing their proposed constitutional reforms. Even Edmund BURKE, the future enemy of the FRENCH REVOLUTION, supported the American rebels. It seemed to these observers that the American Revolution was validating their enlightened ideals and dreams about human potential. The American Revolution, then, not only gave birth to the United States, but served also as a symbolic and practical testimony to the power of the Enlightenment.

See also COLONIALISM; EQUALITY; EPICUREAN PHILOSOPHY; FREEDOM; MABLY; POLITICAL THEORY; SOCIAL INSTITUTIONS OF THE ENLIGHTENMENT; WASHINGTON.

Amsterdam Primary city of the Netherlands; present-day capital of the province of North Holland, Amsterdam lies on an inlet of the North Sea. The city is actually built on land reclaimed from the sea, linked by concentric rings of canals. The canals were products of the great rational urban planning projects of the 17th century.

At the beginning of the 18th century, Amsterdam had close to 100,000 inhabitants. Like most European cities, it benefited from the relatively long period of peace and from the associated prosperity that marked the 18th century. By the end of the century, the city had grown to about 221,000 inhabitants.

Shipping, finance, and commerce made Amsterdam a prosperous economic center. The powerful Dutch East India Company and the Bank of Amsterdam had headquarters in the city. Although Amsterdam had dominated world trade and finance in the 17th century, it slowly ceded that position to LONDON during the 18th century.

Religious TOLERATION and relatively lax censorship made Amsterdam a center of book publishing. Works denied publication in FRANCE or other European countries found both sponsors and publishers in Amsterdam. In this manner, the city played a crucial role in spreading the ideas of the ENLIGHTENMENT throughout Europe by making them available in printed form to the general reading public.

When, in 1685, LOUIS XIV of France revoked the Edict of Nantes that had granted limited toleration to French Calvinists (HUGUENOTS), thousands of them fled their homes and settled in the Calvinist UNITED PROVINCES OF THE NETHERLANDS. The city of Amsterdam received an infusion of talented, prosperous merchants and businessmen as a result.

Amsterdam was one center of the small, idiosyncratic Dutch Enlightenment and, also, of the revolutionary Dutch Patriot movement.

See also PUBLISHING.

ancien régime French term meaning "old regime." It refers specifically to the social and political order in FRANCE prior to the FRENCH REVOLUTION. The ancien régime consisted of a monarchy supported by a corporate social structure. French law did not recognize individual rights, but rather the rights and privileges of specifically organized groups (corporations). The concept of EQUALITY before the law had no relevance in the old French system. The corporations included the three legal estates (clergy, nobility, and bourgeoisie), organizations such as the law courts, guilds, and universities, and many other groups.

Each group held special legal privileges that were theoretically granted in accordance with the duties they performed. But in reality, by the 18th century, the relationship between duty and privilege had thoroughly broken down, and the corporate system was seen by many PHILOSOPHES as a hindrance to political justice and PROGRESS.

During the 17th century, the French kings had consolidated much political power into their own hands, or into the hands of their ministers. The reign of LOUIS XIV saw the climax of this centralizing process. Bolstered by a POLITICAL THEORY known as the DIVINE RIGHT OF KINGS, he tried to convert the French monarchy into a true system of ABSOLUTISM. But his efforts to extend his powers had enemies in many quarters. Even at the height of his reign, Louis XIV could not fully control the lawyers and judges of his PARLEMENTS (royal courts of justice), nor could he enforce certain tax reforms in his kingdom. His successors, LOUIS XV and LOUIS XVI, met with even greater difficulty.

Opposition to absolutism stemmed in part from the various corporate groups of the ancien régime. *Parlements* played the greatest role, but they were not alone in blocking monarchical reforms aimed at streamlining, rationalizing, and extending central control.

The successful opposition to royal policies stemmed at least partly from the custom of selling offices in the royal bureaucracy. Venality (*venalité*), as this system was called, allowed officeholders to purchase an office for a considerable sum of money, to hold it as private PROPERTY, to sell it, and in some cases, to pass it on to legal heirs. Instituted originally as a measure for filling the royal coffers, venality bred a host of political problems for the French kings. Since officeholders could not be removed from office except in extraordinary circumstances, they enjoyed a great deal of political and legal independence.

French kings tried periodically to eliminate venality, but they were consistently prevented from doing so by opposition from powerful groups of officeholders. They sometimes resorted to creating whole new groups of offices, in an effort to short-circuit entrenched officeholders. This practice usually brought them new funds, but also created extra layers of bureaucracy, making the system ever more cumbersome.

Fiscal problems bedeviled the royal governments of the ancien régime. The tax structure consisted of a web of exemptions for special groups. The nobility enjoyed exemption from the *taille*, the most hated tax in France. The acquisition of noble status, either by buying noble land or by purchasing an ennobling office, also exempted many members of the bourgeoisie from the most burdensome forms of taxation. The clergy could not be directly taxed, except for certain commodities. Instead, they voted to donate a certain sum to the king each year. This *don gratuit* (free gift) was the source of much tension between king and clergy.

Taxes were collected by a group of wealthy private fiscal agents called tax farmers. They assumed the duty of collecting taxes and promised to deliver specific sums of money to the royal treasury. However, they could legally collect as much additional money as they could extract from the populace. Many tax farmers grew enormously wealthy, and they were one of the most hated groups in France. Antoine LAVOISIER, the great French chemist, was beheaded during the French Revolution on account of his tax-farming activities.

The ancien régime was thoroughly rooted in an alliance between ROMAN CATHOLICISM and the state. The church served as a kind of avenue for the communication of royal policies; new decrees were officially read in the pulpits of parish churches. The traditional Catholic teaching orders—the JESUITS and Oratorians—carried primary responsibility for EDUCATION. The Catholic Church also enjoyed powers of censorship and exercised justice over clergymen. In short, certain important administrative functions were controlled by the church or at least shared with it. The clergy served in many instances as an effective and troublesome source of opposition to Crown activities.

French Protestants, most of whom followed CALVINISM, enjoyed limited toleration between 1598 and 1685. But after 1685, they could be imprisoned, sent to the galleys, or banished for openly practicing their faith. During the ENLIGHTENMENT, prosecution still occurred, although instances decreased in number. Civil liabilities for Protestants were not officially removed, however, until the French Revolution dissolved the formal ties between church and state.

The French legal system not only differentiated between various corporate groups, but also varied by region. France was not a united nation under one law.

Instead, the king ruled in various regions according to long-established customary law. This meant that Languedoc, for example, had different laws than Brittany. But these differences were not the result of general principles or of a federal structure. They were simply accident, agreements hammered out between the king and a province at the time the province became part of France.

French peasants labored under varying conditions. They had been personally free for many years, although vestiges of the old feudal structure hung on in some areas. Some were prosperous farmers, owning large farms. But most were subsisting from small plots, working as tenant farmers or day laborers. The peasants bore the burden of taxation but had no legal recognition as a separate estate.

During the Enlightenment, the basic principles underlying the ancien régime were thoroughly criticized. Calls for religious TOLERATION, for the SEPARATION OF CHURCH AND STATE, for equality before the law, for office-holding based on talent rather than on heredity and venality, for limited monarchy, for tax reform, and for the establishment of a representative advisory or legislative body, stemmed as much from the abuses of the ancien régime as they did from any theoretical or philosophical convictions on the part of enlightened reformers.

See also CLASS AND RANK; PUBLISHING.

Further reading: J. O. Lindsay, ed., *The Old Regime, 1713–63*, vol. 7 of New Cambridge Modern History (Cambridge: Cambridge University Press, 1970); David Ogg, *Europe of the Ancien Régime (1715–83)* (New York: Harper Torchbooks, 1965); Franco Venturi, *The End of the Old Regime in Europe, 1768–76: The First Crisis,* tr. R. Burr Litchfield (Princeton, N.J.: Princeton University Press, 1989); Alfred Cobban, *A History of Modern France, Vol. 1: 1715–1799. Old Régime and Revolution* (Baltimore: Penguin Books, 1963).

Ancients *See* QUARREL BETWEEN THE ANCIENTS AND THE MODERNS.

Anglicans Term referring to members of the Church of England. English Protestants on the periphery of the Anglican Church fell into several overlapping groups known collectively as DISSENTERS or Nonconformists. They included Calvinist groups, such as Presbyterians and Independents (Congregationalists and Baptists), and also Methodists and Quakers. The relations among Anglicans, non-Anglican Protestants, and Roman Catholics strongly colored English politics from the 16th century through the 18th century.

Until the 16th century, the English Christian church was part of ROMAN CATHOLICISM. As in other Catholic lands, tensions and conflict existed between the popes in Rome and the kings of England over the exercise of justice and the collection of revenues. The English kings attempted to gain as much control over the church administration as possible. By the 14th century, they had succeeded in gaining the right to appoint bishops to episcopal sees in spite of the opposition of the papacy. In addition, the statutes of Praemunire (1353, 1365, and 1393) had forbidden the introduction into England of papal decrees (bulls or excommunications) from Rome. Violations of these statutes were punishable according to the king's pleasure.

When Henry VIII (1509–47) succeeded in having the English Parliament pass the Act of Supremacy (1534) that separated the government of the English church from Rome, he was to a great extent merely codifying and formalizing conditions that had existed for many years. The English church became subject to royal control in all administrative or governmental matters. Nevertheless, the church remained organized into parishes, bishoprics, and archbishoprics. Furthermore, in doctrinal matters it remained closely, if informally, aligned with Roman Catholicism.

Henry VIII's defiance of papal control encouraged the growth of an authentic reform PROTESTANTISM in England. Henry himself, however, had no intentions of supporting such a movement and even boasted of his doctrinal orthodoxy. During the 16th century, English reformers tended to look to Ulrich Zwingli in Zürich, SWITZERLAND, for inspiration. A few followed the tenets of LUTHERANISM or CALVINISM. The early Church of England accommodated some doctrinal reform but maintained an essentially conservative framework. Roman Catholicism continued to exist as a separate Christian organization.

The reign of the devoutly Catholic Mary I (1553–58) was largely responsible for determining the strong anti-Catholic sentiment of subsequent English history. Queen Mary attempted forcibly to restore Catholicism in Presbyterian Scotland. Protestants were persecuted, and nearly 300 people were burned at the stake as heretics.

The events of Queen Mary's reign ultimately strengthened the Anglican Church and contributed toward pushing it solidly into the Protestant fold in matters of doctrine. Under Queen Elizabeth I (1558–1603), the transformation was formalized when the Anglican Church created a distinct doctrinal position in the Thirty-Nine Articles of 1571. These articles contained two fundamentally Protestant tenets: the belief in justification by faith and the assertion that the Bible contains all knowledge necessary for salvation. The resulting Anglican Church, or Church of England, was a conservative form of Protestantism that retained many aspects of Catholic liturgy and government. In particular, the administrative structures of the church remained essentially unaltered, with archbishops, bishops, local parishes, and two official universities (Oxford and Cambridge) carrying out the business of the church. Monasticism had been eradicated under Henry VIII, and, of course, the English king had assumed the position as church head formerly occupied by the Catholic pope.

Tensions within the Church of England began to grow during the first half of the 17th century. Calvinism had strongly imprinted itself on the church during Elizabeth's reign. But radical forms of Calvinism with strong democratic implications were beginning to develop. A theological dispute within the Anglican Church among Calvinists, moderate conservatives, and Arminians intertwined with growing tensions between king and Parliament in the English political system. The execution of King Charles I, the English Civil Wars, the Calvinist-dominated Commonwealth (1642–60), and the rule of Oliver Cromwell developed out of this early 17th-century conflict.

When the monarchy was restored in 1660, the Church of England regained and strengthened its privileged official position. The reinstated church defined itself more narrowly than in the past: Calvinist pastors were required to submit to reordination by an Anglican bishop. Many Calvinists refused to obey and set up small independent congregations. These became the core of the Nonconformist movement. In general, Calvinism became a Christian branch outside the boundaries of Anglicanism.

The Anglicans dominated the English Parliament. They secured their political supremacy by passing acts excluding from political office anyone not belonging to the Church of England. These acts, the Act of Conformity (1662) and the Test Act (1673), created a system of real civil disability and discrimination for Calvinists and Catholics.

Both Charles II and his brother James II tried to soften the disabilities faced by non-Anglicans in England. Both favored TOLERATION and suspended the laws that excluded Catholics and Dissenters from political life. But, in order to implement their policies, these kings resorted to using royal prerogative to suspend laws passed by Parliament. In so doing, they were attempting to assert a more absolute royal power in England. Thus, the conflict over English confessional loyalties contained political implications about the form of monarchy—limited or absolute—that would exist in the country.

King James II (r. 1685–88) was overtly Catholic. His actions on behalf of Catholicism combined with the general notion of religious toleration to heighten tensions over both the desired religious configuration of England and the related structure of political power. English Protestants of all persuasions were uneasy with a Catholic monarch, especially since Counter-Reformation Catholicism seemed to be regaining dominance on the European mainland.

Specifically, James II used his royal prerogative, itself a matter of contention, to set aside the provisions of the Test Act and other laws that protected Anglican political supremacy. He appointed Catholic officials, introduced Catholic professors into Oxford and Cambridge, and

William III (1650–1702), prince of Orange, and his wife, Mary II (1664–94), daughter of King James II, ruled England and Ireland as joint sovereigns. *(Courtesy New York Public Library)*

extended the Declaration of Indulgence of Charles II that suspended penal laws against non-Anglican Protestants. In April 1688, James II issued a second Declaration of Indulgence and ordered Anglican parish priests to read it from their pulpits at Sunday services. At the same time, his queen gave birth to a son, thereby raising the specter of a Catholic successor. This conjunction of events provoked a political rebellion in 1688 called the GLORIOUS REVOLUTION.

A group of powerful dissident Englishmen, including some Anglican bishops, invited the Protestant William of Orange (of the United Provinces of the Netherlands) to invade England in order to redress their grievances with King James II. William accepted the invitation and landed in England on November 5, 1688. James II fled, having been deserted by his daughter Anne and his outstanding general, John Churchill. By January 1689, William and his wife, Mary, were asked to assume the English throne and to call a Parliament. Although Mary was a Protestant, she was the daughter of James II, a fact that provided a degree of legitimacy to the offer.

The Parliament negotiated a settlement with William and passed a Bill of Rights that weakened the power of the English king. The English monarchy, although still hereditary, assumed the form of a contract between people and king. The outlines of this settlement played a significant role in determining the content of 18th-century political conflict in England. These events also stimulated John LOCKE to write the TWO TREATISES OF GOVERNMENT, works that made seminal contributions to the development of contract theory in the early ENLIGHTENMENT.

The Glorious Revolution, produced a series of changes in the relations between Anglicanism and the state. On the one hand, it resulted in the Toleration Act of 1689, which granted the right to worship to all Protestant Nonconformists except Unitarians. On the other hand, it further tightened the bonds between Anglicanism and the Crown by denying the English throne to Catholics (Act of Settlement, 1701). English non-Anglicans (Dissenters and Nonconformists) continued to be excluded from political life and public service by law. The practice of Unitarianism (denial of the doctrine of the Holy Trinity) remained a criminal act. Effectively, Anglicans controlled the English throne and political life.

However, the Glorious Revolution also produced a rift within the Anglican church between so-called jurors and nonjurors. All clergymen were required to take an oath of allegiance to William and Mary when they assumed the English throne. Those who acquiesced were called jurors. Certain Anglican bishops and lower clergymen (nonjurors) refused, pointing out that the church forbade civil disobedience. Although they had disliked the Catholic James II (some had even been imprisoned by him in the Tower of London), these men believed that they owed him allegiance as their rightful monarch. For them, William and Mary were usurpers. Eventually, many of the nonjurors seceded from the Anglican Church, setting up independent congregations.

Developments associated with the Enlightenment—trends toward toleration and the search for a NATURAL RELIGION—challenged the orthodox Anglican Church. Specifically, certain theologians and clergymen minimized the importance of strict adherence to Anglican doctrine and ritual. Known as latitudinarians, these men favored a general attitude of tolerance in religious matters. Furthermore, since the tradition of religious dissent had existed for more than a century, reformers such as John WESLEY could break away from the church with relative ease. Deists also supported the idea of toleration and challenged Anglican orthodoxy by offering an alternative form of religious belief stripped of Christian revelation and miracle.

In spite of these challenges, however, the stance of the Anglican Church changed little during the Enlightenment. It retained its traditional doctrine and preserved its status as the official state church. The legal acts that limited the rights of non-Anglicans stayed on the books until the Emancipation Acts of 1828 and 1829, in spite of the tolerance granted to dissenting worship. Thus, while England contributed several central ideas to the Enlightenment, the Church of England remained relatively untouched by the resulting pressure for reform.

See also DEISM; ENTHUSIASM; METHODISM; WILLIAM III AND MARY II.

Further reading: Catholic University of America, eds., *New Catholic Encyclopedia* (New York: McGraw-Hill, 1967–89); *New Schaff-Herzog Encyclopedia of Religious Knowledge,* 13 vols. (New York: Funk and Wagnalls, 1908–14); J. H. Plumb, *England in the Eighteenth Century (1714–1815)* (Baltimore: Penguin Books, 1950).

animalculism A theory developed in the late 17th century and abandoned during the 1740s; posited that the GENERATION of life (i.e., reproduction) is accomplished by a completely developed, preformed individual located in the head of the male sperm. The egg, or ovum, of the female mammal—unobservable by microscopes of the period and hence a merely hypothesized entity—was believed to provide nothing other than nourishment to the embryo.

Sperm had first been observed through a microscope by Antoni van LEEUWENHOEK in 1677. He called them "animalcules" or "spermatick worms." The word *spermatozoon* was not coined until 1827. Leeuwenhoek and Nicolaas Hartsoeker (1656–1725) were the microscopists who most strongly believed in the generative power of animalcules. Other researchers maintained that animalcules were parasites or mere masses of inert matter.

Support for animalculism was undermined by early experiments on regeneration because these experiments showed reproduction occurring in the absence of animalcules. These experimental findings added strength to the criticisms of animalculism that had come from orthodox Christian theologians. The theologians rejected animalculism on the grounds that it contradicted and undermined belief in the biblical story of the Virgin Birth of Jesus Christ. Charles BONNET's discovery in 1746 of female aphid parthenogenesis (asexual reproduction) provided a resounding blow to animalculism. From a solitary female aphid, isolated for its entire life, Bonnet obtained 95 offspring. Obviously, animalcules and male sperm were not involved. The combination of these factors caused animalculism to lose its dominant position in the 1740s. As a result, from the late 1740s until the 1780s, preformation theory became ovist. It now posited that the female egg contained the preformed embryo, and relegated the male sperm to an insignificant role in generation.

animism A theory of the nature of life whose chief 18th-century proponent was the German chemist and physician Georg Ernst STAHL. Animist theories had provided explanations both for life phenomena and for the nature of all creation in earlier centuries. They were particularly popular during the Renaissance. These theories had often been condemned as heretical by Christian theologians of both Roman Catholic and Protestant affiliation. Stahl's animism focused exclusively on living creatures and attempted to provide a solid explanation of life phenomena rooted in observation. His formulation severed the links with natural magic that had characterized Renaissance versions of the theory.

Stahlian theory postulated that life is fundamentally distinct from nonlife on account of its holistic, organic organizational principles. A living organism is characterized by parts that are thoroughly interconnected and mutually dependent. Any change in one part produces related alterations in all other aspects of the organism. In contrast, nonliving entities displayed mechanical organizational principles in which the fundamental parts were independent and interchangeable. Alterations to one part of a nonliving being would not affect the rest of the body.

Animist theory maintained a strict distinction between mind and matter. Matter is composed of motionless particles of substance, whereas mind is immaterial but nevertheless wholly real. Mind is manifested in living beings through the agency of the anima, the source of all motion and of purposeful (teleological) behavior. Both motion and goal-directed behavior are characteristics that distinguish living beings from the nonliving entities of the universe.

The anima directs all the activities of living material organisms. A major source of theoretical difficulty thus lay in the age-old question of how mind, an immaterial entity, could affect body, a material entity. Stahl thought that motion provided the necessary link. He conceived of motion as an immaterial entity that operated on bodily organs. The major life motions were circulation, secretion, and excretion. Emotions produced in the anima by external influences also acted on the body by means of their effects on circulation, secretion, or excretion.

Animism gradually fell into disrepute as the theories of VITALISM gained strength in the latter half of the 18th century. Vitalism occupied an intermediary position between MECHANICAL PHILOSOPHY and animism by preserving the distinctness of life while rejecting belief in an immaterial anima as the directive principle of life.

anthropology A science whose object of study is human beings. It focuses on both physical characteristics (physical anthropology) and sociocultural practices (cultural anthropology). The science of anthropology emerged during the ENLIGHTENMENT as a distinct conceptual field that recognized the complexity of human characteristics and desired to find theories that would account for observed facts.

Anthropology was one of several new social sciences that appeared during the 18th century in response to the scientific culture of the Enlightenment. It was a logical extension of the new drive to investigate the world using the tools of REASON, HISTORY, comparative analysis, and direct observation. Although anthropology did not acquire status as an institutionalized discipline—there were no faculties of anthropology at universities, for example—the word was used in book titles, and the general outlines of the 19th-century discipline began to coalesce into a recognizable form.

Studies in anthropology, drawing inspiration from *l'Histoire naturelle de l'homme* (Natural history of man; 1749) by Georges-Louis Leclerc, comte de BUFFON, attempted to unite the natural (physical) and cultural aspects of human existence into a new theoretical and empirical understanding of humankind. Of major concern were questions about fundamental human nature; theories about the distinctions between human beings and other animals; inquiries into the origins of society; explorations into the nature of "primitive" society and mentality; investigations into the origins of RELIGION; and research into the nature and origin of the distinctions between various human races.

These research topics actually derived from earlier established disciplines such as anatomy and MEDICINE, religion, POLITICAL THEORY, and NATURAL LAW. But the particular overarching interest of enlightened intellectuals in defining the characteristics common (universal) to all human beings from birth tended to separate these topics from their originating disciplines and to bring them together as the new social science of anthropology.

The comparative anthropological study of human cultures developed in response to the information about non-European cultures that was being collected by various explorers and missionaries throughout the world. The vast TRAVEL LITERATURE, both documentary and fictional, helped to create a general interest in exotic cultures. Europeans viewed these cultures as "primitive" because they lacked Western political, technological, religious, and social structures.

European assessments of non-Western cultures extended from the excessively negative to excessively positive. The general outlines of the debate resembled those of the literary QUARREL BETWEEN THE ANCIENTS AND THE MODERNS and the musical BATTLE OF THE BUFFOONS. Interpretations of the primitive often depended on general attitudes toward contemporary culture. A person who believed in natural progress over time usually rated 18th-century European culture superior to primitive ones. Some writers who represented this position were Pierre BAYLE, Bernard de FONTENELLE, Giambattista VICO, David HUME, Charles de BROSSES, Nicolas-Antoine BOULANGER, and Baron d'HOLBACH.

In contrast, if writers believed that the course of history had brought decay and degeneration (a secular version of the Christian story of Adam and Eve in the Garden of Eden), then they often extolled the virtues of "primitive" culture and longed to recapture some of those qualities in modern times. Writers in this category included Jean-Jacques ROUSSEAU, the mature Denis DIDEROT, Baron de Lahontan, and Abbé RAYNAL.

By analogical and imaginative extension, writers transformed "primitive" non-Western cultures into examples of the hypothetical natural state of humankind at the beginning of history. Other analogies were drawn with childhood and with the ancient Greeks. By means of these various comparisons, the investigation of primitive cultures, both ancient and modern, became linked to discussions about PROGRESS, natural morality, natural social order, natural knowledge, and NATURAL RELIGION. At bottom, the Enlightenment was wrestling with the thorny question of the relative importance of human nature (innate qualities, present at birth) as opposed to nurture or history (social and environmental factors that shaped experience) in forming human civilizations.

This nature versus nurture debate extended from cultural anthropology to physical anthropology, where it lay at the center of investigations about the human species. Progressive enlightened thinkers generally believed that the differences between the races developed in response to social and environmental factors; they were thus superficial differences, having nothing to do with essential qualities.

Major figures in the new discipline of anthropology were Buffon, Johann Friedrich BLUMENBACH, Raynal, de Brosses, and Immanuel KANT. But many other figures of the Enlightenment made contributions to the general questions that became subsumed under the discipline of anthropology.

See also RACE.

anticlericalism   Term meaning literally "against the clergy." The period of the ENLIGHTENMENT witnessed much open criticism of Christian clergymen, whether they were Roman Catholic priests or preachers in a Protestant tradition. The clergy in most nations exercised certain powers on behalf of both church and state. Moreover, the clergy in Catholic lands were also landowners who could demand considerable amounts of labor and sizable rent payments from their tenants. Most clergymen were supported through obligatory and sometimes burdensome church taxes called tithes.

Since they were prominent and powerful members of communities, clergymen were subject to much scrutiny, especially when people began questioning religious traditions and authority. During the Enlightenment, clergymen were intensely and publicly criticized for sexual abuses such as keeping concubines or forcing sexual relations on parishioners. Ostentatious displays of luxury were attacked as unworthy of Christians and improper for persons dedicated to spreading the word of God. Clergymen were also attacked for holding rigid, intolerant views; for encouraging beliefs in superstition (the enlightened term

for religious miracles); and for generally obstructing the PROGRESS of human knowledge and REASON.

The JESUITS earned particularly vehement attack on account of their power and widespread influence. Their enemies included Italian and French adherents of JANSENISM, the French PARLEMENTS, the ENCYCLOPEDISTS, enlightened ministers of state, and their enlightened rulers. Anti-Jesuit sentiment resulted in the expulsion of the order from PORTUGAL (1759–61), FRANCE (1761–63), and SPAIN (1767). Pope CLEMENT XIV finally yielded to pressure and disbanded the entire order in 1773. Pope Pius VII reestablished it in 1814.

Anticlericalism came from all geographic regions of Europe and had voices in many intellectual quarters. The attacks by VOLTAIRE against *l'infâme* (infamy, meaning religion) are memorable and renowned, but Voltaire was not alone. Most of the French PHILOSOPHES associated with the *ENCYCLOPÉDIE* project were strongly anticlerical. In ENGLAND as well as in France, the most radical adherents of DEISM criticized clerical abuse as one example of the general corruption of Christianity.

In the hands of other intellectuals, criticism of the clergy was not necessarily paired with general attacks on RELIGION but rather served as a call for internal church reform. Such approaches were common in the Italian peninsula, in the HAPSBURG EMPIRE, and in other German Catholic lands. But the deistic defense of Christianity by the Englishman Matthew TINDAL was also virulently anticlerical.

Among believers, distrust and dislike of the clergy also contributed to the creation of new Christian approaches: Quietism and Quakerism, for example, removed the priest or preacher from any dominant role in religious life and made faith an inner matter concerning the individual and God.

In general, anticlericalism provided a major ingredient of Enlightenment thought and served as a major focus of its reforming efforts.

See also QUAKERS.

Argens, Jean-Baptiste de Boyer, marquis d' (1704–1771) *French writer*

Argens was born in Aix-en-Provence, the son of the *procureur général* (attorney general) of the *parlement* (court of justice) at Aix. The family was well represented in the local legal profession. Argens was something of a rebel and libertine. He defied his father by joining the army, became notoriously popular with women, and created some minor diplomatic scandals during brief service with the French ambassador to the Ottoman Empire. He developed a pronounced SKEPTICISM in matters of RELIGION. Argens studied law and obtained a broad background in the natural sciences, philosophy, and letters. His scandalous lifestyle caused his father to disinherit him. As a result, Argens left FRANCE.

About 1734 he settled in Holland, where he pursued a literary career by writing novels and historical and personal memoirs. By 1740 he had produced a large number of works. His series of "letters," the *Lettres juives* (Jewish letters; 1738), *Lettres chinoises* (Chinese letters; 1739–40), and *Lettres cabalistiques* (Cabalist letters; 1741); the *Mémoires secrets de la république des lettres* (Secret memoirs of the republic of letters; 1737–39); and the *Philosophie du bon sens* (Philosophy of common sense; 1737) earned him a reputation as a skeptic in the style of Pierre BAYLE. FREDERICK II (THE GREAT) and VOLTAIRE particularly liked the *Lettres juives*.

Frederick the Great invited Argens to BERLIN in 1740 shortly after assuming the throne in Prussia. He made Argens his chamberlain and director of the section on literature in the BERLIN ACADEMY. Argens stayed in Berlin until 1766, when, to Frederick's displeasure, he returned to his native Provence. He died in 1771. Frederick helped to purchase his elaborate tombstone in the Minim church at Aix.

Argenson, Marc-Pierre de Voyer, comte de Weil d'
(1696–1764) *French statesman, lawyer, courtier, and intellectual*

Marc-Pierre de Voyer, comte de Weil-d'Argenson was the younger brother of René-Louis de Voyer, marquis d'AR-GENSON. He married Anne Larger, a member of a well-placed Parisian family of nobles of the robe (ennobled magistrates and royal administrators). They had two sons, Marc-René and Louis-Auguste, both of whom became military officers. Blessed with a combination of talent, training, familial connections, and social graces, young Marc-Pierre d'Argenson moved quickly into state service. He worked as a lawyer at the Châtelet in PARIS, councillor in the Parlement of Paris (royal court of justice), intendant both in Touraine and in the Paris region, and, following in the footsteps of his father, as lieutenant general of the police in Paris (1720). Marc-Pierre also acquired positions in the households of the royal heirs, Philippe and Louis d'Orléans. He became a councillor to the king, serving both in the Grand Council and the Bureau of Commerce.

In 1743, d'Argenson received an appointment as secretary of state for war. In this capacity, he reorganized the army in an attempt to offset the negative effects of the ANCIEN RÉGIME practice of selling military commissions. He had fortifications repaired, established a military academy (École militaire), and oversaw the expansion of the military hospital in Paris (Les Invalides). Like his elder brother, his tenure as a minister of state coincided with the military and diplomatic upheavals of the 1740s and 1750s. During this period, the court faction headed by the marquise de POMPADOUR acquired enough power to influence French foreign policy. This faction pressured LOUIS XV to abandon the traditional French alliance with the enemies of the Austrian Hapsburgs. Marc-Pierre d'Argenson opposed the new foreign policy direction and, as a result, lost his appointment as secretary of state for war (1757). He retired to his chateau at Ormes and did not return to Paris until after the death of Madame de Pompadour in 1764.

Marc-Pierre d'Argenson led an active intellectual life, moving in the Parisian circles frequented by the enlightened PHILOSOPHES. He entered the FRENCH ACADEMY OF SCIENCES in 1722 and the Academy of Inscriptions in 1749. He served as a library inspector and amassed an impressive private collection of books. D'Argenson was a friend of VOLTAIRE. He is commemorated to this day as the man to whom Denis DIDEROT and Jean Le Rond d'ALEMBERT dedicated the great ENCYCLOPÉDIE.

See also DIPLOMATIC REVOLUTION OF 1756.

Argenson, René-Louis de Voyer de Paulmy, marquis d'
(1694–1757) *French statesman, lawyer, and political theorist; acquired the nickname "la Bête" (the Beast) because his manners were rough*

He was a descendant of an illustrious noble family whose members had served the French monarchy for several generations. His father, Marc-René, comte d'Argenson, was the famous reforming chief of police under LOUIS XIV. His brother, Marc-Pierre de Voyer, comte d'ARGENSON, served as minister of war in the cabinet of LOUIS XV. René-Louis himself capped his career with a post as minister of foreign affairs under Louis XV. He had prepared himself for high office by obtaining a series of lesser posts as a young man. He served as councillor in the Parlement of Paris (royal court of justice), member of the Council of State (1720), royal intendant in the province of Hainaut (1721), chancellor for the duke of Orleans, member of the Royal Council, and finally, in November 1744, minister of foreign affairs.

D'Argenson assumed his ministerial post during the military and diplomatic upheavals engendered by the WAR OF THE AUSTRIAN SUCCESSION. France had allied itself, as its traditions dictated, with FREDERICK II (THE GREAT) OF PRUSSIA against MARIA THERESA OF AUSTRIA. But Frederick had proved to be unreliable as an ally; he had abandoned the alliance twice when the specific interests of Prussia seemed to favor making peace with Austria.

D'Argenson continued to push for alliances with Frederick, in spite of the evidence suggesting that new policy lines were needed. His vision of European lines of power remained stubbornly wedded to the conditions that had prevailed under Louis XIV. Consequently, he was removed from his position as minister of state in January 1747. He devoted much of his last 10 years to writing.

D'Argenson left several manuscripts on political and related social reforms. These literary works place him squarely within the bounds of the ENLIGHTENMENT.

D'Argenson attended the famous Collège Louis-le-Grand, operated in Paris by the JESUITS. There, he began a lifelong intellectual friendship with VOLTAIRE.

In 1725, d'Argenson joined the Abbé Alary's Club de l'Entresol in Paris. Conceived as a kind of unofficial political academy in the style of the great French Academy, the group met weekly to read foreign newspapers, present essays on assigned topics, and engage in unfettered discussion of political issues. Because censorship prevented open publication and public discussion, manuscripts circulated privately within the confines of this group. Attending the meetings were several prominent French noblemen, the English expatriate Viscount BOLINGBROKE, Voltaire, and perhaps MONTESQUIEU.

D'Argenson presented his manuscript "Jusques où la démocratie peut être admise dans le gouvernement monarchique" ("Where democracy can be admitted in monarchical government") at a Club de l'Entresol meeting. It was published posthumously, in considerably altered form, as *Considérations sur le gouvernement ancien et présent de la France* (Considerations on the ancient and present government of France; 1764). He also circulated other manuscripts, which have been passed on to posterity as the *Journal et mémoires du marquis d'Argenson* (Journal and memoirs of the marquis d'Argenson; 1755–57).

In these works, d'Argenson draws from traditional western European POLITICAL THEORY. But he offers a unique solution to the vexing questions raised by these theories. He suggests that democracy and monarchy need not be viewed as necessarily antagonistic forms. Rather, the best elements in each could be combined within one government to produce a truly utilitarian government capable of safeguarding liberty and EQUALITY. He envisions a state composed of numerous small, local democratic governments unified at the top by a single sovereign, the hereditary monarch. Such a state requires no limits on the absolute monarch, who, it is presumed, will rule according to the dictates of morality, REASON, and justice. Only in his later years, in the aftermath of his personal experiences in the French government, did d'Argenson, like Montesquieu, begin to see a need for an aristocratic, intermediary political body as a guarantor of good behavior on the part of the king. D'Argenson's works also advocate reforms such as implementation of the new LAISSEZ-FAIRE economic doctrine.

aristocratic resurgence Concept developed by historians to illuminate one aspect of the social changes that helped to prepare conditions for the FRENCH REVOLUTION in 1789. According to this view, the French aristocracy made a last attempt in the 18th century to stave off the growing dominance of the bourgeoisie and to limit the power of the king.

The aristocracy had been losing ground since the end of the Wars of Religion in 1589. The French kings had managed to consolidate their political power at the expense of the local powers of the nobility. They had accomplished this, in part, by drawing ministers and administrators from the high bourgeoisie and granting them noble status. The old aristocracy perceived itself as being cut off from its fair share of power. Furthermore, although the aristocracy still enjoyed privileges with respect to taxation, the concept of privilege was being attacked by reforming kings and ministers who viewed it as an obstacle to the exercise of royal power.

Many nobles were wealthy, but an even greater number were feeling strained by the steady increase in prices that occurred during the 18th century. A poor nobleman could not hope to serve in the military, for he would have been required to raise a regiment. The costs of doing that had become prohibitive for all but the wealthiest nobles. Nobles perceived that they were losing access to both high state office and military service. Both had been traditional areas of aristocratic profession.

According to the thesis of aristocratic resurgence, access to high government and military office actually was increasingly reserved for the nobility during the 18th century. Laws were promulgated that required several generations of noble status before a person could enter the military as an officer (except in the artillery). Otherwise, it was necessary to work up through the ranks. Some of the regional justice courts (PARLEMENTS) required nobility on the father's side for admittance to the corporation. High church offices were given to members of the nobility. In fact, in 1789, every French bishop was a nobleman. This situation differed noticeably from the one that had prevailed during the reign of LOUIS XIV. The "Sun King" had routinely tapped influential, wealthy commoners for various forms of high office.

By the end of the 18th century, therefore, the aristocracy actually enjoyed a stronger position than it had during the 17th-century reign of Louis XIV. But members of this group did not perceive their advantages. They were discontented with the encroachments by the central monarchy on their fiscal privileges and desired a formal role in the exercise of power.

The *parlements,* composed increasingly of noblemen by birth, became a center of protest against monarchical reforms and efforts to centralize power. The language of the protests employed both appeals to alleged French tradition and enlightened concepts of the NATURAL RIGHTS of humankind. But the goal of the protests focused more on protecting noble privileges such as tax exemptions than on developing a system that would give political power to all subjects of the king.

Financial crises of significant proportion faced the French government during the 1780s. The government needed larger and more reliable sources of funding. Two controllers general, Jacques NECKER and Charles-Alexandre de CALONNE, tried to instigate tax and other financial reforms. But the existing structures of the ANCIEN RÉGIME prevented any substantive change. As a result, Calonne, with the consent of LOUIS XVI, decided to call an Assembly of Notables to address the crises.

The assembly convened in February 1787. Calonne immediately alienated the notables (clergy and nobility) by attacking their tax exemptions. The assembly accused Calonne of favoring despotic central rule, but reluctantly agreed to accept the principle of equal liability for taxation. However, it refused to accept Calonne's specific proposals and also rejected the idea of a representative body in which all deputies, whatever their rank, would be equal. Consequently, the Assembly of Notables was dismissed in May 1787, having succeeded only in aggravating the antagonism between the aristocracy and the king.

The financial plight of the French kingdom continued unabated. The center of resistance to royal reform now shifted back to the *parlements*. An attempt to impose a stamp tax provoked a revolt in the Parlement of Paris. The king responded in customary fashion by exiling the *parlement* to Troyes (August 1787). This action triggered widespread protests by the courts, the provincial assemblies (such bodies met in certain French provinces), the peers and dukes of France, and the Assembly of the Clergy. The bourgeoisie, especially in Paris, looked on the exiled *parlement* members as victims of an absolute monarchy gone awry. *Parlement* members were recalled to Paris by October 1787. However, their continued opposition to royal policies resulted in the abolition of the *parlements* in May 1788.

French historians refer to these events as the *révolte nobilaire* (revolt of the nobility). The term underlines the fact that open, effective opposition to the French Crown began as a revolt of nobles of the robe (ennobled magistrates) who were claiming the right to limit the actions of the king.

To try to defuse the escalating political and economic crises, the king and the Calonne's replacement, Loménie de Brienne, agreed to call an Estates General meeting at Versailles in May 1789. The Estates General was the traditional advisory body to the French king. It was composed of representatives of the three legal classes in France. The kings of France had not called such a meeting since 1614. Thus, the decision to call the meeting in 1789 constituted a recognition by the monarchy that its absolute aims were unattainable.

The calling of the Estates General was brought about by the united protests of various elements of the aristocracy and represents the acme of the influence of the movement of aristocratic resurgence. However, as the events of the revolution unfolded, leadership rapidly passed into the hands of the middle classes.

Historians debate the extent to which the aristocratic resurgence was a reality. They also disagree about the degree of influence it exerted in the course of events leading to the revolution. Some historians point out that, despite the laws favoring aristocratic access to high office, in fact the non-noble bourgeoisie continued to enjoy upward mobility. The aristocracy may not have been as dominant as the laws would suggest. What cannot be disputed is the fact that the aristocracy perceived the situation in France as threatening to its status and economic privilege. The immediate political instability that led to the calling of the Estates General was caused at least partially by the reaction of members of the aristocracy to the acts of the king. In this sense, the aristocratic resurgence played a major role in creating the environment for the outbreak of the French Revolution.

Further reading: C. B. A. Behrens, *Society, Government and the Enlightenment: The Experience of Eighteenth-Century France and Prussia* (London: Thames and Hudson, 1985).

Arkwright, Sir Richard (1732–1792) *English inventor and cotton manufacturer who contributed to the 18th-century revolution in cloth manufacturing*

Richard Arkwright was a barber by profession. In 1769, he invented the WATER FRAME, a water-driven spinning machine that used a sequence of steps for spinning that differed from both the spinning wheel and the rival SPINNING JENNY. The water frame produced a coarser, firmer yarn than the spinning jenny. The yarn's greater strength made it a valuable commodity because it could be worked without breaking by machines such as the POWER LOOM.

Arkwright opened up factories for producing cotton cloth and introduced a 100 percent cotton calico cloth in 1773.

Arnold, Gottfried (1666–1714) *radical German Pietist and historian*

Arnold trained at the University of Wittenberg for the Lutheran ministry. He drew his primary inspiration from the various unconventional strains in Christian thought and practice: Rosicrucianism, Spener and PIETISM, Jakob Boehme and mysticism, Molinos and Quietism. Upon completing his education, Arnold turned away from the ministry and in 1697 accepted an academic post at the Pietist-influenced University of Giessen. He became disillusioned with that appointment and resigned the same year (1697) in order to pursue a more immediately meaningful Christian life according to his personal understanding of such matters.

Between 1699 and 1700, Arnold published the work that established him as a seminal Pietist and church historian, the *Unparteyische Kirchen-und-Ketzer Historie* (Impartial history of the church and of heresy). He followed this book with the *Geheimnis der göttlichen Sophia* (Mystery of divine Sophia) in 1700.

Arnold conceived the history of Christianity as one of constant degeneration. The sources of degeneration were the development of rational theology, dogma, all aspects of the institutionalization of Christianity, and most important, the establishment of close church-state relations. The only true Christian church to have existed was that of the apostles during the birth years of Christianity. Decline began to set in with the earliest church councils and squabbles over the creeds of Christianity. The most devastating event was the conversion of the Roman emperor Constantine to Christianity, for this conversion produced the subsequent establishment of Christianity as the state religion of the Roman Empire. The Middle Ages continued the process of decline. A regeneration occurred in the 16th century, when Martin Luther set into motion the events called the Protestant Reformation. But soon a new degenerative process set in. Theological disputation, guidelines for worship, and the general paraphernalia of external religious observance gained a foothold in the reformed Protestant churches just as they had in ROMAN CATHOLICISM.

As a corrective to the degeneration in the history of Christianity, Arnold offered an idealistic, universal vision abstracted from his personal experience and observations. Arnold's ideal church was the radical opposite of the practices that existed in churches of his era. His true church was priestless, lacking theology, dogma, Sunday ritual worship, religious instruction, and political affiliation. It was simply the formless, institutionless aggregate of truly reborn believers. True Christianity, thus, was a personal matter shaped by the relationship between the individual and God. This relationship prepared the soul to receive true wisdom (*Sophia*), the inner enlightenment that comes from God.

Despite his definition of true Christianity in terms of the individual, inner spiritual life, Arnold demanded highly ethical behavior from the true believer. Essentially, he posited an identity between the inner and outer lives of the individual: Traditional upright behavior reflected the genuinely enlightened Christian inner state. Arnold's position, thus, in no way favored libertinism.

Arnold's vituperative attacks on rational theology identify him as an enemy of RATIONALISM. But his thought lies well within the parameters of the ENLIGHTENMENT. Arnold's interpretation of the course of church history embodied a highly pessimistic vision that would become common enough in the assessments of human HISTORY during the Enlightenment: Jean-Jacques ROUSSEAU and Edward GIBBON are the two most outstanding examples. In addition, Arnold's use of the concepts of inner light and of intuitive knowledge demonstrates that his thought belongs to one of the significant but lesser-known streams of enlightened thought. This stream fed the German forms of the Enlightenment (*AUFKLÄRUNG*) and played a significant role in the formation of great German cultural figures such as Johann Wolfgang von GOETHE. During the later years of the Enlightenment in Germany and throughout Europe, it also influenced AESTHETICS and philosophy, as well as RELIGION.

See also INTUITION AND IMAGINATION; LUTHERANISM; ROSICRUCIANS; SEPARATION OF CHURCH AND STATE.

art and architecture　*See* AESTHETICS; BAROQUE STYLE; ENGLISH GARDEN; NEOCLASSICISM; PALLADIAN STYLE; ROCOCO.

Asam, Cosmas Damian (1686–1739) *German rococo painter; the leading frescoist in early 18th-century Germany*
Asam was the older brother of Egid Quirin ASAM. His father was the painter Hans Georg Asam; his mother was the daughter of a Bavarian court painter, Niklas Prugger. Cosmas Damian Asam worked first with his father and in 1707 began taking independent projects. In 1713, he visited ROME, where he won a painting prize at the Accademia di San Luca (Academy of Saint Luke). By 1714, he was working in the German Upper Palatinate.

Asam decorated many Catholic churches in southern Germany, the upper Rhineland, Bohemia, AUSTRIA, and Silesia. Major examples of his work can be found in Weingarten, Weltenburg, and Mannheim in present-day Germany; in Prague (St. Nicholas in the old city) in the Czech Republic; in Innsbruck, Austria; and in Einsiedeln, SWITZERLAND. His last work was the decoration of the Chapel of St. John of Nepomuk, designed by his brother and located in MUNICH. The Asam brothers collaborated on this chapel and many other projects. Cosmas Asam died in Munich in 1739.

Asam, Egid Quirin (1692–1750) *German rococo painter, sculptor, architect, and stuccoist*
Son of the painter Hans Georg Asam and younger brother of Cosmas Damian ASAM. The family lived in the lakes district between MUNICH and the foothills of the Alps. Egid Quirin Asam received his first art instruction from his father. From 1711 until 1716, he worked as an apprentice to the Bavarian court sculptor Andreas Faistenberger in Munich.

Egid Asam and his brother, Cosmas Asam, decorated churches throughout Bavaria and the Lake Constance region. Their work represents some of the finest productions in the German rococo style. The major creations credited to Egid Asam are the Chapel of St. John Nepomuk, which was attached to his Munich residence, and altarpieces in Rohr, Weltenburg, and Asterhofen. Egid Asam died in 1750 at Mannheim, where he was in the midst of decorating the Jesuit church.

association movement　A political campaign by English Protestant DISSENTERS aimed at securing civil rights equal to those enjoyed by orthodox ANGLICANS. This campaign intensified during the late ENLIGHTENMENT between 1787 and 1790. The movement failed to reach its goals, and what progress had been made was cut short by the English reaction to the FRENCH REVOLUTION.

Although it stemmed from a question of religious TOLERATION, the association movement borrowed the

POLITICAL THEORY and vocabulary of the liberal Enlightenment. As a result, the campaign to achieve parity with Anglicans was couched in terms of NATURAL RIGHTS and political EQUALITY. Parallels were deliberately drawn between the situation of the Dissenters and the plight of the Third Estate (bourgeoisie) in FRANCE.

Conservative Englishmen reacted negatively to this language, especially since the introduction of reforming bills into Parliament coincided with the onset of the French Revolution. Three attempts to repeal the restrictive Test and Corporation Acts—in 1787, 1789, and 1790—failed by substantial margins. The cause of equality separate from religious confession had to wait in England until the 19th century before it would become law.

astronomy   A scientific discipline that studies the solar system (except for Earth) and the larger universe. Astronomy was one of earliest disciplines to be transformed during the SCIENTIFIC REVOLUTION of the 17th century. The foundations for this transformation had been laid in the 16th century by Nicolaus COPERNICUS in his treatise *De revolutionibus orbium coelestium* (ON THE REVOLUTIONS OF THE HEAVENLY SPHERES; 1534). This work posited that the sun occupies the central position in our solar system while Earth and the other planets revolve around it. Up until Copernicus's time, the dominant and officially condoned vision of the universe postulated that Earth occupies the center position in the universe. All other heavenly bodies were believed to revolve around Earth.

Copernicus's ideas were largely ignored by his contemporaries, but in the early 17th century, Galileo GALILEI, Johannes KEPLER, and other like-minded mathematicians and natural philosophers began to accept the Copernican hypothesis as valid. In spite of Galileo's censure by Roman Catholic authorities (1633) for teaching the Copernican hypothesis, the Galilean writings in support of the HELIOCENTRIC theory spread clandestinely throughout Catholic Europe and openly in Protestant lands. By the 18th century, the Copernican vision had become dominant in astronomy, in physics, and in the popular imagination.

Despite this radical shift in the scientific vision of the universe, many of the general activities of astronomers in the 18th century continued to resemble those of preced-

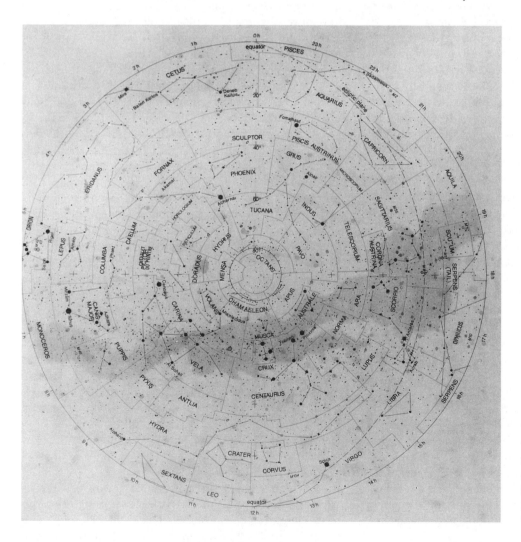

The developments in printing technology of the 17th century and the increasing strength of telescopes helped astronomers map the stars in celestial atlases with greater accuracy and detail.

ing generations. At the beginning of the century, astronomy was still classified as a part of mixed mathematics (applied mathematics). It concerned itself primarily with the study of the positions and motions of objects in the universe.

By the end of the 18th century, however, the invention of more powerful telescopes was allowing astronomers to collect enough light from distant stars to observe previously undetected phenomena. The discovery of stellar spectra, for example, led astronomers to begin asking anew about the composition and structure of bodies in the universe. Furthermore, developments in mathematics allowed the relations observed between heavenly bodies to be expressed in mathematical equations. Thus, the groundwork was laid for later substantial changes in the questions that astronomy could fruitfully address.

Astronomers devised two notable collaborative projects: the worldwide observations of the TRANSIT OF VENUS and the expeditions designed to measure the extent in miles of a degree of terrestrial longitude. Scientists from Europe and America contributed observations to these projects. Both projects demonstrated the usefulness of collaboration in the acquisition of knowledge and confirmed scientific ideals cherished by the ENLIGHTENMENT.

Astronomers made major contributions toward the verification of Isaac Newton's theory of universal gravitation. In particular, they used research results on three problems in astronomy as proof of the idea of universal gravitation: calculating the shape of the Earth; describing the motion of the moon; and predicting the date for the return of Halley's Comet. At the end of the century, Pierre-Simon, marquis de LAPLACE, demonstrated that the solar system in stable in spite of the periodic fluctuations in observed planetary motion that had suggested instability to earlier astronomers. Laplace summed up the work of 18th-century astronomy in his five volumes entitled *Mécanique celeste* (Celestial mechanics; 1799–1825).

Major figures who contributed to astronomy during the late 17th century and through the 18th century included Edmond HALLEY, William HERSCHEL, Pierre Louis Moreau de MAUPERTUIS, César CASSINI, Alexis CLAIRAUT, Joseph-Jérôme Le Francais de LALANDE, Joseph-Louis LAGRANGE, and Laplace.

See also COPERNICAN REVOLUTION; GEOCENTRIC; MATHEMATICS AND MECHANICS; RITTENHOUSE; SCIENCE; TECHNOLOGY AND INSTRUMENTATION; TELESCOPE.

atheism   The belief that God does not exist. Because the structure of political power in Europe was intertwined with Christian religious institutions, persons suspected of atheism had nearly always suffered at the hands of authorities. The charge of atheism was sometimes used like that of heresy against anyone whose publicly expressed views did not conform to orthodox theology. This situation existed in both Catholic and Protestant areas of Europe.

The ENLIGHTENMENT has sometimes been presented by its critics as a period of rampant atheism, but this image seriously distorts the reality. In fact, very few enlightened intellectuals, even when they were vocal critics of Christianity, were true atheists. Rather, they were critics of orthodox belief, wedded rather to SKEPTICISM, DEISM, VITALISM, or perhaps pantheism.

Without a doubt, aspects of the new scientific view that emerged in the SCIENTIFIC REVOLUTION hinted at the possibility of a godless universe. Subsequent developments during the Enlightenment definitely gave some weight to these fears. For example, although Isaac NEWTON, the natural philosopher whose theories of physics formed one of the building blocks of the Enlightenment, was a dedicated Christian, his theory of universal gravitation eventually yielded a vision of the universe that could be godless. Newton believed that God not only created the universe but also intervened occasionally to keep it running properly. His theories required this external intervention because they contained no way of explaining how the motion of the universe could be maintained naturally. At the end of the 18th century, however, the marquis de LAPLACE and the Joseph-Louis LAGRANGE developed the mathematical tools and equations that seemed to eliminate the need for outside sources of motion in a Newtonian universe. Their universe was self-correcting and stable without external help. It did not need an active God, although it still needed a creator. The role of God was thus severely diminished, if not completely eliminated.

MATERIALISM, another philosophical position that received attention during the Enlightenment, posed additional threats to belief in a God or gods. Materialism grew logically from the MECHANICAL PHILOSOPHY of the 17th century. It also had ancient Greek sources in the writers of EPICUREAN PHILOSOPHY. Materialism denied the existence of spirit, soul, or mind, explaining all such phenomena as manifestations of physical matter. Christianity, of course, concerned itself ultimately with the fate of the human soul after death. Other religions tended to see the soul as some manifestation of the spiritual world of the gods. If soul was simply the action of matter, then perhaps the whole world of God or gods did not exist.

These developments, however, were only one possible set of responses available to enlightened individuals. Most enlightened people struggled to find some new form of religious belief that would at least preserve the possibility that God or gods existed. Only a handful of the most radical PHILOSOPHES—Julien Offray de LA METTRIE, Paul-Henri-Thiry d' HOLBACH, Claude-Adrien HELVÉTIUS, Denis DIDEROT, and Nicolas-Antoine BOULANGER, for example—can accurately be called atheists.

Like many moderate philosophes, avowed atheists were critics of institutions such as CENSORSHIP, the privileged clergy, ecclesiastical courts, and mandatory church taxation (tithes), which preserved the political and spiritual power of churches. If RELIGION could not be totally abolished, then they desired at least a clear separation between church and state. Avowed atheists also wished to undermine all belief in supernatural beings, whether stemming from Christianity or from PAGANISM. They held that belief in supernatural deities blocked the path of human PROGRESS, and they wished to rid the world of religion in order to advance the quality of human existence. Their attack on religion was thus wedded to the general secular humanitarianism of the Enlightenment.

Atheism provided one possible intellectual position for enlightened individuals. But it was never representative of the main body of enlightened thought. Critics of the Enlightenment, nevertheless, often accused the philosophes of atheism in order to discredit their ideas; the term functioned well as a pejorative even in that relatively tolerant era. As a result, when the accusations of atheism or atheist are encountered in 18th-century treatments of a writer, care must be taken to determine whether they accurately describe that person's ideas.

See also LONGITUDE; SEPARATION OF CHURCH AND STATE.

Aufklärung German word for the ENLIGHTENMENT. In historical texts, *Aufklärung* refers specifically to the forms of the Enlightenment that developed in the various German states. It had two very broad forms distinguished on the basis of geography and religion: the form of the primarily Protestant, northern German principalities and the form of the Catholic, southern German lands.

As a general culture, the *Aufklärung* resembled its French and European counterparts. The institutions that lay at the center of the Enlightenment—COFFEEHOUSES, salons, reading clubs, SCIENTIFIC ACADEMIES, and the periodical press—all flourished in the various German states. The FREEMASONS were particularly strong in Germany, and their program was supported by the Bavarian ILLUMINATI. However, UNIVERSITIES in Germany also played strong roles in the creation and dissemination of enlightened thought. This characteristic sets Germany somewhat apart from FRANCE and from ENGLAND, where the universities tended to be conservative institutions defending the pre-enlightened order.

The *Aufklärer*, as enlightened German thinkers were called, studied and utilized the RATIONALISM and EMPIRICISM of the French and British Enlightenments. They believed in the power of reason as an aid to human progress; they called for religious TOLERATION, not only of all forms of Christianity but also of JUDAISM; they desired intellectual freedom, humanitarian reforms, universal education, and a host of other reforms generally associated with the Enlightenment. But the *Aufklärer* added ingredients drawn from their specific philosophical, political, and religious heritage to create a unique German movement.

Perhaps the most fundamental distinguishing characteristic of the *Aufklärung* lay in its debt to the philoso-

phy of Gottfried Wilhelm LEIBNIZ and his disciple Christian WOLFF. This philosophy offered a systematic vision of the world based on distinctive forms of rationalism and the MECHANICAL PHILOSOPHY. It differed markedly from the philosophies of NEWTON and DESCARTES that underlay most aspects of British and French enlightened thought. Leibnizian-Wolffian philosophy stimulated German thought in nearly every realm, from SCIENCE to PSYCHOLOGY to POLITICAL THEORY.

Four sets of German religious and political practices also added unique ingredients to the blend of ideas that was the *Aufklärung*: PIETISM, CAMERALISM, ENLIGHTENED DESPOTISM, and particularism (the existence of hundreds of tiny independent states within the HOLY ROMAN EMPIRE). Each of these traditions tended to stress the importance of fostering the common good of society over unbridled individualism. The value of individual freedom of thought was recognized but subordinated in the sphere of public behavior to communal needs.

As a result, the *Aufklärung* generally lacked the strong elements of political opposition and of the potential for revolution that characterized the late Enlightenment in France. The *Aufklärer* tended to be members of the government bureaucracy working in various offices or in state-run universities such as HALLE and GÖTTINGEN. They were generally more successful at securing reforms than were their enlightened bureaucratic counterparts in France or England. Their activities were supported and furthered by enlightened despots such as FREDERICK II (THE GREAT) OF PRUSSIA, JOSEPH II OF AUSTRIA, the duke of Weimar, and Elector Dalberg of Mainz.

Finally, although the *Aufklärung*, like its counterparts in other European cultures, praised the role of REASON in the attainment of truths about nature, it specifically denied the power of reason alone to reach creative artistic heights or religious truths. German thinkers created a powerful new theory of AESTHETICS that assigned dominant creative roles to the mental processes of INTUITION AND IMAGINATION. *Aufklärer* also preserved a role for inner revelation, intuition, and emotion in religious practice. They generally retained respect for religious belief and avoided the extremes of ANTICLERICALISM promoted by VOLTAIRE and his fellow French PHILOSOPHES.

Germans in the 18th century carried on a lively public discussion about the Enlightenment. They wondered how to define the term, whether or not the phenomenon existed in Germany, and whether specific ideas or actions could be labeled "enlightened."

The fundamental question *Was ist Aufklärung* (What is the Enlightenment?) had many answers. One famous definition came from Immanuel KANT, who suggested that *Aufklärung* ultimately referred to moral and intellectual freedom, not necessarily paired with political liberty. Another answer, that of Moses MENDELSSOHN, transformed *Aufklärung* into the process of acquiring reason, thereby linking it to the notion of BILDUNG (development through EDUCATION). Mendelssohn, like most of his German contemporaries, feared the dangers to society inherent in creating thoroughly independent enlightened individuals.

These two definitions of *Aufklärung* contained the main elements of the German approach: a stress on process, education, or Bildung and an ambivalence toward unrestricted FREEDOM that resulted in an explicit denial of the goal of political EQUALITY. The result was an *Aufklärung* dedicated to seeking reform, to bettering human living conditions, and to increasing levels of education but also wedded to the modification rather than to the destruction of the existing social and political order.

When attention is focused on the differences between the Protestant and Catholic forms of *Aufklärung*, one distinction assumes major importance: In Catholic Germany, church-and-state relations dominated enlightened discussion. The inspiration for southern German thought on this matter derived more from Italian enlightened thinkers (ILLUMINISTI) than from French anticlericalism.

In general, southern German reforms aimed at redefining the realms appropriate for church interference. The secular rulers of the state attempted to assert their rights to control education, marriage, and other realms that had previously been the domain of the church. When the JESUITS were disbanded, for example, universities were restructured and placed under the state control. Their curricula were revised to include contemporary enlightened subjects approved by the secular rulers.

The Catholic *Aufklärung* also produced reform movements within the church. FEBRONIANISM, for example, called for restructuring the government of the Catholic Church to spread power between the pope and the bishops. JANSENISM helped to create calls for a return to simple teaching and pious practices.

In spite of the vitality of the Catholic *Aufklärung*, it was the northern Protestant movement that left the most renowned enlightened German legacy. The impassioned pleas of Moses Mendelssohn and Gotthold Ephraim LESSING for toleration; the powerful new theories of aesthetics proposed by Lessing; the educational reforms of Johann Bernhard Basedow and the Halle Pietists; the medical reforms of Johann Christian REIL; and the scientific and literary innovations of the young Johann Wolfgang von GOETHE all grew from the soil of German PROTESTANTISM.

In past scholarly works, this German Enlightenment in both Catholic and Protestant forms was often treated as a weak and largely insignificant phenomenon, rapidly overshadowed by the STURM UND DRANG literary movement and by ROMANTICISM. Today, this view is rejected, and the *Aufklärung* receives credit for its rich and varied contributions to enlightened thought.

See also PUBLISHING; SEPARATION OF CHURCH AND STATE.

Further reading: Peter Hans Reill, *The German Enlightenment and the Rise of Historism* (Berkeley: University of California Press, 1975); Hajo Holborn, *A History of Modern Germany (1648–1840)* (New York: Alfred A. Knopf, 1967).

Aulnoy, Marie-Catherine d' (ca. 1650–1705) *French writer of fairy tales, novels, and memoirs*
D'Aulnoy is best known today for her fairy tales, but novels and memoirs made her famous during her lifetime. Fairy tales were a fashionable literary genre of the period, intended not for children, but for adults. Unlike the most successful male compiler and author of fairy tales, Charles Perrault, d'Aulnoy put more emphasis on the role of the heroine in her works.

Many aspects of the author's life are not known, but she experienced scandal and adventure early on. Married young to the baron d'Aulnoy, a much older man, she acquired a bad reputation for extramarital affairs. D'Aulnoy attempted to have her husband denounced for *lèse-majesté* (a threat to the king's honor or power), a very serious offense punishable by death. The plan did not work and resulted in her imprisonment and subsequent separation from her husband.

The most important theme in all d'Aulnoy's works was love. Her first NOVEL, *Histoire d'Hypolite, Comte de Duglas* (Hypolitus, earl of Douglas; 1690) was extremely successful and was reprinted 37 times. In keeping with the literary taste of the times, the narrative told of adventures, disguises, surprising coincidences, and a hero who surmounts many obstacles to be reunited with his true love.

D'Aulnoy was fond of setting her works in England or in Spain, and her most successful memoir, *Relation du voyage d'Espagne* (Account of a journey to Spain; 1691), recounted travels in Spain (though it is not known whether she actually traveled there or simply based her account on books that she had read).

Further reading: Amy Vanderlyn DeGraff, *The Tower and the Well: A Psychological Interpretation of the Fairy Tales of Madame d'Aulnoy* (Birmingham, Ala.: Summa Publications, 1984); Jack Zipes, ed., *Beauties, Beasts and Enchantment: Classic French Fairy Tales* (New York: NAL-Penguin, 1989).

Austria Central European kingdom occupying the eastern Alpine regions and portions of the Danube River plain. Its capital city is VIENNA. As the ancestral territory of the Hapsburg family, Austria served as the center of the Austrian HAPSBURG EMPIRE. Until 1683, with John III Sobieski's great victory at the Battle of Kahlenberg, just outside Vienna, the Ottoman Empire offered a serious threat to Austria. After the victory at Kahlenberg, however, the Turks withdrew and never again directly threatened Austrian territory. But various wars continued to take a toll on the people and lands.

In the middle of the 18th century, population stood at about 6,135,000. The years of peace and prosperity that followed the close of the SEVEN YEARS' WAR produced vigorous growth. The country gained nearly 2.5 million people, reaching an estimated size of 8,511,000 in 1800.

The last half of the 18th century brought noticeable changes to Austria as MARIA THERESA and JOSEPH II pursued their administrative, fiscal, economic, ecclesiastical, and educational reforms. The country thrived, enjoying a surge in cultural activities. Austria was one of the centers of the great German BAROQUE and ROCOCO styles in art and architecture; the visitor today can see fine examples from the period in the cities of Vienna, Innsbruck, and Salzburg. Country estates and monasteries also remain, testifying to the vigorous artistic expression of the period.

Music played a central role, with brilliant classical composers such as Wolfgang Amadeus MOZART, Christoph Willibald GLUCK, and Franz Joseph HAYDN producing their great works for the various princely courts of Austria and its neighbors, HUNGARY and Bohemia. Vienna assumed an ascendancy in the world of music that was not lost until the beginning of the 20th century.

The Austrian Enlightenment produced some unique contributions in the work of Franz Joseph GALL and Catholic reformers. It also helped to produce a great, if controversial, emperor in the figure of Joseph II. The ideas and activities of imperial advisers such as Gerard van SWIETEN and Josef von SONNENFELS mark them unmistakably as figures of the ENLIGHTENMENT. The ecclesiastical policy known as JOSEPHINISM was heavily indebted to enlightened ideas. The FREEMASONS flourished and created a new message by combining the ideas of the Bavarian ILLUMINATI with traditional Masonic teachings. In short, Austria and Austrian culture were deeply colored and formed by currents of the Enlightenment.

Austrian Netherlands Name for the 18th-century northern European territory located on the North Sea between France and the UNITED PROVINCES OF THE NETHERLANDS. Today the region is called BELGIUM.

Until the late 16th century, Belgian territories were joined to those of the Dutch Netherlands in a territorial unit called the Low Countries or the Netherlands. The Spanish branch of the Hapsburg family controlled the region after the mid-1500s.

In 1572, the Low Countries revolted against religious policies that were being enacted by Philip II of SPAIN. The region contained both Catholics and Calvinist Protestants. Ultimately, seven predominantly Protestant provinces in the northern section of the region broke away from Spanish domination and, in 1579, established the United Provinces of the Netherlands. The remaining 10 Catholic provinces in the south remained attached to Spain and became known as the Spanish Netherlands.

When the Spanish line of the Hapsburgs died out at the beginning of the 18th century, the War of the Spanish Succession resulted in the ceding of the Spanish throne to a grandson of the Bourbon French king LOUIS XIV. In the territorial musical chairs that accompanied the war, the Austrian Hapsburgs acquired the provinces of the Spanish Netherlands. As a result, from 1714 until the end of the 18th century, these provinces were called the Austrian Netherlands and were officially part of the HAPSBURG EMPIRE.

The provinces of the Austrian Netherlands had long enjoyed a special status in relation to their Hapsburg rulers. A traditional constitution replete with special privileges protected the subjects from the extremes of monarchical ABSOLUTISM. When the Austrian Hapsburgs assumed control of the region, they continued, out of necessity, to protect these special "Belgian liberties." JOSEPH II, however, proved impatient with this situation and viewed the traditional privileges as obstructions to enlightened, rational, central administration. He imposed a group of reforms on the provinces.

Joseph's actions provoked a revolt in 1787 that soon became a full-scale revolution containing elements and contradictions that would later characterize the FRENCH REVOLUTION. The situation was briefly stabilized in 1815, when peace returned to Europe after the Napoleonic Wars. At that time, the provinces of the Austrian Netherlands were reunited with the northern Dutch provinces to form the kingdom of the Netherlands. The southern provinces revolted in 1830 and, according to treaties signed in 1831 and 1839, were finally recognized as the independent kingdom of Belgium.

automata Mechanical figures that attempted to mimic a living being. Automata were a manifestation of the early modern belief that human beings were, at the basic level, sophisticated machines, an idea posited by René DESCARTES in the 17th century and elaborated by Julien Offray de LA METTRIE in the 18th. The makers of automata used sophisticated clockwork—levers, gears, and other interconnected parts—to try to produce artificial life. Influenced by the empiricism and man-machine ideas of the ENLIGHTENMENT, they believed that their figures might actually replicate the workings of living creatures.

Examples of sophisticated automata of the type produced in the 18th and early 19th century can be found as early as the 1400s. Noted pre-Enlightenment makers of automata included Italian artist and inventor Leonardo da Vinci and Dutch astronomer and mathematician Christian Huygens.

The 18th century saw an increase in interest in automata. Two noted inventors were Jacques de Vaucanson, a French engineer, and Pierre Jaquet-Droz, a Swiss inventor and mathematician. Vaucanson's creations included a mechanical duck that could swim, quack, and imitate eating and defecating, as well as a flute player with a repertory of 12 different melodies. Jacquet-Droz also created a famous musical automaton known as the Lady Musician. It could play five melodies on a harpsichord and displayed a stunning level of detail that included imitating breathing and eyes that followed its hands as it played. Jacquet-Droz also built an automaton of a boy seated at a small table who could write words or sentences containing 40 or fewer characters.

Some automata, such as Wolfgang von Kempelen's Turkish chess player, were too good to be true. The machine, with a lifelike torso, supposedly could play chess, and did so against opponents such as CATHERINE II (THE GREAT), Benjamin FRANKLIN, and Napoleon. The "Turk" toured Europe and America, but was later discovered to be a fraud, nothing more than a puppet whose chess-playing abilities were controlled by a real person.

See also SCIENCE OF MAN.

Further reading: Gaby Wood, *Edison's Eve: A Magical History of the Quest for Mechanical Life* (New York: Alfred A. Knopf, 2003).

B

Babeuf, François-Noel (1760–1797) *French journalist and radical revolutionary democrat*

François-Noel Babeuf was the son of Claude Babeuf, a soldier who deserted and fled from FRANCE in 1738. In 1752, Claude Babeuf received amnesty, returned to France, and became a minor official involved with the collection of salt taxes. Claude lost this job and became a laborer working on the construction of the fortifications at St. Quentin. Babeuf's mother, Marie-Cathérine Anceret, was a spinner whose labor provided major support for the family.

Young François-Noel Babeuf apparently received no formal schooling and taught himself how to read. He began working at the age of 12 and eventually obtained a job with a land surveyor. He opened his own surveying office at Roye in the province of Picardy, but encountered problems with clients who failed to pay their accounts. He also seems to have experienced some social prejudice on account of his personality, background, and obvious sympathies for people of the lower social classes.

In his capacity as a surveyor, Babeuf learned about feudal law and agrarian practices. He began to develop ideas about restructuring the distribution of land and about reforming the manner in which it was cultivated. He read avidly, especially Jean-Jacques ROUSSEAU, Gabriel Bonnet de Mably, and Louis Sébastien MERCIER. He dreamed of reestablishing either a communal agriculture system or an equitable division of land into plots capable of sustaining a family. He believed that the fundamental human right was the right to exist. Under the umbrella of that concept he placed both a right to own property and an equally valid right to work. Babeuf's ideas contained certain general traits that were to become common characteristics of 19th-century socialism and communism.

With the outbreak of the FRENCH REVOLUTION in 1789, Babeuf published a pamphlet entitled *Cadastre perpétuel*; (Permanent land survey), calling for equality in taxation, public assistance for the poor, and universal education. He also published several short-lived journals during the early years of the revolution: *Courrier de l'Europe* (European courier), *Journal de la Confédération* (Journal of the Confederation), and *Correspondant Picard* (Picard Correspondent).

Both in Paris and the region around Roye, Babeuf rapidly emerged as a leader of the lower classes of artisans and workers. He served in various regional administrative positions until January 1793, when he was accused of forging an official document. He tried to hide in Paris, but was arrested in November 1793 and imprisoned until after the downfall of Maximilien ROBESPIERRE.

Shortly thereafter, he began editing the journal *Le Tribun du Peuple* (The People's Tribune). He assumed the name Caius Gracchus Babeuf in direct reference to the famed democratic leader of ancient Rome. Babeuf began attending meetings at the Club électoral (Electoral Club) and persuaded the members to radicalize their revolutionary program. These activities brought a second arrest and imprisonment (1795). Upon release, Babeuf resumed publishing the *Tribun du Peuple*.

Around Babeuf a small group of radical democrats gathered who called themselves the Club du Panthéon (Pantheon Club). Within the club a secret committee, the Directoire secret de salut public (Secret directory for public safety), was formed in March 1796. The committee developed a larger conspiratorial organization whose job consisted of preparing for an insurrection.

The program of the committee called for an extension of the revolutionary ideal of equality from the strictly political sphere into the social sphere. It advocated a social system with nationalized commerce in which the use of money would be abolished. It also proposed that the transmission of property and associated privileges by inheritance would be abandoned. An obligation to work would be established, while both the production and the distribution of goods would be communally organized.

To spread its program, the committee utilized all the common propaganda tools of the period: pamphlets, placards, and songs. For six weeks the group agitated for the overthrow of the official government (also known as the Directory). By May 10, 1796, however, the identity of the conspirators was uncovered, and Babeuf and his companions were arrested. After a three-month trial, Babeuf and one companion were condemned to die. Babeuf was beheaded by the guillotine on May 26, 1797.

The program developed by Babeuf places him as an immediate forerunner of 19th-century socialism. It demonstrates one way that two central concepts of the ENLIGHTENMENT—EQUALITY and NATURAL RIGHTS—could be defined. The rejection of Babeuf's calls for radical social and economic equality demonstrates very clearly that the most common 18th-century definition of equality did not extend to property and wealth, but was primarily limited to legal political rights.

Bach, Carl Philipp Emanuel (1714–1788) *German composer, harpsichordist, and clavichordist*

C. P. E. Bach was the second son of Johann Sebastian BACH and his first wife, Maria Barbara Bach. He was the full brother of Wilhelm Friedemann BACH and the half brother of both Johann Christian BACH and Johann Christoph Friedrich Bach. He had two godfathers, one of whom was Georg Philipp TELEMANN.

C. P. E. Bach received his elementary education at the Leipzig Thomasschule (Thomas School). He studied law at the University of Frankfurt an der Oder in PRUSSIA and earned his law degree in 1735. From his earliest years, C. P. E. Bach demonstrated musical precocity. His father trained him in composition, and the young man produced several works before leaving the Thomasschule. He continued to pursue his musical activities at the university.

A dispute exists among historians about whether J. S. Bach intended his son to follow a legal career and to enter the Prussian bureaucracy. Music won the battle. C. P. E. Bach received an appointment in 1740 to serve as harpsichordist in the court orchestra of FREDERICK II (THE GREAT). Frederick was an avid amateur flutist who put on concerts three times each week at his court. Frederick chose the music and often featured himself as flute soloist.

At first flattered by his post, C. P. E. Bach ultimately found the chore of accompanying Frederick burdensome, especially since Frederick demanded deference even in matters of interpretation. Bach began seeking a new appointment. But in order to accept a different post, he needed the permission of Frederick the Great, and Frederick was reluctant to release such an eminent musician from his staff. Finally, in June 1767, when Telemann's death opened up a prominent position in Hamburg, Frederick relented.

C. P. E. Bach assumed Telemann's post and worked in Hamburg for the rest of his life. He was survived by his wife, Johanna Maria Dannemann, a son (d. 1789), and a daughter. During his Hamburg years, Bach assumed responsibility for his young half brother, Johann Christian Bach. He tutored him in music and provided for his living needs following the death in 1750 of their father, J. S. Bach.

The compositions of C. P. E. Bach clearly mark him as a member of the transitional generation that divides the BAROQUE STYLE of J. S. Bach from the mature classical style of Franz Joseph HAYDN. This transitional German style is sometimes called EMPFINDSAMER STIL (sensitive or sentimental style). Some musicologists liken it to the literary STURM UND DRANG that marked the German transition to ROMANTICISM. Others consider it a distinct style from the *Sturm und Drang* and align it with the French and Italian STYLE GALANT (gallant style).

The uniqueness of C. P. E. Bach's compositional ideas did not fully emerge until after his departure from Frederick the Great's service. Frederick had conservative musical tastes (he especially liked the *style galant* compositions of Johann Joachim Quantz and the Graun brothers). Bach felt constrained to compose for those tastes, but hints of his mature *empfindsamer Stil* were already apparent.

Bach's early *empfindsamer Stil* works treat melody homophonically: One line in a composition carries the melody, and the other lines are subordinate, providing the accompaniment. In contrast, his father's contrapuntal compositions contain many lines of equal weight. Works by C. P. E. Bach display great delicacy of sentiment and form, traits that were generally associated by contemporaries with naturalness. They break with baroque conventions by exploring more than one sentiment within the boundaries of a single piece or movement.

The compositions from C. P. E. Bach's early period are eminently suited for intimate performances in salons or private rooms. They particularly exploit the quiet sounds and musical capabilities of the clavichord, the viola da gamba, and the one- and two-keyed flute. Prominent works include the six Prussian Sonatas and the six Württemberg Sonatas for clavichord or other keyboard instrument, several concertos for flute, the sonatas for violin and keyboard, and the sonatas for viola da gamba and keyboard.

C. P. E. Bach's mature compositions, written in the relative freedom of Hamburg, thoroughly exploit the possibilities of the *empfindsamer Stil*. They use sharp dynamic contrasts, startling harmonies, and sudden periods of silence to emphasize various emotional states. The most outstanding of these later compositions include the Six Symphonies for Strings, Wotquenne 182, written on a commission from the Austrian minister Gottfried van SWIETEN. The complete catalog of C. P. E. Bach's works drawn up by Wotquenne lists more than 700 individual compositions.

In addition to his musical compositions, C. P. E. Bach left two important instructional treatises: the *Versuch über die wahre Art das Klavier zu spielen* (Essay on the true art of playing keyboard instruments; 1753–62) and the *Kurze Anweisung zum General-Bass* (Short introduction to the general-bass). The former work is the first methodical treatment of keyboard technique and stylistic ornamentation. Both MOZART and Haydn acknowledged their indebtedness to this manual. Today it serves as a primary source for musicians interested in learning the intricacies of 18th-century performance practices.

Bach, Johann Christian (1735–1782) *German musician and composer, popularly known as the "London Bach"*

J. C. Bach was the youngest son of Johann Sebastian BACH and his second wife, Anna Magdalena Bach. Little is known about Johann Christian Bach's early education. His older brothers attended the Thomasschule (Thomas School) in Leipzig, but no records exist regarding this youngest member of the illustrious Bach family. The death of his father in 1750 prevented him from attending a university. Instead, he joined his older half brothers, Wilhelm Friedemann BACH and Carl Philipp Emanuel BACH, in BERLIN, where under the tutelage of the latter, he continued his musical training.

Like many of his contemporaries, Johann Christian Bach traveled to the Italian peninsula in search of employment and continued instruction. In MILAN, he obtained the patronage of Count Agostino Litta, who provided him with the means to begin studying music theory and composition under the famed Giovanni Battista Martini (Padre Martini). Young Bach converted, at this time, from his native LUTHERANISM to ROMAN CATHOLICISM, and devoted himself to creating church music.

By 1760, through the continued patronage of Count Litta, Bach acquired a coveted post as organist at the Cathedral of Milan. But his artistic interests were already leading him away from ecclesiastical music toward the composition of secular operas. Therefore, when the opportunity arose in 1762 to take a post in England, Bach quickly accepted. His operatic productions at the King's Theater in LONDON were notably well received. Their success brought him an appointment as music master to Queen Charlotte and her children. In this capacity, Bach pursued a 20-year career as composer, performer, teacher, and impresario. He died at the age of 46 and was buried in London at St. Pancras.

The middle years of the 18th century can be viewed as a great period of ferment and transition in the realm of music. Nothing illustrates this claim more succinctly than the spectacle of Johann Christian Bach, son of the great baroque master, Johann Sebastian BACH, instructing the future master of the classical era, Wolfgang Amadeus MOZART, in the art of writing symphonies. The works of J. C. Bach demonstrate in bold relief most of the major characteristics of 18th-century musical development. They have elegant, witty, yet simple and accessible melodies conforming to the Italian version of the popular STYLE GALANT (gallant style). Lovely in their own terms, they also functioned as important bridges between the baroque and classical periods in MUSIC.

J. C. Bach left an impressive opus of vocal and instrumental works. They include operas, songs, masses, cantatas, symphonies, and chamber works. Perhaps his most significant contributions with respect to the subsequent history of music were his symphonies. The symphonic form was new, still in embryonic stages, and Bach proved to be a master at drawing out its potentialities. He demonstrated adeptness at solving the structural problems of the form. New instruments such as the CLARINET and pianoforte challenged his creative abilities, and he became a master at orchestration.

Johann Christian Bach worked diligently not only as a composer but also as an impresario. Throughout the 18th century, steps were being taken to popularize music by making it more readily accessible to the general public. Whereas stylistic simplifications broadened the appeal of the music, changes in the way it was presented and financially supported made concertgoing a possibility for commoners. Courts, churches, and salons continued to serve as concert sites, but public performances in outdoor gardens and concert halls became more frequent. For a very small sum, anyone, regardless of his or her social status, could hear a performance. Such public concerts freed the pursuit of music from exclusive associations with either church or aristocracy and helped break down the old system of aristocratic patronage for performers and composers. By the end of the 18th century, it became possible, although very difficult, for composers to support themselves without the benefit of traditional patronage. J. C. Bach never lived in this manner, but when he and Karl Friedrich ABEL sponsored their highly successful series of subscribed, public concerts in London, they were contributing substantively to the transformation of the old system.

See also BAROQUE STYLE; CLASSICISM; PIANO; SYMPHONY ORCHESTRA.

Bach, Johann Sebastian (1685–1750) *German baroque composer, organist, and harpsichordist*

J. S. Bach came from a large musical family that produced competent and outstanding musicians in the best "craft guild" tradition for many generations. Johann Sebastian was the youngest son of musician Johann Ambrosius Bach and Elisabeth Lämmerhirt. The deaths of his mother

Portrait of Johann Sebastian Bach (1685–1750), one of the greatest performers and composers in the history of European music. His baroque and rococo influenced compositions fused German, Italian, and French styles. *(Courtesy New York Public Library)*

and father made J. S. Bach an orphan at the age of 10. He and his older brother, Johann Jakob Bach, were taken in by their newly married oldest brother, Johann Christoph Bach. Johann Sebastian Bach attended school at the Gymnasium of Eisenach and at the Ohrdruf Lyceum. He was a good student, and having an outstanding soprano voice, sang in both school and church choirs.

In 1700, at the age of 15, Johann Sebastian Bach set out on his own. Through the references supplied by the music instructor at his school, he obtained a post in the principal choir or Mettenschüler in Lüneburg. Bach had studied both organ and violin. He traveled to Hamburg to hear the organist Johann Adam Reinken and also went to Celle to experience the French-influenced court orchestra concerts sponsored by the duke of Celle. Bach began his regular adult employment at Weimar as a violinist in the orchestra of the reigning duke's nephew. He stayed only briefly since he was able, in 1703, to obtain a position as organist in the Bonifacius-Kirche at Arnstadt.

In October 1705, Bach obtained permission to take a short leave to visit Lübeck to hear the organist Dietrich Buxtehude perform. Under the spell of the great organ master, he stayed away from Arnstadt for four months. When he returned to Arnstadt, he was severely reprimanded by the city's governing consistory, for such absences were illegal under Arnstadt law. The consistory also complained about new compositional techniques that Bach was using. They found his vocal works too difficult for the members of the congregation.

In 1707, Bach obtained a more distinguished post as organist in the free imperial city of Mühlhausen. He stayed just short of one year. The city was embroiled in a theological dispute between Lutherans and Pietists that had implications for his work. Pietists opposed the use of elaborate music in worship services, and Bach found his creativity stifled. During this period, he married Maria Barbara Bach, a cousin from his mother's side of the family.

The year 1708 brought an appointment as court organist and chamber musician at Weimar, where he stayed until 1717, when he moved to Cöthen to direct the prince of Anhalt-Cöthen's orchestra. Maria Barbara died unexpectedly in 1720. Bach married his second wife, Anna Magdalena Wilcken, in December 1721. He remained in Cöthen until 1723, when he accepted a position at the St. Thomasschule in Leipzig. Part of his reason for moving seems to have stemmed from concern about securing a proper Lutheran education for his children in Calvinist Cöthen.

Bach assumed duties as the music master (cantor) at the St. Thomasschule in Leipzig. He remained there writing and producing works for the various churches of the city. The school was responsible for providing both choirs and music to these churches. In 1749, Bach was afflicted by nearly total blindness. The English eye surgeon Chevalier John Taylor, later the eye doctor to King George III, tried unsuccessfully to restore his sight. Bach died in July 1750 of complications from a paralytic stroke. He was buried in the St. Thomaskirche at Leipzig next to the remains of the noted German poet Christian Fürchtegott Gellert.

Not much is known of Bach's private life. He had 12 children, of whom four, Wilhelm Friedemann BACH, Carl Philipp Emanuel BACH, Johann Christoph Friedrich Bach, and Johann Christian BACH, made noted musical careers. Histories of Bach and various town consistory records reveal a colorful, frugal, and independent character. More than once Johann Sebastian was called before a town consistory to explain his behavior. He was imprisoned for one month in November 1717 for requesting release from his Weimar post in a manner lacking the required deference. Bach was a devout Lutheran who considered a career in music as a vocation dedicated to the service of God.

During his life Bach was renowned throughout Germany as a brilliant organist and improviser. His compositions, however, were not widely known outside the courts and towns where they were composed. The beginning of a Bach revival can be traced to the biography written by Johann Nikolaus Forkel (1802), who Bach had visited in Göttingen. Forkel dedicated his work to the Austrian statesman and music patron Gottfried van SWIETEN. In BERLIN, Carl Friedrich Zelter, founder of the Berlin Singakademie (1791), took up the revival cause. Zelter helped to persuade the mature Johann Wolfgang von GOETHE of the value of Bach's works. Finally, Felix Mendelssohn (1809–47) conducted a performance of the SAINT MATTHEW PASSION at the Berlin Singakademie in 1829. The work was published in 1830. These events proved a turning point after which Bach became a popular figure. The Bach-Gesellschaft, an organization formed in 1850, began the long-term task of publishing all known works of the master. These publications remained the standard until 1954, when the music publisher Bärenreiter began the Neue Bach-Ausgabe (New Bach Edition), still in progress.

Bach was a prolific composer whose work represents the culmination of the polyphonic compositional style. He composed almost exclusively according to BAROQUE STYLE conventions, which were already becoming old-fashioned during his life. However, some of his compositions, particularly those modeled consciously on the contemporary French or Italian styles, exhibit ROCOCO inspiration. In general, Bach's compositions achieve a masterful fusion of the specific German, French, and Italian national styles. His polyphony is remarkable for the melodic richness of its thematic material.

The large catalog of his works reveals that most of his vocal compositions are sacred church music. It lists five complete cycles of vocal cantatas, one for each Sunday in the liturgical year. Other great sacred works are the MASS IN B MINOR (sent to Augustus III of Saxony and Poland as application for a job as royal composer), the Saint Matthew Passion (composed on a commission from van Swieten), the Passion according to Saint John, the Magnificat, and the Christmas Oratorio. Bach's numerous organ works were also written to be played in church services. These pieces include the wonderful choral preludes and the masterful organ preludes, fugues, fantasies, and passacaglias. Bach produced outstanding secular works at Cöthen and, in later years, on private commission. Among the works from the Cöthen period are the BRANDENBURG CONCERTOS (written for Margrave Christian Ludwig of Brandenburg), the flute sonatas, the suites for orchestra, the Chromatic Fantasy and Fugue for keyboard, the English suites and French suites for harpsichord, the first part of the Well-Tempered Clavier (written for his son Wilhelm Friedemann Bach), the two-part inventions and the three-part inventions, several concerti for violin or harpsichord, the six partitas for violin, and the marvelous unaccompanied suites for violoncello. The delightful Musical Offering (Musikalisches Opfer) was written in 1747 on a theme provided by FREDERICK II (THE GREAT). Bach also composed secular vocal cantatas for special state occasions such as marriages, coronations, and

funerals. The best known are the two wedding cantatas, the Peasant Cantata, with its authentic Low German text, and the satirical Coffee Cantata, written to poke fun at contemporaries' anxieties over the potential evils of the new drug, coffee.

J. S. Bach stands as one of the greatest composers and performers in the history of European music. His works have been played lovingly by subsequent generations and have been adapted successfully to widely different stylistic interpretations.

Further reading: Donald Jay Grout, *A History of Western Music,* rev. ed. (New York: W. W. Norton, 1973); Christopher Wolff et al., eds., *The New Grove Bach Family* (New York: W. W. Norton, 1983).

Bach, Wilhelm Friedemann (1710–1784) *German organist and composer, known as the "Halle Bach"*
W. F. Bach was the oldest son of Johann Sebastian BACH and his first wife, Maria Barbara. Wilhelm Friedemann received his early musical education from his father, who composed the *Clavier-Büchlein vor Wilhelm Friedemann Bach* (Little Clavier Book for Wilhelm Friedemann Bach), the *Two- and Three-Part Inventions,* and *Das wohltemperierte Clavier* (The Well-Tempered Clavier) for his instruction. Young Bach attended a Lutheran school (gymnasium) in Cöthen, then transferred to the St. Thomasschule in Leipzig when his father became the school's music master (cantor). Wilhelm Friedemann enrolled at Leipzig University in 1729, where he pursued courses in mathematics, philosophy, and law, but also continued his musical pursuits. He met George Frederick HANDEL during this period (1729) in Halle.

In 1733, Wilhelm Friedemann obtained a post as organist of the Sophien-Kirche in Dresden. He carried out his performance duties and had ample time to compose, teach, and continue studying mathematics. Bach became a well-known figure in Dresden musical society. However, he desired a greater salary, more independence, and a post in a Protestant rather than Catholic church. As a result, he took a position in Pietist-dominated Halle in 1746. The job entailed considerably more responsibility. He was both organist and director of accompanied choral music. During his Halle years, W. F. Bach acquired a reputation as the most outstanding organist in Germany.

In Halle, W. F. Bach came into contact with the enlightened philosopher Christian WOLFF. Wilhelm Friedemann seems to have been strongly influenced by Wolff's ideas and also by his contacts with BERLIN. He became dissatisfied with the drab atmosphere of Halle, and his relationship with his employers, the Halle town council, became increasingly tense. In the eyes of the Halle council members, W. F. Bach was growing irresponsible.

In 1770, Bach resigned from his position and, after having sold some of his wife's property, moved the family to Braunschweig (Brunswick). Although he failed to find a permanent position, he supported his family in piecemeal fashion by playing recitals, composing on commission, and selling his father's manuscripts. In 1774, he moved to Berlin, where he pursued his free-lance existence with better results. Nevertheless, when Bach died in 1784, his wife and daughter were left in poverty. They were provided a small endowment through the proceeds of a Berlin performance of Handel's *Messiah.*

Wilhelm Friedemann's most important works are the *Concerto for Two Unaccompanied Harpsichords* and the *Sinfonia in F.* Both display his characteristic vacillation between the old BAROQUE STYLE of his father and the emerging EMPFINDSAMER STIL. Wilhelm Friedemann Bach never achieved a true synthesis of the two approaches, nor did he abandon the older baroque style. W. F. Bach also left numerous solo sonatas for keyboard, chamber music for small groups of instruments, sacred cantatas, concertos for harpsichord and orchestra, and several sinfonias for orchestra. A catalogue of the major musical themes in his work has been published by Martin Falck.

Bacon, Francis (baron of Verulam) (1561–1626) *English philosopher of science*

Francis Bacon, son of the lord keeper of the great seal of England, Sir Nicholas Bacon, attended Trinity College at Cambridge University and entered the legal profession in 1582. His contacts with the English court brought him knighthood in 1603 (with the accession of James I) and the post of lord chancellor of England in 1618. In 1621, however, Bacon lost the chancellorship after being convicted of bribery. He retired to his estate near Saint Albans and devoted himself to studying the philosophy of science.

Although Bacon's life preceded the onset of the ENLIGHTENMENT by nearly a century, his writings nevertheless served as one of its primary intellectual sources. In the spirit of many figures of the late Renaissance, Bacon envisioned a thoroughgoing reform of all human knowledge, based on a new SCIENTIFIC METHOD. Bacon's method was that of philosophical induction. It involved the careful collection of observations (facts) from experience and experiment and their subsequent organization into a new system of knowledge. He equated the collection and description of observations from nature with natural history and called that discipline the "great root and mother" of all scientific endeavor.

The new system of knowledge would include not only the abstract disciplines such as philosophy and mathematics but also the trades and crafts. A group of intellectuals working together (collaborating) at their task would create the new system. Once elaborated, the new system of knowledge would be used to solve practical problems in human life. Knowledge, then, would acquire a certain utility (usefulness) for human society, would serve the cause of PROGRESS, and would play a central role in creating a human utopia, Bacon's New Atlantis.

Bacon's method stood in stark opposition to the deductive method in PHILOSOPHY. Deduction began not with observations (facts) but with a single philosophical principle or axiom. From that principle it created a whole system of knowledge by applying the rules of logic. Deduction had produced the great medieval systems of Scholastic philosophy, and in a revised form, it would create the geometric method and MECHANICAL PHILOSOPHY of René DESCARTES.

Bacon outlined his method and program in several works, the most significant of which were: *Novum organum* (New organon; 1620), part one of the projected *Great Instauration; De augmentis scientiarum* (On the advancement of learning; 1623), part two of the projected *Great Instauration; The Advancement of Learning* (1605), an early English version of *De augmentis scientiarum;* and *New Atlantis* (1627), the presentation of Bacon's utopian vision, published in English for the general reading public.

Bacon's inductive method, and his conceptualization of science as a collaborative project based on inductive reasoning and aimed at achieving complete human knowledge inspired the work of 17th-century experimental scientists in ENGLAND, the UNITED PROVINCES OF THE NETHERLANDS, and FRANCE. His vision of science received institutional form in the creation of the ROYAL SOCIETY OF LONDON. The society's founders consciously modeled their organization on Bacon's vision of collaborative, experimental science.

Through the activities of the Royal Society and of scientists throughout Europe who were committed to experimental methods, the Baconian vision eventually entered into the discourse and vision of the Enlightenment. VOLTAIRE, whose *Lettres philosophiques* (Philosophical letters) introduced the general French public to the experimental science of NEWTON and the sensation psychology of John LOCKE, included Bacon as one of the philosophers who had proved the necessity of experiment in attaining knowledge. Denis DIDEROT planned the ENCYCLOPÉDIE as a comprehensive presentation of human knowledge in the sciences, trades, crafts, and arts. He followed not only Bacon's general vision but also the specifics of his CLASSIFICATION of human knowledge. In addition, Bacon's elevation of natural history to a primary role in creating comprehensive knowledge helped to stimulate the dramatic growth and intellectual development of that discipline.

In short, the Enlightenment in some instances represented an attempt to bring Bacon's New Atlantis, that utopian human society built on knowledge, into actual existence.

See also HISTORY.

Bahrdt, Carl Friedrich (1740–1792) *German theologian and philosopher*

Carl Friedrich Bahrdt was born in Bischofswerda, in the Oberlausitz region east of Dresden. His father was a Lutheran theologian, and Bahrdt began his theological studies at the University of Leipzig in 1757. He became a professor there in 1766. Bahrdt moved around German-speaking Europe frequently, and in 1777, he traveled to England, where he joined the FREEMASONS. He settled at the University of HALLE in 1779. In addition to his activities as a Freemason, Bahrdt founded the German Union of the Twenty-Two as an organization parallel to the Bavarian ILLUMINATI.

Bahrdt was one of the most controversial theologians of his time. His outspoken criticism of Johann Christoph Wöllner's religious edicts, enacted in Prussia in 1788, resulted in his imprisonment in Magdeburg between 1788 and 1790. It his satire of the edicts, published as *Das Religionsedikt* (The edict of religion), Bahrdt claimed that Moses used explosives to create the divine thunder witnessed on Mount Sinai and accused Jesus of working his miracles with secret stockpiles of food and medicine. While in prison, Bahrdt wrote his autobiography. After his release, he was further radicalized by the FRENCH REVOLUTION. Having lost his position at the university, he spent his last decade as an innkeeper and died in Halle on April 23, 1792.

Further reading: Carl Bahrdt, *The Edict of Religion: A Comedy, and The Story and Diary of My Imprisonment* (Lanham, Md.: Lexington Books, 2000).

Banks, Joseph (1743–1820) *English botanist who accompanied Captain James cook on his first voyage around the world (1768–71)*
Joseph Banks enjoyed the privileges and income that derived from his family's position in the English landed gentry. The income, in particular, supported Banks's botany studies throughout his life.

Banks began his higher education at Oxford University, but abandoned his coursework after several years without obtaining a degree. He moved to LONDON and began traveling in order to collect plant specimens for the Banks Herbarium. Banks and Daniel Carl Solander, a Swedish student of LINNAEUS, joined Cook's first voyage to the South Pacific. They gathered more than 800 specimens of previously unknown plants.

In 1766, Banks was elected a fellow of the ROYAL SOCIETY OF LONDON. He served for 41 years as president of the society (1778–1820). Sometimes portrayed as an autocrat, Banks was definitely a dominating force in the Royal Society and in London life.

A 1771 meeting between Banks and King George III resulted in a friendship between the two men that centered on their mutual botanical interests. Banks persuaded the king to make Kew Gardens a botanical research site. He assisted in bringing merino sheep, jealously guarded by the Spanish, to England and helped with the establishment of a colony in Australia. Finally, during the wars that broke out in conjunction with the FRENCH REVOLUTION, Banks used his influence to protect French and English scientists from incarceration and harassment.

See also VOYAGES OF DISCOVERY.

Barlow, Joel (1754–1812) *American poet, businessman, writer, and diplomat*
Joel Barlow was born into a farming family in Connecticut and attended both Dartmouth and Yale Colleges. He delivered a commencement poem, *The Prospect of Peace*, at his Yale graduation ceremony in 1778. During the AMERICAN REVOLUTION, Barlow served between 1780 and 1783 as a chaplain in the Continental Army. After the war, he settled in Hartford, Connecticut, where he joined a group of young writers known as the Connecticut, or Hartford, Wits. With Elisha Babcock, he founded a weekly newspaper in Hartford, *The American Mercury*. In 1786, Barlow was admitted to the bar.

In 1787, the Constitutional Convention began meeting in PHILADELPHIA to hammer out the provisions of a constitution for the new United States. Barlow publicly praised the achievements of the convention, but warned against assuming that the work of the American Revolution was yet completed. Although the United States had won the war, it still needed a viable government. Evoking certain ideals of the ENLIGHTENMENT, Barlow declared that "the present is the age of philosophy, and America the empire of reason."

Barlow gained literary fame in 1787, when he published his epic poem, *The Vision of Columbus*. This poem narrated the story of the discovery of America and portrayed America as a place of hope for future generations.

Barlow traveled to France in 1788, having agreed to sell American land in Europe on behalf of the Scioto Land Company. Although unsuccessful in his official duties, Barlow used the opportunity to make the acquaintance of the leading enlightened French intellectuals of the era. He immersed himself in French politics and, when the FRENCH REVOLUTION broke out in 1789, aligned himself with the men who became leaders of the Girondin faction.

On account of the political instability associated with the revolution, Barlow found it necessary, in 1791, to move to ENGLAND. He was soon mingling with radical reformers such as Joseph PRIESTLEY and Thomas PAINE. He published *Advice to the Privileged Orders* (1792), an essay whose support of the revolutionary ideals of political EQUALITY, of social reform to meet basic human needs, and of SEPARATION OF CHURCH AND STATE earned public attacks from Edmund BURKE. The essay was censored, and Barlow fled back to France in 1792, settling in Chambéry in the Savoy region. He helped to establish the revolutionary administration in Savoy and ran unsuccessfully as the representative of the region to the National Convention. While in Chambéry, Barlow wrote his most popular poem, a mock epic about New England corn-mush entitled *The Hasty Pudding* (published 1796).

Barlow remained in France from 1792 until 1795. He spent some time in PARIS, where his home served as a gathering place for people such as Thomas Paine, Robert Fulton, Count Rumford, Marie-Jean de CONDORCET, and

Mary WOLLSTONECRAFT. Barlow assisted Paine during the latter's imprisonment, by seeing that Paine's book, *THE AGE OF REASON*, was published. He presented his *Letters to the French Convention* to the deputies of the National Convention in 1792 and was received as an honorary citizen of France.

Between 1795 and 1797, Barlow served as United States consul at Algiers in North Africa. He carried out a series of negotiations with the Barbary States, securing the freedom of several Americans who were being held for ransom.

In 1805, Barlow returned to the United States, settling outside Washington D.C., on an estate with extensive gardens called Kalorama. He acted as a political ally of Thomas JEFFERSON and James MADISON. He published a revised edition of *The Vision of Columbus* in 1807, and in 1811 traveled back to France to negotiate a commercial treaty with Napoleon. The trip proved to be his last. While waiting in Vilna, POLAND, to meet Napoleon, Barlow was caught up in the chaos of the French retreat from MOSCOW in 1812. He completed *Advice of a Raven in Russia,* a verse attack on Napoleon, just days before pneumonia killed him.

See also UNITED STATES CONSTITUTION.

barometer   Scientific instrument that measures atmospheric pressure. The barometer aided the development of 17th-century fluid statics and played a significant role in legitimizing both the new MECHANICAL PHILOSOPHY and the experimental SCIENTIFIC METHOD. As a result, the barometer acted as a major factor in the SCIENTIFIC REVOLUTION.

The first barometer, consisting of a glass tube closed at the top, with its open end standing in a water-filled vessel, was built in the early 1640s. In 1644, the Italian Evangelista Torricelli constructed the first mercury barometer. Torricelli conducted experiments that suggested that the barometer acts on the same principles as a simple mechanical balance. The weight of atmospheric air acting on a water barometer produced a column of 34 feet (10.4 meters), whereas the same air acting on a barometer filled with mercury (denser than water) raised the mercury column only 29 inches (74 centimeters). Such results were predicted by mechanical theory and helped to convince European researchers that the mechanical philosophy contained valid views of the natural world. The famous Puy de Dome experiment carried out by Blaise Pascal definitively confirmed the mechanical theory of the barometer.

The barometer also helped to resolve debates over the question of whether vacuums exist in nature and disputes over the nature of air. Torricelli's experiments had suggested that a vacuum exists at the top of the barometer tube. But traditional science rejected the notion and Christian theologians also rejected the idea. Torricelli and Pascal both investigated the question of the vacuum and struggled with the implications of their findings. Later, the chemist Robert Boyle performed experiments with a barometer and air pump that led him to assert that air is a kind of elastic fluid.

baroque style   A style in music, art, and architecture created around 1600 in ROME, and then transmitted throughout Europe. It continued to exercise aesthetic influence in some areas until 1750, well into the era of the ENLIGHTENMENT. Especially in music and architecture, it overlapped with the appearance of the ROCOCO style.

During the late Enlightenment, the word *baroque* entered the language of art critics through the works of Johann Joachim WINCKELMANN, Giuseppe Marc'Antonio Baretti, and Saverio Bettinelli, who championed the newer AESTHETICS of NEOCLASSICISM. These critics derided baroque art as irregular, and hence "unnatural"; they believed that, in contrast, neoclassical forms were "natural" because they were regular and symmetrical, conforming to the geometrical laws of proportion and perspective. Thus, one faction of the Enlightenment considered the baroque its aesthetic enemy, something to be avoided and rejected. However, the relations between the baroque and the Enlightenment were much more complex than this criticism suggested.

The term *baroque* has two distinct etymologies, both of which have influenced its meaning and application. Some scholars attribute the source to the Portugese *barroco,* meaning a kind of rough, asymmetric natural pearl. French critics and dictionaries of the 18th century made explicit use of this meaning. Other scholars attribute the origin of the term of the logical concept of *baroco,* developed in the Middle Ages. By the 16th century, that concept had come to mean any complex, convoluted idea or exceedingly tortuous line of thinking. It was contrasted to the simple, regular forms of thought associated with syllogistic logic.

Baroque style emerged in the late 16th century and early 17th century as the artistic expression of three significant historical developments: the revision of conceptions of the universe implied in the theories of the early SCIENTIFIC REVOLUTION; the retrenchment of ROMAN CATHOLICISM in opposition to PROTESTANTISM; and the development of monarchical ABSOLUTISM.

Scientific changes encapsulated in the COPERNICAN REVOLUTION and the discoveries of Galileo GALILEI offered to human beings the prospect of an immense, possibly infinite universe in which constant motion was the normal state of things. At the same time that human images of the natural world began dramatically to change, the Roman Catholic Church and secular monarchies both emerged as powerful, centralizing forces in Europe. The Catholic Church recaptured some regions that had fallen under Protestant control during the 16th century, and the pope, the head of the church, desired to fill his capital, Rome, with symbols of that new power. In fact, it was the popes whose commissions financed the earliest baroque creations.

The era witnessed the consolidation of the theory and practice of monarchical absolutism. Kings and princes attempted to gather all aspects of political power under their control and used the forms of the baroque style to represent their power and their visions of the world.

Baroque style manifested itself in paintings, sculptures, churches, monumental buildings, and musical compositions. Specific stylistic elements varied widely, but a few characteristics cut across boundaries, thereby providing the unity that justifies speaking at all of a general baroque style.

Four such general traits can be named. First, in spite of what critics said, baroque creations were mostly symmetrical in basic structure. Second, however, they attempted to represent motion rather than rest by means of these forms. Third, baroque productions generally focused on manipulating psychological response by means of artistic expression. They accomplished this goal in two general ways: by using religious, political, mythological, and social symbols for conscious purposes of propaganda or by depicting the human passions, those grand emotions such as terror and ecstasy whose power had been clearly demonstrated in the preceding century. Fourth, themes of grandeur, power, infinity, and universality dominated the intellectual content of baroque works.

Specific technical practices served these general goals. They varied according to the propagandistic and aesthetic aims of an individual work. Architecture offers outstanding examples of the adaptation of technical practices to propagandistic goals.

In general, architectural treatment of interior space and facades began to shift away from straight lines that produced square or rectangular buildings, to curving lines that formed circles or ellipses. These curves dominated both interiors and facades, helping to keep the eye constantly in motion, and therefore creating a dynamic sensation.

In Jesuit church architecture, one major example of baroque achievement, facades curve out into the street, beckoning passersby to enter and to experience religious emotion by contemplating the church interior or by hearing the mass. Inside the churches, the senses are impressed by the massiveness and grandeur of scale. Nevertheless, the interiors create a sense of dramatic motion. Wall lines are broken by columns or niches. The eye is drawn by architectural lines upward to a round dome. Careful attention to sources of light creates theatrical effects, a specialty of the style. For example, the dome is nearly always open so that light rays, representing the divine light of God and his revelations to humankind, filter into the church. In general, interior decoration consisted of a rich combination of painting, sculpture, and architectural elements, all designed to deliver a coherent message.

The era of the baroque produced the first urban planning efforts since antiquity. In Rome, Pope Sixtus V inaugurated the idea of urban planning by commissioning Domenico Fontana to lay out a new street plan. Fontana utilized long, straight roads connecting the seven major Christian churches of the city to unify the city in a manner that made Christian rather than pre-Christian architecture the central focus. The whole plan underlined not only the power of the pope but also the renewed vigor of Counter-Reformation Roman Catholicism.

In FRANCE, a special form of baroque CLASSICISM emerged. In fact, the French generally hesitate to apply the term *baroque* to their 17th-century art, preferring the terms *classicism* and *style of Louis XIV.* However, their 17th-century styles contained prominent baroque elements and served as the source for much baroque courtly architecture in Europe. The most remarkable example is the Palace of Versailles, built by LOUIS XIV in order to escape the necessity of living in PARIS. The palace design demonstrates the manner in which baroque architects manipulated space; in this instance, the manipulation aimed at symbolically representing the might of the French monarchy. The Versailles Palace is a huge, imposing structure, set on a hill with views to the distant horizon that were intended to suggest that French royal power extended infinitely, beyond any horizon. Interiors are large in scale and richly decorated in a manner that also constantly suggests power.

Examples of baroque architecture, interiors, and urban planning may still be observed throughout Europe. In Rome, where baroque buildings are plentiful, Saint Peter's Basilica with its curved colonnade and papal throne by Bernini; the Church of Saint Ignazio; San Carlo alle Quattro Fontane; and Santa Agnese and its Piazza Navona should be mentioned. Also, the Spanish Steps, the Fontana di Trevi, the Church of Il Gesù, and the Collegio di Propagande Fide are outstanding examples. TURIN contains a baroque quarter among whose important buildings are the Palazzo Carignano, the Palazzo Madama, San Lorenzo, and the Chapel of the Holy Shroud. Just outside Turin, the Superga and Stupinigi demonstrate the power of the style. In VENICE, the facade of the Palazzo Rezzonico on the Grand Canal, and the Church of Santa Maria della Salute represent the style. Paris contains the beautiful Place des Vosges (originally called the Place Royale), the Church of Saint Peter and Saint Paul, the church of the Invalides, the Sorbonne, and the East Wing of the Louvre Palace. In Austria, the Melk Monastery and the Church of Saint Charles Borromaeus illustrate the style.

Major architects and sculptors in this tradition were Giovanni Lorenzo Bernini, Francesco Borromini, Carlo Maderno, Guarino Guarini, and Filippo Juvarra of the Italian peninsula; Jules Hardouin Mansart and Andre Le Nôtre of France and Jakob PRANDTAUER, and Johann FISCHER VON ERLACH of the HAPSBURG EMPIRE.

Baroque style in painting and sculpture manifests itself in readily identifiable technical aspects. Diagonal lines with curves organize the compositions and force the eye to move continually. Surrounding material seems to move with sometimes dizzying motion, and strong primary colors such as red, blue, and yellow are common. Thematic materials—drawn from Christian tradition, pagan mythology, or history—depict physical or emotional action, and compositions tend to capture the climactic moment in a story. Clouds, *putti* (plump infant boy angels), and radiant light are present everywhere. Finally, the lighting of the compositions is wholly new. Light is used to reveal the dramatic moment and to display inner emotion. Sometimes the implied source of light in a composition lies outside the frame of the work. In fact, baroque compositions sometimes suggest that the action both begins and ends somewhere beyond the boundaries of the actual composition. The resultant works are dramatic and powerful, offering insight into the deepest meanings of the subjects.

Beyond these common elements, baroque painting breaks down into several types or traditions. The idealist tradition initiated by Annibale and Lodovico Carracci tended to portray mythological or perfect subjects in a manner that emphasized the higher moral or spiritual aspects of the theme. Members of this school generally were experts at the use of color to make statements. In contrast, members of the realist school, following traditions established by Caravaggio, depicted the full humanity of subjects. They concentrated on revealing inner emotion and imperfection, and developed the use of lighting to produce desired dramatic effects. They sometimes portrayed everyday activities or subjects: tavern drinking, peasants at work and play, or domestic scenes. Within the realist tradition, some painters also concentrated on depicting landscapes.

Outstanding painters in the baroque style included Rembrandt van Rijn, Franz Hals, Jan Steen, and Jacob van Ruisdael of the UNITED PROVINCES OF THE NETHERLANDS; Georges de La Tour from the principality of Lorraine; Nicolas Poussin, Louis Le Nain, and Claude Lorrain from France; Anthony van Dyck of Antwerp and ENGLAND; Peter Paul Rubens of Antwerp; and finally Diego Velazquez, Francisco de Zurbarán, and Bartolomé Esteban Murillo of SPAIN.

By the beginning of the 18th century, baroque painting and architecture were beginning the transformation to rococo. The latter style is strongly associated with the Enlightenment. Whatever its similarities to and origins in the baroque, modern scholars tend to treat rococo as a separate aesthetic style.

Baroque MUSIC, like baroque ART AND ARCHITECTURE, began on the Italian peninsula around 1600 with the compositions of Claudio Monteverdi. It spread rapidly throughout Europe, and did not really disappear until 1750, when Johann Sebastian BACH died in Leipzig. However, by the first decades of the 18th century, a new style called STYLE GALANT or rococo had appeared in Italy, spread to France, and subsequently coexisted with

baroque forms. This state of affairs continued until musical CLASSICISM succeeded in establishing itself as an international European style in the 1770s and 1780s.

Baroque music is noticeably formal in its treatment of musical material. The modes for developing themes, the use of key signatures, and the mood presented in music were governed by specific rules. The music is complex; no single line takes the melody, but rather several musical lines coexist, weaving together to create intricate, dynamic, powerful compositions. On account of its complexity, baroque music was often accused of being exceptionally intellectual, especially by its critics in the last half of the Enlightenment. The magnificent organ fugues by Johann Sebastian Bach provide a clear illustration of baroque compositional techniques.

Baroque style was associated with royal courts and churches, performed in palaces, at state ceremonies, in church services, and on other special occasions. The form was easily adapted to the goals of portraying grandeur, representing power, and creating illusion that were so much a part of the era.

The era produced a rich tradition of musical theory, including the theory of the affects (prescribing a special musical key for each emotion); the harmonic theory of figured bass; and countless systems for solving the tuning problems associated with musical scales.

Baroque composition borrowed from the music of common people, developing country dances such as the *allemand* and *saraband* into standard movements for formal compositions. But it also endowed music tradition with original creations such as opera, oratorio, concerto, and sonata.

Some baroque musical instruments—flutes, oboes, bassoons, horns, trumpets, and violins—differed noticeably from modern orchestral instruments. They produced tone colors ranging from the intensely sweet to the raucous that were exploited by the best baroque composers. A baroque composition such as *The Four Seasons* by Antonio VIVALDI evokes different reactions depending on whether the instruments playing it are baroque or modern in structure. Favorite keyboard instruments were the harpsichord and the pipe organ.

Among the major composers who wrote in baroque style were Claudio Monteverdi, Giralomo Frescobaldi, Henry Purcell, Jean-Baptiste Lully, and Heinrich Schütz in the 17th century and Dietrich Buxtehude, Johann Sebastian Bach, Georg Philipp TELEMANN, Antonio Vivaldi, Archangelo Corelli, Giovanni Battista PERGOLESI, Domenico SCARLATTI, George Frederick HANDEL, François COUPERIN, and Jean-Philippe RAMEAU during the 18th century.

See also CORELLI; OPERA.

Further reading: Willi Apel, *Harvard Dictionary of Music* (Cambridge, Mass.: Harvard University Press, 1962); Anthony Blunt, ed., *Baroque and Rococo Architecture and Decoration* (New York: Portland House, 1978);

Manfred F. Bukofzer, *Music in the Baroque Era* (New York: W. W. Norton, 1947); Emil Kaufman, *Architecture in the Age of Reason. Baroque and Post Baroque in England, Italy, France* (New York: Dover Publications, 1955).

Barthélemy, Jean-Jacques (Abbé) (1716–1795) *French archaeologist, antiquarian, and writer*

His book, *Voyage du jeune Anarchasis en Grèce vers le milieu du IVe siècle avant l'ère vulgaire* (Travels of the young Anarchasis in Greece toward the middle of the fourth century B.C.), played an important role in forming the concepts of antiquity in the minds of the young generation that provoked and led the FRENCH REVOLUTION.

Barthélemy was born in Cassis, the son of Joseph and Madeleine Rastis. He entered a seminary with the intention of becoming a priest and became a specialist in the ancient languages of the Near East: Hebrew, Syrian, and Arabic. He also studied archaeology and Christian antiquities. A short time after leaving the seminary, he renounced the priesthood, but continued to call himself *"abbé"* (abbot) throughout his life. Barthélemy became an assistant to Gros de Boze, who was curator of the royal collection of medals and coins. Barthélemy inventoried large sections of the collection. In 1747, the Academy of Inscriptions voted him into its membership. In 1753, Barthélemy replaced Boze as curator of the medals collection.

Étienne-François, duc de CHOISEUL, employed him as an assistant during his ambassadorship to ROME (1755–57), thereby providing Barthélemy the opportunity to purchase items for the royal collection. Barthélemy remained in the private household of Choiseul for the remainder of his life, even after the minister's disgrace in 1770. He refused an invitation to assume the general editorship of the prestigious journal *Mercure,* turned down a position as royal librarian, and declined to assume the French Academy seat of the disgraced Jean-François MARMONTEL.

Barthélemy wrote many learned articles on numismatics and antiquities. Some appeared in the *Recueil d'antiquités* edited by the comte de CAYLUS, a renowned archaeologist, and others were published in the *Journal des Savants.* But Jean-Jacques Barthélemy is primarily renowned for the *Voyages du jeune Anarcharsis en Grèce* (written at leisure between 1757 and 1787, published in 1788). The book narrates the tale of a fictional excursion through the ancient history and lands of Greece. It prompted the French Academy to offer Barthélemy a membership. Widely read in the late 18th century, it remained a standard assignment in French schools until 1859.

Barthez, Paul-Joseph (1734–1806) *French physiologist who believed that the theory of vitalism provided the best explanation of the structure and functions of living organisms*

Paul-Joseph Barthez, son of the chief engineer of Languedoc, Guillaume Barthez de Marmorière, entered the medical school at the University of Montpellier when he was 16. He received his degree three years later, then moved to PARIS, where he established connections with the royal physician, Noel Falconet. Barthez frequented the salons and intellectual circles of Paris, became a friend of the mathematician Jean Le Rond d'ALEMBERT, and contributed to the ENCYCLOPÉDIE.

After two years in the French army, Barthez began working as a royal censor in Paris. He also became an editor of the widely read *Journal des Savants.* (Newspaper of the Scientists). About 1760, Barthez returned to Montpellier, where he became a professor of medicine at the University of Montpellier and ultimately chancellor of the medical school. Barthez championed clinical research and Hippocratic MEDICINE, two causes that were novel for the era. He reorganized the medical curriculum at Montpellier in order to make it reflect his intellectual convictions. Because of his contentious personality, Barthez became embroiled in many power struggles at the university and, as a result, resigned his university posts in 1781. He returned to Paris, resuming his activities on the intellectual circuit. He was nominated to the Royal Academy of Sciences and to the Royal Society of Medicine. During the FRENCH REVOLUTION Barthez lost these honors, but his status was rehabilitated during the Directory period. Barthez received appointments to the new Institut de France (French Institute, an organization that combined all the old academies, restructured, into one organization) and to the Légion d'Honneur. He also served as Napoleon's private physician and provided medical counsel to the government.

Barthez was one of the primary proponents of VITALISM in France. In this capacity he participated in the discussions about NATURE and human nature that were transforming the thought of the ENLIGHTENMENT during the middle decades of the 18th century. Barthez emphasized that life is something distinct from both matter and soul and consequently must be studied and described in unique ways. He rejected the positions of both MECHANICAL PHILOSOPHY (especially Giovanni Borelli and Hermann BOERHAAVE) and ANIMISM (Georg Ernst STAHL and John Baptiste van Helmont). His vitalism occupied a middle ground between the extreme approaches of these doctrines.

Barthez removed the "soul" from its dominant position as governor of the organism and attempted to construct an alternative way of evaluating the interactions that characterized living organisms. In place of the soul, Barthez introduced the concept of a single vital principle (*principe vital*) that directs the processes of the living body. He compared this vital principle, an occult force inaccessible to direct observation, to Isaac Newton's concept of gravity. Operating under the direction of the vital principle were two powers, SYMPATHY and synergy, whose actions facilitated bodily functions. Synergy enabled large-scale, general, and normal body functions to occur, whereas sympathy governed the ability of specialized organ systems (respiratory system, digestive system, and so forth) to react to both external and internal stimuli.

Unlike Albrecht von HALLER, Barthez refused to make a sharp distinction between sensibility and irritability, two properties that distinguished living from nonliving entities according to vitalist theory. The debate over the relationship between these two properties occupied vitalists throughout the 18th century.

Barthez published four major works in which he spelled out his theories: *De principio vitali hominis* (On the vital principle in men; 1773); *Nova doctrina de fonctionis naturae humanae* (New doctrine on the function of human nature; 1774); *Nouveaux éléments de la science de l'homme* (New elements of human science; 1778), his most important work; and the *Nouvelle méchanique des mouvements de l'homme et des animaux* (New mechanics of the movements of men and animals; 1798).

Barry, Jeanne Bécu, comtesse du (1743–1793)
official royal mistress of Louis XV from 1768 until 1774
Jeanne Bécu was the illegitimate daughter of a seamstress, Anne Bécu, and a Capuchin monk, Jean-Baptiste Gomard de Vaubernier (Frère Ange). Between the ages of three and 15, she lived in an orphanage and then resumed residence with her mother. Anne Bécu had family connections with the Parisian world of the high bourgeoisie. She introduced her beautiful young daughter into that society, thereby launching Jeanne in the career that by 1768 would allow her to meet LOUIS XV and become his official mistress.

Besides being beautiful, Jeanne was good-natured, easygoing, charming, and charitable. She seems not to have engaged extensively in the incessant intrigues of the court. However, the foreign minister the duc de CHOISEUL and the members of the *dévot* party (party of the devout that had strong ties to ROMAN CATHOLICISM and a long history in French politics), including the heir apparent to the throne, LOUIS XVI, and his young wife, MARIE-ANTOINETTE, opposed du Barry's presence, largely because of fears that she would exert excessive influence over Louis XV.

Du Barry may have hastened the downfall of Choiseul after he had already compromised his position with military policy mistakes. He was replaced by a triumvirate of du Barry's favorites, René-Nicolas-Charles-Augustin de MAUPEOU, Emmanuel Armand de Richelieu d'Aiguillon, and Joseph-Marie, Abbé Terray. But evidence of extensive intrigue does not exist.

The countess du Barry seems to have exerted her most extensive influence in matters of fine art, fashion, interior decoration, and architecture. She divided her time among Versailles, Louveciennes (a château that was a gift from Louis XV), and various Parisian town houses.

Immediately upon Louis XV's death in 1774, du Barry withdrew from the court. But within two weeks, she found herself involuntarily cloistered by the new king. She spent 13 months in this unofficial prison,

finally obtaining released in June 1775. By October 1776, she had received permission to return to Louveciennes. She entered a relationship with Louis-Hercule-Timoléon de Cosse, duc de Brissac. In 1785, she agreed to testify against Madame Jeanne de La Motte, on behalf of Marie-Antoinette in the DIAMOND NECKLACE SCANDAL.

During the FRENCH REVOLUTION, both du Barry and Brissac remained staunch royalists. Brissac served in the Royal Guards. He was executed on May 29, 1792, at Versailles by an angry mob. To underscore their vengeance, the mob placed his head on a pike, carried it 12 kilometers from Versailles to Louveciennes, and threw it into the countess du Barry's salon. Du Barry herself had been moving between FRANCE and ENGLAND since early 1791. She was probably a secret agent of the royalist party in exile in LONDON. On a visit to France in the spring of 1793, she was denounced by a local patriotic mayor at Louveciennes, arrested, and imprisoned. Released after a petition by residents, she was again denounced, retried in a different location, sentenced to death, and publicly hanged on December 8, 1793.

Batteux, Charles (Abbé) (1713–1780) *French writer and educator*
Batteux was born near Vouziers, child of Jean and Jeanne Stevenin. He entered the seminary at Reims (Rheims), became a professor of rhetoric at the *collège* (secondary school) attached to the University of Reims, and a canon of the cathedral of Reims. He transferred to PARIS as a teacher at the Collèges Lisieux and Navarre. He eventually obtained a teaching post at the prestigious Collège de France. Both the Académie des Inscriptions (Academy of Inscriptions) and the French Academy elected him to their membership (in 1754 and 1761, respectively).

Batteux wrote many works that aimed at popularizing the philosophy and literature of the ancient Greeks and Romans. His point of view caused his name to appear in the 1769 *Dictionnaire des athées* (Dictionary of atheists). His works include: *Les beaux-arts réduits à un même principle* (The unitary principle of the fine arts; 1747), *Cours de Belles-Lettres* (Course on literature; 1765), *La Morale d'Épicure tirée de ses propres écrits* (The morality of Epicurus based on his writings; 1758), *Traduction d'Horace* (Horace, in French translation; 1750), *Histoire des causes premières ou exposition sommaire des pensées des philosophes sur les principes des êtres* (History of first causes or summary of the thoughts of the philosophers on the principles of being; 1769). He served as general editor of two multivolume works, one on the customs and history of China, the other an academic course designed for students at the École Militaire in Paris.

Battle of the Buffoons (French: Guerre des Bouffons)
Parisian war of words about musical AESTHETICS. The popular press (see PUBLISHING) made the issues widely

known and discussed. The conflict broke out in 1752 over the question of the relative merits of French versus Italian musical styles. Champions of the Italian style disliked the old French, state-sponsored operatic traditions.

The immediate cause of this quarrel was an Italian opera company that was producing wildly popular Italian comic operas in Paris. In particularly, LA SERVA PADRONA, a one-act comedy by the Neapolitan composer Giovanni Battista PERGOLESI, created a sensation. This Italian style, called *opera buffa*, lent its name to the ensuing Battle of the Buffoons.

The Battle of the Buffoons stands as a particularly colorful testimony to the cultural ferment that marked the middle decades of the ENLIGHTENMENT. In the end, the French party lost to the Italian party. But a full resolution had to wait until the triumph in 1774 of *Iphigénie en Aulide* by Christoph Willibald GLUCK. Gluck's compositions eliminated the grounds for the dispute by adopting the new style of musical CLASSICISM. It blended elements from French, Italian, and German operatic traditions to create an international style.

In the Battle of the Buffoons, Jean-Philippe RAMEAU, the leading French opera composer of the era, headed the pro-French party, while Jean-Jacques ROUSSEAU headed the opposing pro-Italian party. Rousseau's party included most PHILOSOPHES who were engaged in the publication of the ENCYCLOPÉDIE. The articles on music and musical aesthetics in the *Encyclopédie* generally reflect their stylistic biases.

The Battle of the Buffoons took place in public in the pages of the French periodical press and the *Encyclopédie*. The debate drew responses from nearly every French intellectual in the capital, and provided an excellent instance of the manner in which the press was serving as a new means of shaping cultural opinion during the Enlightenment.

Although it pitted French style against the newly imported Italian style, the Battle of the Buffoons really concerned tensions between late baroque opera forms, and the earliest forms of musical classicism. The opposing parties couched their arguments in terms of NATURE, the key concept around which so much enlightened discourse turned. The two parties espoused two opposing views of nature, both of which played important roles in the Enlightenment. Italian opera, its supporters declared, was more natural; they equated simple, pleasant, easily accessible, melodious music with natural style. By comparison, the French late baroque operas were stiff, formal, and intensely stylized; in other words, they were unnatural according to their critics. The French party, however, maintained that baroque opera forms reflected the magnificent harmony and order in nature; Italian operas were unruly, and hence unnatural.

Supporters of the Italian party favored the new Neapolitan *bel canto* singing styles and the use of the Italian language in librettos. Rousseau, in an extreme

moment, even declared that the French language was unsuited to singing. The French party, in turn, defended the use of the French language and extolled its artistic merits.

At times, the content of the quarrel showed how sharply aesthetic consciousness was becoming associated with notions of culture defined by linguistic and political nationality. This development, of course, countered the tendencies in the Enlightenment that emphasized the universal brotherhood of humankind and the superiority of international and thoroughly cosmopolitan culture.

The War of the Buffoons was simply one of many intellectual quarrels that preoccupied people during the Enlightenment. It had counterparts in LITERATURE with the QUARREL BETWEEN THE ANCIENTS AND THE MODERNS and in SCIENCE with arguments over the principle of least action developed by Pierre-Louis Moreau de MAUPERTUIS, and the concept of *vis viva* (living force) created by Gottfried Wilhelm LEIBNIZ. Each of these instances reflected certain tensions inherent within enlightened thought and demonstrated that the era was far from harmonious. The general historical presentation of the Enlightenment, if it is to be balanced, must recognize these tensions and find satisfactory methods of explaining why and how they could emerge.

See also BAROQUE STYLE.

Baumgarten, Alexander Gottlieb (1714–1762) *German philosopher who specialized in the theory of aesthetics*

Baumgarten, a professor at Frankfurt an der Oder in PRUSSIA, was a philosopher devoted to the systematic philosophy of Gottfried Wilhelm LEIBNIZ and his student Christian WOLFF. He was highly respected for his rigorous analytic skills and ability to create clear definitions in philosophy. Immanuel KANT used Baumgarten's book on metaphysics as the basis for his lectures on that subject. In private, Baumgarten wrote poetry almost daily. Through this experience, he focused on the creative process and tried to bring it into the realm of philosophy.

Baumgarten developed a systematic philosophy of AESTHETICS (the study of beauty and artistic creation). He coined the term *aesthetics*, defining it as the doctrine of SENSIBILITY or of sensitive knowledge (i.e., knowledge gained directly from the senses without the application of REASON).

Baumgarten made a now classic distinction between the logic that governs the operations of reason and the logic that directs imagination. These two forms of logic cannot be collapsed into one form. They are independent, wholly different ways of knowing. The logic of reason (modeled on geometry) analyzes things into component parts in a process that then allows one to proceed from knowledge of basic principles to knowledge of individual things. It assumes that in breaking down an idea or an object into its component parts (as in a scientific experiment), the character of the object is preserved. The logic of imagination, in contrast, does not analyze, but rather perceives the whole just as it is. To analyze a literary work or a piece of art into its component parts is to destroy its beauty and essence. Similarly, if one breaks down a color into its component physical parts, one destroys the color, although one may learn about its causes.

Baumgarten proceeded from this point to discuss the kind of language needed in an aesthetic production, thereby linking the study of language to the study of beauty. He argued that language, traditionally assumed to be the supreme instrument of human reason, also has aesthetic characteristics. The language of reason seeks objective truth, clear form, and correctness, whereas the language of poetry seeks sensitive force, vital insight, and color. Both poetic language and excellent works of visual art inspire vivid intuitions that possess the capacity to inspire insight and to cause pleasure.

Baumgarten was one of the first philosophers of the ENLIGHTENMENT to begin a synthesis of the philosophical traditions known as RATIONALISM and sensationalism, or reason and sensibility. The exercise of the imagination for him created a unique type of experience and knowledge, which together with the knowledge of reason could help individuals achieve their full human potential. He gave philosophical content to the enlightened preoccupation with beauty and linked the perception of beauty with the experience of pleasure. This last linkage provided a mechanism for uniting the emerging hedonistic psychologies, which described human motivation in terms of striving for pleasure, with aesthetics. This linkage gave aesthetics a role to play in the moral and ethical formation of man.

Baumgarten published several significant works including *Philosophical Meditations on Matters Pertaining to Poetry* (1735); *Metaphysica* (Metaphysics; 1739); *Aesthetica acroamatica* (Pleasurable aesthetics; 1750–58); and *Philosophia generalis* (General philosophy; 1770).

See also INTUITION AND IMAGINATION; PSYCHOLOGY; LOCKE.

Bayle, Pierre (1647–1706) *French critic and philosopher of skepticism*

Bayle came from a family of French HUGUENOTS that lived in the county of Foix near the Spanish border. His father, Jean Bayle, was a Calvinist minister. Pierre Bayle received a classical education, learning Latin and Greek. He continued his studies at the Protestant Academy of Puylaurens. He converted briefly to ROMAN CATHOLICISM, studying with the JESUITS at Toulouse, but he returned to CALVINISM and, in 1670, set out for GENEVA to study theology. He obtained a post teaching philosophy in the Protestant Academy at Sedan, but lost it when that academy was closed during the political persecutions of the Huguenots.

Bayle received an invitation to teach philosophy and history at Rotterdam in the Calvinist UNITED PROVINCES OF THE NETHERLANDS after he sent the university officials

his *Lettre sur la comète de 1680.* He devoted himself from then on to reading, writing, and intellectual discussion. He took up journalism, producing the *Nouvelles de la République des Lettres,* which was eagerly read by French intellectuals.

Bayle quickly established himself as a champion of PROTESTANTISM, defending it against the increasingly bitter attacks coming from the FRANCE of LOUIS XIV. He was opposed to any type of compulsion in matters of conscience. Bayle desired to consider and to weigh all ideas, submitting them to the dictates of reason in order to assess their validity. As Bayle developed intellectually, he became a confirmed rationalist, but also a skeptic. He believed that all matters of morality should be evaluated by reference to natural conceptions of equity and subjected to scrutiny by REASON.

This intellectual conviction led Bayle to turn his critical words against both Protestant friends and Catholic antagonists. He engaged in a pamphlet war with the virulent Huguenot pastor Pierre Jurieu during the years from 1690 to 1692. Jurieu ultimately succeeded in securing Bayle's dismissal from the University of Rotterdam. Bayle was also denied a Dutch state pension.

Bayle conceived the idea for his magnum opus, the *HISTORICAL AND CRITICAL DICTIONARY,* in 1690. When it was published in 1697, the French censors forbade its sale in France, and the Roman Catholic Inquisition placed it on the Index of Forbidden Books. Nevertheless, new editions with Dutch imprints followed in 1702, 1715, 1730, and 1734. Furthermore, during the 18th century the book was translated into English and German.

The *Historical and Critical Dictionary* presented scathing, penetrating evaluations of various contemporary and historical ideas and beliefs. Bayle recognized that the new natural sciences and philosophy, which had done away with the notion that certain knowledge is based on sense experience, had created a situation in which a reasoning person would be inexorably pushed to Pyrrhonist SKEPTICISM. This type of skeptic suspended judgment on all matters of reason on the assumption that nothing could be certainly known to be true.

Bayle tended toward this position himself, but he struggled against it. He sketched out a method for making intellectual judgments that was based on a combination of Cartesianism and reliance on experience. But Bayle lapsed back into his skepticism as he considered the difficulties that would face people trying to put this method into practice. He noted that the pursuit of a particular line of reason would always bring the thinker face-to-face with contradictions (philosophical antinomies). In the end, Bayle was willing to assert only one thing, that nothing could be known beyond all doubt.

Bayle attacked all belief in miracles because miracles were opposed to natural reason and law. He maintained that in religious matters, as well as in other areas, knowledge about truth evades human beings. He admonished believers to refrain from claiming that they accepted a particular dogma just because it had been demonstrated by reason to be true. Such a claim was invalid according to Bayle's understanding of the limits of human knowledge. He criticized Catholics, Protestants, Jews, Muslims, and deists for making false claims about the truth of their beliefs.

Despite the overwhelming skepticism of Bayle's position, he himself maintained commitment to the idea that the errors of the past could be avoided. Bayle passionately hoped that humankind could and would put an end to the terrible religious strife whose results he, as a Huguenot, had experienced firsthand. His *Historical and Critical Dictionary* took the plea for religious peace out of the realm of academic debate and presented it to the general reading public. For this reason Bayle is considered one of the great founders of the complex of ideas that would feed the cries for religious TOLERATION in the Europe of the ENLIGHTENMENT.

Bayle's major works include the following: *Dictionnaire historique et critique* (The historical and critical dictionary; 1695); the *Lettre sur la comète de 1680* (Letter on the comet of 1680; 1682); *Critique générale de l'histoire du calvinisme de P. Maimbourg* (General criticism of the history of Calvinism by Father Maimbourg; 1682); *Recueil de quelques pièces curieuses concernant la philosophie de M. Descartes* (Collection of curious pieces concerning the philosophy of Mr. Descartes; 1684); *Nouvelles de la république des lettres* (News from the republic of letters), beginning in 1684; *Avis important aux refugies sur leur prochain retour en France* (Important advice to the refugees on their next return to France; 1690); and *Cabale chimérique ou réfutation de l'histoire fabuleuse qu'on vient de publier touchant un certain projet de paix* (Chimerical cabal, or the refutation of the fictitious history that has just been published concerning a certain peace project; 1691).

Beaumarchais, Pierre-Augustin Caron de (1732–1799) *French playwright*

Beaumarchais started his professional life as a clockmaker, then turned to commerce. As a sympathizer with the causes of the AMERICAN REVOLUTION, Beaumarchais provided funds for the purchase of supplies to aid the colonial revolutionaries.

Beaumarchais first attracted attention as a writer and social critic when he published four *Mémoires* that vindicated his position in a legal suit. He earned great fame and notoriety with his two plays *Le Barbier de Séville* (*Barber of Seville*; first performance, 1775) and *Le Mariage de Figaro* (*The Marriage of Figaro*; first performance, 1784). *The Marriage of Figaro* was banned from performance on account of its political content, but its publication was allowed in 1785.

Both plays turn the existing social order of privilege on its head by making aristocratic employers the victims of their servants' schemes. The plays clearly demonstrate, however, that the servants were acting in self defense, refusing any longer to be mistreated by their noble lords. Beaumarchais became a kind of popular hero whose plays concisely and wittily presented the biting criticism of the existing social order so characteristic of the late ENLIGHTENMENT.

The Austrian composer Wolfgang Amadeus MOZART and his librettist Lorenzo da Ponte turned *The Marriage of Figaro* into a hugely successful opera, LE NOZZE DI FIGARO. In the early 19th century, Giacomo Rossini did the same for *Barber of Seville*.

Beaumont, Jeanne Le Prince de (1711–1780) *French writer of fairy tales and educational stories*

Jeanne Le Prince de Beaumont was one of many French women writers who worked in the genre of the fairy tale. Her most famous story is *La belle et la bête* (*Beauty and the Beast*), although the idea was not originally hers. Gabrielle-Susanne Barbot de Villeneuve published a tale by that name in a collection in 1740, and Beaumont took the narrative and rewrote it in her *Magasin des enfants* (The Young misses' magazine; 1756). Villeneuve's version was soon forgotten, most likely because Beaumont told the tale in a concise format, while Villeneuve's ran to 362 pages. Beaumont was very interested in education and worked in LONDON as a tutor between 1748 and 1763. An English translation of her *Magasin des enfants* appeared in 1761, and she sometimes wrote in English as well as in French.

Further reading: Jeanne Le Prince de Beaumont, *Beauty and the Beast*, tr. and illus. Diane Goode (New York: Bradbury Press, 1978); Betsy Gould Hearne, *Beauty and the Beast: Visions and Revisions of an Old Tale* (Chicago: University of Chicago Press, 1989); Joan Hinde Stewart, *Gynographs: French Novels by Women of the Late Eighteenth Century* (Lincoln: University of Nebraska Press, 1993).

Beccaria, Cesare Bonesana, marchese di (1738–1794) *Milanese (Italian) reformer, jurist, and economist*

The son of an aristocratic family based in MILAN, Cesare Bonesana, marchese di Beccaria, struggled throughout his life to escape what he considered the restrictions of the paternalistic aristocratic world. He married against his father's will in 1761, but found that the specter of losing familial support—both moral and financial—was too much of a burden. He thus reconciled with his father but retained his resentment of the paternal system throughout his life.

Beccaria studied at the University of Pavia, receiving a degree in 1758. His career did not really get established until 1768, after he had published and acknowledged his authorship of *Dei delitti e dell pene* (ESSAY ON CRIMES AND PUNISHMENTS; 1764). The renown earned by this book brought Beccaria the patronage of the Hapsburg rulers of MILAN. As a result he received a professorship in law and economy at the University of Milan (1768–70) and an appointment to the Supreme Economic Council of that city (1771–94).

Beccaria belonged to the social and intellectual world of the Milanese ENLIGHTENMENT. He participated in the Academy of Fists, a club of reformers organized by Pietro VERRI and his brother Alessandro VERRI. Under the influence of the Verri brothers, Beccaria read the major authors of the French and English Enlightenment: David HUME, MONTESQUIEU, Claude-Adrien HELVÉTIUS, Denis DIDEROT, the comte de BUFFON, and Jean Le Rond D'ALEMBERT.

Eventually, at the suggestion of Pietro Verri, Beccaria wrote *Essay on Crimes and Punishments*. He published the work anonymously, fearing prosecution by the Milanese authorities. That government, however, welcomed the book, recognizing that its proposed penal code reforms could fit nicely with a program for enlightened rule. *Essay on Crimes and Punishments* called for a restructuring of punishments to bring them in line with the severity of the crime committed. It also argued against capital punishment, noting that cruel punishments had no deterrent power.

After seeing that the Milanese authorities were not offended by his work, Beccaria acknowledged his authorship and departed in October 1766 on a tour to PARIS. Beccaria received an enthusiastic welcome, and he was invited to the various enlightened salons. He did not, however, possess the social skills to be comfortable in that society. After three weeks, he left his traveling companion, Alessandro Verri, in Paris and returned home to Milan.

To a great extent, Beccaria succeeded because of the prodding and support of the Verri brothers. They contributed many of the materials and ideas for *Essay on Crimes and Punishments* but always insisted on Beccaria's authorship. Whatever the roles played by Beccaria and the Verri brothers, the book helped to bring about a revolution in criminal justice in European nations, and thus stands as one of the most significant gifts of the Enlightenment to modern society.

See also CAPITAL PUNISHMENT; ITALY; JUSTICE AND THE LAW; SOCIAL INSTITUTIONS OF THE ENLIGHTENMENT.

Beethoven, Ludwig van (1770–1827) *German composer*

The son of a family with a tradition of musical service in the Bonn court of the elector of Cologne, Ludwig van Beethoven not only continued that tradition, but also represented its epitome. He began musical instruction with his father and by the age of 11 was serving Christian Gottlob Neefe as assistant organist for the court. Neefe recognized the boy's talent, took him under his wing, and encouraged him to look beyond the boundaries of Bonn for a future.

In 1787 Beethoven visited VIENNA, the musical capital of the HAPSBURG EMPIRE. He probably met Wolfgang Amadeus MOZART and may have had a few lessons with him.

Returning to Bonn, Beethoven received a larger salary as the head of his family. His mother had died in 1787, and his father, whose voice was failing, was withdrawing into increasing alcohol abuse. During his last years in Bonn, Beethoven played the VIOLA in the court orchestra. He circulated in the enlightened society of Bonn, acquiring influential supporters among certain aristocratic families.

In 1792, Beethoven moved to Vienna, having received a pension from the elector of Cologne to study piano and composition with Franz Joseph HAYDN. Haydn esteemed Beethoven, but the two men seem to have had a difficult relationship. After Haydn left Vienna for LONDON, Beethoven turned to Johann Schenk, Johann Georg Albrechtsburger, and Antonio Salieri for various forms of musical instruction.

Beethoven, a transitional figure in the history of musical composition, inherited the forms of fully developed musical classicism from Haydn and Mozart. He wrote his earlier works in that style but gradually transformed it, thus laying the groundwork for ROMANTICISM.

Unlike Haydn and Mozart, Beethoven did not compose with great ease; thus, his output does not match theirs in sheer number of compositions. Nevertheless, his legacy is one of the richest and most important in the history of European MUSIC. Beethoven was and still is one of the most popular composers ever to have lived.

The catalogue of Beethoven's works compiled by Wotquenne lists nine symphonies, 11 overtures, five piano concertos and one violin concerto, 16 string quartets, nine piano trios, 30 piano sonatas, 10 violin sonatas, and five violoncello sonatas. In addition, it contains one opera (*Fidelio*), an oratorio, two masses, and numerous smaller compositions for chamber music performance.

Musicologists customarily divide Beethoven's work into three periods: the first period of marked classicism (to 1802); the middle period of expansive creativity (1802 until 1815); and the third period of reflective but passionate depth, lasting from 1815 until his death. During this last period, Beethoven was struggling not only with disappointment about the fate of the ENLIGHTENMENT after the FRENCH REVOLUTION, but also with personal deafness and ill health.

The middle period contains Beethoven's most renowned works: Symphony no. 3 (*Eroica*) and Symphony no. 6 (*Pastorale*); the *Rasumovsky* Quartets, op. 59; the *Kreutzer* Sonata, op. 47, for violin and piano; the *Moonlight*, *Appassionata*, and *Waldstein* Sonatas for piano; and the *Leonore* Overtures. The first period is well represented by the Symphony no. 1 and the Septet in E-flat for Strings and Winds, op. 20. The last piece became so popular that Beethoven grew to hate it. The last period is, of course, marked by the renowned Symphony no. 9 with its unconventional harmonies and choral setting of the "Ode to Joy" by Friedrich SCHILLER. It served as a last impassioned statement of Beethoven's enlightened faith in the universal brotherhood of humanity.

The Ninth Symphony premiered in Vienna on May 7, 1824, before a large and enthusiastic audience. Beethoven, however, was so deaf by this time that he could not hear the wild applause. He did not turn to acknowledge the audience until one of the soloist singers tugged his arm to direct him to turn around.

The music of Beethoven's last period was intensely personal and idiosyncratic in style. In this respect, it fits well with the values that inspired the German STURM UND DRANG writers. However, subsequent generations of composers turned not to that period when they sought direction from Beethoven's example, but rather to the middle period. That period bequeathed to romanticism an approach that dissolved the formalities of classicism, allowing harmonic structures and compositional forms to expand and to transform into a new style. With Beethoven, music definitely moved away from the styles associated with the Enlightenment toward the uncertain future that we now call romanticism.

See also NEOCLASSICISM.

Beggar's Opera, The

Beggar's Opera, The A ballad OPERA written by John GAY and set to English folk tunes. Johann Christoph Pepusch usually receives credit for arranging the music, but no solid evidence supports this tradition.

The Beggar's Opera was first produced in LONDON at Lincoln's Inn Fields, January 29, 1728. Its heroes and heroines—Peachum, Mrs. Peachum, Polly, Lucy Lockit, and MacHeath—are highwaymen, ordinary thieves, prostitutes, and drunks. A beggar (the "Creator" of the OPERA), and a "Player" offer commentary about the literary structure of the piece. The opera satirizes prominent English politicians such as Robert WALPOLE and traditional social morality. It flirts with themes common to the new, popular literature of the 18th century such as the idea of marriage for love and the fascination with the dark, irrational, ugly sides of life. It pokes lighthearted fun at the conventions of 18th-century Italian opera in which some miraculous resolution of dramatic conflict allows everything to end happily. It also satirizes both the modish cult of SENSIBILITY and British sentimentalism.

The Beggar's Opera enjoyed a long premiere season by the standards of the time (62 performances). As the first example of ballad opera, it took London by storm, and for the next 10 years many similar operas were produced for the London theater. As a cultural artifact, its exploration of various types of villainy and of marginal social groups places it in the same 18th-century genre as the engravings of William HOGARTH and the novels of Henry FIELDING.

Behn, Aphra

Behn, Aphra (ca. 1640–1689) *English novelist, playwright, and poet*
Aphra Behn was the first professional woman writer in ENGLAND. Very little is known about her early life. Even the place of her birth cannot be verified definitively. One theory is that she was born in 1640 and traveled as a girl to Suriname with her family. In Suriname, she witnessed a slave rebellion led by an African named Oroono. After returning to England, she may have acquired the surname Behn through an unsuccessful marriage.

Because Behn lived in poverty, she turned to unusual methods of self-support. She served, for example, in 1666 as a spy in Antwerp on behalf of England's Stuart king Charles II. Behn had many friends who were connected to King Charles and his court, including John DRYDEN, the poet laureate; John Wilmot, the earl of Rochester; and Nell Gwyn, one of the king's favorite mistresses. After some years, Behn turned to writing as a source of income. She was well known to her contemporaries for her plays, poems, and novels as well as for her translations into English of the famed French works *Maximes* (The maxims; 1685) by François de La Rochefoucauld and *Entretiens sur la pluralité des mondes* (Conversations on the plurality of worlds; 1688) by the Cartesian Copernican natural philosopher and writer Bernard de FONTENELLE.

As Behn began her literary career, court patronage for LITERATURE in England was disappearing and being replaced by the literary marketplace. The most profitable form of literature was drama, which was in high demand during the English Restoration (1660–79). Behn produced her first comedy, *The Forc'd Marriage,* in 1670. It introduced a feminist theme that Behn would explore in 16 subsequent plays: a criticism of the practice of arranging marriages for the purpose of securing family property and status. She presents love and physical passion as forces that are stronger than social convention and family ties. Behn derived these themes from libertinism, a set of 17th-century values and practices whose inspiration derived partly from SKEPTICISM and partly from the philosophy of Thomas HOBBES.

In addition to feminist themes, Behn's plays frequently express anti-Puritan sentiments. In the English society of the time, a person's religion—whether Puritan, Anglican, or Catholic—implied unmistakable political views. Behn's anti-Puritanism, coupled with her strong support of the Stuart kings Charles II and James II, mark her as a Tory, which has led many scholars to see her as pro-Catholic. Her plays *The Feign'd Curtizans* (1679) and *The Roundheads* (1682) hint at her political preferences. The former is about a group of roving Cavaliers, loyalists who supported the Stuart king Charles I during the English Civil War (1642–60), while the latter satirizes the Puritan Roundheads, or parliamentarians.

Behn's most famous theatrical works examine gender roles using the dramatic devices of disguise and mistaken identity, favored during the ENLIGHTENMENT by writers wanting to make controversial political and social statements. In the *The Feign'd Curtizans*, two noblewomen, Marcella and Cornelia, disguise themselves as prostitutes. With this device, Behn adds another layer to the play, a critique of the male-dominated world that requires all women to assume disguises. Behn's poetry also explored issues of gender. "The Disappointment" (1684), for example, rewrote the male "imperfect enjoyment poem" by focusing on female pleasure rather than male failure.

Behn's best known fictional work is *Oroonoko, or the Royal Slave,* a NOVEL she published in 1688, the year of the GLORIOUS REVOLUTION in England. This tale focuses on an African prince who is tricked into slavery by a greedy British sea captain. The novel attacks the values of the colonial administrators and members of the merchant class who were profiting by exploiting Africans such as Oroonoko. Although this novel argued for the humane treatment of colonial peoples, a theme that would later enter Enlightenment thought, it also supported the conservative Tory ideas of ABSOLUTISM and the DIVINE RIGHT OF KINGS. Oroonoko served as an allegorical figure symbolizing King James II, the legitimate heir to the English throne, whose rights were being challenged by political groups favoring limited monarchy. Of course, in 1688, the year the novel was published, James II was forced to flee England and was replaced by WILLIAM III AND MARY II in the Glorious Revolution.

The work of Aphra Behn reveals the complexity of positions of early Enlightenment thinkers. In Behn, an outspoken feminist, her preference for a strong monarchy and most likely for Catholicism coexisted with the Cartesian Copernican view of the universe that was condemned by the Roman Catholic Church.

See also CARTESIANISM; COLONIALISM; COPERNICAN REVOLUTION; JACOBITES; LIBERTINE; RACE, WOMEN AND THE ENLIGHTENMENT.

Further reading: Heidi Hutner, *Colonial Women: Race and Culture in Stuart Drama* (New York: Oxford University Press, 2001); Paul Salzman, ed., *Oroonoko and Other Writings* (New York: Oxford University Press, 1994); Janet Todd, ed., *Aphra Behn Studies* (New York: Cambridge University Press, 2000); Janet Todd, *The Sign of Angellica: Women, Writing, and Fiction, 1660–1800* (New York: Columbia University Press, 1989).

Belgium   Northern European kingdom bounded by the North Sea, the Netherlands, and France; its capital city is BRUSSELS. The kingdom of Belgium has existed only since 1830. From 1714 until the end of the 18th century, it was a group of 10 separate provinces ruled by the Austrian Hapsburgs and known as the AUSTRIAN NETHERLANDS.

The territories of Belgium have played important roles in history. During the Middle Ages, Brussels, Bruges, and Antwerp were thriving economic centers noted for their splendid wealth and rich cultural traditions. The Dutch Revolt of the late 16th century altered the political structure of the region but, more significantly, cut off the region's greatest port, Antwerp, from access to the North Sea. As a result, the region experienced economic decline.

During the 18th century, the region was relatively stable until the 1780s when the Hapsburg emperor JOSEPH II began imposing his program of reforms. Inspired by ideals of the ENLIGHTENMENT, these reforms eliminated torture, established TOLERATION for Protestants, forced educational reform at the University of Louvain, closed monasteries, and opened access to crafts and trades by lessening the power of the guilds. Many powerful Belgians objected that these actions constituted an attack on their traditional liberties. Joseph II responded to their opposition by imposing a new constitution on the recalcitrant region. It reorganized the structure of justice and civil administration, abolishing the old system in which judicial offices were private property and the exercise of justice was intermingled with general administration.

By early 1789, initial protests had swelled to become a revolution. Rebels claimed that they were defending constitutional liberties against despotic reforms from above. The situation resembled what was happening in France as PARLEMENTS challenged reforming royal ministers.

By the end of 1789, the Hapsburg government of the future state of Belgium collapsed. Two political parties soon appeared, one headed by H. Van der Noot calling for the reestablishment of the traditional constitution, the other headed by J. F. Vonck calling for moderate democratic reforms. No compromise position could be found, and the subsequent history of the region is one of political instability throughout the era of the FRENCH REVOLUTION. These events provide a means of observing the complicated issues that could arise when reformers attempted to put the political and social ideals of the Enlightenment, with all their internal conflicts, into practice.

Bellotto, Bernardo (1720–1780) *Venetian painter*
Bernardo Bellotto was the nephew of CANALETTO, and sometimes called Canaletto Bellotto or Canaletto the Younger. Art historians believe that he trained with his uncle, then visited other Italian cities such as ROME, Florence, and TURIN. Like Canaletto, Bellotto produced Venetian view paintings and occasional imaginary scenes.

Bellotto went to Dresden (in Saxony, in the HOLY ROMAN EMPIRE) in 1747 and never returned to the Italian peninsula. From 1748 until 1763, he worked as a court painter for August III, Elector of Saxony. Bellotto set out for Russia in 1767 but decided to stay in POLAND after receiving an invitation to settle in that country from King Stanislaw II Augustus PONIATOWSKI.

Bellotto painted under royal commissions for the remainder of his life. He created historical scenes, imaginary scenes, and realistic views of VENICE, Warsaw, Turin, MUNICH, Dresden, and VIENNA. The Warsaw views, his most important collection of works, display the sharp realism that became prevalent in the 19th century. They also illustrate Bellotto's pronounced break with the style of his uncle Canaletto. Many paintings thought to be Bellotto's lack signatures, making identification somewhat problematic. Two signed paintings are *View of Dresden* (1747) and *View of Turin* (ca. 1745).

Benedict XIV (Prospero Lorenzo Lambertini) (1675–1758) *pope of the Catholic Church from August 17, 1740, to May 3, 1758*

The Lambertinis were a noble family from Bologna. Prospero received his education first from private tutors, then at the Collegium Clementinum in ROME. He studied theology and law at the University of Rome, receiving his doctorate in 1694. He entered public service as a lawyer in Rome and held 11 different offices before Benedict XIII awarded him the archbishopric of Ancona in 1727. A cardinal's hat followed in 1728, and the archbishopric of Bologna became his in 1731.

After his election to the papacy, Lambertini, who assumed the name Benedict XIV, devoted himself to the practical needs of the Papal States. His activities resembled the reforms of secular rulers who were his contemporaries. Benedict XIV supported the construction of village granaries, the repair of roads, and the reduction of export tariffs on necessary commodities such as foodstuffs. He also provided substantial patronage for scholarly activities: Four academies were founded during his tenure as pope, the Vatican Library collections received a substantial number of new books and manuscripts, new publications were encouraged, and the University of Rome was improved. MONTESQUIEU called Benedict XIV "the scholars' pope." In matters of church-state relations, Benedict XIV faced delicate negotiations. For example, in FRANCE, when the Jansenist PARLEMENTS challenged the authority of Catholic bishops, Benedict XIV compromised with the government of LOUIS XV to resolve the crisis in the ANCIEN RÉGIME. In this and other conflicts with the energetic absolute monarchs of 18th-century Europe, Benedict XIV demonstrated an awareness of the limits of papal power. Benedict left an extensive correspondence with Pierre Guérin, cardinal de Tencin in France, and with various Italian friends.

See also ROMAN CATHOLICISM; SEPARATION OF CHURCH AND STATE.

Bentham, Jeremy (1748–1832) *English political theorist*
Jeremy Bentham was a prolific critic of England's political and judicial institutions during the late 18th and early 19th centuries. His central contribution as a political thinker was his idea of utilitarianism, which stated that political action should strive to produce the greatest good for the greatest number of citizens.

Bentham was born in LONDON. He came from a family of attorneys and entered Oxford University at the age of 12 in 1760. After graduating in 1764, he studied law, but a substantial inheritance from his parents meant that he never had to practice. Instead, he devoted his life to study, thought, and writing.

Bentham's first writing on law, *A Fragment on Government* (1776), attacked the idea of precedent in law. The work rejected the notion that laws should be based on tradition, arguing instead that they should be derived

Portrait of Jeremy Bentham (1748–1832); engraving by J. Posselwhite from an original picture by J. Watts. A political theorist, Bentham is best known for his concept of utilitarianism, stating that political action should strive to produce the greatest good for the greatest number of citizens. *(Courtesy New York Public Library)*

from universal principles according to REASON. This idea, the use of reason rather than tradition or abstraction, was central to Bentham's later thought.

In 1785, Bentham went to Russia, where his brother Samuel was working as a naval official. There, he began developing his idea of the Panopticon, a prison where guards concealed in an observation tower in the center could watch prisoners arranged in cells surrounding the tower. The fact that the guards could see the prisoners but that the prisoners could not see the guards meant that, psychologically, the prisoners would feel as though they were constantly being watched. Bentham continued to refine his idea of the Panopticon throughout his life, and several prisons modeled on the Panopticon were eventually built (for example, the penitentiary at Stateville, Illinois).

Bentham completed his most important work of political theory, *An Introduction to the Principles of Morals and Legislation,* in 1789. The work reflects the influence of the French PHILOSOPHES as well as John LOCKE and David HUME and is an important contribution to the formulation of early 19th-century liberalism. (Other key liberal thinkers included John Stuart Mill and Benjamin Constant, who were both followers of Bentham.) Bentham's ideas in the *Principles* and other writings proceeded from the assumption that he could rationally work out legal and political programs from universal principles. In the *Principles,* the starting point is the opposition between pleasure and pain. From this, Bentham worked out a system of UTILITY (a term he took from Hume or BECCARIA) in which laws produced the greatest good for the greatest number of people, a pleasurable effect. Bentham critiqued the ENLIGHTENMENT idea that an abstract notion of NATURAL RIGHTS could provide the foundation of legal and political action. In his system, utility replaced natural rights.

Bentham's earlier writings and the *Principles* gained him a devoted following in FRANCE, and he was made an honorary citizen of the French Republic in 1792. His impact in ENGLAND came later, through a number of disciples who came to occupy positions of power in the 1830s. The British Reform Bill of 1832 (which based representation in Parliament on population and was championed by Lord Henry Brougham, one of Bentham's followers) and the many legal reforms that followed (including the Factory Act, which limited children ages six to 13 to a 48-hour workweek and teenagers between 14 and 18 to a 69-hour workweek) reflect the impact of Bentham's ideas.

Bentham devoted the last decade of his life to writing extensively on the British judicial system and constitution. He died in London on June 6, 1832, leaving a large sum of money to fund University College in London, an institution whose mission was to educate people otherwise barred from university—that is, religious nonconformists, including Catholics and Jews. At his request, Bentham's body was embalmed and seated in a chair in a case in the main hall of the college.

Further reading: Jeremy Bentham, *The Principles of Morals and Legislation* (Amherst, N.Y.: Prometheus Books, 1988); Michel Foucault, *Discipline and Punish: The Birth of the Prison* (New York: Vintage Books, 1995).

Bergman, Torbern Olof (1735–1784) *Swedish chemist, physicist, natural historian, and astronomer; acquired international renown for his work in chemistry*
Several facets of Bergman's work resulted in significant changes in the manner of conceiving, practicing, and teaching chemistry.

Bergman was a major proponent of AFFINITY CHEMISTRY and also accepted the tenets of PHLOGISTON THEORY. Affinity chemistry had been created by Georg Ernst STAHL and by Étienne-François Geoffroy. Although neither of these men was a Newtonian, some 18th-century chemists used the Newtonian theory of universal gravitation (attraction between bodies) to bolster the arguments for affinity chemistry. According to this version of chemistry, different substances had inherent attractions for other substances. The degrees of attraction could be organized into tables of elective affinity.

Bergman produced a major treatise on affinity chemistry, the *Disquisitio de attractionibus electivis* (Inquiry on elective attractions; 1775), that contained tables of affinity. In 1783, he published a revision of the tables that contained information on a larger number of substances.

In 1767, Bergman succeeded J. G. Wallerius as the professor of chemistry at the University of Uppsala and set about revising the manner of teaching chemistry. He emphasized the practical applications of chemistry, especially for mining and industry. He organized the mineral collections to demonstrate both their geographical distribution and their chemical properties. He also acquired chemical apparatus and models of industrial equipment.

Bergman developed the foundations of chemical analysis. He concentrated especially on procedures for breaking down (analyzing) substances by using solutions (wet method). He offered methods both for qualitative and quantitative analysis. Bergman presented his methods in three general treatises: *De analysi aquarum* (On the analysis of waters; 1778); *De minerarum docimasia humida* (On the investigation of mineral water; 1780); and *De praecipitatis metallicis* (On metal precipitates; 1780).

During the 1770s, Bergman developed a new system of chemical CLASSIFICATION and a corresponding nomenclature. He published his initial reforms in *Sciagraphia regni mineralis* (An outline of minerals; 1782). The *Meditationes de systemate fossilium naturali* (Thoughts on the natural system of fossils; 1784) presented his final system. Bergman's classification system divided all inorganic substances into classes, genera, and species, following the model developed by Carl LINNAEUS for the animal and plant kingdoms. Bergman's nomenclature attempted to satisfy utilitarian goals by creating names revealing the inner composition of substances.

Bergman's chemical work reflects impulses similar to those that drove Antoine LAVOISIER to create his new theory of chemical elements and nomenclature. The two men produced different systems, but both were engaged in the creation of ordered systems largely based on experimental evidence. Also, both reflected the dominant 18th-century belief in the central importance of language for the production of rational thought. These concerns illustrate how Bergman and Lavoisier were creators of ENLIGHTENMENT science as well as products of enlightened thought.

As a young man, Bergman worked in natural history, physics, and astronomy. He observed the TRANSIT OF VENUS across the sun in June 1761 and from his observations concluded that Venus had an atmosphere. Bergman investigated some aspects of electricity. He developed a two-fluid theory of electricity to counter the single-fluid theory proposed by Benjamin FRANKLIN. Bergman was an early supporter of Franklin's contention that lightning rods could protect buildings from the harm caused by lightning strikes. Finally, Bergman made a collection of local insects that included several unknown to Linnaeus. He sent the collection to Linnaeus and also discovered that the creature called *coccus aquaticus* by Linnaeus was actually a leech's egg.

Bergman was elected to the Royal Swedish Academy of Sciences in 1764. FREDERICK II (THE GREAT) OF PRUSSIA invited Bergman to Berlin to become a member of the BERLIN ACADEMY. Bergman declined the offer in order to remain in Sweden. He died in 1784 at age 49, having suffered throughout his life from poor health.

Berkeley, George (1685–1753) *Irish philosopher, clergyman, and psychologist*

George Berkeley was a major figure in the development of the British EMPIRICISM that dominated the psychological theories of the ENLIGHTENMENT. The son of English parents living in Ireland, Berkeley studied philosophy at Trinity College, Dublin. He became a fellow at Dublin in 1707; then librarian (1709); and lecturer in divinity, Greek, and Hebrew (1721 to 1724) at the same university. Berkeley was introduced to the English court in 1713 by Jonathan SWIFT. He acquired a position in the Anglican Church as dean of Derry (1724). In 1728, Berkeley crossed the Atlantic, armed with a charter for founding a university in Bermuda. The school did not materialize for lack of funding. Berkeley spent the next three years (1728–31) living in Newport, Rhode Island. The town of Berkeley, California, is named after him. Berkeley became the Anglican bishop of Cloyne in Dublin in 1734 and served in this position until 1752.

Berkeley's philosophical interests centered on the problems of the nature of mind and matter, of their mutual relations, and of the certainty of our knowledge. He developed an extreme form of psychological empiricism known as subjective idealism. Berkeley also created an associated theory of meaning as well as a theory of visual perception.

In his writings, Berkeley was responding to the form of psychological empiricism developed by John LOCKE. Locke had rejected the Cartesian concept of innate ideas (ideas present at birth). He had created a new empirical psychology that claimed that sensory experience of objective matter, of the objective world outside the mind, actually produced all the ideas of the mind. For Locke, the mind at birth was a *tabula rasa* (clean slate) on which the experience of life would be written. Locke believed that the ideas created in the mind by sensory experience were certain and true.

Berkeley agreed with Locke in opposing the notion of innate ideas and strongly criticized the excesses of RATIONALISM that he believed were distorting mathematics. He complained, for example, of mathematicians who spoke of lines that could be infinitely divided; such an idea denied sensory experience and was absurd.

Berkeley, however, rejected Locke's claim that experience of the external world of matter produces certain knowledge or true ideas about real objects in the world. He believed that Locke's theory actually would push people toward SKEPTICISM. After all, what convincing argument could be made for Locke's claim that the mind actually creates objectively true ideas from the sensations it receives?

Berkeley claimed to have developed a more accurate hypothesis for explaining the relations between ideas and external reality. He called his new hypothesis "the immaterialist hypothesis," but during the 18th century it became known as idealism. The immaterialist hypothesis maintained that the only reality of which we can be certain is the reality of the mind. We cannot be sure whether the ideas we have about the objects of the world outside the mind are actually true. The Latin phrase *esse est percipi* (to be is to be perceived) summarized Berkeley's hypothesis. In other words, material objects exist only when they are being perceived (sensed) by an individual mind. The guarantee of the correctness of our perceptions derives from the fact that specific sensory experiences will repeatedly yield the same perceptions or ideas.

It is important to emphasize that for Berkeley, as for Locke, our ideas are the product of experience. Unlike Locke, however, Berkeley denies that these ideas necessarily reflect the objective reality of matter in the world.

Berkeley's philosophical ideas were outlined in two important books: *An Essay Towards a New Theory of Vision* (1709) and a *Treatise Concerning the Principles of Human Knowledge* (1710). Although he is best known for his philosophy of mind, Berkeley also wrote a treatise critical of Isaac NEWTON, *De Motu* (On motion; 1721); and a defense of Christianity and theism called *Alciphron, or the Minute Philosopher* (1732).

See also MATHEMATICS AND MECHANICS; PSYCHOLOGY.

Berlin

Present-day capital of GERMANY, formerly the capital of PRUSSIA, located in the northeastern German plains on the banks of the Spree River. A series of canals cross the city and connect the Spree with the Oder River. The city site has been continuously settled since the 13th century, but until the end of the 17th century, the settlement remained very small. The population stood at only 8,000 in 1648.

Berlin was the seat of the German Hohenzollern rulers of BRANDENBURG. They had embraced CALVINISM, but their subjects remained Lutheran. As a result, the Hohenzollerns practiced a policy of TOLERATION in religious matters. They welcomed HUGUENOTS from FRANCE who were fleeing persecution after the revocation of the Edict of Nantes in 1685. Huguenot settlers swelled the town population, introducing more wealth and skilled artisans to it. By the middle of the 18th century, Berlin had reached a population of 100,000; toward the end of the century, it had climbed to 170,000.

Berlin changed dramatically in the 18th century. The Hohenzollerns had acquired sovereignty over the territories of Prussia, and in 1701 Frederick III, elector of Brandenburg, began to call himself King Frederick I of Prussia. Berlin was chosen as the capital of his new kingdom. In order to provide the city with architectural symbols appropriate to its new status, Frederick I embarked on a building program. He had the Schloss Charlottenburg (Charlottenburg Palace) constructed in the early century for his wife, Sophie Charlotte. The architect was Andreas Schlüter, who went on to adorn the new city of SAINT PETERSBURG in Russia. Berlin acquired monumental city squares such as the Leipziger Platz and Pariser Platz under Frederick I's successor, Frederick William I. A new town, Friedrichstadt, was built just outside the old city walls. FREDERICK II (THE GREAT), in turn, continued the work of Frederick William I. He built the famous Unter den Lindenstrasse and the Forum Fredericianum at Bebelplatz. For himself, he commissioned the lovely ROCOCO palace of Sans Souci at Potsdam. The opera house was also constructed in rococo style. NEOCLASSICISM appeared toward the end of the century and is best represented today by the Brandenburg Gate.

Under the ENLIGHTENED DESPOTISM of Frederick the Great, Berlin became an important commercial and industrial center. But cultural and intellectual activities associated with the ENLIGHTENMENT also were nurtured. The BERLIN ACADEMY, the creation of Gottfried Wilhelm LEIBNIZ and the third-oldest scientific academy in Europe, was restructured and provided with an infusion of money and members. It was renamed the Königliche Preussische Akademie der Wissenschaften (Royal Prussian Academy of Sciences). Chamber music and opera also thrived under the auspices of the music-loving king. In fact, the reign of Frederick the Great transformed Berlin into the cultural and intellectual center of northern Europe.

Berlin Academy (Königliche Preussische Akademie der Wissenschaften)

Scientific academy originally founded in 1700 by Frederick III, elector of Brandenburg. The philosopher Gottfried Wilhelm LEIBNIZ drew up the plans for this early academy. This original institution was neglected during the reign of Frederick William I. In 1744, his son and successor, FREDERICK II (THE GREAT) OF PRUSSIA, revived the academy by joining the Nouvelle Société Litteraire to the old academy (Société des Sciences). He called his new institution the Académie des Sciences et Belles-Lettres. Later, it acquired the name Königliche Preussische Akademie der Wissenschaften (Royal Prussian Academy of Sciences). The restructured academy became a prominent scientific institution of the later 18th century.

At the suggestion of VOLTAIRE, Frederick the Great invited the French physicist and mathematician Pierre Louis Moreau de MAUPERTUIS to assume the presidency of the organization. After Maupertuis's years as president, the French mathematician and encyclopedist Jean Le Rond d'ALEMBERT was offered the position. He declined to accept, but provided leadership by means of correspondence.

For most of Frederick the Great's reign, the academy members exhibited strong biases in favor of French science and enlightened culture. Official academy publications, for example, appeared in French rather than in German or Latin.

The academy rosters reveal that members were drawn not only from the German territories, but also from other European nations. Prominent members included Georges-Louis Leclerc, comte de BUFFON, Claude-Adrien HELVÉTIUS, Bernard de FONTENELLE, Thiry d'HOLBACH, Voltaire, Maupertuis, Julien Offray de LA METTRIE, Joseph-Louis LAGRANGE, Jean Le Rond d'Alembert, and Jean-Baptiste de Boyer, marquis d'ARGENS—all associated with the ENLIGHTENMENT in Paris. Other members were Leonhard EULER (president after Maupertuis), Daniel BERNOULLI, Johann Georg Sulzer, Samuel König (instigator of a vicious quarrel between Voltaire and Maupertuis), and Johann Heinrich Lambert. Christian WOLFF, the transmitter of Leibniz's philosophy to the AUFKLÄRUNG (German Enlightenment), Johann Christoph GOTTSCHED, and Alexander Gottlieb BAUMGARTEN were listed as nonresident German members.

Bernardin de Saint-Pierre, Jacques-Henri (1737–1814) *French engineer and writer*

A native of Le Havre, FRANCE, Bernardin de Saint-Pierre moved at the age of 12 to the French colony on the island of Martinique. The experience with native culture on that island strongly colored his subsequent outlook on life.

Having returned to France, Bernardin de Saint-Pierre initially planned to become a Jesuit missionary, but he abandoned that plan rather quickly, taking, instead, a degree in engineering. He served as an army engineer during the SEVEN YEARS' WAR and as an engineer on the island of Mauritius in the Indian Ocean. He also traveled throughout Europe, residing for brief periods in both Russia and POLAND.

In 1769, he returned to France, assumed a position as a civil engineer in the region near PARIS and began writing.

Bernardin de Saint-Pierre soon formed a solid friendship with Jean-Jacques ROUSSEAU. He frequented the salons of both Madame GEOFFRIN and Julie de LESPINASSE, mingling with the PHILOSOPHES who were leaders of the French ENLIGHTENMENT.

With the publication of his *Voyage à l'Île de France* (Journey to Mauritius) in 1773, Bernardin de Saint-Pierre launched his literary career. A second book, the utopian romance *Paul et Virginie* (Paul and Virginia), appeared in 1787. Bernardin de Saint-Pierre modeled his vision of the ideal society partly on the native societies he had encountered in his youth. But he also shaped his descriptions to present his cherished ideals of simplicity, spontaneity, and naturalness.

In addition to fiction, Bernardin de Saint-Pierre wrote about natural history and helped to shape the fledgling science of BIOLOGY. His *Études de la nature* (Studies of nature, 1784–88) presented ideas about the structure of living organisms along with a general philosophical position that made nature the primary testimonial to divine goodness.

A critic of the enlightened position that emphasized REASON and PROGRESS, Bernardin de Saint-Pierre expressed views similar to those of his friend Rousseau. Both men believed in the superiority of human feeling over reason. They also thought that the course of human HISTORY had been one of slow degeneration from an idyllic antiquity. Furthermore, they adopted a view of NATURE that differed substantially from the one favored by partisans of reason. These views mark them as members of the later generation of the Enlightenment. Their ideas would be adopted and transformed by later writers associated with ROMANTICISM.

See also SOCIAL INSTITUTIONS OF THE ENLIGHTENMENT.

Bernoulli, Daniel (1700–1782) *Swiss mathematician, physicist, and physician*

Daniel Bernoulli was the second son of Johann I BERNOULLI and nephew of Jakob I BERNOULLI. Young Daniel studied mathematics with his father, physics and logic in Basel, and medicine at Basel, Strasbourg, and Heidelberg. Throughout his career, Daniel Bernoulli endured the enmity and competition of his father.

After receiving a degree in medicine, Bernoulli spent some time in VENICE, where he published the *Exercitationes quaedam mathematicae* (Certain mathematical exercises; 1724). The work resulted in a call to the SAINT PETERSBURG ACADEMY in Saint Petersburg, Russia. Bernoulli spent eight years (1725–33) in Russia, working with the mathematician Leonhard EULER. Having received an offer (1732) to teach botany and anatomy at the University of Basel, Bernoulli left Saint Petersburg (1733) and returned to Switzerland. He taught first botany, then physiology (1743), and finally physics (1750).

Although Bernoulli loved mathematics, his major scientific contributions lay in the closely related fields of mechanics and physics. In exploring these disciplines, Bernoulli generally followed the principles of physics spelled out by Isaac NEWTON, but in ASTRONOMY and magnetism he retained allegiance to earlier Cartesian MECHANICAL PHILOSOPHY.

Bernoulli left specific treatises on hydrodynamics and on the mechanics of vibrating bodies. The "Bernoulli theorem," one of his major contributions, demonstrated that pressure in a fluid is inversely related to its velocity. In other words, if a moving fluid is constricted, its pressure decreases and its velocity increases. Bernoulli's applications of mathematical probability theory and statistics to problems of political economy, public health (smallpox morbidity), and population represented an attempt to express variable phenomena as a set of mathematical relations.

Bernoulli wrote 10 prize-winning papers for the FRENCH ACADEMY OF SCIENCES. He was a member not only of that academy, but also of scientific academies or societies in Saint Petersburg, BERLIN, LONDON, TURIN, Bologna, Zürich, and Mannheim. Bernoulli is now considered the first mathematician to link Newton's ideas with the calculus of LEIBNIZ.

Of Bernoulli's many scientific papers and treatises, the following must be noted: *Hydrodynamica, sive de viribus et motibus fluidorum commentarii* (Hydrodynamics, or commentary on the forces and motions of fluids; 1738); *Exercitationes quaedam mathematicae* (Certain mathematical exercises; 1724); and "Specimen theoriae novae de mensura sortis," in *Commentarii Academiae Scientiarum Imperialis Petropolitanae* (Sample of the new theory of measuring fate in Commentaries of the Imperial Academy of Sciences of Saint Petersburg).

Bernoulli, Jakob I and Johann I (Jakob I, 1654–1705 and Johann I, 1667–1748) *Swiss mathematicians and brothers*

Johann I Bernoulli was the father of both Daniel BERNOULLI and Johann II Bernoulli.

Jakob I Bernoulli, the older brother, studied mathematics and ASTRONOMY against the will of his father. His formal degrees were awarded in philosophy and theology. He spent some years as a private tutor in GENEVA, then embarked on an extended educational tour, spending two years in FRANCE studying Cartesianism, followed by a similar period of time in the UNITED PROVINCES OF THE NETHERLANDS and ENGLAND. Beginning in 1687, he served as professor of mathematics at the University of Basel in SWITZERLAND.

Jakob I Bernoulli became an early expert on the application of the infinitesimal calculus to problems in MATHEMATICS AND MECHANICS. His paper of 1690 demonstrated his mastery of Leibnizian calculus and used the term *integral* for the first time.

Johann I Bernoulli, the younger of the two brothers, also studied mathematics. In 1695, he was appointed professor at the University of Groningen in the United Provinces of the Netherlands. He assumed the chair in mathematics at the University of Basel in 1705. Jakob I and Johann I first collaborated on the study of the calculus. They worked together on several problems, but over time became bitterly estranged. Professional jealousy and personality differences seem to have caused the rift. In general, Johann I was recognized as the more gifted intuitive mathematician, but Jakob I left broad theoretical formulations of great significance to 18th-century mathematicians.

Jakob I Bernoulli believed that all processes in nature are continuous (like a curve) rather than discontinuous (stepwise). Therefore, calculus, the mathematical branch devoted to the study of curves, was the proper tool for explaining these processes. The value of calculus for engineering was demonstrated by Jakob I Bernoulli when he solved the drawbridge problem (equation describing the curve of a sliding weight on the rope that holds up a drawbridge).

Jakob I Bernoulli's interests extended to other types of phenomena for which calculus was inadequate. He made significant contributions in his *Ars conjectandi* (Art of inferring; 1713) to the development of probability theory, combinatorial theory, and mathematical series, all of which can be applied to so-called discrete (discontinuous) phenomena. His derivation of the "Bernoulli numbers" facilitated the problem of expanding exponential mathematical series.

A complete collection of Jakob I Bernoulli's publications was printed in 1744 as *Opera* (Works). Johann Bernoulli contributed to the first volumes of the collaborative project, *Theory of Series* (1682–1704). The *Acta eruditorum,* a professional journal, contains papers by both Bernoulli brothers.

Berthollet, Claude-Louis (1748–1822) *French chemist, trained as a physician*

Berthollet spent nearly 20 years of his life trying to develop a synthesis of PHLOGISTON THEORY, AFFINITY CHEMISTRY, and the new doctrines of Antoine LAVOISIER. In the course of this enterprise, Berthollet created a new system of chemistry that was sketched first in *Recherches sur les lois de l'affinité* (Research on the laws of affinity; 1801) and expanded in the *Essai de statique chimique* (Essay of chemical statics, 2 vols.; 1803). His new system assumed that the attraction between elements (affinity) was not a constant, but rather varied in strength with temperature and with the relative quantities of reacting substances. Berthollet developed the concept of "effective mass" or "chemical mass" in conjunction with his new affinity theory.

Berthollet was a member of a French family that had immigrated to Savoy in the 17th century. He studied at colleges in Annecy and Chambéry and later took his medical degree at the University of Turin. He practiced medicine in the Piedmont for four years and in 1772 moved to PARIS. Through the patronage of Théodore Tronchin, Berthollet received an appointment as the private physician to Charlotte-Jeanne Béraud de La Haie de Riou, duchesse de Montesson. As the wife (by an officially secret but well-known marriage) of the duc d'Orléans, son of LOUIS XV, the duchesse de Montesson resided in the Palais Royal in Paris. She gave Berthollet access to a private chemical laboratory in the Palais-Royal, where he began serious experimentation. In 1784, Berthollet

became the inspector of dye works and director of the GOBELINS TAPESTRY works.

During the FRENCH REVOLUTION, Berthollet managed to avoid condemnation. He served on the commission for reform of the French monetary system (1792), the scientific commission on war production (1793), and the commission on agriculture and arts (1794). He also received a position as professor at the École normale (a training school for teachers) and assisted with the establishment of the École polytechnique (a school of applied sciences and engineering). These schools were created during the French Revolution (1795) as part of the Enlightenment-inspired reforms that made education the business of the secular state.

Under Napoleon, Berthollet served on a two-year scientific expedition to Egypt. He accompanied the commission sent to the Italian peninsula to select paintings for transfer to France. Napoleon rewarded him with a title of nobility, with membership in the Legion of Honor, and with a Senate seat. In 1807, Berthollet and his friend Pierre LAPLACE established the Société d'Arcueil, which held weekly meetings to discuss scientific problems.

Berthollet began his career in chemistry committed to the phlogiston theory. He criticized certain inconsistencies in Lavoisier's quantitative experiments, but nevertheless helped to spread information about Lavoisier's novel chemical theories and nomenclature. In addition to his theoretical work, Berthollet made important contributions to industrial chemistry. For example, he developed a process for bleaching textiles with chlorine, created a new form of gunpowder, and produced a theoretical and practical treatise on general techniques of dying cloth.

See also CHEMICAL REVOLUTION.

biblical criticism

A discipline that first appeared in the 17th century as students of ancient languages began applying their linguistic skills to biblical texts. It received impetus from the general enthusiasm for rational analysis that characterized the ENLIGHTENMENT. Biblical criticism continued to develop during the Enlightenment, acquiring during that era the outlines that would develop into the mature 19th-century discipline. Biblical criticism emerged as a line of inquiry distinct from theology and often, but not always, served as a tool in the battle against dogmatism within established Christian churches. It drew not only on linguistics and philosophy, but also on the newer approaches of HISTORY, ANTHROPOLOGY, and PSYCHOLOGY.

Biblical criticism began as textual criticism, an endeavor in which comparative analysis of different versions of the Bible was used to uncover discrepancies in texts. Transcription errors by copyists or printers, unreadable manuscripts, fake documents, and translation difficulties were all identified as sources of discrepancies.

Such textual analysis, however, involved a rather restricted approach to language, and in the late 17th century began to be supplemented by broader inquiries about biblical language. Richard SIMON, the French Oratorian who is often credited with starting the trend toward modern criticism, examined the books ascribed to Moses in the Old Testament and, by a combination of textual, historical, and stylistic analysis, concluded that he could not have written all of them.

The context in which biblical language had been spoken also began to receive attention. It was recognized that the meaning of words or stories might depend on the broader cultural environment in which a given text had been produced. Furthermore, it was supposed that meanings might have been lost or blurred in the course of history as cultures changed to make them less apparent. Benedict de SPINOZA, for example, suggested that the Old Testament was simply the history of the ancient Hebrew people.

Some scholars rejected this contextual criticism and, instead, started with acceptance of the literal meaning of biblical language. But they proceeded, then, to demonstrate that these literal meanings were nonsensical according to the criteria of common sense. The English deist Anthony COLLINS and the German scholar Hermann Samuel REIMARUS both resorted to this form of argument. Reimarus raised the particularly vexing question of the historical Jesus. This problem played a central role in 19th-century biblical criticism and continues both to fascinate and to frustrate scholars today.

Enlightened speculation about the stages of human development produced the notion that "primitive" (that is, ancient) human beings thought and spoke differently from "civilized" people. "Primitives," so the argument went, used metaphor and poetry, whereas "civilized" people used prose and logic. Scholars who accepted this viewpoint suggested that the poetic language of the Old Testament Hebrews reflected their specific level of intellectual development, and that God had purposely inspired people to write in this language because it would be understood.

These approaches tended to make the Bible into a historical, human document whose truths might, therefore, be relative rather than absolute. To combat this danger, some enlightened scholars began to interpret biblical language as symbol or allegory. They assumed that although the literal meaning of biblical stories might be rooted in historical context, these stories nevertheless conveyed deeper universal truths. Gotthold Ephraim LESSING and Johann Salomo SEMLER, two leaders in 18th-century German criticism, both adopted this position. Furthermore, they claimed that because of historical PROGRESS, 18th-century enlightened minds were better prepared to comprehend these deep truths than were the original people who heard them. In other words, knowledge of God's words and truths actually increases as history evolves, contributing to the improvement of the human condition.

Biblical criticism served both critics and defenders of Christianity and Judaism. It tended to make the Bible a thoroughly human production, written by inspired, gifted people. In advancing this view, biblical criticism made defense of the Bible as a book of knowledge especially revealed by God more difficult, but it certainly did not eliminate this viewpoint. In fact, it helped to stimulate the search for additional avenues by which revealed religious truths could be received, so that claims for the unique character of the Bible and for the truth content of the Judeo-Christian tradition could be substantiated.

See also BAYLE; DEISM; MICHAELIS; RELIGION.

Bichat, Marie-François-Xavier (1771–1802) *French physiologist, surgeon, and anatomist*
The son of the physician Jean-Baptiste Bichat, young Bichat originally studied philosophy at the Séminaire Saint-Irenée in Lyons, but after 1791, the fields of surgery and anatomy occupied his primary attention. Having studied for three years in Lyons, he moved in 1794 to PARIS, where he became a student and assistant to Pierre Desault at the Grand Hospice d'Humanité (formerly the Hôtel-Dieu). Bichat assumed the task of publishing the *Journal de Chirurgie* (Journal of surgery) upon the death of Desault. He set up private courses in anatomy at which he performed animal vivisections. He also established a private laboratory and, with the assistance of Henri Husson and Guillaume Dupuytren, founded the Societé Médicale d'Émulation (1796). This new society aimed to bring together the young physicians of Paris. Pierre-Jean-Georges CABANIS and the Philippe Pinel were among the early members of the group.

Between 1799 and 1801, Bichat published the three works on which his reputation rests: *Traité des membranes* (Treatise on membranes); *Recherches physiologiques sur la vie et la mort* (Physiological research on life and death); and *Anatomie générale appliquée à la physiologie et à la médecine* (General anatomy applied to physiology and medicine). He died in July 1802 at the age of 31.

Bichat's physiology incorporated certain aspects of the VITALISM that was taught by the faculty of medicine at the University of Montpellier in southern France. Vitalist theory strongly influenced leading biologists and philosophers (Denis DIDEROT, in particular) during the late ENLIGHTENMENT. In keeping with his vitalist sympathies, Bichat rejected the traditional MEDICINE associated with the work of Hermann BOERHAAVE. He credited Georg Ernst STAHL, the creator of early 18th-century ANIMISM, with having rescued the study of biology from its misguided attachment to the MECHANICAL PHILOSOPHY. In his specific studies of tissue anatomy, Bichat found inspiration and guidance from the work of Philippe Pinel.

Bichat believed that the vital properties of organisms could not be reduced to physical, mechanical principles and laws, but rather that "life" was something qualitatively and fundamentally unique. He developed tissue anatomy by integrating an analogy drawn from chemical elements with his vitalist-inspired understanding of life. Bichat argued that studies of tissue pathology should be based on the various elemental structures of membranes rather than on the location of internal organs. The elemental structures of tissues could de differentiated according to their textures, degree of sensibility (or lack of the same), and ability to contract on touch. Bichat distinguished the vital properties of tissues (lost at death) from physical ones (retained after death). His researches helped to found the modern science of histology, the special branch of BIOLOGY that explores tissue structure.

Bildung   German word with the basic meaning of "form" or "formation." Whatever its application, *Bildung* always implies that a process of change or development over time is occurring. Hence, for instance, in its most common meaning, "education," the concept of *Bildung* refers to the entire process of learning by which an individual human being is formed into a mature, thinking adult.

During the period of the German ENLIGHTENMENT (*AUFKLÄRUNG*), the concept of *Bildung* acquired significance in many disciplines. In general, its use reflected the new awareness during the Enlightenment that, over time, people and things, whether living or dead, change. In other words, they have a HISTORY; they do not remain the same throughout their existence. This history, it was believed, was actively formed, shaped, or educated by both natural forces and human intervention.

This general concept of *Bildung* appeared in many new words coined during the Enlightenment: For example, the *Bildungstrieb* of Johann Friedrich BLUMENBACH denoted a formative force that supposedly determined the pattern of growth and development in living beings. The *Bildungsroman* was a form of novel developed by Johann Wolfgang von GOETHE that described the development of its characters over time. Finally, the *Bildungsbürgertum* was the educated class of city dwellers (*Bürgern*) in Germany.

biology   Term used to denote the study of living organisms. It is anachronistic to apply the term to 18th-century scientific investigations of life. The concept of biology is a product of the early 19th century, having appeared simultaneously in works by Jean Baptiste LAMARCK and Gottfried Reinhold Treviranus published in 1802. The appearance of the term symbolizes the transformations that occurred during the 18th century in the sciences concerned with the study of living organisms. It demonstrates that living beings had come to be conceived as fundamentally different from nonliving things and that they consequently deserved a special scientific approach.

At the beginning of the 18th century, the study of life was largely the business of medical doctors. They approached their subject from differing theoretical positions. Some physicians retained the traditional Aristotelian-derived viewpoints. Others explained life processes in terms of chemistry (IATROCHEMISTRY) or mechanics (IATROMECHANICS). The medical approach to life sciences retained dominance in universities throughout the century.

Outside the realms of medicine and university teaching, a form of life sciences called natural history acquired new vitality after 1670. It was largely the domain of amateurs, men trained for the priesthood, law, or other nonscientific professions. Natural history had emerged during the Renaissance as a science describing natural things in terms of their usefulness for humankind. It had slipped into the scientific shadows during the 17th-century SCIENTIFIC REVOLUTION, overwhelmed by the creativity that was occurring in mathematics, physics, and ASTRONOMY. By 1670, however, a new form of natural history, stripped of its focus on humanity, began to be enlisted in ENGLAND in the service of theological arguments for the existence of God (PHYSICO-THEOLOGY). The wonders of the universe seemed to attest to the wisdom and purpose of the Christian God in his creation.

Over the course of the 18th century, this theologically motivated descriptive natural history transformed itself into an empirical science. NATURE acquired an element of temporality: It was recognized that nature was not immutable but had a history of change over time. This recognition stands as one of the most significant intellectual transitions to have occurred during the ENLIGHTENMENT.

Interest in natural history and the history of nature spawned CLASSIFICATION schemes and theories about the transformation (change over time) of species and of the earth. Both types of scientific endeavor aimed at imposing some order (allegedly natural, of course) on the natural world.

During the ferment caused by these changes in thinking about nature and life, the sciences of physiology and comparative anatomy acquired independent existence. In FRANCE, their institutional base lay outside the University of PARIS and barely touched the FRENCH ACADEMY OF SCIENCES. Rather, the Jardin du Roi (Royal Garden) and the renegade but prestigious University of Montpellier served as the centers for such inquiries. In GERMANY, SCOTLAND, and ITALY, the new approaches were more easily integrated into the universities. In England, however, the proponents of the new views had little influence in the traditional Universities of Oxford and Cambridge.

The discussions among life scientists of the 18th century centered on a few major issues: the questions of GENERATION (reproduction), of DEGENERATION and the fixity of species, of the definitive essence of life, and of the nature of nature (active or static). Scientists were puzzling over the processes of generation in arguments between preformationists and epigeneticists, or between ovists and animalculists. Another contentious question concerned whether or not species have changed over time. Finally, the question of what distinguishes living from nonliving creation assumed major significance.

The middle of the 18th century witnessed notable shifts in the orientation of the life sciences. After 1760, VITALISM, with its emphasis on active natural forces, began vying with the MECHANICAL PHILOSOPHY and the older ANIMISM as a dominant explanatory theory of life processes. In wrestling with questions about living organisms, life scientists turned increasingly to experimental methods and to forms of observation. They largely abandoned the search for causes along with the task of constructing rational a priori systems, contenting themselves, instead, with what they conceived as simple descriptions of phenomena. Finally, scientists for the most part turned away from descriptions or theories that relied on the action of God in nature. Rather, they attempted to explain all life phenomena in terms of natural processes. In so doing, they laid the groundwork for the appearance of the new science of biology.

Major life scientists of the period of the Enlightenment included Hermann BOERHAAVE, Paul-Joseph BARTHEZ, Marie-François-Xavier BICHAT, Charles BONNET, Théophile de BORDEU, the comte de BUFFON, Pierre-Jean-Georges CABANIS, and Pieter CAMPER. Also significant were Georges CUVIER, Louis-Jean-Marie DAUBENTON, Denis DIDEROT, Franz Joseph GALL, Johann Wolfgang von Goethe, Nicolaas Hartsoeker (1656–1725), Robert Hooke (1635–1702), John HUNTER and his brother William HUNTER, Jean-Baptiste LAMARCK, Antoni van LEEUWENHOEK, Johann Kaspar LAVATER, Carolus LINNAEUS, Marcello Malphigi (1628–94), Pierre-Louis Moreau de MAUPERTUIS, Alexander MONRO (Secundus), Pieter van MUSSCHENBROEK, John Tuberville NEEDHAM, John PRINGLE, Johann Christian REIL, Lazzaro SPALLANZANI, and Abraham TREMBLEY. In addition, the chemists Joseph PRIESTLEY, Joseph BLACK, William CULLEN, and Stephen HALES contributed significantly to the understanding of life processes.

Major institutional centers for these studies included the University of Montpellier, the University of Leiden, the University of Edinburgh, the University of Glasgow, the University of GÖTTINGEN, the University of HALLE, the Jardin du Roi in Paris, and the various SCIENTIFIC ACADEMIES in LONDON, EDINBURGH, BERLIN, and Paris.

See also EPIGENESIS; JARDIN DES PLANTES; MATHEMATICS AND MECHANICS; MEDICINE; PREFORMATION THEORY; UNIVERSITIES.

Further reading: Stephen F. Mason, *A History of the Sciences*, rev. ed. (New York: Collier Books [Macmillan], 1962).

Black, Joseph (1728–1799) *Scottish chemist, physicist, and physician; helped to develop the quantitative methods characteristic of modern chemistry*

Black identified carbon dioxide as a unique aeriform fluid (gas) and defined the concepts of latent and specific heat.

Black was born in Bordeux, FRANCE, the son of a Scot from Belfast who worked in France as a wine merchant.

Young Black was sent to Belfast for private school instruction, then attended the University of Glasgow, where he studied with William CULLEN from 1748 until 1752. Black transferred to the University of Edinburgh, took courses with Robert WHYTT, Alexander Monro Primus, and Charles Alston, and received his M.D. degree in 1754.

Black replaced Cullen as professor of chemistry at the University of Glasgow in 1756 because Cullen moved on to a position at EDINBURGH. Black stayed at Glasgow for 10 years, again moving to replace Cullen, this time at Edinburgh. He remained in the city for the rest of his life, teaching Benjamin RUSH and other successful students from Europe and the North American colonies.

James WATT consulted with Black about the properties of heat and subsequently developed the condensing STEAM ENGINE. Watt acknowledged that Black provided him with an understanding of heat theory, but he insisted that the idea for the condenser, based on Black's concept of latent heat, was his own creation. Black and his students disputed Watt's position.

Black maintained a small private medical practice in Edinburgh. He was active in the highly significant intellectual life at Edinburgh and associated with Adam SMITH, James HUTTON, David HUME, Adam FERGUSON, and other illustrious figures of the Scottish ENLIGHTENMENT. Black attended the meetings of the Philosophical Society of Edinburgh and the ROYAL SOCIETY OF EDINBURGH and also frequented the informal clubs called the Select, the Poker, and the Oyster. Black died in 1799.

In 1760, Black began experiments on the subject of heat (conceived as a fluid composed of tiny particles) and its behavior during changes of a substance from one physical state to another. He measured the time that is needed to transform ice into water (during the actual melting process, the temperature remains constant at 32° F, even though much heat is used). He compared this time to that required to raise the same amount of water one degree in temperature. He repeated the experiment for the transformation from water to steam. From his observations and experiments he developed the concept of latent heat (the heat energy put into ice during its transformation into water), recognizing that temperature and quantity of heat were two distinct phenomena. Black then turned his attention to the variation in the rates at which different substances could be heated and changed from one state to another. From these observations, he developed the notion of specific heat (the amount of heat required to raise the temperature of a unit mass of a substance by one degree).

Black remained committed to the PHLOGISTON THEORY of combustion and opposed the new theories of Antoine LAVOISIER for many years. However, in 1790 he wrote to Lavoisier to tell him that he was beginning to teach the new theories to his Edinburgh students. Black taught AFFINITY CHEMISTRY but insisted on using the term *elective attraction* rather than the term *elective affinity* favored by continental chemists. Unlike his teacher Cullen, Black did not link his theory to an atomistic or corpuscular theory of chemical substances.

The paper on which Black's renown as a chemist is based—"Experiments Upon Magnesia Alba, Quicklime, and Some Other Alcaline Substances"—appeared in the *Essays and Observations of the Philosophical Society of Edinburgh* in 1756. Black showed that certain substances contained a specific aeriform fluid that differed from common air. This "fixed air" (carbon dioxide) was released when certain substances were heated or subjected to the action of acids. Previously, chemists had believed that the airs (gases) given off in reactions were all the same substance and had called that substance "fixed air." Black's experiments showed that his "fixed air" displayed special properties. His findings suggested to chemists that perhaps more than one kind of "air" existed. Black's experiment helped to open up the subject of gaseous chemistry to the significant discoveries of the later Enlightenment. His findings, one of a series of crucial chemical discoveries made during the Enlightenment, helped to produce the CHEMICAL REVOLUTION of the 1770s and 1780s.

Blackstone, Sir William (1723–1780) *English jurist, legal scholar, and writer*

The son of charles Blackstone, a silk merchant in LONDON, William was educated at Pembroke College, Oxford University. He entered Middle Temple for law study in 1741 and was elected a fellow at All Souls College, Oxford, in 1744. He joined the English bar in 1746, and after 1753 devoted himself to lecturing at Oxford.

Blackstone experienced pronounced success at Oxford, becoming the university's first Vinerian Professor of English Law in 1758 and principal of New Inn Hall in 1761. He received an appointment as solicitor general to Queen Charlotte in 1763. Blackstone sat in Parliament from 1761 until 1769. After 1770, he served 10 years as a judge in the court of common pleas.

Blackstone's prominent position in the history of the ENLIGHTENMENT in England rests on his *Commentaries on the Laws of England* (1765–69). Dedicated to Queen Charlotte, this book presented a compilation of English law in skillful prose intended for students, professional lawyers, and the general reading public.

The *Commentaries* presented Blackstone's interpretation of the legal basis (constitution) of the English government. The events of the 17th century in England—the Civil Wars and the GLORIOUS REVOLUTION of 1688—had provoked much discussion of this topic. Blackstone believed that sovereignty in England rested on the King-in-Parliament. In other words, undivided and unchallengeable authority rested in the union of the king with the House of Lords and the House of Commons.

The *Commentaries* wrestled with the relations among various types of law: common law, civil or Roman law, NATURAL LAW, and divine or revealed law. Blackstone was overtly concerned with common law, that body of customary law that had developed over centuries of English history. He was not content, however, merely to systematize that law, but rather attempted to demonstrate the intimate links between historical English common law and universal natural law. He thus used one of the basic concepts of the Enlightenment—the idea of a universal law derived from the natural order of things in the universe (i.e., natural law)—as a support for the absolute authority of specifically English customary (common) law. English customary law was, in his treatment, a representation or equivalent of natural law.

In a pronounced departure from English tradition and in direct opposition to the theory of John LOCKE, Blackstone claimed that the English constitution, backed by the body of common law, commanded obedience. The constitution was no longer to be conceived either as a statement of custom or as an expression of the will of the English people, but rather as an absolute statement of the fundamental structure of political authority in England. Common law acquired its power not because it was made

Portrait of William Blackstone by Thomas Gainsborough. Sir William Blackstone prepared the elegant *Commentaries on the Laws of England,* an exploration of English legal traditions that was read by both professionals and amateurs. *(Courtesy New York Public Library)*

by representatives of the people in Parliament, but because it reflected universal, absolute natural law.

Within the context of 18th-century English politics, Blackstone's treatment of common law supported the existing order and gave it a legitimacy based not on history or on a social contract, but rather on the alleged order of things in the universe. It reaffirmed not only the post-1688 solution to relations among king, Parliament, and nation, but also the official links between the secular government and the Anglican Church.

The argument for traditional church-state relations rested on the claim that natural law, like divine law, was a creation of God. Since both were created by God, they could not conflict with each other. Now, according to English tradition, divine law decreed the official link between the English state and the Anglican Church. Since natural law could not conflict with divine law, natural law also necessarily supported this link. Extending this line of reasoning, Blackstone claimed that—since the English common law was the equivalent of the natural law that was itself the equivalent of divine law—then common law, by implication, also reflected divine law. Therefore, common law also necessarily upheld the traditional relations between state and Anglican Church. In mathematical terms, the logic of this argument is transparent and takes the following form: Let a equal common law, b equal natural law, and c equal divine law; if $a = b$ and $b = c$, then $a = c$.

Protestant DISSENTERS in both England and the American colonies immediately comprehended this logic and its implications for their position within the English system and reacted against it. In the American colonies, for example, the 1771 publication of the *Commentaries* inspired a series of political pamphlets that addressed Blackstone's interpretation of church and state relations. Entitled *An Interesting Appendix to Sir William Blackstone's Commentaries on the Laws of England* (1771), this pamphlet collection contained several critical essays by the radical Dissenter Joseph PRIESTLEY.

However controversial, Blackstone's *Commentaries* played a central role in shaping political discussion during the later 18th century in both England and the American colonies. They became standard reading for law students in the Anglo-American world. Furthermore, universities assigned the book in general liberal arts courses, thereby helping to return the subject of law to the realm of general intellectual debate.

See also ANGLICANS; CAPITAL PUNISHMENT; JUSTICE AND THE LAW; POLITICAL THEORY.

Blackwell, Thomas (1701–1757) *scholar of Greek and Roman antiquity*

Born in Aberdeen, SCOTLAND, Blackwell studied Greek and philosophy at Marischal College at the University of Aberdeen, where his father occupied a chair of divinity and was later named principal. He received his master of arts degree in 1718, when he was 17 years old. In 1723,

the college appointed him to a professorship of Greek. Although Blackwell never entered the clergy, as was usual for college administrators at that time, King George II named him principal of Marischal College in 1748. That same year, Blackwell married Barbara Black, the daughter of an Aberdeen merchant.

Blackwell is best known for his studies of ancient literature, *An Enquiry into the Life and Writings of Homer* (1735) and *Letters Concerning Mythology* (1748), both of which he published anonymously. The *Enquiry,* Blackwell's most influential work, assumed that no European poet had been able to equal or to surpass the achievements of the ancient Greek poet Homer and asked why that was true.

In answer to his question, Blackwell turned to historical context. He argued that a society has the capacity to create great poetry only at a certain point in its development. For European culture, that great moment had occurred during the ancient era of Greek domination.

Blackwell further argued that poetry is a primitive and fundamental mode of human expression and that highly polished language loses its poetic power. Thus, the most advanced or highly ordered societies lack genuine poetry. This view contradicted the dominant neoclassical theories of art of the time. Blackwell's new vision stimulated an interest in primitivism that soon swept Britain and parts of continental Europe. Later in the century, this development fueled the popularity of works such as James MACPHERSON's Ossian poems.

Blackwell's work on Homer motivated the Swiss aesthetic theorist Johann Jakob BODMER to search for examples of poetry from the earliest eras of German civilization. Bodmer's work, in turn, played an important role in creating a new interpretation of German medieval culture.

See also AESTHETICS.

Blake, William (1757–1827) *English poet, engraver, religious mystic, and visionary*

William Blake is often treated as a figure of post-Enlightenment ROMANTICISM. Some scholars believe that he was possibly mentally disturbed. Recently, however, research has pointed out his strong ties to the late ENLIGHTENMENT; while this new view does not eliminate the possibility of his madness, it helps to place his concerns into a broader perspective.

As a critic of REASON, Blake rejected the theories of rational NATURAL RELIGION associated with enlightened DEISM. He outlined his ideas in the essay *There is No Natural Religion*. An intensely religious man, Blake believed in a natural Christianity that was built on mystical inspiration rather than on reason. His position did not correspond specifically to the organized sects that grew out of the Enlightenment—METHODISM, the QUAKERS, PIETISM, or Quietism—but like them it emphasized the inner, spontaneous, intuitive religious experience rather than the observance of dogma and law. Blake's father had been an enthusiastic follower of Emanuel SWEDENBORG, and

Blake certainly incorporated Swedenborgian ideas into his vision of relations between humankind and the divine creator of the universe.

The *Book of Urizen* (1794), *Book of Ahania* (1795), and *Book of Los* (1795) offered Blake's extended religious allegory of human history. It presented his interpretation of the roles played by reason, intuition, and imagination in determining the contemporary human condition. Blake's allegory restated the biblical story about the expulsion of Adam and Eve from the Garden of Eden (the Fall), assigning responsibility for the Fall to Urizen (Reason). Urizen had taken control of human minds but was powerless to provide complete understanding of the universe. Such understanding could occur only if Urizen reunited with both Los (Imagination) and Luvah (Love, or the bonds of SYMPATHY). If this reunification occurred, then the human intellect could partake of the divine mind and be redeemed from its misery.

Blake's religious beliefs were intimately linked to his revolutionary artistic, social, and political concerns. He moved in a radical circle of artists and writers that included Henry FUSELI, Mary WOLLSTONECRAFT, William GODWIN, Joseph PRIESTLEY, and Thomas PAINE, all of whom were supported by the publisher Joseph Johnson.

Important writings by Blake included *Poetical Sketches* (1783), *Songs of Innocence* (1789), and *Songs of Experience* (1794), which included "The Tyger." In addition, he wrote several longer prophetic poems: *The Book of Thel, The Marriage of Heaven and Hell* (1793), *America: A Prophecy* (1793), *Europe: A Prophecy* (1793), *Milton* (ca. 1808), and *Jerusalem* (ca. 1818).

Blake had trained to be an engraver and followed this profession throughout his life. He was assisted in his work by his wife, Catherine Boucher. Blake became a masterful illustrator, adorning both his own books and the works of other writers with outstanding copper-plate engravings that he colored by hand (his "illuminated printing"). He illustrated the biblical Book of Job as well as works by Mary Wollstonecraft, Thomas GRAY, Arthur YOUNG, John Milton (*Paradise Lost*), and Dante (*Divine Comedy*). His published writings also contain his illustrations.

Blake's most famous drawings include *When the Morning Stars Sang Together, Elohim Creating Adam, Elijah, The Nativity, The Wise and the Foolish Virgins, Pity, The Spiritual Form of Nelson Guiding the Leviathan,* and *The Spiritual Form of Pitt Guiding the Behemoth.*

Blake manifested many of the traits that were used in the 18th century to develop the concept of GENIUS. His mystical vision, his impatience with the limits of reason, his flights of imagination, his tormented emotions, and his extraordinary talent all placed him in that special category. Whatever his idiosyncrasies, however, Blake clearly also shared in the aesthetic and intellectual culture that was created during the late Enlightenment. He was, in short, both a visionary and a representative of his era.

Blanchard, Jean-Pierre-François (1753–1809) *French inventor and balloonist*

Son of a furniture maker and machinist, Blanchard first displayed his talents as an inventor when he built a mechanical carriage that took him from Les Andelys to Rouen. He became a dedicated hot-air balloonist (first flight, 1784) after witnessing an ascent by Pilastre de Rozier. Together with the American physician John Jeffries, Blanchard made the first crossing of the English Channel by air (1785). He carried a package with him for delivery in England, thus making the first successful air-mail delivery.

A skilled popular performer, Blanchard turned each ascent into a crowd-pleasing spectacle. All over Europe, from BERLIN to VIENNA to PARIS, he produced his shows. The phenomenon is a quintessential illustration of the 18th-century penchant for popularizing scientific ideas and technology by means of spectacle. Other well-known performances were staged by Benjamin FRANKLIN, Franz MESMER, and Jean-Antoine NOLLET.

Blanchard belonged to a lodge of FREEMASONS. During the FRENCH REVOLUTION, the Austrians imprisoned him as a purveyor of radical doctrines. Once released, Blanchard traveled to the United States (1792–98), where, in 1793, he made the first balloon flight in the nation's history. Blanchard left the United States in 1798, returning to Europe and continuing his shows until February 1808. He died of complications from a probable stroke in 1809. Blanchard married twice: first to Victoire Lebrun and later to Marie-Madeleine-Sophie-Armand. The latter was also a celebrated balloonist.

Bluestocking An informal social club for women that originated in the 1750s in LONDON. The term literally derives from the blue worsted stockings that were associated with informal attire and the lower middle class. Such stockings may have been worn by various members of the club, or even by one single member, rather than the more formal white or black silk stockings that were associated with upper-class dress. *Bluestocking* thus connotes the rejection of courtly conventions and the adoption of emerging middle-class values in the mid-18th century.

While the Bluestocking gatherings included upper-class and professional men and women, the club achieved and preserved its fame (and, during the 19th and much of the 20th centuries, its infamy) because of the work of its female members. Assembling in the homes of Elizabeth MONTAGU, Frances Boscawen, and Elizabeth Vesey, the club promoted intellectual conversation rather than cards and gossip. It eventually became associated with the polite, literary writings of Montagu, her sister Sarah Scott, Elizabeth Carter, Hester Chapone, Catherine Talbot and, later in the 18th century, with the work of Hannah More, Anna Seward, and, to a certain extent, Clara Reeve, Mary WOLLSTONECRAFT, and others.

Most of the work of these women falls under the socially accepted categories of fiction, essays, conduct books, and poems, but it includes respected accomplishments in such traditional male preserves as extended works of literary criticism, translation, moral philosophy, political commentary, and social criticism. The club was also noted for its philanthropic activities, ranging from the reclamation of abused women and the institution of schools of industry for lower-class females to projects for improving the living conditions of coal miners and for raising social consciousness with respect to the exploitation of London chimneysweeps.

The praise and scorn heaped historically upon the Bluestockings derive from their perceived blurring of codes (such as gender roles) that subsequent generations would define more strictly. Samuel JOHNSON set the tone of this debate when he gave one of the group's exponents, Elizabeth Carter, the backhanded compliment that her skills at baking equaled her powers as a translator from Greek. The intense political and social turmoil that succeeded the FRENCH REVOLUTION led critics to associate the female pursuit of intellectual life with the disruption of tradition and the "monstrous birth" of a chaotic age. Later generations, in contrast, perceived the Bluestockings as upper-class apologists for the status quo.

Many prominent members of the Bluestocking circle were indeed products of the established order, and they later defended it through their political, cultural, and religious conservatism. However, "Bluestocking feminism" illustrates the status and limits of female agency in the latter half of the 18th century. Scholars widely agree that women assumed a new role in the British national imagination during this period. On the one hand, women were considered slaves to their senses, and hence the consumers and promoters of luxury. On the other hand, the idea of female virtue came to signify modesty and restraint in the face of sensuous, consumerist temptation. This contradictory image of women as appetitive and virtuous points toward the ideological position of Bluestocking feminism, which reaffirmed the progressive, market-driven (and yet chauvinist and racist) social tenets of the British Empire while championing the cause of female intellectual and moral agency.

In the early 19th century, the writings of the Bluestocking circle were considered less important than the club's reputation. This reputation was a source of ambivalent opinions during periods that witnessed the matriculation of women at universities, female suffrage, and the increasing prominence and importance of women in professional workplaces. Recently, works by Elizabeth Carter, Sarah Scott, Anna Seward, and other members of the circle have been reprinted. The Bluestockings may thus yet achieve the recognition as writers that they have long held as symbols.

Further reading: Elizabeth Eger, ed., *Bluestocking Feminism: Writings of the Bluestocking Circle, 1738–1785,* 5 vols. (London: Pickering and Chatto, 1999).

Blumenbach, Johann Friedrich (1752–1840) *German physical anthropologist, natural historian, physiologist, and comparative anatomist*
Blumenbach is considered one of the primary founders of comparative scientific ANTHROPOLOGY. Born into a wealthy, educated Protestant family, Blumenbach enjoyed early exposure to literature and the natural sciences as well as the advantages of an outstanding secondary education. For his higher education he matriculated first at the University of Jena and subsequently at the University of GÖTTINGEN. He studied natural history and the related field of fossil mineralogy. His 1776 dissertation, *De generis humani varietate nativa liber* (Book on the natural variety of the human species), earned him international renown as a comparative anthropologist.

Blumenbach immediately received a post as curator of the natural history collection and adjunct professor at the University of Göttingen. By 1778, he had obtained a post as professor of medicine at the same university. A marriage in 1778 to the daughter of a prominent university administrator no doubt facilitated Blumenbach's rapid professional success. He remained in Göttingen for life, obtaining a prestigious appointment in 1816 as *professor primarius* in the faculty of medicine at the university. He trained most of the leading German life scientists (biologists) of the early 19th century.

Blumenbach enjoyed enormous international prestige. He was elected to membership in more than 70 European academies and scientific institutions. Their ranks included the Institut de France (the post-revolutionary successor to the FRENCH ACADEMY OF SCIENCES), the ROYAL SOCIETY OF LONDON, the BERLIN ACADEMY, the Imperial Academy of SAINT PETERSBURG, and the AMERICAN PHILOSOPHICAL SOCIETY. He corresponded with major scientists throughout Europe, including Charles BONNET, Albrecht VON HALLER, and Pieter CAMPER. His publications on physiology, comparative anatomy, and osteology were widely read in German, English, and French.

Blumenbach's fame rested on two sources: his comparative anthropology of the human species and his concept of the *Bildungstrieb* (*Nisus formativus,* formative force). In the comparative anthropology of humankind, Blumenbach argued that the categorization of humanity into races has no authentic, scientific meaning, but that all the variations in human characteristics form a continuous chain of being within the species. However, he believed that categorizing humans into a few varieties served a useful function for some aspects of anthropological research. He denied the popular notion of a GREAT CHAIN OF BEING that unites all created beings in one continuum. In this manner, he guaranteed that a qualitative break exists between humans and the apes.

Blumenbach entered a vociferous debate with Samvee Thomas Sömmerring about the nature of black-skinned humans. Sömmerring claimed that blacks were the form of humanity closest to the great apes. Blumenbach rejected this notion, saying that a definite break separated humans from the apes and furthermore, that no substantive spiritual or intellectual differences separate the varieties of mankind.

Blumenbach, the major opponent of PREFORMATION THEORY in Germany, developed the concept of *Bildungstrieb* to support a rival theory of GENERATION that was called EPIGENESIS. Preformation theory asserted that the human embryo contains a fully developed individual with all adult traits already present. Epigenesis denied this claim, positing instead that the embryo changes and becomes more complex over the period of pregnancy. For Blumenbach, the *Bildungstrieb*, or formative force, was one of several vital forces that acted together to direct bodily processes both in pregnancy and after birth. The *Bildungstrieb* determined the path of development for an embryo. After birth it acted as a constant force shaping the body, directing its nutrition, and compensating for losses caused by wounds, diseases, or birth abnormalities.

Blumenbach specified that the concept of *Bildungstrieb* combined two fundamental and usually opposed principles about the nature of life: the mechanical and the teleological (goal-seeking) principles. He believed that both the observation of reproductive or generative phenomena and sound reason led to the *Bildungstrieb* concept.

Blumenbach was the major supporter of VITALISM in Germany. He derived his concept of *Bildungstrieb* directly from that theory. Blumenbach's general beliefs about NATURE and living beings contain the major elements of the intellectual shift that marked the later decades of the ENLIGHTENMENT. Most important among these elements were the introduction of HISTORY (that is, development or change over time) into the general conception of individual existence; the insistence that living and nonliving organisms are fundamentally different types of existence; and the stress on a dynamic, motion-filled vision of the natural world.

See also BILDUNG.

Bodmer, Johann Jakob (1698–1783) *Swiss writer and literary critic*

Johann Jakob Bodmer was a prominent figure in the ENLIGHTENMENT of SWITZERLAND, a specific movement that significantly affected the formulations of the German AUFKLÄRUNG. As a professor at the Collegium Carolinum of Zürich, Bodmer trained men such as J. K. LAVATER, Henry FUSELI, and J. H. PESTALOZZI. Bodmer was a colleague of Johann Jakob BREITINGER at the Collegium Car-

olinum and was also a member of the cantonal legislature of Zürich.

Bodmer played a significant role in disseminating and popularizing English literature throughout the German-speaking regions of Europe. This he accomplished partially through translation of John Milton's *Paradise Lost* into German (1732). He was instrumental in the revival of interest in Milton, Dante, and Homer, and engaged in a dispute with VOLTAIRE over the relative merits of these three writers compared to Shakespeare.

With Breitinger as a collaborator, Bodmer aroused curiosity about medieval High German literature by presenting an edition of the *Niebelungslied* (Song of the Niebelungen; 1757) and by his study (1758–59) of the minnesingers, the wandering German poet-musicians of the 12th and 13th centuries. Bodmer also assisted Breitinger in the production and writing of a weekly periodical, *Discourse der Mahlern* (Discourse of artists; 1721–23). The two men modeled their journal on THE SPECTATOR, the influential English publication by Joseph ADDISON and Richard STEELE.

Bodmer developed an important theory of AESTHETICS to counter the French-oriented CLASSICISM espoused in the German-speaking world by the powerful critic Johann Christoph GOTTSCHED. Gottsched generally exalted the rational, analytical products of the human mind and expected these traits to be demonstrated in good literature. He condemned the faculty of imagination to a lower rank than that of REASON and denied the imagination any substantive role in literary creativity. Bodmer, schooled in the philosophy of Gottfried Wilhelm LEIBNIZ and Christian WOLFF, created a theory that rescued imagination from its lowly position. For him, imagination was essential to artistic production and complemented the role of reason in creativity. Imagination and reason were equally important in creativity.

Bodmer and Breitinger stimulated thinking about the nature of beauty and provided the groundwork for a rejection of French canons of taste. Bodmer also provided the first definition of the concept of the "wonderful" or "wondrous" in art.

Bodmer's principal treatises included *Briefwechsel von der Natur des Poetischen Geschmacks* (Correspondence on the nature of poetical taste; 1736); *Critische Betrachtungen über die poetischen Gemälde der Dichter* (Critical reflections on the word-painting of poets; 1741); *Von dem Einfluss und Gebrauche der Einbildungskraft* (On the influence and uses of the imagination; 1727); and *Von dem Wunderbaren in der Poesie* (On the wondrous in poetry; 1740).

See also INTUITION AND IMAGINATION.

Boerhaave, Hermann (1668–1738) *Dutch professor of medicine, botany, and chemistry*

Boerhaave was one of the three great medical theorists and systematizers of the early ENLIGHTENMENT, along with Georg Ernst STAHL and Friedrich HOFFMANN. Boerhaave attempted to explain life processes according to the precepts of both Cartesian and Newtonian forms of MECHANICAL PHILOSOPHY. He was also one of the leading 18th-century chemists, prior to the CHEMICAL REVOLUTION of the 1770s and 1780s. He applied his mechanical philosophical chemical theories to disease, therefore helping to create the medical approaches called IATROMECHANICS and IATROCHEMISTRY.

Boerhaave was an outstanding teacher whose courses at the University of Leiden were renowned throughout Europe. He was the last of the great teachers of an international student body. After Boerhaave, medical training tended to be delivered in vernacular languages and to become closely associated with hospitals and clinics. These developments contributed to the fragmentation of European medical education and practice along linguistic and national lines. This process of fragmentation was offset, however, by the publication of medical journals in whose pages physicians could follow developments in other nations. Journals, therefore, tended to replace universities as sources of medical education on an international scale.

Boerhaave was the son of a Dutch clergyman, the reverend Jacobus Boerhaave, and of Hagar Daelder. The young boy was raised by his father and a devoted stepmother, Eva Dubois. Jacobus Boerhaave supervised his upbringing in the physical, spiritual, and intellectual realms. Acceding to his father's wishes, Hermann Boerhaave began studying theology and philosophy at the University of Leiden in 1684, earning his degree in philosophy in 1690. He turned to MEDICINE afterward, attended public dissections, and in 1693 received a medical degree from the academy of Harderwijk. He settled in Leiden, where he began to practice medicine and to give private lessons in mathematics. Boerhaave received his first official appointment in 1701, as a lecturer in medicine at the University of Leiden. This was followed by appointments at the same university to the chairs of botany and medicine in 1709, and to the chair of chemistry in 1718. Boerhaave held these three chairs simultaneously until 1729, when illness forced him to resign. He was elected to the membership of both the FRENCH ACADEMY OF SCIENCES (1728) and the ROYAL SOCIETY OF LONDON (1730). After retiring from university teaching, Boerhaave continued to give private lectures in Leiden until his death in 1738.

Boerhaave was committed to the cause of explaining life phenomena according to mechanical, inanimate principles (iatromechanism). For example, in clarifying aspects of hemolysis and blood circulation, he spoke of the size and shape of blood particles, of the velocity of the blood flow, and of the angle and diameter of blood vessels. All these general concepts were drawn from Cartesian mechanical philosophy, which reduced all natural phenomena to functions of matter (size and shape) and motion. In supporting iatromechanism, Boerhaave opposed the iatrochemists, who claimed that life phenomena could be reduced to chemical principles. He also rejected the ANIMISM of the influential chemist and physician Stahl. However, Boerhaave did not hesitate to incorporate chemical and other viewpoints into his mechanistic vision where such approaches seemed profitable. Thus, to a limited extent, his approach to medicine could be called eclectic.

Boerhaave laid great emphasis on methodical examination of patients and stressed the importance of bedside observation. He reorganized the medical courses at the University of Leiden, establishing a curriculum model that was copied at major 18th-century medical faculties in GÖTTINGEN, EDINBURGH, and VIENNA.

Although Boerhaave trained in medicine and devoted much of his time to that discipline, his contributions in chemistry are perhaps better known to modern scholars. He stressed the usefulness of quantitative methods and exact measurements in his studies on heat and mercury. He isolated the biochemical substance urea and discovered some of its properties.

Boerhaave's position as professor of botany immersed him into problems of classifying and collecting plant specimens from around the world. He gave practical support to the Swedish botanist Carolus LINNAEUS, who was developing a new system of CLASSIFICATION for plant and animal life. At his private estate outside Leiden, Boerhaave established a noted private botanical garden. He also supervised a 1727 edition of Sebastien Vaillant's *Botanicon parisiense* (Parisian botanical species)

Many of Boerhaave's lectures, speeches, and aphorisms were published during his lifetime or shortly afterward by students. Of special note are: *Atrocis, nec descripti prius, morbi historia* (The history of terrible diseases never before described; 1724); *Elementa chemiae* (Elements of chemistry; 1724); *Institutiones medicinae* (Medical methods, 7 vols. published posthumously by Albrecht von HALLER); *Aphorismi* (Aphorisms, 5 vols. published by Gerard van SWIETEN); and the various papers on experiments with mercury in the Philosophical Transactions of the Royal Society of London (1734–36).

Bolingbroke, Henry St. John, viscount (1672–1751)
English statesman, journalist, historian, and political philosopher

Henry St. John was the son of Sir Henry St. John, a Whig member of Parliament. The St. John family had served the kings of England for several generations. Scholars dispute whether young Henry St. John was educated at Eton School and Oxford University, or at an academy operated by DISSENTERS. After a two-year GRAND TOUR through Europe (1698–99), St. John settled into an arranged marriage with Frances Winchcombe, a wealthy widow.

The elder St. John secured his son's election to the House of Commons of the English Parliament as a representative of Wootton Basset. Young Henry shocked his father and uncle, both staunch Whigs, by aligning himself with the Tory Party and by making a scathing attack in Parliament on the Whig Party.

Henry St. John rapidly moved into state office by attaching himself to the fortunes of Robert Harley, a moderate Tory. In 1704, when Harley became secretary of state, St. John received the office of secretary of war and of the navy. After the Tories lost power in 1708, St. John resigned his post. He remained, however, in secret contact with Queen Anne throughout the ensuing period of Whig dominance. In 1710, the Whigs lost power, and the Tories returned to prominence. St. John became secretary of state, and Queen Anne awarded him a peerage in 1712, under the title viscount Bolingbroke.

As secretary of state, Bolingbroke led the English negotiations for the Peace of Utrecht (signed April 3, 1713). This success marked the pinnacle of his political career. In the aftermath of the treaty, the Tory Party split, and Bolingbroke became the political opponent of his former patron, Robert Harley, now earl of Oxford and prime minister of England. Bolingbroke managed to secure Harley's dismissal from office just four days before Queen Anne died.

The house of Hanover (King George I) in Germany assumed the English throne after Queen Anne's death. The Hanoverians were staunchly supported by the Whigs but were opposed by the Jacobites, partisans of James Edward Stuart (the Old Pretender), son of the deposed King James II. Stuart maintained that he was the legitimate heir to the English throne. His position had been given political backing by King LOUIS XIV of France, who had recognized him as James III of England.

Bolingbroke, who had met James III on his youthful travels through Europe, had clandestinely supported the Jacobite cause in the years preceding the Hanoverian succession. After George I assumed the English throne, Bolingbroke's activities came to light, and he was advised in 1715 to flee from England in order to avoid imprisonment and possible execution. He left England and settled in France, where he briefly served as secretary of state for James III.

While he was in France, a Jacobite revolt in England failed (1715). Bolingbroke became disenchanted with the Jacobite cause and began cultivating English contacts in order to pave the way for a return to his native country.

During his French exile, Bolingbroke bought La Source, an estate outside Orléans. He turned to intellectual pursuits in the fields of philosophy, HISTORY, and mathematics. The *Letter to Sir William Wyndham* (begun in 1717, published in 1753) urging the Troy Party to abandon the Jacobite cause, and the *Philosophical Consolations,* a Stoic meditation in the style of the ancient Roman philosopher Seneca, both date from this period of exile.

In 1725, Bolingbroke received a royal pardon from George I and returned to England. Parliament restored his property and noble titles in 1727, but prohibited him from sitting in either the House of Lords or the House of Commons. Bolingbroke purchased a country estate in Middlesex. He decorated the house in a rustic style and indulged himself for a short while in the pleasures of rural life and simple pastimes.

With his friends Jonathan SWIFT, Alexander POPE, and William Pulteney, Bolingbroke launched *The Craftsman,* a journal of political commentary. The journal printed two of Bolingbroke's most important political essays: "Remarks on the History of England" and "A Dissertation Upon Parties." In these essays, Bolingbroke called for protecting national law from the powers that were corrupting it. He pointed out that the old divisions between Tories and Whigs had become obsolete and asserted that the real political division in 18th-century England lay between the country and the court. In other words, he believed that the English monarchs were encroaching on the liberties and rights of English subjects.

Bolingbroke soon became embroiled again in English politics and once more found it necessary to take refuge in France. He settled at Chanteloup in the Touraine region in 1735, where he took up writing in earnest. *The Letters on the Study and Use of History* (published 1752) and the French *Lettres à M. de Pouilly* are products of this period. Both works explore RELIGION from a critical, historical, and philosophical perspective, adopting positions associated with DEISM.

On a brief return to England in 1738, Bolingbroke wrote *The Idea of a Patriot King.* This work defended the interests of the young heir to the English throne, who was, at the time, estranged from his father. Between 1739 and 1744, Bolingbroke lived again in France. Finally, in 1744, Bolingbroke settled permanently in England. He was working on his *Reflections on the Present State of the Nation* when he died of cancer in December 1751.

Bolingbroke participated in the Club de l'Entresol, a group of aristocrats and intellectuals who met for a few years in Paris to discuss political issues. MONTESQUIEU and the marquis d'ARGENSON were both members of this group and friends of the English refugee. Montesquieu's description in THE SPIRIT OF LAWS of the English constitution was inspired partly by Bolingbroke's interpretations of the English system. Both men believed that royal power needed to be limited by a strong aristocracy, and thus were spokesmen for the ARISTOCRATIC RESURGENCE of the 18th century. Bolingbroke's ideas, however, were complex enough that d'Argenson, a supporter of strong, centralized monarchy, also used them to support his position.

Further reading: Isaac Kramnick, *Bolingbroke and His Circle. The Politics of Nostalgia in the Age of Walpole* (Cambridge, Mass.: Harvard University Press, 1968).

Bonnet, Charles (1720–1793) *Swiss natural historian, philosopher, and biologist*
Charles Bonnet made important experimental contributions to the study of biological GENERATION, but he also devoted himself to theoretical questions about the philos-

ophy and methodology of the life sciences. Religious faith strongly influenced Bonnet's positions in the great 18th-century debates over generation (reproduction). His opposition to the theory of EPIGENESIS, for example, stemmed as much from his perception of its implications for theology as it did from his scientific observations. His religious beliefs, furthermore, often colored the way in which he interpreted his experimental data. Nevertheless, he made important discoveries and was respected by scientists throughout Europe, even when they rejected his ideas.

Bonnet was the son of Pierre Bonnet and Anne-Marie Lullin, who lived near GENEVA. As a boy, he was afflicted by partial deafness that interfered with his schooling. By the time he was 35, he had also become almost completely blind. Bonnet's childhood education was provided by a private tutor, Dr. Laget, who played a role in developing his young student's appetite for natural sciences. In spite of his visual problems, Bonnet was able to attend university, where he studied law in order to please his father. He received his doctorate in law in 1744.

Bonnet married Jeanne-Marie de La Rive in 1756 and spent most of his life on her estate at Genthod in the vicinity of Geneva. He worked throughout his life as an independent scholar. He exchanged letters with scientists throughout Europe and, on the recommendation of Bernard de FONTENELLE, was received as a corresponding member of the FRENCH ACADEMY OF SCIENCES.

Bonnet strongly believed in PREFORMATION THEORY, one of two major approaches then used to explain the processes involved in the generation of life. He defended the theory against the attack of contemporaries who supported the opposing theory of epigenesis. Bonnet maintained that the female ovum (egg) contains the completely preformed individual and that the male sperm contributes nothing to the substance of the new life. He believed that germ cells containing these preformed individuals existed throughout the body and thus were not limited to the egg and sperm. He cited the results of his early experiments as evidence to support his preformationist interpretations. These experiments had investigated aspects of both generation and regeneration. Bonnet had, for example, discovered the phenomenon of parthogenesis in aphids. He had also demonstrated that when a live rainwater worm was cut into many pieces, each piece generated a whole new worm.

After his vision deteriorated so that experimental observation was impossible, Bonnet began to address the philosophical and theoretical issues raised by the phenomena of generation and regeneration. He set forth his theories in a treatise called *Palingénésie philosophique* (Philosophical palingenesis; 1769). The word *palingénésie* was Bonnet's creation. It signified all forms of generation and regeneration in which a completely whole organism is the resulting product. It excluded partially regenerative processes such as the healing of tissues after wounds.

Bonnet made extensive investigations into the nutritional and transpiratory functions of the leaves of plants. He also studied insects, publishing a comprehensive *Traité d'insectologie* (Treatise on entomology) in 1745. His investigations in botany, entomology, and physiology left him a convinced opponent of the notion that one species might transform into another (transformism or transmutation of species). But he did accept the idea that individual species might have changed over time in response to environmental influences. Bonnet used the term *evolution,* but without the genetic connotations of modern theory. His ideas resembled those developed a few years later by Jean Baptiste LAMARCK. Bonnet also speculated that the Earth might have experienced several "revolutions" in the course of its HISTORY that had brought changes in species. The biblical story of creation, he suggested, might not be the description of the beginning of Earth's history, but rather a story about the most recent revolution.

From his reading of Gottfried Wilhelm LEIBNIZ Bonnet developed the concept of the GREAT CHAIN OF BEING. This chain linked all species in a continuous ladder with minute gradations. It stretched from the lowest created forms all the way to God. Bonnet believed that all created things were intertwined. This facet of his thought appealed to the supporters of VITALISM and organicism, who nevertheless rejected his preformation theory.

Bonnet also addressed question of PSYCHOLOGY in the treatises *Essai de psychologie* (Essay on psychology; 1754) and *Essai analytique sur les facultés de l'âme* (Analytical essay on the faculties of the soul; 1759). He left a treatise on the truths of Christianity, *Recherches philosophiques sur les preuves du christianisme* (Philosophical research on the proofs of Christianity; 1771).

Bordeu, Théophile de (1722–1776) *French physician, physiologist, and philosophe one of the leading exponents of an early form of vitalism, a theory that developed and dominated the life sciences during the last half of the 18th century* Bordeu, whose father and grandfather were both physicians, studied medicine at the University of Montpellier, received his degree in 1743, and published a thesis that catapulted him into the spotlight of the French intellectual world. The work, *Lettres contenant des essais sur l'histoire des eaux minérales de Béarn* (Letters containing some) essays on the history of the mineral waters of Béarn), was partially the work of his father.

In 1746, Bordeu traveled to PARIS, where he obtained several years of clinical experience. He returned in 1749 to the Béarn region, which was his original home. Bordeu moved to the Aquitaine region when he received an appointment as superintendent of mineral waters in the Aquitaine. He pursued his inquiries into the curative power of mineral waters. In 1747, Bordeu won an appointment as a corresponding member of the FRENCH ACADEMY OF SCIENCES when he submitted a paper on the articulation of facial bones.

Bordeu moved back to Paris in 1752. After being compelled by French law to earn a second medical degree from the Paris Faculty of Medicine in order to set up a private medical practice, he became a popular doctor, attracting a large clientele of prominent people that included King LOUIS XV and his official mistress, Madame DU BARRY. Bordeu's ideas strongly influenced Denis DIDEROT, who made Bordeu a major character in his novel *Le rêve d'Alembert* (D'Alembert's dream). Diderot borrowed much of the vitalist thought of the novel from Bordeu and publicly acknowledged his debt to his friend and colleague.

Bordeu developed a vision of life processes based on the VITALISM that dominated the medical instruction at Montpellier. But his position differed from that of Georg Ernst STAHL, whose thought had served as a major source for developing vitalism. Stahl had believed that all living matter was animated by a soul, a position known as ANIMISM.

Bordeu rejected the idea of a central soul that governs living organisms, and he strongly believed that living and non-living things are essentially different. He located this difference in the traits of sensibility (sensation) and irritability (the contraction of tissues upon touch) possessed by living matter. Sensibility and irritability became major subjects of investigation for Bordeu, and he particularly refined the concept of sensibility. He argued pointedly with the prominent physiologist Albrecht VON HALLER about the functions of and distinctions between sensibility and irritability.

Bordeu tried to develop a middle ground between mechanistic and animist visions of life. He maintained that each bodily organ is a separate living thing and that the life of the large organism is a summation of the many organ lives that exist in the body. The parts of the organism are tied together by the central nervous system into a harmonious and highly complex whole. He used an analogy drawn from music to elucidate his idea: The whole organism can be compared to a stringed instrument such as a violin that is capable of producing a vast number of harmonious overtones. The nerves, muscles, and other tissue fibers in the body have different lengths and widths, like strings, and can vibrate in myriad ways that produce harmonious or sympathetic relations. In these descriptions, Bordeu blended an old mechanical vision (the whole is equal to the sum of its parts and parts differ only in size, shape, and motion) with a vitalist vision that stressed the unique, vibrant qualities of living organisms.

Bordeu contributed several articles to the ENCYCLOPÉDIE of Diderot and d'Alembert. His major scientific papers included *De sensu generice considerato* (On the senses, considered generically; 1742); *Chilificationis historia* (History of chilification; 1742); *Recherches anatomiques sur la position des glandes et sur leur action* (Anatomical research on the position of the glands and on their action; 1752); *Recherches sur les maladies chroniques* (Research on chronic illnesses; 1775); and *Recherches sur le pouls par rapport aux crises* (Research on pulse in relation to crises). These and other papers were collected and published as *Oeuvres complètes* (Complete works; 1818).

See also SYMPATHY.

Boscovich, Ruggiero Giuseppe (1711–1787) *natural philosopher and mathematician of Serbian-Italian parentage, born in Dubrovnik*

Ruggiero Giuseppe Boscovich (Serbian: Rudjer Josip Bošković) was an expert in several areas of NATURAL PHILOSOPHY that included mathematics, ASTRONOMY, physics, and geodesy (the branch of mathematics dealing with the size and shape of the Earth). His breadth of interest and activity made him one of the last genuine polymaths (experts in many areas of study) of the 18th century.

Boscovich entered the Jesuit order in 1725. He received his advanced education in ROME at the Collegium Romanum, where he subsequently worked as a professor of mathematics. Conflicts arose between Boscovich and his superiors that caused him to leave the Collegium Romanum and to embark on a four-year study tour of Europe. He carried out several short diplomatic assignments during these years (1759–63).

Upon returning to Italy, he secured a post at the newly reorganized University of Pavia (1765) in the Duchy of MILAN and ran the observatory at Brera. He transferred to a post in Milan in 1769. When the Jesuit order was disbanded by Pope CLEMENT XIV in 1773, Boscovich moved to Paris, where he worked as director of optics for the navy. He returned to Milan in 1783, remaining in that city until his death in 1787 from lung disease.

The interests of Boscovich focused on central questions raised by the work of Isaac NEWTON. Boscovich thus explored optics, studied the paths of comets, and devoted attention to the question of the size and shape of the Earth. He displayed a characteristic enlightened conviction that improvements in scientific instrumentation would facilitate research.

But today Boscovich is remembered for his theory of matter and his universal force law. Boscovich accepted the notion that matter is composed of tiny particles, but he conceived of these particles as tiny points that actually lacked extension (i.e., did not take up space). These elemental points of matter differed from the points of geometry only in their tendency to interact with each other and in their possession on inertia. Boscovich was not the only person to conceive of atoms as points. Gottfried Wilhelm LEIBNIZ, Immanuel KANT, Emmanuel SWEDENBORG, and Giambattista VICO all developed variations on this idea.

Boscovich, a committed supporter of Newton's theory of universal gravitation, combined Newtonian and

Leibnizian ideas to create his theory of matter. This theory postulated that matter arises from the interaction between pairs of points. This interaction is governed by forces that constantly change their effect on the point, one moment attracting and the next moment repelling the points. Their action sets up minute vibrations of the points and causes matter to be filled with activity.

Boscovich's theory, published in 1758 as *Philosophiae naturalis theoria redacta ad unicam legem virium in natura existentium* (A theory of natural philosophy reduced to a single law of the actions existing in nature), was speculative rather than experimental, but its creative potential was quickly recognized. The *Encyclopaedia Britannica* of 1801 included a 14-page article describing the theory. Like Kant's new systematic philosophy, Boscovich's work contains a synthesis of major natural philosophical traditions—the Newtonian and the Leibnizian—of the ENLIGHTENMENT. From that synthesis, a new vision of NATURE was created that would in turn stimulate scientific creativity during the 19th century.

Bossuet, Jacques-Bénigne (1627–1704) *French bishop of Meaux, historian, divine rights theorist, and defender of the Gallican liberties of the French Catholic Church*
Bossuet came from a family of lawyers and civil administrators. He studied patristics (writings of the ancient Christian church fathers) at the Collège de Navarre in Paris, under the tutelage of the JESUITS and entered the priesthood in 1652.

Bossuet's brilliant preaching brought him to the attention of LOUIS XIV. He received his first bishopric (Condom) in 1669. In 1670, he was asked to serve as the preceptor for the Dauphin, the young heir to the French throne, and in 1671 received an appointment to the prestigious French Academy. He was awarded the bishopric of Meaux in 1681.

Hoping to secure the reunification of Christianity, Bossuet entered into long discussions with Gottfried Wilhelm LEIBNIZ, the Lutheran German philosopher, about the issues that divided Catholics and Protestants. Bossuet could not envision a reunification except under the auspices of the Roman Catholic pope; for Leibniz, that condition was unacceptable. As a result, the negotiations failed.

In the 1680s, Bossuet emerged as a leading theoretician in the numerous disputes among king, PARLEMENTS, pope, and French bishops over control of the French Catholic Church. The French bishops opposed papal claims of supremacy on the grounds that the early Christian church had not been governed by the pope, who was only the bishop of Rome, but rather by a council of bishops. They insisted that they should be the predominant power in the French church. Their form of Gallicanism is known as episcopal Gallicanism. The French king and members of the *parlements* meanwhile maintained that secular authorities should make appointments in the church and exercise justice in cases

involving the clergy. But they could not agree about whether king or *parlements* should be the primary authority. Their positions are known as royal Gallicanism and parliamentarian Gallicanism.

Actions by LOUIS XIV brought the Gallican disputes to the forefront of both French and papal concerns. An extraordinary Assembly of the Clergy (the meeting devoted to general business of the French clergy) was called in 1681–82 to try to resolve the crisis. Bossuet received the task of writing a declaration outlining solutions to the crisis. He proposed a series of compromises—a modified Gallicanism—that would split power among the various parties.

Bossuet's declaration earned the approval of both the French Assembly of Clergy and Louis XIV, but Pope Innocent XI rejected it. When Innocent XI's successors, Alexander VIII and Innocent XII, maintained this opposition, Bossuet wrote an extensive defense of the Gallican position, *Defensio declarationis cleri Gallicani* (Defense of the declaration of the Gallican clergy, written 1683–85).

Bossuet wrote two famous and significant works, the *Discours sur l'histoire universelle* (Discourse on universal history; 1681) and *La politique tirée des propres paroles de l'Ecriture Sainte* (Politics drawn from the actual words of the Holy Scriptures; 1679), for the edification of the Dauphin. The first work portrays the history of humankind as the unfolding of God's will on Earth, placing the reign of Louis XIV at the highest point of development. The latter work spells out the doctrine of the DIVINE RIGHT OF KINGS, one of the primary theoretical supports of Louis XIV's attempts to make ABSOLUTISM the form of the French monarchy.

Bossuet was a staunch defender of the official theology of the Catholic Church. He was alarmed by the implications for religion contained in the works of René DESCARTES, Benedict de SPINOZA, and Nicolas de MALEBRANCHE. He led the attack on the Quietists, a group of Catholics who practiced a mystical form of spirituality, and challenged their chief supporter, François FÉNELON. Bossuet believed that the Quietist emphasis on the inner subjective state of the spirit would undermine sound religious practice and weaken the commitment of the mystic to the external church.

Richard SIMON, the great founder of biblical exegesis, also earned Bossuet's disapproval. Simon helped to create the modern discipline of BIBLICAL CRITICISM by approaching the Bible as a piece of literature subject to historical and textual analysis. According to Bossuet, Simon's approach attacked the authority of the Bible as the revealed truth of God and, moreover, constituted a direct threat to Christianity and to its view of the world.

Bossuet, thus, clearly recognized the revolutionary possibilities contained in the intellectual movements of the late 17th century. The traditional flavor of his work made it a ready target for criticism during the ENLIGHTENMENT. Nevertheless, even the most outspoken opponents of

RELIGION—Voltaire, for example—admired Bossuet's style and his universal, if seemingly misguided, vision of HISTORY.

Boswell, James (1740–1795) *Scottish lawyer, essayist, chronicler, and biographer*

Son of Lord Alexander Boswell (Lord Auchinleck), a Scottish judge, Boswell was born in EDINBURGH. He was given a strict Calvinist upbringing, and his youth was marred by conflict with his father over professional and personal choices. Boswell ran away from home to LONDON in 1760 but was soon escorted back to SCOTLAND by his father. Boswell suffered from mild bouts of depression throughout his life that are believed to have been at least partially caused by his familial problems.

After some resistance, Boswell acquiesced to his father's wishes by entering the legal profession in Scotland. He gained acceptance to the English bar only in 1786. He made a GRAND TOUR of Europe in the 1760s, exploring FRANCE, BERLIN, SWITZERLAND (where he met VOLTAIRE and Jean-Jacques ROUSSEAU), and Italy. Boswell also visited Corsica, where he established a friendship with the Corsican patriot General Paoli.

A 1768 publication, *An Account of Corsica, the Journal of a Tour to That Island, and Memoirs of Pascal Paoli,* launched Boswell on his literary career. Quickly translated into French, Italian, German, and Dutch, the work exposed British and French Corsican policy and proved to be an embarrassment to foreign ministers of both nations.

In 1773, Boswell was elected to the Literary Club, a private London club founded by the English painter Joshua REYNOLDS for his friend, the writer and critic Samuel JOHNSON. Boswell had met Samuel Johnson in 1763, on his second trip to London. After Boswell began working as a lawyer, he continued to make nearly annual trips to London in order to visit Johnson. His journal materials from these visits provided the substance of his famous biography, the *Life of Samuel Johnson* (1791). This work still stimulates heated debate about the accuracy of its portrayal of its famous subject.

During his lifetime, Boswell was also noted for "The Hypochondriack" (1777–83), a series of periodical essays, and for his *Journal of a Tour of the Hebrides* (1785), reporting on a trip with Johnson to those Scottish islands. Many of Boswell's private papers, assumed lost, actually remained in his family until the 1920s. The first papers were sold for publication in 1927 and 1928; other papers were discovered between 1930 and 1940. The famous *London Journal* contains material from these papers.

Böttger, Johann Friedrich (1682–1719) *German alchemist*

Böttger practiced the art of ALCHEMY in the employment of Elector August of Saxony. During the first decade of the 18th century, Böttger used his alchemical knowledge and technical skills to unravel the secret of the Chinese recipe for fine porcelain. With a collaborator, E. von Tschirnhaus, Böttger began to produce fine white porcelain. He also manufactured a reddish-brown stoneware called Böttger.

Elector August of Saxony immediately capitalized on the discovery of the secrets of porcelain by establishing the first European porcelain factory in his capital city of Dresden. Böttger directed production. A second factory, established in 1710 at Meissen, produced porcelains that dominated the European market until the second half of the 18th century.

The secret porcelain recipe was soon pirated out of Saxony by alchemists who sold it to other European rulers eager to establish their own porcelain works.

See also MEISSEN WORKS; SÈVRES.

Boucher, François (1703–1770) *French painter, engraver, and designer of tapestries, porcelains, and opera costumes*

Boucher was a major artist of the ROCOCO period in FRANCE. He was the foremost designer of CHINOISERIE pieces of that era. The Académie Royale de Peinture (Royal Academy of Painting) accepted him as a member in 1734. Boucher received primary patronage from his student Madame de POMPADOUR and her brother the marquis de Marigny. LOUIS XV gave him several commissions at the royal palaces of Versailles, Choisy, and Fontainebleau and also provided him with a handsome royal pension. Boucher succeeded Jean Baptiste OUDRY to the directorship of the GOBELINS TAPESTRY works in 1755. In 1765, he was made *Premier peintre du roi* (chief royal painter). He was invited to join the Academy of SAINT PETERSBURG in 1769.

Boucher was the son of Nicholas Boucher, an ornamental painter, lace designer, and merchant of prints. François began his study of art with his father. The painter François Le Moyne noted Boucher's youthful painting, *Jugement de Suzanne,* and took the young man as a student. Boucher received further training in the studio of the engraver Jean François Cars and in the painting courses offered at the Académie Royale de Peinture in PARIS. In 1723, Boucher won the prestigious Prix de Rome, a prize that provided a stipend for study in ROME. Since the prize money was not immediately available, he had to postpone his study in that city until 1727 and 1728.

Boucher left a prodigious number of works. Notable paintings include: *Le lever du soleil* (Sunrise), *Le coucher du soleil* (Sunset), *Le déjeuner* (Lunch); *Le triomphe de Venus* (The triumph of Venus); *Madame de Pompadour* (Portrait of Madame de Pompadour); and *La naissance et la mort d'Adonis* (The birth and death of Adonis). Boucher's four ceiling paintings in the queen's bedroom at the Palace of Versailles are titled *La générosité* (Generosity), *La fidelité* (Fidelity), *La prudence* (Prudence), and *La* charité (Charity). The Hôtel de Soubise in Paris (National Archives) contains the Oval Salon decorated by Boucher and paintings of ancient mythological subjects called *Les trois graces entourant l'Amour* (The three Graces surrounding Love), *L'Aurore et Céphale* (Aurora and Cephalus), *L'Éducation de l'Amour par Mercure* (The education of Love by Mercury), *Vénus s'appuyant sur Cupidon pour entrer au bain en descendant de son char* (Venus leaning on Cupid while descending from her chariot in order to enter her bath); and *Léda avec le cygne* (Leda with the swan). The Cabinet des Médailles in the Bibliothèque Nationale contains four Boucher medals called *L'Histoire* (History), *La Tragédie* (Tragedy), *L'Éloquence* (Eloquence), and *L'Astronomie* (Astronomy). At Fontainebleau, Boucher decorated a dining room as *Deux nymphs de Diane au retour de la chasse* (Two of Diana's nymphs returning from the hunt).

Boucher also designed costumes for *Les Indes galantes*, an opera-ballet by Jean-Philippe RAMEAU. He created several famous tapestry series for the Beauvais tapestry factory. They include the *History of Psyche, Loves of the Gods, Pastoral Scenes, Fragments from the Opera*, and a group of Chinese-inspired designs. Boucher's finest models for SÈVRES porcelains include *La lanterne magique* (The magic lantern), *Le chien qui danse* (The dancing dog), and *Jupiter et Léda* (Jupiter and Leda).

Boucher's paintings are noted for their delicate pastel colors, soft rounded sentimental figures, and idealistic treatment of subjects. Toward the end of his life, rococo style had definitely lost favor. Boucher tried to adapt somewhat to the new tastes for NEOCLASSICISM and realism, but his later works were not well-received. Denis DIDEROT harshly criticized his exhibit at the 1765 Salon (public show). Boucher died in his apartments at the Louvre in May 1770. He was survived by his wife, Marie-Jeanne Buseau, who was often his model and was herself an engraver, and by his two sons, Juste-Nathan and Juste-François. The latter produced hundreds of drawings and a number of engravings sometimes erroneously credited to his father.

Bougainville, Louis-Antoine de (1729–1811) *French explorer, geographer, and mathematician*

Bougainville, son of a Parisian notary, studied mathematics and began a career as a mathematician. Under the influence of Jean Le Rond d'ALEMBERT, he wrote the two-volume work *Traité du calcul-intégral* (Treatise on the integral calculus; 1754–56) that presented both the 18th-century additions to the differential calculus and the subject of integral calculus. The publication received praise from the FRENCH ACADEMY OF SCIENCES and earned Bougainville election to the ROYAL SOCIETY OF LONDON in 1756.

In order to escape his father's demands that he enter the notarial profession, Bougainville joined the French army (1754). He served in Canada from 1756 until 1759, during the French and Indian War, a conflict in which the British and the French struggled for control of North America. In 1764, Bougainville decided to settle in the Falkland Islands off the southeastern coast of South America, where he founded a French colony at his own expense. He hoped to provide a place for the Acadians, French Canadian settlers who were displaced after France ceded its Canadian colonies to the British. In 1767, Bougainville had to relinquish control of the colony to Spain; at the same time he received a commission from the French government to circumnavigate the Earth. On the three-year voyage, Bougainville explored the South Pacific islands, touching land in Tahiti ("discovered" eight months before his arrival by Samuel Wallis, an Englishman), locating several islands previously unknown to Europeans, and nearly reaching the great Barrier Reef off Australia. He "discovered" two of the Treasury Islands, then proceeded to the Solomon Islands, where he located a previously uncharted island now called Bougainville Island.

During his travels, Bougainville recorded information about native plants and animals. He also made systematic records and observations of longitude and produced charts that greatly aided later sailors. He published an account of his explorations, the *Voyage autour du monde* (Voyage around the world), in 1771.

Bougainville returned to PARIS and served again in the French army and navy, providing assistance to the American colonists during the AMERICAN REVOLUTION. Although the Americans and French eventually won the war, Bougainville was reprimanded and banished from the French court as punishment for his role in the losses at the Battle of Saintes (1782).

During the FRENCH REVOLUTION, Bougainville supported the cause of the king. He was incarcerated in 1792 but freed after the fall of Maximilien ROBESPIERRE brought an end to the Terror. Subsequently he enjoyed the prestige of election to the new Institut de France (revolutionary reincarnation of the former French royal academies). Napoleon appointed him to both the Senate and the Légion d'Honneur. Bougainville's death in 1811 was followed by burial with full honors in the Panthéon in Paris.

Bougainville's *Voyage autour du monde* played a leading role in the ENLIGHTENMENT by providing accounts that supported the tendency to treat "primitive" peoples as representatives of the natural state of humankind, uncorrupted by civilization. The *Voyage* inspired Denis DIDEROT to write the *Supplément au Voyage de Bougainville* (Supplement to the voyage of Bougainville; 1773), the work that depicted the South Pacific as an idyllic spot where humankind lived moral, yet uninhibited, lives.

See also TAHITI; TRAVEL LITERATURE; VOYAGES OF DISCOVERY.

Boulainvilliers, Henri de (1658–1722) *French historian and writer, whose name is associated with deism, materialism, and the aristocratic resurgence in France*

Henri de Boulainvilliers came from a noble family of northern FRANCE. He was the son of François de Manneville and his wife, Suzanne. Boulainvilliers' parents lived separately, as François had entered a long-term relationship with another woman. This arrangement burdened the family with financial difficulties.

After brief military service, Boulainvilliers settled in his native town (Saint-Saire) and devoted himself to historical research on early French institutions and families. He developed an intense admiration for feudal structures and customs, which led him to oppose the attempts by LOUIS XIV to move France toward absolute monarchy. Boulainvilliers became a champion of the aristocracy, one of the literary leaders of the ARISTOCRATIC RESURGENCE. He developed the theory of the feudal origins of the French nobility and justified revolt by aristocratic nobles against absolutist reforms, on the grounds that these changes were destroying the ancient French constitution.

During the reign of Louis XIV, Boulainvilliers participated with François FÉNELON, Abbé de Saint-Pierre (1658–1743), Sébastien Le Prestre de Vauban (1633–1707), and Louis de Rouvroy, duc de Saint Simon (1675–1755), in producing a series of recommendations for reform of the royal administration. Boulainvilliers contributed two works, *L'état de la France* (The state of France; 1727–28) and *Mémoires présentés à Mgr le duc d'Orleans, contenant les moyens de rendre ce royaume très puissant et d'augmenter considérablement les revenus du roi et du peuple* (Memoirs presented to the duke of Orléans containing the means for making this kingdom very powerful and for considerably enlarging the revenues of the king and the people; 1727), to this reform project.

Tradition has made Boulainvilliers the head of an informal group of freethinkers and deists, whose manuscripts criticizing traditional RELIGION circulated clandestinely throughout French intellectual circles. Modern scholars still speak of the Boulainvilliers circle, but are unsure whether Boulainvilliers actually led this group. Many of the manuscripts circulated in his name may not have been written by him. One famous example is the diatribe against ROMAN CATHOLICISM entitled *Dîner du comte de Boulainvilliers*, in reality a creation of VOLTAIRE.

Boulainvilliers' reputed authorship of the deist tract *Traité des trois imposteurs* (Treatise of the three impostors), is questioned by modern scholars. The unorthodox *Abrégé d'histoire universelle* (Summary of universal history) is probably his work. In addition, he may have authored *Essai sur la noblesse de France, contenant une dissertation sur son origine et abaissement* (Essay on the nobility of France, containing a dissertation on Its origin and decline; 1732); *Mémoire pour la noblesse de France contre les ducs et pairs* (Memoirs for the French nobility against the dukes and peers; 1732); and *Histoire de la pairie de France et du parlement de Paris* (History of the French peerage and of the Parlement of Paris; 1747).

Boulainvilliers married twice, first to Marie-Anne-Henriette Hurault des Marais and later to Claude-Cathérine d'Alègre. He had one son who perished in battle and two daughters.

See also DEISM; MATERIALISM.

Boulanger, Nicolas-Antoine (1722–1759) *French engineer and philosophe*

Although Nicolas-Antoine Boulanger was an engineer by training and profession, he earned his place in the history of the ENLIGHTENMENT as a collaborator on the ENCYCLOPÉDIE, and as an ardent critic of RELIGION. He was closely associated with Claude-Adrien HELVÉTIUS, Madame HELVÉTIUS, and Paul-Henri Thiry d'HOLBACH.

Boulanger planned to write a *Spirit of the Religions*, intended as a counterpart to the *Spirit of Laws* by MONTESQUIEU. To this end, he sought out the principles underlying the religious impulse in human beings. He maintained that all human religious belief had roots in historical traumas and focused specifically on the great flood reported in the Bible as the primary stimulus. According to Boulanger, human beings experienced the tragedy of the flood and reacted with fear at the destructive powers of the universe. They projected their fears out into the universe, embodying them as God or as gods. Over time, elaborate systems of belief developed and then decayed. Overall, the history of religion presented a series of cycles each marked by trauma, the beginnings of belief, development, and then decay.

Boulanger believed that he was writing a history of primitive religion rooted in fact; he scorned symbolic or deistic approaches to religious history, aligning himself with EMPIRICISM. In this belief, he resembled fellow historians of religion Giovan Battista VICO, Charles de BROSSES, Holbach, David HUME, and Johann Gottfried HERDER.

Boulanger died at the age of 37. His books appeared after his death, published in AMSTERDAM and in SWITZERLAND at the urging of Holbach. They included: *Recherches sur l'origine du despotisme oriental* (Researches on the origins of Oriental despotism; 1761), a book translated into English by the radical John WILKES; and *L'antiquité devoilée par ses usages, ou examen critique des principales opinions, cérémonies et institutions religieuses ou politiques* (Antiquity unveiled by Its customs, or critical examination of principal religious or political ceremonies and institutions; 1766). A book entitled *Le christianisme devoilée, ou examen des principes et des effets de la religion Chrétienne* (Christianity unveiled, or examination of the principles and effects of Christian religion; 1767) printed under Boulanger's name was actually composed by Holbach and his associates. The content of these works, as well as the association with the Holbach circle of

PHILOSOPHEs, caused Boulanger to be accused of ATHEISM by conservative contemporaries and later historians.

In addition to these histories of religion, Boulanger wrote three articles for the *Encyclopédie:* "Déluge" (The Flood) "Corvée" (The corvée), and "Société" (Society).

Boulogne, Joseph, chevalier de Saint-Georges

(1745–1799) *French composer, violinist, and revolutionary* Joseph Boulogne, chevalier de Saint-Georges, was a prominent figure in the musical life of Paris during the last third of the 18th century. He also participated in the FRENCH REVOLUTION and the HAITIAN REVOLUTION.

Boulogne was born on the Caribbean island of GUADELOUPE, the son of a planter and his African slave. He grew up primarily in France, living there with his parents from 1747 to 1749 and returning permanently with his father in 1753. As a teenager, Boulogne trained with a master of arms and excelled at fencing. At 19, he became a member of the king's guard and acquired the title of chevalier.

The details of Boulogne's early musical education are sketchy. In 1769, he joined the orchestra of the famous violinist and composer François-Joseph Gossec, becoming its concertmaster later the same year. Boulogne made his debut as a solo violinist with the group in 1772, playing two of his own concertos, and became its musical director the next year. He went on to lead the Concerts de la Loge Olympique, where he commissioned music from Europe's most prominent composers, including Franz Joseph HAYDN, whose six Paris symphonies Boulogne premiered in 1787. During this period, Boulogne composed and published the majority of his instrumental music, including 12 violin concertos, 10 *symphonies concertantes* (works for two or more solo instruments and orchestra), and six string quartets. His music reflects the pervasive influence of the classical style, having much in common with contemporary works by Wolfgang Amadeus MOZART and Haydn.

In 1776, Boulogne was suggested for the post of music director of the Paris Opéra, the most prominent musical position in the city, but racially motivated machinations on the part of ladies at court prevented him from getting the job. Undeterred, Boulogne composed an OPERA, *Ernestine,* which premiered at the Comédie-Italienne, another Paris theater, in 1777. From this point onward, Boulogne concentrated his compositional efforts on opera, having his greatest success with his comic opera *La fille-garçon* (The girl-boy), which premiered at the Italienne in 1787. He also worked as music director of Mme de Montesson's private theater (the duc d'Orléans's wife), composing a comic opera-ballet *L'amant anonyme* (The anonymous lover) for her theater in 1780.

The connection to Orléans also awakened revolutionary sympathies in Boulogne. In 1789, he joined the French National Guard. The National Assembly named him colonel of the Légion des Américains et du Midi, a regiment of black citizens, and he helped stop Charles François Dumouriez's plot to capture Lille in 1793. Boulogne was accused of misappropriation of public funds during the Terror and spent 18 months in prison. After his name was cleared and he was released, Boulogne sailed to Haiti, where he participated in the slave revolt. Upon his return to Paris in 1797, Boulogne spent the final two years of his life directing the newly established Circle of Harmony, an orchestra that performed in the former residence of the duc d'Orléans.

Boulogne's life provides an interesting example of the possibilities open to a black man during the last third of the 18th century. He found success in both the military and musical arenas, and though he encountered racially motivated resistance, he rose to prominent positions in both spheres.

See also CLASSICISM, MUSICAL.

Further reading: Emil Smidak, *Joseph Boulogne, called Chevalier de Saint-Georges* (Lucerne: Avenira Foundation, 1996).

Boulton, Matthew

(1728–1809) *English manufacturer and engineer*
Matthew Boulton was a member of the LUNAR SOCIETY OF BIRMINGHAM. He acquired substantial capital through financial dealings. The STEAM ENGINE factory that he established with James WATT at Birmingham was an example of the linkage between money and inventive talent that stimulated the enormous British inventiveness during the 18th-century INDUSTRIAL REVOLUTION. Boulton himself patented inventions for a steel inlay process and a steam-powered coin press. He produced new copper coinage for Great Britain in 1797.

Bradley, James

(1693–1762) *English astronomer*
Bradley succeeded Edmond HALLEY as royal astronomer at the Greenwich Observatory. James Bradley, an Anglican minister, pursued astronomy as an avocation. Bradley impressed Halley, whom he had met through a relative, with his skillful telescopic observations. The two men collaborated for many years, and Halley laid the groundwork for Bradley to succeed him as astronomer royal. Bradley filled that post for 20 years, from 1742 until his death in 1762.

As astronomer royal, Bradley persuaded the British government to provide funds for the purchase of the best available instruments. As a result, the observations made at Greenwich Observatory during his tenure set a new standard of accuracy for astronomy.

Bradley provided the first direct observational proof of the theory of Nicolaus COPERNICUS about the motion of the Earth around the Sun. His instruments and observational skills allowed him to record aberrations in the light received from stars, and thus to detect the parallactic displacements of stars (shifts in their position as viewed from the Earth and produced by the motion of the Earth around the Sun). Copernican theory had suggested that such shifts should be observable, but until Bradley's time, it had been impossible to observe and to measure them. Bradley also measured the nutation (wobble) of the Earth about its axis, a motion attributable to the effects of the Moon's gravitation on the Earth. In this case, his findings provided support for Newton's theory of gravitation.

With these two contributions, Bradley assisted in the validation of the theories of the SCIENTIFIC REVOLUTION, a process that in turn helped to provide a firm natural philosophical foundation for the theories of the ENLIGHTENMENT.

See also ASTRONOMY; TECHNOLOGY AND INSTRUMENTATION.

Bramah, Joseph (1748–1814) *English engineer and inventor*

Joseph Bramah invented a number of devices of utility in manufacturing and business. These include a pickproof lock (1784), precision machine tools (with Henry Maudslay), a hydraulic press (1795), and a numbering machine for use with bank notes. In 1778, Bramah designed the modern water closet (toilet), thereby contributing to the establishment of better sanitation in cities.

Brandenburg North German principality, which was part of the HOLY ROMAN EMPIRE; its capital and primary city was BERLIN. Brandenburg had no outlet to the sea. The western part of the principality covered a region that is incorporated today in Germany. The eastern lands of the principality have been part of POLAND since 1945. In the 18th century, Brandenburg was bordered on the north by Mecklenburg-Schwerin and Pomerania, on the west by Hanover and Braunschweig-Wolfenbüttel, on the south by Saxony and Saxony-Anhalt, and on the east by the kingdom of PRUSSIA.

Brandenburg was the territorial seat of the Hohenzollern family. Its ruler was one of seven electors of the Holy Roman Empire whose duty and right it was to elect the emperor.

After the Thirty Years' War (1618–1648), Brandenburg, together with the Hohenzollern territory known as East Prussia, began to experience great change under a series of energetic, reforming princes. In 1701, Frederick III, elector of Brandenburg and prince in Prussia, assumed the title of king in Prussia. He merged the administration of Brandenburg with that of Prussia, thereby creating the kingdom of Prussia, with Berlin as its capital. Under the rule of Frederick's successors, Frederick William I and FREDERICK II (THE GREAT), the new kingdom of Prussia expanded and became a major power in 18th-century Europe.

See also DYNASTIC STATES.

Brandenburg Concertos *a series of six works for groups of solo instruments with orchestral accompaniment written by Johann Sebastian Bach*

In 1721, BACH dedicated and sent the *Brandenburg Concertos* to Margrave Christian Ludwig of BRANDENBURG, in the hope of gaining his patronage. Modern scholars postulate that they were actually written over a period of time during Bach's years at Weimar and Cöthen.

The *Brandenburg Concertos* marked an important point in the stylistic development of 18th-century music. They were solidly baroque in compositional style, but departed from the standard concerto form (a piece for a solo instrument with orchestral accompaniment) by featuring two or more solo instruments, joined at varying places by the full orchestra. They called for high levels of professional, technical, and interpretative skill. *Concerto no. 5* represented Bach's first use of the transverse flute in place of the more traditional recorder. The same concerto, which used flute and harpsichord as solo instruments, marked the beginning of the harpsichord concerto as a distinct musical form. *Concerto no. 3* has unusual three-way symmetries that display Bach's love of complex but balanced structures. As a group, these concertos also demonstrate a blending of Italian and German national compositional styles.

See also BAROQUE STYLE.

Breitinger, Johann Jakob (1701–1776) *Swiss literary critic*

Breitinger was the colleague of Johann Jakob BODMER and taught Hebrew at the Collegium Carolinum in Zürich. With Bodmer, Breitinger founded a periodical weekly, *Discours der Mahlern* (Discourse of artists). Although inspired by THE SPECTATOR, the influential English publication by ADDISON and STEELE, the *Discours der Maler* tended to lay greater stress on the importance of communal values than its English counterpart. In fact, Breitinger and Bodmer envisioned their paper as an instrument for reinforcing the unique aspects of Swiss culture.

Breitinger and Bodmer collaborated on many projects in the realm of arts criticism and AESTHETICS. Together, they created the movement that undermined the power of Johann Christoph GOTTSCHED, the German critic and champion of French CLASSICISM. Classicism made REASON the most important creative factor in writing. In contrast, Breitinger and Bodmer gave that honor to the imagination. Their new aesthetic theory helped to stimulate the 18th-century flowering of German as a literary language.

Breitinger contributed to the new literary theory with his *Critische Dichtkunst* (Critical poetics; 1740), a book that presented the history of German poetry, and *Critische Abhandlung von der Natur, den Absichten und dem Gebrauch der Gleichnisse* (Critical treatise on the nature, the purposes, and the use of imagery; 1740). He also published

Fabeln aus der Zeiten der Minnesinger (Fables from the time of the minnesingers; 1757).

Breitinger applied critical historical tools to the Bible, assisting with the publication of a new edition of the Septuagint (a Greek version of the Old Testament of the Bible, predating Christianity) and with the preparation of the *Thesaurus Historiae Helveticae* (Thesaurus of Swiss history; 1735).

See also INTUITION AND IMAGINATION.

Brosses, Charles de (1709–1777) *French jurist and scholar of antiquities, anthropology, and geography*
Beneficiary of a Jesuit education, he entered the *parlement* (royal law court) of Dijon as a councillor in 1730. In his leisure time, de Brosses pursued scholarly interests. He was a close friend of David HUME and actually translated portions of Hume's *Natural History of Religion* into his own *Du culte des dieux fétiches* (Of the cult of the fetish gods; 1760). From 1739 until 1740, de Brosses traveled with friends throughout ITALY. Upon his return to Dijon, he resumed his career as a lawyer and judge.

During the ministry of René-Nicolas-Charles-Augustine de MAUPEOU, de Brosses accompanied his colleagues of the Dijon *parlement* into exile. Upon their reinstatement in 1775, after the downfall of Maupeou, de Brosses became first president of the *parlement*. During his tenure as first president, he became embroiled with VOLTAIRE in a dispute over payment for 40 cords of wood. The two men lived on adjoining estates in Burgundy; according to Voltaire, de Brosses had agreed to pay for the wood. The dispute so angered Voltaire that he reputedly acted to ensure that the French Academy would not admit de Brosses into its membership.

As a scholar, de Brosses contributed to the growth of knowledge about the antiquities of Greece and Rome. In particular, he wrote of the ruins of Herculaneum in the *Mémoire sur les antiquités d'Ercolano et sur l'état du mont Vesuve* (Memoir on the antiquities of Herculaneum and on the state of Mount Vesuvius; 1749) and in the *Lettres sur l'état actuel de la ville souterraine d'Herculée* (Letters on the present state of the buried city of Herculaneum). De Brosses also wrote a series of *Lettres familières sur l'Italie* (Intimate letters on Italy), whose vivid descriptions of VENICE and other Italian cities provide modern scholars with an important historical source for the study of the 18th century.

De Brosses's interest in geography led him to collect existing TRAVEL LITERATURE about the Southern Hemisphere and to publish it in his *Histoire des navigations aux terres australes* (History of navigations to southern lands; 1756).

Questions about the origin of things such as human society, RELIGION, and language fascinated many writers during the ENLIGHTENMENT. De Brosses was no exception. His comparative investigations of ancient Egyptian animal worship and so-called primitive fetish religions led him to the provocative theory presented in *Du culte des dieux fétiches*. This book plunged into interpretations that previous scholars of fetish religions had avoided, declaring that animal worship indeed involves the deification of beasts. These beast gods are not symbols of human aspirations and moral qualities, nor are they allegorical representations of ancient great individuals. They are animals and nothing more. Moreover, fetish worship occurs as a natural stage in the development of religion within any culture.

De Brosses knew that his theory would offend French Catholic authorities because it suggested that human beings were capable of prostrating themselves before beasts. For traditional Christian theology, such a proposition definitely upset the order of things established by God. Consequently, in order to avoid trouble with French censors, de Brosses arranged to have *Du culte des dieux fétiches* published in Calvinist GENEVA and then transported secretly into FRANCE.

Reception was mixed, colored both by the book's daring content and by Voltaire's open derision. The previously noted quarrel between Voltaire and de Brosses moved onto a new level as Voltaire attacked de Brosses for degrading humankind. For 19th-century social scientists, however, de Brosses's work proved highly significant. August Comte (1798–1857) made fetishism one of the universal stages of human consciousness, and Karl Marx (1818–83) invented his concept of "the fetishism of commodities" after reading de Brosses.

De Brosses also investigated the origins of language, publishing the *Traité de la formation méchanique des langues et des principes physiques de l'étymologie* (Treatise of the mechanical formation of languages and of the physical principles of etymology; 1765). Anne-Robert-Jacques TURGOT, the philosophe and reforming general controller of finances under LOUIS XV, adapted materials from de Brosses's treatise for his articles on language in the ENCYCLOPÉDIE.

See also ANTHROPOLOGY; PHILOSOPHES.

Brown, Lancelot "Capability" (1715–1783) *English landscape gardener and architect*
Lancelot Brown was born in Kirkharle, Northumberland, England. He worked as a gardener's assistant when he was a young man. Soon after, he began to work with the landscape architect William KENT in Buckinghamshire on the estate of Lord Stowe. Brown was close to his mentor and married Kent's daughter. He began his own landscaping practice in 1749 and quickly became successful.

Brown was given the nickname "Capability" because he usually assessed his clients' gardens as having "capabilities of improvement." He is credited with doing away with French and Italian geometric gardens in favor of artificially "wild" landscapes in English gardens. The trademark of Brown's gardens was their natural appearance. Groups of trees and rolling lawns would suddenly give way to views of constructed monuments, bridges, or temples.

His clients were by necessity the wealthy landed classes. Although criticized for destroying existing landscapes to create his own, Brown earned much acclaim from his patrons. Brown's clients and admirers included aristocrats, the British royal family, and prominent politicians such as William Pitt.

Brown died in 1783, leaving behind a vast natural legacy for all lovers of nature. Approximately 200 of his gardens survive today. Among the best places to view his work are the gardens at Blenheim Palace, Warwick Castle, the STOWE Landscape Garden, and the Hampton Court Palace, which supposedly contains the oldest existing grapevine planted by Brown.

Through his artistic vision, "Capability" Brown made the garden another 18th-century work of creative genius to be sold as well as appreciated.

See also LANDSCAPES.

Further reading: Dorothy Stroud, *Capability Brown* (London: Faber, 1975).

Brussels   Officially bilingual (French and Flemish) but mainly French-speaking city, capital of modern BELGIUM. The Treaty of Utrecht (1713) transferred Brussels and the surrounding region (then called the Spanish Netherlands) from Spanish control to Austrian Hapsburg control. Thus, for most of the 18th century, Brussels served as a seat of Austrian Hapsburg administration, and the surrounding region was called the AUSTRIAN NETHERLANDS. Toward the end of the century, Brussels served as a center of political activity for the Belgian Patriots, a group whose 1787 revolt received much inspiration from enlightened political theories. The general revolutionary upheavals at the end of the 18th century brought a brief period of independence (December 1789 to December 1790), domination by France (1792–1814), and reunification with the northern, Protestant United Netherlands as the kingdom of the Netherlands (1815–30). In 1830, a revolution created two separate nations, the kingdom of Belgium, with Brussels as its capital, and the Netherlands.

A proud town, whose prominence dated from the 15th century, Brussels had a rich tradition as a center of art, trade, learning, and administration. Its inhabitants and its official loyalties were staunchly Catholic even during the ENLIGHTENMENT. Toward the end of the 18th century, the city had about 80,000 inhabitants.

Brussels today presents the visitor with examples of 18th-century urban planning and architecture. The Grand' Place, despite its medieval appearance, is actually a creation of the early Enlightenment (end of the 17th century). The design, baroque in inspiration, aimed to evoke the splendors of the earlier medieval city, which had served as capital of the magnificent and powerful lands ruled by the duke of Burgundy. The old center of the lower city had been destroyed by fire in 1695. The reconstruction remained faithful to the historic layout and architecture. To the north of the Grand' Place, the lower city underwent marked modernization when Place St.-Michel (today, Place des Martyrs) was constructed. Although the facades again mimic the late medieval Gothic style, the regularity and uniform construction of the square betrays its later roots. In the 1760s, the city received further enhancement with the creation of the public square and park known as La Place Royale (Royal Square).

See also UNITED PROVINCES OF THE NETHERLANDS; BAROQUE STYLE.

Budapest   Capital of modern HUNGARY, located on the banks of the Danube River; the modern city consists of two older cities: Buda, on the right bank, and Pest, on the left bank. The towns were not united until 1873. In the 18th century, Buda served as the capital of the kingdom of Hungary, one of the largest territories of the HAPSBURG EMPIRE.

The Budapest region has been settled since Neolithic times. About 70 B.C. the Eriviscans, a Celtic people with Illyrian culture, settled the area. It came under Roman rule in 9 B.C. The Romans called the city Aquincum and depended on it to defend the outer reaches of the empire. The region lost population after the collapse of the Roman Empire but was resettled in the ninth century A.D. by Magyar, Slavonic, and German peoples. Trade and commerce thrived at Pest. By the 14th century, Buda had become the capital of the Hungarian state. The Ottoman Turks, having conquered the region in 1542, made Buda the center of the territories under their occupation. Turkish rule lasted until 1686, when Christian forces seized Buda. The battles for control of Buda largely destroyed it.

During the 18th century, Buda was rebuilt in the BAROQUE STYLE. Major architectural monuments from that era include St. Anne's Church (1740–70), the former church of the Elizabethan nuns (1731–41), the Trinitarian Monastery (1745–60), the Zichy family castle (1746–57), and the royal palace on Castle Hill (1715–70).

Buffon, Georges-Louis Leclerc, comte de (1707–1788) *prominent French natural historian, one of the major figures of the science of the Enlightenment*
Buffon was one of the most famous natural scientists of the 18th century. He was the son of bourgeois parents, Benjamin-François Leclerc and Anne-Cristine Marlin. Money from his mother's family enabled Buffon's father to purchase a noble title, seigneur de Buffon et Montbard (lord of Buffon and Montbard), and to buy an office as a councillor in the Parlement of Burgundy (court of law) at Dijon. Young Buffon attended the Jesuit *collège* at Dijon, then studied law (1723–26) at the University of Dijon.

He spent two years in Angers (1728–30), but it is unclear what he was studying. After participating in an illegal duel in 1730, Buffon had to leave Angers. He embarked on a GRAND TOUR of southern FRANCE and ITALY in the company of two Englishmen.

Buffon returned to France in 1732, acquired his deceased mother's fortune over the opposition of his father, and began to frequent Parisian scientific and political circles. He pursued a successful career in finance but simultaneously began carrying out research in botany and forestry. By 1734, he had earned a seat as an adjunct in mechanics at the FRENCH ACADEMY OF SCIENCES in PARIS. He became an associate academician in 1739 and transferred to the section on botany.

In 1739, Buffon also obtained the post of *intendant* (superintendant) of the Jardin du Roi (Royal Gardens). Buffon remained in this position for nearly 50 years until his death in 1788. He divided his time between Paris and his estate near Montbard. In his work at the gardens, Buffon was assisted by another Montbard native, Louis-Jean-Marie DAUBENTON. The two men collaborated on the monumental *Histoire naturelle, générale et particulière, avec description du Cabinet du Roy* (Natural history, general and specific, with a description of the royal collection; 1749–67). Buffon received appointments or was elected to academies throughout Europe including the French Academy, the ROYAL SOCIETY OF LONDON, the BERLIN ACADEMY, and the Academy of SAINT PETERSBURG. He received the title of *comte* (count) from King LOUIS XV.

Buffon shared with his contemporaries a general rejection of metaphysical speculation in the natural sciences. He denied that God intervenes directly in nature and rejected the idea that development in nature is teleological (moving toward a preordained goal). Although Buffon paid particular attention to the abundant variety and seeming disorder of life, he ultimately believed that nature is ruled by fundamental laws. He also believed that scientific theory should be directly derived from informed observation of natural phenomena (a form of EMPIRICISM).

Buffon criticized Carolus LINNAEUS for creating an artificial CLASSIFICATION of living things. During his early career, Buffon rejected the Linnaean idea of the family (a large group of supposedly related genuses) and also believed that using resemblance as a criterion for determining groups was invalid. In opposition to Linnaeus, Buffon developed a natural classification of the species that allegedly reflected the real order in nature. It recognized as valid groupings only species, defined in terms of reproductive capacity. The members of a given species are creatures that can produce fertile offspring together.

Buffon played a major role in the controversies about the nature of GENERATION (reproduction) that dominated the life sciences during the later 18th century. In his ear-

Portrait of Buffon by C. Baron, 1761. Georges-Louis Leclerc, comte de Buffon, the author of the widely read *Histoire naturelle* (Natural history), served as superintendent of the Jardin des Plantes (Botanical Garden) in Paris. *(Courtesy Hunt Institute for Botanical Documentation, Carnegie-Mellon University, Pittsburgh, Pennsylvania)*

lier works, he developed a theory of EPIGENESIS that postulated the existence of an interior mold (*moule intérieure*) that directs development in individual creatures. The interior mold preserved the integrity of the species, preventing crossbreeding between species and the transformation of existing species into new species.

As Buffon continued his studies of generation, he began to favor the notion that species change over time in a process he called DEGENERATION. He also decided that the concepts of genus and family could be valid in a natural classification scheme. Buffon believed that degeneration occurred as a result of environmental influences. He presented this theory in an essay entitled *De la dégénération des animaux* (Of the degeneration of animals; 1766).

Buffon devoted considerable energy to the study of geology and fossils. He believed that the Earth had existed for longer than the period indicated in biblical accounts. He calculated the age to be about 75,000 years, considerably greater than the 6,000 to 8,000 years that was the generally, accepted figure.

Buffon also believed that the surface of the Earth and the life it supported had experienced transformations over time. He emphasized the gradual nature of these changes and emphatically denied that cataclysms such as the biblical flood had ever occurred. He asserted that the causes of these changes were always natural rather than acts of God. Buffon's cosmogony (creation theory) reflects these underlying convictions. It suggests that the solar system was created by the impact of a comet that hit the Sun and projected some solar matter, to which a spinning motion had been imparted, into space. This spinning matter slowly coalesced into the planets and their satellites. These views mark Buffon as a highly original contributor to the science of his era. The specific contents of Buffon's theories about the history of the Earth changed during his life. They can be read in the *Histoire et théorie de la terre* (History and theory of the Earth) and the *Époques de la nature* (Epochs of nature), both treatises contained in the monumental *Histoire naturelle* (Natural history).

Finally, Buffon studied the relationship of the human species to other animal species. He believed strongly in the unity of the human species, denying that any substantial differences separated white people from those of other skin colors. He also asserted that REASON, the mental faculty that separates human beings from all other living creatures, is made possible through the physiological organization and normal development of sensory organs. In adopting such a position, Buffon built upon the ideas of John LOCKE. Étienne-Bonnot de CONDILLAC, the French theorist of sensation psychology, in turn built his theories on the ideas of both Locke and Buffon.

Buffon stressed that reason develops only through the acquisition and use of LANGUAGE and that language in turn grows from the sociability of human beings, a trait necessitated by long years of childhood.

Buffon was one of the most influential scientists of the later ENLIGHTENMENT. Not only did he wield great power and patronage by virtue of his position at the Jardin du Roi, but he also gained popular renown through the strength of his literary style. The comprehensive and richly illustrated *Histoire naturelle,* the most widely read scientific book in France, was also translated and disseminated throughout Europe in the 18th century. Buffon's various theories, whatever their flaws in modern terms, provided a framework for natural history that dominated the intellectual landscape until the middle of the 19th century.

See also RACE.

Further reading: Thomas L. Hankins, *Science and the Enlightenment* (Cambridge: Cambridge University Press, 1985).

bureaucracy A body of officials charged with the tasks of securing and maintaining governmental power and authority. The rudimentary forms of modern Western bureaucracy first appeared in the late 17th century in conjunction with the emergence of monarchical ABSOLUTISM, and continued to develop during the 18th century. Enlightened rulers and their reforming ministers tended to believe that the establishment of absolutism

supported by a well-organized bureaucracy would serve the causes of REASON and utility in government.

Bureaucratic development occurred in western Europe, the HAPSBURG EMPIRE, and RUSSIA, but the experiences of FRANCE and PRUSSIA provide especially illustrative examples of the nature and complexity of the phenomenon. In each of these political units, the process displayed unique qualities. These differences, however, were largely offset by the existence of unifying elements such as common sets of ideal goals and associated practices. These elements included the establishment of permanent bureaus staffed by salaried, removable, specialized professionals; the selection and subsequent advancement of officials on the basis of talent rather than birth; and the resulting tendency to exclude hereditary nobles from new offices in order to draw bureaucrats from the ranks of commoners. Other unifying elements were the reorganization of bureaucratic functions in an effort to rationalize administration at both central and local levels; the attempt to overcome particular local interests and privileges by the establishment of universal administrative regulations; the extension of the concept of legitimate government activity to include utilitarian and humanitarian goals when these would serve to enhance the powers of the central state; and finally, the emergence of a conscious distinction between public and private pursuits that redefined rights and duties in the realm of office-holding. Although never fully realized in practice, these ideals helped to motivate enlightened administrative reforms.

Initially, the new type of bureaucracy appeared as a set of practical responses to forces that were threatening to thwart the interests of absolute monarchs. These rulers were asserting their rights to reign as unchallenged sovereigns with all functions of power united in themselves. Such claims required radical reforms within state structures in order to be realized in practice. Naturally, the entrenched hereditary aristocracies and privileged corporations challenged these claims. To carry out their reforms, ambitious absolute rulers needed reliable administrators.

Existing practices had produced bodies of government officials who could be controlled only minimally. One notorious source of difficulty lay in the common practice, perfected in ANCIEN RÉGIME France, of venality (selling government offices). These offices were treated legally as forms of private property, which, in some cases, could be inherited. The purchase of many offices conferred legal noble status upon the buyer, thus making officeholding a vehicle for social mobility into the upper ranks of society. Offices also provided lucrative sources of income because officials were free to collect extra fees and perquisites, and officers tended to develop networks of political influence that were reinforced by formal marriage alliances and friendships. In fact, it was partly these perks of officeholding that allowed the PARLEMENTS to become so powerful in 18th-century France.

This structure of officeholding made the removal of incompetent or unnecessary officers nearly impossible. A reforming ruler, desirous of concentrating more power in his own person, could scarcely turn to these individuals for support. At best, he might circumvent them by establishing new offices that co-opted the older functions. This tactic, however, often complicated the exercise of central control by producing a confusing repetition of administrative jurisdictions.

Into this labyrinthine and unwieldy system, the absolute monarchs attempted to introduce rational reforms. They tackled the problem from two directions: by reorganizing the structures of administration and by establishing new methods for procuring personnel. In France, LOUIS XIV relied on the appointment of special salaried officials, the ill-famed *intendants,* who were charged with the duties of regional administration. Nobles were excluded from such appointments in an effort to circumvent established networks of local power. Intendancies could not be bought or sold. Appointments could be revoked at any time. Unfortunately, these early attempts at administrative centralization and reform were confounded by the continuation of the practice of selling other offices. The incipient, rationalized bureaucracies were, therefore, undermined or co-opted by existing corps of entrenched, hereditary officials. This situation continued unchanged for the most part until the outbreak of the FRENCH REVOLUTION.

The case of Prussia provides a counter-example of brilliant, if temporary, success in the matter of administrative centralization. Under the rule of the Hohenzollern princes and kings (Frederick William I and FREDERICK II [THE GREAT]), the reform of bureaucratic structure and practice paved the way for the establishment and effective maintenance of enlightened absolutism. The Prussian rulers created a professional bureaucracy based on a hierarchical, military model in which merit served—theoretically—as the criterion for advancement.

This bureaucracy worked to secure the interests of the king; officials were not public servants in the modern sense. Initially, tasks centered on narrowly defined military and fiscal issues. During the 18th century, the realm of activity expanded to include the regulation and policing of many facets of daily life. A growing body of public law, applicable throughout the Prussian realms, aided officials in carrying out their duties. The central bureaus of the reformed Prussian administration were staffed with talented commoners. Local rural administration, however, remained in the hands of Junker nobles, thereby producing the famed Prussian alliance between the central, absolute state and the traditional, rural aristocracy.

Despite the success of Prussian reforms, the new bureaucracy proved a tenuous and unreliable source of support for the monarchy. The merit system remained vulnerable to abuse by persons of status. Certain families developed powerful bases of influence within the bureaucracy. The system tended to become more restricted and to develop a troublesome independence. Frederick the Great recognized the threat to his power entailed in these tendencies. To counter the dangers, he instituted a system of secret surveillance that policed the officials. He also introduced other limiting elements. But, in the end, these precautions proved no more successful than the actions of the French monarchs at curbing unwanted administrative independence. During the Napoleonic era, Prussia actually experienced the substitution of absolute bureaucratic rule for that of the enlightened absolute monarch.

These brief excursions into the history of 18th-century bureaucracy reveal not only the weaknesses of the ancien régime, but also the tensions inherent within the rational ideals of the ENLIGHTENMENT. Bureaucracies were created as tools in the service of enlightened reform from above sponsored by ruling monarchs seeking to consolidate their power. These bureaucracies often degenerated, becoming instruments for the abuse of power. Furthermore, in some cases the new bureaucrats began demanding more power for themselves and became spokesmen for reformers from below who wanted to establish representative governments in their nations. Thus, the institution of bureaucracy helped bring about the downfall of absolute regimes throughout Europe. It became apparent that reason, utility, talent, merit, and professionalization, the enlightened concepts embodied by bureaucracy, could serve many political causes.

Further reading: Walter J. Gleason, *Moral Idealists, Bureaucracy, and Catherine the Great* (New Brunswick, N.J.: Rutgers University Press, 1981); L. J. Hume, *Bentham and Bureaucracy* (Cambridge: Cambridge University Press, 2003); Hans Rosenberg, *Bureaucracy, Aristocracy, and Autocracy: The Prussian Experience, 1660–1815* (Cambridge, Mass.: Harvard University Press, 1966).

Burke, Edmund (1729–1797) *British statesman, political philosopher, and aesthetic theorist*
A native of Ireland, Edmund Burke was born into a family with both Protestant and Catholic branches. His father's Protestant affiliations prevailed in determining young Burke's education. Primary schooling was received from the QUAKERS and was followed by university education at Trinity College in Dublin.

Burke moved to LONDON after completing his education; he studied some law, but devoted himself to a literary career. By 1759, Burke had published two books, *A Vindication of Natural Society* (1756) and *A Philosophical Inquiry into the Origin of Our Ideas on the Sublime and the Beautiful* (1757), and had acquired a post as editor of the *Annual Register.* He also became a charter member of the famous Literary Club organized by Joshua REYNOLDS around the figure of Samuel JOHNSON.

Engraving of Edmund Burke. Although he supported the American Revolution, Edmund Burke sharply criticized the French revolutionaries for violating French tradition and for basing their new political structure on ill-defined, lofty principles such as liberty and equality. *(Courtesy New York Public Library)*

In 1766, Burke escaped the drudgery of working for the London GRUB STREET press by winning a seat in the House of Commons of the British Parliament. Although affiliated with the liberal Whig Party, Burke's political philosophy consisted of a synthesis of liberal Whig principles with conservative Tory ideas. For a time, his positions seemed to provide a political restatement that was helpful to the Whigs, but he eventually broke with the party after the onset of the FRENCH REVOLUTION.

A great believer in the strength of tradition, Burke denied the possibility of PROGRESS and the PERFECTIBILITY of human beings. In fact, he distrusted any political policies that were based on abstract concepts, preferring instead a politics rooted in practicality and caution.

Burke accepted the conservative ideas that placed the family rather than the individual at the base of social order. He insisted that inequality is unavoidable in society and believed that qualities of leadership were embodied in the aristocracy. He also supported established religion.

These conservative principles were tempered, however, by elements borrowed from liberalism. Hence, Burke maintained that religious TOLERATION is desirable, that the possibility of upward mobility into the aristocracy must be preserved, that tradition must change slowly, and that imperial nations must respect the unique characteristics of their colonies.

The English constitution hammered out in the GLORIOUS REVOLUTION of 1688 served as Burke's ideal model of government. The monarchy provided an element of continuity and stability that was balanced by the landed and commercial interests represented in Parliament. Burke believed that the right to hold office derived from the ownership of property and conceived of Parliament as a body representing certain social classes rather than individuals.

Burke criticized English colonial policies in North America and India. He also decried the treatment of Ireland. He supported procedures and reforms that strengthened Parliament with respect to the king but that also protected the electoral process from manipulation.

Burke supported the cause of the AMERICAN REVOLUTION against Britain, but he opposed the French Revolution. He interpreted the American rebellion as an attempt to secure traditional liberties and rights, but he considered the French Revolution dangerous because of its appeal to abstract principles. He outlined these criticisms in his REFLECTIONS ON THE REVOLUTION IN FRANCE (1790).

Burke did not confine himself to POLITICAL THEORY, but also addressed issues in AESTHETICS. His *Philosophical Inquiry into the Origins of our Ideas on the Sublime and the Beautiful* (1756) contained the first treatment of the SUBLIME as a concept distinct from beauty. His treatise argued against the forms and ideals associated with NEOCLASSICISM, emphasizing the power of the unknown, the obscure, and the frightening in creative work.

Burke's position illustrates one direction that could be followed by people who rejected the branch of the ENLIGHTENMENT associated with the ideals of progress, equality, and reform. His work demonstrates that these enlightened ideals were not conceived as necessary ingredients for the preservation of political liberty or for the establishment of representative government. In both aesthetics and politics, Burke offered alternatives that would persist into the 19th century in association with political conservatism and ROMANTICISM.

Burlamaqui, Jean-Jacques (1694–1748) *Genevan legal scholar*

A native and citizen bourgeois of Calvinist GENEVA, Burlamaqui devoted his life to service in the city council and to teaching law. He wrote three books—*Principes du droit naturel* (Principles of natural law; 1747), *Principes du droit politique* (Principles of political law; 1751), and

Principes du droit de la nature et des gens (Principles of the law of nature and of humankind; 1748)—that were reprinted in many 18th-century editions. Burlamaqui and his Genevan compatriot Jean-Jacques ROUSSEAU were the primary forces behind the spread of the concept of NATURAL LAW into the discourse of the Swiss ENLIGHTENMENT.

See also RIGHTS.

Burney, Charles (1726–1814) *English composer, music historian, organist, and harpsichordist*

Burney and his twin sister were the last of the 20 children of James MacBurney, a versatile artist with skills in portraiture, dancing, and violin playing. Charles received his formal education at Shrewsbury School and the Free School (today the King's School in Canterbury). He studied the organ and, at age 18, made the acquaintance of Thomas Arne (1710–78), who took him as an apprentice. Through Arne, Burney received his introduction to LONDON musical life, assisting at Vauxhall, Ranelagh, and other playhouses and pleasure gardens.

In 1746, Lord Greville hired Burney as a musical instructor and companion. In this capacity, Burney entered the circles of LONDON's high society and acquired the polished manners that facilitated his subsequent professional activities. He married Esther Sleepe in 1749 and left the employment of Lord Greville in order to pursue a musician's career in London. At this time, he collaborated with David GARRICK on productions at Drury Lane Theatre. He also played harpsichord recitals under the auspices of various concert organizations. Mrs. Burney died in 1761, and in 1767 Burney married Mrs. Allen, the widow of Stephen Allen, a former friend. He earned a doctorate in music from Oxford University in 1769.

Shortly thereafter, he conceived the idea of writing a history of music. To collect materials, he undertook two distinct tours throughout the major European capitals, much in the style of the GRAND TOUR taken by wealthy young British men. Acquaintances in London provided the letters of introduction that allowed him entry into the musical circles and aristocratic salons of Europe. Burney took two extensive tours, one in 1770, the second in 1772. He visited PARIS, Lyons, GENEVA, TURIN, MILAN, Padua, Bologna, VENICE, Florence, ROME, Naples, and Genoa on the first tour. The second trip took him through the UNITED PROVINCES OF THE NETHERLANDS, the AUSTRIAN NETHERLANDS, to various German cities including BERLIN, and on to VIENNA. He met many of the distinguished musicians, composers, scholars, and writers of the era.

From the materials collected on these tours, Burney produced two wonderful volumes of observations about the music and character of his contemporaries throughout Europe. These volumes, *The Present State of Music in France and Italy* (1771) and *The Present State of Music in Germany, the Netherlands, and the United Provinces* (1773), established Burney's literary career and today serve as rich resources for students of the period. Burney followed these books with his multivolumed *General History of Music* (1776–89). These works reveal him to be a staunch supporter of the new musical trends of his era, although the books convey respect for certain earlier composers. The notion of writing about music as HISTORY was a new development in the 18th century. Burney was one of several historians of music to appear in the late 18th century, and he was always chagrined that the *General History of the Science and Practice of Music* (1776) by his Literary Club friend, John Hawkins, appeared before the final volumes of his own *General History of Music*.

Burney's home in London (formerly the residence of Isaac NEWTON) became a salon of sorts where musicians, writers, politicians, and artists intermingled. Burney was well acquainted with Samuel JOHNSON, Joshua REYNOLDS, David HUME, Edmund BURKE, and David Garrick. Joshua Reynolds painted a large portrait of Burney. Several of Burney's children earned recognition in their own right: Fanny BURNEY as a novelist, Esther as a harpsichordist, the Reverend Charles Burney as an eminent classical scholar, and Rear Admiral James Burney as a friend of Captain James COOK and chronicler of Cook's global circumnavigations.

Burney, Fanny (1752–1840) *English novelist whose christened name was Frances*

Fanny Burney was the daughter of the renowned English musicologist and traveler Charles BURNEY. She lived for many years with her father, frequenting with him the literary gatherings around Samuel JOHNSON. Fanny Burney published her early novel *Evelina* anonymously in 1778. The plot unfolds in a series of letters written by a young, impressionable, unmarried woman making her first visits to LONDON. Fanny Burney introduced the book with a declaration of her intent to take the "field of battle" against the male literary establishment. *Evelina* shows Fanny Burney as a penetrating and critical observer of London social life and of the status of women. It also betrays her dislike of middle-class values and culture.

The success of *Evelina* persuaded Fanny Burney to reveal herself as its author. Subsequently, Queen Charlotte engaged her in 1786 as a lady-in-waiting. She remained in the royal household until 1791. In 1793, Fanny Burney married a French royalist refugee and former general, Alexandre d'Arblay. The couple moved to France in 1802, living there through the years of Napoleon's rule. They moved back to England after the Battle of Waterloo.

Novels by Fanny Burney include: *Evelina* (1778); *Cecilia* (1782); *Camilla* (1796); and *The Wanderer* (1814). The 1832 edition of the *Mémoirs of Charles Burney* was also her work.

See also BLUESTOCKING; WOMEN AND THE ENLIGHTENMENT.

Burns, Robert (1759–1796) *Scottish poet*

Born to William and Agnes Burnes in Ayrshire, a district in southwestern SCOTLAND, Robert was the eldest of seven children. William changed his surname to "Burns" when he settled in Ayrshire. He was a landscape gardener, which means that Robert was raised on the farms where his father worked. His father is said to have instilled in Robert the principles of RELIGION and his mother the seeds of the folk tradition that later blossomed in his work. He received a brief, three-year formal education, but he was drawn to popular ballads and songs. In fact, it was while attending school that Robert was introduced to collections of ballad poetry. His first song, "Handsome Nell," was composed in 1774 in honor of a girl with whom he worked during the harvest that year. His convivial spirit manifested itself in his affection for clubs and societies. In 1780, he helped to found the Tarbolton Bachelors' Club, a debating society; the next year he joined the Masons.

When William died in 1784, Robert and his brother Gilbert rented the farm of Mossgiel, where Robert lived for two years. During this period, Robert began to dedicate himself to poetry, composing a wide variety of songs and lyrics. He also entered into relationships with the local girls. Elizabeth Paton bore Robert a daughter in 1785, and Jean Armour bore Robert two sets of twins before he married her in 1788. When Jean's first pregnancy became public knowledge in 1786, her father brought a suit against Robert that almost forced him to immigrate to Jamaica. During this period, he also had an affair with Margaret Campbell, the famous "Highland Mary" of his verse. She died in October of 1786, either of typhus or childbirth.

Burns published his first collection of poems to raise funds to pay the fare for his passage to Jamaica. The poems appeared as *Poems, Chiefly in the Scottish Dialect* in July 1786. Some of Burns's most famous poems appear in this collection, including "The Holy Fair" and "To a Mouse." The collection sold modestly, but it was favorably reviewed by various Scottish literati, among them Thomas Blacklock and Henry Mackenzie. The latter referred to Burns as the "heaven-taught ploughman" in a review later that year. Inspired by this praise, Burns headed to EDINBURGH, aiming to achieve greater success with a second collection. *Poems* appeared in 1787, and its favorable public reception enabled Burns to pay his brother's debts and, in 1788, to lease another farm.

Burns failed to find a patron in Edinburgh and, during the summer of 1787, set out to visit the Scottish Borders and Highlands. Returning to Edinburgh in the autumn of that year, he set to work editing a collection of songs that had been compiled by James Johnson. This collection, *The Scots Musical Museum*, was published in various editions between 1787 and 1803. Approximately 160 of Burns's songs eventually appeared in the volume.

Burns and his legacy have long occupied a curious relation to matters of culture and state. He served as an excise officer (or tax collector) for the last several years of his life, beginning in 1789. However, his vocal support of the FRENCH REVOLUTION also inspired an official government inquiry into his loyalty. When the reorganized Scottish Parliament opened its doors 200 years later, in 1999, the folksinger Sheena Wellington sang the Burns song "A Man's a Man for a' that." He is most often remembered for revitalizing the Scottish folk tradition, but it may be more accurate to say that he capitalized on and increased the already existing affection for the type of vernacular poetry written by his predecessors Allan Ramsay and Robert Fergusson.

Today, Burns is considered Scotland's national poet. Ironically, he might be considered an English national treasure as well, inasmuch as his use of the Scottish vernacular partly inspired William Wordsworth to speak in "the language really used by men" in the *Lyrical Ballads* (1798). Burns is now recognized as a master of many verse forms. However, it is as the "heaven-taught ploughman" that he continues to generate the most interest among scholars and the most affection from casual readers, as evidenced by Burns Nights, celebrated annually throughout the globe on January 25th, Burns's birthday.

Further reading: John Mackay, *Burns: A Biography* (Edinburgh: Mainstream, 1992); Carol McGuirk, *Robert Burns and the Sentimental Era* (Athens, Ga.: University of Georgia Press, 1985); Fiona J. Stafford, *Starting Lines in Scottish, Irish, and English Poetry: From Burns to Heaney* (Oxford: Oxford University Press, 2000).

Butler, Joseph (1692–1752) *English moral philosopher and theologian*

Joseph Butler, son of a retired draper belonging to the Presbyterian Church, received his secondary education at an academy operated by English Protestant DISSENTERS. He converted to the Anglican Church as a young man and entered Oxford University. Ordained an Anglican priest in 1718, Butler devoted his life to the church, rising to become bishop of Bristol in 1738 and bishop of Durham in 1751. He also served in the royal household during the reign of George II.

As a devout Anglican, Butler desired to defend his Christian faith, morality, and belief in revealed knowledge (knowledge sent directly from God) from the many attacks that were being raised by enlightened theologians and intellectual critics. Butler tried to show that the very arguments that deists and other critics used against Christianity could also be used in its favor.

Butler accepted the argument from DEISM that the design of nature suggests the existence of God, but he argued that a strict analogy exists between the religious knowledge gained from nature and the knowledge gained through revelations from God. Therefore, NATU-RAL RELIGION supports revealed religion and hence also Christianity.

Butler also contributed to building a foundation in NATURE for MORAL PHILOSOPHY. He recognized the partial validity of the argument by Samuel CLARKE that morality rests in the preservation of self-interest. But he granted similar approval to the idea of Anthony Ashley Cooper, third earl of SHAFTESBURY, that morality grows from the natural benevolence (desire to do good) of human beings. Butler believed that both self-interest and benevolence interacted to contribute to moral behavior. But he also claimed that these inclinations (passions), and others that he believed equally powerful, were naturally subject to the rule of conscience.

With these arguments, Butler not only furthered the development of natural religion, natural theology, and moral philosophy, forms associated with the ENLIGHTEN-MENT, he also paradoxically helped to preserve the target of much enlightened criticism, Christianity. His writings demonstrate the ambivalent positions contained in enlightened thought and reveal that the Enlightenment was not uniformly anti-Christian.

Butler's major works included *Fifteen Sermons* (1726) and *The Analogy of Religion, Natural and Revealed, to the Constitution and Course of Nature* (1736).

Byron, George Gordon, sixth baron (1788–1824)
British poet

Until the age of 10, Byron was educated in Aberdeen, SCOTLAND, by his mother, a dour and conservative woman. His father died in 1791, and George Gordon became the sixth Baron Byron on the death of his great uncle in 1798. He and his mother moved to ENGLAND, where Byron attended Harrow School and Trinity Col-

lege, Cambridge University. At Cambridge he published his first volume of poetry, *Hours of Idleness* (1807).

In 1809, Byron and a friend set off on a two-year GRAND TOUR of Europe, visiting PORTUGAL, SPAIN, Malta, Albania, Greece, and Asia Minor. During this tour, Byron began his first major work, *Childe Harold's Pilgrimage* (1812, 1816, 1818). Byron published the first two cantos of this poem soon after his return to LONDON, and their success brought immediate fame.

In *Childe Harold,* Byron presents his archetypal hero, a passionate and mysterious figure who lives outside the conventional rules and social norms. He further develops this figure in his dramatic poem, *Manfred* (1816), in which he portrays a hero who seeks the knowledge of the gods, but who, unlike Faust, disdains to enter into a pact with the darker powers.

Byron wrote *Manfred* while he was living in GENEVA near his friends, the poet Percy Shelley and Mary Wollstonecraft Shelley. Mrs. Shelley was the daughter of Mary WOLLSTONECRAFT and the future author of *Frankenstein; or, the Modern Prometheus* (1818).

Byron, who was interested in the power that new scientific inventions could bring to their possessors, was one of Shelley's models for Victor Frankenstein. Byron was the most celebrated poet of his day. He was the only British poet of the romantic era to enjoy an international reputation during his lifetime. Byron's poetry had a profound effect on the work of many of his European contemporaries, including Johann Wolfgang von GOETHE, Alexander Pushkin, and Stendhal.

Byron's work displayed the themes of ROMANTICISM in clear form. His works show how romanticism, often considered a reaction to the ENLIGHTENMENT, actually derived and transformed its materials from themes of the late Enlightenment.

C

Cabanis, Pierre-Jean-Georges (1757–1808) *French physician, psychologist, philosopher, sociologist of medicine, and medical reformer*

Cabanis was the son of a landowner who experimented with the new agricultural methods and crops that were introduced in the 18th century. The elder Cabanis was a friend of the PHYSIOCRAT Anne-Robert-Jacques TURGOT. Pierre Cabanis moved to PARIS in 1771 after completing his elementary and secondary education in schools near his native town of Cosnac. He obtained a post as secretary to Prince Massalsky, bishop of Vilna, and moved to Poland with the bishop. His tenure in that country lasted two years, from 1773 until 1775.

Having returned to FRANCE, Cabanis studied medicine at Saint-Germain-en-Laye (1777–83). By 1785, he had established his residence in Auteuil just outside Paris. Cabanis frequented the salon of Madame HELVÉTIUS and, through the social contacts made at the salon, received an introduction to one of the leaders of the early phases of the FRENCH REVOLUTION, Count Mirabeau. Cabanis served Mirabeau as his private physician. In 1792, he became a close friend of Marie-Jean de CONDORCET after the latter moved into the Auteuil neighborhood. Tradition maintains that Cabanis prepared the poison that Condorcet used to commit suicide after his arrest during the Terror.

During the French Revolution, Cabanis devoted himself to the causes of hospital reform and education. He served on the Commission de Réforme des Hôpitaux (1791–93); received the chair as professor of hygiene in the new Écoles Centrales established by the Convention; and held various teaching posts at the the École de Santé, the reorganized faculty of medicine in Paris. He was elected to the Institut de France (1795) as a member of the class of moral sciences. In 1797, Cabanis was elected to serve on the Council of Five Hundred, and he supported the coup d'état that brought Napoleon to power. Although Napoleon named him to the senate, Cabanis quickly learned to distrust the ambitions of the new leader and gradually withdrew from public life. In 1808 he died after having suffered several strokes.

Cabanis approached medicine as a philosopher rather than as a clinician. Like his fellow IDÉOLOGUES, Cabanis believed that the more REASON dominated human actions and institutions, the more humankind would PROGRESS. He believed that manipulation of external conditions such as health and EDUCATION would help to nurture greater powers of reason in people. Consequently, he sought to reform the health care institutions and educational processes in France. Cabanis's proposal to introduce clinical training into medical training aimed at producing more knowledgeable physicians by providing them with better medical instruction. He used the hospital teaching clinic created by Gerard van SWIETEN in VIENNA as his model. Cabanis's reforms also addressed the problem of proper conditions for treatment and convalescence and recommended the creation of several smaller hospitals outside cities to replace the usual large ones.

Cabanis was particularly interested in the mind-body problem and, like many of his enlightened contemporaries, attempted to explain the origin of ideas. The solution of this problem would have assisted in strengthening the reasoning ability and enlightenment of people. Cabanis opposed the mind-body theories of Condillac's sensation PSYCHOLOGY because that psychology reduced ideas to a simple summation of sensory experiences transmitted by the nerves to the brain. Cabanis believed that a thorough understanding of the processes by which ideas are formed required considering the organic needs and irritable properties (automatic response to touch stimuli) of living tissues.

Cabanis published several works that included *Observations sur les hôpitaux* (Observations on hospitals; 1790); *Rapport sur l'éducation publique* (Report on public education; 1791); *Rapports du physique et du moral de l'homme* (Relations of the material body and morality of man; 1802); *Du degré de certitude de la médicine* (On the degree of certainty in medicine; 1798); and *Coup d'oeil sur les révolutions et sur la réforme de la médecine* (A look at revolutions and medical reform; written 1795, published 1804).

See also CONDILLAC.

Cagliostro, Alessandro, conte di (1734–1795) *Italian adventurer, self-proclaimed magician, and alchemist*

Alessandro, count of Cagliostro, was born in Palermo, Sicily, as Giuseppe Balsamo. Cagliostro caused a sensation in PARIS during the 1780s, holding theatrical seances in the fashionable salons of that city. Cagliostro reputedly possessed magical powers and claimed to have studied ALCHEMY in Alexandria, Egypt. He knew the teachings of the FREEMASONS and practiced the art of hypnosis. His enormous but short-lived success is an outstanding example of the fascination with the hidden and irrational that marked the closing years of the ENLIGHTENMENT. With the careers of the comte de SAINT-GERMAIN and Franz Anton MESMER, the success of Cagliostro shows how the lure of the irrational could be wedded to the love of demonstration and spectacle that also characterized enlightened culture.

Cagliostro was sponsored in Paris by Cardinal Louis de Rohan, one of the casualties of the 1785 DIAMOND NECKLACE SCANDAL. The scandal had serious political repercussions by undermining the reputation of Queen MARIE-ANTOINETTE, but it also ruined Cagliostro's French career and caused him to be banished in 1786 from FRANCE.

Cagliostro and his wife subsequently settled in ROME. In 1789, she denounced him before the Inquisition of the Catholic Church as a heretic. The Inquisition found Cagliostro guilty as accused and sentenced him to death, but commuted the sentence to life imprisonment. Cagliostro died in the prison of San Leo in 1795.

See also SOCIAL INSTITUTIONS OF THE ENLIGHTENMENT.

Calas, Jean (1698–1762) *Protestant cloth merchant of Toulouse who was found guilty of murdering his son and executed*

The Calas case gained notoriety throughout FRANCE as an example of the injustices of the ANCIEN RÉGIME. Jean Calas's eldest son, Marc-Antoine, was found one night behind the family home hanging and dead. Jean Calas was accused of having murdered him and was brought to trial before local officials in Toulouse. The case generated immense public interest and intense public opinion. It contained all the elements likely to appeal to popular curiosity: a Protestant father with a rebellious son who desired not only to abandon the family's traditional profession but also to convert to ROMAN CATHOLICISM; a mysterious murder, that of the son, after an evening spent with his family; family members who first told police that their son had been killed, but the next day declared that they had lied in order to hide the reality, a shameful suicide; and testimony by city officials that a suicide by hanging in the place where the body had been found was impossible. The facts were obscure, and, furthermore, the case touched the raw nerves of a society still wracked by religious tension between Catholics and Protestants.

Public opinion sided with the version of the story that made the dead son a victim of his vengeful Huguenot father. Local Catholic officials elevated the dead son to a martyr's status, buried him in a public spectacle attended by 50 Catholic clergy, and thereby conveniently turned the case into a propaganda tool against recalcitrant Protestants. In this charged atmosphere, the Calas case came to appeal before the *parlement* (court of justice) of Toulouse. The *parlement* found Calas guilty of the alleged crime, sentencing him to torture on the wheel and to death. Jean maintained his innocence throughout the procedures. He was strangled in a public execution on March 10, 1762, and his body was then burnt at the stake. The Calas family members were dispersed and their wealth confiscated.

VOLTAIRE entered the picture when he met the youngest son of Jean Calas in GENEVA. They discussed the case, and Voltaire became convinced that Calas had been wrongfully executed. The case seemed to highlight the weaknesses of the judicial system, and Voltaire used it as the starting point for a public campaign on behalf of criminal law code reform. The case also provided him with useful ammunition in his impassioned attacks on *"l'infâme"* (infamy), religious intolerance.

Voltaire began a campaign to have the Calas family rehabilitated. Ultimately, by making personal appeals before Madame de POMPADOUR (official mistress of LOUIS XV), Chancellor Lamoignon, and the duc de CHOISEUL, he succeeded in having the issue brought before the royal council. A royal tribunal reversed the decisions of the *parlement* of Toulouse, rehabilitated the reputation of Jean Calas, and paid compensation to the family.

See also CALVINISM; HUGUENOTS; *PARLEMENTS*; TOLERATION.

Calmet, Antoine (1672–1757) *Benedictine monk from the province of Lorraine, who was a biblical scholar and historian*

Antoine Calmet, or Dom Augustin as he was known in the clergy, studied with the Benedictine Maurists and

JESUITS before taking religious orders. His superiors sent him to Saint-Epyre to study Cartesian philosophy and the Münster in Alsace for theology, Greek, Latin, and biblical studies.

Calmet held various positions within his order, serving at the abbeys of Moyenmoutier, Lay-Saint-Christoph, Saint-Léopold, and Senones. He held the important post of general visitor to various congregations of the Benedictine order and also served as superior general of the order.

Calmet traveled throughout northern FRANCE, visiting various libraries to collect materials for his biblical studies and historical treatises. He spent some time in PARIS, where he lived at the Jansenist-influenced Abbaye des Blanc-Manteaux. In 1748, he also visited SWITZERLAND, again gathering scholarly materials.

An early practitioner of BIBLICAL CRITICISM, Calmet used both textual and historical forms of analysis to examine the books of the Bible. He published four major biblical studies: *Commentaire littéral sur tous les livres de l'Ancien et du Nouveau Testament* (Literal commentary on all the books of the Old and New Testament; 1715); *L'histoire de l'Ancient et du Nouveau Testament* (History of the Old and New Testament); *L'histoire de la vie et des miracles de Jésus-Christ* (History of the life and miracles of Jesus Christ; 1737); and *Dictionnaire historique, critique, chronologique, géographique et littéral de la Bible* (Historical, critical, chronological, geographical, and literal dictionary of the Bible; 1722, published in French, Latin, German, English, and Dutch).

Calmet was a devout Catholic who wished to provide support for the authority of the Bible as a source of divine revelation. VOLTAIRE, however, found in Calmet's detailed studies ample ammunition for his campaign against revealed religion. In fact, he used a copy of Calmet's *Dictionnaire . . . de la Bible* as one of his major sources in preparing the DICTIONNAIRE PHILOSOPHIQUE (Philosophical dictionary), a work famed for its scathing attacks on Christianity. This incident reveals clearly how the critical intellectual approaches developed in the 17th century and elaborated during the ENLIGHTENMENT could be used to support opposing attitudes about RELIGION.

Calmet was also commissioned by the duke of Lorraine to write the *Histoire de Lorraine,* but, as a result of censorship, the published text differed significantly from Calmet's original manuscript. Calmet also wrote a *Traité historique des eaux et bains de Plombières* (Historical treatise on the waters and baths of Plombières; 1748) and *Diarium Helveticum* (Dairy of Switzerland; 1756).

Calonne, Charles-Alexandre de (1734–1802) *general controller of finances in France from 1783 to 1787*

Calonne was educated in law and began his rise in state administration by purchasing an office as lawyer for the council of Artois in Flanders. He became the legal representative of that council to the *parlement* (court of law) of Flanders in 1759. He earned the undying enmity of lawyers in PARLEMENTS throughout France when he aided King LOUIS XV in the suppression of the resistance of the *parlement* of Brittany. The event cast Calonne as one who would support royal attacks on privileged groups in France.

The affair of the Brittany *parlement* probably aided Calonne's career in the royal administration. In 1766, he became a superintendant in the region of Metz, then assumed the same position in the important province of Flanders. There he devoted himself to industrial and commercial problems. He also followed the political situation in PARIS and may have written an anonymous pamphlet. *"Les comment?"* which harshly criticized the financial policies of the general director of finances, Jacques NECKER. Calonne assumed the position of general controller of finances in 1783 after Necker's disgrace.

Calonne's first acts as general controller helped to ease the financial crisis that faced FRANCE. But Calonne saw that nothing lasting could be accomplished without substantial structural reforms of the financial system. Therefore, in 1786 he submitted to LOUIS XVI the outlines of a reform designed to place royal finances on a rational and secure basis. At its center lay a concerted attack on privilege. It proposed spreading the tax burden equitably on the people of France by removing the myriad tax exemptions enjoyed by the nobility, the clergy, and other privileged groups. It proposed economic policies inspired by the PHYSIOCRATS: the abolition of internal customs barriers and regulations detrimental to free trade.

Calonne knew that his plan called on the privileged groups of society to make personal sacrifices. But he hoped to enlist their support by calling a general assembly where he could explain the rationale of the plan and appeal to the commitment of the assembly members to the common good of the nation. Calling a meeting of the Estates General (representative national advisory assembly), something no French king had done since 1614, carried implications dangerous to the absolute claims of the monarchy, and turning to the recalcitrant *parlements* would have been a futile exercise. Therefore, Calonne proposed a more circumscribed meeting, an Assembly of Notables, which was summoned to meet in February 1787. The Assembly of Notables proved anything but pliant. In fact, resistance to Calonne's proposals was so virulent, that the king removed Calonne from office. The affair clearly demonstrated the intractable nature of the problems within the ANCIEN RÉGIME. Reform from above appeared impossible.

Calonne lost his post in 1787 after the Assembly of Notables meeting failed to produce reform. He left France, establishing himself in England, where he married a wealthy widow and acquired a handsome townhouse in LONDON as well as the beautiful estate of Wimbledon. With the outbreak of the FRENCH REVOLUTION, he offered his services to the exiled French princes and aristocracy. He negotiated throughout Europe on their behalf and attempted to formulate a plan that would save Louis XVI. He also impoverished himself by providing his own funds to finance the émigré party. He died in 1802, one month after having received permission from the revolutionary government to return to France.

See also ABSOLUTISM; ABSOLUTISM, ENLIGHTENED; ARISTOCRATIC RESURGENCE.

caloric   A term invented by Antoine LAVOISIER to define the phenomenon of heat. Caloric (i.e., heat) was conceived as a type of matter or substance in the form of a fluid composed of minuscule particles. It was, in fact, an outstanding example, along with electricity, of the use of theories of SUBTLE FLUIDS by 18th-century scientists. The particles of caloric were deemed so subtle that they escaped detection by weighing (gravimetrics).

Since caloric could not be measured by using weighing techniques, Lavoisier developed an experimental instrument, the calorimeter, that provided an indirect measure. The calorimeter consisted of a double vessel in the inner portion of which a wire basket filled with a chemical substance was placed. Ice was packed directly around it. In the outer vessel, ice was also packed to keep the external temperature at freezing point. The substance was heated, and the ice surrounding it began to melt. The resultant water was collected, weighed, and used to determine the amount of heat that had been used in the melting process.

The calorimeter is considered a classic example of an experimental apparatus. It illustrates the process of which the experimental techniques of the SCIENTIFIC REVOLUTION allowed scientists to assume that certain quantifiable things could be used as indirect measurements of a physical phenomenon.

See also RUMFORD.

Calvinism   Branch of Protestant Christianity founded by the French humanist Jean Calvin (birth name, Jean Cauvin, 1509–64). Calvin studied law, THEOLOGY, Latin, and Greek at the universities in Bourges and PARIS. An intense religious experience in his early 20s led him into church reform. Calvin's activities caused him to be indicated in 1533 for heresy. As a result, he went into hiding for nearly one year, taking refuge in the Swiss city of Basel.

In early 1536, Calvin published, in Latin, his *Institutes of the Christian Religion*. The book presented what Calvin believed were the universal tenets of the Christian RELIGION, applicable within any Christian land where people desired to reform the practices of Roman Christianity (ROMAN CATHOLICISM).

In late 1536, the citizens of GENEVA, whose ruler for centuries had been a Catholic bishop, revolted, threw out their current bishop, and invited Calvin to their city to establish a new Christian government. As a result, Geneva became the center of an international, highly organized Calvinist movement.

In the various European countries, the adherents of Calvinism acquired different names: HUGUENOTS in FRANCE, Dutch Reformed in the UNITED PROVINCES OF THE NETHERLANDS, and Presbyterians, DISSENTERS, Puritans in SCOTLAND, ENGLAND, and the American colonies. Calvinist groups also developed in HUNGARY, Bohemia, POLAND, and certain territories of the HOLY ROMAN EMPIRE such as the Rhineland Palatinate.

The teachings of Calvin developed out of criticisms of the standard practices of Roman Catholicism. Like Martin Luther, Calvin claimed that salvation comes through faith in God, rather than through the accumulation of a record of good works, but Calvin also taught that God chooses a select group of people in advance who will enjoy eternal life (theory of predestination). Calvin followed the practices of Renaissance humanism by prescribing a return to written ancient sources in efforts to reform the churches. For Christianity, this meant relying primarily on the Bible as the authority for views on theology and church polity.

One of the major disputes that divided Calvinists, Lutherans, and other Protestants from Roman Catholics centered on the interpretation of the Eucharist (the principal Christian ritual). Calvin argued that the ceremony was a remembrance of the Last Supper shared by Jesus with his disciples. According to Calvin, during the ceremony, the body and blood of Christ are present spiritually but not physically in the shared bread and wine. Other major interpretations of this central Christian ritual were transubstantiation, in which the bread and wine actually become the body and blood of Christ in a miraculous transformation (Roman Catholicism); consubstantiation, where the bread and wine acquire the physical attributes of the body and blood of Christ, but remain bread and wine (LUTHERANISM); and symbolism, in which bread and wine only symbolically represent the body and blood (Zwinglianism).

These theological issues became critically important in the churches because the interpretation of the Eucharist actually stemmed from basic concepts about the role of God in the world. Catholics insisted that miracles were still occurring in the world; to deny miracles involved denying that God, as the absolute ruler of the universe, could cause anything no matter how unusual, to happen. Protestants tended to accept some biblical miracles, but generally denied that they were occurring with any frequency in the modern world. Their God did not need to intervene in this way to govern his world or to display his power.

The acceptance or rejection of miracle obviously affected interpretations of the Eucharist. For Catholics, a miracle occurred (the changing of the bread and wine into the actual body and blood of Jesus Christ) each time the Mass (Eucharist) was celebrated. Protestants, however, had no need of a miracle at the Eucharist because no absolute physical transformation of the bread and wine was believed to occur.

These arguments about miracle and the Eucharist contained obvious implications for the role of the priest or minister. The Catholic Eucharist ritual, in particular, gave a powerful role to the priest, who acted as the intermediary between the faithful and God. His words and actions in the Mass helped the ordinary bread and wine to transform miraculously into the actual body and blood of Christ. For the Catholic conception of the world, protection of this special role for the priest (illustrated also in his power in granting absolution for sins) was essential, and much Catholic opposition to Protestant theology revolved around this threat to priestly status.

The fact that interpretations of the Eucharist implied certain beliefs about the actions of God in the world and the role of priests as shepherds of the faithful helped to make Eucharist disputes impossible to resolve. Even in the late 17th and early 18th centuries, when Jacques-Bénigne BOSSUET and Gottfried Wilhelm LEIBNIZ were discussing the possibility of reunion between Catholics and Protestants, no compromise on these issues could be reached.

In general, Calvinism approached theology from a rational, legalistic viewpoint. It developed a correspondingly severe notion of worship, stripping services of most emotional or purely aesthetic elements. In this realm, it bore greater similarity to Swiss Zwinglianism than to Lutheranism, Anglicanism, or Catholicism. The lifestyle prescribed for a Calvinist was one of discipline, severity, austerity, and industry. It appealed to motivated, resolute individuals and meshed particularly smoothly with the outlook of ambitious merchants and businessmen. But it also appealed to artisans, poorer townspeople, and women, who found in its messages and practices inspiration for political and social reforms as well as religious insight.

As often happens with religions, the theological views of Calvin had a political side that dealt with matters of power and church-state relations. Calvin did not accept the idea that the church should be subordinate to the state. In fact, he stated the opposite idea, that the church should dominate the secular state, determining what laws and practices would be tolerated by the state. A government in which church dominates is called a theocracy. That is the form of government that Calvin established in Geneva.

Within the boundaries of the church, Calvin favored representative government with local elected officials and a hierarchy of representatives all the way to the pinnacle of power. The elected representatives were both clergymen and laypersons. By giving a role to the laity, Calvinism introduced an element of secularism within the church government.

Wherever Calvinism became the official church (Geneva, the United Provinces of the Netherlands, Scotland), the government could at times be as harsh and as intolerant of dissent as any Catholic government. But in most countries, Calvinism never gained complete ascendancy and remained a minority or unofficial religion. In these countries, its adherents tended to support political theories of limited monarchy or of divided sovereignty and to oppose monarchical ABSOLUTISM. In fact, the Calvinist tradition of government actually provided one of the major sources of republicanism in the centuries between the Protestant Reformation and the FRENCH REVOLUTION.

From its inception of 1536, Calvinism posed dilemmas for rulers and churches throughout Europe. The challenge was especially potent in the United Provinces of the Netherlands, England, and France. During the 16th century, Genevan-dominated Calvinism became so well organized and powerful that it existed virtually as a separate state within the kingdom of France. The question of whether Catholicism or Calvinism would dominate France was one of the central issues at the heart of the bloody Wars of Religion (1562–98). A compromise, introduced in the Edict of Nantes (1598), temporarily resolved the religious tension by granting very limited tolerance and civil rights to Calvinists.

The Edict of Nantes troubled the 17th-century Catholic kings and ministers of France; they slowly limited its extent and finally, in 1685, LOUIS XIV revoked it altogether. This act initiated a wave of religious repression, causing the flight of thousands of Calvinist Huguenots from France to England, to the North American colonies, to the United Provinces of the Netherlands, and to BERLIN.

In England, the challenge of Calvinism came to a head during the great Civil War of the 17th century (1642–48). A Calvinist republic, the Commonwealth, was established in 1649 but was preempted in 1660 with the restoration of the Stuart monarchy. Religious tension among Calvinists, ANGLICANS, and Catholics continued into the 18th century.

In the Holy Roman Empire, the Peace of Augsburg (1555) established an uneasy solution to the problem of religious differences by allowing each territorial sovereign prince to determine the form of Christianity that would exist in his lands (principle of *cujus regio, ejus religio*). This privilege, however, held only for Lutherans and Catholics. Calvinism was not accepted as a legitimate religious form and continued to be a source of conflict and instability throughout the 16th century and well into the 17th century.

Religious tensions in the Holy Roman Empire partly fueled the terrible Thirty Years' War (1618–48). The 1648 Peace of Westphalia established an order that minimized religious conflict and helped to allow a *de facto* religious TOLERATION to develop in certain territories of the empire.

By the dawn of the 18th century, the European desire to define rights and identity strongly in religious terms was beginning to wane. The century witnessed the last waves of persecution with the brutal suppression of the CAMISARDS and the execution of Jean CALAS, but it also produced laws establishing toleration in specific nations.

In addition to fostering republicanism and religious toleration, Calvinism contributed to the development of intellectual positions associated with the ENLIGHTENMENT by encouraging both critical scholarship and general lay reading. Calvinist nations in the 18th century tended to have more lenient censorship regulations than their Roman Catholic counterparts. In fact, the presses of England, the United Provinces of the Netherlands, and Geneva printed many books that could not be published in other nations.

In England, Calvinist Dissenters set up academies to provide their children with university-level educations, since they were barred from the universities at Oxford and Cambridge. These schools offered courses in the newest fields of study and produced several notable enlightened intellectuals. The Scottish Enlightenment, now recognized as one of the most important branches of the whole enlightened movement, was partially indebted to the secular values, ideals, and lifestyles fostered by Calvinism (Presbyterianism) as practiced in EDINBURGH and Glasgow.

In the predominantly Calvinist United Provinces of the Netherlands, Pierre BAYLE, whose *HISTORICAL AND CRITICAL DICTIONARY* provided an early example of the critical power of REASON, worked and published in relative freedom. Moreover, the MECHANICAL PHILOSOPHY, unwelcome in the Catholic-dominated University of Paris, was taught freely at the University of Leiden.

In short, Calvinism helped to create a political atmosphere in which the novel and often troubling ideas of the Enlightenment could survive and see the light as printed books, to be disseminated throughout Europe. Furthermore, it encouraged a practical, rational, critical approach to questions from all facets of life. These characteristics made Calvinism an ally of the Enlightenment, even when enlightened ideas were tearing at the fabric of its religious beliefs.

See also LITERACY; PUBLISHING; SEPARATION OF CHURCH AND STATE; SOCIAL INSTITUTIONS OF THE ENLIGHTENMENT.

Further reading: Catholic University of America, eds., *New Catholic Encyclopedia* (New York: McGraw Hill, 1967–89); *New Schaff-Herzog Encyclopedia of Religious Knowledge,* 13 vols. (New York: Funk and Wagnalls, 1908–14).

Calzabigi, Ranieri Simone Francesco Maria de' (also: Raniero da' Calzabigi) (1714–1795) *Italian poet, librettist, editor, and adventurer*
Ranieri de' Calzabigi was born in Livorno, a city in Tuscany. He lived in PARIS for a few years, jointly operating a lottery with Giovanni CASANOVA. He was eventually expelled from FRANCE for his shady financial dealings. In 1761, he moved to VIENNA, where he worked as a privy councillor in the audit office handling affairs of the UNITED PROVINCES OF THE NETHERLANDS. Casanova left a rather colorful account of Calzabigi that describes his physical disfiguration, keen wit, business acumen, and sharp intelligence.

Calzabigi aligned himself in the Parisian cultural world with Jean-Jacques ROUSSEAU and the ENCYCLOPEDISTS. This placed him squarely on the side of aesthetic reform during the transition years of the mid-18th century. He preferred literary and operatic forms with natural, thoroughly human characters and clean, symmetrical plots, shorn of the complicated structures that had characterized the BAROQUE STYLE and *opera seria*.

Calzabigi wrote librettos for three operas by Christoph Willibald GLUCK: *ORFEO ED EURYDICE* (1762), *Alceste* (1767), and *Paride ed Elena* (1770). The Gluck-Calzabigi operas took Paris by storm, helping to resolve the quarrel between RAMEAU and Rousseau over operatic style, known as the BATTLE OF THE BUFFOONS. While in Paris, Calzabigi also published an edition of librettos by Metastasio.

cameralism Economic theory and associated administrative practices developed by German economists an bureaucrats in the late 17th century. Cameralist theory continued to shape the activities of German and Austrian governments throughout the 18th century. In fact, the tenets of cameralism admirably dovetailed with and even shaped the goals pursued by enlightened rulers such as MARIA THERESA OF AUSTRIA and FREDERICK II (THE GREAT) OF PRUSSIA. The University of HALLE served as a center of cameralist thought. Major cameralists included Johann Justi, Johann Jakob Moser, and the 18th-century Austrian statesman Josef von SONNENFELS.

Cameralism grew out of a conception of society rooted in organic metaphors. Society was depicted as an organism in which all parts, though strongly differentiated, worked harmoniously together. The purpose of the state administration lay in facilitating the harmonious operation of society. The theory assumed that a strong, centralized, and fiscally sound state was necessary as a guarantee of societal harmony. The existence of such a state depended on its having a healthy and productive population. Consequently, the central state was obliged to assume responsibility for the economic welfare of all its population.

By the middle of the 18th century, enlightened cameralist theory also addressed the broad question of policing society. Cameralists assumed that the economic welfare and productivity of society required a morally sound and well-educated (i.e., enlightened) population. Therefore, the state also needed to intervene in order to shape and to protect the moral well-being of its people.

The theoretical tenets of cameralism spawned a wide series of state-directed policies, reforms, and bureaucratic controls. Economic policies resembled those of MERCAN-TILISM in fostering self-sufficiency, protection from outside competition, and the acquisition of precious metals. Education reform received much attention, and many aspects of public and private behavior were regulated and policed. Cameralist policies contributed toward creating the unique social and political forms of the highly centralized German and Hapsburg territories.

Camisards French peasants and artisans from the mountainous Cévennes region, adherents of CALVINISM who engaged in a revolt against the central French authorities. The name *camisard* refers to the white shirts worn as a uniform by these peasants.

The Camisards had been forced to convert to ROMAN CATHOLICISM in 1685, when King LOUIS XIV ordered the revocation of the Edict of Nantes. The Edict of Nantes, a decree dating from 1598, had provided limited toleration for Calvinists in FRANCE. Louis XIV was convinced that the presence of religions other than Roman Catholicism in his kingdom represented a threat to his absolute rule. He therefore determined to make all French people Catholic, by military force if necessary. Heavily armed soldiers (dragoons) were sent into Protestant regions such as the Cévennes to carry out these forced conversions.

Many HUGUENOTS converted to Catholicism, but others fled to the UNITED PROVINCES OF THE NETHERLANDS, to BERLIN and other Protestant regions in the HOLY ROMAN EMPIRE, or to ENGLAND. The culture and economy of the Cévennes region were seriously disrupted by this religious persecution. As early as 1688, certain individuals in the region began speaking in apocalyptic terms about the approaching return of the Messiah and the end of the papacy. There were prophecies, visions, miraculous events, and a growing number of incidences of religious ecstasy, convulsions, and speaking in tongues.

At the same time, the published pastoral letters of the émigré pastor Pierre Jurieu were circulating throughout the region. Jurieu was trying to instigate a revolt by Protestants against the French government. He based his calls for rebellion on Protestant traditions that spoke of government as a social contract between people and ruler and that asserted the right of a people to overthrow any ruler who violated that contract.

The religious frenzy escalated at the turn of the century, and by 1702 a full-fledged revolt had broken out in the region. It was triggered when a man named Abraham Mazel murdered Abbé Du Chayla, a priest who was actively involved in prosecuting people suspected of harboring Huguenot sympathies. The critical phase of the Camisard revolt occurred between 1702 and 1704, but the region remained subject to unrest throughout the first decade of the 18th century.

After the revolt was finally halted by French military forces, many Camisards moved to ENGLAND, where they became known as the French Prophets. In England, they continued to preach about the second coming of Christ and the impending end of the world. They joined with other 18th-century radical religious groups in England, eventually gathering around METHODISM.

The revolt of the Camisards was one of several events—the persecution of the WALDENSIANS, the execution of the Chevalier de la Barre, the hanging of Jean CALAS, and the spectacle of the Jansenist convulsionaries at the Parisian parish church of St. Medard—that helped to shape the critical stance toward RELIGION that characterized the French ENLIGHTENMENT. For many PHILOSOPHES these phenomena served as outstanding examples of the evils wrought upon society by religion. Whether they were criticizing the dogma of Christianity or the intertwined relations between church and state, the philosophes and other critics used the Camisard revolt as an example of the need for reform. They called for TOLERATION rather than for bloodshed and supported a political vision that placed matters of religious faith in the realm of private rather than of public affairs.

See also SEPARATION OF CHURCH AND STATE.

Camper, Pieter (1722–1789) *Dutch anatomist, surgeon, obstetrician, ophthalmologist, and anthropologist*
Camper, the son of a prosperous minister, displayed talents in several areas as a child and received training in the arts, painting, and carpentry as well as academic subjects. He entered the University of Leiden at the age of 12, graduating 12 years later (1746) with degrees in science and MEDICINE. His teachers included Willem Jacob's GRAVESANDE and Pieter van MUSSCHENBROEK.

Camper established himself as a respected scientist of international fame. He was restless, hence he traveled extensively, acquiring a network of acquaintances throughout Europe. Camper changed his official jobs frequently. He worked briefly as a practicing physician, and then in 1749 received a professorship in philosophy at the University of Franeker. He assumed that post in 1751, held it four years, and then moved to the Athenaeum Illustre in AMSTERDAM as professor of anatomy and surgery. By 1758, he was also professor of medicine at the Athenaeum. For two years, beginning in 1761, Camper retired from teaching and wrote in the seclusion of his wife's country estate near Franeker. Then, he accepted a post at Groningen University as professor in anatomy, surgery, theoretical medicine, and botany. He remained at Groningen from 1763 until 1773, when he again retired to his wife's estate.

After the death of his wife in 1776, Camper became active in Dutch politics. He was elected to the States (Estates) of Friesland and was sent to represent that province in the States General at The Hague. Camper was a devoted supporter of the Orangist Party. During the political ferment in the UNITED PROVINCES OF THE NETHERLANDS that marked the last quarter of the 18th century, Camper was subjected to bitter partisan attacks. He died in 1789.

Camper made contributions to the development of comparative anatomy and physical ANTHROPOLOGY during the late ENLIGHTENMENT. He argued about similarities and differences between animals and plants in terms of structural and functional analogies. He also described specific human anatomical structures. His facial angle theory posited that differences between and within species could be determined by measuring the width of an angle formed by drawing one line from the teeth to the opening of the ear and by drawing a second line from the teeth to the most prominent protuberance on the forehead. Smaller angles (more acute) were allegedly associated with more brutish creatures.

Camper was not alone in using characteristics of the skull to determine species. Louis-Jean-Marie DAUBENTON, the powerful Parisian anatomist at the Jardin du Roi, had a similar theory that relied on an angle constructed with the nose as its apex to provide differentiating measurements. The Scottish anatomist John HUNTER developed a theory of skull gradations, and Johann LAVATER used facial angles in his theory of physiognomy. These approaches seemed to their creators to offer not only reliable measurable criteria for distinguishing between species (Daubenton, Hunter, and Camper), but also mechanisms for linking external appearances with internal, hidden qualities (Lavater and Camper).

Camper believed that facial angles varied characteristically within the races of human beings, and his ideas were misinterpreted during the 19th century to support white-supremacist racist ideologies. But Camper actually argued against making strong qualitative distinctions between the races; he was concerned to demonstrate that all human races differ markedly from the apes and orangutans, and so to preserve for humankind the unique status in the world that had been assigned it by Christian theology. Camper believed that a basic EQUALITY underlies all human races, and that the original human couple (Adam and Eve) might have been black.

Camper also discovered the air pockets in the bones of birds, researched hearing in fishes, and investigated sound production in frogs. He studied midwifery in England with William Smellie and later provided the anatomical illustrations for Smellie's book on MIDWIFERY.

Among Camper's writings and orations, the following should be noted: *Demonstrationum anatomico-pathologicarum* (Demonstrations of pathological anatomy; 1761–62); *De analogia inter animalia et stirpes* (On the analogy between animals and plants; 1763); and *De quibusdam oculi partibus* (On some parts of the eye; 1746). Certain works were translated and published in England and Germany during the 18th century. These were: *Sämmtliche kleine Schriften, die Arzney-, Wundarzneykunst und Naturgeschichte betreffend* (Collected short works that link medical arts, healing practices, and natural history; 1784–90); and *The Works of the Late Professor Camper, on the Connexion between the Science of Anatomy and the Arts of Drawing, Painting, Statuary* (1794).

Canaletto (Giovanni Antonio Canal) (1697–1768) *Venetian painter and etcher*

Canaletto was born in VENICE, the son of a theater set painter, Bernardo Canal. After training with his father, young Antonio Canal traveled to ROME in 1719, where he became fascinated with the Dutch paintings of classical ruins. He supported himself by painting OPERA sets but soon turned to producing scenic architectural and LANDSCAPE paintings. Canaletto moved back to Venice, where he supported himself by painting Venetian scenes for the burgeoning tourist trade. Most of his commissions came from English visitors through the auspices of Joseph Smith, a merchant, art collector, and British consul at Venice.

Canaletto visited ENGLAND in 1746 and remained working in that country until 1755. He painted many views of LONDON. The British Crown purchased Smith's impressive collection of Canaletto paintings in 1763. Canaletto returned to Venice in 1755, was elected to the Venetian Academy in 1763, and died in his native city in 1768.

Canaletto used the camera obscura in preparing sketches for his paintings. This device permitted the reflection of large objects to be cast against a surface, where their outlines could be traced. As a result, Canaletto's paintings were nearly photographic, presenting lucid, linear, highly accurate images of Venetian architectural monuments. Canaletto occasionally departed from intense realism to produce impressionistic or fanciful scenes. Besides paintings, he also created a series of 31 plates for etchings. Bernardo BELLOTTO was Canaletto's nephew and pupil. Francesco GUARDI may also have worked briefly in Canaletto's studio.

Canaletto's large opus of paintings included several works entitled *Saint Mark's Square, Saint Mark's Square Seen from an Arcade,* several paintings bearing the title *The Grand Canal,* and *The Feast of the Ascension,* all depicting Venice. London scenes included *Views of Whitehall, The Gardens of Vauxhall,* and *The Badminton Court.*

Candide   Satirical novel by VOLTAIRE. First published in 1759, it appeared simultaneously in the cities of PARIS, GENEVA, and AMSTERDAM. The full title of the book is *Candide ou l'Optimisme* (Candide or optimism). The book enjoyed immediate success, appearing in 20 French editions, two English translations, and one Italian translation in less than a year.

Voltaire began writing *Candide* in 1757 and worked on it continuously through 1758. He used the tale of Candide, the illegitimate nephew of Baron Thunder-ten-tronckh, as a vehicle for ridiculing ideas and institutions he considered barriers to human enlightenment. In particular, he singled out for criticism the philosophies of Gottfried Wilhelm LEIBNIZ and Christian WOLFF, two prominent figures in German intellectual tradition. But he also mocked the JESUITS and the institutions of ROMAN CATHOLICISM. Finally, he questioned the simple faith of the ENLIGHTENMENT in PROGRESS and in the goodness of HUMAN NATURE.

The young boy Candide has been tutored by Doctor Pangloss, a naive proponent of the Wolffian idea that this world is the best of all possible worlds. As a young man, Candide is pressed into military service, but deserts after a brutal campaign. Having sought refuge in Holland, he meets his old tutor Pangloss, who tells him of a series of misfortunes: The family chateau has been destroyed in war, Candide's cousin Cunégonde has been killed, and Pangloss himself has contracted syphilis.

Hearing these stories, Candide resolves to tour the world in search of a perfect place. During the ensuing journey, he encounters many evils perpetrated both by NATURE and by human beings. He experiences an earthquake in Portugal, falls afoul of the Catholic Inquisition, and is forced to flee. Pangloss is not so lucky; he is executed, or so it seems, at the order of the Inquisition. One bright note occurs when Candide discovers Cunégonde, who has miraculously escaped the soldiers who tried to kill her.

Further journeys take Candide to the New World, where he thinks he finds the perfect land, El Dorado. In spite of El Dorado's delights, Candide chooses to leave it, taking with him some of its fabulous wealth. Candide meets the brother of Cunégonde, who is a nobleman and who refuses to give her in marriage on account of Candide's illegitimacy. To defend his honor, Candide kills the brother in a duel.

Back in Europe, Candide experiences more troubles in Paris. He betrays Cunégonde by having an affair with a Parisian noblewoman, then finds himself imprisoned, the victim of a well-executed conspiracy. He loses contact with Cunégonde.

Finally, Candide travels to VENICE in the company of a wise man, Martin, whom he first met on the voyage back to Europe from the New World. In Venice, the pair find not only Cunégonde, but also Pangloss, the young Baron Thunder-ten-Tronchk, and Candide's former valet Cacambo. Candide retires with his friends to a small farm that he has bought with the last of the diamonds taken from El Dorado. He spends the rest of his life not in contemplating the truths of the universe but in pursuing the simple pleasure of cultivating his garden in the company of friends.

The parade of misfortunes encountered by Candide and company offers a glimpse into the major issues that preoccupied Voltaire throughout his life: abuses by the Catholic clergy, religious intolerance, the noble custom of dueling, the treacheries of Parisian society, and the brutality of war. It reflects his newfound pessimism, acquired in the aftermath of experiences such as the LISBON EARTHQUAKE and unpleasant encounters in the BERLIN OF FREDERICK II (THE GREAT). The book is one of the outstanding novels of the Enlightenment, containing within its brilliant, witty pages, impassioned appeals on behalf of TOLERATION, peace, and simple, but nevertheless satisfying, modes of human existence.

See also LITERATURE; OPTIMISM TRAVEL LITERATURE.

Canitz, Friedrich Rudolf Ludwig, baron von (1654–1699) *German poet and diplomat*

Canitz came from a Prussian noble family with a tradition of state service. He studied law and statecraft at the Universities of Leiden and Leipzig. From 1675 to 1677, Canitz went on a GRAND TOUR through ITALY, FRANCE, ENGLAND, and the UNITED PROVINCES OF THE NETHERLANDS. He entered the foreign service of Frederick II, elector of BRANDENBURG, serving as a diplomat in VIENNA and Hamburg.

Canitz wrote poetry and presented it in public readings. His themes and writing style set out an aesthetic that became the common property of 18th-century lyric poetry. Canitz strove to write with simplicity, clarity, and gracefulness. He wrote individualistic satire and burlesque poetry. Canitz's most famous poem is *Klagode über den Tod seiner ersten Gemahlin* (Ode of lament over the death of his first wife; 1700). This poem adopts a Stoic outlook, one that Canitz also used for his religious poetry. A group of his poems were published in 1700 as *Nebenstunden unterschiedener Gedichte.*

Canova, Antonio (1757–1822) *Italian sculptor who produced works in the neoclassical style*

Canova came from a family of stonemasons living near VENICE in the town of Possagno. As a young artist, he established himself in Venice. In 1779, Canova visited ROME, Naples, and the ruins of the ancient cities of Herculaneum and POMPEII, an experience that stimulated his interest in antiquity.

Canova settled in Rome and began producing neoclassical sculptures in 1782. Several important papal commissions followed, including the tombs of Pope CLEMENT XIII and Pope CLEMENT XIV. In 1798, when the upheavals of the FRENCH REVOLUTION reached Rome, Canova moved to VIENNA. In 1802, he accepted an invitation from Napoleon to settle in PARIS. There, he became a court sculptor and exercised significant influence on French artists. He created several sculptures of Napoleon.

When Napoleon fell from power, Canova headed a papal commission whose aim was to recover Italian works of art from the French. As a reward for his work, he received the title marquese of Ischia. The English aided the recovery enterprise, thereby providing Canova with an opportunity to visit Great Britain. Shortly after their arrival in LONDON, he saw the Elgin Marbles, sculptures that had been taken by the English from the Parthenon in Athens. Canova died in Venice in 1822 and was buried at Possagno in a tomb designed to imitate the Pantheon in Rome.

Canova's major works include *Theseus and the Minotaur* (1781–82, his first important neoclassic piece); *Perseus with Medusa's Head* (1801); the *Pugilists* (1802); and the *Venus Victrix* (1805–07), a study of Marie Pauline Borghese, Napoleon's sister.

capitalism An economic system arising in 17th-century Europe; based on the principle of private (as opposed to state) investment in and ownership of the means of production and distribution of goods; characterized by the offer of goods for sale in a free market based upon the voluntary exchange between supplier and purchaser for mutual profit. Capital is accumulated wealth in the form of money ready to be invested, or a stock of consumable goods produced by labor and distributed to potential buyers for the purpose of acquiring profit for reinvestment.

The laws of supply and demand govern exchanges within the market. The law of supply states that the quantity of a good supplied rises as the market price rises and falls as the price falls. The law of demand states that when the price of a good rises, the amount demanded falls, and when the price falls, the amount demanded rises. The markets determine the equilibrium point in pricing, which occurs when the supply of and demand for goods are balanced. The factors employed in production (the availability and cost of raw materials and labor) are paid for with money, which is also accepted in exchange for goods and services. Ideally, capitalism permits the freedom to trade without government-imposed restrictions. To succeed, capitalism requires wide-ranging networks of distribution and production. The rise of capitalism is closely connected to the VOYAGES OF DISCOVERY and COLONIALISM.

Economic Theorists

Developing from MERCANTILISM, capitalism is an ENLIGHTENMENT economic practice peculiar to the West. To Adam SMITH, the mercantilist policies of European states seeking silver and gold and monopolizing colonial trade in the New World unnecessarily destroyed the benefits that

might have accrued to all parties—natives, colonists, and the colonial powers. In the 18th and 19th centuries, economists debated the reasons that "backward countries" or "unimproving nations" were economically stagnant, and many believed that European colonialism in these countries would encourage PROGRESS. Native peoples, including the Irish, were frequently characterized by Enlightenment economists, such as David Ricardo, Jean-Baptiste Say, James Mill, and Thomas MALTHUS, as improvident, lazy, and ignorant and thus unable to profit socially or economically from capitalism. John Stuart MILL established his philosophy of capitalism in *The Principles of Political Economy* (1848) and in other works. Like Malthus, Mill believed that the favorable natural conditions in the "backward" countries eliminated indigenous people's need to labor systematically in order to amass surplus. Like his father, James Mill, Mill also saw that oppressive political institutions in colonial lands—such as India—undermined motivation. Despite obvious injustices of colonialism, most economists considered the European presence a civilizing force in these regions, capable of teaching the "lazy" and "ignorant" natives more productive habits. It is a commonplace of modern capitalist thought that efficiency in production and the consequent increase in wealth worldwide have "trickled down" to benefit all people materially, educationally, and physically in terms of health and longevity. However, in his works *Historical Capitalism* and *Capitalist Civilization,* published together in 1995, the modern historian Immanuel Wallerstein, with the benefit of hindsight, argues that the lives of precapitalist peoples were probably more satisfactory on the whole than the lives of the mass of unprivileged people living in modern capitalist states.

One important 18th-century French theorist was François QUESNAY, founder of physiocracy, who provided a capitalist model for agricultural production in *Le tableau économique* (The economic table; 1758). England's Adam Smith disputed the centrality of agricultural production and provided a model for industrial production in *An Inquiry into the Nature and Causes of the Wealth of Nations* (1776). At this point, the competitive capitalism that characterized the international market from 1700 to 1860 had not yet been defined or named.

The two principal thinkers who identified the components of what is now termed the "classical political economy" were the English philosophers Smith and Ricardo, who positioned their arguments against the feudal policies of the past and the mercantile system of the 17th century. Smith proposed that international commerce could overcome the limitations of the internal market by disposing of surplus production overseas (a surplus facilitated by the use of machinery) and by expanding the use of the division of labor in both manufacturing and distribution. The division of labor in manufacturing was a crucial factor in increasing the speed of

Engraving from the *Universal Magazine,* 1749, representing domestic clothmaking *(Courtesy New York Public Library)*

production and thus overall productivity and profitability, which in turn could expand both domestic and international markets. Smith argued that a capitalist society was divided into three interdependent classes: landowners who lived by rents, workers who lived by wages, and manufacturers who lived by entrepreneurial profit. Ricardo, however, perceived landowners and manufacturers as antagonistic rather than interdependent in *Principles of Political and Economic Taxation* (1817). In *An Essay on the Influence of a Low Price of Corn on the Profits of Stock* (1815), Ricardo argued against increasing the tariff on grain imports because he perceived that tariffs increased rents payable to landowners but decreased the profits of manufacturers. He built a case against protectionism by demonstrating that national laws restricting free trade caused imbalances that interfered with profits and the accumulation of capital. In the case of the Corn Laws of 1815, Ricardo showed that the limited supplies of fertile land for agricultural production and inexpensive

wheat artificially raised the demand for and cost of wheat and stimulated the growth of the population, all to the benefit of the landowner who collected rents and to the detriment of the manufacturer who had to raise wages to cover the workers' increased cost of living.

If Ricardo gave little thought to working people caught between contending landowners and manufacturers, Thomas Malthus identified the poverty of the working class as inevitable. States had always legislated labor control of the poor, for example by condoning or abolishing forms of coerced labor (slavery, public labor obligations, indentured servitude) and controlling the movement of laborers from place to place. With state cooperation, capitalists continued to exploit the working poor. Thus, class struggle was a corollary effect of capitalism.

Capitalism in England

Capitalism flourished in 18th-century ENGLAND by virtue of certain political and economic institutions already in place or in the process of emerging. The accession of WILLIAM III AND MARY II (1689) following the GLORIOUS REVOLUTION and the reestablishment of Parliament as a forceful governmental power required substantial funding. This funding was acquired in the form of loans from wealthy Englishmen, both Whigs and Tories, whose investment in the new regime served to mitigate political discord and buttress the authority of the state. Public credit institutions developed in this period; the Bank of England (a joint-stock company) was established in 1694. Companies chartered by the Crown and regulated by a corporation of merchants trading overseas had long been in existence throughout Europe. But these enterprises, by which both interested merchants and speculators jointly invested in foreign trade, became increasingly common in the 18th century. Most English joint-stock companies chartered by the Crown—for example, the EAST INDIA COMPANY (1600) and the Royal African Company (1672)—were profitable investments. England's SOUTH SEA COMPANY, chartered in 1711 to transport slaves to Spanish America, was initially an attractive speculation. The legal institutions established in England contributed to the maintenance of property rights and the enforcement of contracts underlying public finance, and by 1712 a stock market had emerged to facilitate further investment. When the SOUTH SEA BUBBLE ("bubble" means an inflated speculation) burst in 1720, however, it temporarily discredited investment and ruined the financial market.

Continental Economies

The capitalist economies of other European countries had varying degrees of success depending on the basis of their domestic economies, political structures, and financial and legal systems. Eastern Europe, like the East generally, remained on the periphery of the capitalist core, but its interconnectedness was as essential to capitalism as were colonial networks in that these regions provided raw materials, labor, and markets for manufactures. SPAIN, too, was peripheral in capitalist economics. Until 1765, Cadiz held a monopoly over shipping bound for Spanish America, and this isolation of potential markets in the Spanish colonies restricted trade and the establishment of industry.

THE UNITED PROVINCES OF THE NETHERLANDS, on the other hand, had been a 17th-century pacesetter. It established finance, banking, and insurance long before England. Without significant natural resources, the Dutch became highly urbanized, agriculturally productive, and commercially oriented. Even in the 17th century, AMSTERDAM was a global entrepôt (center of commerce). Despite these advantages, however, the United Provinces, as a federation of autonomous provinces, possessed an unwieldy, decentralized political structure and separate systems of taxation that hampered the establishment of national policies. Additionally, the Dutch never invested in large-scale colonial settlements that might have provided markets to spur 18th-century industrial growth.

FRANCE, too, was militarily strong and wealthy. To all appearances, it had the ability to lead the world's economy: Its tax base was substantial, and LOUIS XIV was an absolutist ruler with the theoretical power to do as he wished. However, wars in Europe and colonialism in the New World and India were costly, France's agricultural economy was unstable, and domestic administrative control was ineffective. Until the emergence of the French Civil Code in 1806, administration involved a patchwork of discrete institutions, and the political and legal systems were applied arbitrarily, often operating at cross-purposes. Local corruption further complicated administration. Moreover, unlike English creditors, who felt relatively safe lending money to the government in order to stabilize financial operations, the French elite were unwilling to invest in capital enterprises that served to subsidize a sovereign who was above the law and fully capable of reneging on his debts.

In sum, the development of 18th-century capitalism was highly dependent on political, legal, and economic institutions, both domestic and international, as well as technological advances in shipping and manufacture. Its early proponents were moral philosophers interested in the effects wealth had on a nation, many of whom were familiar with the practicalities of trade.

See also CHINA; JUSTICE AND THE LAW, POLITICAL THEORY; SCIENTIFIC METHOD; TECHNOLOGY AND INSTRUMENTATION.

Further reading: Fernand Braudel, *Civilization and Capitalism, 15th–18th Century* (Berkeley: University of California Press, 1992); Karl Marx and Friedrich Engels, *The Communist Manifesto* (New York: Verso, 1998).

capital punishment Punishment by execution. The term *capital* derives from the Latin *capitalis*, itself derived from *caput*, meaning "head"; the English concept of capital punishment thus originally referred to the punishment of death by beheading. It is used now to refer to any method of execution used as punishment for a crime. European penal codes all included punishment by death in the 18th century. Some nations reserved this extreme penalty for the most serious of crimes, particularly treason. Others, however, prescribed the death penalty for crimes that today are not even considered breaches of the law. For instance, a person could be put to death for denying certain tenets of Christian doctrine. The SEPARATION OF CHURCH AND STATE had yet to be articulated, and religious TOLERATION was considered a denial of truth. Another type of crime that received capital punishment was violating certain rules about public behavior. In ENGLAND, a man could be put to death for blackening his face as a form of disguise. There was no common viewpoint about the circumstances that properly called for such punishment, nor was there agreement about the mode of execution; beheading, breaking on the wheel, and hanging were all commonly used.

Principles of MORAL PHILOSOPHY, POLITICAL THEORY, PSYCHOLOGY, and JUSTICE AND THE LAW that developed in the ENLIGHTENMENT spawned a powerful, impassioned movement against all forms of the death penalty. The argument against execution was first articulated by the Milanese Cesare BECCARIA in his slim volume *Dei Delitti e delle Pene* (*ESSAY ON CRIMES AND PUNISHMENTS*), published anonymously in Tuscany in 1764.

Beccaria wrote his essay at a time when European states were being faced with the need to reform their legal codes and to restructure their systems for meting out justice to reflect the broader socioeconomic changes of the 18th century. He was neither a philosopher nor an expert on the criminal system in his native MILAN, but he was committed to some of the greatest and most influential principles of the Enlightenment: FREEDOM and EQUALITY, the SOCIAL CONTRACT, and UTILITY. In applying these principles to the task of penal reform, and especially to the matter of capital punishment, he produced an argument against excessive punishment that still resonates today.

Beccaria argued that the death penalty is ineffective as a punishment, even for the most heinous of crimes. Not only is it inhumane, it also fails to meet the criteria of usefulness and necessity, which, he argues, should determine the shape of all interventions against crime. Only these criteria will lead to just punishment. Capital punishment fails to meet these criteria because it effectively allows a convicted criminal to avoid suffering any pain on account of his or her actions. It thus fails to punish adequately, even while it violates all humane principles, and, furthermore, it fails to act as a deterrent to others who might consider such crimes. It is not the intensity or barbarity of a punishment that makes a lasting impression on human minds, but the duration. Thus, depriving a criminal of his or her freedom, for life in the worst cases, is much more effective, for no human being can bear the thought of losing his or her liberty forever.

This argument was rapidly embraced by PHILOSOPHES such as Abbé Morellet, who translated the book in 1766 into French, and Claude-Adrien HELVÉTIUS, Jean Le Rond d'ALEMBERT, the comte de BUFFON, Baron d'HOLBACH, and VOLTAIRE, who read the translation and discussed it in their favorite salons or wrote about it in their own publications. Other consequential figures who adopted his ideas were enlightened heads of state such as FREDERICK II (THE GREAT), MARIA THERESA, her son Leopold, then grand duke of Tuscany, where Beccaria's book first appeared, and CATHERINE II (THE GREAT). Among the English, William BLACKSTONE and Jeremy BENTHAM, the influential theorist of utilitarianism, were particularly influenced, while in the British colonies of North America, John ADAMS used arguments from the book in his defense of the British soldiers accused of murdering colonists in the Boston Massacre of 1770. For a brief time in the latter decades of the 18th century, the death penalty was abolished in several German states and in the Duchy of Milan, but the social and political upheavals of the FRENCH REVOLUTION and the Napoleonic Wars brought its reinstitution throughout Europe until the 20th century, when countries began, one by one, to abolish the practice once again. Today, capital punishment is forbidden in the European Union.

The argument against capital punishment stands today as one of the greatest examples of enlightened ideals and theory applied to the practical problems of civilization, and Beccaria's small book still provides one of the best entry points into the language of the Enlightenment.

Further reading: Cesare Beccaria, *On Crimes and Punishments,* tr. Henry Paolucci (Indianapolis: Bobbs-Merrill, 1963).

Caribbean revolutions *See* GUADELOUPE; HAITIAN REVOLUTION.

Carnot, Lazare (1753–1823) *French revolutionary leader and military engineer*
Lazare Carnot played a key role in securing victory for the revolutionary forces during the FRENCH REVOLUTION. A military engineer, Carnot also wrote extensively on mathematics and military matters.

Carnot was born in Nolay, FRANCE. He attended the school of engineering in Mézières, completing his studies in 1773. While serving in the army as an engineer, he devoted his intellectual energies to the study of mechanics. Carnot completed an essay on friction and power in 1780 and published it three years later. He became a captain in the French army that year and a member of the Dijon Academy in 1787. He was elected to the National Assembly in 1791 and to the National Convention the next year. His abilities as a military strategist brought him victory in northern France in 1793. During the Terror, Carnot was a member of the Committee of Public Safety and was responsible for organizing the revolutionary forces into the 14 armies of the republic.

Carnot escaped the backlash against Maximilien ROBESPIERRE and the other radicals after the Terror, primarily because his military expertise made him indispensable. He was a member of the Directory until the coup of 18 Fructidor (September 1797) forced him into exile in SWITZERLAND and Nuremburg, but he returned the next year and served as war minister under Napoleon Bonaparte in 1800.

Carnot spent the latter part of his life writing treatises on geometry, mathematics, and military strategy. In 1803, he revisited his 1783 essay, and the revised version circulated widely and won its author recognition for his observations concerning what is now recognized as the law of conservation in physics. His most important contribution in the field of military strategy, *De la défense des places fortes* (On the defense of fortifications; 1810), had a lasting influence on warfare in the 19th century. He went into exile after Napoleon's defeat at Waterloo in 1815 (Carnot had been military governor of Antwerp during the Hundred Days), fleeing to Magdeburg, Germany, where he died in 1823.

Further reading: Huntley Dupre, *Lazare Carnot: Republican Patriot* (Philadelphia: Porcupine Press, 1975).

Cartesianism *See* DESCARTES; EPISTEMOLOGY; MECHANICAL PHILOSOPHY; RATIONALISM; SCIENCE; SCIENTIFIC REVOLUTION.

cartography Science of making and revising maps. The creation of maps has been a human pursuit from the earliest civilizations, but it was not until the Renaissance that rigorous standards began to be developed in Europe for such work. The term *cartographia* is first credited to the Portuguese nobleman vicomte de Santarem, who used it in 1839 to describe map analysis. Its use grew rapidly thereafter. Accuracy in mapmaking developed as a result of advances in mathematics during the 17th and 18th centuries that helped to resolve the difficulties of projecting the globular surface of the Earth onto a flat plane. These efforts were also linked to debates in the fields of geography and physics concerning the shape of the Earth and the effect of gravity on the planet.

FRANCE and ENGLAND were major centers of cartographic research and relied on a network of scholars from many countries. In France, Jean Picard and Jean-Dominique Cassini greatly advanced accurate map making. Picard, assigned by the FRENCH ACADEMY OF SCIENCES to assist in the scientific determination of the Earth's size, measured an arc (a portion of a curved line) using wooden rods laid along the road from Fontainebleau to PARIS. Using surveying techniques, he accurately calculated that one degree of the meridian is 110.46 kilometers from the next, thus helping to determine the Earth's circumference.

Cassini immigrated to France from his native ITALY in 1669 after being invited to join the French Academy. An established member of the European scientific community, Cassini was approached by LOUIS XIV's minister of finance, Jean-Baptiste Colbert, to help accurately map France as an aid to its economic development. A reliable map of the nation was seen as important for several reasons: to maintain military security, to facilitate commerce among the French provinces, and to manage the land more successfully. Cassini accepted French citizenship in 1673 and would build upon Picard's work.

The project of a national map of France became linked to a larger effort to determine the shape of the Earth. Picard's later efforts with Cassini's son Jacques in 1720 extended the meridian's calculation through Paris. It was necessary to make calculations over larger distances in order to draw firm conclusions as to the shape of the Earth, which Picard and Cassini determined to be ellipsoidal. Englishman Isaac NEWTON built upon this research when he challenged their conclusion that the Earth was elongated at the poles, asserting that centrifugal force would actually flatten its surface there, as later surveys by members of the French Academy in Lapland and Peru bore out by 1738. Newton's and Gottfried LEIBNIZ's simultaneous development of calculus provided the means for cartography's next evolutionary step. Englishman J. H. Lambert's application of this mathematical field to map creation in 1772 enabled him to create more accurate projections of the Earth's surface.

It was the grandson of Jean-Dominique Cassini, known as Cassini III, who finally met the long-sought goal of establishing a detailed map of France. Building on the work of his father and grandfather, and with the help of hundreds of military surveyors, he published the first pages of this map in 1756. It was not completed until the early 19th century, after Cassini's death.

Interest in mapmaking was also stimulated at this time by the colonial interests of many European nations. One of the best cartographers in France, J.-B. Bourguignon d'Anville, never traveled abroad, but relied on voyagers' accounts and other maps to construct a map of the world in 1761. Although there remained many unknowns on his map, he attempted to reflect as accurately as possible the most recent explorations of territories in the New World. Better navigation techniques also resulted in more accurate maps. The 18th century saw the resolution of a problem that had plagued navigation for centuries: the correct measurement of degrees of LONGITUDE at sea. In 1735, John HARRISON built what Isaac Newton proposed in 1714 as a solution to this problem: a seaworthy and consistently accurate chronometer that allowed sailors to determine their position by comparing local time with that of the prime meridian.

See also MATHEMATICS AND MECHANICS; TECHNOLOGY AND INSTRUMENTATION.

Further reading: Phillip Allen, *The Atlas of Atlases: The Map Maker's Vision of the World* (London: Marshall, 1997); Edward H. Dahl, Jean-François Gauvin, et al., *Sphaerae Mundi: Early Globes at the Stewart Museum* (Sillery, Que.: Septentrion, 2000); John P. Snyder, *Flattening the Earth: Two Thousand Years of Map Projections* (Chicago: University of Chicago Press, 1993); John Noble Wilford, *The Mapmakers* (New York: Alfred A. Knopf, 2000); David Woodward, ed., *Five Centuries of Map Printing* (Chicago: University of Chicago Press, 1975).

Cartwright, Edmund (1743–1823) *English inventor and clergyman*
The son of an English gentryman, Cartwright graduated from Oxford University and entered the Anglican clergy; he served in a country parish. After a visit to a power spinning mill in 1784, Cartwright decided to create a

machine-driven loom for weaving. Between 1785 and 1787, he invented the first POWER LOOM. He built a weaving mill in 1787, and in 1789 created a combing machine for wool. Cartwright later patented an alcohol engine.

The power loom, however revolutionary in the long term, did not immediately replace hand weavers. The loom had certain mechanical difficulties that caused thread breakage.

Cartwright went bankrupt in 1793, but revived his business activities. By 1809, he was honored by the English Parliament with a monetary award of £10,000.

Casanova, Giovanni Giacomo (1725–1798) *Venetian adventurer, priest, diplomat, spy, and writer*

The son of a Venetian actor, Casanova began his career of scandalous behavior as a young man when he was thrown out of the seminary of St. Cyprian. He embarked on a career as a violinist in VIENNA and began traveling in the service of a Roman Catholic cardinal. He joined the FREEMASONS in 1750 during a trip to Lyons, FRANCE.

In 1755, Casanova was accused in VENICE of being a magician, arrested, and imprisoned in the Doge's Palace. He managed to escape in 1756, fled to PARIS, and established himself there as a financial wizard and speculator. He became the director of the state lotteries in Paris. However, he accumulated many debts and in 1760 had to flee. Under the name of Chevalier de Seingalt, he traveled throughout Europe visiting SWITZERLAND, southern GERMANY, SAVOY, ROME, Florence, BERLIN, and LONDON. Further sojourns in Russia and Scandinavia produced more scandals and flights. The Venetian government allowed him to return home from 1774 to 1782, but he spent his last years (1785–98) in Bohemia in the service of Count von Waldstein.

Casanova possessed a charismatic personality that charmed the gullible members of aristocratic and upper-middle-class society, even impressing leaders such as FREDERICK II (THE GREAT). Casanova served in Venice (1774–82) as a spy for the Venetian inquisitors.

Casanova left an autobiography entitled *Mémoires de J. Casanova de Seingalt*, first published from 1826 to 1838, and republished in a complete edition as *Histoire de ma vie* (History of my life) between 1960 and 1962. These volumes provide rich and colorful descriptions of 18th-century cities, towns, and social gatherings. Their presentation of the author's escapades, while undoubtedly exaggerated, reveals him to have belonged in that group of colorful charlatans and adventurers who traveled across Europe during the closing years of the ENLIGHTENMENT.

Cassini de Thury, César-François (Cassini III) (1714–1784) *French astronomer and cartographer*

Cassini III was the son of the prominent astronomer Jacques Cassini (Cassini II). The Cassinis lived in the Paris observatory.

Cassini de Thury assisted his father in making the measurements that determined the shape of the Earth. A dispute had arisen between followers of Newtonian physics and those still loyal to Cartesian ideas. Cartesians, including Cassini II, claimed that the Earth must be elongated at the poles, whereas Newtonians, such as Pierre-Louis MAUPERTUIS, Alexis-Claude CLAIRAUT, and John DESAGULIERS, insisted that the rotation of the Earth must result in a flattening of its spherical shape at the poles. The question derived from the different theories of physics spelled out by René DESCARTES and Isaac NEWTON. Ultimately, the debate about the shape of the Earth was resolved in favor of the Newtonian position. The research findings provided a proof of the validity of the Newtonian theory of universal gravitation. In the course of the research, Cassini III abandoned the Cartesian position of his father and espoused the Newtonian vision.

Cassini III contributed to the production of the first modern map of France. He developed a method of triangulation and trained various specialists to carry out the actual measurements. The map was produced with both royal and private funds. The project was completed by Cassini III's son, Jacques-Dominique de Cassini (Cassini IV) after the death of his father in 1784. The map was published in 1793.

See also CARTOGRAPHY.

Catherine II (the Great) (1729–1796) *German princess and Russian empress; wife and second cousin of Czar Peter III of Russia*

Peter III was the grandson of PETER I (THE GREAT). In 1762, Catherine usurped the Russian throne from her husband by means of a palace coup d'etat in which she had him assassinated. She ruled Russia as czarina (empress) from 1762 to 1796. Catherine's activities during the early years of her reign marked her as one of the enlightened despots of the 18th century.

Catherine the Great was born Sophie Friederike Auguste von Anhalt-Zerbst. Her father was a minor German prince, Christian Anhalt-Zerbst, who stemmed from an impoverished junior branch of the ruling family of Anhalt. Christian had entered the service of FREDERICK II (THE GREAT) OF PRUSSIA. He had married Johanna Elizabeth of Holstein-Gottorp, whose family had ties by marriage with the ruling dynasties in both SWEDEN and Russia. Their daughter Sophie received a simple upbringing under the tutelage of a French Huguenot named Babette Cardel. Through this governess, the intelligent young Sophie learned the manners, language, and graces of French culture, but seems to have cared more for vigorous tomboyish play than for those activities normally assigned to young girls.

Sophie's mother took her to Russia in 1744 with hopes of securing a marriage alliance between Sophie and the heir to the Russian throne, Peter. The plan succeeded. The young Sophie made a public conversion to Russian Orthodoxy, and under her new name, Catherine (Yekaterina) Alekseyevna, she began her life in Russia. The marriage in 1745 between Catherine and Peter began badly and deteriorated. Both spouses took lovers, Catherine, most notably, with the elegant and intelligent Polish count Stanislaus Augustus PONIATOWSKI. As a young and unhappy wife, she began to pursue her intellectual interests. The works of VOLTAIRE, MONTESQUIEU, Pierre BAYLE, the PHYSIOCRATS, and the volumes of the great French *ENCYCLOPÉDIE* became her companions. Montesquieu, in particular, would guide her thinking about political reform in Russia.

Peter did not inherit the Russian throne as Peter III until December 25, 1761. He ruled for just six months. Catherine aspired to the throne and with the support of Russian troops had herself proclaimed empress. Peter III was forced to abdicate and was placed under arrest. On the morning of July 9, 1762, he was murdered with Catherine's connivance.

Catherine set out immediately to consolidate her shaky hold on power and to continue the great Westernizing process begun by Peter the Great. For assistance in her tasks, she set up a series of official commissions to review policies toward the church and the military. Then, in 1767, she assembled the Legislative Commission, a group whose members supplied her with information about the conditions of the country and thus helped her to assess the extent of possible reform. Subsequently, she initiated decrees that provided some legal codifications, restrictions on the worst forms of torture, and a degree of religious TOLERATION.

In 1773, the great Pugachev rebellion broke out in Russia's Ural region and rapidly spread into both the southeastern provinces and central Russia. This was a large and violent mass uprising of Cossacks, serfs, and workers in mines and factories, one of the worst rebellions that occurred anywhere in 18th-century Europe. Catherine responded to the crisis with severe repression. She began to see the noble landlords as allies in maintaining central state control. This shift in her thinking resulted in the famous 1785 decree (*ukaz*) called the Charter of the Nobility. Its terms granted to the Russian nobility the privileged status that was enjoyed by the nobility of European countries. The charter contained the following provisions: Nobles were relieved from the compulsory military and state service imposed on them by Peter the Great; they were guaranteed hereditary noble status; they received certain legal and fiscal immunities such as exemption from personal taxation and corporal punishment; they were granted economic privileges; and finally, they were given the right to meet together in provincial assemblies. In short, Catherine, much like Frederick the Great, struck a bargain with her nobles in

Portrait of Catherine the Great of Russia. An enlightened absolute ruler, Catherine II attempted during the early years of her reign to introduce certain important reforms into Russian political, social, and intellectual institutions. *(Courtesy Hillwood Museum, Washington, D.C.)*

return for their support of her rule. With this charter she transformed the Russian nobility into a Western-style aristocracy and laid the grounds for the later claims by the nobility to greater political rights. But Catherine herself ruled throughout her life, to the extent it was possible, as an absolute monarch.

Catherine the Great pursued foreign policies that profoundly affected the European political landscape. Her territorial acquisitions created an expanded Russian Empire that stretched south all the way to the shores of the Black Sea and west to the boundaries of ethnic POLAND. In the west, Catherine, in conjunction with AUSTRIA and PRUSSIA, shocked European sensibilities with the three partitions of Poland that dramatically altered the European balance of power.

Eighteenth-century Russian high culture borrowed much from the ENLIGHTENMENT in western Europe, and Catherine actively encouraged the dissemination of Western ideas into Russia. She herself read the works of the French, German, and English Enlightenment avidly. The theoretical background for many of her reforms can be found in the *Encyclopédie,* in the writings and practices of German CAMERALISM, and in the treatises of Sir William BLACKSTONE, Montesquieu, and the Physiocrats. Catherine maintained a long-term correspondence with both Voltaire and Melchior GRIMM. Efforts in 1762 to woo Jean Le Rond d'ALEMBERT to Russia as the tutor for her son failed, but she corresponded with him until 1772. Catherine purchased Denis DIDEROT's library in order to help him raise a dowry for his daughter, provided him with a substantial annual pension, and invited him to visit Russia. Diderot accepted the offer in 1773, and spent six months (October 1773–March 1774) in SAINT PETERSBURG meeting several times weekly in private sessions with the empress. Diderot praised Catherine highly, calling her the "Semiramis of the North." Catherine admired Diderot but rejected most of his reform suggestions as unrealistic.

Catherine encouraged the translation of important 18th-century European works into Russian; although she kept watch over the press, she did not establish any rigid censorship. She reformed the Russian educational system by closing the private schools and setting up a new group of national, public teaching institutions. In 1764, she founded the first school in Russia for girls, the famous Smol'ney Institute for Noble Girls. She then created the Novodevich'ye Institute for Girls of the Third Estate (bourgeoisie) and reformed the military program at the Army Cadet Corps. Catherine followed the ideas and activities of the German pedagogue Johann Basedow with great interest. She invited Christian Heinrich Wocke, one of Basedow's disciples, to Saint Petersburg to set up a school (called a *philanthropin*) on Basedow's model.

However genuine her enthusiasm for the Enlightenment, Catherine balked at its more radical manifestations. For example, the FREEMASONS and ROSICRUCIANS were flourishing in Russian cities. Their members controlled the Moscow University Press under whose auspices books of the rational Enlightenment were published, along with mystical and occult works. Catherine, at first amused by the Freemasons, later grew to despise them. But they remained in Russia and would play a critical role in the formation of the early 19th-century revolutionary intelligentsia.

Finally, Catherine provided substantial support for ART, THEATER, architecture, and MUSIC. She collected a large number of outstanding European paintings, laying the foundation for the magnificent collections of the modern Hermitage. Among the private collections that came to Russia through her purchases were those of the duc de CHOISEUL and Sir Robert WALPOLE. Catherine sponsored numerous theatrical productions and even tried her hand at writing plays. She commissioned the construction of the lovely PALLADIAN-STYLE Hermitage theater, where she had her own dramatic creations performed. In 1762, she set up a commission on building that supervised public building in Saint Petersburg and MOSCOW. Substantial private construction also occurred as the nobility rushed to provide itself with palaces in the style of the European aristocracy.

Like most absolute and enlightened rulers, Catherine recognized the role that the arts could play in supporting centralized government policies. She organized *fêtes* and theatrical events with an eye toward underscoring her political power. Perhaps the most famous example of this use of spectacle took place in the winter of 1787, when Catherine arranged to have JOSEPH II of Austria, King Stanislaus II Poniatowski of Poland, and emissaries from all the major European capitals escorted on a GRAND TOUR through her newly acquired southern lands. The aim was to impress the visitors with the colonization and building achievements that Potemkin, her former lover and lifelong companion, had accomplished as governor of the new region. The achievements were significant and duly noted by Catherine's illustrious visitors, but the propagandistic nature of the spectacles arranged along the tour route was all too transparent. Furthermore, some of the new villages were not even completed. The prince de Ligne, one of Catherine's guests on the tour, quipped about the unreality of the claimed achievements and referred sarcastically to "Potemkin's villages." The phrase even now is used to refer to overblown, unrealistic claims of achievement. The theatrical element of the planned political spectacle, in this instance overdone, had backfired, creating a tradition of ridicule.

Catherine lived to witness the most violent periods of the FRENCH REVOLUTION and to see aspects of the revolutionary political message being spread by force throughout Europe. She, like many of her contemporaries, reacted with dismay and in the 1790s began to instigate repressive measures designed to counterbalance any radical influences. She instituted strict censorship of the press in 1793, began arresting political dissidents and writers, and even publicly condemned the Enlightenment. Alexander Radischev was arrested, imprisoned in the Peter and Paul Fortress, tried, and sentenced to death for having written and published *A Journey from St. Petersburg to Moscow* (1790), a work critical of Russian serfdom. The repression instituted by Catherine helped to bring about a rupture and estrangement between the government and the intelligentsia that colored the subsequent development of the 19th-century revolutionary movements in Russia.

Further reading: Geoffrey Brunn, *The Enlightened Despots,* 2nd ed. (New York: Holt, Rinehart and Winston, 1967); Aleksandr B. Kamenskii, *Russian Empire in the Eighteenth Century: Searching for a Place in the World,* tr. David Griffiths (Armonk, N.Y., M. E. Sharpe, 1997); Isabel de Madariaga, *Catherine the Great: A Short History* (New Haven, Conn.: Yale University Press, 1993); Marc Raeff, *The Well-Ordered Police State: Social and Institutional Change Through Law in the Germanies and Russia, 1600–1800* (New Haven, Conn: Yale University Press, 1984).

Cavendish, Henry (1731–1810) *English natural philosopher*

Cavendish demonstrated outstanding skill at formulating experiments. His inspiration derived from the scientific philosophy and methodology of Isaac NEWTON.

Henry Cavendish was born in Nice, FRANCE, of aristocratic English parents. Cavendish's father, Lord Charles Cavendish, was a distinguished scientific experimenter and member of the ROYAL SOCIETY OF LONDON. Henry Cavendish studied at Cambridge University but did not receive a degree. Because of his familial wealth, he never formally prepared for a profession but rather pursued his scientific interests throughout his life. In this life course, he was encouraged and assisted by his father.

Cavendish carried out numerous careful experimental inquiries in fields ranging from chemistry through electricity, mechanics, magnetism, optics, geology, and industrial sciences. He published only a fraction of his findings and is most renowned for his studies on gas chemistry, electrical theory, and changes in physical states (freezing points). The gas studies of 1766, for which Cavendish won the Royal Society's Copley Medal, suggested that more than one air (gas) exists in nature. In 1784, Cavendish reported on an experiment in which he had created water from a synthesis of inflammable air (hydrogen) and dephlogiscated air (oxygen). As a committed believer in the PHLOGISTON THEORY, he concluded that inflammable air was really phlogiston united with water, while dephlogiscated air was water deprived of phlogiston. The experiment had been performed previously by Joseph PRIESTLEY and a collaborator, but the pair had not recognized that the dew produced when the two airs (gases) were subjected to electrical activity was actually common water. Cavendish's findings from both sets of gas experiments helped to provide the data on which Antoine LAVOISIER built the subsequent CHEMICAL REVOLUTION.

Cavendish is also noted for his development of a single-fluid theory of electricity that allowed him to quantify electrical force, and for his determination of the density of the Earth (1798). In general, Cavendish stood as an outstanding 18th-century representative of the blending of experiment and mathematics that underlay Newtonian science.

See also MATHEMATICS AND MECHANICS; SCIENCE.

Caylus, Anne-Claude-Philippe de Tubières de Grimoard de Pestel de Levis, comte de (1692–1765) *French aristocrat, amateur antiquarian, painter, engraver, and writer*

Comte de Caylus was the son of Jean-Anne, comte de Caylus, and of Marthe-Marguerite Le Valois, marquise de La Villette. His mother was the niece of Madame de Maintenon, morganatic wife of LOUIS XIV during the last 20 years of his reign. Caylus's father was a soldier who was unwelcome at court because of his alcohol-induced rude manners. Anne-Claude became a soldier at the age of 17 and served in the War of the Spanish Succession, but dropped that profession to pursue his interests in antiquities, art, and literature. He traveled to ITALY, Asia Minor, the AUSTRIAN NETHERLANDS, and ENGLAND as a young man. In Asia Minor he searched unsuccessfully for the ruins of the ancient city of Troy.

At the end of these travels, Caylus settled in PARIS and remained there for the rest of his life. He lived for some time with his mother at her house near the Luxembourg Palace and frequented the salons of Mademoiselle Quinault-Dufresne and Madame GEOFFRIN.

Caylus produced hundreds of engraved reproductions of works by Peter Paul Rubens, Leonardo da Vinci, Anthony Van Dyck, the Carracci brothers, Parmigianino (Girolamo Francesco Mazzola), Raphael, and Antoine WATTEAU. In 1731, the Académie Royale de Peinture et Sculpture rewarded him for this work with an honorary membership. The Académie des Inscriptions et Belles-lettres elected him to its membership in 1742.

Caylus developed considerable power within the academies. Because he was an amateur, his colleagues often resented his influential position. Caylus fostered the career of the artist Vien, who in turn inspired Jacques Louis DAVID and the French school of neoclassical painters.

Caylus published several books under his own name, but doubts exist about their originality. One work, *L'histoire de M. Guilleaume, cocher* (The story of Mr. Guilleaume, coachman), is considered his authentic work; it offers rich details about the life of ordinary Parisians. His seven-volume compendium, *Recueil d'antiquités égyptiennes, étrusques, grecques, romaines et gauloises* (Collection of Egyptian, Etruscan, Greek, Roman, and Gallic antiquities; 1752–67), provides valuable descriptive information. The ENCYCLOPEDISTS, especially Denis DIDEROT, disliked Caylus intensely. They considered his antiquarian interests rather useless and generally disparaged him as an amateur. Their assessment illustrates their intolerance for older forms of descriptive, detailed knowledge based on copious memorization. The new, enlightened thinker paid little concern to systematic, detailed knowledge, but aimed rather to create generalizations and insights based on common sense analyses and first-hand observations.

See also NEOCLASSICISM.

censorship *See* ANCIEN REGIME; PORNOGRAPHY; PUBLISHING; SEPARATION OF CHURCH AND STATE.

ceramic arts Decorative art form that became a popular medium for the expression of the ROCOCO aesthetic. Fired earthenware ceramics have been produced since ancient times throughout the world. In Europe, at the dawn of the 18th century, glazed pottery called majolica was produced in nearly every nation. Europeans knew and loved the fine, hard porcelains that came from CHINA, but they were unable to produce copies. The Chinese fiercely guarded the secret of the chemical composition of their fine porcelains.

In the first decade of the 18th century, the Saxon alchemist Johann Friedrich BÖTTGER finally unraveled the chemical recipe. Using the kaolin clay found in Saxony, he created the first European porcelains for Augustus the Strong, elector of Saxony and king of POLAND. In 1710, Augustus established the first European hard porcelain works at Meissen, with Böttger as its head. The MEISSEN WORKS product dominated European markets throughout the first half of the 18th century.

Rival manufacturers appeared as European princes began to view the possession of such a factory as a form of symbolic status. In 1718, the first competitor appeared at VIENNA; VENICE followed in 1720, Florence in 1735, and Naples in 1743. Soon every major European capital possessed a porcelain manufactory.

The French lagged somewhat. They already had a strong tradition of soft porcelain production, especially at the Vincennes Manufacture Royale established in 1738. This factory moved to SÈVRES in 1758, but it was not until 1768, when a source of kaolin clay was found near Saint-Yrieux, that the Sèvres porcelains began to appear. Madame de POMPADOUR, official mistress of King LOUIS XV, played a central role in the development of the Sèvres works, helping with financial patronage and influencing the style of the Sèvres products. French rococo Sèvres creations soon replaced Meissen porcelains as prized objects in the European market.

The Sèvres dominance disappeared only with the advent of the neoclassical style toward the end of the 18th century. If any producer dominated that later period, it was the Englishman Josiah WEDGWOOD. At his ETRURIA WORKS, Wedgwood produced ivory creamware and colored jasperware with neoclassical lines and decorative motifs. With the close of the 18th century and the onset of the FRENCH REVOLUTION, the era of porcelain ceramics' popularity in Europe ended, although production has continued to the present day.

Ceramic arts became fashionable during the era of the rococo, in part because they could be easily and beautifully adapted to the intimate interiors, refined but sensual tastes, and intense love of decoration characteristic of the rococo aesthetic. Factories produced delicate, intricate groups of figures; single figurines; porcelain representations of natural objects; standard dinnerware settings; and some ornate, highly fanciful decorative table pieces. Meissen styles differed somewhat from those of Sèvres. The Meissen pieces were heavier, darker in color, and more ornate than the later Sèvres pieces. The neoclassic designs of Wedgwood exhibited simple, geometric lines.

Chamfort, Sébastien-Roch-Nicholas (1741–1794) French writer

Chamfort took minor orders in the Catholic Church but never pursued a clerical career. Instead, Chamfort turned to LITERATURE, writing comedies, poems, essays, and journalistic essays. The French Academy awarded him a prize in 1769 for his *Éloge de Molière* (Eulogy of Molière). He was accepted as a member of the academy in 1781. He received income not only from his publications, but also from various secretarial posts in the royal household.

Chamfort was especially noted for his brilliant, biting wit. He regularly attended the salon of Madame HELVÉTIUS, a gathering place for the radical, enlightened PHILOSOPHES of PARIS.

At the beginning of the FRENCH REVOLUTION, Chamfort aligned himself openly with the moderate revolutionaries Honoré Gabriel Riqueti, comte de Mirabeau and Charles Maurice Talleyrand-Pengord, but he also flirted with more radical positions, attending the meetings of the Jacobin Club and serving as the club secretary. He collaborated on revolutionary journals, prepared the *Tableaux de la Révolution* (Tables of the Revolution), and served from 1792 as director of the Bibliothèque Nationale. Chamfort's politics always remained moderate, and during the Terror, the ruling Committee of Public Safety placed him under surveillance. The experience caused Chamfort to attempt suicide. He died after surgical intervention failed to reverse the self-inflicted wounds.

Chamfort's literary work includes *La jeune indienne* (The young Indian; 1764), a comedy produced at the Théâtre-Français; *Épitre d'un père à son fils sur la naissance d'un petits-fils* (Letter of a father to his son on the birth of a grandson; 1764); *La grandeur de l'homme* (The greatness of man; 1767), a series of odes; and the tragedy *Mustapha et Zéangir* (Mustapha and Zeangir; 1776). He wrote two prize-winning eulogies: *Éloge de Molière* (Eulogy of Molière) and *Éloge de La Fontaine* (Eulogy of La Fontaine). His famous work *Pensées, maximes et anecdotes* (Thoughts, maxims, and anecdotes), was published in 1795, the year after his death.

Chardin, Jean-Baptiste-Siméon (1699–1779) French painter

Chardin painted primarily still-life scenes of humble objects used in the daily lives of middle-class people. He was a dedicated realist, reproducing in exquisite detail the forms he chose as objects. He had a keen eye able to discern the visual composition and attributes of an inanimate object. As a portrait painter, he was less successful and produced only a few such paintings. Denis DIDEROT esteemed Chardin highly for his approach to art and for his choice of subjects.

Chardin was the son of a Parisian carpenter and master cabinetmaker, Jean Chardin, whose primary job was to keep the king supplied with billiard tables. His mother was Jeanne-Françoise-David Chardin. Chardin had two brothers and two sisters. The family lived in modest circumstances.

Chardin studied painting technique in the studios of Pierre-Jacques Cazes, Noël-Nicolas Coypel, and Jean-

Baptiste Van Loo. Next, Chardin enrolled at the Académie de St.-Luc. He showed some paintings in 1728 at a student exhibition. Since they were well received, Chardin decided to try to gain entrance to the Académie Royale de Peinture (Royal Academy of Painting). He set up his canvases in the courtyard of the academy just before a session was to begin. The various academy members noted the quality of his work and decided to admit him that very day. They accepted two paintings, *La Raie* (The Skate) and *Le Buffet* (The Buffet) as his admission pieces.

Chardin showed paintings annually at the Salon Carré exhibitions in the Louvre. He received commissions from CATHERINE II (THE GREAT) of Russia, the prince of Liechtenstein, and other foreigners. He obtained a decent royal pension through the patronage of the marquis de Marigny, brother of Madame de POMPADOUR. Chardin became treasurer of the Royal Academy of Painting in 1755 and held that post until illness forced him to resign in 1774. He spent his last few years in severe pain due to kidney disease. Ultimately, in 1779, the loss of kidney function brought about his death.

Chardin left many fine still-life paintings that demonstrate a masterful understanding of the effects of light. Among the most notable are *La table de cuisine* (Kitchen still-life); *Bocal d'olives* (Glass jar of olives); *Le gobelet d'argent* (Silver goblet); *Le singe peintre* (The painter monkey); *Le singe antiquaire* (The antiquarian monkey); *Le panier de pêche* (Basket of peaches); and *Le lapin* (The rabbit). The painting commissioned by Catherine the Great, *Les attributs des arts et les recompenses qui leur sont accordées* (The attributes of the arts and their rewards), hangs in the Hermitage Museum in the Winter Palace at SAINT PETERSBURG. Also notable are Chardin's many scenes of family life, examples of which are *Mère laborieuse* (The hard-working mother); *Le negligé ou la toilette du matin* (The negligé or morning dressing); and *Le Bénédicité* (Grace).

Chardin married twice. His first wife, Marguerite Saintard, died as a young woman. His second wife, Françoise-Marguerite Pouget, occasionally served as his model. Only one son survived to adulthood, and he died before his father.

Charles III of Spain (Spanish: Carlos III) (1716–1788)
king of Spain from 1759 to 1788
Charles III was the son of King Philip V (Felipe V) and Isabella Farnese of Parma, Philip's second wife. He was the great-grandson of King LOUIS XIV of FRANCE. Charles III became king of Naples and Sicily (the KINGDOM OF THE TWO SICILIES) in 1734.

In Naples, Charles benefited from the advice of an energetic lawyer, Bernardo, marchese TANUCCI. The two men instituted a series of reforms aimed at consolidating the control of the Crown over Naples and Sicily. The reforms curbed the feudal privileges of the Neapolitan nobles, attacked the privileges of the entrenched Catholic Church, and imposed judicial, administrative, and fiscal changes. Charles III encouraged a revival of the sciences and provided significant patronage to the arts. Under his rule, Naples became the center of a notable southern Italian ENLIGHTENMENT, producing individuals such as Ferdinando GALIANI and Antonio GENOVESI. The university at Naples flourished, and the conservatory of music provided musical training rivaled only in VENICE.

In 1759, Philip V died and Charles inherited the Spanish throne. As a result, Charles ceded Naples and Sicily to his third son, Ferdinand, and moved to MADRID. Tanucci, his trusted minister, remained in Naples to assist Ferdinand.

Charles is considered the greatest of the Spanish Bourbon kings. He pursued policies characteristic of enlightened despotism (see DESPOTISM, ENLIGHTENED), although they were stimulated more by practical concerns than by any commitment to ideals associated with the Enlightenment. Hence, the desire to increase Spain's military strength, to enhance the prosperity of his subjects, and to centralize his control over institutions such as the Catholic Church and the nobility provided the driving force behind Charles's actions. Comparison with the policies of FREDERICK II (THE GREAT), MARIA THERESA, JOSEPH II, or CATHERINE II (THE GREAT) reveals broad similarities, but conditions in the vastly differing lands governed by these sovereigns ensured that the results would differ widely.

Charles III's early reforms were intensely unpopular. When, in 1766, he decreed that certain traditional clothing could no longer be worn in public, a revolt broke out, the Hat and Cloak Riots. Charles fled Madrid by night to avoid being attacked by the angry mobs. He considered moving his capital from Madrid to Seville but ultimately decided against it. By the end of 1766, he was back in Madrid. Charles expelled the JESUITS from Spain and its colonies in 1767, confiscating their lands and other possessions. Some of the income from confiscated lands went to support schools, hospitals, and orphanages. The departure of the Jesuits left the Spanish educational system without teachers. Charles took advantage of the situation by instituting a series of curriculum reforms in the former Jesuit universities that introduced instruction in modern mathematics and the sciences.

Charles instituted a series of economic reforms aimed at limiting internal controls on trade, removing legal stigmas associated with the practice of certain skilled crafts, and establishing government-sponsored manufacturing enterprises. He tried to improve commerce by building roads and canals. He also set up a postal system and a national standard of weights and measures, opened up Spanish colonial ports to free trade, and instituted a program of ambitious reforms in Spain's American colonies.

The extent of reform and change was great, but it nevertheless was limited by several factors. In particular, the Spanish aristocracy retained its economic strength. Noble lands remained free from taxation, even though higher taxes were needed to pay for reform programs. Industry continued to be weak in spite of government interventions to stimulate growth. Ultimately, Spanish reformers began to lose faith in the ability of an enlightened despot to make effective, substantive change. That conviction was sharpened with the accession of Charles IV, Charles III's rather ineffective son. Spain began to experience the ferment that marked political life throughout Europe at the end of the 18th century.

Charles III was a concerned, astute ruler. He lived a simple, unostentatious life, indulging himself only by hunting. He was an active patron of the arts. He brought the painters Francisco de GOYA, Giovanni Battista TIEPOLO, and Anton MENGS to his court and financed a beautification program in Madrid.

Châtelet, Gabrielle-Émilie Le Tonnelier de Breteuil, marquise du (marquise du Châtelet-Lomont)

(1706–1749) *French writer, specializing in commentary on the science of Isaac Newton and Gottfried Wilhelm Leibniz*

Madame du Châtelet was the daughter of a noble official in the royal household. She received a literary, scientific, and musical education somewhat unusual for her era. Her marriage in 1725 to Florent-Claude, marquis du Châtelet, was merely formal after the first few years. The marquis, a military man and royal governor, visited his wife sporadically.

Madame du Châtelet settled in PARIS in 1730, where she participated vigorously in the life of the enlightened salons. After she met VOLTAIRE in 1733, she became his lover for many years and remained his lifelong friend even after their passion waned. She also befriended Alexis-Claude CLAIRAUT and Pierre-Louis Moreau de MAUPERTUIS, both, like Voltaire, champions of Isaac NEWTON's science. She began studying Newtonian ideas with Clairaut and Maupertuis.

In 1734, when Voltaire was facing arrest for the publication of his *Lettres philosophiques* (Philosophical letters), Madame du Châtelet arranged to shelter him at her estate of Cirey. At Cirey, Madame du Châtelet and Voltaire began a collaborative project designed to introduce the French public to the NATURAL PHILOSOPHY of Isaac Newton. They were inspired by the example of their guest Francesco ALGAROTTI, who was preparing a popularization of Newton's optics. They published the *Éléments de la philosophie de Newton* (Elements of the philosophy of Newton) in 1738 under Voltaire's name.

Madame du Châtelet had immersed herself in Newtonian science during this project and had begun preparing an independent book on physics. She studied not only Newtonian ideas but also the rival theories of Gottfried Wilhelm LEIBNIZ.

When Madame du Châtelet published her *Institutions de physique* (Institutions of physics) in 1740, she

Engraving of the marquise du Châtelet. Gabrielle-Émilie Le Tonnelier de Breteuil, marquise du Châtelet, renowned as the mistress of Voltaire and as a defender of Maupertuis, was herself a natural philosopher, the translator of Isaac Newton's *Principia mathematica* into French, and a central figure in enlightened scientific circles. *(Courtesy Archive Photos)*

included a chapter that championed the Leibnizian concept of *vis viva* (living force) and rejected the related Newtonian idea. Her publication intensified a scientific debate (the *vis viva* controversy) that had been brewing for some time, turning it into one of the celebrated scientific quarrels of the ENLIGHTENMENT. Madame du Châtelet corresponded with Leonhard EULER, Pieter van Maupertuis, Clairaut, Pieter van MUSSCHENBROEK, Willem Jacob's GRAVESANDE, and others seeking a resolution to the complicated dispute.

In 1745, Madame du Châtelet began a French translation of Newton's *PRINCIPIA MATHEMATICA* (Mathematical principles) that was published posthumously in 1756 and 1759. It remains even today the only French translation of Newton's seminal work. In the course of this activity, Madame du Châtelet spent some months at the Lunéville court of the former king of POLAND, Stanislaw I Leszczynski, who was also the duke of Lorraine and Bar. At the court, she met a young military officer named J. F.

de Saint-Lambert, with whom she had an affair. A pregnancy resulted, and after successfully delivering a child in 1749, Madame du Châtelet became ill with childbed fever and died.

Voltaire was distraught at her death, and his friends feared for his life. He revealed his affection and devotion to Madame du Châtelet in a letter sent to the comte d'Argental after her death: "J'ai perdu la moitié de moi-même, une âme pour qui la mienne était faite . . ." (I have lost half of myself, a soul for whom my own soul [la mienne] was made . . .).

Madame du Châtelet was one of a handful of women who, despite exclusion from formal institutions, actively participated in the scientific life of the Enlightenment. Both her successes and the limitations of her career help to reveal the boundaries of the enlightened vision of human EQUALITY that prevailed in most of Europe (Bologna, Italy, was an exception). While women could participate actively in intellectual life, they were denied formal professional careers, membership in academies, and the privileges that accompanied that status.

See also WOMEN AND THE ENLIGHTENMENT.

Chemical Revolution Descriptive term for the transformations of chemical theory, associated laboratory practice, and nomenclature that occurred in Europe after 1750. The Chemical Revolution was shaped by the general trends fostered by the ENLIGHTENMENT toward reordering ideas about NATURE and toward creating clear, precise, descriptive scientific language. Major contributors to the Chemical Revolution were Antoine LAVOISIER, Joseph PRIESTLEY, Joseph BLACK, Henry CAVENDISH, Stephen HALES, Carl Wilhelm SCHEELE, Abbé NOLLET, Torbern BERGMAN, Anne-Robert-Jacques TURGOT, and William CULLEN.

Before 1750, the study of chemical phenomena fell to practitioners of either ALCHEMY or MEDICINE. A form of the MECHANICAL PHILOSOPHY espoused by Hermann BOEREHAAVE and the PHLOGISTON THEORY of Georg Ernst STAHL dominated chemistry. After 1750, theoretical problems generated by these older theories combined with various newer threads of Enlightenment science to facilitate major shifts in the study of chemical processes. By the end of the 18th century, the rudiments of the modern science of chemistry had appeared. The old systems of elements—Aristotle's earth, air, fire, and water and the alchemists' varied theories of three elements—were slowly being replaced by a new system that recognized the existence of many elements. A new methodology of chemical analysis based on the quantification of substances (measuring and weighing) had largely replaced the older qualitative methods. Several new systems of nomenclature had been developed including the well-known creation of Lavoisier and less familiar ones invented by Torbern Bergman and Louis-Bernard Guyton de Morveau (1737–1816). In general, the new chemistry

aimed at producing accurate, empirical descriptions of phenomena rather than hypothesizing about causes or essential attributes of substances.

The PHILOSOPHES of the late Enlightenment were conscious of the magnitude of these changes in chemistry and described them as a revolution in the making. That concept has stuck with most historians of science, although arguments exist over the degree of continuity or abrupt change that underlay the revolutionary transformations.

Three key conceptual changes prepared the ground for the theoretical shifts of the Chemical Revolution. One was the formulation of the theory that any physical solid can be transformed into a vapor (gaseous state) if it acquires a sufficiently high temperature. A second key conceptual shift occurred with the discovery of several new "airs" (substances in vaporous states) and with the realization that these airs could actually be mixtures of different substances rather than pure substances. The third major change was the development of a new theory of combustion.

Turgot, the French controller general of finances, developed ideas that challenged traditional theories of matter. He was not a chemist but was intrigued by the research on evaporation that had been carried out by Abbé Nollet and Johann Gottschalk Wallerius. Turgot coined the term *expansibilité* (expansibility) to describe the properties of air and then concluded that such properties would exist in any vaporized substance. The term *vaporisation* was also his invention and designated a state of matter now called the gaseous state. Turgot wrote an anonymous article on *expansibilité* for the French ENCYCLOPÉDIE.

At the same time, Scottish scientists were exploring the nature of air and discovering that it was actually a mixture of different substances. Stephen Hales had paved the way by first collecting the air that was given off when a substance was heated. He had believed that this air was a substance fixed in solid matter and accordingly named it "fixed air." Joseph Black recognized that fixed air (carbon dioxide) was actually a substance with different properties from those of common atmospheric air.

Black's findings stimulated other British researchers to search for new airs. Consequently, Henry Cavendish identified "inflammable air" (hydrogen, 1766), and Joseph Priestley isolated "nitrous air" (nitric acid), "marine acid air" (hydrogen chloride), "alkaline air" (ammonia), "vitriolic acid air" (sulfur dioxide), "phlogisticated nitrous air" (nitrous oxide, laughing gas), and "dephlogisticated air" (oxygen). Carl Wilhelm Scheele in SWEDEN and Antoine Lavoisier in FRANCE also independently isolated oxygen.

In the 1770s, Lavoisier, Scheele, and Priestley were investigating the nature of gases and the process of combustion. In 1772 and 1774, Lavoisier made the experiments that led him to develop a new theory of combustion. The prevalent theory of combustion derived

Portrait of Antoine Laurent Lavoisier and his wife, Marie-Anne Pierrette Paulze, by Jacques-Louis David, 1788. With the assistance of his wife, Lavoisier set up an elaborate chemistry laboratory at the Paris Arsenal, where he carried out the series of experiments that provided the basis for his claim to have created a Chemical Revolution. *(Courtesy Metropolitan Museum of Art; purchase of Mr. and Mrs. Charles Wrightsman Gift, in honor of Everett Fahy, 1977)*

from the phlogiston theory of the German chemist Stahl. Phlogiston theory posited that a substance called phlogiston was given off when charcoal was burned (combustion) and also that the processes of respiration and calcination involved the same substance.

The phlogiston theory provided a satisfactory qualitative description of all three processes. But Lavoisier was committed to measuring and weighing chemical products before and after reactions. This penchant for measuring led him to results that could be interpreted as challenging the validity of phlogiston theory. Phlogiston-producing processes sometimes caused weight loss and other times caused weight gain in chemical products. Lavoisier's measurements suggested that if phlogiston really existed as a substance, then it had the puzzling ability occasionally to have negative weight.

This anomaly, produced by applying quantitative methods to an essentially qualitative theory, prompted Lavoisier to investigate combustion processes in a systematic, quantitative manner. Lavoisier determined that a specific "air" played a role in combustion, isolated it, and

eventually named it oxygen. Joseph Priestley carried out related experiments independently. The findings of the two men eventually resulted in Lavoisier's oxygen theory of combustion.

Lavoisier's dedication to the notion of measuring and weighing all input and output in chemical reactions contributed to the dominance, in laboratory practice, of quantitative techniques. But the Swedish chemist Torbern Bergman also must be credited for building the foundations of quantitative chemical analysis. The emphasis on quantitative description of chemical experiments not only helped to solve the basic problem of combustion, but also later facilitated the reacceptance of temporarily discredited atomistic ideas in chemistry.

The desire for increased rigor and accuracy in experimentation stimulated not only the development of quantitative analysis but also the creation of a new LANGUAGE of chemistry. Lavoisier designed a radical new nomenclature, based on the linguistic theory of Étienne-Bonnot de CONDILLAC, as a replacement for the chemical language inherited from alchemy and medicine. Condillac had argued that a language can be rationally constructed so that its words and grammar represent reality in a clear and accurate manner. He considered the mathematical language of algebra, also called analysis, the outstanding example of such a perfect language. Condillac believed that speaking a well-constructed language would also guarantee correct reasoning.

Lavoisier tried to create an analytical chemical language in which the names of substances would reveal their fundamental composition and other central chemical properties. He set oxygen at the center of his new nomenclature. Indeed, anyone who accepted his new language, also implicitly accepted his oxygen theory. He named the air responsible for combustion "oxygen." The manner in which Lavoisier applied the concept of algebraic analysis to this language is revealed in the term *oxygen*. If the word is broken down (analyzed) into its constituent parts, *oxy* and *gen*, its meaning becomes clear. *Oxy* is Greek for acid and *gen* is a suffix derived from the Greek term for generating (forming). Lavoisier believed that oxygen was involved in the formation of all acids, and therefore named it accordingly. Lavoisier named other substances according to the amount of oxygen they contained. For example: acids with names ending in *ic*

(i.e., sulfuric acid) contained more oxygen than those whose names ended in *ous* (i.e., sulfurous acids). Names for chemical salts similarly reflected their relative oxygen content. Metal "oxides" (formerly called calxes) were metals mixed with oxygen.

Lavoisier was not alone in recognizing the desirability of a new chemical nomenclature. Rival systems were developed by Bergman and the French chemist Guyton de Morveau.

The Chemical Revolution illustrates two important general facets of Enlightenment science. First, the experimental results obtained by Lavoisier and others were made possible in part by the development of new instruments such as the calorimeter, for collecting, weighing, and carrying out other aspects of chemical experimentation. Without the instruments and other technology, the measurements could not have been obtained that supported the radical departures in conceptualization that characterized the Chemical Revolution. Second, the diffusion of Lavoisier's new theory of the elements and chemical nomenclature was in large part carried out through an organized collaborative propaganda effort. Chemists such as Claude Louis BERTHOLLET, Antoine de Fourcroy (1755–1809), and Guyton de Morveau accepted

Alchemical-chemical laboratory. The science of alchemy, with a centuries-long tradition, continued to be practiced into the Enlightenment, but was ultimately replaced by chemistry in the professional scientific world as a consequence of the 18th-century Chemical Revolution. *(Courtesy Metropolitan Museum of Art; purchase of Mr. and Mrs. Charles Wrightsman Gift, in honor of Everett Fahy, 1977)*

Lavoisier's findings and banded together to disseminate the new views. They received assistance from Pierre LAPLACE and Gaspard Monge (1746–1818). They jointly produced the *Méthode de nomenclature chimique* (Method of chemical nomenclature; 1787), whose major author was Lavoisier; also, an annotated edition in French of Richard Kirwan's *Essay on Phlogiston* (1788); and a new journal, the *Annales de chimie* (Annals of chemistry; volume one, 1789). Lavoisier capped these projects with his *Traité élémentaire de chimie* (Elementary treatise of chemistry; 1789).

Further reading: Frederic Lawrence Holmes et al., eds., *Instruments and Experimentation in the History of Chemistry* (Cambridge, Mass.: MIT Press, 1999); Mi Gyung Kim, *Affinity, That Elusive Dream: A Genealogy of the Chemical Revolution,* Transformations: Studies in the History of Science and Technology Series (Cambridge, Mass.: MIT Press, 2003); J. R. Partington, *A Short History of Chemistry* (New York: Harper & Row, 1960).

Chesterfield, Philip Dormer Stanhope, fourth earl of (1694–1773) *English statesman and man of letters*

The earl of Chesterfield achieved posthumous literary renown through his *Letters to His Son,* published by his widow in 1774, just one year after his death. They contain scintillating observations and purport to give his son instruction in the manners and ways of the high social world to which the Chesterfield family belonged. In this respect, they belong to the genre of LITERATURE that was written with social and moral educational purpose. However, Chesterfield's letters differ, for example, from the essays of THE SPECTATOR in their presentation of aristocratic rather than middle-class manners and values. A second set of letters, *Letters to His Godson,* written for Chesterfield's formally adopted godson, first appeared in print only in 1890.

During his lifetime, Chesterfield moved in both literary social circles and in the world of politics. He was a friend of Alexander POPE and Jonathan SWIFT. He earned the dubious honor of being snubbed in a letter by Samuel JOHNSON. Johnson, whom Chesterfield had protected with his patronage, refused to dedicate the *Dictionary of the English Language* to his patron. Johnson was insulted that Chesterfield had ignored the project for the eight years of its creation, only to offer his patronage and money when it promised to be a success. Johnson used the opportunity to assert his desire to be independent of funds or protection provided by aristocratic patrons. The incident graphically portrays one of the key developments in the organization of the literary world: the demise of patronage and its replacement by the independent though often poverty-stricken artist.

childhood, ideas about   *See* EDUCATION.

China The Chinese Empire of the Qing (or Ch'ing) dynasty. Territories claimed by China are bordered by Russia in the west, Burma in the southwest, Vietnam and India in the south, the South China Sea in the southeast, and the East China Sea in the east. Modern China (The People's Republic of China), which incorporates the whole of Mongolia, covers more than 3,500,000 square miles, only slightly larger than the territory acquired during the Qing dynasty. China proper, or the "China of the 18 Provinces," is located below the Great Wall of China, which stretches for 4,000 miles from east to west. This region fell to invading Manchus, who founded the Qing dynasty in the early 1600s, and they subsequently pushed the borders outward to incorporate Inner Mongolia in the north, Tibet in the west, Manchuria in the east, and Taiwan in the south. During the 18th century, the population grew from about 200 million to 300 million people.

Ruled by the Son of Heaven from his Great Dragon Throne in the imperial palace in Beijing, known as the Forbidden City, China was administered by a vast BUREAUCRACY. The emperor was not protected by the DIVINE RIGHT OF KINGS that absolutist European monarchs claimed. He could legitimately be deposed by public revolt. The emperor's delegates arbitrated disputes, conducted military action, and maintained social order. Governor-magistrates were appointed by merit after taking public examinations on the vast canon of Confucian philosophy. Administrators (mandarins) were required to set an example of high moral standards. Codes of criminal conduct existed, but social order in China relied on the practice of natural morality. Confucianism was an ancient, family-centered, secular code. All members of society recognized the structure of authority, and at all levels—political, civic, and domestic—the inferior person kowtowed to his or her superior in a symbolic rite of subordination. To some European philosophers, such as the baron de MONTESQUIEU, this social system represented an enlightened despotism (see DESPOTISM, ENLIGHTENED).

Various religions were practiced in China. Buddhism and Taoism had been assimilated; their emphasis on simplicity and individual enlightenment supplemented the Confucian code. Nearly all the Chinese revered ancestral gods. Islam had also penetrated certain regions adjacent to Muslim countries, and French JESUITS in the 17th century had converted courtiers to ROMAN CATHOLICISM. In 1692, the emperor granted toleration to Christianity. Barely a decade later, a protracted intra-Catholic conflict ensued. The pragmatic Jesuits' failure to use standard Catholic rites with their Chinese converts was condemned by papal bulls in 1715 and 1721. Immediately thereafter, the emperor withdrew his edict of toleration. Other European missionaries—Franciscans and Dominicans from FRANCE, Eastern Orthodox priests from Russia, Protestants from ENGLAND—had little effect on the courtly or local populations. Islamic militants in the 18th

Watercolor of a tea warehouse in Canton (Guangzhou), ca. 1790. Chinese porters carry tea from the storeroom while Europeans examine the tea. *(By permission of the British Library)*

century generated a Muslim neo-orthodoxy (known as *hsin-chiao*) and, perhaps, introduced the Muslim habit of using opium. This taste for opium was to have severe consequences for China in the 19th century.

Local rebellions against state authority occurred with regard to RELIGION, land use, and commerce, especially in the second half of the 18th century. But regional communities were sheltered from radical European influence by Chinese traditionalism combined with the emperor's policy of segregating foreign merchants in separate towns. As the ultimate authority, the emperor perceived his country as self-sustaining, and he was uninterested in forging closer ties with Europe either by increased trade or by conquest. Traditionally, China traded its tea, silk, and porcelain by sea and land with Muslim states and distant provinces, but trade was far less significant to the Chinese economy than it was to European economies driven by colonial expansion, MERCANTILISM and, later, CAPITALISM. From the 15th century onward, Europeans began arriving via the Cape of Good Hope, the Pacific, and the far north, their governments intent on trade with this newly accessible empire of the East.

Europeans in China

Europeans had three objectives in China: to convert its people to Christianity, to obtain diplomatic recognition, and to establish reciprocal commercial relations. The missionary Jesuits, who proved themselves interested in Chinese culture and useful as technological advisers and translators, were successful with conversions only in the 17th century. By the 18th century, foreigners were not welcome at the imperial court. Only traders were tolerated. However, trade was restricted to Canton, and merchants were segregated from the local population by their enforced residence at specific regions of the coast. For much of the year, traders were required to live in Macao, without their families or any weapons, and were subject to close regulation of their activities. The Chinese rarely came into contact with foreigners whose influence was so firmly contained. Local people were never subordinate to European authority, and, despite the naval technology and advanced weaponry of the visitors, the Chinese secured themselves from aggressive Europeans, who were nevertheless valued for their willingness to curb local piracy.

China was at a crossroads when it confronted the West in the 17th and 18th centuries. The Qing dynasty could have expanded as an imperial power by adopting Western science and economic strategies to compete with European empires, but it chose to remain in its relative isolation, committed to traditional ways. By the 18th century, China had already fallen from its earlier state of almost universal literacy and technological prominence. Unlike Europe, which became ever more urban as the population increased, the growing Chinese populace was emigrating from the cities to rural regions where literacy and technical invention declined. As China stagnated, content with its own wealth and ways, the Western naval powers—subject to contentious religious, political, and colonial competition—vied for wealth and international prestige. Domestically, the ENLIGHTENMENT states encouraged universal education; fostered MATHEMATICS AND MECHANICS, SCIENCE, and technological innovation; and initiated measures to improve the lot of common men and women. These measures included better medical treatment, reformation of legal systems, and toleration of religious dissent (even as ancient rights were wrested from the poor and the dispossessed were summarily shuttled into urban factories or reformatories).

Despite these changes at home, French and German philosophers tended to be Sinophiles, lovers of Chinese culture, a culture that seemed to embody superior social systems and values than did those of European culture. Gottfried LEIBNIZ admired Chinese NATURAL RELIGION, the secular, practical application of ethics and politics to social organization. Pierre BAYLE admired China as the exemplar of moral ATHEISM. VOLTAIRE admired what he considered Chinese DEISM, the culture's lack of dogmatism in matters of religion. European PHYSIOCRATS (economists committed to free trade as a path to prosperity) believed the Chinese government practiced a model form of LAISSEZ-FAIRE economics. In 18th-century England, however, the Chinese were more often dismissed as servile and barbaric. Samuel JOHNSON was able to appreciate only their CERAMIC ARTS.

Nonetheless, China's influence on Western artistic taste was remarkable. Houseware design throughout Europe drew on Chinese simplicity. In England, gardening was transformed by Chinese naturalism. Joseph BANKS, president of THE ROYAL SOCIETY OF LONDON from 1788 to 1820, introduced a number of Chinese plants to England, including the now-familiar tree peonies, chrysanthemums, hydrangeas, magnolias, and tiger lilies. Later botanists introduced forsythia, rhododendrons, and wisteria. In turn, the Chinese imported practical American food plants: potatoes, maize, sweet potatoes, and groundnuts. In the early 19th century, Europeans also brought cholera, which devastated the population of Chinese ports.

Western Trade with China

Russian, Armenian, Jewish, and Persian traders prospered in the China trade during the 18th century, but Western Europeans were also interested in China's porcelain, tea, and silk exports. All major European commerce was controlled by East Indies monopoly companies, which covered the costs of voyages and handled negotiations. Initially, China's interest in the West was restricted to exporting its own goods and importing silver bullion. The Portuguese were the first European traders, operating from 1497 under a Crown monopoly but losing their advantage to later competition. The Spanish had Pacific access from the Philippines, but did not maintain a regular trade.

From 1660, the English EAST INDIA COMPANY was immensely influential: It sponsored the consumption of tea as a national habit, and England was, indeed, the principal European consumer of Chinese tea exports. At first, tea was deemed to have medical benefits; later, drinking tea became a social accomplishment; and, in its third phase, between 1800 and 1833, it was naturalized into the daily English diet as teatime. Its great social benefit was the substitution of tea for alcoholic beverages. The porcelain (or china) from which tea was drunk and from which teatime meals were served was originally imported from China but later produced in European factories. About 1707, Johann Friedrich BÖTTGER discovered kaolin, the secret ingredient of Chinese porcelain, and invented European hard-paste porcelain. The elector of Saxony and king of POLAND, Augustus the Strong, forced Böttger to work on improving European porcelain at the Meissen factory in GERMANY. Later, Josiah WEDGWOOD and his successor, Josiah Spode, developed and marketed fine English porcelain.

Dependence on Chinese exports without significant imports into China created trade imbalances in Europe. For some states, this imbalance was rectified by the immoral expedient of carrying opium to China. After the failure of Lord Macartney's 1792–93 diplomatic mission to increase trade and improve Britain's ties with China, the East India Company (sanctioned by the government) vastly facilitated Chinese addiction in the early 19th century by trading Indian opium as an exchange commodity.

Other European monopolies trading in China were based in France (although its interests lay primarily in India), SWEDEN (whose company incorporated merchants displaced from the Ostend trade), and Denmark. The Ostend trade, chartered in 1722 by Charles VI as an AUSTRIAN NETHERLANDS monopoly, was actually an international consortium of Antwerp merchants and various European refugee groups. Its acquisition of Chinese tea for smuggling into England provoked international sanctions, and the company was liquidated in 1731. The Dutch East India Company was able to boost its shipping to China in the first half of the 18th century, but the English overtook the Dutch in the second half. Dutch decline may be accounted for by its slow vessels, but the UNITED PROVINCES OF THE NETHERLANDS chiefly focused its resources on the colonization of Indonesia.

Chinese Independence

To stem its outflow of silver after 1760, China remained active in the international commodity market. It encouraged a coalition of Muslim states to resume trade along the land route through Central Asia, and this coalition provided horses, opium, furs, and other goods in exchange for Chinese tea, pepper, silk, and ceramics.

Unlike many countries discovered or rediscovered by Europeans in the 18th century, China, by and large, remained immune to European ideas and products. Influence clearly filtered from East to West: Chinese imports, both material and philosophical, were readily assimilated by the West, but European goods and culture had little effect on China.

See also CHINOISERIE; COSMOPOLITANISM; ECONOMICS; ENGLISH GARDEN; JUSTICE AND THE LAW; MERCIER DE LA RIVIÈRE; POLITICAL THEORY; QUESNAY; TRAVEL LITERATURE; VOYAGES OF DISCOVERY.

Further reading: Albert Feuerwerker, *State and Society in 18th-Century China: The Ch'ing Empire in its Glory* (Ann Arbor: University of Michigan Press, 1976); John S. Gregory, *The West and China Since 1500* (New York: Palgrave Macmillan, 2003).

chinoiserie A style of decoration. The word *chinoiserie* comes from the French and refers to the Chinese inspiration behind this style. Chinoiserie developed as part of the 18th-century ROCOCO style in art and architecture and was especially popular in FRANCE, GERMANY, and ENGLAND. It utilized motifs copied from Chinese porcelains—birds, flowering branches, and other natural objects—as elements of decoration for art objects and interior design. The color palette tended toward pastels, and designs were ornate but delicate.

Rococo decorators applied these designs to porcelains, tapestries, musical instruments, furniture, clocks, and upholstery fabrics. Wall coverings and interior decorations also proved adaptable. In fact, for a brief period during the middle decades of the 18th century, chinoiserie appeared on nearly any surface that could be decorated. The French painter Antoine WATTEAU was an innovator in chinoiserie, and, under his influence, François BOUCHER popularized the style in the fine arts. Boucher's delightful figures were copied in ceramic designs throughout Europe.

Chinoiserie had very little influence on architectural design, but it had a great impact on interior decorative arts. The style became fashionable in France when Alexis Peyrotte (1696–1769) created designs for the royal palaces at Versailles, Fontainebleau, Choisy, and Bellevue. The fad spread to Germany. On the Nymphenberg Palace grounds in Munich, Josef Effner built the Pagodenburg (ca. 1726) and the Amalienburg hunting lodge designed by François de Cuvilliés (1734–39); both structures display masterful use of chinoiserie interiors. The fashion also appeared in many English gardens, manifest in pagodas and other exotic garden structures.

Consumer interest was driven by new trade between Europe and CHINA during the 18th century, not only for tea but also for the porcelain that was deemed essential in its service. The British EAST INDIA COMPANY encouraged the consumption of tea over the consumption of coffee, both foreign commodities introduced in the latter half of the 17th century that Europeans rapidly adopted. The domestic tea table, especially in England, was a space for cultured ladies to indulge their aesthetic taste, and they frequently criticized the lower classes for expending money and time they could ill afford on the luxury of tea drinking. In a bizarre reversal of cultural transmission, in 1823 Britain's Spode factory exported English chinoiserie to China: it sent 1,300 pieces of the famous porcelain with the blue willow pattern that represented a Chinese landscape.

As a facet of rococo style, chinoiserie illustrates one manner in which the enlightened culture of SENSIBILITY was expressed in art. The objects decorated with these fantastic designs were intended to please the eye and to evoke images of exotic places far removed from Europe. The popularity of chinoiserie in England and on the Continent is not evidence of fascination with Chinese culture but simply a European affectation of style.

See also ENGLISH GARDEN.

Further reading: Madeleine Jarry, *Chinoiserie: Chinese Influence on European Decorative Art, 17th and 18th Centuries,* trans. Gail Mangold-Vine (New York: Vendome Press, 1981).

Chippendale, Thomas (1718–1779) *English furniture maker*

Thomas Chippendale's furniture designs influenced a generation of furniture makers, especially in ENGLAND and North America, to such an extent that the name Chippendale has become synonymous with furniture built in the middle of the 18th century.

Thomas Chippendale was born in Otley, Yorkshire. His father was a carpenter. Chippendale married in London in 1748, where he opened his furniture workshop and storefront in 1753. He lived and worked there for the rest of his life.

In 1754, Chippendale published a collection of furniture designs, *The Gentleman & Cabinet-Maker's Director.* The work made Chippendale's reputation and was responsible for his pervasive influence as a furniture maker, especially in the English-speaking world. His designs were inspired by 18th-century CHINOISERIE, French ROCOCO, and neo-Gothic influences. One of Chippendale's signature designs, the carefully carved geometric chair back, was derived from Chinese patterns and exemplifies his use of chinoiserie.

In the 1760s, Chippendale partnered with the neo-classical architect Robert ADAM, creating furnishings for several of Adam's projects, including Harewood House, which continues to house a valuable and representative collection of Chippendale's furniture. Very few pieces of so-called Chippendale furniture can actually be attributed to Chippendale himself, making collections such as that of Harewood House doubly important. When Chippendale died in 1779, his workshop and business passed to his son, Thomas Chippendale, Jr.

Further reading: Thomas Chippendale, *The Gentleman & Cabinet-Maker's Director* (New York: Dover, 1966).

Chodowiecki, Daniel Niklaus (1726–1801) *Prussian painter and engraver of Polish descent*

Born in Danzig, POLAND and employed in BERLIN, the capital of PRUSSIA, Chodowiecki moved to the latter as a young man in order to apprentice himself with his merchant uncle. He was largely self-taught in drawing and painting. He took a few private drawing lessons in 1743 from Bernhard Rode.

Chodowiecki established himself first as a miniaturist and then as an engraver. By 1758, he had earned public recognition. The Berlin Academy of Arts received him in 1764 as a member; in 1790, he became vice director of that institution, and in 1797 succeeded Rode as its director.

The *Calendar of the Berlin Academy,* containing Chodowiecki's miniature series *Life of Jesus Christ,* introduced his work to a broader audience. Chodowiecki subsequently became a fashionable book illustrator, adorning works by Johann Wolfgang von GOETHE, Laurence STERNE, Shakespeare, Gotthold Ephraim LESSING, and Johann LAVATER. He also left numerous etchings that capture aspects of 18th-century life in Berlin. His witty portrayals of daily existence have been compared to those of William HOGARTH. His paintings include *Les adieux de Calas à sa famille* (Calas's farewells to his family), a depiction of the execution of Jean CALAS, and a portrait of Joseph BANKS. Chodowiecki died in Berlin in 1801.

Choiseul, Étienne-François, comte de Stainville, duc de (1719–1775) *French statesman, military officer, protector of the philosophes, and protegé of Madame de Pompadour*

Choiseul made his early career as a soldier and acquired the rank of brigadier by 1746. In 1750, he married Louise-Honorine Crozat du Châtel, the wealthy sister of his deceased lover, Madame de Gontaut.

Choiseul made the acquaintance of Madame de POMPADOUR and intervened to prevent her from being ousted at court by a rival. She rewarded him with substantial patronage, securing him his first diplomatic appointment as ambassador to the Vatican in ROME (1753–57). Choiseul helped to persuade Pope BENEDICT XIV to modify the papal bull *Unigenitus* (1713), which had aimed at discouraging JANSENISM in FRANCE.

Choiseul's success earned him the prestigious of ambassador before the imperial Hapsburg court in VIENNA (1757–58). His new duties included cementing the fragile alliance with Austria that had been worked out in the DIPLOMATIC REVOLUTION OF 1756. He helped to negotiate the second treaty of Versailles (May 1, 1757), in which France and AUSTRIA formed an offensive alliance against PRUSSIA.

From 1758 until 1761, Choiseul served LOUIS XV as minister of foreign affairs. In this capacity, Choiseul grappled with the problems caused by the SEVEN YEARS' WAR and tried, in the third treaty of Versailles (1759), to limit the financial impact of the war on the nation. He also negotiated the so-called Family Pact (1761), an alliance among French, Spanish, and Neapolitan rulers, all of whom were members of the Bourbon family.

Choiseul served as director of the office of the admiralty from 1761 until 1766 and as minister of war between 1766 and 1770. He secured the expulsion of the JESUITS from France in 1762. He expanded the French navy and instituted major reforms in the army, concentrating especially on military training. He also helped to negotiate the marriage between MARIE-ANTOINETTE, the daughter of MARIA THERESA of Austria, and the Dauphin, the future LOUIS XVI.

In domestic affairs, Choiseul was a secret supporter of the PARLEMENTS in their battle against royal ABSOLUTISM. Thus, he generally favored policies that aimed toward establishing a limited monarchy in France. He was a friend of VOLTAIRE, supported the publication of the *ENCYCLOPÉDIE,* and generally protected the PHILOSOPHES from harassment by royal officials. Choiseul lost his ministerial position in 1770, a victim primarily of court intrigues by Madame DU BARRY and friends of the exiled Jesuits. Choiseul divided his time during his remaining years between his chateau at Chanteloup (to which he was exiled from 1770 until 1774) and his town house in PARIS. He died in 1785, having lost the great fortune that had once belonged to him and his wife.

Christian VII of Denmark and Norway (1749–1808) *king of Denmark and Norway from 1766 until 1808*

Christian VII, the son of Frederick V of DENMARK, was poorly educated and brutally treated as a child. As he matured into adulthood, he began to display signs of the mental disturbance that would prevent him from ruling his kingdom effectively. During his reign, his court physician and chief councillor, Count Johann Friedrich STRUENSEE, took over the government.

In 1771 Struensee instituted a series of far-reaching reforms in the style of enlightened despotism (see DESPOTISM, ENLIGHTENED), but he compromised his authority by having an affair with the queen, Caroline Mathilda. Christian VII, acceding to pressure from parties offended by Struensee's reforms, signed a warrant for his arrest and had him executed for adultery in 1772. After Struensee's death, the government of Denmark fell largely to Christian's advisers.

Christian VII became progressively more insane, and by 1784 was no longer able to rule. He ceded his royal authority in the royal council to his son, Crown Prince Frederick, who ruled as the regent from 1784 until Christian VII's death in 1808. Frederick, under the title Frederick VI, ruled Denmark from 1808 until 1839 and Norway from 1808 until 1814.

civil society A term intimately associated with the work of the historian and moral philosopher Adam FERGUSON and his contemporaries in 18th-century SCOTLAND. Ferguson's *Essay on the History of Civil Society* (1767) was widely read and influential, not only in Scotland but also in FRANCE and GERMANY. Scottish writers gave the term *civil society* variable meanings. Sometimes it simply acted as a synonym for the word *civilization;* at other times it referred more specifically to polished, polite society, and at still others, it indicated a society of highly structured political institutions in which the use of power was regulated by law. In its guise as a synonym for *civilization,* the concept of civil society was also a focus for writers outside Scotland. The social contract theorists Samuel PUFENDORF, Thomas HOBBES, John LOCKE, and Jean-Jacques ROUSSEAU and the historians Giambattista VICO and Pietro GIANNONE are principal among the many writers who speculated about the shrouded origins of human societies and the motives that might have led to their creation. The birth of civil society for these writers was tied up with central matters and institutions such as basic HUMAN NATURE, JUSTICE AND THE LAW, property, FREEDOM, EQUALITY, and RIGHTS. Their writings reflect the great passion of the ENLIGHTENMENT for finding rational, natural explanations for all things human.

Ferguson and his Scottish contemporaries David HUME, Lord Kames, John MILLAR, William ROBERTSON, and Adam SMITH in EDINBURGH and Glasgow, while sharing this general interest, were largely concerned with understanding their 18th-century urban world. Today, it is commonly understood among scholars of the Enlightenment that "civil society" is a complex signifier for a peculiarly Scottish ideal of society: a polity made up of self-interested, free, and equal individuals who are motivated by the pursuit of wealth and who seek that wealth in commerce and trade and a society whose justness is guaranteed by the operation of natural psychological laws and universal philosophical principles. Seen from another perspective, this Scottish concept of civil society is shorthand for the sociopolitical forms of organization that developed during the Enlightenment and that were associated with the early INDUSTRIAL REVOLUTION, with the emergence of classic liberalism and the middle classes of successful businessmen, professionals, and intellectuals; and with the collapse of the social, political, economic, and intellectual structures of the old European order. That the concept of civil society played such a central role in Scotland is explained at least partly by the fact that that country, even more than ENGLAND in the 18th century, was a predominantly urban, commercial society whose political structures were changing dramatically on account of the 1707 union of Scotland and England. Before 1707, the two countries had been independent kingdoms, linked only in the person of the king. (The personal union had occurred in 1603, when King James VI of Scotland inherited the throne of England and became James I of England.) After 1707, the two kingdoms were merged to form Great Britain and given a single, common Parliament. The old Scottish Parliament was dissolved, not to be reconstituted until the last decade of the 20th century.

Like many of their contemporaries, Scottish thinkers were particularly anxious to develop an understanding about how morality, VIRTUE, and healthy public life might be preserved in the new world of individual, private, commercial, self-interested, utilitarian relations. The solution offered by Dutch moral philosopher Bernard MANDEVILLE in *Fable of the Bees,* in which the naked pursuit of self-interest creates industrious societies akin to beehives and anthills, did not appeal, nor did Mandeville's vision seem realistic. Ferguson, for one, believed that the ancient virtues, which stress the good of the whole community, remained valid even in the modern world, and he argued that the private pursuit of happiness and the exercise of freedom must be limited where they conflict with the public good. But he also held that the greatest happiness comes to individuals when they are engaged in the public affairs of the civil society, exercising their duties as citizens as well as pursuing their individual talents and interests. Other writers, among them Hume, turned away from the tradition of civic virtue and made human SYMPATHY, a hypothetical faculty of the human mind, the natural principle that ensures harmony between individual SELF-INTEREST and the common good. Adam Smith's famed "invisible hand" is nothing other than sympathy working together with "unintended consequences," another favorite philosophical principle of this Scottish group, to ensure that the unencumbered pursuit of wealth serves the interests of the community.

As they grappled with this conundrum, the Scottish writers turned to many sources for inspiration: to the baron de MONTESQUIEU for his discussion of various government forms and their guiding principles; to the ancient Stoics for the republican tradition of the virtuous citizen-soldier; to Renaissance civic humanism, itself a neo-Stoic articulation of the idea of the active, virtuous citizen; to Pufendorf and other writers in the NATURAL LAW tradition; and to their own moral philosophers Francis HUTCHESON and David Hume for psychological and moral philosophical concepts.

See also MORAL PHILOSOPHY; SOCIAL CONTRACT; UTILITY.

Further reading: Christopher J. Berry, *Social Theory of the Scottish Enlightenment* (Edinburgh: Edinburgh University Press, 1997); Adam Ferguson, *An Essay on the History of Civil Society,* ed. Fania Oz-Salzberger (Cambridge:

Cambridge University Press, 1995); Charles L. Griswold, Jr., *Adam Smith and the Virtues of Enlightenment* (Cambridge: Cambridge University Press, 1999); J. G. A. Pocock, *The Machiavellian Moment: Florentine Political Thought and the Atlantic Republican Tradition* (Princeton, N.J.: Princeton University Press, 1975); Roy Porter, *The Creation of the Modern World: The Untold Story of the British Enlightenment* (New York: W. W. Norton, 2000); Quentin Skinner, *The Foundations of Modern Political Thought*, 2 vols. (Cambridge: Cambridge University Press, 1978); Adam Smith, *Lectures on Jurisprudence*, eds. R. L. Meek and D. D. Raphael (Indianapolis: Liberty Press, 1982); Adam Smith, *The Theory of Moral Sentiments*, eds. A. L. MacAfie and D. D. Raphael (Indianapolis: Liberty Press, 1982).

Clairaut, Alexis-Claude (1713–1765) *French mathematician*

Clairaut was one of the early French supporters of Newtonian physics and therefore an important figure in the cultivation of the scientific soil that nurtured the early French ENLIGHTENMENT. Clairaut's works all demonstrated how Newtonian principles could be used both to solve practical problems and to develop viable scientific theories.

Clairaut accompanied Pierre Louis de MAUPERTUIS in 1736 on his expedition to Lapland to measure the meridian (any great circle on the surface of the Earth that passes through both poles and another spot). The exercise aimed at measuring the length of an arc of one degree along the meridian. This measurement from the Lapland region was then compared with measurements taken at the equator in order to determine whether or not the Earth was flattened slightly at the poles. Newtonian theory predicted such flattening, whereas Cartesian theory predicted a polar elongation. The results of the expedition helped to establish the ascendancy of Newtonian physics over Cartesian theories. After this expedition, Clairaut published *Théorie de la figure de la terre* (Theory of the shape of the Earth; 1743).

Having been introduced to Madame du CHÂTELET by VOLTAIRE, Clairaut assisted her with her French translation of Newton's PRINCIPIA MATHEMATICA (Mathematical principles) and allegedly became her lover. Clairaut wrote his *Eléments de la géometrie* (Elements of geometry) for Madame du Châtelet, and she prepared her *Solution analytique des principaux problèmes concernant le système du monde* (Analytical solution of the principal problems concerning the system of the world) under his direction.

Clairaut made additional important contributions to Newtonian physics and ASTRONOMY by addressing the problem of determining gravitational influences among three bodies and by accurately predicting the 1759 return of Halley's comet. Twice, the SAINT PETERSBURG ACADEMY OF SCIENCES awarded Clairaut its annual prize: in 1752 for *Théorie de la lune* (Theory of the Moon), a treatise that derived a complete theory of the motion of the Moon based on the Newtonian principle of attraction; and in

1761 for *Recherches sur la comète des années 1531, 1607, 1682 et 1759 pour servir de supplément à la théorie par laquelle on avait annoncé le retour de cette comète* (Research on the comet of the years 1531, 1607, 1682, and 1759 to supplement the theory by which the return of this comet was foretold).

See also DESCARTES; NEWTON.

clarinet Single-reed woodwind instrument that first appeared in Europe between 1690 and 1720. Eighteenth-century instrument makers were modifying many existing instruments. They were striving for more reliability and also, in some cases, for different types of sound. The clarinet was developed by Johann C. Denner and his son, Johann Denner. The Denners modified an instrument called the chalumeau by adding keys for fingering and one key (speaker key) that vents the instrument to make certain notes easier to obtain. The chalumeau was a single-reed keyless instrument with six finger holes.

Early 18th-century clarinets sounded more like oboes than the modern instrument. Johann Walther, in his *Musikalisches Lexikon* (Musical dictionary; 1732), described the sound as trumpetlike. This characteristic of the sound may explain the name "clarinet." It probably refers to the clarino style of playing the valveless baroque trumpet, in which style the player overblows to produce notes in a high, penetrating range.

During the 18th century, both chalumeaux and clarinets were used by composers. Christoph Willibald GLUCK called for the chalumeau in his opera *ORFEO ED EURIDICE* (Orpheus and Eurydice; 1762). Jean-Philippe RAMEAU in PARIS and Johann Wenzel Anton Stamitz (1717–57) of the MANNHEIM SCHOOL are among the composers who first used the clarinet in orchestral works. By the end of the century, the clarinet had become a standard member of the SYMPHONY ORCHESTRA.

Clarissa, or The History of a Young Lady British epistolary novel (in the form of letters) in eight volumes published between 1747 and 1748 by Samuel RICHARDSON. The novel tells the story of Clarissa Harlowe, a young heiress whose family wants her to marry Solmes, a man she despises, in order to increase the Harlowe family's social and political prestige. The family has recently risen from the middle class and would like to gather enough social prestige and political power to obtain a peerage. They are also anxious to separate Clarissa from a handsome, aristocratic young rake named Lovelace, who was originally introduced into the family as a suitor for Clarissa's sister, Arabella, but soon made his preference for Clarissa known. The Harlowe family persecutes Clarissa by locking her in her room and intercepting her letters. When they threaten to force her to marry Solmes against her will, Lovelace persuades her to leave the house and travel to LONDON under his protection.

Once in London, Lovelace takes Clarissa to a brothel populated by other women he has seduced. Persuaded that she is staying at a respectable lodging house, she remains at the brothel and seeks a reconciliation with her family, which they refuse. She continues to resist Lovelace's increasingly forceful advances, and this resistance serves to increase his desire for her. After he physically attacks her, she runs away, but he finds her and brings her back to the house. With the help of the other women of the house, Lovelace drugs Clarissa and rapes her. By doing so, he expects to break down her resistance and reveal the artificial nature of the sexual virtue upon which she had resisted his earlier advances. Instead, this loss of physical chastity destroys Clarissa's sense of identity. The letters she writes immediately after this attack suggest madness or the loss of reason.

When she begins to recover her senses, she attempts to escape from Lovelace once again. This time the owner of the brothel has her arrested for debt. Even after her friends obtain her release, she refuses to leave the prison, choosing instead to waste away and die in the squalid room where Lovelace's machinations have placed her. Lovelace himself dies after fighting a duel with Clarissa's cousin, Colonel Morden. Most of the final letters of the novel are written by Lovelace's friend Belford, a young man who had been Lovelace's confidant in the beginning of the novel. Clarissa's story persuades Belford to resume a virtuous life, and thus the novel can be read as a triumph of middle-class morality over the aristocratic libertinism of the Restoration period.

Clarissa created a sensation not only in ENGLAND, but also on the European continent, where it rapidly appeared in translation. It was disdained by certain members of the aristocracy—Lord CHESTERFIELD for one—as middle class and devoid of depth. But it was read, nevertheless, by literate persons from all social classes. With its predecessor, *Pamela,* it established a fashion for heartrending novels in which characters bared their inner sentiments and soul. These novels served as one facet of the literary expression of the culture of SENSIBILITY and reveal the interest during the ENLIGHTENMENT in the hidden thoughts and feelings of individuals.

Clarke, Samuel (1675–1729) *English theologian and philosopher*

Clarke, the son of an alderman, attended Cambridge University, acquiring his B.A. in 1695. In 1697, through his acquaintance with William Whiston, an English theologian and mathematician, Clarke received an appointment as chaplain to Dr. John Moore, bishop of Norwich. Cambridge University awarded Clarke an M.A. degree in 1698.

Clarke's sermons were highly regarded for their clarity and significant intellectual content. As a result, he was invited to give the Boyle lectures in 1704 and 1705.

Robert Boyle, chemist and member of the ROYAL SOCIETY OF LONDON, had established these lectures in London for the express purpose of addressing the relationship between SCIENCE and THEOLOGY. He believed that the new science of the SCIENTIFIC REVOLUTION, founded on REASON, Mathematics (see MATHEMATICS AND MECHANICS), and experiment, could provide the foundations for a Christian natural theology.

While at Cambridge University, Clarke had devoted himself to studying the *PRINCIPIA MATHEMATICA* by Isaac NEWTON. He became an ardent champion of Newtonian science, helping to disseminate its ideas by translating them into the international scientific language of Latin and by defending them against the criticisms of the German philosopher Gottfried Wilhelm LEIBNIZ.

Clarke's commitment to Newtonianism grew at least partially from his desire to defend a vision of the universe constructed on principles of LIBERTY and free will. He believed that Newton's NATURAL PHILOSOPHY supported his position and objected to any theory of the human mind or soul that reduced action to mechanical laws. If soul or mind operate like "meer [sic] machines," then human actions are determined in advance; freedom of choice, thus, would not exist, and human beings would be absolved of responsibility for their actions.

Clarke defended the concept of free will in three different, renowned exchanges with the Anglican materialist Henry Dodwell, with the deist Anthony COLLINS, and with Leibniz. In the exchange with Leibniz, the most important for the ENLIGHTENMENT, Clarke defended the ideas of Newton against Leibniz's criticisms. Leibniz believed that the Newtonian philosophy had undermined NATURAL RELIGION by making God into a "watchmaker" who must periodically wind up his world to keep it running. Leibniz also criticized Newton for making gravity into either an occult (hidden) principle or a magical phenomenon; for treating space and time as real (absolute) things, rather than as concepts derived from observing the relations between objects; and for misunderstanding the philosophical principle of sufficient reason.

Clarke answered Leibniz by defending positions derived from Newton. Clarke believed that the differences in the philosophies of the two men actually involved a conflict between FREEDOM and necessity in the operations of the universe. Clarke believed that Leibniz was proposing a kind of philosophical necessity that would eliminate liberty and choice from the universe and from the actions of people. He also opposed the Leibnizian position in the famous *vis viva* (living force) controversy over the quantity of force contained in a moving body.

Clarke, whose interests lay precisely in the arena of reconciling science and RELIGION, argued that the concepts of the new science strongly supported traditional Christian views about God's active presence in the world. Clarke's political affiliations were consistent with his positions in theology and natural philosophy: The Whig Party received his support because it championed the cause of political liberty.

Clarke was a major figure in the early Enlightenment, one whose concerns amply illustrate how the era was struggling over the philosophical and religious implications of new forms of science. His theological and philosophical writings, as well as his correspondence with Collins, Dodwell, and Leibniz, were published in the 18th century as *The Works of Samuel Clarke* (4 vols., 1738). Clarke's writings identify him as one of many enlightened individuals who remained committed to traditional forms of religion. The vision of the Enlightenment as an era of virulent attacks on Christianity and other traditional religions has validity, but only when it is complemented by an understanding of the vast spectrum of positions that were actually held by enlightened people.

class and rank in the 18th century   At the base of ANCIEN RÉGIME European political structures lay a concept of social structure in which people were grouped into ranks according to their function in society. These ranks were called orders or estates; they were legal constructions. They were not conceived as economic divisions according to wealth (classes). The identity and status of a person was tied to his or her corporate identity (membership in a particular order). The most common system divided society into three groups, but sometimes the division was fourfold. FRANCE offers a classic example where the three estates in order of decreasing status were the clergy, the aristocracy, and the bourgeoisie. In some parts of the HOLY ROMAN EMPIRE (e.g., Swabia), a fourth estate, the peasantry, received official recognition. But in most states, the peasants and urban lower classes lacked an official political rank.

Membership in a given order or estate brought with it attendant privileges (called liberties). In the theoretical scheme of things membership in a specific order or estate also entailed the fulfillment of certain responsibilities. The nobility protected the state from harm by giving military service, the clergy cared for souls, and the bourgeoisie furthered commerce, business, and financial activities. At the bottom, peasants, artisans, and other groups of poor people owed labor, money, and goods to the state and to their lords, who in return theoretically provided protection. The entire scheme was hierarchical and based on an analogy that compared human society to a living creature.

Theory and reality never wholly coincided, but by the 18th century, the economic and attendant social structures of society had changed such that this traditional scheme was jarringly removed from reality. A division of society according to lines of wealth, with an accompanying emphasis on talent and on individual rather than corporate identity, was becoming increasingly evident. Economic class was beginning to be more significant in practice than social and legal rank. But political structures and opportunities for advancement remained largely tied to ranks, to membership in a functional order.

The disparity between theory and practice—in the realms of legal status, political power, and economic reality—created significant tensions in ancien régime societies. Calls for recognition of talent rather than birth and for the abolition of privilege gave voice to this tension. The members of the privileged orders intermarried with newcomers, and noble rank, for example, could sometimes be acquired by purchasing a high office or by being rewarded for outstanding service. In spite of this social trend, the members of high orders generally rejected the idea of giving up their special status and, in fact, frequently tried throughout the 18th century to restrict upward mobility.

European states adopted several types of policies to try to mitigate the social conflict and instability resulting from the disparities between class and rank. One policy direction involved reform from above in an effort to eliminate the worst abuses of privilege. This line of attack was followed in France during the reigns of LOUIS XIV, LOUIS XV, and LOUIS XVI. The ministers, Jacques NECKER, Anne-Robert-Jacques TURGOT, and Charles-Alexandre de CALONNE tried with little success to attack fiscal privilege by instigating universal taxation.

Resistance came from all quarters of privilege in the form of the ARISTOCRATIC RESURGENCE, the opposition of the PARLEMENTS, and resistance from members of other privileged institutions. The development of a POLITICAL THEORY of monarchy limited by intermediate powers (for example, *see* MONTESQUIEU) assisted the cause of resistance.

A second general policy direction also involved reform from above by a central authority, but it incorporated the newly wealthy and educated into a special new privileged rank. It thus co-opted the potential discontent of the new classes to support the old system of ranks. While innovative, this solution proved ultimately to be a powerful conservator of the structural status quo. This solution appeared in PRUSSIA (Frederick William I and FREDERICK II [THE GREAT]) and RUSSIA (PETER I [THE GREAT] and CATHERINE II [THE GREAT]) with the creation of state civil services. In each state, the civil service provided a new hierarchy of service nobility open to talented individuals that paralleled the one of the hereditary, military nobility. The two lines were separate yet provided similar status and privileges.

A third solution to the tensions in the old system consisted of revolution or a radical restructuring of the old society of orders and ranks. In its place a new system was constructed in which all individuals enjoyed equal legal status under universal law and tax codes. The vision of an aggregate of individuals coming together into a government whose duty it was to preserve the natural rights of the individual provided the formative analogy for society. Liberal social contract theory and FREE TRADE theories (John LOCKE and Adam SMITH) put forth this view and, of course, both the AMERICAN REVOLUTION and the early phases of the FRENCH REVOLUTION attempted to put it into practice.

See also JUSTICE AND THE LAW; RIGHTS.

classicism A literary style of the 17th century associated with FRANCE under the ABSOLUTISM of LOUIS XIV. It coexisted in Europe with the BAROQUE STYLE, generally replacing that style in France and ENGLAND. The principles of classicism were spelled out in France by Nicolas Boileau in *L'art poétique* (The poetic art; 1664); by François Hédelin, abbé d'Aubignac; and by René Rapin. In England, the great exponent of classicism was Alexander POPE, while in GERMANY, its ideals were defended into the 18th century by Johann Christoph GOTTSCHED.

With roots in the model of NATURE and the geometrical method of reasoning developed by René DESCARTES, classicism offered literary ideals that reflected the assumed links between nature and human REASON. The model for both nature and reason in Cartesian thought was provided by geometry, a branch of mathematics concerned with two-and three-dimensional forms. The method used to prove theorems in geometry was a rigorous one based on the logic of deductive reason.

Classicism translated this geometric model into LITERATURE by stressing clarity of style and content, symmetry and simplicity of form, the existence of universal rules for composition, and the presentation of abstract truths. It aimed at directly imitating the rational order of nature. It abhorred strong emotion or any hint of imperfection and irrationality.

The result was literature written according to rules clearly specified for each specific literary genre. Themes were general in nature, and characters revealed their common human traits, not their uniqueness. Classicism did not suggest directly copying the forms of Greek or Roman antiquity, but rather drew inspiration from ancient subject matter.

The rules and doctrines of classicism were raised to special protected status through the activities of the Académie Française (French Academy), established during the later years of the reign of Louis XIII. LOUIS XIV supported the academy, viewing it as a means for extending his absolute rule into the realm of culture.

The formulas of classicism began to come under attack in the later years of Louis XIV's reign by writers interested in greater freedom and in contemporary content. The famous QUARREL BETWEEN THE ANCIENTS AND THE MODERNS, a dispute that dominated the literary salons of PARIS during the 1680s, pitted the elderly Boileau against Charles Perrault and other innovators. After the death of Louis XIV in 1715, classicism was generally abandoned in favor of the sentimental literature that had originated in early 18th-century England.

See also NEOCLASSICISM.

classicism, musical *See* HAMILTON, SIR WILLIAM; MUSIC; NEOCLASSICISM.

classification The act of organizing objects into systems based on a predetermined set of criteria. The desire to impose order on the chaos in the world, one of the chief stimuli of the 17th-century SCIENTIFIC REVOLUTION, continued into the ENLIGHTENMENT in a marked tendency to create classification systems. Examples abound: Carolus LINNAEUS developed the beginnings of our modern system for classifying plants and animals; Pieter CAMPER classified human races according to the measurement of their facial angles in order to simplify their treatment in works of art; anthropologists argued over whether the classification of living beings should include one or several species of human being; physicians developed systems of diseases, dividing them according to symptoms, origin, and other criteria; linguists spoke of the classification of world languages according to various criteria; and chemists such as Antoine LAVOISIER and Torbern BERGMAN developed new systems of elements and compounds.

The spirit of RATIONALISM persisted during the Enlightenment in these new systems, all of which reflected the belief that language and artificial categories could, indeed, accurately mirror the natural order of the world. Classifications provided a way for human beings to impose some order on the complex world, to have concrete evidence of the lawful structure of nature. They organized the objects of the world, suggested the nature of their relationships, and simplified the task of recovering information. In this manner, they helped to create the optimistic expectation that human beings would one day achieve absolute mastery over nature.

Cleland, John (1709–1789) *British novelist, journalist, and philologist*
He may have been the son of William Cleland (1674?–1741), but no records of his family background exist. Cleland attended Westminster School between 1721 and 1723. He traveled as a young man, eventually joining the EAST INDIA COMPANY in Bombay, India. A quarrel of unknown nature caused him to leave that position, whereupon he resumed traveling throughout Europe.

Cleland returned to ENGLAND in 1741, penniless and without any prospects for regular employment. He reputedly was put into debtors' prison several times. In 1749, during one of these incarcerations, he completed his novel *Fanny Hill, or the Memoirs of a Woman of Pleasure*. Cleland received the paltry sum of 20 guineas for the book from a publisher named Griffiths. The fantastic success of the work brought Griffiths £10,000 in sales earnings.

Fanny Hill is the story of a young woman who falls into prostitution, but who eventually recovers her mid-

Birds, beak varieties. The careful differentiation of birds according to the shape and function of the beak illustrates the 18th-century passion for imposing classification systems and order on the natural world. *(Courtesy New York Public Library)*

dle-class respectability. Fanny herself narrates the story in a series of letters to a friend who has inquired about the more scandalous episodes of her past.

Fanny tells how she journeyed to LONDON after the loss of her parents, hoping to find respectable employment as a servant. The owner of a brothel, who the 15-year old Fanny mistakes for a gentlewoman, hires her with promises that she will lead the life of a servant to the upper classes. The other prostitutes in the brothel quickly initiate Fanny into the pleasure she will enjoy as a member of their sisterhood.

Having escaped an attempted rape at the hands of one of the brothel patrons, Fanny runs away with Charles, a handsome young gentleman who keeps her as his mistress until his family intervenes. She then embarks on a lucrative career as a "woman of pleasure" until chance brings Charles back into her life.

In this novel, Cleland combines the conventions of 18th-century SENTIMENTAL FICTION with a philosophy drawn from the late-17th-century LIBERTINE literature of FRANCE and England. *Fanny Hill* was condemned by the Anglican bishop of London immediately after it appeared. The arrest of Cleland and his publisher Griffiths only increased popular demand for the book. Cleland was released after questioning, having pleaded poverty as his excuse for writing such a book. Lord Granville, a member of the privy council, procured Cleland a pension of £100 per year, hoping that this would free Cleland to use his talents for more edifying literary pursuits.

Cleland turned to journalism and theater after the *Fanny Hill* episode. He produced dramas such as *The Ladies' Subscription* (1755), *Titus Vespasian* (1755), and *Timbo-Chiqui, or the American Savage* (1758). His articles for the journal *Public Advertiser* appeared over the signatures of "Modestus" or "A Briton." He also wrote *Memoirs of A Coxcomb* (1751) and *Surprises of Love* (1765).

In the 1760s, Cleland began studying English linguistics and devoted himself especially to the relations between the English and Celtic languages. These investigations resulted in an essay entitled *The Way to Things by Words and to Words by Things* (1766). Cleland spent his last years in relative obscurity.

Clement XII (1652–1740) *pope*

Clement XII worked to restore the reputation of the Roman Catholic Church after the papacy of Benedict XIII. He was responsible for a number of reforms as well as physical improvements to ROME, though he also positioned the Church against ENLIGHTENMENT-influenced movements such as Freemasonry and JANSENISM.

Clement XII was born Lorenzo Corsini in Florence. The Corsini family had been prominent in the city since the middle of the 12th century; Lorenzo's ancestors included ambassadors, a bishop (subsequently a cardinal), a prince of the Holy Roman Empire, and a saint. His mother hailed from the Strozzis, another prominent Florentine noble family. Lorenzo studied at the Roman College and completed his doctorate in law at the University of Pisa. He returned to Rome and practiced law for his uncle, Cardinal Neri Corsini.

Following the death of his father and his uncle in 1685, Lorenzo gave up his right to inherit as eldest son and entered the priesthood. He devoted his time and money to enlarging the library he had inherited from his uncle. In 1691, he was made archbishop of Nicomedia and selected papal representative (nuncio) to the imperial court in VIENNA. Corsini did not go, however, because of a struggle between the emperor and Pope Alexander VIII over the selection of representatives. Instead, Corsini was appointed to the office of treasurer general and governor of the Castel Sant' Angelo, a key papal administrative position.

Under Pope Clement XI (pontiff 1700–21), Corsini showed himself to be skilled in matters requiring diplomacy and good judgment. In 1706, Corsini was made a cardinal deacon. He continued to advance under Pope Benedict XIII (pontiff 1724–30), securing a position as cardinal and bishop of Frascati.

Corsini was elected pope in 1730 at the age of 78. He took the name Clement XII in honor of Clement XI, who had been a benefactor and was also a distant relative. Clement XII was nearly blind (he lost his sight completely within two years of his election) and was not in particularly robust health, but what he lacked in youth and vigor he made up for with other abilities.He rooted out corruption, punishing one cardinal with imprisonment and a heavy fine. He modernized laws, especially those dealing with commerce, which, in turn, helped spur manufacture. He also reinstated the public lottery and used the money it generated to beautify Rome and improve its infrastructure. In matters of RELIGION, Clement XII devoted his energies to two causes—bringing the Roman Catholic and Eastern Orthodox Churches closer together and defending Catholicism from movements influenced or encouraged by the Enlightenment, such as Freemasonry and Jansenism.

See also FREEMASONS.

Clement XIII (Carlo della Torre Rezzonico) (1693–1769) *pope from July 6, 1758, to February 2, 1769*

The family of Clement XIII resided in VENICE, where it belonged to the ruling aristocracy. The future Pope Clement XIII studied first with the JESUITS at Bologna, then pursued a course in THEOLOGY and canon law (Catholic church law) at Padua. He went to ROME intent on a diplomatic career in the church. He was ordained a priest in 1716. He spent the next 10 years working in the provincial administration of the Papal States, then received a call to Rome to serve in the central papal administration.

Under Clement XII, Carlo entered the cardinalate, and by 1743 he had also become bishop of Padua. His contemporaries regarded him as conscientious, candid, benevolent, and generous. Carlo became Clement XIII in the papal election that followed the death of BENEDICT XIV. He was a compromise candidate, acceptable to the various factions within the church.

Rezzonico assumed the papal tiara at the point when European absolute monarchs were beginning strong attacks on both church privilege and the Jesuits within the boundaries of their kingdoms. The marquês de POMBAL in PORTUGAL, the *PARLEMENTS* in FRANCE, and CHARLES III in SPAIN forced the banishment of the Jesuits from their respective kingdoms. Papal power within Spain and the kingdom of Naples experienced further diminution when priests were forbidden to read papal bulls (decrees from the pope in the form of a letter accompanied by the special papal seal) in church pulpits without prior authorization by secular authorities.

Clement XIII responded to these attacks with papal bulls defending the Jesuits and asserting papal rights, but these had no effective power over the secular absolute monarchs. He also tried using censorship to gain control of the situation. Thus, many major works of the ENLIGHTENMENT were condemned and placed on the Index of Forbidden Books. Among the condemned works were *ÉMILE* by Jean-Jacques ROUSSEAU, *De l'esprit* by Claude-Adrien HELVÉTIUS, and the *ENCYCLOPÉDIE* edited by Denis DIDEROT and Jean Le Rond d'ALEMBERT. A tract by Febronius (Johann Nikolaus von Hontheim, 1701–90) that laid down the outlines of FEBRONIANISM also was banned. Another line of defense occurred in art when Clement ordered the nude body parts of the figures in Michaelangelo's Sistine Chapel frescoes painted over with clothing.

In a more positive vein, Clement patronized the artists Anton Raphael MENGS and Giovanni Battista PIRANESI. He expanded the Vatican Library collections by purchasing oriental manuscripts and by supporting various publishing projects. During the great drought of 1763–64, he provisioned Rome with supplies and had shelters built for the thousands of starving people from the countryside who crowded into the city. Clement XIII died of a stroke in 1769.

See also ABSOLUTISM; ABSOLUTISM, ENLIGHTENED; ROMAN CATHOLICISM; SEPARATION OF CHURCH AND STATE.

Clement XIV (Giovanni Vincenzo Antonio Ganganelli) (1705–1774) *pope of the Roman Catholic Church from May 19, 1769, to September 22, 1774*

He came from a town near Rimini where his father, Lorenzo, was a surgeon. Ganganelli studied with the JESUITS at Rimini and the Piarists at Urbino. He entered the Franciscan monastic order as a novitiate in 1723 and became a Franciscan priest in 1724; at that time he took the name Lorenzo as his religious name. Ganganelli studied THEOLOGY in ROME at the College of St. Bonaventura, received a doctorate in that subject, and carried out teaching duties at Franciscan convents in Bologna, MILAN, and Ascoli. Twice he refused nominations to head the Franciscan order. He received encouragement and support from the Jesuits as he advanced in his career. By 1759, CLEMENT XIII had awarded him a cardinal's hat. At the time, Clement XIII noted that Ganganelli seemed a Jesuit in Franciscan clothing. Ganganelli's election as pope came 10 years after his cardinalate.

In spite of his indebtedness to the Jesuits, Ganganelli, as Pope Clement XIV, did not hesitate to follow pragmatic policies that eased the tensions between the church and anti-Jesuit secular rulers. In 1773, he published the papal brief "Dominus ac Redemptor" (Lord and Savior), which fully suppressed the Society of Jesus, or the Jesuits. This brief legitimized the actions that had already been taken in FRANCE, SPAIN, and PORTUGAL. It disbanded the Society of Jesus throughout ITALY and POLAND, closing its many convents, colleges, and seminaries. But it did not actually extinguish the order, for both FREDERICK II (THE GREAT) and CATHERINE II (THE GREAT) refused to enforce the instructions of Clement XIV's bull. To have done so, of course, would have meant granting legitimacy to papal actions in their kingdoms, something they were unwilling to do. But also, both rulers valued the educational expertise of the Jesuits. Thus, the Society of Jesus continued to exist, but only in the non-Catholic states of PRUSSIA and Russia.

Clement XIV, like his predecessors, saw danger to ROMAN CATHOLICISM in the writings of the ENLIGHTENMENT. He condemned the works of Julien de LA METTRIE and some minor works by VOLTAIRE. He continued patronizing the arts in Rome by commissioning Anton MENGS to decorate the Vatican Museum. He expanded antiquities collections at the Museo Clementino and added to the papal coin collection. He also heard the 14-year-old Wolfgang Amadeus MOZART perform on the fortepiano and decorated him with the Order of the Golden Spur. Clement XIV died in 1774. Rumors circulated that he had been poisoned, but subsequent autopsies and historical inquiry have confirmed that he died of natural causes.

Clementi, Muzio (1752–1832) *Italian-born English composer, keyboard player, music teacher, piano manufacturer, and music publisher*

Muzio Clementi was born in ROME and began his musical studies at an early age. As a teenager, he attracted the attention of Englishman Peter Beckford, from a prominent LONDON family. Beckford took Clementi to ENGLAND and supported the young man's studies and musical education for the next seven years. In 1774, Clementi moved to London and began to appear publicly as a harpsichord player. The publication of a set of keyboard sonatas in 1779 bolstered his career and increased demand for his solo appearances. He undertook the first of three continental tours between 1780 and 1783, playing in PARIS, VIENNA, and other important centers. Upon returning to London, Clementi appeared regularly as a soloist with the orchestra at the Hanover Square Concerts, but he left for FRANCE abruptly in the middle of the 1784 season to elope with a French pupil (although her father put a stop to it). He also visited his family in Rome. He returned to London in May 1785, remaining there until 1802.

Beginning with the 1786 season, Clementi was at the height of his popularity as a performer and would remain there for several seasons. He played concertos, gave recitals, and conducted at the Hanover Square Concerts, and was named principal composer and performer of the latter. He continued to compose, especially for the piano. His music circulated widely and influenced, among others, the young Ludwig van BEETHOVEN. Clementi's popularity as a performer and composer began to erode with

Joseph HAYDN's two visits to London (1791–92 and 1794–95). Clementi stopped playing publicly sometime in the early 1790s and ceased conducting for nearly two decades beginning in 1796.

While his popularity as a composer and performer was waning, demand for Clementi as a teacher was growing. He summed up his pedagogic ideas in his *Introduction to the Art of Playing on the Piano Forte* (1801). He also established a music firm, Longman, Clementi & Co., in 1798, which, despite several changes of partners, survived until Clementi's death in 1832. The company manufactured pianos and published music, including works by Beethoven, Haydn (*The Seasons,* in 1813), and Clementi himself. Clementi visited the Continent for a third time in 1802 on behalf of his firm and remained abroad until 1810. After returning to London, he resumed conducting in 1813, leading several of his recent works from the keyboard at London's Philharmonic Society concerts and on visits to the Continent, notably to Paris in 1816 and 1817 and to Leipzig in 1822. He was, however, again eclipsed—this time by Beethoven—and retired from concert life after 1824. His work as a composer and teacher, which had spanned six decades, had a lasting influence on many of the 19th century's notable pianist-composers, and much of his piano music still remains in the repertory today.

Further reading: Leon Plantinga, *Clementi: His Life and Music* (Oxford: Oxford University Press, 1993).

coffeehouses *See* PUBLISHING; SOCIAL INSTITUTIONS OF THE ENLIGHTENMENT.

Coleridge, Samuel Taylor (1772–1834) *English poet, critic, philosopher*

The youngest son of a clergyman in rural Devonshire, Coleridge was sent to school in LONDON at Christ's Hospital, where he met Charles Lamb. In 1791, he entered Jesus College at Cambridge University, where he found little intellectual stimulation. He left the university without a degree in 1794. He became a friend of Robert Southey, with whom he planned to create a utopian democratic community in Pennsylvania.

To earn money for this project, Coleridge and Southey gave lectures on radical political subjects and collaborated on a verse drama, *The Fall of Robespierre* (1794). After the failure of the American venture, Coleridge met the British poet William Wordsworth. The friendship between Coleridge and Wordsworth became one of the most important literary partnerships in the history of British letters. Together, they published *Lyrical Ballads and Other Poems* (1798), a collection that served as the foundation of literary ROMANTICISM in ENGLAND.

The first edition of this collection opens with Coleridge's "Rime of the Ancient Mariner," a poem that tells the story of a sea voyage haunted by strange, unexplainable phenomena. This collection also contains "The Nightingale," "Frost at Midnight," and "France: An Ode." The poems "Kublai Khan" and "Christabel" also date from this period, although they were not published until 1816.

Coleridge began to experiment with opium around the turn of the century and, after 1803, fought addiction to that drug. He suffered periods of depression that left him unable to support his family.

Throughout his life, Coleridge attempted to create a philosophical system that could account for all natural phenomena, a project that conflicted with his strict Christian upbringing. Toward the end of his life, Coleridge published an account of his literary philosophy and intellectual development, which he called *Biographia Literaria* (Literary biography; 1817). In this work, he outlined his disputes with Wordsworth over the role of the human imagination in creating poetry. Coleridge divided the process of the imagination into two stages, the primary imagination (the perceiving mind) and the secondary imagination (the creating mind). He linked the creative mind to the powers of God.

Like other philosophers of romanticism, Coleridge criticized the power of REASON that had been proclaimed by some philosophers of the ENLIGHTENMENT. Coleridge believed that human reason is severely limited in contrast with the infinite potential of the human imagination. He thus expressed a conviction that had first developed in the late decades of the Enlightenment, as thinkers struggled with the increasingly obvious limits of RATIONALISM.

See also INTUITION AND IMAGINATION; LITERATURE; SUBLIME.

Collins, Anthony (1676–1729) *English judge and free-thinker, a major contributor to the development of deism*

Educated at Cambridge University, Anthony Collins became a close friend of the aging John LOCKE, who made Collins one of three trustees of his estate. One of Collins's primary intellectual opponents was Samuel CLARKE, the theologian who defended the NATURAL PHILOSOPHY of Isaac NEWTON in debates with Gottfried Wilhelm LEIBNIZ.

A committed believer in intellectual liberty and freedom of the press, Collins developed and published his own radical ideas regarding religious doctrine, the clergy, and the relationship between human will and necessity. His *Discourse of Free-Thinking, Occasion'd by the Rise and Growth of a Sect call'd Free-Thinkers* (1713) presented his argument about the right to think freely. Earlier works, *Essay Concerning the Use of Reason* (1707) and *Priestcraft in Perfection* (1709), developed the various threads that would compose the argument of the *Discourse.*

Although Collins championed intellectual freedom, he rejected the belief in the free human will that was common to most deists. Instead, he favored a doctrine of necessity that limited the action of the will in directing human behavior. He presented this position in his

Philosophical Inquiry Concerning Human Liberty (1715) and defended it against the criticisms of Samuel Clarke in the *Dissertation on Liberty and Necessity* (1729).

Collins's books generated much controversy. They were widely read and discussed in theological circles. He revived the idea that biblical stories and prophecies were intended as allegories rather than as historical reports of actual events. He developed these ideas in *A Discourse of the Grounds and Reasons of the Christian Religion* (1724) and *The Scheme of Literal Prophecy Considered* (1725). The former book generated especially intense interest and elicited more than 35 different replies within two years of its publication.

Collins also contributed to the discussions of the nature of the soul that were so much a part of enlightened PSYCHOLOGY, philosophy, and life science. He believed that it was conceivable that the soul was a material substance and insisted that if it is immaterial, it still is not necessarily immortal. Collins outlined these ideas in *A Letter to Mr. Dodwell* (1707).

Collins's books illustrate the manner in which the turn to REASON as the major source of human knowledge generated religious controversies during the formative years of the ENLIGHTENMENT. As the Enlightenment progressed, Collins's ideas and those of his fellow freethinkers would not only be extended but would also help to stimulate antirational forms of religious doctrine in response.

See also BIBLICAL CRITICISM; DEISM; FREEDOM; MATERIALISM; RELIGION; PUBLISHING.

Cologne (German: Köln)

German city located on the banks of the lower Rhine River. Cologne has a long and rich history that is intimately associated with ROMAN CATHOLICISM. In the fourth century, the Roman emperor Constantine made Cologne the seat of a Catholic bishopric. Charlemagne elevated the city to the higher status of archbishopric in the eighth century.

During the Middle Ages, Cologne was one of the preeminent European cities and the largest city in German lands. Roughly 40,000 people lived within its walls. As one of the great intellectual centers of Roman Catholicism, the city sheltered Albertus Magnus, teacher of Thomas Aquinas, Master Eckhart, and Duns Scotus, all prominent and original medieval philosophers. The city was economically powerful because of its location on the great Rhine River. It rivaled Lübeck, then the greatest of the Hanseatic League cities. Cologne became a free imperial city in the HOLY ROMAN EMPIRE in 1475, but the archbishop of Cologne remained a powerful element in the city's affairs, serving as an elector of the Holy Roman Empire until its demise in the 19th century. Since Cologne itself was a free city, the seat of the archbishop-elector actually lay in Bonn.

In the late 15th century, Cologne served as one center of the Catholic revival and reform movement that preceded the Protestant Reformation. By the 18th century, the Wittelsbach archbishops of Cologne could scarcely be distinguished from their secular counterparts. The last Wittelsbach archbishop-elector, Clementus-Augustus von Wittelsbach (1723–61), was a staunch ally of LOUIS XV and modeled his lifestyle after that of the French king. He built the Schloss Brühl (Brühl Castle; 1724–28) a few miles from Cologne. The palace was largely the work of the ROCOCO master François de CUVILLIÉS, but its central staircase was designed by Balthasar NEUMANN.

In 1784, the youngest son of the Hapsburg empress MARIA THERESA, Maximilian Francis, was elected archbishop of Cologne. He followed the pattern of his brother, Emperor JOSEPH II, in trying to reform the archbishopric. The University of Cologne, a stronghold of Catholic orthodoxy, exerted considerable conservative influence. To counter its power, Maximilian Francis transformed an academy at Bonn into a new university dedicated to teaching the reforming ideas of the ENLIGHTENMENT.

The city of Cologne was badly damaged (90 percent of the old town was destroyed) in World War II. It has been rebuilt, partially in the old style, but little that dates from the 18th century can be seen.

colonialism

The subjugation of one people or nation for the economic or political benefit of a dominant state. The term designating the practice is modern, but its rationale was argued in many 18th-century philosophical tracts concerning ECONOMICS, JUSTICE AND THE LAW, RACE, POLITICAL THEORY, RELIGION, and SLAVERY. Colonialism, as the state machinery of Europe's overseas territorial expansion, was driven by VOYAGES OF DISCOVERY, MERCANTALISM, CAPITALISM, and international competition among nations striving for economic wealth and world dominance.

Colonial acquisitiveness was by no means an 18th-century nor even a solely European or Christian phenomenon. Powerful military states from antiquity through the 17th century had subjected adjacent and distant lands to colonial control. In the 18th century, established colonial empires of the East included the Turkish Ottomans, the Chinese Qing dynasty, and the Indian Moguls.

A great part of the known world in the 18th century was partitioned out to imperial powers, whether Christian, Muslim, or Confucian. The Christian states most interested in new colonial acquisitions during the ENLIGHTENMENT were FRANCE and Great Britain, but SWEDEN, Finland, and RUSSIA acquired some colonies in the New World. The UNITED PROVINCES OF THE NETHERLANDS had been an active colonizer in the early 17th century, but its power declined in the 18th century. SPAIN and PORTUGAL had initiated Europe's grab for overseas colonies in the 15th century with the discovery of the New World and warfare in North Africa, but these states stagnated during the 18th century. At that time, Spain possessed

Bombay, ca. 1731. Illustration by George Lambert and Samuel Scott. Trade ships of the East India Company sail in front of the company warehouse. *(By permission of The British Library)*

several garrison cities in North Africa, the Canary Islands, Mexico, the greater part of southern North America, Venezuela, Colombia, Peru, Paraguay, Argentina, the Philippines, Cuba, and part of Hispaniola. Portugal governed Brazil, the Azores, and Madeira. The United Provinces still controlled several West African forts, Mauritius (in the early part of the century), and Indonesian plantations or trading posts as well as colonies in Guyana, Suriname, Curaçao, and several southern African towns, the most important being Cape Town. France had outposts in India and Madagascar and colonies in Hispaniola, Louisiana, Nova Scotia, Newfoundland, Quebec, and Montreal.

Internally, ENGLAND effectively colonized SCOTLAND in 1707 and Ireland in 1801. From its foothold in the New World in Virginia (1607), England had acquired the New World territories of Barbados, Connecticut, Delaware, Georgia, Maryland, Massachusetts, New Hampshire, New Jersey, New York, North Carolina, Pennsylvania, Rhode Island, South Carolina, and Virginia. In the Caribbean, England also held Jamaica. Britain gained control of French Canada in 1763. In the Mediterranean, Britain acquired Gibraltar, Minorca, and the Ionian Islands, and in the Pacific, it maintained trading posts in West Africa, Bencoolen, Ceylon, Singapore, and Hong Kong and colonies in New Zealand and Australia. The appointment in 1773 of the governor-general of Bengal, an administrator who was finally responsible to Parliament as well as to the EAST INDIA COMPANY, augured the beginning of colonization proper in India and stripped the Moguls of any real power. The East India Act of 1784 consolidated British activities by setting up a board of control.

Other European states had less success. Sweden and Finland founded small colonies in North America. Russians had explored Alaska in pursuit of the fur trade, but only in 1784 did Grigori Shelekhov (1747–95) establish the first permanent Russian settlement in Alaska, on Kodiak Island. The Russian American Company (chartered in 1799), influenced by Shelekhov's deputy, Aleksandr Baranov, extended the fur trade down the west coast and founded a settlement in California in 1812. However, Russian colonists never numbered above a few hundred, and the native Alaskans who resisted colonial domination contained the spread of Russian influence.

As might be expected from such a complex international nexus, European systems of colonial control were varied. However, the two major types of colonial governance can be characterized by the assimilation or exclusion of indigenous people. Spain and Portugal, both Roman Catholic countries, were assimilationist, claiming, in theory at least, a mission to Christianize and civilize native people in the New World. In practice, the mission served to justify the plunder of the land and the slaughter of the indigenous people. Ultimately, the Iberians introduced relatively benign governments administered by a viceroy and backed by the Catholic Church. Iberians practiced plantation agriculture, but Iberian colonial wealth chiefly came from precious metals stolen from or mined by Native Americans. Also Roman Catholic and assimiliationist, France attempted the conversion of Native Canadians and employed them in exploration and in military actions against the English. But France lost its Canadian territories to Britain in 1763, and French Canadians who had sought refuge from the British in French Louisiana were transferred by the Louisiana Purchase of 1803 to the jurisdiction of the UNITED STATES OF AMERICA.

New World European arrivals in the 17th century— the English and Dutch—were primarily exclusionary with respect to the native population. Their interest in permanent settlement, plantation agriculture, and international trade resulted (often despite governmental directives from home) in the displacement or slaughter of Native

Americans, a practice justified by John LOCKE's concept of land use. His concept granted possession of land to the person or persons who improved it through their labor. British New World colonialism expanded unchecked until the AMERICAN REVOLUTION, when the 13 North American colonies claimed independence. The United Provinces still held colonies in the New World, but in the 18th century Dutch interests lay primarily in Indonesia.

Besides gold, silver, and minerals, New World commodities included furs, sugar, tobacco, rice, coffee, and cotton. Colonists (France excepted) exchanged their agricultural products for African slaves and manufactures from the home country. Some states, such as England, controlled colonial shipping so firmly that colonists were entirely dependent on government supplies and credit.

Colonialism initiated the traffic of African slaves to the New World. Because European immigrants were not numerous enough to provide sufficient labor for plantations and indigenous populations often proved intractable, by the late 17th century large-scale agriculture demanded the labor of African slaves. Commodity SLAVERY—that is, the sale of slaves in open markets—had long been operating in the East and in various forms throughout Europe. After the introduction of African slavery into America, Spanish, Portuguese, Dutch, and English colonies made use of slave labor. This reliance on slaves had dire results for Africa and, indeed, for the United States. Whereas most 18th-century Europeans would have conceived their influence as enabling native and African PROGRESS, current opinion holds that the effects on indigenous peoples and slaves have been entirely pernicious. Thomas JEFFERSON recognized the negative effects that slavery had on slaves as well as slave masters. Europeans spread European disease (sometimes deliberately), introduced deadly firearms and alcohol, oppressed ethnic peoples physically, linguistically, politically, legally, and sexually, and, in the English and Dutch colonies at least, refused to acknowledge their own hybrid children fathered on native or slave women.

Even as Europeans became more firmly entrenched in the New World during the 18th century, colonialism laid the ground for revolts. Slaves rebelled regularly throughout the century. Innumerable insurrections occurred in colonial territories, and in French Saint Domingue rebels managed to establish the free state of Haiti in 1804.

Colonialism was threatened not just by slave revolt, but also by the revolt of colonial subjects against home rule. Britain's American colonies revolted in 1776 and achieved independence in 1783; Spain's Mexican colony rebelled from 1810 to 1811 and achieved independence in 1821.

In the 18th century, the territorial acquisitiveness that came to be known as colonialism expanded eastward from Europe. Colonialism in the East was facilitated by discoveries in the Pacific and Australasia, better navies and safety at sea, the suppression of piracy, and the eco-

nomic return on rampant consumerism at home. Besides providing economic wealth, colonialism permitted relief from overcrowding at home by the placement and employment of Europeans in eastern colonies.

In the East, European policy was directed by trade interests rather than the permanent settlement of emigrants. Valuable trade goods included spices, coffee, tea, silk, inexpensive cottons, and, later, opium. Virtually all European states chartered East Indies trading monopolies and established their own culturally distinct outposts.

New colonial projects arose in the early 19th century. Britain acquired South Africa, and France subjugated Algiers. Colonialism throughout Africa surged in the late 19th century, when BELGIUM, ITALY, and GERMANY joined in the grab for territory. Apart from the 18th-century revolutions by slaves and colonial subjects, the dismantling of colonial empires was primarily a 20th-century phenomenon.

See also NATURAL LAW; NATURAL RIGHTS; *TWO TREATISES OF GOVERNMENT*.

Further reading: Norman Davies, *Europe in History* (Oxford: Oxford University Press, 1996); O. W. Frost, ed., *Bering and Chirikov: The American Voyages and Their Impact* (Anchorage: Alaska Historical Society, 1992); George Raudzens, *Technology, Disease and Colonial Conquests, 16th to 18th Centuries* (Boston: Brill, 2001).

Common Sense A revolutionary pamphlet published by Thomas PAINE in January 1776. In 1775, the first battles of the AMERICAN REVOLUTION had already been fought, but a declaration of complete independence from Britain had not yet been issued by the American rebels. The leaders of the American colonies were attending the Second Continental Congress in PHILADELPHIA. Paine, who had arrived in the colonies from ENGLAND two years previously, decided to write a series of articles arguing the case for independence. At the urging of his friend Dr. Benjamin RUSH, Paine collected his articles and published them as a pamphlet called *Common Sense*. Rush suggested the title.

Common Sense quickly created a sensation, selling more than 150,000 copies in the colonies within two months. Paine reduced the price from two shillings to one shilling so that unskilled workers and poor people might be able to buy it.

In the pages of *Common Sense,* Paine attacked the basic notion of rule by a monarch, called for independence from Britain, and suggested that defeating Britain would constitute PROGRESS for humankind. He depicted the colonies as a haven for people needing to escape civil and religious persecution. He asserted that the colonists were being driven by the actions of the British government into rebellion. His ideas elicited a flurry of Loyalist pamphlets, but none could compete with the popularity of Paine's masterful piece. Paine's suggestions were ultimately adopted by the committee headed by Thomas JEFFERSON that prepared the formal DECLARATION OF INDEPENDENCE.

Common Sense is just one example—a particularly influential one—of the hundreds of pamphlets whose publication helped to fuel revolutionary actions in Europe and America at the end of the ENLIGHTENMENT. Because LITERACY rates reached new highs during the 18th century, these pamphlets reached a widespread audience that cut across normal social and economic boundaries. They provided a potent weapon for propaganda, but also helped to democratize political culture by engaging a wide segment of the population in political dialogue.

See also PUBLISHING.

Condillac, Étienne Bonnot de (Abbé de Condillac) (1714–1780) *French philosophe, psychologist, and theorist of language*

Condillac was the third son of Gabriel de Bonnot, viscount of Mably, who was a judge in Dauphiny. His brothers, Jean Bonnot de Mably and Gabriel Bonnot de Mably, both lived in PARIS. Gabriel Bonnot de Mably established a reputation as a philosophe with special interest in economic issues.

As a young adolescent, Condillac lost his father and subsequently moved to Paris, where his oldest brother, Jean, supervised his education. Condillac studied at the seminary of Saint-Sulpice and received his degree in theology from the Sorbonne, the faculty of theology of the University of Paris. He took minor orders and became an abbot (abbé). His surname, Condillac, was the name of a family estate in the Dauphiny.

Condillac moved easily into the social world that supported the French ENLIGHTENMENT. He attended the weekly salons of Madame du Tencin, Madame d'ÉPINAY, Mademoiselle de LESPINASSE, and Mademoiselle de La Chaux. Jean-Jacques ROUSSEAU introduced Condillac to Denis DIDEROT.

Condillac made significant contributions to the development of a psychological theory of knowledge based on sensation. He built on the twin legacies of the physics of Isaac NEWTON and the association PSYCHOLOGY of John LOCKE. His psychology rejected the RATIONALISM of DESCARTES that had informed earlier French theories and spurred on the process of separating psychology from philosophy. Condillac perceived a serious weakness in Locke's sensation psychology. Locke had distinguished between the physical perception of an object and the idea (consciousness) of the object, thereby implicitly leaving open the possibility that innate ideas exist. Condillac was committed to banishing innate ideas from psychology and to demonstrating that all knowledge comes from outside sensory experience.

Condillac attempted to place Lockean sensation psychology on a sounder basis. To do so, he reexamined the question of how the mind passes from physically perceiving an object (perception) to formulating ideas about the object (consciousness). For him, the mediator in this process was LANGUAGE; in fact, he believed that language

Portrait of Condillac. Étienne Bonnot de Condillac helped to establish the sensation psychology of John Locke as the most influential approach to human understanding during the Enlightenment. He presented his own interpretation of these psychological principles in his *Treatise on Sensations.* (*Courtesy New York Public Library*)

served as the underlying cause of all higher intellectual functions of the mind such as attention, memory, imagination, intuition, reason, and reflection.

Armed with these basic convictions and concerns, Condillac studied the development of language. He established a theory that asserted the identity (one-to-one correspondence) between perception and idea. Condillac's theory left no room for mental interpretation of perceptions in the process of idea formation, for varying perceptions, or for innate ideas.

In developing his concepts of language, Condillac used algebra (mathematical analysis) as a model. Algebra consisted of a set of unambiguous symbols and rigorous rules that yielded certain knowledge about mathematical and physical relationships. Drawing an analogy with algebra, Condillac treated language as a set of similar symbols (letters and words) and rules (grammar) that also yields certain forms of knowledge. The MECHANICAL PHILOSOPHY provided him with a theory of sensation that could explain how identity between the perception of any object and its idea is achieved. This theory posited that in perception, a physical likeness of the image is actually impressed on the nerves and mechanically transmitted to the brain.

Condillac sketched these ideas in *L'essai sur l'origine des connaissances humaines* (Essay on the origin of human knowledge; 1746) and then elaborated them in the *Traité des sensations* (Treatise on sensations; 1754). The latter work contains his renowned description of the manner in which a statue, organized internally like a human being, attains complex knowledge from the accumulation of individual sensations. The book posits that the experience of pleasure and pain helps the statue to decide how to respond to various external stimuli. This pleasure and pain experience would later become a fundamental source of morality in utilitarian MORAL PHILOSOPHY.

Condillac elaborated his ideas about language as an algebra in two later works: *La logique* (Logic; 1780) and *La langue des calculs* (The language of calculations; published posthumously in 1798). He proposed that all sciences must have foundations in rigorously constructed languages. During the late Enlightenment several such language projects—the new chemical nomenclature developed by Antoine LAVOISIER and the species classifications by Jean Baptiste de LAMARCK and Carolus LINNAEUS—appeared. Furthermore, Condillac's work directly stimulated the advances in linguistic science made by Wilhelm von Humboldt (1767–1835).

Condorcet, Marie-Jean-Antoine-Nicolas Caritat, marquis de (1743–1794) *French mathematician, social scientist, and philosophe*

Condorcet came from an old noble family of the principality of Orange. After converting to CALVINISM in the 16th century, his ancestors settled in the Dauphiné, where the Calvinist HUGUENOTS had a strong territorial base. During the 17th-century repression of French Protestants by LOUIS XIV, the family reconverted to ROMAN CATHOLICISM.

As an infant Condorcet lost his father, who died in a battle. An uncle who was the bishop of Auxerre became the child's guardian. Condorcet's mother was Marie-Madeleine-Catherine Gaudry, madame de Saint-Felix, daughter of a financial official in the region of Soissons. According to tradition, she surrounded her son with Catholic piety, dedicated him to the Virgin Mary (hence the name Marie), and forced him to wear white dresses until the age of eight.

At 11, Condorcet took his first steps away from provincial culture by entering the Jesuit school at Reims. This was followed by training at the Jesuit Collège de Navarre (secondary school). Nothing is known of Condorcet's feelings during his youth, but as an adult, his thinking contained strains of a rabid ANTICLERICALISM. He completely rejected the teaching tradition of the JESUITS, claiming that the custom of educating children under church auspices perfectly guaranteed that they would be reduced to the intellectual level of beasts.

In 1758, against the wishes of his family, Condorcet elected to study mathematics in PARIS rather than to pursue a military career. He submitted a paper on integral calculus to the FRENCH ACADEMY OF SCIENCES in May 1765. In 1769, he gained a seat in the academy and after four years became the assistant to the perpetual secretary of that institution. By 1775, he had received the position of perpetual secretary, which he kept until 1793, when his political enemies during the FRENCH REVOLUTION forced him into hiding. From 1773 until 1793 Condorcet wrote the official eulogies (*éloges*) of deceased academy members. These literary sketches earned him a seat in 1782 in the French Academy (Académie Française).

Condorcet espoused revolutionary ideas about public EDUCATION, financial reform, and the constitution of governments based on his convictions about the PERFECTIBILITY of the human mind and the NATURAL RIGHTS of all people. He believed, however, that changes should occur in small steps and felt that the calling of the Estates General to a meeting in 1789 was an unwise action. In his opinion, the citizens of FRANCE were not yet enlightened enough to vote judiciously. However, as the events of the French Revolution began to unfurl, Condorcet joined the National Guard and then worked briefly in his local Paris neighborhood (commune). He joined revolutionary clubs like the Société de 1789 (1789 Society) and the JACOBINS. He also served in the Legislative Assembly and the National Convention.

Condorcet voted to condemn King LOUIS XVI of treason, but he opposed the death penalty as punishment. He did not hesitate to criticize the constitution proposed in the National Convention at the session of July 24, 1793. In the environment of rapidly escalating revolutionary fervor, a fellow academician, Chabot, used the occasion of the criticism to accuse Condorcet of being an enemy of the young French Republic. Condorcet, fearing for his liberty and life, hid at the home of his friend Madame Vernet. Then, concerned that he would implicate her in the eyes of the accusers, he fled from Paris. He was denounced by a patriot in the town of Clamart, arrested, and imprisoned at Bourgla-Reine. On March 29, 1794, he committed suicide in his prison cell by swallowing poison.

Condorcet was a disciple of VOLTAIRE, Jean Le Rond d'ALEMBERT, and Anne-Robert-Jacques TURGOT. His ideas helped to shape many facets of social and political theory and action during the closing years of the 18th century. He championed and helped to create the new social sciences that were developing in the atmosphere of the late ENLIGHTENMENT. He believed that rational laws govern human relations and that these laws can be discovered by the use of REASON and applied to human affairs. He dreamed of establishing a social mathematics that would contain the certainty and predictability of algebra, geometry, and calculus.

The term *social science* first appears in a letter addressed by a member of Condorcet's circle to him. It entered normal usage through the activities of the IDEO-LOGUES, who, in 1795, oversaw the establishment of a new system of French public education inspired largely by Condorcet's writings. The early 19th-century creators of sociology such as Claude-Henri de Rouvroy de Saint-Simon and Auguste Comte claimed Condorcet as their predecessor. The marquis de LAPLACE, Poisson, and Cournot worked to actualize Condorcet's dream of a rational science of decision making. Finally, Condorcet developed strong views about the manner in which the "doing of science" should be organized. He conceived of science as a vocation that should be the central occupation of a scientist's life. He therefore began developing the ideas that would ultimately remove science from the realm of amateurs and reserve it to professionals.

Condorcet's major works included the following: *Esquisse d'un tableau historique des progrès de l'esprit humain* (Outline of a historical view of the progress of the human mind; 1795); *Rapport et projet de décret de l'organisation générale de l'instruction publique* (Memo on the general organization of public instruction; 1792); *Examen du gouvernement d'Angleterre, comparé aux constitutions des États-Unis* (Examination of the government of England, compared to the constitutions of the United States; 1789; contributor). Also, many articles appeared in the *Supplément à l'Encyclopédie, où Dictionnaire raisonné des sciences, des arts, et des métiers* (Supplement to the Encyclopedia, or rational dictionary of the sciences, arts, and crafts; 1776); *Du calcul intégral* (On the integral calculus; 1765); and *Du problème des trois corps* (On the three-body problem; 1772). Condorcet edited the periodical *La Républicain* (The republican) with Thomas PAINE and Achille Duchâtelet. He also assisted with the *Chronique de Paris* (Chronicle of Paris). Condorcet published editions of the *Pensées de Pascal* (Thoughts of Pascal), the *Oeuvres complètes de Voltaire* (Complete works of Voltaire), and the *Lettres de M. Euler à une princesse d'Allemagne sur différentes questions de physique et de philosophie* (Letters of Mr. Euler to a German princess on different questions about physics and philosophy; 1795). Condorcet's widow edited his complete works in a 21-volume French edition (Paris, 1804).

See also MATHEMATICS AND MECHANICS; EULER; PHILOSOPHES.

Further reading: Keith Michael Baker, *Condorcet: From Natural Philosophy to Social Mathematics* (Chicago: University of Chicago Press, 1975); Edward Goodell, *Noble Philosopher: Noble Philosopher: Condorcet and the Enlightenment* (Amherst, N.Y.: Prometheus Books, 1994); Ian McLean and Fiona Hewitt, eds., *Condorcet: Foundations of Social Choice and Political Theory* (Northampton, Mass.: Edward Elgar, 1994); Emma Rothschild, *Economic Sentiments: Adam Smith, Condorcet and the Enlightenment* (Cambridge, Mass.: Harvard University Press, 2002).

Bust of Condorcet by J. A. Houdon. Marie-Jean Caritat, marquis de Condorcet, mathematician, academician, social scientist, revolutionary, believed that reason and human perfectibility would guarantee progress for civilization. *(Courtesy Musée Versailles. © Photo R. M. N.)*

Confessions Autobiography by the Genevan philosophe Jean-Jacques ROUSSEAU, an outstanding revelation of subjective experience and of the intricacies of the social culture of the ENLIGHTENMENT. The *Confessions* consists of 12 parts that describe Rousseau's life from his childhood up to the year 1765. The book appeared posthumously in 1782 (parts one to six) and 1789 (parts seven to 12).

Unlike many memoir writers of the 18th century, Rousseau intended in the *Confessions* to reveal his inner development rather than merely to chronicle events of his era. Rousseau's life had always been difficult, marked by intense friendships, bitter quarrels, trouble with authorities, public criticism, and persecution. His innovative stances on a broad range of topics had made him vulnerable to vicious attacks in the press. For example, an anonymous pamphlet by VOLTAIRE entitled *Sentiments of a Citizen* had accused Rousseau of madness, indecency, irreligion, megalomania, ingratitude, subversive behavior, and debauchery.

The *Confessions* served not only as a personal revelation, but also as Rousseau's response to his enemies. The book sought to counter his negative reputation by describing the large conspiracy, directed by Melchior GRIMM, Denis DIDEROT, Madame d'ÉPINAY, and David HUME, that he believed was driving the public attacks against him.

Using the model of the *Confessions* by Saint Augustine (354–430), Rousseau presented his understanding of his own development from childhood to adulthood. He discussed the mistakes he had made and the paths he could have taken to secure more desirable results. Augustine had organized his work to reveal not only his personal sins, but also to convey his profession of faith. God was the ultimate judge of his life and the source of his salvation. Rousseau, in contrast, set up his readers as his judges. He sought salvation, understanding, and acceptance in the act of baring his soul before his contemporaries.

If confession and salvation form one set of themes in this book, a second set revolves around the relationship between self-knowledge and pleasure. In the 17th century, René DESCARTES had transformed EPISTEMOLOGY by making knowledge of the self (his famous *cogito ergo sum*, or I think, therefore I am) the foundation of all knowledge about God and the world. The Enlightenment had developed this approach to knowledge. In presenting his subjective ideas of himself Rousseau was to some extent merely playing on this theme, offering his life as a source of general information about human nature and behavior. He was also, however, indulging himself by reliving the passionate, pleasurable moments of his past, using this remembrance to balance equally powerful, but painful, memories.

Rousseau's *Confessions* closely parallels *ÉMILE* (1762), his famous *Bildungsroman* (novel of EDUCATION and formation), but the *Confessions* narrates his personal, subjective, flawed experience rather than outlining an ideal path of development.

Although the *Confessions* was finished in 1770, Rousseau did not want the book to appear until after his death. In fact, he asked his publishers to wait until 1800 before putting it into print. It appeared posthumously, as Rousseau wished, but before 1800, and evoked a mixed response. Many readers in FRANCE found Rousseau's revelations—about his sexual activities, petty thefts, and abandonment of his children—shocking. His admirers thought that he had ruined rather than rescued his reputation. In Britain, reception was lukewarm, and Edmund BURKE castigated the book as an "unparalleled monument of vanity and folly." It seems that the *Confessions* was most appreciated by German writers such as Johann Wolfgang von GOETHE, Friedrich SCHILLER, and Christoph Martin WIELAND, who spoke enthusiastically of its daring content.

Despite this ambivalent initial reception, the *Confessions* stands out as one of the key texts of modern LITERATURE and as a monument to important trends in the Enlightenment. It broke new ground by relating the inner development of an individual personality. Its concentration upon childhood as the central formative period in life reflected the Enlightenment's "discovery" of the special nature of childhood. Its willingness to be embarrassingly frank underscored the importance given to private spheres of life in 18th-century thought. Thus, the book presents several important traits of the Enlightenment and can serve as an entertaining and educational introduction to this era.

See also BILDUNG; HISTORY; PHILOSOPHES.

Congreve, William (1670–1729) *English writer and dramatist, noted for his brilliant Restoration comedies of manners*

Although born in ENGLAND, Congreve grew up in Ireland, where his father was serving in a garrison of the English army. Congreve attended Trinity College in Dublin. During his university years, he established what would be a lifelong friendship with the writer Jonathan SWIFT. He also enjoyed the friendship and admiration of John GAY, Alexander POPE, and Richard STEELE.

Congreve studied law at Middle Temple, but he never entered the legal profession, choosing writing instead. He launched his dramatic career at Drury Lane Theatre with the highly successful comedy *Old Bachelor* (1693). In 1695, his play *Love for Love* inaugurated the new theater at Lincoln's Inn Fields. Congreve became one of the production managers at the theater.

Restoration comedy concentrated on interpreting the world of the aristocracy. It specialized in witty presentations of foppish young lords and mined the subject of sexual intrigue for humorous material. Congreve excelled in this genre, although his last play, *The Way of the World* (1700), begins to explore love from more serious perspectives. As the 18th century opened, English audiences began to lose interest in the subject matter of Restoration comedy and to demand themes taken from middle-class life and values.

In 1698, the critic Jeremy Collier published an attack on Congreve entitled *A Short View of the Immorality and Profaneness of the English Stage*. Collier's criticisms underlined the shift in values that was occurring within the consumers of English THEATER and LITERATURE. This incident apparently demoralized Congreve; at any rate, he abandoned writing for theater after 1700 and turned to a career in the English civil service.

In addition to his Restoration comedies, Congreve left one novel, *Incognita* (1692); collaborated with John DRYDEN on the translations of the satires of Juvenal (1692) and Persius (1693); and created a blank verse tragedy, *The Mourning Bride* (1697).

Although he never married, Congreve had a long and close friendship with his leading actress, Mrs. Anne Bracegirdle. He is also alleged to have been the lover of the second duchess of Marlborough and to have fathered a daughter, Lady Mary Godolphin, by her. He left most of his fortune to the duchess.

Cook, James (1728–1779) *English explorer*
Popularly known as Captain Cook, he served as a sailor in the English navy and merchant marine before embarking on his famous voyages around the world. Cook was an excellent seaman and student of the mathematics of navigation.

Cook's first voyage on the ship named *Endeavour* lasted from 1768 until 1771. It was billed publicly as a voyage to Tahiti for the purpose of carrying out observations on the TRANSIT OF VENUS that occurred in 1769. However, Cook also had secret instructions to sail south, in order to search for the rumored huge southern continent. In the course of his travels, Cook charted New Zealand (first reached by Europeans in 1642), charted the east coast of Australia, and found Torres Strait. Among the passengers who sailed with Cook was Joseph BANKS, the botanist whose collections and observations vastly expanded 18th-century knowledge of world flora.

Cook's second voyage, with the ships named *Resolution* and *Adventure,* occurred from 1772 until 1775. Again, he searched for the great southern continent, "discovering" in the course of his travels Easter Island, Tonga, the Marquesas, the New Hebrides, New Caledonia, part of Tierra del Fuego, South Georgia, and the South Sandwich Islands. Traveling with Cook on this voyage were Johann Georg FORSTER and his father Johann Reinhold Forster.

Cook's practices at sea—his demand for shipboard cleanliness, the provision of time for exercise, and the use of lime juice or lemon juice to ward off scurvy—became the model for the Royal Navy and acted as proof of the benefits to be gained by attention to practical human needs. As a reward for his achievements, Cook was promoted to captain. The ROYAL SOCIETY OF LONDON received him as a fellow and awarded him the Copley Medal for his paper on the prevention of scurvy. Cook left an account of his travels that was published as *A Voyage Towards the South Pole, and Round the World Performed in His Majesty's Ships the Resolution and Adventure, in the years 1772, 1773, 1774, and 1775* (1777).

Cook began a third exploring voyage, designed to find the rumored Northwest Passage through the North American continent. He sailed east toward Alaska with the *Resolution* and the *Discovery,* landing on the island of Hawaii and charting much of the Bering Strait. Upon returning to Hawaii to overwinter, Cook was killed by Hawaiians in an incident involving a dispute over a boat.

Cook's exploits amply illustrate the manner in which the technological and mathematical advances spurred by the scientific spirit of the ENLIGHTENMENT led to significant discoveries and advantages for European nations. His travel memoirs, like those of other travelers, were read avidly by Europeans. The new cultures and worlds that were constantly being discovered helped to stimulate discussions in fields as widespread as comparative RELIGION, ANTHROPOLOGY, and the natural sciences.

See also TAHITI; VOYAGES OF DISCOVERY.

Copernican Revolution
Term used by historians to describe the great shift in conceptualization of the universe that developed from the middle of the 16th century through the 18th century. This revolution had implications not only for ASTRONOMY but also for physics, THEOLOGY, and PHILOSOPHY. It stands as one of the fundamental changes in European thinking and helped to lay the foundations for our modern world. The Copernican Revolution served as a major stimulus for the SCIENTIFIC REVOLUTION of the 17th century without which the science of the ENLIGHTENMENT—and indeed many general concepts of that 18th-century intellectual movement—could not have existed.

The Copernican Revolution takes its name from the Polish astronomer Nicolaus COPERNICUS, who in 1534 published a technical mathematical treatise, ON THE REVOLUTION OF THE HEAVENLY SPHERES, in which he proposed a theory of a HELIOCENTRIC (Sun-centered) universe. Traditional beliefs about the universe, derived from the ancient Greeks, Aristotle, and Ptolemy, posited an Earth-centered universe in which the Sun and planets revolved around the Earth on crystalline spheres. This universe was finite, bounded by an orb in which all the stars were located. It was conceived as bipartite in structure. The terrestrial realm, containing the Earth, differed fundamentally from the celestial realm in which the Moon, planets, and stars resided. The terrestrial realm was a world of change over time and of imperfection governed by a set of physical laws based on motion in straight lines. In contrast, the celestial realm was a realm of perfection in which change did not occur and which was governed by perfectly circular, self-sustaining motion. This system had been used for centuries to explain celestial phenomena and to structure astronomy, physics, cosmology, and related theology. But it contained weak points that Copernicus considered intolerable. It could not in his view satisfactorily explain the paths of the planets as observed from the Earth. And it was a complex, messy theory, something that Copernicus found distasteful.

Copernicus proposed that if the Earth were conceived as simply another planet, moving with all the planets around the Sun, then the problem of observed planetary motion would be more satisfactorily explained than in the Ptolemaic system.

This shift in conception provided the jumping off point for what over time became the Copernican Revolution.

ASTRONOMY Plate LXXXVII
Fig. 207 The GRAND ORRERY by Rowley

Fig. 208

Grand orrery by John Rowley. Orreries, mechanical instruments prized by wealthy amateur astronomers and public lecturers, reproduced the motions of the heavenly bodies according to the Copernican heliocentric theory. *(Courtesy Bettmann Archive)*

Changing the position of the Earth in relation to the center of the universe and giving it motion (Copernicus actually assigned three motions to the Earth) created new theoretical problems in astronomy. It raised questions about the size of the universe and the source of planetary motions, questions that would eventually affect physics as well as astronomy. It also challenged the old concept of a bipartite universe in which the terrestrial realm was governed by laws different from those that ruled in the celestial realm. It suggested that a single set of uniform laws might govern all bodies in the universe.

Still another critical question centered on the issue of whether or not Copernicus's theory actually described the physical reality of the universe. At the time of the publication of *On the Revolutions of the Heavenly Spheres,* a preface by Andreas Osiander was attached that asserted that the theory should be construed as nothing more than a useful hypothesis. This ploy allowed the book to pass by the censors and protected it until the beginning of the 17th century, when the work of Galileo GALILEI with the TELESCOPE made it increasingly difficult, though not at all impossible, to deny the physical existence of the Copernican universe. This issue became a major concern not only for astronomers, physicists, and other natural philosophers, but also for Christian theologians. If the Copernican system were indeed real, then centuries of theological dogma, whether Catholic or Protestant, would be challenged and would require revision. The Copernican vision thus challenged fundamental aspects in many realms of human thought and belief.

The Copernican Revolution as a scientific phenomenon was scarcely begun by Copernicus. It was much more the product of later astronomers, mathematicians, physicists, and philosophers. Major contributions were made prior to the 18th century by Johannes KEPLER, Galileo Galilei, Giordano Bruno, René DESCARTES, G. A. Borelli, Robert Hooke, and, of course, Isaac NEWTON. In resolving problems raised by Copernican theory, these men and their lesser-known contemporaries developed a new concept of SCIENCE and NATURE that established universal mathematical laws as the immediate source of order in the universe. They developed the associated MECHANICAL PHILOSOPHY to describe the world as they conceived it. They created the new science that the PHILOSOPHES of the Enlightenment hailed as a great revolution and that modern parlance calls the Scientific Revolution.

By the beginning of the 18th century, the old Earth-centered, finite, bipartite Ptolemaic universe had been replaced by an infinite, vastly populated, Sun-centered universe governed by universal mechanical mathematical laws.

Copernicus, Nicolaus (Polish: Mikolaj Kopernik) (1473–1543) *Polish astronomer*

Copernicus authored *De Revolutionibus Orbium Coelestium* (ON THE REVOLUTIONS OF THE HEAVENLY SPHERES; 1543). This book proposed the revolutionary but not wholly unprecedented idea that the Earth moves around the Sun. It laid the theoretical foundations of and provided detailed observations and technical mathematical support for the HELIOCENTRIC (Sun-centered) theory of the universe. During the half-century following its publication, the book precipitated the COPERNICAN REVOLUTION in ASTRONOMY.

Nicolaus Copernicus was raised by a maternal uncle, himself a bishop in the Catholic Church, who provided for Copernicus's education at the University of Cracow and who secured his election as a canon in the cathedral chapter of Frombork. The position provided a steady income that allowed Copernicus to enroll in a course of canon law at the University of Bologna and to pursue his private interests in astronomy. The cathedral chapter also granted Copernicus permission to travel to ITALY in order to study medicine at the University of Padua and to finish his canon law studies at Ferrara. Copernicus returned to POLAND in 1503 and spent the remainder of his life serving the cathedral chapter and working as an astronomer. In 1513, with the support of the chapter, he constructed the small observatory from which he conducted the astronomical observations that underlay his heliocentric theory of the universe.

Copernicus developed his heliocentric theory relatively early but declined to publish it for fear of its heretical implications. To upset the traditional Ptolemaic cosmology in which the Earth stood at the center of the universe was to challenge the traditional doctrines of Christianity. Instead of publishing his early ideas and observations, Copernicus circulated them among astronomers in a manuscript entitled *De hypothesibus motuum coelestium a se constitutis commentariolus* (Short treatise on the hypothesis of the heavenly motions, having been established from [the motions] themselves; 1514). One of his students and earliest disciples, Georges Joachim Rheticus (1514–76), also published an advanced report of the Copernican theory, the *Narratio Prima* (First report), in 1540 and again in 1541.

Rheticus finally persuaded the reluctant Copernicus to publish *De Revolutionibus Orbium Coelestium*. The first edition, which appeared in 1543, was allegedly placed in Copernicus's hands as he lay on his deathbed. It spelled out a basic heliocentric theory of the universe. More important, at least for Copernicus's contemporaries, the book provided pages of detailed measurements of planetary positions and associated mathematics.

The potential of the book for spearheading a revolution in astronomy was not fulfilled until the opening years of the 17th century. By that time, astronomers and mathematicians were beginning to make celestial discoveries that gave increasing authority to the Copernican heliocentric vision. In those early decades of the 17th century, it is possible to see an incipient Copernican Revolution. But that revolution, with all its implications for RELIGION, NATURAL PHILOSOPHY, and general interpretations of the place of humanity in the universe, would not be completed until well into the period of the 18th-century ENLIGHTENMENT.

Corelli, Arcangelo (1653–1713) *Italian composer and violinist*

Arcangelo Corelli composed a fairly small number of works by 17th- and 18th-century standards. His output was restricted to instrumental genres such as the concerto grosso and the trio sonata. This small body of work, however, is not indicative of Corelli's profound influence on several prominent 18th-century composers and musicians.

Corelli was born into a prosperous family of landowners in Fusigano, midway between Bologna and Ravenna, on February 27, 1653. He began studying music with a local priest, and at the age of 15, went to Bologna, where he continued his studies. In 1675, he went to ROME, where he was engaged to play as an orchestral violinist in several church performances. He gradually gained recognition for his performing abilities. He entered the service of Queen Christina of Sweden, who lived in Rome, sometime before May 1679, and he dedicated to her his first published collection, the 12 Trio Sonatas, op. 1. These were chamber pieces for two violins and bass instruments written to showcase the individual talents of the performers. He continued to appear frequently and regularly as the leader of the violin section of orchestras at prominent performances in Rome, including, from 1684, concerts organized for his patron, Cardinal Benedetto Pamphili, who was the dedicatee of Corelli's 12 Trio Sonatas, op. 2. Pamphili hired Corelli as his music master in 1687, and the composer-violinist remained in his service until 1690.

When Pamphili left for Bologna in 1690, Corelli entered the service of Cardinal Pietro Ottoboni, the nephew of Pope Alexander VIII. Corelli performed at regular musical academies held in the cardinal's palace on Monday evenings and dedicated his op. 4 set of trio sonatas to his new patron. Corelli's performing technique began to decline during the first years of the 18th century, and he retired as a violinist in 1708. He died on January 8, 1713, and was interred in the Pantheon in Rome.

Corelli's influence both as a violin teacher and as a composer was important and widespread. Several famous violinists of the early 18th century studied with him, among them Francesco Gasparini, Francesco Geminiani, Pietro Locatelli, and several others from both ITALY and the rest of Europe. The 1680s saw the beginning of Corelli's wider influence as a composer. The Bavarian composer Georg Muffat imitated Corelli's style in his *Armonico tributo* (Harmonic tribute), a series of sonatas published in 1682. Several other imitations and tributes appeared, including works by Antonio VIVALDI, Baldassare Galuppi (*Concerto in the Manner of Corelli*), Georg Philipp TELEMANN (*Sonates corellisantes*), and François COUPERIN (*Le Parnasse, ou l'Apothéose de Corelli* [Parnassus, or the apotheosis of Corelli]). In 1695, the Englishman John Ravenscroft composed a group of trio sonatas so similar to Corelli's work that they were republished in 1730 as Corelli's posthumous "op. 7." Corelli also exercised an influence over the young George Frederick HANDEL, who visited Rome from 1707 to 1708. During Handel's stay, Corelli played in the orchestra in performances of the young composer's early oratorios: *Il trionfo del tempo e del disinganno* (1707) (later revised and published as *The Triumph of Time and Truth*) and *La resurrezione* (The resurrection; 1708). He apparently collaborated closely with the young composer, offering advice on several stylistic and technical matters. The concerts were among Corelli's final appearances as a violinist.

Further reading: Peter Allsop, *Arcangelo Corelli: New Orpheus of Our Times* (Oxford: Oxford University Press, 1999).

Cort, Henry (1740–1800) *English ironmaster*

Henry Cort developed techniques for puddling (transforming pig iron into wrought iron) and for moving iron between grooved rollers. Both improvements created a malleable product and yielded the finished iron at least 15 times faster than existing manufacturing practices. Cort's inventions allowed the use of cheap coal fuel in iron mills. The grooved rollers permitted iron to be performed in the refining process, thereby permitting the production of standardized shapes for beams, bars, and rails. The development of new methods for iron and steel production was a significant factor in the later 18th-century phases of the INDUSTRIAL REVOLUTION.

Così fan Tutte

Two-act opera buffa (farcical comic opera with dialogue in recitative form) by Wolfgang Amadeus MOZART (K588). Lorenzo da Ponte wrote the libretto. The opera was commissioned in 1789 after the widespread success of *LE NOZZE DI FIGARO*. *Così fan tutte* (Thus do they all) premiered in the VIENNA Burgtheater on January 26, 1790. The death of Emperor JOSEPH II caused the production to be closed after only five performances. It reopened in 1790, playing from June through August of that year. Shortly thereafter, it appeared in Prague, Leipzig, Dresden, Frankfurt, Mainz, and AMSTERDAM.

The plot of *Così fan Tutte* deals with favorite themes of the late ENLIGHTENMENT: the questions of female loyalty, love, and the nature of the two sexes. These issues are explored through the medium of a bet. The action requires disguises and complicated comic twists highly popular with 18th-century audiences. As the plot unfolds, the inconstancies of both sexes become clear. However, the behavior of Dorabella, the disloyal female, receives the most attention. The piece is one of many late-Enlightenment works that present the feminine as something dark, irrational, and opposed to REASON-based enlightenment. Nevertheless, it also shows the feminine as the one source of constancy in human relations, for the second lead female character, Fiordiligi, is the only character who does not betray a lover.

See also MUSIC.

cosmopolitanism   An ENLIGHTENMENT philosophical and intellectual idea that sought to transcend national loyalties and local prejudices. Adherents to cosmopolitanism were called "cosmopolites" or "citizens of the world." They were to be found in ENGLAND, FRANCE, GERMANY, SWITZERLAND, ITALY, and America. These intellectuals believed that the formation of the individual's moral, cultural, and artistic intelligence depended on an open attitude to different places and people. Of course, even important cosmopolitan philosophers sometimes failed to live up to the ideal: VOLTAIRE disliked Jews, and David HUME disliked the Irish. Nevertheless, the ideal derived from an eclectic mix of philosophical, scientific, religious, economic, and political thought that stressed the unity of all humankind and sought to promote humanitarian compassion in every individual.

At its least imposing level, cosmopolitanism became a social aspiration of the urban elite, manifest as a fashionable regard for the clothes, cuisine, and furnishings of the cosmopolitan centers of PARIS and LONDON. At its highest level, cosmopolitanism fostered a truly international movement in Western intellectual history, a movement that attempted to redress social inequities and undermine constricting traditions.

The 18th century ushered in the third phase of cosmopolitanism. Its proponents are too numerous to enumerate in full, but some major figures in cosmopolitan moral PHILOSOPHY were Voltaire, Hume, Benjamin FRANKLIN, Adam SMITH, Joseph PRIESTLY, Marie-Jean de CONDORCET, Paul-Henri-Thiry d'HOLBACH, Immanuel KANT, Thomas PAINE, Cesare Bonesana BECCARIA, Edward GIBBON, and Denis DIDEROT. Some cosmopolitan works are Paine's *RIGHTS OF MAN*; Hume's *DIALOGUES CONCERNING NATURAL RELIGION*, and *Enquiry concerning the Principles of Morals*; Voltaire's *CANDIDE*, and *Élémens de la philosophie de Newton* (Elements of Newton's philosophy); Franklin's *Experiments and Observations on Electricity*; and Kant's *Foundations of the Metaphysics of Morals*.

The canon of 18th-century cosmopolitan writing was founded on two earlier phases of the ideal. The first phase was classical. In post-Aristotelian philosophy, Diogenes the Cynic and the Stoics adopted cosmopolitanism (cosmos = world, polis = city state) as a doctrine of world citizenship in opposition to the traditional, hierarchical distinction Greeks made between themselves and barbarians. The focus on individualism, the ethical concern for humanity, the consciousness of political pluralism, and the artificial nature of the state remained basic to later forms of cosmopolitanism. The second phase arose in Europe and lasted from the Renaissance to the 17th century. Its major proponents were Erasmus, Francis Bacon, John LOCKE, Isaac NEWTON, Pierre BAYLE, and Gottfried LEIBNIZ. Cosmopolites in the 18th century integrated the intellectual premises of these two sets of precursors, in particular, knowledge of classical history, Newtonian cosmology, and the philosophy of NATURAL RIGHTS. They also took into consideration 18th-century historical realities—the development of international commerce, the information collected about other peoples from exploration and VOYAGES OF DISCOVERY, and contemporary political systems.

Cosmopolitan philosophers met in the salons, COFFEEHOUSES, and clubs characteristic of the age; they communicated by letters and books, and they traveled widely. They were interested in science and promoted the SCIENTIFIC METHOD, which applied universal procedures in the investigation of natural phenomena and universal categories in the CLASSIFICATION of results. They promoted moral philosophy as an alternative to traditional theology, and in religion sought to transcend local beliefs, sectarian loyalties, and even Christianity itself. Often the term *deism* is applied to their unorthodox approach to theology. Cosmopolites also discussed and wrote about current affairs. In economics, they were critical of the protectionist policies that characterized 17th-century mercantilism, and put forward a constructive theory of FREE TRADE. In politics, they stripped governments of their traditional power to oppress and awe the people.

Concerned about the incessant warfare among nation states in Europe and America, cosmopolites presented theories of international cooperation for the mutual benefit of humankind. A number of projects to avoid interstate warfare were proposed, including the French Abbé de Saint Pierre's *Project for Perpetual Peace* (1713). Responding to St. Pierre in *Perpetual Peace: A Philosophic Sketch,* Kant proposed that the relations among polities had to be controlled if moral life were to be possible within the polity. Kant first proposed the suppression of wartime practices and peace treaty negotiations that fostered continuing enmity (the principle behind the United Nations today and our modern code of international legal order). He supplemented this principle with three "Definitive Articles" that set out the precise relationship between the individual and the just (or republican) state; the relationship of polities to one another; and the relationship of states and individuals to one another on the understanding of a common humanity.

A corollary to the intellectual and political effects of cosmopolitanism was its effect on ordinary people. European manners shifted from the strictures imposed by religious authorities, and the 18th century saw a new interest in artistic SENSIBILITY and a decline in legal restraints on morality and religious practice. Additionally, explorers, travelers, and writers had revealed to Europeans the intriguing physical, cultural, and spiritual differences among the peoples of the contemporary world, and many people coasted on these currents of adventure and experimentation.

The decline of cosmopolitanism around 1790 came about primarily from the deaths of nearly all its major figures. It was supplanted in the 19th century by ROMANTICISM in the arts and nationalism in politics.

See also COLONIALISM; DEISM; PUBLISHING; SOCIAL INSTITUTIONS OF THE ENLIGHTENMENT; TOLERATION; TRAVEL LITERATURE; VATTEL; WOLFF.

Further reading: Thomas J. Schlereth, *The Cosmopolitan Ideal in Enlightenment Thought* (Notre Dame, Ind.: University of Notre Dame Press, 1977.

Cottin, Sophie (1770–1807) *French novelist*

Born Sophie Risteau to a well-to-do Bordeaux family, Cottin was a successful and widely read novelist whose literary career was tragically halted by her premature death from breast cancer in 1807. Living only to the age of 37, Cottin produced a body of work all the more remarkable for the short period of time in which she produced it: Her first published NOVEL, *Claire d'Albe* (1799), was immensely popular, and was followed by four other novels; a prose poem titled *La Prise de Jéricho* (The fall of Jericho); and a historical novel, *Mélanie,* which was left unfinished at her death.

Cottin's life followed the same tragic path as the lives of her characters. She was able to marry for love in an age when arranged alliances were the norm, but two months after she and the wealthy Parisian banker Jean-Paul-Marie Cottin were wed in 1789, the Bastille fell, sparking the FRENCH REVOLUTION. Cottin's husband supported a constitutional monarchy, and when this viewpoint became dangerously unpopular, the couple fled to ENGLAND. Between 1791 and 1793 they moved between England, SPAIN, and FRANCE, as they attempted to maintain control over their property in France while ensuring their personal safety. Jean-Paul-Marie Cottin's health was already fragile, and the stress of emigration and a dangerous political climate proved too much for him; he died in 1793. After his death, most of Cottin's fortune was lost, and she was exiled from PARIS by the repressive regime known as the Terror. Cottin was eventually able to buy a house in the French countryside and find some semblance of security living with her cousin Julie and her two nieces. Cottin's close relationship with Julie is reflected in the intense fictional friendship between Claire d'Albe and her cousin Elise.

Claire d'Albe, published in 1799, remains her best-known work. It established the subject matter and tensions of her literary output: love, virtue, and the situation of women. The title character, a young woman in an arranged marriage to a much older man, discovers true love with his adopted son Frédéric. Loyal to her sense of virtue and responsibility, Claire nevertheless finds herself drawn to the promise of happiness and fulfillment with this younger man. Like many sentimental novels, which were frequently authored by women, *Claire d'Albe* discusses conflicting issues of personal liberty versus familial and moral responsibility; Cottin's frank acknowledgment of women's sexuality is more unusual. In the early 19th century, *Claire d'Albe* was a best seller; today, it is still appreciated for its dramatization of the ENLIGHTENMENT concern with individual happiness, its emphasis on the innate goodness of the uncultured Frédéric, which is reminiscent of the work of Jean-Jacques ROUSSEAU, and its scenes of emotional plenitude and despair. Claire's position as wife and mother imposes a conflict between virtue and desire; in this way, the novel also provides a thoughtful treatment of gender roles, and its epistolary format gives the reader a sense of intimately knowing the heroine.

Cottin's novel *Elisabeth, ou les exilés de Sibérie* (Elisabeth, or the exiles of Siberia; 1806) was translated and adapted more than any of her other works. The story of a devoted daughter who goes to Siberia to save her exiled father, the novel inspired reworkings by other artists as a play and an OPERA. Scenes from the novel were reproduced as engravings for home decoration, as well as appearing on household items such as wallpaper and clocks. The immense popularity of Cottin's novels was for some time overshadowed by later writers' rejection of the sentimental genre, but she has been rediscovered in recent years by critics seeking to understand the influence of women authors and the connection of the sentimental novel to intellectual and literary movements of the 18th and 19th centuries.

See also WOMEN AND THE ENLIGHTENMENT.

Further reading: Michael J. Call, *Infertility and the Novels of Sophie Cottin* (Newark: University of Delaware Press, 2002); Margaret Cohen, *The Sentimental Education of the Novel* (Princeton, N.J.: Princeton University Press, 1999); Sophie Cottin, *Claire d'Albe,* tr. Margaret Cohen (New York: MLA, 2002); David Denby, *Sentimental Narrative and the Social Order in France, 1760-1820* (Cambridge: Cambridge University Press, 1994); Janet Todd, *Sensibility: An Introduction* (New York: Methuen, 1986).

Coudray, Angélique-Marguérite Le Boursier du (ca. 1714–1794) *French midwife*

Madame du Coudray traveled exhaustively throughout FRANCE, teaching women about childbirth and challenging the male-dominated medical establishment. Her modern techniques, ability as a teacher, and ability to navigate the hazardous political waters made her efforts a great success.

Coudray established herself as a midwife in PARIS in 1740. She spent the next decade building her reputation and acquiring apprentices. In 1751, she traveled to the Auvergne, which was facing a depopulation problem. Her work there allowed her to refine her teaching and to perfect her visual aids, including the "Machine," a model of the pelvic region that included a uterus and an extractable baby, with all of the anatomy clearly labeled.

In 1759, faced with infant mortality and population loss, LOUIS XV called on Madame du Coudray to travel through the country, educating women about MIDWIFERY and childbirth as she had in the Auvergne. This was a controversial move on the part of the king because of the tension at the time between midwives and the university-trained physicians usually deferred to in such matters. Coudray spent 23 years traveling through France with her assistants, and estimates place the number of women she spoke to at around 10,000. Demonstrations on her "Machine" and pamphlets handed out to women helped Coudray convey her message. Her efforts are credited with helping to bring about population growth during the second half of the 18th century in France. She died during the Terror in April 1794.

Further reading: Nina Rattner Gelbart, *The King's Midwife: A History and Mystery of Madame du Coudray* (Berkeley: University of California Press, 1998).

Coulomb, Charles-Augustin de (1736–1806) *French physicist*

A member of a successful family of judges, Coulomb was prepared for a career as a military engineer. He spent some time on the island of Martinique in the West Indies helping with the construction of Fort Bourbon. Upon return to FRANCE, Coulomb spent time near Rochefort and Cherbourg before finally being assigned, in 1781, to PARIS.

Coulomb was elected as a corresponding member of the FRENCH ACADEMY OF SCIENCES in 1774, named adjunct mechanician in 1781, and associate mechanician in 1784. He won a prize in 1781 for his paper entitled *Théorie des machines simples* (Theory of simple machines). He was appointed to the Institut de France in 1795. Coulomb retired from his duties as a military engineer with the outbreak of the FRENCH REVOLUTION and settled in the region of Blois. Napoleon appointed him inspector of public instruction during the first years of the 19th century, but Coulomb died in 1806, before he could accomplish much in his new position.

Coulomb's fame derives from his work in the field of electricity. He formulated certain laws that helped to untie the puzzles that electrical and magnetic phenomena had posed for earlier generations of scientists. In particular, Coulomb developed the mathematical law bearing his name that describes the relations between electrical charge and attraction or repulsion. He demonstrated that electrical charge collects on the surface of a conductor and established the inverse square law of magnetic attraction and repulsion. The unit of electricity used in modern physics is called the coulomb.

Coulomb thus acted in several areas of significance for the ENLIGHTENMENT. He furthered the process of mathematization of the sciences by developing equations for electrical phenomena. He also contributed to the endeavor of measuring that accompanied mathematization by developing a sensitive instrument, the torsion balance. This device permitted him to make the measurements that produced Coulomb's law. The whole series of events demonstrates the reciprocal causal relations that existed between TECHNOLOGY AND INSTRUMENTATION on the one hand, and theoretical innovation on the other. This relationship was one of the primary driving forces behind developments in SCIENCE during the Enlightenment.

Couperin, François (1668–1733) *French composer, organist, and harpsichordist, called the "Great Couperin" (le Grand Couperin)*

Couperin was a member of a family that produced several generations of musicians. He was the only son of Charles Couperin and Marie Guérin. He studied organ, harpsichord, and composition with Jacques-Denis Thomelin at the parish church St. Jacques-la-Boucherie in PARIS. After the death of his father, who served the church of Saint-Gervais as its organist, young François Couperin received the post. In 1693, at age 25, he succeeded his former master as organist for the royal chapel. Members of the court, including LOUIS XIV, esteemed Couperin highly; he was asked to play harpsichord concerts (the famed *concerts royaux*) at the court and to compose for various occasions. In 1694, he acquired the office of master harpsichordist and composer for the duke of Burgundy and the royal princes. The post of harpsichordist for the Kings's Chamber became his in 1717. His students included sons and daughters of various prominent aristocrats as well as the members of the royal family.

Couperin helped to create the early 18th-century STYLE GALANT (gallant style) music, which is closely related to the ROCOCO in the visual arts and architecture. His music combined elements of the traditional French BAROQUE STYLE with conventions borrowed from contemporary Italian composition. The music is lively and filled with delicate ornamentation.

Couperin published several collections of pieces among which the best known are the four volumes of *Pièces pour clavecin* (Pieces for harpsichord), the *Concerts royaux* (Royal concerts), *Nouveaux concerts* (New concerts), *Les goûts réunis* (Tastes reunited), *Les apothéoses* (Apotheoses), *Les trios* (Trios), and *Sonates pour violon* (Sonatas for violin). Couperin's sacred choral works included the well-known *Leçons des Ténèbres* (Lessons of Tenebrae), written for the special Catholic Masses of the last three days of Holy Week. Couperin published a method for learning harpsichord, *L'art de toucher le clavecin* (Art of playing the harpsichord), which, for the first time, suggests that the thumb might be used in playing the harpsichord.

Couperin played a role in freeing organists, harpsichordists, and composers from the restraints of guild organization. He bought himself a noble title after a royal decree in 1696 allowed 500 distinguished persons to "ennoble" themselves (i.e., purchase the title). Couperin died on September 12, 1733, in Paris. His daughter, Marguerite-Antoinette (1705–78), succeeded him in his post as harpsichordist for the King's Chamber. She also received an appointment as master of the harpsichord for the royal ladies of France. She was the first woman to receive such honorable offices.

Cowley, Hannah (1743–1809) *English playwright and poet*

Hannah Parkhouse was born in Tiverton, ENGLAND, the daughter of a bookseller and classical scholar who encouraged her intellectual development. In 1772, she married Thomas Cowley, a government clerk who later became a captain in the EAST INDIA COMPANY.

She commenced her writing career by chance when she remarked during the performance of a play that she could do better and then met her husband's skepticism by writing *The Runaway*. Only two weeks in composition, it was produced in February 1776 by David GARRICK, the famous actor and manager of the Theatre-Royal in Drury Lane. The play proved itself both a popular success and an economic windfall for Cowley, who earned more than £500 (nowadays about $35,000). Cowley followed up with 12 more plays, most of them comedies about fashionable people involved in courtship negotiations. Among these works was *The Belle's Stratagem*, which premiered in 1780 and wittily satirized the world of upper-class manners and morals.

A married woman with four children, Cowley presented herself as a model of female propriety and, like many of her contemporaries, was dismayed by the moral tone of the fashionable crowd. She quarreled with several theater managers and retired from the stage in 1801. Some contemporaries condemned her as a hypocrite, and Cowley, in turn, somewhat censorious of women intellectuals in general, condemned Mary WOLLSTONECRAFT for her political interests and publicly accused Hannah MORE of plagiarism.

Cowley also wrote poetry, which critics have treated unkindly. The name "Anna Matilda," which she adopted in a platonic, poetical correspondence with Robert Merry (writing as Della Crusca) in a highly popular work entitled "The British Album" (1790), ultimately became a figure of speech to denote an overly affected and sentimental style.

See also MORAL PHILOSOPHY.

Cowper, William (1731–1800) *English poet, a dominant figure in English literature during the late 18th century*
William Cowper, member of a prominent English family of judges, studied law and entered the legal profession in 1754. He began shortly afterward to experience the symptoms of the mental depression that would plague him throughout his remaining years. He worked for a few years in the English civil service as commissioner of bankrupts (1759–64). A suicide attempt in 1763 was apparently provoked by fear that his bid to obtain a clerkship in the House of Lords of the British Parliament would be blocked. Cowper entered the asylum of Dr. Nathaniel Cotton for two extensive periods of treatment: The first lasted from 1763 to 1765, and the second from 1773 until 1774. Cowper was protected and cared for by his close friends the Unwins. He lived unmarried with their daughter Mary Unwin for several years. After her death in 1796, Cowper slipped into a deep depression that lasted until he died in 1800.

A deeply religious man, Cowper excelled at producing poetry on themes related to his faith. His *Olney Hymns* (1779), written with John Newton, became standard popular Protestant hymns. Cowper's religious poetry included "The Progress of Error," "Truth," "Hope," "Charity," "Conversation," and "Retirement." He also wrote *The Ballad of John Gilpin* (1782) and *The Task* (1783).

Cowper excelled at writing blank verse, and his letters set a new standard for that art in the English literary world. The romantic poets William Wordsworth and Samuel Taylor COLERIDGE revered Cowper's work. His literary activities delved into many of the realms that would characterize later ROMANTICISM—Homer, Milton, and melancholy—themes that were already staple elements of the English GOTHIC REVIVAL.

Creation, The Large-scale religious composition (oratorio) for choir and full orchestra by Joseph HAYDN. Haydn's inspiration for this work came from a hearing of Handel's *Messiah* in LONDON. He was stunned by the huge choir (nearly a thousand singers!) and the large orchestra. The "Hallelujah Chorus" moved Haydn to tears. After this performance, Haydn decided to write such a work. He spoke with his agent in London, Johann Peter Salomon, who provided him with a text. The origin of the text remains unknown. Haydn asked his patron and friend Baron Gottfried van SWIETEN to revise the text and to translate it into German. The finished oratorio premiered in a private concert, April 29 and 30, 1798, at the VIENNA palace of Prince Schwarzenberg. The Associierte, a group of aristocratic patrons of music headed by van Swieten, underwrote the performances. The official public premiere occurred in Vienna at the Burgtheater in March 1799. *The Creation* was a triumphant success and soon was being heard throughout Europe.

The text of *The Creation* is definitely permeated with the DEISM and optimism of the ENLIGHTENMENT. The work extols the magnificent design of God's creation. It contains none of the Christian ambivalence toward humankind, no hint of the expulsion of Adam and Eve from the Garden of Eden, or of the related notion of original sin. The music offers highly programmatic elements (the superb choral proclamation in C-major at the words "and there was light") and is written in a style closely related to Haydn's creative approaches to the symphony.

Crèvecoeur, Michel-Guillaume-Saint-Jean de (1735–1813) *French writer who lived in colonial North America*
Michel-Guillaume-Jean de Crèvecoeur, also known as J. Hector St. John de Crèvecoeur or as the "American Farmer," was born near Caen, FRANCE. He served as a soldier on the Canadian front during the SEVEN YEARS' WAR (French and Indian War). Afterward, he traveled in the western regions of the British colonies (Ohio and the Great Lakes region) and settled in New York in 1759. He obtained citizenship in New York in 1765.

During the AMERICAN REVOLUTION, Crèvecoeur's personal loyalties caught him between the opposing factions. He was imprisoned in New York for some months, then, in 1780, he returned to Europe, settling in LONDON. In 1784, having been appointed consul to three states in the fledgling UNITED STATES OF AMERICA, he returned to America. In 1790, after completing his diplomatic service, Crèvecoeur traveled back to Europe, where he finished his years living in France and GERMANY.

In London, as J. Hector St. John, Crèvecoeur published his *Letters from an American Farmer* (1782). The book served enlightened Europeans as a primary source of information about the new political and social experiment called the United States of America. It also earned him an appointment to the FRENCH ACADEMY OF SCIENCES. Crèvecoeur also published *Voyage dans la haute Pennsylvanie et dans l'État de New York* (Travels in Upper Pennsylvania and New York; 1801).

Crèvecoeur wrote a second group of essays about America, but these were not published until 1925 as *Sketches of Eighteenth Century America, or More Letters From an American Farmer.* These essays contain penetrating observations about American religious life, sketch out the melting pot theory of the young nation, and offer rich documentation about the complexities and tensions in American existence.

criticism *See* AESTHETICS.

Crompton, Samuel (1753–1827) *English inventor*
Samuel Crompton was the son of a prosperous farmer who also produced cloth. Crompton created the SPINNING MULE in 1779, but sold the invention for £60 as he could not afford to patent it himself. The spinning mule helped

to transform the cotton industry by greatly increasing the quality of spun yarns and the efficiency of output. In 1812, Crompton received a monetary reward of £5,000 for his invention from the British Parliament.

Cruikshank, George (1792–1878) *English artist, illustrator, and caricaturist*

Born in LONDON of an artistic family, Cruikshank displayed great natural aptitude and never had formal technical training. Family circumstances required him to begin working as an assistant to his father, Isaac, who designed etchings for a living. By his late teens, George Cruikshank's talents had already attracted some attention.

Cruikshank possessed a fine eye, wit, and intellect that enabled him to incorporate biting political satire in his etchings. Cruikshank's approach continued the tradition of William HOGARTH. His prints offer modern students a valuable commentary on the politics of early 19th-century England. They were published both individually and as illustrations to various books. Cruikshank died in London in 1878. He is buried in St. Paul's Cathedral.

Cruikshank's political satirical prints can be found in *The House that Jack Built* (1819) and *Facetiae and Miscellanies* (1827). Other witty illustrations can be found in *The Humorist* (1818–21), Grimm's *Collection of German Popular Stories*, *Bentley's Miscellany* (contains the prints that illustrated *Oliver Twist* and *Guy Fawkes*), the *Ainsworth Magazine* (volumes one to six), and the *History of the Irish Rebellion in 1798*. Cruikshank himself published several books of his drawings: *George Cruikshank's Omnibus*, *George Cruikshank's Table Book*, *Cosmic Almanack*, and *The Life of Sir John Falstaff*. Cruikshank's productions, designed for widespread consumption and produced independently without public or private patronage, provide one example of the lasting nature of the changes wrought under the influence of the ENLIGHTENMENT in the aims and modes of artistic production.

Cudworth, Ralph (1617–1688) *English philosopher and theologian, a prominent member of the group known as the Cambridge Platonists*

Educated at Cambridge University, Cudworth devoted his life to that institution. During the English Revolution and Civil Wars (1647–60), Cudworth supported the cause of religious TOLERATION. He originally backed the revolutionary Commonwealth but turned against it when the Puritan factions began to show increasing rigidity. In 1654, Cudworth became master of Christ's College, Cambridge, a post he retained until his death in 1688.

Cudworth contributed to the development of rational theology, DEISM, and rational systems of ethics in ENGLAND. He was the leading systematic philosopher among the Cambridge Platonists. His major work was *The True Intellectual System of the Universe* (1678).

This treatise attacked the ATHEISM implied in philosophies of MATERIALISM. Its targets were both the ancient Greek Epicureans such as Democritus, and contemporaries such as Thomas HOBBES and Benedict de SPINOZA. In developing his alternative to materialism, Cudworth combined Renaissance Neoplatonism with Cartesian MECHANICAL PHILOSOPHY.

At issue was the question of the independent existence of a spiritual soul. Materialists described all activities of the soul as products of the mechanical motion of matter. Cudworth, in contrast, believed that some sort of spiritual principle had to exist in order to give life and motion to the universe. But Cudworth also rejected Cartesian dualism, the system that posited a stark division between mind and body or between soul and matter. He developed a middle position, proposing that a spiritual principle called the "plastic nature" actually exists in all matter and provides life. This concept of the "plastic nature" was adopted during the ENLIGHTENMENT by the supporters of VITALISM.

Cudworth held that religious belief could be founded on human REASON, but he rejected any notion that made reason the product of the simple mechanical action of matter. He believed that materialist philosophies were actually unreasonable and irrational because they failed to recognize the spiritual attributes of reason.

Cudworth also wrote a treatise on MORAL PHILOSOPHY that was published posthumously in 1731. Entitled *Treatise Concerning Eternal and Immutable Morality*, it rooted morality in NATURAL LAW rather than in the revealed laws of God. The development of such forms of ethics helped to separate the realm of ethical behavior from that of religious faith and assisted in building the foundations for a secular rather than religious moral social order.

Cudworth's theories had implications not only for theology but also for SCIENCE and PSYCHOLOGY because they addressed fundamental questions about the nature of matter, of life, of soul, and of morality. Cudworth's work contributed to the intellectual currents that emerged full-blown during the 18th-century Enlightenment. His work was particularly useful to Isaac NEWTON as Newton struggled to develop his concept of universal gravitation.

See also EPICUREAN PHILOSOPHY; RELIGION.

Cullen, William (1710–1790) *Scottish physician and chemist*

Cullen studied MEDICINE and chemistry first at the University of Glasgow and later at the University of Edinburgh. Cullen began working as a private physician in 1734, receiving his M.D. degree from Glasgow only in 1740. After 1744, Cullen gave private lectures in Glasgow and persuaded the university to provide him with funds for a chemistry laboratory to supplement his independent lectures in that subject. Cullen became officially affiliated with the University of Glasgow in 1751, when he accepted the chair in medicine. In 1755, he assumed the chair of chemistry at the University of Edinburgh and then, in 1766, the chair of the theory (institutes) of medicine. The chair of physics was added in 1773. Cullen helped to found the ROYAL SOCIETY OF EDINBURGH and the Royal Medical Society of Edinburgh. The ROYAL SOCIETY OF LONDON elected him to its membership in 1777, but he seems never to have played an active role in that group.

Cullen's scientific reputation rests on his skill as an innovative and clear teacher. He taught in English rather than in Latin, which was still the normal language of instruction. Among his many students was Joseph BLACK. Cullen and his Edinburgh contemporary Robert WHYTT numbered among the early critics of the MECHANICAL PHILOSOPHY in medicine. Cullen incorporated his views in a work on the CLASSIFICATION and diagnosis of diseases entitled *Synopsis Nosologiae Methodicae* (Synopsis of nosological method; 1769), and in a textbook on medical practice, *First Lines of Physic* (1776). The latter book was widely used during the late 18th century and translated into several languages.

Cullen wrote one important research paper, a report of experiments on evaporation entitled "Of the Cold Produced by Evaporating Fluids and of Some Other Means of Producing Cold." The paper was published in 1756 in the *Essays and Observations Physical and Literary Read Before a Society in Edinburgh and Published by Them*. His investigations along with those of Johann Gottschalk Wallerius, Johann Theodore Eller von Brockhausen, Abbé NOLLET, Charles Le Roy, and Antoine Baume provided certain background material for the CHEMICAL REVOLUTION of the later ENLIGHTENMENT.

Cuvier, Georges (Baron Cuvier) (1769–1832) *Alsatian natural historian, paleontologist, and zoologist, especially known for his contributions to the development of classification theory and comparative anatomy*

Cuvier was the son of a poor retired soldier, who lived in an Alsatian region under the control of the duke of Württemberg. Young Cuvier demonstrated remarkable intellectual gifts. On the strength of his promise, he received a position at the Hohen Karlsschule, a recently established academy near Stuttgart. He studied at the Hohen Karlsschule from 1784 until 1788, distinguishing himself by earning the golden cross of the chevaliers. This honor allowed Cuvier to live with the students of noble extraction. In this manner, Cuvier learned social skills that aided his subsequent career in PARIS. Cuvier graduated from the Hohen Karlsschule in 1788 after studying administrative, juridical, and economic sciences, a series of courses that contained a strong element of natural history. Cuvier studied primarily with Karl Friedrich Kielmeyer.

From 1788 until the beginning of 1795, Cuvier worked as a private tutor in Normandy for the Protestant d'Héricy family. In 1795, he moved to Paris. He had already established a correspondence with Étienne Geoffroy Saint-Hilaire, a professor at the Muséum d'Histoire Naturelle. The two men collaborated for one year. Cuvier remained affiliated with the museum throughout his professional career. He vastly expanded the specimen collections of the museum and reorganized the comparative anatomy collections according to his own classificatory criteria.

Cuvier rapidly established himself as a dominant figure in Parisian society. He was appointed professor of zoology at the Écoles centrales (established by the FRENCH REVOLUTION to replace the old universities) and was received as a member of the Institut de France (class of physical sciences) in 1796. He obtained a position at the prestigious Collège de France in 1800 and became the permanent secretary for his class at the Institut de France in 1803. During the Napoleonic era, Cuvier continued to receive honors and positions, especially in the area of secondary school organization. With the restoration of the Bourbon monarchy in 1814, Cuvier became a councillor of state and presided from 1819 until his death in 1832 over the Interior Department of the Council of State. The French Academy received him as a member in 1818. Cuvier was made a baron of France in 1819 and an officer in the Légion d'Honneur in 1824. He was nominated to the peerage of France in 1831.

In the natural sciences, Cuvier made contributions to the theory of CLASSIFICATION of species. Underlying the conflicts about classification were various questions about the age of the Earth and about the issue of whether new species had appeared after the original creation (conceived in biblical terms). Additional disputes focused on the hypothesized existence of a GREAT CHAIN OF BEING linking all species and on the issue of whether to classify biological specimens according to morphology (form and structure) or to function. Answers to these questions seemed to threaten Christian beliefs derived from the Bible and sharply divided natural historians.

Cuvier vacillated about the question of the great chain of being. He opposed the idea as a young man, shifted toward supporting the idea after 1792, then after 1802 returned to his original position, bolstering it with religious, scientific, and political arguments. Cuvier rejected the idea that species had varied over time. He engaged in a notorious dispute after 1802 with his former friends Jean Baptiste de LAMARCK and Geoffroy Saint-Hilaire over this question of the transformation of species.

In general, Cuvier grounded his classifications on the notion that a harmony exists between the physical structure of an animal and its manner of living. He held an organic, holistic view of life. His view stressed that life is more than physical and chemical laws and that each organism constitutes a closed system composed of parts highly organized and interrelated. A change in one part would trigger changes throughout the organism. He complemented this concept of the individual organism with a related notion that conceived of an immense network linking all species. This model diverged sharply from the mechanistic model for life that had dominated ENLIGHTENMENT science before the 1760s.

Besides his contributions to natural history, Cuvier also played a role in the education reforms established during the later years of the French Revolution. He helped not only to reorganize the Sorbonne, but also to establish provincial secondary schools and to reform secondary education in European territories that fell under French domination during the revolutionary wars.

Cuvier left many publications, of which the most notable are *Discours sur les révolutions du globe* (Discourse on the revolutions of the globe; 1812); *Description géologique des environs de Paris* (Geological description of the environs of Paris; 1822, 1835); *Tableau élémentaire de l'histoire naturelle des animaux* (Elementary table of the natural history of animals; 1797); *Leçons d'anatomie comparée* (Lessons of comparative anatomy; 1800 and 1805); *La regne animal* (The animal kingdom; 1817); *Histoire des poissons* (History of fishes; 1828–32); and the posthumously published *Anatomie comparée, recueil de planches de myologie* (Comparative anatomy, collection of plates on myology; 1849–56).

Cuvilliés, François de (The Elder) (1695–1768)
architect and decorator who worked in Germany

Cuvilliés was born in the Hainault region, an area now part of BELGIUM. He trained in PARIS with Jacques-François Blondel from 1720 until 1724. Cuvilliés was one of the masters of ROCOCO and was largely responsible for introducing the French forms of this style into southern German territories.

Cuvilliés first major commission came from the archbishop of COLOGNE, Clementus Augustus von Wittelsbach, who hired Cuvilliés to redesign his summer residence at Brühl beginning in 1728. Cuvilliés remodeled the entire palace and designed the dependent buildings. The Yellow Apartment in the Brühl Palace shows Cuvilliés's mastery of the French style. This palace would later receive a significant addition in the form of a central staircase designed by Balthasar NEUMANN.

Residenztheater, Munich, designed by François de Cuvilliés, 1751–1753. A brilliant example of rococo architecture and interior design, the Residenztheater provided a center for theatrical and musical productions in 18th-century Munich. *(Courtesy Bildarchiv Foto Marburg/Art Resource, New York)*

Cuvilliés also worked as chief architect to the Bavarian elector Carl Albert von Wittelsbach. For Carl-Albert, Cuvilliés designed the Reiche Zimmer in the Munich Electoral Residence and the exquisite Amalienburg Hunting Pavilion (1734–39) on the Nymphenburg Palace grounds just outside Munich. The Mirror Room in the Amalienburg is considered the supreme achievement of Bavarian rococo palace architecture. The Residenztheater (1750–53) and the facade of the Theatinerkirche (1765–68), both in Munich, complete the list of Cuvilliés's major achievements. François de Cuvilliés had a son, also named François (the Younger), who became an architect and worked in the rococo tradition.

D

Dale, David (1739–1806) *Scottish industrialist, philanthropist, and chief minister to the religious sect called the Old Independents*
With Richard ARKWRIGHT, inventor of the WATER FRAME, Dale set up a revolutionary cotton mill at NEW LANARK, SCOTLAND, in 1785. He sold the mill in 1799 to Robert Owen, the prominent 19th-century industrial reformer and socialist.

Damiens, Robert-François (1715–1757) *French domestic servant who attempted to assassinate King Louis XV in January 1757*
Damiens had a history of trouble in his various jobs and may have been somewhat unstable. In 1756, he fled from FRANCE to the AUSTRIAN NETHERLANDS after stealing money from an employer. He returned to PARIS in December 1756 and tried to assassinate the king with a knife at the Palace of Versailles on January 5, 1757. Damiens did not attempt to escape but rather submitted willingly to arrest.

In the interrogations and torture that followed his arrest, the police tried to elicit information about possible accomplices. At that time, Damiens made references to JANSENISM and to Cardinal Noailles (1651–1729), the deceased archbishop of Paris, who had reputedly been a Jansenist. Damiens also mentioned the PARLEMENTS (royal courts of justice) and their acts of resistance to the absolute authority of the king. But the police never uncovered any hard evidence implicating either group.

The *parlement* judges, however, were alarmed at being mentioned in connection with regicide attempts. They made a great public spectacle out of Damien's execution in March 1757, trying in this manner to demonstrate their loyalty to the king and to deter similar attempts by disgruntled subjects.

LOUIS XV might have used the occasion to place some limits on the *parlements,* but instead, he dismissed his anti-*parlement* ministers, the comte de Weil-ARGENSON and Jean Baptiste de Machault d'Arnouville Machault. In their place, he appointed the duc de CHOISEUL, who supported the *parlements* and was a protégé of Madame de POMPADOUR. This decision has been treated as one of several critical errors made by Louis XV in his attempts to stabilize his control over France. His action implicitly gave permission to the *parlements* to continue their course of action, thereby allowing the continued development of a major source of opposition to royal ABSOLUTISM.

News of the torture and execution of Damiens spread quickly throughout France. The incident was used to support the arguments against torture and CAPITAL PUNISHMENT presented by Cesare BECCARIA in his *ESSAY ON CRIMES AND PUNISHMENTS.*

Darby, Abraham (1678?–1717) *English forgemaster*
At his Bristol Iron Company in 1709, Darby developed a technique for smelting iron with coke. The invention was one of the earliest of the technological advances that ultimately produced the steel-based INDUSTRIAL REVOLUTION. The process produced a higher quality product than could be obtained with existing techniques and made coke-blast iron a viable commodity. Darby's invention helped to transform the Shropshire area of England into a major iron-producing region. The first Newcomen STEAM ENGINE (1712) was made of iron from Darby's mill.

Darwin, Erasmus (1731–1802) *English physician, botanist, poet, and inventor*

The grandfather of the famed naturalist Charles Darwin, he stands as one of the outstanding English representatives of the ENLIGHTENMENT. Darwin combined rational, analytic approaches to the study of natural phenomena, with a fervent appreciation of nature as an aesthetic object. He was committed to the ideal of human PROGRESS and shared the common belief in the ability of industrial technology to further that cause. He was a founding member of the LUNAR SOCIETY OF BIRMINGHAM, formed to further the cause of enlightened philosophical, scientific, and technological goals. Committed to radical DEISM and thus convinced that the design of the natural world testifies to the existence of a divine wisdom, he turned away from traditional English Protestantism toward a personal religion created from a blend of paganism, science, and philosophy. These beliefs, combined with his speculations about possible evolution of species over time, caused him to be called an atheist by his conservative countrymen.

Darwin was the son of a lawyer of independent means. He received a high quality education during which he earned a medical degree from Cambridge University. His medical studies included two years at the University of Edinburgh and private study with William HUNTER in LONDON.

As a physician, Darwin committed himself to the new clinical practice of medicine that was a chief contribution of the Enlightenment to the healing arts. He carefully observed patients and tried to formulate individual treatments that addressed their special situations. He published the first reports on the treatment of heart disease (dropsy) with digitalis, although credit for the innovation usually goes to William Withering. Darwin's skill as a physician was quickly recognized and rewarded in 1761 by election to the ROYAL SOCIETY OF LONDON.

His second major set of interests centered on botany. An avid supporter of the new system of CLASSIFICATION developed by Carolus LINNAEUS, Darwin also addressed practical issues such as the control of plant disease, the use of manure as fertilizer, and methods for land reclamation and irrigation.

Darwin's practical inclinations led him to design several inventions. One, a windmill that operated grinding machinery, was used by Josiah WEDGWOOD in the production of colors for his pottery. Others never were realized, but they included such intriguing devices as a speaking machine and a copying machine.

In the course of pursuing all these interests, Darwin developed one of the earliest clear statements of evolutionary theory. He believed that the Earth was millions of years old, that species can change over time as they strive to respond to environmental conditions, that acquired characteristics can be passed along to later generations, and that all of life might conceivably have developed from a single source. Darwin published two major scientific treatises: *Zoonomia* (2 vols., 1794 and 1796), which presents his ideas on both medicine and the natural sciences, and *Phytologia: The Philosophy of Agriculture and Gardening* (1800).

Darwin also wrote long philosophical nature poems in which he turned his poetic imagination to the service of science. The poems provide the best evidence of his deism and general philosophy of nature. The first poem was *The Botanic Garden,* with two parts entitled "The Loves of Plants" (1789) and "The Economy of Vegetation" (1791). Probably for political reasons, this poem was viciously satirized in *The Loves of Triangles* by George Canning, foreign under-secretary of state in the government of Prime Minister Pitt. On account of his radical philosophical and political beliefs. Darwin and his colleagues at the Lunar Society of Birmingham were hated and feared by English authorities.

Darwin wrote a second long nature poem, *The Temple of Nature* (posthumously published in 1803). It presented classical pagan myths as an example of the ancient understanding of natural truths. Darwin died in 1802, after a year of illness.

Daubenton, Louis-Jean-Marie (1716–1800) *French physician, natural historian, and animal husbandry expert (zootechnist)*

He came from the same town, Montbard, as his contemporary and colleague Georges-Louis Leclerc, comte de BUFFON. Daubenton's father, Jean Daubenton, was a notary. Young Daubenton attended the Jesuit college at Dijon and also studied at the school run by the Dominicans. He began a course of theological studies at the Sorbonne in PARIS but soon began pursuing a greater interest—medicine—by attending the anatomy and botany lectures at the Jardin du Roi (Royal Garden). He entered formal medical training only after his father's death and received his degree from the medical faculty of Rheims in 1741.

After a brief return to Montbard to practice medicine, Daubenton was called by Buffon to assume a position as curator and lecture-demonstrator (*garde et démonstrateur*) of the natural history collection at the Jardin du Roi. He remained at the Jardin du Roi until his death in 1800. He held several different positions at the gardens.

During the FRENCH REVOLUTION, Daubenton assisted with the planning and founding of the Muséum National d'Histoire Naturelle (National Museum of Natural History, founded 1793). Daubenton became the first director of the museum, but chose not to put himself forward for reappointment at the end of his first term as director. In addition to his post at the gardens in Paris, Daubenton held chairs in natural history at the prestigious Collège de France and in rural economy at the veterinary school in Alfort. Buffon's patronage helped Daubenton receive an adjunct appointment to the FRENCH ACADEMY OF SCIENCE in 1744. This was followed by several promotions in the departments of botany and anatomy. When the academy was reorganized during the French Revolution to become part of the new Institut de France, Daubenton received an appointment as *membre résident* (resident member) in the sections of anatomy and zoology (1795). Daubenton died of a stroke in 1800 and was buried at the JARDIN DES PLANTES (new name given to the Jardin du Roi during the French Revolution).

Daubenton collaborated with Buffon on the first edition of the influential *Histoire naturelle, générale et particulière, avec description du Cabinet du Roy* (Natural history, general and specific, with a description of the royal collection; 15 vols., 1749–67). Daubenton contributed hundreds of anatomical descriptions to the many volumes of this important work. He was recognized as a skillful comparative anatomist, although lacking in the theoretical boldness of his more illustrious and dominating colleague. The collaboration with Buffon ended in 1766, when Buffon declined to include Daubenton's descriptions in subsequent editions of the *Histoire naturelle.*

Daubenton turned his attention to technical problems of animal husbandry, publishing an *Instruction pour les bergers et les propriétaires de troupeaux* (Instruction for shepherds and proprietors of flocks; 1782), which dealt with various aspects of breeding and maintaining flocks of sheep. Daubenton became renowned for this work and, in 1793, during the Reign of Terror, received a certificate from the revolutionary government guaranteeing his good citizenship as a "shepherd." Daubenton also published a *Tableau méthodique des minéraux* (Methodical table of minerals; 1784), which helped to disseminate the current knowledge of mineralogy throughout France.

Daubenton married his first cousin Marguerite Daubenton in 1754. Madame Daubenton was a writer whose novel, *Zélie dans le désert* (Zélie in the desert; 2 vols., 1786–87), enjoyed some success. Daubenton spent his leisure time reading literature with his wife. The couple had no children.

See also BIOLOGY; HISTORY.

David, Jacques-Louis (1748–1825) *French painter, the major artistic figure during the French Revolution*

David was born into a wealthy bourgeois family. He studied art in PARIS at the Royal Academy from 1766 until

The Death of Socrates by Jacques-Louis David, 1787. A leader of neoclassicism in France, David created paintings inspired by themes from ancient Greece and Rome. *(Courtesy Metropolitan Museum of Art, Catherine Lorillard Wolfe Collection)*

1774. In the latter year, David won the coveted Prix de Rome, which provided him with the opportunity to study in ROME, where he fell under the influence of Johann WINCKELMANN, Anton MENGS, and Gavin Hamilton. David developed a strong interest in antiquity, and his painting assumed the characteristics of NEOCLASSICISM. Once he returned to FRANCE, his paintings helped to popularize that new style.

David painted historical subjects with didactic themes aimed at improving the intellectual and moral condition of the French middle classes. Examples include *Belisarius Asking for Alms, The Horatii,* and *The Death of Socrates.* When the FRENCH REVOLUTION broke out in 1789, David quickly committed his talents to its service. He produced various works commemorating major revolutionary events, such as *The Oath of the Tennis Court* and *The Death of Marat.* These works demonstrated that David was beginning to move away from neoclassical conventions and toward realism.

David, a friend of ROBESPIERRE, served as a representative to the National Convention in 1792. He became the director of artistic affairs for the fledgling French Republic, a position that he held until the downfall of Robespierre in 1794. Like other associates of Robespierre, David was imprisoned after 9 Termidor (the date of Robespierre's downfall) but was eventually released. His career went into eclipse, although he continued to paint. The neoclassical *Rape of the Sabine Women* dates from this period.

When Napoleon assumed the reins of government in 1799, David won renewed popularity and prestige. He served as first painter to Napoleon until the fall of the empire. David spent the last nine years of his life (1816–25) in BRUSSELS, having been exiled there by the restored French monarchy.

In addition to historical paintings, David created a number of important portraits. They are notable for their penetration of character. His subjects included Antoine LAVOISIER and his wife, Pope Pius VII, Madame Recamier, and Monsieur and Madame Seriziat. The work of David greatly influenced the younger generation of painters that included Théodore Géricault, Eugène Delacroix, Jean INGRES, and A. J. Gros.

Declaration of Independence The document in which 13 colonies established by ENGLAND in North America declared their independence from their parent country, Great Britain, and became the UNITED STATES OF AMERICA. The colony of Virginia set the process in motion by instructing its delegates to the Second Continental Congress in PHILADELPHIA to introduce a motion for independence. Virginia delegate Richard Henry Lee (1732–94) made the motion on June 7, 1776, and the Declaration of Independence was drafted by a committee of delegates including Thomas JEFFERSON, John ADAMS, Benjamin FRANKLIN, Roger Sherman of Connecticut, and Robert R. Livingston of New York. On July 2, 1776, the Second Continental Congress adopted the resolution. It was the formal announcement of the legal act of separation from Britain. The 13 colonies involved were Connecticut, Delaware, Georgia, Maryland, Massachusetts, New Hampshire, New Jersey, New York, North Carolina, Pennsylvania, Rhode Island, South Carolina, and Virginia. Initially, only John Hancock, the presiding officer, signed the document, but its aims and philosophical content derived from the drafting committee who saw themselves as representatives of the American point of view.

Early in 1776, several months after the first battles of the AMERICAN REVOLUTION had been fought, Thomas PAINE published his series of essays called COMMON SENSE. In the last section of his book, Paine suggested that the colonies prepare a written declaration of their independence. In May, the Virginia Convention at Williamsburg adopted a resolution calling for the confederation of the Brittish colonies and declaring those colonies free states capable of forming foreign alliances on their own behalf. On June 3, John Adams reiterated the major points and proposed the establishment of a constitution for the confederated states. After receiving a draft of the proposed declaration, Congress adopted a resolution on July 2, 1776, calling for independence. Two days of debating followed. Some colonial leaders questioned the need for a formal document, but Paine's position and Virginia's resolution prevailed. On July 4, 1776, "The Unanimous Declaration of the Thirteen United States of America" was approved. The official signing ceremony involving all participants in the Congress took place on August 2.

Thomas Jefferson wrote most of the Declaration of Independence, and Benjamin Franklin and John Adams suggested changes in terminology. The document contains a brief section on the philosophy behind the American Revolution, followed by a list of grievances against the British king and Parliament, and concludes with a section declaring the right and intention of the colonies to be free. The document drew on common ideas from the ENLIGHTENMENT for philosophical and theoretical support. The concept of the universal NATURAL RIGHTS of humankind, whose truth is supported by the fact that all people understand them, appears in the opening phrases of the declaration: "We hold these truths to be self-evident, that all men are created equal, that they are endowed by their Creator, with certain unalienable rights."

The Declaration borrows from enlightened SOCIAL CONTRACT theory, stating that governments are formed by men in order to protect these rights, and that when governments fail in this duty, they may be justly overthrown. The main sources for these ideas were the *Second Treatise of Government* by John LOCKE, and the interpretations of Lockean liberalism developed by radical Protestant DISSENTERS such as Joseph PRIESTLEY and Richard Price, a moral philosopher and friend of Benjamin Franklin. But social contract theory had roots in the ideas of Thomas HOBBES, Samuel PUFENDORF, and Jean-Jacques ROUSSEAU.

Appeals to natural rights and the social contract received reinforcement from the interpretation of the English political system that stressed the roles of Parliament and of common law as protectors of ancient English liberties. Associated with the *Commentaries on the Laws of England* by Sir William BLACKSTONE, this interpretation provided strong arguments that could be used to challenge the actions of King George III in the colonies. Together, all these arguments, even though they contained incompatible views, strengthened the American claim that British policies abused colonial rights and privileges, thereby giving the colonists cause to rebel.

The committee did not address the controversial issues of SLAVERY and abolition. British law—in the famous but ambiguous Somerset case of 1772—initiated the end of slaveholding in Great Britain, and public sentiment at this time tended to discredit the slave trade and the institution of slavery. However, the institution was vital to the economic health of the southern states in North America, and Jefferson, a southerner with well-known views about racial difference and slavery, did not accord African slaves in America with the right to their liberty. Nevertheless, from 1777 until 1804, all states north of Maryland abolished slavery.

The Declaration of Independence incorporated innumerable well-known ideas from contemporary and classical European thought, not only philosophical and political but also religious. Jefferson's DEISM, revealed in his term *Nature's God,* derives from contemporary British writings by John Locke and the earl of SHAFTESBURY, but Jefferson transformed concepts to fit American perceptions and contexts. Perhaps the most notable instance of transformation occurred in the treatment of natural rights. Whereas Locke, for example, had listed life, liberty, and property as the inalienable (natural, nontransferable) rights of humankind, Jefferson chose to list life, liberty, and the pursuit of HAPPINESS. The substitution of the *pursuit of happiness* for *property* as the third natural right reveals that the framers of the declaration were acquainted with the way principles

"The Signing of the Declaration of Independence," engraving by Edward Savage. The American Declaration of Independence gave certain principles of the Enlightenment a concrete political form. *(Courtesy American Antiquarian Society)*

derived from EPICUREAN PHILOSOPHY were interpreted during the Enlightenment.

Originally called the State House of Pennsylvania, the Georgian building now known as Independence Hall and located in Philadelphia housed the assembly, council and supreme court of the province (later the commonwealth) from 1735 until 1799. It is the place where the Declaration of Independence was adopted, where the Articles of Confederation were enacted (1781), and where the UNITED STATES CONSTITUTION was drafted (1787). Across the street is the famous Liberty Bell (now silenced). The original bell was sent from England to mark the 50th anniversary of William Penn's Charter of Privileges (1752). It was engraved with a verse from Leviticus 25:10: "Proclaim liberty throughout the land, unto all the inhabitants thereof." Recast in 1753, it rang on July 8, 1776, when it summoned Philadelphians to the State House to hear Colonel John Nixon, a veteran of the French and Indian Wars, read the Declaration of Independence.

The Declaration of Independence had a direct influence on the French DECLARATION OF THE RIGHTS OF MAN AND CITIZEN. As well as Jefferson, who served as the American ambassador to FRANCE, the English firebrand, Thomas Paine helped cement French and American cooperation in this revolutionary period. Outlawed from England, he dedicated himself to the American Revolution, and later sat in the French Convention, escaping the guillotine by a whisker. Not only did the Declaration of Independence influence political change, it later became the basis for other efforts to resist oppression, including the movements for women's rights and abolition.

See also COLONIALISM; JUSTICE AND THE LAW; LIBERTY; NATURAL LAW; POLITICAL THEORY; PUBLISHING; *TWO TREATISES OF GOVERNMENT.*

Further reading: Julian P. Boyd, *The Declaration of Independence: The Evolution of the Text* (Hanover, N.H.: Library of Congress in association with Thomas Jefferson Memorial Foundation, 1945); Allen Jayne, *Jefferson's Declaration of Independence: Origins, Philosophy and Theology* (Lexington, Ky.: University Press of Kentucky, 1998).

Declaration of the Rights of Man and Citizen A proclamation of constitutional principles written during the first months of the FRENCH REVOLUTION. The National Assembly adopted the declaration on August 26, 1789. At least in part, the declaration was inspired by and modeled on two documents of the AMERICAN REVOLUTION, the DECLARATION OF INDEPENDENCE and the Virginia state legislature's 1776 Declaration of Rights.

Intended as a guide for the men charged with writing a French constitution, the Declaration of the Rights of Man and Citizen (*Déclaration des droits de l'homme et citoyen*) highlights the central position of the concept of RIGHTS in late 18th-century political thought. As a public statement, the document had both pedagogical and disciplinary functions: to remind people of their rights and duties and governing bodies of the constitutional limits to their powers.

The declaration enumerates the principles on which a legitimate constitutional government must rest: universal rights and laws (a radical departure from the ANCIEN RÉGIME system of privilege and particularism); representative government; and structural safeguards, that is, taking legislative power from the king to prevent abuses. Moreover, sovereignty resides in the "nation," not in the king.

The fundamental NATURAL RIGHTS—liberty, property, security, and resistance to oppression—derive from the principle that "men are born and remain free and equal in rights." Neither the government nor the individual may lawfully infringe on any of these rights. The government, for example, may not arrest a person unless he or she has violated a specific law (the infamous *lettre de cachet* would henceforth be abolished), nor may authorities persecute people for expressing their opinions or practicing their religions. The government may not tax its citizens without their consent, and it must apportion taxes "equally among all citizens according to their capacity to pay." The civic society envisioned here is an organic body, composed of equal parts, in which the actions of one part affect the good of the whole, positively or negatively. Liberty, for example, is specifically defined as "the ability to do whatever does not harm another," and law, the "expression of the general will," is the mechanism that preserves the balance between individual rights and the collective good.

The declaration utilizes abstract concepts from the ENLIGHTENMENT traditions articulated for the French by PHILOSOPHES, ENCYCLOPEDISTS, and PHYSIOCRATS. But it also reflects the experience of a people weary of living with ABSOLUTISM. Drawing on the Enlightenment concepts of natural rights, EQUALITY, FREEDOM, UTILITY, SOCIAL CONTRACT, and the SEPARATION OF POWERS and also on older French traditions of constitutionalism, the declaration states the philosophical principles necessary to a well-regulated government, legitimized by the rational, egalitarian natural order of the universe rather than by the will of a king. Both its vision and form (it utilizes the Cartesian model of deductive reasoning) testify to the creative power of enlightened discourse, while the public exchange of ideas in which it was generated demonstrates the social institutions of the Enlightenment in action.

Even so, the subsequent history of the declaration also reveals the limits of enlightened reform projects in late 18th-century France. When French deputies to the National Assembly and to the later Constituent Conventions tried to define the concept *citizen* in real political terms, they found the universal model of rights unpalatable. In principle, all men are free and equal and have natural rights, and all natives of France are citizens. But did universal principles require that all citizens have equal political (voting and office holding) rights to complement their natural rights as citizens? Were women, blacks, non-Catholics, non-French speakers, the unpropertied poor, and slaves to be given political rights alongside the French-speaking, Catholic, propertied male members of society? The answers were many, and intense feelings gave rise to impassioned debate, many constitutional revisions, and sometimes violence. The deputies were not all equally prepared to grant political rights to all members of society. The declaration, nevertheless, was and still is an inspiration to people the world over.

See also LETTRES DE CACHET; JUSTICE AND THE LAW; POLITICAL THEORY; SOCIAL INSTITUTIONS OF THE ENLIGHTENMENT; UNITED STATES BILL OF RIGHTS.

Further reading: Lynn Hunt, ed., *The French Revolution and Human Rights* (Boston: Bedford Books, 1996); Dale Van Kley, ed., *The French Idea of Freedom: The Old Regime and the Declaration of Rights of 1789* (Stanford, Calif.: Stanford University Press, 1994).

Decline and Fall of the Roman Empire, The History of the

A HISTORY of the ancient Roman Empire written by Edward GIBBON. The first volume appeared in 1776, the last three volumes in 1788. The book covers the period from about A.D. 100 to the fall of Constantinople in 1453. Although not especially methodologically innovative when compared with the work of other historians of the ENLIGHTENMENT, the *Decline and Fall* was widely read and thus highly influential.

The History of the Decline and Fall of the Roman Empire combines two approaches to history: the old method associated with antiquarian research that concentrates on description of detailed fact and the enlightened philosophical history that explained development over time in reference to some overarching philosophical principle.

Gibbon focused on the principle of FREEDOM, showing how the events that unfolded in Roman history related to that principle. He believed that the history of the Roman Empire represented a slow abandonment of freedom in the political, intellectual, and religious spheres of life. This abandonment of freedom represented for him a path of decay and degeneration, one that ultimately led to the death of the great Roman state.

Gibbon needed to identify a force that could have caused this negative development in Roman history. He suggested that Christianity had provided that negative force. Before 313, when the Roman emperor Constantine the Great (Flavius Valerius Aurelius Constantinus) converted to Christianity, thereby granting it official status, the dominant attitude in the Roman Empire had been one of religious TOLERATION. Christian leaders became ambitious, eager for power. Their religion encouraged believers to spread the message of Jesus Christ. According to Gibbon, when Christian leaders obtained political power in ROME, their mission to convert the world transformed Christianity into a distorted RELIGION that persecuted anyone who disagreed with its doctrines. The Roman Empire under Christianity thus abandoned its commitment to freedom and toleration.

Gibbon presented this interpretation in Chapters 15 and 16 of the first volume of *Decline and Fall*. He was praised by the enlightened historians David HUME and William ROBERTSON. But he was harshly criticized by more conservative readers who were offended by his treatment of Christianity. Feeling compelled to defend his position, Gibbon published *A Vindication of Some Passages in the XVth and XVIth Chapters of the Decline and Fall of the Roman Empire* (1779).

Gibbon's historical vision changed as he prepared the later volumes of *Decline and Fall*. These volumes treated the long history of the Roman Empire in the East (Byzantium), covering the period from about 480 to 1453. The material on this subject was less familiar to Gibbon, and its complexities seemed to defy the philosophical treatment he had applied to the years of Rome's glory.

Gibbon explored many facets of Byzantine history, offering subsequently renowned chapters on the emperor Justinian and the history of Roman (written, codified) law. But, in the end, he still viewed the whole course of Roman history as a "triumph of barbarism and religion." The course of history, then, was not one of upward PROGRESS, but of continual decline.

Deffand, Marie de Vichy-Chamrond, marquise du
(1679–1780) *French salon hostess*

A rival of Madame GEOFFRIN for dominance in the Parisian social world that supported the ENLIGHTENMENT, Marie de Vichy-Chamrond was the daughter of Gaspard de Vichy and Anne Brûlart. Her parents sent her to a convent to obtain a basic education, but she seems to have been rebellious—a skeptic and LIBERTINE—from her youth. In 1691, she married Jean-Baptiste-Jacques-Charles du Deffand, a military officer who served as governor of the Alsatian town of Neuf-Brisach and as royal lieutenant in the Orléanais region. The marriage was unhappy, and the couple finally separated in 1722. Madame Du Deffand became the mistress of the regent of France, Philippe, duc d'Orléans, from whom she received a substantial pension. She spent some time at La Source, the French estate of Lord BOLINGBROKE, where she mingled with VOLTAIRE and Madame de Tencin. She also frequented gatherings at the home of the duchesse de Maine in Sceaux. She entered an intimate but tension-filled relationship with the *parlement* president Charles Hénault that lasted until his death in 1770.

When she was in PARIS, Madame du Deffand held a weekly salon at which major enlightened intellectual figures gathered. Their number included Bernard de FONTENELLE, Voltaire, Pierre-Louis de MAUPERTUIS, Morellet, Sébastien-Roch-Nicolas CHAMFORT, MONTESQUIEU, Hénault, Jean Le Rond d'ALEMBERT, and Anne-Robert-Jacques TURGOT. Mademoiselle Julie de LESPINASSE, her illegitimate niece, assisted her at these gatherings.

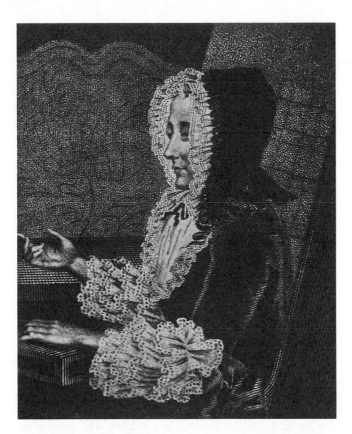

Madame du Deffand. The marquise du Deffand hosted one of the most influential enlightened salons in Paris. *(Courtesy New York Public Library)*

Eventually, the two women quarreled, and Mademoiselle de Lespinasse left the service of the marquise Du Deffand, taking her admirer d'Alembert with her. The two began to frequent Madame Geoffrin's salon, which became known as the salon of the ENCYCLOPEDISTS. Thereafter, the marquise du Deffand became a bitter antagonist of the encyclopedists, and her salon reflected these sentiments.

Madame du Deffand corresponded regularly with Voltaire, with Louise Honorine de Crozat, duchesse de Choiseul, and with Horace WALPOLE. Her witty, often brilliant letters provide instructive glimpses into sociocultural aspects of the Enlightenment. At her death, Madame du Deffand left both her papers and her beloved dog Tonton in the care of Walpole.

See also WOMEN AND THE ENLIGHTENMENT.

Defoe, Daniel (1660–1731) *English novelist and political pamphleteer, whose penetrating observations of 18th-century English social conditions have caused some scholars to treat him as an early social historian*

Daniel Defoe was the son of a LONDON tallow chandler of Flemish (Belgian) descent. His family members were Protestant Nonconformists and therefore subject to certain legal discrimination. Young Defoe, for example, could not enter the powerful Anglican universities at Oxford or Cambridge on account of his religious affiliation. In response to this situation, the Nonconformists and DISSENTERS had established some excellent private academies, and Defoe received a strong basic education at Charles Morton's Academy. Defoe abandoned plans to become a Presbyterian minister and instead entered commerce. He remained interested in trade throughout his life even after he suffered serious losses in several ventures.

Defoe's commercial interests stimulated his concern for politics, and he began writing political pamphlets in the 1680s. He opposed the Catholic King James II, and, during the GLORIOUS REVOLUTION of 1688, he was one of the party that rode out to welcome the Protestants WILLIAM III AND MARY II as the new rulers of ENGLAND. Defoe remained a committed supported of William III throughout his reign and produced several pamphlets defending various Crown positions.

Defoe's political concerns and personal history naturally made religious TOLERATION one of his principle concerns. Consequently, he allied himself with the liberal Whig Party during the early 18th century. His most famous pamphlet, *The Shortest Way with the Dissenters* (1702), adopted literary irony to ridicule the Tory Anglican party, which favored increasing restrictions against Dissenters. The pamphlet resulted in Defoe's being sued for libel, fined, and sentenced to stand three times in the public pillory. He used the occasion to his advantage, writing the *Hymn to the Pillory* (1703). The pamphlet turned his public punishment into a public celebration of his cause.

Defoe eventually opted for a career as an official government pamphleteer, producing tracts on behalf of both Tory and Whig leaders. He edited periodicals with widely varying political positions, such as the *Review* (1704–13) and the *Mist's Weekly-Journal*. Defoe allegedly believed that by writing for various opposing causes, he was actually helping to prevent bitter divisions and religious strife.

Defoe acquired a reputation as a novelist only in 1719, when he published *Robinson Crusoe*. This NOVEL used its protagonist, Robinson Crusoe, to demonstrate the power of certain enlightened values such as self-reliance and independence. It showed Crusoe mastering potentially dangerous situations by relying on his natural common sense and by creating useful forms of technology to assist him in his labors. The book was an immediate success with the middle-class and lower-class reading public in England. It was also a favorite novel of countless enlightened figures throughout Europe.

Defoe spent the next three years writing several outstanding works. He expanded *Robinson Crusoe* into a trilogy, with *Farther Adventures* (1719) and *Serious Reflections* (1720). The year 1720 brought *The Life and Adventures of Duncan Campbell, Memoirs of a Cavalier,* and *The Life of Captain Singleton*. Defoe then created *Moll Flanders, A Journal of the Plague Year,* and *Colonel Jack* in 1722. *Roxana* appeared in 1724.

After this tremendous burst of fictional creativity, Defoe returned to his political writing. During his last years, he produced such works as *The Complete English Tradesman* (1725–27), *The Political History of the Devil* (1726), and an *Atlas Maritimus et Commercialis* (Maritime and Commercial Atlas; 1728).

Defoe is renowned for his penetrating portrayals of the relationships between fear of poverty and crime. *Moll Flanders* and *Colonel Jack* both explored these themes and provided sharp criticisms of 18th-century English social and economic structures.

degeneration   A term used by natural historians and life scientists in the later 18th century to describe the processes that produce variations among living organisms. Although the term bears negative connotations in modern language, it did not necessarily have such meaning in the 18th century. It was, indeed, contrasted to the notion of a process of perfection, but the two processes—degeneration and perfection—were not routinely given qualitative or moral connotations. They were simply developments in different directions. Geology served both as the stimulus and as a major testing ground for the theory of degeneration. Fossil remains provided disturbing evidence that species no longer in existence had once thrived on the Earth.

The possibility that species had actually disappeared raised major questions about the nature of creation. The idea of degeneration implied that the natural world has a HISTORY, that is, that it changes over time. Today, such a notion is commonly accepted, but that was not the case in the 18th century. In fact, one of the major conceptual shifts that occurred under the influence of the ENLIGHTENMENT involved the acceptance of this novel idea of natural history.

The idea of degeneration played a major role in the discourse of the life sciences in the second half of the 18th century. The French natural historian George-Louis Leclerc, comte de BUFFON, began the theoretical discussion of degeneration in his 1744 publication, *Théorie de la terre* (Theory of the Earth). He used the concept to explain variations in species thought to have occurred because of natural environmental influences. For example, Buffon believed that the mule is simply a degeneration of the horse produced centuries ago by the influence of climate, nourishment, and other local factors. Jean Baptiste de LAMARCK extended this approach by making degeneration (conceived as the result of natural chemical processes) the central agent in the transformation of animal and plant species and in the creation of new species. The concept was also invoked in discussions of reproduction as an explanation for birth deformities ("monsters" in 18th-century language). The concept of degeneration was closely allied to the equally popular notion of the GREAT CHAIN OF BEING, a notion that posited the existence

in creation of myriad species separated only by nearly undetectable variations.

The possibility that natural transformation and generation occur in nature embroiled scientists of the Enlightenment in sharp theological and philosophical disputes. The idea of change over time suggested not only that God had not created all things at the beginning of time but also that some of his creations might have altered or disappeared over the centuries. If such were the case, then the biblical account of the Creation in the book of Genesis could no longer be taken as a literal presentation of facts. Furthermore, the relationship between God and his creatures would require reconceptualization. The theory of degeneration required a radical rethinking of the nature of the world and of the role of God within its daily operations.

deism   A term derived from the Latin word *deus,* meaning "god." The term *deism* designates a form of NATURAL RELIGION that arose as an alternative to the traditional theology of Protestant and Roman Catholic Christianity during the formative years of the ENLIGHTENMENT. It stressed belief in God as the creator of the universe. In its disparate forms, deism played a significant role in the Enlightenment as an attempt to preserve religious faith by wedding it to human REASON. It was particularly important in ENGLAND and in FRANCE, but eventually became an international element of the Enlightenment.

Deists, like many other committed Christians, were sensitive to the challenges to Christianity raised by the SCIENTIFIC REVOLUTION, by philosophical SKEPTICISM, and by 17th-century RATIONALISM. These intellectual movements had not only produced a new vision of the universe, but had also spawned new disciplines such as BIBLICAL CRITICISM and comparative RELIGION that threatened to undermine traditional Christian beliefs.

The HELIOCENTRIC theory of the universe developed by Nicolaus COPERNICUS, and later substantiated by the findings of Galileo GALILEI and Isaac NEWTON, seemed to conflict with the Earth-centered (GEOCENTRIC) universe depicted in the Bible. The new image of a universe running according to impersonal laws based on mathematics seemed to leave little room for a God who was actively involved in its daily affairs. The subjection of the Bible to textual and linguistic analysis seemed to reduce its authority as the vehicle for the revelations of God to humankind. And familiarity with many world religions raised the possibility that Christianity might not contain the only form of religious and moral truth.

This intellectual ferment of the 17th century raised disturbing questions for Christians. If reason, for example, was such a powerful intellectual tool for understanding both the natural and the moral world, then what role was left for the revelations of God that Christians believed were contained in the Bible? If Copernicus was right about the structure of the universe, and the Bible consequently wrong, then what other errors did that great book contain? If the testimony of the Bible could not be trusted, then what other avenues existed for proving the existence of both God and of morality in the universe? To what sources could people turn for knowledge of moral and spiritual truths?

Deism tried to answer these questions and concerns by turning reason—the very source of the threats to religious belief—into its major support. Most deists believed that reason and the related lawful, orderly, mathematical, rational universe presented by the Scientific Revolution actually testified to the existence of God. The very elegance and simplicity of the design of the universe proved that it had been created by a wise God, and the operation of the universe according to law ensured its morality, its basic goodness, and its benevolence. The God of the deists, however, was not the judging and forgiving God of Christian theology. Rather, he was a watchmaker who had produced a beautiful piece of machinery largely capable of operating without his intervention.

Since they viewed the universe as a rational place governed by laws instituted by God, deists tended to challenge aspects of Christianity that could not be explained by the laws of nature. They often rejected the authenticity of miracles and of the other "supernatural" aspects of Christianity. This category included the story of the resurrection of Christ, a central Christian belief. Thus, although deists often considered themselves Christians, they were attacked by orthodox Christian theologians as atheists or heretics.

The earliest known use of the term *deist* was pejorative: Pierre Viret (1511–71), a follower of CALVINISM, wrote that deists believed in God, but because they rejected belief in Jesus Christ as the son of God, in miracles, and in other Christian dogma, he considered them atheists and monsters.

Pierre BAYLE, the great French critic whose skepticism directly stimulated the thought of the early Enlightenment, passed this negative stereotype of deism to the early Enlightenment. He used the term throughout his *Dictionnaire historique et critique* (1697) (English translation, HISTORICAL AND CRITICAL DICTIONARY, 1710). Bayle, for all his skeptical inquiry into the grounds of religion, probably still favored belief based on an act of will or faith (fideism). The deistic reliance on reason as a ground for belief did not impress him, and he disliked the tendency of deists to ignore the doctrines of redemption and salvation through Jesus Christ. Consequently, Bayle's treatment of deism in articles such as "Viret" and "Socin" was negative. His *Dictionnaire* popularized the pairing of deism with ATHEISM and the vision of deism as dangerous free thought.

The deism that eventually became part of enlightened religious discourse grew in the intellectual soil of 17th-century England and France. It seemed to offer a rational basis for religious belief that could make obsolete the impassioned doctrinal quarrels that were tearing at the fabric of Christian society.

In England, the term *deist* first appeared in Robert Burton's *Anatomy of Melancholy* (1621). Principles resembling deism existed in the works of Lord Herbert of Cherbury (1583–1648), but the concept of deism did not flower until the latter part of the 17th century. At that time, currents as varied as the philosophy of Thomas HOBBES, the SCIENCE of Isaac Newton, the ideas of Benedict de SPINOZA about universal religion, calls for TOLERATION, the force of biblical criticism, corruption within the established church, the writings of the Cambridge Platonists, and the philosophy of John LOCKE came together in England to stimulate the development and spread of the deistic approach to religion.

Major English deists were Charles Blount, Anthony COLLINS, Samuel CLARKE, John TOLAND, Matthew TINDAL, Ralph CUDWORTH, and Lord BOLINGBROKE. The earl of SHAFTESBURY and Bernard MANDEVILLE were considered deists, and many other innovative English thinkers, such as Thomas Chubb, Thomas Morgan, and Peter Annet, were given the label of their enemies.

Many English deists had theological training and remained within traditional English Christian churches, a fact that sets them apart from their French counterparts. Press censorship was more lenient in England than in France, making it possible for deists to publish their ideas in open, direct form. Prosecution was also less of a danger in England than in France, although deists, even in the 18th century, were occasionally charged and convicted of blasphemy.

In France, the presence of stricter censorship by the Catholic Church and by royal officials created a specific form of deistic literature: the travel account or series of letters purporting to come from non-European observers in Europe or pretending to describe non-European societies. This literary device allowed writers to evade censorship, while openly utilizing deistic forms to criticize ROMAN CATHOLICISM and to offer alternative natural religions. The *Lettres persanes* (PERSIAN LETTERS; 1721), a book by MONTESQUIEU, was only the most famous example of this genre. Other examples were *L'espion turc* (The Turkish spy) by Giovanni Paolo Marana, to which Montesquieu was explicitly indebted; the *Histoire de Calejava* (History of Calejava) by Claude Gilbert; and the *Dialogues curieux* (Curious dialogues) by the baron de Lahontan.

Important deist tracts also circled clandestinely in France. Many influential pieces were anonymous, such as the *Difficultés sur la religion proposés au père Malebranche* (Difficulties about religion proposed to Father Malebranche) by an author who signed himself as the "Militaire philosophe" (militant philosopher); or the *Examen de la religion* (Examination of religion) and the *Analyse de la religion* (Analysis of religion). Several secretly circulating influential works were attributed to Henri de BOULAINVILLIERS.

As French deism developed, it acquired a particularly strong element of ANTICLERICALISM, presenting vehement attacks on sexual abuses by priests, on luxury in the church, or on Catholicism's intolerance toward Protestants and Jews. VOLTAIRE, converted to deism during his years in England, used its ideas in his attacks on the Roman Catholic establishment in France. Voltaire's most famous deist tract was the DICTIONNAIRE PHILOSOPHIQUE (Philosophical dictionary) published in 1764.

Voltaire's use of deism in the campaign against Christianity was continued by the more radical leaders of the Enlightenment, the atheists and materialists headed by Baron d'HOLBACH and his circle. These PHILOSOPHES printed some of the earlier deist manuscripts and adapted them to their critical purposes.

Deism as a substitute for Christianity continued in France in a new form given by Jean-Jacques ROUSSEAU. Rousseau accepted the argument for God's existence that was based on the design of the universe, but he relied on his feelings or sentiments in the face of this design to bring him to faith. Reason stepped aside to the replaced by emotion as the primary source of religious inspiration. This twist reveals how Rousseau, by combining the tradition of rationalism that had stimulated original deist thought with the culture of SENSIBILITY, developed during the Enlightenment, produced a new argument for religious faith. Rousseau presented his ideas most clearly in a chapter of his novel *Émile, ou de l'éducation* (Emile, or on education; 1762) entitled "The Vicar of Savoy."

Deism also played a role in the thought of the German *AUFKLÄRUNG* (Enlightenment). In the hands of Hermann Samuel REIMARUS, deism functioned as a tool for strengthening attacks on miracles and revealed religion. It motivated him to begin the search for the authentic historical Jesus, to make an effort to strip away elements of the biblical account that might be later additions. Moses MENDELSSOHN used deist thought in the service of pleas for toleration. Finally, Immanuel KANT used its arguments to formulate an idea of religion that was intensely practical and was concerned primarily with moral behavior and the shaping of individual conscience.

Major leaders in the AMERICAN REVOLUTION such as Thomas JEFFERSON, George WASHINGTON, and Benjamin FRANKLIN were deists who used their position to support their pleas for toleration and for the SEPARATION OF CHURCH AND STATE. Thomas PAINE, on the other hand, used his strong deistic principles to attack Christianity in his famous book THE AGE OF REASON: *Being an Investigation of True and Fabulous Theology* (1794–96). He was attempting to rescue deistic thought from accusations of atheism at the hands of critics of the radical French philosophes.

Deism persisted throughout the Enlightenment in the teachings of the FREEMASONS. In this manner, it pro-

vided an alternative to established churches: a formal organization and institution under whose auspices universal rational religion, toleration, and the goal of PROGRESS through Enlightenment spread throughout Europe.

In all its manifestations, deism beautifully represents the complexities of the Enlightenment. In the name of toleration, humanitarianism, and universal reason it attacked traditional dogmatic Christianity. It applied critical methods and skepticism to received religious tradition and indicted religion as something opposed to the orderly, rational structure that natural science had revealed as God's design for the universe. Deism also revealed the ambivalence in enlightened thought toward religion, for it allowed enlightened but religious people to continue to believe in God and in a moral universe. Thus, it used the tools of the Enlightenment to preserve basic belief in God. If the Enlightenment was sometimes the enemy of religion, then enlightened deism was also one source of its survival.

See also MATHEMATICS AND MECHANICS.

Further reading: C. J. Betts, *Early Deism in France: From the So-Called Déistes of Lyon (1564) to Voltaire's Lettres Philosphiques (1734)* (The Hague: Martinus Nijhoff, 1984).

Delille, Jacques (1738–1813) *French poet and student of ancient Latin poetry; played a role in popularizing Latin classics during the Enlightenment*

Delille worked as a professor in two provincial *collèges* before gaining a chair as professor of Latin poetry at the prestigious Collège de France in PARIS. He also obtained the Catholic abbey of Saint-Séverin as abbot *in commendam*, a situation that granted him the revenues from the abbey but did not require him to live at the abbey.

Delille made his initial literary reputation with his versiform *Épîtres* (Epistles). His popular translation of Virgil's *Georgica* (Géorgiques; 1770) helped him to earn election in 1774 to the French Academy. Delille was arrested during the early part of the FRENCH REVOLUTION, but was soon released so that his poetic talents could be tapped for the cause of the revolution. Delille wrote the *Dithyrambe sur l'immortalitée de l'âme* (Dithyramb on the immortality of the soul) for the celebration of the Cult of the Supreme Being during the years of Robespierre's dominance. After the downfall of Robespierre, Delille immigrated to ENGLAND, where he remained until 1802, when the political situation in France no longer threatened his life and livelihood. He resumed teaching at the Collège de France and continued writing until his death in 1813.

In addition to the works mentioned above, Delille was noted for translations of Virgil's *Aeneid* (1804) and Milton's *Paradise Lost* (published during his English sojourn) and for *Trois règnes de la nature* (Three kingdoms of nature; 1808).

Delisle, Joseph-Nicolas (1688–1768) *French astronomer and cartographer*

Delisle studied at the Collège Mazarin. In 1708, at the age of 20, Delisle began frequenting the Paris Observatory, where he assisted members of the Cassini family with their work. By 1709, he had obtained permission to install a small observatory in the cupola of the Palais du Luxembourg. He worked at that site until 1715, when the duchesse de Berry, the eldest daughter of the duc d'Orléans, who had moved into the Palais, asked him to leave. In 1718, Delisle obtained a teaching post at the prestigious Collège de France. The FRENCH ACADEMY OF SCIENCES accepted him into its membership in 1714.

In 1724, Delisle traveled to ENGLAND, where he met Edmond HALLEY, Isaac NEWTON, and other members of the ROYAL SOCIETY OF LONDON. In 1725, he accepted an offer from PETER I (THE GREAT) (originally extended in 1721) to move to Russia. He was charged with setting up an observatory and school of ASTRONOMY to be associated with the Academy of SAINT PETERSBURG. Delisle taught at the academy from 1725 until 1747, where his colleagues included the illustrious mathematician Leonhard EULER. In 1747, upon returning to FRANCE, Delisle assumed a position as geographical astronomer to the French naval department and resumed teaching at the Collège de France. He died in 1768 of a stroke.

Delisle helped to formulate the international scientific project for observing the TRANSIT OF VENUS across the Sun. His proposal for the project identified the locations all over the Earth that would be best for observing the transit phenomenon. In addition, while in Russia, Delisle developed a plan that never reached fruition for mapping the vast regions of the Russian Empire. He perfected a technique for determining terrestrial LONGITUDE that had originally been proposed by Halley and also corrected Halley's planetary tables.

Publications by Delisle include *Abregé des mathématiques pour l'usage de S. M. impériale de toutes les Russies* (Summary of mathematics for the use of His Imperial Majesty of All the Russias; 1728); *Projet de la mésure de la terre en Russie* (Project for the measurement of the land in Russia; 1737); and *Mémoire présenté au roi . . . pour servir à l'explication de la mappemonde au sujet du passage de Vénus sur le soleil . . . le 6 juin 1761* (Memoir presented to the king . . . for helping the interpretation of the map of the world on the occasion of the transit of Venus across the Sun; 1760). He also left the *Mémoires pour servir à l'histoire et au progrès de l'astronomie, de la géographie et de la physique . . .* (Memoirs for assisting with the history of astronomy, geography, and physics . . .) that was published in 1738. Many of his scientific papers were published in the *Commentarii Academiae imperialis scientiarum petropolitanae* (Memoranda of the Imperial Academy of Sciences in Petersburg).

See also TECHNOLOGY AND INSTRUMENTATION.

democracy Specific form of government in which all persons designated as citizens have the right to vote on political affairs. Sovereignty is considered invested in all citizens rather than in any single individual or group. The term *democracy* (Greek: *demokratia*, from *demos*, people + *kratia*, rule by) comes from the ancient Greek political philosophers. Democracy was one of several general types of government in their typologies of government.

In the 18th century, the word *democracy* appeared frequently in treatises on POLITICAL THEORY and philosophy. A few cantons in SWITZERLAND and several free cities of the HOLY ROMAN EMPIRE were considered democracies. In general, however, it was accepted that democracy (meaning direct vote by all citizens) could not exist in any but the smallest sovereign states. Few PHILOSOPHES of the ENLIGHTENMENT favored direct democracy. Claude-Adrien HELVÉTIUS was one outstanding exception. The marquis d'ARGENSON was another, although he argued that democracy and monarchy could be intertwined in a politically potent manner. Most French revolutionaries preferred to establish an indirect democracy or republic with representative government and with the voting franchise limited to male property owners. But radical revolutionaries such as Maximilien ROBESPIERRE and François-Noel BABEUF championed democracy. The association of the term *democracy* with the excesses of the National Convention and Reign of Terror during the FRENCH REVOLUTION helped to reinforce a conservative, antidemocratic political position in FRANCE.

The concept of "democrat," defined as a partisan of direct democracy, was a product of the late Enlightenment. Although the term is alleged to have appeared in English in the 1740s, it did not become common in European languages until the 1780s and was not used in the AMERICAN REVOLUTION. Radical patriots in the Dutch revolt of 1784 were called *democraten* (democrats). And in the 1789 revolt in the AUSTRIAN NETHERLANDS, the most radical left-wing party preferred to be called democrat. In many instances the democrat was contrasted to the aristocrat in an effort to highlight differences in theoretical outlook. In this manner, *democrat* and *aristocrat* came to refer to political party lines.

As use of the term *democrat* spread throughout Europe, it acquired both positive and negative connotations that depended on the political alignment of the individual user. In ENGLAND and SCOTLAND, however, the term *democrat* nearly always carried a negative connotation and was used primarily by the opponents of the French Revolution.

demography Study of population growth and composition. European citizens of the 18th century were witnesses to huge alterations as large numbers of people moved from the countryside to burgeoning cities in search of work, yet the European population remained overwhelmingly rural; modern research estimates that no more than 10 to 11 percent of the population lived in urban centers. This seeming contradiction can be explained by the return of young provincials to their villages to marry and settle down after earning sufficient savings working as domestic servants in cities.

Not all those who sought work in the cities were so successful. Those who could not find or keep work were reduced to begging, prostitution, or crime. In late 18th-century PARIS, Louis Sébastien MERCIER, in his *Tableau de Paris* (Sketch of Paris), reported large numbers of prostitutes on the streets and decried the human suffering that he witnessed. LONDON and Paris were the largest cities in western Europe. Although disease spread more rapidly in urban centers due to overcrowded conditions, cities continued to grow over the course of the 18th century due to an influx of workers from the provinces. Illnesses such as typhoid, dysentery, and smallpox were widespread and frequently fatal, and only at the end of the 18th century was an effective vaccine for smallpox discovered.

Despite the presence of disease and a high infant mortality rate, the European population continued to grow during the 18th century. Although approximately 400,000 French and English citizens immigrated to the colonies over the course of the 18th century, these countries' populations continued to increase. This can be explained by the large families that were common in rural areas. Even if one in four French children died, as is estimated by modern researchers, a couple who married young could still have numerous children. Indeed, Europeans at the time were aware of this fact, and the strategy of late marriage was used as a form of birth control. Knowledge of contraceptives was kept away from the public because both political and theological authorities objected to them. Although many young people did not wish to postpone marriage, this strategy complied with a number of social, moral, and economic imperatives. Having children out of wedlock was frowned upon (a social and moral restriction), and couples were expected to have earned some income and set up their own household before marrying and having children (an economic restriction). Nevertheless, children were frequently conceived outside marriage, resulting in abandonment or even infanticide. When considering population growth in the 18th century, it should also be remembered that wars, plague, and famine were much more severe in the 17th century, causing more fatalities. The bubonic plague was no longer a threat in the 18th century.

At the time, most people were unaware of this increase in population. On the contrary, they believed that Europe had been much more populous during ancient times and that its numbers were declining in the modern era. Some authors, such as VOLTAIRE and Guillaume-Thomas-François de RAYNAL, were skeptical of the notion of large ancient populations, but their critiques fell on deaf ears. A large population was seen as a sign of the strength of a nation, both in military and economic terms, and European countries saw depopulation as a serious threat.

Real efforts were made during the 18th century to understand population growth and composition, as the ENLIGHTENMENT drive to classify and measure the natural and human worlds turned to a consideration of the changes in size and makeup of human groups. As the term *demography* did not yet exist, those who studied population called this undertaking *political arithmetic*. They believed that their efforts could lead to a more accurate understanding of population size, which would help European nations to gauge the strength of their economies and to develop strategies for the future. There was also a religious element to some of this research: By disproving the notion that population was in decline, many scholars, such as Johann Peter SÜSSMILCH, hoped to show a regular pattern of population that would support the idea of a divine order. Most significantly, led by scholars such as Leonhard EULER in GERMANY, Enlightenment thinkers began to apply the tools of mathematics to an understanding of human population.

It was not until Thomas MALTHUS published his *First Essay on the Principle of Population* in 1798 that overpopulation, rather than depopulation, became a concern. Whereas earlier thinkers such as Süssmilch posited an equilibrium between population and food supply, Malthus claimed that population growth always outpaces food production. Coming at the end of the Enlightenment, his theories would greatly influence the understanding of demography and its significance for political theory during the 19th century and beyond.

See also MATHEMATICS AND MECHANICS; MEDICINE; SMITH; STATISTICS.

Further reading: Richard Lawton and Robert Lee, eds., *Population and Society in Western European Port Cities c. 1650–1939* (Liverpool: Liverpool University Press, 2002); E. A. Wrigley, *Population and History* (New York: McGraw-Hill, 1969).

Denmark   Northern European kingdom located on the Baltic and North Seas. In the 18th century, the Oldenburg kings of Denmark ruled over territories including modern Denmark, Norway, and parts of the German-speaking territory of Schleswig-Holstein. Contemporaries called this large territorial conglomerate the Twin Kingdoms. The great Northern War (1700–21) established a balance of power in the Baltic region among Denmark, SWEDEN, the northern German principalities of the HOLY ROMAN EMPIRE, and RUSSIA that lasted until the end of the 18th century. However, conflicts over the Schleswig-Holstein area continued to dominate Danish foreign policy toward both Sweden and Russia.

The many years of external peace in the 18th century allowed Denmark to prosper. The Oldenburg kings and their ministerial advisers concentrated on restoring their kingdom after the devastation brought on by the earlier wars. The theory of MERCANTILISM guided economic policies. Attempts were made to stimulate shipping, commerce, and industry, to foster population growth, and to support agriculture. As the century progressed, the government introduced some elements of free trade and agricultural reform inspired by the PHYSIOCRATS and by related English economic doctrines.

Reformers inspired by the critical, rational spirit of the ENLIGHTENMENT focused in Denmark on issues of social and economic structure. Followers of PIETISM also dedicated their efforts to reform. Of particular concern was the relation of the peasantry to land. Peasants were legally tied to the land where they were born until they reached the age of 35. This system, a variant of SERFDOM, had been designed in 1733 to prevent flight from the countryside to cities and to ensure a steady, readily available supply of soldiers for the military forces. During the later 18th century, the system received heavy criticism for its inhumane treatment of peasants and for its basic violation of human dignity. Widespread land reform and peasant freedom, however, did not become reality until the end of the 18th century.

Denmark is noted for the political tranquility it enjoyed throughout the 18th century. Unlike the neighboring Swedes, the Danes accepted the ABSOLUTISM and enlightened despotism (see DESPOTISM, ENLIGHTENED) that the Oldenburg kings had imposed on them by a coup d'état in 1660. This absolute monarchy lasted until 1848. For a brief period from 1770 until 1772, conflict occurred between the king (the mentally unstable CHRISTIAN VII) and his council of advisers. A political reform experiment, inspired by certain ideals of the Enlightenment and carried out under the sponsorship of the minister Johann Friedrich STRUENSEE, brought about conflict with traditionally privileged groups in the advisory council. These groups forced Struensee's removal from office, after which the country returned to the centralized absolutism that had dominated its government policies through most of the 18th century.

Desaguliers, John Theophilus (1683–1744) *French-born experimental natural philosopher*

An early supporter of Isaac NEWTON, Desaguliers established the demonstrative lecture as a popular form in ENGLAND. These lecture-demonstrations were depicted in two paintings by Joseph Wright of Derby.

Desaguliers was the son of HUGUENOTS who emigrated from France to England after King LOUIS XIV promulgated the revocation of the Edict of Nantes in 1685. Having received a primary education from his father, Desaguliers entered Oxford University. He received a B.A. in 1709 and an M.A. in 1712. He began lecturing in experimental philosophy at Oxford while he earned his M.A. By 1712, Desaguliers was living in LONDON, lecturing, and enjoying remuneration from several royal pensions. He joined the FREEMASONS and became grand master of the Grand Lodge in 1719. The ROYAL SOCIETY OF LONDON elected him to its membership in 1714.

Desaguliers demonstrated many experiments for the Royal Society of London, lectured at the royal court, and taught courses in his home. For his various audiences, Desaguliers reproduced Newton's experiments on heat, as well as numerous experiments on optics and electricity. The content of his lectures appeared in 1734 as the *Course of Experimental Philosophy*. Desaguliers improved many scientific instruments and machines. He participated in the controversies over the shape of the Earth that pitted French Cartesians against English Newtonians. All parties in this controversy accepted the HELIOCENTRIC vision of the universe, in which the Earth revolves annually around the Sun and rotates daily on its axis. As a champion of Newton's theory of universal gravitation, Desaguliers believed that the Earth's rotation should produce a slight flattening of its spherical shape at the poles. Cartesians predicted the opposite, that the poles would be slightly elongated. In the end, expeditions sent out to measure the geographical distance between degrees of longitude at the poles and at the equator returned with data that supported the Newtonian predictions.

Desaguliers also tried to resolve the *vis viva* controversy in physics (a dispute over the definition of the concept of force) by portraying the dispute as a matter of semantics. His treatment was widely accepted at the time, but is now routinely challenged by historians of science. As part of his campaign to spread knowledge of Newtonianism, Desaguliers translated the Newtonian-inspired *Mathematical Elements of Physics* by Willem's GRAVESANDE from Latin into English.

Descartes, René (1596–1650) *French mathematician and systematic philosopher*

Born into the robe nobility (lawyers and officeholders), Descartes was the son of Olympe-Joachim Descartes and Jeanne Brochard. Descartes's middle name, Du Perron, comes from the estate of Du Perron ceded to him by his father. In 1606, Descartes entered the prestigious Collège La Flèche, founded by the JESUITS at the request of King Henri IV. The college provided Descartes with an education steeped in mathematics, philosophy, physics, and Latin classics. After his graduation in 1612, Descartes spent a few months in PARIS acquiring the social skills required of his status, then pursued a law degree at the University of Poitiers.

In 1616, with law degree in hand, Descartes volunteered for military duty in the army of Prince Maurice of Nassau. He spent the winter of 1618–19 at the garrison in Breda, where he met the mathematician Isaac Beeckman. Under Beeckman's influence, Descartes began exploring mathematical problems, making his first discoveries in what would become analytical geometry. He also wrote a brief treatise on music theory, the *Compendium Musicae*

Portrait of René Descartes (1596–1650) engraved by W. Holl from the original pictures by Frans Hals. Descartes's geometric method of reasoning ("I think, therefore I am") became the basis of his method to prove the existence of God. *(Courtesy New York Public Library)*

(Compendium of music), published posthumously in 1650.

The winter of 1619–20 found Descartes quartered near Ulm in southern GERMANY, having passed into the service of the elector of Bavaria. For four years, he would participate in the bloody battles of the Thirty Years' War. But the first winter in Ulm had significance far beyond his military career, for it was during that time that Descartes claimed to have gained his most important philosophical insights. He published nothing of his ideas, however, until 1637.

In 1622, Descartes returned for a few months to Paris and then settled in the countryside. He arrived in Paris during the height of the Rosicrucian scare, an episode in which rumors were circulating in the French capital about the infiltration of the city by a clandestine group bearing a radical religious and political philosophy. Descartes was accused by some people of having joined that secret and allegedly subversive organization. Descartes denied relations with the ROSICRUCIANS, insisting later in life that he learned about the organization only in the 1640s.

In 1628, Descartes left FRANCE for reasons that remain unclear. He seems to have feared persecution, either because of his philosophical ideas or perhaps because of undeclared religious convictions. At any rate, he lived in the UNITED PROVINCES OF THE NETHERLANDS from 1628 until 1649, returning to France between July 1644 and November 1646, again for a few months in 1647, and finally for a few weeks in 1648. He moved frequently within the United Netherlands, residing in Franckeren (1628–29), AMSTERDAM (1630), Deventer (1633), Utrecht (1635), Leiden (1636 and 1640), Sandwoert and Haarlem (1637), Endegest (1641), and finally Egmont (1643–49).

During these years, Descartes developed the systematic philosophy that made him renowned throughout Europe. Publication of parts of this work was delayed until 1637, for Descartes definitely feared prosecution after hearing of Galileo GALILEI's fate at the hands of the Roman Inquisition. His works, however, were circulating before 1637 in manuscript form. In Paris, Father Marin MERSENNE was overseeing their dissemination and providing various criticisms.

Descartes ended his years in Stockholm, SWEDEN, where he had settled in 1649 after accepting a post as philosopher to Queen Christina of Sweden. He instructed the queen in philosophy but also composed poetry and court ballets at her request. Unfortunately, the bitter climate of the Swedish winter caused Descartes to fall ill. He died in February 1650 and was buried as he had requested, in the orphans' cemetery of Stockholm. His remains were moved to France in 1666 but did not reach their final resting place until 1819, when they were interred at Saint-Germain-des-Près.

Philosophical Origins of Rationalism

Descartes, whose name is associated strongly with the earliest years of the SCIENTIFIC REVOLUTION, constructed the first of the three great 17th-century philosophical systems of RATIONALISM. The other two were developed by Benedict de SPINOZA and Gottfried Wilhelm LEIBNIZ later in the century, partly in an effort to respond to problems in the Cartesian framework. The ENLIGHTENMENT would inherit not only the faith in REASON of these three philosophers and their concept of a world based on mathematical law but also a set of thorny philosophical problems in EPISTEMOLOGY (human knowledge), PSYCHOLOGY, NATURAL PHILOSOPHY, NATURAL RELIGION, and MORAL PHILOSOPHY, which these 17th-century systems failed to address adequately. Thus, as a set of ideas and methods for understanding the universe, the physical world, God, and man, the Enlightenment is rooted in and grows out of 17th-century innovations.

When Descartes began his work in 1619, European philosophers and theologians were wrestling with problems about epistemology that were being forcefully stated or restated by skeptics. Skeptics were thinkers who followed several forms of philosophical SKEPTICISM that were part of the intellectual inheritance from antiquity. Skepticism claimed that all knowledge obtained through our senses and intellect is unreliable and necessarily subject to doubt. People of Descartes's generation were deeply disturbed by these claims, as they seemed to call into question all tradition and knowledge, even knowledge of God. Descartes was one of many who tried to answer the skeptics in order to restore a sense of intellectual and psychological security. His approach was novel in that he used the very strategy of the skeptics—radical doubt and criticism—to overturn their claims. He resolved to subject all his own ideas to critical doubt, retaining only those that were "clear and distinct," that is, "self-evident" and impossible to deny. This exercise yielded one self-evident truth, the bit of intuitive knowledge encapsulated in the famed phrase, *cogito ergo sum* (I think, therefore I am). Starting with this simple idea, Descartes proceeded to formulate additional reliable ideas about humankind, the world, and, ultimately, God. He determined that body and mind are distinctly different, the former made of matter, the latter of spirit (not-matter); that all the phenomena of the universe can be explained in terms of matter and its motion; and that God does indeed exist. The process by which he arrived at these ideas is his famous geometrical method of reasoning, which he sketched out in the *Discours de la méthode* (DISCOURSE ON METHOD; 1637).

Geometrical Method

The geometrical method relies wholly on a disciplined form of reasoning to arrive at reliable knowledge. It consists of four simple rules: start only with clear and distinct ideas; divide any complex idea into small, simple ones (analysis); think in an orderly process, moving from the simplest to the most complex ideas; and, finally, subject the process at every point to thorough criticism and evaluation so that nothing escapes your attention.

The term *geometrical* in this method reveals its roots in Descartes's formal Jesuit education at La Flèche, specifically his acquaintance with the deductive reasoning used in Euclidean geometry. This geometry constructs a complex system of reliable knowledge about two- and three-dimensional figures from simple axioms such as "two points define a line." That Descartes turned to mathematics as an intellectual model is no surprise, for he believed that only mathematics and theology, both rooted in philosophical logic, provide reliable knowledge, the former about the world, the latter about God. Descartes was not alone in seeking refuge within these two disciplines. The project of mathematizing all human knowledge about the world became a sort of collaborative effort in the 17th century as thinkers all over Europe exchanged their ideas and actual mathematical discoveries through the unofficial network called the REPUBLIC OF LETTERS.

The assertion that knowledge gained by rigorous deductive reasoning can be accepted as true made Descartes vulnerable to accusations of ATHEISM; the Cartesian world seemed to have no need of God as guarantor of truth. Descartes, however, actually believed that his method could play a role in supporting Christianity, and he is believed to have begun writing the *Discours de la méthode* after a discussion to that effect with the French Oratorian Cardinal Pierre de Bérulle. Descartes sought to demonstrate that his system actually could be used to prove the existence of God. However, the proofs (there were three) turned out to be variants of medieval scholastic demonstrations of God's existence.

Descartes has often been hailed as a radical who broke with tradition, but modern scholarship provides a more balanced perspective and reveals the many ways he drew on the past for his ideas, even as he restated them in novel form for his contemporaries. Whatever his indebtedness to the past, it must be emphasized that Descartes took a radical step when he made the thinking, reasoning human being (the *subjective self,* in philosophical language) the final judge of truth. Many scholars believe this step prepared the way for the later emergence of INDIVIDUALISM in western European thought and society.

The geometrical method was just one tool used in a comprehensive work, *De mundo* (On the world), written between 1627 and 1633, in which Descartes used the method, mathematics, and Copernican theory to demonstrate the unity of all knowledge—that is, the applicability of a few simple principles about matter, motion, and geometrical reasoning to all disciplines. The desire to prove precisely this unity is one of the threads that links 17th-century thinkers to the early Enlightenment.

Although Descartes finished *De mundo* by 1633, he did not publish it as a whole; Galileo had just been condemned for writing from a Copernican perspective, and Descartes did not want to suffer the same fate. Thus, he began testing the mood of the censors by issuing the four sections separately. The sections on optics and meteors came first, followed by the seminal *Traité de géométrie* (Treatise on geometry). It spelled out the basic tenets of Descartes's new coordinate geometry, which demonstrated that geometry (lines, planes, and solids) and algebra (numbers and their relationships) could be combined and even made interchangeable. This treatise provides an excellent, still valid example of the results that could be obtained in the search for unified knowledge. Finally, Descartes decided to publish *De mundo* as a whole in 1637, with its preface, the famed *Discours de la méthode.* He went on to expand his system with works such as the *Meditationes de prima philosophia* (Meditations of the first philosophy; 1641), *Principes de philosophie* (Principles of philosophy; 1644), *Traité des passions* (Treatise on the passions; 1647), and *Les passions de l'ame* (Passions of the soul; 1649)—all of great importance for later writers. Two works appeared posthumously: *De l'homme* (On man; 1644), and *Opuscula posthuma: Physica et mathematica* (Posthumous opuscules: Physics and mathematics; 1701).

Mechanical Philosophy

The unified natural philosophy developed by Descartes is called MECHANICAL PHILOSOPHY. It begins with the two simple ideas of matter (defined as extension, the ability to occupy space) and motion, then goes on to explain all natural events in the universe in terms of matter moving according to mathematical laws. It addresses the movement of bodies in space as well as the physiology of human bodies, and much more. From our contemporary perspective, much of Descartes's work is imaginary, an exercise in "armchair science," but this view overlooks the fact that Descartes actually developed his ideas by applying his method to the basic mechanical principles he had outlined in the *Discours de la méthode*. He did not resort to observation because he believed it would produce inferior and unreliable knowledge.

One of the foundations of mechanical philosophy was the Cartesian principle of inertia, the notion that an object (matter) in motion continues to move so long as something does not interfere. Changes in the direction of motion occur only as a result of impact between two objects, and the quantity of motion is always conserved in these collisions.

Any theory of motion must account for circular motion. In the scientific philosophy of Aristotle, circular motion was considered "natural," "perfect" motion. Galileo changed that conception, making linear motion the natural motion. Descartes accepted Galileo's idea, but then had to explain how circular motion arises. He attempted to explain it by resorting to the impact between particles, and offered a picture of the creation of the universe that was dominated by swirling vortices. Descartes's theory was never very satisfactory but it nevertheless had many adherents throughout the 17th century and into the 18th century. Isaac NEWTON was addressing the problem of circular motion when he developed his substitute theory of universal gravitation with its associated concepts of centripetal and centrifugal motion.

Descartes also applied his mechanical model of the universe to human beings. The resulting treatise, *De l'homme*, strongly affected the subsequent development of physiology and MEDICINE. It offered the model of the machine for human biological functions, providing explanations derived from hydraulics, statics, and other forms of mechanics. The Cartesian vision directly influenced 18th-century MATERIALISM.

Like the geometric method, mechanical philosophy contained troubling implications for Christian theology. If the universe operated according to a set of mathematical laws as Descartes claimed, then it seemed to have no need of God. The later representations of God as a watchmaker and the universe as a clock point to this reduced role. Lacking a deity, humankind would need something other than divine law to provide a basis for morality. This problem would not only bedevil natural philosophers but would also stimulate the development of DEISM and other

contributions of the Enlightenment to the disciplines of natural theology and moral philosophy.

Yet another perplexing problem was raised by the implications of Descartes's philosophy for human psychology. At the very outset of his work, in the *Discours de la méthode*, Descartes claimed that the distinction between soul and body, one of Christianity's central tenets of orthodoxy, follows immediately from the idea of *cogito*, of knowing oneself directly only as a thinking being. The mind, which is equivalent to the soul, recognizes the body, a type of matter, as something separate. Moreover, it does this without knowing anything about the rest of the external world. Therefore, the mind is distinct from all matter, just as it is from its own body. Descartes wished to refute the claims of the various animist and occult philosophies that were legacies of the Renaissance. The material world he envisioned was dead, stripped of the unruly, capricious forces and the MAGIC present in these Renaissance views. Without a soul, Descartes's mechanical, rational world functioned only according to the orderly, mathematical laws created by God.

While this system worked passably for matter, it failed to explain how, in human beings, a nonmaterial soul could act through a material body. Descartes thought that the site of intersection and interaction lay in the brain, in the tiny pineal gland, but he could not develop an adequate explanation of the way in which mind-body interactions occurred. The body-mind (body-soul) problem would challenge philosophers throughout the 17th century and the Enlightenment. Cartesian dualism spawned many counter theories, among them the monism of Spinoza, the parallelism of Leibniz, the neo-Cartesianisms of Nicolas de MALEBRANCHE and the Cambridge Platonists, the mechanical theories of John LOCKE, the animism of Georg Ernst STAHL, the VITALISM of the later 18th century, the skepticism of David HUME, and eventually a daring synthesis of Immanuel KANT.

The Cartesian geometric method had enthusiastic popular support, and the importance of Cartesian mathematics was readily recognized. The mechanical philosophy contained troubling implications for Christian theology, but it eventually entered the European mainstream by way of UNIVERSITIES in the United Provinces of the Netherlands and ENGLAND. By the dawn of the Enlightenment; Cartesianism had widespread support, but also influential critics. The discussion of its various tenets engaged scientists during the 18th century in a number of important investigations. If in the end many Cartesian ideas were surpassed, they nevertheless served as important stimuli for the science of the Enlightenment.

See also ANIMISM; COPERNICAN REVOLUTION; MATHEMATICS AND MECHANICS; SCIENCE.

Further reading: René Descartes, *The Philosophical Writings of Descartes,* tr. John Cottingham, Robert Stoothoff, and Dugald Murdoch (New York: Cambridge University Press, 1984); René Descartes, *Principles of Phi-*

losophy, tr. Valentine Rodger Miller and Reese Miller (Boston: D. Riedel Publishing, 1984); Genevieve Rodis-Lewis, *Descartes: His Life and Thought* (Ithaca, N.Y.: Cornell University Press, 1998).

Desmarest, Nicolas (1725–1815) *French geologist, expert on industrial technology, friend of Jean Le Rond d'Alembert and Anne-Robert-Jacques Turgot, and member of the enlightened circle of French encyclopedists*

Nicolas Desmarest worked first as an editor in PARIS, then for the royal French BUREAUCRACY as an inspector of manufacturing. With the outbreak of the FRENCH REVOLUTION, his official post was abolished. He worked in several minor positions and finished his professional career as a teacher at the new École Normale.

Desmarest developed his interests in geology as an adult by studying independently and by following the public lecture series on that subject given by Guillaume-François Rouelle. He carried out much of his geological fieldwork in the course of his official travels as a government inspector.

As a geologist, Desmarest developed a complicated theoretical position that reflected the controversies of his era. He was basically a Neptunist: He believed that most land formation occurred as a result of the deposit of sediments on the ocean floors. He rejected the opposing Plutonist viewpoint that volcanoes were the primary formative forces on Earth.

However, Desmarest did recognize that volcanic action plays some smaller role in creating geological structures. In fact, Desmarest argued in the basalt controversy that basalt is a rock of volcanic origin. He opposed the Neptunist position of Abraham WERNER on this subject.

Desmarest was elected to the FRENCH ACADEMY OF SCIENCES in 1771. He wrote two articles—"Fontaine" and "Géographique physique"—for volume seven of the ENCYCLOPÉDIE. The primary substance of his report on the basalts of the Auvergne region appeared in the sixth volume of the supplement to the *Encyclopédie.* He also published an article on earthquakes, *Conjectures physico-méchaniques sur la propagation des secousses dans les tremblemens de terre, et sur la disposition des lieux qui en ont ressenti les effets* (Physico-mechanical conjectures on the propagation of shaking in earthquakes, and on the arrangement of places that have felt the effects of them; 1756), shortly after the great LISBON EARTHQUAKE of 1755.

despotism, enlightened   Term used by historians to characterize one form of 18th-century political practice and theory. The term is closely related to enlightened ABSOLUTISM. In fact, historians argue about whether valid distinctions can be made between the two concepts.

AUSTRIA under JOSEPH II, PRUSSIA under FREDERICK II (THE GREAT), and RUSSIA under CATHERINE II (THE GREAT)

provide the most outstanding and generally accepted examples of the practice of enlightened despotism. These rulers were considered enlightened because they were designing state policies aimed at the realization of humanitarian and utilitarian goals. They were despots because no political body within their realms could effectively act as a check on their behavior. Theoretical and critical treatments of despotism or enlightened despotism may be found in the writings of MONTESQUIEU, Denis DIDEROT, Abbé RAYNAL, the marquis de MIRABEAU, Claude-Adrien HELVÉTIUS, Baron d'HOLBACH, Anne-Robert-Jacques TURGOT, Jeremy Bentham, Marquis d'ARGENSON, Paul-Pierre MERCIER DE LA RIVIERE, Baron von GRIMM, Frederick the Great, VOLTAIRE, Ludwig von SCHLÖZER, and various German theorists of CAMERALISM.

The term *enlightened despotism* is not an 18th-century creation, but rather a concept developed by historians who study the government structures of European nations during the ENLIGHTENMENT. Political theorists and critics of the 18th century wrote either of "despotism" or of "enlightened despots." Their collective attitude toward these phenomena was one of ambivalence. In *Esprit des lois* (SPIRIT OF LAWS; 1748), Montesquieu wrote that despotism is a corruption of government in which power is exercised by one individual or institution. According to his interpretation, any form of government, whether monarchy, aristocracy, or DEMOCRACY, can become despotic if its dominant ruling groups fail to respect the fundamental laws, natural laws, or divine laws that constitute the tradition of a state. Most 18th-century theorists, however, treated despotism as a species of monarchy and distinguished between despotism and absolutism. In the former, power was unlimited; in the latter, it was checked by fundamental NATURAL LAW or by divine laws. Political theorists described certain princes and kings, especially the three central and east-European rulers Joseph II, Catherine the Great, and Peter the Great, as enlightened despots. Through the middle of the 18th century, these rulers often received much public praise. Voltaire, Diderot, and Raynal, for example, admired the reforms of Frederick the Great and Catherine the Great.

Throughout the Enlightenment, political theorists recognized the contradictions inherent in the idea of an enlightened despot. The very notion of an unlimited ruler seemed to violate the cherished ideals of individual rights, liberty, and freedom, highlighting the tension inherent between individual liberties and central control. Writers sidestepped these contradictions by emphasizing that enlightened despots were forcing rational, progressive reforms on a reluctant populace in a kind of benevolent patriarchal rule. Furthermore, by forcing their subjects (with compulsory education) to acquire basic reading skills and practical knowledge, they were helping to realize the goal of a political society peopled with "enlightened" (i.e., literate) subjects. That these rulers were treading on traditional rights and ignoring certain liberties was deemed justified by their humanitarian and utilitarian goals. Rousseau spelled out this type of apology for enlightened despotism in *Du contrat social* (THE SOCIAL CONTRACT; 1762).

As the 18th century progressed, the positive assessment of despotism began to be challenged by observers who had experienced the negative effect of despotic practice or who had seen its inherent limits as an effective government form. Voltaire and Diderot both changed their minds, and the majority of writers began calling for some form of limited, parliamentary monarchy.

See also MONARCHS, ENLIGHTENED; GUSTAV III OF SWEDEN; POLITICAL THEORY.

Destutt de Tracy, Antoine-Louis-Claude, comte

(1754–1836) *French philosophe who with his friend Pierre-Jean-Georges Cabanis established the movement of the Idéologues during the French Revolution*

Destutt de Tracy belonged to a military family with a long tradition of royal service. After studying at the University of Strasbourg, Destutt de Tracy became a musketeer in the Maison du Roi (household of the king) and then a colonel in a regiment under the duc de Penthièvre. In 1789, he was elected to the Estates General as a representative of the Second Estate (nobility). During the earliest convocations of the Estates, however, he demonstrated his sympathy with the cause of reform, joined the delegation of the Third Estate (bourgeoisie), and voted on the night of August 4, 1789, in favor of abolishing the social titles and privileges of the ANCIEN RÉGIME.

Destutt de Tracy served in the revolutionary army under Lafayette. After Lafayette emigrated from FRANCE, Destutt de Tracy was imprisoned (November 1793–October 1794). He used the time in prison to study the psychological theories of John LOCKE and Étienne de CONDILLAC. Under the influence of these theorists, Destutt de Tracy began to develop his own ideas about the relationships between LANGUAGE, psychological development, and general moral EDUCATION. These ideas were central to the theory of IDÉOLOGIE (ideology) developed by the IDÉOLOGUES.

The downfall of Maximilien ROBESPIERRE brought freedom for Destutt de Tracy. He received an appointment to the new Institut de France in the class of moral and political sciences. In 1799, he was named to the Council of Public Instruction. The council established a system of universal public education following plans that had been developed during the years of the National Convention. The program of the Idéologues, based on the utilitarian notion that the proper formation of language produces rational, enlightened people, played a central role in the new curriculum.

Destutt de Tracy received the assignment to prepare textbooks for the important course on general grammar and legislation that was offered in the new Écoles Centrales. By 1805, he had completed three volumes: *Éléments d'Idéologie. Projet d'éléments d'Idéologie à l'usage des écoles centrales* (Elements of idelogy. Plan of the elements of ideology for use in the central schools; 1801); *Grammaire* (Grammar; 1803); and *Logique* (Logic; 1805). These works described the analysis of sensations and ideas, the principles of language, and the logic of sciences that underlay the theory of the Idéologues. A fourth volume, the *Traité de la volonté et de ses effets* (Treatise on the will and its effects) appeared in 1815. It outlined the elements of a novel social science that would help individuals direct their actions effectively and efficiently.

Destutt de Tracy also published the *Commentaire sur l'Esprit des lois* (Commentary on the Spirit of Laws; 1807), a work that claimed to elucidate the complete system of social science hidden within the disorder of the *Esprit des lois* (SPIRIT OF LAWS) by MONTESQUIEU. Under the auspices of Thomas JEFFERSON, who favored the programs of the Idéologues, Destutt de Tracy's commentary was translated into English and published in the UNITED STATES OF AMERICA. The volume contained an introduction by Jefferson.

See also CABANIS; PHILOSOPHES; PSYCHOLOGY.

Dialogues Concerning Natural Religion   Book by the Scottish philosopher David HUME. Hume began writing the *Dialogues Concerning Natural Religion* in the 1750s but did not complete it until 1776, the year of his death. It was published posthumously in 1779. The arguments of the *Dialogues Concerning Natural Religion* complement those in the *Natural History of Religion* (1757). Both works treat RELIGION as a human creation rather than as something given from God.

In the *Dialogues Concerning Natural Religion*, Hume examines the various proofs for God's existence associated with NATURAL RELIGION and philosophy. He does not address the doctrines of revealed religion (i.e., Christian revelation). Hume casts his analysis in the form of a dialogue among three speakers: Philo, the skeptic, Demea, the orthodox theologian, and Cleanthes, who occupies a middle position between these two extremes. The dialogue model had been frequently used in ancient Greek and Roman literature to explore difficult philosophical questions. In fact, a treatise by Cicero, *The Nature of the Gods,* apparently served as Hume's model. But Hume was doing more than just mimicking the respected writers of antiquity, for the dialogue model offered him a delicate vehicle of addressing sensitive topics without making open statements about his personal beliefs. In this respect, the dialogue model allowed Hume's work to escape censorship.

Building on the philosophy of knowledge (EPISTEMOLOGY) that he had outlined in A TREATISE OF HUMAN NATURE (1739–40) and AN ENQUIRY CONCERNING HUMAN UNDERSTANDING (1758), Hume uses the *Dialogues* to examine the various traditional proofs—from EMPIRICISM, RATIONALISM, and MORAL PHILOSOPHY—for the existence of God.

Philo the skeptic begins the main analysis by pointing out the logical fallacies in the popular empirical argument from design associated with the name of Isaac NEWTON. He points out that even though we see evidence of design and order in the world, that evidence tells us nothing with certainty about how the world was created. A deity might have created it, but it is also possible that the world generated itself through some unknown process.

Hume's critique of proofs continues by pointing to problems with rational arguments based on self-evident propositions, the type of proof associated with the philosophy of René DESCARTES. It then examines a third type of proof that was enjoying a vogue during the ENLIGHTENMENT: the proof based on the apparent benevolence in the world. Philo again plays the major role and shows that experience seems to suggest that the world is morally neutral.

Hume seemed to be leading his readers to gloomy conclusions about the validity of belief in a deity. But, at the close of the *Dialogues,* he backed away from the implications of his arguments and acknowledged, through Philo, that some beliefs are practically justified even if philosophically uncertain. It is acceptable, therefore, to believe that an intelligent being might have created the ordered universe that we experience on a daily basis. Philo's final position comes close to that of fideism (belief based on a leap of faith rather than on reasoned knowledge) and grows from Hume's earlier epistemological arguments for the practical value of belief in human existence.

In contrast to the *Dialogues,* the *Natural History of Religion* examines the psychological foundations for religion, linking its appearance to fundamental traits of human nature and to the irrational aspects of the human mind. In particular, it assigns the creation of the gods to human fear and to the propensity to personify those fears in the figures of gods and goddesses. The gods (or God) do not reveal finished, exclusively true religions to people. Rather, people created their deities in the course of coping with unknown aspects of life on Earth.

The *Natural History of Religion* also treats religious belief from the perspective of HISTORY, assuming that the basic religious forms—polytheism and monotheism—are linked to each other in naturally occurring cycles of flux and reflux.

In both these works on religion, Hume was questioning not only revealed religions such as Christianity (ROMAN CATHOLICISM and PROTESTANTISM), Judaism, or Islam, but was also criticizing the foundations of DEISM. His work disturbed English Protestant theologians such as William Warburton and Richard Hurd, both of whom condemned his dangerous ideas. Yet Hume's views were shared by others during the Enlightenment. His equation of religious ENTHUSIASM with fanaticism drew on the writings of the earl of SHAFTESBURY, Pierre BAYLE, and David HARTLEY. His explanation of the birth of the gods in terms of human PSYCHOLOGY had counterparts in works by Bernard de FONTENELLE, Nicolas-Antoine BOULANGER,

Hartley, and Baron d'HOLBACH. Furthermore, his explorations of the limits of human REASON and of the inadequacy of rational proofs for the existence of God provided materials for the seminal work of the late Enlightenment offered by Immanuel KANT.

diamond necklace scandal A petty scandal that broke out in August 1785 in the court of LOUIS XVI and MARIE-ANTOINETTE. Although small in comparison to other events and issues of the era, the scandal made Marie-Antoinette look intensely frivolous and seriously undermined public respect for her. It had an impact on public opinion that far outweighed its actual seriousness. Napoleon dated the outbreak of the FRENCH REVOLUTION from this episode because of its effect on public attitudes toward the royalty of France.

The outline of events is as follows: A group of court intriguers wished for various reasons to bring about the downfall of Cardinal de Rohan. They included Marie-Antoinette; the minister of state, the baron de Breteuil; and the presumed instigator of the plot, the comtesse Jeanne de La Motte. The comtesse convinced the hapless Cardinal de Rohan to use his credit in order to purchase an expensive diamond necklace (over 600 stones with a total weight of 2,800 carats and a price tag of 1.6 million livres) for the queen. Rohan agreed because he wished to mend his shaky relations with the queen. When the necklace was delivered to Rohan, the comtesse had one of her agents, posing as a courier of the queen, take it away. The necklace never reached the queen, of course, but was instead broken up into smaller parts and sold. Breteuil, in the meantime, had Rohan arrested and charged him with falsely using the queen's name to procure the necklace. The duped cardinal was brought to trial. He was found innocent but banished from court. The comtesse de La Motte was flogged and imprisoned, but she managed to escape to ENGLAND after two years in prison.

Public opinion placed central blame for this affair on Marie-Antoinette, the consensus being that she had promised favors to Cardinal de Rohan if he would procure the necklace, but that she had then balked at paying the price. In fact, historians have ascertained that she had expressly rejected the necklace as gaudy and reminiscent of the excesses of the reign of LOUIS XV.

The fact that the queen could not escape having her reputation tarnished by this bit of trickery reveals how little esteem and trust she had acquired with the French public. Modern historians tend to see the episode as an illustration of the growing tendency in the late ENLIGHTENMENT to reject female influence in politics.

Dictionnaire philosophique Book by VOLTAIRE, begun in 1752 and finally submitted for anonymous publication in 1764 under the title *Dictionnaire philosophique portatif* (Portable philosophical dictionary). The *Dictionnaire* appeared in GENEVA with a false LONDON imprint. It enjoyed immediate success and provoked intense outrage from ecclesiastical and secular authorities. Baron Melchior GRIMM announced its appearance in his *Corréspondance littéraire* (Literary correspondence), noting that copies were already difficult to find. The city of Geneva condemned the book shortly after its appearance. Authorities in The Hague, PARIS, and ROME followed suit between December 1764 and July 1765.

These official condemnations did not hinder the success of the book. New editions appeared in December 1764, 1765, 1767, and 1769. The 1769, the largest edition, appeared under the title *La Raison par alphabet* (Reason by [the] alphabet). It was reprinted several times under the title *Dictionnaire philosophique*.

The *Dictionnaire* is a polemical and propagandist tract whose positions are revealed in a series of alphabetical articles treating various subjects. Articles bear titles such as: ENTHUSIASM, abbot, the GREAT CHAIN OF BEING, TOLERATION, miracles, SUPERSTITION, the Mass, luxury, fanaticism, Inquisition, and FREEDOM of thought. Voltaire used these topics as vehicles for an attack on his primary enemy, Christianity. In his view, Christianity not only encouraged superstition, but also spawned intolerance, fanaticism, enthusiasm, clerical abuses, and distortions of political power. He particularly disliked ROMAN CATHOLICISM, the official religion of his native FRANCE. Voltaire preferred a world view wholly different from the one espoused by Christianity—the one embodied in English EMPIRICISM and DEISM in the ideas of John LOCKE, Isaac NEWTON, David HUME, and Thomas WOOLSTON. Voltaire's brilliant writing, his wit and masterful use of irony, his tactical inventiveness in the service of his ideas, and his impassioned commitment to religious toleration, Newtonian science, and British empiricism make his *Dictionnaire* a masterpiece of the French Enlightenment.

See also RELIGION; SEPARATION OF CHURCH AND STATE.

Diderot, Denis (1713–1784) *French philosophe, encyclopedist, novelist, playwright, and literary and art critic*
Denis Diderot ranks with MONTESQUIEU, VOLTAIRE, and Jean-Jacques ROUSSEAU, as a leader in the French ENLIGHTENMENT. Within this intellectual circle he was known by the nickname "Pantophile."

Like Rousseau, who was first a friend and later a bitter critic, Diderot came from an artisan family—his father was a master cutler—and gave voice to the discontents and aspirations of middle-class groups. But the content of his thought extended far beyond any narrow bounds that might have been imposed by his socioeconomic origins. Diderot was an intellectual rebel, thoroughly committed to MATERIALISM, to ATHEISM, and to revolution in AESTHETICS and POLITICAL THEORY.

As a youth in Langres, Diderot received a secondary education from the JESUITS and took preliminary steps toward entering that order by receiving his tonsure. At the age of 16 (1728) he moved to PARIS, where he matric-

ulated at the University of Paris, receiving an M.A. degree in 1732. He abandoned his plan to enter the clergy and also declined to take degrees in law or medicine, actions that angered his family. During the years from 1728 until 1740 Diderot may have worked briefly as a law clerk, and he most certainly continued his independent studies in a wide range of fields. He supported himself by tutoring and translating books from English into French. But not much more is known of his life until 1740, when his literary career began to blossom.

In the eyes of his family, Diderot was behaving irresponsibly. His father cut off all financial support and also refused to assent to his son's request in 1743 for permission to marry Anne-Toinette Champion. In an effort to show his displeasure and to enforce his will on his son, the elder Diderot resorted to a standard practice of the time: He had his son incarcerated for a short period in a monastery near Troyes. Upon his release, young Diderot returned to Paris, where he and Mademoiselle Champion were secretly married.

During the early 1740s, Diderot was circulating in various cafes and coffeehouses, making contacts with PHILOSOPHES such as Rousseau (1742 in the Café de la Régence) and Étienne de CONDILLAC. His translations from English began to appear in 1742, but the year 1745 marked the solid establishment of his career. In that year, he published a translation of the *Essai sur le mérite et la vertu* (Essay on merit and virtue) by Anthony Ashley Cooper, third earl of SHAFTESBURY.

The Shaftesbury translation helped to secure Diderot a position with the publisher André Le Breton as a translator of the Chambers *Cyclopedia*. Although never completed, the Chambers project gave birth to the great ENCYLOPÉDIE (Encyclopedia), one of the major publications of the Enlightenment. Diderot became its general editor in 1747, with assistance from Jean Le Rond d'ALEMBERT in the realms of mathematics and SCIENCE.

Diderot devoted the next 25 years to the *Encyclopédie*. He also began publishing independent essays whose ideas quickly brought him under surveillance by CENSORSHIP authorities. The "Lettres sur les aveugles à l'usage de ceux qui voient" (Letters on the blind for the use of those who can see; 1749) was condemned for its materialist ideas, and, as a result, Diderot spent July through November 1749 incarcerated in the dungeons at Vincennes. In 1759, censorship also forced a temporary suspension of the publication of the *Encyclopédie*.

After these experiences, Diderot refrained from publishing his more radical philosophical writings such as *La réve de d'Alembert* (D'Alembert's dream, written 1769) and the *Réfutation de l'ouvrage d'Helvétius* (Refutation of the work of Helvétius). These works did not appear in print until the 19th century. The novels *Le neveu de Rameau* (Rameau's nephew), *La religieuse* (The nun), and *Jacques le fataliste* (Jacques the fatalist) were published posthumously during the FRENCH REVOLUTION.

operations of the mind. He rejected the dualism between mind and matter contained in Cartesian forms of mechanical philosophy and explained all functions of the mind—sensation, perception, memory, the sense of self, REASON, and imagination—in terms of the activity of bundles of nerve fibers.

Diderot adapted the sensation psychology of John LOCKE and Abbé CONDILLAC to his materialist vision by adding the concepts of SYMPATHY and harmony, drawn from musical acoustics, to explain the production of ideas. According to Diderot, the brain consists of fibers of matter that act like the strings on a violin. A set of fibers that has received an external sensation begins to vibrate. Its vibrations set up a series of sympathetic vibrations in nearby fibers, causing associations of ideas to occur. Various other harmonic phenomena produce other types of association, thus building up a store of connected ideas in the brain.

The brain serves as the central organ of the body, exerting control over all functions. In waking hours, it also controls the nature of its internal vibrations, thereby regulating the type of ideas that are generated. During dream states, or in cases of insanity, however, the brain relaxes this control. Associations begin occurring at random, producing the bizarre images and ideas of dreams and psychosis.

Diderot adapted this theory of psychology to questions of aesthetics and MORAL PHILOSOPHY. Like Shaftesbury, whose treatise he had translated as a young man, Diderot believed that emotions are the source of our ideas about what constitutes beauty, goodness, and truth. Events and objects that produce strong feelings of desire are called beautiful, good, or true. Things that produce strong aversion become defined as bad, ugly, or untrue.

Creative GENIUS involves experiencing strong emotions while maintaining complete control over them. In the act of creating a work of art, literature, or music, the artist first experiences a strong emotional sensation that activates the imagination. The artist perceives RELATIONS between things in a manner that is unusual and faces the challenge of communicating this insight to others. Successful communication occurs in a second event, involving a burst of ENTHUSIASM as the artist discovers the way to express himself or herself. Diderot thus parted ways with the critics of enthusiasm, rehabilitating it by assigning it a central role in creative processes. He also rejected the idea put forth by Helvétius that proper EDUCATION could form genius in people. Genius was not an acquired trait, but rather something inborn, related to the physiological functioning of individuals.

Diderot expanded his aesthetic ideas into a theory that stressed the differences between various art forms. He became a prominent art critic, offering evaluations of the biennial painting exhibitions (salons) held at the Louvre. He championed art that combined both aesthetic beauty with the presentation of some moral vision. His favorite artists—Jean-Baptiste GREUZE, Jean-Baptiste-Siméon CHARDIN, and Claude-Joseph Vernet—painted simple scenes of middle-class activities and environments.

Situated as he was at the center of the *Encyclopédie* publication, Diderot exercised significant influence over the form in which ideas of the Enlightenment were spread beyond the boundaries of the Parisian salons to the broader reading public. His many articles in the *Encyclopédie,* however, do not reflect the scope of his inventiveness. Diderot formulated an enlightened discourse that differed significantly from those associated with his fellow philosophes in Paris. He carried materialism and atheism to extremes but imbued them with elements drawn from the German Enlightenment (AUFKLÄRUNG) that give them a unique character. Diderot helped to bring these ideas into the mainstream of French intellectual life. In the process, he began approaching and exploring realms that would prove to be the boundaries of the Enlightenment.

See also ANCIEN RÉGIME; INTUITION AND IMAGINATION; MATHEMATICS AND MECHANICS; PORNOGRAPHY; RADICAL ENLIGHTENMENT; PUBLISHING; RIGHTS; SEPARATION OF CHURCH AND STATE; SOCIAL INSTITUTIONS OF THE ENLIGHTENMENT.

Further reading: Robert Darnton, *The Literary Underground of the Old Regime* (Cambridge, Mass.: Harvard University Press, 1982); Denis Diderot, *The Nun,* tr. Leonard Tancock (New York: Penguin Books, 1972); Denis Diderot, *Rameau's Nephew and Other Works,* tr. Jacques Barzun and Ralph H. Bowne (Indianapolis: Bobbs-Merrill, 1964); Aram Vartanian, *Diderot and Descartes: A Study of Scientific Naturalism in the Enlightenment* (Princeton, N.J.: Princeton University Press, 1953); Arthur Wilson, *Diderot: The Testing Years, 1713–1759* (New York: Oxford University Press, 1969).

Diplomatic Revolution of 1756 The historical term used to describe the radical reshuffling of European alliances that occurred in the middle of the 18th century. The changes caused major shifts in the European balance of power. FRANCE and Hapsburg AUSTRIA initiated the changes. The old order rested on a system in which France and Austria were traditionally enemies. Britain usually allied itself with France against Austria. However, as the 18th century progressed, the British and French conflicts in the American colonies produced increasing tension between them. The emergence of PRUSSIA as a major power provided Britain with an alternative to France for alliances against Austria. Prussia's rise meant that Austria now had a new, more threatening enemy than the French. In the meantime, the French, who had supported FREDERICK II (THE GREAT) in his wars against Austria, were annoyed with his arrogance and Machiavellian tactics in war and diplomacy. The stage was set for the great reversal of alliances.

Diderot's reluctance to publish his ideas did not, of course, mean that they were unknown. His presence in various enlightened salons, his open associations with the atheistic group around Baron d'HOLBACH, and his earlier publications such as the *Pensées philosophiques* (Philosophical thoughts; 1746), the "Lettre sur les aveugles," and the *Pensées sur l'interprétation de la nature* (Thoughts on the interpretation of nature; 1754) assured knowledge of his positions. Besides, his ideas in somewhat censored form could be encountered in the many articles he wrote for the *Encyclopédie*, in the volumes of the *Correspondence littéraire* (Literary correspondence) published by Melchior GRIMM, and in the famous pieces of art and literary criticism that appeared under the title *Salons* (Salons; 1759–81).

Diderot's activities brought him into contact with all the major intellectual figures of his era. He assisted Grimm with the *Correspondance littéraire,* Holbach with the *Système de la Nature* (System of nature), Abbé RAYNAL with the HISTOIRE DES DEUX INDES (History of the two Indias), and Madame d'EPINAY with the *Histoire de Madame de Montbrillant* (History of Madame Montbrillant). He regularly attended enlightened salons at the homes of Madame Suzanne NECKER, Madame Louise d'ÉPINAY, Baron d'Holbach, and others.

Diderot corresponded with CATHERINE II (THE GREAT) of Russia for many years and spent a few months during 1773 in SAINT PETERSBURG. He was elected to membership in the Academy of Saint Petersburg, an honor that had also been bestowed by the BERLIN ACADEMY. Catherine assisted Diderot by buying his library and by rewarding him with a lifelong pension to serve as its curator. She failed, however, to act on the various suggestions for legal reform contained in his *Mémoires pour Cathérine II* (Memoirs for Catherine the Great) and thoroughly suppressed their circulation in Russia.

Upon his return to France in 1774, Diderot divided his remaining years between leisure and writing. He died in Paris in 1784, just a few months after the death of his mistress, friend, and correspondent, Sophie Volland.

Diderot developed a philosophy rooted in materialism that provided the foundations both for his theory OF PSYCHOLOGY and for his concepts in aesthetics. He drew on the contemporary theories of AFFINITY CHEMISTRY and VITALISM, and also on the works of the comte de BUFFON, Louis-Jean-Marie DAUBENTON, Pierre MAUPERTUIS, Albrecht von HALLER, and Théophile de BORDEU to develop a theory of matter that sharply contrasted with the vision offered in the MECHANICAL PHILOSOPHY. According to the mechanical philosophy, matter is a substance that occupies space (is extended) and lacks the ability to move unless acted upon by some force outside it. For Diderot, however, matter was a dynamic substance, possessing inner forces; motion was essential to its nature. The source of this motion lay in chemical activity. All matter, whether living or nonliving, also

Engraving of Denis Diderot. A leader of the philosophes in Paris, Denis Diderot served as general editor of the *Encyclopédie,* risking imprisonment and financial difficulty in order to ensure its publication. *(Courtesy New York Public Library)*

possessed sensitivity (*sensibilité*), the ability to react to external stimuli, as happens in the nervous system. The whole universe was a kind of organism composed of active, living particles of matter.

Diderot's world was one of constant flux and transformation. Birth, life, and death were merely changes in form, something like chemical changes that transform substances from gaseous to liquid to solid states.

The idea that the world is ordered according to some design was for Diderot a mere illusion. He believed instead that the world was constantly changing in a random manner that made possible the appearance of infinitely many new and different creatures. According to Diderot, species were not constant, and the entire concept of CLASSIFICATION, in which living beings were arranged into groups, was artificial.

The fundamental characteristics of matter contained everything Diderot needed to explain the creation of the world, the appearance of the species, and even abnormal phenomena such as birth defects. His world did not need a creator God in order to acquire its form or orderly ways of functioning. Thus, Diderot's conception rejected the foundation for DEISM and overtly favored atheism.

In claiming that his idea of matter could account for all phenomena in the world, Diderot was including the

The chief architect of the new alliance between France and Austria was Maria Theresa's adviser, Wenzel KAUNITZ. As early as 1748, he had seen the desirability of alliance with France as a means of protecting Austria from Prussian predation, but attempts at negotiation with the French had always failed. The turning point came in January 1756, when Frederick the Great made an unexpected alliance with Britain that violated an existing treaty between France and Prussia. The French were furious and moved quickly to establish the alliance with Austria in May 1756.

The immediate result of the French and Austrian move was a new war, the SEVEN YEARS' WAR. The war forced France to cede all its Canadian colonies to Britain and saddled the French government with enormous debts. Difficulties in financing these debts contributed substantially to the general crises that brought the downfall of the Bourbon monarchy in the FRENCH REVOLUTION. In spite of these long-term consequences, the end of the Seven Years' War was followed by nearly 30 years of peace in Europe. That peace was, in part, produced by the new, more stable system of alliances negotiated in the Diplomatic Revolution.

Discourse on Method

Discourse on Method René Descartes's groundbreaking philosophical work that attempts to define principles for scientific methods of thought and inquiry. The energetic debates and publications of 17th-century philosophy established principles essential to ENLIGHTENMENT thinking and practice. One of the most influential figures of this period was the French philosopher René DESCARTES, whose works sparked discussions in his homeland and across Europe that helped to establish modern PHILOSOPHY. The roots of his theoretical work lay in his *Discours de la méthode pour bien conduire sa raison et chercher la vérité dans les sciences* (Discourse on the method of rightly conducting reason and seeking truth in the field of science; 1637), an exhaustive analysis of the nature of scientific reasoning that paved the way for later 18th-century researchers and philosophers.

Building on Descartes's previous work in SCIENCE and mathematics, the *Discourse* was designed to lay out the rules for discovering the truth of any idea or situation. It was published as a preface for three scientific essays: *La Dioptrique* (Dioptrics), *Les Météores* (Meteors), and *La Géometrie* (Geometry). The *Discourse* provided a philosophical justification for the accuracy of Descartes's notions in the realms of physics and mathematics developed in these essays. Descartes had been working on these writings for many years; when they first appeared, the three scientific essays received more attention than the *Discourse* itself, but it was the latter text that would profoundly influence Western philosophy.

Divided into six parts, the text asserts in Part One the innate rational ability of all individuals. For Descartes, everyone is endowed with common sense, or REASON; if individuals learn to hone this ability, they will be capable of engaging in philosophical speculation and following philosophical arguments. The fact that Descartes first published the *Discourse* in French, instead of in Latin, the language of scholarly investigation, shows that he intended to reach an audience of nonspecialists in his own country. (Afterward, in 1644, Descartes oversaw a Latin translation for the European scholarly community.) To a modern reader, this scientific text begins with an unusual approach: Descartes describes the beginnings of his own intellectual trajectory and suggests reading the *Discourse* as a "story" or a "fable." The philosopher recounts his struggle to find some sure basis for knowledge over the course of his formal education.

Part Two continues the personal tone, as Descartes describes the influence of travel on his intellect. The variety of customs and beliefs that he discovered abroad, as well as the contradictions in the systems of different philosophers, led him to search for some method by which he could ascertain the true from the false. Starting from a position of doubting everything, he decided that he would accept only those ideas that presented themselves to him "clearly and distinctly" as true. This is the first of four precepts that he establishes. Second, he finds it necessary to break down all difficulties in reasoning into as many components as possible, in order to achieve a solution with the least effort; third, to order the reasoning process from the most basic ideas to complicated theories; and fourth, to perform all research and consideration as exhaustively as possible. Using mathematics, especially geometry, as his model, Descartes wished to move from the simplest propositions to the most complex, as in a geometrical theorem that builds from a basic axiom to more complex assertions.

In the next two sections he considers the wider philosophical implications of this new method. In Part Three, Descartes explains that he did not subject morality and religion to the same scrutiny as other intellectual matters, believing that it was wiser to accept the religious tradition into which he was born. While accepting the customs and beliefs of his country, Descartes maintains that his personal mission is to attempt to perfect his reason by following his own method, as this philosophical practice is a source of great satisfaction.

Part Four investigates the realm of metaphysics. Although Descartes established in Part Three that religion was off-limits in this inquiry, he nonetheless seeks some foundation for understanding human knowledge and existence. Claiming that the senses are unreliable sources of knowledge because they can deceive, he turns within and decides that the first single thing of which he can be certain is that *Je pense, donc je suis* (I think, therefore I am). Even if he imagines that the whole world is only a dream, or does not exist, he cannot doubt his own ability to think. Therefore, he must have a soul that allows him to think and that is separate from the flawed body.

Finally, Descartes reflects that knowledge, something perfect, and doubt, something imperfect, coexist in the human mind; he concludes that knowledge has its origin in God, who is perfect.

In the last two sections, Descartes shows the results of his method and reflects on its usefulness. Part Five reviews contemporary thinking in numerous branches of scientific inquiry, including Descartes's thoughts on the circulation of the blood and the heart in the human anatomy. In Part Six, Descartes looks to the future of scientific research and its potential questions and issues. He reviews his own paths of inquiry and evaluates his ability to follow scientific methods. Descartes asserts the end result of philosophical inquiry as a new form of pragmatic thinking that leads to improvements in both human understanding and existence. He contrasts it with Scholastic philosophy (the philosophical system of the medieval Catholic Church), which has no practical application.

The *Discourse on Method* established the principles of the philosophy that would come to be known as Cartesianism. These principles are deductive in nature, that is, they start from basic principles such as distinctness and clarity of ideas and build upon them to arrive at more general conclusions. This method was extremely influential for Western thought, especially in terms of Descartes's positing of hypotheses and his insistence on clear proof through logic. However, Cartesianism was to fall from favor in light of the discoveries of Isaac NEWTON, whose science used an inductive method, based on observations. Enlightenment thinkers of the 18th century were suspicious of the abstract nature of Descartes's speculations and saw the effort to come up with systems that could explain the workings of the universe as less productive than a gradual development of human knowledge based on observation and experiment. Indeed, it is the latter that gave rise to modern scientific method. Although Descartes's science was contested, and often disproven, during the Enlightenment, he has remained a challenging author in the field of philosophy and must be considered one of the innovators in the development of a modern approach to science and knowledge.

See also MATHEMATICS AND MECHANICS; MECHANICAL PHILOSOPHY; NATURE.

Further reading: Harry M. Bracken, *Descartes* (New York: Oxford University Press, 2002); Desmond M. Clarke, *Descartes' Philosophy of Science* (University Park, Penn.: Pennsylvania State University Press, 1982); René Descartes, *Discourse on Method and Meditations* (Indianapolis: Bobbs-Merrill, 1960).

Discourse on the Origins of Inequality　An essay by the Genevan philosophe Jean-Jacques ROUSSEAU, written in 1755 for a contest sponsored by the Academy of Dijon. Rousseau emerged in this work as an original thinker who refused to embrace the conclusions accepted as commonplace by his enlightened contemporaries. But his rejection of their specific ideas about human EQUALITY and its relation to civilization did not mean that he rejected the basic values of the ENLIGHTENMENT.

Like his enlightened contemporaries, Rousseau turned to NATURE as the best source of knowledge and wisdom for people. But he believed the task of uncovering such knowledge was difficult for people living in civilized societies. He maintained that civilization actually separated people from their natural abilities to read the "book of nature."

Rousseau located the source of these difficulties in the HISTORY of humankind. This history had entailed not constant PROGRESS toward perfection, but rather a pattern of progress followed by decline.

Three different stages of historical development had brought European society to its unfortunate 18th-century condition. At the beginning of time, people had lived as savages in a state not much different from animals. They had surpassed animals only in possessing free will and the related ability to make choices about behavior. People had also possessed three other basic characteristics: PERFECTIBILITY, the faculty of SYMPATHY, and SELF-INTEREST. The operation of these basic characteristics had set in motion a certain course of upward human development, a process that had inevitably brought people to the second stage of history.

The second stage was the primitive or barbaric stage, for Rousseau the ideal state of humankind. Original characteristics were somewhat modified, but they were not warped beyond recognition. The primitive state offered a delicate balance between the natural characteristics of people and the needs of larger groups.

The unfortunate and indeed tragic invention of private PROPERTY had brought this idyllic state to an end. One person set aside some land and said, "This is my property." As a result, the foundations were laid for the appearance of inequality based on material possessions and the social status or political power that such possessions could bring. Rousseau believed that certain earlier human inventions had laid the groundwork for the creation of private property: institutions such as the family, metallurgy, agriculture, and the concept of self-esteem.

Property, then, created the third stage of history, the social stage in which inequality became institutionalized. Property had to be protected, and thus laws were created along with the judges and courts to enforce them. Furthermore, legitimate power tended to become corrupt and to transform into arbitrary tyranny. This third stage of history saw the slow decline of people back toward their original, anarchic savage state.

Embedded in this pessimistic vision of history was a criticism of the arts, of modern science, and of technology. Rousseau also decried luxury, declaring that it corrupts because of its roots in the concept of property.

Rousseau's vision parallels that of John LOCKE by ascribing the foundations of civil society to property. But where Locke sees property as the guarantee of political freedom and equality, Rousseau sees it creating inequality and the division between master and slave. The celebrated progress of mankind that contemporaries believed they saw in 18th-century developments was an illusion in Rousseau's eyes.

Rousseau, then, stands as a severe critic of his contemporary world and as a pessimist with respect to the course of history up to his era. His works overall, however, display the same faith in human potential that stamps the writings of his enlightened friends and acquaintances. To find that positive vision, the reader must look beyond the *Discourse on the Origins of Inequality* to the SOCIAL CONTRACT and to ÉMILE. Without the balance provided by these later works, readers can easily gain a distorted vision of the ideas of this complex and inventive man.

Dissenters   English Protestants who stood outside the boundaries of the official Church of England (Anglican Church). They refused to take Communion on account of disagreements over the theological interpretation of that central Christian ritual. They also refused to subscribe to the Thirty-Nine Articles, a document that defined the beliefs of ANGLICANS. In the 18th century, Dissenters included Calvinists (Puritan Independents and Presbyterians), Unitarians, Quakers, Congregationalists, and Baptists. They were drawn largely from the English merchant and business classes.

Dissenters are sometimes also called Nonconformists, a term that dates back to the 16th-century Protestant Reformation, when people were attempting to define the ritual and polity of the new Church of England. Nonconformists wished to push reforms beyond the minimal ones that had been established when Henry VIII removed the English church from the control of ROME. Their positions stimulated the development of the many Puritan sects of the 17th century whose members were the forefathers of the Dissenters.

Although worship by Dissenters had been tolerated since 1689, choosing to be a Dissenter still carried severe disabilities in the 18th century. This situation had grown partially from the excesses, including the execution of King Charles I, committed by extreme Puritans during the 17th-century Civil War (sometimes called the Puritan Revolution). When the Stuart monarchy was restored in ENGLAND, legal restrictions were placed on Dissenters in order to prevent the recurrence of revolution.

Restrictive laws such as the Test Act of 1673 and the Corporation Act of 1661 excluded Dissenters from appointments in the civil government, forbade their attendance at either Oxford University or Cambridge University, and prohibited them from joining the municipal corporations that acted as the foundation for all English representative politics. Dissenters were also excluded from the Bank of England and the South Sea, East India, and Russia Companies.

In spite of these restrictions, or perhaps because of them, Dissenters made major contributions to the development of enlightened thought in England. Their academies, established to provide the education denied them at Oxford or Cambridge, became strongholds of the new SCIENCE and philosophy associated with the ENLIGHTENMENT. They were the first schools in England to teach HISTORY and ECONOMICS. Prominent English dissenters included Joseph PRIESTLEY, Daniel DEFOE, and Richard PRICE.

divine right of kings   Political theory formulated in the 17th century to justify absolute monarchy. The French Catholic bishop Jacques-Bénigne BOSSUET provided the clearest and best-known statement of this theory. He spelled out his ideas in a book written for the edification of the heir to the French throne. The book is titled *Politique tirée des propres paroles de l'Écriture Sainte* (Statecraft drawn from the actual words of the Holy Scriptures; 1679). It combines arguments from the Bible, law, and traditional political theory, with contemporary ideas derived from theorists of ABSOLUTISM.

Underlying the entire argument is the analogy between God in his universe and the king in his kingdom. According to Christian theology, God is the creator and king of the universe. All things are contained in him, and all individual things come from him. He shares power with no one, but he does not rule arbitrarily. Rather, he rules according to his own self-imposed laws. Similarly, the king in his kingdom contains the entire nation in his being. The king is holy, rules as a father in his family, and is absolute. All authority, whether legislative, judicial, or executive, comes from him. It cannot be divided or shared with other individuals or groups. This does not mean that the king rules arbitrarily. Rather, like God, the king is bound by the laws that he makes.

Law has its foundation in the law of NATURE, that is in right REASON and natural equity (not to be confused with EQUALITY). But, of course, the law of nature is God's law, created by him. And thus, having begun with God, Bossuet skillfully brings his argument back to him. The conclusion to be drawn is that the absolute authority of the king derives from God himself, and that the rule of the king through law reflects the natural order of things as created by God.

Bossuet bolsters his divine rights theory with historical arguments and appeals to pragmatic SELF-INTEREST. Thus, he states that monarchy is the oldest and most common form of government. Furthermore, monarchy is the best government form because it provides the best protection against strife and division. Monarchy guarantees perfect liberty for its subjects because such liberty consists not of participating in government but of being protected from oppression and exploitation.

Bossuet's theory of divine right bolstered the absolutism of LOUIS XIV throughout his reign. However, with the arrival of the 18th century and the development of increasingly secular views of nature and the universe, absolutism began to need other forms of support. These would be supplied by secular theories of NATURAL LAW, and by appeals to utilitarian and humanitarian ideals, thereby transferring the theory of divine rights absolutism into that of enlightened absolutism.

See also ABSOLUTISM, ENLIGHTENED; HOBBES.

Dobrovský, Josef (1753–1829) philologist

Josef Dobrovský is credited with establishing Slavonic studies as a legitimate field of research. Perhaps more important, his study of Czech language and literature helped establish Czech on an equal footing with German in Bohemia.

Dobrovský was born of Bohemian parents. He went to Prague to study in 1773 and by the 1790s was known as an expert in Slavic languages. In 1791, at a session of the Royal Academy of Sciences in Prague, Dobrovský delivered an address in the presence of Emperor Leopold II arguing for the preservation of the Czech language and against Germanization. His first important publication, the History of the Czech Language and Its Literature, appeared a year later. Dobrovský spent the rest of the 1790s preparing his monumental Czech-German Dictionary (1802). His codification of Czech grammar, the Short Instruction on the Czech Language, appeared in 1809.

Dobrovský spent the latter part of his career studying ancient Slavic languages and challenging the authenticity of The Judgment of Libuse, an early Czech text discovered in 1817. He died in the Bohemian city of Brno in 1829. His linguistic explorations were part of an early 19th-century movement to study the origins of LANGUAGE. Significant figures in this undertaking included Johann Gottfried von HERDER and Wilhelm von HUMBOLDT. Dobrovský's work also had significance for later Czech nationalist movements, in that it provided a cultural and linguistic basis for Czech national aspirations.

Don Giovanni

Dramma giocoso (opera blending comic and dramatic elements) of two acts in Italian by Wolfgang Amadeus MOZART (K. 527). Lorenzo da Ponte wrote the libretto; it is partly original and partly drawn from earlier treatment of the Don Juan theme. The complete title is Il dissoluto punito, ossia Il Don Giovanni (The libertine punished, or Don Giovanni). The opera premiered in Prague at the National Theater on October 29, 1787. It had been commissioned by the Prague-based impresario Guardasoni after the brilliant success of Mozart's LE NOZZE DI FIGARO (December 1786).

Don Giovanni (Don Juan) is treated in this opera as a serious character. He is a consummate seducer of women, unrepentant and driven by his love of "universal" woman. But he is not a comical or scandalous character. Rather, he is a bold rebel, unrepentant even as he meets his death at the hands of a vengeful ghost (in statue form). He is said to be an early example of the 19th-century romantic hero. Mozart's music underscores his daimonic character. The plot structure unfolds in the manner typical of opera buffa (comic opera), with intrigues and disguises. But the conclusion is starkly different, lacking an unambivalent happy ending. Only the death of Don Giovanni, the bold individual, brings resolution for the other characters, and this resolution is one that lacks its hero who, although villainous, was also loved. The character of Don Giovanni fascinated several 19th-century and 20th-century writers, including Stendahl, Ernst Theodor Amadeus Hoffmann, George Bernard Shaw, and Søren Kierkegaard.

Dryden, John (1631–1700) English poet, playwright, and critic, the third poet laureate of England

Dryden was an older cousin of Jonathan SWIFT. Dryden dominated the literary world of Restoration England (1660–1714). His writing provided models (satire) and new forms (the poetic couplet) that became standard vehicles of literary expression for the next generation of English writers.

Dryden's enormous output spanned the range of literary forms. During the 1660s and 1670s, he wrote many classicist theatrical pieces such as All For Love (1677), Secret Love, or The Maiden Queen (1666), and Tyrannick Love 1669. His oustanding comedy, Marriage à-la-Mode (1672), was later depicted in a popular series of engravings by William HOGARTH.

Dryden turned increasingly to anti-Whig satire in the 1680s, wielding his pen against the duke of Buckingham and fellow political conspirators in Absalom and Achitopel (1681), satirizing the subsequent trial of the first earl of Shaftesbury in The Medall (1682), and mocking Thomas Shadwell in Mac Flecknoe (1682). He entered the religious controversies of his era with Religio Laici or A Laymans Faith (1682), a book that explored the authoritarian and rational grounds for religious belief. Just a few years later, Dryden converted to ROMAN CATHOLICISM, an act that he justified in terms of his newfound conviction that fideism (belief rooted in faith rather than in authority or reason) could resolve SKEPTICISM toward religious doctrine. He outlined his new position in The Hind and The Panther (1687).

Dryden returned to dramatic writing in his later years. He also produced translations and English paraphrases of Roman classics such as the satires of Juvenal and Persius and Virgil's Aeneid. He performed similar services for the fables of Ovid, Chaucer, and Boccaccio. In his later years, Dryden wrote "Alexander's Feast" as an ode for Saint Cecilia's Day.

Dryden was a member of a strictly Puritan family. He attended Westminster School on a royal scholarship, then matriculated at Trinity College, Cambridge. In 1654, after graduating from Cambridge, he moved to LONDON to pursue a literary career. His earliest important poem was

"Heroique Stanzas" written to eulogize the deceased soldier, revolutionary, and statesman Oliver Cromwell.

Except during the GLORIOUS REVOLUTION of 1688, Dryden nearly always excelled at shifting politically so that his patronage was secure. Thus, after 1660, when the Restoration brought the Stuart monarchs back into power, Dryden abandoned his support of radical Puritanism and adopted a Tory royalist stance. He marked the shift by publishing poems—"Astraea Redux" (1660) and "To His Sacred Majesty on his Coronation" (1661)—that quickly brought him the desired royal patronage. He received the titles of poet laureate in 1668 and royal historiographer in 1670.

Dryden's staunch support of the Catholic king James II during the Glorious Revolution caused him to refuse to take an oath of loyalty to the new Protestant rulers WILLIAM III AND MARY II. As a result, he lost his poet laureateship.

Dryden's work demonstrates his debt to the intellectual trends that helped to define the early ENLIGHTENMENT in England. He formulated his dramatic works along the lines of French CLASSICISM, drawing from the examples of Molière, Corneille, and Quinault. His religious tracts wrestled with the skeptical and epistemological problems that had arisen in the late 16th and early 17th centuries. If his ultimate solutions to religious and political crisis tended to oppose the general trends that would prevail during the Enlightenment, they only reveal the wide range of intellectual positions that were available to educated, enlightened individuals.

See also EPISTEMOLOGY; LITERATURE; RELIGION.

Du Bos, Jean-Baptiste, Abbé (1670–1742) *French writer, known for his theoretical contributions to aesthetics, art criticism, and history*

Abbé Du Bos, a widely traveled and broadly educated intellectual, served the French government for many years in diplomatic assignments. Admired by VOLTAIRE and criticized by MONTESQUIEU, Du Bos was one of the more important contributors to the early ENLIGHTENMENT in FRANCE. Du Bos was a member of the French Academy and served in the powerful position of perpetual secretary of the academy for several years.

Of many works by Du Bos, two—one on AESTHETICS and the other on HISTORY—were his most important contributions to enlightened theory. The *Réflexions critiques sur la poésie et sur la peinture* (Critical reflections on poetry and painting; 1719) drew on the skeptical critical approach of Pierre BAYLE to argue for a new definition of beauty. Du Bos maintained that beauty is not produced by allegiance to preordained rules, as was claimed by French classical theory, but rather is a relative matter determined by national culture, weather, and mores. Thus, at an early date, Du Bos stated one of the major themes of the Enlightenment: criticism of the role of REASON and rules in the arts coupled with appreciation of the influence exerted by general context and subjective imagination in creative processes.

The *Réflexions critiques* theorized about beauty, but they also contained implicit views of the structure and function of the human mind. For modern scholars, Du Bos's ideas provide an example of the intimate linkages between aesthetics and PSYCHOLOGY that set enlightened ideas apart from their predecessors. Du Bos's treatise pointed toward theories of mind that were going to concentrate not only upon the formation of ideas, but also upon the whole range of mental functions outside the realm of reason.

In 1734, Du Bos published a book on the history of France entitled *Histoire critique de l'établissement de monarchie française* (Critical history of the establishment of the French monarchy). Like several contemporary works, it addressed the question of the historical foundations of the political structures of France. In particular, it explored the question of the relations between king and hereditary nobility in France during the years of ancient Roman rule. Du Bos argued that the first Frankish king, Clovis, had not conquered Roman Gaul, but rather, that he had entered the region and assumed control over it as an ally and agent of the Roman emperor. Clovis had possessed, therefore, the same absolute authority as the Roman emperors. Consequently, the authentic tradition in ancient France had been that of monarchical ABSOLUTISM, and the claims of nobles and bourgeoisie that they had legitimately shared sovereignty in early French government were spurious.

In THE SPIRIT OF LAWS, Montesquieu expressly rejected Du Bos's *thèse royale* (royal thesis) about the origins of the French monarchy, but he also opposed the alternative *thèse nobilaire* (thesis of the nobility) that was associated with the works of Henri de BOULAINVILLIERS. Montesquieu tried to rise above this dispute. In contrast to Du Bos, he believed that Clovis had indeed conquered Gaul, but that he had also been co-opted by the old Roman system of law. Thus, the original "constitution" of France had been a hybrid produced by blending ancient Frankish and ancient Roman political traditions.

See also CLASSICISM; POLITICAL THEORY.

Duclos, Charles Pinot (1704–1772) *French writer*

Orphaned as a youth, Duclos led a tumultuous life until he finally settled in PARIS and devoted himself to literary and intellectual pursuits. He entered the circle of Secretary of State Jean Frédéric Phélippeaux, comte de Maurepas, which met habitually at the Parisian coffeehouse Café Procope. These connections served Duclos well, for Maurepas secured him an appointment to the Académie des Inscriptions et Belles-lettres in 1739, before he had published a single literary work. By 1742, Duclos had published two successful novellas: *Histoire de Mme de Luz* (History of Madame Luz; 1741) and *Les confessions du comte de **** (*The confessions of Count ****; 1742).

Maurepas protected and advanced Duclos on several subsequent occasions, securing him a commission to write the *Histoire de Louis XI* (History of Louis XI; 1745–46). This work propelled Duclos into the French Academy and helped to secure him the post of royal historiographer as successor to VOLTAIRE.

Duclos became a friend of the men who were writing the ENCYCLOPÉDIE. He contributed to the critical culture of the ENLIGHTENMENT with a commentary called *Mémoires pour servir à l'histoire des moeurs du XVIIIe siècle* (Memoirs for use in the history of morals of the 18th century; 1751). He also wrote the *Essai de grammaire française* (Essay on French grammar; 1754) and a series of personal *Mémoires* (Memoirs; published 1790) concerning his travels in ITALY.

Dupont de Nemours, Pierre-Samuel (1739–1817)

French Physiocrat and businessman who lived and worked both in France and the United States

Dupont came from a Protestant family. His father, Samuel Dupont, worked as a royal watchmaker. His mother, Anne de Monchanin, died before Pierre-Samuel reached adulthood. After a rather stormy adolescence, in which he considered possible careers as a preacher, military officer, physician, or actor, Du Pont settled on studying economics.

Dupont's writings on the utility of agriculture brought him to the attention of François QUESNAY, who invited him to Versailles. From that point, Dupont became a Physiocrat, acquiring friends and patrons from that circle of economists. Victor de Riqueti, marquis de MIRABEAU, stood as godfather to Dupont's firstborn son. During his tenure as general controller of finances (1774–76), Anne-Robert-Jacques TURGOT offered Dupont a post as general inspector of commerce.

During the FRENCH REVOLUTION, Dupont played active roles in a variety of situations. He participated in dismantling the ANCIEN RÉGIME by serving in Charles-Alexandre de CALONNE's Assembly of Notables, the 1789 Estates General, and the National Constituent Assembly. However, during the more radical phases of the Revolution Dupont went into hiding (in the astronomer Joseph-Jérôme de LALANDE's observatory) and was twice imprisoned. Madame de STAËL intervened to free him from the second incarceration. A brief return to favor, before the 1796 coup d'etat of 18 Fructidor, resulted in Dupont's obtaining a chair in the new Institut de France (Institute of France). This organization restructured the old royal academies by combining them into a single institution that was charged with continuing the prestigious intellectual traditions of those academies.

Toward the end of the 18th century, Dupont turned to the new UNITED STATES OF AMERICA, where the political system seemed to embody many of his ideals. He arranged to leave FRANCE and arrived in the United States on January 1, 1800, intending to set up an agricultural enterprise. He abandoned that project, however, turning instead to manufacturing. Although Dupont chose the site for a planned gunpowder factory, it was his son Eleuthère Du Pont who purchased the land (near Wilmington, Delaware) and established the factory and associated village called Eleutherian Mills.

At the request of Thomas JEFFERSON, Dupont returned in 1802 to France to engage in some preliminary negotiations with Napoleon about the purchase of the Louisiana Territory. From 1803 until 1814, Dupont resided in Paris, where he served as the secretary of the Parisian Chamber of Commerce. In 1815, he chose to move permanently to the United States and died at Eleutherian Mills in 1817.

Dupont de Nemours left an important treatise of physiocratic theory: *Physiocratie, ou constitution naturelle du gouvernement le plus avantageux au genre humain* (Physiocracy, or the natural constitution of government most advantageous to humankind; 1767). Other works include *De l'origine et progrès d'une science nouvelle* (On the origins and progress of a new science; 1768); *Table raisonnée des principes de l'économie politique* (Systematic description of the principles of political economy; 1773); *Examen du gouvernement de l'Angleterre, comparé aux constitutions des Etats-Unis* (Investigation of the government of England compared with the constitutions of the United States; 1789; contributor); *Philosophie de l'univers* (Philosophy of the universe; 1796); *Sur l'éducation nationale dans les Etats-Unis d'Amérique* (On national education in the United States of America; 2nd edition, 1812); and a multivolumed edition of *Oeuvres de Turgot* (Works of Turgot; 1801–11). Dupont's correspondence with Thomas Jefferson can be found in English.

See also PHYSIOCRATS.

dynastic states

Form of most 18th-century monarchies and empires. The various territories in such states belonged to the ruler in his or her capacity as the king or queen, duke or duchess, archduke or archduchess of the region. Thus, the unity of a dynastic state derived from the person of the hereditary ruler. The territories were unified only in the sense that the same individual ruled in each of them. For example, SCOTLAND and ENGLAND became a dynastic state in the 17th century when the Scottish king James VI inherited the English throne, thereby also assuming the title King James I of England. In FRANCE, the hereditary ruler was king in central France but ruled in Provence as the count. In the HAPSBURG EMPIRE, the emperor was the archduke of AUSTRIA and the king of HUNGARY; in PRUSSIA, the ruler was king in Prussia but elector in BRANDENBURG.

Within a dynastic state the separate territories retained many unique laws, customs, and privileges. These determined the relations between the region and its ruler. For example, laws in central France did not necessarily apply to Provence. Rulers who wished to govern as absolute monarchs in centralized, unified territories thus faced a confusing and obstructive set of variations within the boundaries of their possessions.

Throughout Europe, monarchs during the 18th century attempted to impose some uniformity and universality over the disparate lands within their kingdoms. They all enjoyed some degree of success but were limited by traditional local powers and privileges. Dynastic states were certainly more highly centralized than their predecessors, but they were not yet the unified nation-states of the 19th century and should never be so construed. This peculiar nature of the 18th-century state must be kept in mind in order to understand the political conflicts of the period and to appreciate the radical transformations that occurred in Europe as a result of the FRENCH REVOLUTION.

See also ABSOLUTISM.

E

East India Company British trading company charged with the administration of India in the 18th century. The East India Company was chartered by Queen Elizabeth I of ENGLAND on December 31, 1600. The royal charter granted the company £70,000 for a 15-year period, with the aim of increasing English presence in the East Indian spice trade, but also made the company subject to parliamentary control. The powers of the company were transferred to the British Crown in 1858, after the Mutiny of 1857, also known as the Sepoy Rebellion in the West and as the First War of Independence in India. The company was dissolved in 1873.

The coat of arms of the East India Company, ca. 1730. *(By permission of The British Library)*

The first ships of the East India Company landed in the Indian port of Surat in 1608. The company began establishing trading posts throughout the Asian subcontinent—in Machlipattanam in 1611, Surat in 1612, and later in Madras in 1641 and Calcutta in 1699. In 1615, English diplomat Sir Thomas Roe visited the court of the Mughal emperor Jahangir, who granted the British the right to build a textile manufactory in Surat. This marked the beginning of a series of concessions made to the British by the Mughal court, allowing the East India Company's influence on the subcontinent to grow. In 1688, another decisive event occurred when the company acquired its first territory, the island of Bombay (now Mumbai), from King Charles II.

By the beginning of the 18th century, the East India Company had established trading outposts up and down both the east and west coasts of India. Bombay, Calcutta, and Madras were home to sizeable English settlements. In 1717, Emperor Farruk-Siar issued a decree exempting the company from paying customs duties in the province of Bengal. The definitive moment in the company's history came in 1757, with the Battle of Plassey. The battle marked the culmination of a decades-long process on the part of the company to consolidate its power in Bengal. The British victory transformed the company from a trading outfit into a full-fledged governing body. The Mughal emperor Alamgir granted the British permission to administer three provinces, including Bengal, which meant that the company now collected taxes on behalf of the emperor and made a fixed tribute payment to him from this revenue.

The company used the local governing apparatus already in place to collect taxes and took control of the local army to enforce their rule. The consequences were dire for both the provinces and for the company. A widespread famine in 1769–70 may have killed as many as a third of the residents in the company's east coast holdings, which, in turn, had a devastating effect on tax revenues. The cost of maintaining an army and an administration edged the company close to bankruptcy. Parliament rescued the company, but the Regulating Act of 1773 gave Parliament more control over the company and created the office of governor-general to administer the British holdings in India.

The second governor-general, Lord Charles Cornwallis, reached an agreement, the so-called Permanent Settlement, with local landlords that gave the British the right to collect taxes and revenues in perpetuity. The closing decade of the 18th century in India saw the beginning of further British expansion and consolidation of power. The company defeated the forces of Tipu Sultan in 1792, annexing the territory of Mysore (Karnataka) as a result.

The East India Company was significant because of the role it played in Britain's ascendancy as a colonial power. During the 16th century, SPAIN and PORTUGAL had been Europe's dominant colonizers. Their systems had focused on the extraction of natural resources and wealth from their overseas holdings, the primary example of this system being their approach to colonies in the Americas during the 1500s. The British East India Company marked an important change in European attitudes with respect to colonies. The company secured British dominance in India over the Portuguese, who had first arrived there in 1498, more than a century before the company's ships. By founding permanent settlements, the company not only gained a foothold for the extraction of wealth from the Asian subcontinent, but also opened up new markets in India for goods from Britain and its other colonies. The idea that colonies could become part of a trade scheme involving both raw materials and manufactured or agricultural products rather than just a source of gold, silver, and other forms of raw wealth marked a change in the European colonial system.

See also COLONIALISM, HASTINGS, MERCANTILISM.

Further reading: Anthony Wild, *The East India Company: Trade and Conquest from 1600* (London: Harper Collins, 1999).

economics *See* CAMERALISM; ENLIGHTENED DESPOTISM; INDUSTRIAL REVOLUTION; LAISSEZ-FAIRE; MERCANTILISM; PHYSIOCRATS; SMITH; and individual countries such as FRANCE, ENGLAND, PRUSSIA, HAPSBURG EMPIRE, KINGDOM OF THE TWO SICILIES, UNITED PROVINCES OF THE NETHERLANDS.

Edgeworth, Maria (1767–1849) *Anglo-Irish novelist and educational writer*
Edgeworth was the eldest daughter of Richard Lovell Edgeworth, a wealthy Anglo-Irish landowner and friend of Erasmus DARWIN, whose liberal political views and interest in experimental SCIENCE greatly influenced his daughter. Maria became her father's close companion and assistant in a variety of projects. One of their joint ventures consisted of a series of educational experiments with Richard Edgeworth's 20 younger children. Maria kept notes of the children's reactions and progress during their exposure to the new pedagogical practices. Drawing from these notes and experiences, father and daughter published *Practical Education* (1798), a pedagogical work that was influential among contemporaries in both Britain and FRANCE.

Maria Edgeworth also published a series of didactic tales for children entitled *The Parent's Assistant* (1796–1800). She was, however, better known for her many novels and other works of adult fiction. Her most famous work is *Castle Rackrent* (1800), the first of several Irish novels. In this work, she tells of the life of an Anglo-Irish family like her own. Contemporaries praised the novel for its subtle representation of the different regional and social dialects that existed in Ireland at the time of the FRENCH and AMERICAN REVOLUTIONS.

In her next novel, *Belinda,* Edgeworth satirized what she believed were extreme beliefs about the proper role and education of women. She aimed her criticism at two ENLIGHTENMENT writers, Mary WOLLSTONECRAFT and Jean-Jacques ROUSSEAU. Her unflattering representation of the rash and masculine Harriott Freke reminded her contemporaries of Mary Wollstonecraft, whose *Memoirs* had caused a scandal when William GODWIN published them in 1798. The hero in *Belinda* is a misguided disciple of Rousseau who finds a beautiful young child and educates her to be his wife by using the model of Sophie in *ÉMILE*. The central conflict in Edgeworth's novel arises when the hero falls in love with the more worldly and intelligent Belinda but feels honor-bound to marry the child he has reared to be his "ideal" wife. Other novels by Edgeworth included *Leonora* (1806), *Tales from Fashionable Life* (1809–12), *The Absentee* (1812), *Ormond* (1817), and *Helen* (1834).

See also EDUCATION.

Edinburgh City in SCOTLAND that played a major cultural role in the ENLIGHTENMENT as the center of Scottish intellectual life. Edinburgh has been continuously settled since the 11th century. It is located on the south side of the Firth of Forth and is served by the seaport of Leith. The city is dominated by a hill topped with the old fortress castle. Edinburgh became the political capital of Scotland during the reign of James II (1437–60). When the Scottish king James VI also became James I of ENGLAND (1603), the royal court moved from Edinburgh to LONDON. A Parliament and law courts remained in Scotland. The complete union between England and Scotland occurred in 1707 and brought with it the abolition of the Scottish Parliament.

Edinburgh lost its political significance after 1707, but during the second half of the 18th century it experienced an artistic, literary, scientific, and general intellectual flowering, serving as the center of the highly significant Scottish Enlightenment. The University of Edinburgh and the scientific societies such as the ROYAL SOCIETY OF EDINBURGH and the Philosophical Society of Edinburgh served as the formal institutional supports of this cultural activity. Informal gatherings occurred under the auspices of the Oyster Club. Several of the most important figures in the development of the Enlightenment lived, studied, or taught in Edinburgh. Any list must include the political economist Adam SMITH; the skeptical philosopher David HUME; the historians Adam FERGUSON and William ROBERTSON; the chemists Joseph BLACK and William CULLEN; the geographer James HUTTON; the physicians and physiologists Alexander MONRO (both primus and secundus) and Robert WHYTT; the poet Allan Ramsay; and the architect Robert ADAM.

During the 18th century, Edinburgh expanded to the north and south. The northern New Town was laid out according to a rational gridiron plan in which major streets culminated at Charlotte Square. Robert Adam adorned the city with two major architectural monuments: the General Register House (1772–90), which was the first public record office in Scotland, and the old University Building (begun in 1789 but not completed until 1834). The town council focused on several public works and public health projects typical of the utilitarian goals of the Enlightenment.

Further reading: James S. Buchan, *Crowded with Genius: The Scottish Enlightenment: Edinburgh's Moment of the Mind.* (New York: HarperCollins, 2003).

education   A term that encompasses both the process of acquiring knowledge and the methods, theories, and institutions developed to sustain the learning process. The ENLIGHTENMENT gave birth to educational theories, methods, curriculum contents, and institutions that have survived into the modern era.

The attention given to education by enlightened intellectuals developed quite logically from concepts of HUMAN NATURE associated with SCIENCE, PSYCHOLOGY, and MORAL PHILOSOPHY. From Francis BACON, the Enlightenment inherited a vision of the power that human knowledge possesses when it is systematically acquired and applied to practical human needs. From the sensation psychology of John LOCKE, the Enlightenment received the idea that infants come into the world without any innate (inborn) ideas. Their minds are like blank slates (*tabula rasa*) waiting to record sensory experiences that will then be transformed into ideas. From moral philosophy, the era acquired the idea that PROGRESS is possible for individual human beings as well as for society. Certain human mental abilities—REASON, emotion, and the moral sense—facilitate the process of advancement toward perfection.

These beliefs about human nature and the power of knowledge stimulated new assessments of the nature of childhood. If the experiences of young, impressionable children could be controlled and directed, then, it was reasoned, the children could be molded to be more perfect and knowledgeable (enlightened) human beings. Education seemed to provide one means for intervening to direct the processes of individual development toward these lofty goals.

For enlightened intellectuals, childhood became a long period of development, of gradual change over time during which the young human being passed through a distinct series of stages. At each stage, children displayed specific mental and moral capabilities. Educational practices were expected to recognize these stages and to provide appropriate curriculum materials.

Many individuals and organizations associated with the Enlightenment offered ideas about the theory and practice of education. The Abbé CONDILLAC was an acknowledged expert on pedagogy. Radical and highly optimistic theories about the power of education came from the pens of Claude-Adrien HELVÉTIUS, the marquis de CONDORCET, the comte DESTUTT DE TRACY, and Pierre-Jean-Georges CABANIS. The FREEMASONS and IDÉOLOGUES made educational reform one of their primary goals. And Jean-Jacques ROUSSEAU captivated imaginations when, in *ÉMILE,* he spelled out an idealized method for preserving positive natural qualities while still producing civilized young adults.

Shifts in the theoretical foundations of education were matched by reforms in practice. The Pietists August Hermann FRANCKE and Christian THOMASIUS initiated this trend with their experiments at the orphanage in Halle. They introduced teacher training, approved textbooks, group instruction, and strict discipline in an effort to mold both the minds and moral characters of their students. In other regions, alternative schools offered teaching methods and curriculum materials directly inspired by the ideas of the Enlightenment. The Dessau Philanthropin created by Johann Basedow in 1774 tried to implement the educational theories of Jean-Jacques Rousseau. It received widespread financial support (Immanuel KANT helped to raise money for the school), but floundered for lack of strong administrative leadership. In SWITZERLAND, Johann Heinrich PESTALOZZI set up his famous Rousseauist experimental school outside Lausanne. It, too, attracted international visitors and support. In BERLIN and Hamburg, free schools were established for poor children and for the children of the Jewish communities.

Reformers in western Europe such as the French Physiocrat and minister Anne-Robert-Jacques TURGOT proposed compulsory education, but their plans were generally not implemented until the end of the century, during the era of the FRENCH REVOLUTION. In central Europe, however, where the tradition of compulsory religious education had existed since the 16th-century Protestant Reformation, FREDERICK II (THE GREAT) OF PRUSSIA and MARIA THERESA OF AUSTRIA and her son JOSEPH II translated the idea of universal, compulsory secular education into reality. They issued edicts requiring children to attend primary schools in an attempt to ensure that all their subjects acquired basic utilitarian knowledge. Their actions met with mixed success and much resistance from groups who resented having a certain cultural and educational formula imposed upon them.

Theoretical support for compulsory education rested not only in the *tabula rasa* theory of Locke, but also in the related notion that all human beings at birth are intellectual and moral equals. Rulers who required education of their subjects believed that universal requirements were not only more enlightened but that they also would assist in raising standards of living. These rulers were motivated by humanitarian values, but they also recognized that education might provide an avenue through which the central state government could exercise control over the ideas and moral formation of subjects.

During the Enlightenment, systems of schools still largely fell under the administration of the various official state churches. In ENGLAND, for example, the Anglican Church operated primary and secondary schools as well as the Universities of Oxford and Cambridge. Protestant DISSENTERS and Roman Catholics were excluded from the higher-level schools on account of their religious beliefs. Dissenters opened alternative academies where modern subjects joined the curriculum beside the older traditional courses. These academies trained several major leaders in the English Enlightenment. In Roman Catholic countries, local parishes provided most primary teaching, while the JESUITS, Oratorians, and a few other monastic teaching orders handled secondary education. Universities closely linked to the church hierarchy offered higher education.

The disbanding of the Jesuits in 1773 created a vacuum in the 18th-century world of education. The Jesuits had provided the most visible, successful, and prestigious secondary schools in Catholic Europe. In 1749, for example, they had eight operating *collèges* (secondary schools) in FRANCE, 133 in the Italian peninsula, and 105 in SPAIN. The HOLY ROMAN EMPIRE, HAPSBURG EMPIRE, and other regions of eastern Europe boasted between 200 to 300 Jesuit schools. Students received a rigorous but old-fashioned education in philosophy, classics, and mathematics. The Jesuits resisted including newer subjects in their 18th-century teaching programs, despite the fact that they had been innovators in the 16th century and 17th centuries.

When the Jesuit order was dissolved by Pope CLEMENT XIV, their schools and other properties were confiscated by secular authorities. A few other Catholic orders picked up their teaching responsibilities in France, but the secular authorities stepped in to meet the needs in the German principalities and the Hapsburg Empire. The French Revolution spawned many radical educational experiments and the total restructuring of the French educational system by secular authorities.

On the subject of education, as elsewhere, the thought of the Enlightenment contained tensions. People embraced the idea of human EQUALITY suggested by Locke's theories of the mind, but balked at providing truly universal education to both males and females of all religions and social classes. This ambivalence was especially prominent in England, but also bedeviled reform efforts in France. The enlightened despots of central Europe forced such reforms on their subjects, but they too encountered resistance.

As a result, the legacy of the Enlightenment to subsequent education remains mixed. Its ideas about the stages of childhood and the related design of curriculum persisted, as did Pietist teaching methods. The notion of compulsory education also survived, but was stripped in most areas of its association with the idea of equality. Perhaps the greatest legacy from the educational experiments of the Enlightenment lay in the inspiration provided by the ideal of using education to further humanitarian forms of progress.

See also HUMBOLDT; TRIMMER.

Further reading: Harvey Chisick, *The Limits of Reform in the Enlightenment: Attitudes toward the Education of the Lower Classes in Eighteenth-Century France* (Princeton, N.J.: Princeton University Press, 1981); R. A. Houston, *Literacy in Early Modern Europe. Culture and Education, 1500–1800* (London: Longman, 1988): Robert Palmer, *The Improvement of Humanity: Education and the French Revolution* (Princeton, N.J.: Princeton University Press, 1985).

Edwards, Jonathan (1703–1758) *American Congregationalist clergyman and theologian who was one of the leaders of the Great Awakening*

Edwards, the son of a pastor in the Congregational Church, was the fifth child and only son in a family of 11 children. He graduated from Yale College in 1720, continued his divinity studies for two years, and served for one year as a pastor in New York before receiving an M.A. degree in 1723. Edwards began working with his grandfather, who was a pastor in a Northampton, Massachusetts, church, and upon the elder man's death received an appointment as head pastor of the church (1729).

Edwards was convinced of the truth of the theory of predestination, a major theological doctrine of CALVINISM.

This theory claimed that God, as the supreme power in the universe, determines in advance which people will be saved and which damned for eternity. Faithful Christians can practice the sacraments and prepare themselves mentally to receive God's grace, but these activities do not guarantee that they will receive eternal salvation.

Edwards's sermons and publications combined predestination theory and other Calvinist teachings with ideas drawn from the NATURAL PHILOSOPHY of Isaac NEWTON, from the PSYCHOLOGY of John LOCKE, and from the Cambridge Platonists. Edwards accepted the claim made by Locke that all human knowledge comes from sensory experience. He proposed that sense perception is God's way of communicating with human beings, and that the knowledge derived from sense experience thus comes from God. We are able to receive this knowledge, just as we receive salvation, only through the grace and will of God, who decreed the laws according to which the universe operates.

Edwards developed a form of religious piety that stressed the importance of a special kind of knowledge, that derived through the faculty of intuition. Intuition allows direct experience of God, tinged with special emotional qualities, and can assist people in receiving the grace of God that guarantees salvation.

From his Northampton pulpit, Edwards began denouncing the moral ills of New England society, reserving special condemnation for the famed attitudes of religious and moral self-reliance that characterized so many residents of the region. In 1731, he published *God Gloried in the Work of Redemption, by the Greatness of Men's Dependence upon Him, in the Whole of It.* He followed this in 1734 with his sermon *Justification by Faith Alone,* a work that began a religious revival (1734–35) in the Connecticut River valley. His *A Faithful Narrative of the Surprizing [sic] Work of God in the Conversion of Many Hundred Souls in Northampton, and the Neighboring Towns and Villages* (1737) had a profound effect on readers in the North American colonies and in Great Britain.

Edwards's sermons helped to pave the way for the Great Awakening, the religious revival movement of the 1730s and 1740s. This movement grew as a response to the open-air sermons preached by the itinerant Anglican preacher George Whitefield. Whitefield and his friend John WESLEY eventually founded METHODISM, a Protestant sect whose approach to faith directly reflected aspects of the ENLIGHTENMENT.

Whitefield preached that the grace of God could be obtained by anyone who had a genuine ecstatic religious experience, and he designed his sermons to evoke strong emotional responses. Edwards adopted these tactics in sermons such as the famous *Sinners in the Hands of an Angry God* (1741), but he eventually grew critical of the excesses of revivalist practices. He published several works—*Thoughts on the Revival* (1742) and *A Treatise Concerning Religious Affections* (1746), for example—that criticized the Great Awakening and suggested ways to purify its techniques.

In 1749 Edwards entered into a theological dispute at his Northampton church over the requirements for admission to the central Christian observance of the Eucharist. His grandfather had allowed people who had been baptized, but who were not fully converted to Christian beliefs, to accept communion (the Halfway covenant). Edwards rejected this practice, insisting that people must be fully committed to Christian doctrine and experience before they can participate in the Eucharist observances.

By 1751, this dispute forced Edwards to resign his position at Northampton. He settled in Stockbridge, Massachusetts, then a frontier town, where he served as a pastor and missionary to Native Americans in the region. During these years, he completed the *Careful and Strict Inquiry into the Modern Prevailing Notions of Freedom of the Will* (1754).

In 1757 Edwards accepted the presidency of the College of New Jersey, an institution that eventually became Princeton University. His last work, *Great Christian Doctrine of Original Sin Defended,* was published in 1758, the same year that he died of smallpox.

See also ENTHUSIASM; INTUITION AND IMAGINATION.

Émile   Educational novel by the Genevan philosophe Jean-Jacques ROUSSEAU. The complete title of the book is *Émile, ou Traité de l'education* (Émile, or treatise on education). Its date of publication was 1762, the same year as Rousseau's masterwork of POLITICAL THEORY, *Le contrat social* (THE SOCIAL CONTRACT).

Émile was greeted enthusiastically in enlightened intellectual circles, but it created a storm of protest from religious censors. The archbishop of PARIS condemned it, and the Parlement of Paris, desiring to make a show of its Catholic orthodoxy, both condemned the work and issued an order for Rousseau's arrest. Rousseau was able to flee before it was enforced. The Genevan Council of Twenty-Five ordered both *Émile* and *The Social Contract* publicly burned, condemning them as scandalous, impious, and threatening to both religion and government.

The cause of these reactions to *Émile* lay not in its educational theory, but rather in a chapter entitled "Profession de foi du vicaire savoyard" (Profession of faith of the Savoyard vicar). This chapter presented an argument for religious faith based on the arousal of feelings of reverence in response to the wonders of the natural world. It thus espoused a form of DEISM, but a deism rooted less in REASON than in the ability to respond emotionally to the beauty and order of the universe.

Émile and *The Social Contract* should be read together, for both treat the general problem of the effects

Engraved illustration for *Émile,* 1779. Jean-Jacques Rousseau offered his ideas about proper education in this widely read and admired book. *(Courtesy New York Public Library)*

of civilization on natural humankind. *Émile* approaches the problem from the standpoint of the formation of individual character, while *The Social Contract* deals with the creation of society. Both books paint utopian visions, and both exercised profound influence over reform activities during the late ENLIGHTENMENT.

Rousseau based his pedagogical ideas on two novel assumptions: the idea that both childhood and youth consist of several phases of development culminating in mature adulthood, and the conviction that the molding of feeling and sentiment should precede the formation of reason. In ascribing a developmental process to children, Rousseau was challenging the conventional practice of treating children as if they were simply little adults. By postponing the training of reason or intellect until later childhood years, he was reversing the customary prescription for EDUCATION.

According to Rousseau, the development of the individual child parallels the development of humankind throughout the course of HISTORY. The infant is similar to an animal, lacking both language and consciousness of self. Between the ages of two and seven years, the child acquires LANGUAGE and a sense of self, and then begins developing the emotional aspects of mind (*raison sensitive*). The rational mind begins to develop between the ages of seven and 12. Adolescence completes the process, providing the full development of mental capacities, the appearance of sexuality, and the understanding of the relations between the individual and the larger society. As he traced the formation of his protagonist, Émile, Rousseau sketched an educational program with activities tailored to the abilities and needs of a young man progressing through the various developmental stages of childhood.

The theory and procedures outlined in *Émile* marked a turning point in the conceptualization of education during the Enlightenment. Rousseau's vision inspired not only the reforms and programs of Johann Heinrich PESTALOZZI in Switzerland, but also the model school established by Johann Bernhard Basedow (1724–90) in Dessau.

empfindsamer Stil   German term for the "sensitive" or "expressive" style in MUSIC. It derives from the verb *empfinden*, meaning "to feel." The German term is commonly used in English literature about the music of the ENLIGHTENMENT.

Empfindsamer Stil arose after 1730 in German-speaking lands and was particularly associated with the compositions of Wilhelm Friedemann BACH, Carl Philipp Emmanuel BACH, Karl Heinrich Graun, and Johann Joachim Quantz. It functioned as a musical form of the enlightened culture of SENSIBILITY. It attempted to adapt musical composition to the tasks of portraying feelings and sentiment rather than of presenting architectonic forms. Music also no longer aimed primarily at giving glory to God or to monarchs, but rather sought to touch hearts and move feelings. In this sense, *empfindsamer Stil* represented a rejection of baroque ideals. After 1770, *empfindsamer Stil* gave way to the musical CLASSICISM of Christoph Willibald GLUCK, Franz Joseph HAYDN, Wolfgang Amadeus MOZART, and the young Ludwig van BEETHOVEN.

Structurally, the *empfindsamer Stil* functioned as a transitional form between BAROQUE STYLE polyphony (many voices moving in complex lines) and classical monophony (melody line with simple harmonic support). The soprano line began to predominate in the composition and eventually was transformed into a real melody line with harmonic accompaniment, a hallmark of fully developed classical style.

The goal of producing intimate music was reflected in preferences for instruments. C. P. E. Bach, for example, loved not only the harpsichord, but also the clavichord, a very soft-spoken keyboard instrument suitable only for small rooms. He also liked the viola da gamba, a quiet, fretted stringed instrument. As *empfindsamer Stil* gave way to classicism, however, the PIANO replaced the softer harpsichord or clavichord, and the violoncello, a member of the violin family, replaced the viola da gamba.

The *empfindsamer Stil* tended to be less decorative than the related French STYLE GALANT, but it still relied on ornamentation derived from baroque performance practices to advance musical ideas. *Empfindsamer Stil* abandoned the baroque theory of the affections that had limited composers to expressing one sentiment in any given piece or movement of a longer piece. Multiple sentiments could be juxtaposed, expressed by highly chromatic harmonies; by sudden contrasts between soft and loud passages; and by the strategic use of either the "melodic sigh" (a melody fragment ending on a weak beat) or the sudden pause. Outstanding examples of this style can be heard in C. P. E. Bach's *Sonaten für Kenner und Liebhaber* (Sonatas for connoisseurs and amateurs; 1779) or in his *Six Symphonies for String Orchestra,* Wq. 182.

In the 1760s and 1770s, the development of *empfindsamer Stil* reached its height. The period is sometimes called STURM UND DRANG (storm and stress) in music history in order to point out its similarities to the literary movement of that name. Six symphonies by Joseph Haydn, numbered 26, 41, 43, 44, 48, and 52, provide delightful and outstanding introductions to the peculiarities of this mature form of the *empfindsamer Stil.*

empiricism   A theory that claims that all knowledge grows from experience. Empiricism, especially as presented in the sensation PSYCHOLOGY of John LOCKE and the SCIENTIFIC METHOD of Isaac NEWTON, provided one of the primary intellectual building blocks of the ENLIGHTENMENT.

Before the era of Locke and Newton, a different theory of knowledge called RATIONALISM had dominated 17th-century intellectual pursuits. Rationalism asserted that people can uncover truths about the world solely by utilizing their ability to REASON. The mind, according to this theory, contains inborn ideas such as Descartes's "I think, therefore I am." By applying reason (meaning the rules of deductive logic), wider truths about the world would be reached.

Empiricism denied the existence of inborn ideas. Its image of the mind was most clearly symbolized in Locke's assertion that the mind at birth is a white paper (Pierre GASSEND actually introduced the now famous term *tabula rasa*). Ideas developed through a process called induction, as the mind stored up and transformed the information acquired through the senses. Reason, the key to all truth for rationalists, simply represented one type of mental activity for empiricists. Reason could provide some truths, but it was always working with information obtained by sensory experience.

Empiricism provided a foundation for the innovations of the Enlightenment in psychology and in most SCIENCE (NATURAL PHILOSOPHY). John Locke's sensation psychology placed experience at the center of all human knowledge. The idea that the mind grows and develops through experience (i.e., that it has a HISTORY) was revolutionary. The mind had previously been conceived as basically formed at birth.

Empiricism suggested that since the mind changes over time with experience, human development could be shaped by controlling that experience. This notion stimulated interest in EDUCATION both as a process and as a specific body of knowledge intended to influence the ideas and behavior of people. In other words, the theories of empiricism, in the form of Lockean sensation psychology, made possible the goal of creating an enlightened population. The psychology of Abbé CONDILLAC, the reform programs of the marquis de CONDORCET and the IDÉOLOGUES, and the rapid development of various pedagogical theories all derived their initial impetus from empiricism.

Newton adapted empiricism to the needs of scientific investigation. He, like many of his contemporaries who had been inspired by the visionary program of Sir Francis BACON (1561–1626), favored a scientific method that placed the observation of natural phenomena at the center of the scientific process. In this case, observation was the equivalent of sensory experience in PSYCHOLOGY. The collection of observations about natural events could lead, by processes of induction (a special form of reasoning), to adequate theories about the laws of nature. When Newton stated that he would not make hypotheses, he was rejecting the approach of reasoning about natural phenomena without first collecting observations.

Newton never claimed that the resulting scientific theories were ultimately true but only that they could be assumed to be true until further observations proved them wrong. The goal of science became the attainment of useful knowledge; the search for ultimate truths, of the type known only to God, was abandoned as a proper scientific pursuit.

Scientific empiricism dominated nearly all scientific pursuit during the Enlightenment. It did not, however, completely eliminate rationalism. In fact, the great advances made in theoretical mechanics at the end of the Enlightenment by Joseph-Louis LAGRANGE and the marquis de LAPLACE were inspired by mathematical rationalism. Thus, the doing of science during the Enlightenment involved both empiricism and rationalism, blended together to create exciting new ideas with great potential for human progress.

See also EPISTEMOLOGY.

Encyclopédie French encyclopedia published in PARIS in 28 volumes (17 volumes of text, 11 volumes of illustrations) between 1751 and 1772. The complete title was *Encyclopédie, ou dictionnaire raisonné des sciences, des arts et des métiers, par une société de gens de lettres* (Encyclopedia, or rational dictionary of the sciences, arts and trades, by a society of men of letters). The project was officially dedicated to Monsieur le comte de Weil-ARGENSON. In form, content, and manner of production, the *Encyclopédie* stands as one of the outstanding creations of the ENLIGHTENMENT in FRANCE.

The project began with the plans of John Mills, an English bank clerk, and G. Sellius, a professional translator, to produce a French translation of the 1728 English *Cyclopaedia; or an Universal Dictionary of Arts and Sciences* by Ephraim Chambers. The two translators offered the project to the Parisian printer André Le Breton, who obtained royal permission in 1745 to proceed with publication.

Le Breton quarreled with Mills, and as a result, the original project was scrapped. Having secured a new royal

Title page from the first of 12 installments of engraved plates published with the *Encyclopédie,* 1762. The engravings published in conjunction with the *Encyclopédie* depicted machines, tools, instruments, and craft techniques used in the various applied arts and sciences. *(Courtesy New York Public Library)*

permission in 1746, Le Breton embarked on an expanded plan for the work. Jean Le Rond d'ALEMBERT was enlisted on the project in 1754, along with a second mathematician, Abbé Jean Paul de Gua de Malves. Denis DIDEROT joined the project in 1746 as an adviser and by 1747 had assumed responsibilities as general editor. D'Alembert retained control of the sections on mathematics.

Diderot and d'Alembert conceived of the *Encyclopédie* as a huge compendium of all the knowledge of humankind. Their model was inspired by the comprehensive system of human knowledge that Sir Francis BACON had sketched in *De Dignitate et Augmentis Scientiarum Libri IX* (Nine books on the dignity and advancement of learning; 1623). The *Encyclopédie,* however, departed

The *Encyclopédie* reflects the great faith of the French PHILOSOPHES in the PERFECTIBILITY of humankind and in the possibility of PROGRESS obtained by means of expanded knowledge. Its authors hoped to further the general cause of enlightenment by making the vast body of human knowledge available to general readers. Its contents were heavily weighted toward the applied sciences, technology, trades, and crafts, a fact that reflects the enlightened emphasis on the utility of knowledge.

The long list of contributors contains nearly every notable philosophe of the 18th century, as well as a host of lesser-known writers. Among the authors were VOLTAIRE (who was always ambivalent toward the project), Diderot, and d'Alembert; Jean-François MARMONTEL, Morellet, Nicolas-Antoine BOULANGER, Paul-Joseph BARTHEZ, François QUESNAY, Nicolas DESMAREST, Jean-Jacques ROUSSEAU, Jacques NECKER, the marquis de CONDERCET, Théophile de BORDEU, and Charles DUCLOS. The editors also relied heavily on two general writers: M. de Jaucourt and M. Boucher d'Argis.

The *Encyclopédie* appeared in spite of several sensitive battles with the official CENSORSHIP institutions in FRANCE. The JESUITS attacked the prospectus for volumes one and two in their official periodical, *Journal de Trévoux*, and in the *Dictionnaire de Trévoux*. The adherents of JANSENISM complained about the manner in which an article on "Certitude" advanced the EMPIRICISM of John LOCKE; they objected to the failure of the author to acknowledge revelations from God as an equally valid source of human knowledge.

KING LOUIS XV's *conseil d'état* (council of state) voted to suppress the publication of the project in 1752 and ordered the manuscripts seized by the police. The plans for confiscation were confounded by none other than the royal director of the press, Chrétien-Guillaume de MALESHERBES (1721–94). Malesherbes, a supporter of reform, was sympathetic to the program of the philosophes and not only warned Diderot of the confiscation order, but also hid all the *Encyclopédie* manuscripts in his own house.

In the meantime, the royal government began to realize the prestige for France implied in the project and ordered it to resume. Volume three appeared in 1753, with publication proceeding fairly smoothly until late in 1757. At that time, an article by d'Alembert on GENEVA managed to praise and to criticize the great Calvinist city in a manner that enraged both Catholic and Protestant clergy. Rousseau, who was still in Geneva, publicly denounced d'Alembert, and a noisy public quarrel of the type that was so common during the Enlightenment ensued. In the meantime, Claude-Adrien HELVÉTIUS rocked the established authorities even further by publishing his materialist treatise *De l'esprit* in 1758. The philosophes had overstepped the limits, and the threat of official prosecution loomed.

Birds, an illustration from the *Encyclopédie*. Curiosity about the natural world inspired enlightened scientists to compile information and provide descriptions of the variety of living creatures on Earth. *(Courtesy New York Public Library)*

somewhat from the Baconian example, a fact that Diderot was careful to point out to critics. D'Alembert spelled out the plan and the ideas behind it in his renowned *Discours préliminaire* published in 1751 with volume one of the work.

The *Encyclopédie* presented not only the contents of various abstract disciplines such as EPISTEMOLOGY, NATURAL PHILOSOPHY, and mathematics, but also the practical sciences such as mechanics, MUSIC, MEDICINE, visual perspective, and the techniques of various arts and crafts. The reader could consult practical articles on the proper measurements and design for a high-quality harpsichord and then turn to essays on the truth and certitude of human knowledge. In other words, the range of materials presented in the *Encyclopédie* was enormous, and did, indeed, cover a substantial portion of the knowledge of the era.

D'Alembert, who was disturbed and frightened by the whole episode, resigned as an editor on the *Encyclopédie* in 1758, leaving Diderot to cope with the problems alone. The project was included in a general list of dangerous books condemned in a February 1759 decree. Diderot, however, remained in Paris and managed to secure permission to continue the project in a more carefully edited form.

Censorship from official organs was not the only source of trouble. Diderot learned in 1764 that the publisher Le Breton had been censoring and revising articles all along. As a result, many of the articles did not reflect the original position of the writers and must be read with that limitation in mind.

The *Encyclopédie* was certainly not the first great compendium of knowledge to be published in Europe. It had 18th-century antecedents in works such as John Harris's *Lexicon technicum, or an Universal English Dictionary of Arts and Sciences* (1704); the *Reales Staates- Zeitungs- und Conversations Lexicon* (1704), with its important preface by Johann Hubner; Ephraim Chambers's *Cyclopaedia; or an Universal Dictionary of Arts and Sciences* (1728); Johann Heinrich Zedler's *Grosses Vollständiges Universal Lexicon* (Great complete universal lexicon; 64 vols.; 1732–50); and Gianfrancesco Pivati's *Nuovo dizionario scientifico e curioso sacro-profano* (1746–51).

The French *Encyclopédie* departed from tradition in two significant ways by adding materials on the arts, crafts, and trades and by relying on a wide group of writers to create a truly collaborative effort. It stands as a great tribute to the dreams of the people who created the French Enlightenment, and as a magnificent source for modern scholars of the era.

See also ANCIEN RÉGIME; MATHEMATICS AND MECHANICS; PUBLISHING; RIGHTS; SEPARATION OF CHURCH AND STATE.

Further reading: Jean Le Rond d'Alembert, *Preliminary Discourse to the Encyclopedia of Diderot*, tr. and ed. Richard N. Schwab (Indianapolis: Bobbs-Merrill, 1963); Robert Darnton, *The Business of Enlightenment. A Publishing History of the Encyclopédie, 1775–1800* (Cambridge, Mass.: Harvard University Press, 1979).

encyclopedists   A term used to describe the group of writers who were associated with Denis DIDEROT and Jean Le Rond d'ALEMBERT in the production of the ENCYCLOPÉDIE (1751–72). This group included Jean-Jacques ROUSSEAU, Anne-Robert-Jacques TURGOT, VOLTAIRE, Paul-Joseph BARTHEZ, Jean-François MARMONTEL, Nicolas-Antoine BOULANGER, Nicolas DESMAREST, André Morellet, and Baron d'HOLBACH, as well as a host of other writers.

England   A region of the modern United Kingdom. England occupies the southern portion of the island of Britain. It is bounded by Wales on the west, SCOTLAND on the north, the North Sea on the east, and the English Channel on the south. The nation has a long tradition of economic activity based on trade and other maritime activities.

English history dates back to the era before written records exist. The region fell under Roman control, serving as the northern outpost of the ancient Roman Empire. Christianity arrived in the early seventh century when Pope Gregory sent a band of monks to convert the Anglo-Saxons to ROMAN CATHOLICISM.

The English monarchy was constituted in the early Middle Ages following the collapse of Roman authority in the west. English political history paralleled that of other European monarchies; kings and groups of noble lords struggled over issues of power. In 1215, King John was forced to recognize certain basic English liberties by consenting to sign the Magna Carta (Great charter). This document placed certain activities outside the limits of royal control, and established the right to taxation only with consent. However limited its extent, the Magna Carta created an early precedent in England for a constitutional government with some degree of representation.

By the 13th century, the great council of advisers to the king had transformed itself into the institution of Parliament. Again, such developments occurred in other European countries, but the English Parliament was unusual in its ability to survive royal encroachments and to extend its power.

The Protestant Reformation produced a marked change in English church-state relations. King Henry VIII separated the English church from Roman Catholicism, establishing himself in place of the pope as head of a new Church of England. From that point on, the Anglican Church fell under secular administration, although its doctrines did not depart substantially from those of the Roman Catholic Church.

With the separation from Rome, the English began to create many splinter Protestant groups. CALVINISM gained great influence, giving rise to the Puritan sects that played great roles in the 17th century.

Tension between king and Parliament had never been eliminated in the English system. It grew to unsupportable intensity during the first half of the 17th century. Disputes centered on issues of taxation, justice, and church-state relations. Civil war finally broke out in 1642. For the next 18 years, England experienced violence and political instability. King Charles I was beheaded in 1649, and England came under the control of politically and socially radical Puritans led by Oliver Cromwell. Cromwell tried unsuccessfully to establish a constitutional government in England and to guarantee religious TOLERATION for Protestant sects; Roman Catholics and ANGLICANS, however, were excluded. Cromwell's death in 1660 brought the end of the English revolution and the return of the Stuart monarchy in the person of Charles II.

Determined to ensure that England should never again experience such upheaval, Charles II sought to extend his control over various facets of English political life; his goal was the establishment of ABSOLUTISM. In actual fact, he enjoyed less power than his father, Charles I. The Parliament contained a group of strong Anglicans who opposed most of his actions. Charles II had close ties with the Catholic monarch of FRANCE, LOUIS XIV. He tried to remove the civil disabilities that weighed on English Catholics, but Parliament would have none of it, and forced Charles to sign the Test Act, imposing Anglican beliefs on all military and civil servants in England.

Much of the tension between king and Parliament centered on fears that Catholicism would regain control of England. These fears combined with the usual conflicts about taxation to create a vocal opposition to the king. When James II, Charles II's overtly Catholic brother, inherited the throne, tensions once again came to a head. James was admitting Catholics to his royal privy council, encouraging their acceptance as military officers, and supporting the appointment of Catholics to university professorships. He tried to broaden support for his policies by removing laws that restricted the rights of Protestant DISSENTERS as well as Catholics.

Opposition to James was organized and, in 1688, culminated in a brief military action that forced him to abdicate the throne. Rebel leaders, members of the Whig Party, invited William, the Protestant prince of Orange, to the English throne. His wife, Mary, the Protestant daughter of King James II, provided an aura of legitimacy to the succession. When William accepted this offer, he was forced to sign a Declaration of Rights that eventually became the English bill of rights. It imposed a series of conditions on William that limited his power as monarch; he could not abolish laws at will, and was required to summon frequent Parliaments. This declaration established limited monarchy in England on clear grounds, and was treated by later generations as a statement of the constitution of English government. The whole affair in which WILLIAM III AND MARY II assumed the English throne is known as the GLORIOUS REVOLUTION.

This 17th-century history of England inspired the great political treatises that became one foundation of enlightened POLITICAL THEORY. Thomas HOBBES wrote the *Leviathan*, a treatise that offered a rational base for absolutism in the aftermath of the Civil War and Puritan Revolution. John LOCKE developed the liberal ideas of the *TWO TREATISES OF GOVERNMENT* as he was working for the first earl of Shaftesbury, a chief architect of the Glorious Revolution. English political theories passed easily into the French intellectual world through the medium of Latin and French translations. For the PHILOSOPHES, the

theories of Locke and the example of England after the Glorious Revolution, interpreted by VOLTAIRE and MONTESQUIEU for French conditions, proved especially potent.

In fact, England became an ideal model for many enlightened writers. Not only its political structures, but also its economic vitality and its relatively unobstructed press seemed to demonstrate that FREEDOM could exist hand in hand with internal peace.

England, moreover, was the home of vibrant innovation in natural SCIENCE and technology. It had given the world Isaac NEWTON, the man whose formulation of the SCIENTIFIC METHOD, invention of mathematical calculus, and discovery of universal laws of motion represented great scientific achievement. The ROYAL SOCIETY OF LONDON provided an institutional base for English creativity and was free of the state control that dogged its cousin, the FRENCH ACADEMY OF SCIENCES in PARIS.

English writers bequeathed a persuasive form of EMPIRICISM to Europe, elaborated by Francis BACON, John Locke, and Newton. Locke's empirical PSYCHOLOGY transformed the understanding of the operations of the human mind, stimulating 18th-century work in EPISTEMOLOGY, MORAL PHILOSOPHY, and psychology.

The English economy of the 18th century was thriving, blessed with prosperous commercial ventures, agricultural experimentation, and industrial innovations. Both the INDUSTRIAL REVOLUTION and the Agricultural Revolution took root in England, in the liberal social and political atmosphere that encouraged and protected private business enterprises. English inventiveness and prosperity seemed to testify that human knowledge applied to practical problems could result in human PROGRESS.

The ideal descriptions of England that can be found in the works of the early ENLIGHTENMENT by continental writers seldom discussed the darker sides of reality in the nation. Economic restructuring was causing great social dislocation. Cities were teeming with people from the countryside who had been removed from their ancestral lands as lords enclosed the property for private exploitation. Urban poverty was widespread, and the English system was being challenged to find ways—in both private and public spheres—to address the social, moral, and public health problems associated with low wages and unemployment. Even in the countryside, the Industrial Revolution changed the organization of work, forcing people out of their homes and into oppressive, unhealthy workplaces.

Religious tension and certain forms of intolerance continued unabated. Neither Catholics nor Dissenters could attend the two major English UNIVERSITIES, and they were still barred from officeholding. DEISM flourished, especially in the early Enlightenment, giving rise to various forms of criticism of Christian tradition. Protestant sects continued to proliferate, causing some factional strife, but also producing vibrant new sects such as METHODISM.

The British colonies provided wealth, but they also pulled England into costly wars. Colonial policies of various sorts proved a source of dissension at home. So too did policies toward Ireland. Although England and Scotland had been formally united in 1707, the Scottish people periodically rebelled, ushering in brief periods of instability in the northern portions of the island.

Developments in 18th-century England created a host of problems that would persist into the 19th century. The ideals of the Enlightenment, so varied in their content, proved in England, as elsewhere, to have ambivalent effects in reality. Embodied in economic liberalism, they produced progress and overall prosperity, but they also encouraged radical political concepts and social criticism. Liberal theory encouraged EQUALITY and EDUCATION, two ideas that seemed dangerous in many eyes when applied universally across the social and political order. The ideas of the Enlightenment could actually support several different political and socioeconomic structures. In England, as the Enlightenment came to an end in the upheavals of the FRENCH REVOLUTION, the state, although still a constitutional, representative monarchy, emerged as a bulwark of conservative policy wedded to a stratified social system.

See also COLONIALISM; EAST INDIA COMPANY; JACOBITES; LONDON CORRESPONDING SOCIETY.

Further reading: J. S. Bromley, ed., *The Rise of Great Britain and Russia, 1688–1725*, vol. 6 of New Cambridge Modern History (Cambridge: Cambridge University Press, 1971); J. H. Plumb, *England in the Eighteenth Century (1714–1815)* (Baltimore: Penguin Books, 1950); Sir Leslie Stephen, *History of English Thought in the Eighteenth Century*, 2 vols. (New York: Harcourt, Brace & World, 1962); A. S. Turberville, *English Men and Manners in the Eighteenth Century* (New York: Oxford University Press, 1957).

English garden A landscape style that developed in the 1740s in ENGLAND. It was the creation of Lord Burlington, William KENT, and their circle of friends, who installed an English garden at Chiswick House. English gardens soon appeared throughout England and on the European continent. Outstanding examples include the gardens at Stowe and Stourbridge in England, the Englischer Garten of MUNICH, and the grounds of the Schloss Eremitage just outside Bayreuth.

The English garden adapted ROCOCO aesthetics to landscaping and was directly derived from descriptions of Chinese gardens transmitted to Europeans in the TRAVEL LITERATURE and official reports of Portuguese traders. The typical English garden consisted of grounds laid out with curving paths, streams, waterfalls, grottos, artificial ruins, and plantings designed to seem as if they had grown up naturally. It reflected the new definition of NATURE that developed when the concept of nature as the embodiment of REASON began to seem inadequate and constricting. The new concept introduced irregularity, feeling, and even irrationality into the idea of nature, transforming these previously disparaged characteristics into positive ideals.

enlightened absolutism *See* ABSOLUTISM, ENLIGHTENED.

enlightened despotism *See* DESPOTISM, ENLIGHTENED.

enlightened monarchy *See* MONARCHY, ENLIGHTENED.

Enlightenment, the Term for the major intellectual and cultural movement of the 18th century, characterized by a pronounced faith in the power of human knowledge to solve basic problems of existence. Scholars disagree over the precise dating of both the beginning and end of the Enlightenment. Most now accept the date of 1680 as a rough beginning point. Some scholars believe that the era concluded in 1789 with the beginning of the FRENCH REVOLUTION, while others extend it through the revolutionary and Napoleonic periods to 1815. An argument can also be made for extending it, at least in the German intellectual world, beyond the 1815 date.

Enlightenment is an English translation of the French word *lumières*, meaning "lights." *Lumières* appeared frequently in 18th-century discussions, referring both to an intellectual program and to the people who were creating it. Everyone claimed to possess light, a symbol borrowed from ancient philosophy by 17th-century intellectuals because of its reference to wisdom. The German term corresponding to *lumières* was AUFKLÄRUNG. Enlightened intellectuals were *Aufklärer* in German regions and ILLUMINISTI in the Italian peninsula.

The Enlightenment possessed complexities that have given rise to several different scholarly interpretations since the 18th century. Today, above all, scholars stress its international scope. Manifestations of the Enlightenment could be found not only in ENGLAND and FRANCE, where it was born, but throughout Europe: in the German territories of the HOLY ROMAN EMPIRE, in AUSTRIA, MILAN, and other regions of the HAPSBURG EMPIRE, in SWITZERLAND, the KINGDOM OF THE TWO SICILIES, RUSSIA, POLAND, SWEDEN, DENMARK, PORTUGAL, SPAIN, SCOTLAND, and the North American colonies. If PARIS was the undisputed center of the Enlightenment, the intellectual milieu in that city was mirrored in places as far-flung as BERLIN, LONDON, VIENNA, GENEVA, Milan, Naples, ROME, Florence, EDINBURGH, SAINT PETERSBURG, and PHILADELPHIA.

Intellectuals during the Enlightenment turned a critical eye on nearly all received traditions in Europe. Political traditions; social and economic structures; attitudes toward the past; ideas about human nature; theories of knowledge, science, philosophy, aesthetics, and morals; and, above all, the doctrines and institutions of Christianity were subjected to analysis. Enlightenment writers aimed at tearing down old structures, rebuilding human society, institutions, and knowledge, and providing them with firm foundations in the presumed natural order of things.

The spirit of critical inquiry was not indulged in by isolated scholars locked up in dusty studies with their books. Rather, the investigations occurred within a remarkable framework of sociability. Intellectuals, journalists, writers, government officials, and other interested people met together to discuss their ideas in places like salons, coffeehouses, and SCIENTIFIC ACADEMIES. In France and England, UNIVERSITIES played minor roles; but in other areas such as Scotland and the Holy Roman Empire, universities acted as important enlightened centers.

The various forms of sociability helped to further the great enlightened cause of disseminating knowledge beyond the boundaries of highly educated society. Professional journals, newspapers and periodicals, and active book PUBLISHING also helped to spread ideas. So, too, did the activities of local scientific societies, political clubs, reading clubs, and lending libraries. Secret societies such as the FREEMASONS, Bavarian ILLUMINATI, and even ROSICRUCIANS incorporated aspects of enlightened thought into their rituals and organization. They provided another avenue for disseminating ideas and served in some areas as important institutional bases for the Enlightenment.

The SCIENTIFIC REVOLUTION of the 17th century had created the basic intellectual milieu in which the Enlightenment was born. Broad shifts in conceptions about the order of the natural world raised a host of questions not only for SCIENCE, but also for most other areas of human intellectual inquiry. The MECHANICAL PHILOSOPHY and RATIONALISM provided explanations of natural phenomena that could even be extended to human behavior and function. The mechanical philosophy proposed to explain all natural phenomena in terms of matter and motion, and to express the relations between things in mathematical language. Rationalism assigned great powers to human REASON, so long as it operated according to the rules of deductive logic as evidenced in the proofs of geometry.

Toward the end of the 17th century, the mechanical philosophy received a potent new form in the work of Isaac NEWTON, and rationalism was joined by a rival system called EMPIRICISM. Empiricism asserted that the exercise of reason yields knowledge, but relied on a method of reasoning drawn from inductive logic. Observing facts from experience and experiment, the empirical approach allowed people to use reason both to impose order and eventually to uncover the underlying structure of things.

These three strands—mechanical philosophy, rationalism, and empiricism—provided the basic cornerstones for the intellectual structures of the Enlightenment. The implications that could be drawn from them and the ten-

sions inherent within them shaped the discourse of the Enlightenment as people struggled to give substance to the major concepts of reason and NATURE.

But why these two concepts? Reason provided both an intellectual tool for acquiring knowledge, and also an analogy for the underlying order of the universe. A world structured according to reason was a world of NATURAL LAW, of orderly, discoverable, and manipulable RELATIONS. Nature provided the basic metaphor on which all artificially constructed forms of human society were to be based. Nature was to be analyzed, understood, and imitated so that natural forms could be constructed in human realms.

Reason and nature, then, provided the two basic models, metaphors, and standards against which all theory and institutions, enlightened or not, were to be judged. But this fact should never be construed to mean that uniform definitions of these two concepts existed. They didn't! In fact, both reason and nature possessed a wide variety of meanings that often produced confusion and conflict. To complicate matters further, a significant shift from one general definition of nature to another occurred between 1740 and 1760. This brought in its wake renewed inquiries into the nature of reason, its limits, and its powers. In fact, as the Enlightenment closed, Immanuel KANT was engaging in an extensive investigation, once again, into the basic foundations of human knowledge about all aspects of existence.

Although the mid-century shift produced noticeable dichotomies in enlightened thought, tension and downright paradox had existed all along. In fact, some scholars like to characterize the Enlightenment as an era of dialectics between pairs of opposing poles in thought. Writers might choose one or another pole; or they might try to find some middle ground between the extremes. The first major enlightened dialectic involved reason and feeling. Both mechanical, material models of things and the cult of SENSIBILITY coexisted during the Enlightenment. Sensation, the result of sensory experience, was made the source of all basic ideas by John LOCKE. The Enlightenment elaborated this basic idea—exploring sensation and its broader meaning, feeling, and often giving them priority over reason. A second dialectic between reason and intuition assumed major significance at mid-century. Reason analyzed a problem, producing a string of statements about it that eventually solved it (discursive thought). Intuition, on the other hand, immediately grasped the whole problem and all its facets, yielding understanding without the analytic process.

The Enlightenment also introduced the concept of HISTORY into many disciplines by emphasizing that the passage of time brings changes in its wake. The Earth, Christianity, the Bible, the human species, and individuals all acquired a historical facet that stressed processes of change and directional development (PROGRESS or decline). Closely related to the concept of history, the German idea of BILDUNG dealt with the appearance of specific forms in the course of historical development. *Bildung* applied not only to biology and geology but also to EDUCATION and to HUMAN NATURE.

The critical inquiry conducted by enlightened intellectuals did not exclude the realm of RELIGION. In fact, questions ordinarily treated in religious doctrine and theology assumed pressing significance for the Enlightenment. If Christianity was subjected to scathing analysis, and to occasionally strong ANTICLERICALISM, it also received support in some enlightened quarters. Reason and critical inquiry could be used to destroy religion or to bolster the grounds for faith. They could also create new ways of examining the Bible and writings of the church fathers that would help to make it more palatable to enlightened believers.

Many enlightened intellectuals sought religious substitutes for the revealed traditions of Christianity. They turned to PAGANISM, replacing Christian values with those of EPICUREAN PHILOSOPHY or of dechristianized Stoicism. Some people tried to develop models of NATURAL RELIGION, such as DEISM and PHYSICO-THEOLOGY, that made religious truths accessible to human reason and therefore universal, capable of rising above doctrinal disputes. The most radical of the enlightened PHILOSOPHES adopted outright ATHEISM and its scientific and ethical equivalents, MATERIALISM and determinism.

Natural religion and the mechanical philosophy allowed enlightened persons to remove the Christian God from his prominent role in the universe. Rather than being intimately involved with the direction of events and of human lives, God became the distant but still all-powerful and wise creator. At best, he intervened occasionally in his world to adjust its mechanisms (the Watchmaker God).

As appealing as this view was to people who were tired of religious conflict and intolerance, it raised a host of serious questions about the moral qualities of the world. The Christian world made God the creator of moral standards and the ultimate judge of conformity to them. Natural religion needed to substitute natural explanations for morality, if such morality was to be retained in the concepts of the world. And it must be emphasized that for most enlightened intellectuals, the preservation of moral qualities was paramount. Questions were asked about the nature of the good, the beautiful, and the true, qualities that were inextricably linked in enlightened MORAL PHILOSOPHY. Did these exist in the external world as real things? Or were they relative to time, place, and person? What is the origin of moral behavior; what kind of natural psychological mechanism could explain moral decisions in human beings? All these problems demanded attention and received innovative answers during the Enlightenment.

The problems of moral philosophy reveal a third enlightened dialectic, between freedom and necessity, or choice and determinism. To what extent, people wondered, were human actions freely chosen, and to what extent were they determined by the natural laws governing human functions. The question demanded answers, especially since most people assumed that ethical behavior had no meaning unless it was freely chosen. Some of the bitterest conflicts within the community of enlightened intellectuals revolved around this problem, and attempts to address it frequently brought out the censoring authorities.

If any model of the Enlightenment has dominated our traditional ideas, it is the model that makes the Enlightenment an era ruled by faith in reason, progress, INDIVIDUALISM, universal brotherhood, and humanitarian values. But these concepts by no means represent the whole body of enlightened thought. Furthermore, they had variable definitions that sometimes produced discrepancies and mutually exclusive theories and practices.

Above all, the intellectuals of the Enlightenment believed in and tried to act on the idea that knowledge should be pressed into the service of humankind. Knowledge was expected to yield practical results—new institutions, new practices, new technologies—all of which would contribute to general human progress. Beautifully encapsulated in the contents of that quintessential creation of the Enlightenment, the ENCY-CLOPÉDIE, this value drove activities throughout Europe on behalf of social, political, educational, economic, and intellectual reform.

The Enlightenment produced practical reforms at all levels of life. Whether driven from below by the actions of intellectuals or other social groups or instituted from above by royal ministers and practitioners of enlightened despotism (see DESPOTISM, ENLIGHTENED), these reforms changed the way in which certain basic human activities were structured. The INDUSTRIAL REVOLUTION, LAISSEZ-FAIRE economics, the controlled police states of central Europe, the political republics created during the AMERICAN REVOLUTION and the French Revolution, all derived inspiration from enlightened ideals.

In the end, the Enlightenment brought the world of Europe into the modern era, even though it was eventually supplanted by ROMANTICISM. During its course, the old institutions of early-modern European society disappeared or were transformed into institutions recognizable to modern eyes. The era presented the modern world with a political, social, economic, and intellectual legacy within whose boundaries we continue to carry on our modern discussions. For this reason, and because it contains so much provocative and fascinating material, the Enlightenment deserves to be studied.

See also INTUITION AND IMAGINATION; LITERACY; POLITICAL THEORY; SOCIAL INSTITUTIONS OF THE ENLIGHTENMENT.

Further reading: Robert Anchor, *The Enlightenment Tradition* (Berkeley: University of California Press, 1967); Ernst Cassirer, *The Philosophy of the Enlightenment*, tr., Fritz C. A. Kolln and James P. Pettegrove (Princeton, N.J.: Princeton University Press, 1951); Norman Hampson, *The Enlightenment*, vol. 4 of the Pelican History of Human Thought (Baltimore: Penguin Books, 1968); Roy Porter, *The Enlightenment* (London: Macmillan Education, 1990); Roy Porter and Mikulas Teich, *The Enlightenment in National Context* (Cambridge: Cambridge University Press, 1981).

Enquiry Concerning Human Understanding, An

Short treatise by the Scottish philosopher David HUME, first published in 1751. *An Enquiry Concerning Human Understanding* was Hume's second revision of part one of his large and initially unappreciated early work, the TREATISE OF HUMAN NATURE. The *Enquiry* was a much shorter book, intended for a broad, unspecialized audience. It was read enthusiastically, and Hume devoted himself during his later years to refining its arguments. He authorized 10 different editions during his lifetime.

Long disparaged as a popularized version of the *Treatise of Human Nature*, the *Enquiry* is now respected as a significant development in Hume's thought. Hume himself always liked the *Enquiry* and openly dismissed the *Treatise* as the work of his youth. However, it is unclear whether his public pronouncements about the two works actually reflected his private opinions and evaluations.

In the *Enquiry*, Hume largely abandons the goal of creating a certain science of HUMAN NATURE and scarcely discusses the three laws of mental association that had been central components of the *Treatise*. Youthful optimism, so evident in the *Treatise*, has been replaced by a more balanced, modest assessment of human capabilities.

Hume continues to explore the limits of systematic RATIONALISM in the *Enquiry* by pointing out that human REASON can produce only flawed knowledge about the world. He carefully tempers his SKEPTICISM, however, for he recognizes that extreme doubt can rob people of guidelines for both belief and action. He suggests that the best intellectual stance for people to adopt is one of moderated skepticism, in which the accumulated experiences of life (custom or common sense) provide the guidelines for action.

Hume uses the epistemological arguments of the *Enquiry* to attack Christian beliefs in miracles and other supernatural events. But his criticisms also extend to reports about supernatural occurrences in ancient Greek and Roman texts and to contemporary manifestations of religious enthusiasm and ecstasy.

In short, the *Enquiry* subjects the revered texts of Christianity and classical antiquity to scrutiny, asking enlightened readers to be wary of accepting all that is claimed in their pages. In this respect, the *Enquiry* bears resemblance to the famous HISTORICAL AND CRITICAL DICTIONARY by Pierre BAYLE. But Hume cannot be wholly content with tearing down received tradition because he recognizes that this tradition has provided needed prescriptions for moral behavior. He therefore points in the pages of the *Enquiry* toward a new MORAL PHILOSOPHY, one that will rely on experience and custom to provide guidelines for human action.

See also ENTHUSIASM; EPISTEMOLOGY; PSYCHOLOGY.

enthusiasm A general term that encompasses the various expressions of intense religious feeling that were common during the ENLIGHTENMENT. The PHILOSOPHES, who were generally critical of such phenomena, labeled as enthusiasm any aspect of religious practice that built on emotion, passion, or spontaneous behavior. They believed that enthusiasm was a manifestation of a passion-dominated mind and a sign of psychopathology. The label *enthusiasm*, therefore, almost always carried negative connotations during the Enlightenment.

The concept of enthusiasm included such behaviors as convulsions, speaking in tongues, prophesying, spontaneous expressions of joy or woe, and active attempts to convert believers. It was used in both Protestant and Catholic states to refer to any religious manifestation that departed from orthodox THEOLOGY by emphasizing emotional rather than rational engagement with the divine. Specific examples in the 18th century included Quakerism, METHODISM, the Great Awakening in America, and the Catholic Jansenist convulsionaries at Saint-Médard in Paris.

The criticism of enthusiasm emerged first in 17th-century Restoration ENGLAND as a response to the upheavals of the Civil War and the Puritan Commonwealth. English Anglican theologians, appalled at the radical and rigid positions taken by Puritans, decried the fanatical intolerance that had characterized the era. They believed that human passions, disguised as religious commitment, had reigned without check during this era.

These early attacks on enthusiasm were accompanied in England by attempts to develop a rational NATURAL RELIGION. Such religion would be rooted in REASON rather than in the passions. Because of its rational foundation, such a religion would not be prone to fanaticism and intolerance. DEISM, the most common enlightened rational religion, developed partly as a result of the abhorrence of enthusiasm.

The theological response to enthusiasm was mirrored in other cultural realms. Anthony Ashley Cooper, third earl of SHAFTESBURY, laid grounds for a psychological inquiry into enthusiasm in his *Soliloquy: or Advice to an Author* (1710) and his *Characteristicks of Men, Manners, Opinions, Times* (1711). David HARTLEY and David HUME developed Shaftesbury's ideas, while William HOGARTH satirized fanaticism and superstition—enthusiasm, for him—in satirical engravings.

The tendency to pair religious enthusiasm with rigid intolerance and fanaticism continued throughout the Enlightenment. It translated easily from the English environment into FRANCE and other continental European states, where criticisms of enthusiasm came from the pens of Pierre BAYLE (*Letter Concerning Enthusiasm*), VOLTAIRE, Julien de LA METTRIE, Claude-Adrien HELVÉTIUS, and Baron d' HOLBACH.

In the later years of the Enlightenment, some philosophes relaxed their negative attitudes toward enthusiasm. They believed that both creative GENIUS and the experience of the SUBLIME depended in some measure on the ability to partake of enthusiasm. As an irrational form of behavior, enthusiasm, like INTUITION AND IMAGINATION, allowed human beings to transcend the ordinary limits of existence and to soar to new heights of creativity and understanding.

See also QUAKERS.

Epicurean philosophy A system of philosophy from ancient Greece based primarily on the writings of Epicurus (341–270 B.C.) and his school of followers. Epicurus constructed his philosophy on intertwined theories of atomism, MATERIALISM, and an EPISTEMOLOGY (theory of knowledge) rooted in experience. He believed that all objects in the universe are made of tiny, indivisible particles called atoms. These atoms combined to produce various material objects; their means of combination produced not only their specific form but also nonessential qualities such as color or taste. Atoms move about freely, influencing each other only in direct contact. No interaction is possible between bodies not in contact.

The human being consists of body and soul, but soul like body is created from material atoms; hence, Epicurean philosophy is materialistic, denying the separate existence of an immaterial soul or spirit. The atoms of the soul resemble those that make up the winds, air, and heat. The atoms of the soul exist throughout the body, and their interaction with the external world produces sensory experience.

Epicurus built a MORAL PHILOSOPHY from the experience of the senses. Pleasurable sensory experiences are good; painful experiences are evil, harmful for the body. The goal of the human being is the attainment of pleasure. But this does not mean simple self-indulgence in the physical pleasures of food, drink, or sexual activity. These activities have positive value, but the primary goal of people must be to obtain longer-lasting pleasures that result from producing a condition of stability in the body. Epicurus believed that the good life can be attained only by philosophers who can combine intellectual wisdom with the practical wisdom that correctly assesses the relative pain and pleasure in any activity.

The revival of Epicurean philosophy in 17th-century ENGLAND and FRANCE acquainted philosophers anew with Epicurean principles. The original philosophy had been born out of the desire to find a basis for human knowledge and behavior that would avoid idealism and escape the pitfalls of SKEPTICISM. Similar epistemological goals motivated Pierre GASSEND and Thomas HOBBES in their use of Epicurean philosophy to develop 17th-century versions of materialist, atomistic NATURAL PHILOSOPHY and moral philosophy.

The ENLIGHTENMENT owes a great debt to Epicurean philosophy. The corpuscular philosophy of Isaac NEWTON, the sensation psychology of John LOCKE, the pleasure-pain psychology and moral philosophy of Claude-Adrien HELVÉTIUS, and POLITICAL THEORY based on HAPPINESS and utility, all represent Epicurean ideas, transformed and, indeed, recreated for the 18th century.

epigenesis Theory of GENERATION (reproduction) first developed in the 17th century. The theory of epigenesis posited that all individuals begin life as a homogeneous bit of matter (the egg or ovum) from which the various organs and body parts develop according to a predetermined potentiality. This process of generation and development was called epigenesis. It derived from the ideas of the ancient Greek philosopher Aristotle and from Hippocratic MEDICINE.

William Harvey first spelled out the 17th-century version of the theory in the *Excercitationes de generatione animalium* (On the generation of animals), published in 1651. Harvey believed that all life came from "eggs" and developed in the manner just outlined.

During the 18th century, the theory of epigenesis became more complex and sophisticated. It incorporated the methodological ideals of the ENLIGHTENMENT, refusing to speculate about the causes of phenomena or about embryological structures that could not be observed. Epigeneticists emphasized careful, direct observation and limited their activities to describing the macroscopic embryonic processes accessible to them. It must be noted that the realm of the directly observable was limited since MICROSCOPE technology was still relatively undeveloped. The ova of mammals were not observed until 1826, and the fertilization of an ovum by sperm was not witnessed until 1875.

The theory of epigenesis was opposed in the 17th century and 18th century by supporters of the more common PREFORMATION THEORY. During the last half of the 18th century, epigeneticists and preformationists engaged in an intense debate about generation that helped to transform both theories. By the end of the 18th century, preformation theory was largely abandoned as inadequate, and epigenesis was adopted by most students of BIOLOGY.

Major 18th-century supporters of epigenesis were Caspar Friedrich Wolff, a follower of the Leibnizian philosopher, Christian WOLFF; Georges-Louis Leclerc, comte de BUFFON; Pierre Louis Moreau de MAUPERTUIS; John Turberville NEEDHAM; physicians trained at the University of Montpellier such as Paul-Joseph BARTHEZ, Théophile de BORDEU, and Louis Roussel; the brothers William HUNTER and John HUNTER; Johann Friedrich BLUMENBACH; and William CULLEN. Albrecht von HALLER began his professional life as a believer in ANIMALCULISM, then converted to epigenesis, and reconverted in the mid-18th century to ovist preformation theory.

Épinay, Louise-Florence-Pétronville de la Live, madame d' (1726–1783) *French writer and salon hostess*

Madame d'Épinay, wife of Dénis-Joseph de La Live de Bellegarde, marquis d'Épinay, compensated for the frequent absences and amorous adventures of her husband by immersing herself in the literary and intellectual world of PARIS. She frequented the SALONS of Madame GEOFFRIN and the marquise du DEFFAND.

Madame d'Épinay established a salon at her estate of La Chevrette, near Épinay-Saint-Denis. She sheltered Jean-Jacques ROUSSEAU for several years while he was writing *LA NOUVELLE HÉLOISE*. Rousseau and Madame d'Épinay later quarreled, becoming rather outspoken enemies. Madame d'Épinay also counted Denis DIDEROT, Jean Le Rond d'ALEMBERT, Charles DUCLOS, and VOLTAIRE among her friends. Her liaison with Friedrich Melchior GRIMM sustained her for more than 25 years through her many financial and emotional troubles with her estranged husband.

A writer of some talent, Madame d'Épinay left several works worthy of consultation by students of the ENLIGHTENMENT. They include *Portrait de Mme**** (Portrait of Madame ***; 1755); *Les conversations d'Emilie* (Conversations with Emilie; 1774), written for the education of her granddaughter; and *Mémoires et correspondances* (Memoirs and letters; 1818), a posthumous autobiography in the form of a romance novel. Madame d'Épinay died in relatively difficult circumstances after a long illness.

epistemology

The branch of philosophy that explores the nature of human knowledge, the philosophical and empirical grounds of our knowledge, its limits, and its validity or truth. The word *epistemology* stems from the Greek *epistanai*, meaning "to understand" or "to know." Traditionally, epistemology lay within the boundaries of philosophy, but during the ENLIGHTENMENT, PSYCHOLOGY and SCIENCE became the chief intellectual sources of theories about knowledge.

The 18th-century Enlightenment inherited a set of problems about the limits of knowledge from the 17th century. These problems contained implications for nearly every form of human knowledge, ranging from revealed religion to natural science.

At the beginning of the 17th century, Europeans were longing for some sort of peace, stability, and certainty about the world. They had experienced the breakdown of monolithic Christianity (as Protestants and Catholics became hopelessly divided), bitter religious wars, the perplexing but stimulating discovery of non-Western cultures and beliefs, and the breakdown of the traditional view of the universe by astronomers, physicists, and physicians. Philosophers had realized that every traditional form of knowledge, including the revealed knowledge contained in the Bible, could be questioned. They were confronted with an epistemological crisis regarding the validity of all human knowledge.

A strong current of philosophical SKEPTICISM emerged to give form to these doubts about knowledge. But neither philosophers nor official institutions were satisfied with the answers of skepticism. For human beings to operate with a feeling that reliable knowledge could not be obtained was too unsettling. Therefore, in the 17th century, philosophers developed several new approaches to the problem of knowledge.

One new form of epistemological theory was RATIONALISM, a form of epistemology that used REASON and mathematically modeled logic to develop complete systems of knowledge. The most influential 17th-century rational philosophies were created by René DESCARTES, Benedict de SPINOZA, and Gottfried Wilhelm LEIBNIZ.

A second theoretical approach to epistemology has been called mitigated skepticism. It accepted the fact that human knowledge is limited when it attempts to deal with the ultimate causes of things. Only God can have such knowledge. But mitigated skepticism asserted that reliable forms of knowledge could be obtained by using mathematics as the basis for understanding the world. It tended to blend into empiricism because of its emphasis on observing nature as a valid scientific activity. The theory of mitigated skepticism was developed by Father Marin MERSENNE as he wrestled with the problem of reconciling new scientific knowledge with revealed religious truths.

A third theory, that of EMPIRICISM, received a powerful formulation in the works of Francis BACON (1561–1626) and gave rise to experimental science. During the 17th century, it was especially powerful in ENGLAND, where it acquired an institutional base in the ROYAL SOCIETY OF LONDON. By the end of the 17th century, empiricism had become a favored theory of knowledge in England. It substituted experience for reason as the base of reliable human knowledge. Through the psychological theories of John LOCKE and the natural philosophy (science) of Isaac NEWTON, empiricism entered the discourse of the Enlightenment, where it exerted a powerful influence.

However powerful the answers of rationalism and empiricism to the problems of skepticism, the sense that human knowledge was untrustworthy continued to exist. In fact, the Enlightenment opened with one of the greatest works of skepticism in history: the *Dictionnaire critique et historique* (Historical and critical dictionary; 1697) by Pierre BAYLE. The skeptical spirit continued to manifest itself in the seminal works of David HUME: *A TREATISE OF HUMAN NATURE* (1739–40) and *AN ENQUIRY CONCERNING HUMAN UNDERSTANDING* (1758).

Hume offered a restatement of epistemological skepticism that underlined the subjective nature of all knowledge. His works, both disturbing and inspiring, provoked especially creative responses in psychology. Thomas REID and his student Dugald Stewart, for example, developed the philosophy of common sense in an effort to respond to Hume's skepticism. Immanuel KANT, the great epistemologist of the late Enlightenment, certainly knew Hume's work and credited it with awakening him to the inadequacies of philosophical rationalism.

Bayle questioned received traditions, whether religious, scientific, philosophical, or cultural. His *Dictionary* helped to establish the spirit of criticism, based on a skeptical attitude toward tradition, as a primary stance of the Enlightenment. In fact, some scholars believe that this critical spirit is the single most important unifying element in the Enlightenment.

Criticism entailed the use of reason, not primarily to build systems of belief about the world, but to scrutinize, question, analyze, and tear down accepted views of European civilization. Criticism, applied to all aspects of life, helped to produce the great reform programs of the Enlightenment.

When criticism turned against its source, the faculty of reason, it produced the noticeable shifts in enlightened culture that marked the middle decades of the 18th century. Rationalism had to share center stage not only with Lockean empiricism and Humean skepticism, but also with common sense philosophy and with the culture of SENSIBILITY, all of which offered distinct interpretations of epistemology.

In German-speaking lands, the criticism of reason produced a special epistemology in which the INTUITION AND IMAGINATION, also faculties of the mind, received as much attention as reason. The new field of AESTHETICS made imagination and intuition the chief mental means for arriving at creative ideas or knowledge. According to the new theories, intuition and imagination provided the creative insights and inspiration that allowed an artist possessed of GENIUS to transcend the ordinary limits of human existence. The role of reason in creative processes became secondary.

The enlightened examination of the foundations of knowledge reached a culmination in the works of Immanuel Kant. In his three treatises, *Kritik der reinen Vernunft* (Critique of pure reason; 1781 and 1787), *Kritik der practischen Vernunft* (Critique of practical reason; 1788), and *Kritik der Urteilskraft* (Critique of judgment; 1790), Kant investigated all major forms of mental activity. He developed a complex and immensely rich epistemology that attempted to eliminate the gulf between rationalism and empiricism. Kantian epistemology provided the logical climax of the critical spirit of the Enlightenment. And the new emphasis on roles for imagination and intuition provided some of the seeds that produced 19th-century ROMANTICISM.

Further reading: Francis Bacon, *A Selection of His Works,* ed. Sidney Warhaft (New York: Odyssey Press, 1965); Pierre Bayle, *Historical and Critical Dictionary, Selections* (Indianapolis: Bobbs-Merrill, 1965); René Descartes, *The Philosophical Writings of Descartes,* 2 vols., tr. John Cottingham, Robert Stoothoff, Dugald Murdoch (Cambridge: Cambridge University Press, 1984); David Hume, *An Enquiry Concerning Human Understanding,* ed. Eric Steinberg (Indianapolis: Hackett Publishing, 1977).

equality Fundamental concept of the ENLIGHTENMENT that helped to bring about the destruction of the old hierarchical political order in Europe. The notion of equality is an ancient one that has had many historical applications. It has ethical, ontological (i.e., based on the philosophical nature of being and existence), and mathematical components. Fundamentally, it asserts that two distinct objects can be alike (this concept is, of course, open to wide interpretation) and that, when this equality holds, the objects deserve the same treatment. The notion of human equality goes back to ancient Greece, to the era when the axioms of Euclidean geometry also first appeared. The Judaeo-Christian tradition contributed to the concept by stressing that all humans are created by God, hence on some fundamental level they are equal.

Prior to the 19th century, however, Christian-dominated European societies were constructed according to hierarchical principles, which assigned people to functional groups and gave each group different privileges. Such privileges were considered to be proportional to the contribution made by each group to overall society. The notion of human equality received a major thrust forward during the Reformation, when Protestants began asserting to varying degrees that all believing Christians have equal status. Protestants minimized, and in some cases eliminated, differences between the clergy and the laity. They stressed that all individuals could read the Bible and understand the truths of God without assistance from priests or ministers. This religious notion of human equality translated easily into political realms, as the German Peasant Rebellion (1525), the Anabaptist movement headed by Thomas Münzer, the extreme Catholic radicalism of the French Wars of Religion (1560–98), or the Puritan parties of Levellers and Diggers during the English Civil War (1642–49) and Commonwealth (1649–60) all made clear. In general, however, the notion of equality as a political concept had to wait for 17th-century RATIONALISM, for new theories of NATURAL LAW, for John LOCKE'S empirical PSYCHOLOGY, and for 18th-century humanitarianism to acquire the theoretical and emotive force that made it dominate the political theory of the Enlightenment.

Rationalism and natural law provided the first impetus for modern notions of political equality. These related intellectual phenomena posited that reason governs in the universe according to universal, unchanging laws. These laws operate equally and impartially, without any regard for artificial distinctions. All men (the idea did not often extend to women) possess an innate, natural ability to reason and therefore are psychologically, if not socially, equal.

In the late 17th century, the Englishman John Locke gave egalitarian theories additional legitimacy when, in *An Essay Concerning Human Understanding* (1690), he proposed his theory of psychological EMPIRICISM. This book established new psychological grounds for the idea of equality. Locke rejected the notion that men are born with innate ideas (this notion of innate ideas characterized some natural law theories). Rather, he believed they were born with blank minds (*tabula rasa*) on which sensation and experience inscribe a content and impose a shape. Thus, all men are created equal. Any inequalities of mind or condition are the result of personal history and environmental influence. The sources of such inequality could be eradicated.

Locke himself developed the implications of his psychology for POLITICAL THEORY in his *TWO TREATISES OF GOVERNMENT* (1690). His idea of the social contract made basic human equality the foundation of all civil society. According to Locke, people had entered freely into a contract to live together under laws, and they had determined by majority vote the specifics of that contract. They did not give up their natural rights but only limited them to the degree necessary for the preservation of the whole.

The Lockean form of natural equality underlay much of the political thought of the liberal Enlightenment and of the centralized political reforms of that era. Attempts were made to equalize taxation, to create universal (i.e., equally applicable) law codes, and to eliminate certain political and social privileges. These policies were pursued by rulers and their reforming ministers no matter whether the constituted state was a limited or an absolute monarchy. But egalitarian reforms were mostly blocked by the traditional social groups whose SELF-INTEREST led them to call for the preservation of their political privileges.

The idea of equality did not belong exclusively to liberal theorists of the Lockean school. Radical writers of the later Enlightenment also theorized about establishing and preserving equality. But their ideas about how to proceed differed dramatically from those of Locke. Jean-Jacques ROUSSEAU was the most outstanding and influential proponent of this radical approach. In his *Discours sur l'origine et les fondements de l'inégalité parmi les hommes* (DISCOURSE ON THE ORIGINS OF INEQUALITY; 1755), Rousseau suggested that the state of equality among men had existed only in the Golden Age of primitive, natural man. All subsequent history, but especially the development of private property and the influence of the passions, had conspired to eliminate equality, replacing it with hierarchical systems of institutionalized inequality. Rousseau did not believe that it was possible or desirable to return to the pristine state of nature. But he desired to recover man's lost equality. In *Du contrat social* (THE SOCIAL CONTRACT; 1762) Rousseau outlined a plan for a contractual society, akin somewhat to the one that Thomas HOBBES had described in LEVIATHAN (1651). But in the place of Hobbes's submission to an absolute sovereign (ABSOLUTISM), Rousseau prescribed voluntary submission by individuals to the abstract "General Will." This General Will, a benevolent force that protects the communal good, transcends all individual wills, allowing the creation of an organic society. According to Rousseau, the General Will would be given practical expression by a "Legislator," a supremely wise person who would make laws that would guarantee political equality. Economic equality would not exist, although Rousseau hoped that some leveling of economic differences in society would occur. In contrast to the aggregate, individualistic society created by Locke's social contract, Rousseau's social contract produced an organic, indivisible whole in which individualism tended to be lost.

The FRENCH REVOLUTION witnessed a tug-of-war between the liberal and radical philosophies of equality. Most moderate liberal revolutionaries called for the establishment of legal equality, but shied away from democracy in either direct or indirect form. They wished to make political rights and equality dependent on the ownership of property. American liberals, in contrast, thought about creating a property qualification but ultimately rejected the idea. All political rights in both revolutions were exclusively reserved for males. Only a handful of revolutionaries called for the extension of political rights to women.

Radical French revolutionaries such as Maximilien ROBESPIERRE and François-Noel BABEUF adopted the ideas of Rousseau. In their zeal to impose equality on French citizens, they suppressed individual freedoms and lapsed into a terrorizing control.

Certain theorists of the Enlightenment had always remained chary of government based on equality. MON-

TESQUIEU, the upholder of limited monarchy, is perhaps the most important example. He believed that the privileged aristocracy had a critical role to play in preventing tyranny, and that equality could only produce tyranny in the form of corrupt democracy. It is a mistake, therefore, to see the Enlightenment as a movement in which intellectual leaders unanimously supported notions of political equality. Whatever their philosophical views, many of them ultimately shied away from egalitarian policies when such policies were being considered for practical application.

See also LONDON CORRESPONDING SOCIETY.

Further reading: John Locke, *An Essay Concerning Human Understanding,* ed. A. D. Woozley (New York: New American Library, 1964); Jean-Jacques Rousseau, *The Social Contract and Discourses,* tr. and intro. G. D. H. Cole (London: Everyman's Library, 1973); Franco Venturi, *Utopia and Reform in the Enlightenment* (Cambridge: Cambridge University Press, 1971).

Equiano, Olaudah (1745–1797) *slave, later free man, and abolitionist*

According to his autobiography, Olaudah Equiano was born in Africa, in what is now Nigeria. His autobiography provides an account of his capture, his experiences as a slave, and his views on slaves' rights and the abolition of SLAVERY. Though questionable in the veracity of some of its details, Equiano's autobiography is valuable nevertheless because its compelling account of the hardships suffered by a slave had a profound impact on movements to abolish slavery in the latter part of the 18th century.

In his narrative, Equiano states that he lived peacefully in the Kingdom of Benin until he was 11, when he and his sister were kidnapped while the adults in his village were at work in the fields. He was separated from his sister and transferred from master to master until he ended up on the coast. There, he was put on board a slave ship bound for Barbados.

From Barbados, Equiano was transported to Virginia, where he briefly worked on a plantation before he was bought by Michael Henry Pascal, a lieutenant in the Royal Navy. Equiano accompanied Pascal to ENGLAND in 1757. While there, Equiano attended church for the first time and was baptized in February 1759 during a brief stay in LONDON. He also began attending school, but his formal education was cut short when Pascal returned to sea.

During his time at sea, Equiano traveled extensively around the Mediterranean, surviving combat on several occasions. He also learned to write and picked up some basic arithmetic. After his time with Pascal, Equiano was sold twice in quick succession, and he ended up in the West Indies, where his experiences as a slave on a large plantation shaped his criticisms of the institution and laid the foundation of his abolitionist stance. In 1763, his master put Equiano on one of his ships, and Equiano

Frontispiece of Olaudah Equiano's autobiography. The book provides an account of his capture, his experiences as a slave, and his views on slaves' rights and the abolition of slavery. It had a profound impact on movements to abolish slavery in the latter part of the 18th century. *(By permission of The British Library)*

managed to save enough money through small-scale mercantile activity to buy his freedom in July 1766.

Freedom for Equiano was just as perilous as slavery. He justifiably feared that he would be kidnapped and reenslaved. Equiano gradually made his way back to Europe, and, after a brief stay in London, which he made his home base, he traveled extensively. He sailed around the Mediterranean and to the Caribbean, and he traveled as a member of John Constantine Phipps's expedition to the area around the North Pole in 1773.

Equiano met an important figure of the English antislavery movement, Granville Sharp, in 1774. During the mid-1780s, Equiano became increasingly active as an abolitionist. He addressed a congregation of QUAKERS in PHILADELPHIA in 1785 and served as the government commissioner for an English expedition to Sierra Leone in 1787. He first published his autobiography, *The Interesting Narrative of the Life of Olaudah Equiano,* in 1789. He died on March 31, 1797, with Sharp at his bedside. His autobiography had gone through eight English-language editions and had been translated into Dutch, German, and Russian.

The autobiography not only narrated Equiano's life in rich detail, it also lent his eloquent voice to the anti-slavery movement. Some of the details of the *Narrative,* such as Equiano's claim that he was born in Africa, have been called into question. Even so, the work makes a powerful case against slavery, and its author's claim that it was autobiographical no doubt added to its impact. Equiano wrote from a viewpoint strongly influenced by his experiences and by his devout Christianity. He often contrasted the behavior of Europeans with that of Africans, for example, in his forthright criticism of the Europeans he encountered on the African coast and in Barbados who behaved with "brutal cruelty," unlike the African masters who treated him humanely. He also did not hesitate to criticize the hypocrisy he saw in Christian civilization, where slaves were abused and tortured by Christian masters. English abolitionists acknowledged the galvanizing effect Equiano's account had on their movement, crediting it with helping to bring about the motion for the abolition of the slave trade in the British Parliament in 1791. Although it failed, the motion marked an important step in the move toward abolition.

Further reading: Olaudah Equiano, *The Interesting Narrative and Other Writings* (New York: Penguin Classics, 1998).

Essay on Crimes and Punishments (Italian title: *Dei delitti e delle pene*)　A treatise on criminal justice, originally published anonymously in 1764 by a Tuscan printer. Its author was the Milanese aristocrat, Cesare Bonesana, marchese di BECCARIA. Beccaria did not produce the book in isolation. He was a member of a group of intellectuals in MILAN who regularly met for discussions at the coffeehouse operated by Pietro VERRI and his brother Alessandro VERRI. There, Beccaria honed his ideas about reform of the legal system. Pietro Verri prodded Beccaria to publish the treatise and served as a kind of editor and publicity manager for the project. The decision to publish anonymously stemmed from fear of prosecution by the authorities in Milan. When, instead, they received the book favorably, Beccaria publicly admitted his authorship.

The *Essay on Crimes and Punishments* generated animated public discussion immediately after its appearance. In just 18 months, it passed through six Italian editions, numerous French ones, and was being prepared for English publication. Widespread diffusion occurred throughout Europe after the appearance of the 1766 French translation by Abbé Morelly. Reform-oriented monarchs greeted the work no less enthusiastically than the PHILOSOPHES. Beccaria became the hero and darling of enlightened society.

Beccaria structures the arguments of the *Essay* according to the geometric method of René DESCARTES. He begins with one general utilitarian principle, the notion of "the greatest happiness shared by the greatest number." According to Beccaria, human laws, necessary for the preservation of the social contract, should be derived from this maxim. Furthermore, if laws violate the social contract, they are by nature unjust. Beccaria then proceeds to derive certain consequences for the administration of a legal system from his general principle. First, he stresses the necessity of a SEPARATION OF POWERS; legislative and judicial functions must not be combined in the same person or institution. The legislator may not determine whether a crime has been committed; that is a matter for the magistracy. Similarly, judges must not usurp legislative functions by interpreting the law or meting out punishments. In court, points of evidence must not be derived one from another. Rather, the summation of independent proofs will determine whether a crime has been committed. Verdicts should be delivered by juries of peers, drawn by lot. If laws are clear and proofs precisely constructed, then the formation of a fair judgment requires only the exercise of that innate human quality, "ordinary good sense." Thus, ordinary people are wholly capable of rendering just verdicts.

The major portion of Beccaria's treatise explores the relationships between crimes and their punishments. Throughout this section, the argument continues to draw on geometric reasoning for its structure, pointing out general characteristics of crime-punishment relationships, and then adding specific details. Beccaria offers a classification of crimes and appropriate punishments that includes a stinging criticism of capital punishment.

Beccaria offered arguments against the death penalty based on the POLITICAL THEORY and sensation PSYCHOLOGY of John LOCKE, on historical experience, and on utilitarian principles. He compared the death penalty to war, asserting that it is nothing more than a state engaging in war against its errant citizens. He pointed out the absurdity of systems that make suicide a crime but that nevertheless allow governments to kill their citizens. He also argued that the death penalty has very little deterrent power, being much less frightening to most people than the spectacle of a long, painful imprisonment. Finally, he argued that the transformation of executions into public spectacles actually undermines respect for laws, for lawmakers, and for the justice system.

The section on crime-punishment relationships closes by stressing the importance of crime prevention. Clear laws, EDUCATION, the reward of VIRTUE, and proper control of the magistracy will function to prevent criminal behavior. The treatise concludes, in the Cartesian spirit, with a concise statement of the theorem yielded by the general utilitarian principle with which the book began. Punishments, Beccaria declares, must be "public, prompt, necessary, proportionate to the crime, the least possible in the given circumstances, dictated by laws."

The *Essay on Crimes and Punishments* draws on theories fundamental to 18th-century thought. The notion of social contract, the stress on law as a creation of human convention rather than of divine revelation, the use of the psychological theory of the passions as an explanation for the effects of law on behavior, the application of the geometric method of reasoning, and the adoption of UTILITY as the central governing principle of human relations all identify this work as one belonging to the ENLIGHTENMENT. As such, it stands as a monument to the creative potential of 18th-century intellectual convictions. But the *Essay* is more than a relic of this earlier era. Its criticisms of traditional European forms of criminal justice remain fresh and relevant in the modern world. The *Essay*, indeed, stands as one of the lasting contributions of the Enlightenment to the modern world.

See also CAPITAL PUNISHMENT; JUSTICE AND THE LAW.

Esterházy, Miklós József (English: Nicholas Joseph) (1714–1790) *Hungarian nobleman, prince of the Hapsburg Empire, and patron of Franz Joseph Haydn*

Prince Esterházy was called "the Magnificent" on account of the opulence of his lifestyle. He was part of a family of dedicated amateur musicians and music patrons, four of whom aided HAYDN: Miklós himself, his son, his grandson, and his brother. Miklós's great-grandfather Prince Pál (Paul) had been a composer. Like many members of the Hungarian nobility, the Esterházy family adopted German, the language of their Hapsburg overlords, as their court language. The family took the name Esterházy in the 16th century, when one of their members, Ferenc Zerházy (1563–94), received a title of nobility. Esterháza, the source of the name, was the family's summer estate on the Neusiedler See. Prince Miklós Jószef constructed a magnificent new residence at Esterháza that included two music rooms, an OPERA house, and a marionette theater. The design of the estate echoed the BAROQUE STYLE and magnificence of Louis XIV's Versailles Palace. After its completion, Miklós spent most of his time there, accompanied by his household staff, his orchestra, and his opera singers. He himself played the cello, the viola da gamba, and the baryton (viola di bordone).

Franz Josef Haydn first received employment from Miklós's elder brother, Prince Pál Anton, in 1761, and when Miklós succeeded his brother in 1762, he continued the composer's tenure. Haydn directed the Esterházy orchestra, produced operas, and composed hundreds of compositions that included 82 symphonies and nearly 200 baryton trios. When Miklós died in 1790, Haydn was released from his duties in the princely household and moved to Vienna. Later generations of the Esterházy family continued the tradition of music patronage by supporting musicians such as Wolfgang Amadeus MOZART, Franz Peter Schubert (1797–1828), and Franz Liszt (1811–86).

ethics *See* MORAL PHILOSOPHY.

Etruria works English ceramics factory established by Josiah WEDGWOOD and Thomas Bentley in 1769. The factory specialized in producing neoclassical ornamental ceramics. Its focus on the legacy of antiquity was reflected in the name *Etruria*, which was intended to evoke images of ancient Etruscan artifacts. Wedgwood developed an interest in antiquity through contact with Bentley. He adapted his ceramic shapes and decoration to classical ideas. His designs were simple and inspired by geometric symmetry. Specific pottery lines included the black basalt and jasperware designs, both of which utilized classically inspired forms and motifs. During the 1770s, the Etruria works began producing all the Wedgwood products including the famed ivory-colored Queen's ware pottery.

See also NEOCLASSICISM.

Eugène of Savoy, Prince (1663–1736) *brilliant military general, commander in chief of the Austrian Hapsburg armies, president of the Hapsburg imperial war council, regent of Milan, governor of the Austrian Netherlands (1716–24), and renowned patron of the arts and architecture*

Prince Eugène was one of the greatest military commanders in Europe during the late 17th century and early 18th century. FREDERICK II (THE GREAT) OF PRUSSIA and Maurice of Saxony, both outstanding military leaders, considered themselves pupils of Prince Eugène.

François-Eugène de Savoie-Carignan (Prince Eugène of Savoy) was essentially a mercenary soldier. His father was Eugène-Maurice de Savoie-Carignan, count of Soissons, head of the French branch of the Savoyard ruling family and cousin of Charles Emmanuel II of Savoy. His mother was Olympia Mancini, niece of Cardinal Mazarin, the last great prime minister of FRANCE. Prince Eugène spent his childhood and youth at Versailles learning military skills and other skills considered essential for princes of the era. LOUIS XIV declined to give him a commission in the French army, so Prince Eugène offered his services to the Austrian Hapsburgs in their struggles against the Ottoman Turks. When he distinguished himself in the great Battle of Kahlenberg (1683), the battle that saved VIENNA from Turkish conquest, he was fighting as an unpaid army volunteer.

Having revealed his military expertise at Kahlenberg, Prince Eugène received the command of the Kufstein dragoon regiment and embarked on what would become an outstanding career. He was promoted to major general in 1685, to lieutenant field marshal in 1688, and to lieutenant general field marshal of the HAPSBURG EMPIRE in 1706. He was named president of the imperial war council during the War of the Spanish Succession (1700–13) and held that position for the remainder of his life.

Prince Eugène earned military fame by gaining significant victories at Zenta (1697), Blenheim (1704), Turin (1706), Oudenaarde (1708), Malplaquet (1709), Peterwardein (1716), and Belgrade (1718). He advised the Hapsburg emperor Charles VI to accept the terms of peace proposed at Utrecht in 1713 and participated in the negotiations for the Treaty of Rastatt in 1714. His many victories in the War of the Spanish Succession gained the Italian duchy of MILAN and the Spanish Netherlands (subsequently called the AUSTRIAN NETHERLANDS) for the Hapsburgs. His victories in the eastern parts of Europe extinguished the persistent threat to the Hapsburg Empire posed by the Ottoman Empire and brought HUNGARY, Transylvania, northern Serbia, Belgrade, and Little Wallachia into the Hapsburg fold (Treaty of Carlowitz, 1699, and Peace of Passorowitz, 1718). Thus, Prince Eugène of Savoy was a major actor in the early 18th-century consolidation of Hapsburg power.

As a mercenary soldier, Eugène could have offered his services to any European prince. The practice of maintaining standing armies was only beginning to be established. Thus, rulers turned to great independent soldiers to provide them with troops and leadership. Eugène chose to serve the Austrian Hapsburgs, in part, because they offered opportunities to him unavailable in France, but also because he considered the Hapsburgs the key protectors of Christian Europe.

Prince Eugène, although reputedly a rather simple and markedly pious man, was a great art connoisseur. Johann FISCHER VON ERLACH and Lukas HILDEBRANDT built his Viennese town palace, and Hildebrandt created the beautiful Belvedere Palace for him in the Viennese suburbs. Both buildings are outstanding examples of 18th-century Viennese late BAROQUE STYLE architecture.

Prince Eugène was also a substantial patron of the intellectuals who helped to create the early phases of the ENLIGHTENMENT. He protected and supported the German philosopher Gottfried Wilhelm LEIBNIZ, who thanked him by dedicating the *Monadologie* (Monadology) to him. As governor in the Austrian Netherlands, Prince Eugène protected adherents of JANSENISM and facilitated the spread of those doctrines into German-speaking lands. With his French origins and education, his Austrian and German loyalties, and his Italian and French artistic tastes, Prince Eugène served as one of the great international, cosmopolitan figures of his era.

Euler, Leonhard (1707–1783) *Swiss mathematician*
Euler was a figure of major importance for the development of mathematics during the ENLIGHTENMENT, for the dissemination of Western scientific discoveries to Russia, and for the popularization of physics and mathematical philosophy. The marquis de LAPLACE, acknowledging Euler's great role, called him the tutor of all the mathematicians of his time.

Leonhard Euler grew up in a small village outside Basel, SWITZERLAND, where his father was a Protestant minister. He received his early mathematical instruction from his father, who had been a student of Jakob I BERNOULLI. At the University of Basel, Euler studied the humanities, philosophy, and theology in addition to mathematics. He maintained his broad intellectual interests and religious commitment throughout his life.

Euler began teaching physics and mathematics at the SAINT PETERSBURG ACADEMY OF SCIENCES in 1730 and remained active as a teacher even after losing the sight in one of his eyes. His colleagues included Daniel BERNOULLI, Johann II Bernoulli, and Joseph-Nicolas DELISLE. In 1741, wary of the Russian political situation, Euler transferred to BERLIN, where FREDERICK II (THE GREAT) installed him as director of the mathematics section of the BERLIN ACADEMY. As a friend of Pierre de MAUPERTUIS, the first president of the academy, Euler also served in a variety of administrative capacities and assisted with the library and PUBLISHING ventures.

Relations between Frederick the Great and Euler cooled on account of their personal and philosophical differences. As a result, in 1766, Euler returned to SAINT PETERSBURG, where he continued an active scientific life. He died suddenly in 1783 of a massive stroke.

Euler, one of the greatest mathematicians of the Enlightenment, demonstrated in several areas how the enlightened goal of viewing the universe in mathematical terms could be approached: He used mathematics to solve both theoretical and practical scientific problems. His greatest contribution, however, lay in his systematic elaboration of mathematics.

Specifically, Euler developed calculus to new levels and contributed to number theory, introduced many notational forms still in use—e for natural logarithms, f and parentheses to denote functions, and i as symbol for the square root of -1—and contributed to mechanics and ASTRONOMY with his theories on the motion of solid bodies and on lunar or planetary orbits. He also published contributions to ballistic theory (principles of artillery); prepared a book with tables on insurance mathematics; and wrote a treatise on navigation and shipbuilding.

Euler served the equally enlightened cause of popularizing mathematics and natural philosophy by making it available to the general reading public. His *Lettres à une princesse d'Allemagne sur divers sujets de physique et de philosophie* (Letters to a German princess on diverse topics of physics and philosophy; 1765) went through multiple 18th-century editions in French, English, German, Russian, Dutch, and Swedish. In addition, because he maintained correspondence with the Academy of Saint

Petersburg during his 25 years in Berlin, Euler also served the cause of spreading western European scientific knowledge into Russia.

Euler played a role in several significant scientific debates of the Enlightenment. These focused not only on disagreements over scientific principles, but inevitably also raised questions of broader religious, theological, and philosophical implication. SCIENCE in the Enlightenment was not a wholly secular enterprise.

In the dispute (1747) over the monadology of Gottfried Wilhelm LEIBNIZ and Christian WOLFF, Euler, as a mechanical philosopher loyal to CARTESIANISM, opposed the Leibnizian party. In the quarrel (1751) over Maupertuis's principle of least action, Euler defended Maupertuis against attacks by VOLTAIRE and partisans of Leibniz.

Euler published prolifically: More than 500 books and articles appeared during his lifetime. Of special importance or interest are *Introductio in analysin infinitorum* (Introduction to the analysis of infinites; 1748); *Institutiones calculi differentialis* (Methods of differential calculus; 1755); *Theoria motus corporum solidorum seu rigidorum* (Theory of the motion of solid or rigid bodies; 1765); *Gedancken von den Elementen der Cörper* (Thoughts on the elements of bodies; 1746); and the *Exposé concernant l'examen de la lettre de M. de Leibnitz* (Statement concerning the examination of the letter of Mr. Leibniz; 1752). Other notable works were *Theoria motuum lunae* (Theory of lunar motion; 1772); *Institutiones calculi integralis* (Methods of integral calculus; 1768–70); *Scientia navalis* (Naval science; 1773); and *Éclaircissemens sur les établissemens publics* (Explanations about public establishments; 1776). Euler corresponded with more than 300 individuals throughout Europe, including Johann I Bernoulli, Daniel Bernoulli, J.-N. Delisle, Alexis CLAIRAUT, Jean Le Rond d'ALEMBERT, Joseph-Louis LAGRANGE, J. H. Lambert, and M. V. Lomonosov.

See also MATHEMATICS AND MECHANICS.

F

Fahrenheit, Daniel Gabriel (1686–1736) *instrument maker and experimental physicist*

Fahrenheit was a native of GERMANY who settled in the city of AMSTERDAM in the UNITED PROVINCES OF THE NETHERLANDS. The inventor of the Fahrenheit temperature scale, he built his work on that of an unknown Danish experimenter named Olaus Roemer. Roemer had invented an alcohol thermometer and a temperature scale but had not published his findings. Fahrenheit learned about them in 1708 when he met Roemer in Copenhagen. Fahrenheit built both an alcohol thermometer and a mercury thermometer. He adapted Roemer's temperature scale to create his own Fahrenheit scale. The peculiarities of Fahrenheit's scale, that is, the adoption of 212 degrees for boiling point and 32 degrees for freezing point, stemmed from his interpretation of Roemer's scale.

Fahrenheit recognized that the boiling point of water varies with atmospheric pressure. He invented a hypsometric thermometer that allowed the determination of atmospheric pressure directly from the boiling point of water. He also invented a hydrometer. His work illustrates the close relationship that existed between instrument technology and experimental SCIENCE during the ENLIGHTENMENT. Fahrenheit's instruments assisted in making the quantification of natural phenomena a possibility.

Fahrenheit was elected to the ROYAL SOCIETY OF LONDON and also worked personally with the great Dutch scientists Hermann BOERHAAVE, Willem Jacob's GRAVESANDE, and Pieter van MUSSCHENBROEK.

See also TECHNOLOGY AND INSTRUMENTATION.

Falconet, Étienne Maurice (1716–1791) *French sculptor*

Falconet trained first as a carpenter, then studied sculpture under J. B. Lemoyne. In 1744, he was elected to the Academy of Fine Arts.

Falconet became an outstanding ROCOCO sculptor and was particularly favored by Madame de POMPADOUR. With her support, he became director of sculpture (1757–66) at the new SÈVRES porcelain factory. Falconet lived in Russia from 1766 until 1778, then returned to PARIS, where he died in 1791.

Falconet produced many models for Sèvres porcelains. The *Pendule des trois Grâces* (Clock of the three Graces) is particularly noted for its delicacy. Other notable creations were *Milon de Crotone* (1754), *La baigneuse* (The female bather; 1757), *Pygmalion et Galatée* (Pygmalion and Galatea; 1763), and *L'hiver* (Winter; 1765). Falconet's outstanding bronze equestrian statue of PETER I (THE GREAT) in SAINT PETERSBURG was commissioned by Czarina CATHERINE II (THE GREAT). Falconet also left writings about art and AESTHETICS that were published as *Oeuvres Littéraires* (Literary Works; 1781–82). He corresponded with Dénis DIDEROT about a statue of Emperor Marcus Aurelius in ROME. These letters were not published until the 20th century.

Faust A versiform drama by the German writer Johann Wolfgang von GOETHE, first published between 1808 and 1832. The complete text carries the title *Faust: Eine Tragödie* (Faust: a tragedy). The first English translation appeared in 1838 as *Faust Rendered into English Verse*.

Faust reflected a lifetime of thought about the relations among knowledge, power, the masculine and the feminine, and divine truths. The story is based on the legends of Dr. Johann Faust, a practitioner of ALCHEMY and astrology who lived in GERMANY during the first half of the 16th century. Like many astrologers and alchemists, Faust was reputed to practice magic.

The Faust legends were collected and printed in 1580 as *The History of Dr. Johann Faustus.* They told the story of a scholar who made a pact with the devil, exchanging his soul for knowledge and power. Christopher Marlowe, the Elizabethan dramatist, used the legends for his play *Doctor Faustus* (1604), and in the 19th century, the romantic composers Hector Berlioz and Charles Gounod based famous operas on them.

In Goethe's drama, Faust seeks transcendent knowledge, that knowledge of essences and of the whole course of HISTORY that normally eludes the human mind. This is the knowledge known only by God and occasionally glimpsed by people of GENIUS in contact with the SUBLIME. It is not the simple knowledge of daily existence, dependent on sensation and REASON. Faust makes a bargain with Mephistopheles, the devil, who promises to give him the desired transcendent knowledge. But Mephistopheles also warns Faust that once he has obtained this knowledge, he will necessarily die.

A female figure, Margarete (also called Gretchen), represents for Faust and Goethe a degree of desired but unattainable perfection. Faust cannot possess Margarete sexually without corrupting her and destroying the very perfection he desires. Nevertheless, he enters into a sexual relationship with her. Margarete conceives a child and kills it because it is illegitimate. For this act she is condemned to death by earthly authorities, but she is forgiven by God and allowed to enter heaven after her death. Faust, however, cannot enter heaven because he has bound himself to earth in making the bargain with Mephistopheles.

Faust's bargain with the devil gives him powers denied normal men, and he does not hesitate to abuse them at times. However, as his life draws to a close, he begins to understand the mistakes he has made by wishing to transcend the knowledge and laws of the natural world in which human beings live. He begins to recognize the value of human relationships (he had failed to treat Margarete in human terms) and generally breaks through to a deeper form of wisdom. Upon his death, Faust is not damned as might have been expected, but rather, through the intercession of Margarete (the perfect feminine), experiences a kind of salvation in which he progresses to a higher level of existence.

Readers of the Faust legends in the 16th and 17th centuries saw the tale as a warning about the dangers of overstepping human limits. But Goethe and his generation viewed the legends as an example of the natural dilemmas that face human beings striving for PROGRESS

and perfection. For them Faust represented the heroic individual who frees himself from the shackles of authority and begins the long ascent toward perfection, no matter what the potential consequences.

Faust, then, served as a literary symbol of the striving of German intellectuals during the closing decades of the 18th century. In his retelling of the Faustian legend, Goethe joined major themes of the German AUFKLÄRUNG to create a drama with stimulating and compelling messages. His themes would eventually be picked up and transformed during the era of ROMANTICISM, but they owed their inspiration and specific form to the ENLIGHTENMENT.

Favart, Charles-Simon (1710–1792) *French dramatist and theatrical producer, a master of vaudeville*
The Favart family had a tradition in vaudeville, which Charles-Simon Favart's father abandoned. Instead, he took work as a pastry chef, a trade his son also entered. The young Favart, however, used his earnings to support forays into theater and eventually returned to the long-standing professional traditions of his ancestors.

Favart established his career with a series of vaudeville pieces, but fame eluded him until 1741, when he produced *La chercheuse d'esprit* (The female seeker of mind). One of his innovations involved the use of historically correct costumes. In 1743, Favart became stage manager of the Opéra-Comique in PARIS and produced such successful shows that in 1745 his competitors, the directors of the Comédie-Italienne and the Comédie-Française, banded together to secure closure of the Opéra-Comique.

The theater reopened in 1752, but it was not until 1758 that Favart assumed the directorship of the company. In the interim, he had developed his talents to their height with productions such as *Les amours de Bastien et Bastienne* (The loves of Bastien and Bastienne; 1753, later set to music by MOZART), a parody of the opera *Le devin du village* (The village fortune-teller) by Jean-Jacques ROUSSEAU, and *La noce interrompue* (The interrupted wedding), a parody of Philippe Quinault's *Alceste*, set to music by Jean-Baptiste Lully.

When he resumed work at the Opéra-Comique, Favart found that the taste of the Parisian public had moved away from vaudeville toward *comédie à ariettes* (light opera). Favart never really mastered the form, but his career continued to flourish. Under his direction, the Opéra-Comique and the Comédie-Italienne became one enterprise. During these years, Favart wrote the *Correspondance avec le Comte Durazzo* (Correspondence with Count Durazzo), a form of theater criticism and poetry for the enlightened literary salons. He also directed productions for the royal family at Versailles, Fontainebleau, and Marly. Favart died in 1792.

See also SOCIAL INSTITUTIONS OF THE ENLIGHTENMENT.

Febronianism An 18th-century German version of JANSENISM. A published work by Johann Nikolaus von Hontheim, under the pseudonym of Justinus Febronius, spelled out the position of the doctrine. It concerned the constitutional organization of the Catholic Church. This book, *De Statu Ecclesiae et Legitima Potestate Romani Pontificis* (Concerning the state of the church and the legitimate power of the Roman pope), was published in 1763.

Throughout the history of ROMAN CATHOLICISM, conflicts had occurred over the nature of its constitution and the respective roles of the pope and the bishops. The conflicts can be summarized in the question that follows: Would the church be constituted as an absolute monarchy or as a species of aristocracy, governed by its equivalent to the nobility, the council of bishops? Although the popes tried to function as absolute monarchs, their assertions were often opposed by the bishops. The latter could appeal to the tradition of church councils to assert that, at most, the pope should be a limited monarch, responsible to a council of bishops. This conciliar organization, with sovereignty lying in the hands of the bishops, was called an episcopal constitution. Clearly, the outlines of these arguments between pope and bishops resembled the 18th-century secular quarrels about the constitution of governments.

Febronius, following one tendency in 18th-century Jansenist thought, combined calls for an episcopal constitution of the church with support for the idea that the national Catholic churches should control their own affairs. This idea of national control dovetailed nicely with imperial and monarchical claims to the right of dominating the churches within their realms. Full-blown Febronianism called for control of each national church by its separate council of bishops and for concerted action between these councils and secular rulers in order to protect the churches from papal domination.

JOSEPH II OF AUSTRIA and Prince KAUNITZ readily recognized the utility of this Febronianism for their ecclesiastical policies. Hence, they supported the movement, combining its Jansenist vision of ecclesiastical polity with the rational ideals of the ENLIGHTENMENT to produce JOSEPHINISM.

Fénelon, François de Salignac de la Mothe
(1651–1715) *French Roman Catholic archbishop who was a supporter of Quietism and its major practitioner, Madame de Guyon*

Fénelon was the scion of an old but impoverished noble family from the Périgord region of southwestern FRANCE. He was the 13th of his father's 15 children. Fénelon attended the seminary of Saint Sulpice in PARIS and entered the priesthood as a young man of 24. He served three years as a priest for the parish of Saint-Sulpice before he received an appointment as head of the Convent of New Catholics, a school for girls recently converted to ROMAN CATHOLICISM from CALVINISM. He worked at the convent from 1678 to 1689.

In 1687, Fénelon published his *Traité de l'éducation des filles* (Treatise on the education of girls), which brought him quickly to the attention of Madame de Maintenon, the companion of LOUIS XIV. From 1685 to 1686, Fénelon served in a Catholic mission to the Huguenot regions of southwestern France. Designed by Bishop BOSSUET in the aftermath of the revocation of the Edict of Nantes (1685), this mission aimed at converting French HUGUENOTS back to Catholicism.

Fénelon cherished the ideal of reuniting all Protestants with the Catholic Church, but he disapproved of the forced conversions and other military tactics that were being used. The PHILOSOPHES revered his memory on account of the gentleness of his approach to the perceived problem of religious disunity. He counseled the approach of making France a more attractive, economic place for Huguenots so that they would not feel compelled to emigrate. Yet his attitude toward the Huguenots themselves was one of impatience and contempt. His tolerance stemmed more from pragmatism than from moral conviction.

Fénelon served from 1689 until 1699 as the preceptor (tutor) to Louis, duke of Burgundy, grandson of Louis XIV and heir apparent to the throne of France, and transformed the spoiled child into a devoted, respectful admirer. He also gained a seat in the French Academy (1693) and a nomination to the archbishopric of Cambrai. Bishop Bossuet consecrated him in the latter position on July 10, 1695.

For the duke of Burgundy, Fénelon wrote his philosophical novel *Les aventures de Télémaque* (The adventures of Telemachus; 1699). It aimed at preparing the young, future king for the duties of royal office. The book describes the imaginary journey of Telemachus in search of his father, Ulysses. The goddess Minerva (wisdom) accompanies Telemachus throughout his travels in a disguise as Mentor. In the course of the journey, the young Telemachus gains wisdom by observing people and places but also by making his own errors. He sees the sorry results of the acts of the wicked king, Pygmalion, and savors the delights of an earthly utopia, Bétique. He also experiences more realistic situations in the kingdom of Salente. Salente can be viewed as an allegorical allusion to the kingdom of France. The king of Salente, Idomeneo, has fallen into a baroque love of grandeur, but he is open to suggestions for reform. He accepts the counsel offered by Mentor. Mentor outlines a series of economic policies and basic social values that are, in fact, the policies Fénelon believed should be instigated in France.

What happens in Salente when Mentor's policies are implemented illustrates Fénelon's vision of what could happen in a reformed France. Agriculture flourishes as a result of state support, business and commerce operate without restrictions, and foreigners are welcomed into the kingdom. As a result, the kingdom prospers and its people become wealthy. But life is simple, devoid of ostentation and luxurious consumption.

Salente demonstrates the economic benefits to be derived from the reforms proposed by the PHYSIOCRATS. It also represents a kingdom whose ruler avoids the evils of ABSOLUTISM, opting instead for a limited monarchy. Furthermore, it is a kingdom where the evils of warfare are recognized and therefore avoided whenever possible.

Fénelon had already developed his reform proposals in a 1694 manuscript, the *Letter to Louis XIV*. It is not known, however, whether the letter was ever delivered to Louis XIV. Jean Le Rond d'ALEMBERT referred to it in his 1774 *Éloge de Fénelon* (Eulogy of Fénelon), and the first known publication of the letter was in 1785, in a posthumous edition of d'Alembert's *History of the Members of the French Academy*.

Fénelon spelled out a definite reform program in two additional works written for the duke of Burgundy, the *Examination of Conscience on the Duties of Royalty* and the *Chaulnes Tables, or Plans of Government*. He never published these works himself, but in 1746 the *Examination* appeared in French and English editions, both published out of London. In 1775, LOUIS XVI requested its publication in France.

In 1688, just before he began his service as preceptor to the heir apparent, Fénelon met the religious mystic Madame de Guyon, a follower of Quietism. Under her influence Fénelon became a strong supporter of the subjective, inward Christian piety practiced by Quietists. Fénelon introduced Madame de Maintenon to the Quietist aproach, and for a brief time, she allowed him to teach its principles at Saint Cyr, her school for girls.

Bishop Bossuet opposed Quietism, believing that its inward, individual piety constituted a threat to the established institutions of the Catholic Church. Bossuet and Fénelon became embroiled in a bitter public quarrel over the merits and dangers of Quietism. The dispute permanently ruptured their friendship, robbing Fénelon of the support of one of the most powerful clergymen in France.

Louis XIV sided with Bossuet in this quarrel. In this period of his reign, Louis XIV tended to view any religious dissension, whether from Protestants or from Catholics, as a threat to his absolute rule. Consequently, he exiled Fénelon from Versailles, confining him in perpetuity to Cambrai. Fénelon, indeed, never returned to the French court, but rather devoted his remaining years to the spiritual and administrative work of his archdiocese.

However, the consequences of the quarrel over Quietism continued to unfold, and in early 1699, the pope, under pressure from French diplomats, reluctantly condemned Fénelon's masterpiece of Quietist inspiration, *Explications des maximes des saints sur la vie intérieure*

(Maxims of the saints on the interior life; 1697). Fénelon himself, however, was neither punished nor imprisoned. The condemnation caused him to make a public announcement of his total submission to papal authority.

In general, Fénelon was a man of innovative intellectual convictions. Historians consider him a key figure in the early 18th-century ARISTOCRATIC RESURGENCE. He was a supporter of modernism in the literary and aesthetic QUARREL BETWEEN THE ANCIENTS AND THE MODERNS. His acceptance of Quietism placed him solidly in the camp of an emerging form of religious piety that stressed subjective, personal, and direct experience of God as the most fruitful approach to Christian spiritual practices. His pragmatic condemnation of forced religious conversions and his gentle manner of handling the followers of JANSENISM, whose religious positions he believed were erroneous, helped to promote the idea of religious TOLERATION within certain French Catholic circles. In short, Fénelon proposed reforms and supported positions whose general outlines suggested the programs that would emerge during the ENLIGHTENMENT. As such, he is one of the great transitional, creative figures who helped French intellectuals move from the 17th century into the century of *les lumières*.

See also PIETISM; QUAKERS; RELIGION.

Further reading: Gerald R. Cragg, *The Church and the Age of Reason, 1648–1789* (New York: Penguin Books, 1970); Robert Palmer, *Catholics and Unbelievers in Eighteenth-Century France* (New York: Cooper Square, 1961).

Ferguson, Adam (1723–1816) *Scottish historian and moral philosopher*
Ferguson followed his father's footsteps into the Scottish Presbyterian ministry, having first received an education at St. Andrew's University and the University of Edinburgh. He served as both deputy chaplain and chaplain of the Scottish Highland "Black Watch" regiment. Ferguson was related to the chemist Joseph BLACK both by descent through his mother's family and by marriage.

Ferguson received a position in 1757 replacing David HUME as the chief librarian for the Advocates' (Lawyers') Library in EDINBURGH. The University of Edinburgh appointed him in 1759 to a chair in NATURAL PHILOSOPHY and in 1764 to the chair of pneumatics and MORAL PHILOSOPHY. Ferguson taught moral philosophy at the university until 1785, when ill health forced him to retire. He spent the next 30 years in semiretirement, writing and continuing his various other activities on behalf of the Scottish intellectual community.

Ferguson was a founding member of the ROYAL SOCIETY OF EDINBURGH and counted among his friends people such as David Hume, Henry Home, Lord Kames, William ROBERTSON, Adam SMITH, and Edward GIBBON. He was also an honorary member of the BERLIN ACADEMY.

Ferguson wrote four major works: an *Essay on the History of Civil Society* (1767); *Institutes of Moral Philosophy* (1769); *The History of the Progress and Termination of the Roman Republic* (1783); and *Principles of Moral and Political Science* (1792). Of these books, the *Essay on the History of Civil Society* was the most influential during the ENLIGHTENMENT and is still considered Ferguson's most important work.

Ferguson conceived of himself as a student of human nature and approached the subject from the standpoint of disciplines as diverse as ANTHROPOLOGY, HISTORY, PSYCHOLOGY, RELIGION, and ECONOMICS. He believed that the only way to understand humanity is to study the individual as a member of a community. In fact, for Ferguson community defines the essence of what it is to be human, for it is in community that people exercise their special gift of language.

Ferguson's *History of Civil Society*, consciously modeled after the SPIRIT OF LAWS by MONTESQUIEU, offered a natural history of human society, tracing its supposed development from the savage state through stages of animal grazing, agriculture, and commerce. In the theory of society that emerged from this history, Ferguson drew sharp distinctions between physical law and moral law and between the cultural factors and the biological factors that act in human beings. He therefore rejected any tendency on the part of moral philosophers to reduce moral behavior to the simple operation of natural physical laws.

Ferguson envisioned society as a place of conflict between two principles, one of union and one of "rivalship," whose interaction drives social developments. He also provided what Karl Marx considered the first modern statement of the division of labor in society.

Ferguson's books were translated quickly from English into both French and German. Some appeared also in Italian and Russian. In GERMANY, translations by Christian GARVE created an enthusiastic following that included Friedrich SCHILLER, Friedrich Heinrich JACOBI, and Johann Gottfried HERDER. The radical French PHILOSOPHES associated with Baron d'HOLBACH also admired his work. Thus, although Ferguson is only beginning to receive much attention from modern scholars, his works enjoyed a high reputation and exercised notable influence during the Enlightenment.

See also CIVIL SOCIETY.

Fielding, Henry (1707–1754) *English novelist, playwright, political journalist, and judge*

Fielding began a professional career in the THEATER. Among his successful early dramatic works, the *Historical Register,* a satire on the government of Robert WALPOLE, contributed to creating the political climate that caused Walpole to establish CENSORSHIP of English theater. Field-

ing turned away from drama as a result and entered the profession of law. He served in the LONDON courts throughout his life. Fielding continued his literary pursuits by editing and writing for journals such as *The Champion* (1739–41), *The True Patriot* (1745–46), *The Jacobite's Journal* (1747–48), and *The Covent-Garden Journal* (1752).

In 1740, Samuel RICHARDSON published PAMELA: OR VIRTUE REWARDED. The novel lauded the virtues of a simple, strict morality and enjoyed immense success throughout Europe. Fielding, incensed at the simplistic vision of morality contained in its pages, reacted by writing a burlesque of *Pamela* called *Shamela* (1741). He followed it with *Joseph Andrews* (1742) and *Jonathan Wild* (1743). His triumphant masterpiece, *Tom Jones,* appeared in 1749, and his last novel, *Amelia,* in 1751.

In developing his ideas, Fielding consciously tried to create a new art form, "a comic epic in prose." As models of form he turned to the ancient epics of Homer, to the picaresque novel *Don Quixote* by Miguel de Cervantes, and to the Bible. Fielding is considered one of the early masters of the NOVEL, a writer who helped to convince the critics and the reading public of the potential contained within that new literary form. He was a cogent and insightful social critic who drew his characters and plots from his gentrified background and from his experiences in a London courtroom.

Fielding is an outstanding example of the critical spirit of the ENLIGHTENMENT. His work reveals the complexity of the discourse that was developing in enlightened intellectual circles around the middle of the 18th century. On the one hand, in the manner of many of his enlightened contemporaries, Fielding criticizes the clergy and unearned social or political privilege, thereby showing himself sympathetic to the interests of the English middle and lower classes. On the other hand, he rejects the maudlin sentimentalism that was a dominant characteristic of the enlightened AESTHETICS and moral values that were developing in these classes, and therefore also rejects one of the major themes of the era.

See also SELF-INTEREST.

Fielding, Sarah (1710–1768) *English novelist*

For most of the 20th century, Sarah Fielding was primarily identified as the younger sister of the famous English novelist Henry FIELDING and as a minor novelist in her own right. Recently, though, scholars have helped to restore her reputation. Today, she is recognized as an innovative literary figure whose significance stems almost as much from her role as a female writer as it does from the work she produced.

Sarah was born at East Stour, Dorset. Her father was a lieutenant general in the army; her mother died when she was seven. Her maternal grandmother sued for custody of the Fielding children when Sarah's father remarried. Sarah was educated at a girls' school in Salisbury, where she began to acquire her extensive knowledge of English and French literature. Neither Sarah nor her sisters ever married, and they lived together in Prince's Court, LONDON, from 1739 to 1744.

Receiving little inheritance and struggling to make ends meet, Fielding turned to writing. Her first and most famous NOVEL, *The Adventures of David Simple,* was published in 1744. She called this work a "moral romance" in which the title hero, a kind-hearted, sentimental soul, confronts a wide range of good and mostly bad characters. The episodic nature of the plot enabled Fielding to criticize multiple facets of London society. She already had experience as a writer, having composed an episode that appeared in her brother Henry's popular novel *Joseph Andrews* in 1742. Samuel RICHARDSON, the printer and novelist, considered Sarah a sharper observer of human and social nature than her brother.

Sarah Fielding wrote a total of six novels. One of them, *The Governess* (1749), is considered the first children's novel. A later novel, *The Countess of Dellwyn* (1759), relates the adventures of a woman whose adulterous life causes her remorse rather than death from shame, a deviation from the narrative conventions of the mid-18th century. Her last publication was a translation of the Greek historian Xenophon's *Memoirs of Socrates* (1762). This work was probably inspired by Elizabeth Carter's successful 1758 translation of Epictetus; and indeed, Sarah had much in common with the female intellectuals of the BLUESTOCKING circle to which Carter belonged.

Filangieri, Gaetano (1752–1788) *Neapolitan economist and state adviser*

Gaetano Filangieri spent most of his life as a scholar of ECONOMICS and law. Filangieri served briefly, just before his death in 1788, as a member of the council of finances in Naples. During his last years, confined to his country estate by illness, Filangieri corresponded with many intellectuals, including Benjamin FRANKLIN.

In his work, Filangieri drew from the ideas of the French PHYSIOCRATS. Their emphasis on the economic primacy of agriculture seemed well suite to the situation in the predominantly rural kingdom of Naples. He began publishing his multivolume *Scienza della legislazione* (Science of law) in 1780. Its success caused Filangieri to be praised as the Italian incarnation of both John LOCKE and MONTESQUIEU. The book was translated into German, French, and English. It denounced various structures and practices of the Neapolitan system such as torture, government surveillance of citizens, and feudal rights. It pleaded for national public education and presented a systematization of enlightened views on penal reform. It

criticized the preoccupation with war ("killing men") that characterized the European monarchies and called for government in the service of humanitarian goals.

Filangieri's book stands as a landmark of the Italian ILLUMINISTI movement, a worthy successor to the renowned work *ESSAY ON CRIMES AND PUNISHMENTS* by Cesare BECCARIA. The Roman and Spanish Inquisitions of the Catholic Church both condemned the first volumes of Filangieri's work. In 1790, when the turmoil inspired by the FRENCH REVOLUTION began to threaten the government of Naples, Neapolitan officials reacted by publicly burning the works of their former colleague.

Fischer von Erlach, Johann Bernhard (1656–1723) *Austrian architect, sculptor, and architectural historian*

Fischer von Erlach created a uniquely Austrian BAROQUE STYLE out of an idiosyncratic blending of architectural elements borrowed from various historical periods. He drew particularly from classical, Renaissance, and baroque traditions. Fischer von Erlach learned his trade in the workshop of his father, who was a sculptor and turner. He moved to ROME at the age of 16 and spent a like number of years living, studying, and working in that city. The great baroque sculptor and architect Gian Lorenzo Bernini (1598–1680) invited Fischer von Erlach to work in his studio. The young man also mingled with the group of archaeologists and antiquarians who surrounded Queen Christina of Sweden (1626–89) during her years in Rome. Fischer von Erlach studied the history of architecture and its theory, ultimately creating his unique style from the experience.

In 1683, after VIENNA had been freed from the siege of the Ottoman Turks, Fischer von Erlach moved to that city. The emperors and leading nobility of the HAPSBURG EMPIRE were embarking on an ambitious program of building and restoration to repair the damages caused by the Turkish wars. Fischer von Erlach became the court architect for three emperors, Leopold I, Joseph I, and Charles VI. He also designed buildings for the archbishop of Salzburg and for EUGÈNE OF SAVOY.

Of all the buildings Fischer von Erlach produced, his designs for various country estates and for city palace facades had the most widespread influence on subsequent architects. The country houses synthesized elements of the PALLADIAN STYLE with aspects of the French baroque. These houses had powerful curving lines and oval central pavilions with detached low wings. Outstanding examples include Schloss Neuwaldegg near Vienna and Schloss Engelhartstetten in Lower Austria. The city palaces presented a different synthesis of elements drawn from the same sources, but the result was impressive facades with strong, clear lines. The Winter Palace of Prince Eugène of Savoy in Vienna is an outstanding example.

In addition to these buildings, Fischer von Erlach created the Schönbrunn Palace, the facade of the Bohemian Chancellery, and the Trautson Palace, all in Vienna; the Holy Trinity and University churches in Salzburg; and Schloss Klesheim, the archbishop's summer residence just outside of Salzburg. In 1712, Fischer von Erlach published his comparative history of architecture, *Entwurff einer Historischen Architektur* (Outline of a historical architecture). This was the first book of comparative architecture to appear in Europe.

At his death in 1723, Fischer von Erlach was working on a great baroque aesthetic and propagandistic monument, the Karlskirche (Church of St. Charles Borromeo) in Vienna. The church was intended to represent the extensive power of the emperor and his role as the defender of Catholicism. This church was completed by Fischer von Erlach's son, Joseph Emanuel Fischer von Erlach. This son also implemented his father's design for the Viennese Imperial Stables and the Imperial Library.

flying shuttle   A device for mechanical weaving, patented in 1733 by the Englishman John KAY. The flying shuttle was developed for use in the wool industry and was one of the earliest technological innovations in the series that ultimately revolutionized the production of textiles. Since the flying shuttle increased the speed at which weavers could produce wool cloth, it stimulated a demand for greater quantities of yarn. In this manner, it helped to produce the *de facto* yarn shortages that, in turn, spurred the invention of the earliest spinning machines, the SPINNING JENNY, SPINNING MULE, and WATER FRAME.

See also INDUSTRIAL REVOLUTION.

Fontenelle, Bernard Le Bovier de (1657–1757)
French scientific writer and academician
Fontenelle was the son of the lawyer François Le Bovier and of Marthe Corneille. He was the nephew on his mother's side of the French authors Pierre Corneille and Thomas Corneille. These Corneille uncles introduced Fontenelle to the literary, intellectual, and social worlds of PARIS.

Trained by the JESUITS at the college in Rouen, Fontenelle decided to follow his uncles into a literary career. He settled in Paris, establishing himself in the salons of the late 17th century.

Fontenelle's career began flourishing after 1678, when he started exploring philosophical questions that were being raised by the SCIENTIFIC REVOLUTION. Fontenelle became a staunch supporter of the philosophy of René DESCARTES, clinging to that view even after most French scientists had abandoned it in favor of Newtonianism.

Fontenelle acquired fame with the 1686 publication of his *Entretiens sur la pluralité des mondes* (Conversations on the plurality of worlds). In a highly entertaining series of evening conversations between a fictional noblewoman and a scientist, the book explained various models of the universe: the HELIOCENTRIC universe of Nicolaus COPERNICUS, and the GEOCENTRIC models of Tycho Brahe and the ancient Greek astronomer Ptolemy. Fontenelle speculated about the possibility that other heavenly bodies might be inhabited, about the possibility that the universe might be infinite in size, and about most of the important questions and discoveries that were preoccupying astronomers of the 17th century.

The *Entretiens* was an instant success, enjoying rapid translation and dissemination throughout Europe. It played a major role in spreading knowledge about the heliocentric model of the universe, and it helped to popularize that view. Thus, Fontenelle assisted the acceptance of certain key ideas of the Scientific Revolution, making them acceptable and intelligible to the educated public. In this manner, he helped to create an audience that would later be receptive to the ideas of the ENLIGHTENMENT.

The publication of the *Entretiens* brought Fontenelle the honor of election in 1691 to the prestigious French Academy. In 1697, he was also received into the FRENCH ACADEMY OF SCIENCES and assumed the post of perpetual secretary to that organization. For the next 50 years, he prepared the annual academy reports and *éloges* (commemorations of deceased members). Fontenelle retired from the French Academy of Sciences in 1741 at the age of 84. His long tenure as perpetual secretary made him a major figure in spreading knowledge of the work of academy members to outside readers.

Fontenelle died on January 9, 1757, just one month and two days before his 100th birthday. He had continued to participate actively in Parisian salons even in his 90s. In the course of his long life, he sampled the salon culture at the gatherings of Ninon de Lenclos, of the marquise de LAMBERT, of Madame de Tencin, and of Madame GEOFFRIN.

Besides contributing to the general dissemination of the new SCIENCE, Fontenelle also wrote about the origins of RELIGION. He suggested that religious belief is grounded in human fears and powerlessness and is, therefore, an expression of human PSYCHOLOGY. He developed his position by comparing the myth-making activities of the ancient Greeks and Romans to the product of contemporary "primitive" peoples presented in TRAVEL LITERATURE. He identified certain common traits among these widely separated groups and suggested that their understanding of the world was like that of young children.

Fontenelle believed that humanity progress over the course of HISTORY, gradually acquiring the ability to use REASON. Reason provides an alternative way of viewing the universe that will eventually free people from the psychological dependence on religious faith.

Fontenelle, therefore, was one of the early spokesmen for a party of modernity and for the Enlightenment.

He believed that his European contemporaries were superior to their ancestors. It should not be surprising, then, to learn that Fontenelle also supported the Moderns in the literary QUARREL BETWEEN THE ANCIENTS AND THE MODERNS.

Of his many works, those most significant for the Enlightenment were *Entretiens sur la pluralité des mondes, Doutes sur la système physique des causes occasionelles* (Doubts on the physical system of occasional causes; 1686), a criticism of the occasionalism of Nicolas de MALEBRANCHE; *Poésies pastorales de M.D.F., avec un traité sur la nature de l'églogue et une digression sur les anciens et les modernes* (Pastoral poetry of M.D.F., with a treatise on the nature of the eclogue and a digression on the ancients and the moderns; 1687); *Histoire des oracles* (History of oracles; 1686), an exploration into the psychological foundations of religious faith; and *De l'origine des fables* (On the origins of fables; 1724), a further exploration of religion and myth. Fontenelle's work for the French Academy of Sciences lies in the *Histoire de l'Académie royale des sciences . . . avec les mémoires de mathématique et de physique pour la méme année, tirés des registres de cette Académie* (History of the Royal Academy of Sciences . . . ; vols. for the years 1699 to 1741). In 1733, he also published the *Histoire de l'Académie royale des sciences. Tome 1er. Depuis son établissement en 1666, jusqu'à 1686* (History of the Royal Academy of Sciences.: Vol. I, From its origins in 1666 to 1686).

See also SOCIAL INSTITUTIONS OF THE ENLIGHTENMENT.

Forster, Johann Georg Adam (1754–1794) *German naturalist and writer, an active supporter of the political ideals of the Enlightenment*
Johann Georg Adam Forster—or Georg Forster, as he was commonly known—traveled extensively with his father, Johann Reinhold FORSTER, through ENGLAND and RUSSIA. The pair also accompanied Captain James COOK on his second voyage around the world from 1772 until 1775. After the Cook expedition returned, Georg Forster wrote and published *A Voyage around the World* (1777 in English, 1778–80 in German), thereby establishing a reputation as a careful observer and talented writer.

Forster subsequently taught natural sciences at the Carolinum in Kassel (1779–84) and at the University of Vilnius (1784–88). He moved to Mainz in 1788, having accepted the post of university librarian. With the outbreak of revolutionary ferment following the events of 1789 in FRANCE, Forster became politically active as a supporter of the ideals of FREEDOM, EQUALITY, and TOLERATION. He served in PARIS as a representative of Mainz, became a citizen of France and died in Paris in 1794.

Besides his report on the Cook expedition, Forster wrote essays on AESTHETICS, literary criticism, politics, natural history, and SCIENCE. In a dispute with Immanuel KANT over classifying the human races, Forster argued a liberal position, stating that all human races are equal in the realm of intellectual potential and capability. He outlined his position in "Noch etwas über die Menschenracen" (Something more about the races of humankind), published in the periodical *Deutsche Merkur* (1786). Forster also left a second travel book, the highly praised *Ansichten von Niederrhein* (Views from the lower Rhine; 1791–94).

Forster was a close associate of Johann Wolfgang von GOETHE and Friedrich SCHILLER, two of the leading figures of the late German Enlightenment. His circle of colleagues and friends also included the archbishop of Mainz, Karl Theodor Anton Maria von Dalberg (1744–1817), a supporter of the Bavarian *illuminati* who was dedicated to the more radical goals of that organization. In addition, Forster moved in the circles of Wilhelm von Humboldt, the philologist and diplomat whose work preserved and transmitted enlightened ideas into 19th century German culture. Forster's wife, Therese Heyne Forster, the daughter of Göttingen philologist Christian Gottlob Heyne, was herself a respected writer.

See also AUFKLÄRUNG; TRAVEL LITERATURE.

Forster, Johann Reinhold (1729–1798) *German clergyman, traveler, and writer*
Johann Reinhold Forster and his son Johann Georg FORSTER accompanied Captain James COOK on Cook's second voyage around the world (1772–75). The elder Forster recorded and published his experiences as *Observations made During a Voyage Around the World* (1778).

Johann Reinhold Forster did not support the FRENCH REVOLUTION as did his son Georg. In fact, Johann Reinhold declared that, in the event of his son's return to GERMANY, Georg should be put to death as a traitor.

Four Seasons, The A set of four concerti for solo violin and strings (opus 8, nos. 1–4) written by Antonio VIVALDI. The MUSIC is consciously intended as program music designed to evoke certain images, experiences, and feelings. It is an early example of 18th-century descriptive pastoral orchestral work. Many similar works would appear later, including the famous Pastoral Symphony (no. 6) by Ludwig von BEETHOVEN. Vivaldi published *The Four Seasons* concertos in 1725 in *Il cimento dell'armonica e dell'inventione* (The contest of harmony and invention) with a dedicatory letter to the Bohemian Count (Graf) Wenzel von Morzin. In the letter, he pointed out that he had added specific notations to the score and parts about the programmatic nature of the music. These notations were Vivaldi's own additions to the sonnets on the seasons that provided the major setting for the music. The published version also contained the texts of these sonnets.

The Four Seasons portrays the various aspects of life and nature in each of the four seasons of the year. One concerto is assigned to each season. Each of these concerti is a complete work, able to stand alone. The scene is pastoral, presenting the listener with the marvels of springtime in the countryside, with the languid days of summer heat (complete with annoying, buzzing flies), with the festivities of the autumn harvest, and with the cozy warmth of the fireside in the comfort of a house that provides shelter from the winter rains. Vivaldi was a master at drawing out the potential tone colors in stringed instruments. He produced his suggestive effects by utilizing different combinations of stringed instruments and by requiring different bowing techniques to vary the articulations of the notes and musical phrases.

Fourier, Jean-Baptiste Joseph (1768–1830) *French mathematician*

Orphaned by the age of nine, Fourier came under the guardianship of the archbishop of Auxerre, who placed him in the local military school. Fourier received additional education in a Benedictine school at Saint-Benoit sur Loire. The outbreak of the FRENCH REVOLUTION interrupted his plans for a university education in mathematics. Instead, he returned to his native town of Auxerre and assumed duties as a teacher in his former military school.

Fourier played a role in local political affairs during the revolution and was arrested in 1794 after openly defending victims of the Reign of Terror. Released after the downfall of Maximilien ROBESPIERRE, he moved to PARIS. Brief studies in the short-lived École Normale resulted in an appointment in 1795 as assistant lecturer in courses offered by Joseph-Louis LAGRANGE and Gaspard Monge (1746–1818). In 1798, Monge secured a position for Fourier in the entourage that Napoleon led to Egypt. Fourier remained in Egypt until 1801.

Napoleon subsequently tapped Fourier for administrative work in France, sending him to a post as prefect of the department of Isère. Fourier carried out several civil engineering projects such as draining marshes and constructing roads. In 1808 Napoleon rewarded him for his work with the title of baron.

Fourier's close association with Napoleon compromised his career for a brief period after 1815, but eventually he obtained a new administrative post and election to the reconstituted FRENCH ACADEMY OF SCIENCES. In 1822, Fourier became the perpetual secretary of that institution, then in 1827 was elected to the prestigious French Academy. He was also a foreign member of the ROYAL SOCIETY OF LONDON. He died in 1830 from the complications of a chronic illness acquired during his years in Egypt.

Fourier made a significant contribution to MATHEMATICS AND MECHANICS by developing differential calculus techniques that allowed calculus to be applied to new areas of scientific analysis. In particular, he discovered

ways of applying calculus to problems about heat flow (diffusion) and developed mathematical techniques known today as the Fourier series and as the Fourier integral. He also generalized the rule of signs that had been developed by René DESCARTES and addressed various other problems in dynamics and mathematics.

By extending the applicability of mathematical analysis (calculus), Fourier continued the rational approaches developed in the early ENLIGHTENMENT to problems that had previously evaded solution or comprehension. Unlike his contemporary the marquis de LAPLACE, Fourier insisted that every mathematical statement must have a real physical meaning, evidenced in real motions and in accessibility to direct measurement. He rejected what he considered the speculative theories of Laplace.

Fourier's major scientific publications included *Théorie analytique de la chaleur* (Analytic theory of heat; 1822) and *Analyse des equations determinées* (Analysis of determinant equations; 1831). He also wrote and published a *Description de l'Egypte* (Description of Egypt; 1808–25) based on his years in that country, and assisted in a translation of Pliny's *Natural History*.

Fragonard, Jean Honoré (1732–1806) *French painter*

Son of a glovemaker from Grasse in the region of Provence, FRANCE, Fragonard was destined by his father to become a notary. However, his earliest employer recognized his talent for painting and encouraged him to change his professional plans. Apprenticeships followed in PARIS with François BOUCHER and Jean-Baptiste CHARDIN. At the age of 20, Fragonard won the Prix de Rome from the French Academy of Painting. He spent three more years studying art at the Écoles des Élèves Protégés. He finally traveled to ROME in 1756, spending five productive, creative years in that inspirational city, returning to Paris by way of VENICE in 1761.

Fragonard obtained membership in the Academy in 1764, with the painting *Le Grand prêtre Corésus se sacrifie pour sauver Callirhoe* (Coresus sacrifices himself to save Callirhoe). King LOUIS XV bought the painting but delayed payment for several years. Fragonard entered paintings in the annual salons held at the Louvre until 1767, but after that date, he devoted himself to painting privately for wealthy financiers and society ladies. He preferred the secure living these patrons could provide to that of the struggling exhibiting artist. As a result, Fragonard lost his reputation as a serious artist. Nevertheless, he remained intensely active, producing paintings and interiors for Madame de POMPADOUR, Mlle. Guimard, and Madame DU BARRY. Fragonard enjoyed a trip to ITALY, VIENNA, and Mannheim with a rich patron in 1773.

During the FRENCH REVOLUTION, the social world in which Fragonard was so intimately embedded came under attack. But because he had befriended the young radical painter Jacques Louis DAVID, he was protected

A Young Girl Reading by Jean Honoré Fragonard. This painting captures its sitter engaged in the fashionable activity of reading. *(Courtesy New York Public Library)*

from the consequences of his lifelong affiliations and was even appointed to the committee of the new revolutionary Museum of Arts. Fragonard died in Paris in 1806.

Major works by Fragonard include the Louveciennes panels painted for Madame Du Barry entitled *Le Progrès de l'amour dans le coeur des jeunes filles* (The progress of love in the heart of young girls), *Le baiser à la dérobée* (The furtive kiss), *La chemise enlevée* (The stolen chemise), and *La balançoire* (The swing). These paintings depict lighthearted, sometimes frivolous subjects. They lack the emotional depth of the paintings by the earlier ROCOCO master Antoine WATTEAU. Nevertheless, their pastel colors and delicate figuration convey the sensuality that typified rococo AESTHETICS.

France Western European nation bounded in the 18th century by the kingdoms of SPAIN, PIEDMONT, and SAVOY; the republican city-state of GENEVA and the Swiss Confederation (SWITZERLAND; the HOLY ROMAN EMPIRE; and the Hapsburg-ruled AUSTRIAN NETHERLANDS (BELGIUM). France had thousands of miles of coastline along the English Channel in the northwest, the Atlantic Ocean in the west, and the Mediterranean Sea in the south. France was an overseas power with colonies in North America

(French Canada and the Louisiana Territory) and the Caribbean (the western half of Hispaniola, then called Saint Domingue, now Haiti).

A major center of the ENLIGHTENMENT, France was the birthplace of several of its leading figures, among them René DESCARTES, VOLTAIRE, the baron de MONTESQUIEU, and Denis DIDEROT. PARIS, where the PHILOSOPHES pursued projects such as the *ENCYCLOPÉDIE* and women as well as men met in salons, was the symbol of enlightened activity and sociability for people all over Europe and North America.

Until the end of the 18th century, France was officially a Roman Catholic kingdom, and its history cannot be separated from the complex chapters in the history of SEPARATION OF CHURCH AND STATE that were written in the 18th century. The Calvinist HUGUENOTS who had not fled the kingdom in 1685, when LOUIS XIV reversed the laws that had made France a model of 17th-century TOLERATION, were subject to civil liabilities and to sporadic persecutions well into the 18th century. Jews were subject to discriminatory personal taxes and other civil liabilities.

The population of France grew during the course of the 18th century. It stood at approximately 22 million in 1700, 24.6 million in 1740, and nearly 28 million in 1789. Paris was the cultural, financial, and administrative center of the kingdom. Other principal cities included old provincial administrative centers such as Bordeaux, Aix-en-Provence, Toulouse, Rennes, Rouen, Dijon, and Grenoble and university towns such as Montpellier and Bourges. Important commercial towns were located alongside bodies of water: La Rochelle on the Atlantic, Caen on the English Channel, Marseille on the Mediterranean, Lyons on the Rhone, and Tours on the Loire. Louis XIV's great baroque palace at Versailles was the site of the royal court.

Economic Factors

Fertile agricultural lands, decent roads, navigable rivers (the Seine, Loire, Rhone, and their main tributaries), an excellent system of canals, extensive forests, ocean resources, and a particularly mild climate sustained the largest population in 18th-century Europe. From the point of view of contemporaries, France should have been the richest state in Europe: A large population could have provided the labor needed to grow food and to produce necessities; rich lands could have allowed the population to sustain itself without relying on imports; and navigable rivers and coasts could have allowed products to be transported from one region of the state to another. Agriculture, practiced according to centuries-old traditions through the manual labor of peasants, was the mainstay of the French economy throughout the 18th century and well into the 19th century. Had the ideas of the PHYSIOCRATS, who saw agriculture and the free exchange of agricultural products as the primary source of wealth in a nation, been incorporated into policy,

France might have enjoyed economic primacy. The wealthiest states in Europe were two seafaring, trading nations, ENGLAND and the UNITED PROVINCES OF THE NETHERLANDS.

The economic problems in France had certain social structural causes, among them an inability to circumvent the restrictions associated with the trade and craft guilds or to accumulate capital for business ventures, and a system of privilege that favored the status quo. Limiting, too, was the allegiance of the French kings and many ministers to MERCANTILISM, a theory that stressed economic self-sufficiency and the accumulation of wealth (in the form of gold, not of agricultural or manufactured goods) rather than the exchange (repeated circulation) of goods and money via trade. Policies guided by these ideas helped to keep manufacturing rare and focused on the creation of luxury goods for aristocratic consumption. They also reduced the colonies to little more than sources of raw materials.

Mercantilist policies tended to reinforce the traditional, hierarchical structure of French society, with the Catholic clergy and aristocratic landowners at the top; a small class of professionals, merchants, financiers, and petty officeholders in the middle; and at the bottom a large class of peasants, who supported the whole edifice with their labor and taxes. In retrospect, allegiance to mercantilism was one of the sources of the economic crises that plagued 18th-century France and eventually helped to bring the downfall of the ANCIEN RÉGIME. The system could not support the fiscal needs of the government or the social and material needs of a changing society. France during the Enlightenment was a state faced with the need to make structural economic changes but unable to do so.

Political Structure

Politically, France was not a uniform entity. It was a collection of regions that had been united over centuries, according to feudal practice, in the person of the king. Certain areas in the north (the Ile de France and its major city, Paris, for example) had belonged to the kings since medieval times as their personal domain, or property. The king was charged with protecting these areas, administering justice, and making laws. He also had the right to the products of the land, and it was this right—not the consent of the people—that legitimized the practice of collecting taxes. Other regions of France had come under royal control through marriage dowries (Brittany, for example). Still other regions reverted according to feudal law to the direct control of the king when their overlords, who were bound to the king by feudal oaths of allegiance, died without heirs. Some regions were joined to the Crown at the time of dynastic changes, such as when Henry IV brought his kingdom of Navarre into the French domain. Other areas came under direct royal control as a result of military conquest. There were also church-owned territories (according to the *Encyclopédie*, 18 archbishoprics, 112 bishoprics, and thousands of monastic institutions) answerable to the king but also to the laws of the Roman Catholic Church.

The conglomeration of ever more distant, distinctive regions took place over centuries. No single constitutional moment, such as the signing of the Magna Carta, defined the fundamental relation of the French king to his subjects. Instead, the conception and exercise of royal sovereignty in France was a historical product. Thus, constitutionalism in France, though it did exist and would emerge as one of the forces behind the calls for reform at the end of the 18th century, was weaker and dependent on the different historical experiences of the various French provinces and territories.

Equally important was the fact that the powers of the king had emerged gradually over time in a long process that had involved wars, rebellions, negotiations, and gradual extension of royal control from the center to the periphery of the kingdom. Each region in France had its own unique history, proud and relatively autonomous institutions, and powerful lords with juridical powers. Each French province, to a greater or lesser extent, was granted privileges and given laws derived from centuries-old unique traditions, so France was a pastiche of institutions, locally entrenched officials, and legal codes. Customary law reigned in the northern regions, while Roman law shaped the codes of the south. Some provinces, such as Burgundy and Provence, had their own sovereign courts of law (PARLEMENTS), and others answered directly to the courts in Paris. There was nothing like American federal law, conceived as a set of universal laws that apply according to the dictates of the U.S. Constitution to every state in the union. And there was certainly nothing like a constitutionally protected structure of government at the center, based on the concepts of SEPARATION OF POWERS and representation.

Nevertheless, the France of the Enlightenment did have a legacy, derived from the medieval monarchy, of institutions with powers that could limit the authority of the king. Foremost were the estates (the kingdomwide Estates General and several provincial estates), or representative institutions of the ancien régime. These were composed of delegates elected by the three legal social orders: the clergy, or First Estate, the nobility, or Second Estate, and the bourgeoisie, or Third Estate. The estates gave advice to the king and had often acted to limit the powers of medieval and Renaissance kings by protecting the privileges of the three legal orders. They did not, however, make law. Moreover, the estates could meet only when the king asked them to convene; they had no constitutional right to meet. After the decades of civil war in the name of RELIGION that tore apart 16th-century France, the kings began to try to eliminate the estates simply by not calling on them to meet. Before LOUIS XVI convened the Estates General in 1789, that body had not met since 1614.

In the absence of estates meetings, the *parlements,* which were sovereign courts of law, not elected legislative bodies such as the English Parliament, assumed the task of trying to place limits on the monarchy. In 18th-century France, there were 12 *parlements,* the most important of which was the one in Paris, which had existed since the 13th century. With the protections brought to members by the system of office ownership called *vénalité* and the fact that members could pass these posts on to their heirs, the *parlements* were, to some degree, free to use judicial processes to oppose the wishes of the king. In the face of ambitious monarchs, the most important power of the *parlements* derived from their historic duty to register and have read in public the edicts (laws) of the king. If they refused to register an edict, it could not become the law of the land. The nature of royal sovereignty in France, therefore, was not clear and distinct.

At the beginning of the 18th century, Louis XIV (assisted by his chancellors, secretaries of state, and various royal councils) was ruling very nearly as an absolute monarch. Supporters and critics alike in France and throughout Europe perceived his power as absolute and considered his kingdom a model of ABSOLUTISM. Louis's predecessors had centralized the government of France to some degree, but Louis refined and extended the power of the center to an extent that made his kingdom unique among the large states of Europe. He sent an administrative "army" of appointed officials (*intendants*) into the Crown lands and provinces to administer in his name and circumvent the power of local officials. He subdued the nobility and lured them to the court, where their activities could at least be watched, if not always controlled. A system of royal academies shaped, to a great extent, the content and practices of the fine arts, architecture, music, and the natural sciences; censors controlled what was being printed, although never completely; and the new professional royal army made rebellion on the part of princes and other restive members of the sword nobility more difficult than ever before.

However, Louis's centralized state was simply grafted onto the old system of privilege and particularism in France. He was never able to tax his citizens to the degree needed to bring various domestic reforms and foreign policies to fruition. His infatuation with absolute power and his vision of the role that France should play in Europe lured him into the financially disastrous SEVEN YEARS' WAR, led him to quarrel with the papacy in ROME, and inured him to the suffering of the peasantry.

The beginning of the 18th century was the pinnacle of the years of the French ancien régime monarchy. The combination of entrenched powers and particularism, along with the fact that the kings of France were sworn to uphold the legal order of privilege, made further reform from above all but impossible. Louis's successors inherited a brilliantly crafted but financially unstable and politically weakened state whose centralized structures proved to be fragile. Before LOUIS XV even reached adulthood, the nobility and officeholders began reasserting their power in a phenomenon that historians call the ARISTOCRATIC RESURGENCE. Reforms could not be implemented, as several royal finance ministers discovered to their regret. In 1787, when the plans of ministers Charles-Alexandre de CALONNE and Jacques NECKER to recall the Estates General were put into action, the government of France was bankrupt and unable to raise taxes to finance the state debt.

In the countryside, the effects of absolutism and the aristocratic resurgence meant that more money, goods, and services were being demanded from peasants. The burden of taxation grew until no more could be squeezed from them. Meanwhile, landlords, usually noblemen, began trying to reassert their old rights to certain dues. Despite innovations in agricultural science and theory, farming practices and crop yields had not changed; crop shortages and famines were still a threat. It was just such a series of famines in the 1780s and 1790s that helped to produce the conditions under which the ancien régime and the earliest revolutionary governments collapsed.

Intellectual Climate

However much life remained the same, potent forces for change were at work in France. Commerce and trade were increasing, giving birth to a new moneyed, politically ambitious class. New roads were being constructed (with forced peasant labor), so that news as well as people and products moved more quickly. The number of educated people in towns and cities was increasing, and reading was becoming a favorite pastime. To meet the demand, presses churned out books, newspapers, and pamphlets, with and without the approval of the royal censors. Salons, official academies, reading clubs, and libraries provided places for people to meet and discuss ideas. In short, the residents of France were being brought together more than ever before.

Among the subjects of discussion was reform of the basic structures of the French state. Reformers considered everything from English-style limited monarchy to the enlightened forms of absolutism and despotism at work in PRUSSIA and AUSTRIA. Eventually, as the French people embarked on a project to reform their state, replacing ancien régime privilege and absolute monarchy with a constitutional government based on egalitarian, universal principles, JUSTICE AND THE LAW, and RIGHTS, the territory of France became a laboratory for political experiment in which leaders tried to put some of the ideas of the Enlightenment into practice. Revolution took the nation from monarchy to republicanism (first in liberal representative form and later in despotic form) to empire and finally to the restoration of monarchy and a return to the old order in somewhat modified form. With that, the era of the Enlightenment came to an end.

In many respects, France dominated 18th-century Europe, even when its real political and economic powers were waning. In the development of Enlightenment thinking, France played a preeminent role.

See also ABSOLUTISM, ENLIGHTENED; DESPOTISM, ENLIGHTENED; FRENCH REVOLUTION; HAITIAN REVOLUTION; POLITICAL THEORY; ROCOCO; ROMAN CATHOLICISM; SOCIAL INSTITUTIONS OF THE ENLIGHTENMENT.

Further reading: Alfred Cobban, *A History of Modern France*, vol. 1: *1715–1799 Old Régime and Revolution*, 3rd ed. (Baltimore: Penguin Books, 1963); Pierre Goubert, *Louis XIV and Twenty Million Frenchmen*, tr. Anne Carter (New York: Vintage Books, 1966); Daniel Roche, *France in the Enlightenment*, tr. Arthur Goldhammer (Cambridge, Mass.: Harvard University Press, 1998).

Francke, August Hermann (1663–1727) *German Pietist theologian and professor at the University of Halle*
As a young man, Francke studied at the universities in Kiel and Leipzig. At Leipzig, he became active in setting up Bible study groups (*collegia biblica* or *pietatis*) under the influence of the founder of PIETISM, Philipp Jakob SPENER. Francke became a strong proponent of Pietism after he experienced a personal rebirth in 1687. In 1690, Francke was forced to leave the University of Leipzig, which did not wish to tolerate the deviance represented by Pietist ideas.

In 1694, the elector of BRANDENBURG founded a new university at Halle and extended his patronage to the Pietists. He called Francke and his friend Christian THOMASIUS to teach at the new university. They established HALLE as the center of Pietist teaching and publishing. Francke built up the theological faculty at the university. He also established a number of charitable foundations intended to serve as outward signs of inner spiritual renewal enjoyed by Pietists. These foundations included a school for poor children (1695), an orphanage (1698), a print shop, an apothecary, and a foreign missionary organization.

Francke's publishing house produced aids for private devotion and public worship: hymnals, inexpensive German Bibles and prayer books, and devotional works. In the last category, Francke released an edition of the major tract of Quietism, the *Spiritual Guide*, by Miguel de Molinos. Francke's Halle schools developed new approaches to EDUCATION in the form of curriculum revisions and creative pedagogical techniques.

When Christian WOLFF, the proponent of Leibnizian RATIONALISM, arrived at Halle, Francke emerged as his bitter enemy. Consequently, Halle became an academic battleground between Pietism and the rational philosophy of the early German ENLIGHTENMENT (*AUFKLÄRUNG*). For some years, Wolff was actually obliged to leave Halle, but after FREDERICK II (THE GREAT), the ruler of the region, assumed patronage of the university, Wolff was able to return. The conflicts between Pietist spirituality and rationalism played out between Francke and Wolff hinted at one of the major sources of tension within the Enlightenment in GERMANY. Eventually that tension would help to create the new EPISTEMOLOGY and AESTHETICS that were hallmarks of the German contribution to the era.

Frankfurt (Frankfurt-am-Main) German city on the Main River, located a short distance upstream from the confluence of the Main with the Rhine. In the 18th century, Frankfurt was a free imperial city (self-governing city) that served as the coronation site for the emperors of the HOLY ROMAN EMPIRE.

The city originated as a Celtic settlement. During the period of the Roman Empire, it lay on the boundary between that empire and the lands of the barbarian Frankish tribes. The name *Frankfurt* dates from the early sixth century. It means "the crossing place of the Franks." During the Middle Ages, Frankfurt developed into a central trade center. It was ideally located to serve as a focal point for river and overland trade. By the 16th century, it had become a financial center, having gained the right to coin money for the Holy Roman emperor. It had also become a center of book publication and trade. The annual international Frankfurt book fair provided a focal point for transactions between publishers and book-buyers from all over Europe. The fair still exists and performs crucial services to the modern international book trade.

Frankfurt served as a major European banking center in the 18th century. The financier Mayer Amschel Rothschild (1743–1812), a member of the large Jewish community, centered his activities there. His five sons would move out later to found the Rothschild banks in LONDON, PARIS, VIENNA, and Naples. The great German writer Johann Wolfgang von GOETHE was born and grew up in Frankfurt. While living there, he witnessed the coronation of JOSEPH II OF AUSTRIA as Holy Roman emperor.

Franklin, Benjamin (1706–1790) *American printer, publisher, diplomat, scientist, inventor, writer, and political leader*
Benjamin Franklin was born in Boston, the 15th of 17 children. His father, an English immigrant, was a soap and candle maker, and his mother the daughter of an indentured servant and her master. Franklin had only two years of formal schooling, but was an enthusiastic reader. His literary tastes ranged from Greek classics such as the biographies by Plutarch to contemporary works such as the *Essays to Do Good* by Cotton MATHER.

Franklin used THE SPECTATOR, the journal produced by Joseph ADDISON and Richard STEELE, as a model for improving his writing skills, first copying essays from the paper and then rewriting them. Franklin entered a printing apprenticeship with his older brother and published his first literary work, a series of satirical letters printed under a pseudonym, for his brother's newspaper.

In 1723, Franklin left Boston and found work as a printer in PHILADELPHIA. A business venture during the years between 1724 and 1726 took him to LONDON, where he also worked as a printer. Shortly after returning to Philadelphia, Franklin set up the Junto (1727), a debating club for artisans who wished to discuss politics, philosophy, and practical business matters.

In 1728, Franklin started a printing business and within a year began publishing *The Pennsylvania Gazette,* soon to become one of the most popular newspapers in the American colonies. He also began printing currency for the colony of Pennsylvania and eventually became the official public printer for the colonies of Delaware, New Jersey, and Maryland. Another profitable venture was the annual publication of *Poor Richard's Almanack* (1732–57), a calendar of information and popular lore designed for the general reader.

Through the influence of the Junto, Franklin was able to pursue a variety of practical plans for improving life in Philadelphia. He set up a circulating library, founded the police force, and established both a militia and a volunteer fire company for the city. He also assisted in securing improvements in the lighting of Philadelphia streets.

In 1743, Franklin organized the AMERICAN PHILO-SOPHICAL SOCIETY in order to foster the exchange of both philosophical and practical information in the colonies. Its statement of purpose revealed its roots in the ENLIGHTENMENT by emphasizing its desire to spread light (knowledge), to increase the power of humankind over nature, to improve the quality of life, and to increase its pleasures. Franklin also founded the Academy of Philadelphia in 1751, an institution that eventually became the University of Pennsylvania.

Franklin served in a number of important public posts. He was clerk of the Pennsylvania legislature (1736–51), postmaster of Philadelphia (1737–53), and deputy postmaster of the British North American colonies (1753–54). In 1754, when the British Board of Trade called for a congress of delegates from the colonies to discuss their defense needs in the impending war with FRANCE, Franklin presented, but could not obtain approval for, his Albany Plan of Union, a document that proposed setting up a loose confederation of colonies in America.

Franklin moved to London in 1757, to serve first as the colonial agent for Pennsylvania (1757–62), and later in the same capacity for the colonies of Pennsylvania, Georgia, and Massachusetts (1764–75). He was to remain

Benjamin Franklin, portrait by Chappel. A major intellectual and political leader in the American colonies, Benjamin Franklin was also a well-known, highly regarded amateur scientist welcomed in enlightened European circles. *(Courtesy New York Public Library)*

in London for nearly 20 years. During this period, he published *The Way to Wealth* (1758), a book that offered practical advice, in the form of witty maxims, to those who wished to be self-reliant. In London Franklin gradually became disillusioned with British colonial policies. He expressed some of his views publicly in 1773, in the ironic *Rules by Which a Great Empire May Be Reduced to a Small One.*

The beginning of the AMERICAN REVOLUTION found Franklin serving as a delegate to the Second Continental Congress (1776) and sitting on the committee that assisted Thomas JEFFERSON in drafting the DECLARATION OF INDEPENDENCE. In 1776 Congress also appointed Franklin to represent the UNITED STATES in France. In this capacity, Franklin helped to negotiate both the alliance with France (1778) that was so crucial to the success of the American Revolution and the Treaty of Paris (1783), in which Great Britain recognized American independence.

The French received Franklin enthusiastically, and he participated avidly in the various social activities that were so much a part of the Enlightenment. Thus, he could be found discussing ideas in salons, giving or listening to public scientific lectures, and attending meetings of the FREEMASONS at the Loge des Neufs Soeurs, the famous center of enlightened Freemasonry in PARIS. Even with all these activities, Franklin found time to invent bifocal glasses (1784) and to continue writing the *Autobiography* that he had begun in ENGLAND.

Having returned to the United States in 1785, Franklin attended the Constitutional Convention in Philadelphia (1787) and signed the new UNITED STATES CONSTITUTION. During his last years, Franklin actively supported the abolition of SLAVERY, serving as president of the Pennsylvania Society for Promoting the Abolition of Slavery. In fact, just three weeks before his death in 1790, he published an essay entitled "Against the Slave Trade."

Franklin was a noted amateur scientist, famous for practical inventions such as the Franklin stove and bifocal lenses, but also noted for his work on electricity. During the 18th century, electricity was believed to be one of several SUBTLE FLUIDS that existed in nature. The ether (a fluid that Isaac NEWTON proposed could account for gravitational actions) and heat were others. In the study of electricity, experimental scientists were struggling to find a theory that would explain the phenomena of attraction and repulsion. Franklin espoused a one-fluid theory of electricity in contrast to the more common two-fluid theory. He believed that the observed phenomena of electricity were caused by variations in pressure within a single electrical subtle fluid. Two fluid theories, in contrast, asserted that two different electrical fluids existed. When like fluids met, they repelled each other, thereby causing electrical repulsion. But when a fluid of one type encountered a fluid of the second type, attraction occurred.

Franklin's fascination with electricity eventually led to his invention of the lightning rod. But it also provided him with material for popular lecture demonstrations that were half entertainment and half science. His activities offer an outstanding example of the manner in which technological inventions and scientific theories interacted to produce new discoveries during the Enlightenment. He also provides a colorful example of the practical scientist in action, exploring and manipulating nature for the purpose of human PROGRESS. Franklin communicated his ideas about electricity to the ROYAL SOCIETY OF LONDON, and the papers were published as "Experiments and Observations on Electricity" in the 1751 edition of the society's *Philosophical Transactions*.

In general, the activities of Benjamin Franklin make him an outstanding representative of the Enlightenment. His wide range of interests, his practical scientific orientation, and his commitment to progress for humankind embodied the values of that era and were admired by both Americans and Europeans. For the French, moreover, Franklin symbolized the great American experiment, which they believed was bringing the ideas of the Enlightenment into reality. Furthermore, they viewed him as a symbol of the rustic man, who, unprejudiced and untainted by debased civilized society, could discover truths about nature by using his natural ability to REASON. Franklin loved to play this role and frequently appeared in elegant Parisian salons dressed in appropriately simple, rugged clothing. He was, in short, a symbol and source of inspiration for the PHILOSOPHES, and one of the most widely admired foreigners in Paris during the later years of the Enlightenment.

See also PUBLISHING; SOCIAL INSTITUTIONS OF THE ENLIGHTENMENT.

Further reading: John L. Heilbron, *Electricity in the 17th and 18th Centuries: A Study of Early Modern Physics* (Berkeley: University of California Press, 1979); Henry F. May, *The Enlightenment in America* (New York: Oxford University Press, 1976).

Frederick II (the Great) of Prussia (1712–1786) *king of Prussia (1740–86)*

Frederick, or "old Fritz," was renowned among his European contemporaries as a model of successful enlightened despotism (see DESPOTISM, ENLIGHTENED). He was a brilliant military strategist and tactician, an energetic, capable state administrator, and a patron of the arts and sciences. He was also an amateur philosopher, poet, flutist, composer, and music critic. He left major legacies as the ruler of PRUSSIA and many creations in the arenas of his amateur interests. He is remembered today as both an illustrious example of the Prussian soldier-king and as an 18th-century incarnation of the ideal of the PHILOSOPHER KING.

Frederick was the son of King Frederick William I of Prussia and of the Hanoverian princess Sophia Dorothea. The relationship between Frederick and his father was marked by enormous tensions that stemmed primarily from sharp differences in temperament, values, and ideas about the nature of rulership. Frederick William represented the traditional German Protestant ideal of the king as a benevolent and absolutely powerful father to his subjects. A devout Calvinist, he approached his tasks with a zealous attention to detail and with an intolerance of frivolity. The young Frederick seemed to embody precisely what his father despised, for Frederick preferred to spend his time reading philosophy and literature, playing the flute, or writing poetry rather than hunting, practicing military drills, and drinking.

But this conflict of personalities only partially explains the tension between the two men. The young Frederick also participated in the schemes of his Hanoverian mother and the English-Hanoverian faction at court.

This faction wished to see Prussia align itself with EN-GLAND and Hanover, rather than with its traditional ally, AUSTRIA. To achieve the desired alliance, negotiations were being carried out behind Frederick William's back. Young Frederick personally made some contacts and definitely favored the idea of marriage with an English princess.

The combination of personal conflict with his father and political intrigue proved so explosive that in 1730 the future Frederick the Great tried to flee from Prussia, only to find himself captured, court-martialed, and imprisoned by his enraged father. The episode resulted in at least a superficial public reconciliation between father and son. Frederick began to dedicate himself to learning the business of governing a state. He began to exercise the political imagination that would mark his subsequent years as Prussian king.

On May 31, 1740, King Frederick William died. Frederick immediately assumed the throne and plunged into war with Austria by grabbing Silesia (the Silesian Wars, 1740–42 and 1744–45). The act precipitated the larger European war known as the WAR OF THE AUSTRIAN SUCCESSION (1740–48). In pursuing his Silesian aims, Frederick showed that his vision of Prussia's position in Europe consisted of one in which Prussia would operate as a major power to counterbalance the HAPSBURG EMPIRE. He also showed that he considered territorial aggrandizement necessary for the establishment of secure Prussian borders. People began to call Frederick, "the Great." The Treaty of Aix-la-Chapelle ended the fighting in 1748. It confirmed Prussia as a new major force within Europe. The negotiations and outcome also put into motion the process that would bring about the great reversal of European alliances known as the DIPLOMATIC REVOLUTION OF 1756.

Upon completion of the Silesian campaigns, Frederick turned to the business of internal government. Between 1746 and 1756, he initiated nearly every major reform of his reign. Later years would see the development and maturation of these policies. Frederick inherited a state already provided with the outlines of an absolute, highly centralized government. Much of his work consisted of intensifying the level of control within Prussia by extending and developing the possibilities contained within the structure left to him by his father. However, in several areas he quickly displayed the creative nature of his thinking about state policy. First, he immediately called several prominent ENLIGHTENMENT figures to his capital, BERLIN. Among them, VOLTAIRE was outstanding, if also one of the more difficult to handle. Plans were made to rejuvenate the BERLIN ACADEMY, and Pierre de MAUPERTUIS, the French astronomer, was invited to become its president. Julien Offray de LA METTRIE, the exiled French philosopher of MATERIALISM, obtained Prussian protection. Several musicians received royal appoint-

ments. They included C. P. E. BACH, the eldest and highly original son of J. S. BACH, Johann Joachim Quantz, the famed flutist who provided Frederick with flute lessons, and the OPERA composer Karl Heinrich Graun, who immortalized Frederick's Machiavellian invasion of Silesia in an opera allegory entitled *Montezuma*.

Frederick also embarked on a major building campaign in Berlin. The Opera House (1743), the state buildings along Unter den Linden Strasse, the Forum Fredericianum (now, Bebelplatz), and the Platz der Akademie (Academy Place) all date from Frederick's reign. Frederick also had Charlottenburg Palace expanded by adding an east wing, and he commissioned the construction of Sans Souci, his summer palace at Potsdam.

Judicial reform ranked high for Frederick, and he outlined four major reform goals as early as 1746: to establish one state court in each Prussian province, thereby reducing the numerous courts whose jurisdictions clashed; to reduce the number of judgeships and to pay each judge substantially, while forbidding the practice of receiving private dues and fines; to require the seignorial courts of private landowners to use state-approved judges; and to create a uniform law code applicable to every territory within Prussian control. The first two reforms enjoyed swift implementation. The universal law code had to wait until 1795 for fruition. Very early in his reign, Frederick liberalized state control of the press and issued an official decree of religious TOLERATION, which established as law the actual Prussian practice.

In 1756, Frederick again plunged Europe into a war, the SEVEN YEARS' WAR, by moving against the electorate of Saxony. Following the destruction and chaos engendered by this, the last great European conflict before the Napoleonic Wars, Frederick turned to the business of rebuilding and restoring his state. In 1766, he reorganized the central administration, replacing the old General Directory with a smaller council and establishing separate ministries for mining, forestry, the mint, the state bank, and the tobacco and coffee monopolies. Foreign affairs and justice were already separate departments. With this reform, Frederick attempted to streamline and to rationalize the government BUREAU-CRACY, while still maintaining personal control of business. He issued regulations directly to each department and provided no opportunity for official interdepartmental consultations.

Through various largely mercantilistic policies, Frederick attempted to invigorate trade, industry, and agriculture. He established a program of colonization and land reclamation in the marshy areas of Pomerania, BRANDEN-BURG, and the Oder River and introduced new English agricultural methods and products such as the potato. He even considered relieving Prussian peasants of the burdens of SERFDOM, but, ultimately, he instituted such changes only in his extensive private domains—even

Frederick did not believe it possible to tamper with the privileges of his powerful serf-owning nobles, the Junkers. In manufacturing, Frederick encouraged private ownership, although he did take over an ailing porcelain factory and convert it into a state enterprise.

As Frederick aged and the task of ruling Prussia grew ever more complex, he became increasingly cynical and suspicious. In an attempt to maintain thorough control over government affairs, he instituted a system of internal surveillance, whereby individual bureaucrats surreptitiously observed and reported on each other. The extension of absolute control became an obsession that began to demonstrate how the ideals that had driven his reforms—RATIONALISM, the location of all aspects of sovereignty in the kingship, and *raison d'état,* all central to one strain of the Enlightenment—could be warped beyond recognition.

In spite of the developments of his later years, Frederick must be seen as an outstanding example of enlightened despotism. Like his father, Frederick believed that the position of king above all entailed a duty to govern the state responsibly, to observe strict economies of time and money, and to ensure military efficiency. But Frederick William's concepts derived from the old Calvinist notion of responsible rule, whereas Frederick's inspiration grew out of the application of the philosophy of the Enlightenment. Rationalism, the associated notion of NATURAL LAW, utilitarianism, and humanitarianism, all enlightened concepts, informed Frederick's attempts to rule as the "First servant of the State" and to ensure that foreign policy, justice, state bureaucracy, the arts, and culture all served the interests of the state. If contradictions exist between Frederick's theories (so eloquently stated in his earlier POLITICAL THEORY and MORAL PHILOSOPHY) and his practices as king of Prussia, then these contradictions stem at least in part from the tensions inherent within the Enlightenment.

In addition to his achievements as a ruler, Frederick left some writings of interest to students and scholars. His political writings include the *Anti-Machiavel* (1740, published 1767), the *Histoire de mon temps* (History of my time; 1740–45), and the *Testament politique* (Political testament; 1768). He also left an extensive correspondence. An avid, if not particularly accomplished, flutist, Frederick wrote more than a hundred sonatas for that instrument, some of which can be obtained in modern editions, and he left a small body of music criticism.

See also ABSOLUTISM; ABSOLUTISM, ENLIGHTENED; MERCANTILISM.

Further reading: Leonard Krieger, *Kings and Philosophers, 1689–1789* (New York: W. W. Norton, 1970); Gerhard Ritter, *Frederick the Great: A Historical Profile,* tr. and intro. Peter Paret (Berkeley: University of California Press, 1968); Rudolf Vierhaus, *Germany in the Age of Absolutism,* tr. Jonathan B. Knudsen (Cambridge: Cambridge University Press, 1988).

freedom The state of being free; the absence of constraint or coercion. Questions about freedom stood at the center of discourse about power, economic organization, and morality during the ENLIGHTENMENT. For many PHILOSOPHES, freedom, in various forms, seemed a necessary ingredient for prosperity and PROGRESS.

Social and legal structures of the 18th century regulated individual choices about occupation, marriage, places of residence and employment, religious beliefs, educational opportunity, and intellectual activity. In most countries, social status and religious affiliation determined whether one would enjoy legal privileges or civil disabilities.

In FRANCE, for example, noblemen enjoyed certain tax exemptions because of their birth status. Marriages were arranged by families, and young people could be prohibited by their fathers from marrying a desired person. Fathers could also incarcerate their sons at will or send their daughters to convents. HUGUENOTS, the French followers of CALVINISM, could not openly practice their faith without risking imprisonment and persecution. Laws with similar restrictions existed throughout Europe. In ENGLAND, Protestant DISSENTERS and Catholics were forbidden to attend the UNIVERSITIES at Oxford and Cambridge. They also lacked certain political rights that were enjoyed by ANGLICANS.

When the philosophes called for freedom, they were asking for the removal of these discriminatory laws based on social status. In the place of such laws, they wished to establish EQUALITY before the law and the right to choose occupation at will.

In conjunction with the calls for greater social, political, and occupational freedom, certain enlightened groups—the PHYSIOCRATS and English liberal political economists—called for the removal of tariffs, guild regulations, and other restrictions against the free exchange of commercial goods.

But the philosophes wanted more than the removal of legal limitations in these practical spheres. They also wanted to see European rulers embrace the cause of freedom of thought. They believed that the free exchange of ideas would further the cause of general enlightenment by allowing people to examine their own ideas critically. Such criticism and exchange would facilitate human progress; restrictions on thought, in contrast, would hinder the good of humankind.

Religious intolerance and prohibitions against the expression of the varieties of religious faith also were believed to hinder progress by giving power to favored ecclesiastical groups who were likely to abuse it. Only by removing formal RELIGION from any position of political power could freedom and progress be guaranteed.

In idealizing freedom, most enlightened intellectuals were not favoring anarchy. Freedom had a moral component. In fact, the existence of free will, another form of freedom, seemed for many a necessity if the world were to retain its moral character. For people committed to the idea of free will, the MATERIALISM embodied in the radical ideas of Claude-Adrien HELVÉTIUS, Julien Offray de LA METTRIE, or Denis DIDEROT and the tendencies toward materialism in the philosophies of Gottfried Wilhelm LEIBNIZ and Benedict de SPINOZA suggested that people were not responsible for their actions. This notion was unacceptable to most people, and reactions to the idea of an amoral world fueled most of the negative criticism of various materialist theorists.

Questions about individual freedom of action inevitably raised problems about how the individual was related to society. Solutions ranged from the radical anarchism favored by William GODWIN and the glorification of individual freedom in the *STURM UND DRANG* to the total subjection of individual will to the General Will advocated by Jean-Jacques ROUSSEAU in the *SOCIAL CONTRACT*. Numerous intermediary positions also existed, in which political and moral philosophers struggled to work out conceptions of the proper relationship between the individual and society. In fact, most enlightened theorists tried to find some balance between the extremes. Varying treatments of the theme of freedom can be found, for example, in John LOCKE, Thomas HOBBES, MONTESQUIEU, VOLTAIRE, Edward GIBBON, Thomas JEFFERSON, Immanuel KANT, Johann Gottfried HERDER, Friedrich SCHILLER, Johann Wolfgang von GOETHE, Gotthold Ephraim LESSING, Moses MENDELSSOHN, Adam FERGUSON, Adam SMITH, David HUME, and John MILLAR.

At the end of the 18th century, the struggle for freedom erupted into the political action of the revolutionary era. In both the AMERICAN REVOLUTION and the FRENCH REVOLUTION, political LIBERTY, religious TOLERATION, freedom of thought and press, and economic freedom were embedded into new political frameworks. The French also freed their colonial slaves.

The practical results of these political changes were mixed, and strong limits on the extent of freedom continued to exist. The right to vote in France, for example, was linked to PROPERTY and to gender. Even the ideal of EQUALITY in the Enlightenment could not overcome certain built-in prejudices. The concept of freedom and its applications in reality provide inspiring examples of the humanitarian impulses behind the Enlightenment, but they also yield a clear measure of its boundaries.

See also AESTHETICS; LAISSEZ FAIRE; MORAL PHILOSOPHY; PUBLISHING.

Freemasons

Freemasons An organization that originated in 17th-century ENGLAND and SCOTLAND. During the 18th century, the Freemasons spread throughout Europe, functioning as an active and highly influential institutional embodiment of the ideals, ideas, and sociability of the ENLIGHTENMENT.

The details of the origins of Freemasonry remain unclear, shrouded in the secrecy that has always surrounded the activities and records of its lodges. The earliest lodges appear to have emerged through a transformation of the Scottish and English stonemason guilds from trade organizations into speculative, philosophical societies. The earliest record of this speculative Freemasonry dates from 1641 in EDINBURGH, Scotland, while the first reference to an English organization lies in an October 1646 diary belonging to the Oxford professor Elias Ashmole.

The history of the organization that has relevance for the Enlightenment begins in 1717, when four LONDON Masonic lodges united to create the Grand Lodge of London. Its early leaders were drawn from the ranks of philosophers and pastors committed to spreading the ideas of Isaac NEWTON, of MECHANICAL PHILOSOPHY, and of DEISM. The Grand Lodge quickly established power over English lodges, but the Scottish and Irish lodges refused to recognize its claims to dominance.

One of the earliest grand masters (highest leaders) of the London lodge was John Theophilus DESAGULIERS, the experimental scientist who was curator and demonstrator for the ROYAL SOCIETY OF LONDON. With J. Anderson, Desaguliers drafted the first constitution of the Freemasons, published in 1723 as *The Constitutions of the Free-Masons containing the History, Charges, Regulations, etc., of that most Ancient and Right Worshipful Fraternity, For the Use of the Lodges*.

The *Constitutions of the Free-Masons* provides a mythologized history of the organization that traces it back to the first man, Adam, and to the ancient Egyptians and Greeks. This "history" illustrates the strong links between Freemasonry and deism, especially in the vision of God as the architect of the universe.

Freemasons were searching for the universal religious beliefs rooted in the natural feelings and ideas of earliest primitive human beings. Freemasons hoped that such a NATURAL RELIGION could act as a substitute for dogmatic forms of Christianity. This natural, universal set of beliefs would bring men (no women were originally admitted) from conflicting religious and socioeconomic backgrounds together into a common brotherhood of humanity. The ideals of the Enlightenment—religious TOLERATION, the universal brotherhood of humankind, REASON, PROGRESS, PERFECTIBILITY, and humanitarian values—find early expression in the teachings of English Masonic organizations. And the rites of the organization were designed to ensure that these ideals would be realized.

Freemasonry grew rapidly in England and in Scotland, but the English lodges remained markedly distinct from the Scottish lodges, separated on political rather than philosophical grounds. The Scottish lodges served as sources of institutional support for the JACOBITES. These people supported the claims of the Stuarts to the 18th-century British throne. From their exile in FRANCE, the

French Freemasons in the 18th century. The Freemasons, an international secret organization whose members dedicated themselves to attaining wisdom and virtue, championed the causes of the Enlightenment and actively backed various reform programs of the era. *(Courtesy New York Public Library)*

Jacobites and the Stuart pretender to the throne marshalled support for their claims. Between 1700 and 1720, they also established the first French Masonic lodges to provide a secret organization through which to disseminate their political claims.

In England, meanwhile, the Masonic lodges loyal to the Grand Lodge of London (called Blue Lodges) had developed strong ties to the Hanoverian dynasty and to the political principles of the Whig Party. They repudiated the radical republicanism of the 17th-century English Commonwealth, favoring instead a monarchy with firm constitutional limitations. They also dedicated themselves to philanthropic activities.

The membership of English Freemasonry included several high-ranking aristocrats, Whig Party members and sympathizers, deists, and members of the Royal Society of London. Among their number were Desaguliers, Brook TAYLOR, John TOLAND, and Robert WALPOLE.

Freemasonry spread throughout Europe and North America wherever the English were living and wherever enlightened English ideas were admired. Lodges were founded in Ghent (1722); PARIS (1726); the American colonies and Russia (1731); Florence (1733); The Hague (1734); POLAND and Lisbon (1735); Hamburg, Mannheim, GENEVA, and SWEDEN (1737); and Copenhagen (1743). From these points they proliferated until Freemasonry

became an international network of loosely affiliated groups.

As Freemasonry grew, the number of distinct rites (rituals and teachings) also proliferated. This phenomenon accounts for the vast and confusing complexity of enlightened freemasonry. It also helps to explain the kaleidoscope of reactions to the organization that occurred across Europe.

Certain lodges in German-speaking states incorporated the teachings of the ROSICRUCIANS, while others, especially in Bavaria and AUSTRIA, joined with the Bavarian ILLUMINATI. The result was the creation of both a conservative Rosicrucian Freemasonry and of a progressive and actively revolutionary Illuminist Freemasonry. Similarly, in France, the progressive, deist Loge des Neuf Soeurs existed alongside lodges devoted to mystical, esoteric rites. The latter, inspired in some instances by the comte de SAINT-GERMAIN, Louis-Claude de SAINT-MARTIN, and Emanuel SWEDENBORG, included the Scottish rites, the Cohen Elect (Élus Cohens), Adhonimarite Masonry, the Philalètes, and the rites of Benedict Chastanier.

Progressive Freemasonry in German and Austrian regions counted many influential figures as members, such as FREDERICK II (THE GREAT) OF PRUSSIA; Josef von SONNENFELS; Wolfgang Amadeus MOZART; Franz Joseph HAYDN; Gotthold Ephraim LESSING; the Hapsburg emperor

Francis I of Lorraine, husband of Empress MARIA THERESA; and possibly Gerard van SWIETEN.

In Paris, Freemasonry became intimately associated with the French Enlightenment, counting many prominent PHILOSOPHES as members. Among them were MONTESQUIEU, Sebastien-Roch-Nicolas CHAMFORT, Claude-Joseph Vernet, Jean HOUDON, VOLTAIRE, Joseph-Jérôme LALANDE, the marquis de CONDORCET, Jacques-Pierre Brissot de Wanville, Georges-Jacques Danton, Abbé SIEYÈS, and Benjamin FRANKLIN. The most influential enlightened lodge was the famous Loge des Neuf Soeurs.

In the American colonies, Freemasonry flourished and claimed leaders of the AMERICAN REVOLUTION such as George WASHINGTON and Benjamin Franklin as members. FRANKLIN's contacts with European Masonic lodges greatly assisted the process of creating support for the American rebel cause.

Masonic lodges did not limit their activities to their initiated members. They also founded various societies dedicated to humanitarian and educational pursuits. The Loge des Neuf Soeurs, for example, sponsored both the Société des Amis des Noirs (Society of Friends of the Blacks), dedicated to the abolition of SLAVERY, and the Société Apollinaire, a teaching organization. Many Masonic lodges held open meetings where lectures on science and philosophy could be attended by anyone, male or female, with an interest in the subject. Some lodges also sponsored reading clubs. The organization of Freemasons thus played a conscious and decisive role in disseminating the message of the Enlightenment by means of educational programs and reform activities.

Throughout the 18th century, the Freemasons endured attacks from political, religious, and social adversaries. They were accused of practicing HOMOSEXUALITY and of encouraging alcoholism, of defending ATHEISM, and of engaging in subversive political activities. One 19th-century historical tradition hostile to the FRENCH REVOLUTION claimed that the Freemasons plotted the whole affair.

This claim is no longer considered valid; the French Revolution had multiple causes and social sources that make conspiracy theories ridiculous. Nevertheless, the role of the Freemasons as a prominent institutional support for liberal political programs cannot be denied. As a result, the Freemasons were persecuted on various occasions throughout the 18th century. The French government tried unsuccessfully to limit their activities between 1736 and 1738, and the Hapsburgs outlawed Illuminist Freemasonry in 1785. However, the currents that were supporting the ideals of the Enlightenment extended far beyond the boundaries of this secret organization. Freemasonry was just one actor in the great human drama that unfolded during the 18th-century Enlightenment.

See also SECRET SOCIETIES; SOCIAL INSTITUTIONS OF THE ENLIGHTENMENT.

Further reading: Bernard Fäy, *Revolution and Freemasonry, 1680–1800* (Boston: Little, Brown, 1935); Margaret C. Jacob, *Living the Enlightenment: Freemasonry and Politics in Eighteenth-Century Europe* (New York: Oxford University Press, 1991); Margaret C. Jacob, *The Radical Enlightenment: Pantheists, Freemasons, and Republicans* (London: George Allen & Unwin, 1981).

free trade Economic philosophy advocating the exchange of goods and services without government regulation. The period of the ENLIGHTENMENT saw its pursuit of reasoned models of operation filter into all aspects of society, including economic philosophies and practice. Free trade was a significant issue at this time, especially since international trade was increasing due to the beginning of industrialization, improved navigation routes, and the establishment of colonies whose goods could be sold as well as enjoyed by colonial powers. Policies concerning trading arrangements and tariffs imposed on goods imported from other nations thus reached critical significance.

Tariffs were not only an issue in international trade but also in domestic commerce and in relations between nations and their colonies. The AMERICAN REVOLUTION of 1776 was triggered by the British government's attempt to enact higher tariffs upon both imported and exported goods. In France, there were many internal customs barriers, as provinces traditionally operated almost like individual countries within the nation to which they all belonged.

The period ending in the late 18th century was one of MERCANTILISM, which wedded the pursuit of national power to economic development and manipulation. Wealth was measured by the amount of gold and silver a country possessed. Nations that could not produce wealth locally were driven to obtain it via favorable trading relationships. To increase their wealth, nations sought to maximize exports of goods to foreign countries while minimizing imports, and governments used regulations to protect their national economic interests above those of rival states. An intensified version of this philosophy emerged in Germany in CAMERALISM, from the German term *Kammer,* which meant the vault of the royal treasury. Government intervention at all levels was intended to protect and advance the entirety of the nation's wealth. The nation was analogized as a family farm in which the economic interests of the state superceded those of individual relatives, or citizens.

The shift away from mercantilism was already underway by the time of the Scottish Enlightenment of the mid-18th century. Philosophers such as David HUME followed a rational approach to politics and ECONOMICS in their writings that remains influential in contemporary economic thought. Hume's *Political Discourses* of 1752 challenged mercantilist notions in the essays "Of the Balance of Trade" and "Of the Jealousy of Trade," in which he asserted that the flow of currency between nations was self-correcting and that nations could prosper in common with one another rather than necessarily bankrupting one another. He likened this process to a series of connected chambers filled with water: The water will flow into all the chambers and its level will be equalized.

Adam SMITH, another thinker of the Scottish Enlightenment, was the first person to arrive at an exhaustive analysis of trade and commerce within a theoretical framework. His *Inquiry into the Nature and Causes of the WEALTH OF NATIONS* of 1776 extended Isaac NEWTON's vision of the universe as an elegant, self-regulating machine to the analysis of the root forces of economic growth and interaction. Bernard de MANDEVILLE had already argued in his *Fable of the Bees* at the beginning of the 18th century that private vices led to public benefits. Comparing society to a beehive, Mandeville argued that each individual operates according to personal impulses, but that the group benefits nevertheless. Individuals' desire to become rich and successful should naturally lead to a prosperous and happy society. Smith made a similar argument: People working to improve their own economic standing, guided by sound rational and moral principles, would necessarily improve the economic standing of the nation as a whole, and on an even larger scale, that of the world. He used the phrase "the invisible hand" to describe the operation of such an economic system: It functions smoothly on its own, as if an invisible hand were regulating its workings. Smith supported this claim with observations of commercial enterprises and governmental legislation. To him, economic intervention by the government was not only pointless but frequently destructive, as tyrannical influences sought to rob people of their wealth as well as LIBERTY. Smith's work proved so influential that it is still cited by economic policy makers today.

Further reading: John Brewer, *The Sinews of Power: War, Money and the English State, 1688–1783* (New York: Alfred A. Knopf, 1989); Johannes Overbeek, *Free Trade versus Protectionism: A Source Book of Essays and Readings* (Northampton, Mass.: Edward Elgar, 1999); Richard Semmel, *The Rise of Free Trade Imperialism: Classical Political Economy, the Empire of Free Trade, and Imperialism, 1750–1850* (London: Cambridge University Press, 1970).

French Academy of Sciences   Official state institution for the study and dissemination of natural sciences; established in 1666 by LOUIS XIV and his controller general of finances, Jean-Baptiste Colbert. It was called the Académie Royale des Sciences (Royal Academy of Sciences). The academy met weekly at the Bibliothèque du Roi (now the Bibliothèque Nationale) in PARIS. Its mem-

bers were elected after submitting research papers in any of several scientific fields. Members received a royal stipend whose size varied according to the specific membership category to which they belonged. The academy transferred its meetings to the Louvre in 1699. Although still under royal control, it changed its name to the Académie des Sciences (Academy of Sciences). It published official *Mémoires* of each year's activities and also the influential *Journal des Savants*.

The Academy of Sciences functioned as a kind of official arbiter of scientific thought in FRANCE. It assisted the absolute French monarchs in their drive to establish state guidance and control over all arenas of intellectual and artistic life. As a result, the academy sometimes stifled the more innovative facets of French scientific life. At the time of its foundation, however, it became a place for the adherents of the new MECHANICAL PHILOSOPHY that was revolutionizing scientific thought. Mechanical philosophers acquired teaching posts in the French UNIVERSITIES only with difficulty, and the academy provided them with another forum and source of support.

Many of the major scientific figures of the ENLIGHTENMENT were active members of the Academy of Sciences. The long list of outstanding members illustrates the extent to which the activity of science was linked to the French state. Their ranks included Jean Le Rond d'ALEMBERT; Paul-Joseph BARTHEZ; Claude Louis BERTHOLLET; Napoléon Bonaparte; Louis Antoine de BOUGAINVILLE; George Louis Leclerc, comte de BUFFON; César-François CASSINI DE THURY; Alexis-Claude CLAIRAUT; Marie-Jean-Antoine-Nicolas Caritat, marquis de CONDORCET; Charles-Augustin de COULOMB; Georges CUVIER; Louis-Jean-Marie DAUBENTON; and Joseph-Nicolas DELISLE. Also included were Nicolas DESMAREST, Bernard Le Bovier de FONTENELLE, Claude-Adrien HELVÉTIUS, four members of the Jussieu family, Joseph-Louis LAGRANGE, Joseph-Jérôme Le Français de LALANDE, Jean Baptiste Pierre Antoine de Monet de LAMARCK, Pierre-Simon LAPLACE, Antoine LAVOISIER, Gottfried Wilhelm LEIBNIZ, Pierre Louis Moreau de MAUPERTUIS, Gaspard Monge, Jean-Antoine NOLLET, Philippe Pinel, François QUESNAY, and Félix Vicq d'Azyr.

During the FRENCH REVOLUTION, the Academy of Sciences and all the other ANCIEN RÉGIME academies were disbanded because of their corporate form of organization and elite membership. The first action against the academies occurred in November 1792, when a decree was passed forbidding new members to be elected to replace those who had died. Many academicians fled from Paris to escape imprisonment, and others were so busy with revolutionary activities that they had no time to attend meetings. Activities at the Academy of Science, consequently, came to a near halt.

On August 8, 1793, despite intense efforts by Lavoisier and Condorcet to convince enemies that the academies served the causes of UTILITY and PROGRESS, the Convention abolished all academies. The functions of the

Academy of Science were divided between three different types of institution: Advice to the government was to be provided by specially appointed individuals or commissions; the task of education went to new institutions such as the Muséum d'Histoire Naturelle and the public schools; and the job of advancing science was given to private voluntary associations, the so-called *sociétés libres* (free societies). This new organization was designed to reflect republican ideals and to foster science as a democratic rather than elite enterprise.

The new system failed to survive the downfall of Maximilien ROBESPIERRE and the end of the Jacobin-led Terror. On August 22, 1795, the Convention ratified an act that established a new super academy, the Institut de France. Inspired both by the radical ideas of the IDÉO-LOGUES and by recognition that the old academic system had embodied some desirable approaches to the problem of creating and disseminating knowledge and culture, the new Institut had several sections or classes, each of which was devoted to a different pursuit. The arts, science, and literature were all brought under its jurisdiction. The Institut de France was reorganized by Napoleon Bonaparte in 1803 and continues to exist today.

French Revolution   The term used to cover the comprehensive political and social upheavals that began in FRANCE in 1789. The French revolutionary era lasted from 1789 until 1815, when the Congress of Vienna restored the Bourbon monarchy to power. During these years, French subjects overthrew the political and social order of the ANCIEN RÉGIME. In its place, they first established a constitutional monarchy, followed by a republic with several different forms of executive leadership, and, finally, the empire of Napoleon.

During its course, the French Revolution produced many changes of government and policy. Historians usually break the revolutionary era up into several distinct phases that can be characterized as follows:

> *Phase I* (July 1788–June 1789). Elections to the Estates General and the beginning of the conflict pitting the Third Estate (bourgeoisie) against the First and Second Estates (clergy and nobility).
>
> *Phase II* (June 1789–October 1789). The Third Estate declares itself the National Constituent Assembly, takes the Tennis Court Oath (June 20, 1789), abolishes feudal privilege (August 4, 1789), and produces the DECLARATION OF THE RIGHTS OF MAN AND THE CITIZEN. The National Assembly declares its intent to reform France as a constitutional monarchy. The storming of the Bastille (July 14, 1789) and other manifestations of popular insurrection take place.
>
> *Phase III* (October 1789–September 1791). The clergy are required to take an oath upholding a new Civil Constitution of the Clergy (July 12, 1790). This

Louis XVI and the Paris mob at the Tuileries. On several occasions, mob action helped to tilt French revolutionaries toward more radical positions. *(Courtesy New York Public Library)*

constitution reorganizes the Catholic Church parishes and bishoprics, transforms the clergy into civil servants paid by the secular state, and confiscates church properties. The Constituent Assembly also prepares the Constitution of September 1791. The document sets up a constitutional monarchy based on the concept of the SEPARATION OF POWERS. A representative legislature is to be elected by "active" citizens (citizens who owned a certain amount of PROPERTY). During this period, trade and craft guilds are also abolished.

> *Phase IV* (October 1791–August 1792). A Legislative Assembly is elected under the constitution. The Girondin faction of the Jacobins dominates the assembly proceedings. France declares war on the HAPSBURG EMPIRE in April 1792. August 10, 1792, brings an urban insurrection by working-class people, responding to economic distress. The Tuileries palace is stormed, and King LOUIS XVI is imprisoned with his family. The new revolutionary

à Versailles à Versailles du 5. Octobre 1789.

"To Versailles, to Versailles!" During the French Revolution, groups of lower-class Parisian women transformed the traditional urban bread riot into an act with political overtones. In October 1789, led by a group of revolutionary leaders, women marched to Versailles and forced King Louis XVI to return to Paris with his family. *(Courtesy New York Public Library)*

"Commune" in Paris forces the election of a new legislative body to be called the National Convention. The name is drawn from the American Constitutional Convention that was held in PHILADELPHIA in 1787.

Phase V (September 1792–1795). This is the most radical period of the revolution. A revolutionary republic is established by the National Convention that replaced the Legislative Assembly. In Paris, the working-class "sans-culottes" press for more radical, democratic reforms. The Convention abolishes the French monarchy on September 21, 1792, and, after condemning Louis XVI for treason, has him executed in January 1793. In April 1793, the victorious revolutionary military leader General Dumouriez defects to Austria. The specter of counterrevolution seems to be an increasing threat. Girondin leaders are arrested in May 1793 under pressure from the sans-culottes. The Mountain faction of the Jacobin Party assumes control of the Convention. Tension heightens in Paris and fears

of foreign intervention grow stronger. In early September 1792, more than 1,300 prisoners suspected of royalist sympathies are massacred in Paris by an angry mob of people. The Convention reacts to the specter of anarchy by creating the Committee of Public Safety to oversee domestic affairs. The Committee includes Maximilien ROBESPIERRE and Louis-Antoine-Léon de SAINT-JUST. Under their leadership, the Terror begins. Imprisonments and executions are ordered for political opponents. About 40,000 people are guillotined and many thousands more imprisoned. Economic regulations such as price controls aim at helping the lower classes. Peasants are relieved of the last vestiges of manorial obligations to their lords. A program of dechristianization is instituted and the Cult of REASON established as the official secularized creed of France (1793), both advocated by the radical Parisian Commune leader Jacques René Hébert. Finally, political opposition to Robespierre and the Committee of Public Safety brings their downfall on July 27, 1794 (9 Thermidor). The most radical revolutionary reforms are abandoned. This period, known as the Thermidorean reaction, produces the Constitution of Year III (1795) that sets up a new government called the Directory.

Phase VI (1795–1799). The era of the Directory was that of the first formally structured French republic. Adult males vote for electors (propertied males) who choose all members of the national legislature and high state officials. A bicameral legislative assembly is established consisting of a Council of Five Hundred and a Council of Ancients (250 men over age 40). The elections of 1797 are overturned on September 4, 1797, by the coup d'etat of 18 Fructidor, instituted by some Directory leaders with military support from General Napoleon Bonaparte. The Directory degenerates into an ineffective dictatorship, which is overturned by Napoleon's coup d'etat of 18 Brumaire (November 9, 1799).

Phase VII (November 1799–1804). The Consulate is established. Napoleon sets himself up as first consul of France. Although the forms of a republic are retained, power is effectively concentrated in his person. Peace is reached with the pope, and the Concordat of 1801 restores ROMAN CATHOLICISM in France. The Napoleonic Code of 1804 and other reforms attempt to preserve some revolutionary changes. The Consulate brings the end of the French Revolution internally, but the years of the empire see a continuation of international war.

Phase VIII (1799–1815). The Napoleonic Empire extends its control into Italy and the German territories on the Rhine and attempts to conquer all of Europe. The HOLY ROMAN EMPIRE is finally dissolved. PRUSSIA experiences humiliating and devastating defeats at Jena (1806) and Auerstädt, leaving Napoleon with a free rein in northern Europe. The Russians, aided by the brutal winter cold, defeat Napoleon in 1812 and force his retreat. Additional defeats at the battle of Leipzig (Battle of Nations, October 1813) and in Paris (April 1814) result in Napoleon's exile to the island of Elba. The French Bourbon monarchy is restored. Napoleon makes a dramatic escape from Elba, reappears in Europe (March 1815) at the head of an army, and is finally defeated at the Battle of Waterloo (June 18, 1815). European peace is restored by the Treaty of Vienna in 1815.

From the beginning, interpretations of the French Revolution have included discussions of the ENLIGHTENMENT, and attitudes toward the revolution have colored assessments of enlightened ideas. But historians have argued over the extent to which enlightened ideas actually caused the revolution. Most modern historians tend to give more causal weight to the budgetary crises, social stresses, political paralysis, and economic upheavals that preceded the outbreak of revolt. Nevertheless, certain ideals and values of the Enlightenment definitely provided inspiration and ideological garb in which various revolutionary groups presented their goals and demands.

The various political conflicts of the French Revolution reveal obvious debts to the Enlightenment. In each phase, leaders drew on enlightened political theory for general ideals. The famous slogan, *liberté, egalité, et fraternité* (LIBERTY, EQUALITY, and brotherhood), derived directly from enlightened beliefs in the universal qualities of human nature. The philosophy of John LOCKE, for example, suggested that people are born as intellectual equals and that inequality arises from personal historical circumstances. Equality, then, was the natural condition of humankind, a situation that revolutionaries believed should be preserved in human political institutions.

Problems arose when people began trying to give these values concrete forms of existence. They could not agree on specific concrete reforms and political structures. What did equality mean in political terms? Should the idea extend beyond political bounds to include social and economic equality? Were women truly the equals of men?

At first, the French Revolution was moderate, seeking only to eliminate the remnants of feudal privilege that were embedded in the legal, fiscal, and political structures of the ancien régime. On August 4, 1789, a group of noblemen and bourgeois delegates to the Estates declared the abolition of all feudal privileges. Henceforth, French men (women were not included) would enjoy legal equality; all laws would apply to all men, regardless of their social status or wealth.

Such extensive change could not, of course, be instituted without opposition from the groups whose privileges were being abolished. Furthermore, certain groups wished to see far more radical changes that involved broader reforms in the name of equality. As a result, the declaration of August 4, 1789, escalated the political crisis in France, opening the door not only for open discussion of change but also for active rebellion.

The early revolutionaries not only disliked the French legal system, but also wished to abolish royal ABSOLUTISM. It proved impossible, however, to reach agreement on the form for a new government. Moderates wanted to retain the monarchy, but to transform it into a limited and constitutional monarchy modeled after ENGLAND. More progressive groups favored a republic in which elected officials would rule the nation. Finally, a small group of radical reformers desired to see direct democracy take root in France.

The Enlightenment had prepared the ground for these disputes with its lively intellectual queries and debates about POLITICAL THEORY. The *SPIRIT OF LAWS* by MONTESQUIEU and the *Lettres philosophiques* by VOLTAIRE had popularized the English model, while the AMERICAN REVOLUTION provided immediate inspiration for moderate republicans. Radical democrats turned to the *SOCIAL CONTRACT* by Jean-Jacques ROUSSEAU for their theoretical arguments. On one level, the French Revolution witnessed the playing out in practice of the conflicts between these various theories.

Although the political arena provided the most dramatic and obvious stage on which people attempted to put their enlightened ideals into practice, these attempts also transformed other aspects of French life. From the beginning, revolutionaries turned their energies to the reform of French EDUCATION. Faith in PROGRESS and the power of REASON inspired Marie-Jean de CONDORCET, the IDÉOLOGUES, and other reformers to formulate plans for a compulsory and free system of education in France. Church-controlled schools were replaced by state schools offering education at all levels. The royal academies were also disbanded and a new comprehensive Institut de France set up in their place.

The revolutionaries also abolished the links between the secular state and Roman Catholicism that had characterized the ancien régime. They believed that the SEPARATION OF CHURCH AND STATE was essential to political freedom and wished to rid the state of a hierarchical organization with ambivalent political allegiances.

The enlightened passion for reason translated into attempts to bring order and uniformity into the French monetary system. The metric system of weights and measures replaced old units, and a new calendar built on natural agrarian cycles replaced the old Julian calendar.

As happens in most truly revolutionary situations, none of the new political regimes in France was able to establish its legitimacy and authority in a lasting manner. Social discontent, international war and opposition, economic hardship, and a host of other factors destabilized the situation. When the Mountain (radical Jacobins) under Robespierre assumed leadership, they began resorting to terror and totalitarian measures in efforts both to push more radical change and to protect the revolution from enemies, both real and imagined. These actions, however, created further upheaval and strong opposition to revolutionary values.

Eventually, Napoleon assumed power, establishing first a government of enlightened despotism (see DESPOTISM, ENLIGHTENED) and then the empire. His reforms tried to create a composite of ancien régime and revolutionary structures and revealed strong affinities with the Enlightenment. Public offices were no longer private property; holders received salaries from the state and supposedly obtained their positions on the basis of their talents. The Napoleonic Code provided the French with their first universal code of laws, applicable to every citizen. It also provided a clear legal framework for free private enterprise and for the protection of private property. It also contained laws that aimed at suppressing any tendencies on the part of French labor to organize for its protection against exploitation. Thus, Napoleon's code placed strict limits on the extent to which the enlightened concept of equality was to be institutionalized in France.

In the end, the French Revolution left France with a complicated legacy that continues to affect the manner in which historians assess the Enlightenment. It provides material for discussion about the relationship between ideas and actions, for social history, for examinations of the relationship between economic condition and political attitude, and for inquiries into the general conditions that produce radical upheaval in nations.

See also CARNOT; GREGOIRE; JACOBINS; RADICAL ENLIGHTENMENT.

Further reading: Roger Chartier, *The Cultural Origins of the French Revolution,* tr. Lydia G. Cochrane (Durham, N.C.: Duke University Press, 1991); François Furet, *Interpreting the French Revolution,* tr. Elborg Forster (Cambridge: Cambridge University Press, 1981); Simon Schama, *Citizen: A Chronicle of the French Revolution* (New York: Knopf, 1989).

Fréron, Élie-Cathérine (1719–1776) *French critic, journalist, and poet, the avowed enemy of the Philosophes*
Élie-Cathérine Fréron, son of a Quimper silversmith, studied with the JESUITS and entered that order in 1735. In 1739, he left the order and apprenticed himself to the critic Desfontaines, who had established himself as an enemy of VOLTAIRE. Fréron continued the tradition, becoming the principal adversary of Denis DIDEROT, Jean Le Rond d'ALEMBERT, and the project of the ENCYCLOPÉDIE. Fréron maintained an extreme independence, attacking even Madame de POMPADOUR in print. For his efforts, he earned a period of imprisonment at Vincennes.

Fréron began his career collaborating with Desfontaines and François Marius Granet on periodicals such as *Observations sur les écrits modernes* (Observations on modern writings) and *Jugements sur quelques ouvrages nouveaux* (Judgments on some new works). In 1745, he inaugurated his own journal, *Les lettres de Mme la Comtesse de *** sur quelques écrits modernes* (The letters of madame, the countess of *** on some modern writings).

In 1746, after his release from Vincennes, Fréron launched a new periodical, *Lettres sur quelques écrits* (Letters on some writings), in which Jean-François MARMONTEL and Voltaire received biting criticisms. Voltaire, never tolerant of his critics, secured the suspension of the periodical and prevented Fréron from becoming the literary correspondent of FREDERICK II (THE GREAT).

King Stanislaus Augustus PONIATOWSKI of POLAND offered Fréron his protection, enabling the journalist to continue his work. *L'année littéraire* (The literary year, 1754–75) and *Journal étranger* (Foreign journal), the latter edited first by Abbé PRÉVOST, enjoyed popular success and respect. Fréron died in 1776, the day that *L'année littéraire* was suppressed by royal decree.

Friedrich, Caspar David (1774–1840) *German Romantic painter*

Caspar David Friedrich came from Greifswald in the Prussian-controlled territory of Pomerania. He studied art at the University of Greifswald in Pomerania with Johann Gottfried Quistorp and, in 1794, moved to Copenhagen for further study at the Royal Art Academy. He left Copenhagen in 1798 and, after a brief stay in BERLIN, settled in Dresden. Although that city became his permanent home, Friedrich did travel frequently, visiting the Harz Mountains, the Baltic coast, and the Riesengebirge.

The city of Dresden had a group of young writers and artists who were adherents of the movement that would eventually be called ROMANTICISM. Friedrich joined the group, thus becoming acquainted with Novalis (Friedrich von Hardenberg), Johann Ludwig Tieck, and Heinrich von KLEIST.

Although a somewhat shy and reclusive individual, Friedrich nevertheless was known and appreciated by some of his contemporaries. Johann Wolfgang von GOETHE, who was working in Weimar, recognized his talents and awarded him a prize in 1805 for a sepia drawing. The BERLIN ACADEMY elected Friedrich to its membership in 1810, and the Dresden Academy followed in 1816. The Dresden Academy made Friedrich a professor in 1824. In 1825, Friedrich became ill, a stroke crippled him in 1835, and death followed in 1840.

The paintings and drawings of Friedrich mark him as a transitional figure between the realism of 18th-century German neoclassicists such as Anton Raphael MENGS and fully-developed romanticism. Friedrich's notable paintings include *The Wreck of the "Hope," Graveyard in the Snow, Alpine Scenery, Two Men Contemplating the Moon,* and *Rest in a Hayfield.*

Fuseli, Henry (Swiss German: Johann Heinrich Füssli) (1741–1825) *Swiss painter*

Henry Fuseli was a native of Zürich. He was the son of the portrait painter, theorist, and art historian Johann Caspar Füssli (1706–82) and godson of the painter and writer Salomon Gessner. The young Füssli studied AESTHETICS with Johann Jakob BODMER at the Zürich Collegium Carolinum. He also took courses in theology and English and, after graduation, entered the ministry (1761) as a Zwinglian preacher. In 1762, Zürich officials ousted Füssli and his friend Johann Kaspar LAVATER for political reasons.

Füssli moved to BERLIN and developed an association with his Swiss compatriot Johann Georg Sulzer. The two men collaborated in producing the *Allgemeine Theorie der schönen Künste* (Universal theory of the fine arts). In 1764, Füssli translated the neoclassical treatise *Gedanken über die Nachamung der griechischen Kunst* (Reflections on the imitation of Greek art) by Johann Joachim WINCKELMANN into English. In the same year, having obtained a position that served as a link between German and English aesthetic theorists, Füssli traveled to ENGLAND and anglicized his name to Henry Fuseli.

At the suggestion of a new friend, Joshua REYNOLDS, Fuseli spent the years from 1768 until 1778 in ITALY, where he studied the works of Michelangelo and the great masterpieces of antiquity. He developed a great admiration for the heroic aspects of humanity. Like many artists, Fuseli traveled throughout the Italian peninsula. A bout of fever in VENICE (1772) partially affected his right hand.

Fuseli left ROME in 1778 and settled permanently in England. William BLAKE, the painter and poet, became his friend, and Fuseli assisted Blake in finding a publisher for some of his works. The Royal Academy accepted Fuseli as an associate member in 1778 and as a full member in 1780. He served as a professor at the Royal Academy from 1799 until 1805 and again from 1810 until his death in 1825. He was buried in St. Paul's Cathedral in LONDON.

Fuseli had a significant impact as a painter. Although he moved in circles with neoclassical painters, he himself moved toward the aesthetic of the newer ROMANTICISM. He was particularly fascinated with portraying the irrational and wholly subjective but nevertheless heroic sides of the human mind. He drew his artistic inspiration from the Italian late-Renaissance Mannerists and especially from Michelangelo. His most famous painting is *The Nightmare* (1781). Other important paintings are *Death of Cardinal Beaufort* (1774) and *The Oath on the Rütli* (1778).

G

Gainsborough, Thomas (1727–1788) *English portrait and landscape painter*

Gainsborough, the son of a woolen goods maker, demonstrated talent at landscape painting from his early adolescence. For that reason, his father consented to send him to LONDON to work as an apprentice with Hubert Gravelot, a French painter and engraver. Gravelot introduced Gainsborough to the aesthetic and techniques of French ROCOCO painting, which, along with the designs and techniques of 17th-century Dutch landscape painters, were most influential in forming Gainsborough's early style.

Gainsborough always preferred landscape painting to portraiture; he turned to the latter only as a means of earning income and often placed his subjects in pastoral landscapes. These portraits, natural and spontaneous in mood, were highly regarded, and soon Gainsborough was receiving commissions from highly placed clients in the fashionable circles of Ipswich. Gainsborough had settled in this town in 1746, after marrying Margaret Burr, the illegitimate daughter of the duke of Beaufort.

In 1759, the Gainsboroughs moved to the resort town of Bath. This new location allowed Gainsborough to meet numerous wealthy English families who subsequently commissioned him to do portraits. Gainsborough began exhibiting regularly in London in the 1760s and won election to the Royal Academy in 1768.

Upon moving to London in 1774, Gainsborough received both royal and aristocratic commissions. A 1781 commission from King George III provided the opportunity to paint both the king and Queen Charlotte. Gainsborough died in London in 1788.

Notable portraits by Gainsborough include *The Blue Boy, Mr. and Mrs. Andrews, Mrs. Siddons, Mr. William Woollaston, Mrs. Graham, C.F. Abel,* and *Isabella, Countess of Sefton.* Of his many landscape paintings, *Cornard Wood, Peasants returning from Market, The Market Cart, The Woodcutter Courting a Milkmaid,* and *The Cottage Door*

Mrs. Garrick, portrait by Thomas Gainsborough. Gainsborough became an expert at translating aspects of personality onto the painted canvas and left an invaluable legacy for students of prominent 18th-century figures. *(Courtesy New York Public Library)*

provide a glimpse of the painter's range of conceptualization and talent.

Galiani, Ferdinando (1728–1787) *Neapolitan economist who opposed the economic theories of the French Physiocrats* Galiani, the son of a Neapolitan gentleman and royal official, studied at the University of Naples during the tenure of Antonio GENOVESI. Pope BENEDICT XIV made Galiani a canon at the cathedral of Amalfi. In 1751, Galiani published an anonymous book, *Della Moneta,* on the circulation of money.

Galiani served from 1759 until 1769 as the secretary to the Neapolitan ambassador in PARIS. Throughout this period he corresponded regularly with the Neapolitan minister Bernardo TANUCCI. Galiani was received into the major Parisian salons where he made the acquaintance of PHILOSOPHES such as Anne-Robert-Jacques TURGOT, VOLTAIRE, Denis DIDEROT, and André Morellet. Galiani returned to Naples by royal order in 1769 where, as secretary of the Board of Trade and adviser to the treasury, he helped to formulate and implement Neapolitan economic policies. He died in Naples in 1787.

Galiani published his ideas on commerce in the *Dialogues sur le commerce des bleds* (Dialogues on grain commerce; 1770). The book's criticisms of free trade and related economic reforms provoked a heated debate in the French press between the supporters of the PHYSIOCRATS and those favoring Galiani. Diderot eventually sided with Galiani, making his support publicly known by publishing the *Lettre à M.***sur l'abbé Galiani* (Letter to Mr.*** on Abbé Galiani). Diderot also wrote, but never published, an *Apologie de l'Abbé Galiani, ou réponse à la réfutation de Dialogues sur le commerce des bleds par l'abbé Morellet* (Apology of Abbé Galiani, or response to the refutation of the Dialogues on the Commerce of Grains by Abbé Morellet).

The *Dialogues* grew out of Galiani's bitter experiences with the Italian famine of 1764. From his post in Paris, he had provided advice to Tanucci, but the interventions had failed to prevent the deaths from starvation and disease of thousands of Neapolitans. Galiani developed a deep sense of pessimism after this experience that helped to shape his critical opinions of French attempts, in 1763 and 1764, to establish a free grain trade. The bitter resistance of privileged groups of the ANCIEN RÉGIME to economic reforms ultimately forced them to be abandoned. From these French events, Galiani derived lasting lessons about political possibilities in his own nation.

In the *Dialogues,* Galiani spelled out a position of political pragmatism that opposed the stringent application of theory or principle to a specific problem. He argued that because grain is a necessity for human survival it must not be treated in the same manner as unessential commodities. Furthermore, he argued that the physiocratic concept of LAISSEZ FAIRE, with its

Ferdinando Galiani, engraving by Gillberg after Lefèvre. The Italian economist Ferdinando Galiani served as an important critic of the French Physiocrats and helped to transmit the ideas and writings of the French Enlightenment to the Italian peninsula. *(Courtesy Bildarchiv Preussischer Kulturbesitz, Berlin)*

underlying concept of the balanced harmony that exists in unfettered NATURE, could not properly be applied to human affairs. Over long periods of time, nature does indeed establish perfect balance, but individuals do not live long enough to reap the benefits of this long-term trend. If people wish to survive as individuals, they must intervene in the course of events, living in a state of conflict rather than of harmony with nature.

See also ITALY; SOCIAL INSTITUTIONS OF THE ENLIGHTENMENT.

Galilei, Galileo (commonly called Galileo) (1564–1642) *Italian mathematician, physicist, and astronomer who was a major contributor to the shift in the practices and theories of science commonly called the Scientific Revolution* Galileo's work contributed to the dissemination and acceptance of the theory of the HELIOCENTRIC universe, to the establishment of mathematical equation as the means for expressing universal physical laws (mathematization of the universe), and to the spread of experimental approaches to specific scientific problems. Galileo was a contemporary of René DESCARTES, Johannes KEPLER, William Harvey, Marin MERSENNE, and Pierre GASSEND, each of whom made contributions considered seminal to the development of a new scientific vision and related set of practices.

Galileo was the son of Vincenzo Galilei, an Italian musician and important theorist of MUSIC. Galileo received his primary education from a tutor in Pisa and later form the monks at the monastery of Santa Maria at Vallombrosa in Florence. He studied medicine at the University of Pisa from 1581 until 1585, but he supplemented his medical course work with private instruction in mathematics. He gave private lessons in mathematics from 1585 to 1589 in Florence, before occupying the chair of mathematics at the University of Pisa (1589–91). In 1592, the University of Padua awarded Galileo its mathematics professorship. A few years later, he took a Venetian woman, Marina Gamba, as his mistress. She gave him three children, two daughters, Virginia and Livia, and a son, Vincenzio. The daughters both entered a nunnery near Florence as very young women, whereas Vincenzio was eventually legitimized. Both Virginia and Vincenzio assisted Galileo after 1633, during his long years of house imprisonment.

Galileo remained in his teaching post at Padua until 1610, at which time his astounding discoveries with the TELESCOPE helped to win him an appointment as philosopher and mathematician extraordinary to the grand duke of Tuscany. At the same time, Galileo became the head mathematician at the University of Pisa. A journey to ROME in 1611 to demonstrate his telescopic discoveries resulted in the honor of election to the Lincean Academy.

In 1610, Galileo turned a telescope toward the night sky and made shocking discoveries about the celestial world. He saw that the surface of the Moon was marked by craters and shadowy spots, observations that severely challenged the prevailing notion that the Moon was one of the perfect, incorruptible bodies of the celestial realm. He also discovered the phases of Venus, the four moons of Jupiter, and myriad stars that had been invisible to the naked eye.

These discoveries, published in 1610 as the *Siderius Nuncius* (The starry messenger), provided evidence that could be viewed as substantiation for the heliocentric universe posited by Nicolaus COPERNICUS. At the time, Copernicanism was beginning to receive more public discussion, and Galileo contributed to that process with his *Letters on Sunspots* (1613) and with a private letter to his student Benedetto Castelli that fell into the hands of the Roman Inquisition. An official Catholic commission appointed early in 1616 investigated the theological correctness of the Earth's motion and ruled against it. As a result, in late February 1616, faithful Catholics were forbidden to believe in or to teach Copernicanism, and Galileo was instructed to cease his activities on behalf of

the theory. In addition, Copernicus's 1534 treatise *ON THE REVOLUTIONS OF THE HEAVENLY SPHERES* was censored for the first time, and a book by Paolo Antonio Foscarini that attempted to reconcile biblical passages with Copernican theory was condemned and placed on the Index of Forbidden Books.

Galileo defied these prohibitions in 1632, when he published his *Dialogue on the Two Principal Systems of the World*. The *Dialogue* used subtle arguments to criticize Aristotelian and Ptolemaic views of the universe, focusing specifically on areas whose discrediting would strengthen Copernican arguments. The preface adopted an equivocal position that even today has scholars divided about the extent of Galileo's commitment to Copernicanism. The *Dialogue* contained a number of arguments for Copernicanism invented by Galileo, including references to annual variations in sunspots and the ocean tides. It also used the law of falling bodies, the relativity of motion, the conservation of motion, and the composition of motions—all concepts created by Galileo—in defense of heliocentrism.

Shortly after the *Dialogue* appeared in 1632 in Florence, Galileo was instructed to travel to Rome to appear again before the Inquisition, but he postponed his journey until February 1633. The trial began in April 1633 and resulted in Galileo's abjuration of the contents of the *Dialogue*. The book was placed on the Index and Galileo was sentenced to house arrest for the remainder of his life. The printing of any books by Galileo, whether old or new, was also forbidden.

Despite this fate, the books and manuscripts of Galileo circulated freely although clandestinely throughout the European intellectual community. Some were summarized, translated, and printed in PARIS by the Catholic Minim monk Marin Mersenne, who had received a copy of the manuscript smuggled from Galileo's house in the security of a French diplomat's pouch. Other Galilean books—the *Discourse and Mathematical Demonstrations Concerning Two New Sciences* (1638), known as *Two New Sciences,* for example—were published in the UNITED PROVINCES OF THE NETHERLANDS by the Elzeviers of Leiden.

The popular fame of Galileo rests on his spectacular discoveries and the equally notable Inquisition trial. But Galileo made equally important contributions to physics, particularly to mechanics and kinematics (the science of motion). The *Two New Sciences* explores the law of levers as the basis for a science of the strength of materials, examines both uniform and accelerated motion (the inclined plane experiments), and presents a law relating the period of a pendulum to its length. These subjects are treated mathematically by the presentation of equations that describe the phenomena. Galileo also made a noted contribution to physics and by implication to PSYCHOLOGY, when in *Il Saggiatore* (The assayer; 1619) he distinguished between the physical properties of objects and their sensory effects. In that book, a polemic with the Jesuit mathematician Orazio Grassi, Galileo also claimed that only mathematicians can decipher the "book of nature" (as opposed to the Bible, the "book of revelation") since it is written in mathematical language. Finally, he claimed that received tradition or authority must be repudiated in any matters accessible to direct investigation.

Galileo spent the last years of his life, from early 1634 to his death in 1642, at his villa at Arcetri near Florence. He became totally blind in 1638. At his death his remains were buried in the Church of Santa Croce in Florence, but the tomb that today commemorates Galileo was not erected until the middle of the 18th century.

Galileo was a major figure in the creation of the SCIENTIFIC REVOLUTION, and a scientific figure revered during the ENLIGHTENMENT. The MECHANICAL PHILOSOPHY, the theory of NATURE that dominated the early Enlightenment, owed much to Galileo's work, and Copernicanism began to take root outside narrow scientific circles as a result of his work. Both developments, of course, helped to determine the future outlines of NATURAL PHILOSOPHY and SCIENCE. The fact of Galileo's trial and house imprisonment by Catholic Church authorities underscored, for both his contemporaries and later generations, the obstacles to free intellectual inquiry posed by intertwined church-state relations. In short, Galileo was one of the great father figures of the Enlightenment, even though he lived nearly a century before the beginning of that era. It is fitting that his monumental tomb in Florence was erected not in the 17th century, but during the years of enlightened rule in Florence.

See also MATHEMATICS AND MECHANICS.

Further reading: Mario Biagioli, *Galileo, Courtier: The Practice of Science in the Culture of Absolutism* (Chicago: University of Chicago Press, 1993); Thomas L. Hankins, *Science and the Enlightenment* (Cambridge: Cambridge University Press, 1985); Thomas S. Kuhn, *The Copernican Revolution: Planetary Astronomy in the Development of Western Thought* (Cambridge, Mass.: Harvard University Press, 1957).

Gall, Franz Joseph (1758–1828) *German-born psychologist, neuroanatomist, and proponent of phrenology, who worked primarily in Vienna and Paris*

Gall studied MEDICINE at the University of Strasbourg and received his medical degree from the University of VIENNA. He established a medical practice that included many prominent individuals. He worked first in Vienna, but moved to PARIS in 1807. He became a French citizen in 1819 and died in Paris in 1828.

Gall argued that theories of mind and the brain based on sensation psychology—those of the French IDÉOLOGUES and Abbé CONDILLAC, for example—failed adequately to explain the origins of individual character and personality. Like so much science of the ENLIGHTENMENT,

Gall's theory carried implications not only for PSYCHOLOGY and BIOLOGY but also for EPISTEMOLOGY and ontology (the philosophical study of the nature of existence). Gall's ideas reflected the radical, antimechanistic philosophy that emerged during the late Enlightenment. His ideas were related to and partially derived from Johann Gottfried HERDER and early German *Naturphilosophie*.

Gall drew on comparative and developmental theories as well as organic and holistic ideas for his theory of mind-body relationships. He returned to an old concept, that of brain organs (a concept drawn by analogy from other internal organs), in an effort to describe the RELATIONS between cranial structures and observed behavior. In the list of functions and associated brain organs, Gall included not only recognized physiological processes such as digestion, or traditional brain functions such as speech and thought, but also sexuality, emotion, passions, and RELIGION.

In determining the locations of the brain organs, Gall assumed that an analogy exists between the qualities of a specific brain function and observable physical structure. In other words, character and personality can be read from external physical characteristics. Gall, therefore, was asserting that both moral and intellectual faculties are innate and that their expressions in a given individual are determined by the physiological organization of the body. These beliefs differentiated him sharply from the sensation psychologists who argued that experience determines personality and intellect. Gall's ideas formed the basis for his highly popular, but controversial, PHRENOLOGY, a theory that was criticized heavily by traditional psychologists, scientists, and church theologians. Largely on account of their opposition to this "nonscientific" aspect of his work, Gall failed in 1808 to gain the honor of admission to the Institut de France (the organization that replaced the FRENCH ACADEMY OF SCIENCES during the FRENCH REVOLUTION).

Gall developed his brain theory before 1791 and published its basic principles in the *Philosophische-medicinische Untersuchungen über Natur und Kunst im kranken und gesunden Zustände des Menschens* (Philosophical-medical investigations about nature and art in the sick and healthy conditions of human beings; 1791). In conjunction with Johann C. Spurzheim, a research assistant, Gall later developed a program of neuroanatomical investigation that yielded results of importance for anatomical theories in later generations. Gall conceived of the nervous system as a hierarchy of structures, in which the higher structures developed from lower ones. This theory led him to differentiate between the active tissues (higher order gray matter) and the conducting tissues (lower order white matter) of the brain. Gall and Spurzheim published the results of their work in four volumes accompanied by an atlas of a thousand plates bearing the title *Anatomie et physiologie du système nerveux en général, et du cerveau en particulier, avec des observations sur la possibilité de reconnoître plusieurs dispositions intellectuelles et morales de l'homme et des animaux, par la configuration de leurs têtes* (Anatomy and physiology of the general nervous system and of the brain in particular, with some observations on the possibility of knowing several intellectual and moral traits of humans and animals by the configuration of their heads; 1810–19).

See also LAVATER.

Gallicanism   Religious and political movement proclaiming the independence of the French Catholic Church from ROME. While the word *gallicanism* comes from the Latin *ecclesia gallicana* (the French church), the phenomenon can be linked to similar attempts in other countries to subordinate religious authority to political authority. However, in FRANCE the struggle between the monarchy and the Catholic Church was particularly bitter.

This struggle came to the forefront in the 17th century while the church faced other challenges to its authority from the developing power of PROTESTANTISM. Under the stewardship of Pope Paul V, who spoke out against increasing calls for independent administration of the French church in the early part of the century, ROMAN CATHOLICISM faced further rebellion when the authority of France's king was proclaimed to be independent of Rome, proceeding directly from divine authority. This debate continued over the century as Paul V's successors faced mounting resistance from French religious authorities. King LOUIS XIV asserted increasing political autonomy, to the point of seizing church funds in France and refusing military aid to Rome in the face of the Turkish invasion of Europe in the second half of the century.

When Pope Innocent XI took power in 1676 and condemned these stirrings of autonomy, the French clergy, responding to Louis XIV's wishes, proclaimed the Four Gallican Articles of 1682. These articles denied the pope's authority over worldly matters, asserted the superiority of councils of bishops over the pope, declared that the authority of papal decrees depended on their acceptance by the church, and rejected the notion of the pope's infallibility. All four articles placed limitations on the pope's authority, with the intention that French bishops, under the control of Louis XIV, would acquire more power. The king proclaimed that these articles would be taught as official church doctrine in all seminaries and universities. Naturally, Innocent XI rejected this encroachment on papal authority, and this dispute verged on producing a schism between the French church and the Roman Catholic Church. In retaliation, Innocent XI refused to approve the king's nominees for vacant bishoprics, and many positions remained unfilled.

Bitterness on both sides of the conflict continued into the following centuries, but the rift was at least partially healed by a compromise under Pope Innocent XII. The pope ratified the king's appointments of bishops, and Louis XIV no longer required French bishops to subscribe to the Gallican Articles. Nevertheless, the Gallican Articles remained in force. Thus, the compromise amounted to a grudging acceptance of Gallican church authority on the part of the pope. Gallicanism would remain the norm in France until the FRENCH REVOLUTION and Napoleon I.

See also DIVINE RIGHT OF KINGS; JESUITS.

Further reading: Thomas Bokenkotter, *A Concise History of the Catholic Church* (New York: Doubleday, 1979); Austen Gough, *Paris and Rome: The Gallican Church and the Ultramontane Campaign, 1848–1853* (New York: Oxford University Press, 1986); P. G. Maxwell-Stuart, *Chronicle of the Popes: The Reign-by-Reign Record of the Papacy from St. Peter to the Present* (New York: Thames & Hudson, 1997).

Galvani, Luigi (1737–1798) *Bolognese anatomist and physiologist*
Galvani spent most of his life in that city, studying MEDICINE, practicing clinical and surgical medicine, and teaching and researching at the University of Bologna and the Istituto delle Scienze.

Galvani is credited by modern historians of science with discovering current electricity (galvanism) during experiments with the nerve and muscle tissue of frogs, but it is important to note that he never spoke of his discoveries in these terms. When he designed his frog experiments, Galvani was investigating the property of irritability in animal tissue. The subject lay at the center

Engraving of Luigi Galvani. In experiments with frog tissue, Galvani discovered "animal electricity," a phenomenon now known as current electricity. *(Courtesy New York Public Library)*

of controversies between adherents of VITALISM and more traditional mechanistic approaches to the explanation of life. Galvani believed that his experiments demonstrated the existence of a special "animal electricity." Throughout the 1790s, he defended this conceptualization against the attacks of his contemporary Alessandro VOLTA. Galvani reported his experiments and findings in his *De viribus electritatis in motu musculari commentarius* (Commentary on electrical forces in muscular motion) published in 1791. His other scientific papers were published in 1841 as *Opere edite et inedite* (Published and unpublished Works).

Garrick, David (1717–1779) *English playwright and theater director*

David Garrick was a legendary actor during his lifetime and one of the outstanding English actors of all time. David Garrick was the son of Peter Garrick, an officer in the English army, and his wife, Arabella Clough. As HUGUENOTS, the Garrick family had fled from FRANCE in 1685 when King LOUIS XIV reinstituted religious persecution with the revocation of the Edict of Nantes. Young Garrick enrolled in the school at Edial operated by Samuel JOHNSON. When that venture failed, Johnson set out for LONDON with Garrick as a companion.

From boyhood, Garrick demonstrated talent for and interest in the THEATER. In London, he set himself up as a wine merchant after a brief stint in law school, but continued to pursue his real love, theater, on the side. His first comedy, *Lethe, or Esop in the Shades,* played at Drury Lane Theatre in 1740. Garrick made his acting debut one year later as a substitute in the role of Harlequin. His career bloomed after his outstanding 1741 performance as Richard III in Shakespeare's tragedy of the same name. He was immediately hired to act at the prestigious Drury Lane Theatre and, in 1747, became the director of that institution. Under his leadership, the theater flourished.

Garrick brought a new acting style to London theater, one that seemed natural in comparison with the formal French style that was then dominant in English theater. At Drury Lane Theatre, Garrick devoted himself to productions of Shakespeare's plays, altering them, however, to fit contemporary tastes. He also produced contemporary plays and other English classics.

Garrick played a major role in creating the English passion for Shakespeare. Through his efforts, the late-16th-century bard acquired preeminence as England's national poet and playwright. Garrick established the first Shakespeare festivals and held meetings at Shakespeare's home, Stratford-on-Avon, to commemorate him. He even arranged for the sale of souvenir twigs plucked from the great oak under which Shakespeare was allegedly buried.

In 1749, Garrick married a Viennese dancer named Eva Maria Veigel whom he had met at the home of Lord Burlington. The marriage was apparently a happy one, and the Garricks' hospitality was renowned. Garrick was a member of the Literary Club, whose center was Samuel Johnson. He sat for portraits by many artists, including Thomas GAINSBOROUGH, Joshua REYNOLDS, and William HOGARTH. Garrick died from the complications of kidney disease in 1779. His wife survived him until 1822.

See also COWLEY.

Garve, Christian (1742–1798) *German translator and popular philosopher*

Christian Garve was born in the Silesian city of Breslau. He studied in Frankfurt an der Oder and at HALLE, receiving his degree in philosophy in 1766. From 1770 to 1772, Garve was professor of philosophy at the University of Leipzig.

In 1772, Garve returned to Breslau, where he opened a book store and concentrated on writing and translation. He produced a number of important translations, rendering works by Adam SMITH, Adam FERGUSON, Edmund BURKE, Cicero, and Aristotle into German. He also participated in the Berlin ENLIGHTENMENT, offering a criticism of Immanuel KANT's *Critique of Pure Reason* and contributing to Friedrich NICOLAI's *Allgemeine Deutsche Bibliothek,* a German publication similar in its aims to the French ENCYCLOPÉDIE.

Garve was a "popular philosopher" in that he contributed to popularizing the ideas of the Enlightenment through publications such as the *Bibliothek* and various journals. Garve's own ideas were influenced by English EMPIRICISM and freemasonry—he was active as a member of the Golden Scepter lodge in Breslau. He died there in 1798. His importance lies in his commentaries on the works of others, which helped to bring the ideas of Gellert, Kant, and those whose works he translated to a wider audience.

See also FREEMASONS.

Gassend, Pierre (also: Pierre Gassendi) (1592–1655) *French philosopher and astronomer*

Gassend played a major role, together with Thomas HOBBES, in reviving MATERIALISM and EPICUREAN PHILOSOPHY for 17th-century Europeans. Pierre Gassend studied at the Jesuit college in Digne and at the University of Aix-en-Provence and was ordained as a Roman Catholic priest in 1615. He taught rhetoric at Digne (1612–14) and philosophy at Aix (1617–23) before being honored with election as canon and provost of the cathedral chapter at Digne (1634–ca. 1655). Gassend taught mathematics at the prestigious Collège Royal in PARIS from 1645 until 1648, then returned to southern FRANCE, where he pursued the philosophical writing that made him renowned. He returned to Paris in 1653, participating in Habert de Montmort's fledgling scientific academy. Gassend died in 1655 at Montmort's home.

Gassend was an early but cautious supporter of Galileo GALILEI, hence of both the HELIOCENTRIC theory of the universe and of the MECHANICAL PHILOSOPHY. He affiliated himself with a circle of scientists and general scholars affiliated with Nicolas-Claude Fabri de Peiresc in Aix and Marin MERSENNE in Paris. These men actively supported the philosophical and theological views that would eventually be called the SCIENTIFIC REVOLUTION. Gassend assisted Mersenne in countering the ANIMISM and occult philosophy of Robert Fludd and also in responding critically to René DESCARTES.

Gassend left work in ASTRONOMY and mechanics that aided the gradual development of these disciplines. But his major contributions, those that earn him a place in an account of the ENLIGHTENMENT, lay in the broader realms of general NATURAL PHILOSOPHY and EPISTEMOLOGY. Through the work of Gassend, both experimental science and Epicurean philosophy acquired support. Gassend's support of experiment meshed with calls from other quarters—Francis Bacon, Christian Huyghens, and Robert Boyle for example—for basing SCIENCE in observation and inductive reasoning. His explorations into Epicurean philosophy provided an account of atomistic theories of the universe and a moral vision that placed HAPPINESS and utility at the center of human existence.

Epicurean materialism provided ideas that facilitated the separation of physics (study of the natural world) from metaphysics (the study of the world in its relationship with God). Realizing that his position conflicted with the doctrines of ROMAN CATHOLICISM, Gassend tried to harmonize the two by suggesting that the all-powerful God of Christianity certainly could have chosen, if he had wished, to create the world according to an Epicurean model.

The work of Gassend entered ENGLAND in the 17th century through the writings of his friend Thomas HOBBES. Scholars know that it was read by Isaac NEWTON, Isaac Barrow, and Robert Boyle. Gassend's works were published in 1658 in Lyons as *Opera omnia* (Complete works) and reprinted in 1727 in Florence. Specific treatises of significance for the Enlightenment were *Exercitationes paradoxicae adversus Aristoteleos, in quibus praecipua totius Peripateticae doctrinae atque dialecticae excuntiuntur* (Exercises against Aristotle in the form of paradoxes; 1624 and 1658, vol. 3 *Opera omnia*) better known by its short title *Exercitationes paradoxicae adversus Aristoteleos; Disquisitio metaphysica seu dubitationes et instantiae adversus R. Cartesii metaphysicam, et responsa* (Metaphysical disquisition or doubts and objections in opposition to R. Descartes metaphysician, and the responses; 1644 and 1658, vol. 3 of *Opera omnia*); *De vita et moribus Epicuri libri octo* (Eight books on the life and death of Epicurus; 1647 and 1658, vol. 5 of *Opera omnia*); and *Syntagma philosophicum* (Philosophical Treatise; published posthumously in 1658, vols. 1 and 2 of *Opera omnia*).

Gatterer, Johann Christoph (1729–1799) *German historian*

Gatterer was a native of Altdorf. Together with his colleague August SCHLÖZER, he helped make the UNIVERSITY OF GÖTTINGEN the leading center of professional HISTORY in the 18th-century German world. Like many of his contemporaries, Gatterer believed that disciplines whose object of study was human behavior could be transformed into genuine sciences.

In the interests of this goal, Gatterer tried to formulate an EPISTEMOLOGY of history and an accompanying method that would support its claims to offer valid scientific knowledge. He concentrated on carefully defining the objects of historical investigation, expanding the traditional focus on political events to include social, economic, and cultural facets of human activity. To support the professional pursuit of history, Gatterer created several institutions: the Historisches Institut in Göttingen (1764) and the journals *Allgemeine Historische Bibliothek* (General historical journal; 1761–71) and *Historische Journal* (Historical journal; 1772–81). Thus, Gatterer assisted in an important intellectual development of the ENLIGHTENMENT, the transformation of history into a respected profession, rooted in scientific EMPIRICISM.

In conceptualizing a scientific discipline of history, Gatterer did not try to make it identical to the abstract physical sciences or to mathematics. Rather, he claimed that historical knowledge rests on a different philosophical base. Historians enter into an intuitive, empathetic relation with the past in order to understand it. Like physicists, they uncover RELATIONS of cause and effect, but historians cannot simply apply REASON based on mathematical deduction in this process. The intuitive understanding is essential and, according to Gatterer, actually a superior form of understanding.

This approach to knowledge places Gatterer squarely within the German Enlightenment (AUFKLÄRUNG). Gatterer demonstrated the creative power of the German approaches to epistemology, linguistics, and PSYCHOLOGY by using them to formulate his revised theory and practice of history.

See also INTUITION AND IMAGINATION; MATHEMATICS AND MECHANICS.

Gay, John (1685–1732) *English poet, librettist, inventor of the ballad opera, and member of the Scriblerus Club*

John Gay was born in Barnstaple, England. He wrote dramatic verse and OPERA libretti, but aside from a few private commissions, such as the one from George Frederick HANDEL for the libretto of *Acis and Galatea*, he did not succeed in getting much work. He was reportedly disappointed and bitter about not receiving an appointment in the English royal court.

Gay translated his bitter sentiments into a satirical attack on BAROQUE STYLE Opera, creating a new dramatic form called ballad opera in the process. THE BEGGAR'S OPERA (1728), the first example of this genre, turned opera conventions upside down by inverting traditional morality and by substituting protagonists drawn from the LONDON underworld—thieves and highwaymen, for example—for the usual mythological heroes. Gay's scenes contain political and social satire that was wholly transparent to his contemporaries. The music consisted of a collection of well-known, popular Scottish, English, and French folk tunes, which the composer John Pepusch supplied with accompaniment. Altogether, *The Beggar's Opera* is an excellent example of the manner in which the culture of the lower classes could be used to illustrate and to criticize upper-class and middle-class customs and values.

The Beggar's Opera enjoyed tremendous success with London audiences, but its transparent political satire embroiled Gay with London theater censors. *Polly* (1729), the sequel to *The Beggar's Opera,* was prohibited from appearing in English theaters and had to wait until 1779, more than 45 years after Gay's death, before it could be produced. The opera libretto and music was, however, published during Gay's lifetime and in this form brought him financial returns.

Other works by Gay include *Rural Sports* (1713), *Shepherd's Week* (1714), and *Fables* (in two series, 1727 and 1738), all verse creations; *Three Hours after Marriage,* a play written by Gay with Alexander POPE and John Arbuthnot; and *Achilles,* a ballad opera that Gay completed shortly before his death.

generation   General term that refers to processes of reproduction and healing. It is important to note from the outset that nothing was known of genetics in the modern sense of the term and that the mammalian egg was simply a theoretical postulate still undetectable even with the aid of the MICROSCOPE.

The subject of generation assumed major significance in the second half of the 18th century as exponents of the PREFORMATION THEORY quarreled with adherents of EPIGENESIS. Preformationists believed that all individual beings were created at the beginning of time. They were believed to be contained in miniature form in the semen or eggs of creatures. Epigeneticists believed that only the potential individual existed and that the process of gestation entailed real changes in the individual organism. They were challenged, therefore, to explain how fully developed individuals could be created in the gestation process. Epigeneticists often but not always subscribed to vitalist ideas about the nature of life, whereas preformationists tended to align themselves with mechanistic visions of living beings.

All major life scientists of the second half of the 18th century dealt with questions of generation. Their number included the comte de BUFFON, Charles BONNET, John NEEDHAM, Abraham TREMBLEY, Pierre de MAUPERTUIS,

Albrecht von HALLER, Caspar Friedrich Wolff, and Lazzaro SPALLANZANI. These men built on the earlier studies of generation by scientists such as Nicolaas Hartsoeker, Jan Swammerdam, Marcello Malphigi, and Antoni van LEEUWENHOEK. Their discussions entered the general discourse of the ENLIGHTENMENT through the writings of Denis DIDEROT and the other ENCYCLOPEDISTS.

The question of generation contained implications for traditional Christian THEOLOGY that were seriously troubling to some life scientists and to certain groups of lay persons. If one accepted the notion that new life is somehow created in the generation process, then God cannot have created all the universe at the beginning of time, and the question arises whether and to what extent God is involved in the generation of individual creatures.

See also ANIMALCULISM; BIOLOGY; DEGENERATION; VITALISM; MECHANICAL PHILOSOPHY.

Geneva (French: Génève: German, Genf) French-speaking city located on the southwestern tip of Lake Geneva at the point where the Rhone River leaves the lake. Today, it is a part of SWITZERLAND, but in the 18th century it was a free city-state, constituted as a republic. The site of Geneva shows evidence of early settlement by the Celts. It became a city of the Roman Empire and the seat of the bishop of Geneva in A.D. 379.

In the 16th century the city became the center of the branch of Protestantism called CALVINISM. The Catholic bishop was expelled, and John Calvin, founder of the Protestant sect, was invited to assume the leadership of the city. He transformed Geneva into a genuine theocracy and gave it the constitution that continued to govern it in the 18th century. The 16th-century city provided a haven for persecuted Calvinists fleeing their native lands.

During the 17th century, Genevans began to resent newcomers although they did not turn them away. They simply refused to grant the newcomers citizenship, thereby relegating them to second-class status. This policy harshly affected the many French HUGUENOTS who fled to Geneva after LOUIS XIV revoked the Edict of Nantes in 1685.

Geneva, although sometimes offered by contemporaries as an example of an ideal republic, seldom held up as such under close scrutiny. Practice did not match theory. In theory, its citizens, acting in assemblies and councils, ruled the city as a republic. However, citizenship was highly restricted, and control of the city rested in the hands of a small, ruling elite who ruled it as an oligarchy. Factional strife marred political relations, and the city experienced a small, mostly unsuccessful democratic revolution in the 1760s.

The ruling oligarchy in Geneva practiced harsh censorship and strict policing of individual behavior. This caused difficulties for PHILOSOPHES who chose to settle in and around the city in order to escape worse conditions elsewhere. The rebellious Jean-Jacques ROUSSEAU, for example, was constantly in trouble with the city authorities, and his books were banned and burned. Although he was a Genevan native, he left the city twice in order to avoid trouble. VOLTAIRE, another example, was an early admirer of Geneva who had moved to the city to avoid harassment at the hands of French officials. He, however, encountered difficulty with the Genevan censors when he started producing his plays before private guests in his home at Ferney. The censors ordered him to stop his activities, declaring that they were dangerous to the morals of Genevan citizens.

At Voltaire's suggestion, Jean Le Rond d'ALEMBERT took up the public defense of the cause of theater in Geneva. His essay on the subject appeared in the ENCYCLOPÉDIE, angering not only Genevan officials but also Rousseau, who entered the fray against both Voltaire and d'Alembert.

In spite of the variety of difficulties that could be encountered with Genevan authorities, the region around the city provided one major focal point for the Swiss ENLIGHTENMENT, supporting, besides Rousseau and Voltaire, Benjamin Constant, Charles BONNET, Charles Tronchin, Madame de STAËL, Abraham TREMBLEY, and Horace-Bénédict de Saussure.

genius   A quality possessed by people with unusual intellectual or artistic gifts. The modern concept of genius first appeared during the second half of the ENLIGHTENMENT. The term derived originally from the Latin word *genius,* which means "guiding spirit or guardian of a person or place." It also had some etymological roots in the oriental concept of the *jinn* or elemental spirit. The term was carried from antiquity into modern times in Christian lore and astrology.

In the 18th century, English and German writers and philosophers, inquiring about the nature of art and of human creativity, began to develop a new meaning for the word. They wished to understand not only how creative work can occur, but also the nature of the relationship between creative artists and society.

Traditional concepts of art and the artist had treated the issue of creativity from the perspective of the crafts. An artist, musician, or writer was simply a well-trained craftsman. Innate talent was recognized, but generally no great distinctions were made between skilled artists and other skilled craftspersons.

This vision of the arts began to shift as the forms of French CLASSICISM gave way in GERMANY to the *STURM UND DRANG* movement in LITERATURE. Writers began to reject the highly formal, rule-bound formulae of classicism, turning instead to literary expressions that stressed individuality and freedom in creation.

In the meantime, philosophers of AESTHETICS were developing the theory that placed INTUITION AND IMAGINATION above REASON in creative processes. Reason had reigned supreme in classicism, and the resulting forms had stressed order, symmetry, clean lines, and other qualities associated with the mathematical model of reason. Reason yielded insights based on analysis, on taking things apart in order to understand them.

In contrast to reason, intuition and imagination were forms of instantaneous, comprehensive insight. They owed nothing to mathematics but were rather linked to the kind of immediate, all-encompassing knowledge possessed by God. This link was critical to the concept of genius, for it suggested that an artist was capable of rising above ordinary human understanding and participating in the kind of knowledge that had always been reserved for God. The artist acquired divine qualities in a manner that made him or her an instrument of and spokesperson for God.

The idea that the artist possesses certain divine qualities was not new; it had been expressed in ancient Greek philosophy by Plato. But it had fallen into disuse and was first brought back into 18th-century philosophy by Edward Young in his *Conjectures on Original Composition.* Young was an English poet whose work helped to create the English Gothic poetic form known as "graveyard poetry," best represented by the work of Thomas GRAY. Young's essay on genius was widely read in Germany and helped to initiate the use of the term in that culture.

A related, but slightly different source for the concept of genius derived again, in the first instance, from England, but later was incorporated into German and French culture. English writers—Thomas BLACKWELL, for example—were inquiring about the nature of genius in primitive literature. In general, they believed that the classical Greek poet Homer and the ancient Hebrew writers of the Bible had possessed an insight and original genius born from superior intuitive and imaginative abilities. These people had intuited truths that could be expressed only through the medium of poetic, symbolic language. The modern genius was, in this interpretation, an individual possessed of such extraordinary gifts.

The idea of the divinely inspired creative genius fit beautifully with another theme central to German intellectuals, that of the individual artist struggling to attain FREEDOM from the constrictions of human institutions. The combination of the idea of the genius as the possessor both of unusual insight and of the responsibilities attendant with true freedom produced the fully developed idea of genius that has since become our common concept of the artistic person.

Within the 18th-century context, this concept of genius asked enlightened intellectuals to wrestle with various questions of MORAL PHILOSOPHY. In particular, they had to work out a satisfactory answer to the question of whether an individual genius was authorized and, indeed, charged with the responsibility to challenge and break social norms and laws. Both Johann Wolfgang von GOETHE and Denis DIDEROT, for example, struggled with this question throughout their lives, occasionally living

"Ancient of Days," hand-colored, metal relief etching by William Blake. Published as the frontispiece for *Europe, A Prophecy,* the "Ancient of Days" symbolized Blake's vision of creative genius and inspiration. *(Courtesy Metropolitan Museum of Art, Rogers Fund, 1930)*

the rebel role and suffering the consequences within their respective societies.

This modern concept of genius was intimately linked to beliefs in the PERFECTIBILITY and PROGRESS of humanity. The genius was, as a result, sometimes defined as nothing more than a person who had reached a higher than normal level of perfection. This twist to the meaning of the concept inspired Claude-Adrien HELVÉTIUS, for example, to write of producing genius in people simply by educating them properly. Helvétius's vision was shared to some extent by Moses MENDELSSOHN and Christoph Friedrich NICOLAI but was not the most common application of the idea. Rather, the concept of genius was generally reserved for the lone figure

at the pinnacle of human development who already had one foot in the realms of the divine. The 18th-century genius was an individual who helped to forge human links with the divine through the medium of his or her art.

The concept of genius liberated its adherents from uneasiness in the face of religious ENTHUSIASM, allowing them to embrace such expressions of faith as an example of inspiration and genius. It generally also gave renewed validity to the expression of intense human passions, suggesting that the expression of intense emotion was a sign of the superhuman status of the artistic genius.

Further reading: Edmund Burke, *A Philosophical Enquiry into the Origins of Our Ideas of the Sublime and*

Beautiful, ed. Adam Phillips (New York: Oxford University Press, 1990).

Genlis, Félicité de (1746–1830) *French tutor and writer of educational treatises and fiction*

While many women worked as tutors or governesses, Genlis's success was extraordinary: She was the first woman to tutor princes of FRANCE. When she was hired in 1779 to teach the five children of the duc de Chartres, Genlis's fame spread, and she acquired many other pupils. She wrote several books on EDUCATION, including *Théâtre à l'usage des jeunes personnes* (Theater of education; 1779) and *Adèle et Théodore, ou lettres sur l'éducation* (Adelaide and Theodore, or letters on education; 1782). Genlis was even proposed for membership in the Académie Française—a remarkable tribute, especially given that a woman was not finally elected to the Académie Française until 1980.

In keeping with many of the pedagogical reforms of her day, Genlis believed in practical, hands-on learning. Her rigorous schedule for her pupils included physical exercise, charitable works, and field trips in addition to traditional subjects of study, such as RELIGION, foreign languages, mathematics, HISTORY, and LITERATURE. For Genlis, the tutor was a maternal figure who combined complete authority over her pupils' lives with affection and understanding.

In 1785, Genlis went to ENGLAND, where Oxford University granted her an honorary degree for her writings, which had been translated into English. There, she met many prominent English personalities of the time, including Edmund BURKE, Fanny BURNEY, and Horace WALPOLE.

When the FRENCH REVOLUTION began in 1789, Genlis played a role in political reform, hosting a salon that was attended by political theorists such as Emmanuel SIEYÈS and even attending some sessions of the National Assembly. Her enthusiasm for the revolution was dampened by the manner in which the National Convention governed and especially by the execution of King LOUIS XVI. When she made another trip to England in 1791, her name was placed on the list of *émigrés* (people who had emigrated from France and were considered enemies of the French republic), and she did not return to France until nine years later. During that time, she gave lessons and published works on public education in order to support herself. After returning to France, Genlis lived out the rest of her life there and maintained her status as a respected thinker on education. Her fictional output dates from this period, including sentimental and historical novels, most of which focused on themes of motherhood and child rearing.

See also WOMEN AND THE ENLIGHTENMENT.

Further reading: Elizabeth Eger, ed., *Women, Writing, and the Public Sphere: 1700–1830* (New York: Cambridge University Press, 2001); Joan Hinde Stewart, *Gynographs: French Novels by Women of the Late Eighteenth Century* (Lincoln.: University of Nebraska Press, 1993).

Genovesi, Antonio (1712–1769) *Italian philosopher and economist, one of the most influential figures of the Enlightenment in Italy*

A native of Castiglione, near Salerno, Genovesi entered the priesthood in 1737 and settled in Naples, where he assumed duties teaching metaphysics at the University of Naples. Genovesi sought new philosophical materials in the ideas of the ENLIGHTENMENT then current in ENGLAND and FRANCE. Isaac NEWTON, John LOCKE, VOLTAIRE, and John TOLAND served as his major sources. He also turned to the German philosopher Gottfried Wilhelm LEIBNIZ for inspiration, and, in general, tried to reconcile RATIONALISM (systematic philosophy) with EMPIRICISM. When his new ideas embroiled him with Catholic authorities, however, Genovesi abandoned the study of philosophy and turned instead to ECONOMICS. In 1754, he received an appointment to teach commerce and mechanics (political economy) at the university.

As an economic theorist, Genovesi borrowed the pragmatic approach stimulated by British and French empiricism and the PHYSIOCRATS, and wedded them to MERCANTILISM. The result was a new form of mercantilism that focused specifically on the unique social and economic conditions that shaped Neapolitan agricultural practices.

Genovesi argued strongly against the temporal power of the Catholic Church. He gained favor with the government of Bernardo TANUCCI, when he asserted that church-owned lands in the Kingdom of Naples should be taken over by the secular state. Genovesi published his economic views in two major works: *Discorso sopra alcuni trattati d'agricoltura . . .* (Discourse on some treatises on agriculture; 1753) and *Delle lezioni di commercio* (Some lectures on commerce; 1765; 2nd edition, 1768).

Genovesi's philosophy can be found in *Disciplinarum metaphysicarum elementa* (Elements of metaphysics; 1743–52) and *Meditazioni filosofiche sulla religione e sulla morale* (Philosophical meditations on religion and moral philosophy; 1758).

See also ILLUMINISTI; KINGDOM OF THE TWO SICILIES; MORAL PHILOSOPHY; RELIGION; ROMAN CATHOLICISM.

geocentric
Term that literally means having the Earth at the center. The model of the universe that dominated European thought from the era of ancient Greece until the long years of the unfolding COPERNICAN REVOLUTION was a geocentric model.

This geocentric model was derived primarily from the physics and cosmology of Aristotle and from the astronomy of Ptolemy. It posited a universe in which the stationary Earth stands at the center of a finite, small, spherical universe. The planets, Sun, Moon, and stars revolve around the Earth on invisible concentric spheres. The planetary spheres were sometimes endowed with deferents and epicycles (smaller circles riding on the larger one) to account for their motions in the night sky as observed from the Earth. The sphere of the stars lay at the outer edge of the universe. All the spheres and the celestial bodies, including Moon and planets, were usu ally conceived as solid, composed of a pure, perfect, weightless, transparent, changeless substance called "aether." This universe contained no void spaces (vacuums). The spheres revolved in a perpetual motion that was guaranteed by the Prime Mover.

This Earth-centered universe was divided into two realms, the terrestrial and the celestial. Each was governed by a separate and unique set of physical laws. In the terrestrial realm, linear motion dominated and all objects strove to reach a state of rest. This terrestrial realm was marked by change over time and physical corruption (decay). In contrast, the celestial realm was the realm of perfection, incorruptibility, and perpetual circular motion.

The geocentric universe differed greatly from the modern, Copernican-based HELIOCENTRIC model. Although individual philosophers and scientists had, on occasion, challenged it before the time of Copernicus, it was not until the arrival of the 16th and 17th centuries that European SCIENCE was receptive to the notion of a vast revolution in cosmological and astronomical conceptions.

Geoffrin, Marie-Thérèse Rodet, Madame (1699–1777) *French hostess, chief social rival of the marquise du Deffand for dominance of the Parisian salons*

Madame Geoffrin, the wife of François Geoffrin, a bourgeois man of commerce, presided over one of the most brilliant literary and artistic salons of the French ENLIGHTENMENT. Her widowed daughter, Marie-Thérèse Geoffrin, marquise de la Ferté-Imbault, assisted her with the gatherings.

An intelligent, beautiful, strong, and practical woman, Madame Geoffrin not only drew intellectuals and artists to her home at the already famous Hôtel de Rambouillet, but she also provided them with pensions

Salon of Madame Geoffrin, by P. L. Debucourt. Madame Geoffrin (1st row, 3rd seated figure from the right) was one of several powerful female patrons of the philosophes. She provided substantial financial support to projects such as the *Encyclopédie.* *(Courtesy Culver Pictures, Inc., New York)*

and other forms of support. In fact, it was Madame Geoffrin who ensured the publication of the ENCYCLOPÉDIE. The project had been halted in 1759 because of financial difficulties and censorship. Madame Geoffrin secretly gave money to the printer to ensure the resumption of the project.

Madame Geoffrin reserved Monday afternoons and evenings for artistic gatherings. Her regular guests included prominent painters and architects such as Jacques SOUFFLOT, Edmé Bouchardon, Étienne-Maurice Falconet, François BOUCHER, Jean-Baptiste GREUZE, Louis-Michel VanLoo, Maurice LA TOUR, and Claude-Joseph Vernet. They also included the antiquarian comte de CAYLUS and the powerful superintendent of buildings, the marquis de Marigny, brother of Madame de POMPADOUR.

Wednesdays were devoted to literary discussion. Madame Geoffrin welcomed Frenchmen such as Pierre de MARIVAUX, Jean-François MARMONTEL, Abbé Morellet, MONTESQUIEU, Bernard de FONTENELLE, VOLTAIRE, Jean Le Rond d'ALEMBERT, and Saint-Lambert. Other guests were Baron d'HOLBACH, Claude-Adrien HELVÉTIUS, Abbé RAYNAL, Denis DIDEROT, and Anne-Robert-Jacques TURGOT. Foreigners visiting PARIS also attended enthusiastically, and at various times, King GUSTAV III OF SWEDEN, the young Stanislaw PONIATOWSKI, Ferdinando GALIANI, Horace WALPOLE, and David HUME added their presence to the gatherings. In short, the Geoffrin salon regularly brought together the major figures of the French Enlightenment and points out the importance of the role of women in that era as powerful protectresses of intellectual and artistic pursuits. This role, so frequently played by wealthy women of the Enlightenment, was taken away from them during the French Revolution, in a move that reflected the desire to eliminate all social and institutional forms associated with the ANCIEN RÉGIME.

See also SOCIAL INSTITUTIONS OF THE ENLIGHTENMENT; WOMEN AND THE ENLIGHTENMENT.

Germany Central European state bordered today by FRANCE, SWITZERLAND, AUSTRIA, the Czech Republic, POLAND, the Netherlands, DENMARK, and the Baltic Sea. The modern state did not exist until 1871. Hence, it is improper to speak of Germany in a political sense, unless one is discussing late-19th-century and 20th-century history. The term is used in the present book only as a convenient shorthand expression. In the 18th century, the lands of modern Germany were fragmented into 343 sovereign kingdoms, principalities, bishoprics, archbishoprics, free cities, and other independent territories—all loosely connected under the largely moribund, Hapsburg-ruled HOLY ROMAN EMPIRE. The chief German principalities of the 18th century were the kingdom of PRUSSIA (capital, BERLIN), Saxony (capital, Dresden), Bavaria (capital, MUNICH), the Rhineland Palatinate (capital, Heidelberg), and Hanover.

In the course of the 18th century, the superficial union of these states receded in importance, and the major principalities developed independent, often conflicting lines of foreign policy. Prussia emerged as a major European power, on a par with France, the HAPSBURG EMPIRE, and RUSSIA.

The German territories were divided along religious lines. Northern principalities and cities tended to be officially Lutheran Protestant. The southern and Rhineland regions remained in the fold of Catholicism. In certain highly fragmented areas—the southwest, for example—the map of religious affiliations resembled a crazy quilt of differing loyalties. In other regions, such as Prussia, religious TOLERATION was practiced as a pragmatic matter. But most states expected their subjects to conform to the official religion selected by the ruler.

Culturally, the German territories created a special form of ENLIGHTENMENT that is distinguished from its French counterpart by calling it the AUFKLÄRUNG (German word meaning Enlightenment). Chief cultural centers were Berlin, Halle, Königsberg, Weimar, Göttingen, Leipzig, and Munich. The period produced some of the greatest writers and philosophers of the German language: Johann Wolfgang von GOETHE, Friedrich SCHILLER, Christian WOLFF, Gotthold Ephraim LESSING, Gottfried Wilhelm LEIBNIZ, Moses MENDELSSOHN, Samuel PUFENDORF, Johann Gottfried HERDER, and Immanuel KANT. Southern Germany witnessed a great Catholic revival that left the landscape dotted with graceful ROCOCO churches and palaces. MUSIC thrived, especially in the north, leaving the legacy of the BACH family, Georg Philipp TELEMANN, and a host of lesser-known composers. Both Ludwig van BEETHOVEN and George Frederick HANDEL were born and partly trained in German territories, but spent their careers in other states. The burst of German musical creativity would continue into the 19th-century, although Austrian VIENNA would act as its center.

In the early 19th century, after the wars brought about by the FRENCH REVOLUTION had come to an end, the German territories were consolidated into several large kingdoms and placed into a loose union called the German Confederation. Complete unification of the country did not occur until 1871, when Otto von Bismarck imposed Prussian rule over the entire region.

Giannone, Pietro (1676–1748) *Italian historian, one of the major figures of the Enlightenment of southern Italy*
The history of Giannone's career reveals the complexity of political power relations in ITALY during the period of the ENLIGHTENMENT. It also provides an excellent example of the manner in which reform programs, inspired by the enlightened goal of placing government on a sound basis of law, necessarily raised the question of church-state relations.

Pietro Giannone studied law in Naples and turned his legal skills to the subject of relations between the KINGDOM OF THE TWO SICILIES (Naples and Sicily) and ROMAN CATHOLICISM. Giannone attempted to establish a legal basis for challenging the temporal powers of the church in Naples.

Giannone researched the history of Neapolitan law, publishing his findings in two important works: *Istoria civile del regno di Napoli* (Civil history of the Kingdom of Naples; 1723) and *Il Triregno, ossia del regno del cielo, della terra, e del papa* (The triple crown, or the kingdom of heaven, of earth, and of the pope; not published until 1895). His *Istoria* was placed on the Index of Forbidden Books of the Catholic Church, and Giannone himself was excommunicated from the church.

Giannone fled to VIENNA, where the Hapsburg emperor, Charles VI, awarded him an imperial pension. In 1734, when Naples came under Spanish rather than Austrian control, Giannone moved to VENICE. There, his views on maritime law caused conflict with Venetian authorities. As a result, in 1735, he decided to flee to the safety of GENEVA, but he was kidnapped along the way by an agent of the Sardinian government, then under the control of the kingdom of SAVOY. Giannone spent his remaining years as a prisoner in Ceva and TURIN.

See also ANCIEN RÉGIME; ILLUMINISTI; PUBLISHING; SEPARATION OF CHURCH AND STATE.

Gibbon, Edward (1737–1794) *English historian*

Son of an independently wealthy member of Parliament, Gibbon always claimed that his maternal aunt, Catherine Porten, played the greatest role in shaping his mind. As a child, Gibbon experienced a series of illnesses that prevented him from attending school regularly. Nevertheless, he became an avid reader and developed his lifelong fascination with HISTORY as a young adolescent. Gibbon's health improved during his teen years, allowing him to enroll at Magdalen College, Oxford University, in 1752.

Gibbon was raised as an Anglican but converted to ROMAN CATHOLICISM in 1753 after exploring Catholic THEOLOGY. His alarmed father rushed him off to Lausanne, SWITZERLAND, where under the watchful eye of a Calvinist minister, the Reverend Daniel Pavillard, he received further education and returned to Protestantism. During his years in Lausanne, Gibbon attended gatherings at the home of VOLTAIRE. He met and fell in love with Suzanne Curchod, the future Suzanne NECKER, a pastor's daughter whose hand he asked in marriage. She refused his offer, but the two remained devoted friends thereafter.

Gibbon returned to ENGLAND in 1758, began his historical writing, served (1762–63) in the English militia during the SEVEN YEARS' WAR, and then departed in 1763 on a two-year GRAND TOUR of FRANCE and ITALY. During his stay in ROME, Gibbon decided to write the story of the rise and decline of the great Roman Empire. Having returned to England in 1765, Gibbon lived with his father, moving to LONDON only in 1772, after the elder Gibbon's death.

In London, Gibbon quickly made the acquaintance of people in the fashionable intellectual circles. He was received into the Literary Club, headed by Samuel JOHNSON, and entered the House of Commons of the Parliament.

Gibbon published the first volume of his DECLINE AND FALL OF THE ROMAN EMPIRE in 1776. The work received mixed reviews. David HUME and William ROBERTSON praised it, but people who disliked Gibbon's argument that official Christianity had brought the demise of the empire vilified the book. The last three volumes of the *Decline and Fall* appeared in 1788, having been written in Lausanne, where Gibbon lived between 1782 and 1793 in the house of his old friend Georges

Engraving of Edward Gibbon. Gibbon acquired both fame and notoriety when, in his *The History of the Decline and Fall of the Roman Empire,* he claimed that the establishment of Christianity as the official religion of the empire had precipitated its eventual disintegration, corruption, and decline. *(Courtesy New York Public Library)*

Deyverdun. Gibbon returned a final time to England in 1793 and died in 1794.

Gibbon displayed an interest in antiquity that was common to educated people of the ENLIGHTENMENT. He knew his classical Latin sources extremely well and also was well acquainted with the later commentaries on those sources. His personal library contained between 6,000 and 7,000 volumes. He was thoroughly grounded in the fact-gathering style associated with antiquarians, but also knew and liked the emphasis on development and on nonpolitical factors associated with the new "philosophic" history of the Enlightenment. The result was a creative blend of the antiquarian and philosophic approaches: a collection of facts woven together into a story about the fate of the ideal of FREEDOM in the course of Roman civilization.

Gibbon's story is energized and shaped by his personal hatred of SUPERSTITION and intolerance; by his commitment to intellectual and political freedom; by his faith in the power of human REASON; and by a mild form of DEISM. If Gibbon resembled his contemporaries of the French and English Enlightenment in holding these views, he departed from the belief in PROGRESS that was also common to the era. He believed that the general course of history has followed a path of decline from the glorious days of early classical civilization. He hoped, however, that his own era of Enlightenment might be able to reverse that trend.

Besides *The Decline and Fall of the Roman Empire,* Gibbon left the *Memoirs of My Life and Writings.* These were published posthumously (1796) in a collection of his *Miscellaneous Works.*

Gilbert, Nicolas-Joseph-Laurent (1750–1780) *French writer and an outspoken critic of the Enlightenment*

A native of the eastern French territory of Lorraine, Gilbert stemmed from a peasant family. He received a basic education in the classics and humanities under the auspices of the local Catholic church. Gilbert remained forever reverent toward his schoolmasters. After completing school, he settled in Nancy, the capital of Lorraine, where he began offering both private lessons and public lectures on literature.

Gilbert wrote both poetry and prose. He enjoyed some literary success in Nancy but was disappointed by the reception of his works in PARIS. He became an outspoken critic of Parisian enlightened literary culture, considering the writers of the ENCYCLOPÉDIE special enemies. Partial motivation for Gilbert's stance seems to have derived from his unsuccessful showing in a poetry competition at the French Academy.

Gilbert's primary public attacks on the Enlightenment came in the form of two satires: *Dix-huitième siècle* (Eighteenth century; 1775), dedicated to Elie-Cathérine FRÉRON; and *Mon apologie* (My apology; 1778). These pieces attracted favorable attention and pensions from the archbishop of Paris, from LOUIS XVI, and from the

journal *Mercure de France.* Gilbert died in 1780 at the age of 30, victim of an injury acquired in a fall from a horse.

Glorious Revolution   Rebellion of 1688 in which a coalition of English Tories, Anglicans, and Whigs forced the Catholic king James II to abandon the throne of ENGLAND in favor of the Protestants WILLIAM III AND MARY II.

The Glorious Revolution established a strong precedent for the idea of the contractual nature of the English kingship. The *TWO TREATISES OF GOVERNMENT,* written by John LOCKE about 1680 but published only in 1689, provided a theoretical justification for the settlement between William III and Parliament. The treatises spelled out a contractual theory of monarchy in which the power of the king was limited significantly by that of Parliament. They helped to justify the right of rebellion against political tyranny and stimulated many political discussions of the 18th-century Enlightenment.

The Glorious Revolution also established a firmer basis for the sovereign rule of law in England and greater power with respect to the monarchy for the members of Parliament, England's lawmakers. In strengthening the Parliament, the Glorious Revolution made it more difficult for monarchical ABSOLUTISM to secure a foothold in the English political system. The English kings relinquished their powers to suspend or to dispense with laws passed by the Parliament. They were required to call Parliaments frequently, and free elections were mandated.

The Glorious Revolution also stimulated a series of legal changes in the relations between the state and various English religious confessions. It established formal laws that strengthened the political power of Anglican Protestantism in England by denying the right of participation in political and public life to both non-Anglican Protestants and Catholics. It resulted in the Act of Settlement of 1701 that reserved the English throne to persons of Protestant belief. But, in a more liberal vein, it also stimulated passage of the 1689 Act of Toleration that granted the right to worship to non-Anglican Protestants (DISSENTERS and Nonconformists).

It was this English form of government that so fired the imaginations of PHILOSOPHES such as MONTESQUIEU and VOLTAIRE. Their interpretations of this structure, outlined in books such as the *Esprit des lois* (THE SPIRIT OF LAWS,) by Montesquieu and the *Lettres anglaises ou philosophiques* (English or philosophical letters) by Voltaire, translated the English system into an ideal model of rational, legal, well-balanced government that exercised a powerful influence in Europe.

See also JACOBITES.

Gluck, Christoph Willibald (1714–1787) *Bohemian-born composer who made his primary career in Austria*

Gluck was the son of Alexander Gluck, a successful and prosperous forester who tried to suppress his son's musical interests. At about the age of 13, in reaction to this parental disapproval, young Gluck ran away from home. He journeyed to Prague, where, with the help of a clergyman's letter of recommendation, he was able to find work as a musician. Eventually, he was reconciled with his father, who thereafter agreed to provide some financial support. Gluck was largely self-trained as a musician, and his lack of systemic, formal education was sometimes used against him by later critics.

Gluck moved to VIENNA sometime in 1734 or 1735, where he met Prince Antonio Maria Melzi of MILAN. At the invitation of the prince, he moved in 1737 to Milan, where his OPERA *Artaserse* (1741) with a libretto by Pietre Metastasio, met with great success. This triumph brought a series of commissions and performances throughout ITALY.

At the end of 1745, Gluck moved to ENGLAND, where he met both Charles BURNEY and George Frederick HANDEL. The English style of vocal writing, which tried to express human affections and passions in a natural manner, appealed to him, and he spent some time studying its various techniques and forms. His compositions were not, however, appreciated by English audiences, and he departed from the country after about six months. For the next six years, Gluck traveled throughout Europe, hearing Opera performances and staging his own productions. His first success in Vienna came with the 1747 production of *Semiramide riconosciuata,* an opera he had originally composed for the official celebrations in the city of Prague of the coronation of MARIA THERESA.

In 1750, Gluck settled in Vienna and married Maria Anna Bergin, the daughter of a wealthy merchant and member of the circle of ladies in waiting who surrounded Maria Theresa. Maria Bergin's connection with the Viennese court served Gluck well. The imperial advisers charged with control of Viennese cultural affairs, Count KAUNITZ and Count Durazzo, became interested in Gluck's work. Count Durazzo hired him to adapt French comic opera for production at the Viennese Burgtheater. Gluck began composing arias and overtures to add to these French works. From 1758 until 1762, Gluck directed the orchestra and productions at the Burgtheater. His immensely successful collaboration with Ranieri de CALZABIGI began in 1761 with *Don Juan ou Le Festin de Pierre* (Don Juan or the banquet of stone).

Together, Calzabigi and Gluck created the Italian reform operas—ORFEO ED EURIDICE (Orpheus and Eurydice), *Alceste,* and *Paride ed Elena* (Paris and Helena)—that created a new, universal, cosmopolitan operatic form constructed of blended elements from the distinct French, Italian, and German national styles. This new universal idiom, one aspect of the musical expression of CLASSICISM, was Gluck's chief contribution to the culture of the ENLIGHTENMENT. Gluck's innovations were noted at the time by the critic and imperial Austrian minister Josef von SONNENFELS, but audience responses to these works were mixed. In Paris, his operas provoked a quarrel in the press, reminiscent of the earlier BATTLE OF THE BUFFOONS, between admirers of Gluck's style and those who preferred the operas of the Italian composer Niccolò Piccini.

In addition to the three Italian reform operas, Gluck wrote French operas, which, thanks to the patronage of Queen MARIE ANTOINETTE, he was able to produce in PARIS. These were *Iphigénie en Aulide* (Iphigenia in Aulis), *Iphigénie en Tauride* (Iphigenia in Tauris), *Echo et Narcisse* (Echo and Narcissus) with text by Baron von Tschudi, and *Armide.* Gluck also revised *Orfeo* (*Orphée et Euridice*) according to a French text by P. L. Moline and added ballet *intermezzi* to satisfy the French love of ballet-opera combinations. Gluck left very few compositions other than opera. Of some interest are his songs to odes by Friedrich KLOPSTOCK, which were published (1774–75) in the *Göttingen Musenalmanach* (Göttingen almanac of the Muses).

Gluck's marriage was childless, but he adopted his orphaned niece, Maria Anna Rosina (Nanette), to whom he became devoted. She became a singer and together with her adoptive father entertained guests with *Hausmusik* concerts. Gluck provided significant support and patronage to Antonio Salieri, the chief competitor of the young Wolfgang Amadeus MOZART in Vienna. Gluck died in 1787 after suffering several strokes. Salieri conducted Gluck's own composition, the *De Profundis,* at the funeral services.

Gobelins tapestry French tapestry manufactory, founded in PARIS in 1662 by order of King LOUIS XIV. During the 18th century, Gobelins tapestries dominated the European market. They were bought by clients in all lands and copied by workshops in other countries.

The Gobelins were a family of skilled dyers and clothmakers who had established themselves in the Faubourg Saint-Marcel of Paris in the 15th century. Jehan Gobelin, the first head of this old firm, had discovered scarlet dyestuff and, with heavy personal investment in the business, had made it enormously successful. His descendants kept the dye and cloth business but also began to purchase royal and municipal offices. By the end of the 16th century, they had abandoned their traditional trade, devoting themselves, instead, to royal service and finance.

In 1662, Jean-Baptiste Colbert, Louis XIV's chief of finances, purchased the old Gobelin dye and clothmaking works and transformed them into a new state-sponsored tapestry and upholstery manufactory called the Manufacture Royale des Meubles de la Couronne (Royal manufactory of furnishings for the Crown). This was the Gobelins manufactory, a project designed to put the theory of MERCANTILISM into practice. Production was highly organized and controlled by royal officials. During the 17th century, the manufactory produced not only tapestries but also upholsteries and other decorative items. Most of the production went to the royal Garde Meuble (furnishings repository).

Tapestry weaving in Europe dated back to the 12th century. Private workshops existed throughout the continent, although artisans in FRANCE and Flanders (part of modern BELGIUM) produced the most notable creations. At its foundation, the Gobelins manufactory was unique in that it was owned by the state. State-owned factories were created in imitation of Gobelins in other European countries, but private manufactories also continued to exist. Nevertheless, Gobelins dominated the tapestry weaving business throughout the 18th century, preempting the earlier prominence of workshops in Brussels and other Flemish towns.

When the Gobelins manufactory opened, its superintendent was the French artist and academy member Charles Le Brun. Sometimes he drew the cartoons (sketches of the designs) for tapestries, but even when others performed this task, he chose the subject matter. The Gobelins tapestries depicted stories taken from the past that could be transformed into allegories about the power of Louis XIV. This approach to subject matter was typical of the baroque era, during which aesthetic style was pressed into the service of political propaganda in all European states. Examples of this genre include series such as the History of Alexander, Life of the King, and Royal Palaces.

The Gobelins factory closed in 1694 as a result of the financial difficulties that were plaguing the royal budget, but it reopened in 1697. The first tapestries produced after reopening followed the baroque tradition of symbolic storytelling. But soon the emphasis changed, and newer tapestries featured purely decorative, ornamental designs. The tapestries were smaller, reflecting the fact that they were being purchased and hung in Parisian town houses rather than in the monumental chateaux of old. The focus on ornamentation and on smaller-scale design reflected aspects of the emerging ROCOCO style. It also reflected the fact that new social groups were purchasing tapestries. Changes in weaving technology had allowed the production of cheaper tapestries, thereby expanding the market of potential buyers.

In the 18th century, during the reign of LOUIS XV, Jacques SOUFFLOT directed the Gobelins manufactory. It was Soufflot who introduced the new technologies that allowed the vast expansion of the Gobelins production. During this period, cartoons were supplied by François BOUCHER, Alexander-François Desportes, Claude Audran III, Jean Baptiste OUDRY, and Charles Antoine Coypel. The styles and subjects chosen by Oudry and Boucher strongly influenced 18th-century tapestry designs throughout Europe. Toward the end of the century, historical and didactic themes inspired by NEOCLASSICISM were applied to tapestries with disappointing results. With the outbreak of the FRENCH REVOLUTION, the Gob-

elins manufactory, like so many other institutions closely associated with the ANCIEN RÉGIME, was closed. It was reopened during the Napoleonic era.

The Gobelins manufactory had privately owned French rivals throughout the 18th century at Beauvais and Aubusson. Their tapestries matched those of Gobelins in quality, but Gobelins dominated the market in large part because of its favored position as a state-owned enterprise. The tapestry manufactory in Naples followed the French model closely. Tapestry production during the 18th century also flourished in SPAIN (MADRID), ITALY (TURIN and Florence), and GERMANY (BERLIN and MUNICH).

Godwin, William (1756–1836) *English social philosopher and journalist, the second husband of Mary Wollstonecraft*
Godwin grew up in a strict Calvinist family and entered the ministry himself. He eventually affiliated himself with a theologically extreme group of Calvinists called the Sandemanians.

Godwin worked as a parish pastor until 1782, when he settled in LONDON and began writing. He met Mary WOLLSTONECRAFT in 1796, married her in 1797, and lost her in childbirth a few months later. Their daughter, Mary, a writer noted for her novel *Frankenstein*, eventually became the wife of the poet Percy Bysshe Shelley. In 1801, Godwin remarried and entered the publishing business. He specialized in producing historical works and children's books, but also published the memoirs of his deceased wife Mary Wollstonecraft and his own *Life of Chaucer*. Always in need of money, Godwin obtained a small salary and an apartment in 1833 by working as usher of the exchequer. He died in 1836.

Godwin believed in the possibility of PROGRESS and in the PERFECTIBILITY of humankind. He devoted himself and his political tracts to two ideals associated with the ENLIGHTENMENT: the attainment of social justice and the pursuit of truth. But he did not believe that these ideals could be realized by actual governments. He opposed the popular POLITICAL THEORY that made the social contract the basis of society. In his principal work, *An Enquiry Concerning Political Justice, and Its Influence on General Virtue and Happiness* (1793), he asserted that no matter how a government was constituted, its power would inevitably produce corruption and repression. Godwin thus began to embrace both anarchy and a primitive form of communism.

In addition to the *Enquiry*, Godwin wrote the anonymous *Imogen: A Pastoral Romance* (1784); *Caleb Williams, or Things as They Are* (1794); *Considerations on Lord Grenville's and Mr. Pitt's Bills* (1795); *Saint Leon* (1799); *Mandeville, a Tale of the Times of Cromwell* (1817); and *Of Population, an Answer to Malthus* (1820). Mary Wollstonecraft's memoirs appeared as *Memoirs of the Author of the Rights of Woman* (1798).

Godwin was one of the most radical spokesmen of the Enlightenment. He carried the implications of enlightened ideals such as FREEDOM and perfectibility to their extremes, yet displayed a distrust in the ability of formal human institutions to bring them about. Godwin thus presented a combination of optimism and pessimism that reflected the tensions inherent within the thought of the Enlightenment.

See also HAPPINESS; MALTHUS; MORAL PHILOSOPHY; RADICAL ENLIGHTENMENT.

Goethe, Johann Wolfgang von (1749–1832) *German novelist, poet, playwright, natural scientist, and statesman; considered Germany's greatest writer and one of the most versatile intellectuals of his or any succeeding age*
Goethe was born in FRANKFURT am Main of wealthy bourgeois parents. Although Goethe showed evidence of his multifaceted talents as a youth, his father nevertheless prevailed upon him to study law. Goethe wished to enroll at the UNIVERSITY OF GÖTTINGEN, but his father thought it too radical and insisted that he matriculate at the University of Leipzig. Goethe spent three years in Leipzig and then came down with a serious illness that forced him to return to Frankfurt in 1768. Susanna Katharina von Klettenberg, whose acquaintance Goethe made after resettling in Frankfurt, directed him to a Pietist doctor who helped cure him. With Klettenberg, Goethe studied cabalistic philosophy and the works of the Renaissance physician Philippus Aureolus Theophrastus Bombast von Hohenheim, better known as Paracelsus. These studies are presumed to have laid the foundations for his later intense interest in the natural sciences.

After recovering from his illness, Goethe moved to Strasbourg to finish his studies. Strasbourg, an Alsatian city that had at one time belonged to the HOLY ROMAN EMPIRE, was officially a French city in the 18th century. Its university, however, attracted many German students, who were granted the privilege of practicing their own RELIGION. At Strasbourg, Goethe met Johann Gottfried HERDER, who introduced him to the writings of Homer, Shakespeare, and Ossian. Goethe found the beauties of the Strasbourg cathedral captivating, and he became convinced that its "Gothic" architecture expressed the GENIUS of the German national character. He presented his new conviction in *Von deutscher Baukunst* (On German architecture; 1773). Goethe also fell in love with a pastor's daughter, Frederike Brion. As with many of his infatuations, this proved to be an unrequited love but one that, nevertheless, inspired several love poems. Some of these poems—"Mailied" (May song), "Willkommen und Abschied" (Welcome and farewell), "Kleine Blumen, kleine Blätter" (Little flowers, little leaves)—belong in the list of his best poetic creations.

Goethe finished his legal studies and received his doctorate in law in 1771. He then returned to Frankfurt

Johann Wolfgang von Goethe, portrait by Joseph Karl Stedler, 1828. A brilliant novelist, playwright, and poet, Goethe led the younger generation of German intellectuals in their explorations of the creative forces of life. *(Courtesy Bayerische Staatsgemäldesammlungen, Munich)*

to establish a legal practice. He spent some time in Wetzlar, studying the workings of the *Reichskammergericht,* one of the central law courts of the Holy Roman Empire. While at Wetzlar, Goethe met a young man named Karl Wilhelm Jerusalem, who was serving at the court and was, at the same time, a promising writer. Jerusalem committed suicide because of unrequited love, and Goethe used this incident as the basis for his novella, *THE SORROWS OF YOUNG WERTHER* (1774). This work, which explored questions of love, genius, rejection, and suicide in the context of a critical examination of existing society, was an immediate success: It captured the imagination of a whole generation. The tale was told so powerfully that a number of young men copied Werther's last desperate act of defiance (suicide). The book also became an object of attack, satire, and imitation, producing a subcategory of literary works including *The Joys of Young Werther* by Christoph Friedrich NICOLAI and two novellas, *Allwill* and *Woldemar,* by Friedrich Heinrich JACOBI. The influence of Goethe's *Werther* was so great that even dressing *á la Werther* (in Werther's style) became obligatory for admiring young men of Goethe's generation.

In 1775, Goethe was offered a position at the court of the duke of Weimar. The 18-year-old duke, Karl August, was impressed more by Goethe's legal experience than by his literary fame and pushed through Goethe's appointment as a high civil servant in the Weimar administration. Goethe remained employed at the Weimar court for the rest of his life.

Goethe soon justified the young duke's trust by proving himself a deft and efficient administrator. He took over the ministry of mines, reformed the way in which the mines operated, became head of the department of war, and finally also served as chief minister of finances. Through these activities, Goethe was able to help balance the Weimar duchy's budget, to reduce the size of the army, and to improve the state's economy. At the same time, he continued writing and developed his natural scientific interests. He took courses in comparative anatomy at the nearby University of Jena and began his important collections of plants and minerals. He also assisted the duchess of Weimar, Anne Amélie, with her efforts to bring the culture of the ENLIGHTENMENT to Weimar. Together with Christoph Martin WIELAND, Goethe formed a loosely constituted circle of artists and writers that became increasingly important in German intellectual life. In 1776, Goethe was able to convince the duke to call Herder to Weimar as superintendent of the churches. In all these ways, Goethe helped to lay the foundations for the spectacular emergence of both Weimar and Jena as major intellectual centers during the years of the late Enlightenment and of early ROMANTICISM.

By the late 1780s, however, Goethe felt that he had reached a dead end. He had experienced a number of unsuccessful affairs, including a broken engagement, all of which produced major pieces of poetry but did nothing for his emotional well-being. He decided that he needed to renew his literary career and asked Karl August for a paid leave from his duties in order to travel to ITALY. The duke consented.

Goethe's GRAND TOUR to Italy lasted two years and became one of the most important experiences of his life. His encounters with the remnants of ancient classical culture and with the Italian countryside impressed upon him a sense of the strong connection between NATURE, GENIUS, and the manifold variety and greatness of the human spirit. While in Italy, Goethe met a host of new friends, especially artists, architects, and poets, sketched out new literary works, and delved deeply into natural history. He also convinced himself that his greatest gifts lay in literature and in the natural sciences. Goethe notified the authorities in Weimar of his intention to pursue writing and the natural sciences professionally.

When Karl August heard of this decision, he decided to make Goethe the director of the cultural institutions of the duchy of Weimar in order to honor Goethe's newfound determination but also to retain his services. Thus, Goethe received responsibility for directing the University of Jena, the Weimar court theater, the Weimar school of drawing, several libraries, and parks.

Upon his return to Weimar in 1788, Goethe settled into his new life, devoting himself to his official duties and to his creative work. He founded a new theater in Weimar and also published several essays from his travel journal. One of these essays, "The Roman Carnival," presented a stirring portrayal of popular festivities that captured the imagination of succeeding generations. Hector Berlioz, for example, attempted in his *Roman Carnival Overture* (1844) to translate the moods evoked in Goethe's essay into music. Goethe also fell in love with the 23-year-old factory worker Christiane Vulpius. The two soon began living together, and Christiane bore Goethe a child named August in 1790. The pair finally married in 1806.

This second Weimar period of Goethe's life was extremely productive. Goethe's new friendship with Friedrich SCHILLER proved to be one of the stimuli for his remarkable burst of creative energy. Schiller had arrived in Weimar in 1787 and, although hailed as one of the most imaginative poets of the time, had been unable to establish good relations with Goethe. This situation changed after Schiller asked Goethe to contribute regularly to his new journal, *Die Horen*. Schiller dedicated the journal to the task of improving German culture and society by providing an education in AESTHETICS. He believed that such an education would gradually lead humanity to FREEDOM. Schiller's offer to Goethe led to meetings and to an exchange of letters between the two men, which, in turn, laid the groundwork for a growing friendship. For Goethe, the new contact with Schiller enabled him to experience "a second youth."

Many scholars believe that the joint activities of these two literary giants produced what is sometimes called German CLASSICISM, an attempt to use the classical past (especially the Greeks) as inspiration for a new German literary style. German classicism proved to be an intensely productive literary mode, at least in part because its creators—Schiller and Goethe—approached their goal of elevating humanity from different perspectives. Schiller, on the one hand, emphasized the subjective nature of writing and the liberating aspects of intellectual and artistic freedom. Goethe, on the other hand, was attracted to the objective side of knowledge and used the natural sciences, as he understood them, as a model both for literature and for knowledge. Schiller, nevertheless, was more comfortable with basic questions of philosophy, while Goethe was more an intuitive thinker and natural poet. Goethe's application of German classical style can be encountered in his two plays, *Iphigenie auf Taurus* (Iphigenia in Taurus; 1787) and *Torquato Tasso* (Torquato Tasso; 1790).

During the years of his friendship with Schiller, Goethe wrote his essay "Die metamorphosen des Planzen" (Metamorphosis of plants); *Lehrjahre des Wil-*

helm Meisters (Wilhelm Meister's apprenticeship), the first example of a *Bildungsroman* (novel of character formation); a number of narrative poems including the *Magician's Apprentice* (transformed into the tone poem *Sorcerer's Apprentice* by Paul Dukas in 1897); *Hermann und Dorothea* (Hermann and Dorothea); "Winckelmann und sein Jahrhundert" (Winckelmann and his century), his masterful essay on classical culture; a large number of lyrical poems; and a host of articles on science ranging from geology to meteorology.

Goethe became ever more convinced that Nature provides the grand analogy for human thought and development. But his idea of nature was not the one sketched out in the popular Newtonian MECHANICAL PHILOSOPHY of the early Enlightenment. Instead, he drew from VITALISM, a theory of organic life developed in the late Enlightenment. According to Goethe, nature is constantly experiencing metamorphosis (change), but these changes are not random. They occur within well-defined limits, which Goethe conceived as defined by pairs of polar opposites. Goethe's favorite metaphors for the polar opposites were male and female, exhalation and inhalation, expansion and contraction, and positive and negative charges. Change proceeds through a series of developments from one extreme to another, always progressing in an upward spiraling motion. He argued in the "Metamorphosis of plants," for example, that the development of a plant occurs by a series of transitions from "male" forms to "female" forms until the mature plant appears. Similar processes occurred throughout nature and in the formation of adult humans.

For Goethe, forms repeat over time in nature, but each reappearance of a form represents a higher level (*Steigerung*) of development. The repetition of forms occurs because all parts of living nature are designed after a few simple plans, *Urformen* (prototypes) in Goethe's language. These prototypes acted as the regulating principles of nature, ensuring nature's uniformity while still allowing the prototypes to express themselves in reality in many variations.

As Goethe worked out his vision of nature, Schiller's critiques and recommendations played a stimulating and provocative role. When Schiller died in 1805, Goethe was distraught. Shortly afterward, FRANCE and PRUSSIA resumed the fighting that had first broken out with the onset of the FRENCH REVOLUTION. As an ally of Prussia, Weimar was drawn into the conflict. The French won several decisive victories, occupying Jena and Weimar and imposing stringent conditions upon the losers. These two events—Schiller's death and the resumption of the war—caused Goethe to begin doubting his optimistic conviction that human beings could conquer the darker sides of nature.

Wahlverwandschaften (Elective affinities), his novella of 1809, testified to these somber feelings. Its title was drawn from 18th-century AFFINITY CHEMISTRY, which posited that the various chemical elements have different degrees of attraction (affinity) for each other. The operation of these forces of affinity causes some chemical compounds to dissolve and new ones to be formed. *Elective Affinities* described how a seemingly happy marriage was destroyed by the introduction of two new persons, each of whom unintentionally drew one of the marriage partners away from the other spouse and to them. The results were catastrophic for all involved, attesting to the power of natural impulses that act beyond the control of the will or of reason.

Goethe's literary explorations of the darker sides of human life was paralleled by his intense reflections upon his own life. The result was one of the great autobiographical works of the period. Entitled *Dichtung und Wahrheit* (Poetry and truth; published in three parts, 1811–12), the book charted Goethe's development through his youth. The title attests to Goethe's fascination for polarities and their resolution into higher forms. The work is beautifully constructed, modeled after his image of the spiral path of natural development. *Dichtung und Wahrheit*, Goethe's other autobiographical works—*Italian Journey, Campaign in France*—and the *Talks with Goethe* by Johann Peter Eckermann, all offer rich sources for reconstructing Goethe's life and thoughts.

During these later year, Goethe also became increasingly interested in the culture and literature of the Far East, viewing it as representative of ancient Western civilization prior to the arrival of the Greeks in the Mediterranean regions. Goethe's interest was nourished by a love affair with Marianne von Wilemer. The result was *West-Oestliche Divan* (1820), which was both a celebration of the East and a love poem to Marianne. It is now known that this work includes two poems she had written to him.

Goethe remained productive as he aged. Not only did he edit his collected works (which ran to over 40 volumes), but he also continued to write poetry, completed the *Wilhelm Meister* project with *Wilhelm Meisters Wanderjahre* (Wilhelm Meister's journeying years), and finished the dramatic poem FAUST (1831), his greatest literary achievement. He had been working on *Faust*, the greatest single work in the German language, for almost 40 years.

Part One, influenced greatly by Christopher Marlowe's *The Tragicall History of Dr. Faustus* (1604), describes Faust's pact with the devil. Faust receives the capacity to acquire the infinite knowledge of God in return for promising to yield his soul to Mephistopheles (the devil) at the point where he, Faust, becomes satisfied with what he has learned. Part One also contains the Gretchen story, in which Faust falls in love with Gretchen and impregnates her. When the child is born, Gretchen kills it because it is illegitimate and will have no chance to live an ordinary life. She is then executed for having committed infanticide, but God forgives her and allows her to enter heaven.

Part Two of *Faust* concentrates less upon Faust's actions and more upon major questions concerning aesthetics (whether modern culture and ancient Greek culture can be joined), POLITICAL THEORY, and the development of an educated person within society. This part is extremely complicated, drawing both from Goethe's knowledge of cultural traditions and from his poetic genius. It includes one scene where Faust meets Helen of Troy and another scene depicting the Witches' Sabbath. Toward the end of Part Two, Faust finally announces that he is satisfied with the knowledge he has attained. He has used it to help bring wealth, security, and peace to his homeland. He has thus fulfilled one of the central ideals of the Enlightenment, that of using his knowledge to aid the PROGRESS of humanity. Honoring his pact, Faust yields to Mephistopheles and goes to hell. Gretchen, however, reappears at this point, and she successfully intercedes with God to save Faust's soul.

Faust's salvation occurs because of the action of both the feminine and the masculine principles in his life. The feminine, for Goethe, acts as the ordering force in the world, whereas the masculine produces typical human striving toward goals. As Goethe put it in a famous phrase with biblical echoes, "He who forever strives, he shall be saved." After he had completed *Faust*, Goethe remarked that the poem was his legacy to the world. He died a year after its publication at the age of 83.

Goethe was shaped during the Enlightenment and actively tried to live its many ideals and reach its goals. As is true with all great thinkers, he nevertheless cast the legacy of the Enlightenment into highly original forms. For this reason, he is sometimes seen as a critic of the Enlightenment, as a founder of romanticism, or as the creator of what is called German classicism. Still, in the broadest sense, in his critiques of pure subjectivism and of romantic excess, in his belief in the close analogy between nature and human development, and in his cosmopolitan commitment to human welfare, he expressed the highest ideals of the Enlightenment, albeit in a rich, poetic language uniquely his own.

See also AUFKLÄRUNG; BILDUNG; LITERATURE; MACPHERSON.

Further reading: W. H. Bruford, *Germany in the Eighteenth Century: The Social Background of the Literary Revival* (Cambridge: Cambridge University Press, 1971); John Gage, ed., *Goethe on Art* (Berkeley: University of California Press, 1980); Johann Wolfgang von Goethe, *Faust: A Tragedy,* tr. Walter Arndt, ed. Cyrus Hamlin (New York: W. W. Norton, 1976); Johann Wolfgang von Goethe, *Goethe,* ed. John Whaley (Boston: Charles E. Tuttle, 2001); Lesley Sharpe, ed., *Cambridge Companion to Goethe* (Cambridge: Cambridge University Press, 2002).

Goldoni, Carlo (1707–1793) *Italian playwright, often called the father of modern Italian comedy*
A native of VENICE, Goldoni attended a Jesuit secondary school and then studied philosophy at Rimini. His pas-

sion for comic THEATER, however, soon began to dominate his life. Nevertheless, Goldoni did obtain a law degree, and for three years, from 1745 until 1748, practiced law as a means of support.

Goldoni helped to create a new form of Italian comedy. He introduced unmasked characters in his comedies, thus departing from the older Italian commedia dell'arte practices. He provided these characters with completely written out dialogues, removing the improvisation that had been part of the earlier Italian comedic traditions.

Goldoni produced about 150 comedies whose number include *Belisario* (Belisarus; 1734); *La famiglia dell'antiquario* (The antiquarian's family); *La bottega del caffè* (The coffeehouse); *La putta onorata* (The respected young girl; 1759); *La Pamela* (Pamela; 1750); and *La Locandiera* (The innkeeper; 1753). Later works were *I rusteghi* (The rustics) and the trilogy *Villeggiatura* (Country holidays). He also wrote 283 *opera buffa* libretti such as *La buona figliuola* (The good daughter) and *Il talismano* (The talisman). Set to music by composers such as Baldasarre Galuppi (1706–85), Franz Joseph HAYDN, Giovanni Paisiello (1740–1816), Niccolò Piccini (1728–1800), Florian Leopold Gassman (1729–74), and Antonio Salieri (1750–1825), the Goldoni libretti formed the backbone of the comic OPERA repertoire in late 18th-century Europe. Goldoni left a handful of serious operas, several one-act *intermezzi* (comic pieces customarily inserted between the acts of serious operas), and his *Mémoires* (1787).

Goldoni worked from 1748 until 1758 in Venice. In 1762, he moved to PARIS, where he worked as the Italian tutor to Princess Adelaide, the daughter of King LOUIS XV. Goldoni received a government pension and remained in FRANCE until his death in 1793. His plays helped to shape the French taste for modern Italian-style comic theater. His Paris productions included *La Femme de tête* (The resourceful woman) and *Le Bourru bienfaisant* (The beneficent peevish man).

Goldsmith, Oliver (ca. 1728–1774) *Irish playwright, novelist, and poet*
Although educated at the UNIVERSITIES of Edinburgh and Leiden in the field of MEDICINE, Oliver Goldsmith's youth was marked by a series of failed business and professional ventures. One of his more colorful adventures consisted of a GRAND TOUR of the European continent on foot with his flute in hand. Finally, at the age of 26, he settled in LONDON, having chosen to devote himself to LITERATURE. He began his career as a hack writer on GRUB STREET, but his talents soon attracted the attention of more established writers such as Samuel JOHNSON. Goldsmith entered Johnson's most intimate circle of friends and became a charter member of the club that met weekly at the Turk's Head in Soho. Besides Johnson and Goldsmith, members included David GARRICK, Joshua REYNOLDS, Richard SHERIDAN, Edmund BURKE, and Charles BURNEY.

Goldsmith produced some of the best-loved literature of the middle ENLIGHTENMENT years. He criticized the sentimental style, associated with the broader cult of SENSIBILITY, that had developed in 18th-century literature. Himself something of a vagabond and rake, he turned a satirical eye toward contemporary culture, exposing both its foibles and injustices. Goldsmith occasionally borrowed materials and critical techniques from continental writers such as MONTESQUIEU, Pierre de MARIVAUX, and the marquis d'ARGENS.

The Goldsmith opus included the outstanding comedy *She Stoops to Conquer* (1773), the widely-read novel *The Vicar of Wakefield* (1766), and an important poem, *The Deserted Village* (1770). He also wrote *An History of the Earth and Animated Nature* (1774), *Enquiry into the Present State of Polite Learning in Europe* (1759), and "Chinese Letters," published in the *Public Ledger* and later printed as *The Citizen of the World* (1762).

See also ROWLANDSON.

Gothic revival An architectural style that developed in England during the middle of the 18th century. It had a literary counterpart in the GOTHIC ROMANCE. The creation of both Gothic revival architecture and Gothic romance LITERATURE is most strongly associated with Horace WALPOLE, Thomas GRAY, and their friends at the estate of Strawberry Hill in Twickenham, ENGLAND. Walpole "gothicized" Strawberry Hill by adding interior and exterior elements of medieval inspiration to the basic structure.

In part, the Gothic revival occurred as a reaction against the formal, severe, geometric aesthetic associated with English neoclassical PALLADIAN STYLE architecture. It turned to the conventional forms of medieval Gothic architecture—pointed arches, lacy openwork ornamentation, and narrow columns—utilizing them as primarily decorative elements rather than structural devices. But Gothic revival did not turn exclusively to the Middle Ages for its inspirations. The name was attached to any structure that appeared exotic. Hence, the Royal Pavilion built by John Nash at Brighton was called Indian Gothic.

Gothic revival style adapted the ENGLISH GARDEN to new purposes, incorporating artificial ruins (medieval rather than classical), grottoes, and representations of uncontrolled nature into its designs. From England, the Gothic taste spread to the European continent.

The Gothic revival is one of many manifestations of the transformation in the culture, philosophy, SCIENCE, and AESTHETICS that marked the middle decades of the ENLIGHTENMENT. The earlier concern with REASON, geometric form, PROGRESS, and order began to be supplemented by renewed interest in the irrational, in irregular forms, in HISTORY (both ancient and medieval), and in cyclical processes that involved not only progress but also decay.

Gothic romance A literary style of the last half of the ENLIGHTENMENT, associated with that period's explorations of the limits of human REASON. Gothic romance had a counterpart in architecture and landscape design usually called the GOTHIC REVIVAL.

Most critics and historians date the origin of the vogue for Gothic romance to the publication of the *Castle of Otranto; A Gothic Story* (1765) by Horace WALPOLE. Utilizing material from a dream, Walpole fashioned a rather simple story about an evil and corrupt nobleman who attempts to separate two lovers. It takes place in an ancient castle filled with vaults and mysterious passageways, peopled with ghosts, giants, and living statues.

The castle setting and the fantastic figures of the novel are the elements that make this story Gothic. But, although the term refers to the style of the Middle Ages, coupling it with irrationality, Walpole was implying much more in his choice of setting and plot mechanisms. In fact, Walpole was using Gothic elements as a metaphor for the human mind and for NATURE. He was not depicting the mind solely in terms of its capacity to reason, the model favored by the early Enlightenment, but rather the mind filled with irrational thoughts, with passions, with "feminine" modes of thinking and sexuality, and even with evil. This fascination with the irrational, and the depiction of it as a convoluted, haunted, weird place became a fixture of Gothic romance and of other Gothic-inspired art forms.

Walpole's story reflected the fascination with these nonrational sides of human existence that was moving to the forefront of consciousness in enlightened circles. It grew, in part, from the earlier, fashionable sensation PSYCHOLOGY. The living statues at the Castle of Otranto, for example, were borrowed straight from Abbé CONDILLAC, whose *Traité des sensations* (1754) had adopted a living statue as a metaphor for the processes of mind formation.

Gothic romance, however, picked up its explorations of mind where sensation psychology and the associated culture of SENSIBILITY had stopped. These approaches had emphasized refined feelings and the relationship between sensory perception (feeling) and reason. The creators of Gothic romance recognized that feeling often becomes passionate, unrefined, uncontrollable, and frightening. The power of these darker or unpredictable aspects of mind could no longer be ignored.

Gothic fiction not only explored the irrational and the associated concepts of the "feminine," but also tried to evoke sensations of the SUBLIME, that is, feelings of terrified awe when confronted with the powers of the irrational in mind and nature. In this sense, Gothic romance became part of the larger aesthetic movement of the sublime whose appearance marks both a culmination of the Enlightenment and the beginnings of ROMANTICISM. Gothic romance was enormously popular in England, especially among women. It soon also became fashionable on the European continent. The most popular English works of Gothic fiction were *Castle of Otranto,* Charlotte Smith's *Emmeline; or the Orphan of the Castle* (1788), Ann Radcliffe's *The Mysteries of Udolpho* (1794), M. G. Lewis's *The Monk* (1796), Mary Shelley's *Frankenstein; or the Modern Prometheus* (1818), and C. R. Maturin's *Melmoth the Wanderer* (1820). Jane Austen satirized the excesses of Gothic romance in *Northanger Abbey,* a novel written during the final years of the 18th century and published posthumously by the author's family in 1818.

Göttingen, University of

Göttingen, University of   University in the city of Göttingen, officially founded by George II, King of ENGLAND and Elector of Lower Saxony, in 1737. Professors actually began giving courses three years earlier, in 1734. The University of Göttingen was the most modern university in the 18th-century HOLY ROMAN EMPIRE (modern Germany) and provided major institutional support for the German ENLIGHTENMENT (*AUFKLÄRUNG*).

Göttingen offered a new model of university structure and curriculum, closely resembling that of our modern research universities, that was subsequently perfected by Wilhelm von HUMBOLDT and his supporters at the University of BERLIN. In the UNITED STATES OF AMERICA, late-18th-century administrators at Harvard University also remodeled their university after the example of Göttingen.

The educational experiment at Göttingen actually expanded on reforms that had begun 40 years earlier at the UNIVERSITY OF HALLE. The traditional structure of the four teaching faculties (law, MEDICINE, THEOLOGY, and PHILOSOPHY) was restructured so that philosophy acquired equal footing with theology. The power of censorship was removed from the faculty of theology, thereby separating the university from the church. Religious TOLERATION was adopted as an official policy so that believers in ROMAN CATHOLICISM, JUDAISM, and CALVINISM could attend classes along with Lutherans and worship in private.

German universities had traditionally been filled with students from the ranks of the middle classes. Göttingen continued to recruit from these classes but also actively pursued young noblemen. In fact, the first building erected at the university was a riding hall; classes were held in the private homes of professors.

The University of Göttingen established seminars in philosophy and philology (study of language). Professors were encouraged not only to teach but also to do original research. Several faculty members established professional journals, the most famous of which were the *Göttinger Gelehrte Anzeige* and the *Staatsanzeige.* These publications were read throughout the Holy Roman Empire, SWITZERLAND, AUSTRIA, and Hapsburg-dominated Italian territories.

The University of Göttingen exercised notable influence in several areas during the *Aufklärung.* Mathematics, the life sciences (physiology, anatomy, medicine), social sciences (ANTHROPOLOGY, political science, HISTORY), and textual criticism (the Bible and Homer) were particularly strong disciplines. The university established several practical facilities in keeping with its interests in the applied sciences. Among the notable foundations were a women's medical clinic, a botanical garden, an anatomy laboratory, and an observatory.

Major intellectual figures at the University of Göttingen were Albrecht von HALLER, Georg Christoph LICHTENBERG, Carl Friedrich Gauss, August Ludwig von SCHLÖZER, Johann Christoph GATTERER, Johann David Michaelis, Georg FORSTER, Johann Friedrich BLUMENBACH, and Samuel Sömmering. Renowned students of the 18th-century university included Alexander von HUMBOLDT and his brother Wilhelm von Humboldt, Johannes von MÜLLER, Johann Christian REIL, the Schlegel brothers, and the early 19th-century Prussian reformers Prince Karl August von Hardenberg, Friedrich von Gentz, and Baron Heinrich Friedrich Karl vom und zum Stein.

Finally, the daughters of many Göttingen professors played important roles in the literary and cultural life of enlightened German salons. Dorothy Schlözer was the first woman to receive a Ph.D. (nonmedical degree) at any German university; Therese Heyne Forster became a well-known writer; and Carolina Michaelis was the companion and wife of both August Wilhelm Schlegel and of Friedrich Wilhelm Joseph von Schelling.

See also MICHAELIS.

Gottsched, Johann Christoph

Gottsched, Johann Christoph (1700–1766) *German literary critic and theorist of aesthetics*
Born in East Prussia, he studied at the University of Königsberg. He settled in Leipzig in 1730 after receiving an appointment as professor of poetry at the University of Leipzig. In 1734, Gottsched supplemented this position with additional appointments in logic and metaphysics. He developed the Leipzig school of acting and criticism in conjunction with the actress and theatrical manager Karoline Neuber and founded the Deutsche Gesellschaft, an organization devoted to the advancement of German culture. Through his various journals of literary criticism, Gottsched developed into a powerful critic hated by the younger generations of German writers. Gottsched died in Leipzig in 1766.

Gottsched championed the cause of French literary CLASSICISM as formulated by Nicolas Boileau by introducing the rules of this highly formal and rational literary mode into Germany. He fought energetically against its critics, especially during the 1740s dispute with the influential Swiss theorists Johann Jakob BODMER and Johann Jakob BREITINGER.

Gottsched provided German translations of French dramas in his *Deutsche Schaubühne* (German theater, 6 vols.; 1740–45) and prepared a bibliography of German drama entitled *Nötiger Vorrat zur Geschichte der deutschen dramatischen Dichtkunst* (Necessary stock for the history of German dramatic poetry; 1757–65). He thus helped to build a formal repertoire for use in German theater. Gottsched's play *Der sterbende Cato* (The dying Cato), an adaptation of a work by Joseph ADDISON, offered German audiences an example of English classical dramatic style. Gottsched's theoretical works supplemented his work on stage repertoire and poetry by presenting an interpretation of classical aesthetics applicable to German poetry and dramatic literature. They include *Versuch einer kritische Dichtkunst für die Deutschen* (Essay on critical poetry for the Germans; 1730) and *Grundlegung einer deutschen Sprachkunst* (Foundation of a German linguistics; 1748).

In spite of his dedicated work, Gottsched's position was eclipsed in the German literary world by the middle of the 18th century. In place of his formal classical style, built on the rigid application of REASON and rule to literary production, midcentury theorists such as Bodmer, Breitinger, Gotthold Ephraim LESSING, and Moses MENDELSSOHN offered an aesthetic based on the creative power of INTUITION AND IMAGINATION.

Gournay, Jacques-Claude-Marie-Vincent de (1712–1759) *French Physiocrat, businessman, and government official*

Gournay was a disciple of François QUESNAY and believed strongly in the principle of free trade, but he rejected the Physiocrats' notion that agriculture is the source of all wealth. He maintained that industry and commerce are equally potent primary sources of wealth and thus should also be freed from regulation. His teachings were adapted by several 18th-century economists, such as Ann-Robert-Jacques TURGOT and the Abbé Morellet. Gournay is credited by some scholars with having coined the famous phrase, *laissez-faire, laissez-passer* (allow to do, allow to happen), which summarizes the liberal economic ideal of free, unregulated trade. Gournay's published works included a *Mémoire sur la Compagnie des Indes* (Memoir on the East India Company; 1769) and *Considérations sur le commerce* (Considerations on commerce; 1758).

Gournay was the second son of the merchant and royal official Claude-Vincent de Gournay and his wife, Françoise-Thérèse de Sère. Jean-Claude-Marie-Vincent de Gournay entered commerce as a young man and spent 15 years working in SPAIN (1729–44). He also traveled (1745–46) in the HOLY ROMAN EMPIRE, Holland, and ENGLAND. During these business-related sojourns, he collected observations about commerce, navy, and law. In 1746, after inheriting goods from his former associate, Jamets de Villebarre, Gournay retired from business and

moved to PARIS, where he assumed the title marquis de Gournay. He took advantage of the prevalent ANCIEN RÉGIME practice of venality (selling government offices) by purchasing a spot in the great royal council and a position as superintendent for commerce with the Companies of the Levant and East Indies. Gournay died in Paris on June 27, 1759. Turgot delivered the memorial address at his funeral.

See also LAISSEZ FAIRE; MERCANTILISM; PHYSIOCRATS.

Goya y Lucientes, Francisco José de (1746–1828) *Spanish painter and engraver*

A native of Saragossa, Goya studied art in that city, in MADRID, and in ROME. His first important art commission came from his native city, where he was asked to paint frescoes in the cathedral. Goya executed the paintings in the ROCOCO style that had been introduced to SPAIN by Giovanni Battista TIEPOLO.

In 1775, Goya obtained a post as a cartoon designer for the royal tapestry factory, Santa Barbara, in Madrid. His work was supervised by A. R. MENGS, the German neoclassical painter who had assumed prominence in Madrid after Tiepolo's death. In spite of these various influences, Goya always cited the 17th-century painters Rembrandt van Rijn and Diego Velázquez, as well as NATURE, when discussing his primary artistic models.

Goya worked at Santa Barbara until 1792, but in 1780 he also obtained a position at the Royal Academy of San Fernando in Madrid. He was appointed its deputy director in 1785, director in 1795, and first court painter in 1799. He continued in these positions through the period of French occupation during the Napoleonic Wars and after the 1814 restoration of monarchy. Goya fled from Spain after a rebellion in 1824 failed to establish a liberal limited monarchy in that nation. He subsequently painted several works that depicted King Ferdinand VII as a tyrant. He died in exile in Bordeaux, France.

Goya lived through the period of transition from the ENLIGHTENMENT to ROMANTICISM. His art reflects these developments, displaying an intensely personal and revolutionary element.

The experience of the Napoleonic Wars had a profoundly disturbing effect on him. Napoleon, in one sense, represented the high point of enlightened rationalism. He not only codified laws, but he also introduced a number of educational reforms and other improvements that had been championed during the Enlightenment. On the other hand, he engaged in a Europe-wide war of conquest, brutally attacking and repressing other nations. Goya, feeling betrayed by this apostle of the Enlightenment, captured the horrors of Napoleon's wars in his renowned series of etchings, *Los Desastres de la Guerra* (The disasters of war). These were not published until 1863.

Goya was a masterly caricaturist but also could paint with brutal realism. As his style developed, he minimized detail and color, producing simple yet powerful forms. He remained a passionate opponent of political, religious, and social abuses throughout his life, attacking them through the skillful use of artistic satire.

Goya left numerous masterful works among which are the following: *Los Desastres de la Guerra; Family of Charles IV; Charles III as Huntsman; Madhouse; Procession of Flagellants; Tribunal of the Inquisition; The Execution of the Defenders of Madrid; The 3d of May;* and *Proverbios* (Proverbs).

grand tour   Travel undertaken by the children of 18th-century nobles and wealthy families to broaden their experience and complete their educations. Grand tours ranged over itineraries that almost always included the Italian peninsula, SWITZERLAND, and FRANCE, but they could also encompass major cities in the HOLY ROMAN EMPIRE and the UNITED PROVINCES OF THE NETHERLANDS. The cities most frequently visited were PARIS, ROME, Florence, MILAN, and VENICE. Other destinations included GENEVA, BERLIN, AMSTERDAM, and The Hague. These journeys could extend from a few months to several years. The term *grand tour* is associated with ENGLAND, where the phenomenon was most widespread, but young people from other countries pursued similar itineraries.

The grand tour was commonly used as a capstone to a young man's EDUCATION. It provided him with a degree of worldly cultural sophistication deemed highly desirable in a man of high social standing. He would learn of foreign customs, experience great works of art and ancient ruins, and become conversant in foreign languages. While the grand tour was generally pursued by young men, it was not unheard-of for women to undertake such a journey, as did Mary MONTAGU and Mary WOLLSTONECRAFT. Letters of introduction and an ever-expanding network of contacts allowed the travelers to receive hospitality and guidance from local aristocrats. Although the grand tour was mainly purused by those of aristocratic or wealthy backgrounds, young men of more modest financial means were sometimes able to participate, especially if their artistic talents earned them some kind of sponsorship.

Although the educational aspects of the grand tour may often have been eclipsed by other pleasures, such as idleness, merry-making, and pursuing women, these journeys helped to introduce young men to new ideas and customs. John Milton's travels to ITALY, for example, where he spent nearly 15 months, exposed him to a variety of classical and vernacular literary, musical, and visual art forms that influenced his own poetry. In Naples, Milton was able to meet Giovanni Battista Manso, an elderly patron of Torquato Tasso, one of the epic poets whom he most admired. It was during this inspiring journey to Italy that Milton first decided to write an epic himself and became convinced that his poetry would survive for future generations. During his Italian travels between 1786 and 1788, Johann Wolfgang von GOETHE was able to combine pleasure seeking with his literary development. In his famous *Römische Elegien* (Roman elegies) published in 1795, he described love affairs with Italian women using poetic forms and allusions that showed his ability to engage with the poetic tradition of ancient Rome.

The grand tour could frequently lead to interesting social encounters and intellectual developments. Many young composers traveled to Italy in order to study music theory in Milan with Padre Giovanni Battista Martini or to study Italian styles of composition. Wolfgang Amadeus MOZART and J. C. BACH are among the most famous of Martini's students. The English musicologist Charles BURNEY made a stunning musical discovery during his Italian tour. He managed to obtain a copy of Gregorio Allegri's *Miserere*, a piece of Easter music which, according to orders from the pope, could be performed only in the Sistine Chapel and was not to be circulated. Some scholars have wondered whether Martini aided Burney in obtaining the music, but others find it unlikely that the Italian composer would flout the orders of the pope. Thus, it remains a mystery how Burney acquired this intriguing piece of music. In 1771, Burney published an account of his travels in Italy and included the transcription of Allegri's composition, which could thenceforth be enjoyed by English audiences.

The ancient sites of Italy were the most celebrated aspect of the grand tour. Young painters, architects, and sculptors traveled to Rome, where they studied magnificent artifacts and drew upon ancient sites for their subject matter. A primary impetus for this phenomenon came from the German art historian and archaeologist Johann Joachim WINCKELMANN, who helped to start the neoclassical movement in art. In 1755, Winckelmann published *Gedanken über die Nachahmung der griechischen Werke in der Malerei und Bildhauerkunst* (Reflections on the imitation of Greek works in painting and sculpture), in which he called for artists to seek inspiration and refine their skills by imitating ancient works.

As the 18th century progressed, certain new destinations were added to grand tour itineraries. Of special importance were the newly excavated ruins of POMPEII and Herculaneum, where visitors could see artifacts from the lives of ordinary ancient Italian people. Toward the end of the century, tourists also began to linger in the Swiss Alps. These mountains had once been considered merely an inconvenient obstacle to traverse, but the late 18th-century fascination with wild and unruly NATURE changed that; the Alps began to be appreciated for the SUBLIME experiences they offered to visitors. Over the course of the 18th century, English attitudes placed increasing importance on the familiarity with continental Europe gained through the experiences of a grand tour. This trend continued until the FRENCH REVOLUTION, which disrupted travel as well as the social and political networks of Europe as a whole.

See also REPUBLIC OF LETTERS.

Further reading: Jeremy Black, *The British Abroad: The Grand Tour in the Eighteenth Century* (New York: St. Martin's Press, 1992); Edward Chaney, *The Evolution of the Grand Tour: Anglo-Italian Cultural Relations Since the Renaissance* (Portland, Ore.: Frank Cass Publishers, 1998); Brian Dolan, *Ladies of the Grand Tour: British Women in Pursuit of Enlightenment and Adventure in Eighteenth-Century Europe* (New York: HarperCollins, 2001).

Gravesande, Willem Jacob's (1688–1742) *Dutch natural philosopher, physicist, and mathematician*
Gravesande was one of the earliest continental European proponents of both the NATURAL PHILOSOPHY of Isaac NEWTON and of British EMPIRICISM. Together with his compatriots Hermann BOERHAAVE and Pieter van MUSSCHENBROEK, Gravesande disseminated these new scientific approaches by means of lectures and textbooks to younger generations of European students.

Gravesande received his primary education at home from a private tutor. He studied law at the University of Leiden from 1704 until 1707 and graduated with a dissertation on suicide. He established a law practice in The Hague. In 1713, he helped to establish the *Journal littéraire de la Haye* (Literary journal of The Hague) and thereafter contributed essays and book reviews to its issues. Having acquired a post as secretary for a Dutch ambassador, Gravesande spent a full year (1715–16) in ENGLAND. He was elected to the ROYAL SOCIETY OF LONDON on the strength of recommendations from his friend Gilbert Burnet. At the meetings of the Royal Society, Gravesande encountered John DESAGULIERS and John Keill, both committed Newtonians. He probably also made the acquaintance of Newton himself.

In 1717, Gravesande received an appointment as professor of mathematics and ASTRONOMY at the University of Leiden. He became an influential and renowned teacher and, like his colleague Boerhaave, attracted students from many European countries. The university further honored Gravesande in 1734 by giving him a second chair in PHILOSOPHY. From that time, following a practice that was not unusual at the time, he held two chairs jointly.

Gravesande published the content of his Leiden courses in three textbooks: the widely disseminated *Physices elementa mathematica, experimentis confirmata. Sive, introductio ad philosophiam Newtonianam* (Mathematical elements of physics, experimentally confirmed, with an introduction to Newtonian philosophy; 1720, 1721); *Mathesis univesalis elementa* (Elements of universal mathesis; 1727); and *Introductio ad philosophiam, metaphysicam et logicam continens* (Introduction to philosophy, containing metaphysics and logic; 1736). These works were translated from Latin into Dutch, English, and French. The *Physices elementa mathematica* presented basic Newtonian ideas and served as the primary textbook of its kind until the 1750s.

Gravesande accepted Newton's theories of gravity, matter, and light. He specifically attacked the reliance by René DESCARTES and his followers on a priori hypotheses and systematic rationalization. He also adopted an anti-Cartesian position in the *vis viva* controversy, the noisy 18th-century dispute over the proper conceptualization of forces in NATURE. Gravesande taught that scientific procedures must be empirical, drawing their truths from experiment aided by instrumentation and mathematics. Gravesande stands as one of the major early figures to disseminate the fundamental scientific ideas without which the 18th-century ENLIGHTENMENT could not have developed as it did.

See also MATHEMATICS AND MECHANICS.

Gray, Thomas (1716–1771) *English lyric poet, one of the early representatives of the Gothic revival*
Gray produced some of the finest English-language poetry of the 18th century. The son of a prosperous scrivener of LONDON, he was a shy, reclusive individual. His childhood was marred by his father's physical and emotional abuse of his mother. At Eton school, Gray met young Horace WALPOLE, and the two men became fast friends. Between 1734 and 1738, Gray pursued his education at Peterhouse College, Cambridge, but never received a degree. In 1739, he embarked on a GRAND TOUR of the European continent with Walpole, visiting FRANCE and ITALY. At the monastery of Grande Chartreuse in France, Gray wrote the stanzas "O Tu, severi Religio loci" (O you, the awe before an austere place) to reflect the impact of the monastery on his mood.

Upon returning to ENGLAND, Gray established residency at Peterhouse College, where he pursued law courses unenthusiastically. During these years, he produced excellent poems such as "Ode on a Distant Prospect of Eton College," "Hymn to Adversity," and "De Principiis Cogitandi" (On the principles of thinking, begun in Florence, Italy). About 1742, Gray began work on the famous "Elegy Written in a Country Churchyard" (published 1751). In 1757, Horace Walpole published a small volume of Gray's odes on his private press at Strawberry Hill. Its poems, the odes "The Progress of Poesy" and "The Bard," were coolly received by critics.

Gray wrote very little poetry afterward, having been disappointed by the success of these odes. Instead, inspired by the publication of the "ancient odes" of the Scottish bard Ossian (actually written, if Samuel JOHNSON can be believed, by the Scottish poet James MACPHERSON), Gray turned to a historical investigation of the Celtic and Scandinavian poetic traditions. In 1768, he secured an appointment at Cambridge University in modern HISTORY. He taught seldom and died after a sudden illness in 1771.

Many scholars treat Gray and the GOTHIC REVIVAL as a precursor to ROMANTICISM. Certainly Gray's characteristic themes and literary moods were developed by the romantics. His poetry, moreover, was highly esteemed by

English romantic poets such as Lord BYRON and William Wordsworth. But Gray's poetry actually reflects trends that were developing within the boundaries of the culture of the ENLIGHTENMENT during the last years of the 18th century. The shift in mood, the corresponding focus on darker aspects of NATURE, and the development of interest in historic subjects drawn from traditions other than those of classical antiquity all illustrate these trends.

Great Awakening   Religious movement in 18th-century North American colonies characterized by a desire to revive fundamental Christian beliefs, strengthen the influence of such belief in communities, and reemphasize the importance of personal salvation. The Great Awakening was sparked by the 1739 appearance of English preacher George Whitefield in churches and communities throughout the British colonies. Believing that the Christian faith had grown cold and ineffective in the hands of church bureaucrats, Whitefield drew upon the beliefs of German Pietistic sects to reform Anglicanism and other Christian denominations. He advocated a faith spread through conversion experiences that reformed people's beliefs and morality based on the emotional experience of God's love.

Whitefield found a ready audience in American listeners, many of whom had reached similar conclusions about established churches in places such as New England and were generally concerned with the dangers of life in their new home. American preachers such as Jonathan EDWARDS were themselves employing new styles of preaching in an attempt to awaken their communities from the spiritual dangers of self-satisfied complacency. Whitefield's cause was further aided by the fact that many Pietists had themselves already emigrated to the colonies seeking religious freedom. As the movement spread, interest grew in regions associated with religious radicalism, such as the city of PHILADELPHIA, with its Quaker background. In 1740 the city established a "New Building" intended to provide a space where Whitefield and likeminded ministers could hold revivals.

Dissent against Whitefield and his followers soon grew among various groups. Debates between Whitefield's detractors, who were designated by the name "Old Lights," and his supporters, the "New Lights," were vigorous. The "Old Lights" were a far from homogeneous group, ranging from orthodox church authorities who had always distrusted his program to Americans who wished to take his ideas in new and more radical directions, such as the theologian John WESLEY's followers, the future Methodists.

Accusations were leveled that the excesses of Whitefield's movement showed it to be ultimately a work of evil. People caught up in the descriptions of the threats of hell at revival meetings had severe emotional reactions to the point of unconsciousness, and some theologians saw little, if any, spiritual benefit in the riotous meetings. The radical elements of revival movements in places such as New England, on the other hand, saw Whitefield's work as merely an initial step. They continued to question church traditions and reject them when they appeared to contradict fundamental principles, such as the eventual movement against providing newborn babies with the sacrament of baptism.

See also ANGLICANS; DISSENTERS; METHODISM; MILLENARIANISM; PIETISM; QUAKERS.

Further reading: J. M. Bumstead, ed., *The Great Awakening: The Beginnings of Evangelical Pietism in America* (Waltham, Mass.: Blaisedell Publishing, 1970); Frank Lambert, *Inventing the "Great Awakening"* (Princeton, N.J.: Princeton University Press, 1999); G. A. Rawlyk, *The Canada Fire: Radical Evangelism in British North America, 1775–1812* (Buffalo, N.Y.: McGill-Queen's University Press, 1994); Nina Reid-Maroney, *Philadelphia's Enlightenment, 1740–1800: Kingdom of Christ, Empire of Reason* (Westport, Conn.: Greenwood Press, 2001).

great chain of being   Philosophical theory of NATURE that depicted the universe as a continuum in which the inorganic is linked with the organic and the terrestrial with the celestial by a series of minute, nearly imperceptible steps. The idea of a great chain of being, an old medieval scholastic notion, had been restated in a 17th-century form by the German philosopher Gottfried LEIBNIZ. It passed into 18th-century natural history through the works of Leibniz and of the Swiss naturalist Charles BONNET.

The theory conceives of the species as minute building blocks, the sum of which creates a continuum. In conceptualizing the idea, an analogy should be made with calculus (one of whose inventors was Leibniz). The method of deriving a continuous curve from differences of increasingly minute size provides a mathematical representation of the idea of the great chain of being. The theory of the great chain of being was adaptable both to mechanistic and organic visions of nature and was used by partisans of both visions during the 18th century.

The 18th-century theory implied that no significant gaps existed between the organic and the inorganic, between the animal and the vegetable, or between man and the other animals. Some Christian theologians, whose doctrines insisted that a substantial qualitative gap, created by God, separates human beings from lower animals (such as the great apes), treated the theory of the great chain of being as heretical. Others disliked the antimechanistic version of the theory because its insistence that all nature is alive supported pantheism. In all instances, theologians saw that the implications of the theory seriously challenged traditional Christian views about the fixed nature of species and about the relation of the creator God to his universe.

See also RELIGION.

Gregoire, Henri, Abbé (1750–1831)

Abbé Henri Gregoire was born in Lorraine, france, and was educated by the jesuits in Nancy. He became a priest in 1776. After his ordination, he was assigned to a parish in Lorraine, where he reformed and improved both the education and the social conditions of the peasants. This early work was only a sign of things to come.

An effective writer, Gregoire used his talent both before and after becoming a priest. In 1773, he won an essay contest about poetry in Nancy. Another prize followed in 1788 in Metz for his essay on the restrictions against the Jews. He argued that Jews should be allowed to participate in the state as full citizens and be fully assimilated into French society. In these early writings and in those to come, it became clear that Gregoire was determined to intermingle his radical politics, his Roman Catholic ideals, and public service.

Gregoire was a representative of the lower classes in the 1789 meeting of the Estates General, the French representative body. There he made various speeches for the joining of the clergy with the lower classes to make reforms in government, as well as speeches and legislation to grant full rights to Jews and blacks.

Gregoire became a firm supporter of the FRENCH REVOLUTION and its ideals of liberty, equality, and brotherhood. A member of the Jacobin Club, Gregoire began to support political and social reforms in his pamphlets and in speeches in the National Assembly. The most radical reforms he supported were for the abolishment of primogeniture laws, SLAVERY, and the oppression of racial and religious minorities.

He also supported reforms of the church in France, such as the Civil Constitution of the Clergy, a radical piece of legislation that put the church under the National Assembly's authority. This move was condemned by the conservative members of the Catholic Church in France and by the pope. Despite his support for this law, Gregoire remained dedicated to the active use of his faith to help others and to his Catholic beliefs.

Under the revolutionary government Gregoire became the bishop of Blois in 1791. From this position, he continued to crusade for social reform, especially for the end of the aristocracy as a class.

Perhaps the greatest contribution of Gregoire to history was his work on civil RIGHTS for ethnic and religious minorities and for the poor. Arguably, his most successful work was for the abolition of slavery. Gregoire first became involved in the slavery issue when he served on a committee to decide whether blacks and those of mixed RACE in the French colonies should enjoy equal rights with whites. Gregoire, ever a champion of equal rights, spoke out in favor of abolition. Outside the assembly, he also worked with the Society of Friends of Blacks to do away with slavery and to promote social equality.

Portrait of Henri Gregoire (1750–1831), French priest and author. He fought for the civil rights of the poor and of ethnic and religious minorities and for the abolition of slavery. *(Courtesy New York Public Library)*

After the end of the Reign of Terror, Gregoire remained in office. He continued as part of the government of the Directory in 1795. When Napoleon Bonaparte came to power, Gregoire made it clear that he opposed the idea of empire. However, Napoleon still wanted Gregoire to work for France and made him both a senator and a count. Gregoire declined the title of nobility on principle.

There were other principles that Gregoire felt Napoleon's government violated. The Senate was basically a puppet assembly, as it was clear that Napoleon held the real power in government. In addition, in 1801, Napoleon ended the Civil Constitution of the Clergy and placed ecclesiastical control back in the hands of the pope. At this point, Gregoire resigned from office and gave up his position as bishop.

Reform Work

Even worse in Gregoire's eyes was the worsening situation blacks and mulattoes faced under Napoleon's government. In response, Gregoire published his work on the history of the black people, *De la littérature des nègres, ou recherches sur leurs facultés intellectuelles, leurs qualités morales et leur littérature* (An enquiry concerning the intellectual and moral faculties and literature of negroes), in 1808. It was translated quickly into German and English and published in America. In the book, Gregoire says that civilization is the process of making humanity one. Slavery and the oppression of races are actually not acts performed by a CIVIL SOCIETY. Rather, they are the acts of a barbarous society designed to exclude others from humanity. Europeans, therefore, were the real savages.

Gregoire earlier had expressed similar sentiments in his work on Jewish rights. In *Essai sur la régéneration physique, morale, et politique des Juifs* (A treatise on the physical, moral, and political regeneration of the Jews; 1789), he outlined a plan for the full assimilation of French Jews into the rest of French society. Part of this plan was the extension of full rights and citizenship to Jews. In another part of the plan that seems more controversial today, Gregoire advocated that Jews dissolve their political and social societies, hold only religious meetings, and cease to speak their own dialect. According to Gregoire, the dissolution of political meetings would erase people's fears that Jews were trying to change government or society. Gregoire also claimed that the assimilation of Jews into society would make it easier to convert them to Christianity. However, it is unclear whether Gregoire believed all Jews should convert or whether he used this idea simply to convince the more skeptical among his contemporaries of the social benefits of granting rights to the Jews. For instance, Gregoire used the millenarian arguments of the neo-Jansenists that the conversion of the Jews was necessary for the promises of the Old and New Testaments to be fulfilled to gain the support of his fellow clergymen.

Gregoire continued his writing and political work even under changing regimes. In 1815, the French monarchy was restored, and Gregoire's political views were not viewed favorably. Although he was elected to the Chamber of Deputies in 1819, he was not allowed to take his seat. Gregoire continued his work despite being stripped of his pension by the new government, corresponding about the RACE issue with a number of political leaders at home and abroad, such as Thomas JEFFERSON.

Gregoire worked tirelessly for other causes as well. He led the fight to pass legislation against the defacement of France's historic buildings. In fact, it was Gregoire who first used the term *vandalism* to refer to the wanton destruction of beautiful things. He also worked for the eradication of local dialects in order to have a universally understood French. Gregoire wrote more than 400 works covering a wide range of issues. Among his religious subjects are church reform (1814), women and Christianity (1821), and the history of religion (1828).

The Abbé Gregoire died in 1831 after a struggle with cancer. He still would not renounce the oath he had sworn to be part of the Civil Constitution of the Clergy. Although the archbishop of Paris had decreed that no last rites be said for the priest, the Abbé Marie-Nicolas-Silvestre Guillon heard his last confession and officiated at his last rites. More than 20,000 people attended his funeral. Gregoire, the self-described "friend of men of all colors," left an important legacy for all those who were to fight slavery and racial prejudice after him.

See also JEWS AND JUDAISM.

Further reading: Ruth F. Necheles, *The Abbé Gregoire: The Odyssey of an Egalitarian* (Westport, Conn.: Greenwood, 1971); Jeremy Popkin and Richard Popkin, eds., *The Abbé Gregoire and His World* (Dordrecht: Kluwer Academic, 2000).

Greuze, Jean-Baptiste (1725–1805) *French painter*

Greuze came from a poor Burgundian family. His father disliked his son's interest in painting but agreed to provide some lessons with Charles Grandon in Lyons. Grandon took young Greuze with him to PARIS in 1750, where the latter enrolled in courses at the academy. Greuze exhibited his first paintings in the 1755 Salon (art show) sponsored by the academy. His work entitled *Un père de famille expliquant la Bible à ses enfants* (A father explaining the Bible to his children) won praise from critics. In the same year, Greuze was admitted to the Royal Academy of Painting. Shortly afterward, he traveled to ITALY for two years of study but, unlike many of his contemporaries, found himself unmoved by contact with classical antiquities or with the art of the Italian Renaissance and baroque periods.

Back in Paris, Greuze devoted himself to turning out his intensely personal paintings. Denis DIDEROT, whom he met in 1759, encouraged him to develop his highly emotive, didactic, moralizing style and subject matter. Common people and scenes served as the subjects, set in a manner akin to the "dumb show" narratives by William HOGARTH, but Greuze did not use the biting, penetrating eye of his English counterpart in depicting his subjects. Greuze's paintings, nevertheless, were enormously popular. They included pieces such as *L'accordée du village* (The village bride), *L'aveugle trompé par sa femme* (The blind man tricked by his wife), *La mort du paralytique* (Death of a paralytic), *Jeune fille au canari mort* (Young girl with a dead canary), *La malédiction paternelle* (Paternal curse), and *Le fils puni* (The punished son). Despite his popularity, Greuze lived in severe

Broken Eggs, painting by Jean-Baptiste Greuze. Greuze departed from rococo-style conventions by painting incidents drawn from the lives of simple, lower-class people. *(Courtesy Metropolitan Museum of Art; bequest of William K. Vanderbilt, 1920)*

economic straits and died, poverty-stricken, at the Louvre, where he had lived in one of the apartments provided for artists.

Grimm, Friedrich Melchior, baron von (1723–1807)
German critic and diplomat

Friedrich Melchior, baron von Grimm, or Melchior Grimm, as he was also known, was the son of a Protestant pastor in the city of Regensburg in the HOLY ROMAN EMPIRE. Even as a secondary school student, Grimm knew that he wanted to pursue a literary career, and, consequently, he established contact with the powerful German critic Johann Christoph GOTTSCHED. In 1743, Gottsched published Grimm's dramatization of the novel *Asiatische Banise* (Asian banise) in his influential journal *Deutsche Schaubühne* (German theater). The piece failed on stage, and Grimm was persuaded by this experience to turn to the profession of literary criticism.

In 1748, Grimm moved to PARIS as an employee of an aristocratic German family that was living in the French capital. By 1755, he was working as a tutor in the service of the duke of Orléans. In later years, Grimm acted as the Parisian emissary for the duke of Sachsen-Gotha and was also sent to SAINT PETERSBURG to negotiate various issues with CATHERINE II (THE GREAT) of Russia.

Grimm lived in Paris during the height of the ENLIGHTENMENT and moved regularly in the salons and coffeehouses that were meeting places for the PHILOSOPHES.

He was welcomed not only because of his status but also because of his intelligence and wit. In 1753, he contributed two significant essays to the BATTLE OF THE BUFFOONS: "Let petit prophète de Boemisch-Broda" (1753) and "Lettre sur la musique française." Among his closest friends were Denis DIDEROT, Jean Le Rond d'ALEMBERT, Baron d'HOLBACH, Jean-Jacques ROUSSEAU, Madame d'ÉPINAY, and VOLTAIRE.

Grimm made his greatest contribution to the Enlightenment through his nearly 40 years (1753–92) as editor of the private newsletter entitled *Correspondance littéraire, philosophique, et critique, adressée à un Souverain d'Allemagne* (Literary, philosophical, and critical correspondence, addressed to a ruler in Germany). He ceased publishing the newsletter only when events during the FRENCH REVOLUTION forced him to flee from Paris.

The *Correspondance littéraire* reported on all the latest publications, news, and gossip associated with the Enlightenment. It served, in fact, as the single most important vehicle for spreading enlightened ideas into the German territories, Scandinavia, and Russia during the last half of the 18th century. Furthermore, because it was a private document, the newsletter could offer criticisms and opinions that would have been censored in regular publications. Grimm thus left a legacy of incomparable value for modern students of the Enlightenment.

See also PUBLISHING; SOCIAL INSTITUTIONS OF THE ENLIGHTENMENT.

Grub Street   A street in LONDON whose name serves as a metaphor for the 17th-century and 18th-century periodical press. The development of this popular press was a major event in the English 18th-century ENLIGHTENMENT.

Grub Street in London was the traditional residential area of struggling independent writers, journalists, and publishers. It had acquired notoriety during the 17th-century Puritan Revolution and Civil Wars (1647–60) when resident writers turned to creating political pamphlets and satirical illustrated broadsides. These unfettered activities were severely restrained during the subsequent years of the Stuart Restoration (1660–1714). Specifically, a censorship law was passed in 1662 that essentially squelched the budding periodical press.

The situation changed in 1695, when Parliament allowed the licensing laws to lapse, thereby effectively restoring English freedom of the press. As a result, periodicals once again appeared, and journalism became a respectable outlet for writers. During the early years of the 18th century, periodicals such as the *Gentleman's Magazine*, the rival *London Magazine*, *The Tatler*, and THE SPECTATOR flourished, if only for short periods.

Grub Street once again became the center of political and social journalism, a place where so-called writers-of-all trades could make a living at their craft. Grub Street journals aimed to disseminate information about political debates and issues to the general English reading public, but they also offered critical commentary. The journals also served as organs for the articulation of middle-class manners and morality. Among those who contributed to the Grub Street press were the writers Daniel DEFOE, Oliver GOLDSMITH, Samuel JOHNSON, Joseph ADDISON, and Richard STEELE.

The Grub Street press represents one of the major paths by which political and social commentary was transmitted during the Enlightenment. Unfettered by the restrictions associated with traditional patronage, the presses of Grub Street could hire writers to produce highly sensitive and even provocative materials. Grub Street had its counterparts throughout Europe, in spite of the greater degree of censorship that existed in continental countries. These presses could survive owing to a demand for their materials that was at once a product of the intellectual culture created by the Enlightenment and also a result of the increase in general LITERACY that marked the 18th century in Europe.

Guadeloupe   French territory in the West Indies made of a group of several small islands. Originally claimed by the Spanish in the 15th century, the islands of Guadeloupe became a part of the French colony of Martinique in 1693 and a separate French territory in 1775.

In 1695, Dominican missionary priest Jean-Baptiste Labat was sent by the French to explore the islands. He founded the capital city of Basse-Terre in 1703 and was the first governor of the colony. He also encouraged the sugar industry that was the island's principal economic product during the 18th century. In 1691, the British launched the first of several invasions against Guadeloupe during Labat's tenure as governor, which were all defeated. The 1703 British invasion is remembered both for Labat's participation in the fighting and fortification of Basse-Terre and for his arming of the slaves. Guadeloupe became the first place in the New World where slaves were allowed to bear arms.

Between 1756 and 1759, during the SEVEN YEARS' WAR, Guadeloupe endured continued battles between the British and the French for control of the island. The French governor surrendered in 1759. The British exploited the natural resources of the island and used it as a trading center until 1763, when the French regained the island through the Treaty of Paris.

Although occurring far away, the FRENCH REVOLUTION had serious consequences for Guadeloupe. In 1793, slaves at Three Rivers killed 23 whites. In their own defense, the slaves maintained the whites were royalists and that they were simply defending the new French state. The slaves were calling for equal application of the liberty, equality, and brotherhood advocated by the revolution.

Further upheaval ensued in 1794, when French royalist soldiers joined forces with the British and retook Guadeloupe. In FRANCE, the Committee of Public Safety appointed black French patriot Victor Hugues to retake Guadeloupe for France. Outnumbered by the British, Hugues fled to the countryside after several skirmishes. There he rallied his troops and armed 2,000 slaves. The combined slave and French forces forced the British to surrender and return the island to French control.

Hugues then took responsibility for the colony. He decided to subdue the unrest that was spreading throughout the islands through brute force. With the guillotine in tow, he visited the major cities of the islands. He was responsible for beheading more than 1,000 local French aristocrats and royalists there.

Unrest on the islands continued. The French government had outlawed SLAVERY in 1794, which caused large slave rebellions in Guadeloupe. The British intervened to aid the French royalists but were defeated again by Hugues and his army of free men and slaves in December 1794. Hugues abolished slavery in the islands before the end of the year.

After his victory, Hugues used Guadeloupe as a center from which to launch campaigns to recapture the rest of the Indies from Britain. He succeeded in repelling the British in the late 1790s by arming and patrolling Guadeloupe, instituting conscription of able-bodied men, and sending out raiders against British ships. However, the raiders also attacked American ships, leading to tension between France and the UNITED STATES OF AMERICA.

The residence of the sieur de Poincy, governor-general of the West Indies, on Guadeloupe Island. *(Courtesy New York Public Library)*

Guadeloupe became the site of a social experiment of sorts as slaves were granted freedom and citizenship. These new rights posed many problems for blacks and whites alike. Because the slaves had been denied all rights and citizenship under the old law, whites in the government had difficulty seeing how blacks would overnight be able to use and defend their rights. Hugues followed a policy of gradual emancipation, limiting the rights of the newly freed slaves, as proposed by the marquis de CON-DORCET and Abbé Emmanuel SIEYÈS. They argued that gradual rights were best for former slaves in order to maintain the peace of the state and that blacks were not necessarily capable of full citizenship. This posed a problem for blacks who had fought for Guadeloupe's freedom and were still being denied full rights.

Despite the limits imposed by Hugues, the former slaves of Guadeloupe did improve their material existence. They were now able to own property, and their marriages were recorded, ensuring their children's rights to inherit. Blacks and mulattoes in the army enjoyed equal status with their white counterparts.

In 1801, Napoleon's troops arrived in the islands and tried to limit the rights of the blacks in the army. Many black soldiers gathered with their supporters to stage an uprising at Matouba. After the insurgents, led by Louis Delgres, saw that their situation was hopeless, they set off barrels of gunpowder, killing many hundreds of people. The French reinstituted slavery on the island in 1802. Most of the people who had temporarily enjoyed freedom were forced to become slaves again.

Guadeloupe was reclaimed by the British during the Napoleonic Wars. However, the French regained the island through the Treaty of Vienna of 1816.

The freedom of Guadeloupe's slaves, though short lived, had a large impact on history. Abolitionists in America and Europe were encouraged by the early example of the new citizens.

See also SPAIN.

Further reading: Marian Goslinga, *Guadeloupe* (New York: ABC Clio, 1999); Jan Rogozinski, *A Brief History of the Caribbean* rev. ed. (New York: Facts On File, 1999).

Guardi, Francesco (1712–1793) *Venetian painter*

The Guardi family produced several painters in the 18th century. Francesco's sister Cecilia was the wife of the great Venetian frescoist Giovanni Battista TIEPOLO. Francesco Guardi and his brother Niccolò trained under their elder brother, Giovanni Antonio Guardi. The two young brothers established a studio where they painted on ecclesiastical commissions. The *Story of Tobias* (Church of the Angelo Raffaele, Venice) was created in the studio.

At some point around 1750, Francesco Guardi began painting landscapes and scenes of VENICE in a noticeably romantic style. They portray Venice through a veil of dark gloom that contrasts with the brighter, architecturally detailed works of Guardi's older compatriot CANALETTO. Guardi's many works include the *Feste Dogali* (Festival of the doges and the *Santa Maria della Salute* (Church of Santa Maria della Salute). Guardi was elected to the Venetian Academy in 1784.

See also ROMANTICISM.

Gulliver's Travels   NOVEL by Jonathan SWIFT first published in 1726. Swift wrote this satirical travel narrative after working many years as a writer of political propaganda and journalism for the Tory Party. *Gulliver's Travels* was influenced by his friends Alexander POPE, John GAY, John Arbuthnot, and Henry St. John, viscount BOLINGBROKE.

Swift divides his novel into four books, each depicting a different adventure and stage in the hero's development. The hero, Lemuel Gulliver, begins his first voyage as a naive and idealistic ship's doctor. As the plot unfolds, Swift turns his satirical pen against the policies of Prime Minister Robert WALPOLE and his ruling Whig Party. Swift presents Walpole as a wily acrobat whose rise to political power is based on his skill in dancing on a tightrope.

Gulliver lands eventually on Lilliput, an island inhabited by people who are only 10 inches tall. We later realize that their littleness is more than just size, but also reflects their attitudes. The Lilliputians constantly quarrel over petty matters with the people of a neighboring island, Blefuscu. The quarrel between the people of these two islands symbolizes the religious quarrels between ENGLAND and FRANCE.

Having set sail again, Gulliver reaches an island inhabited by the Brobdingnagians, a race of giants ruled by a benevolent PHILOSOPHER KING. This king is horrified when Gulliver offers to share European technologies of war, such as cannon and gunpowder. The contrast between the values of Gulliver and those of the Brobdingnagians serves to reveal Swift's criticisms of the modernizing trends in British culture.

Gulliver's final voyage takes him to the island of the Houyhnhnms, a land occupied by rational horses who keep a race of apelike humans, Yahoos, to work in their fields. Gulliver is horrified by his biological affinity with the Yahoos and attempts to imitate his Houyhnhnm masters, learning to whinny like a horse. Eventually, the Houyhnhnms evict Gulliver from his newly found paradise, and he is forced to return home to his wife and family. His experiences have left him thoroughly disillusioned with his culture and way of life; as a result, he treats his family with a new contempt.

Many critics have read the final book of *Gulliver's Travels* as a celebration of the perfectly rational Houyhnhnms and a rejection of the nonrational aspects of human nature represented by the Yahoos. Contemporary scholars favor a radically different interpretation. They believe that the satire is directed against the Houyhnhnms, those rational beings who regard themselves as the perfection of nature.

According to this interpretation, Swift uses the Houyhnhnms as a vehicle for satirizing REASON, whether used in deductive or inductive fashion, as a means for attaining human PROGRESS and perfection. He thus adopts a position opposed to what was then the mainstream of the scientific ENLIGHTENMENT.

In place of reason, Swift proposes that simple Christian humanism and charity will better serve humanity. He presents his position through the character and actions of the Portuguese sea captain, Don Pedro, who rescues Gulliver from the boat in which the Houyhnhnms have set him adrift.

Gulliver's Travels, then, reveals that the Enlightenment contained a strong element of distrust in reason and its ability to secure progress. Swift offers one solution, the return to simple, spontaneous human sentiment. Like Pierre BAYLE, the author of the HISTORICAL AND CRITICAL DICTIONARY, Swift used his critical abilities to undermine the cult of reason. While he rejects some hallowed ideas of the Enlightenment, Swift nevertheless is an enlightened figure because he displays the critical spirit that provides the underlying unity for the many facets of that era.

Gustav III of Sweden (Gustavus) (1746–1792) *king of Sweden from 1771 until 1792*
Gustav was the son of King Adolph-Frederick of SWEDEN and of Louisa Ulricke, the sister of FREDERICK II (THE GREAT). The Swedish Diet supervised Gustav's EDUCATION. The strained relations between the Diet and his father, the king, created great tension for Gustav. He began to play a political role in 1766, displaying his commitment to ABSOLUTISM by 1768. At that time he helped to stage a temporary abdication by his father, aimed at pressuring the Swedish Diet to give up some power to the king.

When Gustav assumed the throne in 1771 upon the death of his father, the Diet was split between various factions. In August 1772, Gustav engineered a bloodless coup d'etat in which he forced the Diet to make significant concessions to his royal power; from that point on, the Diet could meet only at the invitation of the king. The king could, therefore, control the Diet by refusing to call it into session, but the Diet did retain its legislative power and control over taxation. Thus, even at its most highly centralized stage, the Swedish monarchy shared some power with the Diet. A monarch could rule without the Diet for some time, but eventually political pressures would force him or her to call the Diet into session.

For six years, Gustav refused to call the Diet and governed as an absolute king. During that period he imposed a series of reforms, establishing greater freedom of trade and granting TOLERATION to non-Lutheran Protestants residing in Sweden. A new law on CENSORSHIP stiffened control but still left the Swedish press freer than its counterparts throughout Europe.

Gustav had strong cultural interests that he expressed by writing plays and participating in court theatricals. He generously patronized the arts and literature and founded the Swedish Academy in 1786 for the purpose of furthering the cause of Swedish-language literature (Gustav himself wrote mostly in French). Finally, he established the opera house at Stockholm.

Gustav continued to rule as a nearly absolute monarch from 1778 until 1789, although he did call the Diet for regular sessions in 1778 and 1786. In 1788, he led Sweden into an unpopular war against Russia, and by 1789 he again felt compelled to call the Diet into session. This time, however, he managed to obtain approval of a constitutional amendment that granted him nearly absolute power. The nobility was deprived of its privileges with respect to officeholding and land ownership.

These changes, of course, engendered opposition. In 1792, an assassin hired by members of the nobility shot Gustav at a masked ball (commemorated in Giuseppe Verdi's 19th-century opera *Un Ballo in Maschera*) in the opera house at Stockholm. The king died a few days later and was succeeded by his son Gustav IV Adolph.

See also MONARCHS, ENLIGHTENED; SCIENTIFIC ACADEMIES.

H

Hadley, John (1682–1744) *English instrument maker*
John Hadley developed a method of producing mirrors for a reflecting TELESCOPE that made the instrument superior to refracting telescopes. He presented his invention to the ROYAL SOCIETY OF LONDON and was elected to the society as a fellow in 1717.

Hadley shared his technological secrets with James BRADLEY and Samuel Molyneux. These astronomers had a reflecting telescope built that allowed Bradley to make his important measurements of apparent star displacements. These measurements provided the first direct observational proof of the HELIOCENTRIC theory of the universe that had been proposed in the 16th century by Nicolaus COPERNICUS.

Hadley also invented an improved quadrant (Hadley's quadrant), which measured the altitude of the Sun or a star above the horizon. This instrument enabled sailors to determine their geographic position at sea with greater accuracy.

Hadley's technological skills greatly assisted the progress of ASTRONOMY. This close interaction between scientific theory and instrumentation was one that assumed major significance during the ENLIGHTENMENT.

See also TECHNOLOGY AND INSTRUMENTATION.

Haitian Revolution (1791–1804) A slave revolt against French colonial rule in Saint-Domingue that began in 1791 and ended with the creation of the Republic of Haiti in 1804. The Haitian Revolution—fundamentally a slave revolt complicated by civil war, the FRENCH REVOLUTION, and war on the European continent—resulted in the first republic to be established by former slaves of African descent and the second republic (after the UNITED STATES OF AMERICA) to be created in the New World.

The French had been present in Haiti since the middle of the 16th century, when French buccaneers raided a Spanish settlement that would later become Port-au-Prince, one of Haiti's population centers. In 1665, Frenchman Bertrand d'Ogeron was dispatched to the Carribean as governor of the nearby island of Tortuga. He immediately set about organizing the scattered buccaneers, and, by 1675, Saint-Domingue was a French colony and a center of bustling agriculture. The Spanish recognized the colony in 1697, and, nearly a century later, Saint-Domingue had become a wealthy center of commerce and agriculture with a fully articulated colonial administration.

Agriculture in Saint-Domingue was organized according to the plantation system, which relied on large numbers of slaves brought from Africa and nearby Carribean islands. By the end of 1780s, plantation owners were importing just under 30,000 slaves a year, and, by 1791, three-fourths of the 50,000 people living in Le Cap François, the capital of Saint-Domingue, were slaves. The economy's reliance on SLAVERY created a stratified social system that separated wealthy white planters (*grands blancs*), middle- and lower-class whites (*petits blancs*), mulattos and free blacks (*gens de couleur*), and slaves.

Slave resistance predated the revolution in Saint-Domingue. For nearly a century, small slave uprisings and organized resistance had been suppressed in the colony. The influence of the ENLIGHTENMENT and the social upheaval of the French Revolution acted as cata-

François-Dominique Toussaint Louverture (1743–1803) was the key leader of the Haitian slave revolt (1791–1804) that ended slavery in the French colony of Saint-Domingue (Haiti) and brought about Haiti's independence from France. *(Courtesy New York Public Library)*

lysts, transforming these scattered incidents of rebellion into a larger movement.

Attacks on slavery came from several Enlightenment thinkers. Jean-Jacques ROUSSEAU cited slavery as an example of the inequality found in societies no longer governed by NATURAL LAW. The ENCYCLOPEDISTS, among them Denis DIDEROT, were also fervent abolitionists. The *HISTOIRE DES DEUX INDES* (1770) of the Abbé RAYNAL and Diderot criticized the institution of slavery and did not discourage slaves from securing their freedom through violence. The work influenced, among others, François-Dominique-TOUSSAINT LOUVERTURE, the most important leader of the Haitian slave revolt.

The events of the French Revolution also helped spur events in Saint-Domingue. The DECLARATION OF THE RIGHTS OF MAN AND CITIZEN, approved by the French National Assembly in August 1789, affirmed the EQUALITY of all men and the inviolability of property, concepts that conflicted in the case of slaves, who were both men (and women) and property. To complicate matters fur-

ther, the National Assembly passed the May Decree in 1791, extending the equality of the Declaration of the Rights of Man only to *gens de couleur* who met specific property requirements and were born to free parents. The practical result of this affected only a few hundred people, but it caused great resentment among whites and among the *gens du couleur*. Struggles for control between the *gens de couleur*, many of whom were wealthy landowners but were trapped beneath the whites in the social hierarchy, and the *grands blancs* eventually led to civil war in the colony.

Pamphlets popularized the Enlightenment's attacks on slavery and spread ideas about emancipation, abolition, and equality among Saint-Domingue's slave population. Many slaves also felt a deep hatred of their white masters because of overwork, mistreatment, and other types of abuse. Religious practices among slaves, such as voodoo, expressed this sentiment. Thus, on the eve of the Haitian Revolution, every segment of society was aggrieved—whites over attacks on slavery and the enfrachisement of *gens de couleur; gens de couleur* over their third-class social status and restrictions placed on emancipation; and slaves.

Tensions could no longer be repressed, and a rebellion, led by a Voodoo priest and escaped slave from Jamaica, broke out in August 1791. The rebellion involved slaves from several plantations around Le Cap and soon encompassed an estimated 100,000 slaves in the northern part of Haiti. Whites fled their plantations for the fortress at Le Cap. At first, the *gens de couleur* sided with the whites, and their combined forces made a successful assault on the slave insurgents outside Le Cap in September. But the slave insurgents quickly undermined the military predominance of the combined forces of the whites and the *gens de couleur*. The slaves were becoming better organized and had several advantages, including their skills as guerrilla fighters and their superior knowledge of the terrain. France, mired in unrest and instability, also failed to send reinforcements to bolster white and mulatto strength. Finally, outside the northern area of the colony, in the south and west, the rebellion was a three-way fight among whites, mulattos, and blacks, and this undermined the alliance of the whites and mulattos in the north.

European nations with interests in the Carribean quickly became involved in the fighting. The British sent arms to French planters in Saint-Domingue and banned French slaves from entering English holdings in the Carribean in order to keep the ideology of revolution from spreading. The Spanish sent arms and aid to the slaves. The United States wanted to avoid a spread of the revolt to the southern states and to maintain trade with Saint-Domingue, so it supported the whites as long as they held onto power. The arrival of the representative of the revolutionary French government, Léger Félicité Sonthonax, in September 1792 and his rapid move to establish himself as dictator of Saint-Domingue marked the beginning of white decline. He purged his white opponents, whom he accused of sympathizing with LOUIS XVI, and relied on the mulattos for support. Initial victories over the slave insurgents soon turned to defeat, and the constant purges left the anti-insurgent forces disorganized. Threatened by black and Spanish forces, Sonthonax abolished slavery in August 1793.

France was at war with AUSTRIA, PRUSSIA, SPAIN, Holland, and Great Britain, and no longer had control of its colonies in the West Indies. The British negotiated a treaty with the white planters, giving them control of Saint-Domingue in August 1793; British forces landed in September. The British believed that, with the support of the planters, they would easily quash the slave rebellion and restore order. Meanwhile, with Spanish help, black forces under Toussaint's leadership quickly captured several key positions and split the French forces. The planters did not join the British, seeing them as invaders, and continued to fight alongside French forces under Sonthonax's control. Disease also wreaked havoc on the British forces, and the British had to conscript slaves, promising to guarantee their continued freedom once the revolt was over.

Thus, by the end of 1793, three competing forces were fighting one another in Saint-Domingue: the blacks, supported by Spain; the French, led by Sonthonax, who had abolished slavery; and the English. In May 1794, Toussaint and his forces, which numbered some 4,000 men, defected to the French. He was enticed partly by the French National Convention's abolition of slavery in March of that year. By 1795, the British were in disarray, having lost GUADELOUPE to French forces and trying to put down rebellions all over the Caribbean. In June of that year, Spain also withdrew from the fighting after a series of defeats at Toussaint's hands.

In the relative calm that followed, Sonthonax, who had been recalled to France in June of 1794, returned as head of a commission to govern Saint-Domingue. Rather than openly attack Sonthonax, Toussaint decided to undermine him by portraying him as scheming to bring about Saint-Domingue's independence from France. In May 1797, Sonthonax made Toussaint governor of Saint-Domingue and commander of the French armies there, hoping to protect his own position, but a month later, he was again recalled to France. In August, Toussaint and his forces marched on Le Cap and forcefully evicted Sonthonax, who was trying to stay in violation of the recall order. The British saw the struggle between the two as an opportunity, but Toussaint continued to thwart them as well, and they finally withdrew in May 1798.

In April 1799, Toussaint began fighting the mulattos, who were under the leadership of André Rigaud. This extremely violent and bloody stage of the revolt was known as "the war of knives," with forces on both sides torturing and killing large numbers of their adversaries. In July 1800, Toussaint defeated Rigaud, and the mulatto leader and 700 of his men sailed from the island. The victorious Toussaint invited whites to return to their plantations—the upheaval of the preceding eight years had displaced many—and instituted a system of forced labor to stabilize the economy.

On July 16, 1801, Toussaint issued a constitution concentrating power in himself and omitting any significant recognition of France's sovereignty in Saint-Domingue. In October, France made peace with England, which freed up the forces thought necessary to return Saint-Domingue to French control. The French soldiers returned to the island and initially had better luck than the British, taking control of the north and Le Cap by April 1802. Toussaint and his generals surrendered, and the leader died in prison in April 1803.

War and fever quickly decimated the French forces; of the initial 17,000, only half remained by the summer of 1802. France's restoration of slavery in nearby Guadeloupe sparked more rebellions in Saint-Domingue, and the French were powerless to put them down. Although additional men were sent from France, by September of that year, two-thirds of the 28,000 soldiers had died, the majority of them from disease. Napoleon's reinstitution of legal discriminations against mulattos sparked further unrest. In Le Cap, where mulattos made up the garrison, this effectively put the city under anti-French control. Napoleon promised to send reinforcements, but England's declaration of war and blockade of Saint-Domingue in May and June of 1803 rendered this impossible. The blacks quickly conquered the colony, including the important cities of Port-au-Prince and Le Cap. The last French forces evacuated on November 28, and, on December 31, 1803, the Republic of Haiti declared independence. One of Toussaint's generals, Jean Jacques Dessalines, took control of the republic. Despite his guarantees to protect whites who returned, he started a wholesale massacre of whites in March 1804.

Further reading: C. L. R. James, *The Black Jacobins: Toussaint Louverture and the Santo Domingo Revolution* (New York: Vintage Books, 1963); Thomas O. Ott, *The Haitian Revolution, 1789–1804* (Knoxville: University of Tennessee Press, 1973).

Hales, Stephen (1677–1761) *English physiologist and specialist in public health*

Son of a distinguished family from Kent, Hales acquired his university education at Cambridge, after which he entered the ministry of the Church of England. He became the pastor of the parish at Teddington, remaining there his entire life. His scientific interests developed at Cambridge, partially under the influence of a friend, William Stukeley.

Although he attended some lectures at Cambridge, carried out a few experiments, and participated in field trips, Hales did not begin his serious scientific investigations until about 1712. He was elected to the ROYAL SOCIETY OF LONDON in 1717, largely because of the recommendation of Stukeley. During his later years, Hales received many honors. Oxford awarded him a doctorate in divinity in 1733; he became a trustee of the colony of Georgia in North America; a new genus of plants from the Americas received his name (Halesia); and the FRENCH ACADEMY OF SCIENCES elected him a foreign associate (1753). Hales helped in the founding of the Royal Society of Arts in London. He also developed an air ventilator for use in hospitals, prisons, and ships, on the assumption that poor air was contributing to the high mortality rates of such places. Hales was acquainted with both Alexander POPE and Horace WALPOLE as well as with prominent scientists of his era.

Early in 1719, Hales began a quantitative investigation of the mechanics of sap circulation in plants. His *Vegetable Staticks,* published in 1727 under the auspices of the Royal Society of London, reported the results of 70 chemical experiments. Hales turned next to the subject of animal circulation, taking up an investigation that he had begun during his Cambridge days. His results appeared in the book *Haemastaticks* (1733).

Both of these works started with the assumption that the science of mechanics could provide models and explanations of circulatory phenomena. They also posited that an analogy could be made between sap circulation in plants and blood circulation in animals. He eventually published both books together as *Statical Essays* (1731).

Chapter six of the *Vegetable Staticks* was called "The Analysis of Air." This chapter reported Hales's experiments collecting and measuring the air (gas) given off in various chemical reactions. Hales called this air "fixed air" because it had once been part of other substances. He believed that all substances contained such fixed air. Hales did not recognize that he had actually collected several different airs in his experiments. In designing his experiments, Hales invented several devices, among them the pneumatic trough, which served later chemists in making significant experiments. Hales's chemical experiments for chapter six of the *Vegetable Staticks* provided valuable material for Joseph BLACK, Joseph PRIESTLEY, and Antoine LAVOISIER, whose activities and theories revolutionized chemistry in the 18th century.

See also CHEMICAL REVOLUTION; ENGLAND; MATHEMATICS AND MECHANICS; SCIENCE.

Halle, University of

Halle, University of   German university, located in the city of Halle, founded in 1694 by Frederick III, elector of BRANDENBURG and ruler of PRUSSIA. Among the professors who accepted positions at the new institution were August Hermann FRANCKE, Christian THOMASIUS, and Christian WOLFF.

Under Francke's influence, Halle became the center of academic PIETISM in the German-speaking world and gradually hardened its position against those who did not accept Pietist beliefs and practices. The teachings of systematic philosophical RATIONALISM offered by Christian Wolff, for example, were not tolerated, and Wolff received orders to leave both the university and the town.

After 1740, however, FREDERICK II (THE GREAT) became king in Prussia and hence the ruler of Halle. He provided strong active support for the AUFKLÄRUNG (German ENLIGHTENMENT), and Wolff was able to resume his teaching at the university.

Throughout the last half of the 18th century, the University of Halle served as an important center for the Enlightenment in Germany, matched only, perhaps, by the new University of GÖTTINGEN. Halle was especially noted for the strength of its faculties of MEDICINE, natural sciences, law, and PHILOSOPHY.

See also SPENER.

Haller, Albrecht von

Haller, Albrecht von (1708–1777) *Swiss anatomist, physiologist, botanist, and poet*
Von Haller was a major 18th-century physiologist whose research contributed to several central debates in 18th-century physiology.

Haller contributed major research in physiology, a subject he conceptualized as *anatomia animata* (animated anatomy), and thus a part of anatomy. His distinction between sensibility and irritability in animal tissue lay at the center of a major scientific debate between mechanists and vitalists about the nature of life. Haller's ideas provided a foundation for VITALISM, although Haller himself was not a vitalist. In fact, his inspiration derived from the IATROMECHANICS of his professor at the University of Leiden, Hermann BOERHAAVE. Haller accepted Boerhaave's idea that fibers are the basic building block of organisms and developed the concept of the *tela cellulosa* to designate the structural tissues of the body.

Haller also contributed to the 18th-century study of GENERATION. He began his career as a believer in EPIGENESIS, but ultimately altered his viewpoint and supported PREFORMATION THEORY. Haller investigated birth deformities in a search for answers about the constancy of species. He believed that deformed individuals were unique life forms rather than aberrations from the normal, and argued that the appearance of deformities proved the ability of the divine power to create new life forms at will.

Haller also conducted important research on the heart and circulatory system. He demonstrated that the heart can continue to beat even after it is removed from the body. This finding was used to refute Georg Ernst STAHL and other adherents of ANIMISM who believed that the soul caused the actions of the heart.

Haller was a precocious child, gifted in languages as well as sciences. He wrote poetry throughout his life but devoted his public career to anatomy. Haller studied medicine at Tübingen in GERMANY, and at Leiden in the UNITED PROVINCES OF THE NETHERLANDS. He received his M.D. degree in 1727, and promptly embarked on a study tour to LONDON, Oxford, PARIS, Strasbourg, and Basel. Haller worked as a physician and private instructor in Bern, Switzerland, from 1729 until 1736, when he received the chair of anatomy, surgery, and medicine at the new University of GÖTTINGEN in Germany. He remained in Göttingen until 1753, when he returned to his native city, Bern, as an elected official (*Rathausammann*). Haller combined political service with his scientific and literary pursuits for the remainder of his life.

Haller's major publications include the following: *Elementa physiologiae corporis humani* (Elements of the physiology of the human body; 1757); many book reviews in the *Göttingische Zeitungen von gelehrten Sachen* (Göttingen journal of learned subjects; directed by Haller from 1747 to 1753); transcriptions of Boerhaave's lectures entitled *Hermanni Boerhaave praelectiones academicae in proprias institutiones rei medicae edidit . . .* (Academic lectures of Hermann Boerhaave . . . [7 vols.]; 1739–44); the *Prima lineae physiologiae* (First lines of physiology; 1747); and the *Historia stirpium indigenarum Helvetiae inchoata* (A beginning history of indigenous Swiss plants; 1768). Haller's most renowned poem was "Die Alpen" (The Alps), one of the first literary works to celebrate the beauty and serenity of the great mountain range that made passage from northern Europe into the Italian peninsula so difficult. This poem hinted at the elements that would later coalesce into the concept of the SUBLIME. Haller outlined his political ideas in three pieces of fiction: *Usong* (1771), *Alfred* (1773), and *Fabius und Cato* (1774).

Halley, Edmond (1656–1743) *English astronomer, mathematician, and geophysicist*

As the eldest son of a prosperous manufacturer and landowner, Halley enjoyed access to a prestigious education at St. Paul's School in LONDON and at Oxford University. By royal order, Oxford University awarded Halley an M.A. degree (1657) although he had not filled the normal residence requirements at the university. Halley had attracted royal attention when he named a newly identified constellation of stars in the Southern Hemisphere after King Charles II. Halley also had dedicated a planisphere (a special type of map of the stars) of the Southern Hemisphere to the king.

The ROYAL SOCIETY OF LONDON elected Halley to its membership in 1678. From 1685 until 1699 he worked as a paid assistant to the honorary secretaries of the Royal Society, engaging in an extensive correspondence with scientists throughout Europe and editing the *Philosophical Transactions of the Royal Society*, the official journal of the organization.

As an astronomer, Halley faced competition from the first astronomer royal of England, John Flamsteed. The latter was an expert observer whose skills surpassed those of the younger man. But Halley compensated for his deficiencies in the observational realm with his ability to impose order on large masses of experimental data. Tension between Flamsteed and Halley somewhat hindered Halley's early career, but, nevertheless, in 1720 Halley was appointed as Flamsteed's successor at the post of astronomer royal. He had earlier (1704) obtained the chair of geometry at Oxford University. The FRENCH ACADEMY OF SCIENCES in PARIS nominated him to its membership in 1729.

Halley produced notable observations and theories in ASTRONOMY and geophysics. Major contributions in astronomy included calculating the orbit of the bright comet of 1682 (subsequently named "Halley's Comet") and correctly predicting the year of its return to visibility from the Earth (1758); and proposing the 1761 and 1769 observations of the TRANSIT OF VENUS across the face of the Sun as a means of calculating the distance between the Sun and the Earth. In geophysics Halley produced the first meteorological chart of the monsoons and trade winds, completed a survey of the English Channel (1701), and developed a theory of terrestrial magnetism. Halley believed that the Earth was much older than the age given in the Bible, an unusual but not unknown position during his era.

Halley was also a mathematician of some skill who made contributions to geometry, trigonometry, and social statistics. He published a *Breslau Table of Mortality* (1693) and Latin translations of two ancient treatises by Apollonius of Perga.

Without Halley's efforts, it is unclear whether Isaac NEWTON would have chosen to publish his PRINCIPIA MATHEMATICA. Halley encouraged the reluctant Newton to put his work into print and paid for its production and printing. When Robert Hooke challenged Newton about priority in certain findings, Halley encouraged Newton to continue his work. He also defended Newton in the controversy with Gottfried Wilhelm LEIBNIZ over priority in the discovery of the calculus.

Hamann, Johann Georg (1730–1788) *Prussian philosopher, an outspoken critic of the rationalism of the Enlightenment*

Hamann was called by his contemporaries the "Magus of the North" (wise man of the North). Major figures in the German intellectual world—Johann Wolfgang von GOETHE and Johann Gottfried HERDER—paid tribute to his influence on their thought. But Hamann was also acknowledged as an inspiration by the German philosopher and writer Friedrich Heinrich JACOBI, by the Swiss pastor Johann Kaspar LAVATER, and by the "German Burke," Friedrich Karl von Moser.

A native of the old Hanseatic League city of Königsberg, Johann Georg Hamann grew up in a Pietist Lutheran family. His father, the supervisor of the municipal bathhouse in Königsberg, is believed to have been a barber surgeon by profession. Hamann received a somewhat irregular and lax early education, which did not, however, prevent him from gaining admission to Königsberg University. He studied HISTORY, PHILOSOPHY, THEOLOGY, mathematics, and Hebrew; but he was especially drawn to the literature of antiquity and of enlightened FRANCE. He emerged from the university as a disciple of the French ENLIGHTENMENT and as a spokesman for the middle class of merchants and businessmen.

After completing his university education, Hamann traveled to Riga, then the capital city of Livonia in Russia. He entered the service of the wealthy Berens brothers who sent him in 1756 on a secret diplomatic mission to LONDON. It is believed that Hamann was charged with contacting the Russian ambassador in London, in order to enlist support for a secession of the Baltic states from Russia. The mission failed, but Hamann's experiences in London provoked a spiritual crisis that transformed his life.

Hamann returned to Prussia committed to challenging the faith in REASON that characterized the mainstream of the Enlightenment. He brought back the works of English millenarians and the theological writings of Isaac NEWTON, rather than books by English rationalists and deists.

He began to develop a complicated, often convoluted set of ideas that attacked the basic ideas of the French and English Enlightenment. His writings addressed language theory, AESTHETICS, the origins of RELIGION, PSYCHOLOGY, and MORAL PHILOSOPHY. He attacked DEISM, the sensation psychology of John LOCKE and Abbeé CONDILLAC, and the aesthetics embodied in French CLASSICISM and NEOCLASSICISM. He rejected INDIVIDUALISM, Utilitarianism, and RATIONALISM as legitimate bases for both human moral behavior and social organization. He also criticized the enlightened belief that PROGRESS and even GENIUS could be obtained through socially engineered education.

Much of Hamann's work turns on the desire to preserve religion from the destructive attacks of rationalism, ATHEISM, and MATERIALISM, all of which were advanced during Hamann's lifetime by the BERLIN ACADEMY of FREDERICK II (THE GREAT). Hamann maintained that the sole origin of religion lies in revelation. According to his interpretation, religion and the human capacity for language that allows the communication of religious truths, were both gifts from God. Neither these religious truths nor linguistic ability could have arisen solely from the operation of natural physical laws. By making this claim, Hamann effectively removed religion from the realms of reason and NATURAL LAW, thereby making irrelevant the discussion of its roots in HUMAN NATURE.

Hamann's ideas produced a fresh approach to the Bible that extolled its poetic power and reasserted its status as an example of divine revelation. Hamann rejected any attempt to treat the Bible as the simple history of an ancient people. For him, the Hebrew texts displayed the special human quality of genius that is also revealed in other primitive epics and myths. Hamann insisted that the Biblical story of Jewish experience is actually an allegory revealing the inner spiritual history of every individual.

Hamann's interpretation of the Bible rested on his vision of human psychology and aesthetics. His criticism of reason resulted in a reassessment of the importance of INTUITION AND IMAGINATION in creating human knowledge. His position resembled that of Alexander Gottlieb BAUMGARTEN, Johann Jakob BODMER, and other German enlightened theorists of language and aesthetics.

For Hamann, the concrete stories of the Bible, contained, for example, in the episodes about Eve and the serpent in the Garden of Eden, about Joshua making the sun stand still, or about Jonah in the belly of the whale, provided the most natural way of writing about truth and about the world. Such graphic, pictorial representation is powerful but never crude. In contrast, the abstract explanations, characteristic of writing based on reason, are impotent and artificial (i.e., unnatural).

This concrete imagery was not a way of watering down truths for unenlightened, ignorant primitives, but rather was a powerful, divinely derived presentation of truth that could not be equaled by the abstract language of reason. For Hamann, God speaks in images, not in mathematical equations or in abstract language.

Abstract reason thus lost the primary role and status that it enjoyed in French and English rational approaches. For Hamann, the introduction of abstract explanations was a sign of degeneration. Hamann, thus, actually turned the values of the Enlightenment upside down, defining progress as the restoration of primitive sensibility and poetic expression, rather than as the slow triumph of human reason.

This revulsion against abstraction drove Hamann's work in all areas. He rejected the enlightened vision of human nature in which human beings are rational animals operating according to the natural law of reason. He reasserted an older image of people, as creatures of emotion and passion, whose most authentic experiences were rooted in the imagination and in feelings.

Hamann publicly criticized all the major champions of reason in the culture of the AUFKLÄRUNG, including Gotthold Ephraim LESSING, Moses MENDELSSOHN, Christoph Friedrich NICOLAI, Claude-Adrien HELVÉTIUS (who was living in Berlin), Johann David Michaelis, and even his old friend Immanuel KANT. He also attacked the German poet Christoph Martin WIELAND and the English novelist Laurence STERNE. Hamann admired the brilliance of VOLTAIRE, even while he condemned his doctrines.

Denis DIDEROT received praise for his stance regarding rigid rules, and Jean-Jacques ROUSSEAU received fluctuating assessments.

Hamann is often treated as an early example of ROMANTICISM, but this view needs qualification. He is, in fact, a highly creative product of the Enlightenment. The complexity of his thought reveals a lifelong struggle with the enlightened dialectic between reason and feeling. In the end, his ideas contributed not only to enriching the legacy of the *Aufklärung*, but also to inspiring the development of German romanticism.

Hamann left volumes of publications that include *Gedanken über meinen Lebenslauf* (Thoughts about my life; 1758–59), *Sokratische Denkwürdigkeiten* (Socratic memorabilia; 1759), *Kreuzzüge eines Philologen* (Crusades of a philologue; 1762), and *Golgatha und Scheblimini* (Golgatha and Scheblimini; 1784).

See also BIBLICAL CRITICISM.

Further reading: Isaiah Berlin, "The Magus of the North," *The New York Review of Books,* XL (17:64–71); Hajo Holborn, *A History of Modern Germany (1648–1840)* (New York: Alfred A. Knopf, 1967).

Hamilton, Alexander (1755–1804) *American soldier, politician, essayist, and statesman who favored establishing a strong central government in the new United States*
Hamilton was born an illegitimate child on the island of Nevis in the British West Indies. His father abandoned both mother and son when Alexander was about 10. Young Hamilton began working in a St. Croix counting-house to support himself and his mother. In 1772, four years after the death of his mother, he was sent by relatives to New York City.

Hamilton studied at King's College (now Columbia College) in New York City. He supported the Continental Congress and colonial protests against Great Britain by writing pamphlets. During the AMERICAN REVOLUTION, Hamilton first served as a captain in a New York artillery company and then as aide-de-camp and secretary to General George WASHINGTON (1777–81). Hamilton commanded some of the troops at the decisive siege of Yorktown.

During these war years, Hamilton wrote a series of letters to the *New-York Journal* attacking civilian war profiteers. He supported the cause of abolishing SLAVERY, even suggesting to John Jay that African-American slaves should be armed to fight in the war and then freed as a reward for their service. In 1780, after his marriage to the wealthy Elizabeth Schuyler, Hamilton freed the slaves that were included in the marriage dowry. He also helped to set up the New York Manumission Society, which worked to bring about abolition. After a brief disagreement with George Washington, Hamilton retired from military service.

Hamilton then began studying law and was admitted to the New York bar in 1782. He served in the Congress of the Confederation (1781–82) and published several articles calling for a stronger central government. In 1784, in another series of newspaper articles, Hamilton decried the harsh treatment that was being given to Loyalists, those American colonists who had supported the British during the war. Part of his effectiveness as a writer stemmed from his conscious adoption of the style used in THE SPECTATOR, an immensely successful English journal that had been published in the early 18th century by Joseph ADDISON and Richard STEELE.

Hamilton represented New York at the Constitutional Convention in PHILADELPHIA and was one of the signers of the new UNITED STATES CONSTITUTION. In the debates from which the Constitution was shaped, Hamilton continued to argue for a strong central government and suggested that the rich and well-educated should be given a large share of power. Like MONTESQUIEU, who provided one of his theoretical models, Hamilton believed that this class of people would act as an intermediary power, protecting the government from the potential excesses of democracy and also checking abuses of power by the executive.

During 1787 and 1788, when the Constitution went before the various state legislatures for ratification, Hamilton joined with John JAY and James MADISON to write *The Federalist Papers* (1787–88). This series of 85 essays outlined the new government for readers and offered clear arguments in favor of the Constitution. The essays were extremely important in winning support for ratification and are considered a classic of constitutional theory. The essays echo the ideas of John LOCKE as well as those of Montesquieu, all adapted to fit the American context. They are indebted, therefore, to the ENLIGHTENMENT for their basic POLITICAL THEORY.

George Washington, as the first elected president of the United States, appointed Hamilton secretary of the treasury (1789–95). Hamilton, thus, helped to shape the economic and fiscal policies of the new nation. In particular, he addressed the problem of the national debt, suggesting that the foreign debt be funded at face value and that old wartime bond issues be recalled. He laid out the plans for the first Bank of the United States, which was set up in 1791 to provide short-term loans to the central government and to increase the amount of capital available to businesses. Madison also supported the establishment of a federal excise tax on distilled liquor as a means of reducing the debt and of demonstrating the power and effectiveness of the central government.

In 1791, Hamilton presented his *Report on Manufactures* to Congress. Following the basic practices of MERCANTILISM, he proposed that the federal government play an active role in promoting and regulating industry and commerce. He also recommended investing in infrastructures such as roads and canals. Most of the recommendations in this report went unheeded.

All of these economic proposals formed what came to be called "the Hamiltonian system," and they aroused criticism from those who believed that they overstepped the constitutional limits of the federal government. Hamilton claimed that the Constitution implicitly authorized the federal government to take an active economic and fiscal role and formed the Federalist Party to back his position.

Many people in the opposing Anti-Federalist group— the members of the Democratic-Republican Party led by Thomas JEFFERSON and James Madison—supported an agrarian rather than industrialized society and tended to support more democratic visions of government.

Hamilton left his cabinet post in 1795 but remained a close adviser to President Washington. In fact, Hamilton wrote much of Washington's famous *Farewell Address* (1796), which was never delivered as a speech but was printed, instead, in a newspaper. When war seemed imminent between the United States and FRANCE, Hamilton was appointed inspector general of the army with the rank of major general (1798–1800).

Complex factional divisions within the Federalist Party caused Hamilton to throw his support against Federalist President John ADAMS in the presidential elections of 1800. When a tie of electoral votes occurred between the candidates Jefferson and Aaron Burr, Hamilton helped persuade members of the House of Representatives to vote for his old political enemy Jefferson rather than for the Federalist-supported Burr.

Hamilton worked successfully against Burr again in the 1804 elections for the governor of New York. Angered by his loss of the election and insulted by remarks that Hamilton allegedly made at a dinner party, Burr challenged Hamilton to a duel. Hamilton was shot and killed.

Further reading: Henry F. May, *The Enlightenment in America* (New York: Oxford University Press, 1976); Robert R. Palmer, *The Age of Democratic Revolution: A Political History of Europe and America, 1760–1800*, 2 vols. (Princeton, N.J.: Princeton University Press, 1959 and 1964).

Hamilton, Sir William (1730–1803) *British ambassador to the court of Naples, geologist, and art collector*
Sir William Hamilton spent 36 years as British ambassador to the KINGDOM OF THE TWO SICILIES, but his lasting contributions were as a writer on geology and archaeology and as a collector of antiquities.

Hamilton was born into an impoverished noble family in SCOTLAND. He married his first wife, Catherine, a cultivated woman from a wealthy family, in 1755. In 1764, he was appointed ambassador to the Kingdom of the Two Sicilies, and he lived in Naples until 1800. As a diplomat, Hamilton's most important achievement was to negotiate the kingdom's neutrality during the AMERICAN REVOLUTION.

The kingdom was not in the front rank of European powers during the period of Hamilton's assignment to Naples, so he was able to devote most of his energy to other pursuits. Immediately upon his arrival, Hamilton visited Mt. Vesuvius (outside of Naples) and Mt. Etna (in Sicily) and began a lengthy and detailed exploration of the volcanoes and the land around them. In a series of regular reports to the ROYAL SOCIETY OF LONDON between 1766 and 1779, the *Observations on Mount Vesuvius, Mount Etna, and Other Volcanoes in the Two Sicilies* (1772) and *Campi Phregi* (1766), Hamilton formulated his main geographic theory, which argued that the formation of the Earth's crust was the result of volcanic and seismic activity.

Hamilton also amassed a rich collection of antiquities during his time in Naples, including Greek, Roman, and Etruscan objects. Several volumes of engravings of pieces in his collections were published and circulated widely; Hamilton eventually sold the collections to the British Museum.

The last years of Hamilton's life were overshadowed by his second wife's affair with Admiral Horatio Nelson. Hamilton's first wife died in 1782, and he married Emma LYON in 1791. In 1800, Hamilton left Naples to join an expedition to Egypt. His findings were published posthumously, in 1809, as *Aegyptiaca, or Some Account of the Ancient and Modern State of Egypt*. He died in April 1803 at the age of 73.

Hamilton's work as a diplomat should be seen as a means to an end. It was thanks to his posting to the Kingdom of the Two Sicilies that he could pursue his interests in antiquities and in science and make his important contributions to geographic theory.

See also CLASSICISM; WINCKELMANN.

Further reading: David Constantine, *Fields of Fire: A Life of Sir William Hamilton* (London: Weidenfield & Nicolson, 2001).

Handel, George Frederick (1685–1759) *German-born composer who worked most of his life in England*
A native of Halle, Saxony, George Frederick Handel (spelled Georg Friedrich Händel until 1715) was the son of a surgeon and the grandson, on his mother's side, of a Lutheran clergyman. The family encouraged the young Handel's musical talents by providing him with instruction on keyboard instruments, violin, and oboe and by securing him opportunities to hear musical performances. Although Handel lost his father at the age of 11, arrangements had been made to ensure his education, and he was, therefore, able to enroll at the University of HALLE. Handel studied law but supplemented his income by playing organ at the

George Frederick Handel, engraving by J. Bankel after C. Jager. One of the masters of late baroque musical composition, Handel enjoyed enormous popularity after he settled in England. *(Courtesy Archive Photos)*

Reformed (Calvinist) Cathedral in Halle. After only one year at the university, he moved to Hamburg, where greater opportunities in music presented themselves. Handel joined the Hamburg Opera orchestra as a violinist and soon was also fulfilling duties as a harpsichordist. He wrote and produced four operas in the years 1705–06: *Almira, Nero, Florinda,* and *Daphne.* The music for all these works except *Almira* has been lost.

In Hamburg, Handel met Ferdinando de' Medici, the heir of the grand duke of Tuscany, who invited the talented young composer to visit Florence. Encouraged by this offer, Handel embarked on a GRAND TOUR to ITALY, spending time in Florence, Naples, VENICE, and ROME. During these Italian years (1707–10), Handel composed many works remarkable for their dramatic harmonies and tone colors. His operas *Rodrigo* and *Agrippina* enjoyed great success, and the oratorio *La Resurrezione* (The Resurrection) is recognized even today as one of his outstanding creations.

In 1710, through the patronage of a friend, Agostino Steffani, Handel acquired a position as director of music for the court of the elector of Hanover. Handel held the post officially from 1710 until 1716, although during most of this period he was actually living and working in ENGLAND. He visited the European continent on a few occasions in subsequent years, but England became his permanent home. In 1715, Handel formally changed the orthography of his name from the German Händel to the English, Handel.

From the very beginning, Handel enjoyed great popularity with English audiences. His OPERA *Rinaldo,* performed early in 1711 in LONDON, was enormously successful. By 1713, he had gained the favor of Queen Anne with his compositions celebrating the Treaty of Utrecht that had ended the War of the Spanish Succession. The death of Queen Anne in 1714 brought Handel's German employer, George Louis, the elector of Hanover, to the English throne as King George I. From that point on, Handel could stay in England without any neglect of his duties to the Hanoverian court.

Handel obtained an official post as director of music to the duke of Chandos in 1718. In 1726, he became a British subject, an act that enabled him to receive an appointment as composer for the Chapel Royal. From 1720 until 1728, Handel served as director of the Royal Academy of Music. Most of the operas staged by the academy during that period were Handel's creations. Handel continued to compose Italian operas until 1741, when opera in London began to decline in popularity. After 1741, Handel turned to composing oratorios and incidental instrumental music.

The list of Handel's works includes the major oratorios: *Alexander's Feast* (1736); *Messiah* (1741); *Samson* (1741); *Belshazzar* (1745); and *Jephtha* (1751). It also includes the beloved *Water Music* (1717) and the *Music for the Royal Fireworks,* the latter written for a huge public display in Vauxhall Gardens to celebrate the end of the Silesian Wars (1749).

In 1751, Handel began to go blind. A surgeon operated on his eyes, providing some relief, but the condition handicapped Handel's last years. He died in 1759 and was buried in the Poets' Corner of Westminster Abbey at a service attended by 3,000 people.

Handel became a widely known and beloved popular figure for the English people. With his great oratorios, he established large-scale choral works as a major English institution. The production of oratorio became associated in English consciousness with the concomitant attacks on moral laxity that characterized the last half of the 18th century in that country. Oratorio also became associated with charitable work, a pairing produced at least in part by Handel's productions of *Messiah* on behalf of the London Foundling Hospital. Handel is considered one of the great 18th-century pioneers who transformed the world of music, extending its audience and sources of support from the small circle of aristocracy and royalty to the wider middle-class public.

See also CORELLI.

happiness A state of good fortune and well-being. The ENLIGHTENMENT moved the concept of happiness from the realm of the Christian afterlife into the secular world of everyday life. The attainment of happiness became a goal that individuals could hope to reach by pursuing normal human activities at work and in play. Government and society were charged, in theory, with the responsibility of ensuring the happiness of humanity.

During the course of the Enlightenment, the concept of happiness acquired several different shades of meaning. In earlier decades of the era, it was often derived from moral concepts and thus defined as the attainment of a more perfect individual character. The happy individual was made to serve the social good through the operations of SYMPATHY.

Under the influence of popularized sensation PSYCHOLOGY, this moral state of happiness gradually became identified with sensual pleasure. The cult of SENSIBILITY gave particular support to this interpretation of happiness. Early utilitarian MORAL PHILOSOPHY provided a more sophisticated interpretation. It made the pursuit of pleasure and the avoidance of pain the primary motivations of human behavior. Pleasure was equated not only with happiness but also with the moral quality of goodness.

During the middle years of the Enlightenment, happiness acquired a strong communal dimension by being explicitly related to social utility. The society that best protected and ensured happiness was the one that procured the greatest good for the greatest number of people. The moral dimension thus returned, but it was given a strong social component.

In this later utilitarian form, the concept of happiness entered the POLITICAL THEORY of the Enlightenment. The famous invisible hand that operated in Adam SMITH's version of political economy derived directly from this usage of the idea of happiness. The American DECLARATION OF INDEPENDENCE, of course, raised happiness to new levels by making its "pursuit" one of the natural rights of humankind.

See also EPICUREAN PHILOSOPHY.

Hapsburg Empire One of the great 18th-century DYNASTIC STATES, which, after the final defeat of the Turks in 1685, emerged as one of the major players in 18th-century international politics. The territories of the empire lay primarily in south-central and eastern Europe but also included far-flung holdings elsewhere. VIENNA was the dynastic seat of the empire, but BUDAPEST, Prague, MILAN, and BRUSSELS also functioned as major centers of power. The Austrian branch of the Hapsburg (German: Habsburg) family ruled in most territories of the Hapsburg Empire by hereditary rights. In HUNGARY, however, they ruled as elected kings or queens. They also customarily ruled as the elected emperors of the HOLY ROMAN EMPIRE.

It is important not to confuse the Holy Roman Empire with the Hapsburg Empire or to consider them as interchangeable; they are distinct political entities, whose rulers happened to be the same individual. As such, their existence strikingly represents the bewildering complexity that typified 18th-century European political systems.

At the beginning of the 18th century, after the Treaty of Utrecht (1713), the Hapsburg Empire, or Hapsburg dominions as they are more properly named, consisted of AUSTRIA; Bohemia (including Silesia); the kingdom of Hungary (including Croatia, northern Serbia, and Transylvania); parts of Galicia; Wallachia; the AUSTRIAN NETHERLANDS; Naples, Sicily, Milan, and Tuscany in ITALY; the tiny but strategically important Rhine River principalities of Breisgau and Sundgau; and the kingdom of Sardinia. In the course of the century, the Hapsburgs permanently lost several territories such as Naples, Serbia, and the Bohemian land of Silesia. But they also gained territories as a result of the PARTITIONS OF POLAND. In the typical manner of the dynastic state, the Hapsburgs ruled their various dominions in disparate capacities. Thus, for example, they were archdukes or archduchesses in Austria, and kings or queens in Hungary and Bohemia.

The welter of Hapsburg territories provided numerous challenges to rulers bent on consolidating power, centralizing administration, or applying the rational and humanitarian values of the ENLIGHTENMENT to practical government. But that is exactly what the greatest of the 18th-century Hapsburgs, MARIA THERESA and her son JOSEPH II, set out to achieve. The transformation of the Hapsburg Empire into a military-bureaucratic state occurred in two stages: a moderate, pragmatic stage under Maria Theresa, which established the basic outlines of all the 18th-century reforms, and a subsequent, more radical, ideological one under Joseph II.

Much of Maria Theresa's reform activity derived from her desire to build a strong military state that would prevent further humiliations such as that caused by the Prussian annexation of Silesia. To achieve her goals, she decided to wrest control of taxation from the various territorial diets (representative bodies); to improve the EDUCATION, training, and living conditions of her troops; and, since armies required able-bodied men, to raise the standard of living of the common people who provided ordinary conscripts for the army. On the advice of Prince KAUNITZ, she sought to isolate the Prussian king, FREDERICK II (THE GREAT), on the international scene. As a result, Hapsburg needs helped to trigger the DIPLOMATIC REVOLUTION OF 1756 and the ensuing SEVEN YEARS' WAR. Following the Seven Years' War, Maria Theresa turned her attentions increasingly to domestic reforms. The plight of peasant serfs, the outlines of church-state relations, education, and the provision of basic human needs increasingly occupied her attention.

Joseph II continued the activities of his mother. However, both his personality and his strong, committed belief in certain enlightened ideals produced in him a rigid, uncompromising attitude, which was effective at producing reform results, but which also engendered intense hatred and opposition. For all his humanitarian idealism, Joseph, like Frederick the Great, distrusted his administrators and moved over time toward limiting certain freedoms in the name of the interest of the state.

By 1787, only seven years after Maria Theresa's death, revolt broke out in the Austrian Netherlands. When Joseph II died in 1790, Hungary, Lombardy (Milan), and Wallachia (modern Romania) were also engaged in rebellion. The diets (estates) in all territories registered their discontent and their intention to limit absolute imperial power. Leopold II, Joseph's brother and successor, began his reign by yielding to the demands of the diets. He wanted to continue the process of reform, but wished to elicit the support of the diets rather than to alienate them. Death, in 1792, cut short his reign. His son, Francis II, did not have the will or the strength to carry on his forebears' legacy. The chaos engendered throughout Europe by the FRENCH REVOLUTION and the subsequent Napoleonic Wars occupied center stage. In the end, the reformed Hapsburg Empire, product of the various strands of the European Enlightenment, reverted to its condition prior to the rule of Joseph II.

Hargreaves, James (unknown–1778) English inventor of the spinning jenny

Hargreaves was a weaver and mechanic by trade. He invented the SPINNING JENNY that revolutionized the production of cotton yarns in ENGLAND. His invention was patented in 1770. The spinning jenny was one of the earliest technological innovations in the 18th-century INDUSTRIAL REVOLUTION. English spinners recognized that their livelihood was threatened by the new device, and a group of them destroyed Hargreaves's house and machinery. Hargreaves then moved to Nottingham, where he set up a small mill that relied on the jennies to produce cotton yarn.

Harrison, John (1693–1776) English clockmaker and inventor

Harrison, by adapting the theories of the Dutch mathematician and mechanician Christian Huyghens (1629–95), created an accurate, reliable chronometer. The device measured time more accurately than ordinary clocks and aided navigation at sea by facilitating precise measurements. With its assistance, global circumnavigation became safer and more successful.

The example of John Harrison illustrates two facets of the manner in which the ENLIGHTENMENT served the cause of human technological PROGRESS. First, the thoughtful application of scientific theory to practical, technical questions produced positive advancement for human commerce, navigation, and industry. Second, craftsmen like John Harrison, with practical skills and training, represented a typical English mode of enlightened activity. By a combination of tinkering, skill, inspiration, and knowledge, English craftsmen, although lacking formal theoretical training, produced significant numbers of important technological innovations.

See also LONGITUDE.

Hartley, David (1705–1757) English philosopher and psychologist

Hartley was the son of a minister and prepared himself to become a clergyman. He could not, however, bring himself in good conscience to sign the Thirty-Nine Articles required of orthodox Anglican clergymen. These articles spelled out the formal dogma of Anglicanism, and Hartley objected specifically to the doctrine of eternal damnation. Having turned away from the church, he studied MEDICINE at Cambridge University and practiced that profession throughout his lifetime. His major contributions to the intellectual life of the ENLIGHTENMENT lay in the field of PSYCHOLOGY. He tried thoroughly to ground psychology in a physiological theory of nervous system action. He also developed a form of psychology known as association psychology, which was formulated by means of a fusion of the psychology of John LOCKE with the physics of Isaac NEWTON.

John Locke, the founder of British psychological EMPIRICISM, had outlined the notion of association in one chapter of his *Essay on Human Understanding*. The concept, however, was not the central focus of his theory. Hartley developed the idea of association, making it the dominant organizing concept of his psychology. As a result, Hartley is considered the founder of association psychology, if not the creator of the original notion. As a branch of psychological empiricism, association psychology shared in the general popularity of all empirical theories of mind and EPISTEMOLOGY during the earlier Enlightenment and dominated psychology in the second half of the 18th century. It provided the psychological and philosophical underpinnings for the faith of the Enlightenment in the formative powers of human experience.

The theory of association tries to explain how the simple ideas derived from sensory experience are compounded and shaped into more complex notions. A form of psychological dualism (mind and body are distinct), the theory postulates that mind and body operate according to parallel sets of laws (psychophysical parallelism). Sensory experience of an external object sets up vibrations of small particles in the nerves (an adaptation of Newton). Corresponding to these vibrations in the body are similar but minute vibrations in the mind that give rise to ideas. The relationship between vibrations in body and in mind is a 1:1 ratio. The minute vibrations in the mind are exact replicas of the physical vibrations in the bodily nerves. As a result, the ideas in the mind are exact copies of the sensory experiences of the body, which are, in turn, exact copies of the world of external objects.

Association occurs when two or more distinct sets of vibrations occur simultaneously and repeatedly. The associated vibrations and their corresponding ideas add together, according to strict laws of arithmetic, to become a complex idea. These ideas can be easily broken down into their constituent parts (analyzed). Association psychology is a clear example of the analytic method that was spawned by the MECHANICAL PHILOSOPHY during the SCIENTIFIC REVOLUTION.

Like many of his enlightened contemporaries, Hartley realized that sensation psychology contained implications for the understanding of human FREEDOM and morality. For him, an action that occurred in response to a complex idea, rather than as a simple reaction to a sensation, was a voluntary act for which a person could be held accountable. He recognized that feelings of pleasure or pain could reinforce the power of certain ideas and, therefore, help to shape behavior. Among the feelings whose roles he recognized were sensation, imagination, ambition, SELF-INTEREST, SYMPATHY, theopathy (feelings about God), and the moral sense. The last three feelings—sympathy, theopathy, and moral sense—were, for Hartley, emotions of especially high moral value.

Hartley published his theory of psychology in a large treatise entitled *Observations on Man, His Frame, His Duty, and His Expectations.* (1749). His ideas were adapted by Joseph PRIESTLEY, Erasmus DARWIN, and William GODWIN to fit their own, sometimes quite different, philosophical and psychological theories. Priestley, in particular, aided in the dissemination of Hartley's ideas by publishing an abridged version of the *Observations* entitled *Hartley's Theory of the Human Mind on the Principle of the Association of Ideas* (1775).

See also EPICUREAN PHILOSOPHY; MORAL PHILOSOPHY.

Haskalah   The Jewish ENLIGHTENMENT. The movement of Haskalah developed in the 1770s in the northern German states of the HOLY ROMAN EMPIRE, in AUSTRIA, in eastern Europe, and in RUSSIA, all states with significant Jewish populations. Moses MENDELSSOHN, the Jewish writer and advocate of the Enlightenment, is generally credited as its founder. Other 18th-century leaders were David Friedländer in BERLIN and Naphtali Herz Wessely in the HAPSBURG EMPIRE.

Haskalah encouraged Jewish assimilation to the broader European cultures in which Jews were embedded, expressing in this manner the enlightened belief in the universal qualities of humankind. To this end, Haskalah leaders encouraged Jewish communities to reform educational programs by introducing secular subjects such as world history and mathematics, by abandoning the study of the Talmud (the Jewish law), by teaching the language of the secular state rather than Yiddish, and by studying Jewish history. They did not, however, generally advocate the EDUCATION of Jewish children in non-Jewish schools. Rather, they hoped to bring cultural awareness and some assimilation to Jews, but to avoid the total loss of the culture of Judaism.

The first such reformed school was the Freischule founded in 1778 in Berlin. Others followed throughout central and eastern Europe. In the Hapsburg lands, Wessely encouraged communities to found reformed schools so that they would not be compelled to integrate into the compulsory state schools.

Haskalah programs meshed comfortably with the aims of enlightened despots such as JOSEPH II, FREDERICK II (THE GREAT) in PRUSSIA, and CATHERINE II (THE GREAT) in Russia. In general, the Haskalah movement developed in connection with the phenomenon of Jewish emancipation, which, in the countries where it occurred, ended discriminatory laws against Jews. As restrictions that had confined Jews to ghettos and had prohibited their public worship were lifted, the process of assimilation to the general culture could begin to take over.

Sometimes, this process, aimed at integrating Jews into the society, actually created new limitations on free expression. For example, Joseph II issued edicts ordering compulsory education for Jews in Bohemia (1781), Moravia (1782), Hungary (1783), and Galicia (1789). But this education could not include the study of the Talmud. Violators were imprisoned. Furthermore, if people tried to evade the law by refusing to attend school, they would be penalized in other ways. Legal marriage, for example, was forbidden without a certificate of school attendance.

Haskalah helped to promote the cause of education for women. Whereas girls had always been educated at home, Haskalah encouraged their enrollment in community schools. Such schools, segregated according to sex, were established in the 1790s in the German cities of Breslau, Hamburg, Dessau, and Königsberg.

Haskalah was an important manifestation of the enlightened doctrines of EQUALITY and universality. Its appearance in the German states led to levels of assimilation and emancipation that were unmatched in other areas of Europe. If, in the end, the movement did not achieve its aims, that is due at least in part to the fact that the enlightened vision of the universal brotherhood of humanity was replaced by movements stressing nationalism, linguistic and cultural uniqueness, and separatism.

Hastings, Warren (1732–1818) *first governor-general of British India*
Warren Hastings was born to the educated but relatively poor Penyston and Hester Hastings, landowners in Worcestershire. Despite a lack of resources, Hastings was still able to receive a good education and was first in his class at Westminster School.

Upon leaving school, he was appointed a lower-level clerk for the EAST INDIA COMPANY in 1750 and went to India. He soon rose to become the trading manager in Bengal. In 1756, the nawab of Bengal, Siraj-ad-Dawlah, captured Calcutta from the British, and Hastings was imprisoned, but he was later released. The British retook the city in 1757. Hastings continued to serve in the company's government and was eventually appointed to the Calcutta Council in 1761. Disillusioned by the large-scale corruption he saw in the governance of Bengal, he returned to ENGLAND in 1764.

Hastings returned to India in 1769 as a member of the Madras Council and became governor of Bengal in 1771. As governor, Hastings reformed the financial, legal, and judicial systems of Bengal. These steps helped secure British rule in India. He also passed measures to make Bengal both more safe and efficient by suppressing banditry and reforming the collection of land taxes. In 1773, he was appointed governor-general of India by Lord North. However, governing the colony was no easy task. Sir Philip Francis, who served on the company council and had been wounded once by Hastings in a duel, continually undermined his work and encouraged a local financier to bring charges of corruption against the governor-general.

Hastings resigned his post in 1784 and returned to England after control of the company went to the Crown. But he was not allowed to retire peacefully. Francis, who was now in Parliament, brought charges against him, and Hastings was impeached in 1787 on charges of extortion. His trial lasted from 1788 until 1795. Politicians Edmund BURKE and Charles James Fox were among his accusers. Hastings was also criticized for interfering in the affairs of provincial Indian governments. His interference was blamed for the outbreak of war in Mysore and Madras.

The lengthy trial left Hastings in financial ruin, but the East India Company provided for his upkeep. Despite the evidence and considerable eloquence of his accusers, Hastings was acquitted by the House of Lords. Although he would not accept the peerage offered to him, Hastings remained in favor with the government and, in 1814, became a privy councilor. He died four years later at the age of 86.

Hastings's legacy is a mixed one. While he did increase administrative efficiency and brought prosperity not only to the East India Company but also to Bengal itself, he did not always deal fairly or humanely with the Indian people. Debate remains as to whether the charges brought against him were partially legitimate or wholly a function of the political struggles between the company and different factions in Parliament.

Further reading: Jeremy Bernstein, *Dawning of the Raj: The Life and Trials of Warren Hastings* (Chicago: Ivan R. Dee, 2000).

Haydn, Franz Joseph (1732–1809) *Austrian composer, affectionately nicknamed "Papa Haydn" by his contemporaries*

Haydn and Wolfgang Amadeus MOZART stand out as the greatest composers of the late 18th century. Both men exploited the possibilities of the MUSICAL CLASSICISM that dominated their era. The two men knew each other as friends, and Haydn was deeply saddened by the death of the young Mozart in 1791.

Franz Joseph Haydn was the second of 12 children born at Rohrau in Lower Austria to Mathias Haydn, a master wheelwright, and his first wife, Anna Maria Koller. Music played a central role in the Haydn family, and besides Joseph, Johann Michael also became a composer. Young Joseph Haydn left his family for school in Hainburg at the age of six. He studied the usual school subjects but also received training on several musical instruments and sang in the boys' choir. In 1740, at the age of eight, he earned a coveted position with the Boys' Choir of St. Stephen's Cathedral in VIENNA. Haydn lived in Vienna for the next 20 years. After his voice changed and he could no longer sing in the Boys' Choir, he began struggling to support himself as a musician, teacher, and occasional composer. Haydn rented a room in a serendipitous location, in the Michaelerhaus across from the entrance to the Hofburg in Vienna. The building had two important occupants: Pietro Metastasio, the court librettist of the era, and the dowager princess Esterházy. Metastasio introduced Haydn to Nicola Antonio Giacinto Porpora (1686–1768), an Italian composer living in Vienna, from whom Haydn learned much about composition. The sons of the dowager princess Esterházy, Prince Paul Anton Esterházy and his younger brother, Prince Miklós József (Nicolaus Joseph) ESTERHÁZY, became Haydn's patrons for nearly 30 years.

Haydn began his service with the Esterházy court in 1761 after having spent a brief time as music director for Count Morzin in Bohemia. The Esterházy family, which had its traditional territorial base in Eisenstadt, was one of the richest and most influential families of the Hungarian nobility. Prince Miklós József Esterházy, who became head of the family in 1762, especially loved ostentatious festivities. He built a sumptuous new estate at Esterháza, which, beginning in 1766, became the primary residence of the prince and his household. Haydn's duties entailed playing in the princely orchestra, directing its performances, and composing new symphonies or other works for the two weekly concerts required of the orchestra. Haydn also composed trios, string quartets, and anything else desired by his employer. In particular, he composed more than 125 trios for baryton, violin, and cello because Prince Esterházy was particularly fond of playing the baryton, a large stringed instrument equipped with two sets of strings, a gut set that were bowed and a metal set that simply resonated. Haydn produced 92 symphonies during his years at Esterháza, mostly at the request of the prince.

Haydn became increasingly involved with OPERA after 1776, when he began supervising performances at the Esterháza opera house. His name became famous throughout Europe, for Prince Esterházy had a constant stream of notable visitors at his magnificent estate. With his growing reputation, Haydn was able to secure the publication of many compositions. He also began receiving commissions from all over Europe. One notable example was the six *Paris Symphonies* (1785–86), which were commissioned by the Concert de la Loge Olympique, a concert-producing enterprise in PARIS.

Prince Miklós Jószef Esterházy died in 1790, and his brother Miklós II succeeded him. Haydn remained officially in the employment of the Esterházy family, but since the new prince was relatively uninterested in music, the composer was able to move to Vienna. That city became his permanent home, and he left only occasionally to produce concert series in other European capitals. One such venture took Haydn to LONDON, where, in conjunction with the impresario Johann Peter Salomon, he produced two highly successful concert seasons (January 1791–July 1792 and February 1794–August 1795). The London visits gave Haydn a chance to hear performances of the popular oratorio, *Messiah,* by George Frederick HANDEL. The experience inspired Haydn to create two major choral works, THE CREATION (1798) and *The Seasons* (1801), after he returned to Vienna. Haydn's librettist for both works was Gottfried van SWIETEN.

During his last years, Haydn devoted himself to writing string quartets. He published these works and appeared occasionally conducting his creations. His last public appearance occurred December 26, 1803, when he conducted his *Seven Last Words of Christ.* Haydn lived to see Vienna fall to the army of Napoleon in May 1809. The French conqueror ordered a guard of honor for the elderly composer's house, but Haydn died shortly thereafter on May 31, 1809. The *Requiem* mass by Mozart was performed at a great memorial service on June 15, 1809.

Haydn led a fairly regular, precise daily life. His marriage (1760) to Maria Anna Aloysia Apollonia Keller was unrewarding and childless. Haydn himself admitted to being vulnerable to the charms of other women. In 1779, he began a long relationship with the 19-year-old Luigia Polzelli who had been hired as a singer at Prince Esterházy's court. His devotion to her lasted at least until 1800, when, after his wife's death, he declared that he would never remarry unless to Luigia. Haydn also had a close friendship with Maria Anna (Marianne) von Genzinger. His correspondence with her, begun in 1789, reveals aspects of his inner self not otherwise evident.

Haydn lived through the years that witnessed the transition in MUSIC from the late BAROQUE STYLE through the STYLE GALANT and EMPFINDSAMER STIL to full-blown classicism. He made substantial contributions to the development of three musical forms: the symphony, the string quartet, and the keyboard sonata. In fact, it is often claimed that the perfected classicism of the late 18th century owes more to Haydn's work than to that of any other single composer. Haydn's earlier works display certain *galant* characteristics in their light, pleasing melodies and structures.

Like his contemporaries, Haydn used music as a means for exploring emotions that ranged from light-hearted gaiety through the entire spectrum of dark passions, but his music was especially noted for its clever humor. After 1766, he entered a period that has been equated by some musicologists to that of the STURM UND DRANG in LITERATURE. Other experts challenge this characterization, but all admit that between 1766 and 1775 the characteristic moods, forms, and instrumentation in Haydn's compositions changed noticeably. He routinely wrote symphonies in four movements, rather than in the three movements that had typified his earlier works. He also largely abandoned the harpsichord in favor of the new, more expressive fortepiano. In general, the period saw the emergence of his fully developed, mature style.

Even today the number of authentic Haydn compositions is a matter of dispute. The provisional catalog lists 106 symphonies, 68 string quartets, 60 piano sonatas, 20 to 25 operas (15 extant), and 4 oratorios. In addition, numerous chamber music works are attributed to Haydn. Notable symphonies include the six *Paris Symphonies* (nos. 82–87); the symphonies numbered 88 to 92; the 12 *London Symphonies* (nos. 93–104); and the so-called *Sturm und Drang Symphonies* (nos. 26, 41, 43, 44, 48, and 52). The late string quartets (1780s), opus numbers 42, 50, 54, and 64, are considered outstanding. Finally, of Haydn's vocal music, *The Creation, The Lord Nelson Mass* (1798), and the *Mass in Time of War* (1796) must be noted. Haydn's operas were quite successful during his lifetime, but they are scarcely known today.

See also NEOCLASSICISM; PIANO.

Further reading: Donald J. Grout, *A History of Western Music,* rev. ed. (New York: W. W. Norton, 1973); Elaine R. Sisman, ed., *Haydn and His World,* Bard Music Festival Series (Princeton, N.J.: Princeton University Press, 1997); W. Dean Sutcliffe et al., eds., *Haydn Studies* (Cambridge: Cambridge University Press, 1998).

Haywood, Eliza (ca. 1693–1756) *British novelist, playwright, translator, and magazine editor*

Little is known about the early life of Haywood, who was probably the most prolific and popular novelist of early 18th-century ENGLAND. In 1715, she made her theatrical debut in Dublin. Her lack of success as an actress probably led her to turn to writing.

Haywood's first NOVEL, *Love in Excess* (1719–20), was a sensational success, going through five single editions and several collected editions during her lifetime. In this and other early works, Haywood celebrates the triumph of pure, physical passion over REASON, which she represents as a weak means of understanding the more powerful forces of NATURE.

During the 1720s, Haywood published more than a dozen amorous novellas, making her one of the most popular writers of her day. Her popularity and notoriety gained her powerful enemies such as Alexander POPE and Jonathan SWIFT. Pope attacked her by name in his *Dunciad* (1728).

During the 1730s, Haywood returned to the THEATER, working with Henry FIELDING at the Haymarket Theatre in attacking the Whig administration of Robert WALPOLE. Haywood returned to writing fiction after the Licensing Act of 1737 reinstated government censorship of the theater. Like Fielding, she published an attack on Richardson's immensely successful novel PAMELA (1740). Haywood's book was titled *Anti-Pamela, or Feign'd Innocence Detected* (1742).

During this stage in her career, Haywood generally abandoned the amorous themes of her early novellas. Inspired by the emphasis on EDUCATION fostered by the ENLIGHTENMENT, she began to stress the moral and didactic qualities of her fiction. *The Female Spectator* (1744–1746), the first British magazine written entirely by and for women, was one result. Following the example of THE SPECTATOR, whose legacy her periodical title invoked, Haywood published the various issues of *The Female Spectator* in a collection that went through several editions in the 18th century.

Haywood's best and most well-known work is her *History of Miss Betsy Thoughtless* (1751), a novel in which she presents the story of a naive and frivolous young woman who grows into a creature of moral seriousness and intellectual maturity. The vehicle for this transformation in Betsy's character is education. Several female novelists during the later 18th century—Charlotte LENNOX, Fanny BURNEY, and Jane Austen, for example—recognizing the power of education as a means for revolutionizing feminine social roles, borrowed aspects of the plot of *Betsy Thoughtless* for their own novels.

heliocentric   Term that literally means having the Sun at the center. A heliocentric model of the universe was proposed by Nicolaus COPERNICUS and developed during the course of the COPERNICAN REVOLUTION in the 17th century and 18th century. It ultimately replaced the traditional GEOCENTRIC vision that had dominated European intellectual life since the time of the ancient Greeks. The new model placed the Sun at the center of the universe. The planets, including the Earth, revolved around the Sun while stars occupied vast spaces beyond the planets.

The original heliocentric model proposed by Copernicus retained circular orbits, a finite although enlarged size for the universe, and crystalline spheres. Theories and discoveries by later astronomers transformed the Copernican model into a universe characterized by infinite size, countless stars, elliptical planetary orbits, and universal mathematical laws governing both celestial and terrestrial physical events.

During the 17th century and 18th century, this model of the universe gradually replaced the traditional model. The process of diffusion of Copernicanism into the sciences and related branches of philosophy occurred mostly in the 17th century. THEOLOGY and the popular imagination, however, waited until the early decades of the 18th-century ENLIGHTENMENT before yielding, at least partly, to the new vision.

See also ASTRONOMY.

Helvétius, Anne-Cathérine de Ligniville D'Autricourt, Madame (1722–1800) *wife of Claude-Adrien Helvétius and hostess of a major enlightened salon*
One of the 21 children of Jean-Jacques de Ligniville, an officer in the service of the duke of Lorraine, Anne-Cathérine de Ligniville D'Autricourt was sent to a convent for 15 years in order to be educated. About 1738 (the exact date is not known), she moved to PARIS with her aunt, Madame de Graffigny, and began assisting at the enlightened salon sponsored by the older woman. In these environs, Mademoiselle de Ligniville encountered Anne-Robert-Jacques TURGOT, Denis DIDEROT, Jean Le Rond d'ALEMBERT, Baron d' HOLBACH, the comte de BUFFON, Abbé Morellet, and the young Claude-Adrien HELVÉTIUS.

Helvétius married Mademoiselle de Ligniville in 1751. The couple divided their time between Paris (Rue Sainte-Anne) and a chateau at Voré. In Paris, Madame Helvétius established a Tuesday evening salon where the guests included, Jean-François MARMONTEL, Bernard de FONTENELLE, the marquis de CONDORCET, Saint-Lambert, Charles DUCLOS, Melchior GRIMM, and Abbé CONDILLAC, as well as the friends from her aunt's salon.

After the death of her husband in 1771, Madame Helvétius moved to Auteuil, where she continued holding salons. Her guests included Benjamin FRANKLIN, who called her Notre-Dame d'Auteuil and asked for her hand in marriage. Thomas JEFFERSON, Pierre-Jean-Georges CABANIS, Condillac, Comte DESTUTT DE TRACY, Jean HOUDON, and other members of the later generation of PHILOSOPHES also attended. During the FRENCH REVOLUTION, the salon d'Auteuil provided the meeting place where plans were made for the coup d'état that brought Napoleon to power.

See also RADICAL ENLIGHTENMENT; SOCIAL INSTITUTIONS OF THE ENLIGHTENMENT.

Helvétius, Claude-Adrien (1715–1771) *French philosopher*
The son of a physician to the queen of France, Helvétius received his secondary education at the prestigious Jesuit Collège Louis-Le-Grand in PARIS. The income from an office as tax farmer allowed him to support the activities of his enlightened friends. In 1751, Helvétius resigned as a tax farmer but bought a more lucrative position as maître d'hôtel for the queen of France. His activities on behalf of the causes of the ENLIGHTENMENT consumed increasing portions of his time. Helvétius and his wife, Madame HELVÉTIUS, presided over one of the major radi-

cal enlightened salons in Paris. She continued this activity even after her husband's death in 1771.

In 1758, Helvétius published *De l'esprit* (On the mind). The publication created a crisis for the French PHILOSOPHES, for Helvétius's extreme theory of the mind brought the institutions of CENSORSHIP into quick action. Both the Sorbonne (the theological faculty of the University of Paris) and the Parlement of Paris condemned the book, and all copies were ordered burned by the public hangman. The burning also included the works of philosophes such as VOLTAIRE. The Sorbonne censors lamented that the book contained all the poisons characteristic of 18th-century modernity. They specifically drew parallels between *De l'esprit* and books by "atheists" such as Benedict de SPINOZA, Anthony COLLINS, Thomas HOBBES, Bernard MANDEVILLE, Julien de LA METTRIE, and the marquis d'ARGENS. Helvétius was forced to recant his position on three separate occasions, and the publication of the ENCYCLOPÉDIE, with which he was associated, was suspended.

De l'esprit offered an Epicurean and utilitarian vision of the psychological motivation of human beings. It was based on the sensation PSYCHOLOGY of John LOCKE and Abbé CONDILLAC. According to Helvétius, the fact that human beings construct their world on ideas on the basis of sensation implies that basic choices are made according to a pleasure-pain principle. People seek to avoid painful sensation and to maximize pleasure. All human behavior, including moral behavior, is based on this fact and is therefore rooted in self-interest.

Helvétius suggested ways to organize a political society that would capitalize on this basic principle of human morality and motivation. He believed that the creation of a functional political culture required shaping individual perceptions of self-interest so that they would correspond exactly to the general interest of the society. He was not calling for the sacrifice or suppression of SELF-INTEREST, because he did not believe that people could be expected to make such sacrifices. Rather, he was calling for manipulating the way an individual defined his or her self-interest. This would be accomplished by means of EDUCATION and legislation. Through education, certain values would be taught so that they became internalized by young people. Legislation would shape behavior by attaching punishments (pain) to certain behaviors. People would avoid the behaviors that bring punishment, recognizing that inviting punishment was not in their self-interest.

Helvétius's position was so extreme that even his enlightened friends felt compelled, in order to protect themselves from censorship and harassment, to criticize his work. Jean-Jacques ROUSSEAU, Denis DIDEROT, Anne-Robert-Jacques TURGOT, and Voltaire all disputed both his utilitarian view of human behavior and his vision of the organizing principles that should inform a reformed

political culture. Even FREDERICK II (THE GREAT), who offered Helvétius protection in BERLIN, criticized the ideas put forth in *De l'esprit*.

Helvétius left FRANCE in 1764, traveling briefly to ENGLAND before taking up residence in Berlin. He was accepted as a member of the BERLIN ACADEMY and wrote his second major treatise while living in that city. The work, *De l'homme, de ses facultés intellectuelles et de son éducation* (On man, on his intellectual faculties and his education), was not published until 1772, one year after Helvétius's death. This work offered a theory of education based on the assumption that all people are equally capable of learning. He specifically criticized the views that Rousseau had spelled out in his educational novel ÉMILE. Rousseau retaliated by chastising Helvétius for his ATHEISM.

Helvétius dedicated himself to the cause of reforming society on behalf of human PROGRESS. He was a member of the FREEMASONS and in 1766 founded the Parisian lodge known as "Les sciences." The work of Helvétius represents the extreme development of the enlightened vision based on REASON, PROGRESS, human PERFECTIBILITY, and sensation psychology. Helvétius transgressed the boundaries of expression that were possible during his era, and thus, his work helps to define the limits of enlightened thought.

See also ANCIEN RÉGIME; EPICUREAN PHILOSOPHY; MATERIALISM; MORAL PHILOSOPHY; PUBLISHING; SEPARATION OF CHURCH AND STATE; SOCIAL INSTITUTIONS OF THE ENLIGHTENMENT.

Herder, Johann Gottfried (1744–1803) *German philosopher of history and aesthetics*

Herder studied theology and philosophy at Königsberg University, where he became an ardent disciple and admirer of Johann Georg HAMANN. After ordination into the Lutheran clergy, Herder pursued a professional career that combined teaching, preaching, and writing. He worked in Riga (1764–69) and Bückeberg (1771–76) before settling in Weimar as an official under KARL-AUGUST, Duke of Weimar. He died in Weimar in 1803.

Herder presented his historical theory in his major work: *Ideen zur Philosophie der Geschichte der Menschheit* (Ideas on the philosophy of human history; 1784–91) and in his earlier *Auch eine Philosophie der Geschichte der Bildung der Menschheit* (Another philosophy of the history of the formation of humankind; 1774). He derived special inspiration from the works of Gotthold Ephraim LESSING, Benedict de SPINOZA, Gottfried LEIBNIZ, and Hamann. His historical ideas closely resemble those of Giovan Battista VICO, but no evidence has yet been uncovered to show that Herder actually read Vico's work.

Herder combined the French notion of PROGRESS based on the triumph of REASON with the German belief that the world contains inner forces whose action drives change. He also constantly stressed the concept that the

Johann Gottfried Herder, portrait by G. von Kügelgen, 1809. With Herder and his generation, the German Enlightenment (*Aufklärung*) reached its peak and also began to follow paths that eventually produced Romanticism. *(Courtesy Library of Tartu University Estonia)*

world consists of a unity rooted in diversity and that it is characterized by a constant tension between the One and the Many.

Utilizing these general concepts, Herder developed an idea of human progress based on conflict as the force that drives the historical process. For Herder, HISTORY unfolds in a series of necessary stages that bring the gradual triumph of humanity over the forces of NATURE. The development of SCIENCE, technology, and the arts and the gradual attainment of FREEDOM represent this human triumph.

Although Herder offered a universal interpretation of the direction of human history, he emphatically rejected the idea that individual cultures could be reduced to some common content. Rather, he stressed the variety in human societies, asserting that their organization resembles the form of living organisms. Various societies cannot be made the equivalent to one another, or reduced to some abstract universal ideal. They must, instead, be understood on their own terms, as unique forms of human expression.

In conjunction with this position, Herder developed the concept of national character. Derived both from MONTESQUIEU and from his personal experience in Riga,

his concept embodied the notion that a special set of traits rooted in a given people (*Volk*) endows its culture with unique forms of GENIUS, LANGUAGE, and ideas. The *Urvolk,* the original people of any nation, unite the divine, truth, beauty, poetry, music, and art into one harmonious whole.

The job of the historian does not lie in telling the story of great leaders but in depicting the story of a general culture. In this realm, Herder agrees with the major historians of the Enlightenment: VOLTAIRE, Montesquieu, David HUME, August von SCHLÖZER, and Johann GATTERER. But he departs from their position in outlining his idea of historical understanding. For Herder, the job of the historian does not consist of analyzing a culture by breaking it down into components in the style of the SCIENTIFIC METHOD; rather, it consists of entering into a sympathetic understanding of the *Volk* by immersing oneself in its cultural expressions.

According to Herder, the methodology of the historian must rely on the use of the mental faculties of INTUITION AND IMAGINATION rather than on reason. The value of history writing lies in capturing the variety and richness of human life rather than in reducing all forms of human expression to the operation of universal laws.

Herder's history departs from the secularized vision of the world that characterizes other enlightened histories. His account of the RELATIONS between the divinely inspired *Urvolk* and their history tended toward Pantheism, the notion that God is actually contained in everything in the world.

Embedded in Herder's philosophy of history lay a related theory of AESTHETICS that focused on the role played by creative artists in society. Artistic expression, whether in the form of painting, sculpture, literature, or music, represented for Herder the most complete expression by people of both their individual and communal existence. The task of the artist lay in conveying authentically the contents of this existence and experience.

Herder's concern with the role of the artist spilled over into other areas of aesthetics. He championed the German language as a valid vehicle for literary creation, placing himself in line with illustrious predecessors such as Martin Luther, Samuel PUFENDORF, Leibniz, Christian THOMASIUS, Christian WOLFF, Hamann, and Lessing.

Herder expressed special sympathy for the oppressed peoples of the 18th century: for the Slavs of the HAPSBURG EMPIRE, for enslaved people, and for indigenous groups living under European or American subjugation. He supported enlightened absolutism (see ABSOLUTISM, ENLIGHTENED), in the belief that it would guarantee the greatest freedom and progress in contemporary states.

In spite of his preference for enlightened absolutism, Herder, however, also believed that people have a right to rebel against oppression, and that revolution is just a means of achieving progress. He welcomed the initial stages of the FRENCH REVOLUTION in his *Briefen zur*

Beförderung der Humanität (Letters on the progress of humankind; 1792–97), but he was horrified by the execution of LOUIS XVI and by the terror of the JACOBIN period.

Herder rejected certain aspects of the ENLIGHTENMENT even while he was championing some of its most powerful ideas. He was, for example, a strong critic of the French *ENCYCLOPÉDIE*, but he championed the causes of political freedom and human progress. A skeptic about the powers of reason and RATIONALISM, he nevertheless incorporated the rational systematic philosophy of Leibniz into his own thought. He embraced the materialistic and pantheistic monism of Spinoza, yet he was sensitive to the depiction of that system as a kind of ATHEISM in the work of Friedrich JACOBI.

Immanuel KANT, Herder's former philosophy professor at Konigsberg, received incisive criticism, yet both Herder and Kant were struggling with the problem of developing epistemologies that could deal with the recognized limits of human reason. Kant tried to preserve the Enlightenment by reformulating the idea of reason, but Herder helped more to undermine that central idea. His work inspired the writers and artists of the *STURM UND DRANG* movement and greatly assisted the development of ROMANTICISM. Thus, Herder was a major figure of the Enlightenment, but one who stood at its boundaries and who began stepping into new realms.

Further reading: Isaiah Berlin, *Vico and Herder: Two Studies in the History of Ideas* (New York: Viking Press, 1976); W. H. Bruford, *Germany in the Eighteenth Century: The Social Background of the Literary Revival* (Cambridge: Cambridge University Press, 1971).

hermeticism *quasireligious philosophical movement*
Hermeticism in the 18th century was an offshoot of the earlier hermetist movement. Historically, hermeticism refers to beliefs found in the writings of Hermes Trismegistus and his followers. Supposedly, Trismegistus was an Egyptian philosopher writing at the time of Moses and a teacher of Plato. The main hermetic texts are the 17-volume *Corpus Hermeticum* and the *Asclepius*. These writings first made their appearance in Europe in the court of Cosimo de Medici in 1460. Throughout the Renaissance, hermeticism grew as Europeans sought to recover the "lost" writings of the ancients.

Combining the philosophical beliefs of hermeticism with the study of ALCHEMY, astrology, magical systems, and other occult practices and philosophies, hermeticism was a formidable movement. Championed by Giordano Bruno in the 1600s, hermeticism seems to have been viewed as a very credible alternative or complement to the growth of SCIENCE, humanism, and Christianity. Adherents of hermeticism supposedly included Bruno, Johannes KEPLER, Nicolaus COPERNICUS, Galileo GALILEI, and Sir Isaac NEWTON. The movement grew throughout Europe and was denounced by the Catholic Church and other civil and religious authorities. Although Isaac

Casaubon was able to show in the 17th century that Trismegistus's works had in fact been written in the early days of Christianity and not in the time of Moses, hermeticism never fully died out.

Hermeticism saw a revival in the 18th century, especially in ENGLAND. At this time, there was an increase in the number of SECRET SOCIETIES throughout Europe. A part of that growth, the spread of hermeticism can be seen as a reaction to the emphasis on science and rationality of the mainstream ENLIGHTENMENT. Hermeticism was not a rejection of science and rationality in and of themselves, however. Rather, it was an attempt not only to maintain some sort of RELIGION and spirituality, but also to marry it to a form of science.

The Hermetic View of God and Persons

While Enlightenment rationality was used to analyze the visible world of industry and political revolutions, hermeticism emphasized inner enlightenment. It encouraged greater knowledge of both the self and God. But it did so outside the bounds of contemporary traditional European THEOLOGY and PHILOSOPHY.

Hermeticists believed that the world was God's first creation. God himself is good and is knowable through his earthly creation. Humankind was God's second creation. Created by a good God, humans therefore are also good. God and the good are to be discovered in the created world and in the human mind. The human form, which is one with the human mind, is considered to be the ultimate manifestation of God's creation. Therefore, God is knowable through humankind's use of mind to contemplate NATURE and God. Through this contemplation and through ritual, God and goodness are revealed to humankind. The goal of attaining such revelation is to achieve union with and knowledge of the divine and of the universe.

Hermeticism required its believers to change as they passed through several stages of study and initiation. An example of this is evident in the hermeticist view of sexuality. Having children and engaging in procreation were considered a religious duty. However, God is both male and female. Therefore, in the latter stages of initiation, sexuality is to be transcended altogether so that the initiate becomes as close to the Divine as possible.

All levels of hermetic study, whether scientific or magical, were undertaken with the purpose of finding God and good in the world. The final phase of hermetic study was initiation into the mystery of the Divine itself. While it is unclear what this initiation entailed, it is clear that hermeticism required an evolution of the self.

Hermetic "Science"

Because hermeticism stressed the importance of the natural universe as God-created and benevolent, the natural world was important to hermeticists. The use of one's mind to change the natural world was also a major aspect of hermeticist belief. Because the spiritual and the natural worlds were one, divine revelation could be made known through either. Hence, for the hermeticist the application of ritual and mysticism to science was not a contradiction.

Hermeticism, therefore, stressed instruction in the knowledge of the cosmos and of humankind. In the most general terms, hermetic mystical science believed that the world, both divine and natural, could be known through the manipulation of the forms and substances of mercury, sulphur, and solid metals. Various alchemical experiments were used in conjunction with ritual to reveal truths about nature, which pointed back to the Divine. The combination of MATHEMATICS, MEDICINE, and ASTRONOMY with alchemy, ritual, and MAGIC was at the core of hermetic studies.

The Hermetic Legacy

Hermeticism offered an alternative to the early Enlightenment philosophy of mechanism. It also played a role in the growth of later esoteric traditions, such as 18th-century Rosicrucianism and Freemasonry in Europe and America. Although its influence on science subsided in the later 18th century, hermeticism continued to inspire many romantic artists, musicians, and writers, including Samuel Taylor COLERIDGE and William BLAKE in Britain, Victor Hugo in France, and Johann Wolfgang von GOETHE and Johann Salomo SEMLER in Germany. The appeal of hermetic thought is still present today, as many New Age philosophies and sects continue to use hermetic ideas and rituals.

See also FREEMASONS; MECHANICAL PHILOSOPHY; ROMANTICISM; ROSICRUCIANS.

Herschel, William (1738–1822) *astronomer who was born in Hanover but who worked in England*
William Herschel worked initially as a musician playing in the band of the Hanoverian Guards and moved to ENGLAND in 1757 to pursue his musical career. He obtained employment in Bath as a church organist. He was passionately interested in ASTRONOMY and earned enough in his musical post to sustain his investigations of the universe.

Herschel designed and built the largest reflecting TELESCOPE of his era, a 40-foot instrument with a mirror that was 4 feet, 10 inches in diameter. The instrument proved impractical for observations because the weight of the mirror significantly distorted its images. With a smaller telescope, Herschel began mapping the universe in an effort to determine its shape. In this project he was assisted by his sister, Caroline Herschel (1750–1848), who subsequently became a prominent astronomer in her own right. In the course of this study, the Herschels made the first recorded observations of double stars, star clusters, and gaseous nebulae. Herschel also discovered the planet Uranus in 1781 and was rewarded with membership in the ROYAL SOCIETY OF LONDON and with the soci-

ety's prestigious Copley Medal. He also received a substantial pension from King George III in return for devoting himself full-time to astronomy.

See also TECHNOLOGY AND INSTRUMENTATION.

Hildebrandt, Johann Lukas von (1668–1745)
Genoese-born architect
Hildebrandt's major works, in BAROQUE STYLE with some ROCOCO interior elements, were built in AUSTRIA. Hildebrandt studied military and civil architecture in Genoa and worked as a fortifications expert for Prince EUGENE OF SAVOY in the PIEDMONT (1695–96) before moving to VIENNA. He made the move to the Hapsburg capital in order to take advantage of the enormous building fever that gripped the city after the end of hostilities with the Ottoman Empire. Johann Bernhard FISCHER VON ERLACH and Hildebrandt were major rivals, although Hildebrandt was always more of a designer, decorator, and remodeler than his illustrious competitor.

Hildebrandt is most admired today for his country and suburban *Lustgebäude* (summer houses, the German *Lust* means "pleasure"), which treated house and garden as an organic whole. His most famous extant projects include the Belvedere Palace, designed for Prince Eugene of Savoy, and the Stahremberg Palace, both in Vienna; the Pommersfelden and Gollersdorf country estates in modern Bavaria, Germany, designed for members of the powerful Schönborn family; and the remodeled Mirabel Palace, outside Salzburg, Austria, designed for the archbishop of Salzburg.

Histoire des deux Indes French encyclopedia of the European colonies. Edited and, to a large extent, written by Guillaume, Abbé RAYNAL, the *Histoire philosophique et politique des établissements et du commerce des Européens dans les deux Indes* (Philosophical and political history of the institutions and commerce of the Europeans in the two Indies; 1770) provided information about Europe's colonies as well as a critique of their political institutions and, by extension, of the institutions of the European continent as well.

Raynal enlisted the help of several collaborators in compiling the *Histoire,* of whom Denis DIDEROT was the most prominent. In preparing the *Histoire,* Raynal consulted people knowledgeable about other parts of the world, including traders, diplomats, travelers, and soldiers. He also had access to the records of the French colonial office through his friend the duc de CHOISEUL, LOUIS XV's secretary of foreign affairs.

The *Histoire des deux Indes* was first published in six volumes in 1770. The work is organized as an encyclopedia, that is, with separate entries under topic headings. It attempts to encompass all knowledge about the non-European world in a series of articles on subjects such as coffee, cocoa, Indians, and SLAVERY, as well as on several geographic locations and their residents.

Raynal's original intent was to collect knowledge that would be valuable to those interested in commerce. The aim of the *Histoire* was to encourage trade between Europe and the colonies. But the work also had a strong political-philosophical component in its discussion of the political institutions of Europe, especially FRANCE. The *Histoire* contrasts Europe and the colonies, challenging notions of the former as the bearer of civilization and of the latter as backward and needing to be civilized. Raynal offered outspoken criticism of the whole colonial endeavor, accusing its advocates of invading and devastating lands around the globe and subjugating and massacring their inhabitants.

The *Histoire* appeared in revised editions in 1774, 1780, and 1820. An English translation was published in London in 1777. By the time Raynal offered the third edition, the work had gone through 17 printings, and about 25,000 copies were in circulation. This number doubled by 1820. The critical position taken by Raynal with respect to the institutions of Europe in the first two editions was radicalized further by the greater participation of Denis Diderot in the 1780 edition. Its outspoken criticism of the Catholic Church in comparison to the examples of NATURAL RELIGION found among the "savages" incurred the wrath of the authorities in France. Raynal added his name to the title page of the 1780 edition, and he was exiled from France as a result. In 1781, the book was publicly burned. This, apparently, only increased the popularity and fame of both the work and its author-editor.

The impact of the *Histoire des deux Indes* on 18th-century Enlightenment thought was great. The work circulated widely both because of its useful content for those engaged in colonial trade and other activities connected to the colonial enterprise and because of its political discussions. The anticolonial stance, refined and sharpened in the 1780 edition, contributed to debates on slavery, a key institution of the colonial system, and NATURAL LAW.

Further reading: Denis Diderot, *Political Writings* (Cambridge: Cambridge University Press, 1992).

Historical and Critical Dictionary

A multivolume work by Pierre BAYLE, first published in 1697 in Rotterdam. By 1740, five French editions had been published. Johann Christoph GOTTSCHED oversaw a German translation in the 1740s.

The *Historical and Critical Dictionary* (French title: *Dictionnaire historique et critique*) was one of the most important works of the earliest years of the ENLIGHTENMENT. Bayle was a French Calvinist living in the UNITED PROVINCES OF THE NETHERLANDS in order to avoid persecution by the government of LOUIS XIV. His experiences with religious intolerance helped to turn him against all forms of dogma, whether religious or secular in origin. He adopted an intellectual stance of extreme SKEPTICISM known as PYRRHONISM and decided to write a work that would subject all forms of received knowledge to critical analysis. The result was the *Historical and Critical Dictionary,* one of the first books in which REASON was consciously used as an instrument for tearing down tradition.

Bayle's book served both as a source of specific ideas and as a model of a general critical attitude for the Enlightenment. Its fundamental theme consisted of an attack on rational systems of knowledge in which Bayle denied that human reason could reveal the underlying truths of existence. Bayle believed in the power of reason but only as a tool for criticism. He organized his work as a dictionary with entries on subjects from A to Z. They cover such topics as Benedict de SPINOZA (Bayle attacked his ideas), Jupiter, Pyrrho, Zeno the Epicurean, and a host of others.

Bayle was a hero for many enlightened thinkers. His admirers included Edward GIBBON, FREDERICK II (THE GREAT), Thomas JEFFERSON, Benjamin FRANKLIN, David HUME, VOLTAIRE, Jean-Jacques ROUSSEAU, and Denis DIDEROT, to name only a few.

The established authorities were less pleased with Bayle's creation. It was publicly burned in Alsace (Colmar), subjected to critical analysis by the JESUITS, and generally attacked by the upholders of religious orthodoxy.

history

A discipline devoted to the investigation and re-creation of the human past. The word *history* derives from the Latin *historia,* meaning "inquiry, learning, or a story." History writing is an ancient literary form whose choice of subject matter, methods of research, and ways of telling about the past have undergone marked changes over the centuries. The ENLIGHTENMENT proved to be a creative era for historical methodology, one in which the first recognizably modern studies appeared.

On a broader scale, the Enlightenment brought the historicization of many fields of study. NATURE, the Earth, childhood, reproduction, languages, the Bible, society, political structures, and the human mind all acquired a historical dimension as intellectuals began to assume that changes had occurred over time, began to speak of development, and sought to uncover the mechanisms that caused or directed such development. Theories in SCIENCE, EDUCATION, PSYCHOLOGY, RELIGION, THEOLOGY, and ANTHROPOLOGY changed when they began to incorporate history into their conceptual frameworks.

The writers of the Enlightenment inherited several intellectual traditions that dealt with the past: universal history, pragmatic history, antiquarian studies, and studies on the nature and principles of law. From the pen of Bishop BOSSUET, the era had received an influential universal history of the world (Europe and the Mediterranean) that presented all events as the unfolding of God's purpose and design. According to this scheme, ROMAN CATHOLICISM and the ABSOLUTISM of King LOUIS XIV represented the high point of civilization; both institutions thoroughly embodied the laws and purposes of the Christian God.

The work of the ancient Roman historian Livy was the most popular and frequently cited example of pragmatic history. Livy had provided lessons about proper behavior and wise government by using examples drawn from history. Imitations of this form provided guidance for many young European princes during the 17th century and continued to appear in the 18th century.

Antiquarian studies offered rich and detailed descriptions of the architectural monuments, sculpture, coins, epitaphs, and other artifacts left from ancient Greek and Roman civilizations. Antiquarian history writing received official support in France from the Academy of Inscriptions. Studies in this form continued to appear throughout the 18th century, although they were often disparaged by the PHILOSOPHES.

The last received tradition of history writing came from the realm of law and was represented for the intellectuals of the Enlightenment by the works of Jean Bodin, Hugo Grotius, and Samuel PUFENDORF. These men had investigated the manners and morals of nations as one set of indicators about the effectiveness of laws. Studies in this spirit had introduced the idea that climate and environment might have some influence on human behavior and institutions.

The historians of the Enlightenment produced their innovations in the conceptualization of history by blending these various modes together with certain approaches derived from philosophy. Sacred universal history gave way in the hands of Giambattista VICO, MONTESQUIEU, and David HUME to secularized philosophical history. Natural principles such as the spirit of laws or elements of human psychology replaced God as the primary driving forces behind the course of events. In the hands of Edward GIBBON, antiquarian studies experienced a similar transition. With VOLTAIRE and Montesquieu, relatively narrow studies of RELATIONS between manners, morals, and law generalized to encompass inquiries into the broad institutions and structures of human societies. Isolated examples of pragmatic history were woven together by German historians such as Johann Christoph GATTERER to produce a series of orderly events related by cause and effect. Event "A" preceded event "B" and caused it to happen. Finally, Scottish historians such as Hume, Adam FERGUSON, William ROBERTSON, and John MILLAR borrowed concepts from natural history. Just as living bodies went through stages of development, so human societies also moved from one stage to another.

In all these enlightened approaches, history writing turned away from telling stories about great rulers and their military exploits. They examined social structures, economic organization and policies, forms of government, religions, laws codes, customs, and other aspects of general culture in order to produce stories about nations or groups of people.

Altered ways of conceiving history took historians to new types of evidence and posed questions about the nature of historical understanding. It did not seem possible to express the relations between historical events in mathematical terms or to predict the future on the basis of the past. Yet historical understanding seemed to be an important and valid form of human inquiry. It was based, however, on a form of human understanding wholly different from the understanding used by scientists.

According to the theories of Gatterer and his colleagues at the University of GÖTTINGEN, historical understanding relied on intuition (German: *Anschauung*) rather than on REASON for its knowledge. Intuition allowed the historian to enter a relationship with the past based on imagination and SYMPATHY.

In general, the historians of the Enlightenment continued to believe that history could provide valuable lessons and insights to its readers but that the lessons presented were different from those offered in earlier pragmatic histories. They now focused on banishing general ignorance and parochial, prejudiced views. In other words, history served the cause of advancing general enlightenment and human PROGRESS.

It is often claimed that the Enlightenment was an age in which people believed in the march of human progress over time. The examination of enlightened histories, however, reveals that three distinct treatments of the direction of history existed. Some writers, such as Johann Gottfried HERDER and Marie-Jean de CONDORCET, definitely believed in progress. Others, however, were more ambivalent about history. Hume and Vico saw cyclical patterns in which periods of progress alternated with periods of degeneration. Their descriptions of these cycles sometimes suggested spirals that produce very slow upward movement, but at other times they evoked the image of simple waves, having no overall upward or downward motion. Finally, writers such as Gibbon and Jean-Jacques ROUSSEAU believed that history had actually produced human degeneration. For Rousseau, the cause of downward movement was the introduction of private property and of artificial culture. For Gibbon, the cause was the invention and institutionalization of Christianity as a state religion.

Historians, then, turned a critical eye to their own civilization and past, using their particular talents and training to shed light on the basic issues that dominated enlightened imaginations. History, like psychology, science, and other disciplines, seemed capable of clarifying the relationships between human nature and the societies constructed by human beings. It seemed to provide a means for gaining greater insight into the effects of economic, political, social, and religious institutions on human character. And finally, it seemed to offer another avenue by which the goal of human progress could perhaps be attained.

See also BACON; BOLINGBROKE; GIANNONE; INTUITION AND IMAGINATION; MÖSER; MÜLLER; MURATORI; REIMARUS; SCHLÖZER; SEMLER; SPINOZA; WINCKELMANN.

Further reading: Donald R. Kelley et al., eds., *The Historical Imagination in Early Modern Britain: History, Rhetoric, and Fiction, 1500–1800* (Cambridge: Cambridge University Press, 2002); Arnaldo Momigliano, *Gibbons' Contribution to Historical Method,* Studies in Historiography (New York: Harper Torchbooks, 1966); Emery Neff, *The Poetry of History* (New York: Columbia University Press, 1947); Laird Okie, *Augustan Historical Writing: Histories of England in the English Enlightenment* (Lanham, Md.: University Press of America, 1990); J. G. A. Pocock, *Virtue, Commerce, and History: Essays on Political Thought and History, Chiefly in the Eighteenth Century* (Cambridge: Cambridge University Press, 1985).

Hobbes, Thomas (1588–1679) *English philosopher*

The son of an English clergyman, Hobbes was brought up by a wealthy uncle. His father had engaged in a brawl outside his parish church and had fled to LONDON to escape prosecution. Under the tutelage of his uncle, young Hobbes acquired a thorough education capped by study at Magdalen Hall, Oxford University.

In 1608, Hobbes left Oxford and assumed a position tutoring the son of William Cavendish, earl of Devonshire. Hobbes was released from his position when the earl died in 1626, but he found similar employment with Sir Gervase Clinton. Sometime after 1629, he returned to the service of the Cavendish family and remained until 1640, when the political turmoil in ENGLAND caused him to flee to FRANCE.

During his years as a tutor, Hobbes had made two shorter trips to the European continent in 1610 and 1629 and had also made one extended excursion between 1634 and 1637. On the last of these trips, he made contact with the circle of natural philosophers and mathematicians surrounding Father Marin MERSENNE in PARIS. He also traveled to Florence to visit Galileo GALILEI, who was under house arrest after his condemnation by the Roman Inquisition. Hobbes thus acquired contacts with the major figures who were working on behalf of the movement that would eventually be called the SCIENTIFIC REVOLUTION.

When Hobbes returned to France in 1640, he rejoined the Mersenne circle, becoming a close friend of Pierre GASSEND, the French champion of EPICUREAN PHILOSOPHY. Hobbes published his major works on NATURAL PHILOSOPHY and POLITICAL THEORY during these year in France: *De Cive* (On the citizen) in 1642; *Minute or First Draught of the Optiques* between 1642 and 1646; *De Corpore* (On the body) in 1650; and *Leviathan* in 1651.

Frontispiece for *Leviathan* by Thomas Hobbes. A rationally constructed, centralized machine of state, symbolized as the Leviathan, represented for the Englishman Hobbes the best guarantee of political peace and social order. *(Courtesy Culver Pictures, Inc., New York)*

During his years in France (1640–51), Hobbes served for a few months as the tutor of the exiled English king Charles II. With the restoration of the Stuart monarchy in 1660, Charles II granted Hobbes a pension and free access to his person. However, Charles II could not prevent Hobbes from being harassed for his alleged ATHEISM. Thus, in 1666, Parliament forbade him from publishing any more books.

Hobbes embraced the MECHANICAL PHILOSOPHY in its most extreme form, explaining all phenomena in the world as the product of the motion of matter. Even human sense perceptions and feelings were the result of motions: Thus, pleasure was motion about the heart; phantasms, the images produced in the mind during sensation, were caused by the interaction of particles from external objects with particles inside the sense organs;

and thinking was motion about the head. According to Hobbes, human beings were machines, operating according to the same mathematical laws that rule the external world of objects. They did not even have souls, for Hobbes believed that the mechanical philosophy made it possible to dispense with spiritual components in human nature. The Hobbesian man was thus soulless, and the Hobbesian philosophy of man, one based on MATERIALISM.

Hobbes's theories of sense perception contained elements of EMPIRICISM, the theory of knowledge that roots all knowledge in experience. But Hobbes intended his system to support the opposite theory of knowledge: A rationalism in which scientific and philosophical knowledge derived from deductive (geometric) reasoning about matter in motion.

That Hobbes was not a real empiricist is further supported by his nominalist theory of language. He believed that words were just signs agreed upon by convention and custom. They named objects, but the names chosen had no relation to actual, essential reality of the object. True knowledge was obtained rather through the reasoning processes applied to these words, so long as the rules of rigid, geometric, deductive logic are followed.

Hobbes intended to write a trilogy on body, man, and citizen in which each of these aspects of human existence would be derived from mechanical principles by a process of deductive reasoning. He completed two parts: *De Corpore* and *De Homine* (On humankind). The third section, on the citizen, was never completed, although both the *Leviathan* and *De Cive* contain reasoning clearly linked to the mechanical philosophy.

The *Leviathan*, Hobbes's theory of political ABSOLUTISM, earned its author notoriety that lasted long beyond his lifetime. Hobbes developed his theory from two assumptions about HUMAN NATURE, both loosely derived from his mechanical, materialist view of humanity. People are moved (like matter) by two emotions, the desire for power and the fear of death. In the natural, primitive state, the desire for power causes people to lead lives that are "solitary, poor, nasty, brutish, and short." But the fear of death leads them to join together by means of a social contract into a political society or commonwealth. Hobbes called this commonwealth a Leviathan, that is, an artificial machine (in contrast to the natural human machine).

Most social contract theory had supported claims for representative government, but Hobbes turned the social contract idea on its head, using it to prove the necessity of undivided sovereignty (absolutism) in any state. In other words, political power should not be divided between king and Parliament or between various factions in a republic. Instead, power should be concentrated in one individual in order to prevent the formation of warring factions and the outbreak of civil war.

Hobbes, of course, was reacting to the English Civil Wars, whose outbreak in 1640 had caused him to seek exile. He believed that a strong, central monarchy was the only political form that could guarantee peace and prosperity to his nation.

Hobbes's book provoked an outcry of criticism and revulsion. The call for absolutism had serious implications for the political and social structures in England and in all 17th-century states. When Hobbes stated that power could not be divided, he meant to exclude both the established Christian churches and various representative institutions (Parliament in England, estates in other countries) from any role in government. His position, thus, offended representatives of these powerful groups.

Moreover, Hobbes's theory also disturbed the very centralizing monarchs who, it would seem, might have welcomed his arguments. Their dislike rested on the fact that Hobbes pointedly rejected the theory of the DIVINE RIGHT OF KINGS as a foundation for absolutism. Instead, he rooted his claims in human PSYCHOLOGY and secular MORAL PHILOSOPHY. To monarchs and their partisans, this seemed to weaken their ultimate claims to power.

Besides, Hobbes had made a social contract, consent by the people, the basis of his system. True, the people gave up all their sovereignty to the absolute ruler, but what, it was wondered, might happen if they became displeased with their rulers. Hobbes's justification of absolutism seemed flawed on this point.

Hobbes had challenged accepted ideas on other points as well. He had pointed out, for example, that the distinction between RELIGION and SUPERSTITION was really a matter of political power and public policy; beliefs that were publicly allowed were called religion, while those not allowed were called superstition.

Hobbes was one of the 17th-century philosophers whose positions commanded attention during the Enlightenment. His materialist mechanical theory of human sensation appalled his contemporaries in its equation of man and beast and in its denial of a spiritual side to life. But it was his political theory, contained in the *Leviathan*, that most preoccupied enlightened thinkers. The great founders and spokesmen of the political theory of the Enlightenment—Samuel PUFENDORF, John LOCKE, baron de MONTESQUIEU, and Jean-Jacques ROUSSEAU—all had one eye on Hobbesian theory as they developed their own ideas.

Further reading: Thomas Hobbes, *Leviathan, Or the Matter, Forme, and Power of a Commonwealth Ecclesiastical and Civil,* ed. Michael Oakeshott, intro. Richard S. Peters (London: Collier Macmillan, 1962); Alan C. Kors, *D'Holbach's Circle, An Enlightenment in Paris* (Princeton, N.J.: Princeton University Press, 1977); Steve Shapin and Simon Shaffer, *Leviathan and the Air Pump: Hobbes, Boyle, and the Experimental Life* (Princeton, N.J.: Princeton University Press, 1985); Tom Sorell, ed., *Cambridge Companion to Hobbes* (Cambridge: Cambridge University Press, 1996); Richard Tuck, *Hobbes* (New York: Oxford University Press, 2002).

Hoffmann, Friedrich (1660–1742) *German physician and chemist who was the first professor of Medicine at the new University of Halle*

Hoffmann, with Hermann BOERHAAVE, was a major figure in the transmission of IATROMECHANICS (MEDICINE based on the MECHANICAL PHILOSOPHY) to the earliest generations of the ENLIGHTENMENT. A committed teacher who recognized that both older and newer theories of medicine contained valuable ideas, Hoffmann tried to create a viable synthetic system of medicine from components of iatromechanics, IATROCHEMISTRY, and Galenic theory.

Hoffmann combined principles drawn from the mechanical philosophies associated with René DESCARTES and Gottfried LEIBNIZ to create his theory. He accepted the Cartesian vision of the body as machine. But his theory of the animal spirits extended beyond Cartesian dualism in its attempts to explain how the soul operates on the body. Some scholars have argued that his theory incorporated elements of Leibnizian monadology, but this interpretation is a matter of dispute. Hoffmann also retained language about the SYMPATHY between certain organs and humors, which, although derived from older medical traditions, would eventually play an important role in enlightened medicine.

Hoffmann called Georg Ernst STAHL, the physician and chemist whose ANIMISM would later stimulate the birth of VITALISM, to join the HALLE faculty. The two men favored substantially different medical theories, and Stahl eventually left Halle for BERLIN. Stahl always considered Hoffmann his primary professional opponent.

As a young man, Hoffmann had studied chemistry and had worked as a physician in Halberstadt, Saxony, a town renowned for its curative mineral waters. The subject of chemistry fascinated him throughout his life. Although he rejected Stahl's animistic medicine and his PHLOGISTON THEORY, Hoffmann accepted the major portion of Stahl's chemical theory and worked primarily within that framework. He isolated some components of mineral waters and also developed the *Liquor anodynus minerali Hoffmanni* (anodyne liquor of Hoffmann's minerals), better known as Hoffmann's drops.

In 1740, a collection of Hoffmann's works was published in GENEVA under the title *Opera omnia physicomedica* (Complete physical-medical works). This compendium contains his important *Medicinae rationalis systematicae* (Of systematic, rational medicine), which had originally been published in Halle between 1718 and 1720. Hoffmann's works were printed in both French and English translations during the 18th century, and the Latin versions were also reprinted several times before the end of that century.

Hogarth, William (1697–1764) *English engraver and painter*

Hogarth, the son of a schoolmaster, was apprenticed to a silverplate engraver until 1720, then enrolled at St. Martin's Lane Academy for painting instruction. He quickly earned a good reputation as a book illustrator and satirist, possessed of outstanding talents for observing and commenting on aspects of 18th-century English life.

Hogarth created several famous print series including *The Harlot's Progress* (1732); *A Rake's Progress* (1735); *Marriage à la Mode* (1745); *Four Stages of Cruelty* (1751); *Industry and Idleness* (1751); *Four Pictures of an Election* (1755–58); and *Beer Street and Gin Lane*. In addition, Hogarth published individual prints criticizing and highlighting conflicts within English society. These include *The Enraged Musician* (1741); *Strolling Actresses Dressing in a Barn* (1738); and *The Sleeping Congregation* (1736). Hogarth left a satirical print dealing with the politician John WILKES, executed at the time when Wilkes was awaiting trial for libel. He also painted scenes from history and portraits.

Hogarth possessed an acute visual memory. He enhanced it by developing a mnemonic system of shorthand that he used to remember various scenes from the theater and from daily life. He incorporated these scenes into his engravings, using them as a vehicle for his social criticism. Hogarth was a master of psychological penetration and excelled at depicting human feeling. He left an incomplete autobiography and a respected treatise on aesthetic theory, *The Analysis of Beauty* (1753).

The Analysis of Beauty championed aspects of ROCOCO style such as asymmetry, the graceful serpentine line, and other forms of composition that force the eye into constant movement. But Hogarth also liked certain aspects of the BAROQUE STYLE, especially the choice of grand themes as subject matter.

Hogarth's satirical vision of English society was complimented by his social action and his belief that society is responsible for the formation of the individuals within it. He was a life governor of St. Bartholomew's Hospital and also supported the London Foundling Hospital. His paintings hang in both institutions. Having experienced the frustration of having his prints pirated, Hogarth actively championed the 1735 Copyright Act for Engravers, known as Hogarth's Act. The bill provided some protection from pirating for printmakers and helped to establish the concept in law that an individual's artistic, literary, or musical production is a form of private property.

Hogarth was widely known and admired in both England and on the European continent. Horace WALPOLE published a fine assessment of him in the *Anecdotes of*

Marriage à la Mode: "The Marriage Settlement," by William Hogarth, 1745. In the series of engravings entitled *Marriage à la Mode,* Hogarth turned his critical eye to the subject of English aristocratic marriage. *(Courtesy New York Public Library)*

Painting in England. Immanuel KANT, Gotthold Ephraim LESSING, and Georg Christoph LICHTENBERG in Germany all praised Hogarth's works. Some comparisons have been drawn between Hogarth's creations and those of both Jean-Baptiste GREUZE in FRANCE and Pietro LONGHI in Italy.

See also PROSTITUTION.

Holbach, Paul-Henri-Thiry d' (1723–1789) *French philosophe and pamphleteer*

Born Paul Dietrich in the town of Edesheim near Landau in the Rhineland Palatinate, Holbach transcribed Dietrich into French as Thiry or Thierry. Young Thiry moved to PARIS at the age of seven after his mother's death, after having been adopted by a maternal uncle named Holbach. He attended the renowned University of Leiden in the UNITED PROVINCES OF THE NETHERLANDS, where he befriended John WILKES and other progressive English students.

Holbach inherited both the title of baron and a sizable sum of money after his uncle's death. Following normal French practices of the era, he purchased an office as *conseiller-secrétaire du roi* (councillor and secretary to the king) and settled into the intellectual world of Paris.

Holbach served in two ways as a key figure in the French ENLIGHTENMENT. First, he placed his considerable fortune at the disposal of Denis DIDEROT and the project of the ENCYCLOPÉDIE. Second, through the activity of the *coterie d'Holbach,* a circle of like-minded friends, he became a major champion of ATHEISM.

Holbach met Diderot in 1750, just as the latter was preparing the second volume of the *Encyclopédie.* Holbach wrote several unsigned articles for this volume. Later volumes contained his signed articles on subjects from chemistry to religious criticism. His total contribution numbered some 438 articles, excluding those of questionable authorship.

Holbach gathered around him a group of PHILOSOPHES that included Diderot, Nicolas-Antoine BOULANGER, and Jacques-André Naigeon. These men were especially committed to advancing atheism as an alternative to religious faith. They believed that Christianity and, indeed, any RELIGION stood in the path of human PROGRESS and general enlightenment. Acting on this conviction, they produced countless signed and unsigned pamphlets, tracts, and larger works all designed to destroy the grounds for religious belief. Some publications, including Holbach's *Système de la nature* (System of nature; 1770), were original works, but the group also printed atheist tracts that had been circulating throughout France in manuscript form for years. Thus appeared significant works such as *Le militaire philosophe ou Difficultés sur la religion, proposées au P. Malbranche* (The warlike philosopher, or difficulties about religion, proposed to Father Malebranche), the *Traité des trois imposteurs* (Treatise of the three imposters), and the *Lettre de Thrasybule* (Letter of Thrasybulus). The group also drew materials for publication from the writings of English skeptics and deists such as David HUME, John TOLAND, Anthony COLLINS, Thomas WOOLSTON, John Trenchard, and Thomas Hope. Holbach himself had smuggled these works into FRANCE after a 1765 visit to ENGLAND.

Holbach produced many pamphlets attacking Christianity on various grounds. They included *Le bon sens, ou Idées naturelles opposées aux idées surnaturelles* (Common sense, or natural ideas opposed to supernatural ideas; 1772); *J. Brunus redivivus ou Traité des erreurs populaires. Ouvrage critique, historique, et philosophique imité de Pomponace* (J. Brunus Renewed or treatise of popular errors. Critical, historical, and philosophical work modeled after Pomponace; 1771); *Essai sur les préjugés, ou, de l'influence des opinions sur les moeurs et sur le bonheur des hommes* (Essay on prejudices, or of the influence of opinions on the morality and happiness of men; 1770); *Tableau des saints ou examen de l'esprit, de la conduit, des maximes et du mérite des personnages que le Christianisme révere et propose pour modèles* (Table of the saints or research into the mind, conduct, maxims, and merit of the people that Christianity reveres and proposes as models; 1770); *Théologie portative ou Dictionnaire abrégé de la Religion Chrétienne* (Portable theology, or abridged dictionary of the Christian religion; 1768); *Contagion sacrée, ou Histoire naturelle de la superstition, ouvrage traduit de l'Anglois* (Sacred contagion, or natural history of superstition, a work translated from English; 1768); and *Le Christianisme dévoilé, ou examen des principes et des effets de la religion chrétienne* (Christianity unveiled, or investigation of the principles and effects of the Christian religion; 1767, published under the name of Boulanger, but actually written by Holbach).

These pamphlets attempted to discredit religion by linking it with various negative factors. Holbach declared

A Rake's Progress: "Orgy at Rose Tavern," by William Hogarth. This scene was one of a series of engravings by Hogarth commenting on the idleness, banality, and degenerated morality of the English aristocracy. *(Courtesy Culver Pictures, Inc., New York)*

that religion was a product of childlike naiveté and gullibility, the product of fear and of the tendency of people to project their psychological needs onto imaginary gods. These gods, including the Christian God, were capricious or cruel, and the religious impulse in humankind was a kind of contagious disease. Furthermore, religion had not produced moral behavior, but had instead increased vice, had encouraged persecution, and had legitimized fanaticism.

The *Système de la nature ou des loix de monde physique et du monde moral* (System of nature or of the laws of the physical world and the moral world; 1770) offered a novel thesis about the origins of religion built on the tenets of ancient EPICUREAN PHILOSOPHY. Holbach claimed that the religious impulse grows from the human need to avoid pain. In fact, for Holbach, the desire to avoid pain drives all human inquiry about the world. The ultimate goal of such inquiry is to minimize pain and to secure pleasure. Religious belief eliminates certain types of psychological pain, such as anxiety in the face of the unknown and uncontrollable aspects of existence.

Holbach offered SCIENCE and secular authority as antidotes for this pain. Science could explain the unknown and help people to control their environment. Secular authority could provide the government structures needed to ensure tranquil existence and to avoid the evils of religious ENTHUSIASM and fanaticism. For Holbach, such avenues of attack on human anxiety and pain were far preferable to the ignorance perpetrated by religious SUPERSTITION.

Holbach and his circle, then, gave a public voice to the secular trends implicit within enlightened thought. They helped to shape the most radical strands of the French Enlightenment and represent the extremes reached by later enlightened thought.

See also HAPPINESS; MORAL PHILOSOPHY; RADICAL ENLIGHTENMENT.

Further reading: Roger Chartier, *The Cultural Uses of Print in Early Modern France,* tr. Lydia G. Cochrane (Princeton, N.J.: Princeton University Press, 1988); Alan C. Kors, *D'Holbach's Circle: An Enlightenment in Paris* (Princeton, N.J.: Princeton University Press, 1977); Alan Charles Kors, *Atheism in France, 1650–1729,* vol. 1 of The Orthodox Sources of Disbelief (Princeton, N.J.: Princeton University Press, 1990).

Holy Roman Empire Large political entity composed of the multitudinous sovereign German states and of some lands belonging to the HAPSBURG EMPIRE. In the 18th century, the territories of the Holy Roman Empire included most of what are now the nations of GERMANY, BELGIUM, AUSTRIA, the Czech Republic, and Slovenia, as well as parts of modern POLAND, ITALY, and Serbia. On the west, the Holy Roman Empire bordered FRANCE; on the east, the Ottoman Empire and the kingdoms of Poland

and Hungary; on the south, SWITZERLAND and the Italian states; and on the north, the kingdoms of DENMARK and SWEDEN. Originally constituted in the Middle Ages, the Holy Roman Empire had dominated Europe until the terrible Thirty Years' War (1618–48) left it drastically depopulated and physically ruined. The Peace of Westphalia had granted the princes of the empire great freedom of action, including the right to enter foreign alliances separate from the emperor. This allowed the princes in larger kingdoms to develop quite independently from the emperor and hastened the downfall of the empire as an effective power on the European scene.

In the 18th century, the Holy Roman Empire still existed, but it had ceased to play a dominant role in the European balance of power. Instead, its constituent kingdoms, especially Austria, PRUSSIA, and Saxony, were following separate policies based on their specific self-interests.

The Holy Roman Empire was constituted as an elective, limited monarchy. At the beginning of the 18th century, eight German princes and archbishops—the electors—held the right to elect the emperor. During the century, the Bavarian Wittelsbach line died out, and the number of electors was reduced to seven. An imperial diet, which enjoyed the privileges of voting on tax levies and of advising the emperor about legislation, sat at Regensburg. The diet was composed of representatives of the three legal estates of the empire: the nobility, clergy, and townspeople. The position of emperor had been occupied by the Austrian Hapsburgs for centuries, so that it had nearly become a hereditary position. The 18th-century Hapsburgs asserted some central control over the diets, but mostly they concentrated their attentions on ruling their hereditary lands and other territories of the Hapsburg Empire. The Holy Roman Empire and the Hapsburg Empire are not interchangeable names but, rather, denote distinct political entities that happened to have a common ruler.

The Holy Roman Empire existed officially in Europe until 1806, when Francis II, who had assumed the title Francis I, emperor of Austria, relinquished the title of Holy Roman Emperor. At the Congress of Vienna (1814–15), the political structure of Europe was formally revised in the aftermath of the Napoleonic era, and the Holy Roman Empire was officially dissolved. Of its constituent states, 39, including Prussia and Austria, formed the brief-lived German Confederation, while Bavaria, Württemberg, Hanover, and Saxony were recognized as independent kingdoms.

homosexuality Sexual orientation toward people of the same sex. Although the idea of homosexuality in its modern conception as an identity did not exist during the ENLIGHTENMENT, preferences and behavior that we would today designate as homosexual were very much in evidence. Political and religious authorities stigmatized and repressed such homosexual behavior. Enlightenment philosophers, on the other hand, recognized the existence of homosexuality in various periods of history (especially ancient Greece and Rome) and in the animal kingdom. Although their belief in TOLERANCE and individual LIBERTY led some of these thinkers to a certain degree of openmindedness regarding homosexuality, they nonetheless frequently displayed a conservative morality and an emphasis on procreative sex. These two attitudes coexist in the thought of VOLTAIRE, who acknowledged that homosexuality was natural while remaining unable or unwilling to defend it outright.

In the 18th century, there was a general impression that homosexual behavior was on the rise; whether or not this was true, there is evidence of a certain amount of sexual freedom, especially in certain milieus and at certain moments. Shifts in sexual attitudes in ENGLAND at the beginning of the 18th century are due in large part to the Restoration of Charles II, whose French upbringing brought the English court a return to THEATER and increasingly open sexuality. The LIBERTINE ethics of the time allowed homosexuality to feature as simply another kind of pleasure-seeking. Indeed, the earl of Rochester was bold enough, in his play *Sodom; or, The Quintessence of Debauchery*, to imagine the entire court of England as a homosexual paradise.

The Restoration stage could also serve to caricature and mock homosexuals, as frequently occurred through the stock character of the fop, who was depicted as effeminate and occupying an amorphous sexual identity. The poet Alexander POPE used such imagery in his satiric attacks on Lord Hervey, whom he saw as belonging to a "third sex" and whom he declared an "amphibious thing." In this way, the visibility of the homosexual was a double-edged sword: It could lead to acceptance, but it could also provoke hostile reactions seeking to affirm a normative heterosexual notion of masculinity.

Despite the aura of sexual freedom that the English and French courts sometimes displayed, homosexuality remained illegal in both countries and was punishable by death. In fact, the authorities usually preferred to exile homosexuals or to give them prison sentences in order to avoid publicizing their acts, for fear that others might be inspired to imitate them. Nevertheless, CAPITAL PUNISHMENT for committing homosexual acts was not unheard of. In France, for instance, Etienne Benjamin Des Chaufours was burned at the stake for such acts in 1726 (a punishment condemned by Voltaire, despite his ambivalent feelings toward homosexuality).

In this legal climate, it was necessary for homosexuals to establish networks and find strategies that would allow them to engage in sexual behavior in relative safety. According to French police archives of the 18th century, the authorities were aware that several public gardens and boulevards functioned as places of homosexual encounters. In England, the early 18th century also saw transgressive male homosexuality established as a part of the culture in the growth of molly houses, where cross-dressing men gathered. Such establishments were associated particularly with men of the lower classes.

Women's sexual behavior was subjected to closer scrutiny and more stringent standards than was that of men. Female homosexuality was associated with actresses and the theater—a milieu that was already connected to PROSTITUTION. Female homosexuality was perceived as a threat to procreation and to masculine authority, yet the social and financial pressures for women to marry were so strong that they rarely entered into public view as confirmed homosexuals, as was the case with men. Thus, the public interest in male homosexuality frequently revolved around a few prominent figures, whereas female homosexuality, while still a concern of the period, remained more in the background, in a more private and shadowy context.

See also WOMEN AND THE ENLIGHTENMENT.

Further reading: Netta Murray Goldsmith, *The Worst of Crimes: Homosexuality and the Law in Eighteenth-Century London* (Brookfield, Vt.: Ashgate, 1998); George E. Haggerty, *Men in Love: Masculinity and Sexuality in the Eighteenth Century* (New York: Columbia University Press, 1999); Jeffrey Merrick and Bryant T. Ragan, Jr., eds., *Homosexuality in Early Modern France* (New York: Oxford University Press, 2001); Randolph Trumbach, *Sex and the Gender Revolution: Heterosexuality and the Third Gender in Enlightenment London* (Chicago: University of Chicago Press, 1998); Elizabeth Susan Wahl, *Invisible Relations: Representations of Female Intimacy in the Age of Enlightenment* (Stanford, Calif.: Stanford University Press, 1999).

honor Concept of personal worth or status based on a code of behavior and values. This code involved rigid distinctions along class and gender lines. Honor was considered a purely aristocratic phenomenon, and masculine honor was tied up with notions of valor, integrity, and the family line. To a large degree, such notions were inherited from an earlier chivalric model according to which nobility was a result of service to the king through warfare. Impugning a man's courage was not only a personal insult, but also an implicit challenge to his place in his family line. Conversely, attacking a man's ancestors for lack of valor or for impure blood (meaning that they were not truly noble because extramarital affairs had introduced nonnoble elements) was an insult to his status, perceived to depend on his connection to an illustrious family tree.

In this context, it can be clearly seen that the behavior of women played an important role in the concept of masculine honor. A husband who was cuckolded by his wife could not be sure that his children were his own. This was shameful on a personal level and a threat to his ability to preserve the nobility of his family line. It should be noted that in European society a woman's honor was almost always perceived to be the possession of the men of her family, obliged to maintain the nobility of their name and their heritage. If a woman was seduced or raped, it was up to her father or brothers to seek revenge if she was unmarried, and it was up to her husband to repair the injury to his honor if she was married.

The honor of women, therefore, was limited to their sexual conduct, whereas a man's honor could take several different forms. Frequently, the mere appearance of sexual impropriety was enough to threaten a woman's reputation. Such scandal could ruin a family's or husband's reputation, and those women unfortunate enough to lose their honor before marriage had dismal prospects of finding a suitable husband, and, by extension, a secure financial situation. Many female writers depicted the internal struggles that women experienced due to the critical eye of the public, and their characters frequently invoked a personal code of conduct based not on masculine honor, but on notions of virtue and love. In their novels, the English authors Eliza HAYWOOD and Charlotte LENNOX illustrated the unfairness of their society, which imposed a stringent standard of conduct on women, while men were permitted a much wider range of social and sexual behavior.

The concept of honor can best be identified at moments of crisis, when a man was forced to defend his honor against the insult of another man. The most common method for restoring one's honor was to challenge the offending party to a duel. While this practice was officially banned in many countries, it nevertheless persisted, functioning as a public enactment of a man's defense of his reputation. A man's honor did not only depend on safeguarding the honor of the women in his family, it could also concern matters of courage and integrity. In the French writer Laclos's novel *Les liaisons dangereuses* (Dangerous liaisons; 1782), the young Danceny challenges the LIBERTINE Valmont to a duel when he learns that Valmont has seduced Cécile, the girl he loves. Danceny is not motivated by a need to defend Cécile's honor, as she is not part of his family line. Valmont has shown such disregard for Danceny through his treachery that the young man must affirm his self-worth by demonstrating that he cannot be treated in such a disrespectful manner.

The concept of honor often worked against ENLIGHTENMENT notions of EQUALITY, as can be seen in a striking example from the youth of VOLTAIRE. In 1726, Voltaire made a witty remark at the theater that embarrassed the chevalier de Rohan. The aristocratic Rohan would not treat Voltaire, who was of modest origins, as an equal by challenging him to a duel. Instead, Rohan sought revenge by having his servants lie in wait for Voltaire and attack him. After this rude treatment, Voltaire intended to challenge Rohan to a duel, even though his birth did not grant him this prerogative, but the chevalier's family intervened and had Voltaire thrown into prison by the king for this audacity. Voltaire managed to obtain his freedom only by exiling himself to ENGLAND for more than two years.

In the writings of Enlightenment authors one finds tensions in the notion of honor. For MONTESQUIEU, honor can be connected to aristocratic virtue and independence of spirit, as seen in the lives of the ancient Romans. For Jean-Jacques ROUSSEAU, however, honor is an artificial concept that responds to no real human need; it is part of the corruption of modern society, stemming from the same selfish urge for dominance that led to the invention of private property. Although the phenomenon of dueling would continue even into the 20th century, notions of aristocratic honor could never find the same kind of widespread acceptance and fervent belief after the FRENCH REVOLUTION broke with the notion of an inherently noble class.

See also WOMEN AND THE ENLIGHTENMENT.

Further reading: Robert Baldick, *The Duel: A History of Dueling* (London: Chapman & Hall, 1965); Geoffrey Best, *Honour Among Men and Nations: Transformation of an Idea* (Toronto: University of Toronto Press, 1982); Elizabeth A. Foyster, *Manhood in Early Modern England* (New York: Longman, 1999); Robert A. Nye, *Masculinity and Male Codes of Honor in Modern France* (New York: Oxford University Press, 1993).

Houdon, Jean-Antoine (1741–1828) *French sculptor whose works immortalized major figures of the late Enlightenment*
Houdon, born at Versailles, received a formal education in sculpture from the Royal Academy of Fine Arts. He earned the Prix de Rome in 1761 and thus had the opportunity to study at the French Academy in ROME from 1764 to 1768.

Houdon ultimately abandoned the decorative sculptural style of his ROCOCO predecessors and developed a neoclassical style that he believed reflected the artistic aesthetic of ancient Rome. He became a master at sculptural portraiture, receiving commissions from Duke Ernst II of Sachsen-Gotha (GERMANY), CATHERINE II (THE GREAT) of Russia, and Thomas JEFFERSON. He exhibited his creations regularly at the biennial art salons held at the Louvre.

Houdon's work was not hindered by the FRENCH REVOLUTION, and he remained active through the Napoleonic era. He created a portrait of Napoleon for which he was awarded membership in the Légion d'Honneur. He was a member of the Institut de France and taught at the École des Beaux Arts.

Among his famous sculptural portraits are busts of George WASHINGTON, VOLTAIRE (four different versions), Denis DIDEROT, Christoph Willibald GLUCK, Catherine the Great (not created from live sittings), the marquis de Lafayette, Jacques NECKER, and the comte de Mirabeau. In

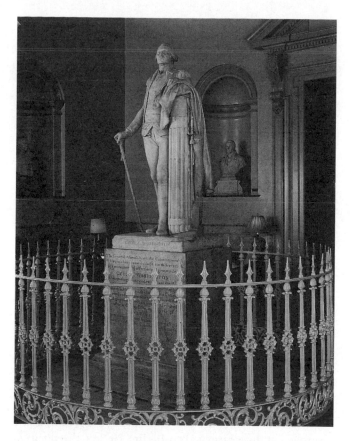

Monument of George Washington by Jean-Antoine Houdon. Houdon left a priceless legacy for students of the Enlightenment, with his numerous full sculptures, busts, and death masks of 18th-century leaders. *(Courtesy Virginia State Library and Archives)*

addition, Houdon created the famous mask of Jean-Jacques ROUSSEAU from a cast of his dead face, the seated figure of Voltaire at the Comédie Française in PARIS, and a famous reclining figure, *Morpheus*. Sculptures of mythological subjects included *Vestale, Minerve, Diane,* and *Apollon*.

See also NEOCLASSICISM.

Huguenots Term, whose origins remain unclear, that was used to describe the French adherents of CALVINISM. A form of PROTESTANTISM created by John Calvin, a 16th-century French theologian and humanist, Calvinism won many converts throughout Europe in the 16th century. Although Calvinism offered a THEOLOGY that differed from that of ROMAN CATHOLICISM, the persecution of French Calvinist Huguenots by central authorities resulted more from the political ramifications of Calvinist theology and from the threats posed by the Huguenots' centralized organization than from the exclusive spiritual content of Calvinist teachings.

Among the French subjects who converted to Calvinism were powerful and often unruly provincial noblemen

with vast resources at their disposal; townsmen engaged in business, crafts, and commerce; peasants; and many women. These people formed a highly structured Huguenot organization built on the political principle of representation, which was, however, directed from the Swiss city-state of GENEVA, the international headquarters of Calvinism. This Huguenot organization presented serious challenges—both religious and political—to the authority of 16th-century French kings. Not only did it encourage republicanism as a political form, but also it was, in fact, a semi-independent political entity operating within the boundaries of the French kingdom.

Attempts at resolving doctrinal differences between Huguenots and Catholics had no success. Likewise, no compromise could be reached regarding either the thorny matter of church polity (government and structure) or the definition of relations between the priesthood and the laity. The Huguenot threat was perceived by the French Crown and by Catholic factions within the kingdom as intolerable.

Finally, in 1560, a bloody civil war broke out in France when it became clear that King Henry III would leave no direct male heir. The nearest male successor was a chief of the Huguenots, Henry of Navarre. Ultra-Catholic factions who also had legitimate, if more distant, claims to the French throne, could not tolerate the idea of a Huguenot (heretic in their eyes) ruler of France. They rebelled in the name of preserving the kingdom of France from heresy. A Catholic candidate for the throne, the duke of Guise, was put forth as the legitimate heir of Henry III and received support from both ROME and SPAIN.

The French civil wars (Wars of Religion) lasted from 1560 until 1598. In 1589, Henry of Navarre claimed the French throne as Henry IV after separate assassinations had removed not only King Henry III but also the duke of Guise from power. The troops of Henry IV fought until 1598 to subjugate internal dissenters within the kingdom and to drive the Spanish out of French territory. The process was aided by Henry's official conversion in 1593 to the Catholic Church, an act that allowed him to be crowned in 1594, with the blessings of the pope.

With the cessation of hostilities in 1598, Henry IV issued the Edict of Nantes, a decree that granted limited civic and religious tolerance to Huguenots living within the borders of his kingdom. Certain cities such as La Rochelle were recognized as Huguenot citadels, thereby preserving a base of power for the group. Huguenots were, however, forbidden to gather for worship or for any other purpose within 20 miles of PARIS. Limited rights of worship were granted in the remaining French cities, and special regional courts were set up to deal with Huguenot legal cases.

After the assassination of Henry IV in 1610, the devout Catholic Louis XIII assumed the throne. With the assistance of his powerful minister Richellieu, Louis XIII began to curtail the already limited political rights of the Huguenots. These rights, particularly the one that preserved certain cities as armed Huguenot citadels, were allowing Huguenots to function as a major source of aristocratic opposition to the central authority of the king. In a series of short civil wars, Louis XIII and Richelieu subjugated the Huguenot fortresses and eliminated most of their independent power base.

The process of curtailing the provisions of the Edict of Nantes continued under LOUIS XIV and his minister, Louvois, but the repression became harsher. To Louis XIV, the presence of Huguenots in his kingdom created intolerable religious disunity and constituted a threat to his absolute rule. Forced mass conversions of Huguenots were carried out by dragoons (soldiers) who were also billeted (quartered) indefinitely in Huguenot households, thereby creating financial hardships. Rights of worship were further curtailed. Finally, in 1685, Louis XIV revoked the Edict of Nantes, thereby authorizing persecution, imprisonment, or banishment for anyone who openly practiced Huguenot forms of worship. The last Huguenot persecutions occurred in the early 18th century with attacks against the CAMISARDS in the Cévennes region of France and against the WALDENSIANS in SAVOY.

The revocation of the Edict of Nantes had serious consequences for France. Great numbers of 17th-century Huguenots were successful merchants, businessmen, lawyers, and intellectuals. They fled from France to states where they would be tolerated: ENGLAND, the UNITED PROVINCES OF THE NETHERLANDS, PRUSSIA, and the British colonies in North America. Their host countries benefited considerably from their talents. Some historians believe that this great Huguenot exodus from France seriously hindered the development of French trade and industry in the ensuing decades, but others believe that the effects have been overstated.

During the ENLIGHTENMENT, the persecution of Huguenots became a symbol for some PHILOSOPHES of the bigotry and error fostered by RELIGION. In this sense, the Huguenot question helped to stimulate an emotional revulsion against religious bigotry and to foster the intellectual discussions that ultimately produced calls for TOLERATION.

See also ABSOLUTISM.

Further reading: R. D. Gwynn, *Huguenot Heritage* (Brighton: Sussex Academic Press, 2001).

human nature   *See* EDUCATION; MECHANICAL PHILOSOPHY; MORAL PHILOSOPHY; NATURE; POLITICAL THEORY; PSYCHOLOGY.

Humboldt, Alexander von (1769–1859) *German naturalist and traveler*
Alexander von Humboldt combined the natural history style of scientific inquiry that characterized the ENLIGHT-ENMENT with the more rigorous empirical SCIENCE of the 19th century in his work as a naturalist. His observations, made during wide-ranging travels around the globe, and the conclusions he drew from them, formed the foundation of modern geography and meteorology.

Humboldt was born in BERLIN. His father was a Prussian military officer, and his mother was descended from a noble family; his older brother was the scholar and statesman Wilhelm von HUMBOLDT. Alexander attended university at Frankfurt an der Oder and GÖTTINGEN, where he heard lectures by, among others, anthropologist Johann Friedrich BLUMENBACH. In 1789, during a break from studies at Göttingen, Humboldt made a scientific journey up the Rhine River, publishing his observations on a wide range of natural phenomena he recorded, including a detailed account of the region's topography and geology, a year later. While at Göttingen, he also met the naturalist Georg FORSTER, who had accompanied Captain James COOK on his second voyage in search of a southern continent thought to keep the world in balance. These events helped Humboldt to focus his efforts on acquiring the training necessary to pursue life as a scientist and traveler. He continued his studies in Hamburg (economics and languages), Freiberg (geology), and Jena (physiology and ASTRONOMY).

In 1792, Humboldt was appointed Prussian assessor of mines, and he returned to Berlin. He left the position following the death of his mother in 1796 and the receipt of an invitation to join a voyage of discovery around the world. When the planned journey fell through, Humboldt went to Marseilles with botanist Aimé Bonpland, who was also to have gone on the failed expedition. In Marseilles, the two were unable to gain passage to Egypt, so they went on to MADRID. With the help of a powerful minister and their own reputations, Humboldt and Bonpland joined an expedition to Central and South America that sailed in June 1799.

For the next five years, Humboldt compiled an astounding and groundbreaking body of scientific observations. His data on meteor showers, which he began collecting in November 1799 in Brazil, showed for the first time that these were periodic, regular natural phenomena. In 1801, the explorers ascended into the Andes, where Humboldt made the observations on which his correlation between temperature and altitude were founded. In November 1802, Humboldt visited the Peruvian guano fields; he was responsible for introducing the substance into Europe through his accounts of its value as a fertilizer.

Upon their return to Europe in 1804, Humboldt and Bonpland immediately began publishing their findings. The work, entitled *Voyage de Humboldt et Bonpland* (Humboldt and Bonpland's voyage; 1805–34), eventually ran to 23 volumes. In the publication Humboldt introduced the use of *isotherms* in 1817 to geographically map climate conditions. He also argued for the relationship between geography and foliage, stating that the types of plants that grow in a particular area depend on its topography.

In 1827, Humboldt returned to Berlin at the request of Friedrich Wilhelm III, king of Prussia. In 1829, Humboldt convinced the Russian government to set up stations to measure magnetism and weather across northern Asia, and he persuaded the British Empire to do the same throughout its dominions in 1836. The resulting data allowed Humboldt to posit, among other things, an increase in magnetic force as one moves from the equator toward the poles.

The last two decades of Humboldt's life were consumed with *Kosmos* (Cosmos; 1845–62), his attempt at devising a universal scientific theory. The work was based on a lifetime of scientific observation and thought, and it reflects the fact that Humboldt, though he had acquired the empirical tools of 19th-century science, was nevertheless rooted in the all-encompassing attempts at understanding NATURE that formed the bulk of Enlightenment inquiry. *Kosmos* had its origins in a series of lectures Humboldt had given in Berlin in 1827 and 1828, in which he proposed a creative and vibrant idea of the physical world rooted in data gleaned from empirical observation. Humboldt stated that the study, which eventually ran to five volumes, was meant to be composed of two parts: a general introduction, followed by detailed discussions of topics such as "outer space," "all of astronomical physics," "the solid body of our earth," "a brief geognosy," and "a geography of animals." When the work first appeared in print, there was nothing else like it. It represents one of the last attempts to encompass the totality of NATURAL PHILOSOPHY from a single vantage point. Humboldt died on May 6, 1859.

Further reading: Douglas Botting, *Humboldt and the Cosmos* (London: Joseph, 1973); Alexander von Humboldt, *Cosmos* (Baltimore: Johns Hopkins University Press, 1997).

Humboldt, Wilhelm von (1767–1835) *German philologist, political theorist, historian, and statesman*

The older brother of Alexander von HUMBOLDT, Wilhelm was born in Potsdam. Following his early education in BERLIN, Wilhelm von Humboldt attended university in GÖTTINGEN and Jena, where he met the poet and playwright Friedrich SCHILLER as well as Johann Wolfgang von GOETHE. Under their influence, Humboldt inclined toward German idealism, rejecting the limiting categories of the ENLIGHTENMENT in favor of a more open approach to life and knowledge that was rooted in realizing the potential of the individual. Humboldt came to believe that the individual could represent the unity of diversity, and that the greatest happiness resulted from the individ-

ual realizing his potential. With his wide-ranging interests and experiences, Humboldt can be seen as an embodiment of this ideal.

Humboldt's earliest publications indicate his extensive interests. His *Ideen zu einem Versuch die Grenzen der Wirksamkeit des Staates zu bestimmen* (Ideas on an attempt to determine the boundaries of state action; 1792) posits Humboldt's version of utilitarianism (see UTILITY), a state in which a maximum of freedom from political constraints allows the individual freedom to pursue education and religious enlightenment. John Stuart Mill directly acknowledged his debt to Humboldt's *Ideen*, which is apparent in Mill's *On Liberty*. Humboldt's translations of Pindar's odes appeared in 1795 and 1797, his commentary on Goethe's *Herrmann and Dorothea* was published in 1800, and Humboldt's epic poem *Rome* appeared during his tenure as Prussian resident and minister plenipotentiary in ROME, which began in 1802.

During the first two decades of the 19th century, Humboldt was consumed with his activities as a statesman. In 1809, after his appointment in Rome ended, he was made Prussia's minister of education. Though he held the position for only a short time (1809–10), Humboldt subjected the Prussian school system to drastic reforms based on the educational ideas of Johann Heinrich PESTALOZZI and rooted in his own conviction that EDUCATION was a means for individuals to realize their potential. He sent Prussian teachers to visit Pestalozzi in SWITZERLAND and observe his educational methods. Humboldt was also instrumental in founding the University of Berlin (now Humboldt University). He went to VIENNA in 1812 as Prussian ambassador, where he helped secure AUSTRIA's alliance with RUSSIA and PRUSSIA against FRANCE. He signed the capitulation of PARIS in 1815 and negotiated a treaty between Prussia and Saxony that helped solidify Prussia's position as a leading German power.

During this time, Humboldt also continued to pursue his interest in LANGUAGE, both as a translator and a philologist. He published a translation of Aeschylus's *Agamemnon* in 1816. His interest in the Basque language also dates from this period. He visited SPAIN and published his *Examination of the First Inhabitants through the Basque Language* in 1821. In the work, Humboldt argues that the commonalities between Basque and the languages of Africa offer proof of the origins of early Spaniards on the Continent.

Humboldt continued to elaborate on his theories about language until the end of his life. His final scholarly work, on the ancient Kavi language of Java, which he left unfinished when he died on April 8, 1835, offers the fullest exposition of his theories. His brother Alexander helped edit the work, which was published between 1836 and 1840 and is Wilhelm von Humboldt's most important contribution to the field of linguistics. In it, Humboldt argues that a language conveys and contains the inner life and collective knowledge of the people who speak it. Words express this inner life and collective knowledge, and that is what separates words from mere sounds. Humboldt posits that philology classifies languages according to differences in their expressions of this inner life, which finds articulation not only in words, but also in grammar.

Further reading: Wilhelm von Humboldt, *Essays on Language* (New York: Lang, 1997).

Hume, David (1711–1776) *Scottish philosopher, historian, economist, and essayist, one of the major figures of the middle decades of the Enlightenment*

Hume investigated problems of human knowledge (EPISTEMOLOGY) that neither the Continental RATIONALISM nor the British EMPIRICISM of the 17th century had satisfactorily answered. In the course of his inquiries, he also restated the problem of SKEPTICISM for intellectuals of the middle period of the ENLIGHTENMENT. He provided the analytical base from which modern empirical philosophy has developed.

Hume's analyses had implications not only for epistemology, but also for PSYCHOLOGY, MORAL PHILOSOPHY, and NATURAL PHILOSOPHY. He is famous for his pioneering

Portrait of David Hume. Hume revived the legacy of skepticism during the middle years of the Enlightenment, giving it new power as a tool for critical inquiry into all varieties of human knowledge. *(Courtesy New York Public Library)*

investigations of the concept of RELATIONS and especially for his analysis of our ideas of cause and effect (causal relations). He laid the foundations for a theory of mental association that provided the materials from which David HARTLEY constructed his association psychology. Hume also inquired into the epistemological and psychological origins of our ideas of self and of individual identity, a problem that acquired increasing urgency as 18th-century philosophers abandoned the Christian concept of the soul.

In conjunction with these investigations, Hume presented a theory of ethics and morality rooted entirely in the natural operations of the human mind. He extended the idea of the moral sense that had been used by predecessors such as Francis HUTCHESON and Anthony Cooper, third earl of SHAFTESBURY.

Hume outlined a youthful version of these ideas in his TREATISE OF HUMAN NATURE (3 vols., 1738–39). Although he later repudiated the *Treatise*, dismissing it as an immature inquiry, it became his most influential work. Hume preferred the later ENQUIRY CONCERNING HUMAN UNDERSTANDING (1758), a revision of the first two volumes of the *Treatise*, and his *Enquiry Concerning the Principles of Morals* (1751), the reworked third volume.

Hume posed a fundamental question: How do human beings gain any knowledge about the external world in which they live? His answer began with sensory experience, borrowing the concepts of sense impression and idea from John LOCKE. Hume believed that the data derived from human sensory experience (impressions) were the fundamental facts in a human science. Any information that is not rooted in this experience is not properly called knowledge but is rather a matter of belief.

But there is a problem with this sensory experience. I look at a tree, for example, and I say that I see a tree. I touch a tree and say that the tree exists. I assume in making these statements that a real material tree exists out in the world. But I really know nothing about this tree except that I have visual images and tactile sensations that I label "tree." I have no way of knowing whether or not these images and sensations have anything to do with the real object in the world, nor do I really even know whether or not it exists. After all, the senses can deceive. We see mirages of water in the desert, and we see a moon in the night sky that appears many times larger than the other heavenly bodies. For Hume, then, sensation is the foundation of our knowledge, but it is a foundation that has nothing necessarily to do with external reality.

What then, is the knowledge that we have about the world and about the order in it? Hume explains that the mind builds knowledge from basic sense impressions by transforming then first into simple ideas (fainter copies of the impression) that then combine freely, creating complex ideas. But although the possible combinations are infinite, the mind tends, as a matter of habit, to join ideas according to three basic patterns of association: proximity in time and space; cause and effect; or resemblance. Hume called these three patterns of association "natural relations."

Hume analyzed the problem of relations, allotting extended time to the subject of casuality (cause and effect relations). He demonstrated that our assumption that event X causes event Y (fire causes heat, for example) is based on the fact that the second event (Y or heat) always follows the first (X or fire) in our experience. We assume that this means that X actually causes Y (fire actually causes heat). However, we cannot know with philosophical certainty that the next time X occurs, Y will follow. Similarly, although the sun has arisen every morning since the beginning of history, we cannot know for certain that it will arise tomorrow morning. We assume that it will because of our experience, but that assumption is actually rooted in faith or belief rather than in certain knowledge.

Hume focused on the relation of cause and effect because it was the single most important foundation upon which empirical systems of knowledge were built. He showed that such systems—indeed all systems of knowledge based on experience—were matters of belief or faith rather than of certainty. He thus called into question the reliability and foundations of all empirical science. Hume, the skeptic, made a powerful negative statement about the program for building comprehensive systems of knowledge that British empiricism had inherited from Francis BACON and John Locke.

Hume turned a similarly critical eye toward rationalism, showing the limits of logic as a tool for gaining practical understanding. According to Hume, neither rationalism nor empiricism yielded true knowledge about the external world. Humans were actually acting on belief in all their dealings with the world of objects and everyday existence. Belief, therefore, was essential to the practical existence of people and the only possible antidote against extreme skepticism. As a result, Hume determined also to investigate the foundations for belief.

Hume used his system of epistemology and psychology as a base from which to examine religious belief. His DIALOGUES CONCERNING NATURAL RELIGION (1779) and *Natural History of Religion* (1757) offered a psychological interpretation of religious forms that was derived in part from the account provided by Pierre BAYLE in the HISTORICAL AND CRITICAL DICTIONARY. Hume was accused of ATHEISM, and in 1761 the Roman Inquisition placed all of his books on the Index of Forbidden Books.

Hume examined the question of belief from the standpoint of natural human psychology, inevitably extending his inquiry to cover religious as well as practical beliefs. He excluded the question of the existence of an immaterial soul from his inquiry, saying that it was a completely unintelligible question. He meant by this statement that neither REASON nor experience could provide knowledge about the question, and that it therefore must be dropped from consideration. Hume similarly excluded from investigation the contents of Christian or other revealed knowledge. These things, having by definition come from God to supplement human understanding, lay outside the realm of human knowledge and, therefore, could not be discussed.

Hume turned his attention to the practical manifestations of belief, to religious institutions, customs, and ritual practices. He rejected all the major arguments of DEISM about natural human religious instincts. He retained the argument for God's existence from design (PHYSICO-THEOLOGY) but was unwilling to equate the being whose intellect was represented in the order of the universe with any God modeled on the Judeo-Christian deity.

For Hume, the gods were created as a result of the fears of primitive peoples faced with a world of incomprehensible events. These early people projected their fears out into the cosmos, embodying them as the various gods and goddesses of antiquity.

The HISTORY of religions in all cultures tended to follow a process of development that began with polytheism (belief in many gods) and resulted in monotheism (belief in one God), but this process was not for Hume one that could be equated with PROGRESS. In fact, for Hume, monotheistic religions—Christianity, Judaism, and Islam—were pernicious corruptions that tended to foster dogmatic beliefs, intolerance, and religious ENTHUSIASM. Only by constant striving, by the application of knowledge derived from experience and carefully pondered, could people hope to rise above this cycle of religious flux and reflux. Human belief, therefore, was a dangerous element, necessary to existence but requiring constant attention to prevent it from acquiring harmful forms.

As an alternative to ethical systems derived from religious dogma, Hume offered a naturalistic theory that founded morality in the operations of the mind. Unlike the rationalists who offered naturalistic moral philosophies, Hume based moral behavior not in reason, but rather in the emotions. Emotions (or passions) can be either calm or violent. Violent emotions, consisting of either pain or pleasure, directly motivate human action. The morally good is that which is pleasurable; the morally bad is that which is painful.

Calm emotions have more complicated sources that involve both feelings of pain or pleasure and rational reflection on the UTILITY (usefulness) of behavior. Utility is not defined solely in terms of SELF-INTEREST, but rather, also takes into account the good of other people.

The psychological mechanism of SYMPATHY allows people to understand the effects of an action on others. The action of sympathy is helped by the fact that human beings possess common sentiments of morality. These common sentiments constitute a sixth sense, the moral sense, that operates like the other physical senses (sight, smell, etc.). Experiences that arouse this sixth sense produce sentiments of benevolence.

Moral sense theory, especially in the form presented by Hume, received considerable criticism within Scottish and English circles. The Scottish school of common sense philosophy developed in direct reaction to Hume. Its adherents—Richard PRICE, Thomas REID, George Campbell, James Oswald, and James Beattie—raised the common sense into a reliable source of knowledge that could address the weaknesses of reason and sensory experience. Aspects of Hume's thought were positively developed by Adam SMITH and by Immanuel KANT, the great Prussian philosopher of the late AUFKLÄRUNG.

The final realm in which Hume helped to shape the thought of his era encompassed both POLITICAL THEORY and history. He published a six-volume *History of England* (1754–62) that covered English history from the time of Caesar's invasion of the British Isles to the GLORIOUS REVOLUTION of 1688. Several essays explored facets of political theory: "Of the Original Contract"; "Of Some Remarkable Customs"; and "That Politics may be reduced to a Science."

For Hume, justice, the original creation of human societies, and law all derived from the emotional impression of their utility. They had no basis in the rational (reason-based) order of things. As a result, legitimacy derived not from some rationally conceived social compact or contract arranged between people and their chosen leaders, but rather arose from the actual ability of leaders to exercise power and to maintain security. The legitimacy of the Glorious Revolution of 1688 lay, for example, in the fact that people had accepted it, not in the fact that a small group of conspirators had offered the throne to WILLIAM III AND MARY II.

Hume's interpretation of English history rejected Whig party attempts to root the limited monarchy and representative government of the English constitution in ancient English history. He pointed out that historical analysis could also support the claims of monarchical ABSOLUTISM and insisted that the most accurate depiction of English history would emphasize conflict between competing political forms.

Underlying all of Hume's work was the ideal of creating a SCIENCE OF MAN rooted like natural SCIENCE in the close observation of actual experience. Observation would reveal facts about human action that could then be subjected to a process of induction in order to identify the few principles that shape the whole system. Hume, of course, often tended to use this close observation to destroy the very ideal of building systems. But he backed away from embracing the total skepticism that his logical positions demanded.

Hume was the younger son of a gentry family from SCOTLAND. He attended the University of Edinburgh, but he found formal education distasteful. He applied himself instead to intense independent reading. In 1729, partly as the result of exhaustion, he suffered a nervous breakdown.

After an unsuccessful and uninspiring business venture, he moved in 1734 to FRANCE. There, at La Flèche, the Loire valley town where René DESCARTES and Marin MERSENNE had been educated, Hume devoted himself to studying and to writing the *Treatise of Human Nature*.

He moved to ENGLAND in 1737, eager to launch his intellectual career. But the reception of his treatise was disappointing. A second venture, *Essays, Moral and Political* (1741–42), received some positive notice. Hume applied for a professorship at the University of Edinburgh, but his detractors accused him of atheism and heresy on account of his philosophy.

Hume worked at several jobs between 1744 and 1763, serving as a tutor to the marquess of Annandale, as secretary and assistant to General James Saint Claire, and as the librarian to the Faculty of Advocates (Law) in EDINBURGH. He continued during these years to write and to publish. The *Enquiry Concerning Human Understanding* appeared in 1758, preceded by his successful *Political Discourses* (1752) and the *History of England* (1754–62).

Hume returned to France in 1763 as secretary to the earl of Hertford, British ambassador to France. In PARIS, Hume joined the enlightened intellectual world, attending salons and arguing his positions. He befriended Jean-Jacques ROUSSEAU, who traveled to LONDON with Hume in 1766. The two men soon quarreled, and Hume, like other PHILOSOPHES, felt obliged to defend himself in print against accusations by Rousseau (see the pamphlet "A Concise and Genuine Account of the Dispute between Mr. Hume and Mr. Rousseau," 1766). After two years in London as undersecretary of state, Hume moved back to Edinburgh in 1769, remaining in that city for the rest of his life. He died in 1776.

Hume was one of the most controversial figures of the 18th century, and his work definitely helped to shape the ideas of the later Enlightenment. He was subjected to sharp criticism and disparagement in British intellectual circles. In France, however, he was received as the leading English intellectual and was enormously popular. Circles of enlightened Germans also revered his work. The mixed reception of his work brings the differences between the Enlightenment in Britain, France, and GERMANY into sharp relief. Whatever their indebtedness to one another, they remain distinct movements. The British movement could not embrace the radical philosophy and criticism of religion contained in Hume's work. It remained for the French and the Germans to recognize the value of his work for their programs of criticism and reform.

See also AESTHETICS; FREE TRADE; RIGHTS; SOCIAL INSTITUTIONS OF THE ENLIGHTENMENT; SPINOZA (for a comparison of ethical systems).

Further reading: David Hume, *Dialogues Concerning Natural Religion and the Posthumous Essays,* ed. Richard H. Popkin (Indianapolis: Hackett Publishing, 1980); David Hume, *An Enquiry Concerning Human Understand-*

ing, ed. Eric Steinberg (Indianapolis: Hackett Publishing, 1977); David Hume, *A Treatise of Human Nature*, ed. L. A. Selby-Bigge (Oxford: Clarendon Press, 1968; reprint of 1888 ed.); Anthony Quinton, *Hume* (New York: Routledge, 1999); Claudia M. Schmidt, *David Hume: Reason in History* (University Park, Pa.: Pennsylvania State University Press, 2003).

Hungary   Large kingdom of eastern Europe, which, in the 18th century, formed one of the major divisions of the HAPSBURG EMPIRE. The capital city of Hungary was Pest, one of two towns—Buda and Pest (hence BUDAPEST)—that flanked opposite banks of the Danube River. The territory of Hungary lay between AUSTRIA, POLAND, and the Ottoman Empire. At the beginning of the 18th century, the population of Hungary was seriously depleted on account of losses during the continual wars with the Ottoman Turks. After the Peace of Passarowitz in 1718, however, the Turkish threat to Hungary was finally removed. The Hapsburg rulers encouraged settlement in the kingdom, and by the end of the 18th century, its population had climbed to about 6,468,000 people. Hungary was a polyglot and ethnically diverse kingdom containing Magyars, Slovaks, Ruthenians, Transylvanians, Romanians, Serbs, Austrians, and southern Germans.

The king or queen of Hungary had been elected traditionally by members of a representative institution called the Diet. The Austrian Hapsburgs had often received the Hungarian crown. In 1687, however, shortly after the Turks had been driven out of Buda, the Hapsburg emperor Leopold I pressured the Hungarian Diet to renounce its rights to elect the Hungarian monarch and to accept a Hapsburg ruler as long as the Hapsburgs continued producing male heirs. This provision created a political crisis in Hungary in the 1720s when MARIA THERESA OF AUSTRIA became the Hapsburg heir apparent. Since no male heir existed, the Hungarian Diet legally regained its right to elect its monarch. The Hungarian Diet eventually agreed to accept Maria Theresa as the queen of Hungary, but it extracted certain concessions from Emperor Charles VI, her father, in return for recognizing her rights of succession. In particular, Charles VI promised that he and every sovereign after him would respect the special freedoms and rights of Hungary. Maria Theresa's coronation provided an opportunity for the Hungarian Diet to negotiate more concessions from the Hapsburgs. Thus, the nation retained numerous privileges and independent institutions within the Hapsburg Empire.

In her earliest years as queen of Hungary, Maria Theresa refrained from instituting reforms. But she also refused to call meetings of the Hungarian Diet, in an effort to prevent them from making new demands against her power. In 1764, her need for more tax income finally drove her to call the Diet. The Diet proved obstreperous, voting only a small increase in taxation and allowing itself to be dissolved rather than be forced to accept other reforms. After disbanding the Diet, Maria Theresa proceeded with her plans for peasant status reform and began sending her own royal commissioners to survey conditions on the estates of Hungarian nobles.

JOSEPH II continued the direct assault on Hungarian privileges by ordering a census of lands for the purpose of establishing a land tax, by eliminating the constitutional authorities who could have obstructed his work, and by introducing a Theresian administrative BUREAUCRACY.

With the death of Joseph in 1790, an aristocratic revolt against Hapsburg rule broke out in Hungary. Peasants, in turn, rebelled against their noble masters in support of the Hapsburgs. Troops brought in from other regions of the empire pacified the kingdom. Hungary would remain linked to Austria until the dissolution of the Austro-Hungarian Empire toward the end of World War I.

Hunter, John (1728–1793) *Scottish-born surgeon and anatomist who practiced his profession in London*
Hunter, the tenth child of farmer John Hunter and his wife Agnes Paul Hunter, had an older brother, William HUNTER, who was also an anatomist and surgeon.

Young John lost his father at the age of 13. He stayed on the family farm, assisting his mother and learning about animal husbandry. In 1748 he moved to LONDON, where his brother William assumed responsibility for securing his education in anatomy and surgery. Most of John Hunter's anatomy training occurred in the dissection room under the tutelage of his brother, but he also attended surgical classes at St. George's, St. Bartholomew's, and Chelsea Hospitals in London. The irregularities in Hunter's education caused by economic circumstances forced him to wait until the age of 40 (1768) to obtain his diploma from the Company of Surgeons.

The difficulties that John Hunter faced in obtaining his formal surgical education left him committed to the cause of facilitating the process for other students. He gave private lectures in anatomy and surgery at his home and founded a student society, the Lyceum Medicum Londinense (London Medical Lyceum). At the weekly meetings of the society, students read papers and discussed their findings with fellow students. They were able to draw on Hunter's private museum of anatomical specimens and paintings. The painter George STUBBS produced four animal pictures on commission for Hunter's museum. Hunter's students included Edward JENNER and other subsequently successful surgeons and physicians.

Hunter's personal career began with 11 years of taxing but useful labor in the Covent Garden anatomy laboratory operated by his brother. Hunter then obtained an appointment with the army surgical staff (1760) and served during the SEVEN YEARS' WAR in the campaign to capture Belle Ileen-Mer and in PORTUGAL. His important *Treatise on the Blood, Inflammation and Gun-Shot Wounds* (1794) recorded his observations about and experiences in treating war wounds. Hunter returned to London in 1763 and set up a private anatomy lab in Golden Square. Although he was already working as a surgeon, the path to senior appointments was blocked because he lacked the required diploma from the College of Surgeons. After he received his surgical diploma in 1768, he procured a post as senior surgeon at St. George's Hospital. He also established a large, influential, and financially rewarding private surgical practice.

Rewards and recognition followed quickly. Already a member of the ROYAL SOCIETY OF LONDON (1767), Hunter also was invited to join the board of the Royal Humane Society (1776); appointed to the Académie Royale de Chirurgie (Royal Academy of Surgery, 1783) in PARIS; elected to the AMERICAN PHILOSOPHICAL SOCIETY (1787); awarded the prestigious Copley Medal (1787); appointed deputy surgeon general (1785) and later surgeon general of England; and retained as surgeon-extraordinary to King George III.

Hunter, a major supporter of the theory of living organisms called VITALISM, believed that the blood is an animated fluid that carries the vital force in living organisms. Because of this conviction, he opposed the common practice of bloodletting. He also believed that animal and vegetable matter were entirely different from nonliving matter because they possessed a vital force. He rejected the medical theories derived from the MECHANICAL PHILOSOPHY and also denied the tenets of IATROCHEMISTRY. Hunter made notable investigations of anatomical pathology, of the anatomy of various animals, and of the human reproductive system. He used the knowledge obtained in dissections for his surgical work. His major publications included the *Treatise on the Blood, Inflammation and Gun-Shot Wounds, Treatise on the Natural History of the Human Teeth* (1771 and 1778), *Treatise on the Venereal Disease* (1786), and *Observations on Certain Parts of the Animal Oeconomy* (1786).

See also MEDICINE; SCOTLAND.

Hunter, William (1718–1783) *Scottish-born anatomist, surgeon, and follower of vitalism who worked in London*

William Hunter was the older brother of John HUNTER and the son of a Scottish farmer, John Hunter, and his wife Agnes Paul Hunter. William Hunter began his higher education in theology at the University of Glasgow. He met the chemist and physician William CULLEN at Glasgow and, having found theological study distasteful, became Cullen's assistant. In 1739, at Cullen's advice, Hunter enrolled for studies in anatomy and MEDICINE at the University of Glasgow. His primary professor was Alexander Monro Primus. After one year at the university, Hunter moved to LONDON, where he obtained a tutorial position in the household of the anatomist and male midwife James Douglas. Hunter continued his training with Douglas until the latter's death in 1742. In 1745, Hunter set up a series of private anatomy lectures. The reorganization of the Company of Barber-Surgeons in 1745 had

split the barbers from the surgeons, and the surgeons, relatively powerless, had been forced to relax their customary restrictions on the holding of private lectures. Hunter's initial lecture courses expanded in the 1760s into a fully developed private school of anatomy with an outstanding museum of specimen collections and a journal, the *Medical Commentaries.* Hunter's collection went to the University of Glasgow after his death.

Between 1747 and 1768 William Hunter earned many important honors and degrees. The Company of Surgeons granted him a diploma in 1747, and the University of Glasgow granted him an M.D. in 1750. At Surgeon's Hall he was received as a master of anatomy in 1752, and the College of Physicians accepted him in 1756. After receiving his position in the College of Physicians, Hunter removed his name from the roles of the less prestigious Company of Surgeons. The ROYAL SOCIETY OF LONDON elected him a fellow in 1767, and King George III appointed him in 1768 as a professor of anatomy at the Royal Academy.

Hunter's surgical practice was lucrative and contained many illustrious patients. He attended Queen Charlotte throughout her pregnancy and the delivery of her first son. He obtained some fame and was painted by several major artists including Joshua REYNOLDS. Hunter published many papers on anatomy, but his most notable work is *The Anatomy of the Human Gravid Uterus* (1774), a large folio with 34 engravings of the pregnant uterus.

Although Hunter assisted his younger brother John in obtaining training and experience as an anatomist, the two men became estranged in a dispute about priority in the discovery of the blood supply to the uterine placenta. They never reconciled.

Huntsman, Benjamin (1704–1776) *English inventor; a clock and instrument maker by trade*

About 1740, he invented a process for making spring steel and later developed a new crucible process for manufacturing cast steel. His steel was a purer and more homogenous product than steels produced by other methods. Huntsman opened a steel foundry at Sheffield and for some time maintained a near monopoly over steel production in England.

See also INDUSTRIAL REVOLUTION.

Hutcheson, Francis (1694–1746) *moral philosopher and theorist of aesthetics born in Ireland of Scottish parents; considered by many scholars to be the earliest major figure of the Scottish Enlightenment*

Following in the footsteps of his grandfather and father, Hutcheson entered the Presbyterian ministry after studying theology at the University of Glasgow. His first pastoral call came in 1719 from a Presbyterian church in Ulster, Ireland. After a short time, he agreed to help found an academy for DISSENTERS in Dublin, where he taught until 1729. From 1730 until his death in 1746, Hutcheson served as a professor of MORAL PHILOSOPHY at the University of Glasgow. Among his many students was the young Adam SMITH. At the time, moral philosophy covered natural theology, ethics, jurisprudence, POLITICAL THEORY, and elementary ECONOMICS. Hutcheson's ideas helped to shape ethical theory and PSYCHOLOGY not only in Great Britain and on the European continent but also in the North American colonies, where they gained admirers such as Thomas JEFFERSON.

Hutcheson made noted contributions to ethics, to the philosophy of human rights, and to the theory of beauty. He opposed the idea championed by Samuel CLARKE that morality can be derived from REASON. Likewise, he rejected the common sense philosophy of his fellow Scot Thomas REID because it asserted that objective moral truths could be uncovered by a rational (reason-based) common sense.

Having borrowed the concept of the moral sense from Anthony Ashley Cooper, third earl of SHAFTESBURY, Hutcheson created a moral sense philosophy that founded ethical notions on subjective human perceptions or feelings about the virtue of specific acts. The moral sense, a universal characteristic of human beings, operated like any other human sense—sight, hearing, smell, taste, or touch—evaluating experiences according to whether or not they produce pleasing ideas. Hutcheson proposed that what motivates people to behave virtuously is the experience of pleasure after engaging in a specific act. In contrast, evil acts that produce personal pain will be avoided. In his first book, *Inquiry into the Origin of Our Ideas of Beauty and Virtue* (1725), Hutcheson denied that reason plays a role in giving us moral knowledge or insight, but he revised this position somewhat in two later books, *Essay on the Nature and Conduct of the Passions and Affections* and *Illustrations Upon the Moral Sense* (both published in 1728). These later works argued that reason does play a small role in helping people to determine moral truths by helping them to distinguish acts that will be approved from those that will be disapproved. Reason also helps us to delineate what actions will tend best to serve the public goods and to understand what things serve to motivate human behavior. Reason thus deepens our knowledge of morality but cannot be useful without the fundamental knowledge brought by the moral sense.

Hutcheson's aesthetic theory roughly resembled his moral sense theory. He believed that beauty is defined by a special sense that yields pleasurable feelings in the presence of certain forms, especially those that are regular, uniform, and harmonious.

In addition to the treatises already mentioned, Hutcheson left the following works: *A Short Introduction to Moral Philosophy* (1747), *Metaphysical Synopsis* (1742), *Logical Compendium* (1756), and *A System of Moral Philosophy* (1755).

See also AESTHETICS.

Portrait of Francis Hutcheson. Hutcheson helped to define the Enlightenment in Scotland with his moral sense philosophy and aesthetic theory. *(Courtesy Hunterian Art Gallery, University of Glasgow)*

Hutton, James (1726–1797) *Scottish geologist and agricultural specialist*
Hutton, a member of a Scottish merchant family, tried both law and medicine as professions, before finally settling on agriculture and geology. Throughout his life, Hutton maintained a wide range of interests that are reflected in his writings.

An active member of the ROYAL SOCIETY OF EDINBURGH, Hutton reflected the general tendency in that organization to specialize in practical applications of science to technology, ECONOMICS, agriculture, and industry. Joseph BLACK became a close friend, and Hutton's broader social group included illustrious contributors to the Scottish ENLIGHTENMENT such as Adam SMITH, Adam FERGUSON, and James Burnett (Lord Monboddo).

Hutton developed an important geological theory of the Earth that vied with the theory of Abraham WERNER for dominance. Geologists of the era were arguing about whether rocks came originally from volcanic or oceanic sources. Most geologists accepted the oceanic theory in some form. When they recognized a role for volcanic action in rock formation, these geologists usually maintained that the volcanic action was very recent, while the primary formation from oceans had occurred in the more distant past.

Hutton's more complicated theory, outlined first in a pamphlet called *Abstract of a Dissertation . . . Concerning the System of the Earth, Its Duration, and Stability* (1785), and later in his *Theory of the Earth: With Proofs and Illustrations; in Four Parts* (1795), accepted the idea that rocks are generally produced by a process of sedimentation at the bottom of oceans. But unlike his contemporaries, Hutton assigned a central role to heat in causing the fusion of the sediments into different mineral forms. He also asserted that the force of expanding heat had caused these sediments to lift upward from the ocean bottom to become dry land.

Hutton also recognized that volcanic action had played a great role in the formation of rocks. He put granite in the category of igneous rock (an originally molten substance, of volcanic origin, that cooled over time). Eventually, the school of geologists who followed Hutton's theory became known as the "Plutonists," and the supporters of Werner became the "Neptunists." Their dispute played a major role in 19th-century geological debates.

Hutton developed an interest in agriculture after reading *Horse-Hoeing Husbandry* by Jethro Tull. He devoted himself for 14 years to farming an estate at Slighshouses in SCOTLAND. He traveled extensively in ENGLAND, FRANCE, and the Low Countries to study agricultural techniques. Hutton wrote a long, unpublished treatise on agriculture that demonstrates his vast knowledge (the work has 1,045 manuscript pages) of agriculture and his interest in the animal-breeding experiments of Robert Bakewell.

Finally, Hutton explored several areas of SCIENCE related to geology. He published a three-part treatise entitled *Dissertations on Different Subjects in Natural Philosophy* in 1792. The work contains discussions of PHLOGISTON THEORY and of the nature of matter. In the latter field, Hutton maintained that the fundamental elements of a body (elements were considered indivisible), called "matter" in his terminology, must be unextended. That is, these elements could not occupy space, for if they did, he believed, they could not be indivisible. This position closely resembled the one adopted by Ruggiero BOSCOVISH and later put to creative use by Pierre-Simon LAPLACE. But Hutton apparently developed the idea independently of these two illustrious scientists.

Hutton was a believer in DEISM, that religious and philosophical position that argued for belief in God on the basis of the wonderful design of the universe. He believed that the Earth had neither a beginning observed by humankind, nor would it have an observable end. But he also believed that the whole Earth is a machine constructed upon both mechanical and chemical principles, which can be understood by humankind. He denied that the biblical account of creation accurately portrays the history of the Earth, asserting, instead, that it deals only with the relatively brief history of human beings. These ideas placed him in conflict with accepted Christian dogma.

As a scientist and philosopher, Hutton reflects major themes of the Enlightenment. His research used techniques of observation in the field characteristic of EMPIRICISM and also reflected concern with developing knowledge that could be put to practical use. His deistic philosophy showed how theories of science were still intertwined with religious questions. But his ideas also demonstrated how the new forms of science could be made to serve the cause of faith in God.

I

iatrochemistry An approach to physiology and MEDICINE that reduces all phenomena to aspects of chemistry. The prefix *iatro* means in Greek "of or relating to" and has historically been used in compound words referring to physicians and medical treatment. Iatrochemistry derived from ALCHEMY and from the chemical medicine of the 16th-century Renaissance physician Philippus Aureolus Theophrastus Bombast von Hohenheim, better known as Paracelsus (1493–1541). Iatrochemists generally tried to explain all life functions as a chemical process, and they relied heavily on chemical preparations for medicines.

At the beginning of the ENLIGHTENMENT, professors such as Hermann BOERHAAVE and Friedrich HOFFMANN merged iatrochemical approaches with the MECHANICAL PHILOSOPHY to create their influential systematic medical theories, but, in general, iatrochemistry as a separate approach to medicine receded into the background.

The influence of iatrochemistry continued, nevertheless, to be expressed during the 18th century in the search for chemical explanations of physiological functions and in the widespread interest in the curative powers of mineral waters. VITALISM, the theory of organic life that became highly influential in the middle decades of the 18th century, also borrowed some elements from iatrochemistry.

See also IATROMECHANICS.

iatromechanics An approach to the science of life that developed in the 17th century out of the MECHANICAL PHILOSOPHY. Iatromechanism had significant influence in the life sciences and MEDICINE, but it never wholly dominated those fields. Rather, it had rivals in IATROCHEMISTRY, ANIMISM, VITALISM, and traditional Galenic medicine.

Iatromechanics reduced all phenomena of organic life to the principles of mechanics. It explained life functions in terms of size, shape, and motion of particles of matter. It also drew heavily on the analogy between life processes and the action of machines.

René DESCARTES had paved the way for the development of this approach in the DISCOURSE ON METHOD (1637), where he explained blood circulation in terms of the mechanical processes of pumping and the action of valves. The heart, for Descartes, was a simple pumping machine. Descartes went further in his *Traité de l'homme* (Treatise on man, circulated in manuscript form for many years before its publication in 1664), in which he described a machine that could perform all the life functions of a man.

Major 17th-century proponents of iatromechanics included Giovanni Alfonso Borelli (1608–79) and Hermann BOERHAAVE. Borelli studied the skeleton and its supportive system of muscles, explaining all motion in terms of the principles of levers. Boerhaave attempted to develop a systematic medical theory based on mechanics. Boerhaave's work—both writing and teaching—provided the major avenue by which iatromechanics was transmitted to the scientists and physicians of the early ENLIGHTENMENT.

By the middle of the 18th century, however, iatromechanics had lost considerable ground to new forms of vitalism that seemed to preserve the unique qualities that differentiate living creatures from nonliving things.

Idéologie Theory of social science and EDUCATION rooted in the PSYCHOLOGY, MEDICINE, and linguistics of the ENLIGHTENMENT. The theory of Idéologie was developed by a group known as the IDÉOLOGUES that included Antoine DESTUTT DE TRACY, Pierre CABANIS, Joseph-Dominique Garat (1748–1833), and Pierre-Louis Ginguené (1748–1815). These men were closely associated with Marie-Jean de CONDORCET, and, like Condorcet, committed themselves to the task of reforming the French system of education. Because the instructional program of Idélogie was implemented during the years of the FRENCH REVOLUTION, it has often been discredited and neglected by scholars hostile to the political and social legacy of that great upheaval. However, the theory actually illustrates one form, although by no means the only form, taken by the Enlightenment when its ideas were wedded to specific social or political goals and associated practices. In many respects, the Idéologues were simply putting into practice the ideals of the Enlightenment as expressed in the ENCYCLOPÉDIE.

The Idéologues participated in the early events of the French Revolution, but they did not obtain the necessary power to implement their educational program until after the downfall of Maximilien ROBESPIERRE in July 1794 (9 Thermidor, according to the revolutionary calendar). After that event, Cabanis, Destutt de Tracy, Garat, and Ginguené received positions in the new Institut de France, and also were appointed to the new Council of Public Instruction. Their educational reforms were briefly incorporated in the system of *écoles centrales* (central schools) that operated in FRANCE between 1795 and 1797. Their instructional program was, however, opposed by Napoléon Bonaparte and was largely dismantled during his years of power.

In its essence, Idéologie was a psychological theory of LANGUAGE. It began with the analysis of sensation and proceeded to posit the construction of ideas from sensory experience. It thus placed experience rather than innate ideas or metaphysics at the center of the process for knowledge formation. This approach derived from a blending of the psychological theories of Abbé CONDILLAC and John LOCKE with vitalist principles of formative processes. Idéologie proceeded in the style of Condillac from the construction of basic ideas to the creation of language. It stressed both the possibility and importance of forming an ordered, rational grammar and associated vocabulary.

Idéologues believed that language and psychology provided the key to understanding and to shaping human behavior. Their theory thus stimulated an educational program with specific courses and texts on psychology, logic, grammar, and the use of will to attain desired ends. Their ultimate goal, highly pragmatic or utilitarian in nature, was the production of an educated, rational, enlightened citizenry in France.

See also BILDUNG; FRENCH ACADEMY OF SCIENCES; VITALISM.

Idéologues A group of French educational reformers whose theory of IDÉOLOGIE was a quintessential example of the social thought of the late ENLIGHTENMENT. The theory of ideology provided one cornerstone for the curriculum of the new system of public EDUCATION established in FRANCE during the FRENCH REVOLUTION. Antoine DESTUTT DE TRACY, Pierre CABANIS, and Joseph-Dominique Garat were prominent *Idéologues*. The *Esquisse d'un tableau historique des progrès de l'esprit humain* by Marie-Jean de CONDORCET (Outline of a historical description of the progress of the human mind; 1795) served as a succinct statement for the Idéologues of the social goals and vision of the Enlightenment.

The Idéologues helped to develop the new concept of social science or the SCIENCE OF MAN and tried to implement a program that would put such SCIENCE to use in the interests of creating an enlightened, rational citizenry fully capable of exercising its political rights. They formulated their theory from the association PSYCHOLOGY of John LOCKE and from the related sensation psychology and language theory of Abbé CONDILLAC. Their specific reforms did not survive the Napoleonic era, but their activities helped to stimulate the development of experimental and educational psychology. Their ideas also directly stimulated the development of early-19th-century positivism, the theory of sociology associated most commonly with the name of August Comte (1798–1857).

Illuminati, Bavarian A secret revolutionary organization founded in 1776 by the canon law professor Adam Weishaupt. It was headquartered in the Bavarian city of Ingolstadt, where Weishaupt held a chair in canon law at the local university. The term *illuminati* merely means "enlightened" or "illumined." Weishaupt modeled his organization on the FREEMASONS, and the founding chapter of Illuminati eventually joined with the Freemasons of the Munich Masonic lodge called Zur Behutsamkeit (Toward Watchfulness). Through the Freemasons, the Illuminati organization expanded its membership and geographical influence.

The Bavarian Illuminati represented the extreme radical wing of the *AUFKLÄRUNG* (German ENLIGHTENMENT). It was born out of the disillusionment that arose in enlightened Bavarian circles when the progressive elector Maximilian III Joseph Wittelsbach (ruled 1745–77) was replaced by the conservative Karl Theodor Wittelsbach.

The members of the Bavarian Illuminati had believed that enlightened despotism (see DESPOTISM, ENLIGHTENED)—centralized rule by strong progressive princes—was the political structure most likely to produce enlightened reform, and the reign of Maximilian III Joseph Wittelsbach had seemed to support their beliefs. But the arrival of Karl Theodor Wittelsbach on the Bavarian throne called that faith into question. Karl Theodor strongly supported the Catholic clergy and even hired an ex-Jesuit as his personal confessor.

The Illuminati also believed that Bavaria was threatened by a conspiracy of JESUITS, ROSICRUCIANS, and other conservatives, all opposed to the spread of the Enlightenment. These groups, in fact, opposed the goals of the Illuminati, played a role in their eventual suppression, and continued to see them as a kind of threatening conspiracy into the 19th century.

The Illuminati were committed to political, social, and educational reform and lamented the turn to conservatism that was occurring in Bavaria. Their teachings consisted of a blending of ideas taken from such enlightened figures as Adam SMITH, Gotthold Ephraim LESSING, Jean-Jacques ROUSSEAU, Gabriel Bonnet de Mably, Baron d'HOLBACH, and Claude-Adrien HELVÉTIUS; with inspiration from the ancient classics of ROME and Greece. Initiates passed through four stages, learning of the revolutionary and subversive aims of the order only upon arrival at the highest stage.

The Illuminati organization contained several prominent members, each of whom adopted a secret name drawn either from ancient history or from more recent figures associated with the SCIENTIFIC REVOLUTION and the early Enlightenment. Members (with their secret names) included Weishaupt himself (Spartacus); his student Franz Xaver von Zwackh (Cato); Karl Theodor Anton Maria von Dalberg Archbishop-Elector of Mainz (Bacon von Verulam); and a Göttingen historian Ludwig Thomas Spittler (Bayle). Other members included the University of GÖTTINGEN philosophy professor Johann Georg Heinrich Feder (Marcus Aurelius), who provided the major intellectual formulations for the group; Adolf, Freiherr von Knigge (Philo); Friedrich Heinrich JACOBI (Sully); Christoph Friedrich NICOLAI (Lucien); Johann Heinrich PESTALOZZI (Alfred); and Josef von SONNENFELS, the Austrian minister under MARIA THERESA and JOSEPH II (Fabius-Numa pompilius romanus). Some evidence suggests that Johann Wolfgang von GOETHE, Johann Gottfried HERDER, and KARL-AUGUST, duke of Weimar, were also members of the Illuminati, but scholars have not yet made a final determination on this matter. Because the Illuminati organization was dedicated to revolutionary aims, the members of a specific local group or cell did not know the names of members of other cells. The cities and nations in which cells were located had code names drawn from antiquity: AUSTRIA was Egypt, FRANCE was Illyricum, MUNICH was Athens, VIENNA was ancient Rome, and Ingolstadt was Eleusis, the place associated with ancient Greek mystery rites. Major leaders of the organization were Weishaupt, Knigge (until a 1784 quarrel with Weishaupt), and Zwackh.

News of the Illuminati reached Bavarian authorities and may have been passed to them by members of the Rosicrucians. Decrees aimed at suppressing the Illuminati and other secret organizations were issued by Karl Theodor Wittelsbach in 1784 and 1785. These were paralleled in 1785 by the decree (*Freimauerpatent*) of Emperor Joseph II that banned the Illuminati and limited the activities of the Freemasons. By 1787, the organization of the Illuminati had collapsed.

Illuministi   A word sometimes used to denote the intellectual leaders of the Italian ENLIGHTENMENT. It derives from the Italian *illuminare,* meaning "to enlighten." The characteristics of the Italian Enlightenment varied according to geographic location and to the political structure of various Italian states. The Italian Enlightenment must not be understood as a single, united movement. Its creators reflected the special conditions and traditions in their various provinces and cities, thereby leaving a rich, multifaceted legacy for students to unravel. For example, the enlightened thought that developed in MILAN differed from that of Naples, Florence, VENICE, or TURIN.

The cultural institutions associated with the French Enlightenment also existed in Italy; reading clubs, salons, coffeehouses, journals, and political societies, for example, all flourished. Professors at traditional universities in Naples, Pavia, and Bologna also played important roles, a characteristic that distinguishes the Italian Enlightenment from that of FRANCE and underscores similarities with the German AUFKLÄRUNG.

Eighteenth-century observers of ITALY often noted that the penetration of enlightened ideas in the peninsula was not deep; a certain element of superficiality prevailed, largely because of the relatively small number of individuals who were involved in the movement. The Italian Enlightenment nevertheless produced works of great significance not only for Italy, but also for many European states.

As examples of the Italian contribution, one need only point to the treatise *ESSAY ON CRIMES AND PUNISHMENTS* by Cesare BECCARIA; to the histories of Lodovico MURATORI and Giambattista VICO; to the political economy of Antonio GENOVESI and Ferdinando GALIANI; to the science of Alessandro VOLTA, Luigi GALVANI, and Lazzaro SPALLANZANI; to the paintings of Giovanni Battista TIEPOLO, Pietro CANALETTO, Giovanni LONGHI, Bernardo PIRANESI, and Antonio BELLOTTO; or to the music of Arcangelo VIVALDI, Corelli, Domenico SCARLATTI, Giovanni Battista PERGOLESI, Baldassael Galuppi, and Giuseppe Sammartini.

Special conditions in Italy helped to stamp enlightened ideas coming from that area with a particular form. Church-state relations, for example, dominated discourse in law, HISTORY, and POLITICAL THEORY. The power of the pope, the head of ROMAN CATHOLICISM, reached widely and penetrated deeply into the political fabric of Italian states. Enlightened economists, historians, and juridical experts worked to develop a legal and historical basis for limiting papal jurisdiction by redefining the areas of legitimate concern to religion. In the process, these writers developed theories that assisted secularizing processes not only in Italy, but also in Bavaria (southern GERMANY) and AUSTRIA.

In the realm of political economy, the special structure of southern Italian agriculture produced a unique set of theories. In particular, the idea of free trade, so central to the liberal political economy developed by the PHYSIOCRATS and by Adam SMITH, was rejected as inappropriate for the Italian case. In its place, Italian thinkers substituted a form of enlightened MERCANTILISM in which central state policies would continue to control economic activity for the good of the whole nation.

Finally, the contributions of Italy to OPERA, to the development of the SYMPHONY, to ROCOCO style and to ART AND ARCHITECTURE and the general stimulus provided by Italy as the ultimate destination on the educational GRAND TOUR, as the place where the artifacts of antiquity could be readily observed, provided basic ingredients for the construction of the general culture of the Enlightenment.

See also ALGAROTTI; FILANGIERI; GOLDONI; KINGDOM OF THE TWO SICILIES; TANUCCI; PUBLISHING; SOCIAL INSTITUTIONS OF THE ENLIGHTENMENT.

imperialism   Political, cultural, and economic domination of other countries by a nation, achieved through military or other means. The voyages of exploration made by Europeans before the 17th century were driven as much by the promise of wealth as the desire to discover. However, as ocean routes were charted and established and colonial settlements were seeded around the globe, the nations of Europe increasingly bound their economic and political success to the domination of native peoples and the expansion of colonial holdings that served as sources of precious metals and raw materials. Ultimately, the establishment of trading empires became the goal.

SPAIN made the earliest large-scale efforts at empire in the 15th and 16th centuries through explorers such as Hernán Cortés. While still an adolescent, Cortés traveled to Spain's territories in the West Indies and was involved in the conquest of Cuba. During the conflict, Cortés made a powerful future ally in the figure of Diego Velázquez de Cuéllar, the colony's future governor who was the force behind the conquest of mainland America

Caricature by James Gillray, 1818. John Bull, a cartoon personification of Britain, was first created as a character in John Arbuthnot's *The History of John Bull* (1712). This cartoon depicts a dispute over paper money versus gold, with the caption, "Bank notes—paper money—French alarmists—of the devil!—ah! Poor John Bull." *(By permission of The British Library)*

and who selected Cortés to lead the expeditionary force. Exploiting native religious beliefs that identified him as a reincarnated god, Cortés's bloody conquest of the Aztecs became the blueprint for Spain's expansion, as he slaughtered and enslaved the local population, carried off huge amounts of precious materials, and started a devastating smallpox epidemic among Native Americans. Cortés's invasion also prefigured other imperial occupations given that part of his mission was to win souls for Christianity by any means available; violence and torture for the purpose of effecting conversions would continue throughout the Spanish conquest of the Americas.

Other European nations followed suit: PORTUGAL, FRANCE, ENGLAND, and the UNITED PROVINCES OF THE NETHERLANDS established their presence in Africa, the Americas, Asia, and the Pacific rim. The Portuguese Empire extended from South America to Indonesia. The Dutch Empire grew in the Americas, Africa, and Asia, with sites in Suriname and Japan, although their African and American possessions were increasingly the sites of conflict with the British. French imperial expansion faced similar British opposition in these regions. In each case, the individual governments brought their own nationals to rule over the local populations, creating in many cases a creole elite whose loyalty to the home country came into increasing doubt.

Military clashes began to dominate relations among imperial powers in the 18th century as the five competitors sought control of the same territories. British expansion illustrates this pattern: In the 17th century, Britain established colonies in North America and the Caribbean and then increased its presence on a global scale, acquiring colonies from France in the Treaty of Paris (1763), which ended the SEVEN YEARS' WAR.

With the growth of colonial populations such as Britain's American colonies, imperial projects entered a new phase. Access to a largely captive market for domestically produced goods and the prospect of wealth from trade among different colonial outposts created closed imperial trading networks. One of the most notorious examples of this process, known as mercantilism, was the "Triangle Trade." European traders would travel to Africa and either buy or capture people, transporting them in crowded and unsanitary conditions to the American colonies, where those who survived the journey were sold as slaves. From the Americas traders would return home with sugar, cotton, tobacco, rice, and coffee that had been grown and harvested by the hands of earlier transported slaves. From European ports slave traders could return their empty ships to Africa and begin the cycle anew. This became a significant spur to industrial development in the European countries, as industries such as textiles had both a ready supply of raw materials and captive markets for selling their finished products.

By the middle of the 18th century, the British imperial presence was dominating that of its competitor nations.

Fleets of trading vessels seconded a growing naval force, and individual British colonies became part of a global trading empire. Many colonies were self-supporting and self-governing, dictating terms to whatever native populations were left, while the British Army and Navy assured loyalty to imperial authority, as in the American colonies. Also important for the future of the Americas, in particular, was the increase of European immigration. As Britain's colonies became more successful, waves of people booked passage from Europe to North America in search of farmland that was no longer to be had in Europe. Here a significant distinction emerged between the British and Spanish Empires: For the most part, settlement in British areas was done by families, whereas in the Spanish realm men tended to come alone. A similar pattern appeared in South Africa, as British settlements soon became large, successful enterprises.

With the turn of the 19th century Britain sought to expand its imperial presence as a means for increasing military strength in its conflict with Napoleonic France. The British Navy grew in capability during the 1790s to the point of invincibility, and French military operations soon focused their energies on defeating their Continental opponents. Recognizing his inability to maintain an overseas empire in the face of Britain's Navy, Napoleon Bonaparte ceded a huge portion of France's American possessions west of the Mississippi to the emerging UNITED STATES OF AMERICA in what was called the Louisiana Purchase (1803).

Britain further extended its colonial reach, reorganizing its remaining possessions in the West Indies and Canada and solidifying control in areas such as India. The British EAST INDIA COMPANY was itself a force with which to reckon, using British-trained native soldiers to intervene in local conflicts and using its considerable wealth and influence to manipulate Parliamentary decision making back home. As the 18th century wore on, however, the cost of its operations began to exceed its profits. In 1771, the company brought government inquiries upon itself with a loan request of a million pounds that was to help it avoid bankruptcy. The inquiries resulted in the passage of the Regulating Act and greater Parliamentary intervention in Indian affairs. With Parliament's takeover of the India venture, Britain truly had an empire on which the sun never set.

Imperialism in the 18th century set the stage for the appearance of global economic and political structures that dominated the 19th century. Beginning in 1776 and running through the 1820s, Creole elites in North and South America rose up against their parent states and founded independent ones. The young United States of America, the first of these independent states, soon showed that it had absorbed Britain's imperial ambitions and practices with the Monroe Doctrine (1823), a declaration that Latin America was now its sphere of influence and the first sign of a long and troubled engagement of the country with its southern neighbors. As the 19th century progressed and Europe's industrial capacity grew, traditional imperial states such as Great Britain and France were joined by Belgium, Germany, and Italy in a search for raw materials. Shut out of the New World, these powers turned to Africa and later the Middle East, which they carved up among themselves, setting economic and political forces in motion whose effects are still felt today.

See also COLONIALISM; FREE TRADE; MERCANTILISM; NOBLE SAVAGE; SLAVERY.

Further reading: Christine Daniels and Michael V. Kennedy, eds, *Negotiated Empires: Centers and Peripheries in the Americas, 1500–1820* (New York: Routledge, 2002); John E. Flint and Glyndwr Williams, eds., *Perspectives of Empire* (London: Longman, 1973); Martin Kitchen, *The British Empire and Commonwealth: A Short History* (New York: St. Martin's, 1996); Phillip Lawson, *A Taste for Empire and Glory* (Brookfield, Vt.: Ashgate, 1997); Trevor Lloyd, *Empire: The History of the British Empire* (New York: Hambledon & London, 2001).

Inchbald, Elizabeth (1753–1821) *English actress and writer*

Elizabeth Inchbald entered the literary world as an actress turned playwright and novelist. She produced more than 10 original plays as well as five novels that offer a critique of ENLIGHTENMENT notions of EDUCATION and the position of women in society.

Elizabeth Inchbald was born Elizabeth Simpson in Suffolk, ENGLAND. Her parents were small farmers, and she came from a devout Catholic background. She wanted to be an actress from early on and moved to LONDON at the age of 18. There, she met the actor Joseph Inchbald, whom she married in 1772 (the same year she arrived in London). She overcame a childhood speech impediment to embark on a career as a performer. Initially, she appeared opposite Inchbald, but his sudden death in 1779 forced her to make her own way as an actress.

Though Inchbald made her Covent Garden debut in 1780 and performed there regularly for the next five years, she quickly realized that achieving middle-class respectability as an actress would be difficult, if not impossible. She took the remarkable step of writing plays herself, something few women before her had done. (The most notable of her predecessors was Aphra BEHN.) Her first play, *The Mogul Tale,* premiered at the Little Theatre in London's Haymarket in 1784 and was published in 1788. A steady stream of works for the stage followed, including original plays and adaptations (primarily of French comedies and works by German playwright August von Kotzebue). Her success as an author allowed Inchbald to retire from the stage in 1789.

Inchbald wrote her first NOVEL. *A Simple Story,* in 1791. Her second novel, *Nature and Art,* was published in 1796. She also edited numerous volumes of plays by other writers, including her most significant collection,

The British Theatre, which was published in 25 volumes between 1806 and 1809 and featured her commentary.

Inchbald's writing took the significant step of moving away from 18th-century strictures and exploring issues that would be of central concern for 19th-century authors. Her comedies and farces discard the broad humor of earlier works rooted in the commedia dell'arte tradition and offer poignant insights into the living conditions of the lower classes. Her novels do this as well, and they also offer complex female protagonists, such as Miss Milner in *A Simple Story.* Inchbald also engages in the discussions about the sexes inherent in Enlightenment thought. For example, she critiques Jean-Jacques ROUSSEAU's argument in favor of limiting education for women.

See also THEATER.

Further reading: Elizabeth Inchbald, *A Simple Story* (New York: Penguin Books, 1997).

individualism   Form of philosophy touching on politics, ECONOMICS, justice, and ethics, that makes the individual human being the center of concern. Prior to the ENLIGHTENMENT, most European theory and practice placed greater emphasis on social groups than on individuals. Legal privileges, rights, and obligations were defined according to a person's membership in a specific group. Thus, nobles, for example, were distinguished legally from bourgeoisie, clergy, or peasants. The job of law and of the government lay in protecting the rights of these groups.

The Enlightenment developed individualism as an opposing approach to human societal problems. Individualism built on the assumptions of EQUALITY and on the belief in universal human traits contained in the psychology of John LOCKE. It also borrowed from the atomistic vision of the world contained in MECHANICAL PHILOSOPHY. Theories stressed the need to preserve individual rights and FREEDOM. But they also attempted to address in novel fashion questions about the RELATIONS between individuals and the groups in which they necessarily live. These issues dominate certain branches of enlightened POLITICAL THEORY, MORAL PHILOSOPHY, EDUCATION, and PSYCHOLOGY.

Industrial Revolution   Term used to signify the changes in technology, production of goods, and organization of labor that began unfolding in 18th-century ENGLAND and SCOTLAND. The impact of the Industrial Revolution was felt later on the European continent. The full effects of the Industrial Revolution were not apparent until the 19th century.

The Industrial Revolution was made possible by a series of converging developments in England: the accumulation of capital resources (i.e., money), the existence of expanding consumer markets in both England and in its overseas colonies, the existence of a large supply of cheap cotton produced in the British colonies by slave labor, and English domination of the high seas. The success of this revolution in the organization and production of goods was also made possible by the existence of attitudes toward work that gave it a place of honor and an important role in human moral formation. The responsi-

bility for creating these attitudes can be assigned not only to CALVINISM, but also to the practical goals of the SCIENTIFIC REVOLUTION and the ENLIGHTENMENT. In fact, the Industrial Revolution was a logical if not a necessary outgrowth of these two intellectual movements. Both its underlying theories and its practical components

Mineral technology. This plate from the *Encyclopédie* depicts the various methods used in extracting and preparing the mineral alum for industrial uses. *(Courtesy New York Public Library)*

developed in the context of attempts to ensure human PROGRESS through the application of SCIENCE and REASON to economic problems.

The creators of the Industrial Revolution—men such as Thomas NEWCOMEN, Abraham DARBY, Edmund CARTWRIGHT, John KAY, James HARGREAVES, Henry CORT, and James WATT—understood that the development of new technologies could streamline the creation of industrial products. They combined practical knowledge with some scientific theory to invent new devices that speeded up output and greatly increased individual productivity. Their inventions concentrated largely in two areas, cloth manufacturing and iron- and steel-making.

The Industrial Revolution produced major dislocations and hardships for the English working classes. The invention of new machines such as the SPINNING JENNY, POWER LOOM, and STEAM ENGINE required new ways of organizing production. Workplaces were thus moved from private homes to large factories, and workers were forced to move into cities near the factories. Hours were long, wages extremely low; poverty, disease, and alcoholism were rampant. Child labor was common as families needed their wages to survive.

Initially, the introduction of new machines put many people out of work, but as production began to pick up, demand for labor increased. This demand was supplied in England by farmers who were being displaced by 18th-century innovations in agricultural organization and techniques. In fact, this Agricultural Revolution helped make the Industrial Revolution possible in another significant way, by increasing crop yields so that fewer farmers could support larger urban populations.

The negative consequences of industrialism were matched by positive developments. New technologies made certain consumer goods—pottery, silverware, and cotton cloth, for example—more widely available by bringing prices within the reach of a wider population. Other inventions, such as the modern water closet (toilet), enhanced the quality of life by rendering daily life more convenient and by increasing sanitation in cities.

The Industrial Revolution grew up in an environment based upon competition, fueled by the investment capital and by the ingenuity of the English middle classes and enterprising gentry. The theory of economic liberalism, whose major proponent was Adam SMITH, tried to provide a general justification for this environment. Using an understanding of economic forces based on INDIVIDUALISM, free trade, LAISSEZ FAIRE, and adaptations of mechanical physical principles to human society, Smith claimed that free economic markets supported by unrestricted competition in both products and wages would ultimately produce benefits for the larger society. Smith's theory melded nicely with the liberal political stance of the Whig Party and its middle-class constituents.

The forms created by the Industrial Revolution matched the rational values of the Enlightenment. But it must be emphasized that the theory of economic liberalism was not the only economic theory sustainable by enlightened ideas. Economic liberalism was challenged during the 18th century in many European states by equally enlightened forms of MERCANTILISM and CAMERALISM. Furthermore, its practical application, seen in the working conditions of the Industrial Revolution, spawned impassioned criticism from humanitarian philosophers and social critics. Writers such as Abbé GALIANI pointed out that free trade policies could not be beneficial in a traditional agrarian, church-dominated culture such as existed in the KINGDOM OF THE TWO SICILIES. Abbé RAYNAL pointed out the injustices of European colonial policies, and abolitionists called for an end to SLAVERY. Ultimately, in the closing years of the Enlightenment, the human costs of the Industrial Revolution helped to give birth to radical economic DEMOCRACY and to the earliest modern formulations of communism.

See also CAPITALISM; NEW LANARK.

Ingen-Housz, Jan (1730–1799) *Dutch physician and physiologist*

Ingen-Housz, from a Roman Catholic family, met the Scottish physician John PRINGLE during the WAR OF THE AUSTRIAN SUCCESSION when British troops were encamped near his childhood home in Breda. After studying at the Catholic University of Louvain, Ingen-Housz matriculated at the University of Leiden, where his course included lectures by Pieter van MUSSCHENBROEK. Persuaded by Pringle to move to Britain, Ingen-Housz became a member of the influential circle of physicians associated with the center of the Scottish ENLIGHTENMENT, the University of Edinburgh Ingen-Housz's friends included William CULLEN, Alexander Monro Primus and his son Alexander MONRO Secundus, William HUNTER and his brother John HUNTER, Joseph PRIESTLEY, and Benjamin FRANKLIN.

Ingen-Housz earned a role in the HISTORY of MEDICINE through his support for the practice of INOCULATION against the dreaded disease of smallpox. The practice was controversial since it introduced live virus under the skins of patients. But at the time, it was the only means of preventing smallpox and remained so until Edward JENNER successfully developed a vaccine derived from cowpox in 1798.

Ingen-Housz built his medical practice on inoculation. He worked in LONDON but was also requested to serve as the inoculator in the Dutch capital, The Hague. In 1768, he was sent to VIENNA to inoculate the members of the imperial family. Empress MARIA THERESA asked Ingen-Housz to remain in Vienna as her court physician. He accepted the post, remaining in Vienna until 1789.

In Vienna, Ingen-Housz worked with Gerard van SWIETEN to reform Austrian medical education and practices. He also made the discovery of plant photosynthesis, publishing a book about it called *Experiments Upon Vegetables, Discovering Their Great Power of Purifying the*

Common Air in the Sunshine and of Injuring it in the Shade and at Night in 1779. In spite of this publication, credit for the photosynthesis discovery has often been given to Priestley and to a fellow chemist, J. Senebier. This quarrel over precedence is one of several that arose during the Enlightenment, the most famous, perhaps being the dispute over whether Gottfried LEIBNIZ or Isaac NEWTON first discovered mathematical calculus.

Ingen-Housz also contributed to plant nutrition studies for the English Board of Agriculture. His friendship with Benjamin Franklin involved active support of Franklin's unusual one-fluid theory of electricity. This theory explained electrical phenomena by using the concept of SUBTLE FLUIDS. For Franklin, electricity was a single fluid within which changes of pressure cause the effects of attraction and repulsion. Certain demonstrations by Ingen-Housz helped to establish some validity for the Franklin theory over the rival and favored two-fluid theory.

In 1789, an outbreak of violence in Vienna, a response to news of the FRENCH REVOLUTION, caused Ingen-Housz to move back to England. He spent his remaining years in that country dividing his time between London and the estate of a patroness, the marquess of Landsdowne. He died at her home in 1799.

Ingres, Jean-Auguste-Dominique (1780–1867) *French painter, trained in the late-18th-century neoclassical style*

Ingres's father, Jean-Marie-Joseph Ingres, was skilled in art, architecture, and music. He trained young Jean in drawing, then sent his son to the Toulouse Academy in 1791. As a teenager, Ingres supported himself by playing the violin in a Toulouse orchestra. Ingres studied painting at the Toulouse Academy with Roques, then in 1797 traveled to PARIS, where Jacques Louis DAVID accepted him into his workshop. In 1799, Ingres enrolled in the program at the École des Beaux Arts, and in 1801 his painting *The Envoys from Agammemnon* won the coveted Prix de Rome. In 1806, the European political scene had stabilized sufficiently to allow Ingres to collect his Prix de Rome funds and travel to ROME. He spent the next four years as a pensioner of the French Academy at the Villa Medici in Rome, remaining in that city until 1820. Between 1820 and 1824 he lived in Florence, and then returned to Paris, where he was taken onto the faculty of the École des Beaux Arts. Eventually Ingres assumed administrative duties at the École, following up this role in 1834 with that of director of the French Academy in Rome. He resided in the Eternal City until 1841, when his work took him back to Paris. He lived in Paris until his death in 1867.

Ingres continued the French neoclassical painting tradition into the 19th century. He remained committed to the notion that art has an eternal value that transcends HISTORY, and he sought to achieve a purity of form. Therefore, he rejected the subject matter and stylistic conventions—the depiction of the forces of the irrational, evocation of strong moods, somber colors, and the evocation of motion through the use of curving lines—associated with the new ROMANTICISM. Intense antagonism existed between Ingres and Eugène Delacroix, who was the leading exponent of romanticism. Significant works left by Ingres include *Envoys from Agammemnon; Bather of Valpinçon; Oedipus and the Sphinx; Vow of Louis XIII; Sainte Germaine de Pibrac;* and *Christ among the Doctors.*

See also NEOCLASSICISM.

inoculation   A method for immunizing people against smallpox. Inoculation involved the introduction of live smallpox virus under the skin. It worked effectively to prevent smallpox by giving patients mild cases of the disease that resulted in lifelong immunity. Unfortunately, the live virus sometimes caused severe forms of the very disease that inoculation meant to suppress.

Inoculation, therefore, proved intensely controversial, and 18th-century physicians engaged in intense debates over the merits of the practice. Mathematicians such as Daniel BERNOULLI and Jean Le Rond d'ALEMBERT used the risks of inoculation as material for discussions about the application of probability theory to human experience.

The risks associated with inoculation helped to stimulate the search for better immunization methods. Ultimately, a vaccine, produced from the virus of cowpox, was invented by Edward JENNER. With that development, Europeans succeeded in eliminating smallpox from the list of disfiguring and threatening diseases. The success of vaccine stands as one of the great contributions of the ENLIGHTENMENT to actual advances in the quality of life.

Among the advocates of inoculation were Lady Mary MONTAGU, the woman who brought the first information about inoculation to Europe from the Ottoman Empire; VOLTAIRE and his friend, the physician Theodore Tronchin; the Dutch physician Jan INGEN-HOUSZ; the French explorer Charles de La Condamine; the British physician Daniel Sutton; the Empress MARIA THERESA OF AUSTRIA; and King George II of Great Britain.

See also PUBLIC HEALTH.

intuition and imagination (German: *Anschauung* or *Verstehen,* and *Vorstellungskraft*)   According to modern English usage, intuition is the act of immediate apprehension, the power or faculty of attaining direct knowledge without the use of REASON. Imagination is the act of forming a mental image of something that is not present to the senses or that has not been perceived by the senses in the past. During the last half of the ENLIGHTENMENT, these terms acquired their present meanings and played significant roles in theories of EPISTEMOLOGY, AESTHETICS, SCIENCE, PSYCHOLOGY, and HISTORY.

The processes by which knowledge can be obtained through intuition and imagination were contrasted to those that characterized reason. The capacities of intuition to yield instantaneous, complete understanding and of the imagination to invent new ideas, made unique forms of human knowledge possible in instances where reason failed to be productive. In history, for example, a researcher who used his intuition and imagination could enter into a sympathetic relationship with the past that would yield insight into its characteristics; reason would not perceive these insights and hence would produce inferior knowledge. In artistic and literary creation, new 18th-century theories placed imagination and intuition above reason. These forms of understanding produced vibrant, creative insights that could then, if necessary, receive refinement through the application of reason.

Epistemological theories of intuition and imagination stressed that these mental faculties produced whole, complete, organic knowledge, difficult and indeed impossible to break down (analyze) into parts. Reason, by contrast, produced linear knowledge, a summation of parts that could easily be analyzed in the style of mathematics or of deductive logic. Imagination and intuition were also closely linked to emotion and sentiment.

Theories that called for the use of intuition and imagination in creative activities often drew also on the concept of GENIUS. The genius allegedly possessed a divine spark, a superhuman quality, which was partially illustrated in his superior intuitive and imaginative capabilities.

Intuition and imagination first acquired prominence in the works of the English moral philosopher and aesthetic theorist Anthony Cooper, third earl of SHAFTESBURY, and in the works of the French naturalist Georges-Louis Leclerc, comte de BUFFON. Buffon's widely read *Histoire naturelle* popularized the notion that these mental activities could yield desirable knowledge. German philosophers and theorists picked up the idea, recognizing its potential for offering an alternative to reason. German application of the concepts can be found in the aesthetics of Johann Jakob BODMER, Johann Jakob BREITINGER, Alexander Gottlieb BAUMGARTEN, Friedrich Heinrich JACOBI, and Gotthold Ephraim LESSING; and in the historical theory of August Ludwig von SCHLÖZER, Johann Christoph GATTERER, Johannes von MÜLLER, and Johann Gottfried HERDER. Immanuel KANT attempted to examine the epistemological grounds for these forms of knowledge in his *Critique of Practical Reason* (*Critik der practischen Vernunft*). The physician Johann Christian REIL and the philosophical anthropologist Johann Friedrich BLUMENBACH both adapted the theory to their research. The Genevan philosophe Jean-Jacques ROUSSEAU believed that intuition resembled the kind of knowledge that God has of the universe. Finally, the theory of VITALISM drew on these ideas for its conceptualization of the living organism.

In short, intuition and imagination posed during the last half of the Enlightenment as potent opponents to the domination of reason in theories of human understanding. Without these concepts, the various human sciences and aesthetics would have lacked epistemological grounds on which to base their claims as valid, true forms of human knowledge.

See also PHILOSOPHES.

Italy Geographic name for the long, boot-shaped, southern European peninsula that extends into the Mediterranean Sea. The nation called Italy today did not come into existence until the late 19th century. In the 18th century, the Italian peninsula consisted of disparate small states with widely varying political and social structures: the republics of VENICE, Genoa, Lucca, and San Marino; the kingdoms of Sardinia and the Two Sicilies; the duchies of Parma and Modena; the small principality of Piombino; the Papal States; the Austrian-ruled duchies of MILAN, Tuscany, and Mantua; and the Savoyard-controlled PIEDMONT region.

During the first half of the 18th century, Italy served as a battleground for the warring great powers of Europe. With the DIPLOMATIC REVOLUTION OF 1756 and the consequent cessation of hostilities between the French Bourbons and the Austrian Hapsburgs, the peninsula embarked on a relatively long period of peace. The rulers of the various states turned to the business of centralization and reform. Localized privilege and power, however, effectively blocked most of their efforts. enlightened absolutism (see ABSOLUTISM, ENLIGHTENED) existed only in SAVOY, Tuscany, and Lombardy. In these three regions, centralization and associated reform developed along the lines laid out in FRANCE and AUSTRIA. The fact that the pope resided in the Vatican in ROME and ruled the Papal States as their secular overlord, significantly colored the content of Italian enlightened reform. Church-state relations dominated literary output, discussion, and reform activity.

A species of the ENLIGHTENMENT certainly developed in the Italian states. In Milan, Naples, and Tuscany, small, but energetic, highly creative groups occupied themselves with the central issues of contemporary POLITICAL THEORY, HISTORY, ECONOMICS, and juridical philosophy. Also, a specifically Catholic body of enlightened thought emerged. The Italian peninsula bestowed to the European intellectual world the seminal works of brilliant historians like Lodovico MURATORI and Giambattista VICO. But, in general, the emphasis of Italian thinkers and reformers was somewhat more practical than that evidenced in the theoretical works of the French PHILOSOPHES. Major representatives of the Italian reform and Enlightenment movements include Antonio GENOVESI, Ferdinando GALIANI, Cesare BECCARIA,

Gaetano FILANGIERI, Bernardo TANUCCI, Pietro and Alessandro VERRI, Pietro GIANNONE, and Carlo GOLDONI.

Typical enlightened social institutions, such as salons, coffeehouses, and reading societies, existed in cities such as Milan, and the periodical press championed enlightened causes in some regions. But these enlightened elements did not permeate life in the various Italian states as thoroughly as in France. In fact, many journals struggled to survive. The most prominent enlightened periodical, *Il Caffe,* lasted only two years, and visitors from northern Europe regularly noted that Italian salons seemed relatively provincial.

Italian enlightened reformers generally worked within the existing system, holding official appointments in the state bureaucracies and instituting reforms in these capacities. Their results did not approach the magnitude of changes achieved, for example, in PRUSSIA or in the personal domains of the HAPSBURG EMPIRE.

To 18th-century Europeans, Italy was less a center of Enlightenment than a center of brilliant art, architecture, and MUSIC; a source of stimulating political and aesthetic models; and a destination for travel. BAROQUE STYLE architecture and art were born in Italy and, from there, disseminated across Europe. Rome, Venice, Naples, Florence, and Milan all drew aspiring young northern European composers who studied the masterful use of color and harmony characteristic of Italian music. Italian OPERA eventually took even 18th-century PARIS by storm. The republic of Venice presented only a vestige of its former glory, yet it still served as a stimulus for political discussion about decadent republics. Rome, as well as other spots in Italy, provided the artifacts of antiquity, whose forms dominated the emerging neoclassical aesthetic of the late 18th century. Finally, to wealthy young northern European aristocrats and bourgeoisie, Italy, however, disdained as backward, provided the place where polished social manners, cultural sophistication, and worldly introductions could be obtained. And so Italy became a sort of tourist destination, the high spot on any GRAND TOUR itinerary.

See also ILLUMINISTI; KINGDOM OF THE TWO SICILIES; NEOCLASSICISM; ROMAN CATHOLICISM; SOCIAL INSTITUTIONS OF THE ENLIGHTENMENT.

J

Jacobi, Friedrich Heinrich (1743–1819) *German novelist, writer, philosopher, and translator*

Jacobi's father was a well-to-do merchant in the city of Düsseldorf who insisted that his son follow in his footsteps. The young Jacobi found the form of PIETISM associated with Nikolaus Ludwig, count von ZINZENDORF (1700–60), especially compelling and developed strong interests in questions about RELIGION, the meaning of existence, and the grounds for faith. In spite of these intellectual interests, he obediently followed his father's wishes by entering a three-year business apprenticeship in FRANKFURT. He then spent an additional three years in GENEVA, where he acquired cosmopolitan skills and became entranced with the leading works of the French ENLIGHTENMENT. The writings of Jean-Jacques ROUSSEAU and Charles BONNET especially intrigued him. In Geneva, Jacobi began a serious study of the natural sciences. He desired to continue these studies at the medical school in Glasgow, SCOTLAND, but his father insisted that he return to Düsseldorf in order to take over the family business. Jacobi complied with his father's wishes in 1764. In the same year he married Betty von Clermont, the daughter of a successful cloth merchant.

Despite his business responsibilities, Jacobi continued his studies, concentrating upon the philosophical problem of the proof of God's existence. Increasingly he found formal proofs unsatisfactory and sought to evolve a form of existential religion in which God's existence can be intuited but not expressed in logical proofs.

In 1774, Jacobi met Johann Wolfgang von GOETHE, whose ideas played a central role in Jacobi's further intellectual development. Inspired by Goethe's novel, THE SORROWS OF YOUNG WERTHER, Jacobi wrote two novels. The first, *Eduard Allwill's Papiere* (Eduard Allwill's papers), was published serially (1774 and 1779) in *Iris* and in *Der Teutsche Merkur,* the latter a journal founded in 1773 by Jacobi and his friend Christoph Martin WIELAND. *Woldemar: Eine Seltenheit aus der Naturgeschichte* (Woldemar: a rarity out of natural history) appeared in 1777. These novels criticized the unchecked expression of both GENIUS and the emotions from philosophical and literary standpoints. Throughout his life, Jacobi improved and expanded upon these books, personally publishing his revised versions.

Jacobi and his wife settled on the Jacobi family's estate at Pempelfort near Düsseldorf and transformed it into one of the centers of the AUFKLÄRUNG (German Enlightenment). Under the direction of Jacobi's wife, a highly educated and interesting woman, Pempelfort became the meeting place for virtually every famous figure of the time, including Goethe, Wieland, Johann Gottfried HERDER, Denis DIDEROT, the HUMBOLDT brothers, Georg FORSTER, and Johann Georg HAMANN. At the same time, Jacobi maintained an extensive correspondence with all of the leaders of German thought until his death. In these roles, Jacobi served as one of the mediators for the exchange of ideas and information in the late Enlightenment.

Jacobi became well known as a philosophical thinker with the publication of the *Briefe über die Lehre des Spinoza* (Letters on the teachings of Spinoza; 1785). It included the correspondence between Jacobi and Moses MENDELSSOHN about Lessing's alleged Spinozism and Jacobi's commentary on the letters. Jacobi asserted that

Lessing had accepted the fatalism and pantheism associated with the rational monistic philosophy of Benedict de SPINOZA. In fact, Jacobi believed that all philosophy based on REASON and on its handmaiden, demonstrative logic, necessarily resulted in fatalism. As an alternative to this position, one that would preserve human FREEDOM of action, Jacobi put forth an alternative EPISTEMOLOGY, which asserted the necessity of making a willful leap of faith in order to understand the truth of certain positions.

Partly because Jacobi published Mendelssohn's letters without Mendelssohn's permission, the book sparked a major intellectual controversy, the so-called *Pantheismusstreit* (Pantheism controversy). Mendelssohn, a self-proclaimed modified Spinozist, provided a strong and convincing defense of Lessing and of Spinozism, but Jacobi's commentary also demonstrated a subtle understanding of Spinoza. Jacobi's analysis and the entire *Pantheismusstreit* helped to shape the conceptions of Spinoza for the following generations of German intellectuals.

Jacobi followed his critique of Spinoza with attacks on the formal philosophical system of Immanuel KANT and on the idealist philosophies associated with Friedrich Wilhelm Joseph von Schelling (1775–1854) and Johann Gottlieb Fichte (1762–1814). In opposition to both kinds of philosophy, Jacobi developed a system in which knowledge and understanding were achieved through the experience of dialogical interpersonal relations. He assigned an important role to feeling and to intuition in the acquisition of knowledge.

With the spread of the Napoleonic wars into GERMANY, Jacobi first had to flee from Pempelfort to escape the advancing French armies and then lost most of his money in bad wartime investments. Financially desperate, he accepted the invitation of the Bavarian minister for education to assist in the reorganization and modernization of the Bavarian Academy of Sciences. He became the new unit's first president. His inaugural address, *Ueber gelehrte Gesellschaften, ihren Geist und Zwecken* (Over learned societies, their spirit and goals; 1807) angered Schelling who was, at the time, the director of the Academy of the Arts in MUNICH. The disagreement between the two men grew in intensity, reaching its peak in another controversy carried out in the press. The major pieces from his controversy included Schelling's work entitled *Über das Verhältnis der bildenen Künste zur Natur* (On the relationship of visual art to nature); Jacobi's critique, *Von den Göttlichen Dingen und ihrer Offenbarung* (Of divine things and their revelation; 1811); and Schelling's scathing answer, *Denkmal der Schrift von den göttlichen Dingen* (Memorandum about the work on divine things). By 1812, the dispute had developed in such a way that Jacobi felt compelled to abandon his position. He spent the rest of his life editing and correcting his collected works.

Jacobi represents a strain of Enlightenment thought that attempted to found a philosophy of being and action upon experience and existence, upon feeling, imagination and intuition. He was not only a critic of most formal systems of thought but was also extremely wary of absolute systems of government whether or not they were headed by enlightened leaders. He thus considered all forms of ABSOLUTISM—whether intellectual, cultural, or political—antithetical to the development of free, morally responsible human beings.

See also INTUITION AND IMAGINATION; RATIONALISM.

Further reading: W. H. Bruford, *Germany in the Eighteenth Century: The Social Background of the Literary Revival* (Cambridge: Cambridge University Press, 1971); Henri Brunschwig, *Enlightenment and Romanticism in Eighteenth-Century Prussia,* tr. Frank Jellinek (Chicago: University of Chicago Press, 1974); Rudolf Vierhaus, *Germany in the Age of Absolutism,* tr. Jonathan B. Knudsen (Cambridge: Cambridge University Press, 1988).

Jacobins Deputies to the Estates General and National Assembly in FRANCE who founded associated radical organizations instrumental in initiating the FRENCH REVOLUTION. The Jacobin societies of France helped to set the revolution in motion, acted as centers of power during its upheavals, and ultimately became infamous for politically motivated massacres in the years that followed.

The Jacobins originated in the Breton Club of Versailles, which was formed in 1789. When the French National Assembly moved to PARIS in 1790, the Breton Club began to meet in a Dominican convent on the Rue St. Jacques, taking the name Society of the Friends of the Constitution. Derived from the convent's street address, the name Jacobin was originally a term of derision applied by the society's enemies. The society soon appropriated the name, however, calling itself the Society of Jacobins, Friends of Liberty and Equality from 1792 until it was disbanded in 1794.

Two types of organizations in prerevolutionary France served as precursors to these clubs: *chambres littéraires,* or literary societies, and SECRET SOCIETIES. Literary societies functioned as both local social organizations and purveyors of intellectual materials, providing members with access to books and newspapers. They increasingly took on a political character prior to the revolution. The influence on Jacobin clubs of secret societies such as the FREEMASONS is apparent in the Jacobins' emphasis on brotherhood and in their use of secret votes. When the revolution began in earnest, however, Jacobin clubs also appeared that had no previous ties to such societies.

The Breton Club rose to prominence with the National Assembly's move to Paris. Provincial branches soon spread across France, and their meeting places became centers of public debate, using parliamentary procedure. Although opening themselves to wider membership after the revolution, they began to practice more selective methods of admission as the societies increasingly came under the influence of the National Convention's tightly controlling committees.

The Jacobins' history is a microcosm of the French revolution's radicalization. Already in 1791, the club split over whether LOUIS XVI should be deposed after being captured while attempting to flee France. The resulting exit of moderate deputies to another club called the Feuillants allowed Maximilien ROBESPIERRE, the future leader of the Reign of Terror, to move into a position of authority. In 1792, as the monarchy was deposed and the National Assembly became the National Convention, the club expanded its membership to include the Montagnards—a radical political faction to which Robespierre belonged—as well as Paris's radical workers' group, the Sans-Culottes. By January 1793, the club was calling for the king's execution.

On September 5, 1793, the Jacobin clubs shifted from centers of public debate to instruments of political despotism with the establishment of the Reign of Terror under Robespierre. A member of the National Convention, the revolutionary governing body, Robespierre had advanced to become president of the Committee of Public Safety in July of 1793. The National Convention was an unwieldy body, so the deputies had formed committees to transact daily business. As the fledgling republic came under attack by foreign powers and confronted internal unrest, the Committee of Public Safety became the most powerful and most radical body in the government. Staffed by prominent Jacobins such as Marie-Jean Hérault de Séchelles and Jean-Nicolas Billaud-Varenne, the committee soon hunted the Jacobins' political enemies.

In this extreme environment, political differences were rapidly transformed into treason. The Girondists, for example, a more moderate group within the Jacobins who had been purged from the government in June of 1793, soon became enemies of the state. Led by Louis de SAINT-JUST, a Jacobin and member of the Committee of Public Safety, the revolutionary government convicted the Girondin leaders Georges Danton and Camille Desmoulins in a show trial and executed them on April 5, 1794.

Robespierre was able to seize power through the Committee of Public Safety by playing to the citizenry's fears of counterrevolution. In this way, the Jacobin clubs became tools of political control under his direction. Ever in search of new enemies, Robespierre encouraged the clubs to kill hundreds, and hundreds of thousands more were arrested by Jacobin mob justice. The clubs themselves also autonomously imposed brutal and senseless ordinances, created at the whims of their ruling members, upon the local population.

Robespierre was finally deposed and executed on July 27, 1794, and the Jacobin clubs were banned for

their roles in the Terror by the following November. Other Europeans reacted with horror to the events unfolding in revolutionary France. In ENGLAND, a wave of anti-Jacobin literature appeared at the end of the 18th century determined to counter the influence of radical political elements.

See also SOCIAL INSTITUTIONS OF THE ENLIGHTENMENT.

Further reading: Clarence Crane Brinton, *The Jacobins* (New York: Russell & Russell, 1961); M. O. Grenby, *The Anti-Jacobin Novel: British Conservatism and the French Revolution* (New York: Cambridge University Press, 2001); John Paxton, *Companion to the French Revolution* (New York: Facts On File, 1988); J. M. Thompson, *Robespierre* (New York: Basil Blackwell, 1988); Caroline Weber, *Terror and Its Discontents: Suspect Words in Revolutionary France* (Minneapolis: University of Minnesota Press, 2003).

Jacobites   Followers of the exiled Stuart kings of Great Britain beginning in the 17th century.

The Jacobites' main goal was to restore King James II (1633–1701) of the house of Stuart and his heirs to the throne of Great Britain. In the GLORIOUS REVOLUTION of 1689, Parliament deposed the absolutist Catholic James in favor of his daughter Mary and her Protestant husband, William of Orange. They were succeeded by Mary's sister, Anne, in 1702. Upon Anne's death in 1714, Parliament settled the crown on the distantly related German house of Hanover, dashing hopes for a Stuart restoration.

James II set up a court-in-exile in FRANCE, which was a center of Jacobite activity. After James II's death, his son James III and his grandson Prince Charles Edward continued the struggle to reclaim the throne.

Both James III and Charles promised to repeal the taxation and penal laws of the Hanoverians, as well as to restore Scottish independence. Regardless of which noble house they believed had the right to rule, many common people were attracted to the Jacobite movement because of its promises of lower taxation and religious tolerance. The largest pockets of support for the Stuarts were in Ireland and Scotland, especially in the Highlands.

In 1715 and 1745, the Jacobites staged major uprisings in an attempt to put the Stuarts back on the throne. Both rebellions depended on French and Spanish aid, which failed to fully materialize. Mismanaged from the start, the campaign of 1715 failed, and James III was forced to return to France. The 1745 rebellion, led by Charles, was successful in capturing the Scottish capital of EDINBURGH. However, poor planning and lack of coordination among the Jacobite leaders and their foreign allies slowed the army's progress.

The Jacobites were defeated in the disastrous Battle of Culloden in 1746. Outnumbered by the army of the English duke of Cumberland, Charles was eventually forced to flee the field. He spent months in hiding in the Scottish Highlands before returning to France, where he died heirless. The Stuart line came to an end with the subsequent death of Charles's brother Henry, a Roman Catholic cardinal.

Although politically unsuccessful, the Jacobites were a diverse group of individuals from every class of society and every Christian religion, many of whom had lived in countries across Europe. Talented and determined, they not only challenged the Hanoverian government, but also contributed to 18th-century culture with their artistic and intellectual achievements. Among many notable Jacobites were the economist Sir James Steuart, the painter Alan Ramsay, and the poet Algernon Swinbourne. Jacobitism and the struggles of 1745 were romanticized in later years by Sir Walter Scott in his *Waverley* series of novels and by Queen Victoria and her court.

See also ENGLAND; ROMAN CATHOLICISM; SCOTLAND; SPAIN; WILLIAM III AND MARY II.

Further reading: Murray Pittock, *Jacobitism* (New York: St. Martin's, 1998); Michael Hook and Walter Ross, eds., *The Forty-Five: The Last Jacobite Rebellion* (Edinburgh: HMSO for the National Library of Scotland, 1995).

Jansenism Religious movement within ROMAN CATHOLICISM with major strength in the Low Countries, FRANCE, GERMANY, and ITALY. The teachings of Jansenism had ramifications for THEOLOGY and for church-state relations in the 17th and 18th centuries. Jansenism appeared initially in the first part of the 17th century when a French clergyman, Jean Duvergier de Hauranne, Abbé de St. Cyran, began actively spreading the ideas of Cornelius Jansen, Bishop of Ypres (1585–1638) and professor at the University of Louvain in Flanders. Jansen had written a book entitled *Augustinus* (1640) that explored various controversial aspects of the philosophy of the ancient church father, Saint Augustine. St. Cyran developed both theological doctrines and a related mode of piety from the teachings of Jansen. In his capacity as a confessor at the convent of Port Royal outside PARIS, he spread his ideas to the nuns and to a group of associated men. The early group of Jansenists included Blaise Pascal, the renowned mathematician and philosopher; Pierre Nicole; Antoine Arnauld and Robert Arnauld d'Andilly, both members of a prominent anti-Jesuit, noble family of lawyers; and several prominent members of the collateral branches of the French royal family. Nicole, Antoine Arnauld, and Pascal became the major defenders of 17th-century Jansenism.

Quite rapidly, the Jansenists found themselves surrounded by controversy on account of their views about free will, predestination, and the necessity of taking frequent communion. They were accused of repeating the doctrinal errors of CALVINISM. They were also viewed as potentially subversive by LOUIS XIII, LOUIS XIV, and their ministers Richelieu and Mazarin. The causes for concern stemmed both from the implications of Jansenist doctrinal positions and from the political positions held by the Jansenists who were members of the high aristocracy or royal family. Jansenists were persecuted by the secular and ecclesiastical French authorities and opposed by the pope. The JESUITS bore them particular enmity. Popes Urban VIII and Innocent X, Alexander VII, Clement IX, and Clement XI all condemned various Jansenist propositions and books over a period from 1643 to 1713. The major Jansenist religious establishment, Port Royal, was finally closed down in 1709 after several earlier incidents during which royal officials forcibly removed certain of the nuns from its premises.

The Jansenist controversies can be divided into two phases. The first, which dealt primarily with doctrinal issues, lasted until 1669 when Pope Clement IX and French officials found a compromise solution to the theological questions and crises it had raised. The second phase of the controversy, the one with specific connection to the ENLIGHTENMENT, began with the publication of a book by the Oratorian scholar Pasquier Quesnel (1643–1719) called *Le nouveau testament en français avec des réflexions morales* (The New Testament in French with some moral reflections; 1692). The theological content of the book was condemned by Pope Clement XI in 1713 in the bull *Unigenitus Dei Filius*.

When the bull reached France, where it had to be registered in the PARLEMENTS (courts of law) to become the law of the land, it raised a political storm. Such was often the case in early modern states where relations between church and state were so intertwined that the simplest issue could threaten to upset precarious arrangements of power. In the case of the *Unigenitus* controversy, the positions associated with Jansenism (represented by Quesnel's book) blended neatly with those of Richerism and Gallicanism. Richerism was a movement whose adherents sought to give more power to the lower clergy in the French church while parliamentarian Gallicanism represented an attempt by the *parlements* to establish secular control over the Catholic Church in France. The 18th-century Jansenism that actually emerged as these movements blended together to create a new Jansenism was quite unlike its 17th-century counterpart. This complex new form of Jansenism soon spread throughout Europe.

Quesnel's book stated several basic themes that remained central to the movement throughout the 18th century. It dealt with issues of FREEDOM (free will), with the nature of grace, with the proper limits of ecclesiastical authority and with the conditions for establishing and preserving morality. In general, Quesnel believed that spiritual truth could be discovered and understood by individual Catholic believers; the pope was not the only individual on Earth who had access to such truths and the role of priests was given less significance than in traditional Catholic teachings. Quesnel claimed that because truth is available to all people, the pope or bishops had no right to impose dogma on believers unless the latter willingly accepted that dogma as truth. If taken seriously, his ideas gravely weakened the absolute authority of the pope in doctrinal matters and tended to support the idea of a representative form of ecclesiastical government.

Eighteenth-century Jansenism became especially popular in Italy and certain German territories. In France, the organization dwindled but took on a clandestine character. Jansenism provided the basic tenets of FEBRO-NIANISM, the enlightened movement developed in the HOLY ROMAN EMPIRE that aimed at reorganizing the central structures of the international Catholic church. Jansenism also provided a continual stream of anti-Jesuit sentiment, helping to fuel the opposition that finally brought about the suppression of that ultramontane order in 1773.

Jansenism is viewed today as one of the great modernizing influences to have come out of 17th-century Catholicism. It contributed to the development of world views that not only stressed the remoteness of God from the everyday affairs of the world, but also emphasized the necessity of individual strength in the resolution of religious crises. It also stimulated certain rational, legalistic approaches to ancient Christian sources. Pascal, its great polemicist, made not only a moving statement about the importance of faith in carrying believers beyond the limits of REASON, but also significant contributions to the development of the mathematically structured universe that underlies modern SCIENCE. Within Catholic lands, Jansenism played a role in intellectual life somewhat similar to that of PROTESTANTISM in the lands outside Catholic influence.

See also RELIGION.

Further reading: Henri Daniel-Rops, *The Church in the Eighteenth Century* (Garden City, N.Y.: Doubleday, 1964); William Doyle, *Jansenism: Catholic Resistance to Authority from the Reformation to the French Revolution* (New York: St. Martin's, 1999).

Jardin des Plantes French royal botanical garden located on the left bank of the Seine River in PARIS. The Jardin des Plantes held one of the largest botanical and zoological collections in 18th-century Europe. Guy de La Brosse, a royal physician for King Louis XIII, created the garden as a place for assembling rare plants of medicinal as well as ornamental value. The garden became a site for public lectures in botany, natural history, and CHEMISTRY. The lectures were vigorously opposed by professors of the University of Paris as an infringement on their special teaching privileges. The garden received substantial support from Colbert, the general controller of finance under LOUIS XIV. Its botanical collections were augmented with collections of animal specimens and fossils so that the whole institution became an important center of natural history.

In the 18th century, natural historians and comparative anatomists such as the comte de BUFFON, Louis-Jean-Marie DAUBENTON, Georges CUVIER, and Geoffroy Saint-Hilaire offered lectures at the gardens. As superintendents of the Jardin, Buffon, Daubenton, and Cuvier expanded and reorganized the collections according to the new CLASSIFICATION theories that were developing in the 18th century.

Research carried out at the Jardin helped to shed light on controversies over GENERATION and DEGENERATION of the species of living things. For example, the Jardin received from Thomas JEFFERSON the skeleton of a mammoth found in North America. Jefferson sent the skeleton to the Jardin to disprove Buffon's theory that degeneration of the species had occurred in the New World. Buffon equated degeneration with several physical traits including small size; therefore, the huge mammoth skeleton served to negate his theory.

During the FRENCH REVOLUTION, the Jardin and collections became the public Muséum d'Histoire Naturelle.

See also VOYAGES OF DISCOVERY.

Jay, John (1745–1829) *American jurist, diplomat, and statesman who was the first chief justice of the United States* Jay was born in Bedford, New York, and graduated from King's College (now Columbia University) in 1764. Besides studying the ancient classics, he also read several major works of the ENLIGHTENMENT, written by John LOCKE, MONTESQUIEU, Thomas HOBBES, and David HUME. He then studied law and was admitted to the bar in the colony of New York.

Jay participated in the events that led up to the outbreak of the AMERICAN REVOLUTION against British rule. As a delegate to the First Continental Congress (1774) in PHILADELPHIA, he supported reconciliation with Great Britain, claiming that colonial grievances against the British could be settled by framing the colonial position in terms of the historic rights of Englishmen. A new constitution was not required, according to Jay, because the traditional British system contained all the rights and guarantees that were needed to end the conflict. A form of this argument would be used later in ENGLAND by Edmund BURKE to explain his support for the American Revolution. Jay wrote his arguments into his *Address to the People of Great Britain* that was approved by the Congress.

Jay was also a member of the Second Continental Congress and continued to serve in the Congress after the outbreak of hostilities with Britain. He served as president of the Congress in 1778 and 1779. He also sat in the

New York Provincial Congress and helped to draft the first constitution of that state. He served as chief justice of New York in 1777 and 1778.

Jay served the United States as its ambassador to SPAIN during the Revolution. Although Spain had fought with the French against the British, nevertheless, as a colonial power in America, it did not wish to see the British American colonies achieve their independence. Jay was unable to obtain either financial support from Spain or to gain access to the southern Mississippi waterways that were controlled by Spain.

After the American and French troops defeated the British at the siege of Yorktown (1781), Jay served with Benjamin FRANKLIN in the delegation that negotiated the preliminary peace agreement of 1782. The final Treaty of Paris was signed in 1783. Jay continued his official duties with the United States by serving between 1784 and 1789 as the secretary for foreign affairs.

During the nationwide debates that surrounded the ratification of the new UNITED STATES CONSTITUTION (1787), Jay joined with Alexander HAMILTON and James MADISON in writing the *Federalist* (1787–88). This series of 85 newspaper essays drew on the works of Montesquieu and Locke in arguing for ratification of the Constitution. It is considered one of the classics of the Enlightenment in America.

President George WASHINGTON appointed Jay as the first chief justice of the Supreme Court of the United States in 1789. Jay served officially in that capacity until 1795 but was actually in Britain during 1794 negotiating a trade agreement and a plan for the withdrawal of British troops from American territories. In spite of its favorable provisions, the Jay Treaty, which was signed in 1794, proved unpopular with Americans. Mobs rioted against it and hanged Jay in effigy but failed to prevent its ratification by the United States Senate in 1795.

Jay resigned from the Supreme Court in order to become governor of New York (1795–1801). In 1799 he signed a bill that provided for the gradual elimination of SLAVERY in New York.

Jefferson, Thomas (1743–1826) *American lawyer, political leader, and philosopher, the principal author of the United States Declaration of Independence and the third president of the United States*

Jefferson was the son of Peter Jefferson, a farmer and surveyor, and of Jane Randolph Jefferson, a member of one of Virginia's most prominent families. Young Jefferson received a classical Latin education and also studied French. He enrolled at the College of William and Mary where, under the tutelage of William Small from EDINBURGH, SCOTLAND, he studied philosophy and MATHEMATICS. After graduating in 1762 from the College of William and Mary, Jefferson studied law and began his public life as the elected surveyor of Albemarle County in Virginia.

Thomas Jefferson, portrait by C. W. Peale. Jefferson helped to ensure that the foundations of the new United States of America rested securely on principles associated with the Enlightenment. *(Courtesy Independence National Historical Park)*

He was admitted to the Virginia bar in 1767 and set up a law practice in that year.

Jefferson served as a representative in the Virginia House of Burgesses from 1769 until 1775. As the dispute between Great Britain and the American colonies grew in rancor, Jefferson acted as one of the organizers of the colonial committees of correspondence. After the harsh British reaction to the Boston Tea Party, Jefferson launched a career as a political pamphleteer, publishing *The Summary View of the Rights of British America* (1774).

Jefferson began to design Monticello, his Federal-style house near Charlottesville, Virginia, in the late 1760s. Construction started in 1770, and the first part of the mansion was completed in 1775. The building strongly resembles estates in ENGLAND that had been modeled after the PALLADIAN STYLE. But it also contained several technological devices—a calendar clock and a revolving desk, for example invented by Jefferson himself.

Jefferson served as a delegate to the Second Continental Congress in its sessions of 1775 and 1776. He headed the committee (1776) that was charged with drafting the DECLARATION OF INDEPENDENCE and wrote most of that document himself. It provided the basic philosophy that justified the seizure of power by American colonists in their revolt against British rule. The famous opening lines of the Declaration—its references to self-evident truths and to EQUALITY among all "men," its definition of the NATURAL RIGHTS (unalienable rights) of men as life, LIBERTY, and the pursuit of HAPPINESS, and its reference to the social contract theory of government—came directly from the intellectual traditions of the ENLIGHTENMENT. They reflected major themes from the POLITICAL THEORY, PSYCHOLOGY, and MORAL PHILOSOPHY of that 18th-century European movement.

Like the political theorist John LOCKE, Jefferson believed that one of the natural rights of humankind is the right to own PROPERTY, but he modified his position by stating that the presence of either unemployed poor people or unused land in a nation indicates that this natural right has somehow been violated by property owners. Having become a member of the first legislature of the new state of Virginia, Jefferson pushed through property laws that ended the English customs of primogeniture (by which the eldest son inherited all property) and entail (restriction of inheritance to an owner's direct descendants).

Jefferson also tried to reform the system of EDUCATION in Virginia, borrowing again from the Enlightenment the notion that a well-planned, universal system of schools will bring prosperity and PROGRESS to a society. In 1796 Jefferson succeeded in securing passage of his bill providing three years of elementary universal education for any willing student in Virginia. But his other proposals—for statewide school buildings, a system of secondary schools, a university, and a state library—all failed.

Although Jefferson, like most wealthy Southern colonists, owned African slaves, he opposed the institution of SLAVERY of humanitarian grounds. His *Notes on Virginia* (1782) not only described the sufferings of Virginia during the American Revolutionary War, but also called for the abolition of slavery.

Jefferson's wife, Martha Wayles Skelton Jefferson, died in 1782, leaving Jefferson distraught and unable to work. He eventually returned to public life to serve in the Continental Congress from 1783 until 1785. He served as the U.S. ambassador to FRANCE in the crucial years (1785–89) leading to the outbreak of the FRENCH REVOLUTION. While in France, he received a draft of the new Constitution of the United States (1787). He insisted that a bill of rights be added to that document in order to make clearer the civil rights of American citizens. Several years later, the UNITED STATES BILL OF RIGHTS was appended to the Constitution.

Jefferson returned to the United States after the beginning of the French Revolution and became the first U.S. secretary of state (1790–93), under President George WASHINGTON. During this period, his political and philo-

sophical differences with Alexander HAMILTON, the U.S. secretary of the treasury, began to grow more intense. Hamilton favored a strong central government based on the rule of "the rich and the wellborn" and wanted U.S. economic policies to foster the growth of industry. Jefferson, on the other hand, believed that average citizens were capable of voting in a representative government and wanted to retain the agrarian character of the United States. The positions of these two men reflected tensions that were inherent in the political theory of the Enlightenment, and their arguments were echoed in discussions throughout Europe. Eventually, Hamilton became the head of the Federalist Party, and Jefferson assumed leadership of the first American party to be called the Republican Party (not a direct ancestor of the modern party of that name).

Jefferson served as second U.S. vice president, under the Federalist president John ADAMS, a situation that caused much tension within the executive branch of the government. Jefferson openly criticized the centrist policies of Adams and drafted the Kentucky Resolves (1798), which opposed the Alien and Sedition Acts. These acts attempted, in part, to restrict the free exchange of ideas, an enlightened cause of which Jefferson was a lifelong champion.

During his years as U.S. president (1801–09), Jefferson purchased the Louisiana Territory from France (1803) and sent the Lewis and Clark expedition to explore the vast Northwestern Territories. During his administration the United States fought the Barbary States and steered a course of neutrality in conflicts between Britain and France.

When Jefferson retired in 1809, he moved back to Monticello. He had enlarged the original house between 1796 and 1809 and continued to make architectural and agricultural experiments on the estate throughout his remaining years. He devoted himself also to his long-held dream of founding a university in Virginia. The resultant University of Virginia in Charlottesville was incorporated in 1819 and offered its first classes in 1825. Jefferson, loyal as ever to the enlightened ideal of pursuing truth, wherever it might lead, intended his university as a place where the FREEDOM of the mind would be protected and encouraged.

In this, his last great contribution to the new United States of America, Jefferson once again revealed his commitment to the ideals of the Enlightenment. Throughout his life, he worked on behalf of freedom of the press, religious TOLERATION, political liberty, and basic human equality. But his efforts did not stop with these well-known causes. Jefferson also accepted enlightened beliefs in human PERFECTIBILITY and in the powers of human REASON. Like the PHILOSOPHES, his counterparts in enlightened Europe, he believed that progress could be attained by the practical application of SCIENCE and technology to human problems. His activities at Monticello all stemmed from this attitude, informing not only his agricultural experiments, but also his botanical collecting activities, his inventions, and his constant intellectual pursuits. Even at the end of his life, Jefferson was, without a doubt, one of the outstanding representatives of the Enlightenment in America.

Further reading: Daniel L. Dreisbach, *Thomas Jefferson and the Wall of Separation Between Church and State* Law and American History Series (New York: New York University Press, 2003); Joseph J. Ellis, *American Sphinx: The Character of Thomas Jefferson* (New York: Random House, 1998; A. Goodwin, ed., *The American and French Revolutions, 1763–93,* vol. 8 of the New Cambridge Modern History (Cambridge: Cambridge University Press, 1968); Robert R. Palmer, *The Age of Democratic Revolution: A Political History of Europe and America, 1760–1800,* 2 vols. (Princeton, N.J.: Princeton University Press, 1959 and 1964); Garry Wills, *Inventing America: Jefferson's Declaration of Independence* (Garden City, N.Y.: Doubleday, 1978).

Jenner, Edward (1749–1823) *English physician*
Apprenticed first to a surgeon, and then educated under the supervision of the LONDON physician John HUNTER, Jenner concentrated on finding a means of immunizing people against smallpox that would be safer than INOCULATION.

Having noticed that milkmaids who had contracted a related mild disease called cowpox did not get smallpox, Jenner reasoned that inoculating with cowpox virus might provide a safe way of preventing smallpox. An eight-year-old boy, James Phipps, served as the subject for an experiment in which live cowpox virus taken from a milkmaid was injected under his skin. After several weeks, the boy received an inoculation of live smallpox virus and did not contract the disease.

Jenner published his results in 1798 as *Inquiry into the Cause and Effects of the Variolae Vaccinae.* Positive reaction to his discovery came only slowly, in spite of a remarkable reduction in deaths from smallpox after vaccination was introduced. Vaccination was sharply criticized by Jan INGENHOUZS, the physician who had devoted his life to furthering inoculation. Jenner, however, was handsomely rewarded for his work by the English Parliament, which granted him a royal pension. Eventually, Jenner's new vaccine revolutionized the medical approach to smallpox, leading to the elimination of the dreaded disease in Europe.

See also MEDICINE.

Jesuits Catholic religious order, founded in the 16th century by the son of a Basque nobleman, Ignatius of Loyola (1491–1556). As a young man, Loyola had served in the army of SPAIN and had frequented the court of Ferdinand of Aragon. A leg wound acquired during the French siege of Pamplona in 1521 ended his military career. During his convalescence, Loyola began delving into religious questions and adapting military analogies to the challenges facing Christianity. He resolved to become a monk in 1522 and retired to a monastery for contemplation. During the 10 months he spent there, Loyola experienced an intense conversion during which he allegedly saw the outlines of both a new religious order and new method of spiritual discipline. From that experience came the first version of his devotional manual *Spiritual Exercises,* which later provided the foundation of Jesuit spirituality. Loyola traveled to the Holy Land during 1523 and 1524, then returned to Spain to study at the university in Alcalá. There, he began gathering a small following of students, but his activities aroused the suspicions of the court of the Spanish Inquisition. Consequently, he left Spain for PARIS, where he pursued his theological studies at the University of Paris.

In 1534, still in Paris, Loyola and a tiny band of followers vowed to create a new order dedicated to the cause of preserving and defending the Catholic faith against onslaughts by infidels (Muslims) and by Protestant "heretics." Loyola obtained an audience with Pope Paul III in 1538, during which he explained the goals of his tiny group. Pope Paul approved the new order in 1540. Thus was born the Society of Jesus, better known as the Jesuits.

The Jesuits had four principal functions: hearing confessions, preaching, teaching, and missionary work. Their activities all focused on protecting and preserving Catholic Christianity. Their vows included the usual monastic vows of poverty, chastity, and obedience to the leader of the order, but they also swore unquestionable loyalty to the pope in Rome. This vow made the Jesuits an arm of papal policy and diplomacy as well as the primary defenders of Reformation Catholicism.

During the 17th century, the Jesuits developed a system of outstanding secondary schools (the *collèges*) and seminaries that trained major thinkers throughout Europe. The course of study in the *collèges* followed the outline of the *Ratio Studiorum* (Plan of Studies; 1559). Humanist disciplines received strong emphasis and the Jesuits played a significant role in spreading such learning throughout Europe. By 1579, the order had founded 144 *collèges* in Europe, and by 1749 that number had increased to 669 *collèges.* The Jesuits also operated 176 seminaries. Scholars such as Francisco Suarez and Luis de Molina, who were affiliated with the order, made lasting contributions to Catholic theology and produced critical editions of the writings of the church fathers. Athanasius Kircher, Christopher Clavius, and, in the 18th century, Ruggiero BOSCOVICH made important contributions to NATURAL PHILOSOPHY and mathematics.

The Jesuits established Catholic missions throughout the American colonies, India, and China. By the mid-18th century, more than 22,000 Jesuit missionaries were at work throughout the world. Members of the order also developed a base of effective domestic power by gaining appointments as confessors to various Catholic kings. In France, for example, they provided royal confessors for all the kings from Henry III through LOUIS XV, a period spanning nearly two centuries. Jesuits served the 18th-century Spanish kings in a similar capacity. Through these sensitive positions, Jesuits could exercise moral power over royal consciences in order to gain policy concessions favorable to ROME. Jesuits were the implacable foes of JANSENISM throughout the 17th and 18th centuries.

Throughout their history, the Jesuits were periodically accused of treason and worse. In France, members of the order were suspected of complicity in the assassination of Henry IV, the former Protestant who, as king of France, had ended the bitter religious strife of the 16th century. As the 18th century unfolded, the loyalty of Jesuits to the papacy became increasingly problematic in the eyes of secular, centralizing monarchs. In France, Madame de POMPADOUR and the duc de CHOISEUL opposed the influence of the order. Jesuits had additional foes in the proponents of Gallicanism, in the Jansenists of all countries, in Jansenist sympathizers (like the French PARLEMENTS), and in the intellectuals associated with the ENLIGHTENMENT. It began to seem imperative to rid secular kingdoms of the Society of Jesus.

Efforts by secular rulers to rid their nations of Jesuit influences began in PORTUGAL in 1758. There, the powerful enlightened prime minister, the marquês de POMBAL, was able to fan anti-Jesuit sentiment by implicating members of the order in an assassination attempt on King Joseph I. In order to gain support for his anti-Jesuit actions, Pombal engaged in an intense literary propaganda campaign throughout Europe. In 1759, he finally issued a decree that took the daring step of expelling the Jesuits from Portugal. The French soon followed the example of Pombal. The Jesuits had been implicated, although not decisively, in the assassination attempt by Robert François DAMIENS against Louis XV.

At about the same time, financial scandals involving a member of the order brought the Jesuits to the attention of the Parlement of Paris (court of law). The Parlement, composed of large numbers of supporters of Jansenism, was hostile to the Jesuits because of the ultramontane (propapacy) policies of the order. Parlement members, therefore, scrutinized the Jesuit constitution and determined that it was incompatible with the laws of the kingdom of France. A royal decree of 1764 expelled the order. Charles III of Spain followed the French example, securing the Jesuit expulsion not only in Spain (1767), but also in Naples (1767) and Parma (1768), which were ruled by his family members. Finally, in 1773, Pope CLEMENT XIV, under enormous pressure from the Bourbon rulers in France, Spain, and Naples, reluctantly issued a

bull that dissolved the Jesuit order. The Hapsburg empress MARIA THERESA implemented it unwillingly.

Prussia and Russia, both non-Catholic nations and therefore outside the reach of papal power, were unaffected by the papal decree. The rulers of these nations—FREDERICK II (THE GREAT) and CATHERINE II (THE GREAT)—recognized that the professional educational skills of the Jesuits were an asset to their nations, and therefore allowed the Jesuit establishments within their boundaries to continue functioning. Their actions protected the order from extinction. In 1814, after the abdication of Napoleon, the order was formally reinstated by Pope Pius VII.

See also EDUCATION; MATHEMATICS AND MECHANICS; ROMAN CATHOLICISM.

Further reading: Gerald R. Cragg, *The Church and the Age of Reason, 1648–1789* (New York: Penguin Books, 1970); Henri Daniel-Rops, *The Church in the Eighteenth Century* (Garden City, N.Y.: Doubleday, 1964).

Jews and Judaism   The extranational group having cultural, theological, or ethnic connections to the ancient tribal peoples of the region of Israel known as Hebrews.

Having been driven out of Palestine in 70 C.E., the Hebrew people scattered around the Mediterranean areas of northern Africa and southern Europe. Their subsequent history as residents of Christian-dominated Europe was marked by periods of relative toleration and harsh persecution. FRANCE, the UNITED PROVINCES OF THE NETHERLANDS, GERMANY, and ITALY all had permanent Jewish populations, their fortunes fluctuating with the political and religious moods of the dominant Christian society.

By the 18th century, Jews were living throughout Europe and RUSSIA, but they were especially concentrated in commercial centers such as the United Provinces of the Netherlands and the various Italian and German free cities. Large communities existed, for example, in AMSTERDAM, FRANKFURT, VENICE, and ROME. The largest Jewish populations, however, were found in the various states of central Europe, eastern Europe, and western Russia. Overall, two cultural Jewish groups—Sephardic Jews and Ashkenazic Jews—emerged. The influence of ENLIGHTENMENT philosophy was felt early among communities of Sephardic Jews living in areas such as Amsterdam, where religious positions such as DEISM became a part of the theological debates, although not without the strong rejection of such heresy by rabbinical leaders. Ashkenazic Jews were influenced more strongly by the German-Jewish version of the Enlightenment, the HASKALAH.

In general, 18th-century Jewish people were subject to special restrictions in their personal lives, economic endeavors, educational opportunities, and public worship. Jews in Italy, VIENNA, and eastern Europe were

Engraving by Bernard Picart, 1725, illustrating Hoshana Rabba, the last day of Sukkot (the Jewish harvest festival) in the Portuguese synagogue of Amsterdam. The celebrants carry tall willow twigs, called hoshana bundles, which they beat to commemorate the end of a period of repentance and judgment. *(Courtesy New York Public Library)*

required by law to live in ghettos, segregated sections of cities or towns. They were forced to wear identifying clothes, such as a red cloth "O" or a piece of yellow cloth attached to their clothing, as was the case in some Italian cities. They were also subjected to various civil disabilities that limited where they could live and what trades they could practice. These measures were not consistently applied, and exceptions were made in individual cases. Although Jews could not generally attend UNIVERSITIES, they were sometimes admitted to faculties of MEDICINE because that profession involved manual labor and was ranked relatively low in the traditional hierarchy of academic professions. As a result, medicine became one avenue along which some 18th-century Jews advanced into the professions and ultimately into higher social rank.

The Enlightenment brought some change in European attitudes toward Jews. Some people believed that religious TOLERATION should be extended to include Jews as well as Christians of varying persuasions. Others, inspired by the ideal of the universal brotherhood of humankind, believed that discriminatory laws should be removed. John LOCKE, Baron de MONTESQUIEU, and Gotthold Ephraim LESSING all made strong pleas for toleration.

A Jewish enlightenment called Haskalah developed in the German states of the north under the inspiration of Moses MENDELSSOHN. A complicated phenomenon, Haskalah began around 1750 in the northern German states as an attempt by Jewish intellectuals to update medieval Jewish traditions by importing philosophical concepts from the German Enlightenment into their scholarship. By 1800, however, Haskalah had become a movement for emancipating and assimilating Jews into the broader national cultures. As such, it became the cornerstone of the movement for Jewish modernization in the 19th century.

Although it began as a German-Jewish phenomenon, Haskalah expanded eastward and stimulated important changes in Jewish educational traditions across a large area. First, it increased interest in the study of Hebrew and of Jewish history throughout central and eastern Europe. Second, it led to the addition of secular education subjects such as mathematics to Jewish schools. This was usually balanced by the removal of Talmudic studies in schools such as Berlin's Freischule, which was established in 1778. Haskalah also helped to advance the cause of Jewish women in its advocacy of their inclusion in the new school systems.

This movement's goals were occasionally seconded by Jewish emancipation on the part of the heads of national governments, such as Russia's CATHERINE II (THE GREAT), who ended long-held discrimination laws. Toward the close of the 18th century, movements for reform stimulated by the Enlightenment produced toleration and emancipation decrees for Jews in several nations. Limited toleration existed in ENGLAND after the GLORIOUS REVOLUTION of 1688, but English Jews did not receive full civil rights until the 19th century.

PRUSSIA led the way on the European continent, establishing limited toleration early in the 18th century. AUSTRIA followed in 1782, when Emperor JOSEPH II issued a decree that freed Jews from the ghetto, suppressed discriminatory clothing laws, and allowed them into public schools in the Hapsburg territories of Austria, HUNGARY, Bohemia, and Moravia. About the same time, however, Joseph and his ministers established compulsory EDUCATION laws that linked the possession of a state-approved certificate of education with the right to obtain a marriage license. These laws extended the control of the secular state into Jewish private life in a new way and evoked strong opposition from Jewish communities. Thus, while Joseph's reforms released Jews from the worst of their civil disabilities, they subjected them along with the rest of the population to new forms of state control. In this context, it was particularly significant for Polish Jews that Austria, Prussia, and Russia dismembered the Polish state in the three partitions of 1772, 1793, and 1795, as their modernizing agendas were then imposed, albeit slowly, on Polish territories.

The FRENCH REVOLUTION and Napoleonic period had a great effect on the process of Jewish modernization. The French government had already issued a toleration edict in 1787, a policy that the revolutionary government continued. But this process was far from easy, since French Ashkenazic Jews and Christians lived in separate communities. (France's Sephardic Jews were few in number and were highly assimilated.) The mutual suspicion and hostility that this separation created led reformers such as Henri-Baptiste Grégoire to advocate dispersing Jews from their communities and settling them around France. This plan was impractical, since it ignored the crucial role Jews played in French finance and underestimated the power of traditionalism among both Jews and Christians. Napoleon Bonaparte, inspired by the ideals of the Enlightenment and ensconced by the revolutionary wars as the ruler of a great European empire, did much to change this situation, decreeing full civil rights for all Jews, Catholics, Protestants, and unbelievers anywhere in the regions under his control. Religious faith would no longer play a role in determining the legal status of citizens. This tendency toward emancipation for Jews, with accompanying pressures for assimilation, would continue in western and central Europe well into the 19th century, to be reversed only in its closing decades.

See also FRANKFURT; HOLY ROMAN EMPIRE; MILLENARIANISM; PORTUGAL; ROME; SPAIN.

Further reading: Glenda Ambramson, David Katz, and Nicholas de Lange, eds., *The Blackwell Companion to Jewish Culture: From the Eighteenth Century to the Present* (New York: Blackwell, 1990); Edward Breuer, *The Limits of Enlightenment: Jews, Germans, and the Eighteenth Century Study of Scripture* (Cambridge, Mass.: Harvard University Press, 1996); David S. Katz and Jonathan I. Israel, eds., *Sceptics, Millenarians and Jews* (New York: E.J. Brill, 1990).

Johnson, Samuel (1709–1784) *English essayist, biographer, poet, literary critic, and lexicographer*
Samuel Johnson (also known as Dr. Johnson) was one of the most influential and colorful literary figures of the English ENLIGHTENMENT and his contributions are honored in the academic world by the rubric "The Age of Johnson," which is often assigned to the second half of the 18th century.

Johnson was a strong believer in the power of LITERATURE to form human moral nature. He shared this belief with many of his enlightened compatriots. Many of his works reflect his commitment to these educational goals. Their number includes the poem "The Vanity of Human Wishes" (1749); various articles in the *Gentleman's Magazine*; the biography *Life of Mr. Richard Savage* (1744); essays in *The Rambler* and *The Idler; Rasselas, Prince of Abyssinia* (1759), a tale in oriental style on a theme from John LOCKE; and *Lives of the Poets* (1779–81), a collection of biographies considered by some scholars to be his most important literary work. Johnson also published a critical edition of Shakespeare (1765) and wrote an account of his travels with James BOSWELL through SCOTLAND entitled *Journey to the Western Isles of Scotland* (1775).

Johnson was the son of a bookseller of modest means. As a young man, he had to leave Oxford University because he lacked funds to support himself. He tried teaching by setting up a school at Edial, where David GARRICK was one of his students. This venture failed, and Johnson subsequently moved to LONDON, becoming part of the GRUB STREET PUBLISHING world. He apprenticed himself to the *Gentleman's Magazine* and, between 1740 and 1743, reported the speeches and debates of the English Parliament (in the guise of transactions of the Senate of Lilliput) in that periodical. The Parliament was not amused at this breach of its right to closed debate. The *Gentleman's Magazine* publisher Cave, and a competitor, Astley, who was printing similar reports in *London Magazine,* were apprehended and made to appear before the House of Commons. In subsequent years, it became more hazardous to print such materials. Johnson's motivation for writing the reports may have been partly political: He was a committed Tory, hostile to the Whig Party that dominated the English government. The accuracy of Johnson's reports is questioned by scholars, and his adaptations of the material may have been inspired by his critical political point of view.

From 1747 until 1755, Johnson wrote his *Dictionary of the English Language,* the first such publication in ENGLAND. The completed work appeared in 1755. In the process, he snubbed the earl of CHESTERFIELD, who had offered his patronage if the work were dedicated to him. Johnson wrote a letter to Chesterfield notorious for its lack of grace but famous as a clear statement of Johnson's intention to free himself from reliance on patrons. The letter reflects a prominent trend during the Enlightenment that appeared in all the arts: the abandonment of the old system of royal and aristocratic patronage and the concomitant appearance of independent artists who earned their living by selling their works in the marketplace.

Johnson presided over various social and literary gatherings in his home during which he evidenced brilliant conversational skills. In the 1760s his friend the painter Joshua REYNOLDS organized the Literary Club for Johnson as a private club where Johnson and his brilliant group of friends could demonstrate their conversational skills. Besides Johnson and Reynolds, its members included James Boswell, Oliver GOLDSMITH, David Garrick, Charles BURNEY, John GAY, and Edmund BURKE.

Throughout his life, Johnson displayed certain peculiar behaviors that included body tics, loud cries, and occasional bizarre utterances. His behavior disgusted some of his contemporaries including the earl of Chesterfield. Boswell, who wrote an important and popular biography of Johnson, left descriptions of Johnson's condition that still stimulate debate among scholars of Johnson's life and students of the history of MEDICINE. Explanations for Johnson's behavior range from poor upbringing, through mental illness, to the now fashionable idea that he had a neurological disorder called Tourette's syndrome.

Joseph II of Austria (1741–1790) *emperor of both the Hapsburg Empire and the Holy Roman Empire from 1765 to 1790*

Joseph II was the son of MARIA THERESA OF AUSTRIA and of Francis Stephen of Lorraine. Maria Theresa succeeded to the throne of the HAPSBURG EMPIRE in 1740 and Francis Stephen became Francis I, Holy Roman Emperor, in 1745. Joseph succeeded his father as Holy Roman Emperor in 1765. He also ruled the HAPSBURG EMPIRE jointly with his mother from 1765 to 1780, the year Maria Theresa died. Joseph continued as sole ruler of the Hapsburg Empire and as Holy Roman Emperor until his death in 1790.

Joseph ruled the Hapsburg lands as an enlightened despot. He was committed to CAMERALISM and to two associated general principles: that humanitarian concerns should guide state policy and that reform processes should be instigated from above by the emperor and his central state officials. Within the Hapsburg dominions, he continued the basic reform policies that had been laid down during his mother's reign. But unlike his mother, Joseph II had a radical commitment to the ENLIGHTENMENT and an authoritarian temperament. Impatient to increase the extent and the pace of reform, he began to abuse his power, acting outside the bounds that were tolerable to the subjects of his empire. The end of his reign was marked with strife and rebellion. If, on the one hand, his reforms embody the radical extremes of the Enlightenment, on the other hand, they show how at these extremes the tensions inherent within enlightened theories could give birth to political practices totally opposed to enlightened ideals. In this respect, Joseph II's reign demonstrates similarities with the rule of FREDERICK II (THE GREAT).

Joseph II was a rigid but extremely idealistic man. The Enlightenment vision of a world based on EQUALITY, humanitarianism, religious TOLERATION, universal EDUCATION, and economic security inspired his many radical reforms. He believed that change must come from the ruler in whose person both executive and legislative powers should reside. Any sharing of sovereignty with intermediate powers, such as the Estates, the guilds, the Roman Catholic Church, or the landed nobility, would only result in an impasse because these special interest groups squabbled among themselves, neglectful of the common good. When Joseph decided that something must change, he proceeded with direct assaults on any institutional or individual obstacles. He had no patience for gradual reforms or for the art of gentle persuasion. His mother, in contrast, had understood that she needed to respect the traditions of outlying Hapsburg territories like MILAN and the AUSTRIAN NETHERLANDS in order to rule them effectively.

Joseph directly attacked the traditional structures of power and privilege in both Milan and the Austrian Netherlands, replacing the old systems with centralized bureaucracies modeled after his mother's administration in Austria. Within the contiguous Hapsburg lands, Joseph II tackled the privileges of the guilds, confiscated Catholic Church lands, and installed a universal land tax divided proportionally according to the income of the proprietors. In contrast, his mother's land tax had recognized legal social status rather than wealth as the ground for determining tax rates.

The religious policies of Joseph II were called JOSEPHINISM by his contemporaries. Joseph's personal beliefs were drawn partly from DEISM and the FREEMASONS, whose enlightened spiritual orientation had roots in the notion of natural religion. He was immortalized by Wolfgang Amadeus MOZART as Sarastro, the wise, enlightened ruler in the opera THE MAGIC FLUTE. Joseph recognized the value of RELIGION as a shaper of social morality, but he wished to limit the ability of the Catholic Church to exert power in secular affairs. He also wished to extend state control into areas such as education and marriage (granting permission to marry) that traditionally lay in the religious domain. He attacked the fiscal privileges and wealth of the Catholic Church and tried to undermine its popularity with the people. By supporting FEBRONIANISM, he quarreled with the pope in ROME over internal church governance. But Joseph also instituted legal toleration and rights of public worship for religious dissidents (Lutherans, Calvinists, and Greek Orthodox), and removed certain civic disabilities aimed at the Jews of the empire. At least at the beginning of his reign, he also relaxed CENSORSHIP of the press.

Not surprisingly, all these activities aroused opposition from the conservative clergy and from the nobles, who believed that Joseph's reforms were undermining their traditional privileges. Minority religious groups also opposed his reforms aimed at cultural integration, fearing that assimilation through education, for example, might threaten their very existence. Joseph II responded to internal resistance by increasing the police activities of his state. He resorted to internal surveillance, to restrictions on academic freedom, and to the reestablishment of strict press censorship. He outlawed the Bavarian ILLUMINATI and associated radical lodges of Freemasons, fearing the program for revolutionary change that they were promoting. Thus, like Frederick the Great in Prussia, the great enlightened reformer Joseph II finished by curtailing LIBERTY and establishing the rudiments of an early police state. Upon Joseph's death in 1790, most of his reforms were dismantled, in spite of the fact that his brother and successor, Leopold II, also believed in their underlying enlightened ideals.

See also CALVINISM; DESPOTISM, ENLIGHTENED; JEWS AND JUDAISM; LUTHERANISM; ROMAN CATHOLICISM; SONNENFELS.

Josephinism   Term coined in the 18th century during the reign of JOSEPH II OF AUSTRIA. Originally it described the enlightened ecclesiastical policy promulgated by Joseph II and Prince Wenzel Anton von KAUNITZ. This group of decrees profoundly changed church-state relations in the Hapsburg lands. It developed into a loose theory whose adherents were called Josephinians. Over time, the term has been extended to cover the whole 18th-century ENLIGHTENMENT phenomenon of a secular, rational BUREAUCRACY working to further the interests of enlightened absolutism (see ABSOLUTISM, ENLIGHTENED).

The ecclesiastical policies of Joseph II consisted of a combination of liberal and authoritarian measures. Pragmatic matters rather than religious convictions originally inspired these policies. One practical problem, that of church challenges to the absolute authority of the emperor, could be solved by tackling the power of the Catholic church. The second set of problems, that of increasing the population in order to extend the tax base, could be tackled by welcoming persecuted dissidents into Hapsburg lands.

In the matter of the Catholic church, Joseph sought to eliminate church interference in secular affairs, thereby restricting its legitimate authority to matters of private belief and social morality. Church and state issues were to be separated as far as possible. Joseph's mother, Empress MARIA THERESA, although a devout and intolerant Catholic, had already considered such a policy. She had recognized that the Catholic church constituted a real limit to her powers and had wanted to limit its authority to the functions outlined in the New Testament of the Bible. Joseph decided to try to implement this plan.

In Austria, this meant tackling the substantial independence and wealth of the Catholic church. PETER I (THE GREAT) had achieved this very goal with the Orthodox Church in Russia, but his tactics could not be used in Austria. Joseph proceeded in several directions. He extended the tax obligations of the clergy; suppressed the common practices of popular piety that had contributed to a great resurgence of faith in the German-speaking Catholic lands; abolished pious lay organizations and contemplative monastic orders transferred ecclesiastical properties to the state, adapting them into granaries, asylums and prisons; regulated public prayer, rituals, and sermons; established state seminaries for training clergy; increased the power of Austrian bishop with respect to the pope in ROME (the program of FEBRONIANISM); and forbade the pope and the Austrian Catholic Church to communicate without the express permission of the emperor. While curtailing the liberties and powers of the Catholic Church, Joseph extended religious freedom to formerly persecuted dissidents. Thus, he granted to Calvinists, Lutherans, and Greek Orthodox believers the right to worship. He expanded the civil rights of Jews, allowing them a broader choice of domicile and occupation than they had traditionally been allowed. Joseph believed that a policy of TOLERATION would draw people to settle his depopulated lands. In fact, his policies regarding religious minority groups were frequently shaped by pragmatic considerations. Despite the protests of conservative clergy, the Josephinian religious policies survived his death.

Josephinism postulated that RELIGION is a political matter. Joseph's policies represent a fusion of Jansenist beliefs about the inner sources of religion with the enlightened belief that moral action is best produced through secular, rational social organization. The result was a new concept of the relations between the church and the state in which the state, in both principle and practice, assumes responsibility for the common good of humanity. The church continues to play an important role in shaping the moral dimension of individual human beings, but the energy of the religious impulse is channeled into the moral service of the state.

See also CAMERALISM; ROMAN CATHOLICISM.

justice and the law   The quality of being fair and equitable; the protection of the rights and properties of individuals or social bodies by a government, whether by legislation or custom, and the punishment of transgressors. The political and economic histories of different European states determined how each stood at the turn of the 18th century with respect to conceptualizing justice and enforcing the laws of the land or enacting new ones. Important variables arose from embedded political, religious, and class systems, including the range of the sovereign's power, parliamentary involvement, the reach and provenance of ecclesiastical courts, the appointment procedures and responsibilities of magistrates, and common law practices.

From medieval times, much of Europe had adopted Roman law, as codified by Justinian, as the law of Christendom. In the early part of the 18th century, the legislative code of the HOLY ROMAN EMPIRE was based on Roman law, although local tribal law and customs were also incorporated. Dutch-Roman law in THE UNITED PROVINCES OF THE NETHERLANDS combined Roman law with elements from cultures in close contact: German, Burgundian, and Spanish. In ITALY, which was still largely administered by feudal institutions that granted privileges to elite classes, the marchese di BECCARIA called for reform in his treatise *On Crimes and Punishments* (1764). He proposed that laws should be applied equitably to ensure "the greatest happiness shared among the greater number," his humanist position influenced by the baron de MONTESQUIEU, Jean-Jacques ROUSSEAU, David HUME, and other philosophers. In 1792, he advocated the abolition of the death penalty.

Despite theories of reform, Roman law remained in effect in most of Europe until it was supplanted by the French Civil Code (or Napoleonic Code) of 1804. The French Civil Code, in a clear, simple, and effective manner, established a virtually complete legal code based on the doctrines of NATURAL LAW. In 2,281 articles, the new law covered the law of persons, including family law; the law of property, including mortgage law; the law of torts and of contracts; the law of donations; and the law of successions.

After the FRENCH REVOLUTION reformists were intent on rearranging the authority behind French legal machinery in order to render punishment more homogeneous, effective, and reliable, and to reduce the economic and political costs to the population. They were successful in consolidating the power to judge and punish, which was assigned to the public sphere in the form of a contract between the citizen and the laws of society.

FRANCE exported its new code by conquest in the United Provinces (1811), Italy (1805–1820), the Hanseatic territories (1810), and the grand duchy of Berg (1811). By local jurists' advice, various German duchies, Swiss cantons, and the grand duchy of Warsaw adopted the code. The code was also revised and adopted in Greece (1827), various Italian states (1812–65), and Romania (1865). PORTUGAL drafted its own code inspired by the French (1867), and SPAIN drafted a code substantially similar to the French (1889). One way or another, the French code came to predominate in areas where "civil" or Roman law had prevailed. In addition to the states mentioned above, it became integral to the legislative process in SCOTLAND, BELGIUM, South Africa, Ceylon, Mauritius, the Spanish and French West Indies, Quebec, Louisiana, Mexico, Cuba, Puerto Rico, countries in Central and South America, and the Philippines.

Generally, a centralized, absolutist state, such as pre-revolutionary France, operated by more arbitrary legal and political methods than did the constitutional state of ENGLAND. In the early 18th century, these two major ENLIGHTENMENT states coincided in the overall means by which the social body (the population) might be best controlled. Laws that were enforced and the manner by which crimes were punished, as one might expect in a philosophically unified and cosmopolitan Europe, were similar, but England's common law system was more reliable and applied more equitably than was the law in France. However, both France and England held to the ancient practice of punishing the transgressor's body to set an example for others: Public execution was routine; traitors were hanged, drawn, and quartered (hanged briefly, eviscerated, and pulled apart by four horses); confessions were often wrested from defendants by torture; and some punishments involved branding.

Early 18th-century France was overrun by roaming gangs whose predatory activities shifted over time from overt violence against persons to the acquisition of property. Despite multiple attempts to unify French law, which varied from region to region, multiple and oftentimes countervailing courts hampered by private or royal interests prevented any fair dispensation of justice in the prosecution of crimes. By midcentury, criminality had increased dramatically. The poor were punished severely for minor crimes such as theft when the moral value placed on property relations conformed to bourgeois patterns of ownership.

After the French Civil Code replaced Roman law, the revision of the penal code followed in 1810. Punishment was transformed; segregation of the shamed malefactor and his or her confinement within the network of prisons (or convict-ships) became the usual penalty for crime. The new system was designed to reform the convict—in mind and soul—as well as to punish, and was accompanied by constant surveillance and pressure toward conformity.

Like France, England also endured a period of high criminality in the 18th century: Robbers on horseback and on foot—highwaymen armed with pistols and footpads armed with cutlasses, knives, or swords—were active everywhere, their daring and violent exploits frequent fodder for the newspapers. (Their fictionalized biographies, supposedly taken as gallows confessions, were also a popular subliterary genre.)

England had maintained a constitutional monarchy that restricted the sovereign from wielding arbitrary power. Each law enacted had to be approved by Parliament in the House of Commons, composed of elected members (though corruption in electoral matters was commonplace), and in the House of Lords, composed of hereditary peers and clergymen. To become law, the bill had to be signed by the monarch. Because the machinery of the powerful Catholic Church had been formally abolished during the Reformation, the Anglican ecclesiastical courts focused almost entirely on religious and moral issues rather than on common or constitutional law. Thus, Enlightenment secular ideals met with little religious resistance. British prison reformers such as William WILBERFORCE, John Howard, and Jeremy BENTHAM experienced less difficulty than did the French in altering the system to accommodate a more humane and just treatment of prisoners and convicts. The cataloging and codification of British law was significantly enhanced by Sir William BLACKSTONE in his *Commentaries on the Laws of England* (1765–69). British common law was the system of justice used in Canada (except Quebec), the UNITED STATES (except Louisiana), and the British colonies.

In the first half of the 18th century, LONDON magistrates convicted about 3,300 people of capital offences; in the second half of the century, they convicted about 3,600. During the century overall, some 3,350 criminals were actually executed (a ratio of nearly half). In 1800, there existed more than 200 capital offences on the statute books. After 1808, a number of common crimes were stricken from the death-penalty list. Between 1800 and 1830, 3,898 criminals were convicted of capital crimes, but only about 500 executed (a ratio of less than 15 percent). The reduction in actual executions reflects, in part, an increased concern with the hardships endured by the poor, but also the availability of alternative punishments, including imprisonment and exile. (Unlike the French, the English had only in rare periods resorted to the penalty of forced labor.) The Transportation Act of 1718 permitted the courts to sentence individuals convicted of serious crimes and some lesser offenses to seven or 14 years of exile to the American colonies. Later, at the instigation of Joseph BANKS, the penal destination changed to Botany Bay, Australia.

Other important legal measures in Britain included the English Riot Act (1715), which was amended in 1769 to include protection of industrial mills; the establishment of the Westminster Watch Act (1735), which permitted London householders to hire their own watchmen to patrol the streets; the establishment of the Bow Street Police Office (1739), which hired the first policeman in 1753; the Combination Act (1800), which established a Thames Police Office at Wapping, an important port district; and the Militia Act (1757), which levied military service from local, able-bodied men in England and Wales to participate in domestic peacekeeping during times of public disorder.

Besides the commission of thefts, robberies, counterfeiting, poaching, assaults, rapes, prostitution, bigamy, murders, witchcraft, and so forth, the English populace at large was inclined over the course of the century to engage in rioting and sedition (the stirring up of political discontent) for a number of causes. As in prerevolutionary France, public disorder arose in reaction to religion, politics, land privileges, food and alcohol shortages, labor disputes, and taxation. In London, even the price of theater tickets created a stir. Most characteristic of the English were riots involving attacks on Catholics, Methodists, and other Dissenters; the enclosure of common lands; elections; food shortages; attempts to control workers and introduce labor-saving machinery; and the Militia Act. Indeed, one or two riots occurred nearly every year throughout the century. Alarmed by the French Revolution, after 1789 the British government pursued prosecutions for sedition and treason. Two proclamations against seditious publications were issued in 1792; in 1795, Parliament passed laws to suppress treason and sedition, which extended the crime of treason to spoken as well as written words and restricted public meetings and political lectures. Thomas PAINE, the English revolutionary, was one of the victims; he was convicted in absentia for seditious libel.

Common crimes, agricultural and industrial unrest, and political upheaval all contributed significantly to the lawlessness of 18th-century Europe. France and England, and later many other European and American states, by civil or common law, attempted to improve the legal protections available to the common man or woman. Equitable legal treatment in unbiased judicial systems became, if not usual, at least a possibility.

See also ABSOLUTISM; CLASS AND RANK; COSMOPOLITANISM; EMPIRICISM; HUME; IDÉOLOGUES; MONTESQUIEU; MORAL PHILOSOPHY; POLITICAL THEORY; REASON; ROMAN CATHOLICISM; ROUSSEAU; SOCIAL CONTRACT.

Further reading: Michel Foucault, *Discipline and Punish* tr. Alan Sheridan (New York: Vintage, 1979); Bernard Schwartz, ed., *The Code Napoleon and the Common-Law World* (New York: New York University Press, 1956).

K

Kant, Immanuel (ca. 1724–1804) *German philosopher*
The son of a saddler in Königsberg, Immanuel Kant was brought up in a home infused with the spirit and outlook of PIETISM. This form of LUTHERANISM had a profound impact on his MORAL PHILOSOPHY, even though he rejected some of its outward forms, beginning with his education at a Pietist school in Königsberg when he was eight years old. Kant's distaste for the school's strict regimen may have shaped his attitudes toward Pietist beliefs. The city, with its diverse population of various European nationalities, was to prove influential in Kant's intellectual development. He attended the university there and then spent a few years as a private tutor in eastern PRUSSIA before resettling in 1755 in Königsberg. He offered private lectures in that city until 1770, waiting for a position at the university and rejecting positions at other schools until he finally received a professorship in logic and metaphysics there when he was 31 years old.

Kant's lectures became so increasingly popular that eventually a seat could be gained only by arriving hours before the presentation. He remained in Königsberg for the rest of his life, receiving distinguished visitors from all over Europe, preparing lectures, and writing the various parts of his masterly synthesis of the philosophical traditions that had informed the ENLIGHTENMENT.

Kant was renowned for the regularity of his daily life, designed to maximize his intellectual development. Each evening at a specific hour, for example, he could be observed taking a walk. Tradition holds that Kant violated this regime only twice in his life: first, on the day that he read the SOCIAL CONTRACT by Jean-Jacques ROUSSEAU and second, when he learned of the outbreak of the FRENCH REVOLUTION. He gained a reputation for condemning music and noise in general, to the point that he filed a complaint with the police against the audible singing of hymns by prisoners. Despite such misanthropic tendencies, Kant also appreciated guests in his home and would invite people for meals, at which his ready wit charmed listeners.

Kant's intellectual life is usually divided into two periods, the precritical period and the critical period. The precritical period includes his work before 1770, the year when he rejected the philosophical tradition associated with Gottfried LEIBNIZ and Christian WOLFF that he had learned at the university, and began working out his new system. Kant's early works included *Allgemeine Naturgeschichte und Theorie des Himmels* (General history of nature and theory of the heavens; 1755), a work on NATURAL PHILOSOPHY; *Der einzige mögliche Beweisgrund zu einer Demonstration des Daseyns Gottes* (The only possible proof of the demonstration of God's existence; 1763); *Beobachtungen über das Gefühl des Schönen und Erhabenen* (Observations on the sensation of beauty and the sublime; 1764), a discussion of AESTHETICS; and *De mundi sensibilis atque intelligibilis forma et principiis* (On the world of sensible and intelligible form and principles; 1770).

Kant's critical period consisted of the years after 1770, when he published the systematic results of his critical inquiry into the foundations of REASON and moral philosophy. These seminal works appeared in print between 1781 and 1797 and include *Kritik der reinen Vernunft* (Critique of pure reason; 1781); *Prolegomena zu einer jeden künftigen Metaphysik die als Wissenschaft wird*

Immanuel Kant, portrait by Hans Veit Schnorr von Carolsfeld. At the close of the 18th century, the Königsberg philosopher Immanuel Kant elaborated a new systematic philosophy that joined the various philosophical traditions of the 17th and 18th centuries into a creative synthesis. *(Courtesy Marburg Art Reference Bureau; original in the Kupferstichkabinett, Staatliche Kunstsammlungen, Dresden)*

auftreten können (Prolegomena to any future metaphysics; 1783); *Grundlegung zur Metaphysik der Sitten* (Fundamental principles of the metaphysics of morals; 1785); *Metaphysische Anfangsgründe der Naturwissenschaft* (Metaphysical first principles of science; 1786); *Kritik der reinen Vernunft* (Critique of pure reason, 2nd ed.; 1787); *Kritik der practischen Vernunft* (Critique of practical reason; 1788); *Kritik der Urtheilskraft* (Critique of judgment; 1790); *Die Religion innerhalb der Grenzen des blossen Vernunft* (Religion within the bounds of reason alone; 1793); *Zum ewigen Frieden* (On perpetual peace; 1795); *Die Metaphysik der Sitten* (Metaphysics of morals; 1797); and *Anthropologie in pragmatischer Hinsicht* (A practical view of anthropology; 1798).

Only once did Kant's ideas cause trouble with the censoring authorities in Prussia. The book *Die Religion innerhalb der Grenzen der blossen Vernunft* had received the approval of the theological faculties both at Königsberg and Jena, but the devout Frederick William II of Prussia, successor to FREDERICK II, attacked it as hostile to Christianity and Scripture. He threatened Kant with prosecution if he published anything further on the matter of

RELIGION. Kant refrained from doing so, waiting until after the king's death to publish his last work, *Der Streit der Fakultäten* (The conflict of the faculties; 1798).

Kant was noted for his moral earnestness and devotion to duty, traits that probably resulted from his Pietist upbringing. He was not devoutly religious, and he rarely attended church services except when necessary for some special occasion. He was committed to the cause of seeing republican forms of government established in Europe and enthusiastically welcomed both the AMERICAN REVOLUTION and the French Revolution. He longed to see peace established in Europe and sketched out a plan for securing it in his book *Zum ewigen Frieden*. He also maintained a lifelong interest in natural history and SCIENCE.

During his critical period, Kant devoted himself to examining and resolving two basic sets of tensions within the philosophical traditions of the Enlightenment. First, he focused on the tension between the contrasting views of knowledge offered by RATIONALISM and EMPIRICISM. These tensions dated back to the Middle Ages but had assumed particular urgency during the Enlightenment. Second, he struggled to resolve the tension between the natural world described by science and the moral world of human action. This tension translated into an investigation of the relationship between determinism and FREEDOM in human nature.

Kant could not accept the theory in John LOCKE's empirical PSYCHOLOGY that all ideas derive ultimately from sensory experience. But he also rejected the opposing rationalist belief in innate ideas, present in the mind since birth. In spite of the latter position, Kant did believe that the operations of reason add something from within the mind to the elemental sensations received from the external world. Kant called these additions from the mind a priori (before facts) concepts and believed that they were produced by the formal structures of the mind.

David HUME had also insisted that a priori ideas exist, but he had ascribed their origins to the psychological habit of associating ideas. Kant rejected Hume's psychological explanation of origins and turned instead to reinvestigating the fundamental philosophical aspects of human reason. At the end of the Enlightenment, he thus asked the epistemological question with which the era had begun: What are the conditions in which the human mind produces knowledge?

Kant began his investigation with an explanation of the possible types of logical statement (judgments). He accepted the Leibnizian division of judgments into analytic a priori and synthetic a posteriori types. Analytic judgments are necessarily true and universally valid. They give no information about the subject that is not already contained in its definition. Kant offered as an example the statement, "All bodies are extended." In the MECHANICAL PHILOSOPHY, from which Kant was drawing his definition of the term *body,* extension (occupation of space) is intrinsic or fundamental to the idea of body. A body cannot exist that lacks extension. Synthetic judgments, in contrast, are the product of experience. They are contingent upon context rather than necessarily true. The statement "All bodies have weight" was for Kant a synthetic judgment. The basic definition of the term *body* did not, in his vision, contain the idea of weight. That bodies weigh something is an idea we derive from our experience with real bodies in the external world. The synthetic judgment thus pairs together two concepts from the world of sensory experience.

Kant created a third type of judgment, the synthetic a priori judgment. These judgments build on sense data just as synthetic judgments do. But they process this data according to a priori concepts in the mind that are activated by the sense data. Kant gave the example of causality. We see two events occur in succession: Pool ball A strikes pool ball B. This experience activates the a priori concept of causality in our minds, making us think that the fact that pool ball A strikes pool ball B causes B to move in a certain direction. Synthetic a priori judgments occur, according to Kant, in mathematics, physics, and ethics. In short, they allow us to extend our knowledge derived from sense data by transforming it according to certain notions contained in the structure of the mind.

Kant eventually developed the general notion of the a priori concept into a system of categories of the mind. The categories were divided into four groups having to do with quantity, quality, relation, and modality. They can be found in the first chapter of the section of the *Critique of Pure Reason* entitled "Analytic of Concepts." All sense data are given a special form, or set of internal RELATIONS, by these categories. As a result, nothing that we know about the world outside us is known as it actually is. All our sensory information has been molded and transformed by these categories, and our minds are thus actively involved in creating knowledge.

Kant maintained that his new treatment of knowledge amounted to a COPERNICAN REVOLUTION in EPISTEMOLOGY. In a manner resembling Nicolaus COPERNICUS's transformation of ASTRONOMY, Kant had, he claimed, thoroughly reversed the basic hypotheses at work in epistemology, assuming not that our knowledge must conform to objects, but rather that objects (in our perception) must conform to our knowledge.

Having spelled out this scheme of the operations of human reason, Kant proceeded to investigate four basic epistemological questions: How are pure mathematics and science possible; how are natural science and physics possible; how is the human tendency to think about metaphysical questions (questions dealing with phenomena beyond the bounds of the world, such as God's existence) possible; and how is a true science of metaphysics possible? In the course of exploring these questions, Kant offered a proof of the validity of Isaac NEWTON's belief in the uniformity of nature. He also developed the concept of Transcendental Ideas, ideas that lead into realms beyond the boundaries of human knowledge. We can assume their reality because facts point to them, but we can never completely prove or understand these ideas. For Kant, the three great Transcendental Ideas were God, freedom, and immortality.

A related concept was that of the antinomies, four pairs of logical propositions, each pair consisting of a thesis and its contradicting antithesis. With the antinomies, both thesis and antithesis can be proved true by logical methods, a situation that leads to ridiculous and contradictory conclusions. Anyone who tries to prove the existence of God or the reality of one of the Transcendental Ideas will fall into the trap of the antinomies. Although Kant developed the antinomies from traditional philosophy by pairing propositions taken from rationalist systems with those drawn from empirical systems, he believed that they actually arose out of the fundamental nature of the human intellect. Kant listed four antinomies whose theses and antitheses dealt with the themes of space, time, causality, and freedom. Antinomies arise whenever people try to reason about the ultimate unity of the universe. Although we can vaguely imagine such unity, the limits of our reason prevent us from adequately conceiving it in logical terms, thereby leading us into logical contradictions.

The issue of freedom, touched both on POLITICAL THEORY and on moral philosophy. Kant, like many of his contemporaries, attempted to understand the origins of human morality. He did not believe in the existence of a natural morality, but rather stressed that the highest morality consists in controlling natural desires and drives. The greatness of human beings resides in their freedom to choose whether to act in a moral manner.

Kant developed the concept of the categorical imperative to explain the origins and nature of morality. The categorical imperative is an unconditional command, one that must always be obeyed. Furthermore, it is universal, applicable to all human beings. Morality consists of categorical imperatives—commands to act at all times in certain ways. One famous categorical imperative consists of the command never to use another human being as a means to an end. The independence, integrity, and value of the other must always be recognized. Morality does not allow people to ask whether a specific action will bring a desired practical result in a given situation. Rather, morality requires us always to ask whether we would want a specific behavior to become a universal law.

The question of morality was closely linked in the Enlightenment with the question of the human will. For Kant, goodwill was the only unqualified good thing in human nature. He insisted that HAPPINESS, another quality considered desirable by many enlightened thinkers, could be valuable only if it were linked with goodwill. Kant went further, however, suggesting that actions have moral worth only if they are performed out of a sense of duty. In other words, human beings must consciously choose to act according to the moral categorical imperatives.

According to Kant, human nature is composed of two conflicting tendencies. The first is a natural drive to join together in a society or community, while the second consists of the drive to live independently. The combination of these drives creates the "unsocial sociability" of human character and produces unresolvable conflicts that make the attainment of happiness impossible. Nevertheless, it is the unsocial sociability that serves as the motor that drives human HISTORY forward, progressing from the early primitive state of nature to the ultimate state of culture in which reason will prevail. The tensions between nature and culture, or between reason and feeling, produce problems for civilization that will finally disappear when the artificial human culture becomes so strong and thoroughly ingrained that it is a second nature of humankind.

Kant was especially concerned with protecting what he believed was the one fundamental right of humankind—the right to freedom. He did not, however, define freedom as the absence of restrictions, but rather believed that freedom can exist only within the context of a civil society structured by a system of public law. Rousseau's political theory—especially the concept of the "General Will" derived from the "Social Contract"—provided Kant with a starting point. He conceived of the General Will as a kind of "idea" that directs practical legislation, and he accepted the notion that society is based on an original contract. Society is thus composed of an assembly of individuals, each of whom possesses the capacity to make free decisions, but each of whom is also responsible to the General Will. The central problem in social life lies in preserving freedom of action while still recognizing the needs of others.

Kant provided one of the greatest 18th-century statements of the positive content of the Enlightenment in his essay "*Was ist Aufklärung?*" But even his contemporaries, such as Moses MENDELSSOHN, recognized that he came to the Enlightenment as a destroyer. Kant denied the existence of a unitary source of knowledge, of the possibility of proofs in metaphysics, of natural morality, and of MATERIALISM, yet he also provided one of the great systematic theories of reason, revealing both its limits and its potential. His work thus renewed aspects of the Enlightenment and formulated a series of major problems for modern philosophy. In the years immediately after his death, however, his ideas were either transformed by the "Idealists" led by Johann Gottlieb Fichte, Friedrich Wilhelm Joseph von Schelling, and Georg Wilhelm Friedrich Hegel, or abandoned by those German intellectuals who turned instead to the lure of ROMANTICISM.

See also ANTHROPOLOGY; *AUFKLÄRUNG*; HAMANN; HERDER; MATHEMATICS AND MECHANICS; RIGHTS; SUBLIME.

Further reading: Martin L. Davies, *Identity or History: Marcus Herz and the End of the Enlightenment* (Detroit: Wayne State University Press, 1995); Immanuel Kant, *Selected Precritical Writings and Correspondence with Beck,* tr. and intro. G. B. Kerferd (New York: Manchester University Press, 1968); Walter Kaufmann, *Discovering the Mind: Goethe, Kant, and Hegel* (New York: McGraw-Hill, 1980); Roger Scruton, *Kant* (New York: Oxford University Press, 1982).

Karl-August, duke of Weimar (1757–1828) *prince of the Holy Roman Empire in his capacity as ruler (1775–1828) of the tiny duchy of Weimar. In 1815, during the European negotiations that followed the Napoleonic Wars, Karl-August became grand duke of an expanded German principality called Sachsen-Weimar-Eisenach.*

Karl-August's father, Duke Ernst-August II, had died in 1758, the year after his son's birth. As a result, Karl-August's mother, Princess Anna Amalia of PRUSSIA, niece of FREDERICK II (THE GREAT), ruled the duchy of Weimar until her son reached the age of 18. Anna Amalia introduced the ideas of the ENLIGHTENMENT into Weimar culture by presiding over a salon and by welcoming various enlightened leaders to the duchy. She provided an outstanding tutor for young Karl-August in the figure of the poet Christoph Martin WIELAND.

In 1775, upon reaching the age of majority, Karl-August assumed the reins of government. He promptly invited Johann Wolfgang GOETHE to join his privy council. Goethe exercised a wide-ranging influence over the policies of the duchy of Weimar. At his urging, Karl-August asked Johann Gottfried HERDER to join his administration. Between 1775 and 1785, Karl-August instituted numerous reforms that were formulated by applying enlightened values to the practical problems of the duchy. These measures affected finances, taxation, mining, roads, and agriculture. Much of their inspiration derived from the teachings of the PHYSIOCRATS, and Goethe provided persuasive arguments to support the changes.

However important these administrative reforms, the most significant contribution made by Karl-August to the German 18th-century legacy lay in his patronage of the arts and intellectual life. Under his rule, and especially with the presence of Goethe, Herder, and Wieland, Weimar became a brilliant cultural center. The university at Jena drew outstanding young scholars and students such as Friedrich SCHILLER, Johann Gottlieb Fichte (1762–1814), and Friedrich Wilhelm Joseph von Schelling (1775–1854). Both Weimar and Jena became major destinations for foreign intellectuals.

Karl-August did not limit his political activities to his tiny principality but also, from 1783 until 1790, energetically participated in the affairs of the HOLY ROMAN EMPIRE. He involved himself in the ultimately fruitless efforts to reform the empire by resurrecting the traditional representative institution known as the Diet (*Reichstag*). He also joined Frederick the Great's Constitutional Association of Imperial Princes, which served to limit the expansion of Hapsburg power in the empire by preserving Prussia as a counterbalance. However, when the Austrian Hapsburg and Prussia reached an accord in the 1790 Convention of Reichenbach, hopes for substantive reform of the empire died. Karl-August left a sort of requiem for the idea of reform in his *Venezianschen Epigrammen* (Venetian epigrams). Goethe likewise noted the "passing" of a dream in the opening verses of his *Huldigungsgedichten* (Poems of homage).

During the upheavals caused by the FRENCH REVOLUTION, Karl-August served as a general in the Prussian armies that were fighting against the French and participated in the important battle of Jena (1806). The year 1814 found him leading the armies that liberated BELGIUM and the UNITED PROVINCES OF THE NETHERLANDS from Napoleon's rule. With the return of peace to Europe, Karl-August, now head of the expanded principality of Sachsen-Weimar-Eisenach, turned his attention to the matter of establishing a constitution in Weimar, as had been mandated by the treaties and articles establishing a new German Confederation (1816). Karl-August's reform activities, including freedom of the press, participation in the Jena *Burschenschaft* (a radical movement composed of university students supported by some professors and intellectuals), and the establishment of a representative, elected assembly in his duchy, advanced beyond limits acceptable to most German rulers in the early post-Napoleonic era. In the aftermath of the assassination of the conservative playwright August von Kotzebue (1761–1819) by a member of the General German Students' Union, the major German princes passed the Karlsbad Decrees (1819), which imposed strict CENSORSHIP in all principalities of the Confederation. As a result, in 1819, Karl-August's reform activities came abruptly to a halt.

Karl Wilhelm Ferdinand, duke of Braunschweig-Wolfenbüttel (1735–1806) *ruler of the duchy of Braunschweig-Wolfenbüttel from 1780 to 1806*

Marriage alliances linked the Braunschweig princes with PRUSSIA, thereby providing them with a powerful ally and protector. Karl Wilhelm Ferdinand exhibited interests as a young man in the intellectual trends of the ENLIGHTENMENT and in state reform. He studied the writings of the French PHILOSOPHES and traveled to Ferney to visit VOLTAIRE. He also read the German systematic, rational philosophers such as Gottfried Wilhelm LEIBNIZ and Christian WOLFF and writers of the *AUFKLÄRUNG* such as Gotthold Ephraim LESSING. Karl Wilhelm Ferdinand brought Lessing to his capital at Wolfenbüttel to serve as curator and librarian of the impressive (and still extant) ducal library.

As the ruler of Braunschweig-Wolfenbüttel, Karl Wilhelm Ferdinand earned an international reputation as an able, energetic, an enlightened leader. He instituted fiscal and educational reforms, improved the roads, liberalized

restrictions on the press, and finally, although personally a Lutheran, practiced TOLERATION of the Jews.

Karl Wilhelm Ferdinand was also a skilled military commander who served in the Prussian army of FREDERICK II (THE GREAT). During the wars brought about by the FRENCH REVOLUTION, the French revolutionary government considered offering him the command of the French armies, but that plan never reached fruition. Instead, Karl Wilhelm Ferdinand, who had already been made a Prussian field marshal in 1787, headed the German armies when they launched their invasion of France in 1792. He was defeated at Valmy and resigned his command but resumed the command of the Prussian army in 1806. Karl Wilhelm Ferdinand's troops were defeated by the French at Auerstädt, but he was mortally wounded during the battle on the very same day that Napoleon defeated another Prussian army unit at the battle of Jena. Karl Wilhelm Ferdinand died a few weeks later.

Kauffman, Angelica (1741–1807) *Swiss painter*

Angelica Kauffman was born in the small Swiss town of Chur. Her father, a painter of modest talents, discovered in Angelica a prodigious gift for both painting and MUSIC. He educated her in these arts as well as in poetry and HISTORY, and her mother taught her to speak fluent German and Italian. Later, she learned English.

The family moved to Como, ITALY, in 1752. The bishop of Como heard about Angelica's talent and commissioned her to paint his portrait. Shortly thereafter, Angelica became renowned as a portraitist, a distinction she carried all her life. In 1766, she moved to LONDON, where she continued to paint portraits. She also turned to mythological and historical subjects. Her work struck a chord because of its SENSIBILITY, expressed in the decorative nature of her figures and the sentimental attitudes, or poses, of her subjects. Eventually, this became the chief criticism leveled against her work as well. Kauffmann, however, was one of the few women to paint mythological and historical scenes. Her peers attested to their respect for her work by making her one of the 36 founding members of the Royal Academy of London in 1768—one of only two women.

Kauffmann was almost as celebrated for her social abilities as for her painting. When she was a young woman in Italy she made the acquaintance of the famous German art historian Johann Joachim WINCKELMANN, who was seemingly as impressed with her beauty and voice as with her artistic talent. In London she became a protégée of the renowned painter Joshua REYNOLDS, a source of flirtatious attraction for the painter Henry FUSELI, and the toast of British royalty. Her scandalous first marriage, to a so-called count de Horn (soon revealed to be an impostor) in 1767, contributed to her fame. Her second marriage, to the painter Antonio Zucchi, was more stable. They left England shortly after their marriage and settled in ROME, where Kauffmann befriended the visiting Johann Wolfgang von GOETHE and once again became involved in high society.

Zucchi died in 1795. The tumultuous conditions in Europe (exemplified and incited by the FRENCH REVOLUTION) made it difficult to collect debts, which brought Kauffmann into financial difficulties. She also suffered from poor health during the last years of her life. She managed to travel and to continue painting, however, until the end.

Further reading: Dorothy Moulton Piper Mayer, *Angelica Kauffmann, R.A., 1741–1807* (Gerrards Cross: Smythe, 1972)

Kaunitz, Wenzel Anton von, Prince von Kaunitz-Rietberg (1711–1794) *chancellor of Austria under Maria Theresa and Joseph II*

One of the chief architects of the Hapsburg reforms, Kaunitz was recognized as an outstanding 18th-century statesman. MARIA THERESA honored his contributions in 1764 by awarding him the title of Prince of Kaunitz-Rietberg. Kaunitz's paternal relatives, including his father Maximilian-Ulrich, Count of Kaunitz-Rietberg (1679–1746), had established a tradition of service as statesmen and diplomats for the Hapsburg emperors. Young Kaunitz allied himself with another family of statesmen when he married Maria Ernestine von Starhemberg in 1736. Kaunitz received a thorough education, capped by studying law in Leipzig. At the conclusion of his formal education, he embarked on a GRAND TOUR of Europe, spending time in BERLIN, the UNITED PROVINCES OF THE NETHERLANDS, ROME, Naples, and PARIS.

Kaunitz returned to his native city, VIENNA, in early 1734 and worked in a series of minor government posts. He entered the Austrian foreign service in 1740 and subsequently represented Empress Maria Theresa at TURIN and BRUSSELS. Kaunitz helped to negotiate the Treaty of Aix-la-Chapelle (1748), which ended the WAR OF THE AUSTRIAN SUCCESSION. He then received an assignment as Austrian foreign minister in Paris (1750–53), where, in conjunction with his diplomatic activities, he held salons and mingled with the PHILOSOPHES. In 1753, Maria Theresa called him back to Vienna to assume the position of Austrian chancellor of state. Kaunitz served AUSTRIA in this capacity until 1792.

Kaunitz was one of the major architects of the DIPLOMATIC REVOLUTION OF 1756 and served as a principal negotiator not only for the treaty of Aix-la-Chapelle (1748) but also for the Peace of Paris (1763). He also represented Austria in the negotiations with PRUSSIA and Russia that brought about the First Partition of Poland (1772). In the realm of domestic policy, Kaunitz gained fame as the designer of the Theresian reforms of taxation and provincial finance. Kaunitz knew the political and economic theories espoused by the writers and philosophers of the ENLIGHTENMENT, but he recognized the formidable obstacles that would be faced by anyone attempting to apply such theories in the Hapsburg realms. As a result, he shaped the various Theresian reforms in a manner that drew elements from enlightened theory but adapted them to the unique situation in the Hapsburg lands. Kaunitz also helped to conceptualize the reforms that restructured church-state relations in the Hapsburg dominions. He played a significant role in reorganizing the institutional bases of the fine arts and sciences, overseeing the foundation of the Brussels Academy of Sciences (1772) and the consolidation of the Viennese academies for painting, sculpture, architecture, and engraving into the comprehensive Akademie der Bildenden Künste (Academy of Fine Arts). Kaunitz also assisted Gerard van SWIETEN with major university reforms but was unable to realize his dream of establishing a Viennese scientific academy.

After the death of Maria Theresa, Kaunitz continued to serve as Austrian chancellor for JOSEPH II, but he strongly disapproved of Joseph's despotic ruling style. Kaunitz later outlined his criticisms in an advisory letter to Joseph's brother and successor, Leopold II (1790–92). Kaunitz resigned as chancellor of Austria in 1792 and died in Vienna in 1794.

See also SOCIAL INSTITUTIONS OF THE ENLIGHTENMENT.

Kay, John (1704–1764) *English inventor, trained as a clockmaker*

Kay, a weaver from Lancashire, was the son of a prosperous farmer. He invented the FLYING SHUTTLE, a device that speeded up the process of weaving cloth from yarn. Kay patented his invention in 1733, but it did not really take hold in industry until the 1750s and 1760s. Kay was engaged by the French government to train weavers in the use of his new device. Kay's invention aggravated the problem of yarn shortages that was facing English weavers and probably helped to stimulate the creation of spinning machines such as the SPINNING JENNY, the WATER FRAME, and the SPINNING MULE.

See also INDUSTRIAL REVOLUTION.

Kent, William (1685–1748) *English architect, landscape gardener and painter; enlivened austere English classicism with baroque and rococo accents*

He allegedly first served as an apprentice with a coach painter, then, because of the largesse of three wealthy English patrons, travelled to ROME to study art and to collect paintings. In Rome, Kent met Richard Boyle, third earl of Burlington, who provided him with significant commissions and other patronage. Through Boyle's interventions, Kent obtained the commission to decorate the interior of the British royal palace at Kensington. In 1726, again with Burlington's assistance, Kent obtained a post as master carpenter of the King's Works, then in 1735 the appointment as master mason and deputy surveyor of the King's Works.

Kent is most renowned for his development of a new, informal landscape style known as the ENGLISH GARDEN.

Kent designed and installed gardens at the earl of Burlington's Chiswick House in Middlesex; Esher Place and Claremont in Surrey; Euston in Suffolk; STOWE in Buckinghamshire; and Rousham in Oxfordshire. His major architectural works, all in the English PALLADIAN STYLE, included the Royal Mews (demolished in 1830) and the Treasury at Whitehall, Stone Hall at Houghton, Worcester Lodge and Badminton House in Gloucestershire, and Wakefield Lodge in Northamptonshire. Kent also designed and produced the interiors of Burlington's two residences: Chiswick House in Middlesex and Devonshire House in Piccadilly.

Kepler, Johannes (1571–1630) *German astronomer and mathematician*

Kepler was an early supporter of the HELIOCENTRIC theory of Nicolaus COPERNICUS and one of the chief contributors to the COPERNICAN REVOLUTION and to the early SCIENTIFIC REVOLUTION. Kepler learned about Copernican theory from Professor Michael Mästlin at the University of Tübingen in southwest GERMANY. Kepler became a professor at the University of Graz in AUSTRIA in 1594. He began corresponding with Galileo GALILEI in 1597. By 1600, he had acquired a post as an assistant to the famed Danish astronomer Tycho Brahe, who was the imperial mathematician and court astronomer for Rudolf II, the Hapsburg emperor of the HOLY ROMAN EMPIRE. In 1601, Kepler succeeded Brahe in both positions. Kepler also served as the mathematician for Upper Austria at Linz (1612). He moved to Ulm in 1626 and there, in 1627, completed the *Rudolfine Tables,* a set of highly accurate astronomy tables begun by Tycho Brahe. Kepler made one final move in 1628, to Saga in Silesia.

Besides being a convinced Copernican, Kepler was also committed to a popular Renaissance philosophy called Neoplatonism that is believed by some scholars to have provided aesthetic and philosophical impetus for the early developments of the Scientific Revolution. Neoplatonic thought maintained that the world is harmoniously structured according to simple, elegant geometric forms and laws. It placed great value on the Sun as a symbol of power and of God. Neoplatonism is believed to have served as a philosophic source of support for Copernicus's decision to place the Sun at the center of the universe. It may also have helped to shape his preference for a universe of simply geometric design. Whatever the truth in Copernicus's case. Johannes Kepler consciously used Neoplatonism to guide his early work in astronomy.

Kepler addressed two related difficulties in Copernican theory. First, planetary motions did not quite correspond to the perfect circles described by Copernicus, and Kepler determined to uncover the true path of their motion. Second, the source of planetary motion, usually considered perpetual motion caused by the movement of solid, crystalline, heavenly spheres, was demanding a more satisfactory explanation. Kepler's earliest treatise, the *Mysterium Cosmographicum* (Cosmographical mystery; 1596), attempted to solve these problems by positing an *anima motrix* emanating from the Sun as the cause of all celestial motion. He also argued that both the number of planets (only five planets were known) and the sizes of their orbits could be derived from the mathematical relations between the five regular geometric solids inscribed one within the other.

In the years following the publication of the *Mysterium Cosmographicum,* Kepler worked out the planetary orbits in minute detail. He concluded that they are elliptical in shape, with the Sun lying at one of the two foci of the ellipse. He also derived the mathematical equations that accurately describe the planetary paths. These results, called Kepler's Laws, were published in the *Astronomia nova* (New astronomy; 1609) and the *Harmonice mundi* (Harmonies of the world; 1619).

In addition to these works, Kepler published the following books: *De stella nova* (On the new star; 1606); *Epitome astronomiae Copernicanae* (Abridgement of Copernican astronomy; 1618–21); and *Somnium seu astronomia lunari* (The dream, or a lunar astronomy; posthumously published in 1634). He also wrote two short works supporting Galileo's discoveries with the TELESCOPE. These were *Dissertation cum Nuncio Sidereo* (Dissertation on the starry messenger) and the *Narratio de observatis a se quatuor Jovis satellibus* (Narrative about the observation of the four moons of Jupiter), both published in 1610.

See also ASTRONOMY; SCIENCE.

Kingdom of the Two Sicilies

An Italian state that consisted of two kingdoms: Sicily (the island) and Naples (southern half of the mainland peninsula). At times these kingdoms were united and at other times they had separate rulers. The original Kingdom of the Two Sicilies was created by the 11th-century Norman conquerors of the region (1072–91). The kingdom fragmented into two parts with different rulers during the 13th century. From the 16th century until the early 18th century, the Spanish Hapsburgs ruled the two kingdoms. When the last Spanish Hapsburg ruler died without competent heirs, a European war over the succession ensued. The Peace of Utrecht (1713) awarded SPAIN and the West Indies to the French Bourbon claimant to the Spanish throne. Naples and MILAN went to the Austrian Hapsburgs, and Sicily went to SAVOY. In 1720, the duke of Savoy yielded control of Sicily to the Austrian Hapsburgs in exchange for Sardinia. The Hapsburgs ruled both Naples and Sicily until 1735 when the kingdoms were once again transferred back to Spanish control. The Spanish Bourbon prince Charles (eventually King CHARLES III of Spain) assumed both thrones. Because he wished to centralize and modernize his kingdom, Charles and his great adviser, the lawyer Bernardo TANUCCI, instigated a series of ecclesiastical, fiscal, and juridical reforms inspired by theories associated with the ENLIGHTENMENT.

However, in 1759 Charles left Naples, having inherited the Spanish throne from his half brother, Ferdinand VI. Tanucci remained in Naples, serving as regent during the minority years (1759–67) of Charles's successor, Ferdinand IV. Tanucci remained in state service until 1776, when difficulties with Queen Maria Carolina caused his dismissal. Except for the six months during which the revolutionary Neapolitan Republic existed (January to July 1799), Ferdinand IV ruled continuously in Naples and Sicily from 1767 until 1825. He was renamed Ferdinand I of the Kingdom of the Two Sicilies after Naples and Sicily were officially unified at the Congress of Vienna (1815). Ferdinand ruled during the 19th century with nearly autocratic power.

The problem of church-state relations particularly concerned the enlightened Neapolitan princes and their advisers of the 18th century. In their attempts to assert secular, royal control over the powerful Catholic church and to clear up areas of conflicting jurisdiction, they refused to appoint new bishops to fill vacant bishoprics (sees). By the end of the 18th century, as a result, many Neapolitan and Sicilian sees remained unoccupied. This, in effect, weakened the administrative capabilities of the church. A second line of attack revolved around efforts begun in 1767 to abolish the Jesuit order within the kingdom.

The city of Naples under Spanish Bourbon rule served as the center of a Neapolitan political and cultural Enlightenment. Antonio GENOVESI taught and wrote PHILOSOPHY, THEOLOGY, ethics, and ECONOMICS. His students, Gaetano FILANGIERI and the Grimaldi brothers, continued his work, delving into the more radical ideas of the Enlightenment. Ferdinando GALIANI, who resided in PARIS as secretary of the Neapolitan Embassy, kept Tanucci supplied with information about the French Enlightenment, the ENCYCLOPÉDIE, and its two creators, Denis DIDEROT and Jean Le Rond d'ALEMBERT. Thus Naples provided a small but brilliant group of intellectuals who expanded enlightened theory to address special Neapolitan conditions and whose works were known to other European readers.

In spite of enlightened reforms and vibrant if circumscribed intellectual activity, the kingdoms of Naples and Sicily remained extremely poor and economically stagnant during the 18th century. Social structure was relatively simple, consisting of a few very wealthy noble families who owned most of the land and a mass of impoverished peasants. The middle classes were insignificant, and the enlightened educated classes were mostly composed of noblemen. In spite of various state attempts to control the Catholic Church, its power and influence remained extensive. All these facts set Naples and Sicily apart from the other regions of ITALY, helping to limit the extent to which enlightened movements could have influence.

See also ROMAN CATHOLICISM.

Kleist, Heinrich von (1777–1811) *German playwright, novelist, and poet of the late Enlightenment*

Bernd Heinrich Wilhelm von Kleist, the son of a Prussian family, followed the family tradition by serving from 1792 until 1799 as an officer in the Prussian army. He refused to pursue a military career further, turning instead to study of the natural sciences, philosophy, and dramatic literature.

In Dresden, Kleist tried journalism and founded a short-lived periodical called *Phöbus* (1808). He became a pamphleteer during the Napoleonic wars and a critic of Napoleon. His experiences during these years of turmoil in Europe turned him against excessive rationalism. From 1810 until 1811, he edited and wrote for the *Berliner Abendblätter*. The paper was suppressed in 1811 by Prince Hardenberg (1750–1822), chancellor of PRUSSIA, for its criticisms of his reform policies. Burdened with poverty and depression, Kleist and his lover Henriette Vogel made a suicide pact and killed themselves in 1811.

Kleist had studied the philosophy of Immanuel KANT as a student and came away convinced that knowing anything with certainty is impossible for humankind. This conviction marked him as a member of the late Enlightenment, a period during which faith in the power of REASON was rejected and replaced by reliance on subjective, intuitive, and, therefore, uncertain knowledge of the world. Combined with his negative assessment of Napoleon, this view moved him strongly toward the ROMANTICISM that marked the end of the era of the Enlightenment.

Kleist's plays include *Das Käthchen von Heilbronn* (Katie from Heilbronn; 1810), *Prinz Friedrich von Hamburg* (Prince Frederick of Hamburg; 1810), *Die Hermannschlacht* (The Hermann battle; 1810), and *Der zerbrochene Krug* (The broken jug; 1812). He also wrote novellas, the most important of which—*Michael Kohlhaus* and *Die Marquise von O* (*The Marquise of O*)—were published together with six other works as *Erzählungen* (Stories; 1810–11).

Klopstock, Friedrich Gottlieb (1724–1803) *German poet*

Klopstock was a devout Lutheran whose literary production reveals the close links between the German ENLIGHTENMENT (*AUFKLÄRUNG*) and religious conviction. After receiving a traditional education in RELIGION and the classics, Klopstock worked as a private tutor (1748–50). He moved to Copenhagen in 1751, where for the next 20 years he received a pension from KING CHRISTIAN VII OF DENMARK. In 1770, Klopstock returned to GERMANY and settled permanently in Hamburg.

Klopstock was inspired as a young man to attempt to become a great epic bard following the model sketched out by the Swiss literary critic Johann Jakob BODMER. Bodmer had especially admired John Milton and had translated *Paradise Lost* into German. Klopstock, in an attempt to write in the style of Milton, produced an epic religious poem of 20 cantos entitled *Der Messias* (The Messiah; 1748–73). The poem enjoyed enormous success in SWITZERLAND and in Germany outside the circles of the mainstream of the Enlightenment. Klopstock is also renowned for his *Oden* (Odes; 1771); for religious dramas such as *Der Tod Adam* (The death of Adam; 1757) and *David* (1772); for the historical trilogy consisting of *Hermanns Schlacht* (The battle of Hermann; 1769), *Hermann und die Fursten* (Hermann and the princes; 1784), and *Hermanns Tod* (The death of Hermann; 1787). He is also remembered for his critical work *Die deutsche Gelehrtenrepublik* (The German republic of letters; 1774).

Klopstock's poetry breathed a passion that was unusual for his era. It also demonstrated the poetic possibilities of the German language at a time when this facet of the language was not appreciated. Klopstock played an important early role in the establishment of German as a literary language, one of the great contributions of the *Aufklärung* to European cultural life.

In spite of his creative contributions to literature, Klopstock was too conservative to appreciate the philosophic and literary movement that was headed by Immanuel KANT, Johann Wolfgang GOETHE, and Friedrich SCHILLER. He resented the rational and anti-Christian French Enlightenment espoused by FREDERICK II (THE GREAT) OF PRUSSIA. However, he welcomed the FRENCH REVOLUTION because it seemed to promise liberation for Germans from rule by petty princes. In these various facets of his personality, Klopstock thus exemplified the complexities and tensions of the German Enlightenment.

L

Laclos, Pierre Ambroise François Choderlos de
(1741–1803) *French novelist and professional soldier*
Laclos achieved the rank of captain in 1778 but lost his army commission in 1786 after he published certain criticisms of the French military in his *Lettre à MM. de l'Académie Française sur l'éloge de M. le Maréchal de Vauban* (Letter to the gentlemen of the French Academy on the eulogy of Field-Marshal Vauban).

During the early years of the FRENCH REVOLUTION Laclos plotted with the party that sought to replace LOUIS XVI with Philippe Egalité, the duke of Orleans. Like many Frenchmen of the revolutionary era, he altered his politics to reflect whatever regime was currently in power. Thus, during the National Convention Years (1792–95), Laclos became a republican and served again in the army. He had just received an appointment as governor general of French possessions in India when the Jacobin regime and Maximilien ROBESPIERRE were overturned. Instead of traveling to India, Laclos went to prison for 13 months. He later served in the Napoleonic army and died in Taranto, ITALY, after an attack of dysentery.

Laclos's fame as a writer rests on one novel, *Les Liaisons Dangereuses* (Dangerous liaisons; 1782), considered one of the most important French novels of the late 18th century. Like CLARISSA by Samuel RICHARDSON, the book consists of a series of letters between various aristocratic characters. Behind their masks of propriety, these people are all engaged in treacherous games of seduction and adultery. The book contained penetrating commentaries on gender roles and observations about the power that can be a part of sexual expression. It turned the mores of popular sentimental novels such as PAMELA upside down by consigning a pious, upright, emotional female to seduction and to death from a broken heart. It criticized the old aristocratic code of honor, which made men vulnerable to the passions aroused by wounded pride. It also offered a scathing criticism of REASON, revealing the negative results that can occur when it reigns supreme in human actions.

The heroine of *Dangerous Liaisons,* Madame de Merteuil, is an intelligent, beautiful woman who recognizes that she can control the actions of people by manipulating their emotions and pride. Her coldly rational stance precludes ever being in touch with her own feelings, but she delights in the power it gives her in traditional society. Madame de Merteuil coolly challenges her former lover Monsieur Valmont to seduce a married woman renowned for her piety. Laclos skillfully turns Madame de Merteuil's challenge into a potential assault on Valmont's honor. If he refuses to accept her challenge, then he is a coward unworthy of his reputation and honorable status. Valmont thus accepts the challenge, carries it out with success, and returns to accept his reward. But Madame de Merteuil has, herself, been seduced by the powers of her cunning reason and therefore persuades Valmont to accept a second challenge. The struggle between the two antagonists continues until its internal logic makes them both lose control. In the end, Madame de Merteuil and Monsieur Valmont are victimized, she by her commitment to reason and he by his commitment to honor. Valmont dies in a duel, and Madame de Merteuil is cast out from society. Thus, with penetrating psychological insight, Laclos gave his readers a lesson in morality and human psychology. His book is an outstanding example of the social criticism and new mores that characterized the late ENLIGHTENMENT.

See also LITERATURE; MORAL PHILOSOPHY; SENSIBILITY; SENTIMENTAL FICTION.

Lagrange, Joseph-Louis (1736–1813) *Italian mathematician, an expert in the application of mathematics to mechanics*

Lagrange lived and worked in TURIN, PARIS, and BERLIN. He is often treated as French because his family had French origins. His great-grandfather, however, had left FRANCE to serve the duke of Savoy, and subsequent generations had continued that tradition. Lagrange was born in Turin, the capital of the kingdom of SAVOY.

Like many of his contemporaries, Lagrange began legal studies, but was lured away from that area into mathematics and physics by influential teachers and by his natural talents. He began writing mathematical papers as early as 1754, corresponding with prominent leaders in the field such as Leonhard EULER and Jean le Rond d'ALEMBERT.

That Lagrange displayed notable talent was recognized quickly by prominent mathematicians and by the authorities in Turin. As a result, he received an appointment in 1755 as a professor at the Royal Artillery School of Turin. Lagrange entered into the intellectual life of that city, helping to found the scientific society that became the Royal Academy of Sciences of Turin.

In 1763, Lagrange won a prize offered by the FRENCH ACADEMY OF SCIENCES in Paris for a paper on irregularities in the observed motion of the Moon. He received a second prize in 1766 for work on the motions of the planet Jupiter's satellites. Lagrange traveled to Paris in 1763 and then to LONDON, where he worked in the service of the ambassador from the kingdom of Naples. He returned to Turin in 1765, then moved to Berlin in 1766 in order to assume the directorship of the mathematics section of the BERLIN ACADEMY. Lagrange remained in Berlin until 1787, when, at the urging of Comte de Mirabeau, he transferred residency to Paris. He lived in Paris for the rest of his life, working closely with Pierre-Simon LAPLACE, Marie-Jean de CONDORCET, Gaspard Monge, and Lazare CARNOT.

During the FRENCH REVOLUTION, Lagrange escaped political censure, unlike his colleagues Antoine LAVOISIER and Condorcet. He served on the commission charged with developing universal weights and measures, worked in the Bureau des Longitudes, and taught at the École Centrale des Travaux Publics (later to become the École Polytechnique). When the French Academy of Sciences was suppressed and reorganized as the Institut de France, Lagrange was appointed to its roster. Lagrange died in 1813, having been honored by Napoleon with a seat in the Sénat Conservateur and with membership in the Légion d'Honneur.

Lagrange's work centered on the application of mathematical calculus to mechanics. He created the calculus of variations, contributed to number theory, and developed new techniques in both differential and integral calculus. His mathematics provided an important stimulus for Laplace's later work in the field of celestial mechanics. Lagrange himself, however, occasionally expressed the fear that calculus had reached the limit of its power as a scientific tool.

Lagrange published many important early papers in the memoirs and collections of the Royal Academy of Sciences in Turin, the Berlin Academy, and the French Academy of Sciences. They included important papers on maxima and minima in calculus, on the propagation of sound, and on various irregular motions in the solar system. One paper addressed the troublesome three-body problem (the question of how to express the forces acting between three heavenly bodies—Sun, Moon, and Earth, for example—and their resultant motions in mathematical terms). Another paper joined the principle of least action (the idea that the amount of action required to accomplish any change in the universe is the minimum possible) outlined by Pierre de MAUPERTUIS with the notion of *vis viva* (living force or the quantity of force that is conserved in the universe and that prevents it from running down) developed by Gottfried LEIBNIZ to create a new foundation for the science of dynamics.

In his later years, Lagrange turned to the task of organizing his many published papers and presenting them in a manner that would facilitate teaching. The resulting *Mécanique analytique* (Analytical mechanics; 1788) attempted to present a system for the mathematical treatment of both celestial and terrestrial mechanics. The work tried to reduce the theory of mechanics to a few general mathematical equations and to show how all aspects of mechanics were both related and mutually dependent. Other works from this period were the *Traité de la résolution des équations numériques de tous les degrès* (Treatise on the resolution of algebraic equations of all degrees; 1798) and the *Théorie des fonctions analytiques contenant les principes de calcul différentiel, dégagés de toute considération d'infiniment petits, d'évanouissants, de limites et de fluxions et réduits à l'analyse algébrique des quantités finies* (Theory of analytical functions containing the principles of differential calculus; 1797). Lagrange's works were collected and published during the later 19th century as *Oeuvres de Lagrange* (Works of Lagrange, 14 vols.; 1867–92).

These later works stand in the science of the late ENLIGHTENMENT as an example of the manner in which the spirit of building rational systems continued to live in a scientific world dominated by EMPIRICISM. In fact, the science of the late Enlightenment actually consisted of a potent blending of the traditions of experiment and empiricism with the approaches of systematic rationalism.

See also MATHEMATICS AND MECHANICS; SCIENCE.

laissez-faire French term said by some scholars to have been coined by the Physiocrat Vincent de Gournay. The complete term is *laissez-faire, laissez passer.* In English, this means "allow to do, allow to happen," or, in paraphrase, "let things be done, let them happen." The term has come to represent, in shorthand, the economic vision of 18th-century liberalism, which championed free, unregulated business and trade as a necessary condition for the production of national wealth.

The French PHYSIOCRATS were the first European economic theorists to build a theory of economic action and organization on such principles. They were reacting to the standard economic theory of the era, MERCANTILISM, which relied on state regulation and on the accumulation of gold as the best methods for acquiring national wealth. In contrast, laissez-faire doctrines relied on free circulation of goods and labor to enrich a nation. The English adopted the Physiocrats' ideas and applied them enthusiastically to their business, manufacturing, and commerce. The classic exposition of English laissez-faire doctrine appeared in 1776 in the WEALTH OF NATIONS by Adam SMITH.

Lalande, Joseph-Jérôme Le Français de (1732–1807) *French astronomer*

Lalande studied with the JESUITS at the Collège de Lyon. He wanted to join the Jesuit order, but his parents determined that he should instead study law in PARIS. He met the astronomer Joseph-Nicolas DELISLE during his student years, attended his lectures at the Collège Royale, and assisted him in making astronomical observations. Lalande also took courses in mathematical physics with Pierre-Charles Le Monnier. With Le Monnier's patronage, Lalande obtained a post in BERLIN.

Lalande remained in Berlin for some time. He met Pierre de MAUPERTUIS, Leonhard EULER, and the marquis d'ARGENS at the BERLIN ACADEMY where he was received as a member. In 1753, he was also received as an adjunct astronomer in the FRENCH ACADEMY OF SCIENCES.

Lalande participated in several major controversies of 18th-century ASTRONOMY. He quarreled with his mentor Le Monnier over the proper application of lunar parallax measurements to problems of lunar motion and assisted Alexis CLAIRAUT in making the measurements that properly predicted the return of Halley's Comet. In the latter episode Lalande acted as a partisan of Clairaut during the dispute between Jean Le Rond D'ALEMBERT, Euler, and Clairaut over the proper method for approximating a solution to the three-body problem in physics. The solar system offered many examples where three bodies—Sun, Earth, and Moon, for example—were interacting, thereby affecting each other's motion, but mathematicians had been unable to find a way to express these relationships in a specific equation. The answers had to be reached by indirect methods. Lalande also helped to organize the scientific expeditions for the observation of the 1769 TRANSIT OF VENUS across the face of the Sun.

Lalande was committed to improving the accuracy of astronomical measurements. He also dedicated himself to disseminating the latest scientific theories by writing textbooks on astronomy. He edited the astronomical almanac called *Connaissance du temps* (Knowledge of time) from 1760 to 1776 and again from 1794 until his death in 1807. He succeeded Delisle in 1760 as professor of astronomy at the Collège de France.

Lalande lived through the FRENCH REVOLUTION without difficulty in spite of his royalist sympathies. He hid both Pierre DUPONT DE NEMOURS and the Abbé Garnier at the Paris observatory when they were being pursued during the Terror. After the fall of Maximilien ROBESPIERRE, Lalande dedicated himself to reestablishing scientific organizations, but he encountered hostility from Napoleon on account of his reputation as a freethinker.

Lalande belonged to the FREEMASONS. He was a founder of the famous Loge des Neufs Soeurs (Lodge of the Nine Sisters) in Paris. Constituted in 1777, the lodge had been conceived by Lalande and Claude-Adrien HELVÉTIUS as an organization for enlightened writers and scientists who had proven their talents by publication. VOLTAIRE and many other PHILOSOPHES were initiated into this lodge. Lalande wrote the article entitled "Franc-Maçon" for the *Supplément* (Supplement) to the ENCYCLOPÉDIE and a *Mémoire historique sur la Maçonnerie* (Historical memoir on masonry).

Lalande's major publications included *Traité d'astronomie* (Treatise on astronomy; 1764, with subsequent editions in 1771 and 1792); *Histoire de la comète de 1759* (History of the comet of 1759); *Abrégé de navigation historique, théorique, et pratique, avec des tables horaires* (Summary of historical, theoretical, and practical navigation, with hourly tables, with calculations by his nephew's wife, Madame Lalande; 1793); *Bibliographie astronomique* (Bibliography of astronomy; 1802); *Astronomie des dames* (Astronomy for women; 1785, 1795, 1806); and the last two volumes of the *Histoire des mathématiques* (History of mathematics; 1802) by Jean Étienne Montucla (1725–99).

Lamarck, Jean Baptiste Pierre Antoine de Monet de (1744–1829) *French botanist, zoologist, paleontologist, and early theorist of the transformation of species*

Lamarck coined the term BIOLOGY in 1802 and called for a unified science of all living things. Intended by his father for the priesthood, Lamarck instead entered the military and fought in the SEVEN YEARS' WAR. After retiring from the military for medical reasons, he obtained a bank post in PARIS and began studying MEDICINE. His career in the natural sciences developed in the 1770s. The natural historian George Louis de BUFFON obtained Lamarck's election to the FRENCH ACADEMY OF SCIENCES in 1779. Lamarck worked in the academy and its successor, the Institut National des Sciences et des Arts (Institut de France), until his death in 1829.

The JARDIN DES PLANTES provided Lamarck with additional minor positions from 1788 until 1793 when it was reorganized as the Muséum National d'Histoire Naturelle. In the new organization, he received a professorship in zoology with emphasis on invertebrates.

During the ENLIGHTENMENT, the novel idea that the Earth changes over long periods of time (i.e., NATURE has a HISTORY) began to receive credibility. Buffon and other theorists of natural history popularized the idea, and the discovery of fossils that seemed to have no modern analogues raised the possibility that some species had died out over time or had, at least, changed substantially.

From the fundamental questions raised by geological research and fossil studies, Lamarck ultimately developed a theory of the transformation of the species of animals and plants. In other words, he proposed that, like the Earth itself, living creatures have a history that shows change over time. Lamarck explained the mechanisms that produce these changes in terms of chemistry and of environmental influences. He favored both chemical and physical explanations of life. In particular, the traditional chemistry of four elements (earth , air, fire, and water), which made fire the central force in life, seemed to Lamarck to provide an adequate account of natural tendencies toward change. The general environment, he believed, also demanded certain adaptations from individual living things. A *sentiment intérieur* (inner feeling), modeled partially on the ideas of Pierre CABANIS, characterized higher animals and facilitated their response to environmental demands by allowing them to develop alterations in their skeleton or organs. These acquired changes were passed on to subsequent generations in the process of reproduction.

Lamarck used these ideas about the transformation of the species (he did not use the term *evolution* because in 18th-century usages, it meant simply expansion without fundamental change) to formulate a natural CLASSIFICATION of living organisms. This system for imposing an orderly set of relationships on living organisms was intended to accurately reflect their presumed historical and reproductive relationships. In general, Lamarck believed that life forms had developed from the simplest to the most complex over a long period of time.

Lamarck made his first public statements about the transformation of species in 1800 and developed the theory extensively over the next three years. He outlined his earliest ideas in the introduction to *Système des animaux sans vertèbres* (1800) and followed with the *Recherches sur l'organisation des corps vivans* (Research on the organization of living bodies; 1802); *Philosophie zoologique* (Zoological philosophy; 1809); *Histoire naturelle des animaux sans vertèbres* (Natural history of invertebrates; 1815); and *Système analytique des connaissances positives de l'homme* (Analytical system of the positive knowledge of man; 1820).

Other important publications included *Flore française* (French flora; 1779); *Dictionnaire de botanique*

(Dictionary of botany, vols. 1–3 and half of 4; 1783–95); and the *Illustration des genres* (Illustration of the species; 1791–1800). The latter two publications became part of the *Encyclopédie methodique* (Methodical encyclopedia, 193 vols., edited by C. J. Pancoucke; 1782–1832).

Lamarck died in 1829, ignored by many scientists and heavily criticized.

Lambert, Anne-Thérèse de Marguenat de Courcelles, marquise de (1647–1733) *French writer and salon hostess*

As a young girl, the future marquise de Lambert received encouragement to read and to pursue literary interests. She began writing and publishing, however, only in her later years, after the death of her husband, the marquis de Lambert. Her works treated the EDUCATION of young children and subjects touching upon the roles and status of women.

In 1710, the marquise de Lambert initiated a salon at her Parisian town house, the Hôtel de Nevers. Her gatherings provided opportunities in the early years of the ENLIGHTENMENT for the aristocracy to mingle with intellectuals. Guests at her Tuesday evening literary salons included Bernard de FONTENELLE, Pierre de MARIVAUX, and the marquis d'ARGENSON. One could also meet artists such as Jean Antoine WATTEAU and musicians such as Jean-Philippe RAMEAU or mingle with actors and actresses, a group often shunned by high society. Finally the salon attracted a number of women passionately involved in literary and intellectual worlds.

The marquise de Lambert's salon provided one site for the playing out of the literary QUARREL BETWEEN THE ANCIENTS AND THE MODERNS. Her salon became associated with a set of attitudes critical of the cynicism and license associated with the period of the French Regency (1715–23). The marquise de Lambert openly supported MONTESQUIEU when his PERSIAN LETTERS began attracting criticism and also helped to secure his appointment in 1727 to the French Academy.

Writings by the marquise de Lambert include *Avis d'une mère à son fils* (Advice of a mother to her son; 1726) and *Avis d'une mère à sa fille* (Advice of a mother to her daughter; 1728), both inspired by the *Télémaque* (Telemachus) of François FÉNELON; *Réflexions nouvelles sur les femmes* (New reflections on women; 1727); *La Viellesse* (Old age; 1732); and *Traité de l'amitié* (Treatise on friendship; 1732).

See also WOMEN AND THE ENLIGHTENMENT.

La Mettrie, Julien Offray de (1709–1751) *French philosopher and physician, one of the most renowned and notorious proponents of materialism during the Enlightenment*

As a young man, La Mettrie studied theology with a distinct bias toward JANSENISM. He then turned to NATURAL PHILOSOPHY and eventually to MEDICINE, obtaining a degree in the latter field from the University of Rheims.

After a short time practicing medicine in Rheims La Mettrie traveled to Leiden, where he studied with the aged Hermann BOERHAAVE.

In 1734, La Mettrie published a translation of Boerhaave's *Aphrodisiacus* (The aphrodisiac) and dared to append some original essays to the work of the illustrious physician. The act offended the sensibilities of established physicians and initiated a period of unfavorable evaluation of La Mettrie, which ultimately brought about his flight from FRANCE. La Mettrie responded to these first criticisms with a provocative second publication—another translation with his original works appended. Reception was equally negative.

La Mettrie moved to PARIS in 1743 and found a position as physician to the guards of the duc de Gramont. In this capacity he experienced the battlefront during the SEVEN YEARS' WAR. He also developed a serious illness with high fever and delirium.

In the course of his illness, La Mettrie came to the conclusion that the function of the mind and reason depends solely on the workings of the body and that mind, in fact, was no different from matter. He had thus moved to a position of philosophical MATERIALISM.

La Mettrie published his initial thoughts as *L'Histoire naturelle de l'âme* (Natural history of the soul) in 1745. The outcry against the book in France was so intense that La Mettrie fled from his native land to the safety of the UNITED PROVINCES OF THE NETHERLANDS. When, however, he followed the 1745 treatise with *L'homme machine* (Man, a machine) in 1748, even the relatively tolerant Dutch were offended. FREDERICK II (THE GREAT) OF PRUSSIA rescued La Mettrie by inviting him to BERLIN to assume a post as court reader. La Mettrie moved to Berlin in 1748 and remained there for the rest of his life. At Frederick's insistence, he was received into the BERLIN ACADEMY.

La Mettrie's materialism reduced mind to matter and extended to human beings DESCARTES's notion that animal are actually machines. In so doing, he denied the existence of the soul and, in fact, suggested that the world would never be happy until ATHEISM dominated the beliefs of humankind.

If La Mettrie extended the ideas of Descartes to humanity, he also adopted a notion of matter that differed from the classic one of Cartesian MECHANICAL PHILOSOPHY. For La Mettrie, as for Descartes, matter was extended (occupying space), but La Mettrie added that matter also has inherent abilities to move itself and to experience sensations. He therefore approached the position of VITALISM. When La Mettrie described the human machine created by this active matter, he spoke of the human "perpetual motion machine," a concept that departed noticeably from the Cartesian model.

During his years in Berlin, La Mettrie developed a doctrine of hedonism that drew on ancient EPICUREAN PHILOSOPHY. He declared that pleasure is the goal of all life and that all motivation is essentially selfish. La Mettrie presented these ideas in *L'Art de jouir ou l'école de volupté* (The art of pleasure, or the school of voluptuousness) and *Vénus métaphysique* (The metaphysical Venus), both published in 1751. They were also contained in his *Oeuvres philosophique* (Philosophical works; 1751), dedicated to the Swiss physiologist Albrecht von HALLER.

La Mettrie died in Berlin in 1751 at the age of 42. Frederick the Great wrote his eulogy and read it at a session of the Berlin Academy.

See also RADICAL ENLIGHTENMENT.

Lancret, Nicolas (1690–1743) *French rococo style painter* Lancret trained under Pierre d'Ulin and Claude Gillot. In the latter's workshop, Lancret met the ROCOCO master Antoine WATTEAU who also provided guidance. Lancret preserved on canvas the life of the Parisian elite during the regency (1715–23) of Philippe d'Orléans and was especially known for his depictions of *fêtes galantes* (gallant celebrations). He received many private commissions to provide paintings and decoration in the homes of the Parisian upper classes. He was elected to the Royal Academy in 1719.

Of Lancret's many works, *Dejeuner au jambon* (Lunch of ham) and *La Leçon de musique, la Conversation galante* (The music lesson, gallant conversation) are outstanding. The latter canvas illustrates the intimate relationship between eighteenth-century rococo art and STYLE GALANT (gallant style) MUSIC.

landscapes Natural settings, often prized for aesthetic qualities, or garden settings that have been artificially enhanced. The natural world held an endless fascination during the ENLIGHTENMENT, as its beauty and order were asserted to be the most visible indicators of the principles of harmony governing the universe; exposure to landscapes promoted contemplation and engendered artistic appreciation. The 18th century's fascination with landscapes represents three fundamental shifts in the early modern approach to the world. First, people began to emphasize the importance of variety and contrast in an image. Second, they began to appreciate irregularity over regularity. Third, an image's importance lay in the effect it had on the viewer. As David HUME believed, beauty was not inherent in the object viewed but was present only in the viewer's mind. A landscape was, therefore, beautiful for the feelings it inspired in the viewer.

Natural landscapes became important during the 18th century in part due to the increase in travel. English travelers, for example, heading to the Continent to finish their educations would often cross the Alps on their way into Italy, returning with stories of these mountains' great majesty. That mountainous landscapes could become beautiful to the 18th-century eye represented an important change in the European approach to nature. Whereas the 17th-century English preacher Thomas Burnet saw mountains as a metaphor for humanity's fall from grace—they were rough, ugly, and broken—later travelers reveled in their beauty. The writer Daniel DEFOE, for example, waxed poetic about the desolate beauty of Scotland's hills in *Tour through the Whole Island of Great Britain, 1724–27.*

The discovery of beauty in mountains and irregular landscapes in general was connected to a deeper change in Europe's approach to the beautiful. In 1757, Edmund BURKE published *Philosophical Inquiry into the Origin of Our Ideas of the Sublime and Beautiful,* which defined beauty as something inherent in small things and sublimity as inherent in vastness. The beautiful implied happiness and security, and the SUBLIME inspired terror and loneliness. Burke's ideas became a theoretical reference point for all future discussions of the beautiful and sublime, particularly influencing such 18th-century figures as Friedrich SCHILLER and Johann Wolfgang GOETHE.

Landscapes also became important on a smaller scale, as the practice of landscape gardening proliferated in the 18th century. Two Englishmen, Lancelot "Capability" BROWN and William KENT, are credited with the development of the new style of English landscape gardening: rearranging plants and trees, at times even physical phenomena such as hills and streams, in order to produce landscapes that were PICTURESQUE, or pleasing to the eye in the manner of a painting. Brown, born in 1715, married Kent's daughter and worked under him at the gardens of Lord Cobham's estate, STOWE. Brown was already making a name for himself by working for other aristocratic families when he left Stowe in 1751. Another Englishman who shared this interest in gardens was Horace WALPOLE, whose *History of the Modern Taste in Gardening* (1780) addressed the contributions of Brown and Kent to the development of the field and promoted landscape gardening from nationalistic motives. He asserted the superiority of English gardens over those of the French as espousing principles of freedom and liberalism through the inclusion of irregular features, in contrast to the highly formalized French designs.

As the 18th century progressed, English landscape gardening grew in popularity and importance, particularly as newly wealthy families from the merchant class sought to create estates for themselves that would parallel or even outclass those of the ancient gentry. The most influential figure in the latter part of the 18th century in the field of landscape design was Humphrey Repton, whose ingenious Red Books, so named for their trademark binding in red leather, were individualized volumes that featured a series of moveable panels that allowed a prospective buyer to view the landscape in both original and altered appearance. Repton is believed to have coined the term *landscape gardening,* using artistic notions and language from painting to manipulate garden design. This new kind of ENGLISH GARDEN soon became the rage on the Continent,

too. The first English garden in GERMANY appeared in 1775 in Wörlitz, which was part of Anhalt-Dessau. This garden greatly influenced the design of the one later built in Weimar under the direction of Goethe.

Landscape gardens confronted, however, a basic paradox. The artificial organization of a natural space was assumed to heighten its inherent beauty. This tension informed other artistic debates of the period such as the need to use craft in writing poetry to produce its "natural" beauty. One of the early figures in English landscape gardening, Alexander POPE, engaged both these creative dilemmas in his work. One of the first literary figures to support himself with his pen, Pope realized enough money from the sales of books such as his translation of Homer's *Iliad* to buy a country estate at Twickenham, where he created a garden and grotto that became legendary in the field of English gardening. Pope's theories of poetry were not divorced from his theories of gardening. His insistence on classical Greek and Roman models for literary form, like many of his literary contemporaries, led him to draw on classical sources for garden design, such as his use of busts of classical authors such as Homer throughout the estate and his inclusion of a classically inspired temple and amphitheater.

Landscapes also played an important role in painting. During the 18th century, landscape painters such as Salvator Rosa and Claude Lorrain became famous throughout Europe. These two painters in particular refer one back to the emerging categories of the sublime and the beautiful. Salvator Rosa, an Italian, was admired for the sublimity in his work. The arid Italian landscapes that he painted captured perfectly the emerging association of the sublime with vastness and terror. The writer Joshua Reynolds, for example, celebrated the "savageness" that he saw in Rosa's landscapes. Claude Lorrain was, however, celebrated for the beauty of his work. His renditions of sunrises, sunsets, and dew on the grass were the foundation of Arcadian feeling. Lorrain's work was considered beautiful because it inspired security.

The tradition of landscape painting highlights the convergence in the 18th century of the aesthetic and the normative. Landscapes of all types became a sounding board for a new individual, one who looked to the world because it inspired feelings in the soul. Whether a landscape was good or bad was a matter of taste, and in the burgeoning 18th-century public sphere, the issues this highlighted provided ample opportunity to debate the issue at length.

See also AESTHETICS.

Further reading: John Dixon Hunt, *Garden and Grove: The Italian Renaissance Garden in the English Imagination: 1600–1750* (Princeton, N.J.: Princeton University Press, 1986); Mark Laird, *The Flowering of the English Landscape Garden: English Pleasure Grounds: 1720–1800* (Philadelphia: University of Pennsylvania Press, 1999); Robert P. Maccubbin and Peter Martin, eds., *British and*

American Gardens in the Eighteenth Century (Williamsburg, Va.: Colonial Williamsburg Foundation, 1984); Horace Walpole, *The History of the Modern Taste in Gardening* (New York: Ursus Press, 1995).

language Symbolic spoken or written systems of meaning used as the principal means by which humans communicate with one another. As a quintessential characteristic of human society, language was a target of attention for ENLIGHTENMENT thinkers. It was particularly important in the context of two recent European trends. First, as members of the elite traveled across Europe, the obvious linguistic differences they encountered invited investigation. Second, European COLONIALISM brought entirely new peoples into the Enlightenment's mental universe, as Europeans encountered peoples and cultures whose assumptions about philosophy and the foundations of civilization differed radically from those of Europe. This variety of languages and the potential multiplicity of thought processes behind them created problems for a worldview that was based on the belief in REASON's universality.

Philosophers such as John LOCKE, who helped characterize words and ideas as relevant objects of study in his *Essay Concerning Human Understanding* (1689), discussed the nature of language and the ways in which it might be improved via rational principles. Much of his discussion on language was based on travel reports, and the varieties of linguistic practices they identified allowed Locke to dismiss notions that ideas were somehow innate in the human mind. He argued, in contrast, that language was an effect of experience. The Scottish philosopher David HUME raised similar difficulties on the relations of words to the physical world in his *Treatise of Human Nature* (1748), which asserted that abstract ideas are necessarily grounded in particular phenomena.

The debate on language in ENGLAND in the early part of the 18th century revolved around its regulation and purification. Historical research into the roots of Anglo-Saxon stimulated increasing interest in early forms of the language and encouraged work that led to descriptive accounts of how Saxon grammar operated and greater numbers of translations into contemporary English. Such work, however, was not welcomed by all members of the intelligentsia. The author Jonathan SWIFT joined many English people in decrying what he saw as the degeneration of the language in his time into slang and abbreviated monosyllablic words, to the point that he published his *Proposal for Correcting, Improving and Ascertaining the English Tongue* in 1712. He asserted that English had not advanced as far as other European languages such as French due to its lack of influence from Latin, and condemned contemporary poets who mangled words through the use of apostrophes, as in the usage "disturb'd."

Swift elicited a counterattack from Saxonists when he took his discussion to a similar condemnation of barbarous "Northern" languages and their "unharmonious sounds," as well as the uselessness of English antiquarian studies in general. The scholar Elizabeth Elstob took him to task in a preface to her 1715 *Rudiments of Grammar for the English-Saxon Tongue,* the "Apology for the Study of Northern Antiquities," which dismissed Swift's attack due to his ignorance of the subject and also questioned his patriotism in attacking the source of his own "Mother Tongue."

Lockean ideas on language exerted a wide influence on 18th-century discussion. In the 1720s, a Jesuit working in Canada, Joseph-Francois Lafitau, studied the language and customs of North American Indians. In *Moeurs des sauvages Americaines* (1724), he used Locke's idea that language was based on experience to argue that Native Americans could express complicated ideas, but in ways that differed from the European pattern. This is the first sign of what would later become a full-blown relativism in European language theory.

There were, however, other language theorists who supposed the reverse. In the 1730s, Charles Marie de la Condamine reported on his travels in South America that South Americans lacked words for such elevated concepts as art and policy, so he concluded that they must never have thought about these elevated issues. This view of native peoples as less culturally advanced was held by many linguistic theorists and led to significant problems that needed explanation. If reason is universal, how does one explain the relative backwardness of other cultures?

In 1746, Abbé Etienne Bonnot de CONDILLAC published his groundbreaking *Essai sur les origines des connaissances humaines* (Essay on the origin of human knowledge), in which he argued that language conditions how people think. This undermined the notion that there was a universal form of reason, but also had important implications for other theorists. First, Condillac held that language could be improved. The application of thought to any language could rid the people's thought of error. Second, Condillac also suggested an idea that would become important later, the belief that less-developed languages were more poetic than the advanced European ones. Condillac's ideas were especially important for another French thinker, Pierre-Louis Moreau de MAUPERTUIS, who argued in his *Réflexions sur l'origine des langues et la signification de mots* (1748; Reflections on the origin of languages and the meaning of words) that although people started out with similar minds, differences in languages made people's minds different.

In 1770, the German theorist Johann Gottfried HERDER extended the work of Condillac and Maupertuis further in his *Über den Ursprung des Sprache* (*Treatise on the origin of language*). Responding to the German theorist Johann Peter SÜSSMILCH's idea that language originated with God, Herder held that language was a communal enterprise, rooted in a people's common history. He also argued, continuing the process begun with

Condillac, that the human mind could not exist without language. A language's structure and the history encoded within its words shaped the individual mind. This meant, first, as a practical matter that languages could not be ranked, since their foundations were dramatically different. Second, it also implied that languages could develop and prosper only within communities. The improvement of language was rooted in a people's daily life.

In the late 18th century, a response to Condillac and Herder came from SCOTLAND. James Burnett, lord Monboddo, responded to the relativistic line of argument by holding that although languages are historical, they do develop in stages, which he called the "barbarous" and "languages of art." In his lengthy work *Of the Origin and Progress of Language* (1773–92), he argued that languages began in simple cries of nature, but as civilizations developed the nature of these cries changed, becoming more abstract. Thus, although languages are particular, it is possible to see them in terms of hierarchy.

The trends toward categorizing languages and seeing them as formative of identity reached its fullest form at the beginning of the 19th century with Johann Gottlieb Fichte. As the Napoleonic Wars got fully under way, language theory combined with national pique to serve as the foundation for a particularistic view of languages. By 1807, French troops had occupied BERLIN, and Fichte, who lived and worked there, used the opportunity to draw sharp distinctions between Germans and the French invaders. In his *Reden an die deutsche Nation* (*Addresses to the German nation*; 1807), Fichte expressly connected linguistic tradition with virtue. Language and culture made the Germans noble and profound and the French ignoble and superficial. The tendency to identify national virtues through exclusive linguistic traditions did not stop with Fichte, however, but became fundamental to public attitudes across Europe in the 19th century.

See also EDUCATION.

Further reading: Joan C. Beal, *English Pronunciation in the Eighteenth Century: Thomas Spence's Grand Repository of the English Language* (New York: Oxford University Press, 1999); Dennis F. Essar, *Studies on Voltaire and the Eighteenth Century: The Language Theory, Epistemology, and Aesthetics of Jean Le Rond d'Alembert* (Oxford: Voltaire Foundation, 1976); Peter Rickard, *The Embarrassments of Irregularity: The French Language in the Eighteenth Century* (London: Cambridge University Press, 1981); Sophia Rosenfeld, *A Revolution in Language: The Problem of Signs in Late Eighteenth-Century France* (Stanford, Calif.: Stanford University Press, 2001); Susie I. Tucker, *Protean Shape: A Study in Eighteenth-Century Vocabulary and Usage* (London: Athlone, 1967).

Laokoon Treatise on AESTHETICS and criticism by Gotthold Ephraim LESSING, first published in 1766. The full title was *Laokoon, oder Ueber die Grenzen der Malerei und Poesie* (Laocoon, or over the boundaries between painting and poetry). The Hellenic sculpture that depicts the agonizing death of Laocoon and his sons, in a dramatic struggle against an overpowering serpent, provided Lessing with a reference point from which to launch his critical discussion of common aesthetic theories. Lessing rejected the claim that a poem is like a picture (*ut pictura poesis*) and also specifically attacked the neoclassical aesthetic theory propounded by Johann Joachim WINCKELMANN. Winckelmann had assumed the similarity between poem and picture proclaimed in ancient texts, but he had developed an elaborate theory of universal, rational rules to support his ideas.

Lessing rejected both the ancient classical and the neoclassical approaches to aesthetics, asserting, instead, that each of the various art forms is governed by a unique set of rules and principles. He supported his claim by comparing painting and sculpture to poetry. The differences between the manner in which objects or events can be linked in space as opposed to time provided the frame-

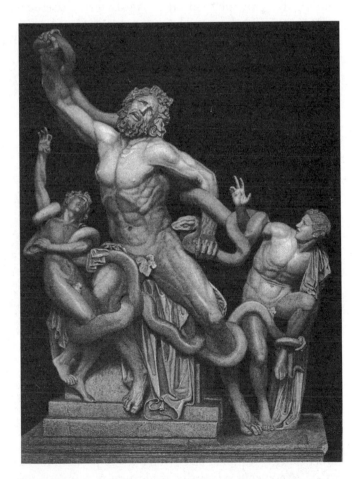

Laocoon, ancient Hellenistic sculpture ascribed to Agesander, Athenodorus, and Polydorus of Rhodes, second century B.C. The sculpture captures a sublime moment as Laocoon and his two sons struggle against impending death. This work inspired Gotthold Ephraim Lessing to write his renowned essay *Laokoon,* exploring aesthetic values and philosophy. *(Courtesy Archive Photos)*

work in which Lessing placed his analysis. Spatial relations do not have a dimension of time; everything in a given space is presented simultaneously. Temporal relations, in contrast, present a sequence or chain of events that often implies they are connected by cause-and-effect relations. The whole sequence cannot be grasped in a single instant, but must be followed as it unfolds with the passing of time. For Lessing, painting and sculpture draw on spatial relations to present creative insights, whereas poetry draws on temporal relationships. Therefore, the plastic arts and the literary arts cannot be reduced to a simple set of universal rules.

Laokoon presented aesthetic theory in a manner that defended the FREEDOM of the artist to create according to inspiration. The prescribed rules associated with CLASSICISM and NEOCLASSICISM were treated as unnecessary constraints on creative imagination. In conjunction with Lessing's many other essays on criticism, this book inspired younger Germans such as Johann Wolfgang von GOETHE to explore new paths in creative work. Although thoroughly grounded in the AUFKLÄRUNG (German ENLIGHTENMENT), Lessing's book eventually played a significant symbolic role in creating the cultural crucible in which ROMANTICISM was born.

See also GOTTSCHED, JOHANN CHRISTOPH; INTUITION AND IMAGINATION.

Laplace, Pierre-Simon, marquis de (1749–1827)
French mathematician, astronomer, and physicist, remembered today as one of the greatest mathematical physicists in history

Laplace has been called "the Newton of France." His work facilitated the process of creating a mathematical language for understanding the universe (mathematization of the universe), a goal that was central to the ENLIGHTENMENT.

As a young man Laplace prepared to enter the Catholic priesthood, but during his early university years at Caen, he decided instead to pursue a vocation in mathematics. In 1768, he left Caen for PARIS, rapidly securing the patronage of the powerful mathematician and *encyclopédiste*, Jean Le Rond d'ALEMBERT. With the patronage of d'Alembert, Laplace obtained a teaching post at the École Militaire in Paris.

During the FRENCH REVOLUTION, Laplace helped design the metric system of weights and measures, served in the Institut de France, and trained mathematical physicists at the new École Polytechnique. Under Napoleon, he served briefly as minister of the interior, but he was rather quickly demoted and given a lower position in the Senate. Napoleon eventually made him a count of the French Empire. With the restoration of the Bourbon monarchy in 1815, Laplace became a marquis.

As a young man, Laplace quickly established his brilliance in mathematics. He was appointed as an associate of the FRENCH ACADEMY OF SCIENCES in 1773; full membership with the accompanying financial rewards came in 1785. He was a member of the ROYAL SOCIETY OF LONDON and other foreign academies.

Laplace developed powerful mathematical tools in the fields of calculus and probability that he then used to solve critical scientific questions. The bulk of his work fell into three major areas: celestial mechanics (the study of forces and motion in the solar system); the theory of probability; and general physics. His research was intertwined with and stimulated by the investigations of his illustrious competitors Leonhard EULER and Joseph-Louis LAGRANGE. He also collaborated with Antoine LAVOISIER in the study of heat, served on a commission with the marquis de CONDORCET that addressed population questions, and worked closely with Claude BERTHOLLET at the Société d'Arcueil, an intellectual club that he had helped to found.

In the field of celestial mechanics, Laplace addressed the knotty problem of variability in the motion of solar system bodies. In particular, the motions of Jupiter, Saturn, and the Moon changed enough over time to challenge the theory of celestial physics created by Isaac NEWTON. Newton himself had struggled with the problem because it seemed to call his universal law of gravitation into question. How, he wondered, could the constant action of universal gravitation cause the changes that were observed in the motion of these troublesome heavenly bodies? Newton tried to resolve the problem by declaring that the action of God in the universe was necessary to keep bodies moving precisely in their orbits. This solution preserved an active role for God in the mathematically designed universe and provided a means by which the aberrant motions of heavenly bodies could be corrected.

Laplace developed mathematical equations that could account for this variability in motion. His papers read at the Academy between 1773 and 1787 showed that the average motions of the planets and the Moon is constant over long periods of time. He showed that variations in motion were periodic in nature and were caused by the fact that the planets and the Moon were acted upon not only by the gravitation of the Sun but also by that of other planets.

Laplace published a monumental five-volume treatise, *Traité de mécanique céleste* (Treatise on celestial mechanics; 1799–1825), which summarized the scientific work on gravitation of three generations of scientists. He also attempted to make this material accessible to the general reader by publishing a popularization called *Exposition du système du monde* (Explanation of the system of the world; 1796).

In the field of probability, Laplace grappled with the problem of the limits of human knowledge. Laplace believed that all phenomena occurred according to laws. Chance, for him, was simply a name for events that seemed, because of imperfect human knowledge, to have no regulating laws. Chance was an expression of our ignorance rather than an actually existing force in the universe. For Laplace, mathematical probability and STATISTICS offered a way of transforming mathematics into a tool for revealing the underlying order in complex, seemingly erratic phenomena.

Laplace had originally turned to probability as a mathematical tool in the study of ASTRONOMY and physics and only later realized its potential usefulness for the SCIENCE OF MAN. He published his research on probability as *Théorie analytique des probabilités* (Analytical theory of probabilities; 1812). He also published the *Essai philosophique sur les probabilités* (Philosophical essay on probabilities; 1814), in order to make knowledge of probability theory accessible to lay readers.

Of the many mathematical techniques invented or extended by Laplace, the following are considered of greatest importance: the generating function, which provided a foundation for his theory of probabilities; the Laplace transform, a method of integration; and the Laplace equation, a second-order partial differential equation.

La Tour, Maurice Quentin de (1704–1788) *French pastel painter*

La Tour trained in PARIS as early as 1723, traveling next to LONDON for three years (1724–27). When he returned to Paris from London, he posed as an Englishman in order to set himself apart from other artists. Little is known of his childhood and youth.

La Tour devoted himself entirely to painting pastel portraits in the sensual style common to French ROCOCO works. His portraits are noted for their penetrating psychological insight into the character of his subjects. His models included members of the royal family and various aristocrats and PHILOSOPHES such as Jean Le Rond d'ALEMBERT, VOLTAIRE, and Jean-Jacques ROUSSEAU. The most important portraits include *Madame de Pompadom Philibert Orry*, and several self-portraits.

La Tour earned membership in the French Academy in 1746 but never attained a high rank within the hierarchy of that organization. The success of his portraits, however assured him a comfortable living. He was admired as a witty, intelligent conversationalist with a wide variety of interests. As an older man, La Tour set up a free drawing school in Saint Quentin, his native city. He also established a scientific prize at the academy in Amiens. La Tour asked in his will that his paintings be sold in an estate sale and the proceeds given to charity. He died in Saint Quentin in 1788, having lost direct control of his affairs because of alleged insanity.

Lavater, Johann Kaspar (1741–1801) *Swiss mystic, writer, and founder of physiognomy, known during his life as "the Protestant Pope"*

Lavater was a Protestant pastor centered in Zürich, SWITZERLAND. In the late 1760s, Lavater entered into a controversy with Moses MENDELSSOHN over the grounds for religious faith. As part of his attack on his opponent, Lavater published (1769) a German translation of a French book by Charles BONNET, to which was added a dedication letter addressed to Mendelssohn. Bonnet's book contained arguments against ATHEISM and DEISM, and Lavater chided Mendelssohn for not accepting the beauty and truth of Bonnet's ideas. In 1770, the dedication letter and Mendelssohn's response were printed together by Friedrich NICOLAI and other publishers with the title *Zueignungsschrift der Bonnetischen philosophischen Untersuchung der Beweise für das Christethum an Herrn Moses Mendelssohn in Berlin und Schreiben an den Herrn Diaconus Lavater zu Zürich von Moses Mendelssohn* (Dedication letter to Moses Mendelssohn in Berlin from Bonnet's philosophical proofs for Christianity and writings to Herr Diaconus Lavater in Zürich from Moses Mendelssohn).

Although he was initially attracted by Lutheran PIETISM, over time Lavater became increasingly interested in occult phenomena, mysticism, and theosophy. He envisioned the science of physiognomy—an attempt to link outer, observable facial traits with hidden (occult) psychological characteristics—as a new statement of the orderly RELATIONS between the physical world and the moral world. His concerns mirrored those of Franz MESMER and of late ENLIGHTENMENT physicians such as Pierre CABANIS who wished to redefine the nature of the links between mind and body, or between the physical world of nature and the moral world of man. Lavater was immensely popular during the later 18th century and received large groups of visitors who flocked to visit him in Zürich and to hear about physiognomy.

Lavater recorded his ideas in *Aussichten in die Ewigkeit* (View into eternity; 1768–78); *Geheimes Tagebuch von einem Beobachter seiner selbst* (Secret diary of a self-observer; 1772–73); and *Physiognomische fragmente zur Beförderung der Menschenkenntnis und Menschenliebe* (Physiognomic fragments for the promotion of human knowledge and love of humankind; 1775–78). His philosophical and theological ideas also appeared in his lyric poems, epics, and dramas.

See also RELIGION.

Lavoisier, Antoine Laurent (1743–1794) *French chemist, agricultural reformer, geologist, and public official who was the major creator of the Chemical Revolution of the late Enlightenment*

Lavoisier was the son of Jean-Antoine Lavoisier, a lawyer in the Parlement of Paris. Young Antoine Lavoisier attended the Collège Mazarin in PARIS, where he studied the liberal arts and law, receiving his law degree in 1763. He pursued the study of chemistry and natural history through courses offered at the JARDIN DES PLANTES.

Lavoisier began his scientific research and writing in the 1760s and obtained admission to the FRENCH ACADEMY OF SCIENCES in 1768 with a paper on hydrometry. In the same year, 1768, Lavoisier became a tax farmer for the French government. Tax farmers collected the indirect taxes such as salt taxes for the royal government. They guaranteed the government a certain payment but were free to extract extra revenues for private use from the populace. Because no official limits existed on the amounts that could be privately collected, the business of tax farming was lucrative and Lavoisier accumulated a fortune. His role as a tax farmer, one of the most hated groups in French society, eventually led to his arrest in 1793 and execution by guillotine in 1794 during the FRENCH REVOLUTION.

In 1775, Lavoisier acquired the post of commissioner for the Royal Gunpowder Administration. He and his wife, Marie Anne Pierrette Paulze, moved to the Paris Arsenal, where Lavoisier set up a well-equipped scientific laboratory. Throughout his career, he combined his official duties with scientific investigation.

Lavoisier made contributions to the study of geological stratification, to the problem of providing a safe water supply to Paris, to the chemical analysis of spa waters, and to the development of better gunpowder. But his fame rests on his creation both of a new chemical nomenclature and of an associated chemical theory symbolized by his novel treatment of oxygen. Lavoisier wanted to ground chemistry in quantification in order to provide it with what he considered a more rational base. He developed new methods for experimentation and special instruments—the calorimeter, for example—for the measurement of chemical products from reactions. He also developed a theory of heat (the CALORIC theory) and a general theory of the chemical elements.

The development of the oxygen theory grew out of experiments on the problems of calcination, combustion, and general gas chemistry. Lavoisier was not alone in applying himself to these problems. His contemporaries Joseph PRIESTLEY in ENGLAND and Carl Wilhelm SCHEELE in SWEDEN also were investigating these issues. Each of these chemists independently isolated oxygen gas and understood that it was a unique "air" (gas) with properties different from those of other airs. Lavoisier definitely knew about the successful experiments of Priestley and Scheele, although he never acknowledged their work. He extended the radical implications of their findings by demonstrating the precise role played by oxygen in combustion and by grounding an entire new chemical theory in his discoveries. Lavoisier's new oxygen theory seriously challenged the preeminence of the PHLOGISTON THEORY in chemistry, although it did not convince all of his prominent 18th-century colleagues.

Lavoisier's combustion experiments are routinely presented as an example of the power of quantitative methods for scientific investigation. But his findings were neither indisputable nor wholly objective, a situation that was frequently noted by his 18th-century opponents.

Lavoisier desired to thoroughly transform the SCIENCE of chemistry and spoke of the "CHEMICAL REVOLUTION" that he was making. In his era, chemistry remained a largely qualitative science burdened with an unclear and haphazard language. Like many of his contemporaries in the Enlightenment, Lavoisier believed that the creation and use of a rational, well-constructed language would engender correct reasoning. Therefore, together with his colleagues Claude-Louis BERTHOLLET, Antoine François, comte de Fourcroy, and de Morveau, he formulated a new language for chemistry whose terms would describe the properties of elements and the composition of complex substances. For example, he coined the term *oxygen* (acid-generating), a name that revealed the central role he believed oxygen played in chemical processes.

Lavoisier's chemistry pointed in the direction of modern quantitative chemistry, and his nomenclature has survived to the present day. But his chemistry was still strongly rooted in received intellectual traditions. Thus it spoke of chemical principles in a manner reminiscent of earlier chemistry and alchemy. Lavoisier believed that he had found new, experimentally verifiable principles that operated consistently in chemical phenomena and determined the outcome of reactions. For example, oxygen (acid-generating) was the acidifying principle and hydrogen (water generating) was the aqueous inflammable principle.

Lavoisier published numerous scientific papers. He is most renowned, however, for the *Méthode de nomenclature chimique, proposée par M. M. de Morveau, Lavoisier, Berthollet & de Fourcroy* (Method of chemical nomenclature, proposed by Messieurs de Morveau, Lavoisier, Berthollet, and de Fourcroy; 1787) and the *Traité élémentaire de chimie* (Elemental treatise on chemistry; 1789).

See also TECHNOLOGY AND INSTRUMENTATION.

Law, John (1671–1729) *Scottish-born financier and reformer who established the Law system in France (1716–20)*
Law, the son of a Scottish goldsmith and banker from EDINBURGH, developed a theory of finance that based wealth on the extension of credit and on a high volume of trade. He outlined a banking reform plan in a 1705 publication, *Money and Trade Considered*. Law was an avid gambler and also developed a mathematical system for winning at cards.

Law attracted the attention of Philipe d'Orléans who was regent in FRANCE during the minority of LOUIS XV. With Philippe's support, Law obtained permission to establish a private central bank in 1716. The bank became a royal bank, and Law also acquired the right to print paper money in order to increase currency circulation in the French economy. Law then established the Compagnie d'Occident (Company of the West, also known as Le Mississippi) in 1717 and procured trading monopolies in Louisiana, Canada, and the West Indies. The Compagnie d'Occident soon absorbed all other French colonial trading companies, extending its control of French trade throughout the Far East, the Americas, and Africa.

Armed with his bank and the Compagnie d'Occident, Law offered to assume the large royal debt that the regency government had inherited from LOUIS XIV. He proposed to eliminate the debt with the profits gained from his trading company. He also proposed that his bank should receive a monopoly on collecting taxes. In this way, the troublesome system of tax farming (private individuals collected taxes and pocketed whatever profits they could extract from the populace) could be eliminated. Tax collection would remain a profit-making enterprise, but because it would be centralized in the bank, collection would theoretically be more efficient and government yields would also increase.

This entire scheme was called the Law system. It operated from 1716 until 1720. Like his English contemporaries who created the SOUTH SEA BUBBLE, Law provoked a wave of financial speculation with his schemes. He was redeeming government bonds and securities with shares of Compagnie d'Occident stock. Prices on individual certificates of that stock rose to nearly 40 times the face amount. The bubble of speculation (MISSISSIPPI BUBBLE) burst when certain key investors became wary and sold their shares. Displaced tax farmers, themselves wealthy financiers, played a role in planting seeds of doubt about the Law system. The stock market fell drastically and suddenly in October 1720. Law fled from France to BRUSSELS. He died, poor and neglected, in VENICE in 1729.

See also ANCIEN RÉGIME.

Leeuwenhoek, Antoni van (1632–1723) *Dutch natural scientist and lens grinder who invented the microscope*
The instrument opened up an unknown world of tiny life forms whose discovery required a revolution in concepts about the extent and nature of creation. Discoveries made with the new instrument severely challenged prevalent Aristotelian biological concepts, and the theoretical problems raised by these new discoveries occupied natural scientists throughout the ENLIGHTENMENT.

Van Leeuwenhoek, the son of a Delft basket-maker, was only six years old when his father died. He was sent to grammar school near Leiden and then took an apprenticeship as a cloth merchant in AMSTERDAM. He never attended university. Leeuwenhoek worked as a shopkeeper until 1660, when he moved into the civil service of the city of Delft. His keen interest in the life sciences motivated him to study scientific texts independently. Despite his lack of formal training, Leeuwenhoek attained international renown as a scientist during his lifetime. The Dutch anatomist Reinier de Graaf (1641–73, discoverer of the ovarian structures called Graafian follicles) assisted him in making contacts with the ROYAL SOCIETY OF LONDON. The Royal Society received Leeuwenhoek as a fellow in 1680, and the FRENCH ACADEMY OF SCIENCES appointed him as a foreign correspondent in 1699.

Leeuwenhoek invented the MICROSCOPE in 1671 when he decided to build a scientific instrument using the ground lenses common in the cloth inspection business. His microscopes were not improved until the 19th century. Thus, they provided the technological basis for all Enlightenment biological research in the critical areas of GENERATION (reproduction) and micro-anatomy.

Leeuwenhoek discovered the existence of minute organisms, invisible to the naked eye, with his new microscope. He believed that the moving objects he was observing with his microscope were living creatures and reported his findings to the Royal Society of London in a letter of October 1676. The letter caused a sensation and generated a strong controversy concerning the actual animal nature of the observed objects.

Leeuwenhoek used the microscope to study animal reproduction after 1677. He believed that sperm, then called animalcules, were normal components of semen and ultimately assigned to them all responsibility for reproduction. In Leeuwenhoek's version of generation theory, the role of the female was limited to that of nourishment. He differed sharply on this question from William Harvey, who believed that the female egg rather than the male sperm was the source of new life.

Leeuwenhoek rejected the Aristotelian theory of spontaneous generation in putrefying matter. He believed that all living forms are functionally similar and therefore searched for analogous structures in animals and plants. His research contributed significantly to the understanding of microscopic plant anatomy.

Having acquired widespread fame in Europe on account of his inventions and discoveries, Leeuwenhoek received visits not only from major scientists but also from PETER I (THE GREAT) of Russia, James II of ENGLAND, Elector August II of Saxony, and Grand Duke Cosimo III of Tuscany. His letters and scientific research were reported in the *Philosophical Transactions of the Royal Society*, the French *Recueil d'expériences et observations sur le combat qui procède du mélange des corps* (Collection of experiments and observations on the struggle which proceeds from the mingling of bodies; 1679), and in the *Journal des Savants* (Scholars' journal). Latin editions of his letters and papers were published between 1715 and 1722.

See also ANIMALCULISM; BIOLOGY; SCIENCE; TECHNOLOGY AND INSTRUMENTATION.

Leibniz, Gottfried Wilhelm (1646–1716) *German philosopher, mathematician, historian, and diplomat, author of one of the three great systems of rationalism contributed by the 17th century to the Enlightenment*
Leibniz was born in Leipzig, a city in the electorate of Saxony, two years before the end of the devastating Thirty Years' War. His father was a professor of MORAL PHILOSOPHY at the University of Leipzig and his mother, the daughter of a professor.

Young Leibniz immersed himself in his father's library, reading ancient classics, medieval Scholastic philosophy, and the writings of the Christian church fathers. After receiving a traditional education in philosophy at the University of Leipzig, he matriculated in 1763 at the University of Jena, where he studied mathematics under the direction of Erhard Weigel. He completed his formal education at the University of Altdorf in 1666.

Having rejected an offer from the University of Altdorf to remain there as a teacher, Leibniz moved to Nuremberg. He entered the local ROSICRUCIANS and met the statesman and diplomat Johann Christian von Boyneburg, who assisted him in establishing his career. At the suggestion of Boyneburg, the archbishop elector of Mainz, Johann Philipp von Schönborn, offered Leibniz a post as a legal researcher and writer. In this capacity, Leibniz assisted in reforming the legal codes of Mainz.

With Boyneburg, Leibniz developed a diplomatic plan designed to divert the attention of King LOUIS XIV from the lands of the Rhine River region of the HOLY ROMAN EMPIRE. This project took the two men to PARIS during the winter of 1671 and 1672. Their diplomatic mission was a failure, but Leibniz used the occasion to make the acquaintance of prominent mathematicians and scientists such as Pierre Carcavi and Christian Huygens. He also met the spokesman for JANSENISM, Antoine Arnauld.

A second diplomatic mission, to LONDON in 1673, extended Leibniz's contacts within the international REPUBLIC OF LETTERS. He was received into the ROYAL SOCIETY OF LONDON where discussions with John Pell, Henry Oldenburg, Robert Hooke, and Robert Boyle proved especially stimulating.

From London, Leibniz returned to Paris, where he remained until 1676. He developed the infinitesimal calculus during these Paris years, publishing his findings in 1684. Isaac NEWTON had already written on the subject but had never published his work. Leibniz was not aware of Newton's discoveries, and, indeed, Newton refrained from publishing them until 1687, three years after Leibniz's findings appeared in print. This chain of events caused a dispute over precedence between Leibniz and Newton, which was resolved only when it was acknowledged that both men had independently invented the calculus.

Leibniz finally returned to Hanover in 1676, having received a post in the service of Duke Johann Friedrich of Braunschweig-Lüneburg. On the trip home, he stopped in The Hague for a visit with the great Jewish systematic philosopher, Benedict de SPINOZA.

In Hanover, Leibniz began preparing a geneology and official history of the house of Braunschweig (Brunswick). This project took him on a three-year research trip to destinations throughout the Holy Roman Empire and ITALY. Although he never completed the project, Leibniz

Gottfried Wilhelm Leibniz. One of the great systematic, rational philosophers of the late 17th century, Leibniz provided some of the ideas from which the unique characteristics of the German Enlightenment (*Aufklärung*) were constructed. *(Courtesy New York Public Library)*

unearthed valuable materials that were used in the successful campaign to elevate the duke of Hanover to the status of an elector in the Holy Roman Empire. Leibniz remained in the service of the Hanoverians Johann Friedrich and Ernst August, but was not retained after the succession of Georg Ludwig (1698).

Through the patronage of Sophia Charlotte, Leibniz was invited to BERLIN in 1700. The daughter of the Hanoverian duke Ernst August, Sophia Charlotte was also the wife of Elector Frederick III of BRANDENBURG. Leibniz submitted plans to Frederick for a scientific organization that resulted in the founding of the first BERLIN ACADEMY. As the first president of the academy, Leibniz guided its operations until his death in 1716. After 1711, however, he did not actually live in Berlin because he accepted a post as privy councillor to PETER I (THE GREAT) that took him to SAINT PETERSBURG. Then, between 1712 and 1714, VIENNA became his home while he worked as an imperial privy councillor to the Hapsburg emperor

Charles VI. Leibniz finally returned to Berlin in 1714, just after George Ludwig had assumed the English throne as George I. Although Leibniz requested to be transferred to ENGLAND, George refused, demanding, instead, that he remain in Hanover in order to complete the long overdue history of the house of Braunschweig.

Leibniz possessed a sharp and wide-ranging intellect that led him to investigate a wide variety of subjects. During his university years, he had supplemented his formal training with independent study of modern natural philosophers such as Francis BACON, René DESCARTES, Pierre GASSEND, Thomas HOBBES, Johannes KEPLER, and Galileo GALILEI. He thus possessed a thorough background in both traditional and contemporary philosophical issues. His extensive contributions to MATHEMATICS, EPISTEMOLOGY, natural SCIENCE, HISTORY, THEOLOGY, and law mark him as a true polymath.

Like Descartes, Spinoza, and the other 17th-century champions of RATIONALISM, Leibniz believed that the architectural model for the world was provided by the kind of logic (REASON) used in mathematics. He developed an early system of language notation that aimed at allowing logical statements (propositions) to be manipulated like mathematical expressions. He also dreamed of developing a new alphabet (*alphabetum cogitationum humanarum*) and language (*characteristica universalis*), which would provide the intellectual tools needed to construct an encyclopedic knowledge of the world.

Leibniz wanted to create a comprehensive system of knowledge based on rigorous logical principles, but he was anxious to avoid the atheistic and materialist implications he believed were contained in both the Cartesian and Spinozist forms of the MECHANICAL PHILOSOPHY. He tried to negotiate a middle path between the dualism of mind and body relationships contained in Cartesian thought and the monism of Spinozism. Leibniz's philosophy offered a synthesis comprising concepts drawn from both medieval Scholasticism and from mechanical philosophy.

At the base of Leibniz's philosophy stood the distinction between truths of reason and truths of fact. This distinction rested on the degree of certainty that is possible with different types of knowledge; truths of reason are absolutely certain, whereas truths of fact are not. It is important to note that this distinction exists only because of the limits of the human mind. If people could know and understand the world from the whole, timeless vantage point enjoyed by God, then all truths, whether concerned with the laws of reason or with factual events, would be known with full and equal certainty.

Truths of reason are "necessary propositions," self-evident statements, capable of being deduced a priori. These truths rest on the "principle of contradiction," which asserts that a thing cannot be both "A" and "not-A." Truths of reason do not, however, reveal anything about actual existence (except in the case of God).

Truths of fact are derived a posteriori. They are the facts of existence or of history. Truths of fact rest, for Leibniz, on the "principle of sufficient reason." They are not logically necessary; their opposites are possible. For example, the statement "the sun rises in the morning" tells a truth that we all recognized from experience. But it is not necessary from a logical standpoint for the sun to rise tomorrow, even though it has risen every day since the creation of the solar system; it is possible that the sun will not rise tomorrow.

The principle of sufficient reason underlies the actual world in which we exist: That is, the world takes the form it has because God decided to create it so. This was not, however, the only world that God could have created; many others were possible, but God chose this world because its overall structure, which is determined by the logical principle of noncontradiction, contains the greatest possible diversity and degree of perfection. It was this complex argument that led Leibniz to conclude that the extant world is the best of all possible worlds.

The description offered by Leibniz of this created world differs in key respects from the views of Descartes or Spinoza. Into the world constructed according to reason, Leibniz introduced a principle of perfection. This principle produces constant striving toward perfection, thus introducing a moral element into the essential physical structure of things. The Leibnizian world consists of a great continuum of beings (the GREAT CHAIN OF BEING) in which all things—nonliving objects, plants, animals, humankind, and even God—are linked together according to a "law of continuity." There are no leaps or breaks anywhere in NATURE.

Leibniz sketched out a physics based on these principles in the famous *Monadologie* (1714) written for Prince EUGENE OF SAVOY. According to Leibniz, the physical world of substances is composed of simple units called monads (Greek: *monas*, signifying one or unity). These monads are not atoms of extended matter like the fundamental particles described by Descartes. Monads are more like spiritual substances that possess both perception and appetite (inner drive or force). Thus, the fundamental building blocks of the universe are mathematical points (unextended, not occupying space) possessing qualities of mind rather than of matter.

Each monad is unique, differing in some way from every other monad. When a series of monads unite together, they create extended matter or bodily objects much as a series of unextended mathematical points on a graph combine to create a two-dimensional form. Because the universe is populated by these monad-containing bodies it is filled with perception and with a tendency toward action (*conatus*).

The world is composed of infinite numbers of monads, each one unique, but also completely related to all the others. Because this infinite set of connections exists, a change in one monad will produce effects on all the others. Leibniz said that monads were windowless; they did not need to observe the world objectively (as we might look at the external world through a window) because their interconnected states meant that they experienced everything that happens in the universe as a set of effects on their individual condition.

Several problems arose from this monadology. First, Leibniz insisted that every monad acts independently. In the interconnected system just described, monads are not acting directly on one another like billiard balls knocking one another about. If this is true, however, then the causes of the interconnectedness must be explained. Leibniz offered the concept of preestablished harmony as a solution. According to this concept, God has constructed the laws of the world so that every monad acting independently will, nevertheless, also act harmoniously with every other monad in the world.

Leibniz developed this notion of independence in an attempt to avoid the consequences of occasionalism as expressed in the works of the French Cartesian Nicolas de MALEBRANCHE and the Dutch philosopher Arnold Geulincx (1624–69). Occasionalism had God acting directly in the world, causing every tiny event to happen by his direct intervention. This vision of God seemed to honor his power to act in the world, but it did not give him much credit for creating an efficient system. Leibniz offered his notion of preestablished harmony as an antidote to occasionalism.

Preestablished harmony, however, raised several new problems for moral philosophy and theology. It seemed to suggest that human behavior is actually predetermined by this God-given harmony. If this is true, then human beings are robbed of the FREEDOM to choose their actions according to principles of good and evil. Leibniz tried to explain in the *Essais de Théodicée sur a bonté de Dieu, la liberté de l'homme et l'origine du mal* (Essays of theodicy on the goodness of God, the liberty of humankind and the origin of evil; 1710, Latin translation 1719) how his system preserved freedom and morality. His account failed to resolve the questions raised by the idea of preestablished harmony.

The desire for religious and international peace motivated Leibniz's activities throughout his life. This fundamental desire manifested itself not only in his diplomatic activities but also in the theme of unity and harmony that informs his philosophical works. As a devout Christian, Leibniz actively pursued Christian reunification. He first tried, through correspondence with Bishop BOSSUET, to establish some areas of agreement that would allow Protestants and Catholics to reunite. When that proved impossible, he turned to facilitating discussions within PROTESTANTISM between the leaders of LUTHERANISM and CALVINISM. The search for peace also motivated his various projects for the creation of a United Europe.

In all his work, Leibniz strove to describe the unity created from infinite diversity, which he believed characterizes the universe. The human world, according to Leibniz, mirrored this broader structure, and the task of political activity lay in preserving individuality within the bounds of a unified state or group of states. He believed that the Holy Roman Empire possessed the potential to realize this political ideal, that the empire could be revitalized if it were transformed into a voluntary confederation united for certain common goals.

Leibniz's death in 1716 was scarcely noted by contemporaries, and his ideas were often criticized during the first half of the 18th century for their excessive rationality and systematic nature. Whatever the problems with Leibniz's system for his contemporaries, certain of its elements played an important role in the Enlightenment. The Leibnizian system of knowledge as interpreted by Christian WOLFF, a student of Leibniz, profoundly shaped the early AUFKLÄRUNG (German Enlightenment). Furthermore, after the 1765 publication of the *Nouveaux Essais sur l'entendement humain* (New essays on human understanding), Leibnizian ideas about epistemology directly entered the mainstream of the Enlightenment.

The famed *vis viva* controversy of 18th-century mechanics pitted the Leibnizian concept of force against the Newtonian view; in the end, most 18th-century thinkers settled for the solution offered by Jean Le Rond d'ALEMBERT, which suggested that the two concepts were simply different ways of expressing the same underlying notion.

The Leibnizian concept of the body as a collection of monads striving toward some goal entered the life sciences through the school of VITALISM. Leibniz's views provided an alternative for people dissatisfied with the Cartesian-inspired vision of the living being as a simple machine operating according to mechanical laws. The Leibnizian view reintroduced the idea that living beings have a purpose, that they are active in the world, and that they are always striving toward some goal, however that goal may be defined.

Immanuel KANT, the philosopher who worked out a major restatement of epistemology in the late Enlightenment, was trained in the Leibniz-Wolff school of philosophy at Königsberg. In developing his positions, Kant both criticized and incorporated concepts derived from Leibniz.

Finally, the Leibnizian vision of the universe as an active, striving whole, a unity created from an infinite variety of independent but interrelated monads, entered the late Enlightenment as a general description of nature. The concept of a striving world helped to introduce the idea that the world and humankind change over time in a direction that is upward, reaching toward perfection.

Thus, in spite of the ridiculous caricature of Leibnizian philosophy painted by VOLTAIRE in CANDIDE, its ideas stimulated the rich transformation of enlightened thought that occurred throughout Europe—even in Voltaire's France—after 1760.

See also BILDUNG; MATHEMATICS AND MECHANICS; PERFECTIBILITY; RIGHTS.

Further reading: H. G. Alexander, ed., *The Leibniz-Clarke Correspondence* (New York: Manchester Press, 1978); C. D. Broad, *Leibniz: An Introduction* (Cambridge: Cambridge University Press, 1975); Gottfried Wilhelm von Leibniz, *Monadology and Other Philosophical Essays,* tr. Paul Schrecker and Anne Martin Schrecker (Indianapolis: Bobbs-Merrill, 1965).

lending libraries   *See* ENLIGHTENMENT; LITERACY; PUBLISHING; SOCIAL INSTITUTIONS OF THE ENLIGHTENMENT.

Lennox, Charlotte Ramsay (1720–1804) *British novelist, poet, playwright, translator, and magazine editor*
Ramsay, the daughter of Colonel James Ramsay, the lieutenant-governor of the British colony of New York, was sent to ENGLAND as a young adolescent to live with an aunt. The arrangement failed because the aunt apparently suffered from some form of insanity, which prevented her from adequately caring for her niece. Charlotte received some support from her father until his death in 1743. After that, she had to support herself. In 1747, she published her first volume of poems. About that time, she also married Alexander Lennox, an assistant to her printer; the marriage failed, and to support herself and her children, Charlotte Lennox began writing plays and miscellaneous pieces. She also worked as a translator.

Early in her literary career, Lennox became a friend of Samuel JOHNSON, who called her the most intelligent of his female contemporaries. She also enjoyed the friendship of Samuel RICHARDSON and Oliver GOLDSMITH. Johnson praised Lennox's first novel, *The Life of Harriet Stuart* (1750), throwing her an all-night party on the occasion of its publication. He also collaborated with her in the translation of *The Greek Theatre of Father Brumoy* (1760). She was also encouraged by Johnson in her publication of *Shakespeare Illustrated* (1753–54), a translation and discussion of Shakespeare's Italian sources. Lennox translated at least five works from the French, including SIÈCLE DE LOUIS XIV (The age of Louis XIV; 1752) by VOLTAIRE; *Mémoires de Maximilien de Béthune, duc de Sully* (Memoirs of Maximillian de Bethune, duke of Sully; 1755); and *Mémoires pour l'histoire de Madame de Maintenon* (Memoirs for the history of Madame de Maintenon; 1757).

Lennox's most famous novel, *The Female Quixote, or the Adventures of Arabella* (1752), focuses on a young woman who grows up in a secluded castle, reading French heroic romances from the 17th century. Like the hero of Cervantes's *Don Quixote* (1605, 1615), Arabella is a victim of illusion, mistaking the stories in these romances for true histories. In a contemporary review of the novel, Henry FIELDING praised Lennox's plot as more probable than Cervantes's original. In Fielding's opinion, this quality made Lennox's work superior. The novel illustrates one of the new uses of fiction in the ENLIGHTENMENT: educating and therefore enlightening readers by providing commentary on human behavior.

Lespinasse, Julie-Jeanne-Eléonore de (1732–1776) *French salon hostess; the illegitimate daughter of a French countess*
She became the companion and assistant of Madame du DEFFAND, serving in this role from 1754 until 1764. During these years, she became the close friend of Jean Le Rond d'ALEMBERT. The friendship was apparently platonic, fueled by spiritual and intellectual links, a rarity among the circles of the PHILOSOPHES.

In 1764, Mademoiselle Lespinasse and d'Alembert left the salon of Madame du Deffand when rivalries between the two women began to surface. Mademoiselle de Lespinasse set up a rival salon at the corner of Rue Saint-Dominique and Rue de Belle Chasse. Her gatherings soon became a focal point for radical enlightened culture and

Portrait of Julie de Lespinasse. As a close friend and intellectual companion of Jean Le Rond d'Alembert, Mademoiselle Julie de Lespinasse presided over one of the central Parisian salons. *(Courtesy Culver Pictures, Inc., New York)*

were attended regularly by the marquis de CONDORCET, d'Alembert, Jean-François MARMONTEL, Anne-Robert-Jacques TURGOT, the writer André Morellet (1727–1819), the archbishop of Toulouse, Loménie de Brienne, and nobles such as the duc de La Rochefoucauld and the comte de Crillon. Other philosophes such as Denis DIDEROT, Melchior GRIMM, Baron HOLBACH, Abbé CONDILLAC, Charles DUCLOS, Abbé RAYNAL, and BERNARDIN DE SAINT-PIERRE sometimes attended.

Mademoiselle de Lespinasse acquired considerable power as a patroness, competing with Madame GEOFFRIN in securing French Academy chairs for favored intellectuals. Her letters to comte de Guibert, published only in 1809, provide insights into the highly influential culture of enlightened Parisian salons during the later 18th century.

See also SOCIAL INSTITUTIONS OF THE ENLIGHTENMENT; WOMEN AND THE ENLIGHTENMENT.

Lessing, Gotthold Ephraim (1729–1781) *German dramatist, critic, and theologian*

Although not the most innovative thinker of the AUFKLÄRUNG (German ENLIGHTENMENT), Lessing was certainly one of the most influential. His plays, essays, and treatises presented major philosophical concerns in an engaging and compelling style, spreading knowledge of these issues to the general educated public in German territories.

A native of Kamenz in the electorate of Saxony, Lessing studied theology and the Leibnizian-Wolffian tradition in PHILOSOPHY at the University of Leipzig. Lessing developed a circle of enlightened friends from BERLIN whose most prominent members were Moses MENDELSSOHN and Friedrich NICOLAI. These men would be his allies and supporters in efforts to spread the Enlightenment throughout German cultural areas.

Until 1769, when he received a position as librarian at the splendid library of the duke of Braunschweig-Wolfenbüttel, Lessing supported himself by writing literary and art criticism. A champion of the artistic potential of the German language, he published a series of letters entitled *Briefe, die neueste Literatur betreffend* (Letters concerning the newest literature; 1759–65) that attacked the artificiality of French CLASSICISM. German writers, he declared, should turn for inspiration to the plays and poetry of William Shakespeare.

Lessing's *Laokoon, oder, über die grenzen der Malerei und Poesie* (Laocoon, or over the boundaries between painting and poetry; 1766) offered an expansion of his literary AESTHETICS. LAOKOON highlighted the forms and style in writing that Lessing was espousing by contrasting them to the elements appropriate for painting. It attacked the theory of NEOCLASSICISM put forth by Johann WINCKELMANN on the grounds that the universal norms prescribed by this theory would limit the FREEDOM of the artist. No single set of aesthetic rules and forms exists, Lessing maintained, that holds good for all types of artistic creation.

After settling in Wolfenbüttel, Lessing turned his attention to the basic questions that were facing the Christian RELIGION during the Enlightenment: religious TOLERATION and the epistemological grounds for belief. Unlike some of his enlightened contemporaries, Lessing could not simply abandon religious belief in favor of a secular vision of the world. But he also could not accept the rigid theological dogma associated with various forms of Christianity. He tried for a while to find a substitute in the enlightened DEISM and RATIONALISM of the FREEMASONS, but that failed to satisfy him.

Lessing could not accept the idea that the Bible is a direct revelation from God. In his eyes, it was simply a human document, the history of the Hebrew people and of early Christians. Lessing pursued this interpretation of the Bible by initiating a series of investigations into the sources for the four New Testament gospels. He also published excerpts from an unfinished manuscript by the deist and biblical scholar Hermann Samuel REIMARUS. They appeared in the *Beiträge zur Geschichte und Literatur* (Contributions to history and literature) as "Wolfenbütteler Fragmente eines Ungennanten" (Anonymous fragments from Wolfenbüttel; 1774 and 1777–78).

Lessing's employer, the duke of Braunschweig-Wolfenbüttel, was anxious to avoid the controversies that Lessing's theological writings were provoking. He forbade Lessing to publish his research on the gospels. Lessing skirted the duke's prohibition by writing the drama *Nathan der Weise* (NATHAN THE WISE; 1779). An impassioned plea for religious toleration, *Nathan der Weise* stressed that true religious belief entails not adherence to dogma, but rather the acceptance of the universal brotherhood of all human beings.

Lessing finally resolved the issue about the roles of REASON and revelation in the presentation of religious truths by adopting a historical explanation. The expression of religious beliefs by human beings became a stage in the general historical PROGRESS of humankind toward greater degrees of perfection. Lessing presented this thesis in a treatise entitled *Die Erziehung des Menschengeschlechts* (The education of the human race; 1780).

In his later years, Lessing turned to the monistic philosophy of Benedict de SPINOZA for ideas regarding the free will of human beings. He agreed with Spinoza that free will is an illusion and that human behavior is determined by the structure of the universe. Rather than bemoaning this situation, Lessing found comfort in it.

Spinoza's philosophy had been treated with suspicion and contempt for its reputed support of determinism and pantheism (or ATHEISM, as pantheism was typically called by its enemies). Word of Lessing's fascination with Spinoza reached the German public in 1785, when Friedrich Heinrich JACOBI published *Über die Lehre des Spinoza in Briefen an der Hernn Moses Mendelssohn* (Letters to Moses Mendelssohn on the doctrine of Spinoza). Jacobi revealed that Lessing had confided to him his acceptance of Spinozist ideas. Such revelations amounted to a libel of Lessing's name in the context of the times. Mendelssohn felt compelled to defend his deceased friend. The ensuing *Pantheismusstreit* (Pantheism Conflict) did not exonerate Lessing, but rather spread knowledge of Spinozism in enlightened German circles. As a result, the accusations against Lessing were ignored in many circles, and Spinozism was praised and incorporated into the ideas of younger generations of German intellectuals.

Lessing was a figure whose work had importance on many levels. He spread the basic humanitarian values of the Enlightenment to his contemporaries, provided a sympathetic reading of Spinoza and pantheism, and championed the cause of the German language and culture, helping to create a national literature. His contributions not only stirred controversy and ferment but also provided several of the critical ingredients whose presence gave the German Enlightenment its unique character.

Further reading: W. H. Bruford, *Germany in the Eighteenth Century: The Social Background of the Literary Revival* (Cambridge: Cambridge University Press, 1971); Paul Hazard, *European Thought in the Eighteenth Century from Montesquieu to Lessing,* tr. J. Lewis May (Cleveland: Meridian/World, 1963); Gotthold Ephraim Lessing, *Lessing's Theological Writings,* tr. Henry Chadwick (Stanford, Calif.: Stanford University Press, 1957).

Letters on Toleration   Three separate letters by John LOCKE that were published anonymously in 1689, 1690, and 1692. The first letter contains the essence of his ideas on religious TOLERATION, a cause that would be championed by spokesmen of the ENLIGHTENMENT. It was originally written in Latin for Locke's Dutch friend Philip van Limborch. It was printed and published in 1689 in both Latin and English editions.

People before Locke had certainly, on occasion, called for religious toleration, but Locke offered a particularly powerful set of arguments that spoke to his contemporaries and to those who followed him in the 18th century. He combined theoretical arguments that had roots in theology and philosophy with practical arguments based on utility and the good of the state.

Locke asserted that a tolerant attitude is the mark of a true RELIGION, for faith should be primarily a matter between the individual and God. In this position, he reflected the trend toward inner forms of religion that was also expressed in PIETISM, Quietism, and Quakerism.

True religion, according to Locke, produces believers who express love toward their fellow human beings and who practice virtue and piety. Arguments about doctrine are futile, especially since no single group can probably ever claim to possess the only path to salvation.

For those who rejected these arguments about the nature of religion, Locke offered a practical argument. Attempts to force people to accept certain beliefs are useless; the mind can always remain independent and efforts to force conformity will merely produce external compliance and hypocrisy.

Locke added a last set of arguments based on the church-state relations, which he derived from his POLITICAL THEORY. Churches are voluntary societies, formed to deal with matters of the spirit. The state has no authority in these realms and must not, therefore, try to control them.

The Letters on Toleration championed the ideals of liberty of conscience and personal FREEDOM, prescribing only that their exercise should not harm another person or group. But Locke could not envision complete freedom of thought and in the end rejected toleration of both ATHEISM and ROMAN CATHOLICISM. He was writing with PROTESTANTISM in mind, hoping to persuade people that the sectarian strife that had ripped ENGLAND apart during the 17th century had no valid reason for existence.

See also QUAKERS.

lettres de cachet   Mechanism for the execution of royal justice in FRANCE. *Lettres de cachet* (sealed letters) were royal orders by which an individual could be summarily imprisoned, exiled, or placed in a monastery, without any stated cause or opportunity to appear before a court of law. For 18th-century French subjects, they represented absolute monarchy at its epitome and were viewed by many people as an abuse of power. Usually, the letters were used rather sparingly. Irate family patriarchs sometimes requested one from the king in order to incarcerate unruly sons. The government sometimes also used them to imprison troublesome political opponents. In the 18th century, the French kings began to resort to them more frequently as they struggled to curtail increasing opposition from the judicial courts (PARLEMENTS) to their central authority. One of the more notorious examples of the use of lettres de cachet occurred when the chancellor René de MAUPEOU used them against the officeholders in the *parlements* who had resisted royal plans for tax reform in an effort to protect their own privileges. The members of the *parlements* were exiled to remote spots in France and their posts filled with judges and lawyers appointed directly by Maupeou. Protests were made against the abuse of judicial power represented by the letters.

See also ABSOLUTISM; ANCIEN RÉGIME.

libertine A free-thinker or someone who leads a dissolute life. Derived from the Latin *libertinus,* meaning a freed slave, the word *libertine* designated someone who claimed intellectual freedom in matters of religion. Libertine thinkers, prominent in 17th-century France, were influenced by SKEPTICISM and MATERIALISM, the idea that everything in the universe—from the movement of stars to the growth of tissues to the workings of the human soul—can be explained as the action of matter in different combinations. They saw RELIGION as a political invention used to control people and maintain the social order. Whether deists or atheists, they questioned the immortality of the soul, the Bible's authority, and the notion of revealed truth. The discoveries of the SCIENTIFIC REVOLUTION confirmed the libertines in their belief that the world could be understood through REASON, without recourse to supernatural or divine phenomena.

In France, the term *erudite libertines* referred to a group of serious thinkers whose best representative was the poet Théophile de Viau. Arrested in 1623 for his beliefs, he was burned in effigy, imprisoned for almost two years, and exiled. This event marked a new phase in which libertines became more careful not to offend the authorities.

During the English Restoration (1660–79), the Court Wits were a visible group of libertines known for writing clever songs and poems extemporaneously. The most famous libertine of the time was John Wilmot, earl of Rochester. While his verses contained serious reflections on love, he also wrote lewd poems and acquired a scandalous reputation. The Restoration stage depicted the libertine as a witty hedonist or a pretentious fool. The plays of Aphra BEHN were inspired by libertine thought in their depictions of the force of love and passion.

By the 18th century, in both ENGLAND and FRANCE, the philosophical meaning of libertine had receded into the background, while the social and moral implications took the forefront. In France, the period of the Regency (1715–23) was seen by contemporaries as a time when libertine behavior flourished. After the death of LOUIS XIV, who had become very devout toward the end of his life, Philippe d'Orléans, a known libertine, became regent and completely reversed the mood at court. A popular anecdote recounted that during Mass one day an acquaintance was astonished to see him following along with a prayer book—until it was discovered that he was actually reading a novel by François Rabelais, a French Renaissance writer famous for ribald scenes.

In the 18th century, the libertine was no longer seen simply as a free-thinker with dubious morals, but as a dishonest seducer of women. Especially in France, libertines were associated with aristocratic decadence. The phenomenon has been frequently explained by the idleness of an aristocratic class that was deprived of its political role by Louis XIV and reduced to seducing women as a means of demonstrating power.

Libertines claimed to be refined, sophisticated connoisseurs of pleasure, but libertine novels frequently portray the cruel and destructive nature of their behavior. The best-known libertines in literature are Lovelace, the sinister seducer in CLARISSA (1747), by Samuel RICHARDSON (1747), and Valmont, the rakish hero of *Les liaisons dangéreuses* (Dangerous liaisons; 1782), by Choderlos de LACLOS. Laclos's novel is exceptional because of the presence of a female libertine character with a powerful intellect, the marquise de Merteuil. In general, when applied to a woman, the term *libertine* did not carry connotations of systematic thinking and intellectual rebellion, as it did when applied to men. Instead, the term was simply a way of condemning a woman's sexual behavior, which was seen as betraying the modesty of her sex.

Many 18th-century observers of society saw libertines as a scourge and bemoaned the terrible times in which they lived. At the same time, libertines continued to exert considerable fascination on the imagination through qualities such as flamboyance, intellect, charm, and wit. The 17th-century libertines had made an intellectual contribution to the ENLIGHTENMENT by their commitment to reason and philosophy; their ideas were disseminated by such important figures as Pierre BAYLE. But in the 18th century philosophers who had absorbed libertine ideals, such as Denis DIDEROT and VOLTAIRE, needed to distance themselves from a phenomenon that was widely seen as a moral threat to society. By the end of this period, two very different figures came to represent the evolution that the libertine had undergone: Giacomo CASANOVA, the charming seducer and adventurer, and the marquis de SADE, the infamous writer and philosopher who spent half his adult life in prison.

See also EPICUREAN PHILOSOPHY; GASSEND.

Further reading: Michael Feher, ed., *The Libertine Reader* (New York: Zone Books, 1997); Lydia Flem, *Casanova: The Man Who Really Loved Women,* tr. Catherine Temerson (New York: Farrar, Straus, Giroux, 1997); Germaine Greer, *John Wilmot, Earl of Rochester* (Horndon, Devon, UK: Northcote House Publishers, 2000); Gillian Manning, ed., *Libertine Plays of the Restoration* (North Clarendon, Vt.: Tuttle, 2001).

liberty *See* ENLIGHTENMENT; FREEDOM; POLITICAL THEORY.

Lichtenberg, Georg Christoph (1742–1799) *German philosopher, mathematician, art critic, and writer*
Lichtenberg studied at the University of GÖTTINGEN and devoted his professional life to that institution, serving as a professor of mathematics. He was a popular teacher whose fame during his lifetime was widespread in German lands. His students included the scientist Alexander von HUMBOLDT and the mathematician Christian Gauss.

Lichtenberg is noted less for his original mathematical contributions than for his literary creations and criticism. Lichtenberg admired English artistic expression as embodied in the satirical engravings of William HOGARTH, the dramas of William Shakespeare, and the acting style of Shakespeare's 18th-century interpreter, the actor David GARRICK. The German STURM UND DRANG movement, in contrast, received his biting criticism. Lichtenberg published most of his critical work in two journals, the *Göttinger Taschencalender* (The Göttingen pocket calendar) and the *Göttingisches Magazin der Wissenschaften und Litteratur* (The Göttingen magazine of sciences and literature).

Lichtenberg developed a philosophy of mathematics and its underlying EPISTEMOLOGY that distinguished sharply between theoretical and practical forms of mathematical expression. Probability theory claimed to be able to predict for example, the odds in reality of having a flipped coin land with heads up. Having noted that sometimes a flipped coin lands neither with heads up nor with tails up but rather on its edge, Lichtenberg concluded that these so-called laws of probability only approached the truth. As a result, in actual experience they lacked the degree of philosophical certainty that they claimed in theory. With his special philosophy of mathematics, now called the theory of scattered occasions, Lichtenberg tried to resolve the problems for theories of human knowledge created by theory-practice discrepancies.

Lichtenberg also addressed the philosophical problems of knowledge in other areas. He noted, for example, that different aspects of nature may display similar patterns in their relationships, but he believed that these patterns (*paradigmata*) should be treated as analogies rather than as evidence of the action of some universal natural law. He also opposed the theory of physiognomy developed by Johann LAVATER, which claimed that outward facial appearances can reliably reveal information about inner human character. Lichtenberg denied that such links between the external and the internal nature of things, between the observable and the occult (hidden), hold true with the certainty of natural law.

Lichtenberg espoused a vision of mind-body RELATIONS related to the monism of Benedict de SPINOZA. His views about how we derive our ideas of self and of other (not-self) developed from his application of monism to the PSYCHOLOGY of sensation. He also tended to see certain philosophical problems as primarily arising from language habits and structures.

Lichtenberg's writings appeared in prints in the early years of the 19th century in collections entitled *Vermischte Schriften* (Miscellaneous writings; 1800–03) and *Physikalische und mathematische Schriften* (Physical and mathematical writings; 1803–06). In earlier years, his impact on thought came primarily through his teaching. Many of his most penetrating ideas, however, were recorded as aphorisms in his private journals. Published in the 20th century as *Aphorismen, nach den Handschriften* (Aphorisms, after the manuscripts; 1902–08), these private musings reveal Lichtenberg to have been a scathing critic of intolerance, of academic pomposity, and of human fallibility. They are now considered one of the outstanding products of the ENLIGHTENMENT in GERMANY.

See also AUFKLÄRUNG; MATHEMATICS AND MECHANICS.

Linnaeus, Carolus (Latinized form of Carl von Linné) (1707–1778) *Swedish botanist, zoologist, geologist, and physician*

Linnaeus constructed the basic system of binomial nomenclature that is still used today for the classification of plants and animals. Each species, whether plant or animal, is identified by a pair of Latin (or Latinized) names; the first for the genus, the second for the species. For example, the white shrub rose that was the symbol of one party in England's War of the Roses was named in Linaeus's system *Rosa alba*. Other members of the genus *Rosa* are *Rosa gallica* (French rose), *Rosa damascena* (damask rose), and *Rosa centifolia* (cabbage rose).

Linnaeus used the reproductive organs as the basis for most of his classifications. This sexual system of CLASSIFICATION was attacked as artificial by Comte de BUFFON and other proponents of VITALISM. Albrecht von HALLER, although not a vitalist, also considered the Linnaean system artificial. In spite of these early negative reactions, Linnaeus's binomial nomenclature ultimately became the standard in biological taxonomy both for plants and animals. But his sexual system for classification later gave way to the system based on general structures and function developed in FRANCE.

The Linnaeus system derived much of its inspiration from aspects of the ENLIGHTENMENT. The controversies concerning the artificiality of his system and the validity of his sexual system of classification, as well as the search for more natural relations as a basis of classification, all derived from conceptual issues that were central for scientists of the era. Linnaeus's binomial nomenclature also manifested in clear form the early Enlightenment passion for ordering, naming, classifying, and thus regulating nature.

Linnaeus, the son of a country pastor, developed his interest in botany as a boy. After an early education at a Latin school, Linnaeus entered the University of Lund in 1727 to study MEDICINE. The next year he transferred to the University of Uppsala. His botanical interests occupied most of his time and energy, and it was only sometime after 1735 that he obtained his M.D. from the University of Harderwijk in the UNITED PROVINCES OF THE NETHERLANDS.

Linnaeus established his reputation as a premier botanist quickly. For three years from 1735 until 1738, he received support and practical assistance from Hermann BOERHAAVE and other Dutch scientists. During these

Lending library, Margate, 1700s. The spread of literacy brought an increased demand for reading materials available at low or no cost. Lending libraries provided such materials and served as a meeting place for the exchange of ideas. *(Courtesy New York Public Library)*

years, he began publishing his botanical findings and ideas on nomenclature. The *Systema Naturae* (System of Nature) appeared in 1735 followed by *Fundamenta botanica* (Foundations of botany; 1736), expanded and published as *Philosophia botanica* (Philosophy of botany; in 1751); the *Hortus Cliffortianus* (Cliffortian garden; 1737); *Flora lapponica* (Flora of Lapland; 1737); *Critica botanica* (Critical botany; 1737); *Genera plantarum* (Genuses of the plants; 1737); and *Classes plantarum* (Classes of plants; 1738).

In spite of this impressive output, Linnaeus could not obtain a university appointment or other official position. He therefore set up a medical practice in Stockholm, SWEDEN. Finally, in 1741, Linnaeus obtained a position as professor of practical medicine at the University of Uppsala. In 1742, he assumed the chair of botany, dietetics, and materia medica. He remained in Uppsala for the rest of his life, teaching at the university and renovating, expanding, and caring for the university's botanical gar-

den. A house in the garden served as home for Linnaeus, his wife, and son.

Linnaeus participated in a series of expeditions in Sweden designed to catalogue all the flora, fauna, and economically useful natural resources of the country. He published Swedish-language reports of these travels in 1745, 1747, and 1751.

Linnaeus received much recognition during his life in Sweden and other countries. He was granted a title of nobility (hence the name, von Linné) in 1762 after having served many years as a court physician. He helped to establish the Swedish Academy of Science and served as its first president. The FRENCH ACADEMY OF SCIENCES accepted him as a foreign correspondent in 1762.

See also BIOLOGY.

Lisbon earthquake Disastrous earthquake that occurred in Lisbon, PORTUGAL, on November 1, 1755. The movement of the earth destroyed most of the city, killing approximately 30,000 people in the structural collapses, fires, and floods that resulted. Many of the victims had been participating in a church service that was honoring departed souls as part of an All Saints' Day observance.

VOLTAIRE, one of the preeminent spokesmen of the ENLIGHTENMENT in FRANCE, was deeply disturbed by the tragedy. As he tried to cope with the emotions and questions raised by the earthquake, he wrote the "Poème sur le désastre de Lisbonne" (Poem on the disaster at Lisbon; 1756), "Poème sur la loi naturelle" (Poem on NATURAL LAW), and his famous novel *CANDIDE* (1759). These works all reflect on the meaning of the disaster for 18th-century views of the universe. They question and ridicule the philosophy of optimism along with beliefs in the benevolence of either NATURE or of God. It no longer seemed possible to Voltaire to believe in goodness when such destruction could be visited on countless innocent souls.

Voltaire was not alone with his feelings. In fact, the Lisbon earthquake was an immediate cause, if not the most important source, of the shift in the enlightened vision of nature that occurred at the middle of the 18th century. After that terrible event, philosophers and natural scientists began trying to find an adequate, but still secularized, way to conceptualize a world vulnerable to cataclysmic natural events.

literacy   The ability to read and to understand what has been read. The period of the ENLIGHTENMENT coincided with a marked increase in literacy in Europe. In some cases—areas where PIETISM or enlightened despotism (see DESPOTISM, ENLIGHTENED) were influential—this increase resulted directly from reforms inspired by enlightened values and goals.

In general, increased ability to read seems to have been produced by the slow extension of opportunities for elementary EDUCATION to new groups of people. PROTESTANTISM continued, as it had since its beginnings in the 16th century, to encourage reading the Bible and other devotional materials. But a passion or vogue for reading developed during the 18th century that cannot be explained simply by pointing to these factors. Books became more widely available, not only for purchase, but even for borrowing. Reading became a social activity as well as something that could be done in private, and people from all walks of life and both genders indulged themselves with books. Lending libraries, both private and public, appeared in cities throughout Europe.

Collecting reliable statistics on the incidence and degree of 18th-century literacy is a difficult matter. Modern historians have used criteria such as the ability to sign a legal document, inventories of libraries, and other indirect measurements in making their judgments.

ENGLAND, SCOTLAND, and PRUSSIA—all formally Protestant states—appear to have enjoyed the highest literacy rates. Some scholars estimate that male literacy rates reached 90 percent of the population and that female literacy rates approached 60 percent of the population in these areas. FRANCE lagged slightly behind, although figures varied markedly by region. Other areas of Europe such as ITALY and the HAPSBURG EMPIRE had lower rates of literacy.

The explosion in printed materials—journals, newspapers, pamphlets, novels, and the famous cheap imprints of the Bibliothèque bleue—helped to bring reading materials to a broader public. As a result, the ideas of intellectuals became available to audiences who were excluded from the salons, SCIENTIFIC ACADEMIES, and various literary clubs that functioned as centers of creative activity.

The various ideals of the Enlightenment stressed the role that knowledge could play in helping humanity reach higher levels of existence. Reading, of course, was one way to acquire knowledge. Both literacy and the enlightenment it could bring were viewed as essential skills for any individuals who were to be given the right to vote or to represent the nation. Thus, beliefs in the importance of literacy lay behind much enlightened POLITICAL THEORY. It is no accident that one of the "fathers" of the Enlightenment, John LOCKE, wrote treatises on both political theory and educational reform.

Few scholars doubt that the spread of literacy was partly responsible for the pronounced effect that enlightened ideas exercised in 18th-century Europe. In the end, the demands of a literate population helped to create strong pressures for change, which broke into the open in the AMERICAN REVOLUTION and FRENCH REVOLUTION. In both instances, political pamphlets, newspapers, and broadsides spread ideas and news to anyone who could read, making public opinion an important factor in determining political actions and events. The ability to read, then, brought with it potential political power and influence, laying a foundation for modern, representative, democratic societies.

See also PERFECTIBILITY; PROGRESS; PUBLISHING; SOCIAL INSTITUTIONS OF THE ENLIGHTENMENT.

literature   Writing in prose or verse. The ENLIGHTENMENT was created by writers, men and women who used their pens as instruments to forge a culture of criticism and new values. The era produced innovations in fiction and in journalism that were directly related to its general intellectual and social ideals. The most significant innovation occurred in prose writing with the development of the NOVEL as a powerful and immensely popular literary form.

A few novels had been written in 17th-century FRANCE, but the form was generally unsuited to the requirements imposed on literature by CLASSICISM. Novel-writing languished until shifts in reading habits and the appearance of a new AESTHETICS combined to highlight the potential and strengths of the form.

These development occurred in the 1730s and 1740s. In prior decades literature remained the domain of classicism, represented, for example, by the elegant poetry of Alexander POPE. Strict rules for composition, spelled out in the influential *L'Art Poétique* (Poetic art) by Nicolas Boileau, were held up as standards for writing not only in France, but also in ENGLAND. From his post in Leipzig, the powerful critic Johann Christoph GOTTSCHED tried to impose classical forms on German writing. But the Enlightenment, already well under way, was producing currents that would undermine the appeal of such formalized style.

Major impetus for literary innovation came early in the 18th century from the literate middle classes. Drawn to reading by the essays of Joseph ADDISON and Richard STEELE, English people began to demand materials of greater complexity, but dealing with similar themes: middle-class activities, problems, and moral sensibilities. The new 18th-century cult of SENSIBILITY, although not limited to the middle classes, tended to provide support for this middle-class literature. Tastes associated with this cult required plots and characters with the ability to appeal to feelings. Lofty subjects with universal value, presented in exquisitely crafted form—the staple of classicism—no longer appealed. People wanted to read about ordinary characters facing the emotional storms of contemporary life.

In 1731, the Abbé, PRÉVOST discovered the success that awaited skillful writers in the new genre. His sentimental novel *Manon Lescaut* enjoyed widespread popularity in France, the HOLY ROMAN EMPIRE, DENMARK, and the UNITED PROVINCES OF THE NETHERLANDS. Prévost's success was eclipsed by the even greater popularity of the novel *PAMELA*, the first by Samuel RICHARDSON. After its publication in 1740, readers throughout Europe began demanding SENTIMENTAL FICTION.

Sentiment sometimes played a secondary role to social criticism in fiction. Fictional TRAVEL LITERATURE, for example, allowed writers to present a story with disguised, but nevertheless accessible commentary on contemporary European situations. *GULLIVER'S TRAVELS* by Jonathan SWIFT and the *PERSIAN LETTERS* by MONTESQUIEU are outstanding representatives of this genre.

The passion for exotic settings grew partly from interest stimulated by European contacts with new cultures and regions of the world. As the 18th century progressed, however, the exotic also began to include previously neglected historical eras and cultures. Thus, by midcentury, GOTHIC ROMANCE novels set in the Middle Ages vied for popularity with ballads and odes written in the style of ancient bards.

Just as they had in the era of classicism, writers again began looking to the past for some forms of literary inspiration, but their models were not limited to the ancient Latin and Greek classics; they also included Shakespeare, Homer, and Milton. Ballads became fashionable, especially after James MACPHERSON succeeded in captivating imaginations with the spurious Ossian poems.

Writers as well as other artists began trying to represent not just the ordinary emotions of people, but also the terror and awe of encounters with the SUBLIME. Theories about GENIUS and the sublime, and about the role of INTUITION AND IMAGINATION in artistic creation acquired prominence. When Edmund BURKE published his seminal observations on the sublime, his work found an especially receptive audience in German cultural areas.

The 18th century had witnessed an upsurge of interest in the literary traditions of the German language. Explorations into medieval German works helped to create a new confidence in the literary potential of the language. When the new theories about genius, the sublime, and aesthetics were taken into this German tradition, they mixed with this resurgent national tradition to produce movements with remarkable artistic force and ingenuity.

The aesthetic theories of Gotthold Ephraim LESSING, the youthful rebellions on behalf of individual freedom espoused by the *STURM UND DRANG* generation, the creation by Johann Wolfgang von GOETHE of the *Bildungsroman* (novel about character formation), the powerful "Ode to Joy" and the celebration of FREEDOM in *WILHELM TELL*, both by Friedrich SCHILLER, all resulted from this productive literary ferment.

Literature in the Enlightenment included several additional forms ranging from the pornographic novels of the marquis de SADE and Restif de la Bretonne through the psychological novels of Heinrich von KLEIST or Pierre LACLOS to the histories of VOLTAIRE and Edward GIBBON. At least in some segments of society where LITERACY had a broad base, reading became a favorite pastime. People visited coffeehouses to peruse the many periodicals and newspapers coming from the presses. They joined reading clubs or barrowed books from lending libraries. They read the *ENCYCLOPÉDIE*, polemical pamphlets, essays, popularizations of SCIENCE, and tracts on EDUCATION, as well as the latest fiction. In short, the period of the Enlightenment saw literature obtain a market of consumers that extended beyond traditional social boundaries and that created new types of reading materials.

See also BLUESTOCKING; HISTORY; PUBLISHING; QUARREL BETWEEN THE ANCIENTS AND THE MODERNS; SOCIAL INSTITUTIONS OF THE ENLIGHTENMENT; and individual writers in addition to those already mentioned in this article:

ADELUNG; ALGAROTTI; BARTHÉLEMY; BAYLE; BEAUMARCHAIS; BEHN; BLACKWELL; BLAKE; BOSWELL; BOUGAINVILLE; Charles BURNEY; Fanny BURNEY; BURNS; CALZABIGI; CASANOVA; CLELAND; COLERIDGE; CONGREVE; COWLEY; DARWIN; DIDEROT; EDGEWORTH; FAVART; FÉNÉLON; Henry FIELDING; Sarah FIELDING; FONTENELLE; FRÉRON; GALIANI; GODWIN; GOLDONI; GRAY; GRIMM; HAYWOOD; Wilhelm VON HUMBOLDT; INCHBALD; JOHNSON; Friedrich Gottlieb KLOPSTOCK; LENNOX; MANDEVILLE; MARMONTEL; Elizabeth MONTAGU; Lady Mary Wortley MONTAGU; MORE; PARINI; PIX; SHAFTESBURY; SHERIDAN; SMOLLETT; STAËL; Laurence STERNE; TROTTER; Horace WALPOLE; WOLLSTONECRAFT; YOUNG.

Further reading: Joseph F. Bartolomeo, *New Species of Criticism: Eighteenth-Century Discourse on the Novel* (Newark: University of Delaware Press, 1994); G. J. Barker-Benfield, *The Culture of Sensibility: Sex and Society in Eighteenth-Century Britain* (Chicago: University of Chicago Press, 1992); Roger Chartier, *The Cultural Uses of Print in Early Modern France,* tr. Lydia G. Cochrane (Princeton, N.J.: Princeton University Press, 1988); Pamela Currie, *Literature as Social Action: Modernist and Traditionalist Narratives in Germany in the 17th and 18th Centuries* (Rochester, N.Y.: Boydell & Brewer, 1995); Robert Darnton, *The Literary Underground of the Old Regime* (Cambridge, Mass.: Harvard University Press, 1982); Hugh Honour, *Romanticism* (New York: Harper & Row, 1979); Thomas M. Kavanagh, *Esthetics of the Moment: Literature and Art in the French Enlightenment* (Philadelphia: University of Pennsylvania Press, 1996).

Locke, John (1632–1704) *English moral, political, and natural philosopher*
Of the several 17th-century figures whose thought may be said to have founded the ENLIGHTENMENT, John Locke stands out for his multifaceted contributions. His LETTERS ON TOLERATION (1689, 1690, 1692), *Essay Concerning Human Understanding* (1690), TWO TREATISES OF GOVERNMENT (1690), *Some Thoughts Concerning Education* (1693), and *The Reasonableness of Christianity* (1695) became standard enlightened reading and helped to stimulate the PSYCHOLOGY and POLITICAL THEORY that provided major building blocks for 18th-century thought.

Locke grew up in a liberal Puritan family, the son of an attorney who fought in the English Civil Wars against King Charles I. Young Locke was enrolled at the elite Westminster School in 1646. The school's location put him within earshot of the execution of King Charles I in 1649, but the schoolmaster refused to allow the students to attend the execution.

In 1652, Locke matriculated at Christ's Church College of Oxford University. He received a B.A. degree in 1656, lectured in Latin and Greek while obtaining a master's degree, and then entered Oxford medical school in order to avoid becoming a clergyman. In 1664, he began serving in an administrative capacity as censor in moral philosophy for Oxford University.

Locke met Anthony Ashley Cooper, eventually to become the first earl of Shaftesbury, in 1666 at Oxford. Shaftesbury had come to take the waters in the town, and Locke, who was working as a physician's assistant, was sent to deliver the required bottles of mineral water. The two men became devoted friends, and Locke quickly entered Shaftesbury's service. As Shaftesbury's personal physician, Locke designed and carried out a liver operation in 1667 that probably saved his employer's life.

From that point, the fortunes of John Locke were tied to those of Shaftesbury and the liberal Whig Party. Locke worked in the Whig administration as a secretary for the committee on ecclesiastical benefices and for the council on trade and plantations. He was received as a fellow of the ROYAL SOCIETY OF LONDON in 1668. But most important, he began to turn his energies to writing.

Between 1675 and 1679, Locke lived in FRANCE for reasons of health. He met the leading scientific and philosophical figures of the period, making especially important contacts with the followers of the EPICUREAN PHILOSOPHY of Pierre GASSEND.

When Locke returned to ENGLAND in 1679, political crisis was brewing over the question of the succession to the throne. Charles II had no heirs except a brother, James, who was an avowed Catholic. Shaftesbury was one of the leaders of a party that wished to exclude the Catholic James from the throne. They were prepared to resort to treason, even to assassination, in order to achieve their purpose. They helped to stir up a scare over an alleged Popish plot to bring England back into the Catholic fold, but their schemes were revealed. Shaftesbury was imprisoned in the London Tower in 1681, then tried for treason. Although he was acquitted, he fled to the safety of Holland in 1682.

Locke, who had returned to Oxford, was suspected of complicity with Shaftesbury, and his activities were being watched closely. The new king, James II, was trying to establish monarchical ABSOLUTISM in England, and consequently he turned his attention to the "dangerous" ideas being taught at English UNIVERSITIES. In July 1683, he ordered what was to be the last book burning in the history of England. Locke watched the spectacle of books going up in flames, and by the fall of 1683, he had joined Shaftesbury in exile in Holland. The Crown, with university officials' complicity, reacted by revoking his position at Oxford.

Scholars for a long time thought that Locke was unjustly suspected by the English Crown, but evidence in his diaries shows that he was working closely with Shaftesbury throughout the years leading up to his voluntary exile. Furthermore, Locke was involved to some extent with the people who brought about the GLORIOUS REVOLUTION of 1688 and the subsequent establishment in

England of a limited constitutional monarchy. He returned to England in February 1689 escorting the deposed King James's daughter, Mary, Princess of Orange. Two days later, she and her husband William, Prince of Orange, were offered the English crown. They accepted the offer and assumed the throne as WILLIAM III AND MARY II of England.

Locke remained in England for the rest of his life. His political influence continued not only through his books, but also through a group of members of Parliament called the "college" who actively supported his ideas. Their patron was Lord John Somers, one of the men whose political fortunes were closely tied to William III and Mary II.

Locke continued to study and to write during these last years, and also devoted himself (1695–99) to tutoring Shaftesbury's grandson, Anthony Ashley Cooper, third earl of SHAFTESBURY. Locke spent much of his time in Oates, the home of Sir Francis and Lady Masham (daughter of Ralph CUDWORTH). He served as a commissioner on the Board of Trade and Plantations until 1700, when ill health forced him to resign. His last years were spent in Oates at the Masham house.

John Locke published nothing until 1689, when he was 57 years old. Furthermore, he insisted on publishing the *Two Treaties of Government* (1690), the Letters on Toleration (1689, 1690, 1692), and *The Reasonableness of Christianity* (1695) anonymously. Having admitted his authorship privately only to a handful of trusted friends, he became angered when they spread rumors about his relationship to the books. In spite of Locke's many precautions to protect his anonymity, it was commonly assumed both in England and on the European continent that these were his works.

Locke was one of the early political theorists of English liberalism and constitutional monarchy. His theories about the origins of political society and about the relations between church and state contain all the basic elements of later liberal theory: the assumption that NATURAL LAW modeled on REASON provides the foundation for human FREEDOM; the related idea that the rule of positive law guarantees freedom in a political society; the notion of the social compact or contract that creates a political structure (government by consent of the governed); the assertion of the right of a people to engage in revolution against any inadequate government; the call of religious TOLERATION and for SEPARATION OF CHURCH AND STATE; the assertion of NATURAL RIGHTS rooted in the concept of PROPERTY; and a strong emphasis on INDIVIDUALISM.

Locke formulated his views in the crucible of the many political crises that occurred during his life. He witnessed the execution of a king, the radical democracy and later anarchy of the revolutionary Commonwealth, the Restoration with its attempts to impose absolutism on an unwilling people, the abdication of a second king, and the acceptance by William III and Mary II of limitations on royal power. Throughout these events, tensions among various English religious groups—ANGLICANS, DISSENTERS, and Roman Catholics—played themselves out in the political realm. Locke tried to develop a theory that would allow variation to exist without creating political instability.

Underlying Locke's political theory and his equally important EPISTEMOLOGY (theory of knowledge) is a philosophical EMPIRICISM based on the ideas of Francis BACON and embodied in the work of the Royal Society of London. *The Essay Concerning Human Understanding* makes this explicit not only by placing experience at the foundation of knowledge, but also by its claim to be using a "Historical Plain Method." By this term, Locke meant that he was describing what he believed were the facts about human sensation, and its relationship to the formation of ideas. He was referring to Bacon's concept of natural history as the process of collecting and describing facts. This process would yield the basic data or building blocks from which a new system of knowledge (based on logical induction) could be constructed. Locke was proposing to carry out this task for a theory of human knowledge and understanding.

In *An Essay Concerning Human Understanding,* Locke put forth the idea that human knowledge is based on two factors: experience and the capacity for reflection. By experience, Locke meant sensory experience, the sensations provided through seeing, hearing, tasting, and touching. By reflection, he was referring to the human ability to exercise reason.

Locke characterized the human mind at birth as a "white paper" or "empty cabinet." It was actually Pierre Gassend, one of the transmitters of Epicurean philosophy to 17th-century England and France, who used the term *tabula rasa* to describe the mind. Locke meant that people are not born with any ideas imprinted in the mind, and he attempted to prove his point by showing how all ideas have roots in experiences after birth. His target in these arguments was the great French rationalist philosopher René DESCARTES, who had argued for the existence of logically certain innate ideas.

On the white paper of the mind at birth, sensory experience begins to write simple ideas. This happens through an unclear process that seems to be rooted in the descriptions of sensation associated with the mechanical philosophy, just as it does for Thomas HOBBES. But Locke does not spell out his ideas clearly.

Complex ideas arise by the simple addition of two or more simple ideas (one simple idea + a second simple idea = a complex idea). Reason (reflection) enters the picture in the production of increasingly abstract ideas. The whole process produces a kind of knowledge that is not certain and true from the standpoint of philosophy, but is nevertheless reliable and usable in everyday life.

Locke's sensation psychology, as his theories are called, stimulated several developments in epistemology and psychology during the Enlightenment. George BERKELEY and David HUME criticized Locke from the standpoints of idealism and SKEPTICISM respectively. David HARTLEY built association psychology from an undeveloped idea in Locke's *Essay*, and Abbé CONDILLAC developed a radical form of sensation psychology from Lockean foundations. Locke's empiricism served also as a general source of inspiration and as an ideal for the French ENCYCLOPEDISTS.

Locke's views on EDUCATION derived partially from his empiricism. He first sketched these ideas in several letters to Edward Clark, an English acquaintance who was seeking advice about rearing his son. Later, Locke transformed the material in these letters into a book, which he published as *Some Thoughts Concerning Education*. His educational theory also begins with the idea that the mind is a white sheet of paper on which experience will be written. Consequently, education becomes in his vision a process by which the entire character and mind of a child are shaped. Locke suggested that the individual needs and strengths of a child should be taken into consideration in planning his or her education. The aim of education is to produce a person of healthy body, virtuous character, and sound mind. Teaching should not rely on memory exercises and rote learning but should engage the child's intellect and include playful activities wherever possible. The intellectual development of sophisticated powers of reasoning is the last task that educators should tackle, after basic skills and language competencies have been acquired. The curriculum should stress modern languages rather than ancient ones (Latin is permissible), geography, arithmetic, ASTRONOMY, geometry, ethics, and civil law. It should also offer MUSIC, dance, and require every student to study accounting and a manual trade. In other words, Locke was recommending that the traditional humanities curriculum based on logic, rhetoric, and ancient languages be revised to introduce modern subjects with value in shaping character, ideas, and practical skills.

Although these ideas may sound commonplace to modern readers, they represented a sharp break from traditional pedagogical practices of the era. Locke's ideas entered into the thinking of educational reformers throughout the 18th century.

Finally, Locke left to the 18th century a set of convincing arguments for religious toleration. These arguments coupled established theoretical arguments drawn from various Christian doctrinal positions with practical arguments that emphasized the benefits of toleration for any nation. His ideas, contained in the Letters on Toleration, eventually joined with other developments in the arena of church-and-state relations to create the impassioned enlightened campaign for religious toleration and freedom.

In these four areas—political theory, psychology, education, and religious toleration—Locke formulated the intellectual building blocks from which enlightened theories were later constructed. No matter how familiar his thought might seem, it acquires new dimensions of meaning when it is placed within the context of the 17th-century English intellectual climate and political ferment. Understanding these dimensions helps to shed light on how these ideas could have seemed so profoundly revolutionary to the men and women of the early Enlightenment.

See also RIGHTS.

Further reading: Richard Ashcraft, *Revolutionary Politics and Locke's "Two Treatises of Government"* (Princeton, N.J.: Princeton University Press, 1986); Peter Josephson, *The Great Art of Government: Locke's Use of Consent* (Lawrence: University Press of Kansas, 2002); John Locke, *An Essay Concerning Human Understanding*, ed. A. D. Woozley (New York: New American Library, 1964); John Locke, *Two Treatises of Government*, intro. and notes Peter Laslett (New York: New American Library, 1965); Nicholas Wolterstorff et al., eds., *John Locke and the Ethics of Belief* (Cambridge: Cambridge University Press, 1996).

Lomonosov, Mikhail Vasilivich (ca. 1711–1765)
Russian chemist and linguist

The wave of reforms enacted by Czar PETER I (THE GREAT) in RUSSIA during the 18th century acted to bring the nation in line with European notions of ENLIGHTENMENT culture, knowledge, and statecraft. One of the greatest figures of this modernization and transformation of Russia was the eminent scientist Mikhail Vasilivich Lomonosov, who is often credited with establishing scientific methods in his homeland.

Like his czar, Lomonosov went to Europe to finish his EDUCATION. After completing his degree at the University of the Imperial Academy of Sciences in the czar's new city of SAINT PETERSBURG, itself a symbol of Russia's embrace of Enlightenment principles, Lomonosov attended universities in GERMANY's Freiburg and Marburg, where he studied the physical sciences. Initially working as a chemistry teacher upon his return to St. Petersburg in 1745, he pioneered such groundbreaking concepts as the conservation of matter and carried out scientific experiments such as the first recorded freezing of mercury. His research also foretold such crucial scientific theories as light's existence as a wave and the kinetic theory of gases. Later in his life, Lomonosov would be a crucial influence in the establishment of Moscow's first university.

Lomonosov's literary achievements were similarly impressive, creating an original metric form in his poetry and inventing a Russian grammar that combined older elements of the LANGUAGE with its contemporary form. One of his most influential literary works, *The Hymn to the Beard* of 1756–57, attacked trends toward the accumulation of wealth and hostility to intellectual inquiry among Russian Orthodox clergy, and this provoked charges of ATHEISM from church leaders.

See also CHEMICAL REVOLUTION; UNIVERSITIES.

Further reading: G. Vasetsky, *Lomonosov's Philosophy* (Moscow: Progress Publishers, 1968).

London   Capital city of Great Britain. London lies in ENGLAND on the Thames River, about 40 miles from its mouth to the North Sea. Archaeological evidence suggests that the site of London has been occupied since prehistoric times, but very little is known about these settlements. By Roman times, a bridge across the Thames had already been built, giving the town strategic importance. It was sacked in A.D. 60 by Icenian tribesmen who were revolting against Roman rule.

The city was rebuilt and by the end of the second century A.D. had acquired a protecting wall. By the fourth century, it had become an important center of Christianity in the British Isles. The Romans left London in the fifth century, and little is known of its history until the beginning of the sixth century A.D. At that time, the city was clearly under Saxon control and was acquiring greater importance as a center of Christian church administration. Saint Paul's Cathedral, the seat of an archbishop, was founded at the beginning of the seventh century.

From an early date, London served both as a commercial and government center. This pattern continued throughout the Middle Ages and Renaissance. By the mid-14th century, it had clearly become the political capital of England, serving as the meeting place for Parliament and the location for major courts of law.

The Renaissance and Reformation period brought population growth and marked changes to London. Between 1530 and 1605, the number of people living in the city trebled, reaching 225,000 (city and surrounding suburbs). By 1660, the city had reached an estimated population of about 460,000, making it one of the largest in Europe.

Epidemics of the black plague occurred several times during the 16th and 17th centuries. The worst of the epidemics, in 1665–66, was also the last. It took 75,000 lives during the 15 months of its duration.

During the 17th-century Civil War (1642–49), London supported the party of the Parliament against the king. But, weary of war and disruption, it also welcomed the return of the Stuart kings in 1660. The Great Fire of 1666 destroyed most of the city, sparing only the northeastern and extreme western areas. In the rebuilding that followed, the city acquired more brick houses, some wider and straighter streets, and improved market sites. Sir Christopher WREN designed 49 parish churches and the new Saint Paul's Cathedral.

London's influence over political affairs was greatly strengthened after the establishment of the Bank of England in 1694. The city generally supported the Crown during the first half of the 18th century, but tensions over royal policy grew during the reign of King George III. London provided significant support for the radical reform program of John WILKES.

During the 18th century, the London population continued to grow, reaching 675,000 in 1750 and nearly 900,000 in 1800. The city served as the major English cultural center of the ENLIGHTENMENT. The ROYAL SOCIETY OF LONDON brought predominance in SCIENCE, and the presence of a flourishing publishing industry made the city the focal point for English literary activities. Clubs, private homes, and coffeehouses served as gathering places for intellectuals and artists. MUSIC flourished under the inspiration provided by Johann Christian BACH, Karl Friedrich ABEL, and George Frederick HANDEL. London was one of the birthplaces of the modern subscription concert series, in which people bought tickets in advance for a series of performances. Theater, too, flourished under the leadership of actor-directors such as David GARRICK.

The importance of London in England resembled that of PARIS in FRANCE. Groups of people in other cities sometimes set up clubs or academies with the expressed intent of providing local centers to counterbalance the influence of the capital city. But London continued to dominate cultural and intellectual life, remaining the destination of most aspiring British intellectuals and a source of inspiration for 18th-century visitors from other nations.

See also PUBLISHING; SOCIAL INSTITUTIONS OF THE ENLIGHTENMENT.

London Corresponding Society   Radical political group. The London Corresponding Society was organized in 1792 with only eight members. The group's purpose was to mount a campaign to extend voting rights and to foster solidarity with other reformist political groups throughout Britain.

The group was called a "corresponding" society because it was illegal to form a national organization as a vehicle for expressing populist discontent. However, the very presence of such a law indicates that the bases of social unrest (food shortages, poor working conditions, lack of political representation and voting rights) were present in Great Britain as they were in revolutionary FRANCE. Hence, the London Corresponding Society membership soon numbered in the thousands. The demonstrations it organized in LONDON between October and December of 1795 attracted more than 200,000 people by some estimates. In the year prior to these demonstrations, three of the group's leaders (Thomas

Hardy, John Horne TOOKE, and John THELWALL) were arrested and tried for treason. The jury found insufficient evidence to convict the men, however, and they were released.

The government reacted to the society's power with a series of repressive measures. In 1794, it suspended habeas corpus, legalizing the detention of prisoners without a fair and speedy trial. Then it issued a proclamation against "seditious assemblies," making open speech against the government punishable by death. Eventually, in 1799, it passed a Corresponding Societies Act, making it illegal for the group to meet for any purpose. Already forced underground, the group disbanded in 1799, although not without inspiring a subsequent generation of reformists.

Further reading: Michael T. Davis, et al., eds. *The London Corresponding Society, 1792–1799*, 6 vols. (London: Pickering & Chatto, 2002).

Longhi, Pietro (1702–1785) *Venetian painter*
Son of a silver caster, Alessandro Falca, and father of the painter Alessandro Longhi, Pietro Longhi (the origin of the name Longhi is unknown) studied art in VENICE with Antonio Balestra and in Bologna with Giuseppe Maria Crespi. Longhi worked in Venice for his entire professional career. In 1756, he was selected as one of the first members of the Accademia di Venezia that was being organized under the auspices of Giovanni Battista TIEPOLO. Longhi taught in alternate years at the academy from 1756 until 1780.

As a young artist, Longhi tried to paint in the grand manner of the high BAROQUE STYLE. Examples from this period include *The Martyrdom of San Pellegrino* (about 1730) and *The Fall of the Giants* (dated 1734, but painted earlier). Longhi abandoned Baroque approaches in the 1740s and established himself as a master of ROCOCO genre painting. His works, drawing on the sensibility of that 18th-century style, portray their subjects with detailed intimacy.

Longhi's paintings, like the plays of his contemporary Carlo GOLDONI, provide a rich chronicle of 18th-century Venetian culture and life. His treatment of aristocratic subjects in the 1740s and 1750s was mostly sympathetic but sometimes contained subtle irony. By the 1760s, Longhi had developed a more openly satirical approach. In general despite the clear parallels between his paintings and those of the French rococo masters Antoine WATTEAU and Nicolas LANCRET or of the English satirist William HOGARTH, Longhi's paintings exhibit a highly original approach to his materials.

Among the notable paintings by Longhi are *The Concert, The Awakening, Visit to the Lord, The Letter, Rhinoceros, The Errand of the Negro, The Sacraments, The Masked Reception, Lion House, Hunt in the Valley, Luncheon in the Gardens by the Lagoon*, and *Duck Hunting*.

longitude   Distance east or west on the Earth's surface, measured between the prime meridian and another meridian. Explorers navigating the seas had no way to determine longitude until the 18th century. As exploration and trade increased during the 16th and 17th centuries, the lack of a way to establish the east-west position of a ship with any certainty caused several accidents whose consequences were lost lives, goods, and revenue.

In 1707, in the Scilly Isles off ENGLAND's southwestern coast, four British warships and almost 2,000 sailors were lost because of the lack of a reliable method for determining longitude. The ships had no way of knowing how far east the islands were, so they were unable to adjust their speed quickly enough to avoid running aground. In response, the British Parliament passed the Longitude Act (1714), which established a prize for the discovery of such a method. The governments of other nations that were invested in maritime trade and exploration had offered similar incentives in the past, but the Longitude Act was the incentive that brought a solution to the problem.

There were two competing schools of thought about the longitude problem. Both approaches to finding a solution were encouraged by the act. One school proposed that ASTRONOMY offered a solution, that careful observation of the stars and calculations based on such observation would allow the seafarer to determine east-west location. The other proposed that an accurate clock, impervious to the ill effects of weather and travel on the high seas, would provide the best way to measure longitude. Sir Isaac NEWTON had suggested that a watch would, theoretically, be the best way to keep track of longitude, but that the vicissitudes of sea travel would render a timepiece useless.

Undaunted, English clockmaker John HARRISON built a series of five sea clocks between 1730 and 1770. The clocks provided navigators with the information they needed to easily calculate their east-west distance from their home port. Knowing the time it was at their home port and the meridian where that port was located, they could calculate longitude by determining the time at their location through observation of the movement of the Sun across the sky. A copy of Harrison's fourth clock, made by watchmaker Lacrum Kendall, accompanied James COOK on his second and third voyages. Cook often praised the clock in the log of the HMS *Resolution*. Harrison never won the actual longitude prize, because the committee that awarded it was dominated by astronomers and their supporters, but Parliament, at the urging of King George III, bestowed the cash equivalent on him in 1773 in recognition of his expert solution to the problem.

Further reading: Dava Sobel, *Longitude: The True Story of a Lone Genius Who Solved the Greatest Scientific Problem of His Time* (New York: Penguin Books, 1996).

Louis XIV of France (1638–1715) *great Bourbon king of France, whose long reign (1643–1715) epitomized absolutism for writers of the Enlightenment*

As the symbol of absolute rule, Louis XIV was both hated and admired held up as a model for emulation by a few writers and as an example of abuse by others. Louis XIV was called both *le Grand* (the Great) and *le Roi Soleil* (the Sun King) during his lifetime. The French, even today, refer to the 17th century, on which he left such an indelible imprint, as *le Siècle d'Or* (the golden century) or *l'Age classique* (the classical era).

Louis was not quite five years old when he inherited the throne from his father, Louis XIII, in 1643. Because he was so young, the actual rule of the country lay in the hands of his mother, Anne of Austria (daughter of Philip III of Spain), who served as regent. Together with her powerful minister Cardinal Mazarin, Anne of Austria directed FRANCE through a period of intense instability during which various factions in France—the PARLEMENTS and the royal princes—used the weakness of the regency as an excuse to rebel. The resultant civil war was called the Fronde and lasted from 1648 until 1653. The unrest forced Louis XIV to spend five years of his youth on the road, moving from one spot to another to avoid hostilities. The experience so disturbed him that

King Louis XIV of France. As ruler of France from 1643 until 1715, the Sun King established a centralized state that symbolized both desirable and detested aspects of absolutism for enlightened political reformers. *(Courtesy New York Public Library)*

he determined to squelch all possible sources of revolt within the country.

Upon attaining his majority, he assumed the throne with his full rights, but Cardinal Mazarin continued to exercise considerable influence until his death in 1661. After that, Louis XIV proceeded to consolidate his royal power and, consequently, brought France as close as it ever came to being an absolute monarchy. He was assisted by several ministers such as Jean-Baptiste Colbert (1619–83), Michel Le Tellier (1603–85), and François-Michel Le Tellier, marquis de Louvois (1639–91).

Louis XIV made important contributions to the art of governing as an absolute monarch. He outlined his philosophy in a document called his *Testament,* written for his heirs. It spelled out the general goals of his reform activities and made recommendations for those who would follow in his footsteps.

Louis's fundamental goal—summed up in the famous dictum ascribed to him, *l'état, c'est moi* ("The state, it is I")—was to unify all sovereign power within his person. To attain this goal, Louis XIV subjugated the sovereign courts of law (*parlements*), abandoned the practice of ruling with a powerful prime minister, quarreled with the Catholic clergy and the pope over control of the French church, attempted to reinstate religious uniformity, established a standing professional army, extended the system of royal superintendents (*intendants*) that had been established during his father's reign, streamlined the central bureaucracy, and attempted to rationalize the French fiscal regime. At Colbert's suggestion, he also founded several royal academies—dealing with SCIENCE, fine arts and inscriptions, architecture, and MUSIC—to complement the French Academy (language and literature). The chief duty of these academies was to establish standards, to provide instruction, and to ensure that all intellectual and artistic pursuits served the interests of the state. Reforms inspired by Louis XIV's actions would appear throughout Europe during the 17th and 18th centuries whenever rulers attempted to centralize or to consolidate their power into absolute form.

In matters of foreign policy, Louis XIV was driven by a desire to protect France from encirclement by Hapsburg-ruled territories. Spain, for example, lying to the southwest of France, and most of the territories of modern BELGIUM, lying on the northern borders of France, were both ruled by the Spanish Hapsburgs. Moreover, the HOLY ROMAN EMPIRE, on the eastern boundaries of France, was controlled by the Austrian Hapsburgs. The threat posed by this situation led Louis XIV into several wars, which had devastating effects, but it also stimulated significant military reforms. Besides creating a professional standing army, ministers under Louis XIV instituted the practice of conscripting members of the nobility, thereby reducing their military independence. Sébastien Le Prestre de Vauban (1633–1707), a military engineer, provided strategic towns in France with a series of formidable forts based on a new design. Finally, under Colbert's direction, new roads and a system of canals not only improved the ability of French troops to move quickly, but also facilitated commerce.

Whatever his military achievements, Louis's wars, especially the series of actions carried out in the Netherlands in 1672 and 1673 and in Alsace in 1689, were notorious, even to contemporaries, for their brutality and atrocity. Their example helped to stimulate the desires for peace and for the reform of international military law that emerged during the Enlightenment.

Louis XIV's many reforms, no matter how successful during his lifetime, did not, for the most part, last after his death. They depended too much for their survival on the force of his powerful personality. His successors would see all the political factions that he had submerged—*parlements,* aristocracy, royal princes—resurface and begin offering obstacles to centralized, rationalized, absolute monarchy.

Furthermore, in one critical area Louis XIV failed to achieve significant reform. That was the area of finance. His inability to overcome the system of tax exemptions for privileged groups or to free the government from the need to rely on the sale of offices for income ultimately hampered all of his reform efforts. In addition, the debts that he accumulated by fighting numerous wars crippled the French budget at a time when the overburdened, poverty-stricken, often famine-stricken, tax-paying population could give no more to the tax collectors. Louis XIV's inability to impose a rational, universal system of taxation on his subjects reveals, in the cold light of retrospection, the structural weaknesses of the ANCIEN RÉGIME. For his successors, fiscal problems would grow worse, eventually bringing about the crises that triggered the FRENCH REVOLUTION.

Louis XIV left his mark on the arts, architecture, THEATER, dance, and music. He hated PARIS because the city represented for him the fickle rebelliousness that had caused the horrors of the Fronde. Therefore, he moved his primary residence from the Louvre to a magnificent new palace at Versailles, about 25 miles from Paris. The Palais de Versailles majestically represents certain aspects of the BAROQUE STYLE. Its style and spatial techniques for symbolizing the absolute power of the king would be imitated throughout Europe by absolute monarchs in great kingdoms and smaller principalities. Louis understood the art of using symbolic, allegorical forms to suggest and to reinforce the image of his power in the minds of his subjects. Hence, he adopted the sun—that circular, perfect center of the universe, source of light and warmth—as the emblem of his power. In all these activities Louis XIV proved himself a master of the art of propaganda that was so much a part of the baroque era.

Louis loved to dance and performed in many ballets, thereby helping to create the French passion for this classical dance form. His reign saw the full flowering of French literary CLASSICISM in the works of Pierre Corneille (1606–84), Jean Racine (1639–99), and Jean-Baptiste Molière (1622–73). Toward its close, the era of Louis XIV produced the QUARREL BETWEEN THE ANCIENTS AND THE MODERNS, which pitted Nicolas Boileau, the champion of classical AESTHETICS, against Charles Perrault, the defender of modern styles. OPERA, that invention of the Italian baroque, developed special French forms, under the direction of Jean-Baptiste Lully, that would govern productions in France well into the 18th century.

Intellectual life in France flourished during Louis XIV's reign, finding expression in the work of the Jansenists Blaise Pascal (1623–62) and Antoine Arnauld; in the religious polemics of Bishop BOSSUET and François FÉNELON; in the vogue for the MECHANICAL PHILOSOPHY stimulated by the work of natural philosophers such as Marin MERSENNE, Pierre GASSEND, and René DESCARTES; and in the scientific popularizations of Bernard de FONTENELLE. The reign thus fostered many of the intellectual forces that helped—either as positive or negative models—to shape the thought of the early Enlightenment.

In matters of RELIGION, Louis XIV hardened the intolerant stance toward non-Catholic minorities that had been started by his predecessor, Louis XIII. He was pushed in this direction by two factors: his belief that the presence of religious diversity in his kingdom constituted a threat to his absolute power and the influence of Françoise d'Aubigné, better known as Madame de Maintenon. Madame de Maintenon was Louis's longtime companion and is believed to have secretly married him either in 1683 or possibly later, in 1697. The facts surrounding the formalization of this relationship are not surely known. Madame de Maintenon encouraged Louis to abandon the wayward ways of his youth (he was 45 years old in 1683) and played a role in shaping his ideas and actions for the last 30 years of his reign.

To rectify what he perceived as the religious problem in France, Louis XIV crushed JANSENISM, hounded the mystical Quietists, repealed Henry IV's toleration decree (the Edict of Nantes) in 1685, and thereafter persecuted HUGUENOTS, CAMISARDS, and WALDENSIANS. Louis's policies forced the Protestant Huguenots either to convert to ROMAN CATHOLICISM or to leave the country. Many chose to leave, thereby becoming valuable, productive settlers in PRUSSIA, the UNITED PROVINCES OF THE NETHERLANDS, the American colonies, or ENGLAND.

In summation, the reign of Louis XIV left a political, economic, social, religious, and cultural legacy to the early 18th century that functioned as the backdrop against which early ideas of the Enlightenment developed in France. His legacy would cast a long shadow over the 18th century, not only pointing the way for reforms, but also highlighting the abuses that could occur under a system of absolutism. In part, the tremendous appeal of English ideas—especially those of LOCKE and NEWTON—for early enlightened French intellectuals derived from the fact that they offered an alternative to the system of the Sun King.

Further reading: F. L. Carsten, ed., *The Ascendancy of France, 1648–1688*, vol. 4 of the New Cambridge Modern History (Cambridge: Cambridge University Press, 1969); Roger Hahn, *The Anatomy of a Scientific Institution: The Paris Academy of Sciences (1666–1803)* (Berkeley.: University of California Press, 1971); John C. Rule, ed., *Louis XIV and the Craft of Kingship* (Columbus: Ohio State University Press, 1969).

Louis XV of France (ca. 1700–1774) *king of France from 1715 until his death in 1774*

He was called *Louis, le Bienaimé* (Louis, the Beloved). Louis XV was the great-grandson of LOUIS XIV of France. In 1725, Louis XV married Marie Leszczynska, the daughter of the exiled Polish king, Stanislaw Leszczynski. The couple produced eight daughters and two sons, only one of whom survived. That son was the father of the future king, LOUIS XVI.

When Louis XIV died, Louis XV was only five years old. Therefore, Philippe, duke of Orléans, ruled as regent until 1723 when Louis was old enough to assume personal control. Regency periods usually were marked by political instability in the ANCIEN RÉGIME, and the regency of Philippe of Orléans was no exception. During his years in power, many privileged groups that had been controlled under the ABSOLUTISM of Louis XIV, reasserted their positions. In particular, the members of the French PARLEMENTS (law courts) began to claim that they were the legitimate heirs of the defunct Estates General, which had, at one time, operated as a representative advisory body to the French kings and queens. The *parlements* thus resumed the old struggles, which Louis XIV had minimized, about the proper form of the French monarchy. Furthermore, they began to expand their demands, claiming a right to share legislative power with the king.

Louis XV allowed Cardinal Fleury to act as his chief minister and to control most government activities from 1726 until 1743. In 1745, Louis XV finally assumed personal control of his government. He inherited a vocal opposition to absolute monarchy and an unstable, debt-ridden financial structure. Yet he desired to rule as an absolute, albeit enlightened, king and wanted to further the process of centralizing the French government, thereby setting the stage for his successes and failures.

Under Louis XV, the foreign policy of FRANCE was radically restructured as the king and his ministers attempted to cope with the novel actions of FREDERICK II (THE GREAT) in PRUSSIA. The result is commemorated in history as the DIPLOMATIC REVOLUTION OF 1756. Louis understood the need in his kingdom for reform of taxation and finance. Cardinal Fleury had been able to maintain stability in the kingdom and to gain some control over the collection of taxes, but his successors had a more difficult time. France was embroiled in wars (WAR OF THE AUSTRIAN SUCCESSION and SEVEN YEARS' WAR) and lost most of its colonial empire. The financial plight of the government was constantly growing worse.

The duc de CHOISEUL, who was Louis XV's primary foreign minister between 1758 and 1770, urged Louis XV to establish a limited monarchy in order to satisfy the increasing demand from the *parlements* for a representative government. But Louis XV chose to follow the advice of another minister, René de MAUPEOU, who recommended the opposite solution: strengthening absolutism by banishing the unruly *parlements*. Consequently, the ministerial triumvirate of Maupeou, Abbé Terray, and the duc d'Aiguillon tried to reform France by absolute decree. Their reforms were solid, clearly addressing the fiscal and social structures that were preventing the government from resolving its financial crisis. But they failed to understand the real limits to enlightened reform from above that existed in the late 18th-century ancien régime. In the end, the reign of Louis XV was littered with the debris of reforms tried and rescinded. The outlines of the ancien régime remained stubbornly drawn, seemingly impervious to change.

Louis XV has been much maligned in history for having kept official mistresses, Madame de POMPADOUR and Madame DU BARRY, with him at Versailles and for having allowed Madame de Pompadour to shape aspects of his state policy. But the practice was quite common in the French court and had precedent in the reigns of both Henry IV and Louis XIV.

The era of Louis XV marks the high point of the flowering of 18th-century French aristocratic culture. Salons formed the center of much of this activity, but, following established traditions, the court also continued to sponsor MUSIC, THEATER, and dance. These art forms received rich patronage, especially from Madame de Pompadour and her circle of friends, and consequently flourished. The period was marked by the kind of lighthearted frivolity and refined sensuality characteristic of the ROCOCO style. But other undercurrents were flowing, and the PHILOSOPHES were continuing to develop their observations and enlightened criticisms of French government and society. In the cultural history of Louis XV's reign, it is possible to see both the epitome of the ancien régime and the outline of the intellectual movements that would help to bring the end of that old world. Louis XV died in 1774 of smallpox, after which his grandson, the unfortunate LOUIS XVI, assumed the throne.

See also ABSOLUTISM, ENLIGHTENED; SOCIAL INSTITUTIONS OF THE ENLIGHTENMENT.

Louis XVI of France (1754–1793) *king of France from 1774 to 1792*

Louis XVI was the grandson of LOUIS XV and Marie Leszczynska. In 1770, Louis XVI married MARIE-ANTOINETTE, daughter of Empress MARIA THERESA OF AUSTRIA and sister of JOSEPH II. Louis XVI ruled in FRANCE during the closing years of the ANCIEN RÉGIME. As he assumed the throne, France was embroiled in financial crisis and political ferment. In 1778, France entered the American War of Independence, fighting on behalf of the American colonists against ENGLAND. The huge expenses of this war further augmented the financial straits of the French government.

The devout, kindly, rather phlegmatic Louis XVI wanted to change what he considered the decadent customs of his court. He was filled with good intentions, but not well suited for the demands of ruling a French court. He preferred hunting and locksmithing to dealing with court intrigues and intractable political problems. Marie-Antoinette further complicated matters for the king. She either would not or could nor bring herself to act according to established rules of etiquette. Her behavior brought constant criticism that slowly undermined the credibility of the institution of royalty. The DIAMOND NECKLACE SCANDAL of 1785 clearly revealed the depths to which the royal couple had sunk in public opinion.

Whatever his faults, Louis XVI recognized the need for fiscal reform in France and enlisted aid from a series of astute, reforming controllers and directors general of finance: Anne-Robert-Jacques TURGOT, Charles-Alexandre de CALONNE, and Jacques NECKER. Their various ideas might have resolved the financial crises facing the kingdom, but among several political factions in French society, opposition directed against any changes instigated by the monarch was so intense that reform efforts from above had little chance of success. Furthermore, the powerful privileged interests, especially the PARLEMENTS, continued to claim the right to play a legislative role in the government and consequently blocked reform programs that failed to meet their demands.

As the political and fiscal crisis intensified, Turgot and Calonne both had to step down from their posts, and Necker, the new director general of finance, felt compelled to call a meeting of the Estates General, the traditional advisory body to the monarch. The Estates had last met in 1614.

The representatives from the Estates gathered in PARIS in May 1789. From that time, the events of the FRENCH REVOLUTION began unfolding at a breathtaking pace. The members of the Third Estate (the bourgeoisie), joined by some liberal nobles and churchmen, declared themselves the National Assembly in June 1789. The prison of the Bastille, hated as a symbol of royal abuses of justice, fell to a mob on July 14, 1789. In the name of

Portrait of Louis XVI, king of France, by Duplessis. Louis XVI reigned during the last decades of the ancien régime in France. His death on the guillotine in 1792, during the French Revolution, became a symbol for conservative critics of the dangers lurking in the political principles of the Enlightenment. *(Courtesy New York Public Library)*

FREEDOM and EQUALITY, the new National Assembly, on the night of August 4, 1789, abolished the social and fiscal order of the ancien régime. Royal control in Paris had clearly collapsed.

Louis XVI, still living at Versailles, cooperated only halfheartedly with the leaders of the Parisian rebellion. In October 1789, a mob of Parisian townspeople marched on Versailles and forced both the king and Marie-Antoinette to return with them to Paris. By July 1790, the National Assembly had crafted a monarchical constitution that sharply curtailed the powers of the king. But the cause of moderate reform was losing ground as the political order in France unraveled.

The political mood in France and the actions of the revolutionaries were shifting continually toward more extreme positions. In April 1792, filled with enthusiasm about the cause of exporting revolution but also intent on defending itself from hostile attacks, the National Assembly declared war on AUSTRIA. Then, on August 10, 1792, a Parisian mob accompanied by provincial militiamen attacked and captured the Tuileries Palace, where the king was residing. Although Louis XVI was unharmed, he was suspended by the National Assembly from his monarchical duties. With this act, the French monarchy was overthrown. In September 1792, the revolutionary National Convention officially abolished the French monarchy.

Following the action of the Convention, Louis XVI and Marie-Antoinette were imprisoned. Louis was tried for treason in December 1792, was found guilty, and condemned to death. He was publicly beheaded on January 21, 1793. Marie-Antoinette met a similar fate nine months later.

See also MALESHERBES.

Louverture, Toussaint *See* TOUSSAINT LOUVERTURE, FRANÇOIS-DOMINIQUE.

Lunar Society of Birmingham An informal society, established in Birmingham, ENGLAND, and devoted to scientific research and technological applications. Its name referred to the fact that its monthly meetings were held on the night of the full moon, in order that members could safely find their way home after the meetings through the unlighted streets of Birmingham. The Lunar Society linked the interests of manufacturers and scientists and is an outstanding example of the creativity of provincial scientific societies in 18th-century Britain. Among those who attended the meetings of this society were Josiah WEDGWOOD, Matthew BOULTON, Joseph PRIESTLEY, Erasmus DARWIN, and James WATT. Other people who could be found at its meetings were William HERSCHEL; William Murdock, the inventor of gas lighting; John Baskerville, a Birmingham printer; and Jon Smeaton, an engineer who designed the Eddystone lighthouse.

The Lunar Society originated sometime before 1760 when Matthew Boulton and Erasmus Darwin became acquainted. They were brought together by their mutual love of science and by their interest in the work of Benjamin FRANKLIN. Links with Franklin, in fact, brought many inquisitive people to the society meetings. Society members addressed themselves to questions of electricity, transportation, steam power, geology, chemistry, and heat. The subjects were linked by the fact that they all involved the application of new scientific knowledge to practical business or civic problems. The intertwined needs of theory and industrial practice spawned important innovations in both realms on the part of Lunar Society participants.

The Lunar Society continued its activities until 1791. In that year riots broke out in Birmingham aimed at Protestant DISSENTERS (Nonconformists) and supporters of the FRENCH REVOLUTION. Several Lunar Society members fell into this group, and Joseph Priestley had his house, library, and chemical apparatus destroyed by angry mobs rioting against progressive ideas. The atmo-

sphere made it no longer safe to hold meetings and the society was disbanded.

See also SCIENTIFIC ACADEMIES; TECHNOLOGY AND INSTRUMENTATION.

Lutheranism A branch of Christianity that follows the religious doctrines outlined by the German monk Martin Luther (1483–1546). Luther belonged to the Augustinian order, a religious order whose members were involved with late 15th-century and 16th-century movements for theological reform within the Catholic Church. He taught at the University of Wittenberg, served as a preacher in a local parish, and, in 1515, became a district vicar charged with administering the affairs of almost a dozen Augustinian monasteries. In 1517, Luther posted a series of 95 theses about aspects of Christian doctrine on the door of the church in Wittenberg. His action was a standard procedure, followed by anyone who wished to initiate an academic debate. Luther's theses, however, dealt with sensitive questions on the doctrines of confession and penance and had implications not only for doctrine, but also for the traditional conceptions of the role of the priest. Luther followed up this original act with an appeal to Pope Leo X in ROME to correct abuses such as the sale of indulgences (documents granting forgiveness of sins) and to institute a broad series of reforms. When Leo did not respond, Luther called publicly for a church council to address the issues. These actions also followed standard procedures within the Catholic Church for dealing with doctrinal disputes.

Luther, however, was unwilling to admit that his positions might be erroneous, and the Catholic authorities, for various reasons, were equally intransigent. Ultimately, the two sides were unable to resolve their differences. The pope excommunicated Luther from the Catholic Church in 1521. Luther and his growing group of followers thus split formally with the church in Rome and started the chain of events that are now called the Protestant Reformation.

The new Protestant church that grew up under Luther's leadership was called Lutheranism. It received early support from the German elector of Saxony, who saw political advantages in supporting the fledgling rebellion. Lutheranism went on to develop strong territorial bases in the HOLY ROMAN EMPIRE, DENMARK, SWEDEN, and Norway.

In general, Lutheran doctrine attacked the authority of Catholic traditions and personnel. It stressed that salvation comes from faith alone, rather than from doing penance or good works. Lutheran positions undermined the traditional role of priests, no longer defining them as necessary mediators between God and repentant sinners. Instead, Lutheranism stressed the importance of the direct relationship between the believer and God, a relationship that could be managed without the intercession of priests and saints. Lutheran clergymen were encouraged to marry and to avoid the ostentatious lifestyle that characterized the higher Catholic clergy. The institution of monasticism was eliminated.

Luther developed a modification of traditional Catholic doctrine about the nature of the sacrament called the Eucharist (Last Supper, Holy Communion), declaring that, during the ceremony, the wine and bread retained their identity as wine and bread but also took on the attributes of the body and blood of Christ. This position lay midway between the Catholic doctrine of transubstantiation, which claims that the wine and bread actually become the body and blood of Christ, and the doctrine of Ulrich Zwingli, which maintains that the wine and bread are only symbolic representations of the body and blood of Jesus Christ. Luther limited the number of holy sacraments to two, baptism and the Eucharist, whereas Catholicism retained seven—baptism, marriage, confirmation, penance, ordination, Eucharist, and extreme unction. Luther also denied the existence of purgatory, the middle realm between heaven and hell. Finally, he encouraged all believers to consult the Bible for themselves and translated the Bible into the vernacular German.

Luther's teachings about the Bible and the priesthood contained radical implications that emerged within a few years of the founding of the new church. A group of peasants in southwest Germany concluded that Luther's teachings supported a democratic vision of the world in which all men should be treated equally. They provoked a mass rebellion in 1525 that Luther was quick to denounce. A group of sovereign petty knights drew different conclusions, using Lutheran teachings to justify annexation of neighboring territories. In Münster, in 1534, a Dutch tailor named John of Leyden set up a radical communist regime, based on his interpretation of Luther's principles, and ruled for over a year by means of terror.

In the aftermath of this unrest, Luther and his church forged strong ties with secular rulers and adopted generally more conservative approaches in doctrinal, social, and political matters. Luther asserted that the FREEDOM of which he had been speaking was a purely internal, spiritual matter and that subjects owed perfect obedience to established authority. As a result, the territories and nations that became Lutheran lands developed a form of church-state relationship at local levels in which church authorities (the local consistory) assumed the duties of policing the behavior and general moral norm of individuals. The secular state willingly left such functions to the consistories, but sometimes co-opted the consistories to their state interests.

Lutheranism in the 18th century dominated the north-central European states: Norway, Sweden, Denmark, nearly all the northern territories of the Holy Roman Empire including Prussia (the Hohenzollern rulers were Calvinists but their state was officially Lutheran), Braunschweig-Holstein, Braunschweig-Wolfenbüttel, Schleswig-Holstein, Saxony (the 18th-century electors, however, as kings of Poland, converted to Catholicism), and most free imperial cities such as FRANKFURT and Nuremberg. Many of the great German figures of the ENLIGHTENMENT, such as Gottfried Wilhelm LEIBNIZ, Gotthold Ephraim LESSING, Christian WOLFF, Samuel PUFENDORF, Immanuel KANT, Johann Wolfgang von GOETHE, Hermann Samuel REIMARUS, and Christian THOMASIUS came from Lutheran backgrounds.

See also PIETISM; PROTESTANTISM; RELIGION; ROMAN CATHOLICISM.

Further reading: Roland Herbert Bainton, *Here I Stand: A Life of Martin Luther* (New York: Plume, 1994); Peter C. Erb, ed., *Pietists: Selected Writings* (New York: Paulist Press, 1983); Hajo Holborn, *A History of Modern Germany (1648–1840)* (New York: Alfred A. Knopf, 1967); Eric W. Gritsch, *History of Lutheranism* (Minneapolis: Augsburg Fortress, 2002).

Lyon, Emma (Lady Hamilton) (1765–1815) *wife of Sir William Hamilton and mistress of Admiral Horatio Nelson*
The life of Emma, Lady Hamilton, provides an example of the opportunities for upward social mobility available to a woman of intelligence during the late 18th century. Born Emily Lyon, the woman who eventually became Emma, Lady Hamilton, went to LONDON at the age of 12. She first worked as a domestic servant in the household of Thomas Linley, Sr., a prominent theater composer, but at 16 Lyon, now known as Emily or Emma Hart, moved into the household of a woman who ran a brothel.

Hart then began as affair with Sir Harry Featherstonehaugh, the first in a series of liaisons with prominent men that would help foster her fame. She gained renown as a great beauty, and her next lover, Charles Greville, commissioned the artist George Romney to paint several now-famous paintings of her. When Greville met a wealthy woman who he thought would make a suitable wife, he sent Emma to stay with his uncle, Sir William HAMILTON, in Naples.

Emma and her mother arrived in Naples in the winter of 1786. It soon became clear to Emma that Greville would not be joining them. She and Hamilton, who was 35 years her senior, went to London in 1791 to marry. Upon their return to Naples, Lady Hamilton became a trusted companion of Queen Maria Carolina of the KINGDOM OF THE TWO SICILIES. She played an important role as a cultural organizer in the city, bringing together leading figures at her salons. One such person was Admiral Horatio Nelson, whom Lady Hamilton met when he passed through Naples during his return from the Battle of the

Nile. They met again in 1798 and became lovers the next year. She bore Nelson a daughter, Horatia, in 1801. Sir William Hamilton died in 1803, leaving his wife a generous annuity (he was apparently pragmatic about her affair with Nelson), and Nelson died at the Battle of Trafalgar in 1805, also providing for his mistress. Her extravagant lifestyle outstripped her money, and she was briefly imprisoned for debt before fleeing to Calais with Horatia. Lady Hamilton died there in 1815.

M

Mably, Gabriel Bonnot de, Abbé (1709–1785)
French philosopher, historian, and writer
Mably was born in Grenoble, FRANCE, in 1709. He was educated in Lyons by the JESUITS and became a priest. His brother Étienne Bonnot de CONDILLAC also became a priest and philosopher. Although not as well known today, Mably was widely read and referenced in the years leading up to the FRENCH REVOLUTION. Despite living a retired life, Mably was well acquainted with several who would play pivotal roles in both the French and American Revolutions, among them Thomas JEFFERSON, Benjamin FRANKLIN, John ADAMS, and Jean-Jacques ROUSSEAU, who was the tutor of his brother's family.

Mably devoted himself to writing, becoming well known for his work in HISTORY, politics, and ECONOMICS. His early work included histories of Greece (1749), France (1765), and ROME (1751), as well as *Étude de l'histoire* (Study of history; 1774), a guide to the exploration of history. Mably's career as a writer was very successful, as his books on all topics were printed in multiple editions and were translated from French into German and English.

Philosophically, Mably's main belief was that all human beings were equal because all had a divine spark. This EQUALITY could not be changed by differences in experience or nation of origin. Therefore, he criticized the existence of both the nobility and the new merchant class. Unlike others of the era, such as Adam SMITH, his emphasis was on equality rather than increased wealth. In his political work, he often praised Roman and Greek antiquity and upheld classical republican ideals against French royal ABSOLUTISM. He was mainly concerned with the RIGHTS of the individual and how government violated those rights, as explained in his 1758 pamphlet *Des droits et des devoirs du citoyen* (The rights and duties of the citizen). His work on Greek history, French politics, government, and human equality was cited in *The Federalist Papers*. John Adams also requested Mably to write his observations on the current constitutions of the states. Mably's commentary appeared in the *Observations sur le gouvernement et les lois des Etats-Unis d'Amérique* (Observations on the government and laws of the United States of America) in 1784. Here Mably made the controversial claim that several of the states still had a tendency toward aristocracy that would be incompatible with a single democratic constitution for the United States.

Ironically, Mably held several views that were contrary to the spirit of the American Constitution. These are seen in the *Observations* as well as in his economic writings. In a 1768 pamphlet on NATURAL LAW and political economy, he had countered many of the theories of the PHYSIOCRATS regarding private property. He felt that private property caused inequality and social conflict and should be abolished. Thus, he can be seen as a critic of existing society similar to Rousseau and the Abbé MORELLY. Mably was read by many French legislators after the revolution, such as François Babeuf, and was celebrated as one of the fathers of the reformed nation.

See also AMERICAN REVOLUTION.

Further reading: Johnson Kent Wright. *A Classical Republican in Eighteenth Century France: The Political Thought of Mably.* (Stanford, Calif.: Stanford University Press, 1997).

Macpherson, James (1736–1796) *Scottish poet, translator, and historian, best known for his "Ossian" poems, which purported to be ancient epics of Scotland*

Macpherson was born the son of a farmer and educated at universities in EDINBURGH and Aberdeen. He published his first book of poems, *The Highlander*, in 1758. Encouraged by Scottish nationalism and the new interest in primitive cultures, Macpherson traveled through rural SCOTLAND collecting materials for his *Fragments of Ancient Poetry, Collected in the Highlands of Scotland, from the Galic or Erse Language* (1760).

The success of this collection led Macpherson to publish another work in which he incorporated fragments of ancient poetry into an entire epic, *Fingal, an Ancient Epic Poem, in Six Books* (1762). Macpherson presented this work as a translation of a complete epic by Ossian, the son of Fingal, which dated from a remote period in Scots history. A year later he published his "translation" of another epic, *Temora*. Both of these works were enormously popular in Scotland and throughout Europe. They earned praise from notable figures such as David HUME, Adam SMITH, Friedrich KLOPSTOCK, Friedrich SCHILLER, Johann Wolfgang von GOETHE, and Napoleon. Goethe admired the Ossian poems so much that he incorporated long passages of them in his novel *Sorrows of Young Werther.*

Nevertheless, the Ossian poems were surrounded by controversy almost immediately after their publication. Critics such as Samuel JOHNSON openly questioned their authenticity and challenged Macpherson to produce the original manuscripts, which he then forged. After his death, a committee chaired by the Scottish lawyer and novelist Henry Mackenzie determined that Macpherson had written the Ossian epics himself by liberally translating and editing fragments of ancient poetry and linking them together with passages of his own verse.

Madison, James (1751–1836) *American philosopher, statesman, and fourth president of the United States*

Madison was born at Montpelier, the Virginia plantation of his mother's family. He received a private education at home before entering the College of New Jersey (now known as Princeton). He completed his college degree in two years rather than the usual four.

Madison entered public service in 1774 as a member of his county's Committee of Safety. He helped to draft the Virginia constitution of 1776, which established the SEPARATION OF POWERS into legislative, judicial, and executive branches as the basic framework of the state government. The Virginia constitution subsequently provided a model for other state constitutions. Madison also served in Virginia's newly created General Assembly, which in late 1776 repealed the acts of the British Parliament that had criminalized certain religious opinions and practices. He worked with Thomas JEFFERSON to make permanent the suspension of laws that had granted government salaries to clergymen. By 1779, through the efforts of Madison, Jefferson, and other revolutionary figures, Virginia had established formal SEPARATION OF CHURCH AND STATE.

During the first years of the AMERICAN REVOLUTION, Madison was a member of the Virginia legislature and of the governor's Council of State. He was selected to represent Virginia at the Continental Congress (1780–81) and then served as a delegate to the Congress of the Confederation (1781–83).

The Articles of Confederation brought the various states of the new United States together into a loose association that lacked a strong central government. Madison, who already believed that the new nation needed to balance the individual interests of the states against the needs of a strong central government, tried unsuccessfully to obtain the power of taxation for the central government. He then returned to Virginia, intending to study SCIENCE, HISTORY, and law from books sent to him from FRANCE by Jefferson. Madison's plans were curtailed when he was again elected (1784–86) to Virginia's legislature (House of Delegates). He led the successful opposition to a bill that sought to establish state salaries for teachers of the Christian religion.

In 1787, Madison attended the Constitutional Convention in PHILADELPHIA as a delegate from Virginia. Madison emerged as a leader in this meeting and played such a prominent role in shaping the outlines of the UNITED STATES CONSTITUTION that he eventually earned the nickname "the Father of the Constitution."

Although the Constitutional Convention had been called to prepare a simple revision of the original Articles of Confederation, Madison steered its delegates toward creating a completely new document. He favored the establishment of a federal government in which power would be shared between state governments and a central national government. He also favored the division of power into legislative, executive, and judicial branches. Madison was building on the general concept of separation of powers that had been put forth by the French political theorist MONTESQUIEU, but his translation of that concept into an actual structure of government departed substantially from Montesquieu's vision.

Madison believed that this federal system would prevent the abuse of power by any one individual or group. He was convinced that a government that balanced the interests of various groups would be stronger than one dominated by special interests. He thus viewed diversity, whether in economic and social status or in political viewpoints, as a strength rather than as a weakness in the new American nation.

The meetings of the Constitutional Convention were closed except to delegates, but Madison kept notes of the proceedings, which were published in 1840. They provide an important record of the debates that shaped the Constitution.

When the completed Constitution was sent to the states for ratification, controversies broke out in the press throughout the young nation. Madison, John JAY, and Alexander HAMILTON wrote a series of letters to various newspapers that were then published as the 85 essays of *The Federalist Papers* (1787–88). *The Federalist* spelled out the political theory behind the proposed Constitution and offered strong arguments in favor of its ratification. Of all the contributions, Madison's were the most original. Perhaps the most famous is "Federalist Number 5," which provides a masterly analysis of the dangers of locating too much power in local communities; the result, he argued would be that the most powerful people in the community would be easily able to bend all others—either through bribes or influence—to their will. Hence, the dangers of corruption were much greater than those generated by a strong central government. Rather than serving democratic ends, local control could result in an oligarchy similar to the abuses perpetrated in 18th-century. Great Britain by English noblemen and wealthy bourgeois.

In the original Constitutional Convention, Madison opposed attaching a bill of rights to the new document. He later changed his position and supported the passage of the first 10 amendments to the Constitution, the UNITED STATES BILL OF RIGHTS (1791). Among the rights protected by these amendments are the rights to peaceful assembly, to petition the government, to trial by jury, and to due process of law. In other words, the United States Bill of Rights translated the fundamental political causes of the ENLIGHTENMENT into a practical program of legal rights.

Toward the end of the 18th century, disagreements about how power should be distributed in American society divided Alexander Hamilton from Madison. Hamilton believed that access to power should be based on the possession of PROPERTY, which he defined to exclude all groups except successful merchants, manufacturers, bankers, and landowners. His Federalist Party dedicated itself to promoting this vision of the United States. Madison and Jefferson, in contrast, championed the rights of those who were less fortunate, such as artisans and small farmers, and created the Democratic-Republican Party to oppose the Federalist Party.

Madison was appointed secretary of state from 1801 to 1809. He was then elected the fourth president of the United States and served in that capacity from 1809 to 1817. He led the United States in the War of 1812 against Great Britain, signed the bill that established the Second Bank of the United States, and approved the Tariff Act of 1816. After leaving public office, Madison retired to Montpelier, his Virginia estate, and devoted himself to agricultural experimentation. He headed the Albemarle Agricultural Society, a group that was encouraging improvements in agricultural crops and techniques. Madison spent his last years as rector of the new University of Virginia (1826–36), which had been founded by his friend Jefferson.

See also POLITICAL THEORY.

Further reading: Joyce Oldham Appleby, *Liberalism and Republicanism in the Historical Imagination* (Cambridge, Mass.: Harvard University Press, 1992); Henry F. May, *The Enlightenment in America* (New York: Oxford University Press, 1976).

Madrid Capital city of SPAIN, located on a high plain in the interior of the Iberian peninsula. The city had a population of roughly 130,000 in 1727. By 1797, that figure had grown to about 170,000. Madrid had fallen to Arab rule during the great Muslim expansions of the early Middle Ages. In 1083, the city was reconquered by Christians. Philip II established his court in the city in 1561.

During the 18th century, CHARLES III OF SPAIN, instigated a program of public works and urban beautification for Madrid. The city had already acquired a lovely botanical garden in 1755, and Charles's plans produced promenades such as the Prado with its BAROQUE STYLE fountains, an observatory, the remodeling and enlargement of the Museum of Natural Sciences (1781), and a modern hospital. The Toledo Bridge (1719–31) is one of the most notable constructions from the era that is still standing.

Eighteenth-century Madrid provided a home to several outstanding artists such as Francisco de GOYA, Giovanni Battista TIEPOLO, and Anton MENGS. The organist, harpsichordist, and composer Domenico SCARLATTI also served for 19 years as master of the chapel in Madrid.

Madrid served as a center for intellectual activities inspired by the ENLIGHTENMENT. The periodical press (*El Pensador; Correo de Madrid; Diario de Madrid*) played a significant role in making ideas available to the educated public. One journal, the *Espíritu de los mejores diarios*, boasted a subscriber list that included John JAY and Benjamin FRANKLIN. Except for the periodical press, however, the Spanish publishing industry remained dominated by the Catholic Church and produced mostly devotional and theological tracts.

See also ROMAN CATHOLICISM.

magic A belief system promising adherents powers over the natural world and other people through the uses of rituals and incantations. Although the cultural currents of the ENLIGHTENMENT sought to move European civilization toward rational models of thinking, older systems of belief persisted throughout the period, including those that involved the practice of magic. Those people who continued to practice magic remained in secret, as the suppression and torture of those suspected of witchcraft continued through the 16th and 17th centuries. Even during these centuries, the accusation of practicing witchcraft alone was often sufficient to bring about punishment.

Nonetheless, actual prosecutions for witchcraft in ENGLAND and FRANCE declined at the end of the 17th century even while popular belief in magical forces continued. Official trials were replaced by mob justice, as people who stood accused of witchcraft could still be hanged by their neighbors. In England, writer and critic Joseph ADDISON considered the question of magic in THE SPECTATOR. He allowed for the possibility of magic while admitting a lack of evidence. Addison also showed an understanding of the grim realities of the situation in his discussion, pointing out that many older women accused of witchcraft were the victims of slander and failing mental acuity. Such accusations continued throughout the period despite decreasing official belief at higher levels of government.

Another famous literary figure of the period involved in the discussion of magic was Daniel DEFOE. He published a book entitled *A System of Magic: or, A History of the Black Art* in 1728, which attempted to survey the subject. The book begins with an attack on current practitioners, who are dismissed as charlatans, although allowing that earlier magicians may have been sincere if misguided. It continues with a discussion of the terminology involved, classifies different styles of magic by the powers assumed to drive them, gives historical examples of different cultural practices, and discusses the contemporary forms the practice takes, such as soothsaying and necromancy. Other contemporary English publications on the subject included John Beaumont's *Treatise of Spirits, Apparitions, Witchcrafts, and Other Magical Practices* of 1705, which catalogued beliefs about spirits and witchcraft, and Bishop Hutchinson's *Historical Essay Concerning Witchcraft* of 1718, which attempted to clarify the significance of instances of magic in the Scriptures.

By 1736, English belief in the existence of witchcraft had declined sufficiently that Parliament passed a law against government officials professing such ideas, setting itself a new role of rooting out superstition and preventing miscarriages of justice such as the aforementioned popular witch executions, and equating the practice of magic with fraud. Popular belief continued through the century, and theological authorities such as John WESLEY, the founder of METHODISM, saw the repeal of earlier punitive witchcraft statutes as a threat to England's moral character. In Italy, figures such as Alessandro, count di Cagliostro, and Giovanni Giacomo CASANOVA profited from the continuing interest in magic among the upper classes by setting themselves up as practitioners of sorcery and alchemy.

Further reading: W. H. Davenport Adams, *Witch, Warlock, and Magician: Historical Sketches of Magic and Witchcraft in England and Scotland* (Detroit: Gale Research Company, 1973); Owen Davies, *Witchcraft, Magic and Culture: 1736–1951* (New York: Manchester University Press, 1999); Kathryn A. Edwards, *Werewolves, Witches, and Wandering Spirits: Traditional Belief and Folklore in Early Modern Europe* (Kirksville, Mo.: Truman State University Press, 2002); Geoffrey Scarre, *Witchcraft and Magic in 16th and 17th Century Europe* (Atlantic Highlands, N.J.: Humanities Press International, 1987).

Magic Flute, The　German opera by Wolfgang Amadeus MOZART with a libretto by Emanuel Schikaneder. It was one of the last of Mozart's compositions. *The Magic Flute* (German: *Die Zauberflöte*) premiered with Mozart conducting on September 30, 1791, at the Freihaustheater in VIENNA. Schikaneder created the libretto by adapting a fairy tale by J. A. Liebeskind entitled *Lulu or the Magic Flute*. The tale had been published in the anthology *Djinnistan* by Christoph Martin WIELAND. Mozart composed most of the music for the opera in the six months preceding its premiere.

The Magic Flute adapted the form of Viennese musical comedy called *Singspiel* into a vehicle for the presentation of a fairy tale allegory on the ENLIGHTENMENT. One of the brilliant creations of that era, *The Magic Flute* is a sophisticated tale that retains its dramatic impact even today.

On the literal level, *The Magic Flute* presents the story of how Prince Tamino successfully completes a number of trials in order to win the hand of Princess Pamina, daughter of the Queen of the Night. The lovers are caught up in a conflict between the Queen of the Night and Sarastro. Tamino first learns that Pamina exists when he is charged by the Queen of the Night to rescue her from the clutches of the evil Sarastro. Tamino sets off on his mission armed with a magic flute and accompanied by a comical bird catcher named Papageno.

Upon arriving in the region controlled by Sarastro, the pair discover that they have been deceived by the Queen of the Night; it is she who is evil and Sarastro who is good. Sarastro has taken Pamina from her mother's clutches in order to raise her in wisdom, love, and goodness.

Sarastro promises that Tamino may marry Pamina, and that he will provide Papageno with a Papagena if the two men successfully endure a series of three trials. These will constitute the proof of their worthiness and nobility of character. After many terrifying and comical adventures, the two men finally attain their goal, and Sarastro rewards them as he has promised. The Queen of the Night in the meantime has attempted to intervene, but Sarastro banishes her for eternity from his kingdom. The whole episode ensures the triumph of love and wisdom over hatred and irrationality.

The Magic Flute offers the observer a rich allegory with several levels of meaning. On the highest philosophical level, Sarastro represents REASON, the brotherhood of all humankind, and the triumph of the forces of light (Enlightenment); while the Queen of the Night represents uncontrolled human passions, irrationality, and the forces of darkness. On a second level, Sarastro functions as a representative of the teachings of the enlightened FREEMASONS, while the Queen of the Night serves as a symbol for the forces of revealed religion and especially of ROMAN CATHOLICISM. A third layer of allegory offers the conflict between masculinity and femininity, in which masculine forces triumph. This symbolism reflects the concepts of gender that appeared during the last half of the Enlightenment. Femininity was linked to irrationality, to intense emotion, and to deceitfulness, whereas masculinity embodied reason and intellect. Finally, the opera presents a political allegory in which the Queen of the Night symbolizes Empress MARIA THERESA, and Sarastro represents her enlightened son, the Emperor JOSEPH II.

Tamino and Pamina, and Papageno and Papagena, represent humankind, whether aristocrat or commoner. They achieve a kind of redemption and fulfillment by embracing the forces of the Enlightenment represented by Sarastro.

Mozart's opera not only presented the general teachings of the Enlightenment to Viennese audiences, but it also offered glimpses of the way that world was embodied in the rites of the Freemasons. The trials of Tamino and Papageno are modeled on the various Masonic rites. Furthermore, the symbolism in Sarastro's garden and the ideals represented by Sarastro reflect the teachings of that secret society. Finally, the great hymns to Sarastro contained in the opera derive directly from Masonic hymns.

The Magic Flute enjoyed immediate and widespread success. Twenty performances occurred in Vienna in October 1791. In 1792, the opera played successfully in Prague, and in 1793, in towns such as Augsburg, Leipzig, and Budapest. Its combination of whimsy and wisdom make it still beloved by modern audiences.

Magnasco, Alessandro (1667–1749) *Italian painter*

Magnasco was the son of a Genoese painter, Stefano Magnasco. During the years 1760–62, Magnasco lived in MILAN, where he studied mathematics and began to learn painting techniques with Filippo Abbiati. Later, he studied with Sebastiano Ricci. After a brief attempt at portrait painting, Magnasco abandoned subjects in which the human figures loomed large and turned out compositions noted for their tiny figures. He worked in Milan, Florence (as court painter for the grand duke of Tuscany), and Genoa.

Whatever their size, Magnasco painted figures whose exaggerated stances communicate irony, pathos, and gloomy emotion. Magnasco figures seem to emerge out of their background colors with imprecise and unstable outlines. They are frequently compared with the figures painted by El Greco, the 16th-century master of the Mannerist style. Magnasco captured the irrational and dark sides of life: gamblers, starving beggars, funerals, tor-

tures, and bacchanals. But he also treated religious subjects: nuns, monks, hermits, and some biblical themes. He is viewed as one of the most imaginative of 18th-century painters.

Magnasco produced more than 400 paintings considered by modern scholars as worthy of note. They include *The Supper of Emmaeus, The Communion of Mary Magdalene, The Old Woman and the Gypsies, The Tame Crow, Don Quixote, The Synagogue, The Refectory, The Meal,* and *The Preaching of the Christian Doctrine in Milan Cathedral.*

See also MATHEMATICS AND MECHANICS.

Malebranche, Nicolas de (1638–1715) *French systematic philosopher*

A native of PARIS, Malebranche studied at the Jesuit *collège* at La Marche. In 1660, he entered the French Oratory, a reformed Catholic order that had been established in France in the early 17th century. Malebranche was ordained as a priest in 1664.

Malebranche created a unique synthesis between the MECHANICAL PHILOSOPHY of René DESCARTES and Catholic orthodox theology derived from Augustinian-Neoplatonic doctrine. He desired always to remain within the bounds of religious orthodoxy, but nevertheless saw his book *Traité de la nature et de la grâce* (Treatise on nature and on grace; 1680) placed on the Catholic Index of Forbidden Books in 1689. Malebranche defended various aspects of his philosophy against attacks from quarters as diverse as Antoine Arnauld, one of the spokesmen for 17th-century JANSENISM; Bishop BOSSUET, the spokesman for orthodox theology and for divine right of kings; and François FÉNELON, the major formulator of Quietism.

Malebranche believed that human REASON is capable of discovering truths about the universe and about God, but he recognized that error and distortion exist in human understanding. He tried to explain these errors by rooting them in the dualism of human nature (division into mind and body) and in the weaknesses of human will.

Malebranche borrowed his concepts of the division between mind and body from Descartes, but he denied that mind and body ever act directly on each other. For example, thinking "I will move my arm" does not cause the arm to move. Mind does not control body. What then, causes the arm to move? For Malebranche, the answer was God, who is everywhere present in the universe. The action of God's will ensures that the thought "I will move my arm" is actually followed by a motion of the arm. Mind and body operate in a series of parallel harmonious actions that are ensured by God's omnipresence in the world.

Malebranche adopted this position, called occasionalism, in part to answer critics of Descartes. The Cartesian image of God in relationship to the world suggested that God had created the world to operate according to mathematical laws and reason and had then stepped back to let the world run without his continuing action. The world was a kind of machine, where the most action demanded from God would be some sort of intermittent maintenance.

Malebranche desired to retain the Christian idea that God is always present in the world and that the operation of the universe and human history reflect the unfolding of his will. Occasionalism, he thought, accomplished this goal. But critics complained that it weakened God, making him a rather poor and inefficient designer.

Furthermore, the idea that God's will was causing every event in the world tended to rob people of any FREEDOM in determining their own fate. This, too, was something deplorable to Christian orthodoxy. Therefore, Malebranche attempted to develop a philosophy of human freedom and free will that would be compatible with his image of God's relationship and activity in the world. The result was his assertion that the human will is free to decide whether or nor it will focus on the attainment of general good or on specific temporary pleasures.

Malebranche also wrestled with the problem that had been posed for philosophy and EPISTEMOLOGY by SKEPTICISM and that would continue to disturb the enlightened thinkers of the next century: How do we know anything for certain about the world external to ourselves? For Malebranche, we have our ideas only through God; we see all things in God. These ideas are pure ideas or archetypes that are represented only imperfectly in the world. The idea of a tree, for example, is an ideal form that is only partially realized in any specific living tree. These ideas that we see in God serve as a kind of corrective for the defective knowledge that we receive through the operation of our senses. The pure ideas also allow us to understand the truth of the RELATIONS (lawful interactions and order of events) between things.

Malebranche developed various aspects of this original position in several books: *De la recherche de la verité* (On the search for truth; 1674–75); *Eclaircissements sur les recherches de la verité* (Clarifications of the search for truth; 1768); *Traité de la nature et de la grâce* (Treatise on nature and on grace; 1680); *Traité de la morale* (Treatise on moral philosophy; 1684); *Entretiens sur la metaphysique* (Conversations on metaphysics; 1688); and *Traité de la communication des mouvements* (Treatise on the communication of movements; 1692).

The *Traité de la recherche de la verité* was translated into English in 1694 and thus entered into English discussions of epistemology. In his *Examination of Malebranche's Opinion of Seeing All Things in God* (written 1694, published 1706), John LOCKE offered a negative evaluation of occasionalism. Wilhelm Gottfried LEIBNIZ developed his notion of preestablished harmony as a way of avoiding the occasionalist vision of God's relation to the universe. He also accused Isaac NEWTON of occasionalism during the debates with Samuel CLARKE over Newtonian ideas. An article on Melabranche in the ENCYCLOPÉDIE praised his inventiveness and GENIUS while still disparaging the philosophy of occasionalism. In general, occasionalism was rejected by enlightened thinkers as an unnecessary and inefficient representation of God's relation to his creation.

See also MORAL PHILOSOPHY; RATIONALISM.

Malesherbes, Chrétien Guillaume de (1721–1794)
French statesman, government official, and defense counsel to Louis XVI during the revolution

Chrétien Guillaume de Lamoignon de Malesherbes was born in PARIS. He was trained as a lawyer and served as a counselor to the Parlement of Paris before joining the body in 1750 upon the promotion of his father, Guillaume de Lamoignon, to chancellor. As chancellor, Guillaume de Lamoignon was responsible for controlling the press, a task he delegated to his son. In his role as royal censor, Malesherbes was one of the most important officials in the French administration. He was in touch with many of the greatest thinkers and writers of the ENLIGHTENMENT, and his support of Enlightenment thought (he was a follower of Jean-Jacques ROUSSEAU, protected the PHILOSOPHES, and believed firmly in the freedom of the press) allowed important publications, such as the ENCYCLOPÉDIE.

Throughout his political career, Malesherbes supported enlightened absolutism (see ABSOLUTISM, ENLIGHTENED) tempered by representation. In 1766, Malesherbes replied to LOUIS XV's high-handed treatment of the Paris Parlement, whose proceedings the king arbitrarily halted, by calling for a convocation of the Estates General. Malesherbes's opposition to the dissolution of the *parlement* in 1771 resulted in his banishment to his country seat. He was recalled to Paris upon the accession of LOUIS XVI in 1774 and was appointed minister of the royal household (*maison du roi*) in 1775. As minister, he was responsible for administering Paris and several provinces, dealing with the church, and overseeing royal appointments. He resigned in 1776 along with Anne-Robert-Jacques TURGOT, whose reforms had faltered.

For the next decade and a half, Malesherbes spent his time in the country, pursuing his scientific and scholarly interests. He wrote an essay on Protestant marriages (1787) that helped gain them legal recognition in France. His *Mémoire sur la liberté de la presse* (Memoir on the freedom of the press; 1790) reflects his strong opinion on the subject. He was briefly recalled to Paris by the king in 1787 to help with the final efforts to reform the monarchy, but soon returned to the country.

In December 1792, Malesherbes volunteered to return to Paris yet again, this time to act as defense counsel to Louis XVI (now citizen Louis Capet), who was to be tried by the National Convention. The king was found guilty and condemned to death. Malesherbes was arrested in December 1793 along with his daughter, son-in-law, and two grandchildren. After being forced to watch their executions, Malesherbes was guillotined on April 23, 1794.

Malthus, Thomas Robert (1766–1834) *English population theorist and political economist*

The sixth of seven children born to Daniel Malthus and Henrietta Catherine Graham Malthus, he received a primary and secondary education at the Warrington Academy operated by English DISSENTERS. Malthus attended Cambridge University, graduating in mathematics in 1788.

Following the customs of the English gentry, Malthus as a younger son entered the Anglican clergy, serving actively as a pastor from 1792 until 1794. He was soon elected a fellow of Jesus College, Cambridge, and spent most of the years between 1793 and 1804 in residence at that school. He traveled through the northern German states and the Scandinavian countries in 1799, gathering materials for his theory of population growth.

After 1805, Malthus occupied the first professorship of HISTORY and political economy in ENGLAND, at a college established by the EAST INDIA COMPANY at Haileybury. His treatise, *Principles of Political Economy* (1820), was written for his course at Haileybury. Malthus was received into the membership of the ROYAL SOCIETY OF LONDON in 1819 and was also a member of the Institut de France and the BERLIN ACADEMY. He was a founder of the Statistical Society, which was established in 1834.

Malthus rejected the mercantilistic assumption that increases in population were always desirable. He was, in fact, one of the first students of population to assert that Europe was not an underpopulated region. He believed that population tends to increase faster than the food supply. Thus, he rejected the notion put forth by Johann Peter SÜSSMILCH and other mercantilists that the two factors—population and food supply—balance each other continually.

In Malthus's pessimistic vision, the human passion for sexual activity will always cause population to increase more rapidly than the food supply. As a result, inevitable periods of critical food shortages will cause high death rates as famine and disease take their toll. Eventually, an unstable and short-lived equilibrium will be restored, until the next cycle of population increase sets the whole cycle once again into motion. The whole process of population change tended to be cyclic, exhibiting repeated episodes of growth and decline.

As a corrective for this situation, Malthus could offer only sexual chastity before marriage and abstinence within marriage. He rejected both birth control and abortion as alternative forms of population control. He thus tied his vision of the population theory to restrictive morality that called for a full reversal of practices during the ENLIGHTENMENT.

Malthus's vision was decidedly pessimistic, built on his sense that the human passions and natural limitations on the food supply could never be fully controlled by well-meaning, reasonable policies or rulers. He supplemented this position with an equally pessimistic assessment of the practicality of poor relief. He believed that such programs aimed at alleviating suffering only cause a deterioration of general economic conditions by stimulating price rises. However, he never called for repeal of the English Poor Laws but preferred to encourage individuals to control their own actions in order to minimize their negative effects on society.

He was one of several English writers at the turn of the century to reject the most pronounced forms of optimism that existed in the Enlightenment, substituting for its belief in human PERFECTIBILITY a gloomy picture of the limits on human action and potential. For Malthus, the visions of earlier theorists such as Süssmilch, Adam SMITH, Bernard MANDEVILLE, William GODWIN, and Marie-Jean de CONDORCET represented a naive misunderstanding of the real forces that determine the conditions of human existence.

Malthus first sketched these ideas in an anonymous publication of 1798, the *Essay on the Principle of Population*. An expanded edition with the same title appeared over his name in 1803. He also published *The Present High Price of Provisions* (1800) and his fully developed political, economic, and population theory, *The Principles of Political Economy* (1820).

See also CAPITALISM; MATHEMATICS AND MECHANICS.

Manchester Literary and Philosophical Society A scientific society founded in Manchester, ENGLAND, in 1785. The various provincial scientific societies of FRANCE provided its model. Its members desired to extend the impact of new scientific findings and theories into the provinces of England by holding local lectures and meetings.

See also SCIENTIFIC ACADEMIES.

Mandeville, Bernard (1670–1733) *Dutch physician and moral philosopher*

Mandeville belonged to a family from Rotterdam, in the UNITED PROVINCES OF THE NETHERLANDS, that had produced three generations of physicians. He followed this path, studying first at the Erasmian School of Rotterdam and matriculating for medical and philosophical studies at the famed University of Leiden. His medical practice focused on the treatment of nerve and stomach ailments.

Mandeville settled in ENGLAND shortly after receiving his medical degree. In addition to his medical work, he began writing. His fame rests primarily on his allegorical *Fable of the Bees*. In its original version, this work was a poem called "The Grumbling Hive: Or Knaves Turn'd Honest" (1705). Mandeville spent the 24 years between 1705 and 1729 rewriting his work, defending and developing certain aspects of his argument in response to scathing critical attacks.

The *Fable of the Bees* began as a reaction to the MORAL PHILOSOPHY of Anthony Ashley Cooper, third earl of SHAFTESBURY. Shaftesbury had offered a vision of HUMAN NATURE that placed the trait of benevolence at its center. He believed that this trait of benevolence provided the natural source of human moral behavior.

Mandeville rejected Shaftesbury's theory of benevolence, stressing instead that human virtue grows directly out of human vices and the pursuit of self-interest. Envy, vanity, and the love of luxury, for example, motivate people to buy products and to spend their money lavishly, thereby promoting individual industry and commerce. Even thieves benefit society by keeping locksmiths in business and by spending the money that they steal. As Mandeville put it "The worst of all the Multitude/Did something for the Common Good."

Mandeville was concerned primarily with the problem of creating national and individual wealth. He criticized normal concepts of virtue on the grounds that such behavior discourages people from spending their money and inhibits the production of wealth. He illustrates this point by introducing virtue into the hypothetical hive of bees that provides his analogy for human society. The productive hive suddenly stagnates and can no longer maintain itself.

Mandeville's stress on the positive benefits of vice, commerce, consumption, and industriousness might seem to suggest that he would favor policies aimed at raising the standard of living for the poor. The opposite, however, was true. Mandeville believed that the poor needed to be kept in place, provided with enough wages to purchase basic necessities and nothing more. Educating them or increasing their buying power would cause disruption and disorder in society.

The theory of economic liberalism developed by Adam SMITH owed much to Mandeville's *Fable of the Bees*. The two works suggest how the special conditions in commercial nations—the United Provinces of the Netherlands and Great Britain, for example—stimulated theories during the ENLIGHTENMENT stressing the interdependency between individualism, self-interest, and the social good.

See also POLITICAL THEORY, SELF-INTEREST.

Mannheim school   A group of composers who worked in Mannheim under the patronage of the elector of the Rhineland Palatinate, Karl-Theodor (ruled 1742–99). Mannheim is a German city, founded in 1609 at the confluence of the Neckar and Rhine Rivers. After the devastation of the surrounding Rhineland Palatinate territories in the Thirty Years' War (1618–48), the Palatinate elector Karl Ludwig (ruled 1648–80) refounded the city in 1652 with the express intent of making it a large commercial center like the great Dutch cities of the era. In the 18th century it was the seat of the ruler of the Rhineland Palatinate. Elector Karl-Theodor was a highly cultured man who liked to live in the highest style. He provided significant patronage to the arts, architecture, THEATER, OPERA and MUSIC.

The composers who made up the so-called Mannheim school—especially Johann Wenzel, Anton Stamitz (1717–

57) and Franz Xaver Richter (1709–89)—developed new approaches to musical form and style that contributed significantly to the emergence of 18th-century musical CLASSICISM. In particular, they developed the practice of writing symphonies for orchestra with four movements rather than the usual three. They introduced the new technique of playing long crescendos (increasing loudness) over long phrases of music. The Mannheim crescendo, as the technique became known, departed significantly from earlier BAROQUE STYLE and STYLE GALANT practices. In these earlier musical styles, dynamic changes had been stepwise rather than gradual. One short phrase in a piece by J. S. BACH, for example, will be loud, and it will be followed by an immediately softer repetition. The Mannheim orchestra was famous for its size (45 players, about double the standard size for the era) and professional expertise. The classical composers, Franz Joseph HAYDN, Johann Christian BACH, and Wolfgang Amadeus MOZART, expressed indebtedness to the Mannheimers for their new ideas.

See also STAMITZ.

Marat, Jean-Paul (1744–1793) *radical French revolutionary, physician, scientist, and critic of the mainstream of the Enlightenment*
Marat came from Boudry in the Swiss canton of Neuchatel. His father, Jean Mara, was a Spanish physician who had practiced medicine in Sardinia. When Mara converted from ROMAN CATHOLICISM to CALVINISM, he moved to SWITZERLAND and set up a medical practice in GENEVA. In Geneva, he married Louise Cabral. Jean-Paul was the eldest of five children. He studied MEDICINE at Toulouse, Bordeaux, and PARIS. After his studies he made an extensive tour of Protestant Europe, visiting Utrecht, AMSTERDAM, The Hague, LONDON, and EDINBURGH. He set up a medical practice in London and, in 1775, received an honorary degree in medicine from the University of Saint Andrews in Scotland.

Marat moved to Paris in 1776 and obtained a medical appointment, which he retained until 1786, in the household of the comte d'Artois. Prior to the outbreak of the FRENCH REVOLUTION, Marat published several scientific papers, which were noticeable for their anti-Newtonian physics. They included *De l'homme, ou des principes ou des lois de l'influence de l'âme sur les corps, et du corps sur l'âme* (On man, either on the principles or on the laws of the influence of the soul on the body; 1775); *Recherches physiques sur le feu* (Physical investigations of fire; 1780); *Découvertes sur la lumière* (Discoveries about light; 1782); and *Recherches physiques sur l'électricité* (Research on electricity; 1782). The last three works were translated into German by C. E. Weigel and published (1782–84) at Leipzig. Other scientific publications included a translation of NEWTON's *Optics* (1787) as *Notions élémentaires d'optique* (Elementary ideas about optics) and *Les charlatans modernes, ou lettre sur le char-*

The Death of Marat by Jacques-Louis David, 1793. Jean-Paul Marat, a physician and radical Jacobin leader during the French Revolution, was assassinated by Charlotte Corday as he sat in his bath. *(Courtesy Musées Royaux des Beaux-Arts, Brussels)*

latanisme academique (Modern charlatans, or letters on academic charlatanism; 1791).

Marat lived in Paris in the parish of St. André des Arts. When the revolution broke out, he became an immediate supporter of the cause of radical democratic reform. He published two pamphlets in 1789, the *Offrande à la patrie* (Offering to the nation) and *La constitution, ou projet de declaration des droits de l'homme et du citoyen par l'auteur de l'Offrande* (Constitution, or project of declaration of the rights of man and of the citizen by the author of The Offering). He also began publishing a journal called *L'ami du peuple* (Friend of the people) in September 1789. Under various titles, more than 1,000 issues of this periodical appeared between 1789 and 1791.

Marat became a champion of the cause of the common people. He called for progressive reforms such as a graduated income tax and vocational training. He also believed that the French monarchy would need to be destroyed before any radical change could occur and advocated the use of violence to achieve revolutionary ends. True to his convictions, he approved of the mob violence of August 10, 1792, that brought the downfall of the monarchy. Marat ran for election to the National Convention in 1792 and won a seat as a representative from Paris. He helped to oust the Girondin faction of the Jacobin Party from power and supported the rival Mountain faction, but he had only 11 days to savor the victory. Marat was assassinated on July 13, 1793, by Charlotte

Corday, a partisan of the Girondins, as he sat in a bath soothing his painful chronic skin disease.

Like many French revolutionaries, Marat was buried and reburied several times. In some cases burial grounds were destroyed, necessitating removal. In others, decisions to move a person from an honored spot reflected fluctuating assessments of the value of a person's contributions. Marat received burial first in the cemetery of the Cordeliers. In late 1793, he was ordered reburied in the Panthéon, the highest place of honor for a revolutionary. But on account of opposition from Maximilien ROBE-SPIERRE, his remains were not actually moved until September 1794, after Robespierre's fall from power. One week later, in the rapidly changing political climate of the Thermidorean Reaction, Marat's remains were again moved to the cemetery of Sainte-Geneviève. The assassination of Marat was immortalized in the painting by Jacques Louis DAVID entitled *l'Assassination de Marat*.

Marat is famous for his revolutionary activities, but his scientific contributions have been mostly ignored, largely because he believed in VITALISM. Although it became prominent during the second half of the 18th century and helped to stimulate certain important developments in later scientific theories, vitalism was mostly disparaged, as Marat, whose work was ridiculed by VOLTAIRE, knew only too well. Marat's anger at the intellectual establishment stemmed largely from the poor reception that was given to his medical theories. In this manner, his vitalist leaning helped to feed his revolutionary social tendencies.

Marggraf, Andreas Sigismund (1709–1782) *Prussian chemist who adhered to the phlogiston theory of Georg Ernst Stahl*

Marggraf studied chemistry at UNIVERSITIES in BERLIN, Strasbourg, and Halle. He directed the chemical laboratory of the BERLIN ACADEMY from 1754 until 1760. Many of his papers were first published in the *Mémoires* (Memoirs) of the Academy. These were read and widely admired by French chemists of his era.

Marggraf developed a process for extracting sugar from sugar beets in 1747. This process stimulated the development of sugar beet cultivation as a major cash crop and was one of the significant events of the 18th-century Agricultural Revolution. Marggraf also pioneered using the MICROSCOPE for chemical investigation. Most of his papers were collected and published together as *Chymische Schriften* (Chemical writings; 1761–67).

Maria Theresa of Austria (1717–1780) *empress of the Hapsburg Empire from 1740 to 1780*

Maria Theresa initiated reforms within the Hapsburg lands that furthered the cause of ABSOLUTISM and laid the groundwork for the enlightened despotism (see DESPO-

TISM, ENLIGHTENED) of her son, JOSEPH II. Maria Theresa was the daughter of Charles VI, who ruled both the HAPSBURG EMPIRE and the HOLY ROMAN EMPIRE.

Charles VI had no male heirs and the law of both empires prohibited the succession from passing to a woman. In view of these restrictions, Charles VI anticipated that his death would lead to a succession crisis. Within his personal domains (the Hapsburg Empire), he warded off trouble by obtaining his Diet's approval of a decree called the Pragmatic Sanction, which provided for the succession to pass to his daughter, Maria Theresa. Within the larger Holy Roman Empire, however, Charles VI had no power to alter succession laws or the electoral process by which an emperor was chosen. As a result, Charles VI was briefly succeeded by the Bavarian elector Charles Albert, who ruled the Holy Roman Empire as Charles VII from 1742 until his death in 1745. Subsequently, Maria Theresa became the de facto ruler of the empire (1745–80), but her husband, Francis Stephen of Lorraine, held the official position as Francis I from 1745

Maria Theresa, empress of Austria. The energetic, determined Maria Theresa set in motion a series of reforms designed to secure her power and to increase the prosperity of her subjects. *(Courtesy New York Public Library)*

to 1765, and her son, Joseph II, followed in the same role from 1765 to 1790. In spite of the precautions taken by Charles VI, the succession of Maria Theresa to the Hapsburg throne plunged Europe into a war known as the WAR OF THE AUSTRIAN SUCCESSION. PRUSSIA, FRANCE, and SPAIN battled against Maria Theresa and her allies, Britain and Holland. Peace returned to Europe in 1748 with the Treaty of Aix-la-Chapelle.

Maria Theresa recognized that the conditions under which she ruled would give her no practical power in the Holy Roman Empire. She turned her attention to the personal domains of the Hapsburg dynasty, with the aim of creating out of them a strong, prosperous, unified nation under absolute rule.

In order to reach these goals, she sanctioned a program of wide-reaching, radical reform. Yet Maria Theresa cannot properly be called an enlightened monarch. Her advisers, Count Friedrich Wilhelm von Haugwitz, Wenzel von KAUNITZ, Gerard van SWIETEN, and Josef von SONNENFELS, however, were well acquainted with the political philosophy of the ENLIGHTENMENT. Their reforms aimed at rationalizing administration and taxation, unifying all aspects of sovereignty under the emperor or empress, and limiting the power of the Catholic Church to interfere in matters over which the secular government claimed control.

Reaching these goals required actions that attacked the system of special privileges, dismantled the right of representative assemblies (the estates) to vote on requests for taxes, and placed limits on the power of the nobility. It also required amelioration of the abject conditions in which most Hapsburg subjects were living.

The practical results included the following: the establishment of a centralized state bureaucracy; the imposition of a tax on all lands (although noble lands paid a lower tax than those in commoners' hands); the exclusion of the estates from decisions regarding military and foreign affairs; and the establishment of a new military academy for training officers (the famed Theresianum). Other reforms resulted in the creation of a new system of courts with unified codes for civil and criminal procedures; the endorsement of a radical new foreign policy designed to isolate FREDERICK II (THE GREAT) of Prussia (the DIPLOMATIC REVOLUTION OF 1756); and the imposition of taxation on the Catholic clergy. Finally, the Roman Catholic order of the JESUITS was dissolved; its properties were confiscated; and its buildings and assets were used to establish a secular system of EDUCATION. By the end of her reign, Maria Theresa was contemplating even more radical reforms, including the abolition of SERFDOM and alteration of the old manorial system in the countryside.

Maria Theresa had begun her reign as a young, vastly inexperienced, embattled young woman. She ended it having provided the basis for a strong, unified nation. Her son, Joseph II, would inherit the throne as a sole ruler, intent on instituting even more radical reform. But within 10 years, the empire, like much of Europe, would be wracked with rebellion as the Continent entered the era of the FRENCH REVOLUTION.

See also CAMERALISM; MONARCHS, ENLIGHTENED; POLITICAL THEORY.

Marie-Antoinette (Marie-Antoinette-Joséphine-Jeanne d'Autriche) (1755–1793) *queen of France (1774–92), wife of King Louis XVI, and daughter of the Hapsburg empress Maria Theresa and her husband, Francis I, emperor of the Holy Roman Empire*
Marie-Antoinette was born on November 2, 1755, the day after the great LISBON EARTHQUAKE. Her mother arranged for her education, providing training in languages (French, English, Italian, Latin), drawing, and music. Christoph Willibald GLUCK provided her music lessons. The marriage between Marie-Antoinette and the future LOUIS XVI was arranged by the duc de CHOISEUL and the Austrian ambassador.

Marie-Antoinette was a young girl of 15 when she left AUSTRIA for her new home in FRANCE. Soon after her arrival at Versailles, she began having difficulties because she was not behaving in the manner expected of a French public figure. She had little patience with her various duties, preferring to amuse herself with her close female friends (Madame de Polignac and the Princess de Lamballe) and to spend time with her paramour, the Swedish Count Fersen. Consequently, she aroused the enmity of powerful court factions, including the one led by LOUIS XV's official mistress, Madame DU BARRY. Marie-Antoinette seems not to have understood that her behavior had both public and private meaning in the closely scrutinized world of the French court.

Louis XVI inherited the French throne in 1774, during a troubled time when extra sensitivity was required of the French royal family. Marie-Antoinette, now the queen of France, failed to have any comprehension of the social, economic, and political instabilities that were shaking her kingdom. Her insensitivity has been passed down in history in the famous, but probably apocryphal statement, made upon hearing that the French people had no bread to eat: "Let them eat cake."

Opposition to royalty and to aristocratic ways was growing in France, and Marie-Antoinette's activities helped to discredit not only herself but also the entire institution of royalty in the eyes of critical and vocal French subjects. The DIAMOND NECKLACE SCANDAL (1785) was particularly damaging, even though the queen was absolved of any wrongdoing.

With the outbreak of the FRENCH REVOLUTION in 1789, the entire royal family was caught up in events that soon passed far beyond their control. For the first phase of the Revolution, negative sentiment toward the person

Queen Marie-Antoinette with Her Children, by Élizabeth Vigée Lebrun. Marie-Antoinette, the young wife of Louis XVI, became for many enlightened critics a symbol of the frivolity, superficiality, and decadence of the French Crown and aristocratic society. *(Coutesy New York Public Library)*

of the king was not high, but critics lambasted Marie-Antoinette. When, on October 5–6, 1789, a Parisian mob of women and militia rode and marched out to Versailles, Marie-Antoinette bore the brunt of the verbal diatribes, partly because a few weeks earlier she had urged the king to resist the National Assembly's demands for abolition of feudal rights and privileges and royal prerogatives. The royal family was escorted forcibly to PARIS. They settled in the Tuileries Palace, but were no longer free to move about at will.

The National Assembly, meanwhile, turned to the task of setting up a constitutional monarchy, which would greatly limit the power of the king. Hoping to prevent the destruction of the French monarchy, the comte de Mirabeau, an aristocrat who gave support and leadership

to the moderate revolutionaries, entered into discussions with the royal couple. But Louis and Marie-Antoinette refused to follow his various counsels. On June 20, 1791, the royal couple fled in secret from Paris. They traveled as far as Varennes, where they were recognized by a local patriot and apprehended. They were forced to return to the Tuileries Palace, this time as prisoners.

On September 14, 1791, Louis XVI signed the new constitution of France. It retained the monarchy in limited form, adding an elected Legislative Assembly in which most sovereignty would reside. Throughout these events, Marie-Antoinette was corresponding secretly with her brother, Leopold II, who had succeeded to the throne of Austria and the Holy Roman Empire in 1790. She was encouraging him toward military intervention in French affairs. Leopold II and Frederick William II, the king of Prussia, signed a manifesto at Pilnitz in August 1791, declaring their support of the French monarchy. The revolutionaries in Paris began to fear armed invasion, and a pro-war party headed by Jacques-Pierre Brissot and the comte de Narbonne acquired strength. France finally declared war on Austria in April 1792, Marie-Antoinette and Louis XVI supported the idea in the hope that the French revolutionary forces would meet with defeat.

Meanwhile, the mood in Paris continued to grow more radical. On August 10, 1792, mobs stormed the Tuileries Palace and massacred the Swiss guards. Urban violence forced the dissolution of the Legislative Assembly and brought the downfall of the constitution, after which elections were called for a National Convention. One of the Convention's first acts, on September 21, 1792, consisted of abolishing the monarchy and establishing a republic in France.

Marie-Antoinette and Louis XVI were immediately imprisoned in the dungeon of the Temple, the former Parisian center of the medieval Knights Templar. Louis was guillotined on January 21, 1793, at the Place Louis XV, then called the Place de la Revolution and now known as the Place de la Concorde. Nine months later Marie-Antoinette, who had been moved to a dismal cell in the Conciergerie, was brought before the revolutionary tribunal. Besides the charge of treason, the list of accusations brought against her included reproaches for extravagance and frivolity and rumors about "unnatural" and immoral behavior. She was also accused of being an incorrigible wife. After this hearing, the former queen was returned to the Conciergerie. The next day, October 16, 1793, she, too, was guillotined.

Marivaux, Pierre Carlet de Chamblain de (1688–1763) *French journalist, playwright, and novelist*

Marivaux was a frequent guest in the enlightened literary salons of the marquise de LAMBERT and Madame Geoffroy. He mingled with writers and patrons such as Jean-François MARMONTEL, Jean Le Rond d'ALEMBERT, Abbé Morellet, Melchior GRIMM, Claude-Adrien HELVÉTIUS, Baron d'HOLBACH, David HUME, and Ferdinando GALIANI.

As a young man, Marivaux participated in the great sense of relief that followed the death of LOUIS XIV. His youthful works such as *Le Télémaque travesti* (Telemachus parodied; written about 1714 but not published until 1736) participate in the lighthearted mood of the era but also reveal Marivaux as an observant critic of his society. Marivaux's novels and plays usually focused on love, chance, and betrayal, all prominent themes in artistic productions of the ROCOCO era. His most famous novel, *La vie de Marianne ou les aventures de Madame la comtesse de **** (The life of Marianne or the adventures of Madame, the countess of ***; serial novel published 1731–41), has its heroine, Marianne, recount the tale of her youth. As an

orphan, she was consigned, according to the customs of the time, to a convent. Marivaux uses Marianne as a vehicle for criticizing French piety and religious practices, and for exploring more adventuresome and emotional female roles. Certain aspects of Marianne's character appeared in *PAMELA* and *CLARISSA*, two novels by the English writer Samuel RICHARDSON. All three books are outstanding examples of the SENTIMENTAL FICTION that emerged in the first half of the 18th century.

Besides writing novels, Marivaux also tried journalism, publishing for a brief time a periodical modeled after *THE SPECTATOR* by Joseph ADDISON and Richard STEELE. Appropriately, it was named *Le spectateur français* (The French spectator; 1722–23). His theater pieces written for the Comédie Française and the Comédie Italienne were not always well received, but they still play today in French repertory theaters. They include *L'amour et la vérité* (Love and truth; 1720); *La surprise de l'amour* (The surprise of love; 1722); *La double inconstance* (Double fickleness; 1723); *Arlequin poli par l'amour* (Harlequin polished by love; 1723); *L'île de la raison* (The island of reason; 1727); *La jeu de l'amour et du hasard* (The game of love and of chance; 1730); and *Les fausses* (False confidences; 1737).

Marmontel, Jean-François (1723–1799) *French writer*

Born in modest circumstances in the province of Limousin, Marmontel obtained his education from the JESUITS. His father intended him for commerce, but Marmontel preferred philosophy and the humanities. He pursued these interests, offering private lessons as a means of self-support, then entered the priesthood with the intention of becoming a Jesuit. The opposition of his mother persuaded Marmontel to abandon his plans for a life in the church, and he began to devote himself to writing. In 1743, disturbed at the cold response his poem *Sur l'invention de la poudre à canon* had received from a provincial literary society, Marmontel began corresponding with VOLTAIRE.

After a few years in Toulouse, Marmontel moved to PARIS. In 1746 and 1747 he won poetry prizes from the French Academy. He moved quickly into the circle of PHILOSOPHES who were preparing the ENCYCLOPÉDIE, gaining the friendship of both Denis DIDEROT and Jean Le Rond d'ALEMBERT and frequenting the salon of Madame GEOFFRIN. Marmontel eventually married the niece of Abbé Morellet.

A poem celebrating the founding of École Militaire (Military School) brought Marmontel to the attention of Madame de POMPADOUR, the official mistress of King LOUIS XV. She secured him an appointment as *secrétaire des bâtiments* under the direction of her brother the marquis de Marigny. In 1758, her patronage also procured for Marmontel the editorship of the journal *Mercure de France* (French Mercury). After that date, Marmontel gave up his post as *secrétaire des bâtiments,* moved out of his Versailles apartment, and assumed residency in the Paris home of Madame Geoffrin.

Marmontel undertook a systematic study of ancient and modern literature in order to prepare articles for the *Encyclopédie.* In his own literary works, he often reset ancient stories and themes. Marmontel's works became extremely popular, and his collection of short stories, *Les contes moraux* (Moral tales), was translated into all major European languages. In 1763, he was given a prestigious appointment to the French Academy.

In 1767, Marmontel published his novel *Bélisaire.* The book delicately delved into politically and theologically sensitive subjects such as religious TOLERATION. As a result, the Sorbonne, the official censoring arm of the French Catholic Church, published a condemnation of the book. The Parlement of Paris and the royal councils, however, failed to follow up the censure of the church, and the book continued to be printed with royal permission.

After this incident, Marmontel became a hero for the philosophes and other enlightened members of the French public. The courts of AUSTRIA, PRUSSIA, and SWEDEN praised him, and CATHERINE II (THE GREAT) of Russia translated his chapter on toleration into Russian. Marmontel became the historiographer of France in 1771 after the death of Charles Pinot DUCLOS. In this position he wrote a poetic history, *Incas,* which he dedicated to King GUSTAV III of SWEDEN.

During this period Marmontel collaborated with Jean-Philippe RAMEAU and André-Ernest-Modeste Grétry in the production of comic operas. With the Italian composer Niccolò Piccinni, Marmontel also collaborated on transforming French operas such as *Atys, Roland, Amadis,* and *Phaéton* into Italian lyrics and style. This activity embroiled him in a press quarrel with the partisans of Christoph Willibald GLUCK over the relative merits of Piccinni's works when compared to Gluck's.

Marmontel assumed duties as perpetual secretary of the French Academy in 1783 after d'Alembert's death. During the early years of the FRENCH REVOLUTION, Marmontel published his *Nouveaux contes* (New tales). In 1792, fearing arrest, he fled from Paris and settled in the countryside near Evreux. In 1797, with a new regime in power, he was appointed to the Conseil des Anciens, but he lost his position a few months later when the coup d'etat of 18 Fructidor (September 4, 1797) forced a restructuring of the government. After that, Marmontel returned to the countryside where, in 1799, he died of a stroke.

In addition to the works already mentioned, the following should be noted: *Mémoires d'un père, pour servir à l'instruction des enfants* (Memoirs of a father to serve for the instruction of children; posthumously published 1804) and *L'histoire de la régence du duc d'Orléans* (History of the regency of the duke of Orléans; posthumously published 1805).

Mass in B Minor   Large-scale choral work with full orchestra accompaniment composed by Johann Sebastian BACH. This work is considered Bach's masterpiece in the large sacred choral form. The complete mass partly follows the outlines of the traditional Latin Catholic Mass and, in two sections—the "Credo" and the "Confiteor"—uses Gregorian chants as the melodic foundation.

The various sections of the *Mass in B Minor* were actually created over a long period of time. The first complete section composed by Bach was the "Sanctus," which he produced at Leipzig in 1724. The "Kyrie" and "Gloria" sections were written in 1733 and dedicated to Augustus III, elector of Saxony and king of POLAND. Bach sent the composition along with a letter applying for a court position. The "Crucifixus" was a reworking of an early cantata from Bach's years in Cöthen (1717–23). Little is known about the composition of the other sections, although it is surmised that the versions we know today were reworked from earlier, lost manuscripts. Bach produced the final version sometime between 1747 and 1749.

The complete *Mass in B Minor* was not intended for use in a church service. Rather, it is a piece for public concert performance. It is not known whether Bach ever actually heard it performed in its entirety. Certain characteristics of BAROQUE STYLE music, besides its obvious contrapuntal lines and highly developed formal structures, are evident in the work. The symbolic use of number, for example, underlies the architecture of some sections, determining whether a given section of the text will be repeated. The "Credo" section is a particularly outstanding example of Bach's use of symmetry. Other sections reveal the masterly use of tonal mode associated with baroque composition. The entire "Crucifixus" section, for example, stays in the key of E minor, modulating only in the last four bars to an ending chord in G Major. By this device, Bach prepares his audience for the joyous outburst that follows immediately in the opening notes of "Et Resurrexit." The tonality of the composition carries the emotions of the listener from the dark despair associated with the crucifixion, to one note of hope, which, in turn, presages the joy to come with the news of the resurrection. In short, Bach's *Mass in B Minor* provides an outstanding example of the dramatic power contained in the formal structures of music from the baroque era.

materialism   A theory that posits that the functions of the body, including those of the mind, all derive from the action of the material substances that compose the body. The name materialism arises from this notion that life is nothing more than matter acting according to natural physical laws. Because it espouses this basic idea, materialism denies the existence of a spiritual (noncorporeal) soul.

During the ENLIGHTENMENT, materialism played a significant role in the development of the life sciences (BIOLOGY), PSYCHOLOGY, and MORAL PHILOSOPHY. Materialist ideas seemed a natural outgrowth of the MECHANICAL

PHILOSOPHY and indeed stemmed from the specific questions that arose in that philosophy about mind and body relationships. Physiologists, psychologists, anatomists, and moral philosophers all struggled to develop theories of mind-body relations that would meet the demands of their modern scientific approaches yet avoid outright materialism.

Materialism was, in some ways, a kind of specter for enlightened scientists, one they struggled to suppress. For in spite of the fact that the Enlightenment has come down to the modern era as a materialist and atheistic era, the actual extent of committed materialist belief was quite limited. In fact, only a few natural philosophers in FRANCE openly espoused materialism. Their number included Julien Offray de LA METTRIE, Claude-Adrien HELVÉTIUS, Baron d'HOLBACH, Jean-Paul MARAT, and the mature Dénis DIDEROT.

Materialists were emphatically criticized by the majority of enlightened thinkers and condemned by the various churches. La Mettrie was forced to flee from both France and the UNITED PROVINCES OF THE NETHERLANDS on account of his beliefs. He finally found asylum in the PRUSSIA of FREDERICK II (THE GREAT).

Believers in materialism were usually considered atheists during the 18th century because their denial of the existence of the soul implied rejection of Christian beliefs. In reading the literary sources from the Enlightenment, however, it is important to treat with caution any accusations of materialism and ATHEISM. The two words, so often paired, were often used indiscriminately to generate negative emotions toward an individual. They were also used by opponents of the Enlightenment to discredit the movement.

Although the number of declared materialists during the Enlightenment was small, the questions they posed about the nature of living matter and about moral existence exerted notable influence. The soul had been treated traditionally, not only as the source of individual emotion, will, and ethical behavior, but also as the source of all motion or decisive action in human beings. If the soul was eliminated from the concept of human beings, then specific material explanations for emotion, will, and action had to be developed. But then several troublesome questions emerged. By what means did the living human being experience a situation and decide to act on it? What mechanisms regulated the bodily functions? What was the source of activity and of conscious behavior with its apparent moral dimensions?

One set of answers came from the life sciences where the theory of VITALISM tried to step in to fill the void left by banishing the soul from consideration. Vitalists proposed that living forces, the source of bodily action and development, exist in all plant and animal matter. By acting according to natural laws, these forces not only regulated all functions of the body and mind but also shaped moral action.

Another set of answers derived from association psychology and theories of UTILITY. These approaches suggested that all behavior is regulated according to the principle of pleasure and pain. They described human beings as naturally motivated to maximize pleasure and to avoid pain. The experience of achieving these goals, it was believed, shaped behavior in both physical and moral realms. The principles of pleasure and pain therefore substituted for the soul as a regulator of action.

mathematics   *See* MATHEMATICS AND MECHANICS.

mathematics and mechanics   Mathematics, the science of numbers, and mechanics, the science of bodies in motion, together provided the fundamental metaphors of the rational branches of the ENLIGHTENMENT. The universe, according to this vision, was constructed according to laws that can be expressed as mathematical equations. All things, whether living or nonliving, could be understood as machines subject to mechanical mathematical laws. Furthermore, since mathematics structured the universe, then the universe was a place that was orderly, lawful, predictable, and comprehensible to human beings. By generalization, this mathematically ordered universe became a world ruled by REASON.

The faith in reason associated with the Enlightenment rested in large part on the structure and content of 18th-century mathematics and mechanics. The linkage among mathematics, mechanics, and reason may seem obscure, but a hint is offered by the French and Latin languages. *Raison,* the French word for reason, also denotes the concept of the mathematical ratio, a strictly determined numerical relationship. The same double meaning belongs to the Latin word *ratio.* Once the idea that the structure of the universe demonstrates an underlying mathematical order became acceptable, the generalization of the notion of mathematical order into a broad discourse about reason became a relatively simple and logical step.

The creators of the SCIENTIFIC REVOLUTION of the 17th century established the idea that the laws governing nature and the whole universe (the book of nature) were expressible in mathematical terms. They tried to uncover (discover) these mathematical laws, thereby making the workings of the universe accessible to the human mind. The success of this approach was remarkable: Johannes KEPLER's laws of planetary motion, Galileo GALILEI's laws of acceleration in free fall, and Isaac NEWTON's universal law of gravitation are only the most famous examples.

In this early period, the specific mathematical discipline of geometry served as the model for the structure of the universe. In the hands of René DESCARTES, the French philosopher who wrote the *DISCOURSE ON METHOD* (1637), geometry also became the source of the rules for the proper use of general reason (thinking).

In conjunction with this emerging belief in the centrality of geometry to the universe, a philosophy called the MECHANICAL PHILOSOPHY appeared. This philosophy, using the science of mechanics as its model, proposed that all phenomena in the universe can be studied in terms of matter (treated as geometric form) in motion. The mechanical philosophy was created not only by Descartes, but also by a group of his contemporaries, scientists dedicated to expressing mechanical principles in mathematical terms. Their number included Galileo Galilei, Pierre GASSEND, Robert Boyle, Christian Huygens, and later, Isaac Newton and Gottfried Wilhelm LEIBNIZ.

In various forms the mechanical philosophy, as an extension of mechanics, influenced nearly all aspects of SCIENCE during the Scientific Revolution. It was this set of beliefs in the fundamental significance of mathematics and mechanics that was inherited and then developed by the Enlightenment.

The two natural philosophers whose thought formed the foundation of enlightened science—Leibniz and Newton—did not, however, simply rely on geometry to solve scientific problems. Both men independently developed a new, powerful mathematics called calculus. This mathematics provided tools for solving problems in mechanics, whether derived from terrestrial or celestial phenomena. Calculus especially assisted the solution of problems concerning both the motion of bodies along curved paths and the action of forces, thereby contributing to the rapid advance of mechanics during the Enlightenment.

The calculus of Leibniz and Newton also began to replace geometry as a general model for correct reasoning and for SCIENTIFIC METHOD. The new model of reason based on calculus was called analysis. Subjecting a problem to analysis involved breaking the problem down (resolving it, analyzing it) into simpler parts for mathematical manipulation and ultimate solution. In the hands of Newton, the process of analysis combined with synthesis (putting together) became the foundation of the scientific method.

As the Enlightenment progressed, the fields of calculus and other forms of analysis experienced rapid development. In the hands of mathematicians such as Leonhard EULER, Daniel BERNOULLI, Johann I BERNOULLI, Pierre LAPLACE, and Joseph-Louis LAGRANGE, analysis was applied to numerous problems of celestial and terrestrial mechanics. Progress occurred in the study of motion along complex curves, in the study of gravitation, in the analysis of vibrating or oscillating motion, and in understanding and predicting the paths of celestial bodies.

But calculus could not explain certain types of irregular events in nature or in the realm of human action. In fact, toward the end of the Enlightenment, the problems that escaped mathematical solution seemed so multitudinous that the great mathematician Lagrange feared that mathematics had already reached its limits. If that were the case, then the goal of the rational Enlightenment—quantifying or mathematizing the universe—appeared unattainable.

Lagrange, however, in assessing mathematics was thinking primarily of calculus. He was not involved in the creation of a second branch of mathematics, probability theory. This theory had developed initially as a study of games of chance. Its power lay in its ability to explain phenomena that seemed erratic and unpredictable. Jakob I BERNOULLI, Leonhard Euler, and Pierre-Simon Laplace transformed probability theory into a tool for solving problems of irregular motions in the heavens and for proving that the universe is a stable dynamic system. The new theory also had practical utility for problems in human affairs such as insurance risk, commerce, and population growth.

Probability theory allowed the mathematization of forms of relationship that were more complex than those of simple cause and effect. It revitalized the enlightened program of extending the realm of mathematics to cover all phenomena of the universe and saved the idea that the universe is lawful, reasonable, and regulated. Probability theory seemed to provide a way to get around the problem of the limits of the human capacity for observation and understanding of complex phenomena.

Probability theory was, in fact, one of the great creations of the Enlightenment. Not only did it extend the power of mathematics in the natural sciences, but also it provided a mathematical foundation for new sciences created during the Enlightenment: the social sciences whose subjects were human behavior, political economy, and DEMOGRAPHY.

Thus, it can be seen that mathematics and the intimately associated science of mechanics were driving forces behind the Enlightenment. It must be emphasized that they not only aided the natural and social sciences but also, as metaphors, provided models for inquiry into all realms of human activity.

See also LONGITUDE; SCIENCE OF MAN.

Further reading: John G. Burke, *The Uses of Science in the Age of Newton* (Los Angeles: William Andrews Clark Library, UCLA, 1983); Thomas L. Hankins, *Science and the Enlightenment* (Cambridge: Cambridge University Press, 1985); Richard S. Westfall, *The Construction of Modern Science: Mechanisms and Mechanics* (Cambridge: Cambridge University Press, 1977).

Mather, Cotton (1663–1728) *American Congregational clergyman, writer, and amateur scientist*

Mather was born in Boston, Massachusetts, the son of Increase Mather, the powerful Congregational minister at Boston's North (Second) Church, and of Mary Cotton, the daughter of a Puritan minister. Cotton Mather graduated from Harvard College in 1678. He then studied

MEDICINE and THEOLOGY, receiving his M.A. degree from the same institution in 1685.

Mather was ordained in 1685 and worked with his father at the Boston North Church. Young Mather was fascinated with supernatural events and carefully collected materials for a book on this subject. It appeared first in 1689 and then in 1691 in a second edition entitled *Late Memorable Providences relating to Witchcrafts and Possessions, Clearly Manifesting Not Only that there are Witches, but that Good Men (as well as others) may possibly have their Lives shortened by such evil Instruments of Satan.* A copy of this book fell into the hands of some girls in Salem Village, Massachusetts. They accused an enslaved family servant of being a witch, thereby setting off the wave of hysteria that led to the notorious Salem witchcraft trials of 1692 and 1693. Before the trials ended, 14 women and five men were hanged as witches. Cotton Mather is often treated as the instigator of the trials, and, indeed, his book obviously contributed to their outbreak. But he was uneasy about trial procedures and pointed out the unreliability of certain forms of evidence that were being accepted as signs of guilt.

Mather remained committed to Puritan forms of religious practice throughout his life. His nearly 500 sermons, books and pamphlets explored aspects of Puritan piety and lifestyle and spread these ideas throughout the American colonies. As would be expected from a Puritan minister Mather emphasized the importance for committed Christians of working industriously, honestly, skillfully, contentedly, and piously. But his ideas extended beyond this simple prescription to embrace a general appreciation of practical activity, whether in a trade, a craft, or applied sciences. None other than Benjamin FRANKLIN, a master of practical invention, acknowledged that Mather's essays had helped to stimulate his interest in practical solutions to human problems.

Mather's interest in supernatural phenomena stemmed not only from theological concerns but also from his medical interests. His *Curiosa America* (1721–24) reported on both supernatural phenomena and natural events in America, earning him election to the ROYAL SOCIETY OF LONDON.

The sensational Salem witch trials, provoked in part by Mather's book on witches, sometimes obscure the fact that Mather's interest in witches was part of a larger scientific and philosophical concern. Mather was, in fact, exploring the relationship between the natural and the supernatural, the rational and the irrational, the material and the spiritual in life. Mather's *Christian Philosopher* (1721) struggles with these relationships, with the proper boundaries and qualities of NATURE, and with the implications of various viewpoints for God's action in the world. It thus reflects certain issues that were central in English tracts on DEISM in the late 17th and early 18th centuries.

Mather was an early proponent of INOCULATION against smallpox, even though the procedure was contro-versial and often feared. He accepted the procedure, in spite of its risks, as something that was likely to assist the PROGRESS of humanity. In this matter, as elsewhere, Mather revealed his commitment to bettering the practical lot of human beings.

In many ways, it becomes apparent, Mather was participating in the intellectual world of the early ENLIGHTENMENT. His reputation as a strict and old-fashioned Puritan sometimes obscures the fact that he was wrestling with difficult and very modern questions, which had many possible solutions in the context of his era.

See also RELIGION; SCIENCE.

Maupeou, René-Nicolas-Charles-Augustin de (1714–1792) *French lawyer, first president of the Parlement of Paris (court of law), and chancellor of France under Louis XV*

Maupeou's father, René-Charles de Maupeou, was also first president of the Parisian *parlement*, vice-chancellor, and keeper of the seals of France. René-Nicolas-Charles-Augustin de Maupeou followed his father's footsteps into the legal profession, becoming a judge in the Parisian *parlement* in October 1743, and first president of the same law court in November 1763. In 1768, he was named chancellor of FRANCE in succession to his father, who had held the office for a mere 24 hours.

The year 1749 witnessed the beginning of a struggle between the king and the French PARLEMENTS. At the center of the quarrel lay a question about the nature of the monarchy: Was the king legitimately absolute or did certain legally constituted groups in France such as the *parlements* have the right to limit royal authority? The lawyers and judges of the *parlements* were claiming the fundamental right to refuse to register the edicts of the king. In earlier centuries they had enjoyed such rights, but under the ABSOLUTISM of LOUIS XIV, they had lost the power to exercise them. By 1749 the *parlements* were beginning to experience a resurgence of strength and thus began overtly challenging royal authority. LOUIS XV responded by trying to silence them or to restrict their activities.

Maupeou's father, as first president of the Parlement of Paris, was heavily involved in negotiations between the *parlement* and the Crown. In the course of the struggles the *parlement* members became dissatisfied with the elder Maupeou's leadership and forced him to give up his presiding position (1753). The king compensated him with a royal pension and in 1763 appointed him as both keeper of the seals and vice-chancellor of France.

The younger Maupeou, René-Nicolas-Charles-Augustin, became committed to royal absolutism as he observed the conflict among his fellow judges, his father, and the king. When he became chancellor in 1768, he soon demonstrated his loyalty to the absolute aims of the king. The conflict between Crown and *parlements* had temporarily subsided after the 1757 assassination attempt by Robert-François DAMIENS against Louis XV. Damiens had hinted that the parliamentarian opposition to the Crown had provided one source of inspiration for him. The members of the Parlement of Paris reacted to this implication by relaxing their position and by using the trial and execution of Damiens as a vehicle for publicly emphasizing their loyalty to the crown.

The truce between the French *parlements* and Crown lasted until 1770 when a dispute broke out in Brittany between the Parlement of Rennes and the duc d'Aiguillon, who was the royal military governor of the province. The case was moved from Rennes to PARIS for hearings. In the course of the conflict, the Parlement of Paris opposed all attempts by the king to impose his will. In return, the king resorted to exiling key opposition judges by *LETTRES DE CACHET* and to enforcing his will by means of a *lit de justice* (his personal appearance in the Parlement of Paris). The conflict displayed the weakness of the Crown with respect to the claims of the *parlements* and exposed the general dysfunction of French political structures.

The duc de CHOISEUL, the minister of foreign policy, generally supported the *parlements* or at least tried to placate them. But he was disgraced in 1770 as a result of a series of foreign policy problems, financial crises, and court intrigues. The king taunted the *parlements* by appointing none other than d'Aiguillon as Choiseul's successor.

Choiseul's disgrace and the appointment of d'Aiguillon put Chancellor René-Nicolas-Charles-Augustin de Maupeou in a strong position. He took up the offensive against the Parlement of Paris by persuading the king to issue a decree that prohibited it from exercising its customary right of refusing to register royal edicts. Of course, for the edict to become law, the *parlement* had to register it. The *parlement* members refused to do so and also declared that they would no longer meet for court sessions until the king withdrew the offending decree.

By a series of subtle provocations, Maupeou had thus lured the Parlement of Paris members into open rebellion against the king. He moved swiftly into action. On January 19 and 20, 1771, by means of *lettres de cachet*, Maupeou had the *parlement* members exiled to distant places. Despite a great outcry in the French periodical press, he proceeded to abolish the practices of selling positions in the Parlement of Paris (venality of office) and of collecting private fees from clients in the court. Justice was to be dispensed free of charge. Maupeou created six new regional courts to replace the inoperative Parlement of Paris. He abolished two other Parisian courts, thereby striking conveniently at his enemy Chrétien-Guillaume de Lamoignon de MALESHERBES, by removing him from office. Ultimately, Maupeou wanted to reform the entire judicial system of France by streamlining jurisdictions, codifying and unifying laws throughout the kingdom,

and reforming trial procedures. But the implementation of this grander plan would wait until the age of Napoleon before it could be realized.

With his attacks on the Parlement of Paris, Maupeou created both a much-needed set of reforms and a firestorm of public protest. Various groups in French society had come to view the *parlement* as the defender of their interests and rights against the encroachments of the monarchy. But VOLTAIRE assessed the situation differently and sided with the chancellor. Maupeou's Parlement, as the new court was called, survived until its creator's disgrace in 1774, the year of Louis XV's death. At that time, Maupeou retired to private life. He died in 1792 at the age of 78.

The drama that surrounded Maupeou's activities graphically shows the forces that were swelling against the cause of enlightened absolutism (see ABSOLUTISM, ENLIGHTENED) in FRANCE. Its details also clearly illustrate how reformers bent on introducing rational enlightened forms of government could be confounded by privileged groups claiming to defend certain liberties against usurpation by the king. Both groups were drawing their arguments from theories common to the ENLIGHTENMENT. Thus, the conflict demonstrates the tensions and contradictory threads contained within the tapestry of the Enlightenment.

Further reading: C. B. A. Behrens, *Society, Government and the Enlightenment: The Experiences of Eighteenth-Century France and Prussia* (London: Thames & Hudson, 1985); Alfred Cobban, *A History of Modern France, Vol. I: 1715–1799. Old Régime and Revolution,* 3rd ed. (Baltimore: Penguin Books, 1963).

Maupertuis, Pierre Louis Moreau de (1698–1759)
French mathematician, physicist, astronomer, and biologist
Maupertuis was one of the early advocates in FRANCE of the scientific theories of Isaac NEWTON. Maupertuis turned to the profession of mathematics after first contemplating careers in PHILOSOPHY and MUSIC. He was appointed to the FRENCH ACADEMY OF SCIENCES at the age of 25 after presenting a dissertation on the structure of musical instruments.

A 1728 trip to LONDON put him in touch with Newtonian theory and resulted in his becoming an outspoken adherent of that new scientific approach. In the famous 18th-century controversy about the shape of the Earth, Maupertuis defended the Newtonian position that the shape of the Earth is a sphere flattened at the poles. The alternative view, supported by CARTESIANISM, predicted that the shape of the Earth is a sphere stretched out at the poles.

Maupertuis participated in the scientific expedition of 1735 that was designed to settle the question by comparing the lengths of a degree along the Earth's meridian at different degrees of latitude. The Cartesian theory predicted that a degree of the meridian would occupy a longer distance at the poles than at the equator, while the Newtonian theory predicted the opposite. Maupertuis traveled to Lapland, to far northern latitudes; another group of scientists traveled to Peru near the equator. Expedition results yielded data that supported the Newtonian position, thereby lending experimental support to Newton's theory of universal gravitation.

About 1732, Maupertuis met both VOLTAIRE and his mistress, Madame du CHATELET. Maupertuis taught Newtonian philosophy to them, and the trio became friends until various conflicts arising from the behavior of Maupertuis's protegé, the Swiss scientist Samuel König, caused estrangement between Maupertuis and his two illustrious friends.

In 1738, while their friendship remained intact, Voltaire began recommending Maupertuis to FREDERICK II (THE GREAT) OF PRUSSIA for the presidency of the newly restructured BERLIN ACADEMY. Frederick responded positively, but Maupertuis hesitated for several years, accepting the post only in 1745. Under Maupertuis's leadership, the academy developed into a major central European institutional base for enlightened science.

Maupertuis developed a metaphysical principle in physics that he called "the principle of least action." He believed that the laws of motion and rest in nature could be derived from this principle. In technical mathematical terms, it asserted that all action in nature is economical and simple.

The principle of least action provided the substance of the public conflict that broke out between Maupertuis and his mentor, Voltaire. Samuel König, again, started the dispute. As a supporter of the philosophies of Gottfried Wilhelm LEIBNIZ and Christian WOLFF, König declared in a Berlin Academy meeting that Leibniz had originally developed the principle of least action. Maupertuis, who had promoted König's career, was incensed. In the ensuing quarrel, Frederick the Great sided with Maupertuis and Voltaire sided with König. The result was a series of vicious satires by Voltaire on Maupertuis and the end of Voltaire's friendships with both Maupertuis and Frederick the Great.

Maupertuis left BERLIN in 1752 as a result of the König affair, but returned from 1754 until 1756. He then moved to Toulouse, France, and died in 1759 while visiting his old friend Johann I BERNOULLI in Basel, SWITZERLAND.

Besides physics, Maupertuis pursued investigations of biological heredity. At the time, the question of how the GENERATION of new life occurs was being hotly debated. PREFORMATION THEORY vied with EPIGENESIS for dominance, and life scientists were unsure about the relative roles of the female and the male in reproduction. Maupertuis was an epigeneticist who believed that both parents contribute characteristics to their children. New life was produced when hereditary particles present in the male and female reproductive fluids joined together by means of the laws of AFFINITY CHEMISTRY.

Maupertuis left many interesting and important works for the history of science in the ENLIGHTENMENT. His theories have been described as an attempt to reconcile the opposing philosophies of nature developed by Newton and Leibniz. His large theoretical works included *Vénus physique* (The physical venus; 1745) and *Système de la natur* (System of nature; 1751), both dealing with biological generation. His principle of least action was put forth in "Les lois du mouvement et du repos" (Laws of motion and rest; 1746), his inaugural paper before the Berlin Academy. Two other works, "Lettre sur le progrès des sciences" (Letter on the progress of the sciences; 1752) and *Lettres* (Letter; 1752), contained speculations about the future of science and specific ideas on various subjects. The satires by Voltaire that deal with Maupertuis were *Diatribe du Doctem Akakia* (Diatribe of Doctor Akakia; 1952) and *Micromegas*. The collected works of Maupertuis appeared in France in 1756 under the title *Oeuvres de Maupertuis* (Works of Maupertuis).

See also MATHEMATICS AND MECHANICS.

McAdam, John Loudon (1756–1836) *Scottish-born engineer who lived and worked in both England and the United States*
McAdam moved to the United States as a young man in 1770 to work in an uncle's New York City accounting firm. He made a substantial fortune in this occupation and was able to return to SCOTLAND in 1783, a wealthy man. He began his public service as a trustee of roads in the Scottish district of Ayrshire. He moved to ENGLAND in 1815 after he was appointed surveyor general of roads in Bristol and, in 1827, became surveyor general of roads for all England.

McAdam developed the technique of building roads with crushed stone (macadamized roads), thus greatly improving the ease of travel. He published two treatises on road construction: *Practical Essay on the Scientific Repair and Preservation of Roads* (1819) and *Present State of Road-Making* (1820).

mechanical philosophy   A form of natural philosophy, derived from the sciences of MATHEMATICS AND MECHANICS. The mechanical philosophy developed in the early decades of the 17th-century SCIENTIFIC REVOLUTION and dominated most scientific disciplines throughout the first two-thirds of the ENLIGHTENMENT. Two fundamental propositions linked all variants of the mechanical philosophy: All natural phenomena can be reduced to problems of matter in motion, and simple cause-and-effect relations between events govern all natural phenomena. In addition, the mechanical philosophy offered the metaphor of the machine as a model for the organization of both the universe and of living beings.

Matter was defined as a substance that occupies space (is extended) and is composed of particles called corpuscles. Most mechanical philosophers believed that all space in the universe is filled with matter; the regions that we now conceptualize as vacuums were believed to be filled with a very finely divided, invisible form of matter called ether. Only a few mechanical philosophers accepted the radical and then disturbing idea that void (empty) space exists.

Mechanical philosophers believed that matter is inert, that is, that it does not contain any active forces capable of moving it. Motion comes rather from the action of external causes (forces), and the ultimate external cause is God. But it was difficult in this version of things to explain how motion is preserved in the universe. To solve the problem, mechanical philosophers invented the concept of inertia, the tendency of matter to stay in motion unless that motion is impeded by some external body or force.

Mechanical philosophers argued over whether external physical forces (not including God) could act at a distance or only through some material substance such as the ether that was believed to fill the universe. Isaac NEWTON himself offered two opposing explanations of the action of the force of gravity: In one instance, he described the action occurring through ether; in the second, he speculated that forces could act at a distance.

The mechanical philosophy first acquired importance through the writings of René DESCARTES in FRANCE. Other early figures of central significance include Pierre GASSEND, Galileo GALILEI, Marin MERSENNE, Christian Huyghens, and Robert Boyle.

The Enlightenment, however, received its mechanical philosophy from three primary sources: Descartes, and two later 17th-century figures, Isaac Newton and Gottfried Wilhelm LEIBNIZ. Each of these men developed a distinct body of thought. Noted scientific quarrels of the Enlightenment often had roots in the allegiance of the various parties to these different traditions in mechanical philosophy. For example, the famous *vis viva* (living force) controversy, involved a conflict between followers of Leibniz and Newton over the fundamental nature of the forces acting upon matter.

The primary scientific opposition to the mechanical philosophy came from the life sciences, where VITALISM offered a powerful alternative theory about the nature of life. In chemistry, the mechanical philosophy had competition from traditional theories based on ALCHEMY and AFFINITY CHEMISTRY.

The mechanical philosophy offered a vision of the world that embroiled this philosophy with religious authorities and caused its followers to be accused, at times, of ATHEISM. To traditional theologians, this new scientific vision offered the specter of a universe regulated by laws and forces that did not need God. It also directly contradicted certain teachings of the Bible and of church fathers, and it even contained implications for the central Christian doctrine about the sacrament of the Eucharist.

Many mechanical philosophers reacted to this situation by making explicit attempts to declare their loyalty to Christianity. Others, uncomfortable with traditional revealed religion, turned to the concept of natural religion. DEISM, for example, provided an alternative foundation for morality and belief in God rooted in the design and laws of nature. Finally, the most radical mechanical philosophers openly espoused forms of MATERIALISM that were, indeed, atheistic in their religious consequences.

The mechanical philosophy, therefore, contained implications that stretched far beyond the boundaries of the natural sciences. It was one major source of fundamental ideas in the Enlightenment and must be understood in order to have a balanced perspective of that great 18th-century era.

medicine The discipline and profession that deals with the study and cure of human disease. During the ENLIGHTENMENT, both the theory and practice of medicine changed. On the one hand, the medical theories and traditions inspired by 17th-century MECHANICAL PHILOSOPHY matured. The primary bearers of this tradition into the Enlightenment were Hermann BOERHAAVE, at the University of Leiden, and Friedrich HOFFMANN, at the University of HALLE. Albrecht von HALLER and Gerard van SWIETEN would continue to develop this tradition. During the 1740s and 1750s, however, a noticeable shift toward VITALISM appeared in medical theory. The vitalist tradition carried into the Enlightenment elements of older medical theories and practice that predated the mechanical philosophy, transforming them to produce a significant alternative medical approach. The chemistry and medicine of Georg Ernst STAHL served as the initial source for this transformation.

Enlightened physicians, whether adherents of mechanical philosophy, vitalism, or some eclectic blend of theories, commonly appealed to experience and observation as the primary sources of their theoretical work. They drew their convictions from the empirical PSYCHOLOGY of John LOCKE and from the clinical medical tradition associated with the ancient Greek physician Hippocrates. Both Locke and Hippocrates, in different ways, had treated environment, climate, and daily experience as critical matters for human well-being. They provided theoretical foundations for medicine that blended beautifully with key components of the Enlightenment: The causes of EMPIRICISM and humanitarianism, of PROGRESS and of rationalization, were all admirably served.

Enlightened medicine was built on changes that had begun in the 17th century. During that earlier century, the century of the SCIENTIFIC REVOLUTION, the form of medicine derived from the ancient theoretician Galen had fallen into disfavor. Galen, a Greek from Pergamum who lived in the second century A.D., had built a medical philosophy and theory based on combining the four physical elements (earth, air, fire, and water) with the four basic qualities of matter (hot, cold, dry, and moist) all derived from the physics of Aristotle. From Aristotle's four elements, Galen derived his theory of the bodily humors. When these humors were balanced, a state of health prevailed; imbalances, in which one humor was deficient or excessive, produced disease. Various combinations of the humors produced the temperaments, basic physical and psychological tendencies in human beings. For Galen as for Aristotle, the heart rather than the brain was the most important organ of the body.

Galen consciously based his theories on those of his predecessor Hippocrates. Thus, the theories of bodily functioning and disease usually presented as Galenic were actually also Hippocratic. Developments in 17th-century medicine caused Galenic/Hippocratic *theories* of health and disease to be abandoned, at least in some medical schools. But Hippocratic medical *practices*, stressing the importance of clinical rather than theoretical medicine, lived on. When physicians of the Enlightenment invoked the tradition of Hippocrates, they were referring to the practice of clinical medicine, an area in which major innovations were occurring. In fact, the advances made in clinical medicine during the Enlightenment provided one foundation of modern medical practice.

But, to return to theory, how, specifically, did the dethroning of Galenic/Hippocratic medical theory (hereafter called traditional medicine) come about? The process was a gradual one, stimulated by general developments in many fields of SCIENCE, but there were two seminal developments.

First, William Harvey proved that the blood circulates through the heart to the body. Galenic tradition had insisted that blood does not circulate and had envisioned the heart, not as a pump for blood, but as a source of bodily heat. Harvey's findings left the Galenic vision of bodily anatomy and physiology severely weakened.

Second, Galileo GALILEI, one of the early creators of the mechanical philosophy, put forth his theory about the primary and secondary qualities of matter. For primary qualities of matter such as shape and weight, he offered a mechanical explanation; these qualities had no independent existence, but were simply manifestations of the quantity of matter in a body. Secondary qualities, including the hot and cold, wet and dry, of traditional medicine, became purely subjective phenomena dependent on human senses, and they also had no independent philosophical or physical existence.

Together, the theories of Harvey and Galileo stripped Galenic medicine of its theoretical foundations.

Frère Jacques (1661–1714) performing a lithotomy by the perineal route. During the Enlightenment, surgery was still performed by barber-surgeons, often in operating theaters filled with young trainees and curious spectators. *(Courtesy Bettmann Archive)*

Consequently, many 17th-century physicians turned to the mechanical philosophy as a source of medical theory. The image of the body as a machine composed of moving parts, operating according to regular laws, replaced the old theory of the humors and temperaments. The Galenic emphasis on the heart and vascular system as the center of life was replaced by an emphasis on the brain and nervous system as the sources of essential physiological activity. As the era of the Enlightenment opened, any medical student who could manage it, traveled to Leiden to study this most advanced form of medicine with the great Hermann Boerhaave.

Boerhaave not only transmitted mechanical and chemical medicine to the Enlightenment, but—following Hippocrates—he also emphasized the importance of basing medical knowledge on experience gained through clinical practice. The physicians of the Enlightenment embraced Boerhaave's approach wholeheartedly. Their observation of patients led to detailed descriptions of specific diseases, to tables outlining symptoms, and to new systematic classifications of disease. They began gathering statistics about treatment, the incidence of disease, and mortality, thereby introducing medicine to the notion of quantifying its experience for further analysis. The spirit of empiricism and the trend toward orderly CLASSIFICATION, both central to the Enlightenment, manifested themselves clearly in these instances.

Clinical medicine stimulated new treatment approaches. Direct observation of patients in clinics or hospitals caused some physicians to begin noticing the effects of environment, climate, and individual habits on health and disease. Remedies for disease involved changing external circumstances, altering diet and residence, or taking mineral water cures. Vitalism, in particular, emphasized the idea that natural powers of healing operate in nature and that medical intervention should build on these powers.

While the new clinical practice of medicine seemed to offer endless possibilities for the progress of medicine, the medical theories derived from the mechanical philosophy attracted increasing criticism as the 18th century progressed. The project of describing all aspects of biological existence in terms of particles of matter in motion simply failed to explain certain phenomena. Besides, the mechanical philosophy could easily lend itself to MATERIALISM, that is, to a vision of life in which the soul was eliminated. This fact troubled many physicians and scientists as much as it disturbed established religious authorities. Despite the reputation of the Enlightenment for secularism and ATHEISM, it was also an era in which most people continued to believe in some form of RELIGION. Thus, theories that placed the existence of the soul in doubt were unwelcome.

As a result of the dissatisfaction with the mechanical philosophy, a new approach, that of vitalism, began in the 1740s to attract prominent advocates. A complex set of theoretical approaches that is difficult to pinpoint precisely, vitalism originated in interpretations of the ANIMISM of the late 17th-century German chemist and physician Georg Ernst Stahl. But its first major institutional base was the University of Montpellier in FRANCE.

Vitalism, in contrast to the mechanical philosophy, claimed that living matter is fundamentally different from dead matter. Living matter contains vital forces that govern the activities of the body through the laws of physiology. Vitalism attempted to mediate between the extremes in medical theory offered by materialism (associated with mechanical philosophy) and animism. Many prominent physicians of the Enlightenment were avowed vitalists. Their ranks included Marie-François-Xavier BICHAT, Lazzaro SPALLANZANI, John HUNTER, Paul-Joseph BARTHEZ, and Robert WHYTT. The theory spread from Montpellier to all nations of Europe.

A final theoretical development that must be noted derived in large part from the work of Philippe Pinel and Johann Christian REIL. Pinel extended the concept of organic disease to disturbances of the mind. As a result, the insane were moved from prisons and workhouses into hospitals where they could obtain medical treatment. While it is fashionable in some modern circles to criticize the conception of mental disturbance as illness, it is important to remember that in the 18th century, the invention of the concept resulted in more humane treatment of sufferers.

Changes in the theory and practice of medicine led to the development of new sites for teaching medicine and to the transformation of older ones. UNIVERSITIES continued to maintain medical schools and to provide the formal training that led to licensing. Prominent university medical schools could be found in Leiden, Montpellier, EDINBURGH, Halle, PARIS, Pavia, Padua, Buda, VIENNA, and GÖTTINGEN. During the Enlightenment, the dominant teaching role that had been exercised by Leiden, Paris, and LONDON, passed to Montpellier, Göttingen, Edinburgh, and Halle.

In response to the emphasis on clinical medicine, important medical training programs also developed in urban hospitals and clinics throughout Europe. The first university clinic was established in Vienna in 1754, under the leadership of Gerard van Swieten. Paris acquired such a clinic only in 1794, at the initiative of reforming revolutionary leaders.

While most medical education was funded by central governments and hospitals were charitable institutions run by churches or philanthropic organizations, private medical schools and entrepreneurial lecture series also came into existence. Young medical practitioners often supported themselves and established viable reputations by offering lecture series for a fee to the public. John Hunter and his brother William HUNTER, for example, ran a highly successful school of anatomy in London, and similar programs existed in Paris.

Major professors of medicine during the middle and later Enlightenment included William CULLEN, Robert Whytt, and Alexander MONRO Secundus in Edinburgh; Johann Christian Reil in Halle; Carl Friedrich Kielmeyer in Stuttgart; Philippe Pinel, Marie-François-Xavier Bichat, Vicq d'Azyr, and Pierre-Jean-Georges CABANIS in Paris; Théophile de BORDEU and Paul-Joseph Barthèz in Montpellier; and Albrecht von Haller and Johann Friedrich BLUMENBACH in Göttingen.

The cause of reform was served by a series of widespread innovations that helped to establish medicine as a distinct and respected profession. Whether undertaken under private or state initiative, the appearance of examinations, the creation of licenses, and the regulation of teaching practices helped to improve the general competence of medical school graduates. Professional journals, presenting clinical observations and experience, proliferated, making it possible for readers of all major European languages to have access to the latest medical research and techniques. Physicians formed new societies, often with the implicit goal of breaking down the hard barriers between medical doctors, surgeons, apothecaries, and other legally defined groups. SCIENTIFIC ACADEMIES in cities such as Paris, London, BERLIN, Göttingen, and SAINT PETERSBURG also sponsored medical research as a serious scientific pursuit.

Of the many specific advances made in medicine, a few deserve special mention. Several diseases—diabetes, typhoid fever, tuberculosis of the bone, and chicken pox—were identified and described for the first time. The conquest of disease stepped into uncharted territory with the introduction in Europe of INOCULATION. For the first time, Europeans had a specific method for preventing a particular disease. General prevention benefited from the emergence of a culture of cleanliness. Originating in Edinburgh, the campaign for cleanliness led to improvements in urban sanitation, to safe water supplies, and to lighted streets, areas vital to the maintenance of public health. Closely related to the public health movement was the drive for reform in hospitals, where conditions were notoriously filthy, crowded, and inhumane. Reformers campaigned for clean wards, for smaller patient populations, for windows to provide fresh air, and for generally better environmental conditions.

The concern with disease prevention and control was intimately linked to the general 18th-century notion of police. This term connotes the practice of developing specific policies for reaching social goals and of providing laws and agencies to enforce them. Toward the end of the 18th century, the notion of policing the health of a community developed into an explicit theory of public health. In the form developed in Vienna by Gerard van Swieten and Johann Peter Frank, the responsibility for preserving the public health rested with the central government. This theory grew quite naturally out of German CAMERALISM, which provided the underpinnings for enlightened despotism (see DESPOTISM, ENLIGHTENED) in the HAPSBURG EMPIRE and in PRUSSIA. But its utility was recognized throughout Europe and public health became a permanent focus of concern as the Enlightenment closed. The theory of public health provides a clear example of the interdependence during the late Enlightenment between humanitarianism, aimed at increasing the quality of life, and the goal of extending state control.

By the close of the Enlightenment, then, medicine had begun to acquire the familiar outlines of modernity. Practice was empirical, based on observation and analysis; the effects of environment were recognized in treatment forms, in public health programs, and in hospital reforms; mental disturbance was defined as a physical illness; and physicians were receiving increasingly rigorous training in

hospitals, universities and clinics, just as happens today. This familiar form, however, masks the fact that 18th-century medicine was very much in flux. Many competing traditions commanded official respect and support. Patients received the most modern drugs or special treatments such as electric therapy, were sent to medical spas for a cure, were advised to alter their lifestyles, and were given homeopathic medicines. But they also were bled, cupped, and purged, and provided with dangerous chemical remedies in the old style. The alternatives were many, some desirable, others wisely abandoned. In any case, enlightened medicine presented a complexity of theory and practice that has largely vanished from official medicine today.

See also BIOLOGY; DIDEROT; IATROCHEMISTRY; IATROMECHANICS; PUBLIC HEALTH; ZIMMERMANN.

Further reading: Lester King, *The Philosophy of Medicine: The Early Eighteenth Century* (Cambridge, Mass.: Harvard University Press, 1978); Z. R. W. M. von Martels, ed., *Alchemy Revisited: Proceedings of the International Congress on the History of Alchemy at the University of Groningen, 17–19 April 1989* (Leiden: E. J. Brill, 1990); Owsei Temkin, *Galenism: Rise and Decline of a Medical Philosophy* (Ithaca, N.Y.: Cornell University Press, 1973).

Meissen works German porcelain factory, the first such establishment in Europe. Elector Augustus II of Saxony founded the Meissen works in 1710 after his jeweler and alchemist, Johann Friedrich Böttger, unraveled the chemical secrets of Chinese hard porcelains. The town of Meissen had an established ceramics industry, but the discovery nearby of deposits of kaolin clay, the type needed for fine porcelain, aided in the decision to locate the new factory at Meissen. The factory was owned by the Saxon elector, and since porcelains were highly prized in Europe, it served as a symbol of the elector's power and wealth.

Augustus II tried to prevent any transmission of the secrets of porcelain-making, but his efforts were subverted by German craftsmen, known as arcanists (from Latin: *arcanum*, secret), who learned the secret and sold both their knowledge and services to rival princes. As a result, rulers throughout Europe emulated the Meissen works by establishing their own state porcelain factories. However, Meissen dominated the European market until late in the 1760s when SÈVRES porcelains captured the European imagination.

At Meissen, the painter Johann Gregor Heroldt (1696–1765) developed a new style for porcelain products. He designed miniature figurines and pieces with rich colors. He also created CHINOISERIE pieces that provided a medium for his inventive imagination. The sculptor Johann Joachim Kändler succeeded Heroldt as a major designer at Meissen. His large porcelain figures, produced as adornments for the palace of Elector August, were especially renowned, but his sculptural table decorations and small figurines were also popular. In 1747 Kändler visited PARIS, where he was favorably impressed by the ROCOCO art of François BOUCHER and Antoine WATTEAU. He adapted their styles and pastoral subject matter to the medium of porcelain design. After 1770, Meissen lost its preeminent position in GERMANY to the products of a factory established in BERLIN by FREDERICK II (THE GREAT).

Mendelssohn, Moses (1729–1786) *German Jewish philosopher, literary critic, and translator*

Mendelssohn, a native of Dessau who was originally named Moses Dessau (until the mid-18th century, many Jews in GERMANY used the city in which they were born as a last name), was the son of Mendel Heymann, a Jewish scribe and teacher at the local Jewish school. As a boy, Mendelssohn was drawn to intellectual pursuits and, because his parents could not afford an extensive formal education, was largely self-educated. He not only taught himself German (the language spoken at home was Yiddish) but also mastered Latin, French, English, and Greek. In Dessau, he attended the school for Talmudic studies (Bet Hamidrasch), which provided basic training in the sacred books of the Jewish faith. Young Mendelssohn was especially beguiled by a work entitled *Guide for the Perplexed* by Moses Maimonides, a renowned Jewish philosopher of the 12th century.

In 1743, when Mendelssohn's teacher David Fränkel, the head rabbi of Dessau, was called to BERLIN to assume similar responsibilities in the Prussian capital, Mendelssohn followed him in order to continue his study of the Talmud. Until 1750, when he was hired to tutor the children of the silk merchant Isaac Bernhard, Mendelssohn suffered extremely difficult financial conditions. Bernhard was pleased with Mendelssohn's work and employed him in 1754 as head bookkeeper for his silk business. By 1762, Mendelssohn was in charge of the whole operation and, after Bernhard's death in 1768, continued to manage the firm jointly with Bernhard's widow.

In 1762, Mendelssohn married Fromet Gugenheim, the daughter of a poor Jewish merchant from Hamburg. This marriage was unusual because it was based on love, an idea that became popular only during the ENLIGHTENMENT. Most marriages of the era were still arranged by parents and aimed at securing both property and status for the contracting parties. Mendelssohn's close relationship with his wife was documented in their letters, later published under the title of *Brautbriefen* (Letters to his fiancée). In 1763, Mendelssohn and his wife received, through the good offices of the marquis d'ARGENS, the status of *Schutzjuden* (protected Jews), which assured them the privilege of living in PRUSSIA. They asked for the same status for their children, but FREDERICK II (THE GREAT) denied the petition; only after Mendelssohn's death in

Moses Mendelssohn. One of the leaders of Haskalah (Jewish Enlightenment), Mendelssohn called for religious toleration and supported efforts to integrate Jewish communities into general German culture and life. *(Courtesy New York Public Library)*

1786 did Frederick's successor grant the children this privilege.

In general, Mendelssohn's life served as a stunning example of upward mobility gained by intense work, talent, willpower, and self-sacrifice. During his life, Mendelssohn forged several deep and lasting friendships, especially with Gotthold Ephraim LESSING, Christoph Friedrich NICOLAI, and Thomas Abbt. Mendelssohn's rise, of course, was largely possible because of his enormous intellectual gifts. He became a renowned figure throughout Europe, one who was sometimes called "the German Socrates." He was also immortalized by Lessing as Nathan in the play NATHAN THE WISE. In all his activities, whether writing, translating, or publishing, four major areas of concern predominated: metaphysics, AESTHETICS, literary criticism, and Jewish studies.

Mendelssohn became an avid student of metaphysics and aesthetics after his youthful encounters with the philosophy of Gottfried Wilhelm LEIBNIZ and Christian WOLFF. His first major publication, the *Philosophischen Gespräche* (Philosophical discourses; 1755), dealt with themes proposed in Leibniz's metaphysics. It was followed by *Ueber die Empfindungen* (On sensation; 1755) and by *Pope ein Metaphysiker* (Pope, a metaphysician; 1755), the latter a critical study written conjointly with Lessing. All three works attempted to chart new terrain within the Leibnizian/Wolffian philosophical school. They modified the strict RATIONALISM of that school by giving some role to sensation in the production of knowledge. They also offered a scathing critique of the argument that "this is the best of all possible worlds," an idea that, in its simplistic form, Mendelssohn and Lessing correctly claimed had first been put forth in the *Essay on Man* by Alexander POPE. It was this idea that Voltaire satirized so mercilessly in his novel CANDIDE, although he incorrectly blamed Leibniz and Wolff for formulating it.

One of Mendelssohn's more striking successes in the area of philosophy was his prize essay entitled *Abhandlung über die Evidenz in Metaphysischen Wissenschaften* (Treatise on evidence in the metaphysical sciences; 1763). The BERLIN ACADEMY had set up an essay contest in which participants were to address the question whether or not metaphysics could ever achieve the degree of certainty found in mathematics. Many of the leading figures of the AUFKLÄRUNG (German Enlightenment) submitted essays, but Mendelssohn won the first prize (Immanuel KANT took second place). Departing from Wolff and Leibniz, Mendelssohn drew a strict line between metaphysics and mathematics, arguing that the subject matter covered by metaphysics and theology precluded the type of formal proof (*Evidenz*) found in mathematical demonstrations.

In his work on aesthetics, especially *Ueber die Empfindungen,* Mendelssohn also modified the Wolffian position. He attempted to mediate between an aesthetics based upon the concept of universal laws and norms for beauty and one that associated beauty with its effect on human feelings. In so doing, he postulated the existence of an active drive in human beings—the power of the soul (*Seelenkraft*)—that linked sensations of beauty with powerful emotional effects.

Mendelssohn, Nicolai, and Lessing were the most important publicists in Germany. Together they produced three great review journals: *Bibliothek der schönen Wissenschaften und der freyen Künste* (Library of great sciences and of free arts), *Briefe die Neueste Literatur betreffend* (Letters concerning the newest literature), and *Allgemeine deutsche Bibliothek* (General German library). To these influential journals Mendelssohn contributed many articles on art, aesthetics, and literature.

One of the most important of Mendelssohn's contributions was a review of the work *Betrachtung über die Bestimmung des Menschen* (Observation on the destiny of human beings; 1752), by the enlightened Protestant theologian Johann Joachim Spalding. In a single sentence Mendelssohn summed up the beliefs of the Enlightenment: "The destiny of a human being: to search for truth, to love beauty, to desire the good: to do the best." In a

similar vein, Mendelssohn composed the work *Phaedon oder über die Unsterblichkeit der Seele* (Phaedo, or on the immortality of the soul; 1767). This piece was modeled on Plato's dialogues of the same name and used a Platonic theme with modern variations. It began with a loose paraphrase of Plato and then proceeded to discuss questions raised by modern philosophers such as René DESCARTES, Benedict de SPINOZA, Leibniz, John LOCKE, and Wolff. Mendelssohn affirmed the immortality of the soul but was careful not to attach any dogmatic religious significance to the question. For him, as for Lessing, religion was more a matter of the heart and of human actions than of any specific dogmatic formulation.

Mendelssohn's interest in Jewish studies was based upon his desire both to purify and to preserve Judaism as a major religious force while, nevertheless, integrating it into the general movement of European and German culture. It is this aspect of Mendelssohn's activity that now, after the experience of the Holocaust, has become so controversial. Some critics decry what they consider the dangerous effects of assimilation, while others praise Mendelssohn's approach for its humanitarian inspiration. Whatever judgment is passed on Mendelssohn, it cannot be denied that his great contributions to religious studies make him one of the major figures of the Jewish Enlightenment (HASKALAH). In his investigations of the Jewish tradition, Mendelssohn followed a double path. First, he sought to expand the field of BIBLICAL CRITICISM and to spread knowledge of the Old Testament by providing translations and commentaries. Second, he offered modern interpretations of the Jewish faith, in a manner that was greatly influenced by the work of the 17th-century Jewish rationalist, Spinoza.

Mendelssohn initially translated the Pentateuch, the first five books of the Old Testament believed to have been written by Moses. Mendelssohn thought that his translations would help Jewish youth to learn a pure German. He then wrote a Hebrew analysis of the Pentateuch text and followed this with a German translation of the Psalms. Although influenced by Luther's German translation of the Bible, Mendelssohn's translations were much closer to the original text and its meaning. His works were harshly criticized by his orthodox co-religionists, yet soon became widely read within the German Jewish community. Just as Luther's Bible had introduced Protestants to literary German in the 16th and 17th centuries, so Mendelssohn's texts introduced Yiddish-speaking Jews to formal German.

In addition to these translation activities, Mendelssohn actively supported the causes of TOLERATION and emancipation for Jews. He persuaded Wilhelm Dohm to write his famous book on Jewish emancipation entitled *Ueber die bürgerliche Verbesserung der Juden* (On civic improvement for Jews; 1781) and convinced his friend Marcus Herz to translate the book *The Salvation of the Jews,* which had been written in ENGLAND in the 17th century by Rabbi Manasseh Ben Israel. As an introduction to Herz's translation, Mendelssohn wrote a sharp condemnation of religious intolerance.

Mendelssohn's attempts to interpret Judaism for the 18th century led him to compose two major works dealing with the general subject of RELIGION. The first, *Jerusalem oder über religiöse Macht und Judenthum* (Jerusalem, or on religious power and Judaism; 1783), addressed the question of the right of the state to regulate religion. Mendelssohn argued that the state had no right to impose religious conformity upon its citizens or to hamper any religious group in the peaceful exercise of its religion. But he also attacked any religious group that tried to enforce a specific interpretation of sacred texts on its adherents. No church should have the right to excommunicate or to punish because of theological dispute or difference within the congregation. In arguing not only for a religion of tolerance but for a religion of the heart and sentiment, based on the concept of brotherly love, Mendelssohn created one of the great religious tracts of the Enlightenment. Thinkers such as the marquis de MIRABEAU, Christian GARVE, Johann Gottfried HERDER, and Immanuel Kant all praised it; others, more desirous of protecting revealed religion, attacked it. Johann Georg HAMANN wrote a spirited critical response entitled *Golgatha und Scheblimini.*

Mendelssohn's second major religious work was the famous *Morgenstunden oder Vorlesungen über das Daseyn Gottes* (Morning hours, or lectures on the existence of God; 1785). The peculiar title of the book grew directly from Mendelssohn's personal experiences. He was suffering from an acute nerve problem, which forced him to curtail his activities almost totally. At the time he wrote this book, he was able to work at intellectual activities only during the morning hours; hence its title. The book reveals Mendelssohn struggling to mediate the conflicts between the thought of Spinoza and that of Leibniz. It first addresses the problem of proving God's existence. This question was closely tied to EPISTEMOLOGY and PSYCHOLOGY, because it required a statement about what kind of knowledge is possible for human minds.

Although centuries old, the problem of God's existence acquired renewed urgency during the Enlightenment, especially after David HUME once again revived negative arguments drawn from philosophical SKEPTICISM. Mendelssohn's proof offered a modification of the proof by design (the world is a highly complicated creation, hence it required an intelligent creator). According to Mendelssohn, everything real must have been first thought by a thinking substance or entity; therefore an infinite understanding must exist. *Morgenstunden* also discussed the omnipotence of God's relationship with the world (theodicy), addressing the question in terms of the goals toward which worldly existence is striving.

Mendelssohn never completed this work, because the last months of his life were taken up by the *Pantheismusstreit,* a controversy with Friedrich Heinrich JACOBI over Lessing's supposed Spinozism and pantheism.

Jacobi began this controversy with *Ueber die Lehre des Spinoza in Briefen an Herrn Moses Mendelssohn* (On Spinoza's teachings in letters to Mr. Moses Mendelssohn; 1785). The book contained the complete correspondence between Mendelssohn and Jacobi concerning Lessing and his alleged acceptance of Spinoza's system. At that time, Spinozism was equated with ATHEISM, and Jacobi thus was suggesting that Lessing had been an atheist. Jacobi had not asked Mendelssohn for permission to publish these letters and Mendelssohn was shocked and humiliated by their appearance, fearing that he would appear to be conspiring in an attempt to discredit his dearest friend. Mendelssohn quickly wrote an answer to Jacobi entitled *An die Freunden Lessings* (To the friends of Lessing), which argued that Lessing had incorporated aspects of Spinoza's thought into his own work without accepting the whole system. This was Mendelssohn's last work and he died before it could be printed.

Mendelssohn was one of the great figures of the German Enlightenment. Although often overshadowed in more recent accounts of the era by the figures of Kant, Lessing, Herder, and Goethe, he evolved an original philosophy and interpretation of religion based upon the fundamental assumptions of the high Enlightenment: toleration, respect for humanity, dedication to critical inquiry, and a deep-seated concern for human betterment.

See also JEWS AND JUDAISM; MATHEMATICS AND MECHANICS.

Further reading: Alexander Altmann, *Moses Mendelssohn: A Biographical Study* Littman Library of Jewish Civilization (Oxford: International Specialized Book Services, 1998); W. H. Bruford, *Germany in the Eighteenth Century: The Social Background of the Literary Revival* (Cambridge: Cambridge University Press, 1971); Moses Mendelssohn, *Moses Mendelssohn: Philosophical Writings* (Cambridge: Cambridge University Press, 1997); David Sorkin, *Moses Mendelssohn and the Religious Enlightenment* (Berkeley: University of California Press, 1996).

Mengs, Anton Raphael (1728–1779) *Bohemian painter, teacher, and theorist of aesthetics*

Mengs was born in Usti nad Labem (German: Aussig) near the 18th-century border between Bohemia and Saxony and now in the Czech Republic. Mengs received his initial training as a painter in his father's Dresden studio and in ROME (1741–44) at the studio of Marco Benefial. Although Mengs returned to Dresden in 1744, a stipend from August III, Elector of Saxony and King of POLAND, enabled him to go back to the "Eternal City" in 1746 for three years of additional training. During that time, he converted to Catholicism in order to marry an Italian woman named Margarita Guazzi. Mengs went back to Dresden one last time in 1749 and rose quickly to become the first painter for the Saxon court. Sometime in the 1750s (the exact year is a matter of debate), he left Saxony permanently, traveled again to Rome, became a member of the Accademia di San Luca, established a working relationship with the noted art critic Joachim WINCKELMANN, and began receiving important painting commissions including the fresco *Parnassus* painted as decoration for the Villa Albani. At the request of CHARLES III OF SPAIN, Mengs moved in 1761 to MADRID, where he worked for the next eight years. In 1771, back in Rome, he assumed the directorship of the Accademia di San Luca and worked in the Vatican for Pope CLEMENT XIV. Between 1773 and 1777, Mengs worked again in Madrid for Charles III and then returned to Rome for what were to be his last two years of life.

Mengs worked with Winckelmann in developing the theoretical aspects of NEOCLASSICISM, making both theoretical and practical contributions to the new aesthetic through his teaching, paintings, and publications. He left an important treatise, *Gedanken über die Schönheit* (Thoughts on beauty), which was published in 1762.

See also AESTHETICS.

mercantilism A term that was suggested by the enlightened political economist Adam SMITH to cover the economic theory and practices developed in the 16th and 17th centuries in Europe. Jean-Baptiste Colbert, controller general of finance in FRANCE during the reign of LOUIS XIV, was especially instrumental in formulating the policies that have come to symbolize the whole mercantilist enterprise. But, in fact, practices varied from one nation to another and no unified body of theory existed.

Behind the various mercantilist policies lay the basic assumption that the wealth of the world—defined as the amount of gold bullion and other precious metals that existed—was a fixed rather than flexible quantity. Given this perception of world economics, it was natural for various states to try to bring ever larger portions of gold and precious metals into their nations. The idea that wealth might be created by increasing the volume of trade or the circulation of currency had not yet been developed. Maintaining a favorable balance of trade was prescribed as one method for ensuring that large amounts of gold remained in a nation. Other approaches included the establishment of privileged trading companies, the foundation of state-run industries, and the exploitation of overseas colonies. The latter were treated primarily as potential sources of cheap raw materials and consumer markets; in other words, their purpose lay in helping to bring wealth to whatever European nation ruled their territories.

The development of mercantilist ideas occurred in conjunction with attempts to centralize power and to create unified states. This process began to quicken its pace in the 17th century with the emergence of monarchical ABSOLUTISM. Absolutist theories and policies recognized that state power and economic prosperity were strongly intertwined and insisted that economic activity should directly help the state. Thus, state regulation and state monopolies were encouraged. Free trade, entrepreneurial speculation, and competition were deemed undesirable and generally prohibited as much as possible. Crafts and skilled trades were highly regulated and often remained formally organized as guilds.

Mercantilism still tended to dominate economic policies in the 18th century, but it was giving way in ENGLAND and the UNITED PROVINCES OF THE NETHERLANDS to more liberal approaches, at least in domestic economic practices. Mercantilism continued, however, to dominate the policies of these nations toward their overseas colonies. It also provided some underpinnings for the economic theories of CAMERALISM and, therefore, continued to shape economic practices in 18th-century PRUSSIA and the HAPSBURG EMPIRE. French and English enlightened theorists—the PHYSIOCRATS and Adam Smith, for example—argued against various aspects of mercantilism in favor of LAISSEZ-FAIRE policies.

See also CAPITALISM; CHINA; COLONIALISM; EAST INDIA COMPANY; DESPOTISM, ENLIGHTENED; ECONOMICS; VOYAGES OF DISCOVERY; WEALTH OF NATIONS.

Mercier, Louis Sébastien (1740–1814) *French writer and revolutionary political figure*
Louis-Sébastien Mercier came from a family of artisans and received a secondary education at the Collège des Quatres Nations. As a youth, he began to frequent the group of enlightened intellectuals that met at Café Procope in PARIS. He believed strongly that writers could and should play a critical role in fighting against abuses of power.

Mercier earned public notoriety when he published *L'an 2440, rêve s'il en fut jamais* (The year 2440, a dream if ever there was one; 1770), a futuristic presentation of a socially just Paris ruled by a PHILOSOPHER KING. He then developed a theory of the educational value of THEATER that he outlined in his *Traité du théâtre* (Treatise on the theater; 1773). He wrote several plays among which were *Jenneval*, published in 1767 and first produced in 1781; *Le déserteur* (The deserter), published in 1770 and produced in 1782; and *Le faux ami* (The false friend; 1772). *La brouette du vinaigrier* (The vinegar merchant's wheelbarrow; 1775) and *La destruction de la ligue* (The destruction of the league; 1782) were not performed until after the end of the FRENCH REVOLUTION.

He began publishing the *Tableau de Paris* (Description of Paris) in 1781. The 12th volume appeared in

1788, completing what was a rich description of many facets of Parisian life, interwoven with critical, enlightened commentary. The *Tableau* was widely read and is recognized today for the important role it played in spreading enlightened ideas to the general reading public.

The *Tableau* was banned by French authorities in 1782 and, consequently, Mercier fled to GENEVA to protect himself from prosecution. There he met Jacques-Pierre Brissot, Etienne Clavière, and Honoré-Gabriel Riqueti, comte de Mirabeau, men who would play leading roles in the French Revolution. Mercier returned to Paris in 1786, more than ever committed to the cause of reform.

When the Revolution broke out in 1789, Mercier began assisting Jean-Louis Carra in publishing *Les annales patriotiques* (Patriotic annals). Although he sided with the ill-fated Girondin faction in the Revolution, he managed, on account of his long record of opposition to absolutism, to escape being victimized during the Terror. He retired from political life after Napoleon, whose ideas he opposed, acquired power.

Other works by Mercier included an attack on the AESTHETICS of 17th-century CLASSICISM entitled *Mon bonnet de nuit* (My nightcap; 1783); the political pamphlet *Notions claires sur les gouvernements* (Clear ideas on governments); and *De Jean-Jacques Rousseau considéré comme l'un des premiers auteurs de la Révolution* (Of Jean-Jacques Rousseau considered as one of the creators of the revolution; 1791). He also left three late works of great value as sources for historians of the Revolution. These were *Le nouveau Paris* (New Paris; 1798); *Néologie ou vocabulaire des mots nouveaux, à renouveler ou pris dans les acceptions nouvelles* (Neology or vocabulary of new words, revived or given new meanings; 1801); and *Mon dictionnaire* (My dictionary; an incomplete work of which one volume appeared in 1802).

Mercier de la Rivière, Paul-Pierre (ca. 1720–ca. 1793–94) *French Physiocrat*

The son of a wealthy financier, Mercier de la Rivière began his career by purchasing an office in the Parlement of Paris. Shortly afterward, he obtained an appointment as royal superintendent in the French island colony of Martinique. Upon his return to France, he began to study the theories of François QUESNAY and became a Physiocrat. Mercier de la Rivière's book, *L'ordre naturel et essentiel des sociétés politiques* (The natural and essential order of political societies), published in 1767, attracted wide response. It spelled out a political philosophy of legal, enlightened despotism (see DESPOTISM, ENLIGHTENED) based on certain conceptions of NATURAL LAW, the theory of ABSOLUTISM, and ideals of humanitarianism. Its practical proposals resembled those contained in the plan of Anne-Robert-Jacques TURGOT and in other published writings of PHYSIOCRATS.

Prince Dmitry Golitsyn, the Russian ambassador in PARIS, considered Mercier de la Rivière's book far superior even to MONTESQUIEU's *Esprit des lois* (SPIRIT OF LAWS). But VOLTAIRE, Gabriel Bonnot de Mably, and Ferdinando GALIANI criticized its contents and ridiculed its writer. Golitsyn's praise of Mercier de la Rivière resulted in his receiving an invitation from CATHERINE II (THE GREAT) to visit Russia. She believed that Mercier de la Rivière could assist her in reforming the Russian system, especially since his book spelled out a theory of enlightened despotism. Mercier de la Rivière accepted the invitation, but dallied in BERLIN before proceeding to Russia. His tardiness complicated Catherine's plans, and Mercier de la Rivière had to face her wrath. He returned to Paris having accomplished little.

Disgruntled by the experience and wary of public criticism of his work, Mercier de la Rivière withdrew into private life. Subsequently, he issued only one public statement, a 1789 letter addressed to the National Assembly's committee on finance. The document warned against the ills that revolution could bring and proposed some means for avoiding it.

Mersenne, Marin (1588–1648) *French mathematician, physicist, music theorist, and theologian*

Marin Mersenne, or Father Mersenne as he was called by most people, was one of the major early supporters of Galileo GALILEI and of the scientific shifts often called the SCIENTIFIC REVOLUTION. Mersenne, a devout Catholic monk, lived in the Minim, monastery in PARIS just behind the Pavillion de la Reine on the Place Royale (Place des Vosges since the French Revolution). He made his early literary career as a Catholic polemicist, and his exaggerated claims about the threat of ATHEISM in the Paris of the 1620s earned him the ridicule of VOLTAIRE over a century later.

Mersenne gradually became committed to the process of placing the natural sciences on a mathematical basis. He believed that mathematics provided the key for solving the thorny conflicts between SCIENCE and orthodox Catholic THEOLOGY. He also supported the cause of experimentation as a method for making new discoveries and generally supported the new MECHANICAL PHILOSOPHY that arose simultaneously with the use of mathematical equations to describe physical laws. Furthermore, he served as a conduit for the international European scientific and intellectual community, forwarding correspondence, posing problems, and encouraging debates between leading intellectuals of his time. Mersenne even proposed the creation of an academy where intellectuals could meet to discuss and solve scientific questions. The idea was noted but not institutionalized in France until 1666, 18 years after Mersenne's death.

Mersenne played a significant role in fostering the publications of many scientists. Galileo Galilei and René

DESCARTES are only the most famous individuals who received the Minim monk's assistance. Mersenne was optimally placed in his Paris monastery to provide such services. He was personally acquainted with prominent officeholders in the royal administration and understood the possibilities as well as limits for publishing in the world of 17th century French censorship.

Besides these general contributions, Mersenne is remembered for having discovered an acoustic law regarding string vibrations (Mersenne's Law) and for the Mersenne prime numbers. He left a monumental treatise of three volumes, the *Harmonie universelle* (Universal harmony; 1636); three popularizations published in 1634 that aimed at introducing the French reading public to the new vision of science and its relation to other disciplines, entitled *Les questions inouyes* (Extraordinary questions), *Les questions harmoniques* (Questions about harmony), and *Les questions théologiques, physiques, morales, et mathématiques* (Theological, physical, moral, and mathematical questions); *Les mécaniques de Galilée* (The mechanics of Galileo), a 1634 transcription of Galileo's work on mechanics; and *Les nouvelles pensées de Galilée* (New thoughts of Galileo; 1639), a translation and paraphrase of the 1638 Elzevier edition of Galileo's *Discourses and Demonstrations Concerning Two New Sciences*.

See also MATHEMATICS AND MECHANICS.

Mesmer, Franz Anton (1734–1815) *German physician who invented the method of magnetic healing*

Born in a village of Swabia (southwestern GERMANY), Mesmer was the son of a forester in the service of the archbishop of Constance. Young Mesmer studied first with the JESUITS in Dillingen, Bavaria, and then entered the University of Ingolstadt. In 1759, he matriculated at the University of VIENNA in the faculty of law. Mesmer soon transferred to MEDICINE, receiving a doctorate in 1766. He was accepted as a faculty member at the University of Vienna.

Mesmer began thinking about animal magnetism in his doctoral thesis, *Dissertatio physico-medica de planetarum influxu* (Medical-physical dissertation on planetary influences). First put forth by Jan Baptista van Helmont (1577–1644), the theory of animal magnetism proposed that a magnetic fluid flows through the bodies of living beings. Mesmer thought that such a magnetic fluid or spirit would perhaps explain the influence of the stars on people.

As Mesmer developed his ideas, he arrived at the conclusion that an active, effective principle exists throughout the universe that acts like electricity or magnetism. In the body, this principle acted on the vital fluids according to the laws of magnetism.

Mesmer began experimenting with metal magnets on patients and discovered how to induce hypnotic trances.

In 1774, he cured a person suffering from what today would be called psychoneurosis. He eventually abandoned the use of magnets, having discovered that he could produce the same effects on patients simply with his presence and words.

Mesmer enjoyed great success in Vienna. He was married to a wealthy woman and thus could afford a lifestyle of some leisure. He was particularly fond of music and was a friend of Wolfgang Amadeus MOZART. In fact, the first production of Mozart's opera *Bastien und Bastienne* occurred in Mesmer's garden. Mozart also incorporated references to Mesmer in his later opera *COSÌ FAN TUTTE*.

In Vienna, Mesmer developed a theatrical style for presenting his cures that offended the medical establishment. Eventually, animosity became so great that Mesmer decided, in 1778, to move to PARIS.

In Paris, Mesmer enjoyed great popularity but again earned the criticism of established physicians. Mesmerism became a kind of cause celebre, generating many pamphlets and testimonials to its powers. Disciples of Mesmer established a secret society modeled on the FREEMASONS called the Société de l'Harmonie Universelle (Society of Universal Harmony) with chapters in most major French cities.

Mesmer contributed to printed debates about animal magnetism with two pamphlets: *Mémoire sur la découverte du magnétisme animal* (Memoir on the discovery of animal magnetism; 1779) and *Précis historique des faits rélatifs au magnétisme animal* (Historical summary of the facts relative to animal magnetism; 1781).

The popularity of this new form of medical cure alarmed both the medical establishment and the French government. A commission whose members included Antoine LAVOISIER and Benjamin FRANKLIN was appointed to investigate mesmerism. It concluded that Mesmer's magnetic fluid did not exist. Subsequently, Mesmer's popularity in France began to decline, and he decided to move to SWITZERLAND, where he spent his last 30 years. His medical approaches remained influential well into the 19th century in Germany, where people such as the philosopher Georg Wilhelm Friedrich Hegel, the theologian and philosopher Friedrich Ernst Daniel Schleiermacher, and the philologist Wilhelm von HUMBOLDT all turned to practitioners of mesmerism for care.

However unorthodox his practices and theatrical his cures, Mesmer's medicine encompassed a theory of disease that was respected in some enlightened circles of medical practice. He believed that disease resulted from the obstruction of the free flow of magnetic fluid through the body. The hypnotic cure broke through the obstruction, restoring circulation and harmony to the body. Much of the opposition to Mesmer seems to have stemmed from his flamboyant style. But, to some extent, he was also opposed by physicians who objected to the apparent reintroduction of MAGIC into medicine. Thus, Mesmer was at once a victim of the empirical scientific spirit of the ENLIGHTENMENT and, at the same time, a notable example of the fascination for the irrational that characterized the later, radical phases of that intellectual era.

Methodism Protestant sect founded in 18th-century ENGLAND by John WESLEY. It emerged from Wesley's personal struggle to achieve an inner sense of peace and salvation. Wesley did not intend to found a separate Protestant sect, but the steady hostility of Anglican authorities to his activities finally caused a break in 1784.

The original Holy Club, derisively called the Methodist Club by its critics, was founded at Oxford University by Charles WESLEY, John Wesley's younger brother. John Wesley joined the club in 1729 and quickly assumed its leadership. Club members believed that prayer, study, and the performance of good works were the most reliable means of obtaining salvation. They also engaged in various charitable activities such as teaching LITERACY and distributing food and clothing in prisons and poorhouses.

The Holy Club was one source of Methodism; the Moravian Brethren, under whose influence John Wesley had a conversion experience, provided the second source. This religious group was an outgrowth of German PIETISM and stressed that salvation is gained in the inner private relationship between a person and God rather than by means of external religious practices or good work.

Wesley combined these two strands to create a set of religious practices based on emotional expression or ENTHUSIASM, in which good works nevertheless provide an estimate of the virtue of a person. Methodist worship services were marked by emotional outpourings in the form of sobbing, weeping, or physical convulsions. The message of salvation was experienced in the heart rather than discovered through the use of the rational mind.

Methodism developed into a tightly controlled, hierarchical, and autocratic organization. Basic membership units called classes received a leader appointed by Wesley, whose job consisted of monitoring the behavior and religious health of his flock. Classes were joined into larger units called bands, and bands were grouped into societies. Over the entire organization, Wesley ruled with such tight control that his detractors called him Pope John.

Methodism aimed at reforming the lives of working-class people by instilling the values of sobriety (the campaign against alcoholism was fueled by Methodism), hard work, and biblical literacy. The organization was wedded to political conservatism, hoping to assist workers in accepting the hardships entailed by the changes of the INDUSTRIAL REVOLUTION rather than encouraging them to protest against those hardships. Wesley and his associates believed that the best way to transform society was to change the behavior of individuals, and some scholars believe that this Methodist attitude helped to produce a notable lack of revolutionary fervor in late-18th-century England.

Methodism was abhorred by enlightened persons wedded to social and political reform or to the ideals of PROGRESS and social EQUALITY. It was also a primary target in the enlightened criticisms of enthusiasm. Yet Methodism was also itself a product of the ENLIGHTENMENT, for it expressed in religious terms the same criticism of REASON that was contained in the widespread secular culture of SENSIBILITY. Methodism, in fact, was one of the great creations of the Enlightenment and clearly demonstrates one pole of the enlightened dialectic between reason and feeling.

See also RELIGION.

Michaelis, Johann David (1717–1791) *German biblical scholar and philologist*
Johann David Michaelis's work on languages, especially his contributions to the knowledge and understanding of Hebrew, were significant for subsequent philologists, especially Johann Gottfried HERDER.

Johann David Michaelis was born in the Saxon city of Halle, which was the center of the Pietist movement. Johann David grew up in the Pietist milieu. His father, Christian Benedikt Michaelis (1680–1764), was a professor at the University of HALLE and schooled the young Johann David in oriental languages. His great-uncle, Johann Heinrich Michaelis (1668–1738), was the director of the Collegium Orientale Theologicum, a body devoted to the study of oriental languages in connection with biblical exegesis, and had produced an annotated edition of the Bible in Hebrew.

Johann David attended the University of Halle, adding to his list of influences the philosopher Sigmund Jakob Baumgarten, who introduced his pupil to the ideas of Christian WOLFF. Michaelis's dissertation looked at the divine origins and meaning of the diacritical vowel marks in ancient Hebrew, a work he later recanted. He also visited ENGLAND (1741–42), where he studied Hebrew poetry and translated and annotated Robert Lowth's *De saecra poesi hebraeorum* while at Oxford University.

In 1745, Michaelis joined the philosophical faculty at the University of GÖTTINGEN, the intellectual center of German-speaking Europe at the time, where he rose quickly through the ranks to become secretary of the Academy of Sciences (Gesellschaft der Wissenschaften) and editor of the Göttingen *Anzeigen von Gelehrten Sachen* (News of learned matters), a position he held from 1753 until 1770. His study of Mosaic law (1777; English translation 1814), his annotated German translation of the Bible (1792), and his series of six supplemental linguistic essays that appeared as appendixes to the Hebrew dictionary (*Suppl. ad Lexicon hebraicum*; 1784–92), published in

Göttingen, occupied him during his later years. His autobiography appeared in 1793, two years after his death in Göttingen at the age of 74.

See also BIBLICAL CRITICISM; PIETISM.

microscope Scientific instrument that uses a system of ground optical lenses to enlarge objects under observation. The microscope was invented about 1624, but the precise date is uncertain. Francesco Stelluti published the first known microscopic observations, made with an instrument capable of enlarging objects only five times. Microscope technology developed steadily during the 17th century, so that, toward the end of the century, Antoni van LEEUWENHOEK could obtain magnifications equivalent to 300 times original size.

Major early discoveries made with the microscope include Robert Hooke's observation of cells in plants; van Leeuwenhoek's discovery of minute, one-celled organisms, bacteria, and human sperm (all called *animalcula*); and his discovery of corpuscles. Another important contribution was made by Marcello Malphigi, who observed the development of embryos through his microscope. Suddenly, the realm of creation had grown dramatically, just as it had when Galileo GALILEI pointed his crude TELESCOPE toward the heavens. But if the telescope had vastly extended the celestial world, the microscope showed that the early realm contained vast numbers of minute objects engaged in various forms of activity.

The discoveries made with this technology not only shocked and excited Europeans but also helped to determine the outlines of several scientific debates during the ENLIGHTENMENT. Most urgent of all was the matter of classifying the new objects that could be observed through a microscope. Were the objects seen in a drop of water, for example, plants, animals, or something in between the two categories? If they were neither plants nor animals but rather intermediate beings, it seemed that the theory of the GREAT CHAIN OF BEING might have more validity. The microscope especially intensified investigations into processes of GENERATION, pitting adherents of PREFORMATION THEORY against champions of EPIGENESIS. The observation of sperm stimulated the creation of ANIMALCULISM, a preformation theory that made the male sperm the carrier of the preformed seeds of new life. Microscopic observations also raised questions about the fixity of the species, for they revealed embryos going through developmental phases that seemed to mimic other species. The resolution of problems and debates in these realms, however, had to wait until the 19th century, when new advances in microscopic technology allowed even more refined observations.

See also BIOLOGY; CLASSIFICATION; SCIENCE; TECHNOLOGY AND INSTRUMENTATION.

midwifery The act of assisting at childbirth. Midwifery, as old as humankind itself, underwent drastic changes and weathered challenges during the 18th century. Whereas the primary attacks against midwives before the 18th century had come in the form of accusations of witchcraft, 18th-century debates about midwifery revolved around gender and professional issues. The 18th century saw the professionalization of obstetrics as both a profession and a field of study.

The introduction and increasingly widespread use of forceps, which began in ENGLAND around 1700, meant a fundamental change in the way childbirth occurred. Forceps were probably invented sometime during the last decades of the 17th century by Peter Chamberlen, surgeon to the queen. Because only men could legally use surgical instruments, a debate about man-midwifery ensued during the mid-18th century. Many of the leading physicians and midwives of the period weighed in, with Chamberlen's sons leading the push for forceps and the Dutch man-midwife Henrik van Deventer declaring the instrument unnecessary.

The forceps issue was one aspect of a larger debate over the inroads men had made into the practice of midwifery. Proponents of men being present during childbirth argued that female midwives should have recourse to physicians if necessary and that the assistance of lifesaving devices such as forceps should be available to mothers during delivery. Those against man-midwives asserted that forceps were dangerous and used too frequently and that man-midwifery transgressed proper social boundaries.

Midwives during the 18th century also undertook to educate women about childbirth. Madame du COUDRAY toured France extensively, lecturing audiences composed primarily of midwives and women, though also containing men, on the subject. For many people living outside large population centers, midwives were the only help available during childbirth. Documents such as the diary of American midwife Martha Ballard, which covers the years 1785 to 1812, underscore how important midwives continued to be for women in countless small communities in Europe and North America during the 18th century.

See also WOMEN AND THE ENLIGHTENMENT.

Further reading: Laurel Thatcher Ulrich, *A Midwife's Tale: The Life of Martha Ballard* (New York: Vintage Books, 1991); Adrian Wilson, *The Making of Man-Midwifery: Childbirth in England, 1660–1770* (Cambridge, Mass.: Harvard University Press, 1995).

Milan Northern Italian city lying on the Lombard plain; capital of the duchy of Milan. Milan became part of the Roman Republic in 194 B.C. A Christian Church was founded in the city in the second century A.D. The city served as a capital of one of the four major regions of the Roman Empire. In 313, Emperor Constantine I recognized the independence of the Milanese Catholic Church.

The city served as capital of the Western Roman Empire from A.D. 354 to 404. Its importance in Christendom was magnified during the years when Bishop Ambrose (374–97) was archbishop of Milan.

After the disintegration of the Roman Empire, Milan was ruled by various tribes, including the Lombard tribe after which the surrounding region, Lombardy, is named. During the Middle Ages, Milan became part of the HOLY ROMAN EMPIRE. It acquired its independence in 1183, when the Peace of Constance recognized several Italian cities (communes) as free cities. Like other Italian cities, Milan was torn in the 13th and 14th centuries by familial conflict between Guelfs and Ghibellines. The Ghibelline Visconti family eventually assumed control of the city. During the 15th century, however, the Sforza family gained control. They were active arts patrons and supported both Leonardo da Vinci and Donato Bramante.

Milan is located in a strategically sensitive spot. The Lombard plain lies just south of Alpine passes into SWITZERLAND. These passes, and the valleys in Switzerland to which they lead, provide the only convenient connections between ITALY and AUSTRIA. The Hapsburg emperors in SPAIN and the Holy Roman Empire believed that controlling the duchy of Milan was essential for their prosperity and security. The Spanish Hapsburgs conquered the region in the 16th century (1535) and controlled it until 1713, when it passed to the Austrian branch of the Hapsburg family. Except during the years of Napoleon's rule (1796–1814), the region remained an Austrian Hapsburg territory until 1859. Thus during the ENLIGHTENMENT, Milan was controlled by the Austrian Hapsburgs and was subjected to some state-directed reform during the reigns of MARIA THERESA and her son JOSEPH II.

The city was a major art and music center during the 18th century with wealthy private patrons anxious to sponsor the creation of new works. The Hapsburg ruler and their ministers such as Wenzel von KAUNITZ, true to the ideals of enlightened despotism (see DESPOTISM, ENLIGHTENED), also provided substantial public support for the arts.

In the world of MUSIC, both OPERA and orchestra concerts thrived. The Regio Ducal Teatro opened in 1717 as an opera center. When it burned down in 1776, a new opera house, the Teatro alla Scala, was built and opened its doors to 1778. Orchestra concerts had large and enthusiastic audiences. In 1758, the Accademia Filarmonica, a large orchestra with stringent entrance tests, was formed. Milan was also home to the composer Giovanni Battista Sammartini and to the music theorist Giovanni Battista Martini (known as Padre Martini). Both men attracted students—Christoph Willibald GLUCK and Johann Christian BACH, for example—from all over Europe and thus helped to make Italian compositional style a major influence in 18th-century music.

During the 18th century, Milan began to assume new architectural character. ROCOCO churches and palaces such as Santa Maria della Sanità (1708), San Francesco di Paola (1728), and the Palazzo Trivalzio (1707–13) were joined later in the century by neoclassical buildings such as the Palazzo Belgioioso (1770) and the Villa Reale (1790–96). The city also acquired large public gardens in 1782.

Under the Austrian Hapsburgs, Milan experienced a general broadening of the scope of its culture. The city became a thriving intellectual center and produced some central figures of the Italian Enlightenment. Among them were Cesare BECCARIA, whose book *ESSAY ON CRIMES AND PUNISHMENTS* stimulated discussions about penal code reform throughout Europe; Pietro VERRI and his brother Alessandro VERRI, who were major supporters of Beccaria; and the historian Lodovico MURATORI, who helped to transform the discipline of HISTORY.

See also ILLUMINISTI; ITALY; NEOCLASSICISM.

Millar, John (1735–1801) *Scottish historian and political theorist*

Millar was a lawyer who taught courses on law at Glasgow University during the second half of the 18th century. He was a close friend of David HUME, Lord Kames, and, especially, Adam SMITH, whose chair he assumed after Smith left Glasgow. Millar's special interests lay in the HISTORY of law and of constitutions. He earned prominence during the ENLIGHTENMENT for two publications: *The Origin of the Distinction of Ranks* (1771) and *Historical View of the English Government* (1787). He was, in fact, one of the outstanding figures of the Enlightenment in SCOTLAND.

Millar used an interpretative scheme, based on natural history, which had been developed by the major Scottish thinkers of the Enlightenment. Histories in this style tended to treat events of the past as illustrations of specific stages in human development, which were believed to characterize development in all societies. Millar emphasized the relationships among historical events, economic organization, and technological expertise. His treatment is typical of the Scottish approach to history and was reflected also in the contextual histories written by German *Aufklärer* (enlightened thinkers).

In all of them society is seen as a human rather than divine construction in which people, driven by certain passions, respond to environmental and social pressures by creating a network of rights and duties. Unlike NATURAL LAW theorists, the Scots assumed that humans were by nature social animals, and they treated the family as the primary social unit lying at the foundation of all societies.

Millar accepted these propositions, but he interpreted them in a unique manner. For him the ruling human passion was sexual attraction, a passion after which all other social passions (emotions) were patterned. However, he refused to draw a distinction between males and females. Both sexes, in his interpretation, shared the same feelings, such as the desire to please the other or the tendency to love their offspring. Differences between the sexes arose because of certain conditions rooted in the necessities of existing in a harsh environment. Forms of family organization, with their specific masculine and feminine roles were, Millar claimed, creations of human history rather than divinely preordained structures. Furthermore, a general tendency had existed in earlier societies to subjugate women.

Because of the centrality of male-female relations in establishing social structure and determining rights and duties, Millar spent over 30 percent of the *Origin of the Distinction of Ranks* on the topic "The Condition of Women." He followed this with chapters about the jurisdiction of fathers, the authority of the chief in the tribe, the authority of the sovereign, changes in government produced by changes in the arts, and masters and slaves. In these sections, Millar argued that commercial societies, as described by Smith, offered women the opportunity to become liberated by developing their talents and abilities. This opportunity contrasted noticeably with the constraints that were placed on women in feudal and primitive societies.

At the same time, Millar warned that any commercial society that generated undue opulence and distinctions based on economic inequality would bring about a return to the subjugation of women. Here, he built his theory on Hume's concept of flux and reflux in history, reflecting the Enlightenment's awareness that human PROGRESS was possible but not automatic. A return to barbarism was also always possible. Such a return would be worse than the first appearance because of the increased technical powers available to humans. Millar's analysis of gender relations and their origins was extremely progressive. In fact, he can be considered one of the most important writers on the condition of women of the period. His treatment still bears reading today.

millenarianism Religious belief that salvation will follow the approaching end of the world and the creation of an ideal society to replace it. Millenarianism in one form or another has existed throughout the history of Christianity. In ENGLAND, the government of Oliver Cromwell followed millenarian policies in the mid-17th century. His administration was motivated in no small part by the drive, evidenced in policies such as his suppression of THEATER, to purify his nation and the wider world through Protestant practices and so prepare the world for the second coming of Christ. The poet John Milton served under Cromwell's administration and was a staunch supporter of this idea, which ultimately cost him his freedom when Cromwell's government fell and Charles II returned from exile in FRANCE. Millenarianism also played an important role in colonial North America, as preachers such as George WHITEFIELD and Jonathan EDWARDS inspired a wave of religious conversions with their often fiery predictions of the world's end. This trend reached its height between 1720 and 1740 with the religious revival known as the GREAT AWAKENING.

Millenarian movements frequently show a desire to aid the process of apocalyptic salvation through direct action in the world. Millenarianist philosophy was not confined to religious groups, however. The eminent scientist and philosopher Isaac NEWTON was occupied with millenarian themes over the course of his life. Influenced by such writers as the medieval Jewish theologian Maimonides, Newton's own work connected religious teachings to science. His mechanistic system, for example, was based on a tinkerer God, who intervened in his creation occasionally to keep it moving. There was, therefore, nothing incompatible in believing both that the universe followed God's rules and that God would change them one day, nor was it unreasonable to seek answers to physical questions in Scripture. For that reason, Newton researched the dimensions of the temple of Solomon's construction, believing they held the key to revealing the universal principles God had created. This mixture of mechanism with millenarianism became the foundation for an alliance between millenarian preachers such as Thomas Tenison and John TILLOTSON with Newtonian science.

Millenarianism also made its presence felt within early modern Judaism. The Sabbatean movement, a Jewish millenarianism, swept through Europe from the 17th into the 19th century. It asserted that the Messiah had finally come in the figure of the Levantine Jew Sabbatai Zevi, although Zevi was later forcibly converted to Islam. There is no intrinsic connection between messianism and millenarianism, but one of Zevi's followers, Nathan of Gaza, spread the message that Zevi had come to "repair" the world and free the Jews. The movement extended into the 18th century, when Jacob Frank, a Polish Jew who later settled in GERMANY, claimed to be the second coming of Zevi. With his death in 1791, however, the movement began to decline.

Millenarian beliefs also informed the philosophy of the FRENCH REVOLUTION. Many people saw the overturning of the old regime as a sign of the second coming of Jesus Christ and justified the revolution's excesses as part of the tribulations expected prior to Christ's return. One of the most influential supporters of these ideas was the radical Suzette Labrousse, who believed so fervently in the religious aura of the revolution that she attempted to gain an audience with the pope in 1792 to convince him of the truth; she became known as the "Prophetess of Perigord." Her beliefs continued afterward in groups such as the Masonically based Avignon Society.

Millenarianism proved to be a broad European movement, extending to Germany, the Netherlands, and across eastern Europe. By the 20th century, millenarianism was taken up by some revolutionary movements in Russia.

See also JEWS AND JUDAISM.

Further reading: James E. Force and Richard H. Popkin, eds., *Essays on the Context, Nature, and Influence of Isaac Newton's Theology* (Boston: Kluwer Academic, 1990); Jack Fruchtman, Jr., *The Apocalyptic Politics of Richard Price and Joseph Priestley: A Study in Late Eighteenth-Century English Republican Millenianism* (Philadelphia: American Philosophical Society, 1983); Hillel Schwartz, *Knaves, Fools, Madmen, and that Subtile Effluvium: A Study of the Opposition to the French Prophets in England, 1706–1710* (Gainesville, Fla.: University of Florida Monographs, 1978).

Mirabeau, Victor de Riqueti, marquis de (1715–1789)
French Physiocrat and writer

Mirabeau's father forced him to pursue a career in the military. The young man entered the French army at the age of 14, rose to become a captain, and received military honors in 1743. Shortly after his father's death, however, he resigned his position and moved to PARIS, intent on obtaining a position in the central royal administration.

Mirabeau became a follower of François QUESNAY and began publishing books on the theories of the PHYSIOCRATS. He also produced works critical of the regime of LOUIS XV. One of them, the *Théorie de l'impôt* (Theory of taxation; 1760), earned him a five-day sojourn in prison and immediately made him a celebrity. Mirabeau acquired the nickname "l'ami des hommes" (the friend of humankind), in reference to his book *Ami des hommes, ou traité de la population* (Friend of humankind, or treatise of population; 1756–58), which contained impassioned humanitarian arguments. With his family, however, Mirabeau patterned his actions after his father's autocratic approach. He fought interminable legal battles with his estranged wife and had his son, Honoré-Gabriel Riqueti, comte de Mirabeau, who had displeased him with his behavior, sent to jail by means of a *lettre de cachet* (sealed royal order). The marquis de Mirabeau died on July 13, 1789, one day before the fall of the Bastille.

Ami des hommes was Mirabeau's most important work. It was immensely popular in ENGLAND and appeared in Italian translation in 1784. The *Économiques* (Economics; 1769), a work in which Mirabeau presented Physiocratic theories, was dedicated to Leopold II, the enlightened Hapsburg ruler of Tuscany. Like many intellectuals of the ENLIGHTENMENT, Mirabeau edited periodicals: *Journal de l'agriculture, du commerce et des finances* (Journal of agriculture, commerce, and finance) and *Éphérémides du citoyen, ou chronique de l'esprit national et bibliothèque raisonée des sciences* (Almanac of the citizen, or chronicle of the national spirit and rational library of the sciences), published jointly with Pierre-Samuel DUPONT DE NEMOURS. Altogether, Mirabeau's writings occupy 20 volumes.

See also ANCIEN RÉGIME; *LETTRES DE CACHET*.

Victor de Riqueti, marquis de Mirabeau. *(Courtesy New York Public Library)*

Mississippi Bubble
Name signifying the French financial speculation crisis of 1720 that was propelled by the schemes of John LAW. It parallels the British SOUTH SEA BUBBLE crisis in many respects.

With the death of LOUIS XIV in 1715, the government of France fell to Philippe d'Orléans, who served as regent until LOUIS XV reached the age of majority. Louis XIV left his state in fiscal disarray. The needs of government had far outgrown the capacity to collect taxes under the system of privilege that dominated the ANCIEN RÉGIME. Attempts by finance ministers under Louis XIV to tax the clergy and nobility on an equal basis with the Third Estate (bourgeoisie) and peasantry had met with stiff opposition. Efforts to repudiate royal debts by forcing French financiers to absorb losses also had accomplished little.

Under these conditions, Philippe d'Orléans was enticed by the ideas of the Scotsman John Law, who proposed a series of major financial reforms. Law believed that the use of credit, based on the constant circulation of money, would resolve the financial impasse. Having earned a solid reputation with a private bank, opened in 1716, John Law was able to obtain the trade monopoly with the North American colony of Louisiana and to establish the Company of the West (popularly called *le Mississippi*). He expanded the trade monopoly by acquiring similar rights in the West Indies and Canada. In the meantime, his bank became a royal institution, and in 1720 Law became the controller general of France.

To finance the Company of the West, Law resorted to issuing paper money from the bank and to advertising the great financial opportunities of Louisiana. In a bid to undercut the French tax-farming system (system of tax collection by private persons who guaranteed that they would deliver certain sums to the treasury but were free to collect whatever else they could for private gain) and the power of the tax-farming financiers, Law assumed the royal debt and offered to pay off private holders of the national debt with shares in the Company of the West. French investors rushed to take advantage of the situation, thereby provoking a steep rise in the paper value of Company of the West stock. The scheme collapsed when some key investors grew wary and pulled out. In October 1720 the whole Law system collapsed, paper money became worthless, and Law fled to LONDON. The regent, Philippe d'Orléans, was badly discredited by the collapse of the Mississippi Bubble and the Law system. He finally resigned in 1723, leaving the government in the hands of Louis XV's powerful minister, Cardinal Fleury.

In the aftermath of the collapse, all of John Law's fiscal reforms disappeared. The event demonstrated the intransigence of the French fiscal system to change and pointed out the risks associated with credit and central banking. But the stimulus the adventure had supplied for trade was not entirely lost, and a new group of wealthy individuals arose from the collapse. In this sense, the Mississippi Bubble and Law's system effected some change in French social and economic structures.

Moderns *See* QUARREL BETWEEN THE ANCIENTS AND THE MODERNS.

monarchs, enlightened Term used by historians to describe the European rulers of the 18th century whose reforms and general policies were guided by their understanding of the RATIONALISM, humanitarianism, utilitarianism, and liberalism of the ENLIGHTENMENT. The term *enlightened monarch* appears in discussions of enlightened ABSOLUTISM and enlightened despotism (see DESPOTISM, ENLIGHTENED). The list of monarchs who can be placed in this category is long. It includes CHARLES III OF SPAIN and Naples, Leopold of Tuscany, LOUIS XV of FRANCE, and Stanislaw PONIATOWSKI of POLAND. Certain kings were assisted by enlightened ministers who functioned nearly as monarchs: Bernardo TANUCCI of the KINGDOM OF THE TWO SICILIES, Johann Friedrich STRUENSEE of DENMARK, and the marquês de POMBAL of PORTUGAL stand out particularly clearly in this respect. If the concept of enlightened monarchy is loosely defined, it can be expanded to include the enlightened despots of the period: CATHERINE II (THE GREAT) of Russia, FREDER-

"John Law Crowned by Folly," a Dutch caricature, 1721. John Law's financial schemes fueled a wave of speculation and a collapse that ultimately helped to deepen the financial crises faced by the French Crown. *(Courtesy New York Public Library)*

ICK II (THE GREAT) OF PRUSSIA, GUSTAV III OF SWEDEN, and JOSEPH II OF AUSTRIA.

See also ABSOLUTISM.

Monro, Alexander (Secundus) (1733–1817) *Scottish anatomist and professor at the University of Edinburgh*
Alexander Monro (Secundus) followed his father, Alexander Monro (Primus), into the anatomy profession. At the age of 21 (1754), Monro Secundus became a joint professor of anatomy with his father at the University of EDINBURGH. The appointment had been arranged by Monro Primus. Monro Secundus obtained his medical degree from the university in 1755. His thesis, *De testibus et semine in variis animalibus* (On the testes and seminiferous tubules in various animals), contained some original research (unusual for the era) on the comparative anatomy of male reproductive organs.

Shortly after graduation, Monro Secundus went to LONDON, where he attended the lectures of William

HUNTER (a former student of his father's) in comparative anatomy. He departed from London in 1757 on a GRAND TOUR of the northern European countries. During his travels (1757–58), he visited PARIS, BERLIN, and Leiden, meeting prominent anatomists and attending medical lectures or dissections. In 1758 Monro Primus became ill and Monro Secundus returned to Edinburgh to teach anatomy. He stayed at the university until 1808 when ill health forced him to resign.

Monro Secundus was active in the vibrant intellectual community of the ENLIGHTENMENT in Edinburgh. He served as joint secretary with David HUME of the Philosophical Society of Edinburgh (1760–63). After the society became the ROYAL SOCIETY OF EDINBURGH, Monro served for 20 more years (1763–83) as its sole secretary. He was active in city of Edinburgh commissions on lighting, street cleaning, and policing of public areas, all aspects of the late-Enlightenment emphasis on public health. Monro also served as the manager of the city's Royal Infirmary. He was a member of the Harveian Society, noted for his skill in oratory and his conviviality. Monro repeated the pattern of his past by securing for his son Alexander Monro Tertius a joint appointment to the faculty of anatomy at the University of Edinburgh. Monro Secundus died in 1817 after suffering a severe stroke.

Most of Monro Secundus's early publications were polemical disputes with William Hunter and Hunter's colleagues over priority in making anatomical discoveries. Monro, for example, had performed the operation of paracentesis of the thorax in Berlin with an anatomist named Meckel, but Mr. Hewson, a colleague of Hunter's who had been a student of Monro's, claimed publicly to have performed the first such operation. Today, scholars believe that Monro performed the first paracentesis of the thorax, but that Hewson must receive credit for the first publication about such an operation.

Monro's major treatises appeared in the 1780s and 1790s. They include *Observations on the Structure and Functions of the Nervous System* (1783; German edition, 1787), the treatise that first identified the foramen in the brain now called the "foramen of Monro"; *The Structure and Physiology of Fishes Explained and Compared With Those of Men and Other Animals* (1785); *A Description of All the Bursae Mucosae . . .* (1788; German edition, 1799); *Experiments on the Nervous System, With Opalline and Metalline Substances; Made Chiefly With the View of Determining the Nature and Effects of Animal Electricity* (1793); and *Three Treatises on the Brain, the Eye and the Ear* (1797).

Monro believed that the action of the nerves stimulates muscle contractions, but he also believed that the nerves carried an "animal electricity" or "animated fluid." Thus, his thinking remained aligned with the 18th-century fluid theories of heat and electricity as well as with the theory of VITALISM. On the problem of GENERATION (reproduction), Monro Secundus supported a PREFORMATION THEORY called ovism, which maintained that the female egg is the source of the preformed embryo and denied any role to the male sperm. In Monro's work, it is thus possible to see a common characteristic of enlightened MEDICINE and life sciences: The discoveries that are recognized today as contributing to the development of modern medicine were, in fact, made within the context of substantially different theoretical frameworks, which, if explored, can extend and deepen our understanding of the Enlightenment.

See also BIOLOGY.

Montagu, Elizabeth [Robinson] (1720–1800) *British essayist, letter writer, and hostess*

Born the eldest daughter to wealthy parents, Elizabeth was educated privately on the Robinson family estates in ENGLAND. In 1742, Elizabeth married Edward Montagu, the wealthy grandson of the first earl of Sandwich and cousin of Edward Wortley Montagu. Thus, Elizabeth Montagu and Lady Mary Wortley MONTAGU, another active female writer of the era, were related through their marriages. After Edward Montagu's death in 1775, Elizabeth managed his estates and coal mines but chose to spend most of her time in LONDON, where her salon became a gathering place for intellectuals of both sexes.

Samuel JOHNSON, a regular guest in her salons, called Montagu the "Queen of the Blues." The Bluestockings were a group of wealthy, well-connected ladies who held evening gatherings devoted to lively and intellectual conversation. Although modeled after the French salons, the English gatherings never succeeded in acquiring the prominence or influence of their French counterparts. Notable members of Montagu's circle were Hester Thrale, Fanny BURNEY, Hannah MORE, Samuel JOHNSON, Edmund BURKE, and Sir Joshua REYNOLDS.

During the ENLIGHTENMENT, Montagu's most famous book was *An Essay on the Writings and Genius of Shakespear* [sic] (1769), a work in which she defended the style of William Shakespeare against criticisms from VOLTAIRE. Montagu compared Shakespeare favorably to the classical Greek and Latin dramatists. Contemporaries such as Samuel Johnson praised her *Essay*, and it was translated into French and Italian. Today, she is more highly regarded for her letters, which her nephew published after her death.

See also BLUESTOCKING; SOCIAL INSTITUTIONS OF THE ENLIGHTENMENT; WOMEN AND THE ENLIGHTENMENT.

Montagu, Lady Mary Wortley (1689–1762) *eldest daughter of Evelyn Pierrepont, first duke of Kingston*

Having been betrothed by her father to a suitable young aristocrat, Lady Mary reacted by eloping in 1712 with Mr. Edward Wortley Montagu, a grandson of the first earl of

Sandwich and cousin of Edward Montagu. Edward Wortley Montagu was a member of Parliament, known to the Whig Party leaders. He was acquainted with Joseph ADDISON and Richard STEELE. Steele, in fact, dedicated the second volume of his journal *The Tatler* to Montagu.

In 1716, Montagu received a diplomatic appointment to Constantinople. Lady Mary accompanied him, learned about INOCULATION against smallpox in Adrianople, and became a committed supporter of the practice. She had her own son vaccinated and took news of inoculation back to ENGLAND. However, it was not until the 1750s that English physicians generally began to accept the new approach to smallpox management.

Upon returning to England, the Montagus studied at Twickenham near the residence of Alexander POPE. At some point relations between the friends soured after Pope was tricked into declaring his love of Lady Mary. She responded by laughing and he answered by caricaturing her in the *Dunciad.* Jonathan SWIFT joined the fray by lampooning Lady Mary in "The Capon's Tale" (1727). Lady Mary retaliated with "Verses addressed to an Imitator of Horace by a Lady" (1733) and continued quarreling in print with Swift.

Lady Mary left her husband in 1739 and lived in ITALY and SWITZERLAND until her death in 1762. From Italy, Lady Mary wrote an outstanding set of letters to her daughter, the countess of Bute. These supplemented the *Letters from the East,* which she had written during her years in Constantinople. Her other literary creations were *Town Eclogues* (1716) and a play, *Simplicity* (about 1735). VOLTAIRE compared her letters favorably with those of Madame de Sevigné, the outstanding 17th-century French epistolary writer. Lady Mary was noted for her intelligence and breadth of learning and was one of the outstanding intellectual women of her era.

See also WOMEN AND THE ENLIGHTENMENT.

Montesquieu, Charles-Louis de Secondat, baron de La Brède et de (1689–1755) *French political theorist, historian, and satirist; one of the most widely read and significant philosophes*

Montesquieu's books, *Les lettres persanes* (THE PERSIAN LETTERS; 1721), and *L'esprit des lois* (SPIRIT OF LAWS; 1748), offered criticism of contemporary French society and helped to popularize the ideals of English constitutional monarchy throughout Europe. Furthermore, his legacy of POLITICAL THEORY, HISTORY, and sociology was one of the chief creations, and certainly one of the most well-known contributions, of the ENLIGHTENMENT to modern Western civilization.

Charles-Louis de Secondat was born at the family chateau of La Brède near Bordeaux in southwestern FRANCE. His great-grandfather, a French Calvinist in the service of King Henri IV, had been rewarded with a noble title. The next generation converted back to ROMAN

Engraving of Montesquieu. Author of the popular *Persian Letters* and the *Spirit of Laws,* Charles-Louis de Secondat, baron de La Brède et de Montesquieu, popularized the idea of political equilibrium guaranteed by a system of checks and balances. *(Courtesy Archive Photos)*

CATHOLICISM and entered the *noblesse de robe* (the judicial nobility) by purchasing offices in the Parlement of Bordeaux (royal court).

The practice of purchasing offices was widespread and allowed the bearer in some instances to pass the office to his heirs as a form of private PROPERTY. In this manner Charles-Louis de Secondat in 1716 acquired the office of *président à mortier* (presiding judge in one section of the court) from a deceased uncle. VOLTAIRE, with his typical biting sarcasm, often ridiculed Montesquieu for having acquired his social standing in such a manner.

Montesquieu served as a presiding judge over the criminal division ((Tournelle) of the Parlement of Bordeaux for 11 years. He had obtained a law degree from the University of Bordeaux and had studied additionally in PARIS. His preoccupation with the role of law in political society thus grew partially from his own circumstances and experience.

Montesquieu married Jeanne de Lartigue, a Calvinist who was openly practicing her religion. She risked civil disabilities, prosecution, and imprisonment for sticking to her faith, a situation that had come into being in 1685 when LOUIS XIV decreed the revocation of the Edict of Nantes (a toleration decree dating from 1598). Throughout his life, Montesquieu openly championed the cause of religious TOLERATION, having seen at firsthand the uselessness of persecution.

Montesquieu divided his time among his judicial duties, his activities as a wine maker and merchant, and his role as director of the Bordeaux Academy. Each of these facets of his life—law, commerce, and science—helped to shape his political theories. In fact, Montesquieu was sometimes criticized for being too transparent a spokesman for the interests of the social groups to which he was linked. That he spoke for these interests cannot be denied, but the fact does not negate the impact, originality, or interest of his ideas.

Montesquieu entered the literary world with a huge splash in 1721 when the *Lettres persanes* (Persian letters) appeared. The book was an instant success, offering at once a juicy piece of entertainment, witty satire, and insightful criticism of French society during the years of the Regency (1715–23).

Montesquieu decided to move to Paris shortly after the publication of *Lettres persanes*. An active social and intellectual life followed, centered on the Parisian salon of Madame DU DEFFAND, the literary and political Club de l'Entresol, and other venues. The French Academy received him into its membership in 1728. Parisian life pleased Montesquieu, and he resigned from the Parlement of Bordeaux, selling the office in the process. He retained, however, the title of *Monsieur le président* throughout his life.

In 1728, Montesquieu embarked on an extended tour with an English friend, Lord Waldegrave, through the HAPSBURG EMPIRE (AUSTRIA and HUNGARY), various German principalities of the HOLY ROMAN EMPIRE, and ITALY. During this trip, he began gathering the materials and exploring the themes that resulted in his two philosophical histories: *Considérations sur les causes de la grandeur des Romains et de leur décadence* (Considerations on the causes of the greatness of the Romans and of their decline; 1734) and *L'esprit des lois* (Spirit of the Laws; 1748). He was particularly impressed with the innovations in historical method that had been developed in Italy by Lodovico Antonio MURATORI, Pietro GIANNONE, and others.

Between 1729 and 1731, Montesquieu resided in ENGLAND. In LONDON, he joined the FREEMASONS, attended Parliament debates, followed the course of political events, and was elected to the ROYAL SOCIETY OF LONDON. These years transformed his life and outlook, convincing him that the rule of law and the preservation of political freedom were indeed possible in real human society. English constitutional monarchy seemed to Montesquieu to embody the ideals of FREEDOM, toleration, moderation, and REASON.

Montesquieu began writing his two philosophical histories after he returned to Paris. The *Considérations sur les causes,* published anonymously in 1734 in Holland, was politely received but not particularly popular. Nevertheless, it did serve as the direct inspiration for the interpretation of the Roman Empire offered by Edward GIBBON in his DECLINE AND FALL OF THE ROMAN EMPIRE. *L'esprit des lois,* published and distributed from GENEVA in 1748, met with an enthusiastic reception and generally created a sensation in Europe. By 1750, some 22 editions had appeared in every major European language.

Montesquieu explored a general set of problems that were perceived by enlightened readers as critical to their era. He wanted to understand the role of law in shaping political society and to find ways to cope philosophically and practically with the specter of despotism. For Montesquieu, despotism was a real nightmare that had plagued France recently in the form of the ABSOLUTISM of King LOUIS XIV (1643–1715). It was Louis XIV who had reinstituted religious persecution of the HUGUENOTS, who had assaulted neighboring states in vicious warfare, who had undermined the power of the PARLEMENTS, and who had taxed his kingdom into rather desperate financial straits. Montesquieu dreamed of finding a way to ensure that such abuses of power would not happen again in France and explored both the problems and potential solutions in his books.

In developing his answers, Montesquieu combined a theoretical model drawn from the VITALISM of the life sciences with an empirical (he thought) description and rational analysis of the English political system. Along the way, he explored other possibilities, in the various states of contemporary Europe, the ancient classical societies of Greece (Athens and Sparta) and ROME, in the Native American societies, and in oriental cultures. He used these cultures for comparative purposes, analyzing the principles that drove their actions and evaluating their successes and failures.

Montesquieu's ideal political culture was built on an analogy with health in the human body. The healthy political body exists in a state of dynamic balance among its various parts. When one aspect becomes too prominent, balance must be restored or the system will deteriorate into an unhealthy state. In political societies, this deterioration brings on abuses of power.

The well-designed political order contains inner mechanisms for self-correction, just like the human body. Montesquieu believed that the English constitutional system based on joint rule by king and Parliament offered the desired self-regulating model. It accomplished this because of the way in which power was divided between the executive and legislative branches. This SEPARATION OF POWERS allows the system to maintain balance or equilibrium by means of a series of checks and balances.

Montesquieu developed a sophisticated theory about the role of law in society. He believed that, in order for the laws of a given state to be effective, they must be rooted in the spirit of its people, that is, in the special combination of environmental and social factors that distinguishes its people. Successful reform of the laws of a state can be accomplished only by first improving the spirit of its people. The imposition of reform from above, a practice that was common among the enlightened despots of central and eastern Europe, would thus be ineffective.

Montesquieu criticized those enlightened writers who believed that the civic virtue of the ancient republic of Rome could be reestablished in 18th-century France. He insisted that civic virtue, defined as the willingness to sacrifice one's well-being and life for the republic, was an anachronism incompatible with life in an 18th-century commercial society. Montesquieu thought that some principle other than virtue must govern modern political behavior. He found the necessary principle in the concept of honor, which he defined as the willingness to do things that appear virtuous in order to win public esteem. In this respect, Montesquieu's ideas about what forces drive modern behavior more closely approached those of Bernard MANDEVILLE than those of idealistic writers such as Jean-Jacques ROUSSEAU.

Montesquieu did believe that properly conceived and prepared positive (human-made) laws protect the freedom of human beings. He also stressed that social and political life consists of a tension between two pairs of opposing principles contained in the very notion of law: liberty versus constraint and necessity versus freedom.

The emphasis that Montesquieu placed on the role played by social and environmental factors in shaping the political possibilities for a nation has led some scholars to call him the father of modern sociology. He also is noted for having helped to develop contextual approaches to history.

Montesquieu prepared his historical interpretations of European nations with the explicit intention of refuting the universal history of Bishop BOSSUET. Bossuet had been the official French defender of absolutism based on the DIVINE RIGHT OF KINGS. His works had provided support for the policies and claims of Louis XIV. Montesquieu wished to undermine Bossuet's approach, to steer history away from telling stories about how the divine will and providence of God are realized through human history. In its place, he wished to substitute a thoroughly human account rooted in the interplay between human nature and the world in which human history occurs. His history was a secular history, a philosophical history rather than a theological history.

The theories of Montesquieu belong to a group of illustrious political models that was created during the Enlightenment. During the 18th century, his ideas, especially as expressed in *L'esprit des lois,* stimulated criticism, praise, further exploration, and imitation. In England, the North American colonies, and GERMANY, Montesquieu was the best known and most influential of all the French enlightened writers. He provided inspiration, for example, to James MADISON, John JAY, and Alexander HAMILTON as they created their vision of a well-formed federal system in the new UNITED STATES OF AMERICA. In particular, the concept of the separation of powers, so central to the new American system, was derived at least in part from Montesquieu. Montesquieu's work also inspired the young German philosopher Johann Gottfried HERDER, even though in his later years Herder believed that Montesquieu had not made a strong enough argument for the links among, environment, tradition, and culture. Antoine DESTUTT DE TRACY, one of the French IDÉOLOGUES, liked *L'esprit des lois* so much that, in 1808, he published his *Commentaire sur l'Esprit des lois de Montesquieu,* a work that tried to update Montesquieu's ideas in the light of the experience of the FRENCH REVOLUTION. After his death, Montesquieu was more than once compared with Isaac NEWTON: by Jean Le Rond d'ALEMBERT in the eulogy he prepared and read at the FRENCH ACADEMY OF SCIENCES; by Charles BONNET, the Swiss life scientist; and by Pierre de MAUPERTUIS, the president of the BERLIN ACADEMY.

On the negative side, Voltaire, for example, criticized Montesquieu's ideas about the influence of climate and environment on national characteristics, suggesting that RELIGION and government were more powerful influences. Voltaire also rejected Montesquieu's treatment of despotism and his claim that English habits of freedom and constitutionalism derived from the heritage of the ancient Germanic (Anglo-Saxon) tribes. He similarly rejected Montesquieu's theory about the Frankish origins of the French monarchy, preferring, instead, to locate its origins in the Roman occupation of Gaul. Voltaire tended, at that time, to believe that real reform in France could come only from the king and his ministers (the Roman model); the *parlements* and other bodies who could claim to be the intermediary bodies so important to Montesquieu's scheme (the Frankish model), were in Voltaire's opinion only interested in securing a privileged position for themselves.

Another critic, Claude-Adrien HELVÉTIUS, pointed out that Montesquieu was merely providing an apology for his own social class, and he also rejected England as a good political model. Rousseau extended that line of thought, arguing that representative governments are mere shadows of authentic self-government; he, too, disparaged the English model. The marquis de CONDORCET and Abbé SIEYÈS, two early leaders of the French Revolution, also rejected Montesquieu's ideal French government model, because of its reliance on the aristocracy as an intermediary body between monarch and people.

The JESUITS, the Jansenists, and the Roman Catholic Inquisition all reacted negatively to Montesquieu's ideas. He was accused of endorsing the philosophy of Benedict de SPINOZA, and, hence, of ATHEISM. *L'esprit des lois* wound up on the Inquisition's Index of Forbidden Books, but that did not prevent it from being enthusiastically read and reprinted.

At his death in 1755, Montesquieu was such a celebrity that the Jesuits and the philosophes engaged in a public quarrel over his last moments of life. The Jesuits claimed that he had received a Catholic confessor for the last rite, had repented his heretical views, and had returned to the arms of the Catholic Church. The philosophes denied all that, insisting that their colleague had remained true to his anticlerical and irreligious ideals to the end. The truth probably lies somewhere in between, but the story illustrates the power ascribed to the man.

See also ARGENSON, MARQUIS D'; BOLINGBROKE.

Further reading: Paul Hazard, *European Thought in the Eighteenth Century from Montesquieu to Lessing,* tr. J. Lewis May (Cleveland: Meridian/World, 1963); Melvin Richter, *The Political Theory of Montesquieu* (Cambridge: Cambridge University Press, 1977); Robert Shackleton, *Montesquieu: A Critical Biography* (Oxford: Oxford University Press, 1961); Judith Sklar, *Montesquieu* (Oxford: Oxford University Press, 1987).

Montgolfier, Jacques-Étienne and Michel-Joseph
(1745–1799 and 1740–1810) *French inventors and technologists who created the first hot-air balloons*

The Montgolfier brothers were the sons of a paper manufacturer. Jacques-Étienne Montgolfier was an architect by training who had studied under Jacques SOUFFLOT in PARIS. He practiced architecture until 1772, when he assumed the directorship of his father's paper factory. Michel-Joseph Montgolfier continued his father's profession by setting up a new paper factory 50 miles away from the family concern.

The Montgolfier brothers, fascinated by the discovery of new gases such as hydrogen, became convinced that a gas-filled balloon could lift a person into the air. They invented the first, small hot-air balloons in 1782, methodically improving the technology until they succeeded in creating a paper and cloth balloon 35 feet in diameter, which rose 6,000 feet into the air.

News of their experiments traveled quickly, and several inventors began trying to repeat the Montgolfier success. The first human ascent, by J. F. Pilatre de Rozier and the marquis d'Arlandes, occurred on November 20, 1783.

The balloon invention earned both Montgolfier brothers positions at the FRENCH ACADEMY OF SCIENCES. The family paper factory also benefited by being named a royal manufactory.

While Jacques-Étienne devoted himself in later years to the paper factory, his brother Michel-Joseph continued to invent practical devices. His hydraulic ram, a machine for raising water in canal locks, proved most useful.

Michel-Joseph eventually abandoned his independent paper factory, moved to Paris, and in 1800 assumed a post with the Conservatoire des Arts et Metiers.

The invention of hot-air balloons stands as a clear example of the marriage between scientific theory and practical invention that marked the ENLIGHTENMENT. The subsequent history of ballooning, with its theatrical forms of presentation, further marks it as a venture of the Enlightenment.

moral philosophy The study of the foundations on which knowledge about morality and definitions of ethical behavior are based. European intellectuals struggled throughout the ENLIGHTENMENT to answer compelling questions about moral knowledge and behavior. People were asking whether good and bad have objective existence or whether they are just subjective values that change with circumstances. They were asking where such values come from and how they can be recognized by human beings. And they were asking what motivates human beings to act one way or another.

Moral knowledge and ethical behavior had previously been the concern of theologians who mostly had derived their ideas from assumptions about the relationship between the Christian God and the universe. The world, according to the Christian vision, was a place created and ruled by God. His eternal, immutable laws, revealed for humanity in the books of the Bible, spelled out both general and specific contents of morality. God had given men the FREEDOM (free will) to choose whether or not to obey his laws. In the end, those who obeyed and who accepted the message of Christianity would be rewarded for their goodness with eternal life while all other people would be condemned. God, then, was the source both of goodness and of the duty to behave in moral ways.

This formula for understanding the moral foundations of the world, like so much else in European systems of belief, had received critical challenges during the era of the SCIENTIFIC REVOLUTION. Seventeenth-century mathematicians and natural philosophers (scientists) had laid the foundations for an alternative vision of the world, one that forced a rethinking of the relationship between God and the world. God's presence and activity were no longer seen as necessary for the daily maintenance of the universe. Instead, a body of NATURAL LAW, modeled after mathematical laws, governed ordinary operations. These rational, mechanical, natural laws could be directly perceived by human REASON; it was not necessary to have revelation from God in order for human beings to discern them.

Although God was moved to the sidelines in this vision of the universe, he still received recognition as the author of the laws of the universe. The real problems for moral philosophy emerged when 17th-century philoso-

The Montgolfier hot-air balloon, September 19, 1783. The Montgolfier brothers turned science to practical purposes, but also endowed their activities with popular, sensational appeal. *(Courtesy New York Public Library)*

phers such as Thomas HOBBES began to describe the actions of the human mind in mechanistic, materialist terms.

Traditional Christian explanations of human nature were dualistic: People had material bodies and immaterial or spiritual souls. Souls were the essence of individuals and lived on after bodies died. Souls directed human action, recognized God's law, and chose whether or not to honor it. They were the seat of the will, of freedom, of choice, of all aspects of human existence that made it possible to speak of moral behavior.

For mechanical philosophers the soul began to seem problematical at best and superfluous at worst. Body-soul relations were difficult to explain in physical terms. If the human body was acting according to the same laws that governed the actions of the planets or of inanimate earthly objects, it seemed unnecessary to have a soul making decisions. The natural action of the laws would direct things. It was actually possible to conceive that the soul does not exist, an implication that some philosophers did not hesitate to explore.

By the beginning of the Enlightenment, an unstable, unsatisfactory, and conflicting set of philosophical solu-

tions had been offered, represented in the RATIONALISM of Hobbes, Benedict de SPINOZA, Gottfried LEIBNIZ, Nicolas de MALEBRANCHE, Samuel CLARKE, and Ralph CUDWORTH. Hobbes had denied that any moral order exists in the universe but had recognized the absolute necessity of moral codes for human society. For him, human beings chose their behaviors according to their perceptions of SELF-INTEREST. Spinoza elaborated the Hobbesian position, developing a philosophy in which all human behavior was determined by human desire; human desire, in turn, was determined by natural, mechanical laws. Both Hobbesian and Spinozist philosophies offered a natural basis for morality that removed it from the realm of RELIGION but that significantly curtailed human freedom of action. Both men were accused of ATHEISM by religious authorities. Their radical MATERIALISM and determinism was too extreme for their century.

Cudworth and his fellow Cambridge Platonists had preserved the dichotomy between body and soul, tending to make soul the seat of reason. They believed that this rational soul could uncover the self-evident moral principles that exist in the universe, just as it could discern natural physical laws. Samuel Clarke accepted the notion of self-evident moral principles, but he believed that intuition (immediate, direct perception) rather than reason played the primary role in discovering these principles. Malebranche tended to agree with these ideas, but he was more concerned to explain what made people act on their moral perceptions. As a Catholic Oratorian, he desired to maintain a role for God in the new, rational mechanical universe; he therefore made God the immediate cause of all human action.

Rationalism tended to dominate thinking as the Enlightenment opened, but British EMPIRICISM, especially in the form offered by John LOCKE, had also developed alternative theories. This psychologically based empiricism tended to equate soul with mind and to root all human ideas and actions in responses to physical sensations. Locke's ideas had some similarities to those of Hobbes and Spinoza. Like Hobbes, he believed that desire motivates human behavior, but Locke expanded the idea by adding to it an explanation of how good and bad receive their definitions. According to Locke, people tend to define things that give pleasure as "good"; those things or events that cause pain are "bad." Locke's theories thus defined moral behavior in terms of its UTILITY or usefulness for individuals.

The moral philosophers of the Enlightenment inherited the problems of moral philosophy implied in rationalism, the MECHANICAL PHILOSOPHY, and empiricism. Most enlightened writers felt compelled to search for a natural foundation for morality that would remove it from the domain of religion. Many, but not all, writers tended still to believe in the existence of a universal, objective standard for good and bad behavior. But PSYCHOLOGY, EPISTEMOLOGY, and physiology rather than theology provided the bases for their understanding. Universal human nature, the operations of the human mind, and the physical structure of the world replaced God as the source of moral ideas and behavior.

Enlightened writers developed their ideas along two general thematic lines: one explored the material, natural origins of human ideas about good and evil; the other struggled to work out the RELATIONS between freedom and necessity in human action.

British philosophers in ENGLAND made the first prominent contributions to enlightened moral philosophy. They had recognized that the fear of pain or punishment is not always strong enough to prevent people from acting in certain ways, but they had also observed that some choices did not seem to be made solely in terms of self-interest. Building on the psychology of Locke, the third earl of SHAFTESBURY asserted that the sense of moral obligation comes from benevolent feelings of love and affection that are as natural as any selfish motives. Bishop Joseph BUTLER expanded the idea within the confines of Christian theology. Bernard MANDEVILLE rebutted these

ideas in his famed *Fable of the Bees* by showing that benevolent behavior leads to weak, ineffective societies.

In SCOTLAND, Shaftesbury's sentiments of benevolence were translated by Francis HUTCHESON into the concept of the moral sense. This moral sense—modeled somewhat on basic senses such as sight or touch—allowed things to be classified as good or bad according to the degree of pleasure that they produced. The moral sense, judged as good any thing that produced pleasure. In this manner it provided the foundations from which the human mind could make judgments about the ethical implications of various actions.

David HUME, David HARTLEY, and Adam SMITH elaborated on Hutcheson's moral sense theory, but they combined it with utilitarian explanations of motivation. These Scottish thinkers emphasized the role of SYMPATHY and "disinterested interest" in motivating moral judgment and behavior. Another group of Scots followed the lead of Thomas REID by theorizing about an inner sense of moral obligation that could help to identify and to motivate good behavior.

French moral philosophy drew primarily from British empiricism but developed its materialism to extreme positions. All moral judgment and action could be explained in terms of the operations of the material mind. Denis DIDEROT, Baron d'HOLBACH, and Claude-Adrien HELVÉTIUS, all writers for the ENCYCLOPÉDIE project, developed particularly clear and sometimes notorious statements of this position. They intended their theories as attacks on the dogmas and theology of ROMAN CATHOLICISM.

In the HOLY ROMAN EMPIRE, moral philosophy followed a somewhat different path by turning its attention to the problem of freedom. Both the philosophy of Leibniz and the German traditions of tight state control over behavior helped to create this focus. Leibniz had posited that the universe is constructed of individual units called monads that possess the quality of PERFECTIBILITY. Monads constantly strive toward greater degrees of perfection and, since they compose all individual things in the universe (including human beings), these things also have the quality of striving toward perfection. This whole system was ordained by God, but it operates according to preestablished laws of harmony without God's direct interference. Since perfection is equated with the moral quality of goodness, a quest for moral purity is fundamental to the whole structure of the universe.

Leibniz maintained that human beings constructed of monads still possessed the freedom to choose their behavior, but critics recognized that the fundamental striving of monads and preestablished harmony tended to take away free choice. Behavior seemed to be determined by the structure of things and by the preordained laws of God.

Immanuel KANT addressed these problems as he attempted to create a synthesis of the various traditions of the Enlightenment. In the process, he also developed a form of moral philosophy that became the major rival to theories based on utility. Kant distinguished between the logic of natural laws and that of ethical laws. Ethical laws or rules are those that can be obeyed freely by any rational human being. They govern the relationship between freedom and duty. Reason guarantees the possibility of freedom rather than serving as a source of determinism. Ethical laws are imposed freely by reasoning human beings on their own behavior and the reward for virtuous behavior is not HAPPINESS or pleasure but freedom and dignity.

The Enlightenment closed with this strong restatement of the duties and obligations owed by individuals to their fellow human beings. But it translated the act of carrying out these obligations into the victory of free rational men over their irrational, natural desires. The Enlightenment was the first era to attempt placing ethical prescriptions and moral judgment on a secular rather than sacred foundation. In undertaking this task, the men and women of the era were inventing some of the basic formulations and creating problems that still demand attention today.

See also CAPITAL PUNISHMENT, CIVIL SOCIETY; INTUITION AND IMAGINATION; JUSTICE AND THE LAW; RIGHTS.

Further reading: Carl L. Becker, *The Heavenly City of the Eighteenth-Century Philosophers* (New Haven, Conn.: Yale University Press, 1959); Michael Hunter and David Wooton, eds., *Atheism from the Reformation to the Enlightenment* (Oxford: Clarendon Press, 1992).

Moravian Brethren   A religious movement revived in the 18th century. The Moravian Brethren, or Brethren of the Common Life, was a revival of the Unitas Fratrum (Brethren's Union) founded in Bohemia in 1457. After two and a half centuries of persecution, the United Brethren had almost disappeared when, in 1722, families fleeing persecution were given sanctuary on the estate of Nicolaus Ludwig, count von ZINZENDORF in Saxony. Zinzendorf was a Pietist, and his deeply held religious beliefs centered on study and the cultivation of individual piety. He gave the Moravians a grant of land at Herrnhut, on his estate, and encouraged them to build a religious community there. In 1727, under Zinzendorf's guidance, the community declared itself the Renewed Unitas Fratrum, and this marked the foundation of the Moravian Brethren.

An important aspect of the Brethren was their missionary work. In 1732 and 1733, the first of the group's missionaries went to the West Indies and Greenland, and, in 1735, the Moravians began to settle in North America. They established settlements in Pennsylvania (Bethlehem and Nazareth) and later, in 1776, founded Salem (now Winston-Salem), North Carolina. During his exile from Saxony between 1737 and 1747, Zinzendorf himself worked as a missionary, founding congregations in ENGLAND, Ireland, North America, and Holland.

The religious foundation of the Moravian Brethren was very simple. The individual had to believe in Jesus Christ as his or her savior and the basic Christian eschatology to be included in the brethren. Like other groups influenced by PIETISM, the brethren emphasized personal piety and justification by faith alone as fundamental tenets of belief. The group consisted of individuals united by these basic beliefs, regardless of confessional differences. Through their missionary work, which included publishing and distributing Bibles, the Moravian Brethren played an important role in the spread of Pietist religious practice, with its emphasis on the cultivation of individual faith and on the importance of meetings for religious study and discussion. The Moravian Brethren were the predecessors of the present-day Moravian Church in America.

See also SPENER; UNITED PROVINCES OF THE NETHERLANDS.

More, Hannah (1745–1833) *English poet, writer and activist*
Hannah More was born in Bristol, ENGLAND, and remained in the region throughout her life. Unmarried and independent, for nearly six decades she built a reputation as a public intellectual, a devout evangelical Christian, and a humanitarian. She is best remembered for her association with the men and women of the BLUESTOCKING circle, whose accomplishments and moral standards she celebrates in her 1786 poem "Le Bas Bleu" (The blue stocking), and for her patronage of the "milk-woman" poet, Anne Yearsley. Yearsley helped with livestock at More's cottage, Cowslip Green, in suburban Bristol. When More learned that the working woman composed poetry, she strove to assist her. Besides food and money to support Yearsley's family, More helped improve her verses and originated a subscription to publish her first volume of poems. However, the relationship eventually collapsed in mutual recriminations.

During her life, More met socially and corresponded with many famous and influential people, including the theatrical manager-actor David GARRICK, writers Horace WALPOLE and Samuel JOHNSON, and the philanthropist-abolitionist William WILBERFORCE, with whom she shared several goals. Champion of numerous reforms, both local and international, More wrote two poems—"Slavery" (1788) and "The Sorrows of Yamba" (1795)—to inspire Britons to support abolition when the issue was debated in Parliament. In her will she bequeathed a substantial sum to the cause. Indeed, SLAVERY in British possessions was abolished in the year of her death, 1833, although it is impossible to assess the extent of her personal influence on this outcome.

Her literary works are many and varied. Besides poetry, she was initially interested in theatrical culture and wrote two tragedies. *The Inflexible Captive* (1774) and *Percy* (1776–77) were both publicly performed, and the latter play was quite successful. More also published sacred drama intended for children's reading; religious, moral, and social tracts; tales; and even a NOVEL. More wrote her novel, *Coelebs in Search of a Wife* (1808), to explore right notions of female education and gender roles. Despite her longstanding distrust of the disturbing effects of light fiction on women readers, she was convinced of the usefulness of moral fiction as well as moral lectures. She sought the reform of her own class in *Thoughts on the Importance of the Manners of the Great to General Society* (1788). For the moral instruction of the poor, she produced in an immensely popular series of inexpensive books entitled *The Cheap Repository Tracts* (1795–98), which bore titles such as "Black Giles the Poacher" and "The Sunday School." Modern feminists have little to praise in More's conservative notion of women's rights, but as a public intellectual she was and, indeed, remains a major figure in ENLIGHTENMENT causes.

See also WOMEN AND THE ENLIGHTENMENT.

Further reading: M. G. Jones, *Hannah More* (Cambridge: Cambridge University Press, 1952); Angela Keane, *Women Writers and the English Nation in the 1790s* (Cambridge: Cambridge University Press, 2000).

Morelly, Abbé (ca. 1715–1778) *French writer and socialist*

Little is known biographically about the Abbé Morelly. His first name is unknown, as are the location and date of his birth. He was a tutor in the northern French town of Vitry-le-François.

What has not been forgotten about Morelly is that he was an early promoter of socialist and utopian ideas. He believed that human nature was essentially good and that most of the evils in society were caused by the greed resulting from private property. Additionally, he believed that the formation of states was unnatural and had caused human society to become more disordered.

He expressed these ideas in several works. The epic poem *Naufrage des Isles Flottantes, ou Basiliade du Célébre* (The Basiliad; 1753) tells of a utopia where private property does not exist. In the *Essai sur l'esprit humain* (Essay on the human spirit; 1743) and the *Essai sur le coeur humain* (Essay on the human heart; 1745) he applies his beliefs on NATURAL LAW to EDUCATION. Morelly's other early works include a treatise on AESTHETICS, *Physique de la beauté* (The form of beauty; 1748) and a critique of MONTESQUIEU, *Le prince* (The prince; 1751).

Morelly's best-known work is the *Code de la Nature, ou le Véritable Esprit de ses Lois* (Code of nature, or the true spirit of the laws; 1755), which was wrongly attributed to Denis DIDEROT. Here he states that all deviations from moral behavior can be traced to the effects on society of the private ownership of resources. The book outlines a program of a state-controlled economy long before these ideas appeared in the 19th century. He wanted to make state legislation reflect the natural state of humans, which he believed was a state of common ownership of goods and resources. Morelly believed that giving the state unlimited power over the resources of a country would heal social ills because the lack of property would eliminate both avarice and poverty.

His ideas that disorder is due to social institutions and that private property should be eradicated were compatible with those of Jean-Jacques ROUSSEAU and his fellow apostate priest Abbé Gabriel Bonnot de MABLY. Morelly's ideas greatly influenced the French revolutionaries and early socialists François-Noël Babeuf and Pierre-Joseph Proudhon.

Moscow City in Russia located on the banks of the Moskva River; at the beginning of the 18th century it was the capital of the Russian state. The Russian chronicles first mention the city in 1147, but archaeological evidence suggests that the site has been settled since the Neolithic era. Yuri Dolgoruki, prince of Suzdal, built the first fortress (*kremlin*) for the city in 1156. Moscow suffered capture, plundering, and burning during the Tatar invasions. The Kremlin fortress area, which contained state administrative buildings and princely palaces, acquired its first stone walls only in 1367. By the second half of the 15th century, Moscow had become the center of the thriving, growing principality of Moscow. Between the 14th and 16th centuries, the city developed into a center for administration, education, book publishing, business, industry, trade, and Russian Orthodox Church administration. During the 16th century, fires destroyed much of the city, and stone structures were built as replacements for the traditional Russian timber buildings.

By the beginning of the 18th century, Moscow was the undisputed center of Russian power, commerce, business, and cultural life. But the city was troubled by religious, social, and political conflicts. It served as the base of power for the old aristocracy who generally opposed efforts by the Russian ruler (*czar*) to centralize the state and to secure absolute power. Czar PETER I (THE GREAT) tired of the difficulties presented by his recalcitrant capital. Much like LOUIS XIV in FRANCE, he solved the problem by simply removing the state administration and power centers from the city to a new site. Louis XIV moved to his new Versailles palace a few miles away from PARIS. But in 1712, Peter moved 400 miles to the northwest, to the newly created city of SAINT PETERSBURG.

Although Moscow lost power and importance when Peter the Great moved away, it nevertheless functioned throughout the 18th century as a great center of ENLIGHTENMENT in Russia. Education flourished with the founding of institutions for teaching mathematics, navigational sciences, MEDICINE, and surgery and with the establishment of the first university in Russia. Many structures were built in a style that is a unique Russian variant of baroque-era CLASSICISM. Major architectural monuments of the 18th century include the Kremlin Arsenal, Church of the Archangel Gabriel, the belfries of the Donskoy and Novospassky monasteries, the Church of St. Kliment, the building of the former Moscow Senate, the university, and the Golitsyn Hospital.

Moscow was occupied by Napoleon from September 14, to October 19, 1812. The Muscovite residents purposefully set the city ablaze and instigated a revolt against the French conquerors. Ultimately Napoleon abandoned the city, embarking upon his now famous, tragic winter retreat from Russia. The Muscovite repulsion of Napoleon served as the turning point of French expansion in Europe and caused the loss of thousands of lives.

See also MATHEMATICS AND MECHANICS.

Möser, Justus (1720–1794) *German essayist and historian*
Möser spent most of his life in his native city of Osnabrück. He served in several administrative posts for the bishop of Osnabrück, who was the ruler of the city and its surrounding territories. Möser also pursued an active writing career, producing the *Patriotische Phantasien* (Patriotic fantasies; 1774–86) and a substantial *Osnabrückische Geschichte* (History of Osnabrück; 1765).

The *Patriotische Phantasien* offered perceptive analyses of contemporary affairs, revealing Möser's roots in the enlightened understanding of the significance of social and economic structures for human PROGRESS. But Möser had no grand, comprehensive scheme for interpreting his materials. Rather, each topic was presented and assessed from a unique perspective. Möser's excursions into the contemporary issues of the day touched on topics such as overpopulation, arts and crafts guilds, and rural standards of living.

In contrast to the *Patriotische Phantasien*, the *Osnabrückische Geschichte* presented a general interpretation of HISTORY that attempted to show the links among social structures, economic conditions, and political organization in Osnabrück. In a departure from the traditional story of the succession of rulers, Möser presented the history of the bishopric of Osnabrück in terms of the development of FREEDOM (*Freiheit*) and of private PROPERTY (*Eigentum*). He examined how climate, crops, the organization of peasant labor, and agricultural techniques actually encouraged the division of society into privileged classes and ranks. Perhaps the most important aspect of his work for later generations was his placement of the origins of German freedom in the forests of Saxony. Here he argued that the roots for modern Western concepts of freedom and liberty were contained in the basic feudal oath sworn by Germanic warriors. This oath established a reciprocal set of rights and duties between the lord and his vassal based upon mutual consent.

Like MONTESQUIEU, Möser denied that the roots of modern concepts of freedom could be discerned in ancient Roman traditions of law and jurisprudence. He argued that "local REASON" (*Lokalvernunft*), based upon a respect for tradition and culture, was a much surer guide than universal reason for those who wanted to see the goals of the ENLIGHTENMENT implemented in the world.

Möser's analyses of society and history inspired Johann Gottfried HERDER and Johann Wolfgang von GOETHE, both major figures of the *AUFKLÄRUNG* (German Enlightenment).

See also ANCIEN RÉGIME; CLASS AND RANK IN THE EIGHTEENTH CENTURY.

Mosheim, Johann Lorenz von (ca. 1694–1755)
German theologian and author
The rise of LUTHERANISM and later Protestant sects in Europe began a process of questioning and evaluating religious authority and practice crucial to the eventual development of many branches of ENLIGHTENMENT philosophy. One of Luther's most erudite theological descendants was the theologian Johann Lorenz von Mosheim.

Born in Lübeck, GERMANY, Mosheim showed great intellectual ability upon his graduation from the University of Kiel and subsequent assumption there of the title of professor of philosophy. His sermons, including seven published volumes, proved influential to later generations of preachers. His reputation grew and, in 1725, he was offered a chair of divinity at the University of Helmstedt by the duke of Brunswick. In 1747, King George II of ENGLAND offered Mosheim the position of head of the theology department and chancellor at the University of GÖTTINGEN.

Mosheim took an active role in 18th-century religious scholarship and debate, publishing orations and sermons, volumes of church history, disquisitions on moral topics, and translations of other seminal theological works. The height of his scholarship came in 1733, when he translated into Latin *The True Intellectual System of the Universe* by the influential 17th-century English divine Ralph CUDWORTH. Mosheim's edition made the work accessible to foreign theologians and included compendious additional notes and related reference materials that established it as a theological classic in its own right.

See also PROTESTANTISM.

Further reading: Johann Lorenz von Mosheim, *Institutes of Ecclesiastical History, Ancient and Modern* tr. James

Murdoch (New York: Harper, 1844); Ralph Cudworth, *The True Intellectual System of the Universe* tr. John Harrison (London: J. Haddon, 1845).

Mozart, Wolfgang Amadeus (1756–1791) *Austrian composer and performer on harpsichord, piano, and violin*

Mozart was born in Salzburg, where he was christened Johannes Chrysotomus Wolfgangus Theophilus Mozart. He had a talented older sister Maria Anna (Nannerl) Mozart, who shared with him some of his earlier musical adventures. Mozart's father, Leopold Mozart, was a violinist, conductor, and composer at the court of the archbishop of Salzburg.

Young Mozart displayed his extraordinary musical gifts from an early age. His father nurtured these talents by providing him with systematic and rigorous training in keyboard technique, improvisational skills, and composition. Between the ages of six and 15, Mozart spent half of his time touring the major European musical cen-

Mozart at Seven, with His Father and Sister, by Louis Carrogis de Carmontelle, 1763. As a boy, Wolfgang Amadeus Mozart and his older sister Nannerl Mozart presented a series of concerts under the supervision of their father Leopold Mozart, in the major European cultural capitals. *(Courtesy New York Public Library)*

ters. His virtuosity in both performance and composition were widely recognized. Mozart seemed to provide an example of GENIUS in the flesh, and he consequently became the hero of the STURM UND DRANG generation of German artists and intellectuals.

Except when he was traveling, Mozart lived and worked until 1781 in Salzburg. He served as organist and concert master for the archbishop of Salzburg. Several tours interrupted these duties. Between 1763 and 1766, the entire Mozart family traveled to PARIS and LONDON, where Mozart met Johann Christian BACH. In 1768, VIENNA was the destination, and from 1770 until 1773, the Italian peninsula. Everywhere he traveled, Mozart met with prominent composers, studied their styles, and incorporated them into his own emerging international classical style.

In 1781, against the advice of his father, Mozart resigned his position in Salzburg and moved to Vienna. He lived there for 10 years, until his early death in 1791. He was actively involved in Vienna with certain organizations such as the FREEMASONS, which were dedicated to implementing the ideals of the ENLIGHTENMENT. The Vienna years began successfully with the production of the *singspiel, Die Entführung auf dem Serail* (The Abduction from the Seraglio), and several acclaimed keyboard performances. However, within two years, the fickle Viennese public had turned its attentions elsewhere, and Mozart was left to struggle with increasing financial debts.

Despite these difficulties, most of Mozart's outstanding compositions date from the Viennese period. Mozart's style continued to evolve. In 1782, for example, he began experimenting with contrapuntal techniques, after having encountered the compositions of Johann Sebastian BACH at music sessions in the home of Gottfried van SWIETEN.

Major compositions from the Vienna period include the six symphonies known as the *Haffner* (K 385), the *Prague* (K 504), the *Linz* (K 425), the Symphony in E Flat (K 543), the Symphony in G Minor (K 550), and the Symphony in G Major (*Jupiter,* K 551). Seventeen piano concertos, the *Haydn* quartets (K 387, 421, 428, 458, 464, 465), and the piano Fantasia show Mozart's mastery of various musical forms. His operas—LE NOZZE DI FIGARO, produced daringly in spite of the censoring of Beaumarchais's play of the same name; *Die Zauberflöte* (THE MAGIC FLUTE), with its Masonic and deist messages; DON GIOVANNI; and COSÍ FAN TUTTE—were widely acclaimed and, of course, still command full houses today.

Mozart's catalogue of compositions, compiled by L. von Köchel, contains over 600 items. He started composing minuets at age six and had completed his first symphony by the time he was nine. Important works from these earlier years include several piano sonatas, the Flute Quartet in D Major (K 285), the Oboe Quintet (K 370), the *Haffner* Serenade, and *Eine Kleine Nachtmusik.* Other delightful works include the Flute Concerto in D Major and the Clarinet Concerto in A Major.

Mozart died at the age of 35, the victim of what was probably rheumatic fever. At the time, he was composing a Requiem Mass on a commission from Count Walsegg. It was completed by Mozart's pupil Franz Xaver Süssmayr and given its first performance under the auspices of Gottfried van Swieten, as a benefit for Mozart's impoverished widow, Constanze. Thus ended the life of one of the greatest composers ever to have lived in Europe. Mozart, the hero of the romantic generation, embodied the best of the Enlightenment, and left a musical legacy that has seldom been matched since.

See also OPERA.

Müller, Johannes von (1752–1809) *Swiss historian, one of the most popular German language historians of the Enlightenment*

The son of a pastor from Schaffhausen, SWITZERLAND, Müller left his native land to pursue courses at the University of GÖTTINGEN. He studied HISTORY with August Ludwig SCHLÖZER, thereby acquiring a thorough grounding in the new historical conceptions and methods that were developing in response to the ENLIGHTENMENT. Müller was strongly influenced not only by Schlözer, but also by the work of Jean-Jacques ROUSSEAU, MONTESQUIEU, Johann Jakob BODMER, Johann Lorenz von Mosheim, and Thomas Abbt.

Müller could not find a university position in Switzerland. After working seven years in GENEVA as a private teacher (1774–80), he finally acquired regular employment in the HOLY ROMAN EMPIRE. He worked as a teacher in Kassel (1781–86) and as librarian and adviser to the archbishop elector of Mainz (1786–89). With the outbreak of the FRENCH REVOLUTION, Müller left Mainz and assumed a position in the imperial chancery of the HAPSBURG EMPIRE. The first decade of the 19th century found him in BERLIN as a member of the BERLIN ACADEMY and as Prussian court historian. In 1807, Müller accepted an appointment from Napoleon as minister of culture in the kingdom of Westphalia. He died in 1809 in Kassel.

Müller helped to transform the manner of writing history from the old chronicle form that had presented a dry listing of political events into a dramatic story built on general themes. He was really the first historian to succeed in casting the critical historical methods developed by the Göttingen school into a narrative form that also incorporated the great 18th-century advances in German literary style. His *Geschichten schweizerischer Eidgenossenschaft* (History of the Swiss Confederation; 1786–1808), for example, reworked the 16th-century chronicles of Swiss history by Aegidius Tschudi (1505–72) and others into this new, intensely researched but nevertheless more readable form. Müller's recasting of the story of Wilhelm Tell not only inspired the version of Friedrich SCHILLER but also served the causes of Swiss national pride and claims of independence.

With his *Vierundzwanzig Bücher Allgemeiner Geschichten besonders der Europaischen Menschheit* (Twenty-four chapters of universal history especially on European humanity; 1809), Müller offered a new tale of the history of humankind, narrated as a gradual unfolding of events, unpredictable and undetermined, but always changing.

Müller also left the *Reisen der Päpste* (Travels of the popes; 1782) and *Darstellung des Fürstenbundes* (Presentation of the League of Princes; 1787), two studies that explore the historical effects of FREEDOM and balance, favorite themes of enlightened historians and students of the human sciences.

Munich   German city on the Isar River, lying on the plains at the northern foothills of the Alps. Munich was the capital city of the German electorate of Bavaria in the 18th century. The original village grew up as support for the Benedictine abbey at Tegernsee; the name, München, simply referred to the monks (German, *Mönche*) who lived in the nearby monastery. The town became a trade center after 1156, when the Isar River was bridged, and shortly thereafter (1157–58) acquired the right to hold a market. The Wittelsbach family became rulers in Bavaria in 1180. From that date until the end of World War I (1918), they controlled Bavaria. Munich became their official residence in 1255. During the Thirty Years' War (1618–48), the Wittelsbachs made Bavaria a staunchly Catholic region. The city remains the premier urban area of modern Bavaria.

In the 18th century, Munich served as one center of a southern German, Catholic form of the ENLIGHTENMENT. The arts and architecture flourished, and the city gained several outstanding religious and secular German BAROQUE STYLE buildings. The Nymphenburg palace, gardens, and outbuildings (Amalienburg, Pagodenburg, and Badenburg); the facade of the Theatinerkirche (Church of the Theatines); the Heiliggeistkirche (Church of the Holy Spirit); the Asamkirche (the Asam brothers' chapel to St. John Nepomuk); and the Residenztheater (Residence Theater) date from the 18th century. The architects and decorators who worked in Munich included François CUVILLIÉS, Egid and Cosmas ASAM, and Johann Baptist Zimmermann. Munich offers a splendid example of 18th-century natural landscaping style in its famous ENGLISH GARDEN.

See also HOLY ROMAN EMPIRE; ROMAN CATHOLICISM.

Muratori, Lodovico Antonio (1672–1750) *Italian historian, librarian, and archivist*

A native of the region near Modena, Muratori received his early education from the JESUITS. He entered the Catholic clergy, taking minor orders in the priesthood in 1688. In the same year he received a degree in civil and canonical law, and in 1695 he became a priest. Muratori worked from 1695 until 1700 as curator of the Ambrosian Library of Milan; he accepted a post as chief archivist to the court of Modena in 1700, a position he retained for the rest of his life.

Muratori's duties at the Modena court included defending the territorial interests of Duke Rinaldo I d'Este against papal claims. These disputes involved conflicts between Catholic church law (canon law) and civil law. Muratori set out to collect as many documents as he could regarding Italian legal and ecclesiastical history. From them, he fashioned a comprehensive history of the Italian peninsula.

The results of this undertaking, the *Rerum italicarum scriptores* (Historians of Italian affairs; 1723–51) and the *Annali d'Italia* (Annals of Italy; 1744–49), presented a narrative of Italian history that included not only political events, but also a consideration of the impact of geographical, social, and economic factors on society.

From 1738 to 1742, Muratori wrote and published his greatest work, *Antiquitatis Italicae Medii Aevi* (Italian antiquities of the Middle Ages, 6 vols.). Muratori presented a vision of the history of the Italian peninsula that stressed the factors that united the region instead of concentrating on its political fragmentation.

Muratori also left some works on religion that attempt to integrate ideas of the ENLIGHTENMENT with the doctrines of ROMAN CATHOLICISM. These works include *Della carità cristiana* (On Christian charity; 1723) and *Della regolata devozione de' cristiani* (On the regulated devotion of Christians; 1747). He turned to political theory with *Della pubblica felicità* (On public happiness), exploring the central enlightened theme of HAPPINESS in the context of the mutual duties that link rulers with their subjects.

Muratori was one of the outstanding historians of the Enlightenment. In gathering materials for his books, he engaged in correspondence with historians throughout Europe. The great German philosopher Gottfried Wilhelm LEIBNIZ served as a major source of inspiration, both for his concept of history and for his ideal of creating an international network of European scholars.

museums Institutions charged with collecting, preserving, and exhibiting artifacts from the past. The first public museums appeared in Europe in the late 17th century. The 18th century saw a proliferation of these institutions. Prior to the establishment of these public collections, kings, queens, princes, and private wealthy individuals had collected art, inscriptions, manuscripts, and a vast array of other artifacts, which they displayed in their homes. The emergence of the idea of collections for public display is intimately linked with the spread of LITERACY, with the strong interest in antiquity, and with the development of historical writing that characterized the 17th and 18th centuries. Concurrently, the passion for organizing and categorizing the vast wealth of human knowledge and production helped to feed the desire to present material objects in a systematic manner. Closely related to the development of museums was the emergence of numerous lending libraries where books and periodicals could be obtained.

The Ashmolean Museum at Oxford University, the first public museum in Europe, opened in 1683. Its holdings consisted initially of two private collections, which had belonged to John Tradescant and Elias Ashmole. The next public museum opened only in 1759, when Sir Hans Sloane offered his private collection to the British Parliament. The Parliament accepted his offer, bought the materials, and used them to open the British Museum.

On the European continent, monarchs began to open their private collections for public viewing. In FRANCE, portions of the royal art collection could be viewed in 1750 at the Palais de Luxembourg in PARIS. The Hapsburgs opened certain collections in VIENNA in 1781. At the Vatican in ROME, the Capitoline Museum was organized in 1734, a picture gallery was founded in 1749 at the Palazzo dei Conservatori, and the antiquity collections in the Museo Pio-Clementino were opened in 1772. In North America, displays for public viewing could be found in Cambridge, Massachusetts, at Harvard College; in PHILADELPHIA, at the Science and History Museum as well as the AMERICAN PHILOSOPHICAL SOCIETY; and in Charleston, South Carolina.

Denis DIDEROT, the general editor of the ENCYCLOPÉDIE, used that great work of the ENLIGHTENMENT as a forum from which he outlined plans for a large public national museum in France. His scheme was partly realized during the FRENCH REVOLUTION with two foundations: the Muséum d'Histoire Naturelle at the JARDIN DES PLANTES, and the Muséum National (1793) at the Louvre.

See also PUBLISHING; SOCIAL INSTITUTIONS OF THE ENLIGHTENMENT.

music Like all other forms of art, music during the 18th century reflected the ideas and values of the ENLIGHTENMENT. Particularly influential were the ideals of COSMOPOLITANISM, popular dissemination, INDIVIDUALISM, and SENSIBILITY. Stylistic innovations, shifts in instrumentation, new types of performing groups, and revisions in the institutional supports for musical activity all bore the imprint of these ideals.

In the realm of musical style, a complex set of overlapping aesthetic ideals and practices existed during the Enlightenment. At the beginning of the 18th century, the BAROQUE STYLE was reaching its epitome in the works of J. S. BACH and George Frederick HANDEL. At the same time, elements of the ROCOCO style, manifested in the music of the *STYLE GALANT* and *EMPFINDSAMER STIL*, were making an appearance. Baroque and rococo forms coexisted until the middle of the 18th century, after which baroque forms generally disappeared and rococo styles began to be supplanted by musical CLASSICISM.

Kassel Wilhelmshöhe, by Johann Eleazar Zeisig. Musical performances in intimate settings such as salons were popular throughout Europe in the 18th century. *(Courtesy New York Public Library)*

The end of the 18th century saw the full flowering of classicism in the compositions of Franz Joseph HAYDN, Wolfgang Amadeus MOZART, and the young Ludwig van BEETHOVEN.

The *style galant* and *empfindsamer Stil* display the earliest signs of the influence of the Enlightenment. Building from the same ideas as the general cult of sensibility, they attempted to transform musical compositions into vehicles for expressing delicate sentiment, abandoning the baroque concern for evoking strong passions. Operas turned away from the mythological subjects of baroque *opera seria,* substituting themes from familiar, thoroughly human situations. These shifts mirror the changes that developed in LITERATURE with the appearance of SENTIMENTAL FICTION.

Musical classicism grew partly from the *style galant* and *empfindsamer Stil,* continuing the trends toward homophonic melodic structures (melody with accompaniment). Its forms strove for balance and simplicity, two ideals that also informed NEOCLASSICISM in art and architecture. It reached for greater expressiveness, introducing, for example, the gradual crescendo and decrescendo into compositions. The era of classicism produced, among other things, the sonata form, the symphony, and the triumph of comic opera.

Prior to the appearance of the classical style, European music could be divided into distinctive national styles. The Italian and German styles were particularly prominent, but the French style also exercised considerable influence. The matter of national styles occasionally generated intense emotions, as happened in the French BATTLE OF THE BUFFOONS. The classical style eventually submerged these national styles into a truly cosmopolitan blend worthy of the enlightened emphasis on the universal qualities that unite all humankind.

Compositional innovations demanded musical instruments capable of putting them across to an audience. The 18th century met these demands by introducing several new instruments to the musical world. These instruments, in turn, allowed composers to continue exploring new styles and techniques. In the course of the century, the PIANO replaced the harpsichord, and the family of violins (violin, VIOLA, and violoncello) replaced the older viols. Transverse flutes took the place of end-blown recorders, and the first true CLARINETS also entered the orchestra.

The music of the Enlightenment was supported by the urban and courtly worlds. It was distinct from the music of lower urban classes and villagers, but it definitely borrowed from those popular forms. During the rococo period, for example, one of the most beloved French court instruments was the *musette,* the simple shepherd's bagpipe. Violins were originally instruments of Italian street musicians, but their impressive expressive capabilities made them attractive to Italian composers seeking to incorporate such qualities into their works. Opera forms such as the Italian intermezzo and the German singspiel developed directly from popular sung comedies.

The cultural structures that supported music composition and performance shifted dramatically during the Enlightenment. At the beginning of the 18th century, composers worked as the employees of kings, princes, high aristocrats, or the churches. In return for a salary, they wrote compositions to suit the needs and tastes of their employers. Private and official patronage of this sort continued throughout the 18th century, but it was slowly disappearing. Composers increasingly worked as independent agents, supporting themselves by selling their compositions to music publishers, giving private lessons, offering series of subscription concerts, and obtaining commissions for specific compositions. This new world, supported by the ideal of individualism, gave composers greater freedom to explore new styles and compositional techniques, but it also brought new difficulties in its wake. Composers and performers struggled to make a living, and all too often, they found that the tyranny of patrons had simply been replaced by the tyranny of popular taste. The insecurities generated during this transition sometimes produced ambivalence toward independence. Mozart, for example, had found the restrictions of working at court (in Salzburg) onerous. Nevertheless, he sometimes expressed disappointment and resentment at not receiving an appointment as official court composer in VIENNA.

Independence was made possible, in part, by changes in the socioeconomic structures of European cities. Increasingly large groups of people from the aristocratic and middle classes had money to spend on consumption. Not only did they buy small luxuries such as porcelains or tapestries, but they also purchased the opportunity to hear musical concerts or to attend operas. The subscription concert, in which tickets for a series of performances were sold in advance, was an invention of the late 17th century and became increasingly popular during the Enlightenment. By the end of the 18th century, these subscribed events had become the standard means for presenting musical performances to the public.

During the last decades of the 18th century, the English provided an entirely new twist to concert repertoire. Performers began presenting so-called classic works. The term *classic works*, not to be confused with the style called classicism, suggested that certain works have lasting value. Rather than presenting newly composed works, as was the standard 18th-century practice, the English series offered works by "old masters" such as Henry Purcell, Handel, and Thomas Arne, who had died only in 1695, 1759, and 1778, respectively.

The Enlightenment encouraged musicians to find ways of making their specialized musical language and training available to the uninitiated. As a result, the first method books and manuals explaining performance practices appeared. Sheet music was produced by music publishers for purchase by interested individuals. However, until the 19th century, printing techniques made costs high. Music CRITICISM also appeared in periodicals and professional journals, where it helped to shape the public taste for certain styles and became a new source of restrictions on the artistic freedom of composers. A critic's words helped to determine whether a new composition became a success—that is, was played, published, or, in the case of opera, staged. Composers in the late 18th century depended on performances, publishing royalties, and commissions for their income. They were, therefore, constrained to some degree to create music that would be praised by critics. The tyranny of the critic replaced that of the patron of earlier eras.

Music continued to play important roles in church services, but many compositions on sacred subjects were presented outside churches. Oratorios by Handel and Haydn, for example, were presented at regular public concerts.

Musical activity tended to center in cities where composers and musicians could not only intermingle but also find audiences. Of greatest importance were Vienna, PARIS, LONDON, BERLIN, Mannheim, MILAN, VENICE, Leipzig, Dresden, and Hamburg. Berlin was home to C. P. E. BACH, Johann Joachim Quantz, Johann Gottlieb Graun, Karl Heinrich Graun (1704–59), and Johann Friedrich Reichardt (1752–1814). Dresden supported Johann Adolph Hasse (1699–1783), one of the most prolific 18th-century composers. Mannheim served as home to Johann Stamitz (1717–57), creator of the so-called MANNHEIM SCHOOL of style, under whose direction the Mannheim orchestra acquired an international reputation.

Composers from the Italian peninsula led the way in creating the symphonic form. Of major importance were Giovanni Battista Sammartini, Baldassare Galuppi, and Niccolò Jomelli. Arcangelo CORELLI, Antonio VIVALDI, and Domenico SCARLATTI left compositions still popular today. ITALY, of course, served as a major destination for eager young composers, and its composers significantly shaped the aesthetics of the classical era.

Paris remained a musical capital, one of the major places where composers staged operas. Christoph Willibald GLUCK and Giovanni Battista PERGOLESI both made their reputations in the French capital. Local musicians included Jean-Philippe RAMEAU, André Ernest Modeste Grétry, and even Jean-Jacques ROUSSEAU. London was home to George Frederick Handel, Thomas Arne, Karl Friedrich ABEL, and Johann Christian BACH. The English capital probably had the most varied musical life in 18th-century Europe. It had a large, wealthy population of eager consumers and musical entrepreneurs such as Johann Peter Salomon, who exploited it. It also possessed several outdoor pleasure gardens, which competed with each other in offering musical attractions.

Vienna supported an active group of composers who were overshadowed by the giants Haydn, Mozart, and Beethoven. Among them were George Matthias Monn (1717–50), Georg Christoph Wagenseil (1715–77), Florian Leopold Gassman (1729–74), Michael Haydn (1737–1806), and Antonio Salieri (1750–1825). Together, these composers helped to make Vienna the center of musical classicism and to secure its leadership into the era of ROMANTICISM.

By the end of the 18th century, both the artistic content of music and the culture that supported it bore scant resemblance to the situation at the beginning of that century. In this realm as elsewhere, the Enlightenment stimulated broadscale changes that helped to usher in the modern era.

See also BOULOGNE; CLEMENTI; CORELLI; OPERA; STAMITZ.

Further reading: Manfred F. Bukofzer, *Music in the Baroque Era* (New York: W. W. Norton, 1947); Charles Burney, *The Present State of Music in France and Italy,* facsimile of 1773 ed. (New York: Broude Bros, 1969); Donald

Jay Grout, *A History of Western Music,* rev. ed. (New York: W. W. Norton, 1973); Charles Rosen, *The Classical Style: Haydn, Mozart, Beethoven,* expanded ed. (New York: W. W. Norton, 1997); Cynthia Verba, *Music and the French Enlightenment: Reconstruction of a Dialogue, 1750–1764* (New York: Oxford University Press, 1993).

Musschenbroek, Pieter van (1692–1761) *Dutch experimental philosopher, mathematician, and physicist*
Musschenbroek (also known as Petrus van Musschenbroek), the scion of a family of prominent instrument makers, studied MEDICINE at the University of Leiden. After receiving his degree in 1715, he embarked on a study tour to LONDON and then returned to Leiden. He worked as a professor of mathematics and philosophy in Duisburg in the HOLY ROMAN EMPIRE (1719–23) and as professor of natural philosophy and mathematics at Utrecht (1723–40). Musschenbroek finished his career at the University of Leiden (1740–61), where he assumed responsibility for teaching experimental physics. Musschenbroek's reputation as a lecturer drew an international student body. Among his students was Jean-Antoine Nollet, the future Abbé NOLLET, who helped to popularize lecture-demonstrations on physics and electricity in FRANCE.

Musschenbroek is renowned for his experiments with the Leyden jar, a device that had been invented by the German scientist Ewald Georg von Kleist (ca. 1700–48). The device became a popular fixture in 18th-century demonstrations of electrical phenomena. In modern terminology, the Leyden jar was actually an electrical condenser that consisted of a glass jar coated on the inside and outside with metal foil. Its inner coating, connected to a conducting rod, passes through the jar's insulated stopper.

In experimenting with the Leyden jar, Musschenbroek and an assistant discovered its capacity to deliver a tremendous shock. Musschenbroek reported the experience in a letter to the French scientist René-Antoine-Ferchault de Réaumur (1683–1757), and his assistant wrote similarly to Abbé Nollet. As a result, the Leyden jar experiments were reported to the FRENCH ACADEMY OF SCIENCES (1746).

Musschenbroek published his lectures and experiments as *Epitome elementorum physico-mathematicorum conscripta in usus academico* (Abridgement of the physical-mathematical elements used in academic practice; 1726); *Elementa physicae* (Elements of physics; 1734); *Institutiones physicae* (Methods of physics; 1748); and *Introductio ad philosophiam naturalem* (Introduction to natural philosophy; published posthumously, 1762).

See also MATHEMATICS AND MECHANICS; NATURAL PHILOSOPHY; SCIENCE; TECHNOLOGY AND INSTRUMENTATION.

N

Nathan the Wise A dramatic poem addressing the question of religious TOLERATION written by Gotthold Ephraim LESSING in 1779. Lessing wrote *Nathan the Wise* (German: *Nathan der Weise*) after he had been forbidden by his employer, KARL WILHELM FERDINAND, duke of Braunschweig-Wolfenbüttel, from publishing on topics of RELIGION. This proscription had come about as the result of Lessing's disputes with the antagonistic and influential Lutheran pastor Johann Melchior Goeze. The plot of *Nathan the Wise* allowed Lessing to evade the duke's orders and to continue addressing religious questions.

Nathan the Wise takes place in Jerusalem during the Third Crusade (1190–92). Nathan, a Jewish merchant of impeccable character, has returned from a trip to find that his house has burned down. His daughter, Recha, would have died in the fire had she not been rescued by a Christian Crusader, the Knight Templar, Curd von Stauffen. Curd himself is a captive of Saladin, a Saracen warrior who, for unknown reasons, has spared his prisoner's life. Nathan seeks out Curd to thank him for rescuing Recha. At first, Curd is rude to the Jew, but gradually his attitude changes as he recognizes Nathan's good qualities.

In the meantime, Saladin has learned about Nathan and summons him in order to procure a forced loan from him. The two men engage in conversation, and Saladin asks Nathan which religion is the true religion: Judaism, Christianity, or Islam. Nathan, fearing a trap, responds by telling the parable of the three rings (inspired by a story in the *Decameron* of Boccaccio). There once was a father who possessed a ring, which not only gave him the right to rule but also guaranteed that he would rule with love, justice, and wisdom. It was the custom of the land for the ring to be passed down to the most beloved son, but this father loved each of his three sons equally. He could not bear to choose one of them over the others and, therefore, he had two counterfeit rings made that were indistinguishable from the authentic one. Each son received a ring. After the father's death, each son claimed the throne and they began to fight with one another. The matter came before a judge who solved the problem by advising the sons that none of them had been behaving as the wise ruler should who would rightfully possess the ring. He suggested that they go out into the world and begin acting in the wise and loving manner that would be expected of the rightful heir to the true ring. He also told them that in the future, a thousand years later, a wiser judge than he would be able to decide on the basis of their actions and those of their successors which of them was the possessor of the true ring.

Nathan, in this indirect manner, advised Saladin that Jews, Christians, and Muslims should all go out and simply act according to the basic ideals of their religions. History and, ultimately, God would judge which religion was true and that judgment would be based upon the presence or absence of loving, tolerant, and wise actions. By implication Nathan was suggesting that all three religions would, in the end, turn out to be the same religion and, therefore, that unity and brotherhood would prevail.

The telling of the parable of the three rings occurs at the highpoint of Lessing's play. What follows is a denouement reminiscent of *Le Barbier de Séville* by Pierre de BEAUMARCHAIS and laced with the ideals of the ENLIGHTENMENT; the universal brotherhood of all people, the desire for a religion based on love and humanitarian sentiments, and the consequent need for tolerance of human differences. Recha turns out to be an orphan, who was adopted by

Nathan when her parents died. Furthermore, she is Curd's sister. Curd and Recha then realize that they are both the children of Saladin's brother, a man named Assad, who traveled to Europe and assumed the Christian name of Wolf. The play ends with the whole family reunited and with Nathan greatly admired and esteemed by all.

Lessing modeled the character of Nathan after his dear friend Moses MENDELSSOHN, a Jewish philosopher who not only helped to found the HASKALAH movement (Jewish Enlightenment) but also championed religious TOLERATION. For Lessing, who viewed religions from the vantage point of the philosophy of Benedict de SPINOZA, the differences among Judaism, Christianity, and Islam were less important than the similarities: They each possess a spark of the divine that compels them to pursue the ultimate truth. God's plan for humankind, Lessing suggests, can best be carried out through toleration of different viewpoints accompanied by virtuous living and generous conduct toward others.

See also AUFKLÄRUNG.

natural history *See* AFFINITY CHEMISTRY; ANIMALCULISM; ANIMISM; BACON; BANKS; BARTHEZ; BERGMAN; BICHAT; BIOLOGY; BLACK; BLUMENBACH; BONNET; BORDEU; BUFFON; CABANIS; CAMPER; CLASSIFICATION; COOK; CULLEN; CUVIER; DARWIN; DAUBENTON; DEGENERATION; *ENCYCLOPÉDIE*; EPIGENESIS; FORSTER, JOHANN GEORG ADAM; FORSTER, JOHANN REINHOLD; GENERATION; HALLER; JARDIN DES PLANTES; LAMARCK; LINNAEUS; MAUPERTUIS; NATURAL PHILOSOPHY; NATURE; PREFORMATION THEORY; RELATIONS; SCIENCE; SPALLANZANI; SYMPATHY; VITALISM.

Further reading: Richard W. Burkhardt, Jr., *The Spirit of System: Lamarck and Evolutionary Biology* (Cambridge, Mass.: Harvard University Press, 1977); William Clark, Jan Golinski, Simon Schaffer, *The Sciences in Enlightened Europe* (Chicago and London: University of Chicago Press, 1999); Christopher Fox, Roy Porter, Robert Wokler, eds., *Inventing Human Science: Eighteenth-Century Domains* (Berkeley and Los Angeles: University of California Press, 1995); Nicholas Jardine, James Secord, Emma Spary, *Cultures of Natural History* (Cambridge: Cambridge University Press, 1996); Ludmilla Jordanova, *Languages of Nature: Critical Essays on Science and Literature* (London: Free Association Books, 1986); James Larson, *Interpreting Nature: The Science of Living Form from Linnaeus to Kant* (Baltimore and London: The Johns Hopkins Press, 1994); John Lyon, Phillip R. Sloan, ed., trans. *From Natural History to the History of Nature* (Notre Dame: University of Notre Dame Press, 1981); Peter Reill, Peter Hanns, *Vitalizing Nature in the Enlightenment* (Berkeley and Los Angeles: University of California Press, 2005); Jacques Roger, *Buffon: A Life in Natural History,* trans., Sarah Lucille Bonnefor (Ithaca, N.Y.: Cornell University Press, 1997); George S. Rousseau, Roy Porter, *The Ferment of Knowledge: Studies in the Historiography of*

Eighteenth-Century Science (Cambridge: Cambridge University Press, 1980); Emma C. Spary, *Utopia's Garden: French Natural History from Old Regime to Revolution* (Chicago and London: University of Chicago Press, 2000); Mary Terrall, *The Man Who Flattened the Earth: Maupertuis and the Science in the Enlightenment* (Chicago and London, University of Chicago Press, 2002).

natural law A legal, moral, philosophical, and theological concept central to RATIONALISM and also to the thought of the ENLIGHTENMENT. The idea of natural law is composed of two separate concepts, NATURE and law. Each of these concepts has a long history in Western thought extending back to the ancient Greeks. These two concepts, which themselves have had varying meanings throughout history, have also been put together in different ways to create the many concepts of natural law that have existed throughout western European history. Natural law theory, then, is not a uniform body of thought, and any attempt to reduce the ideas of its various contributors to one system will result in confusion.

Eighteenth-century concepts of natural law rested on the theories of rational natural law and MORAL PHILOSOPHY that had been built in the 17th century by Hugo Grotius, Samuel PUFENDORF, Gottfried Wilhelm LEIBNIZ, Christian WOLFF, and Benedict de SPINOZA.

Underlying all these theories was the belief that REASON, conceived as a set of rational orderly mathematical RELATIONS (laws), determines the basic structures of the universe. Reason is the "ordering order" (*ordo ordinans*) of the universe in both the physical realm and the realm of human activity. Its laws are not subject to the will of human authorities, whether associated with church or state. Furthermore, even God, who created these laws, is somehow obliged to abide by them. Nature and law, in this vision, are thus intimately intertwined; law is what gives the universe (nature) its order.

The same reason that governs nature also exists as an innate (natural, inborn) faculty of the human mind and enables the mind to detect rational natural laws. It is therefore possible, by careful use of the ability to reason, to discern the natural order of things in the world and to bring positive (human-made) law into accordance with the precepts and principles of this natural law.

Seventeenth-century natural law theorists proceeded from these assumptions to deduce entire systems of rational law that they believed apply universally to all human beings in every cultural or environmental situation. Their systems of natural law were highly abstract and not necessarily intended to provide solutions to the practical problems of their era; they also broke radically, in significant aspects, with earlier concepts of natural law. Perhaps most important, the link that had been established in the Middle Ages between reason and the divine revelations of God was severed.

The 17th-century notion of independent natural law was inextricably tied to theories about the origins and purpose of human society. Writers tended to see natural law as the law that ruled among people before they came together to form societies. As such, it was inextricably linked with the concepts of NATURAL RIGHTS and human nature.

Definitions of these concepts and explanations of their interrelationships varied and, as the writings of John LOCKE and Thomas HOBBES illustrate, could be used to justify everything from representative government to absolute monarchy. But all writers were struggling with the same basic question: defining how human societies and positive laws can best honor the principles of natural law and preserve natural human rights.

Eighteenth-century political theorists—Baron de MONTESQUIEU, Jean-Jacques ROUSSEAU, Immanuel KANT, Jean-Jacques BURLAMAQUI, Emmerich de Vattel, and Christian WOLFF, to name only a few—all worked within the framework of basic 17th-century notions of natural law and struggled with the problem of how to protect natural law and natural rights in civilized societies. They believed that by grounding positive human-made laws in natural law, political systems better than those under which they were living could be created. Their works thus focused on how natural rights such as the rights to FREEDOM, EQUALITY, HAPPINESS, and PROPERTY, could best be interpreted and honored in the context of an actual political society. Toward the end of the Enlightenment, the framers of the American DECLARATION OF INDEPENDENCE (1776), the UNITED STATES BILL OF RIGHTS (1791), various American state constitutions, and the French DECLARATION OF THE RIGHTS OF MAN AND THE CITIZEN (1789) consciously drew on the legacy of natural law and natural rights theory to create new governments and positive law codes.

See also CIVIL SOCIETY; POLITICAL THEORY; RIGHTS.

natural philosophy   The broad discipline that aimed at explaining the philosophical principles and causes that operate in the physical world.

In medieval European universities, a hierarchy of faculties existed with THEOLOGY at the top, law in second place, and MEDICINE in third place. The faculty of liberal arts occupied the bottom rank. The liberal arts included seven subjects clustered as the quadrivium (arithmetic, geometry, MUSIC, and ASTRONOMY) and the trivium (grammar, rhetoric, and logic).

The study of the natural world—that is, natural philosophy—occurred primarily within the context of the quadrivium subjects, all of which dealt with aspects of mathematics. Arithmetic studied discrete numbers and geometry addressed forms (points, lines, planes, and solids). Music studied ratios and proportions, while astronomy dealt with spheres and their motions.

Within this clean division of subject matter, there occurred other classifications that reflected the complexity of certain subjects. A distinction was made, for example, between pure and mixed sciences; astronomy, the fourth member of the quadrivium, was also classified as a mixed science because it actually drew on arithmetic, geometry, and music for its theoretical explanations. Optics and mechanics were also mixed sciences. The concept of a separate discipline called physics did not yet exist, and the subject matter of chemistry fell either under medicine or ALCHEMY.

During the 16th and 17th centuries, curriculum classifications began to be restructured to reflect the increasing importance of mathematics. The subject matter of the various mixed sciences, in turn, tended to be grouped together as natural philosophy.

This system of classification still existed during the SCIENTIFIC REVOLUTION and well into the ENLIGHTENMENT. Newton, for example, was a mathematician and natural philosopher. So were most other major contributors to the important scientific developments of these areas.

Natural philosophy thus encompassed what today we know as natural sciences, especially physics. But during the Enlightenment, the concept of natural philosophy receded into the background as the people studying the natural world moved away from the rational examination of first causes toward the empirical observation of physical events.

See also BIOLOGY; CHEMISTRY; CLASSIFICATION; EMPIRICISM; MATHEMATICS AND MECHANICS; MEDICINE; NATIONALISM; SCIENCE; SCIENTIFIC METHOD; VOYAGE OF DISCOVERY.

Further reading: Lorin Anderson, *Charles Bonnet and the Order of the Known* (Hingham, Mass: D. Reidel, 1982); Francis Bacon, *New Atlantis and the Great Instauration,* ed. Jerry Weinberger (Arlington Heights, Ill.: Harlan Davidson, 1989); Jed Z. Buchwald, I. Bernard Cohen, eds., *Isaac Newton's Natural Philosophy* (Cambridge, Mass: MIT Press, 2001); Susan Liepert, ed., *The Book of Nature: The Eighteenth Century and the Material World* (Edmonton: University of Alberta, 1977); Charles Webster, *The Great Instauration* (New York: Holmes & Meier Publisher, 1975).

natural religion   Form of religious doctrine that developed in the 17th century and continued into the ENLIGHTENMENT. Natural religion was a response to SKEPTICISM, to Christian doctrinal conflict, and to the challenge of non-Christian religions. Theorists of natural religion attempted to find a basis for religious belief and doctrine in the natural order of the universe.

No unified doctrine of natural religion existed, but certain common characteristics did link various formulations together. Most formulations, for example, postulated that human beings have certain religious ideas or feelings from birth. Because these ideas are innate, they are natural, part of the preordained order of things rather than a product of individual experience and EDUCATION. These natural human ideas are also universal (common to every human being), since all things, including the human mind, are constructed after and operate according to universal laws. As universal attributes of human nature, these natural, innate religious ideas or feelings can, therefore, provide a foundation for a universal religion capable of drawing all people together and of ending religious strife.

Belief in the existence of universal religious ideas was intimately linked in the formative years of the Enlightenment to RATIONALISM and its belief that REASON underlies all the human and natural structures of the universe. Reason served not only as the source of all ideas but also as the means by which true ideas could be recognized. By exercising the ability to reason, therefore, people could easily recognize religious truths. They would not be required to make a blind leap of faith or to accept miracles, magic, divine revelation, and irrational events as proofs of the truth of their religious beliefs.

The development of natural religion was intimately associated with the flowering of DEISM in the early years of the Enlightenment. Deism was compatible with both reason and criticism, the two instruments favored by enlightened thinkers for furthering human progress. As a result, deism became a popular religious form for those who could not honestly continue to practice traditional Christianity but who did not want to abandon religion. Natural religion contributed in many ways to the developments that marked the Enlightenment by spurring the search for a rational or natural ethics, by stimulating utilitarianism, by supporting the cause of religious TOLERATION, and by facilitating the separation of MORAL PHILOSOPHY from theology.

Although rationalism underlay the natural religion of the early Enlightenment, feeling and emotion provided the underpinnings for a later natural religion variant, which closely paralleled its enlightened secular counterpart, the cult of SENSIBILITY. Both phenomena emerged in the early Enlightenment and assumed importance during its middle decades. Both recognized that sensation, feeling, and emotion play roles as important as reason in shaping human knowledge. It seemed that certain natural and universal feelings in human beings could be called religious, and that they could provide an alternative to reason and dogma to act as a foundation for natural religion. This feeling-based variant of natural religion expressed itself most strongly in the various forms of religious ENTHUSIASM that appeared during the Enlightenment.

See also RELIGION; UTILITY.

natural rights Central concept of the ENLIGHTENMENT, derived from 17th-century theories of NATURAL LAW and closely associated with the development of INDIVIDUALISM. The theory of natural law posited the existence of ordered, rational RELATIONS in NATURE (natural laws), which govern the physical universe and can be deduced by human beings with their innate ability to reason. Natural laws, rooted as they were in reason, were necessarily true, self-evident, and universal. They prescribed certain fundamental relations and prerogatives for humankind: individual FREEDOM and EQUALITY, the natural rights of mankind. To these two fundamental rights, 17th- and 18th-century theorists added others considered equally natural: PROPERTY and HAPPINESS. In addition, certain derivative rights were discussed such as security and freedom from oppression. The duty of all political government and society lay in protecting and fostering the enjoyment of these rights.

Several forms of government were seen as potentially compatible with natural rights, including enlightened

THE HORSE AMERICA. *throwing his Master.*

"The Horse America, throwing his Master," a British cartoon, 1779. The American colonists justified their overthrow of British rule by appealing to the idea of natural human rights. *(Courtesy Stock Montage, Inc., Chicago, Illinois)*

despotism (see DESPOTISM, ENLIGHTENED), limited monarchy, and republicanism. Theories of social contract by John LOCKE and Thomas HOBBES in the 17th century and by Jean-Jacques ROUSSEAU in the 18th century concerned themselves primarily with describing how these natural rights could be preserved as societies were being constituted. These thinkers recognized that coming together as a society might require the curtailment of absolute liberty, but differed as to how that curtailment could be mitigated or turned into a greater degree of freedom. The American DECLARATION OF INDEPENDENCE (1776), the UNITED STATES BILL OF RIGHTS, and the French DECLARATION OF THE RIGHTS OF MAN AND THE CITIZEN (1789) raised the concept of natural rights into actual organizing legal principles upon which new political structures in the UNITED STATES OF AMERICA and FRANCE were to be constituted.

See also POLITICAL THEORY, RIGHTS.

nature   One of the basic concepts of the ENLIGHTENMENT, a word that served with REASON as the standard against which other ideas, activities, and aspirations were evaluated. Enlightened Europeans tried to bring their concepts of society, their educational programs, and their political structures, art, MUSIC, and LITERATURE into conformity with nature.

Nearly everyone agreed on the importance of using nature as a model, but they parted ways when they began using the term in specific instances. The many definitions of nature reveal the underlying tensions in enlightened thought and assist historians armed with the benefit of hindsight in understanding how its formulas unraveled at the end of the 18th century.

For the history of the Enlightenment, the earliest significant shifts in the use of the term *nature* began to occur during the 17th-century SCIENTIFIC REVOLUTION. The new model of SCIENCE advocated abandoning inquiries about the essences (natures) of things. It proposed, instead, to concentrate on describing events that occur in the terrestrial and celestial worlds.

The nature that scientists were attempting to describe was now simply the world of phenomena observable by human beings. But this nature—the world of stars, planets, the Sun, comets, forests, mountains, oceans, motion, matter, chemical reactions, and living beings—was a nature markedly different from that familiar to Renaissance natural philosophers. Hidden forces (occult qualities) and spirits were banished, or at least deemed unsuitable subjects for scientific inquiry. When such concepts seemed to reappear in scientific theories, as happened when Isaac NEWTON invented the idea of universal gravitation, people exclaimed that occult qualities and the realm of MAGIC were once again threatening to undermine rational human inquiry. Scientists like Newton, who retained certain interests in the realms of magic and ALCHEMY, often concealed their work, leaving only unpublished notes, diaries, and manuscripts for modern scholars to discover.

The new world of nature, the one espoused in the MECHANICAL PHILOSOPHY, was conceived as a giant machine or clock, honed to precision by the expert watchmaker, God. This was the world of René DESCARTES, an image that persisted well into the Enlightenment even after specific Cartesian theories had been displaced by Newtonian models.

In this new world, mathematical laws, put in place by God at the time of creation, actually determined the course of events. God was remote from the world for most theorists, stepping in only occasionally to wind up the clock works. Reason dominated in this world and assured that natural operations would be accessible to the rational minds of human beings.

This was an orderly and benign vision of nature in which conflict, disaster, and passion scarcely existed. Its legal rational basis guaranteed that PROGRESS would occur and that goodness would eventually triumph.

An older vision of nature continued to coexist with this rational view, at least in certain intellectual traditions. This vision retained the notion of nature as an organic unity vibrant with forces and filled with disembodied spirit. Mechanical, mathematical laws described certain aspects of this world adequately, but they could not explain the wondrous phenomena associated with life. Associated with the life sciences, with alchemy, and with the views of the Cambridge Platonists, this vision eventually resurged in the middle of the 18th century when theories of VITALISM began to dominate the life sciences.

The middle years of the 18th century brought another dramatic shift in the vision of nature. In the aftermath of the tragic destruction of the LISBON EARTHQUAKE of 1755, people abandoned their ideas about the benevolence, rationality, and orderliness of nature. They turned with increasing frequency to images that emphasized the violent, destructive, awe-inspiring aspects of nature.

These shifts can be seen in the paintings after mid-century, in the themes of literature, and in the theory of the SUBLIME. Some scholars associate this shift with the beginnings of ROMANTICISM or call the phenomenon pre-romanticism. But the phenomenon has strong roots in the Enlightenment and can be seen as an extension of its basic principles.

In PSYCHOLOGY and the cult of SENSIBILITY, the Enlightenment had recognized the importance of feelings and sensation in forming human experience, and it had wrestled uncomfortably with irrational events. These aspects of existence returned to the forefront of consciousness at mid-century, demanding that intellectuals find ways of accommodating them in their schemes.

In some realms, enlightened theories did succeed somewhat at this task. Insanity, for example, began to be treated as a medical illness rather than as a moral failing. Certain terrifying natural events like electrical storms

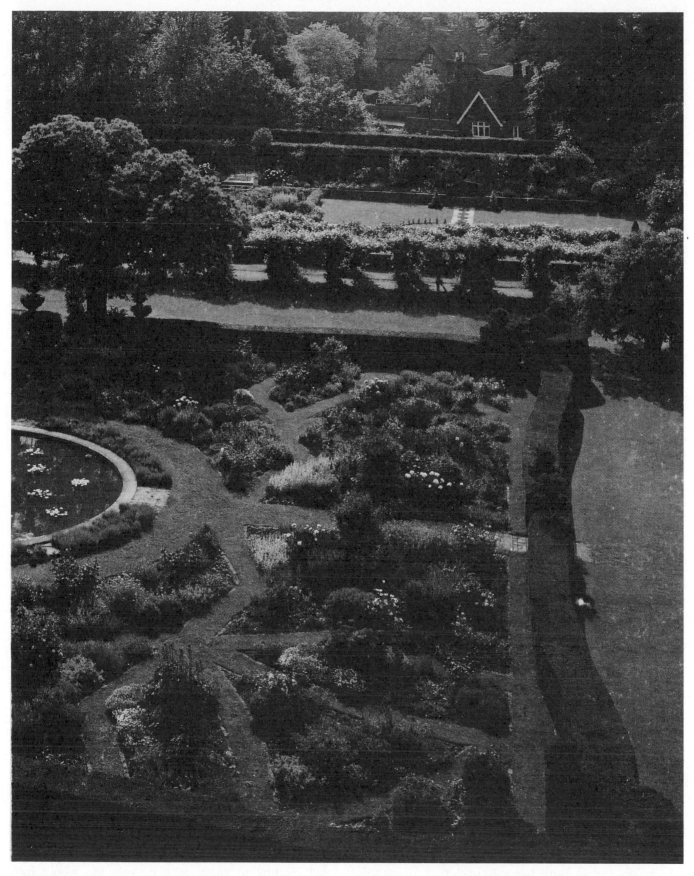

Formal garden, Hatfield House. In the middle years of the 18th century, the formal geometric designs represented by this garden were largely abandoned in favor of the so-called English garden with curved lines and a planned appearance of natural abandonment. This shift in garden styles reflected the basic changes in the conceptualization of nature that began to appear at mid-century. *(Courtesy New York Public Library)*

were given rational explanations. But still, the powers of nature inspired awe, and the passionate, often uncontrolled aspects of human nature captured imaginations. When they joined with renewed demands for individual FREEDOM, they became ingredients for the cultural synthesis and trend called romanticism.

The concept of nature carried with it several related ideas, the presence of which should alert students to the fact that nature is an underlying metaphor. Of the many related notions, the most frequently encountered include "natural," "primitive," and "rational." Most of the concepts associated with the second fundamental value of the Enlightenment, reason, also can refer to the concept of nature. This fact arises out of the intimate linkage between nature and reason that existed at the beginning of the Enlightenment.

The many forms in which the concept of nature enter enlightened discourse reveal the extent to which the Enlightenment was rooted in scientific theory and pursuits. In fact, nearly every significant theme of the Enlightenment—even such notions as progress, HAPPINESS, PERFECTIBILITY, SYMPATHY, and the SEPARATION OF POWERS—have links to the metaphor of nature.

See also STOWE.

Further reading: Lester G. Crocker, *An Age of Crisis: Man and World in Eighteenth-Century French Thought* (Baltimore: Johns Hopkins Press, 1959); W. J. Hipple, *The Beautiful, the Sublime and the Picturesque in Eighteenth-Century British Aesthetic Theory* (Carbondale, Ill.: Southern Illinois University Press, 1957); David C. Lindberg and Ronald Numbers, *God and Nature: Historical Essays on the Encounter between Christianity and Science* (Berkeley, Calif.: University of California Press, 1986).

Necker, Jacques (1732–1804) *Swiss banker who served in France as director general of finance and principal minister of state under Louis XVI*

Necker married Suzanne Curchod de Nasse in 1764; they had a daughter, Germaine Necker, who is renowned in history as Madame de STAËL. Necker was a native of GENEVA. His father, a lawyer and Calvinist, had moved to that city from the electorate of BRANDENBURG. Young Jacques studied PHILOSOPHY, LITERATURE, and business and then, following the wishes of his father, took a position as a banker in PARIS. He rapidly accumulated a private fortune and earned a reputation as a financial genius. In 1768, the republic of Geneva named him its representative to the French court. In that capacity, Necker acquired both business connections and social relations with high court officials such as the duc de CHOISEUL.

Necker began to fashion himself as an opponent of the free-market economic reforms favored by Controller General of Finance Anne-Robert-Jacques TURGOT and the PHYSIOCRATS. Necker preferred the older economic policies associated with MERCANTILISM, which gave the central state administration a powerful role in shaping and regulating economic activity. To underscore his position, Necker wrote an *Éloge de Colbert* (Elegy on Colbert) praising the policies of Jean-Baptiste Colbert, the 17th-century controller general of finance who had championed mercantilistic policies. Necker also published a treatise directly attacking Turgot's policies on free grain trade. When Turgot fell from power, Necker was well placed to assume leadership on account of his business record and literary reputation. But Suzanne NECKER, his wife, seems also to have played a role in securing his first official appointment in 1776 as director of the royal treasury. As a Calvinist, Necker was barred by French law from holding the position of controller general of finance. As a result, when the king decided in 1777 to appoint Necker to that position, he simply ordered the creation of a new office, director general of finance, and left the old position of controller general vacant.

It was Necker's task to rescue the French government from its ever-deepening financial crisis. During his tenure in office (1777–81), Necker proved a master at borrowing money for the regime. He also instituted some important enlightened reforms on behalf of peasants by abolishing mortmain, a remnant of medieval manorial practices that allowed manor owners (lords) to collect taxes on peasant-owned land within their jurisdiction before it could be passed to legal heirs. Necker also abolished the use of torture as a means of extracting a confession from accused prisoners.

In 1781, Necker resigned his post in a state of anger over the disputes that were occurring about his actions as director general. He claimed to have brought the budget deficit under control, but other officials disputed the claim and subsequent investigation has shown that the French debt had actually increased dramatically. Necker had, for example, financed the French fighting against Britain during the American Revolutionary War by borrowing more money rather than by increasing taxation. Unfortunately, Necker's replacement, Charles-Alexandre de CALONNE, proved no more successful than his predecessors in eliminating the structural causes of the French financial crisis.

The fiscal crisis in France was serious aggravating the general political instability of the regime. In the growing atmosphere of unrest, just after he had agreed to call the Estates General meeting that would ultimately bring on the FRENCH REVOLUTION, Louis XVI also recalled Necker to office. Negotiations were being carried out regarding the form that the Estates General would take. Necker supported the so-called doubling of the Third Estate (bourgeoisie representatives). This proposal would have allowed every Third Estate vote in the Estates General meeting to count as two votes but would have counted every First Estate (clergy) and Second Estate (nobility) vote as only one vote. The doubling of the

Third Estate would have strengthened the position of the French bourgeoisie against the privileged clergy and nobility. It was one of the issues that finally provoked the outbreak of revolutionary action.

Necker was dismissed from office on July 11, 1789, and was recalled just six days later. He continued to serve Louis XVI until September 1790, when he left France and returned to his native Geneva. He published an appeal on behalf of Louis XVI (*Réflexions offertes à la nation française* (Reflections offered to the French Nation; 1792), which caused the revolutionary French government to place him on the list of traitor emigres and to sequester his French property and goods. In 1802, Necker published a work criticizing the projects of Napoleon, which caused his daughter, Madame de Staël, who was still living in PARIS, much difficulty with the French regime. Shortly after his death in 1804, Madame de Staël published her memoirs about the private life of her illustrious and controversial father.

Jacques Necker left writings that fill 15 volumes. They were published as *Oeuvres complètes* (Complete works) in Paris between 1820 and 1822.

See also ANCIEN RÉGIME; CALVINISM.

Necker, Suzanne Curchon de Nasse (1739–1794)
wife of Jacques Necker and sponsor of one of the major salons in late 18th-century Paris

Madame Necker was the daughter of an old southern French Huguenot family that had established itself in SWITZERLAND after LOUIS XIV revoked religious TOLERATION for Protestants in FRANCE. Her father was a Calvinist minister in the Swiss canton of Vaud, who secured for his daughter a literary and scientific education of the sort normally reserved for men. Suzanne Necker remained devout throughout her life and pursued discussions on the subject of RELIGION with her many enlightened friends. As a young woman, she had many suitors, most notably the English historian Edward GIBBON. She married Jacques NECKER in 1764. At that time, she gave up her plans to become a writer but continued to record her ideas in long letters with correspondents.

Madame Necker's salon in PARIS provided a meeting place for such prominent individuals of the ENLIGHTENMENT as George-Louis de BUFFON, poet Jean-François de Saint-Lambert, and Jean-François MARMONTEL. She devoted much time to reforms in hospitals and prisons. Jacques Necker praised her publicly for these works, thereby inviting intense criticism by the Parisians who were offended by his open display of pride. After the Neckers left France, Madame Necker published one book, *Réflexions sur le divorce* (Reflections on divorce; 1794). In 1794, after Madame Necker died, Jacques Necker published a collection of her papers entitled *Nouveaux mélanges* (New collection).

See also SOCIAL INSTITUTIONS OF THE ENLIGHTENMENT.

Needham, John Turberville, Abbé (1713–1781)
English-born physiologist and the microscopist

Needham was the son of English recusants (Protestants converted to ROMAN CATHOLICISM) who sent him to the French-controlled region of Flanders (Douai and Cambrai) for his education. He was ordained a Catholic priest in 1738 and began his career teaching rhetoric and directing a Catholic school at Twyford, England. Needham taught PHILOSOPHY at the English College of Lisbon in PORTUGAL and then returned to LONDON in 1745. In 1746, Needham traveled to PARIS, where he met and entered into collaboration with the comte de BUFFON in research designed to challenge the specific PREFORMATION THEORY called ANIMALCULISM. In 1751, Needham began serving as a companion and preceptor for young English noblemen on their GRAND TOURS of the European continent. After working several years in that capacity, he settled in BRUSSELS. In 1768, he accepted a post as director of the academy that would become, in 1773, the Royal Academy of Belgium. Needham remained in Brussels until his death in 1781.

Needham was the first Catholic priest ever elected to the ROYAL SOCIETY OF LONDON (1747). He was also a member of the Royal Basque Society of *Amies de la Patrie* and of the Society of Antiquaries in London.

Needham's broad interests in life sciences, THEOLOGY, and philosophy illustrate the fact that these subjects remained deeply intertwined for 18th-century scientists and PHILOSOPHES. As an apologist for Roman Catholicism, Needham desired to protect the church from the encroachments of MATERIALISM, DEISM, and ATHEISM, and this desire influenced his scientific research. In this respect, he might be usefully compared to the Swiss Protestant physiologist Charles BONNET, although the two men defended widely divergent theories and religious traditions.

Needham rejected the atomistic, mechanistic vision of living matter put forth in the theory of IATROMECHANICS. His vision of living organisms was a dynamic one, more radical even than the view of VITALISM, which made the extension of matter (that is, its occupation of space) a mere appearance rather than an essential quality. For Needham, matter is composed of two simple, opposing, and unextended principles: motion and resistance. The interaction and combination of these two principles or agents produces the appearance of extension. Needham maintained that only this vision of matter as the product of the interplay of active principles could explain the processes and phenomena of GENERATION (reproduction). He believed that the interaction of motion and resistance in the seminal fluid of the male causes the embryo to develop through a series of progressive changes. Needham, therefore, was a supporter of EPIGENESIS who believed that the male sperm plays a role in producing new life. Needham conceptualized embryonic development as a process in which the fetus, during the stages of its formation, takes on the characteristics of other organisms in the GREAT CHAIN OF BEING. Individual embryos were not preformed but their ultimate nature was, in some sense, predetermined.

Needham's theory of reproduction made him a major player in the debates over generation between proponents of preformation theory and epigenesis. Buffon used the results of Needham's experiments with seminal fluids to support a theory of "organic molecules," which he elaborated in the second volume of the *Histoire naturelle*. Charles Bonnet, the major late 18th-century proponent of preformation theory and of the related "*emboitement*" theory of Nicolas MALEBRANCHE (a theory that preserved God's role in individual creation), considered Needham his primary opponent. Lazzaro SPALLANZANI finally refuted the experiments in which Needham had claimed to have observed the spontaneous generation of matter.

In conjunction with his theory of generation, Needham developed a view of the HISTORY of nature based on his interpretation of the biblical verse from the book of Genesis: "the evening and the morning made one day." Needham posited that all the universe and its natural history is the manifestation of the interaction of two opposing principles, one negative and the other positive. Evening in the Genesis account symbolized the negative principle, which preceded the positive principle of day. Each of the biblical days of creation corresponded to a stage in the development of nature toward its ultimate culmination, humankind. Thus Needham, just as his collaborator Buffon, supported the idea that the natural world has a long history in which change has occurred. This was a dialectical and teleological vision of the universe that, nevertheless, retained God as the source and governor of all. The ideas making up this vision had been used in the past, and they would become increasingly common as the various forms of the ENLIGHTENMENT vision of the world gave way to ROMANTICISM and German *Naturphilosophie*.

In a series of polemics with VOLTAIRE over the existence of miracles, Needham supported the belief in miracle that was required by orthodox Catholic theology. Voltaire denied that miracles of the sort reported in the Bible exist. God would not, Voltaire claimed, violate his own natural laws in order to send special knowledge to a few select people. Besides, if one wants to see miracles in the world, one need only observe the marvels of nature.

Publications left by Needham include *An Account of Some New Microscopical Discoveries Founded on an Examination of the Calamary and Its Wonderful Milt-Vessels* (London, 1745); *Nouvelles observations microscopiques, avec des découvertes intéressantes sur la composition et la décomposition des corps organisés* (New microscopic observations, with some interesting discoveries on the composition and decomposition of organized bodies; Paris, 1750); and *Nouvelles recherches physiques et métaphysiques sur la nature et la religion, avec une nouvelle théorie de la terre* (New physical and metaphysical research on nature and religion, with a new theory of the Earth; 1769).

Further reading: John G. Burke, *The Uses of Science in the Age of Newton* (Los Angeles: William Andrews Clark Library, UCLA, 1983); Thomas L. Hankins, *Science and the Enlightenment* (Cambridge: Cambridge University Press, 1985).

neoclassicism An international aesthetic style that appeared in the middle of the 18th century and lasted through the first decades of the 19th century. Neoclassicism was partly a reaction against the forms and content associated with the BAROQUE and ROCOCO styles. Its influence affected creative work in ART AND ARCHITECTURE, MUSIC, and LITERATURE.

Neoclassical ideals restated certain familiar themes of the ENLIGHTENMENT, giving them a form that consisted of a mixture of familiar and new elements. Artists working in this style claimed to be rescuing creative work from the "unnatural" forms of baroque and rococo. In making this judgment, artists were returning to a 17th-century definition of NATURE and beauty that stressed simplicity, order, and geometric form, all alleged manifestations of the REASON that was believed to underlie the structures of the world.

Although founded on reason, actual nature did not provide examples of perfect beauty. Rather, perfection of form had to be abstracted from real objects by the artist. Art did not, therefore, strictly imitate nature but rather acted to purify nature by identifying and representing the pure abstract forms behind natural structures.

These general ideals were translated into a set of concrete aesthetic values and rules for neoclassical composition. Pure, simple, linear forms; restrained feeling or sentiment; and subtle gradations of color were recommended. Painted or sculpted figures were expected to be ideal representations, unblemished and betraying no signs of a particular state of mind or emotion. An outstanding work of art was expected to appeal to the intellect rather than to please the senses.

These values had also characterized 17th-century CLASSICISM, but neoclassicism was not simply a return to that tradition. Classicism had extracted its values and forms from the literature and aesthetic writings of the ancients. The neoclassical artists turned directly to ancient monuments, sculpture, and literature, modeling their own work after these artifacts from the past. Some modern critics degrade neoclassical art as mere copying of the past, lacking any creative inspiration or immediate connection to the milieu in which it was being created. Whatever the assessment, it cannot be denied that neoclassicism had its roots in values associated with certain branches of the Enlightenment.

Model of the Pantheon, Rome. The ancient Roman Pantheon served as one inspiration for the design of the Parisian Church of Sainte-Geneviève (renamed the Panthéon during the French Revolution) by neoclassical architect Jacques-Germain Soufflot. *(Courtesy Metropolitan Museum of Art)*

Neoclassicism appeared in the 1740s and 1750s, in the context of the general interest in antiquity that made ITALY a favorite destination for travelers. The unearthing of the ruins at Herculaneum and Pompeii provided unprecedented glimpses into life during the Roman Empire that increased the fascination with ancient Roman culture.

ROME was the destination of all travelers and aspiring artists, and it became a center of neoclassicism, the home of major theorists of the style, such as Anton Raphael MENGS and Johann Joachim WINCKELMANN. Meng's treatise *Gedan ken über die Schönheit und den Geschmack in der Malerei* (Thoughts on beauty and taste in painting; 1762) and Winckelmann's *Geschichte der Altertums* (History of antiquity; 1763) provided the basic formulations of the new style. Other theoretical discussions of this style were provided by Gotthold Ephraim LESSING in his LAOKOON; and by Joshua REYNOLDS, Johann Sulzer, Saverio Bettinelli, and Francesco Pagano.

French neoclassical architecture is illustrated in the Panthéon of Jean SOUFFLOT, the garden monuments at the Petit Trianon at Versailles; and the Tomb of Rousseau in the park at Ermenonville. Roman examples include parts of the Villa Manfrini by Carlo Marchionne; the Salone d'Oro of the Palazzo Chigi by Giovanni Stern; the Hall of the Greek Cross, Sala Rotunda, and Hall of the Muses at the Vatican Museums; and the Piazza del Popolo. The work of Robert ADAM illustrates the style in SCOTLAND and ENGLAND. The bedroom and study of FREDERICK II (THE GREAT) at Sans Souci in Potsdam and the famous Brandenburg Gate of BERLIN serve as German examples. Finally, the style also appeared in Russia and POLAND under the sponsorship of CATHERINE II (THE GREAT) and Stanisław PONIATOWSKI.

The works of Antonio CANOVA and Jean-Antoine HOUDON represent the translation of neoclassical style into sculpture, while in painting the works of Jacques Louis DAVID, François Gérard, Jean-Baptiste Regnault, Pierre-Paul Prud'hon, and Jean-Auguste-Dominique INGRES provide excellent examples.

In literary realms, neoclassicism led to a resurgence of works based on themes from ancient sources. It also spawned, for a brief time, works constructed according to the principles of unity, simplicity, and symmetry in form. Plays by Johann Wolfgang von GOETHE and Friedrich SCHILLER demonstrate the style.

The musical style that corresponds to neoclassicism is usually called the classical style. Its culmination came in VIENNA with the music of Christoph Willibald GLUCK, Franz Joseph HAYDN, Wolfgang Amadeus MOZART, and the young Ludwig van BEETHOVEN. Favored compositional forms included the symphony for orchestra, the sonata for solo instrument with piano accompaniment, opera, and the string quartet or trio. Each of these types of composition conformed to some extent to customary rules that determined the number of movements, basic harmonic relationships, and other aspects of internal structure. Classical-style compositions strove for universality by avoiding characteristics that were strongly associated with particular national styles. They also aimed at conveying naturalness, where that quality was defined in terms of relative technical simplicity and immediate accessibility for listeners.

The classical-style composition did not rely on models from antiquity for its musical forms. Rather, the debt to classical antiquity appeared in the themes chosen for some operas. Thus, musical classicism differs from its counterparts in literature, art, and architecture. Like them, however, it gave way in the 19th century to the new style called ROMANTICISM.

Further reading: Philip Ayres, *Classical Culture and the Idea of Rome in Eighteenth-Century England* (Cambridge: Cambridge University Press, 1997); Charles Burney, *The Present State of Music in France and Italy,* facsimile of 1773 ed. (New York: Broude Bros., 1969); David Irwin, *Neoclassicism* (Boston: Phaidon, 1997); Wend von Kalnein, *Architecture in France in the Eighteenth Century,* tr. David Britt (New Haven, Conn.: Yale University Press, 1994); Emil Kaufmann, *Architecture in the Age of Reason: Baroque and Post-Baroque in England, Italy, France* (New York: Dover Publications, 1955; Harriet Stone, *The Classical Model: Literature and Knowledge in Seventeenth-Century France* (Ithaca, N.Y.: Cornell University Press, 1996).

Neumann, Balthasar (1687–1753) *German architect and civil and military engineer*

Neumann was one of the masters of late BAROQUE and ROCOCO architecture working in the HOLY ROMAN EMPIRE. Two of his buildings, the Residenz at Würzburg and the pilgrimage church, Vierzehnheiligen, at Langheim, both in the Main River region of modern Bavaria, GERMANY, presented innovative solutions to spatial problems that brought Neumann renown throughout Europe. At Würzburg, Neumann designed a central, free staircase that ascends to an enormous unobstructed vault decorated with magnificent frescoes by Giovanni Battista TIEPOLO. The pilgrimage church of Vierzehnheiligen (Church of the Fourteen Saints) is a rococo masterpiece. Neumann placed the central altar near the physical center of the church and constructed the overhead vaulting with intersecting vaults which produce a visual experience of fluid space with vanishing curves and broken walls. The entire interior is flooded on sunny days with light that plays off the highly ornate interior decoration. The Gnadenaltar (Grace altar) is a large, airy construction, designed by Neumann's successor J. J. M. Küchel, which seems to resemble a porcelain piece.

Neumann was born in Bohemia, son of a clothmaker who apprenticed him in a local foundry. In 1709, he began his wandering years as a journeyman and arrived in 1711 in Würzburg, which was the seat of a sovereign ecclesiastical territory of the Holy Roman Empire. Würzburg had a well-known foundry where Neumann hoped to find work. His talent was quickly recognized, and soon he was receiving training in civil and military architecture. In 1714, Neumann received a military commission as an artilleryman for the bodyguard of the bishop of Würzburg. He worked as a hydraulics specialist in 1716, then became chief of the Würzburg corps of engineers.

During this era, the Schönborn family (not to be confused with Schönbrunn, the name of the imperial palace in VIENNA) held several major ecclesiastical territories in the Holy Roman Empire, including the bishopric of Würzburg, the archbishopric-electorates of Mainz and Trier, and the bishopric of Bamberg. Friedrich-Carl von Schönborn, bishop of Bamberg and Würzburg, was also imperial vice-chancellor in Vienna and Neumann's greatest patron for over 15 years (1729–46). The Schönborn family provided Neumann with most of his major architectural commissions. Buildings created for them include the Würzburg Residenz (Bishop's Residence), the Hofkapelle (Court Chapel) on the residence grounds, and the Brüchsal Palace built for Cardinal Schönborn of Speyer. Neumann was engaged to build a new imperial palace in Vienna for Empress MARIA THERESA and her husband, Emperor Francis I, but the WAR OF THE AUSTRIAN SUCCESSION caused the plans to be abandoned. The Vierzehnheiligen pilgrimage church, built for the Abbey of Langheim, brought European fame to Neumann. Neumann also designed a lovely pilgrimage church at Gössweinstein, the Marienkirche on the old fortress hill outside Würzburg, and the partially completed Abbey Church of Neresheim. The archbishop of Cologne, Clemens August, had Neumann redesign the interior space of his summer palace in Brühl.

Neumann is regarded today as one of the great German baroque and rococo innovators, on a par with the long-recognized masters Johann FISCHER VON ERLACH and Johann HILDEBRANDT. Neumann had a son, Franz Ignaz, who also worked as an architect.

Newcomen, Thomas (1663–1729) *English blacksmith and inventor*

In 1705, with John Cawley (also known as Calley), Newcomen invented the first true STEAM ENGINE that subsequently acted as one of the central technological stimuli of the INDUSTRIAL REVOLUTION. The Newcomen steam engine had a single condensation cylinder that was used to create a vacuum beneath a piston. Ordinary air pressure drove the piston down to fill the vacuum, and the action of the piston drove the machine.

Newcomen established a manufacturing partnership with Thomas Savery, who had built a primitive steam pump for extracting water from mines. After 1712, Newcomen engines appeared in factories and mines and persisted in certain areas even after James WATT invented his double-cylinder engine.

See also ENGLAND.

New Lanark

Site of the cotton mills near Glasgow, SCOTLAND, established by Richard ARKWRIGHT and David DALE in 1785. The mills used Arkwright's WATER FRAME and other machines to produce cotton. New Lanark is a prominent example of the new form for economic production, the factory, that grew out of the INDUSTRIAL REVOLUTION.

The establishment of factories produced drastic changes in the organization of industrial production—changes that, in their earliest decades of existence, seriously degraded the living conditions of workers. Industrial workers, including women and young children, no longer produced goods at home, but rather went to work in the factory buildings where they labored for long hours.

In 1799, David Dale sold New Lanark to the reformer Robert Owen (1771–1858). Owen was strongly influenced by the utilitarianism of Jeremy BENTHAM and by early socialist ideas. He was concerned about the negative social and economic impact produced by the reorganization of work during the Industrial Revolution. He disliked the idea of division of labor, recognizing that it forced workers to perform uninteresting and repetitive task. Owen formulated a series of management practices at New Lanark that aimed at substantially improving the lot of workers. He intended to demonstrate that such improvements would not lessen productive output.

The reforms instituted by Owen concentrated on providing basic EDUCATION, on reducing working hours, and on creating better housing and general living conditions for workers. Owen set up a school, the Institution for the Formation of Character, for the children of New Lanark and kept them in classes until the age of 10. Prior to that, children as young as six years of age had been working in the cotton mills.

Owen believed that environment shapes moral character. His New Lanark school attempted to form young children by exposing them to models of good character, and by introducing them to art, MUSIC, and other desirable cultural objects. His teachers seldom used books for the younger children.

The reforms at New Lanark took place in the twilight of the ENLIGHTENMENT. They illustrate how the humanitarian ideals of that era—its interest in education and its stress on the application of science to foster human prosperity and health—were adapted to the needs of the Industrial Revolution. It also demonstrates how these ideals, so very much a part of enlightened discourse, conflicted sharply with the tenets of the equally enlightened theory of economic liberalism developed by Adam SMITH. Thus, the case of New Lanark demonstrates the tensions inherent in the Enlightenment when economic policy, industrial organization, and labor practices were the subject of concern.

See also UTILITY.

Newton, Isaac (1642–1727) *English natural philosopher and mathematician, one of the intellectual "fathers" of the Enlightenment*

Newton created a major reformulation of 17th-century MECHANICAL PHILOSOPHY, providing it with greater appeal and theoretical power. He revised the theory of colors, creating in the process a new theory of light. His invention of calculus made it possible to represent the laws governing motion in mathematical terms and thus contributed to the development of a mathematical model of the universe. Newton also developed a conception—the SCIENTIFIC METHOD that still underlies basic approaches to scientific inquiry.

Newton developed his philosophy of NATURE and scientific method on foundations provided by René DESCARTES and Francis BACON. Descartes had offered a systematic formulation of the mechanical philosophy that attempted to explain all natural phenomena in terms of matter and its motion. This approach had created a host of scientific, epistemological, and theological problems for natural philosophers. But it exercised strong appeal, because it aimed to make the truths of nature accessible to human REASON.

Specific scientific problems centered on the Cartesian theory of motion and the idea of conservation of quantity of motion. Theological problems were raised by Descartes's attempts to create a self-preserving universe that could operate without the actions of God. Problems in EPISTEMOLOGY and scientific method arose from the strict Cartesian reliance on RATIONALISM and deductive reasoning. Francis Bacon had left a tradition of scientific inquiry that was radically opposed to the one of Descartes. Descartes had believed that human reason, starting with a few basic axioms and following the rules of deductive logic, could uncover scientific truths. His mechanical philosophy represented an attempt to apply his method to the study of the universe and its laws.

Bacon agreed that human reason can uncover truths, but it had to build on experience to do so. After collecting great numbers of facts from experience (experiment), human reason could use inductive logic to arrive at scientific truths and principles. Thus EMPIRICISM, rather than rationalism, provided the basic approach to natural philosophy.

In wrestling with the problems and conflicts inherent in these approaches to science, Newton created a powerful synthesis. He retained empiricism as the starting point for scientific inquiry by emphasizing the importance of gathering experimental data, but he preserved a role for rationalism by demonstrating the power of mathematics as a theoretical tool. He also emphasized that scientific method should combine both analysis (breaking a problem down into parts to solve it) and synthesis (offering formal proof of results in the style of geometry).

Newton agreed with Descartes that the universe operates according to a few basic laws of motion. But he denied the Cartesian claim that this motion could be explained by simple contact between inert bodies moving in a space totally filled with matter. Newton believed that matter was infused by active forces, one of which was

Reflecting telescope. Isaac Newton, the mathematician and natural philosopher, created a theoretical framework for the physical sciences, mathematical tools, and some improved scientific instruments, all of which provided a basic framework for the scientific endeavors of the Enlightenment. *(Courtesy New York Public Library)*

gravitation. Gravitation produced all the motion in the universe, thereby serving as a universal philosophical principle from which the whole system of the world could be constructed. According to Newton's vision, celestial and terrestrial phenomena could be explained with his principles; and the world of microscopic phenomena obeyed the same laws as the world of visible phenomena.

Newton's convictions about the nature of matter and the existence of forces derived in large part from his religious faith. Like many of his contemporaries, he recognized that Cartesian mechanical philosophy made God unnecessary to the world, except in the role of creator. Newton disliked the Cartesian view, for he believed that God is active in the world. The concept of forces represented, for him, one form of this divine presence and activity.

The Newtonian legacy influenced the Enlightenment in two different but occasionally intertwined ways. Its technical scientific theories raised a host of problems for scientists during the following generations. They struggled to find proof of the theory of gravitation by exploring celestial phenomena and by determining the shape of the Earth. They attempted to demonstrate that Newtonian laws of motion could truly explain all phenomena. They developed mathematical techniques to extend the applicability of Newtonian theories. They argued about

his concepts of space and time. And they pursued the fascinating avenues of research that he had spelled out in the famous queries at the end of the treatise on *Opticks* (1704). In short, whether or not they agreed wih Newton, physical scientists were compelled to address his theories.

The impact of Newtonian thought extended beyond the world of the SCIENTIFIC ACADEMIES into the broader culture of the Enlightenment. VOLTAIRE and Francesco ALGAROTTI interpreted Newton for readers throughout Europe. Alexander POPE immortaliized him in heroic couplets. John Theophilus DESAGULIERS presented lectures on Newtonian philosophy under the auspices of the ROYAL SOCIETY OF LONDON. Newtonian concepts formed part of the common cultural baggage of the 18th century, serving with the ideas of John LOCKE and Gottfried Wilhelm LEIBNIZ as major ingredients of enlightened philosophy and discourse.

Isaac Newton was a complex personality whose inquisitive mind examined not only mathematics and natural philosophy, but also ALCHEMY, THEOLOGY, chronology, and BIBLICAL CRITICISM. He was raised by his mother, Hannah Ayscough Newton, for his first three years, and then placed in the care of his maternal grandmother. His father had died three months before his birth, and his mother's remarriage prompted the change in his living arrangements.

The Newtons were yeomen farmers, but young Isaac showed neither aptitude nor interest in farming. His intellectual prowess was recognized by a teacher and an uncle, both of whom encouraged his preparation for university education. As a result, he was allowed to enter Trinity College of Cambridge University in 1661. In 1665, he received a B.A. degree, having devoted himself to mathematics and NATURAL PHILOSOPHY. The M.A. degree followed in 1668, and Newton received the honor of appointment as Lucasian professor in 1669.

Between the summer of 1664 and October 1666, Newton entered an intensely creative period during which he formulated the basic insights and ideas that guided the rest of his professional work. The discovery of the general binomial theorem—expansion of expressions in the form $(a + b)^n$ dates from 1665, as does the general idea of gravity. The method of fluxion (calculus) also was invented during these years.

Newton was reluctant to publish his work, a fact that later helped to create the quarrel with Leibniz over priority in inventing mathematical calculus. But Newton did not hesitate to send papers to the Royal Society of London, and many of his papers were eventually published in the *Transactions of the Royal Society*. In 1672, Newton was elected to membership in the Royal Society, and he served as its president during his later years. Friends and correspondents included Edmond HALLEY, Robert Boyle, Robert Hooke, Christian Huygens, and Gottfried Wilhelm Leibniz.

Newton's duties at Cambridge University consisted of giving one lecture every week during the academic years. He pursued his various researches and also worked actively for the university. He was one of the opponents of King James II when the latter tried to force Cambridge to accept a Catholic Benedictine monk into its fellowship. Newton twice served as a member of Parliament representing Cambridge (1689–90 and 1701–02).

During his Cambridge years, Newton continued working out the details of his natural philosophy and mathematics. He discovered that his idea of gravity could explain Johannes Kepler's law of planetary motion, and developed mathematical equations to express the law of gravitation. At the urging of his friend Edmond Halley, he gathered all his ideas into the PRINCIPIA MATHEMATICA. The Royal Society ordered its publications, and Halley actually paid the printing costs. The first edition appeared in 1687, followed by a second edition in 1713.

Newton pursued his interests in alchemy, theology, and related fields throughout his life. Alchemical theories may have played a role in the development of his natural philosophy, but scholars argue over the point. Newton himself never published anything on the subject, although his notebooks contain extensive evidence of his interests.

In theology and biblical criticism, Newton accepted the general idea that HISTORY had brought corruptions of both biblical texts and theological doctrine. He wrote an anti-Trinitarian essay, but he never published it for fear of prosecution. He believed that disputes over the Christian sacrament of communion (Eucharist), the major doctrinal cause of the splintering of Christianity at the time of the Protestant Reformation, were largely the result of manuscript translation errors dating back many centuries. Like many of his contemporaries, Newton also believed that ancient peoples had possessed a pure and comprehensive wisdom (*prisca sapientia*) that had been lost.

Newton tried to extend his scientific method to areas outside the realm of physical nature. He developed a new chronology of the world on the basis of astronomical observations, one that became the center of a dispute among antiquarians in PARIS. He also tried to unlock the mysteries of the language of biblical prophecy, by making systematic tables and comparisons of various words, but these forays were mostly unsuccessful.

In 1693, Newton apparently suffered a nervous breakdown in the form of a severe depression. Recuperation took some years. By 1696, he was ready to accept a post as warden of the mint in LONDON. He left Cambridge, although he did not resign his Lucasian professorship until 1701.

In London, he pursued activities at the Royal Society, used his position at the mint to secure patronage for various scientists, published the *Opticks* (1704), and engaged in the famed quarrel with Leibniz. He was knighted in 1705 by Queen Anne. Gout and inflamed lungs finally caused his death in 1727 at the age of 85.

See also articles on 18th-century Newtonians: MAUPERTUIS; CLAIRAUT; LAPLACE; LAGRANGE; and Madame du CHÂTELET; also, CARTOGRAPHY; MATHEMATICS AND MECHANICS; NATURAL HISTORY; RELIGION; SCIENCE.

Further reading: John G. Burke, *The Uses of Science in the Age of Newton* (Los Angeles: William Andrews Clark Library, UCLA, 1983); Sir Isaac Newton, *Sir Isaac Newton's Mathematical Principles of Natural Philosophy and His System of the World*, tr. Andrew Motte, ed. Florian Cajori (Berkeley: University of California Press, 1962); Horace S. Thayer, ed., *Newton's Philosophy of Nature: Selections from His Writings* (New York: Hafner Press, 1953).

Nicolai, Christoph Friedrich (1733–1811) *German publicist, publisher, editor, literary critic, and author*

Christoph Friedrich Nicolai, or Friedrich Nicolai, as he was usually known, was the son of a book dealer and publisher. Although he took over the practical duties of running his father's business, Nicolai was also fascinated by the more abstract delights of intellectual activity during the ENLIGHTENMENT. He was largely self-educated but nevertheless mastered the language of Leibnizian/Wolffian philosophy, learned English in order to read Milton's *Paradise Lost* in the original language, taught himself French by reading Bayle's *Dictionaire historique et critique* (HISTORI-CAL AND CRITICAL DICTIONARY), and studied Greek.

Nicolai's position in the German publishing world combined with his intellectual interests to make him one of the most important figures of the AUFKLÄRUNG (German Enlightenment). He had developed a close friendship with Gotthold Ephraim LESSING and Moses MENDELSSOHN as a youth, and together the friends launched three major journals: *Briefe über den jetzigen Zustand der schönen Wissenschaften in Deutschland* (Letters on the current state of the fine arts in Germany; 1755); the *Briefwechsel über das Trauerspiel* (Correspondence over tragedy; 1756/57); and the *Briefe die neueste Literatur betreffend* (Letters, which concern the newest literature; 1759). These three journals became important vehicles for spreading the new aesthetic that Lessing and Mendelssohn were pioneering and were major champions of the ideals of the German Enlightenment.

Nicolai's most important publishing and editorial undertaking was the successor periodical to the *Literaturbriefe* entitled *Allgemeine deutsche Bibliographie* (General German bibliography), which he founded in 1765. It became Germany's leading review journal, criticizing, during the 40 years of its existence (1765–1805), more than 80,000 books. Over 400 writers contributed review articles to the journal with the intent of guiding German readers toward the best books available. The journal attempted to create a large, literate, and critical German reading public that would transcend local and religious differences. If one of the major goals of the Enlightenment lay in spreading knowledge and encouraging critical debate, then the *ADB*, as it is called, was a great success. For many Germans of the era, it was the most important symbol of the German Enlightenment.

In all of his work, Nicolai was an enemy of what he considered overly speculative reasoning and excessive emotional subjectivity. For these reasons he disliked the transcendental philosophy of Immanuel KANT, whom he considered an impractical idealist, and he similarly criticized the subjectivism and idealism in the philosophies of Johann Gottlieb Fichte (1762–1814) and Friedrich Wilhelm Joseph von Schelling (1775–1854). Nicolai also rejected the cult of youthful, tormented GENIUS generated by Johann Wolfgang von GOETHE's immensely successful novel, THE SORROWS OF YOUNG WERTHER.

Nicolai registered his opinions in the *ADB* and in three satirical novels. *Die Freuden des jungen Werthers* (The joys of young Werther; 1755) and the *Vertraute Briefe von Adelheid B. an ihre Freundin Julie B* (Confidential letters from Adelheid B. to her friend Julie B.; 1799), both attacking the cult of genius, and *Leben und Meinungen Sempronius Gundibert's eines deutschen Philosophen* (Life and thoughts of Sempronius Gundibert, a German philosopher; 1798), which mocked the transcendental philosophy of Kant and his followers.

In addition to these satirical works, Nicolai wrote a serious novel that was a great success in his time. Entitled *Leben und Meinungen des Herrn Magisters Sebaldus Nothanker* (Life and thoughts of Master Sebaldus Nothanker; 1773–76), it describes the plight of a Protestant pastor who has enraged the orthodox church officials and is deprived of his post and forced to endure a period of trials and tests that one critic has called a "Prussian Odyssey." Following the new sensibilities of the Enlightenment, the work was written in plain language, the people portrayed were "normal people, both good and bad," and the events described "as they actually take place in daily life." As was to be expected, the novel bristled with criticism of existing society, especially of the nobility and of Protestant orthodoxy. But it also offered a good dose of self-reflection about the dangers of a popular press (which, of course, Nicolai was helping to create). In an important part of the work, Sebaldus has a discussion with a skeptical magistrate, who readers of the time tended to equate with Nicolai himself. The magistrate warns about the commercialization of the press, the creation of a band of writers interested more in fame than in the public weal, and the increasing fascination with the sensational. This could result in the desire for "stories, romances, violent accounts of murder, for trustworthy accounts of things which no one has ever seen, proofs of things that no one believes, thought about subjects that no one understands."

Nicolai's position as one of the most important publishers of his age enabled him to play an important role in BERLIN and Prussian society. He was a member of a secret group called the Wednesday Society (*Mittwochgesellschaft*), composed of the highest Prussian civil servants and leading intellectuals. Members met every Wednesday to discuss important problems facing Prussia and drew up major reform plans, which were presented to the king. The Wednesday Society represented a sort of government within the government, designed to overcome the possible abuses of absolute rule. Nicolai was also a member of the Monday Club, a group of leading intellectuals, writers, artists, and musicians that gathered on Mondays to exchange ideas and conversation. It offers an excellent example of the way in which the sociability of the Enlightenment helped to break down strict class barriers and to enhance critical social thought.

Nicolai was a representative of the practical wing of the German Enlightenment associated with the ideas in Lessing and Mendelssohn's writings. As such, Nicolai presented qualities that included commitment to the expansion of knowledge, opposition to mystification and speculation, a desire to improve the lot of society through reform, and advocacy of an aesthetic ideal in which beauty was defined by the power of its effects on observers.

See also SOCIAL INSTITUTIONS OF THE ENLIGHTENMENT.

Further reading: W. H. Bruford, *Germany in the Eighteenth Century: The Social Background of the Literary Revival* (Cambridge: Cambridge University Press, 1971).

Niebuhr, Carsten (1733–1815) *German explorer*

Carsten Niebuhr was born in Ludingworth, in Hanover. He worked as a farmer and taught himself surveying before going on to study mathematics and NATURAL PHILOSOPHY at the University of GÖTTINGEN, where his teachers included Philologist Johann David MICHAELIS. Through him, Niebuhr heard about an expedition to the Middle East proposed by Michaelis and organized by King Frederik V of Denmark. The expedition was a scientific exploration, the first of its kind, since neither trade nor colonization was a motive. Niebuhr joined the five-man group as an engineer, and they sailed from Copenhagen in 1761.

The expedition landed in Alexandria, Egypt, where the explorers spent a year before sailing down the west coast of the Arabian Peninsula in an open boat. They reached Al Mukha, in Yemen, in 1763. There, a member of the expedition died of malaria. The explorers continued up the eastern coast of the Arabian Peninsula, reaching Basra before sailing to India. Three more men died of fever en route to Bombay, leaving Niebuhr the sole surviving member of the group. He explored India in 1764. From there, he worked his way back across the Middle East, stopping in Baghdad, Babylon, and other important cities and sites. His maps of Persepolis, which he visited in 1765, were long considered authoritative. He spent time in Cyprus and Palestine in 1766 before crossing the Taurus Mountains into Turkey and visiting Istanbul in 1767. He returned to Copenhagen in November of that year.

Niebuhr's report of the expedition, the *Beschreibung von Arabien* (Description of Arabia; 1772), and a follow-up work, the *Reisebeschreibung nach Arabien und andern umliegenden Ländern* (Description of the journey to Arabia and other surrounding lands; 1774–78), were important and influential texts on the Middle East, and his maps of the region were used for more than a century. Not only do the works contain information about the topography, geology, and plant and animal life of the regions he visited, but they also describe the people he encountered, including details such as diet and dress. Niebuhr joined the Danish military in 1773, and in 1778 he took a civil post in Holstein (now part of northern Germany), where he lived until his death in 1815.

Further reading: Thorkild Hansen, *Arabia Felix: The Danish Expedition of 1761–1767* (London: Collins, 1964).

noble savage

Philosophical concept that tribal peoples inherently possessed stronger moral principles as a result of being shielded from corrupting civilization. As European populations increased during the ENLIGHTENMENT and cities and towns expanded to house larger numbers of people, so also grew the sense that the development of Western civilization often did not curb the problems of human existence, and frequently brought new ones such as rising crime rates, wars, and epidemics. Philosophers of the period began to see in accounts of the tribal societies described by colonial traders possibilities of a life unencumbered by civilization's difficulties. The explorations of the Americas in the 17th century seemed to corroborate such notions, with descriptions of harmonious native societies and virtuous Indians published in various newspapers and periodicals. Their moral behavior without the inspiration of Christianity was advanced by groups such as the QUAKERS of Pennsylvania as evidence of God's universal benevolence and inspiration. This fascination with native societies gained further ground in the 18th century with accounts such as those of Captain James COOK's voyages in the Pacific that depicted island communities that seemed to be living in paradise without original sin.

The philosopher who brought these ideas to the forefront of European intellectual discussion was the Frenchman Jean-Jacques ROUSSEAU. A mistrust of the influence of civilization runs throughout his works, beginning with the *Discours sur les sciences et les arts* (Discourse on the sciences and arts) of 1750. Rousseau composed the work in response to the question asked by the 1749 essay competition of the Academy of Dijon: Had the advancement of arts and sciences improved morals? In an age that associated truth, beauty, and virtue, the expected answer was yes, a society that makes progress in the arts and sciences should simultaneously make progress in the realms of virtue and morality.

Rousseau's response was a profound negative: Civilization, which had brought new developments in the arts and sciences, had done nothing to advance the cause of morality. On the contrary, Rousseau argued, the simpler the lifestyle and accomplishments of a people were, the closer its society was to natural goodness and virtue. Rousseau moved the discussion further in his next work, *Discours sur l'origine et les fondements de l'inégalité parmi les hommes* (Discourse on the origin and the foundations of inequality among mankind; 1755). Here he articulated clearly the philosophical notion of the noble savage by imagining a prehistoric state of bliss for humanity before it was corrupted by civilization. Rousseau identified two states of inequality for humans: natural or physical, and moral or political. The first state is the preferable one for humanity: Finding their needs provided for by nature, people are healthy and content. The only inequalities are natural ones: Some individuals may be weaker or stronger than others, but they all live under similar conditions. The second state describes humanity's fall from grace and into complicated social relations that create private property, weakening humanity's physical and moral character. For Rousseau, this moral or political inequality is an artificial one created by human societies. Wealth, luxury, and privilege set up extreme divisions among people: Some have more than they need, while others suffer a miserable existence.

While the concept of the noble savage is particularly associated with Rousseau, it was widespread during the Enlightenment. The power of this notion becomes more apparent when it is contrasted with the impressions that an earlier age had of native peoples. For thinkers of the Renaissance, an essential question to consider was whether native peoples of the New World had souls. Since these tribes had no knowledge of the Christian tradition, it was not clear how they fit into a Christian worldview. During the Enlightenment, there was no question that native peoples were fully human. Instead, the debate revolved around the degree to which they might be superior to Westerners. In his *Nouveaux voyages* (New travels; 1703), the baron de Lahontan, a French explorer, described members of the Huron tribe as being happier and more carefree than were French people, although he recognized that those accustomed to the hectic lifestyle and constant occupations of Parisian life would not be able to adapt to such a radically different notion of happiness.

During the Enlightenment, extensive overseas trade and expanding colonies allowed Western people to have more contact with Native Americans and therefore to acquire more knowledge of them. Nevertheless, the concept of the noble savage remained primarily a reflection of European intellectual concerns and often had little to do with actual native peoples. The idealized image of the noble savage allowed Enlightenment thinkers to posit humanity's basic goodness and to question the rapid development of urban centers, trade, and science that characterized Europe. This image did not go unchallenged, however; those who accepted Thomas HOBBES's notion of the first human societies could not agree with the idea that some innate goodness characterized people untouched by the institutions of European civilization.

See also FRANCE; RACE; *ROBINSON CRUSOE*; TRAVEL LITERATURE; VOYAGES OF DISCOVERY.

Further reading: Peter V. Conroy, *Jean-Jacques Rousseau* (New York: Twayne, 1998); Thomas Hahn, intro., *Upright Lives: Documents Concerning the Natural Virtue and Wisdom of the Indians (1650–1740)* (Los Angeles: William Andrews Clark Memorial Library, 1981); Margaret T. Hogden, *Early Anthropology in the Sixteenth and Seventeenth Centuries* (Philadelphia: University of Pennsylvania Press, 1964); Robert Wokler, *Rousseau* (New York: Oxford University Press, 1995).

Nollet, Jean-Antoine, Abbé (1700–1770) *French experimental physicist, a specialist in the study and public demonstration of electricity*

Nollet was the son of barely literate peasants and obtained his education through the French Catholic church. He studied humanities at the Collège de Clermont and THEOLOGY in PARIS. He became a deacon of the church, but after 1728 abandoned his clerical career. He nevertheless used the title of abbé throughout his life.

Nollet turned to the practical arts and sciences, joining the Société des Arts in 1728. This organization devoted itself to spreading scientific knowledge to artisans. Perceived as a threat by the FRENCH ACADEMY OF SCIENCES, it was dissolved in 1730.

Nollet benefited from the guidance and sponsorship of two academicians, René-Antoine Ferchault de RÉAUMUR and Charles-François de Cisternay Dufay. On a study tour with Dufay to the UNITED PROVINCES OF THE NETHERLANDS, Nollet met the two leading advocates of the theories of Isaac NEWTON: Willem's GRAVESANDE and John Theophilus DESAGULIERS. Nollet returned to Paris determined to pursue Newtonian experimental practices, but still committed to Cartesian MECHANICAL PHILOSOPHY.

Nollet set up a highly successful public lecture course in physics noted for its elaborate and entertaining electrical demonstrations. The course illustrates, for modern students, how serious scientific teaching was blended with public spectacle during the ENLIGHTENMENT in the interests of spreading scientific knowledge to amateurs.

Nollet published an entertaining and informative six-volume summary of his lectures, *Leçons de physique* (Physics lessons; 1743–48). He also published *L'art des expériences* (The art of experiments; 1770), outlining experimental techniques for nonspecialists.

Nollet's talents were recognized in 1739 by an adjunct appointment to the Academy of Sciences in Paris. He eventually assumed the new chair of physics at the prestigious Collège de Navarre in Paris, obtained a full appointment in the Academy of Sciences, and received the position of preceptor to the French royal family.

Like most of his contemporaries, Nollet believed that electricity was a form of moving fluid matter. He developed an elaborate and colorful theory of electricity from aspects of CARTESIANISM, German theory, the work of Dufay, and his own observations. His theory was rooted in the popular two-fluid theories of the era, which posited that two electrical fluids exist, both of which repel fluids of like kind and attract fluids of different kind. In this way, two-fluid theories could partially explain the phenomena of attraction and repulsion. Nollet's system was more complicated, treating the two fluids rather as different currents within the fluid "fiery matter," as electricity was often denoted. The direction and rate at which these currents flowed determined the type of electrical phenomena displayed to the observer. For some time, Nollet's was the outstanding explanation for the phenomenon. His major opponent in the field was the American Benjamin FRANKLIN, whose one-fluid theory of electricity eventually displaced Nollet's ideas.

In the end, however, neither Franklin nor Nollet's theory proved adequate to explain observed phenomena, and experimenters gave up trying to explain the causes of electrical phenomena. Instead, they began simply trying to measure its effects. Nollet, for example, developed a method for measuring the strength of a charge on two threads of silk by casting a shadow of the silk threads onto a wall marked off in degrees like a mathematical protractor. The larger the charge, the farther apart the threads, measured in degrees. Nollet's device is sometimes called the first electroscope, but its novelty lay not in the idea of using the distance between threads as an indication of charge strength but rather in its translation of that distance into a measurable quantity (degrees on the protractor). He thus contributed to the process of developing quantitative methods for handling experimental data that was so central to enlightened science.

See also GALVANI; SCIENCE; VOLTA.

Nouvelle Héloise, La Epistolary novel (*The New Eloise*) by the Genevan philosophe Jean-Jacques ROUSSEAU. The first edition appeared in 1761 with the title *Lettres de deux amans, habitans d'une petite ville au pied des Alpes, recueillies et publiées par J.-J. Rousseau* (Letters of two lovers, living in a small village at the foot of the Alps, collected and published by J.-J. Rousseau). It was an immediate success throughout Europe.

Rousseau intended his novel to represent an incorrupt literary form, free of the artifices normally associated with French fiction during the 18th century. To this end, the book offers two parallel but contrasting plotlines: The first tells the story of the illegitimate love between Julie and her tutor Saint-Preux; the second paints Julie in the calm but uninspiring relationship of an arranged marriage with M. de Wolmar.

Saint-Preux, Julie's tutor, falls in love with her, but marriage is forbidden because of the gap between their respective social statuses. The two engage, nevertheless, in an affair that is assisted by Julie's cousin Claire. Claire, who is a dutiful daughter, meanwhile consents to a marriage arranged by her father to preserve the family position. Julie realizes that she must do the same and agrees to marry M. de Wolmar, her father's choice for her.

Saint-Preux, mad with grief, finds a companion named Milord Edouard Bomston with whom he departs for a GRAND TOUR of Europe. When he returns after a few years, the naive M. de Wolmar invites him to join Julie and himself at Clarens, their home. Saint-Preux accepts and observes the delights of their conjugal existence. But the old love between Julie and Saint-Preux returns, creating difficulties that ultimately bring about Julie's death.

La Nouvelle Héloise, an example of SENTIMENTAL FICTION written in the form of an exchange of letters, adapted these immensely popular literary approaches to the task of offering moral observations about love and family; about ATHEISM, DEISM, and traditional piety; and about suicide. In its stirring pages, Rousseau explored the tensions between social conventions and the aspirations of individuals and between REASON and feeling. In this way, the novel offers a literary representation of the dialectics whose conflict became increasingly tense in the course of the ENLIGHTENMENT.

See also PHILOSOPHES.

novel A new form of prose fiction in the 18th century using realistic plots and character depictions, often for a didactic purpose. The novel as we know it today evolved from multiple genres and influences beginning in the 18th century. What constitutes a "novel" during this period is still actively debated among English literary scholars, with some critics setting the date at the 1719 publication of Daniel DEFOE's *ROBINSON CRUSOE* or even earlier. The date 1740 is a convenient place to begin discussion, as it is marked by Samuel RICHARDSON's publication of what would become his first long-running best seller, *PAMELA, OR VIRTUE REWARDED.* The novel exemplifies the realism and attention to character development generally accepted as the hallmarks of the genre. It gives the details of daily life in its characters and plotlines; this was particularly revolutionary given that many of its characters, including the heroine, are members of the working class. Richardson's narrative also provides credible psychological motivations for character behavior. The book's history of publication and reception shows how important popular reading material had become to an English public that was becoming more and more literate. Its fame spread abroad as well, and after Richardson's death, the French author Denis DIDEROT wrote an essay titled *Eloge de Richardson* (In praise of Richardson; 1762). For Diderot, Richardson provided the best example of what a novel could do: stay true to life through the use of realistic details and allow its readers to experience intense emotion and love of virtue.

The question of virtue was paramount, as novels were frequently blamed for having a bad moral influence on their readership. They were primarily associated with a female reading public, and religious authorities condemned these fictions for corrupting women's minds and, potentially, their souls. This concern stemmed from the popularity of an earlier prose genre against which the novel frequently defined itself, the romance. Romances involved characters born into nobility rather than ordinary people, narrated fantastic circumstances and feats of love and war instead of everyday occurrences, and did not usually contain a moral lesson. Many critics of the romance feared that its fantasy world led young women to have unrealistic expectations about love and marriage and made them likely to make poor moral choices. In the 18th century, novelists tried to counteract this fear with frequent expressions of moral intent, often attaching didactic prefaces to their works. While love was a major concern of the novel, as it had been of the romance, novelists claimed that their goal was to show love in a realistic light, including its potential dangers. Novelists' desire

Cover of Jonathan Swift's satirical novel *Gulliver's Travels*, depicting Gulliver among the Lilliputians, by R. G. Massa. The novel, popular from the time it was first published until today, went through 60 editions between 1726 and 1800. *(Courtesy New York Public Library)*

to describe the world around them allowed the genre's status to improve over the course of the century. Even if the authors' claims to moral purpose were frequently just convenient defenses against criticism, people had to take the novel seriously; it had a claim to social and cultural relevance, unlike the romance.

In many cases, however, the line between the novel and the romance was not so clear. In French, the same word, *roman*, was used for both. The French author Abbé Prévost wrote novels containing many fantastic episodes and settings such as kidnappings and subterranean passages; many of his works closely resembled the romance in tone and plot. In fact, the French novelist Claude de Crébillon made an oblique and unflattering reference to Prévost in the preface to his own novel *Les egarements du coeur et de l'esprit* (The wayward head and heart; 1736–38), in which he sought to describe his society realistically. There is some question whether the English author Eliza HAYWOOD's work *Love in Excess* (1720) should be classified as a novel. Although it contains real-

istic elements, including frank depictions of sexual relationships between men and women, it also shares elements with the romance. In Charlotte LENNOX's novel *The Female Quixote,* the male-controlled world of British society pales in comparison to the fantasy world the heroine, Arabella, constructs for herself after a childhood spent reading romances. These female authors, dismayed by the status of women in their society, were drawn to the romance because of its depictions of powerful women, strong outspoken characters with social and political power who at times would toy with men's affections.

In addition to the romance, other genres also influenced the development of the novel. The popularity of travel narratives inspired many novelists to write fictional accounts of voyages. Defoe's aforementioned widely read *Robinson Crusoe* reflects the same concern with accurate attention to unusual details that characterized the travel narrative. This work also shares elements of the fantastic; even more fantastic was Jonathan SWIFT's *GULLIVER'S TRAVELS* (1726), which used tales of strange, imaginary places as the basis for a satirical look at human foibles and English society.

It should be recognized, therefore, that the novel experienced a number of different influences, and that there was a great deal of variety in the novelistic production of the ENLIGHTENMENT. The novel also developed its own particular types, notably the genres of the picaresque and the epistolary. The picaresque genre takes its name from the Spanish word *pícaro*, meaning a rogue; its hero is a clever, likable rascal who has adventures in the course of traveling and moving through various classes of society. The protagonist relies on intelligence and charm and ends up playing many different roles, sometimes tricking others in an effort to become established. One of the best-known examples is Alain-René Lesage's *Gil Blas,* whose first part, published in 1715, is the most true to the Spanish heritage of the picaresque tradition. Marivaux's novel *La Vie de Marianne* (The life of Marianne; 1731–42) also displays picaresque qualities, as the orphaned heroine finds a place in aristocratic society thanks to her charm, beauty, and virtue. *La Vie de Marianne* is also representative of a popular type of narration, the memoir novel, a first-person account in which the narrator recounts his or her life adventures.

The epistolary novel consists of fictional letters exchanged between two or more characters. Two of the most successful examples are Richardson's *Pamela* and the French novelist Choderlos de LACLOS's *Les liaisons dangereuses* (Dangerous liaisons; 1782), which involved several different letter writers in a complex plot and was remarkable for differences in style that corresponded to each character's personality and education.

Other generic distinctions depend on the content of the novel in question. SENTIMENTAL FICTION, made popular by Richardson, emphasized the language of the heart and sought to have an emotional effect on its readers. Anecdotes of readers shedding tears over the fate of Richardson's characters Pamela and Clarissa abounded. After the mid-18th century, sentimental fiction became popular in France, where Jean-Jacques ROUSSEAU was its most successful representative. His novel LA NOUVELLE HÉLOÏSE (The new Heloise; 1761) was a best seller, appealing particularly to women readers, as attested to by the copious correspondence the author received from his female fans. Many French women authors were influenced by Rousseau and became successful sentimental novelists themselves, such as Sophie COTTIN and Germaine de STAËL. Other women writers had already been successful in the genre before Rousseau, such as Françoise de Graffigny and Marie Riccoboni.

In contrast to the sentimental novel, the LIBERTINE novel told tales of seduction and sensuality. Especially popular in France, it was best illustrated by Laclos's aforementioned epistolary novel *Les liaisons dangereuses*. Crébillon was an early practitioner of the genre, which, as would be expected, was denounced as immoral, but which nevertheless continued to have a great deal of success with the public. The libertine novels that were most shocking to public taste and morality were usually published anonymously, as was the case with the fiction of the marquis de SADE. The name of this most infamous of writers was nevertheless associated with his works, and in 1801 he was jailed for writing the immoral novels *Justine* and *Juliette*.

The novel took on different characteristics in the European countries where it became popular. In ENGLAND, the middle class played a more substantial role in political and cultural life than in France, and the literary developments of the nation reflect this dominance. The British middle class wanted to read about characters who came from their own background and reflected similar values, such as hard work and piety. Middle-class characters were frequently set in contrast with characters from the aristocracy who were clearly less moral. Writers during the midcentury who failed to meet the criteria of morality and virtue in the content of their novels came under increasing pressure and criticism from publishing authorities such as Samuel JOHNSON, who throughout his career remained suspicious of the novel's dangerous potential to teach readers flawed morality. The domestic sphere became an important concern of English novels, which told tales of marriage, family, and child rearing.

In FRANCE, there was also a trend to represent the domestic sphere, but the aristocratic class remained more dominant in French fiction, as it did in French social and political life. The leisured lifestyle of the aristocracy was reflected in the characters of the libertine novel, who spent their time receiving visitors, going for walks, and attending the theater. The genre of the memoir novel was very strong in France, as it grew out of a tradition of historical memoirs published in the 17th century.

The novel developed later in GERMANY, where its first practitioners were very influenced by English and French literature, especially by Richardson and Rousseau. One genre is so associated with German novelists that it has a German name, the *Bildungsroman*, or novel of education. The term BILDUNG refers to the development of an individual's character through formative experiences. Christoph Wieland's *Geschichte des Agathon* (Story of Agathon; 1766–67) helped to establish this genre and was also notable for its psychological observations. Another important innovator was Sophie von La Roche, who wrote the *Bildungsroman Geschichte des Fräuleins von Sternheim* (The story of Miss von Sternheim; 1771) and who was the first woman novelist in Germany. The best-known *Bildungsroman* is Johann Wolfgang von GOETHE's *Wilhelm Meisters Lehrjahre* (The apprenticeship of Wilhelm Meister; 1796), although his most famous novel had been published 20 years earlier. *Die Leiden des jüngen Werthers* (THE SORROWS OF YOUNG WERTHER; 1774) told the story of a melancholy young man who suffered for love and ultimately committed suicide. This novel was tremendously popular both in Germany and abroad; an increase in suicides was even attributed to the appeal of the unhappy hero.

The novel acquired a different character in each country where it took hold, with national traditions as well as foreign influences playing a role. In recent years, critics have paid more attention to the work of women novelists, whose works were often best sellers at the time but who tended to be neglected in the later establishment of a canon of novelists. Current literary scholarship revolves around the fluidity of the novel as a category of writing and finds no easy answers to the questions of its birthdate or essential character. Recent research has also focused on the reading public, as scholars try to ascertain who was reading novels and under what conditions. What remains indisputable is that the novel experienced a true explosion in popularity during the Enlightenment.

See also AULNOY; PUBLISHING; SOCIAL INSTITUTIONS OF THE ENLIGHTENMENT; TRAVEL LITERATURE; TRIMMER; WOMEN AND THE ENLIGHTENMENT.

Further reading: Margaret Anne Doody, *The True Story of the Novel* (New Brunswick, N.J.: Rutgers University Press, 1996); George Justice, *The Manufacturers of Literature: Writing and the Literary Marketplace in Eighteenth-Century England* (Newark: University of Delaware Press, 2002); Michael McKeon, ed., *Theory of the Novel* (Baltimore: Johns Hopkins University Press, 2000); Felicity Nussbaum, *The Autobiographical Subject: Gender and Ideology in Eighteenth-Century England* (Baltimore: Johns Hopkins University Press, 1989); John J. Richetti, *Popular Fiction Before Richardson: Narrative Patterns: 1700–1739* (Oxford: Clarendon Press, 1992); Janet Todd, *The Sign of Angellica: Women, Writing, and Fiction, 1660–1800* (New York: Columbia University Press, 1989).

Nozze di Figaro, Le (*The Marriage of Figaro*) Opera buffa in Italian composed by Wolfgang Amadeus MOZART. The libretto is an adaptation by Lorenzo da Ponte of the play by Pierre de BEAUMARCHAIS, *Le Mariage de Figaro* (1784). The OPERA premiered in VIENNA at the Burgtheater, May 1, 1786. It had nine performances, a normal run for the era. A successful and deeply symbolic revival occurred in 1789, just as the FRENCH REVOLUTION was beginning. Other immediate performance venues included Leipzig, Graz, FRANKFURT, Donaueschingen (in southwestern Germany), and Prague. In the last city, the reception was extraordinarily enthusiastic. Mozart acknowledged that he won the commission for *Don Giovanni* because of this triumph. *Le Nozze di Figaro* established Mozart as a master of the operatic genre, although his operas were not as widely popular as they are today.

Le Nozze di Figaro is considered the epitome of Italian opera buffa, an 18th-century farcical opera form with dialogue in recitative. The plot unfolds with lively, humorous lines carrying various levels of meaning that make the story a biting social commentary. The original play by Beaumarchais was banned in Vienna and elsewhere because of its scathing attack on privileged aristocracy. Mozart and da Ponte disguised these elements somewhat, but they were readily discernible to contemporaries. Emperor JOSEPH II was concerned enough about its subversive qualities that he banned excessive encores after the performances.

The plot focuses on relations between lords and their servants in the context of love and flirtation. Mozart's music is brilliant as it complements and expands the meaning of the text. The Count Almaviva is made to appear ridiculous and unprincipled in numerous situations where his predilection for infidelity is exposed. His actions are revealed through the intrigues of women (his wife and her charming servant, Susanna) and servants (Figaro, Cherubino, and Susanna). The criticism of Count Almaviva's actions and privilege is blunted throughout, however, when he shows various forms of compassion and remorse. The opera is filled with delightful scenes of disguised identity and the ridiculous situations that result. The effects are hilarious and yet deeply moving. The final act presents a denouement filled with the optimism about the universal brotherhood of humanity that characterized the ENLIGHTENMENT.

See also ANCIEN RÉGIME; MUSIC.

Oetinger, Friedrich Christoph (1702–1782) *German Pietist and theosophist*

A native of Göppingen in Württemberg, Oetinger studied theology at the University of Tübingen, was ordained in 1738, taught at the theological seminary in Tübingen, and obtained a pastoral position at Murrhardt in 1752. Oetinger created a theology that was a unique blend of Lutheran PIETISM, mystical spiritualism, and inspirationalism. He drew on the writings of Jakob Boehme (1575–1624), Gottfried Wilhelm LEIBNIZ, and the University of HALLE Pietists to create his ethical, rational, mystical form of religious faith. For this blended spiritual approach, Oetinger used the term *theosophy*. Oetinger traveled extensively within German territories, visiting the mystical spiritual community at Berleburg, the MORAVIAN BRETHREN at Herrhnhut and Jena, and the Pietists at Halle. As an older man, he encountered Emanuel SWEDENBORG, one of the renowned mystics of the ENLIGHTENMENT.

Oetinger believed that the spiritual and physical worlds were fundamentally one, that continuous communication with spirits occurs, and that spirit can be and sometimes is materialized as corporeal body. He tended to reject the common theological and epistemological notion that essential differences exist between the rational knowledge of humanity and that of the heavenly spirits. He believed, instead, that all knowledge is ultimately accessible to human beings. Oetinger's theosophical teachings particularly influenced Swabian Pietism, and seem to have influenced Georg Wilhelm Hegel's formulation of philosophical idealism. Oetinger wrote several works including *Inquisitio in sensu communem et rationem* (Inquiry into the common and rational senses; 1753) and *Theologia ex idea vitae deducta* (Theology deduced from the idea of life; 1765).

See also EPISTEMOLOGY; RELIGION.

On the Revolutions of the Heavenly Spheres (De Revolutionibus Orbium Coelestium)

ASTRONOMY treatise published in 1543 by Nicolaus COPERNICUS of Frombork, POLAND. The book was a technical mathematical treatise aimed at solving the longstanding problem of formulating an adequate astronomical theory to explain the apparent motions of the planets in the night sky. It laid the foundation for the shift to a HELIOCENTRIC model of the universe—the COPERNICAN REVOLUTION—that served as one stimulus for the SCIENTIFIC REVOLUTION. The Scientific Revolution, in turn, helped to provoke the reformulation of traditional concepts of NATURE, RATIONALISM, NATURAL RELIGION, and NATURAL LAW without which the thought of the ENLIGHTENMENT could not have developed as it did. The ideas contained in Copernicus's book, thus, provided one of the intellectual foundations for the Enlightenment.

At the time that Copernicus published *On the Revolutions of the Heavenly Spheres*, the dominant conception of the universe was that derived from the ancient Greeks, Ptolemy and Aristotle. The universe was believed to be finite and full, a plenum without any void space. The Earth lay stationary at the center of the universe while the Sun and planets revolved around it. Invisible, solid crystalline spheres were believed to carry each of the planets, the Sun, and the Moon in their journeys about the Earth. The stars were all believed to be located on a more distant crystalline sphere that lay at the boundary of the universe. The universe was believed to be structured into two distinct realms—the terrestrial and the celestial—that were governed by two equally distinct sets of physical laws: The terrestrial realm (Earth and all areas below the Moon) was the arena of change and imperfection where motion occurred in straight lines; the celestial realm (Moon and all other heavenly bodies beyond it) was the realm of perfection and timelessness where natural motion occurred in circles.

This Ptolemaic and Aristotelian conception had dominated European science for centuries. It explained most of the observed motions of heavenly bodies, and it also allowed for predictions about planetary positions. But it could not adequately explain certain oddities about the paths of the planets across the night sky. Generally, planets seem to move in simple lines eastward across the heavens, but at certain points in their paths, they appear to double back, moving briefly westward before resuming their eastward journeys. This phenomenon, known as planetary retrograde motion, had bedeviled astronomers for centuries, and they had resorted to a complex system of circles with smaller circles (epicycles and deferents) to explain their observations. Yet even with complex systems, the traditional theory failed to explain every aspect of observed planetary paths. Copernicus set out to resolve this problem of planetary motion when he wrote *On the Revolutions of the Heavenly Spheres.*

In his book, Copernicus proposed the radical, but not unprecedented idea, that the Earth, rather than being stationary, actually moves. He suggested, moreover, that the Earth moves with three different motions: that it revolves in a circular orbit around the Sun (annual motion); that it turns once daily on its north-south axis (diurnal motion); and that it wobbles slowly in conical motion around an axis drawn between its north pole and the North Star.

In proposing such earthly motions, Copernicus was reducing the Earth to the status of other planets, thereby removing the Earth from its unique position in the universe. He was also implicitly challenging the belief that Earth was governed by different laws from celestial bodies. But Copernicus did not specifically draw out these implications. His universe was not identical to the infinite, void-filled, heliocentric universe associated with the later full-blown Copernican Revolution. Rather, Copernicus's universe retained important elements from the traditional Aristotelian and Ptolemaic models. It was, therefore, finite, spherical in shape, and a plenum. In addition, its planets and stars were still attached to concentric, nesting, crystalline aether spheres that revolved slowly around the center of the universe. Only the center had changed: Rather than the Earth, it was, for Copernicus, somewhere near the Sun.

Copernicus's theory provided a geometrically harmonious view of the universe consistent with the Neoplatonic philosophy of the Renaissance to which he was committed. But his theory did not really offer a simpler system. In fact, by insisting that the orbits of Earth and the planets are circular, Copernicus created new discrepancies between astronomical observations and theoretical prediction that were as glaring as the older discrepancies. His theory did, however, go a long way toward resolving the thorny problem of planetary retrograde motions by demonstrating that those motions could simply be created by making both the Earth and the planets move around a common center. More significant, at least for his immediate contemporaries, Copernicus supported his theory with pages of technical, mathematical calculations and astronomical measurements whose accuracy was unprecedented.

The initial reception of Copernicus's book was mixed. It was mostly ignored except in the circles of professional astronomers and Protestant theologians. The Roman Catholic Church barely noticed the publication and took no official action against it. The Protestant leaders of LUTHERANISM and CALVINISM viewed Copernicus's ideas as a serious threat to the authority of the Bible since several verses in the Bible seemed to support the traditional view of a motionless Earth. Since one primary goal of PROTESTANTISM was the movement to return Christianity to the alleged pristine purity of the ancient Bible, any challenge to scriptural veracity was also a challenge, by implication, not only to the Bible as the primary source of truth but also to the claims of the fledgling reform movement.

In contrast to the Protestant theologians, astronomers throughout Europe greeted the appearance of Copernicus's book eagerly. They had been made aware of his ideas through an early manuscript, the *Commentariolus* (Short treatise; 1514), which had circulated privately. Also, Copernicus's student, Georges Joachim Rheticus, had published an advanced notice of the findings called *Narratio Prima* (First narration; 1540–41). The astronomers wanted to see the complete Copernican text primarily because his reputedly accurate measurements of planetary positions and his new mathematical techniques were printed in its pages. Most astronomers adopted Copernicus's tables and methods for making measurements while simply ignoring the underlying heliocentric theory detailed in the book.

Only a handful of 16th-century astronomers and other intellectuals accepted the heliocentric theory. Their number included the aforementioned Georges Joachim Rheticus (1514–76), Andreas Osiander (1498–1552), Thomas Digges (1546–95), Giordano Bruno (1548–1600), and Michael Maestlin (1550–1631). Tycho Brahe (1546–1601), a Danish astronomer who worked for the Hapsburg emperor, Rudolf II, developed a highly popular theory that compromised between the Ptolemaic and Copernican systems by borrowing elements from both.

Until the 17th century, it was possible to conceive of the Copernican heliocentric universe as a simple theoretical hypothesis, useful as an explanatory device, but having no relation to the physical reality of the universe. But after 1610, when Galileo GALILEI turned his TELESCOPE to the heavens and discovered evidence of lunar imperfection, countless previously unknown stars, and the phases of Venus, it became more difficult to deny the physical reality of the Copernican universe. Galileo made a public endorsement of Copernicanism in print in his *Letters on Sunspots* (1613). Furthermore, he made some excursions into biblical exegesis (interpretation) in an attempt to wrestle with the increasingly troublesome relations between biblical teachings and those of the natural sciences. These activities and the associated writings came to the attention of Catholic authorities in ROME who began to worry about the revolutionary and heretical potential of Copernicanism. As a result, in 1616, 73 years after Copernicus published *On the Revolutions of the Heavenly Spheres,* the Roman Catholic Church prohibited the teaching or holding of Copernican views. Permission to print or to read *On the Revolutions of the Heavenly Spheres* was suspended, and a book by Paolo Antonio Foscarini, which attempted to reconcile the Bible and Copernicanism, was also placed on the Catholic Index of Forbidden Books. Galileo was instructed to abandon his activities on behalf of Copernicanism.

The action did not halt the diffusion of Copernican theory into European science. In fact, the theory had raised a number of critical and compelling scientific questions. In attempting to address these questions, mathematicians, physicists, and astronomers extended the scope of the Copernican Revolution, and began to spell out the views that became the foundation for the Scientific Revolution and the subsequent science of the Enlightenment. Concomitantly, philosophers, theologians, and other European intellectuals wrestled with the implications for their concepts of humanity and its relation to the universe contained within the Copernican framework. The denial of special status to the Earth threatened to unseat traditional Christian views that placed humankind at the center of the universe, raised the possibility that other populated worlds might exist, and contributed to the proliferation of new methods for substantiating belief in the existence of God.

Even at the beginning of the 18th century, opposition to Copernicus's ideas existed in certain theological circles and also in the general public perception. In fact, it was scientists and lay writers of the Enlightenment who, in championing the ideas of Isaac NEWTON, also finally gained widespread popular acceptance for Copernicanism.

Further reading: John G. Burke, *The Uses of Science in the Age of Newton* (Los Angeles: William Andrews Clark Library, UCLA, 1983); Thomas S. Kuhn, *The Copernican Revolution: Planetary Astronomy in the Development of Western Thought* (Cambridge, Mass.: Harvard University Press, 1957).

opera   A dramatic work in which all roles are sung to instrumental accompaniment. Opera emerged at the beginning of the 17th century in northern ITALY. By the end of the century, most sizable European cities had establishments that performed operas regularly.

In the 18th century, opera was not a uniform genre. Generally, an opera was a work with a dramatic (comic or tragic) plot, performed in a theater by singers in costume and an orchestra. The number of singers and the size of the orchestra varied considerably, and the orchestra changed in terms of both instrumentation and size over the course of the century. A standard opera orchestra at the beginning of the century consisted of strings, oboes, and continuo. The continuo was played by one or more instruments that articulated the bass line, such as a harpsichord or other keyboard, a lute or other plucked instrument, a cello, a double bass, or a bassoon. By 1800, the opera orchestra had changed and resembled something we would recognize today, with flutes, oboes, CLARINETS, bassoons, horns, trumpets, trombones, timpani, and strings.

There were several types of opera with contrasting characteristics: serious and comic, French and Italian, and court and commercial. Well into the 18th century, the two geographically based styles of serious opera, Italian *dramma per musica,* sometimes anachronistically called *opera seria,* and French *tragédie en musique,* exhibited distinct differences. The century can also be divided into two periods. The first, which lasted until the 1760s, was characterized by the dominance of Italian *opera seria* and French *tragédie en musique.* The second, from the 1760s on, witnessed attempts to reform these earlier types along with a proliferation of new operatic forms.

Opera before the 1760s

Until the 1760s, the dominant forms of opera in Europe were the serious operas associated with princely courts. The French *tragédie en musique* was heavily influenced by

Engravings by the Schaffer brothers of costume and scene designs for Mozart's opera *The Magic Flute.*

the works of Jean-Baptiste Lully (1632–87). His operas had deep roots in French court society—they often opened with prologues praising the ruler—and contained a great deal of spectacle, with ballets, choruses, arias, and a wide range of exotic touches. The leading exponent of this school in the 18th century was Jean-Philippe RAMEAU. Several of Rameau's operas are set in exotic locales (Peru, Persia, Egypt, or among the "noble savages" of North America) and include all sorts of gripping musical and visual special effects, such as sea monsters accompanied by a musical depiction of tumultuous seas, supernatural creatures as lead characters, and characters who visit otherworldly realms.

In terms of musical form, French operas of the Lully-Rameau type contain long stretches of music uninterrupted by recitative (sung passages accompanied only by the continuo, meant to imitate the declamatory freedom of the spoken word), although the works do use recitative in places. They also often employ a rich orchestral palette. Whereas the standard Italian opera orchestra of the period used an oboes-strings-continuo combination, Rameau often added other woodwind, brass, and percussion instruments. He had the freedom to do so because of his association with the Académie Royale de Musique (the Opéra) in PARIS, which had greater resources than many other operatic institutions in Europe at the time.

Italian opera traced its lineage back to northern Italy and the period around the turn of the 17th century. Its greatest early exponent was Claudio Monteverdi (1567–1643). Monteverdi's approach freely mixed aria (numbers for voice and orchestra evincing some sort of self-contained musical form), arioso (recitativelike passages of an expressive or melodic, rather than a declamatory, nature), and recitative, especially in his later Venetian works. This freer form gradually developed into the more rigid *dramma per musica* of the 18th century that alternated between recitative and musical numbers for voice and orchestra, such as arias and duets. Most scenes usually consisted of recitative followed by an aria. The arias are sometimes called "exit arias" because the performer had to leave the stage at the end of the scene. The arias themselves were rigidly organized, with careful rules about how many times a composer had to repeat various passages and when he could introduce contrasting musical material. The recitatives housed the dramatic action, moving the plot along, while the arias were the places for reflection and contemplation, the emotional and expressive heart of the works. Well into the 18th century, Italian opera favored stylized expression over dramatic continuity.

Writers such as Louis de Cahusac, Jean-François Marmontel, and VOLTAIRE in FRANCE and Pietro Metastasio and Apostolo Zeno in Italy played a large part in giving opera its distinctive characteristics. In France, librettists (writers of operatic texts) built on the 17th-century dramatic traditions of Pierre and Thomas Corneille and Jean Racine and replicated the structure and style of that era's foremost librettist, Philippe Quinault. Metastasio and his contemporaries embedded the formal rules that governed the MUSIC of 18th-century Italian opera in their libretti, which specified the alternation of recitative and aria and established conventions such as the exit aria.

Both French and Italian serious operas relied on subject matter drawn from antiquity. The subjects chosen for serious operas were meant to reflect on the magnanimity of the ruler. The standard operatic text revolved around a central character, usually a hero or king from the history of Greece or ROME. This hero embodied all the characteristics of a good ruler, victorious in both amorous and political pursuits. Italian opera, more so than French, replicated the social hierarchy in its allotment of arias to characters. The hero (*primo uomo*) and the lead female character (*prima donna*) had more arias than did characters such as their advisers, confidantes, military commanders, or siblings, who, in turn, had more to sing than did servants, soldiers, and the like. These serious operas almost uniformly had a happy ending (*lieto fine*), often brought about by a deus ex machina, some kind of supernatural intervention that helped the hero out of his predicament.

In addition to these two types of serious opera, there were also several examples of comic opera during the first half of the century. In Italy, the most popular example was the intermezzo, which was performed between the acts of the *dramma per musica*. Like its serious counterpart, the intermezzo alternated recitative and aria. The plots of these intermezzi were simple and often revolved around two characters, a man and a woman, with the former usually outsmarted by the latter. One of the most famous examples of this genre was Giovanni Battista Pergolesi's *La serva padrona* (The maid turned mistress; 1733). It was performed throughout Europe in the two decades following its premiere in Naples and instigated the *querelle des bouffons* (BATTLE OF THE BUFFOONS) in Paris in 1752. In France, lighter genres such as the *opéra-ballet* (large-scale work that placed more emphasis on dance than was typical of the *tragédie en musique*), the *pastorale* (smaller-scale work with a pastoral subject), and the *comédie lyrique* (smaller-scale comic opera) were popular.

There were two types of theaters for operatic performances throughout the 18th century, court and commercial. Court theaters were in capital cities of monarchic or princely territories, including Paris and several German and Italian cities such as BERLIN, Dresden, MUNICH, MILAN, TURIN, and Naples. Centers of commercial opera included VENICE, LONDON, and Hamburg. Opera houses in London and the German capitals performed Italian opera, while French opera was restricted to France itself. Other localized operatic traditions also sprang up, including the English ballad opera in London and the works created for the Hamburg Opera, which set polyglot texts to music that combined elements of the Italian and French styles. The most famous example of ballad opera was THE BEGGAR'S OPERA by John GAY (1728), and the leading composers of opera for Hamburg included Reinhard Keiser and Georg Philipp TELEMANN.

Opera after 1760

Although the same types of operas (commercial and court, French and Italian, and comic and serious) were composed during the second half of the 18th century, different types became popular. Attacks on the stilted dramaturgy and inflexible musical structures of serious opera that came from several intellectuals altered the nature of works composed for both commercial and court productions. The spread of commercial theaters and the increase in their popularity, prestige, and influence meant that the tastes of the paying public also took on a greater role in determining the direction of opera. Composers, librettists, and performers had to react to the demands of this new public. Operas performed at court began increasingly to reflect changes that originated at commercial theaters.

Beginning in the 1750s, writers increasingly criticized opera. Foremost among them was Jean-Jacques ROUSSEAU, whose *Lettre sur la musique française* (Letter on French music) appeared in 1753, a year after the *querelle des bouffons*. The *Lettre* attacked the French language as impossible to set to music, and Rousseau turned instead to the example of the Italian style as embodied in *La serva padrona*. He put his theories into practice in two works, *Le devin du village* (The village soothsayer; 1752) and *Pygmalion* (1770). In *Le devin*, Rousseau wrote music radically simpler than that found in contemporary French operas, and in *Pygmalion*, he took the drastic step of abandoning singing altogether in favor of speech interspersed with descriptive orchestral passages, the practical outcome of the position he took in the *Lettre*.

Other figures answered the call for greater dramatic and musical continuity as well as more natural expression in their operas, among them the composers Niccolò Jomelli, who was active in Stuttgart, and Tommaso Traetta, who composed works for Mannheim, Vienna, and SAINT PETERSBURG. These composers tried to soften the rigidity of the *dramma per musica* by incorporating French elements such as choruses, ensembles, and ballets. Another key reformer, Christoph Willibald GLUCK, had a lasting impact because he introduced reform elements in centers of both Italian (Vienna) and French (Paris) opera and because his works were rapidly disseminated to other operatic centers in Europe. Gluck first introduced reform elements in his ballet *Don Juan* (1761) and then in his operas ORFEO ED EURIDICE (1762) and *Alceste* (1767). He outlined the tenets of the reform position in his dedication to the published score of *Alceste* (1769). In lieu of the lack of dramatic continuity, the stultifying repetition, and the damaging emphasis on musical display over natural expression Gluck found in pre-reform opera, he strove to do away with repetition, smooth the break between recitative and aria by orchestrating many of the recitatives and shortening the arias, and include a greater number of choruses and ballets. The musical and dramatic continuity found in *Alceste* is echoed in several later works, notably Wolfgang Amadeus MOZART's *Idomeneo* (1781) and Luigi Cherubini's *Médée* (1797).

Alongside these developments in serious opera, comic opera also underwent several changes during the second half of the 18th century. Many of these were tied less to theoretical developments than to the emergence of new audiences for opera. Theaters opened in many parts of Europe to support travelling troupes that included comic operas in their repertory, and stationary troupes were formed in centers such as Vienna, Berlin, and Paris. Comic works were fairly simple compared to the serious operas of composers such as Gluck, Traetta, and Jomelli. The French *opéra-comique* (comic opera) and the German *komische Oper* (sometimes called singspiel) interspersed spoken dialogue with simple, strophic songs, and Italian intermezzi continued to be popular.

Mozart and his librettist Lorenzo da Ponte brought about opera's final transformation of the 18th century. Their three collaborations—LE NOZZE DI FIGARO (The marriage of Figaro; 1786), DON GIOVANNI (1787), and COSÌ FAN TUTTE (So do all women; 1790)—combined elements of the reform operas, such as more symphonic writing in arias and greater continuity of action, with situations and characterizations from comic opera. The subjects of these works take the stock comic characters of works such as *La serva padrona* and use music and text to infuse them with a rich and complex emotional life, blurring the distinction between comic and serious that had characterized opera from the earlier part of the 18th century. Mozart and Da Ponte even went so far as to label *Don Giovanni* a *dramma giocoso* (comic drama). They also turned to more current subject matter for their works, including Pierre Caron de BEAUMARCHAIS' *Marriage of Figaro* (1784), something that imbued their work with topicality and put characters into opera with whom audience members could more easily identify.

Mozart's *Figaro* marked an early presentation of ENLIGHTENMENT values derived from ideas of NATURAL RIGHTS. Themes of the individual's triumph over tyranny and oppression dominated opera during the period of the FRENCH REVOLUTION. The favorite plot for such works involved the hero's rescue from a tyrannical captor, suggesting the triumph of republicanism over the old regime. Such works included André Grétry's *Richard Coeur-de-Lion* (Richard the Lionheart; 1784), Cherubini's *Lodoïska* (1791), and Ludwig van BEETHOVEN's *Fidelio* (1814).

See also MANNHEIM SCHOOL; NOBLE SAVAGE; SYMPHONY ORCHESTRA.

Further reading: Norman Demuth, *French Opera: Its Development to the Revolution* (New York: Da Capo Press, 1978); Andrew Steptoe, *The Mozart-Da Ponte Operas* (New York: Oxford University Press, 1991); Reinhard Strohm, *Dramma per Musica: Italian Opera Seria of the Eighteenth Century* (New Haven, Conn.: Yale University Press, 1997).

optimism   Philosophical concept that the ultimate outcome of situations was likely to be positive or bring about a desirable state of affairs. Philosophical discussions during the ENLIGHTENMENT proceeded from notions that the universe was knowable through rationality and operated via principles of harmony and order. The role and behavior of humanity within that order was therefore similarly subject to REASON and natural order, and, at least potentially, also subject to improvement through human intervention when it was motivated by ethical and rational principles.

This optimistic attitude toward human endeavors is reflected in the works of thinkers such as Adam SMITH and David HUME of the Scottish Enlightenment, whose works asserted that harmonious natural forces guided human interactions. Smith's *An Inquiry into the Nature and Causes of the* WEALTH OF NATIONS (1776) provides numerous examples of this philosophy applied to the economic sphere. His assertions, such as the idea that the flow of money among different nations was self-regulating and equalizing, provided an optimistic corrective to earlier ideas that countries would need to make war on one another to gain wealth.

Enlightenment notions of RELIGION and the divine were also assumed to proceed from rational optimistic principles. God created the universe to operate according to reasonable laws, and the application of reason allowed individuals to gain greater understanding of these laws as well as to fight more effectively against the forces of corruption. This idea developed in certain intellectual circles into DEISM, the belief in God's creation as a self-regulating mechanism that did not require divine intervention to operate correctly. Another variant saw the natural world as the perfect reflection of divine harmony: Humans could learn the will and lessons of God better by observing NATURE than by studying the Scriptures.

The American statesman Thomas JEFFERSON pursued this notion of rational religion in his ongoing project to edit the books of the New Testament into a form that recaptured the teachings of Jesus unencumbered by historical baggage. He first produced *The Philosophy of Jesus of Nazareth* (1804) and then expanded the scope of the project with *The Life and Morals of Jesus of Nazareth Extracted Textually from the Gospels in Greek, Latin, French and English* (1820).

Another Enlightenment thinker concerned with the principles of reasoned religion was the German Gottfried LEIBNIZ, who also embraced the idea of the universe's regulation and operation by rational principles. He asserted that evil existed as a part of these rational principles, and that human concerns with its existence were the result of the human mind's limited understanding of God's plan. His sense of the universe is summarized by the phrase often attributed to him: "the best of all possible worlds." This phrase asserts that the world and universe constitute God's choice of the best existence possible among a series of alternatives. Everything that exists is as God willed it to be.

Leibniz similarly attributes human evil to a case of misdirected choice, a decision made by a lack of understanding as to what constitutes a true good. The central example of this principle in Christianity is Adam's fall, which nonetheless is transformed into a greater good by God's intervention through the birth, death, and resurrection of Jesus Christ that both corrects Adam's sin and provides a greater glorious opportunity for humanity. Hence, the ultimate human good in Leibniz's system occurs when human beings freely choose the good with an understanding of the available options. In so doing, humans approach the example of divine judgment practiced by God.

Nonetheless, evil's role in the world remained a problem for the Enlightenment's optimists. Natural disasters such as the LISBON EARTHQUAKE of 1755 convinced VOLTAIRE that optimism was folly. His CANDIDE (1759), in part a response to the earthquake, did not refute Leibnizian optimism, but made it irrelevant through ridicule.

Further reading: Charles Vereker, *Eighteenth-Century Optimism* (Liverpool: Liverpool University Press, 1967).

Orfeo ed Eurydice   Italian opera with music by Christoph Willibald GLUCK and libretto by Raineri de' CALZABIGI. The premiere production was staged in VIENNA on October 5, 1762, at the Burgtheater. As part of his program for reforming the arts in Vienna, the Hapsburg minister Wenzel Anton KAUNITZ had assigned the patronage of the Burgtheater to Count Giacomo Durazzo. Durazzo wanted to see Viennese opera move away from traditional opera seria style with its highly stylized plots and strict musical forms. Therefore, he generously supported the activities of Gluck and Calzabigi. *Orfeo* is considered a milestone in the history of opera because it presents a serious subject, yet nevertheless departs from the musical forms and character conceptualizations that had typified opera seria. *Orfeo* represents a melding of the French lyric tragedy tradition with that of Italian dramatic opera.

The myth of Orpheus had been a popular subject for opera ever since Jacopo Peri and Giulio Caccini had created the very first opera, *Euridice*, in 1600. The basic plot revolves around Orpheus's attempt to recover his beloved wife, Eurydice, by crossing over into the land of the dead (Elysium) to secure her release from Hades, lord of that nether world. Hades agrees to release Eurydice to Orpheus but imposes two conditions on the pair: While Orpheus is leading Eurydice out of the underworld, he must not look back at her until both of them have reached the world of the living, and neither of them must speak until they have left Hades.

Gluck's opera stands out from its predecessors because of its treatment of the major characters. The earlier operatic settings emphasize the mythical aspects of the characters, making them stand above ordinary humankind. In those versions, Orpheus's mission tragically fails when he looks back to see if Eurydice is with him before she has completed her exit from that place. Hades's command not to speak plays no part in the tragedy. Gluck and Calzabigi, in contrast, assign responsibility for the failure of the mission to Eurydice. Unable to understand why Orpheus refuses to look at her (she is unaware of the god's instructions), she breaks the required silence by calling out to him. As a result, she is forced to return to the underworld. This treatment of the myth emphasizes the humanness of both characters in a manner that is consistent with 18th-century treatments of natural human passions. Shifting responsibility for failure from the man to the woman also highlights aspects of the redefinition of the nature of the masculine and the feminine that emerged during the last half of the century. Both Orpheus and Eurydice are highly sympathetic, displaying natural joy, fears, doubts, and grief.

Calzabigi's libretto and Gluck's music both place the observer immediately into the dramatic action; the setting is compact, terse, and laden with emotion in a stark departure from opera seria tradition. The music is specifically designed to enhance the poetry of the libretto. Gluck uses a full complement of orchestral instruments. He reworked the opera for the 1774 production in PARIS, adding the well-known "Minuet and Dance of the Blessed Spirits" to accommodate the French love of ballet. Although reaction to *Orfeo* was mixed, performances, nevertheless, occurred throughout Europe in cities such as LONDON, Stockholm, Florence, Naples, Bologna, SAINT PETERSBURG, Lisbon, Warsaw, and Paris.

See also MUSIC.

orientalism The study of Asian societies, philosophies, and arts that significantly shaped ideas of the ENLIGHTENMENT. The great quests of the Enlightenment—particularly finding the age of the earth, discovering the hidden laws of NATURE, recovering the original language of humankind—all were dramatically advanced by exposure to the Orient. Writers of the Enlightenment studied eastern ideas and practices as a way of contrasting them with European culture. They hoped this contrast would ignite governmental, moral, and intellectual reform.

This consideration of new ideas was propelled by a number of causes. Europeans were intrigued by reports carried back by the JESUITS. These missionaries sought to understand and engage the cultures of the peoples they hoped to convert. With sophisticated appreciation for Chinese civilization and Confucian philosophy, the Jesuits translated many classical texts of Confucianism into Latin. In 1678, they published *Confucius Sinarum Philosophus* (Confucius: philosopher of China), effectively and sympathetically introducing this Chinese thinker to Europe. It was followed by the writings of other travelers, so that, by the middle of the 18th century, a considerable body of literature on the great civilizations of the East evoked widespread enthusiasm among European intellectuals. Gottfried LEIBNIZ, in frequent contact with the Jesuits, read widely on China, having more than 50 books on the topic in his own library. He, in turn, compiled *Novissima Sinica* (New China). Published in 1697, it was a compendium of reports and letters from the missionaries.

Commerce also introduced Europe to Eastern culture in the form of exotic goods brought by Portuguese vessels from Macao and spices from Jakarta imported by the Dutch. Oriental motifs were fancifully incorporated into textiles, pottery, furniture, and the decorative arts. This influence is known as CHINOISERIE.

The inflow of ideas and goods elicited an insecurity in Europe about its received truths. Suddenly, Europeans were surprised to discover that they were not the sole possessors of an impressive intellectual and cultural past. China, for example, was shown to be an ancient, advanced, and sophisticated society. Enlightenment thinkers such as Baron de MONTESQUIEU, Denis DIDEROT, Leibniz, and VOLTAIRE found, in China, the perfect foil to reflect on and examine European traditions. China's very antiquity challenged biblical chronology, and its pictograph characters predated the alphabet.

Voltaire's was the loudest voice, praising China in works such as *Zadig* (1748) and *L'orphelin de la Chine* (The orphan of China; 1755), which contributed to the orientalist genre popular during the Enlightenment. This genre used a fictionalized East to mount an assault on both the political and religious institutions of Europe. In his *Essai sur les moeurs* (Essay on morals; 1756), Voltaire wrote of China's moral superiority in philosophy over a degenerate Christianity. He championed its political system, which he saw as based on rational principles, not on inherited positions of influence.

The Jesuit-fueled image of China that Voltaire used to attack the orthodoxy of church and state was taken up and further polished by Diderot, editor of the ENCYCLOPEDIE, and Claude-Adrien HELVÉTIUS. They were part of the RADICAL ENLIGHTENMENT, thinkers who believed the old order of Europe had to be swept away before a new one could develop. China represented the model of this new order for many writers, and Confucius was widely admired by Enlightenment figures. Matthew Tindal (1657–1733), a British deist, saw Confucian moral teachings as equal to those of Jesus Christ. Some historians call Confucius the patron saint of the Enlightenment.

While China was the strongest of oriental influences, it was not the only one. Voltaire became fascinated with India toward the end of his life, believing that India was the world's oldest culture. The craze for oriental fashion, decorative arts, and painting remained strong until the end of 18th century.

See also CHINA; TRAVEL LITERATURE.

Further reading: J. J. Clarke, *Oriental Enlightenment* (London: Routledge, 1997); P. G. Marshall and G. Williams, eds., *The Great Map of Mankind* (London: Dent, 1982); Ziauddin Sardar, *Orientalism* (Philadelphia: Open University Press, 1999); Raymond Schwab, *The Oriental Renaissance: Europe's Rediscovery of India and the East, 1690–1880* (New York: Columbia University Press, 1984).

orrery   An instrument that provided a working model of the solar system according to the theories of COPERNICUS. It was designed so that the HELIOCENTRIC motions of the planets and the three motions assigned by Copernicus to the Earth could be witnessed in detail. An early instrument of this type was designed before 1713 by John Rowley in ENGLAND. It was dubbed the orrery in honor of the English nobleman, the earl of Orrery, who had commissioned its production. Rowley's model may have been derived from an earlier one by Thomas Tompion and George Graham.

Some grand orreries modeled all the planets, along with the Sun, Earth, and Moon. They were expensive instruments and hence available only to the wealthy. During the 18th century, certain instrument makers such as Benjamin Martin created orrery designs that could be produced at lesser expense. These instruments transformed the orrery from a plaything of wealthy princes and aristocrats into a visual aid for general education.

Affordable orreries were used by public lecturers and educators to demonstrate the principal concepts of Copernican theory. These instruments thus helped in the dissemination and popularization of the Copernican heliocentric theory of the universe, which was one of the many important contributions made by the ENLIGHTENMENT to modern visions of the world.

See also ASTRONOMY; COPERNICAN REVOLUTION; RITTENHOUSE.

Ossian   *See* James MACPHERSON.

Oudry, Jean-Baptiste (1686–1755) *French rococo artist, associated with portraiture, animal paintings, and the production of designs for tapestry*
Son of a painter and art dealer from PARIS, Oudry benefited most from his training with Nicolas de Largillière. The French Royal Academy accepted Oudry as a member in 1719. He directed the reorganized Beauvais tapestry works between 1734 and 1736, and later he headed the GOBELINS TAPESTRY works. Oudry was responsible for hiring François BOUCHER as a design artist at the Gobelins manufactory.

Oudry was commissioned by King LOUIS XV to paint official depictions of the royal hunt and received commissions from Czar PETER I (THE GREAT) of Russia. He also illustrated books, including editions of the *Fables* of Jean de La Fontaine and of *Don Quixote* by Miguel de Cervantes.

P

paganism Any religion in which people worship gods or goddesses other than the God of the Judeo-Christian tradition. For 18th-century thinkers, simple condemnation of paganism as heresy, the common approach in earlier eras, was no longer acceptable. Instead, they used paganism as a ground against which they could sketch out their assessments of contemporary society. In this manner, pagan religions, whether those of the ancient Greeks and Romans or of contemporary cults practiced in non-European regions of the world, played a central role in the critical inquiries into RELIGION and society that were carried out during the ENLIGHTENMENT.

The pagans of the ancient world had created magnificent philosophies such as Stoicism, Epicureanism, Platonism, Pythagoreanism, and of course Aristotelianism. Some contemporary pagan societies seemed to European observers to operate more effectively and with greater morality than Christian Europe. Awareness of these factors seemed to call claims about the exclusive truth of Christian beliefs into question. How and why, it was wondered, had God allowed these pagan cultures to exist? And how could they have produced human beings of such high moral, intellectual, and spiritual quality? It seemed that because various pagan cultures and religions had contributed positively to history and to culture, they deserved respectful study and assessment.

European contact with paganism was not a new development in the Enlightenment. Aristotle's philosophy, for example, had been thoroughly Christianized by the scholastic philosophers of the Middle Ages. The centuries of the Renaissance had brought new classic texts to light, creating an explosion of knowledge about ancient pagan cultures. Eighteenth-century scholars continued the queries that had begun during the Renaissance, but people of the Enlightenment brought new sets of concerns to bear on their investigations.

These new concerns centered on questions about essential HUMAN NATURE, about RELATIONS between the material and spiritual worlds, about the role of REASON in uncovering religious truths, and about the best forms of society and political culture. These questions were being asked everywhere by orthodox Christian theologians, by philosophers, by political theorists, by social critics, by doubters, by atheists, and by troubled Christian believers. The answers to these questions provided evidence for or against the possibilities of PROGRESS, of religious TOLERATION, of rational reform, or of general enlightenment. Critical inquiry into the meaning of paganism shed new light on these issues and thus helped to define the major outlines of enlightened discourse about human potential.

Most enlightened thinkers shared the assumption that pagan cultures represented human culture in its earliest stages of development. Their assessments of that stage of development, however, varied widely and depended primarily on the attitude of writers toward their own era. Those who believed that 18th-century culture reflected the positive values of civilization tended to view pagan cultures as inferior and naive, as the era of the childhood of the human race. Others, who were critical of contemporary civilization, looked back to pagan cultures with nostalgia, seeing in them an example of pristine human nature unspoiled by the encumbrances of civilization. Writers seldom examined pagan cultures dispassionately, with the simple goal of describing alternative human social forms. Rather, they used paganism as a symbol for NATURAL RELIGION and the natural state of humankind.

In the last half of the 18th century, one particular form of paganism—pantheism—did begin to receive special attention as an alternative to dogmatic Christianity. Pantheists believe that God or the divine is directly present in everything in the universe; some even believe that the universe is simply an emanation from or facet of divine existence. Christians and Jews, in contrast, envision a God who created the universe as a physical entity distinctly separate from the divine being.

In the 17th century, the philosopher Benedict de SPINOZA incorporated ideas resembling pantheism into his systematic philosophy of monism. He had argued that mind and spirit, world and God are simply different manifestations of the one that is God. These ideas appealed to enlightened German intellectuals such as Gotthold Ephraim LESSING and Moses MENDELSSOHN, who saw in pantheism a way to preserve a religious outlook on life while avoiding the quarrels and hatred that divided Christianity. Pantheistic thought would assume even greater importance as the AUFKLÄRUNG (German Enlightenment) gave way to ROMANTICISM.

The list of enlightened writers who examined paganism includes major figures such as MONTESQUIEU, Jean-Jacques ROUSSEAU, Denis DIDEROT, David HUME, Lessing, Mendelssohn, and Edward GIBBON, but it also encompasses lesser figures such as Baron de Lahontan, Louis de BOUGAINVILLE, and a host of others. The subject of paganism or themes from pagan works appeared in LITERATURE, in criticism, in ART AND ARCHITECTURE, and in MUSIC. In the end, paganism functioned as one of the more powerful creative sources of the Enlightenment.

See also CRITICISM.

Paine, Thomas (1737–1809) *English-American political theorist, propagandist, and writer*

Paine's radical pamphlets and books, including COMMON SENSE (1776), *The American Crisis* (1776), THE RIGHTS OF MAN (1791–92), and THE AGE OF REASON (1794–95), sold more copies than the writings of any other author in the 18th century. His clear presentation of ideas drawn from the POLITICAL THEORY of the ENLIGHTENMENT proved to be very effective in rallying American colonists against Great Britain during the AMERICAN REVOLUTION. They were also welcomed in revolutionary FRANCE. In ENGLAND, however, his writings were greeted with hostility from censoring authorities and members of the elite classes, and his later works, which examined the grounds for religious faith, were reviled in both Great Britain and the UNITED STATES OF AMERICA.

Thomas Paine was born in 1737 as Thomas Pain to Quaker parents in Thetford, England. He did not change his name to Paine until he was 39 years old. His father

Thomas Paine, engraving by W. Sharp. Paine was thoroughly dedicated to the Enlightenment and championed the American Revolution as an expression of its power and potential. *(Courtesy New York Public Library)*

worked as a staymaker—a craftsman who made women's corsets—and owned enough land to make him one of the few people in Thetford (31 out of 21,000) privileged enough to vote. Paine's mother came from one of the leading families of the town. Nevertheless, the family could not afford to send their young son to secondary school, and he was therefore apprenticed to his father.

By the late 1750s, Paine was living in LONDON and attending lectures on mathematics. He married in 1759 only to be widowed in less than a year. Afterward, he took a position collecting excise taxes in towns along the English coast. By 1771, he had remarried and opened a tobacco shop while continuing his tax-collecting duties. His first important political pamphlet, *The Case of the Officers of the Excise* (1772), argued that excise tax collectors should have an increase in pay to lessen corruption and to increase their efficiency. In 1774, Paine was fired from his job, his shop went bankrupt, and he separated legally from his second wife. Following the advice of Benjamin FRANKLIN, whom he had met in London, and armed with important letters of introduction from the influential Philadelphian, Paine set off for the American colonies.

Paine arrived in the colonies just as the tensions that led to the American Revolution were escalating. He obtained work briefly with the *Pennsylvania Journal* and attracted some attention for an article against SLAVERY. He was fired, however, after a dispute with the magazine's owner. Thereafter, he devoted himself to political pamphleteering.

Paine's first outstanding pamphlet was really a series of essays, which his friend, Dr. Benjamin RUSH, encouraged him to publish in pamphlet form. Entitled *Common Sense,* these essays appeared in early 1776 and provided a justification for colonial revolt against Great Britain. He followed this success with *The American Crisis,* a series of propagandistic essays written between 1776 and 1783 while he was fighting in the American army against the British. Several of the essays from 1782 and 1783 were written under a contract signed by General George WASHINGTON, and others were financed from a secret congressional fund.

In 1777, Paine entered public service as secretary to the Committee of Foreign Affairs of the Congress, but he was forced to resign after he exposed the corrupt activities of a high government official, Paine, however, found another position, this time as secretary to the Pennsylvania State Assembly. In 1781, he was sent to France on what was a successful mission to obtain money and supplies for the Continental army.

After the war, Paine settled on a small farm and lived in poverty. He devoted a considerable amount of time to intellectual pursuits, especially those related to SCIENCE and technology. He developed plans and a model for a single-span arched iron bridge that could be built and assembled in sections. When he failed to get financial support in the United States for his project, Paine traveled to Europe, again armed with letters of introduction from Franklin.

Paine arrived in France in 1787 and soon was embroiled in political action. He became renowned as a champion of the FRENCH REVOLUTION in 1791 after he published *The Rights of Man.* Written as a response to the conservative REFLECTIONS ON THE REVOLUTION IN FRANCE (1790) by Edmund BURKE, Paine's book explored the concept of NATURAL RIGHTS, using it as a foundation from which to criticize English social, economic, and political structures. For him, the French Revolution represented an attempt to establish a new, republican political and social order grounded on the natural rights of humankind.

The Rights of Man met with sensational success in Great Britain, the United States, and France, and it made Paine one of the most controversial writers of the period. Cartoonists lampooned his radical, republican ideas in caricatures that depicted "Mad Tom." Paine responded by writing part two of *The Rights of Man* (1792), which offered practical ways to implement political, social, and economic reforms. An astounding 1.5 million copies were sold in Great Britain alone. The pamphlet was especially popular among artisans, unskilled workers, poor people, and small-business owners who did not have the right to vote in British elections. The British government tried and convicted Paine for seditious libel, but he had already fled to the safety of revolutionary France. The trial was held without him.

From the moment he arrived on French soil, Paine was welcomed by enthusiastic crowds. He had been made an honorary citizen of France and was chosen to serve as a delegate to the French National Convention. Although Paine wanted to see the monarchy in France brought to an end, he spoke out in the Convention against the idea of executing King LOUIS XVI. As a result, he gained enemies among the most radical factions in the National Convention. When those factions came to power during the Terror (1793–94), he was imprisoned.

Paine was released at the end of the Reign of Terror (1794) through the intervention of James MADISON, the new American ambassador to PARIS. Shortly afterward he published part one of *The Age of Reason.* This tract explored the various grounds for religious faith and ended by arguing in support of DEISM. Part two of this work appeared in 1795 and applied Paine's critical methods directly to the Bible. It was greeted with cries of ATHEISM in the United States but did not cause much stir in Europe.

Paine resented the time he had spent in French prisons, seemingly abandoned by his former friends in the United States whose intervention could have helped him. In 1796, he vented some of his anger in a pamphlet that attacked both the leadership and character of George Washington. In 1802, he finally returned to the United States, an embittered man. Although he was welcomed at the White House by his longtime friend, Thomas JEFFERSON, he died in obscurity in New York City after suffering a stroke.

Paine's literary career illustrates with great clarity that, when the implications of ideas associated with the Enlightenment were carried to their extremes, the writer was often greeted with ambivalence and outright hostility. His works serve as a kind of litmus test that reveals the subtle differences in political and religious opinion that divided the United States from France and both nations from Great Britain at the close of the 18th century.

See also RADICAL ENLIGHTENMENT; RELIGION.

Further reading: Joyce Oldham Appleby, *Liberalism and Republicanism in the Historical Imagination* (Cambridge, Mass.: Harvard University Press, 1992).

Palladian style   A form of late Renaissance architecture created by Andrea Palladio (1508–80). Palladio believed that architecture must be governed by REASON and by universal rules and that it must imitate the rational

Monticello, Charlottesville, Virginia, erected between 1770 and 1806. Thomas Jefferson modeled his Monticello home after the English Palladian style. In the American colonies, this style was called the Georgian style. *(Courtesy New York Public Library)*

structure of the universe in perfectly proportioned buildings. He spelled out his theories in his treatise *I quattro libri dell'architettura* (Four books of architecture; 1570). Palladio strove to reproduce the plans and proportions of ancient Roman architecture. He incorporated temple porticoes into his designs for both churches and country houses. The Villa Rotunda near Vicenza and the Church of San Giorgio Maggiore in VENICE are two of his most renowned buildings.

In the early 17th century, the English architect Inigo Jones (1573–1652) visited ITALY and became enamored of Palladian style. He adapted the principles in Palladio's treatise to create the symmetrical Banqueting House at Whitehall in LONDON. Jones stimulated the development of a Palladian-derived English CLASSICISM, which, fed by the passionate English love affair with Roman antiquity, dominated 17th-century construction in that nation. Although BAROQUE STYLE elements acquired greater popularity in ENGLAND as the 17th century progressed, by the 1720s a major revival of Palladian style occurred. This movement received its primary impetus from the wealthy amateur architect, Lord Burlington, who designed his Chiswick House after Palladio's Villa Rotunda.

Burlington believed that Palladian designs most closely satisfied the demands of reason because the structural lines were geometric, symmetric, and, therefore, rational. What reveals Burlington's 18th-century mentality, however, was his assumption that, because the dictates of reason were satisfied in Palladian designs, these designs were also more "natural" than others. The classic early 18th-century equation of reason with NATURE is thus vividly portrayed and consciously proclaimed. Burlington explicitly juxtaposed the two concepts—reason and nature—by setting his Palladian geometric house in a vast, naturalistic garden complete with small temples and ruins. This new landscaping style, designed in part by William KENT, became known as the ENGLISH GARDEN. The pairing of Palladian style with naturalistic garden design was copied throughout England. As a separate entity, the English garden was also transported to continental Europe, where, especially in German lands, it became highly popular in the last half of the 18th century.

Although the English proved the most enthusiastic proponents of the Palladian style, other European architects found inspiration in the regularity of Palladian buildings. Johann FISCHER VON ERLACH, for example, created a new country house style, wholly different from the English model, by mixing Palladian designs and baroque elements together. His houses were copied throughout the HAPSBURG EMPIRE. Fischer von Erlach also created a new town house facade of Palladian inspiration. The Palladian style also remained popular in Venice and the surrounding Veneto region throughout the 17th and 18th centuries.

Pamela, or Virtue Rewarded   A novel by Samuel RICHARDSON first published in 1740. The novel presents the correspondence of a 15-year-old servant girl, Pamela. It begins with a letter written by Pamela to her parents informing them that her mistress, an elderly gentlewoman, has just died, leaving her household in the possession of her son. Mr. B., a young gentleman who fancies himself a rake or LIBERTINE of the Restoration school, decides to seduce Pamela. When the heroine resists his subtle attempts at seduction, he goes to more extreme lengths to attain his goal. Bribery, hiding in her bedroom, and attempts to lure her into a sham marriage all fail, and Mr. B. subsequently proposes marriage to Pamela. Throughout the final third of the novel, the heroine wins over Mr. B.'s aristocratic sister and friends with her exemplary conduct.

Richardson intended this novel as a work of EDUCATION. It began as a collection of letters that, in fact, he was compiling and planning to publish as models of epistolary form. Richardson became so very interested in the exchange of letters between a young servant girl, whose employer was making improper sexual advances to her, and her parents, that he developed the letters into the first volume of *Pamela*.

The novel was enormously successful and inspired dozens of responses, adaptations, and sequels. The most famous contemporary response to *Pamela* was the parody *Shamela* (1741) by Henry FIELDING. Fielding's heroine is simply a prostitute feigning sexual chastity and moral virtue in order to entrap the wealthy Mr. B. into marriage.

In response to the many attacks and unauthorized sequels of *Pamela* that appeared, Richardson published a second volume of his own novel, which contains a series of letters that reveal Pamela's behavior as a wife and mother.

An example of the didactic literature of the ENLIGHTENMENT whose goal was improving people through education, *Pamela* also illustrates the social changes that were taking place in ENGLAND during the 18th century. The libertine behavior associated with court and aristocracy during the English Restoration was giving way to new, sterner, simpler moral values associated with the middle classes.

The middle ranks of English society, especially industrialists, merchants, and professionals, were accumulating wealth and had established a powerful political voice in the Whig Party. As a result, the aristocracy was being pressured to lower the social barriers between its members and other wealthy English people.

These developments were provided with a philosophical and psychological base in the works of John LOCKE, which promoted the inborn EQUALITY of all human beings. Pamela voiced this new position when she protested that she was an individual entitled to the same respect as a woman of the aristocracy. The novel illustrates the ability of native intelligence and moral virtue to span the chasms between English social classes, and it provides a strong critique of aristocratic pretensions and behavior.

See also LITERATURE; SENTIMENTAL FICTION.

Parini, Giuseppe (1729–1799) *Milanese poet, an important literary figure in the Italian Enlightenment*
Parini trained for the priesthood but did not pursue that career. Instead, he served as a private tutor for various young aristocrats in MILAN and later (1769–99) taught in Brera. Parini also served briefly (1768–69) as the editor of the Milanese periodical *Gazzetta di Milano* (Gazette of Milan).

His masterpiece, the poem "Il giorno" (The day), contains penetrating critical observations about the lifestyle and values of the Milanese aristocracy. Parini was especially offended by the willingness of the Milanese noble families to accommodate themselves to Austrian Hapsburg rule.

In addition to "Il giorno," Parini wrote *Alcune poesie di Ripano Eupilino* (Some poetry of Ripano Eupilino; 1752) and *Odi* (Odes; 1757–91). He also wrote *Dialogo sopra nobiltà* (Dialogue on nobility; 1757), a satire in prose, and *Ascanio in Alba* (Ascanio in Alba; 1771), a drama set to music by Wolfgang Amadeus MOZART.

See also ILLUMINISTI; ITALY.

Paris Capital of FRANCE, located on the banks of the Seine River. Paris was a major center of the ENLIGHTENMENT, providing the crucible in which the PHILOSOPHES lived, wrote, and worked to transmit their new ideas. It was also the birthplace of the great FRENCH REVOLUTION.

A Gallic tribe, the Parisii, settled the city site in pre-Roman times and left it with their name. Paris became an administrative city during the era of the Roman Empire and has served ever since as the capital of French kingdoms and dynasties. Commercial guilds appeared in the 12th century, and the University of Paris received its founding charter at the beginning of the 13th century. Intellectual and cultural life began flourishing during the late medieval period. The Wars of Religion (1562–98) interrupted intellectual life but by no means extinguished it. In fact, the horrible experiences of confessional strife, civil war, dynastic crisis, and the spectacle of Paris rebelling against its resident king, stimulated some of the thought and associated practical activity that laid the foundation for the later emergence of the Enlightenment.

In the 18th century, Paris remained the official capital of France, but it no longer served as the primary residence of the French kings. LOUIS XIV had moved his court to Versailles, a few miles outside Paris, after the experience of Parisian sedition in the Fronde revolt of 1648–52 had left him permanently distrustful of the fickle city.

Even in the absence of the king, Paris remained the primary intellectual, cultural, diplomatic, and administrative center of the ANCIEN RÉGIME. French aristocrats kept town houses (*hôtels*) in the city, where they held the famous salons that facilitated the transmission of ideas from creators to consumers. OPERA, THEATER, MUSIC, painting, sculpture, and the decorative arts all enjoyed enormous patronage. Construction of public places such as the Place Vendôme and the Place de la Concorde transformed the face of the city. Even today

Paris offers splendid architectural examples of 17th-century classical style and of 18th-century ROCOCO and neo-classical styles.

In the political and intellectual realms, the 18th century brought tremendous excitement and upheaval to Paris. Partly because of the influence of the Enlightenment, the city became a breeding ground for all types of opposition to monarchical ABSOLUTISM and to social, political, and fiscal privilege. On the one hand, the cultural life of the city represented the culmination of the ancien régime and of the Enlightenment; on the other, the same cultural life gave birth to the forces that would destroy the old order.

When the French Revolution finally broke out, Paris played a central role in the unfolding events. It was the place where the National Assembly promulgated its famous DECLARATION OF THE RIGHTS OF MAN AND THE CITIZEN and abolished the ancien régime. As the center of political activity, the city sheltered spokespersons for all points in the political spectrum and brought them together in a protracted confrontation over the ideal structure of a new French regime. The activities of political pamphleteers in Paris demonstrated with undeniable clarity how the spread of LITERACY in the Enlightenment had changed the relationship between political authority and public opinion. Moreover, the various incidents of mob violence, which, at times, moved the Revolution into more radical phases, demonstrated for Europe the potential power of the modern urban lower classes. At the end of the Enlightenment, therefore, the city that had given birth to that powerful intellectual and cultural movement also spawned the elements—both conservative and radical, cultural and political—that would act as its enemies.

See also NEOCLASSICISM; SOCIAL INSTITUTIONS OF THE ENLIGHTENMENT.

Park, Mungo (1771–ca. 1806) *Scottish explorer and naturalist*

Mungo Park was born in Selkirk, SCOTLAND, into a large local family of some means. His unusual Christian name derives from Mungo, the patron saint of Glasgow. Apprenticed to a surgeon in 1785, Park proceeded to medical school at EDINBURGH University three years later and, after studying with some diligence, left in 1792 without taking his final oral examination. His brother-in-law, a renowned botanist named James Dixon, introduced him to Sir Joseph BANKS, who had accompanied James COOK on his early Pacific explorations. Dixon also nominated Park for membership in the Linnean Society of LONDON, which promoted the study of natural history. Banks recommended Park for a post as surgeon's mate on *The Worcester,* a ship bound for the East Indies. Park sailed to Bencoolen, an English outpost on the coast of Sumatra. After his return to ENGLAND, he sought an opportunity to travel in pursuit of scientific knowledge. He was soon assigned by the African Association, in which Banks was a leading figure, to follow the lost explorer Major Daniel Houghton into Gambia in search of the source of the River Niger.

In Pisania with his slave-trading hosts, Park acutely observed all aspects of the West African landscape and culture. In December 1795, he set off into the interior, accompanied by two servants. His journey was difficult, dangerous, and physically punishing. After many hardships and unable to track the source of the Niger, he was forced to return under the protection of an African slave trader. His mission was, however, considered a great success since he returned to ENGLAND alive, and he entertained London society for months with accounts of his adventures. Among his novel anecdotes about African behaviors, he probably described his frequent victimization by beatings, robberies, and incarcerations. With his published account, *Travels into the Interior Districts of Africa Performed in the Years 1795, 1796 and 1797* (1799), Park acquired the reputation of being the first European explorer to reveal that some West African states possessed well-established governments, legal and educational systems, manufactures, commercial networks, and complex spiritual traditions.

Shortly after his return to Great Britain, Park married Allison Anderson, with whom he had two children. The revival of the African mission in 1805 lured him back to Africa. On this occasion, the venture proved fatal. A year later, reports surfaced about the deaths of his entire party. Park's *Journal of a Mission to the Interior of Africa in the Year 1805* (1815) reveals the details of this last, failed mission.

See also VOYAGES OF DISCOVERY; SCIENCE.

Further reading: Peter Brent, *Black Nile* (Tiptree, Essex: Anchor Press, 1977); Kate Ferguson, ed., *Travels in the Interior Districts of Africa by Mungo Park* (Durham, N.C.: Duke University Press, 2000).

parlements French royal courts of law. The Parlement of Paris was one of the most powerful institutions in the ANCIEN RÉGIME during the 18th century. Its area of jurisdiction extended over the central regions that were part of the French royal domain. In the provinces, from the reign of LOUIS XIV until the FRENCH REVOLUTION, *parlements* also existed at Rennes, Toulouse, Rouen, Metz, Bordeaux, Besançon, Arras, Douai, Grenoble, Aix, Pau, and Dijon.

The lawyers and judges of the *parlements* administered royal justice, served as courts of appeal, and registered the royal edicts of the king. Unlike the English Parliament, the French *parlements* did not have the right to make law or to levy taxes. Furthermore, *parlement* offices were not elective but rather could be bought, inherited, and sold as forms of private PROPERTY. They conferred noble status on their holders, a fact that made them highly desirable for wealthy and aspiring bourgeoisie.

From the middle of the 17th century, *parlements* began trying to establish their right to act as true legislative institutions. The civil war known as the Fronde was fought in part over this issue. After the Fronde (1648–53), LOUIS XIV tried to bring the *parlements* under his absolute control. He succeeded in limiting certain of their traditional powers, the most important of which was the right to remonstrance. That right had allowed *parlements* to refuse to register a royal edict or papal decree and thereby had given them a small but significant role in shaping French law.

Despite these setbacks, the *parlements* resumed their opposition to monarchical ABSOLUTISM shortly after Louis XIV's death in 1715. They regained the right of remonstrance and in several important instances, succeeded in blocking the royal will.

Parlement members portrayed themselves as the protectors of French liberties against alleged abuses—usually dealing with taxation matters—by monarchs striving for royal absolutism. In this role, they gained increasing support throughout the 18th century. Certainly, in the absence of an elective representative body, they were one of the major institutions able to limit the activities of the French king.

However, the *parlement* members enjoyed a host of privileges under the ancien régime: noble status, tax exemptions, and other benefits. As the ENLIGHTENMENT progressed, some PHILOSOPHES criticized the *parlements* as groups simply intent on preserving their privileges. The *parlements* were, after all, investing considerable energy in blocking efforts by the king and his ministers to eliminate the system of legal privileges in France. By preventing reforms from above that would have established some EQUALITY before the law, the *parlements* were actually obstructing certain causes of the Enlightenment.

During the French Revolution, the *parlements* were abolished, replaced by a system of courts with appointed judges and by elected representative assemblies.

See also MONTESQUIEU; MAUPEOU; SPIRIT OF LAWS.

partitions of Poland (1772, 1793, 1795) During the 18th century, the kingdom of POLAND, weakened and politically paralyzed by its unique constitution, functioned as a vast vacuum within the European balance of power. Consequently, the kingdom suffered from continual outside interference. The great European powers—RUSSIA, FRANCE, PRUSSIA, and AUSTRIA—meddled blatantly in Polish monarchical elections and maneuvered for influence over the internal and foreign affairs of the kingdom. The three partitions of Poland, in which Poland was carved up by Prussia, Russia, and Austria without declaration of war, present a stunning example of the Machiavellian nature of later 18th-century diplomatic practices. In order to satisfy the SELF-INTEREST of the three partitioning powers, the integrity of Poland was completely violated.

The first partition occurred in 1772. It grew out of attempts by Prussia and Austria to preserve the eastern European balance of power in the face of increasing Russian expansion and domination. At the time, Russia and the Ottoman Empire were fighting in southern Europe over access to the Black Sea. Russia was having great success and seemed likely to emerge from the struggle enormously more powerful than in the past. This created great anxiety on the part of both FREDERICK II (THE GREAT) in Prussia and MARIA THERESA in Austria. Diplomats from these two states approached CATHERINE II (THE GREAT) and offered to give her a large slice of Polish territory if she would give up her conquests in the Black Sea area. Catherine agreed to the plan. Prussia and Austria helped themselves to Polish lands too. Altogether, Poland lost about one-third of its territory. Prussia acquired control of a vast region reaching continuously from the Elbe River to Lithuania.

The Polish aristocracy reacted to these moves by trying to stir up a national revival movement. But their actions had little effect, and they had no realistic option but to acquiesce. In 1793, Russia and Prussia repeated their aggression, helping themselves to greater expanses of Polish land. Austria again joined Russia and Prussia in the 1795 partition, and Poland literally disappeared as an independent state. As a result, Prussia, Russia, and Austria became contiguous states. The balance of power in eastern Europe shifted dramatically but was actually more stable as a result of the removal of the vacuum that had been the Polish state. The partitions ultimately stirred a political movement in Poland, which is generally recognized as the first example of a modern nationalist movement.

perfectibility   To be capable of being perfected. The concept of perfectibility provided a philosophical foundation for the belief in PROGRESS that typified certain branches of the ENLIGHTENMENT. But the specific applications of the notion varied according to both the predilections of individual writers and the dominant intellectual traditions in which they were working.

Some writers applied the concept only to human nature, stressing the perfecting power of knowledge acquired either through the exercise of REASON or through the guidance of an inner moral sense. The sensation PSYCHOLOGY created by John LOCKE reinforced this view by suggesting that the human mind is a blank slate at birth waiting to be written on by experience.

Variations on these themes can be found in the writings of Abbé CONDILLAC, Claude-Adrien HELVÉTIUS, Marie-Jean de CONDORCET, and the young VOLTAIRE. The FREEMASONS, the ROSICRUCIANS, and the Bavarian

ILLUMINATI embedded the notion of perfectibility in their ritualistic degrees. And the MORAL PHILOSOPHY of the third earl of SHAFTESBURY, Thomas REID, and Francis HUTCHESON assumed that the underlying benevolence of NATURE and the innate moral sense of human beings ensure the possibility of human perfection.

Enlightened Christian treatments of perfectibility, in contrast, stressed the role played by inner, divinely inspired enlightenment. This inner light provided a knowledge unlike that resulting from the exercise of reason. It derived from the capacity of the mind to learn through intuition and feeling. Quakerism and METHODISM, as well as the religious teachings of Emanuel SWEDENBORG, the comte de SAINT-GERMAIN, and Louis-Claude de SAINT-MARTIN demonstrate various applications of this approach during the 18th century.

The assumption that human nature is perfectible did not mean that upward notion toward perfection was inevitable. In fact, writers such as Jean-Jacques ROUSSEAU and August von SCHLÖZER stressed that perfectibility and progress can move in negative or backward directions. Human nature, whatever its potential, is also malleable, capable of being molded into any number of forms. As a result, the content and quality of EDUCATION, one of the primary shapers of human character, becomes critically important, not only for individuals but also for societies composed of these individuals. Well-conceived and delivered education taps the quality of perfectibility for the benefit of both the individual and of society. The wise use of social policy enhances the powers of education, helping to create better societies by ensuring and protecting the material and intellectual well-being of individual subjects or citizens. Science, technology, and art aid this process. In addition, the creation of a genuine SCIENCE OF MAN, based on the mathematical laws that govern ordinary events, brings perfectibility into complete control, turning it into a tool for the guarantee of human progress.

The application of these concepts of perfectibility to human society is revealed in the programs of enlightened despotism (see DESPOTISM, ENLIGHTENED), in the educational programs of PIETISM, in the theories of the PHYSIOCRATS and IDÉOLOGUES, in Helvétius, and in the whole conceptual scheme underlying the project of the ENCYCLOPÉDIE.

Some enlightened writers in the German tradition rejected these approaches, however, and tended to view the perfectibility of the individual and the perfectibility of society as somewhat incompatible. These philosophers tended to emphasize that individual needs must give way before the broader needs of the society and that policies and education should, above all, aim at the general good of society. The philosophy of Immanuel KANT represents the most highly developed enlightened statement of this position.

Finally, during the later decades of the Enlightenment, German philosophers used concepts of perfectibility derived from the 17th-century rational philosophies of Gottfried Wilhelm LEIBNIZ and Benedict de SPINOZA. They suggested that the entire universe or created world is striving toward perfection, thus making perfectibility an essential ingredient in the nature of things. Johann Gottfried HERDER and Johann Wolfgang von GOETHE offered the clearest statements of this position. Eventually their ideas were transformed into the 19th-century idealist philosophies of ROMANTICISM.

See also INTUITION AND IMAGINATION; QUAKERS.

Pergolesi, Giovanni Battista (1710–1736) *Italian violinist and composer*
Born in Jesi, where his father was a surveyor, Pergolesi received his first music lessons in his native city, then enrolled in the Conservatorio dei Poveri at Naples, where he continued his studies of the violin and of composition. Pergolesi worked throughout his short life in Naples. He began to enjoy success in 1732 after he met Alessandro Scarlatti. He obtained the post of *maestro di cappella* (choirmaster) to prince Stigliano at Naples in 1732, and by 1734 had moved up to become deputy maestro di cappella for the king of Naples.

In his brief life, Pergolesi wrote a handful of works that suggest that he might have been one of the great composers of the 18th century. His LA SERVA PADRONA, first produced as a comic interlude (intermezzo) between acts of the opera *Il prigioniero superbo,* caused a sensation in its posthumous 1752 production in PARIS. It triggered the critical French press exchanges called the BATTLE OF THE BUFFOONS, in which the relative merits of French and Italian operatic styles were debated. Notable operas by Pergolesi include the comic opera, *Lo frate innammorato* (The enamored friar), and three serious operas: *Il prigioniero superbo* (The proud prisoner), *Adriano ni Siria* (Adrian in Syria), and *L'Olimpiade* (The Olympiad). Pergolesi had just completed the choral oratorio *Stabat Mater* when he died at the age of 26 in 1736.

See also ITALY; MUSIC; OPERA.

Persian Letters Satirical NOVEL by Charles-Louis de Secondat, baron de La Brède et de MONTESQUIEU, first published anonymously, outside FRANCE, in 1721. The book earned instant fame for its author whose identity was actually well known. It was smuggled into France without interference by official censorship.

The *Persian Letters* is an epistolary novel, one of the most popular 18th-century fictional forms. It poses as an exchange of letters between two Persians who are visiting PARIS and their wives and friends back home. The Persians, Uzbek and Rica, serve as the spokesmen for Montesquieu's biting and witty observations about Parisian society. This use of "foreigners" as critics was one convention that authors could use to avoid extreme censorship.

Uzbek is a despot in Persia, the ruler of a large harem (seraglio) of women and eunuchs. He is an observant and intelligent man, who easily puts his finger on some of the absurdities of French society and political life. He speaks of the magicians, LOUIS XIV and the pope, who make people do and believe things they would normally reject. He criticizes the revocation of the Edict of Nantes (1685) that caused thousands of HUGUENOTS to flee from France, stating that Louis XIV decided to "increase the numbers of the faithful by diminishing the numbers of his subjects."

Montesquieu uses the letters also to question common assumptions based on custom, religious faith, or belief in the power of REASON. He wraps his criticisms in entertaining stories drawn from the scarcely restrained social world of the French Regency (1715–23).

Uzbek's harem in Persia plays several roles in the novel. It is obviously an irrational place for Montesquieu, and he uses examples drawn from its operations to make certain points about human behavior. But the harem is also a symbol for the French court and for the religious life of Catholic monasteries and nunneries. These are places where oppression, cruelty, and irrationality prevail.

Throughout his musings, Montesquieu touches on themes that will assume greater importance in THE SPIRIT OF LAWS: the wrongs of the criminal justice system, the need for the reform of punishments and for the abolition of torture, the question of the right to suicide, the oppressive system that subjugates women to men, the evils of intolerance, the abuses of the clergy, and the necessity of preventing despotism.

The *Persian Letters* also deals with the general theme of happiness, or rather, with avoidable unhappiness. Through the letters, the sources of much unhappiness are seen to lie in unreasonable human institutions and laws: One of Uzbek's wives in the harem, for example, writes that she misses their sexual encounters and is unhappy, but she can do nothing about her condition. Harem laws forbid her to be seen or visited by any other man. It seems, on occasion, that Uzbek is a reasonable enough man to escape the limits of these human systems. But in the end, he, too, falls prey to human passion and irrationality. A fit of jealousy, on the news that one of his most dutiful wives has managed to take a lover, sends him running back to Persia and the harem. He locks himself inside, determined to defend his status and honor at all costs. Of course, by acting thus, he has just betrayed himself and consigned himself to continuing a life of unhappiness.

For all its sparkling humor and lasciviousness, the *Persian Letters* contains a dark and pessimistic assessment of human possibilities. Montesquieu's vision would change only after he had encountered ENGLAND, and the result would be *The Spirit of Laws*.

Pestalozzi, Johann Heinrich (1746–1827) *Swiss educational theorist and reformer*

A native of Zürich, SWITZERLAND, Pestalozzi developed a specific method and curriculum for childhood EDUCATION. He derived his model from the ideas spelled out by Jean-Jacques ROUSSEAU in the novel *ÉMILE*.

Pestalozzi advocated incorporating concrete experience into education and, like Rousseau, insisted that the curriculum must be designed to fit the developmental stages of children. In Pestalozzi's plan, students were to receive training in the arts, MUSIC, and physical exercise as well as the usual formal disciplines. Students were to be grouped according to ability rather than age.

Pestalozzi studied THEOLOGY before deciding to commit himself to the simple life idealized in Rousseau's writings. After unsuccessful ventures in agriculture and the spinning and weaving cottage industries, Pestalozzi withdrew to his estate of Neuhof and turned to writing. *Die Abendstunde eines Einsiedlers* (Evening hours of a hermit; 1780) presented his conviction that education must be modeled after NATURE. A second treatise, *Meine Nachforschungen über den Gang der Natur in der Entwicklung des Menschengeschlechts* (My inquiries into the course of nature in the development of mankind; 1797) presented his conviction that education could provide a way of molding individual moral character and intellectual independence.

During the FRENCH REVOLUTION, when the French established the Helvetic Republic in Switzerland, Pestalozzi received a chance to put his ideas into practice. He established his first school at Burgdorf (1800–04) and later moved the school to Yverdon near Neuchâtel (1805–25). The Yverdon Institute, a boarding school, became famous throughout Europe, attracting visitors and inspiring many imitations.

During the last half of the 18th century, the thought of the ENLIGHTENMENT acquired a strongly historical color. Development and change, the stuff of HISTORY, were recognized as characteristics of all natural and human phenomena. Under this influence, the concept of childhood was transformed, acquiring basic outlines that seem familiar even today.

It was recognized that children are not little adults, but rather must grow through a series of emotional, intellectual, and social stages in order to reach maturity. These stages were often equated to the stages that general humankind had experienced over the course of history.

Education came to be viewed as a means by which the development of children could be directed toward desirable ends. Proper instruction could assist the general PROGRESS of humanity by creating individuals fully capable of exercising their emotions and reason. Pestalozzi developed his theories in this context and left a legacy that is still honored today.

Peter I (the Great) *(1672–1725) czar of Russia from 1682 to 1725*

A member of the Romanov dynasty, which ruled in Russia from 1613 until 1917, Peter the Great succeeded his half brother Feodor to the throne of Russia in 1682. Peter was the youngest of the two male children of the deceased Czar Alexis Mikhailovich. Power struggles within the imperial family forced Peter I to share the throne from 1682 until 1689 with another half brother, Ivan V. Since both Peter I and Ivan V were minors at the time they inherited the throne, Sophia Miloslavsky, the sister of Ivan, exercised power as the regent. In 1689, Peter forced Sophia to retire into a convent, and the two half brothers assumed full control of Russia. Ivan V died in 1696 leaving Peter as sole ruler from then until his own death in 1725. By means of forcible reforms from above, Peter the Great proceeded to push Russia into the world of early 18th-century western Europe. Like his counterparts, MARIA THERESA in the HAPSBURG EMPIRE, and King Frederick William I in PRUSSIA, Peter was an absolute monarch and reformer who carried out a vigorous program of centralization. He would eventually be succeeded by a genuine enlightened despot, CATHERINE II (THE GREAT).

Russia occupied a geographical space that lacked natural boundaries. The location of its capital, MOSCOW, encouraged an orientation to the East, toward various central Asian kingdoms. Yet Russia had borders and some contacts with the West. At the time of Peter's accession to the throne, SWEDEN, for example, presented constant threats to Russian security. Peter determined that his European contacts should be expanded and that Russia should borrow what it could from the West in order to strengthen its position at the boundaries of Europe. Thus, the need for external security and the associated requirements of internal peace and adequate financial bases motivated his earliest reforms.

Peter gained his knowledge of western Europe firsthand by traveling in 1697 and 1698 on an imperial version of the GRAND TOUR. He spent considerable time in Holland and ENGLAND, but he also visited the Hapsburg Empire, Prussia, and ITALY. During his travels, he recruited about a thousand technical experts to work on his reform projects.

The reforms accomplished by Peter were monumental in number and significance. By recruiting foreigners as high-level military officers, he transformed his army from an undisciplined horde into a professional force modeled on the Swedish, Prussian, and French examples. He subdued any opposition to his westernizing activities on the part of the Russian Orthodox Church by simply refusing to appoint a patriarch (head of the church) when that position became vacant. Instead, he set up the Holy Synod, a committee of bishops, as administrative head of the church, and he attached a royal official, the procura-

tor, to this new body. As a result, the church became a branch of the secular government.

Peter also attacked the Russian feudal privileges that threatened his central control of the state. He required his nobles to serve either in the military or in his new civil service BUREAUCRACY. Moreover, he enacted laws to ensure that statuses between the military and civil service would be equal so that both forms of employment would be socially desirable. To placate the nobles, Peter strengthened their grip over the peasants whose condition as serfs nearly approached that of the American slaves. He allowed nobles to detach the peasants from the lands they had always tilled and to sell them like chattel. Finally, Peter decreed a new set of taxes on "heads" (the poll tax), land, inns, mills, and a variety of commercial goods. He developed a mercantilistic economic policy for Russia. Stringent controls over the serfs and their degradation to near slavery allowed enterprising industrialists to establish factories staffed by forced labor. Peter himself relied on the forced labor of thousands to build his beautiful new capital city and window on the West, SAINT PETERSBURG. Finally, Peter gained absolute control over the matter of the succession to the throne by decreeing and successfully enforcing a statute that gave a reigning czar the right of naming his successor. Thus, from 1722, the Russian throne was neither an elective nor a hereditary position.

To enforce and to administer all these changes, Peter installed a new state bureaucracy and a hierarchically arranged group of administrative councils that he filled with personal appointments. The idea for this structure was derived from the example of Sweden.

Peter could achieve these radical changes in part because he ruled Russia as an autocrat. Unlike the absolute monarchs of the West, the Russian czars of the 18th century were not limited by any body of law or customary constitution. The will of the czar was law. Some resistance to Peter the Great occurred in the form of the great peasant rebellion under Stenka Razin and in the development of the Old Believers as a sect of the Russian church. But, in general, opposition was limited and Peter was able to carry out government reforms that his Western counterparts could achieve only in their dreams.

See also ABSOLUTISM; DESPOTISM, ENLIGHTENED; MERCANTILISM; SERFDOM; SLAVERY.

Philadelphia   The largest American city during the 18th century; located in Pennsylvania. King Charles II of England had given the province of Pennsylvania to William Penn in 1681 as a proprietary grant in payment for a debt he owed William Penn's father. Philadelphia was laid out in a rectangular grid in 1682 on at site at the confluence of the Delaware and Schuylkill Rivers, an area first inhabited by the Delawares, then in the 1640s by several Swedish families. William Penn named it Philadelphia, based on the Greek word for "brotherly love" because it was intended as a haven for QUAKERS against persecution.

Philadelphia became the capital (1683–1799) of Pennsylvania and was incorporated as a city in 1701. Both its prosperity and its promise of religious TOLERATION attracted many immigrants from ENGLAND, Wales, SCOTLAND, Ireland, and GERMANY. It was soon one of the largest cities in the colonies and a thriving port and manufacturing center.

Benjamin FRANKLIN moved from Boston to Philadelphia in 1723. His formation of the Junto debating society and later the AMERICAN PHILOSOPHICAL SOCIETY (1743) marked Philadelphia as an important cultural and intellectual center in the colonies. Franklin also founded the first circulating libraries in the colonies. The Academy of Philadelphia, founded in 1751, later became the University of Pennsylvania. Important early buildings include Carpenter's Hall (1724) and the State House (1732–41), which was later called Independence Hall. The first medical school in the colonies was established in 1765. Besides being home to Franklin, Philadelphia had other intellectual and cultural leaders such as Benjamin RUSH and David RITTENHOUSE. An ENLIGHTENMENT figure as important as VOLTAIRE even considered, in 1754, the possibility of moving to Philadelphia.

By the mid-1700s, Philadelphia had surpassed New York City and Boston in population. Merchants were involved in prosperous trading arrangements with Great Britain and the West Indies. Lumber, wheat, and other food products were exported; sugar and rum were imported from the West Indies and manufactured goods from Great Britain. Early joint stock companies were established in Philadelphia, including several fire insurance companies. Philadelphia had important shipyards and was a center of charcoal and iron production.

On the eve of the AMERICAN REVOLUTION, Philadelphia was the largest city in the British colonies; only London and Liverpool were more important trading centers of the British empire. In the 1760s and early 1770s, the city was one of the centers of opposition and protest against British policies. The first Continental Congress met in 1774 in Carpenter's Hall. The second Continental Congress met in 1775 in the State House, and the U.S. DECLARATION OF INDEPENDENCE (1776) was signed there. During the American Revolution, the Congress held many of its sessions in Philadelphia, although for a time (1777–78) the British occupied the city.

The Constitutional Convention (1787) was held in Philadelphia, and there Congress adopted the UNITED STATES CONSTITUTION and later the UNITED STATES BILL OF RIGHTS. The city was the capital of the United States from 1790 to 1800. It continued as an important financial center where the First Bank of the United States opened its main office in 1791 and where the first securities exchange was informally organized, also in 1791.

philosopher-king An ideal vision of kingship favored by many PHILOSOPHES during the ENLIGHTENMENT. Originally developed by the ancient Greek philosopher Plato in *The Republic,* the concept was embodied for 18th-century intellectuals in the person of Marcus Aurelius, a Roman emperor and Stoic philosopher who ruled from A.D. 161 to 180. The popularity of the philosopher-king ideal during the Enlightenment provides one clear example of the manner in which the 18th-century interest in antiquity provided inspiration and models for change.

The philosopher-king, were he to become reality, would be a wise and gentle yet powerful ruler, intimately acquainted with intellectual traditions from all facets of philosophy. He would pursue philosophical enlightenment as well as political power, combining both in a reign that would bring prosperity and peace to his subjects.

During the Enlightenment, philosophes such as Jean Le Rond d'ALEMBERT, VOLTAIRE, and Pierre MAUPERTUIS praised FREDERICK II (THE GREAT) OF PRUSSIA as a realization of the philosopher-king ideal. However, their motives in offering such assessments may have derived more from the hope of private gain than from authentic

Frederick the Great, king of Prussia. Frederick II, an enlightened despot, military genius, musician, writer, and patron of the arts and sciences, embodied for some philosophes the ideal of the philosopher-king.

convictions. Certainly Frederick enjoyed a positive reputation for awhile and gave great weight to his intellectual and artistic pursuits. He attempted to meet enlightened goals in Prussia by practicing enlightened despotism (see DESPOTISM, ENLIGHTENED). In the end, however, he alienated most philosophes by his military ruthlessness and rigid control of Prussian intellectual and political life. Even though other rulers such as CATHERINE II (THE GREAT) in Russia and JOSEPH II in AUSTRIA tried also to embody the ideal of the philosopher-king, they failed to offset a progressive disillusionment among philosophes with enlightened monarchy and despotism. As the 18th century progressed, therefore, the philosopher-king concept began to seem unrealistic, for events had shown that kingship allowed too many possibilities for the abuse of power to be compatible with true philosophical wisdom and enlightenment.

philosophes From the French word meaning "philosophers." It is commonly used in discussions of the ENLIGHTENMENT to refer to the various intellectuals actively associated with that 18th-century phenomenon. Although the word is French and obviously applies to VOLTAIRE, Jean-Jacques ROUSSEAU, Denis DIDEROT, and the other ENCYCLOPEDISTS, it also sometimes includes intellectuals from other cultural regions: Any enlightened critic or writer can thus be called a philosophe.

The philosophes were not, for the most part, professionally trained, systematic philosophers. Rather, they were critics of their social, political, and cultural order, who used reason as a tool for evaluating and analyzing the problems that faced 18th-century European civilization.

philosophy See AESTHETICS; EMPIRICISM; ENLIGHTENMENT; EPICUREAN PHILOSOPHY; EPISTEMOLOGY; HAPPINESS; HISTORY; INTUITION AND IMAGINATION; MECHANICAL PHILOSOPHY; MORAL PHILOSOPHY; NATURAL PHILOSOPHY; NATURE; PHILOSOPHES; PHYSICO-THEOLOGY; POLITICAL THEORY; PSYCHOLOGY; RATIONALISM; REASON; RELIGION; SCIENCE; SKEPTICISM. See also DESCARTES; KANT; LEIBNIZ; NEWTON; SPINOZA.

phlogiston theory A theory of chemistry developed in the 18th century by Georg Ernst STAHL. Phlogiston theory provided an adequate qualitative description of the chemical processes of respiration, combustion, and calcination. However, when chemists decided to start using gravimetric quantitative methods (i.e., weighing all the components—gases included—of a chemical reaction both before and after the reaction), phlogiston theory appeared flawed. Sometimes phlogiston seemed to have positive weight and other times it had negative weight. The attempts by chemists to resolve these discrepancies in phlogiston theory ultimately brought about the series of events in the 1770s and 1780s called the CHEMICAL REVOLUTION.

The concept of phlogiston developed as Stahl attempted to create a synthesis of the chemistry of elements with the chemistry of principles. In his endeavors, Stahl borrowed a system and concept of the elements from the German chemist and physician Johann Joachim Becher (1635–82). The elements were three in number: earth, water, and air. Earth existed in three different forms, each of which was associated with a different chemical principle. Oily, moist earth corresponded to the chemical principle of sulfur and had been called *terra pinguis* by Becher. Stahl renamed it *phlogiston*. Phlogiston was definitely a material substance, sometimes the matter of fire, sometimes Becher's second earth or sulfur principle, sometimes invisible particles. All substances contained some amount of phlogiston, which could be separated from a substance in processes of heating (combustion) or calcination. The presence of air was required, in order for the escape of phlogiston to occur.

Phlogiston theory was highly popular among French, German, English, and Swedish chemists during the 1750s, 1760s, and 1770s. Major phlogiston chemists included Pierre-Joseph Macquer, Étienne-François Geoffroy, Wilhelm Homberg, and Guillaume-François Rouelle in FRANCE; Friedrich HOFFMANN, Johann Heinrich Pott, Caspar Neumann, Johann Theodor Eller, and Andreas Sigismund MARGGRAF in the HOLY ROMAN EMPIRE; Joseph BLACK, Henry CAVENDISH, Joseph PRIESTLEY, Richard Kirwan, and William Higgins in ENGLAND; and Torbern BERGMAN, Johann Gottlied Gann, and Carl Wilhelm SCHEELE in SWEDEN. Even after the discovery of oxygen and the development of the oxygen theory of combustion by Antoine LAVOISIER, phlogiston theory continued to have adherents. In fact, Joseph Priestley and Carl Wilhelm Scheele, both of whom discovered oxygen independently from Lavoisier, remained loyal to phlogiston theory. Other chemists such as Joseph Black abandoned phlogiston theory only with great difficulty. In fact, the theory disappeared only over some years as the power of gravimetric quantitative methods became clearer and the new nomenclature invented by Lavoisier, Claude-Louis Berthollet, and their colleagues became simpler.

See also ENLIGHTENMENT; SCIENCE.

phrenology A theory of PSYCHOLOGY developed primarily by Franz Joseph GALL. Gall called his system *Hirnund Schädellehre*. The name *phrenology* was invented by his student and disciple, Johann Christoph Spurzheim (1776–1832).

Phrenology presented a method for linking outer physical appearances with the alleged inner structures and nature of the brain and with dominant personality traits. It thus attempted to provide a link between the physical world of mind and the moral, social world of human behavior. It was immensely popular in the closing years of the ENLIGHTENMENT, offering, it seemed, a key to unlocking the mysteries of individual personality.

To create phrenology, Gall borrowed the scheme of the faculties of the mind associated with the common sense philosophy of Thomas REID, and combined this theory with knowledge of nervous system anatomy and physiology. Certain physical characteristics of the head, such as general shape or special protuberances, were understood as signs revealing the particular dominance or weakness of specific mental faculties. For example, Gall believed that a prominent bump on the forehead was the sign of the mental faculty of acquisitiveness. He extended the theory to include observations on associated personality traits or moral attributes. Thus, the mental faculty of acquisitiveness revealed by the bump on the forehead was also, allegedly, a specific characteristic of pickpockets.

Gall was received with coldness by the French scientific establishment and by Napoleon. Georges CUVIER, for example, was pressured by Napoleon to refrain from making a positive report on Gall's theory to the Institut de France (the reorganized FRENCH ACADEMY OF SCIENCES). The popularity of phrenology was due to its broad popular appeal rather than to acceptance by scientists. In this respect, it stands with the mesmerism practiced by Franz Anton MESMER, as an example of the interest in the seemingly unknowable, which was developing in the culture of the radical, popular Enlightenment at the close of the 18th century. Gall's system seemed to offer a way of extending the powers of human REASON into realms hidden from normal empirical observation.

The system of phrenology was spread as a doctrine less by Gall than by Spurzheim. It retained popularity for more than a century despite criticism from other scientists.

See also MORAL PHILOSOPHY.

physico-theology Term that links the concepts of physical NATURE and of knowledge about God (THEOLOGY). It refers to a form of Christian theology that derives knowledge of God from physics and NATURAL PHILOSOPHY, rather than from rational proofs or from the revelations of the Bible.

During the ENLIGHTENMENT, physico-theologists tried to reconcile the ideas and theories of the SCIENTIFIC REVOLUTION with those of traditional Christianity and metaphysics. They offered a special proof of the existence of God—the physico-theological proof or argument from design—that used the mathematical order and beauty of the universe as evidence.

During the Enlightenment, physico-theology underlay both the philosophy of DEISM and the teachings of the FREEMASONS. Its assumptions can be found in many of the writers of the era: Isaac NEWTON, Alexander POPE, and Jean-Jacques ROUSSEAU are prominent examples. Toward the end of the Enlightenment, Immanuel KANT subjected the logic of physico-theology to a new analysis. His treatment of its claims reveals a kind of allegiance to its basic approach, even while he is criticizing its philosophical validity as a source of knowledge.

See also RELIGION.

Physiocrats A group of French economic theorists and reformers led by François QUESNAY, who formulated a theory sometimes called physiocracy as an alternative to MERCANTILISM. Although Quesnay coined the term *physiocrate,* it did not enter common usage until the 19th century. Quesnay's students and disciples in the 18th century preferred to be called *economistes.* Their number included Anne-Robert-Jacques TURGOT, the marquis de MIRABEAU, Vincent de GOURNAY, Paul-Pierre MERCIER DE LA RIVIÈRE, and Pierre-Samuel DU PONT DE NEMOURS.

The ideas of the Physiocrats developed as a set of criticisms of the older, officially sanctioned theory of mercantilism. The new theory was constructed on the fundamental notion that a natural order, based on NATURAL LAW, exists in the world. This universal and eternal law transcends the realm of human action and reflects the supreme REASON that structures the universe. The relation of humankind to this law is that of the discoverer, rather than that of the creator. Wise rulers and administrators will seek to uncover this law and then will structure their societies according to its principles and prescriptions.

The Physiocrats believed that Quesnay had discovered both the natural law underlying society and the associated economic principles. They maintained that land, rather than gold, provides the basic wealth in a nation. It produces the crops necessary to sustain life and the raw materials from which human labor can create surplus wealth. In order to secure the economic health of a nation, people must be able to trade the products of the land and of industry without hindrance; in other words, a LAISSEZ FAIRE policy should govern trade and commerce.

From these principles, Quesnay and his followers derived a practical program that called for universal, equal taxation of all land and the abolition of internal customs barriers (FREE TRADE). Their program, in actuality, was recommending a radical reform of the system of privileges, exemptions, local duties, state regulation, and private trade barriers that characterized mercantilism under the ANCIEN RÉGIME. But these men were not calling for revolution or insurrection. Rather, they envisioned the reforms coming from above, instigated by an enlightened ruler.

The Physiocrats were enormously influential in 18th-century Europe. Their articles appeared in the

François Quesnay. The creator of the term *physiocrat*, Quesnay led the school of French economists who criticized mercantilist economic policies. *(Courtesy Bettmann Archive)*

ENCYCLOPÉDIE edited by Denis DIDEROT and Jean Le Rond d'ALEMBERT. VOLTAIRE praised their ideas about trade and tax reform. Adam SMITH, who would become renowned for his treatise the WEALTH OF NATIONS, studied with the Physiocrats in FRANCE, and from their economic theory he developed the outlines of classic economic liberalism.

However widespread the discussion of their ideas, the actual implementation of physiocratic programs proved difficult. The enlightened rulers of PRUSSIA and Russia, FREDERICK II (THE GREAT) and CATHERINE II (THE GREAT) respectively, drew much inspiration from the physiocratic program, and elements of physiocratic thought underlay the ill-fated reforms attempted under Turgot in France. The full-blown doctrine of laissez faire also developed out of physiocratic theory. But, except for ENGLAND, most European nations were unready for free trade before the 19th century.

See also CAPITALISM.

piano   Musical keyboard instrument developed in the early 18th century. The piano was one of several new instruments to emerge in the 18th century. Others were the CLARINET, the VIOLA, and the transverse one-keyed flute. The emergence of the piano partly reflects the interaction that existed between changing AESTHETICS and new technological possibilities in the 18th century.

The piano was originally described as a *gravicembalo col piano e forte* (harpsichord with soft and loud). Throughout the 18th and early 19th centuries, the instrument was commonly called the *fortepiano* or sometimes the *pianoforte*. The term *fortepiano* is used today to distinguish the early pianos from their later 19th-century descendants.

Eighteenth-century pianos have small frames, thin strings, and wooden sounding boards. Thus, they produce a smaller, drier sound than their modern counterparts. Each key on the piano activates a felt-covered hammer, which, in turn, strikes one string, eliciting a specific pitch. Performers can produce marked differences in dynamic levels (loudness and softness) simply by varying the force with which they strike the keys. The instrument can also produce a wide range of articulations from very short to nearly legato (smooth and connected). The use of foot pedals can increase the legato effect.

Each of these characteristics clearly separates the piano from its predecessor, the harpsichord. Pressing the keys on a harpsichord activates a wooden plectrum, which actually plucks the string rather than hammering it. All but the simplest harpsichords have several complete sets of strings, which produce different qualities of sound. By coupling and uncoupling these sets of strings, the harpsichordist can produce stepwise changes in tone color and dynamics. But the instrument cannot produce a continuous gradual change of dynamic from loud to soft or the reverse. It also cannot produce a true legato sound because the strings are mechanically plucked, although skilled players can sometimes create the illusion of connectedness.

For most of the 18th century, harpsichords were the dominant keyboard instrument except in churches where the organ reigned. However, the piano existed as early as 1700. The earliest known record of a piano is a reference in a 1700 inventory of the Medici household in Florence. Its creator was Bartolomeo Cristofori, who also created the earliest surviving instrument in approximately 1709. The extant examples resemble harpsichords in size, form, and tonal range. But they possess the rudiments of the new hammer mechanism. Throughout the 18th century, builders struggled to solve the technological problems posed by the new piano mechanism. In the meantime, composers were developing new musical aesthetics that called for dynamic flexibility, tone color variations, and pronounced lyricism. The harpsichord could not meet these demands. The harpsichord and the organ had beautifully met the demands of the 17th-century BAROQUE STYLE MUSIC. *STYLE GALANT* and *EMPFINDSAMER STIL* compositions of the first half of the 18th century had continued to exploit the harpsichord, although they had also popularized the soft, intimate sounds of the piano's cousin, the clavichord. But the emergence of musical CLASSICISM required the abilities of the fortepiano. By the end of the 18th century, the newcomer had replaced the harpsichord as the preeminent keyboard instrument.

Major 18th-century builders in Europe were Andreas Silbermann and his son Johann Heinrich Silbermann, Johann Georg Andreas Stein, and John Broadwood. The reception of the piano varied according to the age and personal predilections of composers and performers. Johann Sebastian BACH did not care for its action; he found it sluggish and unresponsive. His sons C. P. E. BACH and Johann Christian BACH, however, both wrote for the instrument. Wolfgang Amadeus MOZART and Franz Joseph HAYDN wrote most of their keyboard music with the piano in mind. Pianos found their way rather early into some royal courts. FREDERICK II (THE GREAT) owned two Silbermann pianos along with several harpsichords and clavichords.

See also CLEMENTI.

picturesque Possessing the aesthetic qualities of a painting, particularly with respect to LANDSCAPES. The development of English landscape gardening in the 18th century was driven by a group of men who theorized the discipline as akin to another visual art form, painting. Men such as William KENT, "Capability" BROWN, and Horace WALPOLE drew upon concepts of visual art to develop an early vocabulary and practice for garden design. The idea was a sentimental one: Gardens should evoke in the viewer the desire to see the vision painted. Behind the sentimentality was, however, a deep desire to free nature from rigid classical forms, such as those used in the French garden. Brown's redesign of Blenheim Castle's gardens is a classic case of naturalizing a geometrically arranged French garden.

The most important theorists of the picturesque in gardening were Sir Uvedale Price and Richard Payne Knight, who in 1794 began a debate that also included Humphry Repton that is now known as the "picturesque controversy." In his *Essay on the Picturesque* (1794), Price attacked Brown's gardens as boring and formulaic, holding that a garden should be based on roughness, sudden variation, and irregularity. He borrowed this notion from painting, arguing that designers should exhibit the same concerns for arrangement, harmony of colors, and unity of design that painters exhibited. In addition, he gave the picturesque a philosophical structure, inserting it as a middle category between Edmund BURKE's definitions of the SUBLIME and the beautiful. For Price, gardens inspired neither sublime terror nor beautiful passion, but were merely pleasing to the senses.

Richard Payne Knight also scorned Brown's gardens, but his vision of the picturesque was embedded in a complete aesthetic theory. In his *Analytic Inquiry into the Principles of Taste* (1805), a response to Price, Knight located the picturesque not in the garden itself, but in the observer. An educated observer familiar with painting and art would enjoy a garden because of the associations it inspired in the mind. This distinguished sensory pleasure from the picturesque and made it a wholly subjective concept, freeing it from the limits of classical forms while also rooting it in particularities of cultural experience.

The scale of gardening projects grew ever grander as designers drained or moved watercourses, shifted volumes of earth, and cut down and replaced forests in order to reshape the landscape to provide a heightened experience for the viewer. An example of such a large-scale element used by the landscape designer was the ha-ha, a sunken fence or trench designed to separate parts of a garden while remaining hidden from view so as to not interrupt the continuity of landscape for an observer. Garden designers also followed two larger aesthetic trends. First, taking inspiration from the increasingly common GRAND TOUR to ITALY, they added constructions such as Greek- and Roman-themed statuary and temples. Second, anticipating the romantic fascination with the Middle Ages, they incorporated ruins of abbeys and churches. The finest example of this latter trend is Thomas Duncombe III's Rievaulx Terrace, which overlooked the Rievaulx Abbey's ruins.

In the latter part of the 18th century, landscape design was increasingly informed by notions of ROMANTICISM and the Gothic along with the appeal of medieval ruins and classical influences. Central to this shift was the notion of irregularity, that gardens should give the appearance of nature in its free rein through carefully manipulated effects. Earlier garden designs such as Brown's were critiqued for excessive formality by figures such as Price and Sir William Chambers. Chambers's *Dissertation on Oriental Gardening* (1772) asserted that Brown's manipulations removed nature's ruggedness and sublimity.

As notions of the picturesque gained increasing importance in English society, they began to influence other cultural areas as well. The Reverend William Gilpin, another critic of Brown's work, associated these ideas with travel, that a person could take the picturesque perspective associated with carefully planned gardens and use it to enrich the experience of viewing nature in foreign parts. His *Remarks on Forest Scenery* of 1791 clarified theories of the picturesque as being associated particularly with the accidental in nature, with rough elements rather than broad unbroken vistas.

British theories of landscape gardening migrated throughout its empire, influencing design in the American colonies, particularly those in the warmer southern climate. The colonial elite in North America initially followed the lead of English estate planners in the introduction of classically themed statuary and use of English plants and arrangements, but a growing colonial sense of political and cultural separation began to motivate ideas of uniquely American garden design, particularly after the AMERICAN REVOLUTION. Eminent intellectual figures such as John ADAMS and Thomas JEFFERSON looked to America to develop its own models of garden design that would use the grander scale of countryside available and reject English ornamentality in its use of ostentatious elements such as temples. The picturesque, which had been developed in conscious opposition to French models, had now left behind its English roots.

See also ENGLISH GARDEN; POPE; STOWE.

Further reading: John Dixon Hunt, *Garden and Grove: The Italian Renaissance Garden in the English Imagination: 1600–1750* (Princeton, N.J.: Princeton University Press, 1986); Mark Laird, *The Flowering of the English Landscape Garden: English Pleasure Grounds 1720–1800* (Philadelphia: University of Pennsylvania Press, 1999); Robert P. Maccubbin and Peter Martin, eds., *British and American Gardens in the Eighteenth Century* (Williamsburg, Va.: Colonial Williamsburg Foundation, 1984); Horace Walpole, *The History of the Modern Taste in Gardening* (New York: Ursus Press, 1995).

Piedmont Northern Italian territory that lies in the upper Po River valley at the eastern foot of the Alps. TURIN, a city that lies on the Po River, is its capital. The Piedmont (Italian: Piemonte) region was the central territory of the old kingdom of SAVOY. Other territories included in that DYNASTIC STATE were the duchy of Savoy, the duchy of Aosta, Monferrato, and the county of Nice. At times during the 18th century, Sicily (1713–18) and Sardinia (1720–1861) also belonged to the Savoyard dynasty. In 1861, the Savoyard king, Victor Emmanuel II, became the first king of a united kingdom of ITALY.

The Savoyard state occupied a strategically sensitive position in southern Europe since its territories straddled the major Alpine passes that connected Italy and FRANCE. Therefore, the Savoyard rulers were able to play a skillful, but highly opportunistic diplomatic game, allying themselves first with one power, then with another, as reasons of state seemed to dictate.

The Piedmont was a rich agricultural region with wine serving as the most important cash product. Rice provided income in the marshy, malarial Vercelli region. Other grain crops supplied the Savoyard state but were not produced in enough abundance to serve as exports. Turin was by far the largest city in the region. It had a small, high-quality silk-spinning and cloth-manufacturing industry. Metal working, particularly the manufacture of military items, also provided economic sustenance for the city.

The head of the Savoyard dynasty bore the title of king in the Piedmont. Eighteenth-century kings were Victor Amadeus II (ruled 1675–1730), Charles Emmanuel III (ruled 1730–73), and Victor Amadeus III (1773–95). Victor Amadeus II transformed the Savoyard state into a model of ABSOLUTISM. Its administration was centralized, taxation was sufficient to meet budgetary needs, and the potentially rebellious aristocracy was pacified. Victor Amadeus bequeathed this legacy to his son, who maintained the strength of the state. The Catholic Church played a dominant role in the state. In fact, the Inquisition, a Catholic ecclesiastical court, was so powerful that enlightened writers such as Vittorio Alfieri left in order to avoid prosecution.

Pietism A Protestant form of spirituality and religious practice that first developed as a renewal movement within late 17th-century German LUTHERANISM. In 1675, Philipp Jakob SPENER (1635–1705) published some thoughts on Christian renewal, the *Pia Desideria, or Heartfelt Desires for a God-pleasing Improvement of the True Protestant Church,* as a preface to Johann Arndt's *True Christendom.* Spener was the head of the Lutheran pastorate at FRANKFURT am Main. His ideas caught hold rapidly within German Lutheran circles and developed into the movement called Pietism.

The context in which Pietism developed was one of relatively great pessimism about the possibilities of either Christianizing the world or of reconciling the doctrinal conflicts within greater Christianity. Spener and his fellow Pietists consequently focused their attention on the inner, subjective life of the spirit and on an outer concern for practical, charitable works in the community. The experience of repentance and Christian rebirth replaced rational understanding of THEOLOGY or religious law as the primary concern of practicing Christians. Pietists formed groups (conventicles) within which they studied the Bible, practiced prayer, shared personal testimony, and engaged in singing hymns. They believed that the rifts in Christianity had no chance of healing except through the accumulated actions of prayer, moral living, and genuine altruistic love on the part of individual believers. In their communities, Pietists set up charitable institutions such as orphanages, schools, and workhouses for the poor. These served as one outward sign of inner renewal and commitment.

Protestant churches throughout Europe and North America felt the impact of the Pietist approach to spirituality. Most Pietists remained within their traditional Protestant denominations so long as their religious practices were tolerated. Some radical positions developed within Pietism: The MORAVIAN BRETHREN in Saxony under count von ZINZENDORFF provide one well-known example. Through the medium of such radical sects, Pietist ways reached John WESLEY, thereby helping to shape METHODISM in ENGLAND and the UNITED STATES. Pietism had close relatives in Quakerism and Quietism.

Within the HOLY ROMAN EMPIRE, Pietism developed a strong institutional base in the city of Halle. The University of HALLE, established in 1694 by the elector of BRANDENBURG, became a center of Pietist teaching. The faculties of theology, PHILOSOPHY, and law demonstrated strong Pietist leanings under August Hermann FRANCKE and Christian THOMASIUS. However, Thomasius ultimately turned away from Pietism toward the rational aspects of the AUFKLÄRUNG (German Enlightenment). After 1740, when FREDERICK II (THE GREAT) assumed the throne of PRUSSIA, the teachings of the ENLIGHTENMENT received official support, and the Pietist theological faculty slipped from its prominent position. The educational, printing, and charitable foundations that had grown up as a direct outgrowth of Pietist ways continued to flourish, and the town of Halle remained strongly influenced by Pietism. This often produced a devout and rather stern culture that was hostile to musical or artistic expression except when they served as aids to devotional life. As a result, creative artists who worked in Halle—the composer W. F. BACH, for example—often left in frustration.

Pietism is often depicted as a movement antithetical to the Enlightenment. However, it can only be so construed if the notion of the Enlightenment is restricted to exclude anything except the rational, secular streams that are so well known. In fact, in modern scholarship Pietism is generally viewed as an example of an important but rather unfamiliar stream of the Enlightenment, which emphasized individual, subjective, emotional experience and adopted a pragmatic approach to community social problems. The focus on personal religious experience has broad analogs in the secular concern with experience (and experiment) and sensation (SENSIBILITY) in enlightened natural sciences and PSYCHOLOGY.

Pietism played a significant role in stimulating autobiographical approaches to HISTORY, which treated the experience of individuals as primary, replacing the older emphasis on universal history with individual stories. Pietism also helped to pave the way for the radical criticism of religious sectarianism and dogmatism by devout scholars whose subjective spiritual experiences allowed them to transcend doctrinal barriers within Christendom. This development is best represented in the histories of Gottfried ARNOLD.

Finally, Pietism contributed significantly to the development of new approaches to EDUCATION during the Enlightenment. Francke spearheaded this movement, establishing a teachers' training institute at the University of Halle and setting up several different schools in the city. Pietist teaching manuals, which emphasized teaching basic LITERACY skills in a highly disciplined classroom setting, were used throughout the Holy Roman Empire and parts of the HAPSBURG EMPIRE. Furthermore, Pietist educational approaches tended to mesh neatly with the desire of enlightened despots such as Frederick the Great and MARIA THERESA to establish compulsory schooling in their realms. Pietism thus played a major role in spreading literacy, one of the most important social changes associated with the Enlightenment.

See also MICHAELIS; QUAKERS.

Piranesi, Giovanni Battista (1720–1778) *Italian architect and etcher*
Piranesi studied initially in VENICE under the tutelage of his father and uncle. Between 1740 and 1744 he studied etching in ROME. He published his first volume on architecture, the *Prima parte di architettura* (First part of architecture), in 1743, and in 1745 he settled permanently in Rome.

Piranesi was renowned during his life for his etchings. Ruins from ancient Rome and etchings of more recent BAROQUE STYLE buildings provided his most common subject matter. These were not precise, realistic reproductions but rather personal, highly imaginary evocations of earlier eras. Piranesi's prints sold throughout Europe like modern travel posters. In addition to producing these etchings, Piranesi devoted himself to archaeological excavations and to the reconstruction of ancient ruins. His most famous project was the reconstruction of Santa Maria del Priorato on the Aventine Hill (1764–65). He also published a book in 1769, *Diverse maniere d'adornare i cammini* (Diverse ways of decorating rooms), which provided interior designs. Its drawings helped to establish the neoclassical Empire style in early 19th-century Europe. Piranesi's outstanding prints included the *Grotteschi* (Grotesqueries) etchings, the *Carceri d'invenzione* (Prison of invention) prints, and the etchings *Vedute di Roma* (Views of Rome).

See also NEOCLASSICISM.

Pius VI (Giovanni Angelo Braschi) (1717–1799) *pope (head of the Roman Catholic Church) from February 1775 to August 1799*
Pius VI came from an old noble family in the province of Emilia, one of the Papal States. After studying law and obtaining a doctorate in jurisprudence, he entered the papal administration. He advanced rapidly and under CLEMENT XIII became treasurer of the Apostolic Chamber (finance minister for the Papal States). He entered the priesthood only in 1758 and received a cardinal's hat in 1773.

The papal conclave that met to elect a pope upon the death of CLEMENT XIV settled on Pius VI after nearly four and a half months of deliberation. Pius VI assumed the papal dignity at a time when ROMAN CATHOLICISM was being seriously challenged by the forces of RATIONALISM and secularism inherent in the thought of the ENLIGHTENMENT. The pope could no longer depend on the JESUITS to represent his interests in the various Catholic nations of Europe, because the order had been abolished, quite reluctantly, by Clement XIV in the face of strong demands by secular rulers. That act had not, however, eliminated conflict between the papacy and national rulers. Even pious Catholic monarchs like LOUIS XVI in FRANCE and CHARLES III OF SPAIN insisted that the pope refrain from involving himself in the internal affairs of their kingdoms. JOSEPH II OF AUSTRIA was pursuing a series of radical reforms, known today as JOSEPHINISM, at the expense of ecclesiastical privilege and power. Ecclesiastical princes in the HOLY ROMAN EMPIRE, under the stimulus of FEBRONIANISM, were challenging the ABSOLUTISM of the pope within the Catholic Church.

In the face of this overwhelming opposition, Pius VI turned his attention inward to his own territories, the Papal States. He invested in certain public works projects such as draining the malaria-ridden Pontine Marshes, restoring the Capitol in Rome, and building the Pio-Clementine Museum in the Vatican. He also squabbled with the neighboring kingdom of Naples over territories and feudal privileges.

When the FRENCH REVOLUTION broke out, Pius VI quickly reacted against it as a threat to the Christian social order. He condemned the DECLARATION OF THE RIGHTS OF MAN AND THE CITIZEN, the Civil Constitution of the Clergy (requiring the French clergy to take an oath of allegiance to the secular state), and the political principles that supported these two revolutionary documents. He provided financial support and protection to French émigrés, both ecclesiastical and noble. In 1791, he broke diplomatic relations with France and joined the First Coalition in its war against the revolutionary nation. Ultimately, Napoleon invaded the Papal States and Pius VI had to flee. He died, an 80-year-old, physically infirm prisoner, in southeastern France in August 1799.

Pix, Mary (1666–1709) English playwright, translator, and novelist

Born Mary Griffith in Nettlebed, ENGLAND, Mary married a merchant tailor named George Pix in 1684. Their only child died in 1690. Little biographical information about Pix was known even in her own time, and reconstructions of the details of her life rely, in large part, on a contemporary "travesty," or dramatic satire. Travesties were popular entertainments, often quite scurrilous, and always topical.

This travesty, The Female Wits (1696), written by a Mr. W. M. (whose identity has never been definitively confirmed) mocks contemporary female playwrights: Mrs. Pix, Delariviere Manley and Catharine Cockburn

TROTTER. The key to the characters in the printed edition of 1704 identifies Pix as Mrs. Wellfed, an untalented gentlewoman tenaciously clinging to her writing. Mrs. Wellfed satirizes Pix's corpulence but acknowledges her easy going, if not foolish, good humor.

Despite ridicule, Pix did very well for a woman with little education. She came into the public eye in 1696 with two plays, a tragedy and a comedy, which were both well received at the Theatre-Royal in Drury Lane. She was initially mentored by the playwright William CONGREVE, who also took Catharine Trotter under his wing. Following her move to the theater at Lincoln's Inn Fields, Pix wrote another 11 plays that earned her the nickname the "Muse of History." At this time, she forged a mutually beneficial working relationship with the tragic actress Elizabeth Barry, who appeared in most of her plays.

Pix's theatrical debut was a tragedy about the life of Ibrahim, a Turkish emperor whose impulsive self-indulgence and rape of a free woman generated a political coup that led to his assassination and the accession of his seven-year-old son. The play is based on Paul Ricault's sensationalized account of Turkish culture in his Continuation of Turkish History (1687), but Pix misremembered the facts and entitled the play Ibrahim, the Thirteenth Emperor of the Turks (1696), although, as she freely admitted, he was actually the 12th emperor. Her next play was a farce entitled The Spanish Wives (1696), which was well received and revived several times. The other plays attributed to her, many with foreign or historical themes, all met with some degree of success. Her true talent lay in comedy centered on the lives of worthy women, but her final farce, produced in 1706, Adventures in Madrid, failed to duplicate the early success of The Spanish Wives.

Pix evidently emulated the career of Aphra BEHN, writing poetry and translating part of Boccaccio's Decameron as well as producing drama. In turn, Pix influenced the playwright Susannah Centlivre. If Pix's poetics did not merit the accolades earned by some playwrights of her age, she was a familiar playhouse figure, well liked and successful during her productive career.

Pluche, Noël-Antoine (1688–1761) French naturalist

Pluche, who was an abbot, participated in the ENLIGHTENMENT enthusiasm for SCIENCE and attempted to integrate it into a religious worldview. This attempt to reconcile science and faith was known as PHYSICO-THEOLOGY. For Pluche, the movement of the heavenly bodies and the myriad physical properties of plants, animals, and humans testified to the greatness of God. A properly guided understanding of the natural world would lead to a strengthened religious sensibility.

To this end, Pluche published an eight-volume work titled Le spectacle de la nature, ou Entretiens sur les particularités de l'histoire naturelle qui ont paru les plus propres à *rendre les jeunes gens curieux et à leur former l'esprit* (Nature displayed: Being discourses on such particulars of natural history as were thought most proper to excite the curiosity and form the minds of youth; 1732–50). Reprinted numerous times and translated into English, this work was intended to provide the general reader with a grasp of the workings of science and the natural world, and, above all, to demonstrate that their intelligent design proved their source in God. In addition to being a defense of Christian THEOLOGY, Pluche's book imparted real scientific information, especially visually through the accompanying engravings. Written in a conversational style, the book followed the lessons imparted to a young man by his father's learned friend, covering plants and animals, the Earth's surface and interior, the heavens, and, finally, humans' place in society and their relationship to the creator.

While many Christian thinkers decried Enlightenment science, Pluche embraced it and sought to understand it in a Christian context. His observations of the natural world were consistently linked to reflections on its order and goodness as a sign of God's presence. His strongest influence was as a popularizer of scientific developments, for his descriptions of the natural world reached a large audience of nonspecialists.

See also NATURE; RELIGION.

Further reading: John Hedley Brooke, *Science and Religion: Some Historical Perspectives* (New York: Cambridge University Press, 1991); Jacques Roger, *The Life Sciences in Eighteenth-Century French Thought,* tr. Robert Ellrich (Stanford, Calif.: Stanford University Press, 1997).

Pluquet, François André Adrien (ca. 1716–1790)
French theologian
François André Adrien Pluquet was born in Bayeux, a town 150 miles northeast of PARIS, to a devoted family who encouraged his aptitude for hard work and rapid progress. At the age of 16, he was sent to his uncle, the *curé* of San Milo, who encouraged him to attend seminary in nearby Caen to study for the priesthood. He then left behind his beloved country life for the Sorbonne, where he became known for his scholarship. He produced sophisticated research on primitive religions, published in 1762 as *Dictionnaire des heresies, des erreurs et des schismes* (Dictionary of heresies, of errors and of schisms), and was appointed professor of MORAL PHILOSOPHY and HISTORY at the Collège de France in Paris in 1776.

As both a thinker and writer, Pluquet defended his church against ENLIGHTENMENT attack. He joined contemporary theologians Nicolas-Sylvestre Bergier and Claude de Forbin in fighting fire with fire and became fluent in the rational style of argument, taking part in many debates of the day. One of these debates was on the nature of luxury. Bernard MANDEVILLE's widely read *Fable of the Bees* (1714) had elevated luxury to a necessary component of society, for it opened the pockets of the rich. This shocked many who held frugality and simplicity as noble virtues central to a moral government. Mandeville had made the lust for luxury into a philosophical and public bonfire. Pluquet responded with the thoughtful *Le luxe* (On the philosophy and politics of luxury; 1786), written in the reasoned, exacting style for which he was known. While Mandeville regarded luxury as necessary to power and the prosperity of empires, Pluquet held that morally, it was damaging and, finally, deadly to the state.

Among his other writings are *Fatalisme* (Examination of fatalism; 1757), *Traité de la sociabilité* (On sociability; 1767), *Lettres à un ami* (Letters to a friend; 1777), and *Des livres classiques de la Chine* (Classical books of China; 1786). He died in Paris in 1790.

See also RATIONALISM.

Further reading: Christopher J. Berry, *The Idea of Luxury* (New York: Cambridge University Press, 1994).

Poland   Vast eastern European state; at the beginning of the 18th century it stretched more than 1,000 miles from the boundaries of the HOLY ROMAN EMPIRE in the west to RUSSIA in the east and from the Baltic Sea in the north to HUNGARY and the Dniester River in the south. It included the modern states of Poland, Lithuania, Latvia, Estonia, Ukraine, and Belarus. Though its territories were vast, Poland had no geographic barriers to serve as boundaries, which left its territories vulnerable to invasion.

In earlier centuries, under the Jagellon dynasty, Poland had been a vital and powerful state. The monarchy had begun to decline at the end of the 15th century, and ultimately the king had lost his supreme position to the representative body called the Diet. Despite these changes, the 16th-century Polish state had flourished and for some years actually had been the largest state in Europe. It had enjoyed a great period of cultural and intellectual flowering, producing thinkers of the status of Nicolaus COPERNICUS. By the 18th century, however, Poland had degenerated into political impotence.

The 18th-century Polish king was an elected monarch. For this reason, Poland was called a republic. The electors of the king consisted of aristocrats who represented local districts and met in an assembly called the Central Diet. The Central Diet had the right to deliberate and vote on matters of policy, law, and taxation. It met periodically to act on instructions received from approximately 60 regional diets. The members of the diets enjoyed rights that set apart the Polish constitution from all others in Europe. A single, negative vote on an issue prevented it from passing into law. Called the *liberum veto* (free veto), this power of the individual vote had, since 1652, rendered the diets impotent, because the divided Polish aristocracy could not reach unanimous agreement on any issue. Thus, the republican system had grown hopelessly dysfunctional, and Poland represented a kind of power vacuum, whose geographic location made it strategically important. As a result, the kingdom became the eastern European equivalent of ITALY, a region where the greatest states of Europe fought over power.

Foreign countries, intent on controlling Polish policy for their own ends, openly manipulated Polish royal elections, and the fractious Polish aristocracy could rarely agree on native Polish candidates. Thus, various political factions commonly resorted to putting up favored foreign candidates who competed for the vote of Diet members. During the first half of the 18th century, princes from SWEDEN and from Saxony, an electoral principality of the Holy Roman Empire, held the throne. But when Augustus III died, CATHERINE II THE (GREAT's) Russia imposed its candidate, Stanislaw PONIATOWSKI, on the Poles (1764). For the remainder of the 18th century, Russia dominated Poland. The country lost any remnant of independence and experienced the humiliation of being carved up not once, but three times, by the great eastern European powers: Russia, PRUSSIA, and AUSTRIA. At one point, Poland ceased to exist, all its territory having been swallowed up in the diplomatic maneuvering called the PARTITIONS OF POLAND. The last partition, in 1795, triggered a military revolt in the territories that Russia had annexed; large numbers of Poles, inspired by the example of the FRENCH REVOLUTION, rose up to throw off the tyrannical, foreign Russian rule.

The example of the Polish constitution with its *liberum veto* exerted a certain fascination on enlightened political theorists. It served as a symbol for the abuses of aristocracy for most writers, and, sometimes, as an example of democracy gone awry. The one exception to these negative assessments belonged to Jean-Jacques ROUSSEAU, who believed that the Polish constitution could provide the foundation for a revived Polish nation capable of withstanding the Russian onslaught.

politeness   The theory behind and practice of considerate manners and expression, seen as leading to a harmonious social order. Politeness is often synonymous with courtesy, which traces its origin to the word *court* and involves degrees of respect that vary according to an individual's place in the social hierarchy. There is an aspect of politeness that is exclusionary: It can be a way for the aristocratic class to maintain a sense of superiority over other segments of society, which are deemed coarse or unpolished.

During the ENLIGHTENMENT, it was not the term *courtesy* but *politeness* that took on new importance. This change is connected to the growth of the middle class and the public sphere. The period saw new emphasis on the notion of sociability, the belief that humans are social animals and that knowledge, HAPPINESS, and VIRTUE are attained within the sphere of social relations. For this reason, the study of politeness took on special significance as a way of regulating behavior in social settings, in order to ensure social harmony. Although displays of consideration still varied according to the recipient's social status, politeness was, at least in theory, more egalitarian than courtesy.

Politeness was above all a way of making social relationships work well. The 17th-century French moralist Jean de La Bruyére stated that polite behavior left others feeling satisfied with us and with themselves. An important realm of polite society was the salon, a gathering in a private home to discuss art, LITERATURE, and MUSIC. The tone sought in the salons was one of witty and polite exchange, not pedantic, boring analysis. Salons were above all places for conversation, and numerous manuals were published with advice on this art. In the 17th century, salons were primarily an aristocratic phenomenon, but by the 18th century, people of middle-class background were frequently invited to participate, especially writers in the public eye such as Denis DIDEROT, Jean-Jacques ROUSSEAU, and VOLTAIRE. There were even successful salons hosted by women of the bourgeoisie.

Women were often in charge of salons, and they were frequently seen as having a gracious civilizing influence on the men who visited them. Politeness dictated that one try to gratify and please others, a strategy that was deemed necessary not only for a pleasant social experience, but for a civilized exchange of ideas. The notion of a public sphere, the idea that knowledge should be disseminated and discussed by a class of thinkers and writers, relied on conventions of politeness in order to facilitate the free exchange of ideas.

While many treated politeness as a subject of study, others felt that true politeness should be natural, sincere, and come from the heart. Particularly in the 18th century, many thinkers criticized the exaggerated importance paid to the forms of politeness as superficial. The emphasis on domestic life, which was more pronounced in ENGLAND than in FRANCE, led to a perception that simple virtues were more valuable than artificial rules of behavior. The most deeply felt and vociferous critique came from Jean-Jacques ROUSSEAU, who thought that Parisian polite society crushed the goodness of the heart and the simplicity of manners.

Its detractors notwithstanding, politeness was generally perceived as a positive value in Enlightenment culture—a force for order, exchange of ideas, and PROGRESS. The idea that true politeness stems from the heart and the mind reflected the social idealism and humanistic leanings of the Enlightenment. Nevertheless, social interactions continued to be governed by unwritten codes of politeness based on rigid notions of class and gender. But one arena in which the rules of traditional politeness did not apply was the coffeehouse, which dates from the end of the 17th century and which was open to a wide public.

During the 18th century, coffeehouses took on a significant role as places of debate and information gathering, becoming a new cultural model. Viewed from this angle, politeness seemed somewhat outdated, as the public sphere took on more dynamic and open forms.

See also REPUBLIC OF LETTERS; SOCIAL INSTITUTIONS OF THE ENLIGHTENMENT; WOMEN AND THE ENLIGHTENMENT.

Further reading: Peter France, *Politeness and Its Discontents: Problems in French Classical Culture* (Cambridge: Cambridge University Press, 1992); William Bowman Piper, *Common Courtesy in Eighteenth-Century English Literature* (Newark: University of Delaware Press, 1997); Thomas Woodman, *Politeness and Poetry in the Age of Pope* (Rutherford, N.J.: Fairleigh Dickinson University Press, 1989).

political theory The study of government and of the foundations of power in human societies. The ENLIGHTENMENT inherited a set of practical and theoretical political problems from the 17th century that had been created by royal ABSOLUTISM, by civil wars, and by religious strife. These problems centered on fundamental questions about how power should be organized in a state and about whether traditional civic virtue was possible in 18th-century societies. Should sovereignty (the supreme power), it was asked, be located in one person or shared with other constituted groups? Was the sovereign above the law or subject to it; and if subject to law, what law? What should be the relationship between secular and sacred authorities, between church and state? How did political society originate and why? What was the best way of organizing society to ensure that its political life would be marked by stability, prosperity, and PROGRESS? And how could civic virtue, that willingness on the part of individuals to set aside personal desires for the good of the community, be preserved?

Enlightened political theory built on ideas that had been constructed by Thomas HOBBES, John LOCKE, Samuel PUFENDORF, Hugo Grotius, and Gottfried Wilhelm LEIBNIZ. These 17th-century writers had developed their views in response to the upheavals that convulsed their lives. ENGLAND, FRANCE, and the HOLY ROMAN EMPIRE had all experienced bitter wars fueled by both political discontent and by related religious controversies. Hobbes had been forced to take refuge in France during the English Civil Wars while Locke had fled from political persecution during the reign of King James II. Pufendorf and Leibniz had grown up in the decades after the Thirty Years' War, a conflict that had left the Holy Roman Empire decimated. Grotius had been imprisoned by authorities in the UNITED PROVINCES OF THE NETHERLANDS for his religious and political beliefs. It seemed imperative to these men, in the light of personal experience, to find ways of altering political structures in order to prevent a recurrence of violence and disorder.

Because religious strife and factionalism had fueled many 17th-century tragedies, these writers focused considerable attention on desirable relations between church and state. Consequently, even when they maintained an active commitment to some form of Christianity, they consciously tried to separate the principles underlying political power from those of religious doctrine.

In the place of the revealed laws of the Christian God, these writers substituted a set of laws and philosophical principles that they believed had universal validity. These laws and principles were provided by the model of physical NATURE that was being constructed by the MECHANICAL PHILOSOPHY and the SCIENTIFIC REVOLUTION. Divine, revealed law was replaced by NATURAL LAW, rooted in the physical order of the universe. As a result, political theory and positive law, like so many other enlightened disciplines, acquired a foundation in the natural, secular order of things.

From the concept of natural law, the important doctrines of human rights were created. The purpose and duty of government lay in protecting these rights from any form of abuse. Governments that failed in this function were to some degree illegitimate.

Political power always allows its holders to control, reward, or punish the activities of subordinate members of a society. Theorists had long recognized that in order to be respected and to have legitimacy, power needed grounding in something other than the mere exercise of brute force. Might did not necessarily make right, and it certainly did not create desirable forms of government. Seventeenth-century theorists and their enlightened successors believed strongly that the possession of power entailed the duty of ensuring that justice was upheld.

The idea that justice actually exists in the world had always been supported by the Christian belief in a world ruled by a just, righteous, law-giving God. This moral underpinning had, in turn, provided the foundation for societies structured according to positive human law. In setting aside God as the creator and guarantor of morality in the world, political theorists of the 17th century ran the risk of undermining the cause of just government. To avoid this consequence of their beliefs, they turned to a new MORAL PHILOSOPHY, concerned with the natural foundations of human goodness, to provide secular ethical and moral dimensions in the world.

These natural, secular foundations provided the background against which the social contract theories of the 17th century and of the Enlightenment were developed. Whether expounded by Hobbes, Locke, or Jean-Jacques ROUSSEAU, social contract theory posited that human beings had either willingly given up their primitive FREEDOM to join together in societies, or that they might do so in the future, in the event of a radical reform of society. According to contract theory, sovereignty, that is the ultimate power in a society, originally resides with the people. In creating the social contract, people delegate this power to a designated authority, trading their natural freedom for security. Theorists disagreed over whether this original act transfers absolute sovereignty to the designated authority or preserves sovereignty in the people. But they all agreed that the original foundation of society involves a kind of willing agreement on the part of free people to give up some independence in return for the protections offered by a government.

The resulting governments could take any of several forms from absolutism to democracy. For Hobbes, people gave up all individual rights to an absolute ruler in whom sovereignty henceforth resided; Rousseau agreed that all individual rights were given up, but stressed the legal responsibilities and duties of the resulting sovereign. Locke, however, assumed that people possessed certain inalienable natural rights that they retained even after entering the social contract. In fact, the contract could be annulled if these rights were trampled by ruling authorities. In such instances, the people of a nation retained the right to revolt against established authorities and to replace those authorities with new ones.

These theories were all dealing implicitly or explicitly with questions about the extent of individual freedom in societies. Do people retain any individual freedom when they live in a society? If they do enjoy such freedom, is it limited to any extent? What are these limits if any exist? And what are the specific obligations of government. Natural law doctrine was flexible on these issues. During the Enlightenment it was used to support liberal INDIVIDUALISM (Locke, VOLTAIRE), forms of enlightened despotism (see DESPOTISM, ENLIGHTENED) (CAMERALISM), and collective democracy (Rousseau). English theorists tended to favor liberal solutions that made the rights of individuals the cornerstone of freedom. German theorists, building on traditions that dated at least to the Protestant Reformation, emphasized that individual freedoms must be curtailed in the interests of society. Duty toward fellow human beings is more important than individual freedom. In the hands of Immanuel KANT, freedom became primarily a matter of intellectual life. Individuals should "dare to know" but do so while submitting willingly to the laws of society.

Between these two extremes, many intermediate positions were created. MONTESQUIEU, for example, believed that freedom could best be preserved in a traditional society divided into legal orders (nobility, clergy, bourgeoisie). In his vision, the preservation of freedom depended on balancing the claims of absolute monarchs (see ABSOLUTISM) against democratic demands. The nobility could serve as a mediator between these two forces, ensuring that neither obtained so much momentum that political liberty would be lost. His preferred form of government, modeled after his understanding of the English system, involved a division of sovereignty between the king and intermediate powers. This SEPARATION OF POWERS ensured a dynamic political system, stable yet capable of responding to needs without dissolving into anarchy or despotism.

Not all enlightened writers used natural law doctrines to support their views. Theories of UTILITY offered a strong alternative. These theories suggested that the duty of government lies not in upholding rights or natural laws, but rather in guaranteeing pleasure and HAPPINESS, the greatest good for the greatest number of people. Societies were created by human beings in order to satisfy their individual desires. Moral order was an entirely artificial construction, reflecting only the best way of providing satisfaction for the largest number of people.

Utilitarian theories provided the philosophical and moral foundations for works by the English liberal spokesman Adam SMITH, by the Italian champion of legal reform Cesare Bonesana, marchese di BECCARIA, and by the French radical Claude-Adrien HELVÉTIUS. The idea of utility became celebrated in some circles, but was strongly condemned by influential thinkers such as Denis DIDEROT and Rousseau. It would assume a major role in the works of Jeremy BENTHAM and James Mill during the 19th century.

Enlightened political theory was being developed in the context of active and widespread pressures for political change. Until the end of the 18th century, European regimes were relatively stable, but they were, nevertheless, being challenged by forces for reform that stemmed not only from the Enlightenment but also from social and economic changes. Reactions against absolutism drove many of the calls for reform. With respect to the question of absolutism, the Enlightenment inherited certain unresolved issues from the 17th century and then added problems of its own making. It also received the persuasive example of the political solution worked out in England.

The GLORIOUS REVOLUTION of 1688 had ended attempts by the Stuart monarchs to establish royal absolutism in England. When WILLIAM III AND MARY II were invited to assume the English throne, they consented to rule within the bounds of a specific contract; the monarchy was thenceforth limited not only by the Parliament but also by a kind of constitution (a form of social contract). John Locke's TWO TREATISES OF GOVERNMENT spelled out the theoretical underpinnings of this English situation in a form that was disseminated throughout Europe and the American colonies.

In France, the death of LOUIS XIV in 1715 brought the end of his absolute reign and ushered in a renewal of longstanding conflicts between kings and PARLEMENTS over the extent of royal authority. Much of 18th-century political history in France revolved around this conflict, and around the attempts of the *parlements* to gain the same constitutional powers enjoyed by the English Parliament. But the French *parlements* were radically different institutions, populated by lawyers and judges who held their offices as inheritable private property. No elected representatives sat in *parlements,* and the traditional advisory body of elected representatives, the Estates General, did not meet between 1614 and 1789. The French political system was unable to respond to the various pressures for reform, whether they came from within the monarchy or from without. At the end of the century, of course, the whole system broke down in the FRENCH REVOLUTION of 1789.

Only in central and eastern Europe, in PRUSSIA, Russia, and AUSTRIA did absolutism continue to prevail during the 18th century in more than name. Rulers in these states created a new phenomenon, enlightened despotism, that wedded thorough royal control to the cause of human progress and rational government.

For some intellectuals, enlightened despotism seemed to provide an acceptable alternative to the conflicts and paralysis in other political systems. By the end of the 18th century, however, the flaws in this form of government were becoming apparent, and reformers placed their hopes in limited monarchy or in republics.

Absolute rulers, whether enlightened or not, claimed the right to control all traditional functions of government whether executive, legislative, judicial, fiscal, diplomatic, or military. They also attempted to control cultural forms of expression such as MUSIC, LITERATURE, the press, art, THEATER, EDUCATION, and RELIGION. They shared power, at least in theory, with no other groups in society. Enlightened despots generally followed the same policies, although they were aiming to increase the prosperity and enlightenment of their subjects.

In some cases, such as Austria and Prussia, rulers recognized that the SEPARATION OF CHURCH AND STATE would not threaten their absolute control but would, instead, actually strengthen royal control by limiting the institutional powers of established, official churches. Most enlightened writers, however, began to call for the separation of church and state because they wished to see TOLERATION established in Europe.

As the 18th century progressed, a chorus of voices began calling for the separation of powers as a protection against monarchical abuses. The theory of Montesquieu spelled out in THE SPIRIT OF LAWS exercised significant influence on the European continent and in the American colonies. It was possible to separate Montesquieu's major theoretical concepts from their underpinnings in corporative social structure. Leaders of the AMERICAN REVOLUTION, recognizing this possibility, used Montesquieu as one inspiration, if not as a precise model, for their new constitutional government structure.

The example of the American Revolution exerted a significant influence on subsequent political action. The American experience seemed to demonstrate that thoroughgoing reform was indeed possible, that abuses of power could be moderated, and that human and civil rights could be guaranteed in real government structures. It also seemed to validate the idea of the right to revolu-

tion implied in social contract theory. Moreover, it provided an opportunity for intellectuals and statesmen to work out a modern definition of republics and to grapple with the practical issues involved in establishing such a political form.

When the political and fiscal crises of the 1780s engulfed France and the rest of Europe, all these strands in enlightened theory came together, vying for predominance. Human rights such as EQUALITY, happiness, personal security, PROPERTY, political liberty, and government participation would be granted central importance in the early revolutionary constitutions of France and other countries. But it would prove difficult to guarantee them, or to give them concrete forms of interpretation. The enlightened ideals of progress, freedom, individualism, and humanitarianism had the potential to produce social and political transformations with far-reaching implications. As the revolutionary era moved from one form of political experiment to another, reactions revealed the limits beyond which many people, whether enlightened or not, were not yet willing to step.

See also entries for individual nations; ADAMS; ARGENSON, René-Louis d'; ARISTOCRATIC RESURGENCE; BABEUF; BOLINGBROKE; BOULAINVILLIERS; BUREAUCRACY; BURKE; BURLAMAQUI; CALONNE; CALVINISM; CHOISEUL; CLASS AND RANK; CONDORCET; DECLARATION OF INDEPENDENCE; DECLARATION OF THE RIGHTS OF MAN AND THE CITIZEN; DEMOCRACY; DISSENTERS; DIVINE RIGHT OF KINGS; DYNASTIC STATES; EUGÈNE of Savoy; FREEMASONS; GODWIN; HERDER; HISTORY; HUGUENOTS; ILLUMINATI; JEWS AND JUDAISM; LUTHERANISM; JANSENISM; JESUITS; JAY; JEFFERSON; JOSEPHINISM; KAUNITZ; LETTRES DE CACHET; MADISON; MANDEVILLE; MAUPEOU; NECKER, Jacques; PAINE; PARTITIONS OF POLAND; PHILOSOPHER-KING; PHYSIOCRATS; POMBAL; PRIESTLEY; PROTESTANTISM; RAYNAL; ROBESPIERRE; ROMAN CATHOLICISM; SAINT-JUST; SCHILLER; SERFDOM; SEVEN YEARS' WAR; SIEYÈS; SLAVERY; SONNENFELS; STRUENSEE; SWIETEN, Gerard van; TANUCCI; TURGOT; UNITED STATES BILL OF RIGHTS; UNITED STATES CONSTITUTION; VAN DER KEMP; VATTEL; WALPOLE, Robert; WAR OF THE AUSTRIAN SUCCESSION; and WILKES. In addition, consult articles on the following rulers: CATHERINE II (THE GREAT); FREDERICK II (THE GREAT); PETER I (THE GREAT); LOUIS XV; LOUIS XVI; MARIA THERESA; JOSEPH II; KARL WILHELM FERDINAND; CHARLES III OF SPAIN; CHRISTIAN VII OF DENMARK AND NORWAY; PONIATOWSKI; BENEDICT XIV; CLEMENT XIII; CLEMENT XIV; GUSTAV III OF SWEDEN; AND KARL-AUGUST, Duke of Weimar.

Further reading: Joyce Oldham Appleby, *Capitalism and a New Social Order: The Republican Vision of the 1790s* (New York: New York University Press, 1984); Bernard Bailyn, *To Begin the World Anew: The Genius and Ambiguities of the American Founders* (New York: Knopf, 2003); Graeme Garrard, *Rousseau's Counter-Enlightenment: A Republican Critique of the Philosophes* (Albany, N.Y.: State University of New York Press, 2003); Knud Haakonssen,

"Natural Jurisprudence in the Scottish Enlightenment: Summary and Interpretation," in Neil MacCormick and Zenon Bankowski, eds., *Enlightenment, Rights, and Revolution: Essays in Legal and Social Philosophy* (Aberdeen: Aberdeen University Press, 1989); Jonathan I. Israel, *Radical Enlightenment: Philosophy and the Making of Modernity, 1650–1750* (New York: Oxford University Press, 2002); Margaret C. Jacob, *Living the Enlightenment: Freemasonry and Politics in Eighteenth-Century Europe* (New York: Oxford University Press, 1994); Reinhart Koselleck and Maria Santos, *Critique and Crises: Enlightenment and the Pathogenesis of Modern Society* (Cambridge, Mass.: MIT Press, 1998); J. G. A. Pocock, *Virtue, Commerce, and History: Essays on Political Thought and History, Chiefly in the Eighteenth Century* (Cambridge: Cambridge University Press, 1985).

Pombal, Sebastiano José de Carvalho e Mello, marquês de (1699–1782) *Portuguese statesman and reformer*

Prior to 1750, the marquês de Pombal served as a diplomat representing PORTUGAL in LONDON and VIENNA. In these cities, he had ample opportunity to learn firsthand about the government policies that were contributing to vitality in ENGLAND and in the HAPSBURG EMPIRE. By comparison, Portugal seemed backward, a stagnant colonial empire that was squandering the wealth provided by its overseas possessions. With the death of the incompetent Portuguese king John V in 1750, his queen and regent for the young heir called on Pombal to assume the position of secretary of state. Pombal rapidly established thorough control over the young king, Joseph I, and for the next 27 years the enterprising secretary of state ruled Portugal with absolute power. In that brief period, he pushed through a set of central reforms that moved Portugal into the forefront as an example of enlightened despotism (see DESPOTISM, ENLIGTENED).

Pombal began by loosening the stranglehold of the Catholic Church on his country. He was a follower of FEBRONIANISM, a theory derived from JANSENISM that favored the development of strong national Catholic churches subject to secular control. The Inquisition (Catholic ecclesiastical courts) and the JESUITS offered especially difficult problems in Portugal. A series of moves brought the court of the Inquisition under state control, thus removing it as an independent church-controlled judicial system within the state. Pombal also began to challenge the authority of the Jesuits. He dismissed the king's Jesuit confessor, who in the best confessorial tradition had been able to exert influence on state policy by controlling the conscience of the king. Pombal issued a decree forbidding the Jesuits to come to court. When evidence emerged of a Jesuit plot to assassinate King Joseph I, Pombal moved to confiscate all Jesuit property within Portugal and to banish the order from the kingdom. The decree of expulsion appeared September 3, 1759. In this manner, Portugal became the first state to banish the Jesuits. Pombal's action set off a wave of similar activity throughout the Catholic European nations that ultimately forced Pope CLEMENT XIV to dissolve the order in 1773.

In the course of these activities, Pombal also turned against the aristocracy, arresting and imprisoning a group that was involved in the plot to assassinate the king. Once he had subdued the church and the nobles, Pombal was free to reform the kingdom of Portugal at will. He proceeded to reorganize and streamline both the justice and government administration, to build up industries, to promote FREE TRADE between Portugal and the Americas, to strengthen the army, to build up the navy, and to restore civil rights to the Jews. After the disastrous LISBON EARTHQUAKE of 1755, he swiftly mobilized troops and provided hospitals and shelters for the dispossessed and wounded in the devastated city. He subsequently embarked on an ambitious program of reconstruction in Lisbon.

Pombal's energy and ruthlessness have invited comparisons with JOSEPH II OF AUSTRIA. Like Joseph II, he resorted to surveillance to ensure that his decrees were carried out in practice. When his protector King Joseph I of Portugal died, Pombal lost his public office. He was exiled in disgrace and died, embittered, in 1782.

Pompadour, Jeanne-Antoinette Poisson, marquise de (1721–1764) *official mistress of King Louis XV of France and de facto queen of France from 1745 to 1764*

The marquise de Pompadour could not indefinitely hold the fickle LOUIS XV's physical affection, but she succeeded in maintaining their friendship and in actively shaping French policy until she died. Louis XV bestowed the title of marquise de Pompadour on her in 1745.

Jeanne-Antoinette Poisson was the daughter of François Poisson, a successful financier who made a sizable fortune on army contracts and various speculations. In 1725, Poisson had to flee FRANCE to avoid arrest, because he had been involved with the Paris brothers in certain problematic and shady financial deals. In his absence, his wife, Madame Poisson, the beautiful daughter of a butcher, found a wealthy protector, C. F. Le Normant de Tournehem. He arranged for the marriage between his nephew C. G. Le Normant d'Etioles and the young Jeanne-Antoinette de Poisson.

Madame Poisson was ambitious for both her daughter and herself. She introduced her daughter into the social world of the wealthy Parisian bourgeoisie and provided her with a distinguished and unusual EDUCATION, at least by the standards of the time. She also introduced Jeanne to the fine arts, thereby planting the seeds of what would be a lifelong passion. Thus, even before Jeanne-Antoinette (as Madame d'Etioles) met Louis XV in 1745 at a masked ball, she was frequenting Parisian salons and

Jeanne-Antoinette Poisson, marquise de Pompadour, by François Boucher. Madame de Pompadour, the powerful official mistress of King Louis XV, played a significant role as a patroness of the arts and architecture. *(Courtesy New York Public Library)*

demonstrating her interests in ART, MUSIC, OPERA, and THEATER.

During her years at Versailles (1745–64), Jeanne-Antoinette, now the marquise de Pompadour, amassed a splendid cabinet of curiosities, paintings, and engravings. The catalog of her library contained 3,528 entries, most of which were books in either French or Italian. Her taste for refined, gracious, elegant pastel interiors helped to define the parameters of the French ROCOCO style. The painter François BOUCHER was her favorite, and his canvases capture the essence of the contemporary aesthetic. The famous SÈVRES porcelain factory owed its existence to the marquise's love of porcelains and to her determination to establish a French industry that could rival the products both of the MEISSEN factory in Saxony and of CHINA. Theater and opera received her constant patronage.

At Versailles, the marquise de Pompadour—or Madame de Pompadour as she was often called—demonstrated great skill at exercising influence over the policies of state, but her activities earned her many enemies and great notoriety. Sometimes it is difficult to separate her genuine influence from the rumors that have been created about her. It is generally accepted that Madame de Pompadour supported the great change in traditional French foreign alliances that is known today as the DIPLOMATIC REVOLUTION OF 1756. She also seems to have played a role in securing the banishment of the JESUITS from France.

She was devoted to the foreign minister Étienne-François de CHOISEUL, although her death in 1764 probably did not play a major role in bringing about his subsequent disgrace. Her death did, however, rob him of a strong supporter at a time when he was particularly vulnerable. Madame de Pompadour protected and patronized other important figures, most notably VOLTAIRE, François QUESNAY, and the publishers of the ENCYCLOPÉDIE, Denis DIDEROT and Jean Le Rond d'ALEMBERT. Finally, by arranging the appointment of her brother Abel Poisson (awarded the title Marquis de Marigny in 1754) as general director of building for the French government (1751), Madame de Pompadour assured that vigorous support existed for new architectural projects in PARIS. With her support and the direction of her brother, Paris acquired the École Militaire (Military Academy) and the Place de la Concorde (then called Place Louis XV). At Versailles, she arranged for the construction of the Petit Trianon as a retreat.

The marquise de Pompadour remains a difficult figure to evaluate. Her life generated fanciful stories and myths from the very beginnings of her career as Louis XV's official mistress. Numerous spurious publications appeared with her name as authoress. Only a few letters are accepted as authentic. Her role in politics, although substantial, has often been exaggerated, and her activities in the world of fine arts only superficially understood. Scholars of women's history are beginning to reevaluate received interpretations of her life. The enterprise is overdue especially since her political enemies created many of the negative, traditionally accepted views. Whatever emerges in current scholarship, however, it cannot be denied that "the Pompadour" served for 18th-century French people as a symbol of decadence and abuse of power in the ANCIEN RÉGIME. As such a symbol, Madame de Pompadour; her successor as royal mistress, Madame DU BARRY; and her famous younger contemporary, Queen MARIE-ANTOINETTE demonstrate the hold exercised over 18th-century minds by negative images of women.

See also SOCIAL INSTITUTIONS OF THE ENLIGHTENMENT.

Pompeii   Ancient Roman city excavated in the 18th century. Pompeii was an ancient Roman city on the Gulf of Naples at the base of Mount Vesuvius. In 79 C.E., Mount Vesuvius erupted, burying the city and its neighbor, Herculaneum, in up to 10 feet of volcanic ash. The cities would not be seen again until 1748, when a local peasant discovered a buried wall of the city. The Italian authorities were notified, and Charles III, who had inherited Naples in 1734 and was keen to establish his reputation, ordered full-scale excavations to commence on Pompeii and Herculaneum.

Charles hired engineers to carry out the work. Because they were not archaeologists, the engineers neither catalogued nor preserved artifacts carefully. The engineers were mostly interested in excavating treasures for the king. Nonetheless, they uncovered streets, preserved bodies, and buildings. The most important finds of this era of excavation were the Amphitheatre of Herculaneum and several frescoes that were removed to the king's palace.

Excavations continued into the 1750s, and further discoveries were made. In 1755 a large town house the size of a city block was unearthed and the Herculaneum Gate in 1763. The Royal Herculaneum Academy was founded in 1759 to record the discoveries and to invite dignitaries to view the objects uncovered. Due to this public display, the methods of the excavators came to be criticized.

Johann WINCKELMANN, German art historian and archaeologist, was one of the most vocal critics of the disorganization of the excavations. Through his intervention, the work became more systematic.

Under the very able Spanish engineer Francesco La Vega the excavations were conducted more scientifically. Vega led the team that uncovered the Temple of Isis in 1763. In 1765, excavations at Herculaneum ceased, and they intensified at Pompeii. More houses, temples, and other public buildings, such as a large theater and gladiators' barracks, were uncovered. An inscription was found in 1763 that established that Pompeii was a commonwealth.

The finding of ancient artifacts and evidence of how the ancients lived was important for believers in the ENLIGHTENMENT ideal of the PERFECTIBILITY of humans. The findings at Pompeii seemed to provide evidence that the ancients had lived in a golden age of REASON and simplicity, to which people in the 18th century could return.

Representations of Pompeii and its designs, as well as Winckelmann's writings, inspired and popularized a new movement called NEOCLASSICISM. Neoclassical artists and artisans adopted Greek and Roman designs and decorative styles in painting, sculpture, and architecture. Many government buildings and those of commercial and cultural institutions, such as the British Museum, were designed in the neoclassical style. Classical subjects also became popular in 18th- and 19th-century painting.

The excavation of Pompeii also influenced other disciplines. The simplicity of ornamentation found in Pompeiian art and architecture can be seen in literature in the works of English romantic poet Percy Bysshe Shelley and Victorian era poet Algernon Swinburne. In addition, the Enlightenment call for DEMOCRACY and EQUALITY was partly sparked by the rediscovery of ancient art and ideas at Pompeii.

Poniatowski, Stanislaw Augustus (1732–1798) *king of Poland from 1764 to 1795*

Poniatowski had served in various diplomatic capacities before his election to the throne of POLAND and had spent time in ENGLAND and in PARIS. In the latter city, he had frequented the salon of Madame GEOFFRIN. He was well educated and endowed with natural intellect, and also charming and energetic. Poniatowski arrived in RUSSIA in 1755 as an assistant to the British envoy. There he met Catherine, the young wife of the Russian heir, Peter III. Catherine and Poniatowski fell in love and a brief affair ensued. In 1756, when Catherine gave birth to a daughter, Anna, rumors maintained that the child was Poniatowski's. Poniatowski is the only one of Catherine's many lovers who left a description of her. It conveys much of her charm and compelling quality.

When the Polish king, Augustus III, died, Poniatowski became Russia's preferred candidate for the throne. CATHERINE II (THE GREAT), now czarina of Russia and no longer his paramour, ensured that the Russian will would be honored by sending her troops into Poland during the election period. Poniatowski's subsequent election placed Poland solidly under Russian control, but it did not eliminate the diplomatic tensions that centered on the Polish state. He had the misfortune of ruling during the period of the PARTITIONS OF POLAND and had no realistic choice but to sign the treaties by which his kingdom was dismantled by PRUSSIA, Russia, and AUSTRIA. With the third and last partition in 1795, a revolt broke out in the Polish lands that Catherine the Great had annexed, and in November 1796 Poniatowski was forced to abdicate his throne.

Poniatowski had wanted to institute reforms in Poland to revitalize its moribund political system. Above all, he desired to eliminate the *liberum veto* (free veto), substituting a simple majority rule in the Central Diet of Poland. In fact, his reign did witness the slow formation of a rudimentary centralized state to replace the moribund republic.

Poniatowski coauthored the constitution of May 3, 1791, which created a new constitutional monarchy in Poland. It set up a hereditary rather than elective monarchy and specified that the Saxon dynasty should rule after Poniatowski. The constitution divided sovereign power among legislative, executive, and judicial branches. It also abolished the *liberum veto*, which had permitted a single negative vote in the Diet to prevent a law from passing. But the constitution left in place the traditional Polish social order, merely providing legal sanction for certain changes that had occurred over the century.

During his reign, Poniatowski supported economic reforms to stimulate industry, though little could be accomplished. He also encouraged an intellectual and cultural revitalization that was characterized by a return to travel abroad, the circulation of enlightened Polish-language journals, increasing secularization of society and education, and a flowering of literary production. This period of cultural and intellectual revival honors the memory of the intellectual Poniatowski by bearing his name, *epoka Stanisławowska* (Stanislausian era).

Poniatowski recognized that his freedom to act was severely restricted, and he understood the realistic possibilities for effective action in Poland. His pragmatic approach to problems and his support of gradual reform, however, were generally not appreciated by his fellow Poles, who perceived him as weak.

Pope, Alexander (1688–1744) *English poet*

Pope was the son of a wholesale linen merchant. The Pope family was Catholic and therefore suffered from the discriminatory laws that existed at that time in Britain. Young Alexander, for example, was barred from mainline English schools and obtained his education through private tutors, Catholic schools, and independent study.

Pope's allegiance to Catholicism played a significant role in shaping his Tory political sympathies and his concomitant criticisms of his more liberal, commercially minded contemporaries. It also ultimately determined the literary circles in which he moved most comfortably. Among Tory writers, Pope's friends included John GAY, Jonathan SWIFT, and John Arbuthnot, all members with Pope of the Scriblerus Club, and Henry St. John, Viscount BOLINGBROKE, the Tory statesman and historian. Pope's contacts with Whig Party sympathizers such as Joseph ADDISON and Richard STEELE were marred by strained relations owing to competition and differing viewpoints about English politics. His relations with Lady Mary MONTAGU, which have been ascribed to spurned love although the truth of that allegation is not known, were publicly contentious and notorious.

Pope spent his early career at Binsfield in Windsor Forest. In 1718, he moved with his mother to a rented villa at Twickenham and remained there for the rest of his life. At Twickenham, he not only wrote and entertained friends, but also indulged in his passion for designing ENGLISH GARDENS. Pope outlined his landscaping ideas in the *Epistle to the Earl of Burlington* (1731). By choosing that form for his publication, Pope honored Lord Burlington at whose country estate the first garden in the new natural English style had been created.

Pope was one of the outstanding poets during the era of English CLASSICISM (also known as the Augustan Age). In a manner common among writers of the early ENLIGHTENMENT, he used literary models drawn from the heritage of both ancient Greece and ancient ROME. Of his many works in this category, *The Dunciad* (1728), *Imitations of Horace* (1733), and *New Dunciad* (1742) are remarkable for their adaptation of ancient forms to the needs of contemporary English social and political satire. Pope also devoted himself to producing paraphrased translations of certain classics such as Homer's *Iliad* and *Odyssey*.

Pope was a master of the 10-syllable rhymed couplet (heroic couplet) and of the epigram. In the latter category, he contributed to the heritage of the English language such proverbs as: "To err is human, to forgive divine" and "A little learning is a dangerous thing."

In addition to the works mentioned earlier, the following creations by Pope must be noted: the mock-heroic *Rape of the Lock* (1714); *Essay on Man* (1733–34); *Moral Essays* (1732–35); *Epistle to Dr. Arbuthnot* (1735); *Epilogue to the Satires* (1738); and *Essay on Criticism* (1711).

See also LANDSCAPES; PICTURESQUE.

population theories *See* MALTHUS; MATHEMATICS AND MECHANICS; SÜSSMILCH.

pornography
Sexually explicit material intended to arouse sexual excitement. The word *pornography* as denoting a distinct category of obscene material came into widespread use in FRANCE (*pornographie*) during the 1830s and in ENGLAND during the 1850s. During the ENLIGHTENMENT, pornography, when it occurred, was almost always the secondary aspect of a work, most often one attacking political or religious authority. Thus, pornography had not completely emerged as a distinct category during the period of the Enlightenment. What constituted pornography was defined by market forces and the authorities. Print culture and the demand for printed works created pornographic material; the authorities, specifically censors and religious authorities, defined exactly what constituted pornography by regulating and banning it. Because pornographic material could be found in works attacking the church and the absolutist state, scientific treatises, works of NATURAL PHILOSOPHY, and philosophical tracts during the enlightenment, the idea of pornography during the Enlightenment encompassed much more than did the narrow category of the mid-19th century.

Most of the 18th century's prominent examples of pornography were produced in France, where illicit or obscene material became another means of expressing Enlightenment critiques of the church, the state, and society. Pornography in England was tied to the emergence of gentlemen libertines and their pursuit of pleasure. The rest of Europe produced virtually no pornography until the mid-19th century.

The Italian writer Pietro Aretino produced the earliest examples of pornography in modern Europe during the 1530s. In both his series of *Sonnetti lussuriosi* (The lascivious sonnets; 1527) and his prose dialogue *Ragionamenti* (Reasonings; 1534–36), pornographic content characterized what were literary works, the sonnets written to accompany a series of engravings depicting sexual positions. These were widely regarded as pornographic and were joined by such 17th-century works as *L'École des filles* (The school for girls; 1655) and *L'Académie des dames* (The academy for women; 1660). Though both were published anonymously, the *Académie* was probably by a French lawyer, Nicolas Chorier, and the *École* has been assigned variously to the novelist Paul Scarron, Madame de Maintenon (who was Scarron's wife), and LOUIS XIV's minister of finance, Nicolas Fouquet. Both works combine the dialogue style of Aretino's *Ragionamenti* with elements of the emerging NOVEL, and both continued to be popular during the 18th century.

Two mid-century literary phenomena, the emergence of the libertine novel, with its focus on the exploits of the young gentleman, and SENTIMENTAL FICTION, as embodied in Samuel RICHARDSON's extremely successful PAMELA (1740), helped the novel supersede dialogue as the preferred genre for pornographic writing. Richardson's work of sentimental fiction examined the conflicts of female sensibility and sexuality within a male-dominated society. John CLELAND's *Memoirs of a Girl of Pleasure*, also known as *Fanny Hill* (1748–49), is the best example of a work combining the elements of the sentimental novel with pornographic content. Other notable works to emerge from this era included Denis DIDEROT's *Les bijoux indiscrets* (The indiscreet jewels; 1748) and the anonymous *Thérese philosophe* (1748).

There were other factors behind the surge in pornography besides the popularity of *Pamela*. Political and social turmoil as well as the beginning of the high Enlightenment help account for the surge. The appearance of several popular pornographic works in 1748 coincided with the publication of La Mettrie's *L'homme machine* (Man the machine) and MONTESQUIEU's *L'esprit des lois* (THE SPIRIT OF THE LAWS), two texts that marked the beginning of the high Enlightenment in France. Natural philosophy and political critique found expression not only in the works of the PHILOSOPHES, but also in works marked by their pornographic content. The 1740s were also marked by political upheaval on the Continent, with the WAR OF THE AUSTRIAN SUCCESSION (1744–48) finding France unable to successfully prosecute a war. It was no accident that several of the male figures depicted in pornographic images of the time were soldiers, officers whose men were too debauched to win victory on the battlefield.

From the 1740s, French pornography became increasingly more outspoken in its criticism of authority. Pornography attacked the church with imagery of debauched priests and monks engaged in all sorts of illicit sexual activities, another manifestation of the ANTICLERICALISM present in much Enlightenment thought. Attacks on the court in general and on the monarchy in particular increased in frequency, and LOUIS XV, LOUIS XVI, and MARIE-ANTOINETTE were often targeted. Such criticism coincided with the accumulation of tensions that preceded the FRENCH REVOLUTION (1789–99), the era during which the marquis de SADE produced some of his major works—*Justine* (1791), *La philosophie dans le boudoir* (Philosophy in the bedroom; 1795), and *Juliette* (1797). De Sade's writings represent a culmination of the type of pornography that emerged in the 1740s, combin-

ing sexual material with philosophical discussion and reflection on a wide range of topics.

See also LIBERTINE.

Further reading: Robert Darnton, *The Literary Underground of the Old Regime* (Cambridge, Mass.: Harvard University Press, 1982); Lynn Hunt, ed. *The Invention of Pornography: Obscenity and the Origins of Modernity, 1500–1800* (New York: Zone Books, 1993); Marquis de Sade, *Justine, Philosophy in the Bedroom, and Other Writings* (New York: Grove Weidenfeld, 1965).

Portugal   Small kingdom located on the Atlantic coast of the Iberian peninsula, with its capital at Lisbon. It is bounded on the east by SPAIN. Lisbon experienced heavy destruction in the famous LISBON EARTHQUAKE of 1755 and was completely rebuilt in a late-BAROQUE STYLE. A small kingdom of Portugal first appeared in the 12th century after Christian armies began retaking the Iberian peninsula from the Muslims. Navigators from the region spearheaded the period of European explorations that began in the 15th century, eventually establishing a great colonial empire in Brazil and in the East Indies. Portuguese culture flourished during that era, and in the aftermath of the Council of Trent (1545–63) the kingdom also became a bastion of post-Tridentine Catholicism. The Inquisition and the JESUITS gained firm footing in the kingdom, and the University of Coimbra served Europe as a creative intellectual center. At the end of the 16th century, the Spanish monarchy gained control of Portugal by means of dynastic marriage alliances. By 1643, however, the kingdom had regained its independence, and although it had lost its economic dominance of the Iberian peninsula, it continued to reap immense wealth from its colony in Brazil.

Throughout the first half of the 18th century, Portugal existed as a relatively stagnant state largely untouched by the changes that were occurring in neighboring European countries. The population was declining, and the considerable wealth flowing into the country from the colony of Brazil was being squandered in private consumption or foreign investments. With the appearance of the marquês de POMBAL on the scene in 1750, the country was pushed into an era of political and ecclesiastical reform. For 18th-century political theorists and reformers, Pombal's Portugal represented an outstanding example of the practical application of theories of enlightened despotism, (see DESPOTISM, ENLIGHTENED). They admired his direct, successful attacks on the Jesuits and on perceived abuses by the papacy. In the end, however, obstacles deriving from the fundamental social and economic structure of the country and from the internal contradictions of the theory of enlightened despotism eroded Pombal's system. Portugal thus experienced political upheavals similar to those that engulfed the rest of Europe.

See also COLONIALISM.

power loom A weaving machine invented between 1785 and 1787 by Edmund CARTWRIGHT. The adoption of the loom required several decades owing to mechanical flaws and fluctuations in demand.

The tremendous increase in the supply of yarns, brought about by the appearance of the SPINNING JENNY and other machine-driven spinning devices, stimulated the invention of the power loom. It was one of a series of technological innovations that revolutionized cloth production in ENGLAND by transforming the organization of labor and the means of production of certain commodities. The loom thus played an important role in the INDUSTRIAL REVOLUTION of the late 18th and early 19th centuries.

Prandtauer, Jakob (1660–1726) *Austrian architect, one of the first Austrian natives to work in the baroque style*
Jakob Prandtauer worked in the Austrian countryside rather than in VIENNA or other urban areas. He was born in the Austrian Tyrol and trained as a sculptor. He moved to St. Polten in 1689, one of many Tyroleans who resettled the depopulated regions of Lower AUSTRIA. By 1695, he was using the title Baumeister, although little is known of his formal training in architecture. In 1701, he obtained a major commission to rebuild the large Abbey of Melk, on the Danube River. It is assumed that the abbot of Melk, Berthold Dietmayr, assisted Prandtauer in creating the Melk designs. Following his triumph at Melk, Prandtauer succeeded the deceased Carlo Antonio Carlone as monastic architect at Saint Florian near Linz. Prandtauer also received the commission for the Austin Priory at Dürnstein, but he apparently delegated most of the work to his nephew, Joseph Munggenast (1680–1741).

See also BAROQUE STYLE.

preformation theory Theory of GENERATION that dominated 18th-century physiology and embryology until the last third of the century. In the late 17th century, the Dutch scientist Jan Swammerdam (1637–80) articulated preformation theory as an alternative to EPIGENESIS. He claimed that fully preformed individuals exist in embryos. Later preformationists argued about whether the male sperm or the female embryo contained this preformed individual. Most preformationists prior to the 1720s favored the location in the sperm. They were called animalculists; the sperm, animalcules; and the specific theory, ANIMALCULISM. Antoni van LEEUWENHOEK and Nicolaas Hartsoeker (1656–1725) were prominent proponents of this position. In contrast, scientists who believed the female carried the preformed individual were called ovists. Albrecht von HALLER, Charles BONNET, and Lazzaro SPALLANZANI were prominent ovists, as were most preformationists after the 1740s.

At its inception in the late 17th century, preformation theory dovetailed nicely with the scientific vision called the MECHANICAL PHILOSOPHY of nature. Preformation theory removed the need for belief in spontaneous generation, a position that had been strongly associated with the late Renaissance ANIMISM that was so bitterly opposed by mechanical philosophers. Preformation theory could also be made to support orthodox Christian beliefs in the Creator God and in Original Sin. As the philosopher and theologian Nicolas de MALEBRANCHE demonstrated, the seeds of all individual creatures of the past, present, and future had been formed by God at the beginning of time. They simply unfold from one generation to the next. This version of preformation theory, which was supported by devout scientists such as Bonnet, was called divine preformation. The German philosopher Gottfried Wilhelm LEIBNIZ believed that divine preformation theory was actually an essential underpinning of mechanical philosophy.

In spite of these appealing aspects, animalculist preformation theory fell into disrepute after the 1740s. The animalculist form of the theory, in which preformed individuals existed in the head of each of the multitudes of sperm in one male seemed too wasteful. Why, scientists wondered, would God or nature create so many individuals only to have one or a few survive? Furthermore, animalculist preformation theory could not explain how a new individual acquired traits from the mother. Similarly, the ovist theory of preformation could not explain how traits were obtained from the father. Yet clearly, new individuals contained traits from both parents. Even more difficult for preformation theory was the question of "monstrous" births, that is, the coming into the world of malformed and often unviable new lives. How, people wondered, could an omniscient and perfect God willfully bring such beings into existence?

To address these problems, preformation theory had to evolve and to develop altered concepts. This was attempted when René-Antoine Ferchault de RÉAUMUR, Abraham TREMBLEY, and Bonnet published their various findings on regeneration in polyps and flatworms. They offered a new interpretation of preformation in which what was preformed was conceived as a rough form, a "germ." Bonnet, for example, argued that in this germ all organs were preformed but not necessarily in the order that characterizes a fully-formed fetus. Regeneration experiments demanded that preformationists find some convincing way of explaining how each piece of a cut up polyp or flatworm could generate a whole new organism. It seemed that preformed embryos would have to exist throughout the body. Bonnet believed that his germs, containing general prototypes, did indeed exist in all parts of an organism. But the influences of both semen and nutrition were also required to develop specific traits.

At this point, Bonnet's preformation theory began to resemble the tenets of epigenesis, and the maintenance of two separate theories began to have little justification. As the 18th century came to a close, the epigenetic vision took over and both reproduction and regeneration were primarily conceived as processes involving true development and transformation over time.

Preussische Königliche Akademie der Wissenschaften (Royal Prussian Academy of Sciences)
See BERLIN ACADEMY.

Prévost, Antoine-François (1697–1763) *French novelist and journalist*

Antoine-François Prévost (also called Prévost d'Exiles or Abbé Prévost) was an extremely colorful character whose unsettled life resembled those of the characters in his popular novels. He was born in the town of Hesdin in Artois, the second son of a lawyer in the service of the king. Destined for a career in the Catholic Church, Prévost attended a local Jesuit *collège* and then went to PARIS to study. In 1713, he entered the JESUITS as a novice, but he fled the cloister for army life. He served briefly in the army, returned even more briefly to the Jesuits, and then went back to the army as an officer. When he was 22, he entered the order of the Benedictines to recover from an unhappy love affair. He became a priest in 1721 and won a reputation as a good teacher and preacher.

By 1728, Prévost had again tired of the constraints of monastic life. He was helping the Benedictines in their seminal work of HISTORY, the *Gallia Christiana,* but at the same time he was writing secular novels. He left the monastery without permission and, threatened by ecclesiastical authorities with arrest, fled first to ENGLAND and then to Holland.

While he was living in Holland, Prévost began publishing the *Mémoires et Aventures d'un Homme de Qualité* (Memoirs and adventures of a man of quality). The seventh volume of this work, published in 1731, is the work on which his literary fame rests. Entitled *Histoire du Chevalier des Grieux et de Manon Lescaut* (History of Chevalier Grieux and Manon Lescaut), this work has inspired many subsequent plays and OPERAS. *Manon Lescaut,* as the book is most commonly called, reveals Prévost creating a kind of mixed literary genre from a combination of 18th-century SENTIMENTAL FICTION and GOTHIC ROMANCE. It tells of the passionate, unrequited, and ultimately tragic love of the chevalier des Grieux for Manon Lescaut.

In addition to *Manon Lescaut,* Prévost wrote other Gothic novels and helped to popularize contemporary English literature through his translations into French. He also founded a periodical, *Le Pour et le Contre* (Pros and cons), which was modeled on THE SPECTATOR by Joseph ADDISON and Richard STEELE. Prévost's life settled down somewhat after he obtained patronage from Cardinal de Bissy and the prince de Conti. He was one of the first French writers of the ENLIGHTENMENT to make his living through his literary work, and he left a legacy that influenced the later course of 18th-century French fiction.

Price, Richard (1723–1791) *Welsh moral philosopher, mathematician, and political pamphleteer*

By profession, Price was a minister to a congregation of DISSENTERS. He spent his adult life in LONDON.

As a mathematician, Price specialized in the new discipline of PROBABILITY theory. This theory, a product of the ENLIGHTENMENT, applies statistical analysis to a series of unrelated events, in an effort to predict what will happen over a period of time. Price worked specifically to apply probability to risks in insurance and pensions.

Price is best known, however, for his POLITICAL THEORY and MORAL PHILOSOPHY. He wrote *A Review of the Principal Questions in Morals* (1758) to offer a new theory of ethics rooted in REASON. He compared the obvious nature (self-evidence) of moral and metaphysical principles to mathematical truths, and believed that general moral principles exist in the universe.

Price translated his moral philosophy into practical positions that supported both the AMERICAN REVOLUTION in 1776 and the FRENCH REVOLUTION in 1789. He was a friend of Benjamin FRANKLIN whom he met when the American was in London. Price published several political pamphlets supporting the rights of people to revolt against their governments. A February 1776 pamphlet, *Observations on the Nature of Civil Liberty, the Principles of Government, and the Justice and Policy of the War with America,* went through 11 British editions in three months, was reprinted in America, and was translated into Dutch, French, and German. It argued that support of the American revolt was actually a practical position for the British nation.

A moral theory provided the philosophical underpinnings for this position. According to Price, any community, like any individual, has a natural right of self-government that he called the principle of "civil liberty." A nation can choose either independence or partnership in a confederation. Three other types of NATURAL RIGHTS are the right of general choice (physical liberty), the right of moral choice, and the right to religious FREEDOM. Price's concept of natural rights, therefore, provided an ethical basis for political principles.

A second pamphlet published in 1777, *Additional Observations on the Nature and Value of Civil Liberty and the War with America,* answered critics of the first pamphlet. Finally, in 1784, Price published a pamphlet addressed specifically to Americans: *Observations on the Importance of the American Revolution, and the Means of Making it a Benefit to the World.* The pamphlet advised Americans to establish a citizen militia rather than a standing professional army; to strengthen the powers of Congress over the president; to establish a sinking fund for retiring debt; to protect freedom of worship and speech; to promote liberal EDUCATION and EQUALITY of position; and to pursue a simple life. As a result of this work, Price was offered American citizenship, but he declined to emigrate from England on account of his age.

Price believed that the American Revolution was the second greatest event in human history after the birth of Christ. He was equally enthusiastic about the French Revolution. His sermon to a meeting of the Society for Commemorating the Revolution in Great Britain (the 1688 GLORIOUS REVOLUTION) entitled *A Discourse on the Love of Our Country* (November 4, 1789) praised events in FRANCE and repeated the call for liberty and choice. At Price's urging the ROYAL SOCIETY OF LONDON, of which he had been a member since 1761, sent a congratulatory letter to the French revolutionary leaders. Both these acts served as stimuli for the writing of *REFLECTIONS ON THE REVOLUTION IN FRANCE* by Edmund BURKE.

See also MATHEMATICS AND MECHANICS; RADICAL ENLIGHTENMENT.

Priestley, Joseph (1733–1804) *English chemist, natural philosopher, and theologian*

Priestley is remembered for having been one of the first chemists to isolate oxygen and to recognize its unique properties. He also contributed to rational theology and developed a controversial materialist theory of mind-body relations.

Priestley, the son of a Yorkshire cloth merchant, was raised mostly by relatives. Although his family belonged to a strict Calvinist Independent church, young Priestley preferred the milder THEOLOGY of the English Presbyterians. Priestley educated himself in scientific subjects and mathematics before entering the seminary at Daventry that was run by English DISSENTERS. At Daventry, he received encouragement to study John LOCKE, Cambridge Platonists such as Henry More and Ralph CUDWORTH, and Isaac NEWTON. As a result, Priestley obtained a thorough grounding in the British EMPIRICISM, natural theology, and NATURAL PHILOSOPHY that provided foundations for the ENLIGHTENMENT. His thought displayed tendencies toward liberal theological and political positions, and toward utilitarian and reductionist approaches in the sciences.

After being ordained as a minister, Priestley tried working as a pastor, but he was not well received by his congregations. He offset these failures by establishing himself quickly as a successful and respected teacher. He first opened a school at Nantwich and then received a post at the Dissenters's Warrington Academy. In 1767, he accepted a ministerial position with the Mill-Hill Presbyterian Church in Leeds. After 1780, he settled in Birmingham and became a highly popular preacher at the liberal New Meeting House. He participated in the informal intellectual club known as the LUNAR SOCIETY OF BIRM-

Bust of Joseph Priestley. The chemist and theologian Joseph Priestley supported the early French Revolution and consequently saw his home and church destroyed by an angry English "Church-and-King" mob. *(Courtesy New York Public Library)*

INGHAM where his friends included Matthew BOULTON, Erasmus DARWIN, James WATT, and Josiah WEDGWOOD.

Priestley emerged over the years as the primary English defender of Unitarian religious beliefs and as an outspoken champion of enlightened political reform. His writings, preaching, and support of the moderate early stages of the FRENCH REVOLUTION earned him criticism from the ANGLICANS and widespread political enemies. In 1791, a "Church-and-King" mob destroyed not only his home and scientific laboratory but also the Birmingham New Meeting House. The event caused Priestley to immigrate to the UNITED STATES, where he became a friend and supporter of Thomas JEFFERSON. Priestley died in the United States in 1804.

Priestley had served from 1773 until 1780 in the personal household of William Petty, earl of Shelburne. In 1774, Shelburne and Priestley traveled to PARIS, where Priestley met the French chemist Antoine LAVOISIER. Priestley told Lavoisier about his experiments with the calx of mercury. Priestley had collected the "air" (gas) given off in the calcination process and had learned that this air exhibited unusual chemical properties. Because he believed in the validity of PHLOGISTON THEORY, Priestley called the new air "dephlogisticated air." Eventually, Lavoisier, who began experimenting with Priestley's air, dubbed it "oxygen" and gave it a crucial position in his new chemical theory. The meeting between Lavoisier and Priestley has stimulated intense academic debate over the debt of Lavoisier to Priestley in the subsequent development of the CHEMICAL REVOLUTION.

In addition to his significant work on oxygen, Priestley wrote a series of educational texts dealing with physics. These were *The History and Present State of Electricity, With Original Experiments* (1767), *The History and Present State of Discoveries Relating to Vision, Light, and Colours* (better known as the *History of Optics,* 1772), *A Familiar Introduction to the Study of Electricity* (1768), and *A Familiar Introduction to the Theory and Practise of Perspective* (1770). Results of his experiments with electricity were published in the *Philosophical Transactions of the Royal Society.*

Priestley also criticized the Scottish common sense philosophy developed by Thomas REID and the theory of psychological association created by David HARTLEY. In developing his own theory of mind-body relations, Priestley drew on the unusual conceptualization of the atom developed by Ruggiero Giuseppe BOSCOVICH.

Priestley outlined his ideas on RELIGION, PHILOSOPHY, and PSYCHOLOGY in *A History of the Corruptions of Christianity* (1782), *An History of Early Opinions Concerning Jesus Christ* (1786), *Disquisitions Relating to Matter and Spirit* (1777), *Doctrine of Philosophical Necessity, Illustrated* (1777), *Examination of Dr. Reid's Inquiry into the Human Mind* (1774), and *Hartley's Theory of the Human Mind* (1775).

Priestley also wrote books on the general philosophy of EDUCATION, on LANGUAGE, HISTORY, and law. They included *A Course of Lectures on the Theory of Language* (1762), *The Rudiments of English Grammar* (1761), *Essay on a Course of Liberal Education for Civil and Active Life* (1765), *Lectures on History and General Policy* (published 1788), *Essay on the First Principles of Government* (1768), and the pamphlet, *Remarks on . . . Dr. Blackstone's Commentaries on the Laws of England* (a critical treatment of the ideas of William BLACKSTONE, 1769).

Principia mathematica   A treatise by Isaac NEWTON, in which he outlined his reformed version of the MECHANICAL PHILOSOPHY of SCIENCE. Its full title is *Philosophiae naturalis principia mathematica* (The mathematical principles of natural philosophy). It is divided into three books entitled "The Motion of Bodies," "The Motion of Bodies (in resisting Mediums)," and "The System of the World (in Mathematical Treatment)."

The central ideas of the *Principia mathematica* were developed by Newton over a long period of time, but he made his most significant discoveries and wrote the major portions of the treatise between 1679 and 1687. These were the years in which Newton was in isolation from his Cambridge University colleagues, recovering from a severe emotional breakdown. *Principia mathematica* appeared in print in July 1687, having been financed in part through the private support of Newton's friend, the astronomer Edmond HALLEY.

The *Principia mathematica* presents Newton's new system of dynamic mechanics, spelling out the principles of that science in the form of three laws of motion. The first law stated the principle of inertia that Newton had derived from the works of Galileo GALILEI and René DESCARTES. The second law introduced the controversial concept of force into mechanical theory, and the third law stated the principle of action and reaction. Newton demonstrated how these laws could be expressed mathematically using his new techniques of calculus. The treatise also spelled out Newton's version of SCIENTIFIC METHOD.

Newton wrote the *Principia mathematica* at Halley's request, after having demonstrated for Halley how Kepler's three general laws of planetary motion could be derived from the mathematical laws of mechanics. Newton generalized these laws to cover all motion whether on Earth or in the heavens. In the course of describing his new ideas, Newton also proposed the theory of universal gravitation, which assumed that a force called gravitation governs all actions between bodies anywhere in the universe.

Newton's new system of the world challenged and eventually thoroughly undermined the comprehensive system that had been described by René Descartes in *Le système du monde*. The rivalry between the Cartesian and Newtonian systems did not end until the scientists of the ENLIGHTENMENT succeeded in gathering strong evidence from astronomy, which favored the Newtoninan theory.

The *Principia mathematica* eventually replaced Cartesian writings as the primary model of science and scientific method for the Enlightenment. Its ideas, simplified for nonspecialists by VOLTAIRE and Francesco ALGAROTTI, provided the most common vision of the world for enlightened Frenchmen and Englishmen. In its original Latin version, and in the French translation by Madame DU CHÂTELET, the work spread throughout the international scientific community, transforming the fundamental notions on which mechanics and physics were based. The book stands with the treatises of John LOCKE as one of the earliest building blocks from which the thought of the Enlightenment was constructed.

See also CLAIRAUT; MAUPERTUIS.

Pringle, John (1707–1782) *Scottish-born physician who worked in Edinburgh and London*
Pringle, son of Sir John and Magdalen Eliot Pringle, attended St. Andrews and EDINBURGH universities, then

took an M.D. degree at the University of Leiden in the UNITED PROVINCES OF THE NETHERLANDS. He also studied briefly in PARIS. An eight-year period (1734–42) as professor of metaphysics (pneumatics) and MORAL PHILOSOPHY at the University of Edinburgh was followed by a tour of duty in the army (1742–49) during which Pringle headed the British military hospital in Flanders. In this capacity, Pringle campaigned to have military hospitals treated as sanctuaries from enemy attack.

Pringle moved to LONDON in 1749, set up a private practice, and obtained appointments as the physician for both Queen Charlotte and King George III. He was awarded a noble title of baronet at that time. The ROYAL SOCIETY OF LONDON elected Pringle to its membership in 1745. He became a powerful member of the Royal Society, serving as its president from 1772 until 1778. He was also an honorary fellow of the College of Physicians and a member of scientific societies throughout Europe in cities such as Harlem, AMSTERDAM, Göttingen, Kassel, MADRID, Paris, SAINT PETERSBURG, Naples, and Edinburgh.

Pringle is considered one of the primary founders of modern military MEDICINE. His major publication, *On the Diseases of the Army* (1752), went through many 18th-century editions and was translated into French, Italian, German, Dutch, and Spanish before the end of the century. An American edition also appeared with notes by Benjamin RUSH. The book described symptoms and methods for treating such military scourges as malaria, typhus, dysentery, and epidemic meningitis. Following the principles of VITALISM, Pringle assumed that the environment plays an important role in both the prevention and treatment of disease. His book outlined methods for better sanitation in military hospitals and camps and stressed the importance of adequate ventilation in hospitals.

Pringle also contributed significantly toward advancing the cause of general cleanliness in medicine and in daily life. He introduced the concepts of "septic" and "antiseptic" into medical terminology and suggested that some diseases might be caused by microscopic organisms. The papers containing his new terminology appeared in the *Philosophical Transactions of the Royal Society* (vol. 46, nos. 495, 480, 496, 525, and 550).

probability Calculation of the likelihood that a particular event will occur. The work of ENLIGHTENMENT intellectuals to establish and discover rational principles describing the workings of the universe necessitated radical changes in established modes of thought and practice. One of the significant shifts in the conceptualization of the world comes with the development of the idea of probability in 17th- and 18th-century discourse. René DESCARTES and Isaac NEWTON defined knowledge as what was observable and repeatable, but probability considered another aspect of research: what might be possible based on what was already known about a given phenomenon.

The intellectual roots of modern probability lie in the middle of the 17th century, developing from a variety of sources. In France, Blaise Pascal's discussions with the mathematician Pierre de Fermat on processes of gambling grew into the notion of decision theory, the process of giving weight to competing options. European economics increasingly engaged the idea of probability in practices such as the development of annuities. Gottfried LEIBNIZ and Christian Huygens worked in midcentury to advance mathematical models to determine probability, and Huygens took his work a step further in 1657 with his creation of a textbook on the subject. The mathematician Jacob BERNOULLI published his theory of probability in large numbers in 1689.

As the mathematical models to calculate probability grew more advanced, applications in real world situations expanded. The nascent field of STATISTICS drew more and more upon notions of probability as it worked to manipulate public records of births and deaths to establish patterns of length of human life. The 17th century also supported the development of probability study in the establishment of the notion that evidence, or physical phenomena, could impart the weight of authority, just as religious texts and personal testimony had.

The idea of probability also served a crucial function in the development of the NOVEL in 18th-century ENGLAND with its focus on believable details, plots grounded in everyday life, and characters driven by realistic psychological motivations. A test of a successful novel was its ability to live up to a standard of probability for its readers. As Samuel RICHARDSON wrote of his novel *CLARISSA* (1747–48), "I could wish that the *Air* of Genuineness had been kept up. . . ." English prose writing moved away from models such as European romances, featuring fantastic plots and near godlike heroic figures to genres based in the mundane world. Some roots of this shift lay in the appearance of sensational crime depictions in broadsides and other forms of journalism.

Probability in narrative also grew from the development of travel writing related to the growing colonial enterprise, influencing popular fiction of the 1720s such as Daniel DEFOE's novel *ROBINSON CRUSOE*. The book takes great pains to give the appearance of detailed reality down to the inclusion of Crusoe's lists of supplies and plans to improve his island kingdom. This principle of reality in literature gained such importance that midcentury literary critics such as Samuel JOHNSON based a work's merit in part on the quality of its depiction. His concern for reality drew in no small part on the issue of a book's moral message, which was thought to be compromised if it did not give an accurate depiction of life. This issue remained paradoxical, however, since a moral book was also assumed to shape its depiction of life in order to communicate only the correct sorts of moral conclusions.

See also MATHEMATICS AND MECHANICS; OPTIMISM.

Further reading: Paula R. Backscheider, *Probability, Time, and Space in Eighteenth-Century Literature* (New York: AMS Press, 1979); Ian Hacking, *The Emergence of Probability: A Philosophical Study of Early Ideas About Probability, Induction, and Statistical Inference* (New York: Cambridge University Press, 1975); Lorenz Kruger et al., eds., *The Probabilistic Revolution* (Cambridge, Mass.: MIT Press, 1987); Robert Newsom, *A Likely Story: Probability and Play in Fiction* (New Brunswick, N.J.: Rutgers University Press, 1988).

progress An ordered process of change over time. Eighteenth-century thinkers had in mind the simple notion of progression through a set of interconnected stages. Progress could occur in either a negative, downward direction or a positive, upward direction. It could even occur in cycles. Therefore, the common claim that the ENLIGHTENMENT was an era in which people believed that progress was inevitably advancing humankind and society toward greater states of perfection misrepresents the actual breadth of ideas that were common to that era. Upward progress was indeed an article of faith for some writers, but a significant group of important enlightened intellectuals rejected such simple notions and described human HISTORY in more complex, even negative terms.

The concept of progress had not only material dimensions but also intellectual, social, cultural, and moral dimensions for those enlightened thinkers who believed in it. As a result, when writers took a position on the direction of human development over time, they were also, by implication, offering either positive or negative assessments of human nature, of their own civilization, and of the future.

The idea of upward progress rested on assumptions about the PERFECTIBILITY of human nature. Improvements in the human condition would occur over the course of history as human beings capitalized on their perfectible natures. Writers who advanced this view believed that upward progress was guaranteed, either by God or, perhaps, by some secular form of NATURAL LAW. They accepted the idea that the universe operated according to certain mathematical laws whose structures could be uncovered by human beings exercising their REASON.

Illustration of 18th-century public sanitation projects. The ideal of advancing the human condition by creating a higher quality of material existence combined during the Enlightenment with advances in medicine to create practical efforts at bettering public health in European cities. *(Courtesy Baker Library, Harvard Business School, Cambridge, Massachusetts)*

Oxford Canal lock, Warwickshire, England. The construction of canals, an endeavor begun in the 17th century, continued through the 18th century, serving as a realization of the Baconian ideal of mastery over nature. *(Courtesy New York Public Library)*

Knowledge of these laws could yield additional understanding of the universe and of human nature, thereby giving people greater power to control their physical and social environments. Ignorance, according to this viewpoint, was the great enemy of progress.

This positive set of expectations, articulated in the utopian writings of Sir Francis BACON, was transmitted into the Enlightenment through the activities of the ROYAL SOCIETY OF LONDON and of continental scientists committed to the EMPIRICISM associated with the SCIENTIFIC REVOLUTION. But it was also espoused by the creators of 17th-century RATIONALISM, René DESCARTES and Gottfried Wilhelm LEIBNIZ. Progress, it was assumed by all these individuals, could be guaranteed by the extension of scientific knowledge to encompass every aspect of existence.

Some enlightened intellectuals—Jean-Jacques ROUSSEAU, David HUME, and Giambattista VICO, for example—denied that upward progress has occurred, asserting instead that human history displays cyclical growth at best and degeneration at worst. These critics tended to view their contemporary cultures and societies as corrupt and doubted that the simple exercise of reason could bring about positive change. At the end of the Enlightenment, Immanuel KANT attempted to create a synthesis of these conflicting views. He suggested that history is moving the world toward greater rationality and morality but only within the limits of human society. For individuals, upward progress might prove ephemeral, a beautiful but unattainable dream.

Although their views about the nature of the progression of human history varied, most enlightened thinkers believed that human knowledge and action could affect the outcome of history. Therefore, they began to concern themselves about the way in which ideas and insights were communicated and applied, and they turned their attention to reforming EDUCATION, LANGUAGE, and grammar. John LOCKE, the Lutheran Pietists, Claude-Adrien HELVÉTIUS, Jean-Jacques Rousseau, Johann Heinrich PESTALOZZI, Johann Bernhard Basedow (1724–90), and the IDÉOLOGUES all offered programs for educational reform. Efforts to formulate new languages and to organize knowledge according to comprehensive systems of CLASSIFICATION also multiplied throughout the century. All these activities were designed to increase the accuracy with which ideas could be transmitted by their creators to a broad society of educated people. Certain individuals—especially Denis DIDEROT and Johann Wolfgang von GOETHE—also stressed the roles that creative GENIUS, INTUITION AND IMAGINATION could play in advancing the cause of human wisdom and perfection.

Active enlightened reformers tended to hold existing institutions responsible for preventing upward progress.

VOLTAIRE, for example, dedicated himself to demonstrating how SUPERSTITION, RELIGION, and warfare were standing in the way of human advancement. Ministers of state such as Anne-Robert-Jacques TURGOT, Josef von SONNENFELS, and Gerard van SWIETEN joined enlightened rulers such as FREDERICK II (THE GREAT), CATHERINE II (THE GREAT), and JOSEPH II in state-directed efforts to reform social systems, educational institutions, and economic structures. The extension of the powers of the central government over various facets of society actually seemed to some reformers a reliable way of attaining progress. But this approach was countered in some quarters by calls for increasing FREEDOM of thought so that, through the exchange of ideas, human beings could move forward.

Thus, the Enlightenment, so often characterized as a movement created by naively optimistic men, actually offered a spectrum of opinions on the nature of progress and on the best means by which improvements in the human condition could be attained. Its belief in progress was always modified by the realization that the fruits of progress could easily be destroyed through ignorance, barbarism, and even the misuse of reason.

See also COLONIALISM; PIETISM.

property   Something owned or possessed. In the liberal POLITICAL THEORY of the ENLIGHTENMENT, the concept of property served as the guarantee of both political liberty and the general welfare of a society. John LOCKE, who formulated this position, used the concept of property with two variations of meaning. His general definition included not only land and personal goods but also the labor a person performs. His narrower definition treated property strictly as land and material possessions. According to Locke, the need to defend private property caused people to join together to form in the social compact that provided the foundation for political society.

Jean-Jacques ROUSSEAU, the radical philosophe whose works appeared during the middle of the 18th century, treated the accidental invention of private property as the source of degeneration and evil in human HISTORY. Rousseau believed, just as Locke did, that private property had caused people to set up governments, but in Rousseau's opinion this development had produced negative consequences for humankind. Rousseau expressed his convictions in both the *DISCOURSE ON THE ORIGINS OF INEQUALITY* and the *SOCIAL CONTRACT*.

Locke's position was adopted by the framers of the UNITED STATES BILL OF RIGHTS and the French DECLARATION OF THE RIGHTS OF MAN AND THE CITIZEN, who recognized property rights and who also made property ownership a requirement for voting privileges. Rousseau's formulation fed more egalitarian currents in the FRENCH REVOLUTION, which called for the abolition of property requirements in determining citizenship privileges and produced the earliest modern calls for socialism.

A third enlightened treatment of property tended to link the Lockean concept with the structures of the legal estates in ANCIEN RÉGIME France. MONTESQUIEU gave the best-known formulation of this position. For him, the system of privileges associated with noble property and status in France made the aristocracy the natural mediator between the monarch and his subjects. Aristocratic interests would temper absolutist tendencies in the monarchy but would also snuff out dangerous democratic tendencies in the people. If Montesquieu did not explicitly make property the guarantor of political freedom, he nevertheless assigned a special role to the wealthy, noble propertied classes of France.

The inability or unwillingness of most enlightened individuals to treat property in egalitarian terms provides testimonial to the idea that the Enlightenment was partly an ideology that defended the interests of propertied middle classes. Whether or not this interpretation stands the test of detailed examination, it certainly cannot be denied that enlightened intellectuals rarely extended their cherished ideal of EQUALITY to include the material aspects of human existence.

See also CIVIL SOCIETY; RIGHTS; THE SPIRIT OF LAWS; TWO TREATISES OF GOVERNMENT.

prostitution   The public sale of sexual services. In 18th-century Europe, the courtesan or the mistress of a prominent man was generally exempt from prosecution, and some achieved social success, wealth, and even power. However, girls and women who worked in urban taverns, teahouses, brothels (known as bawdy houses), theaters, or on the streets were unprotected and subject to repression, punishment, and reformation over the course of the 18th century. Because sodomy was a capital offense in many nations, male prostitutes who catered to a homosexual clientele worked in secret "molly" houses or private clubs. In 1726, Mother Clap, a bawd, or madam, who ran a homosexual brothel in LONDON, was prosecuted, pilloried, and jailed for two years; three of her prostitutes, however, were hanged.

In the early 18th century, the activities of the ordinary prostitute were tolerated and often poeticized. PORNOGRAPHY, too, was a burgeoning industry. The sex trade was inevitable in a Europe that withheld economic independence from women, and it was one of the few arenas in which women could be self-supporting. Some madams became rich. A famous example is the English madam Mrs. Hayes. One of her staple entertainments was the reconstruction of the "Feast of Venus" based on the erotic story of James COOK and his crew in TAHITI. With Hayes in the role of Queen Oberea, she and her staff danced for and then copulated with the clients.

Prostitutes provided sexual services for men, married and unmarried, but they also catered to those with specific sexual tastes. Brothels often specialized in imaginative scenarios or more sensational desires such as flagellation (whipping), defloration, and lesbian and child sex. Churches, princes, and governments had attempted to regulate nonmarital sexuality for centuries, but the openness of many 18th-century activities spurred greater efforts to control prostitutes' behavior. Initially, poets, in their praise of sexuality, and bawds and pimps who described their girls to clients, represented young prostitutes as healthy, fresh, and lovely. Over time, the consequences of the profession—illegitimate children, disease, and poverty—undercut this image. The illegitimate children of prostitutes were often dependent on charity and, thus, a cause of public concern. Venereal disease, in particular syphilis, with its dire effects on health, became another cause for alarm.

European countries dealt with the problems of prostitution differently, but generally all states viewed the practice as one of fornication rather than the illicit sale of sex. In the absolutist German states, measures to punish fornication escalated in the first half of the 18th century. Increasingly, punishment involved severe penalties, from public humiliation to enforced labor, but harsh legal action proved ineffective. In the second half of the century, German states focused on women's reform rather than punishment. Debate about reform centered on the social causes of and psychological motivation for sexual immorality.

Two of the major cities of the ENLIGHTENMENT, PARIS and LONDON, tended to accommodate prostitution in the early part of the 18th century. Prostitutes advertised their services on cards, which were distributed throughout the cities. But as the idealized image of the mother flourished in the age of SENSIBILITY and concerns for the health of the family overcame the spirit of sexual experimentation, the prostitute was subject to vilification, represented in public discourse—newspapers, pamphlets, and fictions—as dissolute, filthy, and diseased. FRANCE began to repress prostitutes by marginalizing them. The authorities forced them to take cures for syphilis at special hospitals, such as the Sâlpiètre, and incarcerated women in reformatories, known as Magdalene Homes, where they were forced to labor in women's traditional roles, dress modestly, and pray. By the eve of the FRENCH REVOLUTION (1789), the sex trade in France was officially banned.

There were parallel developments in ENGLAND, although venereal disease was not, at first, central to the repression of the sex trade. Indeed, it was clear that many people—infants and wives—were often infected with syphilis through no fault of their own. After the accession of William (1689), English men and women had been free to engage in prostitution and to make use of prostitutes. James BOSWELL, friend and biographer of Samuel JOHNSON, recounts numerous encounters with prostitutes in London.

But by midcentury, several institutions for curbing prostitution or coping with its consequences came into being. The London Foundling Hospital (like its parallel in Paris) nurtured abandoned infants. The mothers of many of these foundlings were prostitutes, and their redemption became a focus of charity. Dr. William Dodd founded the Magdalen Hospital (1758) for this purpose. At about the same time, Parliament passed the Disorderly Houses Act to restrict the sex trade carried out in taverns and brothels. Mary WOLLSTONECRAFT realized that social injustice forced women into prostitution and demanded redress of the cause rather than praise of the Magdalen ethos, but her observations generated no change in official policy, and the problem remained the province of private charities.

A novel institution was the Lock Hospital, founded in 1747 to treat syphilitics. Additional wards created in 1755 and 1766 permitted discrimination among the patients, and women perceived as culpable in their contraction of the disease were separated from the "innocents." A charitable institution, the hospital was supported by luminaries such as David GARRICK and George Frederick HANDEL. Garrick's widow also contributed to the Lock Asylum for Women, a separate institution established by William WILBERFORCE (1787) with the specific purpose of reclaiming prostitutes for ordinary life. Like the French institutions, the Lock Asylum was restrictive and pious, and the women classed by the religious term of "penitents." Its success rate in preventing recidivism was remarkably small, but it continued its mission as a Christian charity quite separate from the Lock Hospital.

The reformation of prostitutes in England arose in part as a health concern, but primarily to safeguard public morals. Led by Wilberforce, Charles Middleton (Wilberforce's mentor in the abolition of SLAVERY) and Hannah MORE, these moralists curbed the freedom of prostitutes but did not prevent the inequities that fostered the sex trade. On the whole, prostitutes were subjects of sympathy as well as objects of degradation. William HOGARTH created a series of engravings entitled *A Harlot's Progress* (1731) to memorialize the history of a prostitute from her innocent arrival in London to her early death from venereal disease. Moralistic but compassionate to the victim, Hogarth reveals the ambiguity underlying England's response to prostitutes.

In the latter part of the 18th century, France, Germany, and England all turned their attention to mitigating the social and medical problems that attended prostitution rather than punishing the offenders. Sympathy and charity aimed at reformation and rehabilitation, but success was limited because the social inequities that drove women into the sex trade were not remedied.

Further reading: Tony Henderson, *Disorderly Women in 18th-Century London* (New York: Longman, 1999); Nickie Roberts, *The Whore in History: Prostitution in Western Society* (London: Harper Collins, 1992).

Protestantism   One of the three major divisions of the religion of Christianity. The other two divisions are ROMAN CATHOLICISM and Eastern Orthodoxy. Each major division has distinct subdivisions. The term *Protestantism* stems from the verb *to protest*. Thus Protestants are those who challenged the dogma and practices of the Catholic Church in ROME. The term was used especially in ENGLAND to identify non-Catholic Christians.

Protestantism developed in the 16th century in response to the intellectual influence of Renaissance humanism and to perceived needs for structural, theological and ritual reforms in the western European Christian church, which was centered in Rome. The movement for church reform also contained strong social and political undercurrents and served as a creative but unsettling force within Europe. By the arrival of the 18th century in Europe, Protestantism had developed many branches. These included the ANGLICANS, as members of the official Church of England were called; the Presbyterians, Puritans, and a host of splinter sects sometimes collectively called DISSENTERS; the HUGUENOTS, followers of CALVINISM; another Calvinist sect called the Dutch Reformed Church; LUTHERANISM; PIETISM; the MORAVIAN BRETHREN; and Anabaptism.

The 16th-century Protestant movement is called the Reformation, or the Protestant Reformation. Its counterpart within the Roman Catholic church is called the Counter-Reformation or the Catholic Reformation. The Protestant Reformation was initiated by Martin Luther in 1517, and ultimately produced an irreparable split within Western Christendom. Luther's actions were soon complemented by those of John Calvin and Ulrich Zwingli. The Christian church in Rome, headed by the pope, attempted to threaten and cajole these reformers to drop their new ideas. A church council, the great Council of Trent (1545–63), met to try to resolve the disputes about THEOLOGY and church organization. In the end, no accord could be reached. The council defined beliefs and practices for those who remained loyal to the Roman Catholic Church, but the new Protestant sects went their independent ways.

This split in the Christian church had momentous effect on the political, social, and economic structure of Europe. Wars broke out between Catholics and Protestants in FRANCE (Wars of Religion, 1560–98), the HOLY ROMAN EMPIRE (Thirty Years' War, 1618–48), and ENGLAND (Civil War, 1642–48). European states had to grapple with the thorny issue of TOLERATION of people with variant views of Christianity. Traditional Christian practices had treated all nonconforming Christians as heretics and had tried to discourage splinter groups from forming within Christianity's ranks. But Protestantism could not be extinguished, and the question of toleration was much more difficult since the various groups not only claimed to represent true Christianity but also established enduring political bases of power. This fact, for example, greatly complicated the French Wars of Religion, because Huguenot princes were not only defending their religion but also competing with Catholic kings and nobility for political control of French territories.

Sixteenth-century states arrived at temporary solutions to the problems raised by the emergence of Protestantism. The Edict of Nantes (1598), for example, granted limited toleration to the Huguenots in France. This edict, however, was gradually abrogated and finally rescinded in 1685 by LOUIS XIV (revocation of the Edict of Nantes) and France returned officially to intolerance. The Peace of Augsburg (1555) in the Holy Roman Empire established the principal of *cujus regio euis religio* (whose the region, his the religion). According to this principle, each prince or other sovereign ruler within a territory of the Holy Roman Empire could determine the religion of his subjects. As a result, certain states became Lutheran and still others remained Catholic. Calvinism and other Protestant sects were officially forbidden, but within certain states, a de facto toleration was practiced. By the 18th century, the religious map in the Holy Roman Empire showed a predominantly Catholic south in Bavaria, AUSTRIA, and the great sovereign ecclesiastical territories such as Mainz, Trier, Cologne, Würzburg, and Bamberg; a predominantly Lutheran north consisting of PRUSSIA (although its kings were Calvinists), Braunschweig-Lüneburg, and Saxony (although its rulers became Catholic to gain access to the throne of POLAND); and pockets of Calvinism in the Rhineland Palatinate, Hesse-Kassel, and Nassau.

As a social phenomenon, Protestantism had particularly strong roots in the emerging middle classes: the merchants, businessmen, tradesmen, and craftsmen of Europe. It helped to encourage the spread of LITERACY as a result of its emphasis on having people consult directly with the Holy Bible rather than relying on a priest for their religious understanding. Protestantism contained potentially radical implications in its suggestion that all men are equally capable of understanding the scriptures.

The early Protestant religious leaders, especially Calvin and Luther, were humanist scholars. They believed that the truth of Christianity is best determined by going directly to its source, the Bible. They opposed the Catholic practice of continually creating new dogma in response to new issues. Innovation was something to be avoided at all costs. Their aim was, instead, to return the church to its early pristine state, to recover the ancient church, which, according to their view, had degenerated over the course of the centuries. Protestant scholars began studying the Bible and associated works from antiquity, and Catholic scholars followed their lead. By the late 17th century, scholarly approaches to the study of Christianity were helping to create innovations in the discipline of HISTORY and had produced a new field called BIBLICAL CRITICISM.

A religious map of 18th-century Europe would appear as follows: Catholicism dominated in the south and west in SPAIN, PORTUGAL, France, ITALY, Austria, Croatia, the southern Holy Roman Empire, and Poland while

Lutheranism dominated the north in SWEDEN, DENMARK, Norway, and the northern Holy Roman Empire. Calvinism ruled in the United Provinces of the Netherlands, GENEVA, and certain western territories of the Holy Roman Empire. It also maintained a strong footing in England and enjoyed protection in Prussia. Other Protestant groups existed in SWITZERLAND and Bohemia, while Russia and much of the Slavic world followed various branches of Eastern Orthodox Christianity.

At the beginning of the 18th century, the issues raised by Protestantism, particularly those of toleration and church-state relations, remained problematic. In the course of the century, persecution slowly died out, and the principle of religious toleration developed a sound base. Nevertheless, church-state relations continued to be a source of tension as Protestant lands grappled with questions about the proper boundaries of state action.

See also RELIGION.

Further reading: E. Gordon Rupp, *Religion in England, 1688–1791* (Oxford: Clarendon Press, 1986).

Prussia One of the regions of the HOLY ROMAN EMPIRE, whose rulers, the Hohenzollerns of BRANDENBURG, made their capital in BERLIN. Most of Prussian territory lay in the northeastern region of the European continent, bordering the Baltic Sea and extending south to the electorate of Saxony and the HAPSBURG EMPIRE. During the 18th century, the Hohenzollern princes of Prussia turned their principality into a kingdom and instituted the military practices and structures that became its hallmark. Under the aegis of FREDERICK II (THE GREAT), who ruled 1740–86, the kingdom emerged as a major European power and eventually forced the realignment of Europe known as the DIPLOMATIC REVOLUTION of 1756. The estimated population grew from 3,617,000 in 1763, to 5,015,000 in 1780.

The term *Prussia* must be carefully interpreted when encountered in 18th-century writings or in histories of that period. In legal political language, the term referred only to the territory of East Prussia, which lay on the Baltic Sea and had its capital in Königsberg. To 18th-century officials and administrators, the term still carried that meaning. To European diplomats, however, Prussia also often referred to the geographically dispersed conglomerate of territories whose rulers were the Brandenburg branch of the Hohenzollern family. It is this meaning that will always be employed in the present volume. This "larger" Prussia consisted of the territories of Brandenburg, East Prussia, Silesia (after 1742), Pomerania, Magdeburg, West Prussia (after 1772), Halberstadt, Minden, Mark, and Ravensberg. It was actually a dynastic construction, like most 18th-century European states, owing its existence to the fact that all its territories belonged by inheritance to the Hohenzollern rulers. The king of Prussia ruled in Brandenburg as the elector; in Pomerania, Magdeburg, and Clèves, as the duke; in Mark

and Ravensberg, as the count; and in Halberstadt and Minden, as the prince. Within each territory, laws and privileges differed according to historical traditions. The business of unifying this conglomerate by establishing centralized control and universal laws preoccupied the great 18th-century Prussian kings, Frederick William I and his son, Frederick the Great.

Prussian rulers claimed absolute power, and the reign of Frederick the Great stands as an outstanding example of enlightened despotism (see DESPOTISM, ENLIGHTENED) in the 18th century. Certainly, the Prussian kings succeeded in exercising power as thoroughly as any ruler of a major 18th-century state. Part of their success derived from the solution they found to the problem of aristocratic opposition. This solution, the famous marriage between crown and nobility, recast state structures to align the interests of the nobility with those of the powerful central state. Although it set Prussia apart from western European states like FRANCE, eastern European states such as Russia and the Hapsburg empire possessed similar structures.

Throughout the 18th century, Prussia remained a largely agrarian state dominated by the nobility. In the few cities of the kingdom, trade, industry, and cultural pursuits received official encouragement. Except in Berlin, however, such middle-class pursuits did not provide the social status that was associated with military service and land holding. Nevertheless, by obtaining a position in the state BUREAUCRACY, a son of the middle class could move upward into the higher ranks of society. At the bottom of the social scale, peasants labored under the onerous strictures of SERFDOM. During the upheavals of the Napoleonic era, the enlightened Prussian minister Baron Karl von Stein succeeded in promulgating an edict abolishing serfdom. But the institution returned with the restoration of the old social order after 1816. Serfdom remained in force in Prussia until 1848, when it was permanently abolished.

As the preceding sketch illustrates, the political regime in Prussia rested on a social order rooted in privilege. Although the monarchs of this land were among the strongest and most absolute in Europe, they were neither able nor willing to alter this structure. In fact, their political power depended to a large extent upon the maintenance of a hierarchical social order based on privilege.

See also DYNASTIC STATES and, for comparison, ANCIEN RÉGIME.

psychology A discipline that attempts to explain both the workings of the human mind and the manner in which mind affects individual behavior. During the ENLIGHTENMENT, the study of psychology underwent dramatic and important conceptual developments. As the era began, the study of the operations of the mind belonged to various sub-disciplines of PHILOSOPHY such as EPISTEMOLOGY and ontology. Human behavior remained largely the concern of RELIGION or of MORAL PHILOSOPHY; and deviant behavior, even severe mental illness, was treated as a sign of moral and spiritual inadequacy. As the 18th century progressed, the philosophical study of the mind began to be complemented and, indeed supplanted in many cases, by psychological and physiological inquiries into the nature of mind-body relations. Eventually psychology replaced epistemology as the chief discipline concerned with questions about human knowledge and mental operations, while disturbances in mental function became the concern of MEDICINE. These shifts are of central importance if one is to understand the substance of the various 18th-century psychological theories, particularly those that developed in ENGLAND, SCOTLAND, and FRANCE.

One of the fundamental aspects of the thought of the Enlightenment arose from the philosophical problems that were posed by systematic RATIONALISM in the 17th century. What, it was queried, were the limits of the human mind, what were its relations to the external world, what was the nature of its understanding and knowledge? During the 18th century, however, deductive logical treatments of these questions were abandoned in favor of empirical theories about mind-body relations. Epistemology and psychology became heavily intertwined. Knowledge of 18th-century psychology is, therefore, fundamental to any understanding of the philosophy of the Enlightenment.

Seventeenth-century rationalism had developed two distinct forms in the systems of René DESCARTES and Gottfried Wilhelm LEIBNIZ. In general, rationalism had proposed that a specific form of logic associated with the human ability to REASON underlies the structure of the entire universe. Furthermore, it had proposed that human reason is capable of accurately discerning this structure and that the application or exercise of reason in all arenas of existence could bring order and satisfaction. Beyond these general positions, there existed more disagreement than agreement.

Cartesian positions were enormously influential during the last half of the 17th century and eventually helped to stimulate rival theories in England and France such as the psychological EMPIRICISM outlined by John LOCKE. Leibnizian ideas informed the psychological philosophy of the AUFKLÄRUNG (German Enlightenment) in central Europe, where they were developed and extended as often as rejected.

The differences between the two basic forms of enlightened 18th-century psychology—the French/British and the German—lay largely in their radically opposed basic conceptualizations of the manner in which the mind relates to the world. British/French empiricists, drawing on Locke, viewed the mind as a primarily passive entity that simply recorded impressions from external reality and from its internal operations. They developed a general form of psychology called empiricism that concentrated on

breaking down (analyzing) ideas into their elemental components. These elements were the simple ideas derived from sensory experience. Complex ideas were created by the orderly addition of two or more simple ideas. The mind contributed nothing creative to this process, which was conceived in simple mechanical terms.

During the Enlightenment, British/French empiricism inspired several new forms of psychology: the association psychology of David HARTLEY, the subjective psychology of David HUME; the subjective idealism of George BERKELEY; the sensation psychology of Abbé CONDILLAC; the MATERIALISM of Julien Offray de LA METTRIE, Denis DIDEROT, Pierre CABANIS, and Claude-Adrien HELVÉTIUS; and the pleasure-pain psychology of La Mettrie, Helvétius, and many other 18th-century thinkers.

Psychologists following the Leibnizian system adopted an entirely different view of the mind based on Leibniz's concept of the monad. According to this approach, the mind was active as it perceived the world. Ideas were formed in a creative synthesis of simple sensation and perception. In other words, as an idea was created, the mind made something new that extended beyond the mere summation of the elemental parts. At the heart of this psychology lay an interest in the concept of RELATIONS, a notion whose definition became a central concern for both psychologists and philosophers. Concurrently, interest focused on describing the various modes by which the mind operated. Reason, if still central to German psychology, was recognized as only one mode, associated with a specific form of logic. Other modes such as INTUITION AND IMAGINATION were also explored. This perspective of German psychological philosophy contributed to the concurrent development of new fields of philosophical inquiry such as AESTHETICS.

In the second half of the 18th century, German theory began to focus more specifically on the function of the faculty of judgment as the mechanism by which the mind transcends its fragmentary bits of knowledge to create a unity. German scholars avidly read the writers of the Scottish school of common sense psychology, especially Thomas REID and Adam FERGUSON. They also read Hume, whose work Reid was attempting to criticize, and Edmund BURKE, whose aesthetic theories were rooted in common sense psychology.

Immanuel KANT, the most profound and significant of the enlightened German philosophers who addressed psychology, formulated a creative synthesis, a form of idealism, out of materials drawn from both the British/French and German lines of development. On the one hand, Kant's philosophy offered a summation of the thought of the Enlightenment, and on the other hand, it spelled out the parameters of much subsequent debate. Enlightened German psychology is commonly called functional psychology and contains within its boundaries the field of faculty psychology. Major contributors to German psychology of the 18th century were Christian WOLFF, Johannes Nikolaus Tetens, Moses MENDELSSOHN, and, of course, Immanuel Kant.

If the psychology of the Enlightenment can be organized according to national or cultural schools, it can also be ordered according to its central investigative questions. Five major themes appeared over the long course of the enlightenment: the nature of reason and the manner by which it is acquired and exercised; the question of whether or not mind and body are distinct; the laws that govern mind and body interactions; the relationships between sensation (nervous system function) and perception (mind function), between the subjective world of thought or sensory experience and the objective, outer world of matter; and the mechanisms whereby mind controls behavior.

Each of these themes had been addressed by the outstanding philosophers of the 17th century: Descartes, Benedict de SPINOZA, Leibniz, and Locke. From their writings, several basic positions emerged, the relative truth of which was the subject of debate and development throughout the Enlightenment.

On the first theme, that of the nature of reason and the manner of its acquisition, debate centered on whether reason is innate (inborn) or acquired through experience. Descartes believed in innate ideas, exemplified by the famous dictum *cogito ergo sum*. Descartes's position provided a major foundation for rationalism. Locke, on the other extreme, claimed that all ideas develop from our sensory experience of the world. His position supplied the foundations for psychological empiricism.

The second theme, the nature of the mind and body relationship, produced debate over three obvious possibilities: Mind and body are distinct (dualism); everything is mind (idealism); everything is matter (MATERIALISM). Of the 17th-century philosophers, Descartes, Leibniz, and Locke believed in dualism. Hartley was a genuine dualist; but gradually, members of the British/French school evaded the question by implicitly or explicitly treating the brain as the seat of the mind. As the Enlightenment progressed, a radical materialism developed in association with medicine and acquired great significance in France. La Mettrie, Helvétius, and Cabanis were the primary proponents of this school. Finally, toward the end of the Enlightenment, a position called idealism began to emerge that made ideas and subjective knowledge the fundamental truth. This position became especially prominent in 19th-century German philosophy. Spinoza, it should be noted, adopted a unique view, now called monism, which posited that mind and matter are simply different manifestations or expressions of a single thing.

With Spinoza's monism, we move to the third theme of enlightened psychological debate: the question of the laws that govern mind and body interaction. Thinkers who accepted the idea of a distinction between mind and body, discussed four general modes of relation. First, Descartes tended to believe that a physical point exists in the brain (the pineal gland) where linkage between mind and body occurred. Many empiricists continued to accept variations of this idea without specifying the precise location of the interaction. Second, Leibniz insisted that no linkage exists: Mind and body operate independently, but in a preestablished set of harmonious relations governed by parallel sets of laws (psychological parallelism). Third, Spinoza's monism assumed that the relationship is not a problem because mind and body are actually different manifestations of an identity operating according to its laws. Fourth, the theorists of medical VITALISM suggested that mind exists in all parts of living bodies, but that mind is nevertheless distinct from the material body. In this formulation, mind and matter interact in a set of harmonious, reciprocal relations.

Most enlightened psychologists adopted some form of psychological parallelism in their theories. However, the materialists and those psychologists with strongly physiological or medical orientations tended to search for a physical location of mind, usually somewhere in the brain. Some simply made the brain the seat of mind.

A fourth theme, that of the relationship between sensation and perception, generated positions along a continuum ranging between two extremes. One extreme, associated with empiricism, posited that perceptions are exact copies of sensations and that complex ideas are mere sums of simple ones. This position was supported by theories of nervous system function arising from Cartesian forms of MECHANICAL PHILOSOPHY. Locke and Condillac both adhered to this position. The opposite extreme within empiricism posited that no guarantee of the accuracy of perceptions exists. This theory was associated with the SKEPTICISM of David Hume and with the subjective idealism of George Berkeley. A third position, that of the Leibnizians, proposed that perception is built from sensation, but that perception actively adds something new to sensations as it creates ideas: Ideas are greater than the sum of their parts.

Rather than focusing on relations between various internal aspects of individual functioning, some psychologists addressed the question of the relation between the individual and the external world in which he or she lives: How, it was asked, do individual subjective perceptions reflect the actual objective world outside us. A continuum of answers, defined by the same extremes that defined discussion of sensation and perception also shaped approaches to the question of relations between the external, objective world and internal, subjective existence. Nearly every psychologist and epistemological philosopher of the Enlightenment addressed this question as it was fundamental to belief in the powers of human reason as a tool for knowing and controlling the world.

Finally, the fifth theme, that of the mechanisms whereby mind controls behavior, helped to generate radical changes in the treatment of serious mental disturbance and other deviant behavior. Mental disturbance began to be treated as a disease of the mind, and the insane were moved from prisons and workhouses into new mental hospitals and clinics. In France, Philippe Pinel contributed significantly to this change, while in Germany, Johann Christian REIL developed similar approaches. It is important to note that this shift in focus grew not only from changes in psychological theories, but also from the general emphasis during the Enlightenment on humanitarian approaches to social problems, on moral philosophy, and on the development of a general SCIENCE OF MAN. Furthermore, the shift was aided by strong criticisms of established Christian doctrines such as sin, and by the associated weakening of the control of the church over individual behavior.

Psychology was a key discipline for the Enlightenment, even though it did not exist as a separately defined profession. It provided foundations for philosophy, moral philosophy, and the social sciences. In addition, it provided a secular basis for understanding the relationships between human knowledge and the world. Thus, psychology provided the theoretical basis for challenging the authority of THEOLOGY and acted as a persuasive substitute for theological and religious explanations of human action.

See also WOMEN AND THE ENLIGHTENMENT.

Further reading: Edwin G. Boring, *A History of Experimental Psychology,* 2nd ed. (Englewood Cliffs, N.J.: Prentice-Hall, 1957); John Bricke, *Mind and Morality: An Examination of Hume's Moral Psychology* (New York: Oxford University Press, 1996); Patricia Kitcher, *Kant's Transcendental Psychology* (New York: Oxford University Press, 1993).

public health The physical welfare of the people of a state. Widespread disease and lack of hygiene brought the issue of public health to the forefront in the 18th century. Smallpox, influenza, tuberculosis, and typhoid fever were all on the rise in early 18th-century Europe. In addition, colonization had increased the spread of diseases between Europe and the colonies in America, Asia, and Africa.

The movement of more people from the countryside to the cities to work in factories increased the spread of disease. Generally poor sanitation, such as the lack of paved streets, trash disposal, bathrooms, bathing, and affordable medicine for the poor all contributed to the problem. The need for improved public health became more apparent.

Reform and Advances

ENGLAND is usually credited as having started the movement for public health by improving hospitals and general health care. In 1789, John Howard, the sheriff of Bedford prison, and Jeremy BENTHAM, among others, made recommendations for prison and hospital reforms in nutrition and sanitation, as well as for the establishment of a health ministry to promote public sanitation.

Advances were made in England in INOCULATION as well. Edward JENNER performed successful vaccinations for smallpox in the 1790s. Inoculation was then used in other parts of Europe and the American colonies. In ITALY, Luigi Sacco, a doctor, was one of inoculation's foremost supporters.

Calls for reform in England usually did not come from those in government or from the Royal College of Physicians. Reformers were usually from local communities, educated in Scottish UNIVERSITIES, and were often also religious dissenters. Army and navy doctors also played an important role in obtaining better health for their soldiers.

Change in the English hospital system began in the 1720s. Earlier, only the wealthy could afford private hospitals. Therefore, charitable voluntary associations began to build hospitals for the poor. Doctors used these hospitals as sites for training and teaching. Army and navy doctors also played an important role in calling for reforms in health care for both civilian and military patients.

Other currents in the ENLIGHTENMENT influenced the spread of public health reform and legislation. Increased incomes for the middle and lower classes meant more people could afford professional medical care. Likewise, the expansion of colleges and guilds of surgeons and physicians made their services more readily available. The presence of such colleges also increased the number of doctors and access to medical training. Advances in chemistry and interest in scientific principles led the way for advances in the production of medicines. The spread of university education also led to improved health as more students were informed of the causes of and preventative measures for disease. Additionally, the increase of commerce and university education increased the supply of traveling doctors and medical services.

The Birth of Public Health Systems

It was Johann Frank, a physician in VIENNA, who in 1780 advanced an actual government health system. Frank promoted the idea that public health is the duty of the state. His collection of works, *System einer vollständigen medicinischen Polizey* (System for a complete state medical policy; 1779–1819) outlined a plan for keeping a population healthy from birth to death. Some of his suggestions for reform included improved safety standards in the workplace and in schools. A system of *Medizinpolizei* (medical policing), which included state-enforced medical education and sanitation standards, was begun. In the 1790s, the German physicist

Scene from a public hospital in Middlesex, England. Widespread disease and lack of hygiene brought the issue of public health to the forefront in the 18th century. England is usually credited with having started the movement for public health by improving its hospitals and general health care. *(Courtesy New York Public Library)*

Count von RUMFORD also campaigned vigorously for improved hygiene for the working poor. Making the connection between disease and poor diet, he initiated the first soup kitchens as a nutritious and low-cost way to feed the poor.

It was not until the 19th century that health systems were implemented elsewhere in Europe. Britain did not begin its public health administration until 1848. FRANCE's Council on Public Hygiene was not established until 1802.

Public Health Legislation

Although ITALY was first to establish laws to prevent the spread of tuberculosis in the 1730s, legislation regarding public health was not widespread. Sanitation laws did not exist in the 18th century in any European country. However, by the 19th century this had changed due to the reforms that began in the late 18th century. Edwin Chadwick, an advocate of utilitarianism and follower of Bentham, had a great impact on the development of public health laws. In the 1830s, Chadwick was part of the commission for the implementation of the New Poor Law. Led by Chadwick, the commission studied how diseases were spread and what could be done to prevent this. His study, *General Report on the Sanitary Condition of the Labouring Population of Great Britain* (1842), set the standard for all health care studies that followed.

The report focused on factors that caused disease and pointed to the connection between poverty and the spread of disease. Chadwick's recommendations to the British government included garbage disposal, ventilation standards for workplaces, a sewer system, increased and cleaner water supplies, and paved roads.

Chadwick's report also had an impact in America, where Lemuel Shattuck, a former teacher and member of the Senate, undertook his own report. In *Report of a General Plan for the Promotion of Public and Personal Health* (1850), he outlined an ideal public health plan and 50 general recommendations for the state of Massachusetts, of which the proposals for improved sewer and water systems were adopted. Although not all their suggestions were implemented, Shattuck's and Chadwick's reports were the model for future public health policy proposals. As a result, public health at all levels of society began to improve.

Further reading: Roy Porter, ed., *The Cambridge Illustrated History of Medicine.* (New York: Cambridge University Press, 2000).

publishing A general term referring to the business of printing and disseminating books, pamphlets, periodical magazines, newspapers, advertisements, playbills, and the like. Publication in all categories expanded dramatically in Europe during the ENLIGHTENMENT, especially in ENGLAND, where innovations in the development of native type founding (the manufacture of type characters) and paper making enabled the English book trade to compete with Continental rivals—predominantly GERMANY, ITALY, and FRANCE—which had been operating successfully since the 15th century.

Throughout Europe, the system of publishing and bookselling, the methods of printing, the workers' jobs, and the influence of craft guilds were essentially the same. The publisher financed production and generally held perpetual copyright in the text (with rare exceptions; an author's right to copyright was a later development); a printer provided the machinery and workers skilled in setting type and operating the press to produce the material book; and a wholesale distributor ensured that retail booksellers acquired copies. The guilds associated with printing and publication were established primarily in the 16th century: VENICE in 1548, LONDON in 1557, and PARIS about 1570. Guilds controlled employment and frequently cooperated with the government in matters of CENSORSHIP. In France, the Paris Book Guild incorporated by the Crown in the 17th century monopolized the legal trade in books and was responsible for the production and distribution of all materials printed in Paris. However, the most restrictive guild was the Stationers' Company of London, whose decline at the turn of the 18th century was instrumental in England's rise as an international venue for publication.

The press was essential for the flow of information among enlightened intellectuals. They believed that human PROGRESS rested on the acquisition of knowledge. PHILOSOPHES assumed that the free exchange of ideas would aid this process. People reading about and subsequently discussing ideas in a public forum might evaluate those ideas critically and use them as guides for action.

New authors depended on contacts in the publishing or periodical magazine trades to enter the market. The *public sphere* is a term coined by the modern German historian Jürgen Habermas to characterize 18th-century society's reliance on printed works for the formation of public opinion and social action. The rise of the public sphere was essential for advertising the array of works available to literate readers: Many 18th-century books contained advertisements listing titles by the same publisher or author. The collected works of well-known writers were often published with a biography of the author, yet another form of advertising for the purpose of increasing sales. Periodicals routinely printed critiques of various works and plays. By these means, works were publicized and marketed. The proliferation of periodical works that included fiction, poetry, history, letters, and news items also provided new opportunities for writers, male and female, to get into print and establish a reputation. Subscription sales (by which the consumers con-

"Louis XVI and Malesherbes." King Louis XVI appointed ministers of state who were dedicated to the principle of introducing rational, enlightened reforms from above. Among them, Chrétien-Guillaume de Lamoignon de Malesherbes was outstanding as a protector of the philosophes and an advocate of freedom of the press. *(Courtesy New York Public Library)*

tributed to the cost of printing) and the serialization of longer works were standard 18th-century practices for offsetting the overall costs of book production.

Lower book prices encouraged purchases and, equally, encouraged the spread of LITERACY. Literacy rates improved dramatically during the 18th century. It is impossible to give precise figures: Literacy has usually been acknowledged to be the ability to sign one's name. However, many people who could not write could, in fact, read. Nevertheless, the only figures available are for signing. In England, the number of men who could sign their names in the 1640s was about 30 percent of the population; in the 1750s, the figure rose to 60 percent for men and about 35 to 40 percent for women. In SCOTLAND, the figure for men rose from 25 percent in the 1640s to 65 percent in the 1750s. German figures vary according to region: in eastern PRUSSIA, only 10 percent of adult men were literate in the 1750s, but in the Duchy of Oldenburg, the figure was 80 percent for men and 46 percent for women. In France, literacy was higher in more densely populated regions, but Provence showed no significant increase in the literacy rate between 1690 and 1740. Overall, European literacy was highest in northern France, western Germany, the UNITED PROVINCES OF THE NETHERLANDS, and Britain, especially in Protestant regions where reading the Bible was encouraged. The number of people who could read, and read at a level that would engender interest in books other than the Bible or religious and moral tracts, depended largely on the availability of schools for boys and girls. By 1819 in Britain, more than 850,000 children received regular schooling. In the 18th century, while many middle-class men and women were literate, the working class had fewer opportunities to learn and less leisure to spend on reading.

The progressive increase in literacy, especially for the lower classes and women, created a greater demand for reading materials. Books had been a luxury item, their purchase the prerogative of the elite class, but pamphlets and very small books (octavos and duodecimos) were sold cheaply. The activist Hannah MORE devoted a good part of her talent and energy to producing inexpensive moral tales for the poor. The establishment of commercial lending libraries and reading societies in the 18th century made printed materials available to the middle class and the educated poor at a small cost. Journals and newspapers (which in Britain were burdened with an expensive stamp tax) were widely available, but they circulated for free in lending libraries and coffeehouses.

Publishers existed in every state in Europe, but censorship difficulties ensured that certain regions played more significant roles than did others in the dissemination of information. Nations under Roman Catholic domination or with absolute monarchs tended to have the most severely restricted presses. Religious authority was vitally concerned with censorship. The Catholic Church kept an Index of Forbidden Books that listed condemned materials. The courts of the Inquisition, in lands where they were allowed (SPAIN, PORTUGAL, and Italy), reviewed books and judged their acceptability. In France, a similar function was carried out by the Sorbonne, the theological faculty of the University of Paris. Condemned books were often collected and publicly burned; authors, when they could be identified and caught, were subject to varying forms of prosecution. Secular authorities under absolute monarchs also exercised censorship functions. In France, for example, both the PARLEMENTS and the royal council could censor books, order book burnings, and punish offending writers. Furthermore, an elaborate system of prepublication censorship required writers and printers to secure royal permission to publish, and works were submitted to censoring authorities for preliminary review.

These controls hampered publishing, but they did not prevent the clandestine circulation of materials. Many forms of subterfuge were practiced in order to escape controls. Authors published anonymously or disguised their commentaries on current events by setting them in exotic lands. Publishers in Paris and elsewhere defied authorities by giving questionable books false imprimaturs (publisher and city information). Censors simply neglected to judge certain books, giving tacit permission for them to be published or circulated, and manuscripts circulated clandestinely.

Wholesalers' international book fairs in cities such as FRANKFURT and Leipzig traditionally facilitated the exchange and dissemination of controversial books. When all else failed, authors turned to foreign presses devoted to publishing new and provocative works. In fact, most of the books associated with the French Enlightenment were published in the United Provinces or SWITZERLAND. When persecuted for their views in their own lands, French authors protected their freedom to think by taking refuge in Switzerland, the United Provinces, England, or Prussia.

The presses that served the Enlightenment to the greatest extent were located in Protestant cities such as London, AMSTERDAM, Rotterdam, the Hague, and GENEVA. In the United Provinces, for example, it was possible to publish nearly anything so long as it did not comment on internal policies. But limits existed even in these liberal regions, as Julien Offray de LA METTRIE discovered in the 1740s. He was driven from France by the widespread condemnation of his views in *Histoire naturelle de l'âme* (Natural history of the soul; 1747), but after the Dutch publication of two more texts on materialistic and atheistic themes, even the Dutch authorities were offended, and La Mettrie was forced to flee the United Provinces.

The perceived role of the printed word in fanning discontent is obvious in the various methods of religious and governmental censorship applied throughout Europe. The FRENCH REVOLUTION brought about a tremendous explosion of printing in the form of pamphlets and short tracts on every possible subject, but even before the Revolution the French censorship system had broken down as the monarchy and church weakened, so that, in the 1780s, it was possible to print nearly anything. The question of cause and effect between the press and the fulfillment of revolutionary goals remains open. It is difficult to prove by historical methods that reading actually changed people's worldview, but the history of successful revolutions shows that revolutionary philosophy circulating among an informed public helped put radical ideas into practice. For example, Thomas JEFFERSON wrote the DECLARATION OF INDEPENDENCE based upon his wide reading of the radical political theory and heterodox (or unorthodox) theology circulating throughout Europe and North America.

The reform of copyright and intellectual property was initiated in England. The copyright law of 1709 granted authors or the purchasers of a work a specific period of ownership. This law did not significantly favor the author because his or her rights in a work generally ended as soon as the text was sold to a publisher, but it did help in the reprinting of his or her works once the copyright period had elapsed. The statute itself lapsed in 1735, and publishers once again claimed perpetual copyright. Publishers' rights to perpetual copyright were finally abolished following a 1774 lawsuit involving a Scottish bookseller who specialized in selling inexpensive reprints of the classics and a London publisher who claimed perpetual ownership of a poem by James Thomson. The decision resulted in the availability of many inexpensive classic texts by authors such as Shakespeare and Milton. Previously, copyrights had been held by publishers who published only classic works in expensive editions. Most disputes arose between publishers and booksellers rather than with authors. William BLACKSTONE set down the argument favoring authors as owners of copyright in his *Commentaries on the Laws of England* (1765–69).

The 18th century was an explosive era for the review of traditional notions about publishing and also for the sheer number of works produced. Works available to the public ran the gamut: literature, politics, philosophy, economics, local commerce, travel, artistic taste, book reviews, and even gossip. More than 1,600 novels were published in Germany from 1791 to 1800, and 735 were published in France. By 1791, some 7,000 authors lived in Germany; by 1789, France had about 3,000 authors; and Britain certainly produced comparable numbers.

Many respected authors, such as John DRYDEN, were partially supported by patrons. The commercial viability of writing during the 18th century undermined the traditional system of aristocratic patronage, both financial and occupational (although men were always at an advantage over women in securing patronage and thus a steady income). However, famous writers routinely dedicated their works to influential and wealthy patrons in the hope of reward, for the profession was treacherous. Many writers with glorious careers—Aphra BEHN, for instance—ended their lives in poverty; others with lucrative patronage positions—William CONGREVE, for instance—lived well until their deaths.

With its stock of works by philosophers, playwrights, poets, and novelists as well as periodical literature, Britain's publication output was high. Most of the minor publications—adaptations of famous plays, literary journals, and literary biographies—were produced by hack writers, but some literary journals were renowned throughout Europe. A popular periodical called THE SPECTATOR (1711–14) rose to daily print runs of 20,000 to 30,000 copies. By 1750, more than 100 journals circulated in Britain. By 1790, 16 newspapers circulated in London. By 1801, more than 16 million people throughout Britain regularly read newspapers. France had more censorship restrictions than did Britain, but nevertheless saw the publication of a *Spectator*-type journal: *Spectateur français* (French spectator; 1722). The first German weekly also emulated the *Spectator* style. By 1750, Germany published some 50 journals. Among the hundreds of journals published in Europe during this period were *The Tatler* and *The Spectator* published by Joseph ADDISON and Richard STEELE; Desfontaine's *Nouvelles littéraires* (Literary news); the *Acta Eruditorum* (Acts of learned people); the *Nouvelles de la république des lettres* (News from the republic of letters), edited by Pierre BAYLE; the *Journal helvétique* (Swiss journal); and the publications of the Société Typographique de Neuchâtel (Typographical Society of Neuchâtel). The ability to read became a vital skill during the 18th century, when the print industry provided news, debate, knowledge, and entertainment essential in the formation of the modern, self-governing individual.

See also COSMOPOLITANISM; *ENCYCLOPÉDIE*; LITERATURE; SOCIAL INSTITUTIONS OF THE ENLIGHTENMENT; WOMEN AND THE ENLIGHTENMENT.

Further reading: David Greetham, *Textual Scholarship: An Introduction* (New York: Garland, 1992); James van Horn Melton, *The Rise of the Public in Enlightenment Europe* (New York: Cambridge University Press, 2001).

Pufendorf, Samuel (1632–1694) *German philosopher of natural law and natural rights, who was also historian to the courts of Sweden (1677–88) and Prussia (1688–94)*

Pufendorf was the third of four sons of a poor Lutheran village pastor. He obtained a classical secondary school education through the generosity of a nobleman who knew his father. After secondary school (gymnasium), Pufendorf attended the University of Leipzig. He was expected to continue the family tradition of serving as a Lutheran pastor, but he soon abandoned his theological studies to pursue courses in law, philology, PHILOSOPHY, HISTORY, and mathematics. He transferred to the University of Jena, where, through the mathematician Erhard Weigel, he became familiar with CARTESIANISM and also with the works of Thomas HOBBES and Hugo Grotius (1583–1645).

Pufendorf obtained work as tutor to the Swedish minister in DENMARK (1658–60), where he served, in a manner common enough for intellectuals of the time, as a part-time spy. He was imprisoned by the Danes, then released. Subsequently, he taught at the Universities of Heidelberg (1660–68) and Lund, SWEDEN (1668–76). He became secretary of state and court historian to the Swedish court (1677–88) and finally returned to Germany to settle in BERLIN as the court historian of PRUSSIA (1688–94).

Pufendorf personally experienced 16 years of the terrible Thirty Years' War in Germany, and the intellectual problems that commanded his attention grew out of that traumatic experience. His writings on NATURAL LAW and NATURAL RIGHTS aimed at developing a system of rational, universal law that he hoped would allow subsequent generations to avoid the horrors brought on by confessional hatred and political particularism. Pufendorf especially sought to free law from links with religious orthodoxy. To this end, he developed Grotius's ideas about natural law, adding a prescriptive moral component to Grotius's concept. According to Pufendorf, the REASON that governs the universe makes clear that certain natural rights must be honored and obligations observed for the protection of human society. His famous analysis of the HOLY ROMAN EMPIRE, *De statu imperii Germanici* (On the constitution of the Holy Roman Empire), published under the pseudonym Severinus de Mozambano (1667), argued powerfully for German unity. Using Aristotelian political categories, Pufendorf demonstrated that the Holy Roman Empire was inviable, a political monstrosity. Banned in the Holy Roman Empire, this book was nevertheless published elsewhere in Europe. Pufendorf's histories of the Swedish and Prussian monarchies were apologetic, partisan presentations, which merely chronicled events rather than offering the insightful analysis of *De statu imperii Germanici*.

In addition to *De statu imperii Germanici*, Pufendorf wrote *Elementa jurisprudentiae universalis* (Elements of universal jurisprudence; 1660), *De jure naturae et gentium* (On natural and human law; 1672), and the separately published introduction to the latter work, *De officio hominis et civis juxta legem naturalem* (On the duty of man and the citizen according to natural law; 1673). These works were translated into every major European languages in the 18th and 19th centuries. They were one major source for the ENLIGHTENMENT of ideas about natural law and natural rights.

See also MATHEMATICS AND MECHANICS.

pyrrhonism   Form   of   philosophical   SKEPTICISM. Pyrrhonism assumed a central role in European philosophy toward the end of the 16th century and shaped the skepticism of the 17th and 18th centuries. Consequently, it played some role in determining the solutions to epistemological dilemmas that were proposed by writers of those two centuries.

Pyrrhonism is one of two forms of skepticism that developed in ancient Greek philosophy. Both forms deal with the nature and limits of human knowledge. Both posit that philosophic certainty, that is, knowledge whose truth value is unquestionable, lies beyond the grasp of the human mind. Pyrrhonist skepticism states that, in the face of overwhelming uncertainty about the validity of human knowledge, judgment should be suspended. A true pyrrhonist would, for example, try to avoid making any statement—positive or negative—about the truth value of some position. He or she would try to maintain an inquisitive but uncommitted stance. Academic skepticism, the second form, shares the general attitude of pyrrhonism. But it is willing to make one positive statement about human knowledge, that one and only one thing can be known, namely: We cannot know anything with certainty. A pyrrhonist would hesitate even to say that with conviction.

Ancient Greek philosophical skepticism, in both its forms, was rediscovered by European intellectuals during the Renaissance. Pyrrhonism was known only through some manuscript fragments ascribed to Sextus Empiricus. According to these fragments, pyrrhonism was founded by the legendary philosopher Pyrrho of Eli (ca. 360–275 B.C.). Pyrrho's student, Timon of Philius (ca. 320–230 B.C.), contributed to the new set of ideas, and the first theoretical formulation of pyrrhonism was allegedly developed by Aenesidemus (ca. 100–40 B.C.).

As revived by 16th-century scholars, pyrrhonism actually aimed at creating a set of mental practices or attitudes that involved continual questioning and suspension of judgment. This set of mental habits appeared in two influential works, the *Apologie de Raimond Sebond* (Apology for Raimond Sebond) by Michel Eyquem de Montaigne (1533–92) and *La sagesse* (Knowledge) by Montaigne's friend and disciple Pierre Charron (1541–1603), both of which applied pyrrhonist attitudes to questions about RELIGION and tradition.

In the 17th century, the inspiration of pyrrhonist skepticism helped to feed the development of a general spirit of criticism and continued to provide a philosophical framework for critics of religious dogmatism. Benedict de SPINOZA was the greatest 17th-century systematic philosopher to apply skepticism to religious questions. But he actually tried to avoid skepticism in matters of EPISTEMOLOGY.

The works of Pierre BAYLE, especially the *HISTORICAL AND CRITICAL DICTIONARY*, provided an early example of the rich and unsettling results that could follow from the application of a skeptical critical spirit to received knowledge. For Bayle and later for David HUME, the skeptical attitude directly fostered creative, compelling new outlooks, but for other philosophers, skepticism produced destructive results and was something to be banished.

When viewed as the enemy, skepticism provided the inspiration for 17th-century RATIONALISM. René Descartes's *Discours de la méthode* (*DISCOURSE ON METHOD*; 1637) was one of the earliest and most influential attempts to provide a rational basis for certain human knowledge. His contemporaries, Pierre GASSEND and Marin MERSENNE, developed alternative methods, which accepted some limits to human knowledge but tried to break out of the intellectual impasse caused by pervasive skepticism. Thus, the great 17th-century theories of REASON and of universal NATURAL LAW, the reliance on mathematics as a means for representing physical natural laws and on empirical observation as a means of obtaining practical knowledge were all different responses to the challenges initially provided by pyrrhonism.

During the 18th century, pyrrhonism continued to fuel criticism and to undermine belief in the certainty of reasoned systems. Pyrrhonist skepticism permeated the philosophy of David Hume, but most 18th-century philosophers abandoned the quest for certainty and simply accepted the idea that certainty could not be guaranteed in many types of human knowledge. They substituted new criteria—utilitarianism (see UTILITY) and humanitarianism, for example—for judging the validity of a set of ideas. They also developed mathematical tools such as PROBABILITY for dealing with chance and random events. They valued reason as a faculty of the human mind that yields immense practical knowledge, even if that knowledge isn't always absolutely true. PHILOSOPHES also developed the habit of observing human societies and describing them comparatively, of detailing differences and criticizing but refraining from condemning according to some allegedly true set of ideals. Furthermore, some writers developed theories about the superior knowledge obtained by exercising the faculties of INTUITION AND IMAGINATION and offered the human GENIUS as an example of humankind transcending its natural intellectual limits. Thus, the writers of the ENLIGHTENMENT created a variety of solutions to the intellectual dilemmas posed by skepticism, most of which accepted the limits of human knowledge, but nevertheless attempted to minimize the negative effects of those limits.

See also MATHEMATICS AND MECHANICS.

Q

Quakers Name given to members of the Society of Friends, a Christian group that was founded by George Fox (1624–91). The Society of Friends grew out of the Puritan movement in ENGLAND and spread to the British colonies in North America, especially after William Penn founded the colony of Pennsylvania as a haven for persecuted Quakers. The English Toleration Act of 1689 afforded them some protection, but their religious practices were better protected in Pennsylvania where religious TOLERATION was written into the colonial charter.

Quaker religious practices emphasize the inner religious experience, which is guided by the "inner light of Christ." The early Quakers possessed no formal creeds, organized clergy, or standard liturgy. Meetings were silent unless a member felt inspired to speak out to the group.

The Quaker notion of the inner light derives from the same intellectual soil that stimulated aspects of the ENLIGHTENMENT. The inner light (enlightenment) is a form of intuitive knowledge similar to that which played a great role in German enlightened theories about creative GENIUS and AESTHETICS. German PIETISM and French Quietism, two religious phenomena that appeared alongside the earliest facets of the Enlightenment, both had links with Quaker beliefs and practices.

Many Quakers were pacifists and humanitarians, committed at an early date to abolishing SLAVERY. In 1688, German Quakers in Pennsylvania declared that slavery violated Christian beliefs. In general, they were committed to reforming the established order of things and stressed the importance of EDUCATION, acting alongside RELIGION, in attaining their goals. They were instrumental in setting up many of the cultural and educational institutions in PHILADELPHIA, the "City of Brotherly Love," which was their major urban center.

Quarrel between the Ancients and the Moderns A quarrel over literary AESTHETICS that preoccupied the Parisian intellectual world between 1685 and 1694. Like many of the famous intellectual disputes of the 17th century and the 18th century, the Quarrel between the Ancients and the Moderns actually had ramifications that extended far beyond aesthetics. The basic issue with which it dealt—whether the traditions associated with CLASSICISM and hence with the Graeco-Roman foundations of Europe were superior or inferior to modern ways—aligned participants not only according to their personal allegiances to the protagonists but also to their assessments of modern civilization, its intellectual authorities, and its history. Thus, the Quarrel between the Ancients and the Moderns actually touched on themes that would remain central intellectual issues as the ENLIGHTENMENT began unfolding in the 18th century.

The protagonists of the literary quarrel were Nicolas Boileau, the champion of the Ancients, and Charles Perrault, defender of the Moderns. The party of the Ancients consisted of the supporters of the forms and rules of classicism. The Moderns, whose number included Bernard de FONTENELLE, criticized both the forms and civilization of antiquity and sought to establish new criteria for literary production. The quarrel spilled over into the salons of PARIS and was especially centered in the gatherings at the home of Madame de LAMBERT. The whole affair came to an end in 1694 when Antoine Arnauld, the leader of

French JANSENISM, effected a personal reconciliation between the two quarreling protagonists.

See also SOCIAL INSTITUTIONS OF THE ENLIGHTENMENT; TEMPLE.

Quesnay, François (1694–1774) *French surgeon, physician, and economist who founded a new school of economics whose disciples were called Physiocrats*

Although Quesnay coined the term *physiocrat,* he always preferred to call his followers *économistes* (economists). Quesnay was the son of a well-trained but impecunious lawyer, who preferred rural life to that of the city. Thus, the Quesnay family lived on a farm and derived a portion of its income and subsistence from it. Quesnay's mother introduced him as a young boy to the practices of agriculture. He retained a lifelong respect for the activity and made it the centerpiece of his economic theory.

As a youth, Quesnay read voraciously and apparently taught himself both Latin and Greek. He decided eventually to go to PARIS in order to study MEDICINE and surgery. He quickly demonstrated skill at treating wounds, a devotion to healing, and a novel way of thinking about medical problems, all of which helped him to receive an invitation to become the secretary of the new Academy of Surgery. When repeated attacks of gout interfered with his ability to do surgery, Quesnay succeeded in getting himself accepted as a doctor of medicine at the University of Pont-à-Mousson. Quesnay also provided medical services to King LOUIS XV and his troops during the 1744 campaigns and was physician to the king at Versailles. The king, who habitually called Quesnay "the thinker," rewarded him by granting him noble status.

In the midst of these professional activities, Quesnay began developing and publishing economic theories. He attracted a group of students and followers that included the marquis de MIRABEAU, who assisted Quesnay with the publication of his works, Anne-Robert-Jacques TURGOT, Jean de GOURNAY, and Paul-Pierre MERCIER DE LA RIVIÈRE. Quesnay died at the age of 80, having remained intellectually active until the end.

In all his writings, he manifested a respect for RELIGION and the monarchy. However novel his ideas, he envisioned that reform would come from within the established system. His most important works include the articles "Fermiers" and "Grains" in the ENCYCLOPÉDIE (1756–57); *Physiocratie, ou Constitution naturelle des gouvernements* (Physiocracy, or the natural constitution of governments; 1768); *Tableau économique* (Economic tableau; 1758); and an early surgical treatise, *Observations sur les effets de la saignée* (Observations on the effects of the practice of bleeding; 1730).

See also CAPITALISM.

R

race The division of humankind into categories determined by similar physical (and sometimes cultural) characteristics. The European concept of race has always been ambiguous and multilayered: At times, the word has been applied neutrally to family, positively to nationality or ethnicity, and negatively to groups considered inferior—for example, the Irish and West Africans.

Science and Philosophy

With no knowledge of the mechanisms of evolution, much less of modern genetic theory, 18th-century natural scientists and philosophers were anxious to pinpoint a scientific basis for racial difference. Categorizing difference was a pressing concern during the ENLIGHTENMENT when VOYAGES OF DISCOVERY and entrenched interests in COLONIALISM and plantation SLAVERY exposed Europeans to ever more people possessing physical traits, languages, and cultural behaviors different from their own. Responses were diverse. It is an oversimplification to think that all Europeans automatically disdained people of different cultures and colors, but the classification of the world's peoples into racial groups belonging to one species (a biological group capable of interbreeding) or into different species became a compelling scientific and philosophical goal.

This goal was significantly abetted by Carl von Linné (or LINNAEUS) of SWEDEN and Jean-Baptiste LAMARCK of FRANCE. Linnaeus published one of the first attempts to classify human races in *Systema Naturae* (The system of nature; 1735). He perceived the purpose of humankind—God's last and best created work in accordance with Genesis—to be the classification of all things in nature by species and genus (a major subdivision of species). He

divided humankind into categories distinguished by physical traits, such as color, and by moral qualities. In *Philosophie zoologique* (Zoological philosophy; 1809), Lamarck put forward the theory that the evolution of species depended on the acquisition of traits developed in response to environmental conditions acting upon the

Theories of racial differences were used to justify the import of individuals to provide agricultural labor in the colonies of European nations. *(Courtesy New York Public Library)*

individual, which traits could be passed on to succeeding generations. Before Lamarck published his evolutionary theory, this idea was implicit in much 18th-century speculation about human difference. For example, it was a commonplace (but mistaken) notion that Africans' exposure to the power of the sun in "torrid," or hot, climates caused dark skin.

Both Linnaeus and Lamarck accepted the existence of the GREAT CHAIN OF BEING, an ancient conception of the universe that celebrated diversity and continuity from the highest existence, God, to the lowest organism. Linnaeus ranked humankind on this chain in a descending order of species, from Europeans nearest to God to Africans nearest the animals. Not all natural scientists and philosophers accepted this notion of multiple human or subhuman species, even if they accepted the basic premises of the great chain of being.

The two major theories of race in the 18th century were polygenesis, which advanced the idea of separate human or subhuman species, and monogenesis, which advanced the idea of one human species marked by racial variation. Georges-Louis Leclerc, comte de BUFFON, favored monogenesis, a theory in line with Enlightenment universalism. In *Histoire Naturelle* (Natural history; 1748–1804), he posited one origin for the human species. However, he suggested that group characteristics degenerated over time from influences such as climate, food, modes of living, diseases, and social admixture, and these acquired traits passed to new generations. In Buffon's theory of race, difference was subject to change under new conditions. Thus, the negative traits that Europeans frequently applied to Africans, Native Americans, and Asians were seen as amenable to improvement, and these races were capable of cultural development equal to that of Europeans. Johann Friedrich BLUMENBACH published the influential text *De Generis humani varietate natura* (On the natural varieties of mankind) in 1775–76. Believing in the existence of only one species, he also accounted for non-European peoples as the products of natural degeneration from an ideal European stock.

Polygenesis was far less well disposed to non-Europeans. From this perspective, human difference was a fixed quality immune to change. The German anatomist Samuel Thomas Sömmerring and the German philosopher Christoph Meiners both posited the essential (or fixed) nature of race. Scottish philosophers of the 1770s also considered race an essential quality that predicted any individual's ability. Lord Kames, David HUME, and Adam FERGUSON all gave intellectual sanction to the notion that certain racial groups were incapable of PROGRESS. Hume's essay *Of National Characters* (1748, 1754, 1777) at first simply claimed the overall superiority of the English, but further revisions led to the denigration of all "the other species of men" as naturally inferior to white people, and, in the last revision (possibly a response to James Beattie's

rebuke) to the idea that Africans in particular were essentially inferior to Europeans. Hume's student James Beattie responded to the essay in *An Essay on the Nature and Immutability of Truth, in Opposition to Sophistry and Skepticism* (1770). He argued, rightly, that white nations had, in the past, been as "savage" as contemporary Africans and Native Americans.

Immanuel KANT was the first philosopher to use the word "race" to describe the typical variations derived from the common human stock. He perceived four distinct categories of human beings, each race endowed with its natural disposition and proclivity to degeneration. He selected the northern Germans as closest to an original and ideal white race. In *Beobachtungen über das Gefühl des Schönen und Erhabenen* (Observations on the feeling of the beautiful and sublime; 1764), he opined that aesthetic and moral sensibilities that permitted the appreciation of the SUBLIME declined sequentially from Germans to other European people to Africans. In various texts, he asserted several preposterous notions about African skin, including the "fact" that whippings, which broke skin and drew blood, were preferable to beatings with sticks because whippings would cause less physical damage. Kant's anti-African stance was directly challenged by Johann Gottfried von HERDER, who attempted to present an impartial evaluation of African people and their cultures. Nevertheless, the theory of racial degeneration was cited time and again to account for differences in physical appearance as well as cultural attainments. In GERMANY especially, the attribute of physical human beauty and the ability to appreciate natural beauty became significant markers of European superiority over the degenerate races.

Whether philosophers believed in the single species or multiple species theory of humankind, very few managed to present an unbiased portrait of Africans. Whether Africans were considered to have degenerated from European stock into a racial variation or to have emerged as a separate species, Africans routinely occupied the lowest niche in the ranks of humankind.

In the late 18th century, the science of comparative anatomy facilitated this unenviable ranking. Blumenbach published a work on the variation in 60 human craniums; Dutch anatomist Petrus Camper assessed the anthropological meaning of facial angles; and British anatomist Charles White, who believed in fixed differences among Europeans, Asians, Native Americans, and Africans, argued, from the continuities visible in skeletal and cranial formations, that some people were endowed with more humanity than were others, and, moreover, that Africans resembled animals more closely than did any other human groups.

Africans

Unlike geographically distant cultural groups, such as Mongolians and Australians, Africans were visible on

European streets and in many European colonies. Their proximity, along with their radical difference in appearance from white Europeans, perhaps spurred the intense 18th-century focus on their attributes. Two 18th-century encyclopedias defined the term *Negro:* the French ENCY-CLOPÉDIE (1751–72) asserted that all Africans were black and bore the same negroid features. Adopting the polygenesis perspective, Denis DIDEROT and his colleagues depicted the Negro as a "new species of mankind." The British *Encyclopaedia Britannica* (1798) was closer to the mark in its privileging of monogenesis. The article identified Negroes as a race and located them within the tropical zone of Africa rather than throughout the continent. The definition, however, emphasized typical physical features at the expense of cultural accomplishments and went on to castigate Negroes with a lengthy catalog of vices.

A salient model for the incompatibility of these 18th- and early 19th-century racial theories is provided by the Cape Khoikhoi people of South Africa, commonly termed "Hottentots," a Dutch word meaning "stutterers." The Cape Khoikhoi were a focal point in Dutch, German, French, and English conceptions of racial difference, and defined in quite contradictory ways. The Dutch at the Cape of Good Hope justified the enslavement and brutalization of the native population on the basis of their supposed inferiority, and they almost destroyed the entire population. Also, for some German philosophers, such as Gotthold LESSING and Kant, the Cape Khoikhoi epitomized the basest and ugliest type of human being. On the other hand, to the German observer Peter Kolb, who lived with the Cape Khoikhoi for two years, they showed themselves a bizarre but interesting people. The English response was also mixed, reactions ranging from gushingly positive to entirely negative from the first encounters in the early 17th century. But the term *Hottentot* came to be used as an epithet for any type of degenerate person. A sad victim of European racial science and philosophy was Sara (Sartje) Baartman (the "Hottentot Venus"), who was displayed in ENGLAND and FRANCE in the early 19th century as a physical curiosity. When she died in 1814, her body was dissected by Georges CUVIER, who thoroughly reviled her as an inferior physical type. Her remains were preserved in PARIS until 2002, when she was finally returned for burial in South Africa at the request of its government.

Slavery

The institution of African slavery held center stage in discussions about racial difference in 18th-century Europe and the New World. Thomas JEFFERSON well perceived the cancerous effects of slavery on the morality of North Americans, but (despite his long-term concubinage of his slave Sally Hemmings) he was, like Kant, entirely critical of Africans in terms of beauty and intellectual capacity. Some Englishmen in the Caribbean colonies argued, as did Richard Ligon and Bryan Edwards, that black women might be strikingly beautiful and sexually desirable, but this praise was often a form of COSMOPOLITANISM based on self-indulgence rather than a belief in racial equality. More often, European colonists denigrated slaves in order to justify their cruelties, and, in their home countries, they manipulated the public by emphasizing the threat posed to European interests by violent slave revolt. The British antislavery movement led by Granville Sharpe and taken up by William WILBERFORCE, a philanthropist and member of Parliament, made slow headway but eventually succeeded in bringing about the abolition of the slave trade in 1807 and slavery on British soil in 1833. Following the DECLARATION OF INDEPENDENCE, the Quaker state of Pennsylvania passed the first United States abolition law in 1779, but the process was so gradual that slavery did not disappear until 1847. However minimal the effects, legislation for the abolition of slavery was later enacted by the states of Connecticut, Massachusetts, New Hampshire, New Jersey, New York, and Rhode Island. During the revolutionary period, France also abolished slavery for a short time. The corollary development to this enthusiasm for abolition was the hardening of negative attitudes toward African slaves as their freedom approached and Europeans and Americans confronted their unwillingness to assimilate free blacks as equals.

Miscegenation

Despite the general reluctance to assimilate Africans into colonial and European societies, the sexual appropriation of slave women by European masters was commonplace throughout the colonial era. The English colony of Virginia established a strange precedent by outlawing marriage or cohabitation between whites and Africans or Native Americans. Interracial sexuality was initially called *amalgamation,* and only in 1863 did the term *miscegenation* (mixing) replace it. In the meantime, colonies, one by one, followed Virginia's example. Eventually, more than 40 states, at one time or another, forbade marriage or cohabitation between whites and blacks, and less frequently between whites and Native Americans and "Orientals" (Asians). These restrictions simply never existed in Europe or even in the Caribbean colonies; the prohibition on interracial marriage was a North American phenomenon. In fact, Alabama excised its antimiscegenation laws from the state constitution only in 2000, despite the 1967 Civil Rights Act that abolished such laws as discriminatory. Despite antimiscegenation laws, innumerable children were born from mixed race unions. This American legacy has produced an ever more complicated network of racial identifications. However, according to the American Anthropological Association, the continual sharing of genetic materials among human groups over the ages invalidates the notion that biologically distinct races actually exist within the human species.

See also ANTHROPOLOGY; CLASSIFICATION; *LAOKOON*; NATURAL PHILOSOPHY; SCIENCE OF MAN; TRAVEL LITERATURE.

Further reading: Linda E. Merians, *Envisioning the Worst* (Newark: University of Delaware Press, 2001); Roxann Wheeler, *The Complexion of Race: Narratives of Polite Societies and Colored Faces in 18th-Century Britain* (Philadelphia: University of Pennsylvania Press, 1999).

radical Enlightenment Submovement in the 18th century to reform politics, RELIGION, and society. The term *radical Enlightenment* refers to the movement aimed at completely changing the traditional society of the 18th century. Unlike those who focused on moderate reforms, adherents of the radical Enlightenment desired sweeping changes in all aspects of life, including the abolishment of monarchy, religious authority, religious intolerance, and other forms of legal, political, and social oppression. Atheists, republicans, materialists, abolitionists, and suffragists can all be classified as part of the radical Enlightenment.

The radical Enlightenment originated with the 17th-century Dutch philosopher Benedict de SPINOZA. Spinoza professed that God and NATURE should be seen as one. This was a direct challenge to European religious tradition and was viewed as either atheistic or pantheistic. Politically, Spinoza favored the abolishment of monarchy and aristocracy, believing a democratic republic would be the best form of government to uphold LIBERTY, EQUALITY, and REASON. Although some of these ideas had appeared in the works Thomas HOBBES, none of the earlier writers simultaneously questioned the status quo in the areas of religion, government, and society. Spinoza's ideas spread from the UNITED PROVINCES OF THE NETHERLANDS throughout Europe.

The main tenets of the radical Enlightenment came to include a rejection of the status quo in all its forms. In terms of religion, this meant a rejection of the Judeo-Christian view of the world as having been created by a provident God who intervenes in human affairs. Socially, this led to the belief that if God did not exist, there could be no divinely ordained social structure. Therefore, the clergy and the nobility did not have the divine right to rule. Economically, this then implied that the distribution of property, with the nobles and churches owning the majority of land, was also unjust and could not have been ordained by God. These key beliefs were also combined with a respect for SCIENCE, mathematics, and republican ideals.

These ideas greatly influenced the PHILOSOPHES and ENCYCLOPEDISTS in FRANCE, including atheist rationalists Julien Offray de LA METTRIE and Denis DIDEROT, Claude-Adrien HELVÉTIUS, and Baron d'HOLBACH. The influence of the radicals in France would culminate in JACOBINISM and the FRENCH REVOLUTION, which saw the end of the monarchy in France and an attempt to institute a radical form of organization of society.

Although the excesses of the French Revolution, such as the beheadings of the royal family and nobility, were abhorrent to many in Great Britain, Britain became another center of activity for radical Enlightenment thought and activity. In the 1790s, Joseph PRIESTLY called for the abolishment of the monarchy and all hereditary titles in England. As a member of the "Friends of the Revolution," he supported the revolution in France. Richard PRICE also spoke in favor of the French Revolution. He called for a similar movement in Britain to fulfill the promise of the GLORIOUS REVOLUTION. Thomas PAINE's THE RIGHTS OF MAN (1791), calling for equality, became the most popular radical text at home and abroad, and his treatise on the follies of Christian tradition, THE AGE OF REASON (1794–96), was also very popular. Mary WOLLSTONECRAFT's A VINDICATION OF THE RIGHTS OF WOMAN appeared in 1792, calling for an acknowledgment of women's equality.

Even more radical than Paine was William GODWIN. Godwin did not just desire to reform government, he wanted to do away with it altogether. Moreover, he advocated the abolishment of the judicial and legal systems. He felt both government and the judicial system were corrupt and unnecessary. He called for the rehabilitation of criminals and for individual and personal judgment to replace law. Godwin's thoughts are reflected in the novel *Caleb Williams* (1794), in which an innocent person is hounded and the true perpetrator goes free. Other radicals who challenged the English government's power and the notion of power altogether include John Horne TOOKE and the doctor Thomas Beddoes.

The differences between the radical and the mainstream ENLIGHTENMENTS were in their notions of PROGRESS. For the mainstream Enlightenment progress was to be attained within the current political and societal framework but would uphold the right and rationality of the individual toward personal enlightenment, rather than reliance on traditional mores of religion and the feudal class system. Radicals also believed in individual rationality and liberty, but did not believe full liberty could be attained in the framework of the current governmental or societal structure. Most radicals wanted full reform, if not completely new social and political institutions altogether.

Although some forms of radicalism, such as Godwin's, can be seen as destructive and extreme, other forms brought benefits to marginalized members of European society. Among the latter were the struggles for civil rights for Jews and other ethnic and religious minorities, for the end of church monopoly over EDUCATION, and for the end of state CENSORSHIP. One of the most important strains of radicalism in the Enlightenment was the movement to abolish SLAVERY. The work of Henri GREGOIRE and the Society of Friends in France did much to bring about the end of slavery. Abolition and suffrage would be two aspects of the radical Enlightenment that would greatly affect America and the world in the very near future.

See also MIRABEAU; ROUSSEAU.

Further reading: Jonathan I. Israel, *Radical Enlightenment Philosophy and the Making of Modernity, 1650–1750* (New York: Oxford University Press, 2001); Margaret Jacob, *Radical Enlightenment: Pantheists, Freemasons, and Republicans* (London: Allen & Unwin, 1981).

Rake's Progress, A   A series of engravings by the satirist William HOGARTH, created in 1734 from earlier paintings. Hogarth waited to release the prints until protection from piracy had been secured by passage of the Engravers' Act of 1735. The act is often called Hogarth's Act on account of his active promotion of its provisions.

A Rake's Progress presents eight engravings illustrating the career of an extravagant young aristocrat, Tom Rakewell. Having inherited his father's fortune, Rakewell proceeds to waste it on traditional aristocratic pleasures of the era, prostitutes, gambling, and revelry. Sizable expenses lead Rakewell to abandon a hardworking, devoted, middle-class young woman in favor of marriage to a wealthy older woman. Rakewell's dissolute life eventually leads him to debtors' prison after he has squandered his wife's estate. He also acquires syphilis and, afflicted with syphilitic madness, ends his days in Bedlam, LONDON's insane asylum.

A Rake's Progress served as companion piece to Hogarth's earlier series, *A Harlot's Progress* (1732). That series presents the career of Moll Hackabout, an innocent young girl who arrives in London from the country to seek employment and is recruited by the manager of a brothel. In depicting her decline from pampered courtesan to common prostitute to inmate of Bridewell, Hogarth represents the fate of an individual struggling against a hostile, predatory world.

Hogarth was a sharp observer of his society, and more than willing to criticize what he saw. *A Rake's Progress* attacked the LIBERTINE values of the English Restoration, suggesting that the ways of the aristocracy can lead only to unreason and madness. By implication, Hogarth supported the middle-class values of sobriety and self-control. The prints thus contain a commentary on English social class divisions hidden behind their specific moralizing content. Hogarth was one of the most powerful representatives of the ENLIGHTENMENT IN ENGLAND, spreading its belief in reason and its call for moral virtue through the medium of his art.

See also PROSTITUTION.

Rameau, Jean-Philippe (1683–1764) *French composer and music theorist*
Rameau received his early musical training from his father who was an organist at Dijon. He made a brief visit to ITALY in 1701, spent a few years as organist at Clermont-Ferrand, then moved to PARIS in 1706. After publishing a book of short compositions for harpsichord, Rameau left Paris, and his activities of the next few years remain unknown. Rameau returned to Clermont-Ferrand after 1715 to resume his organist post. In 1722, he published *Traité de l'harmonie* (Treatise on harmony), the book that established his reputation as a theorist of music. Rameau moved again to Paris in 1723, but had little success until 1731, when he won the support of an important patron, Alexandre-Jean-Joseph Le Riche de La Pouplinière. Rameau served as organist, resident composer, and conductor at La Pouplinière's estate in Passy near Paris.

With the assistance of his generous patron, Rameau began to create and produce operas. His first complete OPERA, *Hippolyte et Arcie,* was produced in Paris in 1733 when he was 50 years old. *Les Indes Galantes* (1735) and the masterpiece, *Castor et Pollux* (1737), established Rameau as a substantial figure in the operatic world. Nevertheless, from the beginning, his pieces also stirred controversy.

The critical quarrel of the Ramists (partisans of Rameau) and Lullists (partisans of his predecessor, Lully) took center stage in Paris during the middle years of the 1730s. The Lullists accused Rameau of undermining French opera with his innovations. Ironically, in 1752 Rameau again found himself in the eye of a critical storm during the celebrated BATTLE OF THE BUFFOONS. This time, however, he was portrayed as the defender of French opera in the face of attacks by supporters of Italian opera. His critics in the War of the Buffoons were his friends Jean Le Rond d'ALEMBERT, Denis DIDEROT, and Jean-Jacques ROUSSEAU. All had supported him in the earlier quarrel but rejected his style as old-fashioned in the Battle of Buffoons.

In the years between these two episodes, Rameau produced a series of works in lighter style. The most outstanding were the comedy-ballet *Platée* (1745) and the serious opera *Zoroastre* (1749). Rameau spent his later years engaged in polemics with Rousseau and the ENCYCLOPEDISTS about his harmonic theory and compositional style.

Rameau's operas are examples of late-BAROQUE STYLE opera-ballet. The plot is reduced to insignificance while the element of spectacle assumes prominence. The evocation of spectacle is accomplished through ballet and through the use of music to evoke dramatic moods and images. Rameau's evocations of thunderstorms, for example, seem to surround the listener with the terrifying force of nature and reveal him to have been a master at French baroque modes of tone-painting.

In the manner of his era, Rameau adhered to the ideal of representing NATURE in his compositions, but his idea of how to realize that ideal differed dramatically from the conceptions of his later critics. The *Traité de l'harmonie* is a major contribution to the development of the homophonic, diatonic compositional style that became a hallmark of musical CLASSICISM. Rameau's theory made the three-note chord the building block of musical structure, whereas earlier theories had given that role to single-note melodic lines. His theory also exploited the particular qualities of various harmonic tonalities and offered a method for deriving melody from chordal structures.

Rastrelli, Bartolomeo (1700–1771) *architect of Italian extraction who created a unique Russian baroque style*
Rastrelli worked for the czarinas Elizabeth and CATHERINE II (THE GREAT). Rastrelli was born in PARIS, the son of an Italian sculptor who had settled in that city. In 1716, PETER I (THE GREAT) invited the Rastrelli family to SAINT PETERSBURG. Young Rastrelli quickly established himself as an architect. He traveled back to western Europe for some training, but it is not known precisely where he studied or with whom.

Rastrelli adapted forms of the late BAROQUE STYLE to create a highly personal form of architectural expression. He used a color palate of blues, whites, and greens, thus leaving buildings whose forms seem to shimmer in the wintry northern light of the often snow-covered Saint Petersburg landscape. Rastrelli's major works include Smolny Convent, the rebuilt Peterhof (1746–58), the Tsarskoe Selo palace (1749–56), the Winter Palace in Saint Petersburg (1754–68), and the Cathedral of Saint Andrew at Kiev.

rationalism A form of EPISTEMOLOGY that makes REASON the source of all true knowledge. During the ENLIGHTENMENT, it was fashionable to attack rationalism and the associated activity of building systems of knowledge. EMPIRICISM, the epistemological approach that makes experience the source of all knowledge, provided an attractive alternative theory of knowledge. But rationalism continued to inform the method of analysis and the mathematical models of natural and human law that were favored by enlightened intellectuals and reformers.

Seventeenth-century rationalism had been created to provided an answer to late-16th-century SKEPTICISM. Rationalism asserted that, contrary to what skeptics declared, people could, by exercising the ability to reason, gain certain and true knowledge about the world.

Seventeenth-century rationalism, derived initially from the philosophy of René DESCARTES, rested on a vision of reason taken from the mathematical discipline of geometry. Following rigid rules of deductive logic, geometry creates an entire system of knowledge from a few basic axioms (assumptions). Rationalists asserted that true knowledge in all areas could be uncovered by using this geometric model.

In his *Discours de la méthode* (Discourse on method; 1634), Descartes outlined an approach to reasoning—his famed geometric method—that made explicit this relationship between rationalism and geometry. According to Descartes, such troublesome philosophical problems as the proof of the existence of God could be solved by the exercise of tightly controlled reason modeled on geometry. Descartes began with the innate (inborn) idea *cogito, ergo sum* (I think, therefore I am). He considered this the one idea in his mind whose truth could not be doubted. From this idea, through a process of geometric reasoning, he arrived at the existence of God.

This method was enthusiastically received not only in FRANCE, but also throughout Europe and the British Isles. It was criticized from various philosophical and theological positions but nevertheless entered the general discourse in Europe about problems of knowledge.

Descartes extended his rationalism to create a system of NATURAL PHILOSOPHY, which he outlined in *Principia Philosophiae naturalis* (Principles of natural philosophy, 1644). In that treatise, Descartes applied his geometric method of reasoning to SCIENCE, creating a complete system called the MECHANICAL PHILOSOPHY. Descartes constructed his system by beginning with the simple axiom that all physical phenomena consist of particles of matter in motion.

Descartes's system received sharp criticism from some of his contemporaries who favored building science on observation (EMPIRICISM). But he was not alone in offering a rational system to natural philosophy. Two competing rationalist systems, developed by Gottfried Wilhelm LEIBNIZ and Benedict de SPINOZA, offered alternatives that would prove especially influential in the development of German enlightened thought.

During the first half of the Enlightenment, intellectuals tended to turn away from systems constructed by the exercise of abstract reason and to favor the construction of knowledge through the accumulation of experience and experimental observations. Nevertheless, they remained indebted to certain aspects of rational method and principles. Without rationalism, for example, the great project of mathematizing the universe, that is, of assuming that scientific laws could be validly written as mathematical equations, likely would not have existed. Scientists who believed that the laws of the world could be expressed mathematically assumed implicitly that reason—that is, a set of lawful, ordered relationships—governs the natural world.

As the thought of the Enlightenment developed, MORAL PHILOSOPHY, theology, and PSYCHOLOGY grappled with issues raised by Spinoza's monism, a philosophy that posited the ultimate identity of body and spirit, matter and mind. Leibniz's monadology, a complicated system that made activity and perception the building blocks of the natural world, colored debates in fields as varied as NATURAL LAW, physics, psychology, and MEDICINE.

The Enlightenment significantly altered all of its inherited forms of rationalism. Following the example of

Pierre BAYLE and other late-17th-century skeptics, enlightened intellectuals conceived of reason as an intellectual tool, just as the 17th-century rationalists had done. But the goal of reasoning was now criticism rather than system-building. Scrutinizing, analyzing, and questioning received knowledge by means of reason were favored intellectual activities. During the Enlightenment, rationalism, defined as the simple exercise of reason, also joined with the questioning stance fostered by skepticism. If any aspect of the Enlightenment can be accepted as universal, cutting across national boundaries and various forms of thought, it was this critical spirit.

Thus, in spite of the prominent criticisms of rationalism contained in enlightened discourse, the spirit of rationalism—in the guise of criticism—lived on. It informed the whole enterprise of reform, affecting theory in virtually every discipline.

See also AESTHETICS; MATHEMATICS AND MECHANICS; SCIENTIFIC METHOD.

Raynal, Guillaume-Thomas-François de (Abbé)
(1713–1796) *French writer, philosopher, and political thinker*

Raynal studied at a Jesuit-operated collège in Rodez and then entered the Jesuit order with the intention of dedicating himself to ROMAN CATHOLICISM. After a few years of teaching for the JESUITS, Raynal withdrew from the order and settled in PARIS, where he pursued a career as a writer.

Raynal's early career was marked by active participation in Parisian intellectual life and financial success. He reviewed and reported on the literary productions of the capital. From 1750 to 1754 he served as the editor of the journal *Mercure de France*. Through this position, he entered the society of the PHILOSOPHES. His friends included Baron de MONTESQUIEU, Denis DIDEROT, Claude-Adrien HELVÉTIUS, and Baron d'HOLBACH.

Raynal is best known today, as he was during his lifetime, for his *Histoire philosophique et politique des établissements et du commerce des Européens dans les deux Indes* (Philosophical and political history of the European establishments and commerce in the two Indies; 1770, revised 1774 and 1780). This was his greatest and most heartfelt project, on which he worked for 20 years.

A best-selling and controversial book, it was an account of commercial practices of European countries in Africa, Asia, and the New World. Basing his descriptions on European travel narratives, Raynal documented the customs and ways of life of foreign peoples, which appealed to readers' curiosity about other lands and their inhabitants. Raynal's study was part of the nascent field of ANTHROPOLOGY being developed at the time. He observed, for instance, the universality of the incest taboo and speculated that it served to link families together through marriage, keeping society peaceful. Although many of Raynal's observations were not new—the view that

human societies vary according to their climate had previously been expressed by Montesquieu—he inserted them into an economic, political, and philosophical vision that displeased authorities. His *Histoire des deux Indes* was condemned in ROME by the censors of the Catholic Church and placed on the Index of Forbidden Books (1774). The Parlement of Paris also condemned the book, ordering it to be burned publicly in 1781.

Histoire des deux Indes was strongly critical of both SLAVERY and the practices of the Catholic Church in the French colonies. It mixed frank discussion of the cruel practices of slavery with idealistic descriptions of the characteristics of native populations who were subjected to its yoke. Its criticisms combined a general humanitarian approach to slavery with practical arguments about the negative economic consequences of the institution. It also affirmed the right of slaves to revolt against those who oppressed them.

At the same time, Raynal saw commerce as a potentially civilizing process. The Europeans could bring ENLIGHTENMENT, talents, and civilized customs to the peoples of less advanced areas. Conversely, commerce could also corrupt Europeans if it made them too wealthy. Raynal pointed in particular to the Dutch and the English as prime examples of colonizers who had become cruel and corrupted. In this way, Raynal saw promise in colonization and international commerce, but he felt that the circumstances under which they took place needed to be radically changed.

Raynal's undertaking also provides a window onto one aspect of Enlightenment writing practices. Raynal made use of a network of European thinkers from whom he received documents, journal articles, and travel narratives that he integrated into his book. He also benefited from extensive contributions by other authors, including Diderot and d'Holbach. For a polemical project such as *Histoire des deux Indes*, intended to inspire debate and reform, the opinions and abilities of several contributors were mobilized in order to give the work more range and authority.

By affixing his name and portrait to the third edition of the book, Raynal took a significant personal risk, and indeed found himself condemned to exile by LOUIS XVI in 1781. He settled first in PRUSSIA, where the increasingly suspicious FREDERICK II failed to welcome him warmly. Raynal moved then to SWITZERLAND but was allowed to return to FRANCE in 1784. He had to wait until 1790 before he received permission to live again in Paris.

Histoire des deux Indes offers an excellent example of the manner in which the major intellectual trends and values of the Enlightenment— humanitarianism, anticlericalism, and impassioned criticism of social and political injustice—combined at the end of the 18th century to produce programs for radical reform. French revolutionaries saw Raynal as an "apostle of liberty" until he criticized the treatment of the king and the Catholic

Church and the strong influence of revolutionary political clubs.

See also COLONIALISM; HAITIAN REVOLUTION; POLITICAL THEORY; TOUSSAINT L'OUVERTURE; TRAVEL LITERATURE.

Further reading: Edward Derbyshire Seeber, *Anti-Slavery Opinion in France During the Second Half of the Eighteenth Century* (New York: Greenwood Press, 1969).

reading   *See* LITERACY; PUBLISHING; SOCIAL INSTITUTIONS OF THE ENLIGHTENMENT.

reading clubs   *See* SOCIAL INSTITUTIONS OF THE ENLIGHTENMENT.

reason   The activity of the mind that produces orderly thought about problems. The ENLIGHTENMENT is often characterized as an age of reason, and indeed, reason served as a kind of standard against which all ideas, theories, and practical programs were judged. However, reason could mean many different things during the Enlightenment. Therefore, students of the period must be careful to determine its precise meaning for any particular author. Otherwise, confusion and misrepresentation will arise.

At the beginning of the Enlightenment, the ambivalent meanings of the term were already apparent. Early "fathers of the Enlightenment" such as Pierre BAYLE were questioning the claims made by the 17th-century rationalists—René DESCARTES, Gottfried Wilhelm LEIBNIZ, and Benedict de SPINOZA—about the abilities of human reason to uncover true knowledge about the world. Rationalist philosophers assumed that the world is built on a system of NATURAL LAW, patterned by God after mathematics and therefore understandable to human reason. They claimed that humans could identify a few simple assumptions about the world similar to the axioms in geometry. Just as geometers derive a complete system of true knowledge from a few simple axioms, so by the process of deductive reasoning, people could derive a complete explanation of all the phenomena in the world. Critics of rationalism were questioning the validity of these rationally based world views; they were thus exploring some of the limits of reason, expressing SKEPTICISM about the philosophical systems it had created.

When indulging in this exercise, however, enlightened writers still claimed that they were using reason in the service of truth. But in this context, reason referred to a generally inquisitive, skeptical mental stance. Reason became an intellectual tool, useful for analyzing problems, and thus was transformed into criticism, the activity that inspired much enlightened thought. Reason as criticism allowed intellectuals to scrutinize traditional ideas and beliefs in the hope of discrediting those that were false.

At the same time that people were criticizing and tearing down inherited traditions, other fathers of the Enlightenment were building new systems of knowledge called EMPIRICISM based on yet another definition of reason. These men, Francis BACON, John LOCKE, and Isaac NEWTON, for example, agreed with the rationalists that the world is structured by mathematical, orderly laws; but they believed that a different method of reason, the inductive method, was the only realistic way for human beings to discover these laws.

In the inductive method, people began the pursuit of knowledge by observing events (experience), making experiments (also called experience), and collecting these observations or facts. Once enough facts were collected, they could be subjected to critical examination and made to reveal their underlying order and lawful RELATIONS. This process of induction would yield reliable knowledge from which further predictions could be made and actions could be planned. This empirical (experience-based) view of the world was the most popular view during the Enlightenment, at least in FRANCE and ENGLAND. It led to a new OPTIMISM about the abilities of human reason, one that recognized its limits but believed that their negative influences could be minimized with proper methods.

As the 18th century progressed, the Enlightenment continued to produce criticism, and thus subjected the claims made for empiricism and induction to the same skeptical attacks it had once aimed at rationalism. Reason was once again on the defensive, especially after the skillful analyses of David HUME.

In response, intellectuals began to search for alternatives to reason, for other avenues by which human beings could acquire knowledge about the world. Sensation, feeling, ENTHUSIASM, INTUITION AND IMAGINATION, and common sense were all offered as alternative paths and given supportive theories.

The Enlightenment seemed to be producing some radically contradictory positions. Rationalist systems continued to have adherents, as did empiricism. Intellectuals struggled to save the faith in reason by inventing new theories and techniques to answer critics. Mathematicians produced new techniques such as the calculus, differential equations, and PROBABILITY theory, to provide certainty for the knowledge obtained by the varieties of reason. Materialists tried to reduce all sensory experience to mechanical operations so that lawful relations and hence reason could still be claimed as the underlying structure of the world.

Toward the end of the century, the claims made for the powers of reason by the marquis de CONDORCET and the IDÉOLOGUES, for example, were being matched by equally strong claims against those powers coming primarily from the regions east of the Rhine River. As the Enlightenment closed, Immanuel KANT tried to resolve the tension by producing a new systematic philosophy of reason, based on a synthesis of the varying enlightened strands. A masterpiece of creativity, Kant's system set the boundaries of debate for much future philosophy. But his system was eclipsed in the general European culture by the philosophies associated with ROMANTICISM.

The many enlightened meanings of reason are closely related to certain other concepts commonly employed by enlightened writers. These include RATIONALISM, deduction, the geometric method, induction, empiricism, natural law, the SCIENTIFIC METHOD, criticism, CLASSIFICATION, and common sense. Discussions about reason and applications of the concept appeared in nearly every enlightened discipline, but they were especially dominant in EPISTEMOLOGY, PSYCHOLOGY, mathematics, RELIGION, and SCIENCE. Enlightened organizations such as the FREEMASONS and the Bavarian ILLUMINATI raised reason to nearly godlike status. Certain religious forms of expression like DEISM and the related PHYSICO-THEOLOGY drew on the concept of reason as support for faith. BIBLICAL CRITICISM used reason to challenge the authority of the Bible. And finally, new religious forms—PIETISM, METHODISM, and Quakerism—sprang up to defend religion from attacks made in the name of reason. In any of these phenomena or areas of thought, the central role played by reason, in its kaleidoscope of meanings, offers insight into the complexities of enlightened thought.

See also MATHEMATICS AND MECHANICS; QUAKERS; WOMEN AND THE ENLIGHTENMENT.

Further reading: Michael Losonsky, *Enlightenment and Action from Descartes to Kant: Passionate Thought* (Cambridge: Cambridge University Press, 2001); John C. O'Neal, *Authority of Experience: Sensationist Theory in the French Enlightenment* (University Park: Pennsylvania State University Press, 1996); Sir Leslie Stephen, *History of English Thought in the Eighteenth Century*, 2 vols. (New York: Harcourt, Brace & World, 1962).

Réaumur, René-Antoine Ferchault de (1683–1757)
French scientist

Réaumur had wide-ranging scientific interests and made contributions to several fields. He is best known for developing a temperature scale in 1730. It divided the range between the freezing and boiling points of water into 80 units, with 0 degrees R as the freezing point and 80 degrees R as the boiling point. During the FRENCH REVOLUTION, Réaumur's system was replaced by the Celsius scale.

Réaumur made many contributions to technology and industry. In 1710, he was asked to begin compiling information on the industrial and natural resources of FRANCE. In this capacity, he reported on the state of many industries, such as gold prospecting and ironmaking. He eagerly explored many industrial processes, demonstrating the importance of carbon in making steel as well as investigating the composition of Chinese porcelain, which led him to develop Réaumur porcelain. After observing a wasp mixing its bodily fluids with a twig to create pulp for a nest, he suggested using wood fiber to produce paper.

Réaumur was also interested in the biological sciences. He wrote a six-volume study of insects, *Mémoires pour servir à l'histoire naturelle des insectes* (Memoirs serving as a natural history of insects; 1734–42). This was the first comprehensive and scholarly work on entomology (the study of insects). Réaumur also designed experiments to confirm his hypothesis that the stomach acts chemically on food during digestion.

See also BIOLOGY; CHEMICAL REVOLUTION; TECHNOLOGY AND INSTRUMENTATION.

Further reading: Jeffrey J. W. Baker and Garland E. Allen, eds., *The Process of Biology: Primary Sources* (Reading, Mass.: Addison-Wesley, 1970); Donald Culross Peattie, *Green Laurels: The Lives and Achievements of the Great Naturalists* (New York: Simon & Schuster, 1936).

Reflections on the Revolution in France   Political commentary by Edmund BURKE, published in 1790. The book contains Burke's harsh criticisms of the FRENCH REVOLUTION. He rejected the revolution as a dangerous exercise governed by abstract principles rather than by practical necessity and predicted that it would lead to despotism.

Burke supported the right of a people to rebel only in cases where they were defending their traditional political liberties and rights. Thus, he defended both the GLORIOUS REVOLUTION of 1688 in ENGLAND and the AMERICAN REVOLUTION. Since the revolutionary French were trying to dismantle the whole structure of their ANCIEN RÉGIME (old regime) rather than to restore tradition, Burke rejected their actions and goals.

Burke attacked the French calls for a new order based on LIBERTY, EQUALITY, and fraternity. According to Burke, the French were ignorant about the meaning of liberty, unaware of the fact that equality cannot be achieved in a society, and gullible enough to believe in the myth of the brotherhood of humanity. By dissolving the old social order that had grouped people into various ranks according to social status and occupation, the French were undermining the structure best designed to guarantee political liberty.

Burke eventually issued calls for an international crusade against the French Revolution and for the suppression of French ideas in the British Isles. *Reflections on the Revolution in France* stands as an indictment of the aspects of the ENLIGHTENMENT that were embodied in the French upheavals and illustrates one direction in which subsequent conservative theorizing would develop.

See also POLITICAL THEORY.

Reid, Thomas (1710–1796) *Scottish philosopher, founder of common sense philosophy*

Reid came from a family of Presbyterian ministers and, like his forebears, entered the ministry. He worked for 10 years as librarian at Aberdeen College, then, in 1737, he obtained a position as a Presbyterian minister at New Machar near Aberdeen. He left that post only in 1751, when he became a professor at King's College, Aberdeen. In 1764, Reid succeeded Adam SMITH at the University of Glasgow in the chair of MORAL PHILOSOPHY. Reid retired from Glasgow in 1781 but remained an active philosopher and writer, publishing major works on common sense philosophy in the 1780s. He died in 1796.

Reid formulated the philosophy of common sense as an answer to the SKEPTICISM expressed by David HUME in the *TREATISE OF HUMAN NATURE* (1739), in the *Philosophical Essays Concerning Human Understanding* (1748), and in the more widely read revision of the *Philosophical Essays* called ENQUIRY CONCERNING HUMAN UNDERSTANDING (1758). Reid declared that Hume was wrong in stating that the mind can know with certainty only its subjective processes. Reid offered common sense, "the consent of ages and nations, of the learned and unlearned, the verdict of the structure and grammar of languages," forms of knowledge he presumed were universally held, as proof of the ability of human minds to know things objectively. Reid published his theory in 1764, in his *Inquiry into the Human Mind on the Principles of Common Sense*. The book established his reputation as a moral philosopher and caused him to be called to Glasgow.

Reid addressed the problem of how sensory experience is translated into conscious ideas (perception). He rejected the idea that reason effects the translation and, as evidence for his claim, pointed to infants and children, who do not yet reason but who nevertheless have perceptions. The validity of human perceptions, according to Reid, has been decreed by the will of God and is guaranteed by the nature and structure of human languages. In other words, the common ability of human beings to understand and to use language creates some sort of common sense understanding, available to all.

Common sense philosophy was rooted deeply in the communal, social aspects of the experience of humankind as expressed through language. This emphasis on the communal nature of understanding places Reid's common sense philosophy squarely in the mainstream of the Scottish Enlightenment.

Reid's new philosophy was received with mixed reviews by Scottish and English intellectuals. It was popularized in England by James Beattie, but the intellectuals of EDINBURGH received it coolly. In 1774, for example, the chemist and physician Joseph PRIESTLEY published a harsh attack on Reid's *Inquiry,* entitled *An Examination of Dr. Reid's Inquiry.*

After 1785, however, common sense philosophy began to dominate moral philosophy in a manner that has been characterized by some scholars as revolutionary. Reid had responded to criticism of his ideas, by seeking a

scientific base for his theory. He elaborated the mechanisms by which common sense operates to produce perception, by drawing on the older psychology of the faculties of the mind. Reid published two late works on this subject: *Essays on the Intellectual Powers of Man* (1785) and *Essays on the Active Powers of Man* (1788). He identified 24 active powers of the mind and about six intellectual powers. These exist in all minds and together produce knowledge common to all human beings.

The new analytic, scientific form of common sense philosophy was popularized by Reid's disciple Dugald Stewart. Through Stewart, the common sense theory of the faculties reached Franz Joseph GALL, who adapted it to his theory of PHRENOLOGY.

See also EPISTEMOLOGY; PSYCHOLOGY.

Reil, Johann Christian (1759–1813) *German physician and physiologist who made an intellectual transition over the course of his life from vitalism to the* Naturphilosophie *associated with German romanticism*

The son of a Lutheran pastor, Reil studied MEDICINE at the University of GÖTTINGEN and the University of HALLE. He graduated from Halle in 1782 and set up a medical practice in Norden, Germany. In 1787, Reil became a clinical instructor at the University of Halle, and in 1788 he succeeded his former teacher, Johann F. G. Goldhagen, as professor of clinical medicine and director of the university's clinical institute. Reil remained at these posts until 1806; when the economic crises precipitated by the capitulation of PRUSSIA to Napoleon (battle of Jena) forced closure of the university. Reil participated in the 1807–08 reorganization of higher EDUCATION at Halle and assumed the deanship of the medical school in 1808. After 1810, he moved to BERLIN, having been invited by Wilhelm von HUMBOLDT to assist with the organization of a medical school at the University of Berlin.

In 1813, when Prussia renewed hostilities against Napoleon, Reil volunteered for military medical duty. He became chief inspector of all lazarettos (hospitals used for patients stricken with contagious diseases) west of the Elbe River. During an epidemic of typhus, he contracted the disease and died in November 1813.

Reil studied with Johann Friedrich BLUMENBACH at the University of Göttingen and adopted Blumenbach's vitalist vision of organisms. He believed that the vital force (*Lebenskraft*) of an organism mediates between the matter and form of an organism, producing the unity that characterizes living things. He also believed that all vital processes—generation, growth, nutrition, and reproduction—obey chemical laws. Reil published this theory in the first issue of his professional journal, *Archiv für die Physiologie* (Archive for physiology).

As Reil matured, he became dissatisfied with the explanatory power of this approach. It seemed that neither mind-body relations nor the uniqueness of organic processes could be adequately explained by arguments from matter and form. Reil adopted the *Naturphilosophie* of Friedrich Wilhelm Joseph von Schelling (1775–1845), seeing in it a more adequate foundation for his medical theory. Reil believed that certain fundamental ideas operate in the natural world and must be used as guideposts for understanding mind and body interactions. In essence, body and mind became different manifestations of an underlying unity.

Reil was particularly concerned with building a system of medical education that could supply trained personnel to all regions of GERMANY. He also devoted himself to the care of psychological disturbances and treated these problems as manifestations of malfunctioning brain activity (oscillations). Reil was one of the important 18th-century pioneers in creating a medical model of mental illness. His work parallels that of Philippe Pinel (1745–1826) in FRANCE.

See also PSYCHOLOGY; VITALISM.

Reimarus, Hermann Samuel (1694–1768) *German scholar and theologian*
A native of Hamburg, Reimarus studied at the University of Jena, lectured at Wittenberg and Weimar, and in 1727 settled back in Hamburg, where he taught Hebrew and Oriental languages at the local gymnasium (secondary school).

Reimarus lived during the time of the bitter intellectual battles at the University of HALLE between the leaders of Lutheran PIETISM and the rational philosopher Christian WOLFF. The experience alienated him from orthodox Lutheran theology. Throughout his life, he continued to practice LUTHERANISM, but inward doubt and disbelief led him toward NATURAL RELIGION and DEISM.

In the writings published during his lifetime, Reimarus explored the truths of natural religions based on reason. The subject led him into inquiries about the fundamental nature of life, and about mind-body relationships. Three books—*Abhandlungen von den vornehmsten Wahrheiten der natürlichen Religion* (Treatises on the principal truths of natural religion; 1754); *Vernunftlehre* (Doctrine of reason; 1756); and *Allgemeine Betrachtungen über die Triebe der Thiere* (General considerations on the instincts of animals; 1760)—contain his theories.

Reimarus declined to publish one major work, the *Apologie oder Schutzschrift für die vernünftigen Verehrer Gottes* (Apology or defense for rational worshippers of God), because he feared that its arguments would embroil him with authorities. Gottfried Ephraim LESSING, however, printed parts of Reimarus's work as the *Wolfenbütteler Fragmenten* in *Zur Geschichte und Literatur* (On history and literature; 1774 and 1777). Lessing, who knew very well who had authored the manuscript, claimed that the *Fragments* had been found in the library at Wolfenbüttel and that they had probably been written by an obscure 17th-century German philosopher. Reimarus's authorship did not become public knowledge until the 19th century.

The publication created great turmoil and ambivalent reactions in German circles. Whereas theologians and orthodox believers lamented the *Fragments'* attacks on revealed religion, many enlightened writers felt that the *Fragments* actually supported a modified form of such religion, shorn of miraculous, mysterious elements. Reimarus had adopted elements from deism, which denied the reality of miracles, mysteries, or other events that do not obey natural laws. But his approach departed from full-fledged deism, because, unlike deism, it strove to defend the possibility of revelation. Reimarus's approach is commonly called neology. It asserts that the fundamental truths of religion (existence of God, immortality of the soul) are accessible to all human beings if they simply use their abilities to reason about the world and about the meaning of life.

Many biblical scholars credit Reimarus with introducing the quest for the historical Jesus, a problem that still fascinates modern researchers. In the *Fragments*, he denies the divinity of Jesus, arguing instead that Jesus was a failed revolutionary whose original message was transformed by the apostles into a mystery religion. Hence, Reimarus drew a radical distinction between the teachings of Jesus and those of the apostles from whose writings most established Christian churches had drawn their dogma.

Reimarus stands as a major representative of the ENLIGHTENMENT in German-speaking territories. His faith in the power of human reason to uncover religious truths was shared by many representatives of the Enlightenment. His fears about publishing reflected the fact that certain subjects were still off limits in the 18th-century world. The organizational, institutional aspects of Christianity could be attacked with relative ease, but authors who ventured into questioning the authority of the Bible—whether fervent Christians, doubting skeptics, or avowed atheists—ran the risk of losing their jobs and even suffering imprisonment.

See also BIBLICAL CRITICISM; RELIGION.

relations A term commonly used in the ENLIGHTENMENT to denote the manner in which two or more natural or human phenomena were connected. The idea of relations is closely related to the general notion of law. It was assumed that underlying laws determined how things happen in the universe. Event *a* would cause event *b* according to a one-to-one principle of cause and effect.

The connection between *a* and *b*, determined by law, was called a relation. Enlightened use of the term in the first half of the 18th century generally followed the principles of one-to-one cause and effect. Toward the middle of the century, however, more complicated relations such as the three-body problem in celestial physics and the complicated interactions associated with organic processes began to assume prominence. The meaning of the term *relations* acquired great complexity and can be quite confusing if these shifts are not taken into account.

The concept of relations appeared in SCIENCE (physics and chemistry) to describe connections between time and motion, between force and directional path, or between one element and another; in PSYCHOLOGY to address ties between sensations and resulting ideas; in MORAL PHILOSOPHY to explain how pleasure and pain shape behavior; in social sciences to explain how the general characteristics of a people reflect their environment or climate; and in HISTORY to describe the links between economic or social factors and political events or to show that the mental stage of human development corresponds to specific forms of cultural expression.

The concept of relations is usually implied whenever language such as "affinity," "sympathy," "antipathy," or "law" appears in an enlightened text. Thus, the notion of relation occurs in all fields of the Enlightenment, and in many guises, wherever people were struggling to devise orderly descriptions of the way in which things happen in the world.

See also AFFINITY CHEMISTRY; MATHEMATICS AND MECHANICS; NATURAL LAW; SYMPATHY.

religion   A set of organized beliefs, usually associated with an external institution, that defines and governs the relationship between humanity and the supernatural world of God or gods. During the ENLIGHTENMENT, religions in the Judeo-Christian tradition dominated Europe: Western Christianity in the two general forms of ROMAN CATHOLICISM and PROTESTANTISM; Eastern Christianity in the form of the various Eastern Orthodox rites; and Judaism (see JEWS AND JUDAISM). But Europe was not insulated from contact with non-Judeo-Christian traditions.

In fact, the isolation of Europeans had broken down dramatically during the 16th and 17th centuries, when explorers and missionaries began traversing the far reaches of the globe. Europeans had begun learning about the variety of religions in the world ranging from Hinduism, Buddhism, and Confucianism to the many small tribal religions of the Pacific islands. Contact with the Muslim religion practiced in the Ottoman Empire had existed for centuries, provoking not only fear and hatred but also curiosity and research.

Contact with non-Christian traditions had raised many disturbing questions about the truth claims that were so much a part of Christianity. The answers of the 16th century and 17th century had centered on asserting the truth of one viewpoint over another with the backing of force, if necessary. Christian Europe defended itself against attack from the Muslims in the east, and Jews were periodically subjected to banishment, violence, or other forms of harassment.

During the 16th century and well into the 17th century, bitter and bloody religious wars had been fought between Christians as they struggled with the implications of the Protestant Reformation. These wars had torn at the political, social, and economic fabric of FRANCE, the HOLY ROMAN EMPIRE, the HAPSBURG EMPIRE, ENGLAND, and the Low Countries.

To end the conflicts, limited forms of religious TOLERATION between Catholics and Protestants had been instituted in France, the UNITED PROVINCES OF THE NETHERLANDS, and in German-speaking states, but few people really welcomed this as desirable; rather it was a matter of practicality, a way to secure political calm.

The 17th century saw a burst of creativity within Roman Catholicism and Protestantism; but it also saw a hardening of positions into rigid forms. Secular rulers in both Catholic and Protestant nations, wedded to the ideas of ABSOLUTISM, attempted to withdraw toleration policies or to force religious conformity on their subjects. In 1685, LOUIS XIV actually rescinded the Edict of Nantes, which had granted limited toleration to French HUGUENOTS (Calvinists), triggering large-scale immigration of Huguenots from France and even the rebellion by the Protestant CAMISARDS. Plans were afoot until the GLORIOUS REVOLUTION of 1688 to return England to the Roman Catholic fold; and Emperor Ferdinand II in AUSTRIA succeeded in forcing many of his Protestant subjects to reconvert to Catholicism. Intolerance continued in the United Provinces of the Netherlands, the American colonies, and other areas, while religious hysteria, persecution of alleged heretics, and witch burnings occurred with disturbing frequency.

These intolerant and dogmatic solutions to religious diversity did not satisfy enlightened individuals in the 18th century; in fact, people increasingly found such attitudes repugnant. Events such as the execution of Jean CALAS, the revolt of the Camisards, and the persecution of the WALDENSIANS greatly disturbed the enlightened world and helped to drive a continuing search for meaningful responses to diversity in the realm of religious belief.

The European exploration and colonization of so-called New World regions brought expanded knowledge about non-Christian religions at the same time that Europe was also experiencing astounding intellectual shifts in concepts about the natural world. The work of Nicolaus COPERNICUS, Galileo GALILEI, Isaac NEWTON, and the many other creators of the SCIENTIFIC REVOLUTION produced a new vision of the universe and new ways of explaining its operations. The role of God in this new universe was not clear, a fact that caused discomfort and stimulated searches for adequate religious responses. In addition, the revised understanding of the human mind entailed in the PSYCHOLOGY of John LOCKE seemed to suggest that the origin of moral behavior might lie more in natural processes than in the laws of God as revealed in the Bible. Finally, the new discipline of BIBLICAL CRITICISM was treating the Bible as an historical document created by human beings and subject to error and change over time. These ideas shook Christianity at its very foundations, calling into question the meaning of human existence, the role of God in the universe, the grounds for morality, and the validity of the Bible as the revealed word of God.

The ferment created by these challenges to traditional views of the world and of humanity caused the period of the Enlightenment to be marked by impassioned scrutiny of all aspects of religious belief. Although Christianity experienced bitter attacks from many fronts, the attackers were nevertheless struggling with issues that had always been treated by religious faith and theology. The questions derived from religion occupy a central place in enlightened discourse.

People who engaged in examining the grounds for religious faith used the basic intellectual tools and ideas of the Enlightenment to create their solutions. REASON, comparative analysis, and historical inquiry admirably served the needs of critics and scholars of religion. These tools aided the goal of dissecting and tearing down tradition, but they also provided means for constructing something new.

Reason, for example, provided the grounds for a universal NATURAL RELIGION such as the deists proposed, for the Jewish movement of the Enlightenment called HASKALAH, and for new systems of natural MORAL PHILOSOPHY. But reason also fueled the criticism of religious ENTHUSIASM, calls for the SEPARATION OF CHURCH AND STATE, various defenses of orthodox Christianity, psychological explanations of the origins of the gods, and attacks by atheists on all religious belief.

Comparative analysis provided evidence that non-Christian peoples could develop cultures of high moral quality. These observations were easily adapted to polemical purposes, supporting arguments in favor of or against the truth of Christianity. They tended, however, to force people into awareness about the varieties of human religious practices and to raise questions about claims that made Christianity the only path to truth.

In conjunction with scrutiny of contemporary "primitive" cultures, enlightened investigators also turned for comparative research to the PAGANISM of the ancient Greek and Roman worlds. Some treated pagan religions as examples of a natural religious impulse common to all people, and they pointed out the parallels between pagan belief and Christian doctrines. Others were appalled at pagan practices, at the blind gullibility and irrationality evidenced in the ancient religions. For these critics, pagan religions provided evidence that religious belief was grounded in fear and vulnerability, and that religious practices tended to encourage distasteful displays of enthusiasm and fanaticism.

The Enlightenment produced several scholars who used HISTORY and textual biblical criticism as constructive tools in an attempt to show that Christianity was a changing rather than static religion. For some writers, history produced progress in religion; for others it brought degeneration; and for still others, it worked in cycles of growth, vigor, and decay. History provided further evidence for theories that rooted religious beliefs in the fundamental psychology of human beings. It also helped to inspire the beginnings of the search for the historical Jesus and for original Christianity.

In the face of doubts and confusion about religion, four basic forms of response were possible for enlightened people. They could refuse to examine the new ideas, appealing instead to tradition, to the Bible, or to institutional authority for justification; or they could maintain their faith, but search for creative ways to resolve the problems raised by new developments. If less wedded to traditional Christianity, they could seek new grounds for religious belief, perhaps inventing new forms of religious practice and new doctrines; or they could reject Christianity and all religion outright, maintaining a skeptical or even atheistic attitude. Each of these forms of response appeared during the Enlightenment, making it a markedly creative, if nevertheless disturbing era for religion and THEOLOGY.

Examination of the actual relations between the Enlightenment and religion reveals that the stereotypical view of the era as one favoring ATHEISM and SKEPTICISM is flawed. Certainly, the PHILOSOPHES of the second half of the 18th century in France were pursuing a campaign to secularize and to dechristianize French society, but their attitude represents only one of the positions regarding religion possible for enlightened individuals. Beyond the well-known Parisian boundaries, one finds that the Enlightenment actually produced a notable group of new religious forms and theologies: PIETISM; DEISM; Hasidism; the various types of illuminism and enthusiasm such as Quietism, Quakerism, and METHODISM; the mystical approaches of Emanuel SWEDENBORG, Louis-Claude de SAINT-MARTIN, or the comte de SAINT-GERMAIN; and neology.

Each of these forms offered a specific solution to the problems that had been raised for religious faith by the intellectual developments of the 17th century. DEISM and neology tended to stray away from traditional Christian doctrine and to locate the grounds for the universal religious impulse in the natural reason of humankind. In contrast, illuminists such as QUAKERS or Pietists stayed within the bounds of basic Christian belief but laid strong emphasis on intuition or a divine spark within people as the source of religious insight and faith. Finally, religious enthusiasm, embodied in Methodism or the American

GREAT AWAKENING, entailed a focus on spontaneous feeling as the primary force behind religious conviction.

Each of these approaches contained implications disturbing to established Christian churches. The turn to reason tended to threaten the specific content of Christian theology that was based on miracles and direct interventions by God. The turn to intuition and the inner light created an intensely private religion immune to control by clergymen and other agents of religious authority. And ENTHUSIASM created intense religious commitment that could fuel subversive social activity and, in some cases, intolerance.

Support for religion during the Enlightenment rested not only on specific allegiance to doctrines or to practices, but also on utilitarian ideals. It was recognized that religion played an important role in maintaining the social and political order. VOLTAIRE, who was renowned for his ANTICLERICALISM, for his support of religious toleration, and for his criticism of enthusiasm, noted this fact. And the enlightened despots of central Europe—FREDERICK II (THE GREAT) OF PRUSSIA and JOSEPH II OF AUSTRIA—consciously shaped their policies with this fact in mind. Only toward the end of the Enlightenment would a line of attack develop in the circle of Baron d' HOLBACH and his associates that effectively challenged this practical view of the value of religion.

One hallmark of the Enlightenment was the emergence of impassioned pleas for religious toleration. Begun in England by John Locke, the campaign for toleration was taken up vehemently on the European continent by Voltaire, Gotthold Ephraim LESSING, Moses MENDELSSOHN, and other philosophes. Toward the end of the century, toleration began to be established as official state policy, with Joseph II in Austria paving the way by formulating the Edict of Toleration of 1781.

The search for new grounds for religion was matched during the Enlightenment by an equally sincere series of attacks on all forms of religion. Although relatively few in number, these attacks nevertheless attracted widespread attention. The French intellectual environment produced several avowed atheists such as Julien Offray de LA METTRIE, Holbach, Claude-Adrien HELVÉTIUS, Denis DIDEROT, and Nicolas-Antoine BOULANGER. Their position colored the whole project for the ENCYCLOPÉDIE with hues of irreligion. But their position was an extreme one, not at all the norm for the wider European Enlightenment.

Not only Christian doctrine, but also the organization of the church and its role as a social and political institution came under scrutiny. The impulse toward reform grew specifically from enlightened POLITICAL THEORY. Within Catholicism, for example, lower clergy began asking for greater power within the political structure of the church (Richerism). And the higher clergy—bishops and archbishops—tried to limit the tendency of the popes to claim the right to rule as absolute monarchs (FEBRONI-

ANISM). They claimed the right to a significant role in church government in a manner that mirrored the claims made by the French PARLEMENTS with respect to the king.

Again, the Enlightenment produced reformers from within as well as critics who wished to destroy traditional church structures. Both the doctrines of Christianity and its institutional aspects received biting criticism. Anticlericalism, expressed in diatribes against abuses by clergymen and priests, in the successful campaign to disband the JESUITS, in the introduction of the principle of the SEPARATION OF CHURCH AND STATE, in the calls for toleration, and in campaigns for FREEDOM from ecclesiastical censorship set the Enlightenment apart from earlier eras in European history.

Whatever the challenges to and criticisms of established Christian churches, they continued to live and to thrive during the Enlightenment. But their relationship to the various European cultures was changing, for the Enlightenment was producing many competitors with answers to the basic religious queries of humankind. Traditional religions were being supplemented by new approaches within the bounds of orthodoxy, by new forms of faith and belief, and by secularized visions of the world that claimed to eliminate all need for religious faith.

See also ANCIENT RÉGIME; ANGLICANS; ARNOLD; BAYLE; BOSSUET; BOULAINVILLIERS; de BROSSES; BUTLER; CALVINISM; CLARKE; COLLINS; COPERNICAN REVOLUTION; CUDWORTH; EDWARDS; EPISTEMOLOGY; FÉNÉLON; FRANCKE; FREEMASONS; GIBBON; HAMANN; HERMETICISM; HUME; ILLUMINATI; JANSENISM; JOSEPHINISM; KANT; LEIBNIZ; LUTHERANISM; MALEBRANCHE; PHYSICO-THEOLOGY; PRIESTLEY; PUBLISHING; ROSICRUCIANS; REIMARUS; SEMLER; SHAFTESBURY; SIMON; SPINOZA; SUPERSTITION; TILLOTSON; TINDAL; TOLAND; VICO; WOOLSTON.

Further reading: C. J. Betts, *Early Deism in France: From the So-Called Déistes of Lyon (1564) to Voltaire's Lettres philosophies (1734)* (The Hague: Martinus Nijhoff, 1984); Gerald R. Cragg, *The Church and the Age of Reason, 1648–1789* (New York: Penguin Books, 1970).

Republic of Letters An ideal community of scholars throughout Europe. The concept of the Republic of Letters was not new to the ENLIGHTENMENT, but it developed new institutions and a different significance during this period. The term does not indicate a real place but rather an imaginary community of scholars made equals by their common love of learning. Theoretically, anyone who was able to engage in scholarly pursuits could be a member of the Republic of Letters, regardless of RELIGION, nationality, class, or gender. The Republic of Letters was strengthened by a number of institutions, such as universities, learned academies, and salons, which reinforced connections made through correspondence or travel, frequently on the GRAND TOUR.

The first permanent learned academies were established in LONDON and PARIS in the mid-17th century. In the 18th century, many provincial cities also set up academies. These institutions offered prizes for works devoted to philosophical and scientific issues, as well as providing prestige to those admitted as members. Jean-Jacques ROUSSEAU won first prize in the essay contest of the Académie de Dijon with his *Discours sur les sciences et les arts* (Discourse on the sciences and the arts; 1750). European UNIVERSITIES, especially the reformed universities of SCOTLAND and GERMANY, also played a role in encouraging learning. The scientist Albrecht von HALLER was connected with the University of GÖTTINGEN, and Adam SMITH taught at Glasgow and EDINBURGH. These universities expanded their activities by offering new courses on popular subjects, paying greater attention to research, and in the case of Göttingen by publishing a review journal and founding a learned academy.

In this guise, the Republic of Letters was dominated by men. Women often had difficulty participating, partly because they usually received an inferior EDUCATION. Still, it was not impossible for women to establish themselves as scholars or translators. René DESCARTES corresponded with several women regarding his philosophical writings, including Queen Christina of SWEDEN. Emilie du Châtelet translated the mathematics of Isaac NEWTON into French and wrote a book explaining the physics of Gottfried LEIBNIZ. Laura Bassi held a professorship of medicine in Bologna and became a member of its learned academy.

Women also played a role in facilitating the exchange of ideas by hosting salons. Parisian salons were imitated elsewhere in Europe, especially ENGLAND, and frequently received foreign visitors, such as Horace WALPOLE, David HUME, and Benjamin FRANKLIN. Salon hostesses served to shape and encourage the intellectual discussions in which they participated, forbidding the use of Latin, the language of learned scholarship, so that participants of different backgrounds could follow the conversation. They maintained the unity of the salon, seeing to it that visitors did not separate into private groups, so that all the guests would be united in a common undertaking. Two of the most successful salon hostesses were Marie-Thérèse GEOFFRIN, who provided financial support to many PHILOSOPHES, and Julie de LESPINASSE, whose salon was a center of philosophical thought and whose correspondence displayed her talent as a writer.

Correspondence was the traditional way for members of the republic to exchange ideas, and interesting letters were frequently circulated to others. Naturally, many members of the Republic of Letters availed themselves of several means of staying connected to other thinkers: In addition to holding a salon in her home, Laura Bassi corresponded with VOLTAIRE. Beginning in the late 17th century, gazettes, or newspapers, also appeared. Between 1684 and 1687, Pierre BAYLE edited in AMSTERDAM a journal of book reviews titled *Nouvelles de la République des Lettres* (News from the Republic of Letters). This publication continued through 1718 under other editors. Erudite journals also appeared in England, Germany, FRANCE, and SPAIN in the 18th century. The salon met the gazette in the *Correspondance littéraire* (Literary correspondence) published by Friedrich Melchior von GRIMM, a friend of Denis DIDEROT. This newspaper kept an aristocratic European audience informed of events in the French capital and reported on conversations in the salon hosted by the baron d'HOLBACH. Information was disseminated to a wider public through the development of the PUBLISHING industry, which expanded throughout Europe but was particularly strong in the UNITED PROVINCES OF THE NETHERLANDS and SWITZERLAND.

Travel allowed scholars to establish connections with others working on similar undertakings and to learn about foreign cultures. England, the United Provinces, and PRUSSIA provided a haven for Protestants, such as Bayle, exiled from France after the revocation of the Edict of Nantes in 1685. Voltaire spent the years 1726 to 1728 in England and wrote admiringly of English tolerance in his *Lettres philosophiques* (Philosophical letters; 1734). Later, Voltaire's own residence at Ferney, near GENEVA, became a popular destination for those on the intellectual scene, counting James BOSWELL and Giacomo CASANOVA among its visitors. Voltaire himself was a guest of FREDERICK II in Prussia, who also invited other European thinkers and writers to his court.

Through its origin as a model of erudite learning dating from the Renaissance, the Republic of Letters can appear conservative and exclusive. In the 17th century, the typical member of the Republic of Letters was engaged in correspondence with other scholars, but was generally uninterested in public opinion, controversy, or political subversion. The Republic of Letters took on a different and more complex range of meanings in the 18th century. The category of man or woman of letters (*gens de lettres*) became much broader, including those who made a living by writing books or newspaper reviews. *Gens de lettres* defined their status in different ways: Some relied on traditional mechanisms of patronage such as royal pensions while others saw publishing as a means of disseminating ideas, making a living, or both. Many thinkers saw this change as a decline. For Voltaire, the republic was destroyed by the presence of petty scribblers who lowered its standards. If the notion of the Republic of Letters is expanded to include wider participation, different means of dissemination of ideas, and an emphasis on public opinion, then the process of ENLIGHTENMENT as it developed in the 18th century can be seen as a new stage in the republic's history.

See also COSMOPOLITANISM; POLITENESS; SOCIAL INSTITUTIONS OF THE ENLIGHTENMENT; WOMEN AND THE ENLIGHTENMENT.

Further reading: L. W. B. Brockliss, *Calvet's Web: Enlightenment and the Republic of Letters in Eighteenth-Century France* (New York: Oxford University Press, 2002); Anne Goldgar, *Impolite Learning: Conduct and Community in the Republic of Letters, 1680–1750* (New Haven, Conn.: Yale University Press, 1995); Dena Goodman, *The Republic of Letters: A Cultural History of the French Enlightenment* (Ithaca, N.Y.: Cornell University Press, 1994).

revolution   A radical shift in culture, society, or politics, particularly with respect to the violent overthrow of an established authority. The modern concept of revolution emerged from the 18th century and owes much of its current form to the ENLIGHTENMENT. Whereas revolution once connoted a cyclical progression through types of government, by the end of the 18th century it meant the permanent replacement of one system of government by another. The American statesman Thomas JEFFERSON, for example, conceived of his new nation's revolution partly in such terms, seeing the AMERICAN REVOLUTION as a necessary response to the tyranny of the British monarchy. He did not, however, completely rid revolution of its cyclical connotations, as he also believed that regular revolutions may be necessary at regular intervals to keep a nation free of tyranny.

Allegorical representation, 1782, of America's struggle for independence from Britain, led by George Washington. *(Courtesy New York Public Library)*

The 18th century's understanding of revolution finds its origins in English political struggles during the 17th century. The Puritan Revolution (1640–60) was a revolution in the modern sense of the word, bringing both political and social change. Led by Oliver Cromwell, the revolutionary government beheaded the Stuart monarch Charles I, created a standing army—something new for England—and altered political power's social foundations by confiscating and redistributing the opposition's lands. Cromwell also changed the nature of religious politics, using Puritan religious ideals to stamp out perceived immoral influences such as theatrical performances.

The Puritan Revolution was short-lived, as after Cromwell's death Parliament recalled the king's son Charles II from his exile in FRANCE. The Stuart restoration was equally brief, however, as James II's incipient Catholicism led to his exile in the Glorious Revolution of 1688, which placed the Protestant WILLIAM III AND MARY II on the English throne. Despite its association with permanent change, the Glorious Revolution actually harkened back to older conceptions of revolution, as theorists such as John LOCKE held that the revolution returned England to its traditional arrangements.

In looking back on the 17th century, the 18th century also discovered a dramatic change in conceptions of intellectual authority that we now call the SCIENTIFIC REVOLUTION. This revolution marked a shift in Europe's approach to the natural world, as scientists such as Galileo GALILEI, Johannes KEPLER, and Sir Isaac NEWTON taught the European world that the universe was governed by natural laws and that humanity could uncover them. Thinkers such as VOLTAIRE, Denis DIDEROT, and Jean Le Rond D'ALEMBERT then took the notion of a rational, knowable universe and applied it to the political and social realm, criticizing institutions and social arrangements that appeared to them irrational.

The next great political revolution, the uprising of ENGLAND's colonies in North America under the kingship of George III, put this enlightened rationalistic criticism into effect. The American Revolution was guided by philosophers and intellectuals such as Benjamin FRANKLIN, John ADAMS, and Thomas Jefferson, all of whom wished to recreate government along rational lines. The clearest example of this is the nascent American government's publication on July 4, 1776, of the DECLARATION OF INDEPENDENCE, which listed the king's excesses and asserted the right of the colonists to revolt in the face of inadequate methods of redress. This call to establish reasonable democratic methods in government also provided the rebellion with its rallying cries against arbitrary interference, such as the Stamp Act, which placed a tax on all printed materials.

American forces were victorious in part due to support from England's enemies, such as France, and that country soon proved ripe for revolution with the

FRENCH REVOLUTION of 1789. A growing debt load from France's wars with England and the spread of starvation among the French populace drove the French to rebellion in PARIS in July of that year, with the storming of the infamous prison the Bastille. This set off a series of power struggles that culminated in 1792 with the deposing of the king. Initial receptions among radical European intellectuals to the revolution were positive, as comparisons were drawn to the English and American examples. However, whereas the aforementioned revolutions led to stable governments, the French Revolution shocked other European nations with its violence and aggression, and they mobilized to contain the anarchy. The greatest violent excesses of this revolution fell during the period of the Terror in 1793, when the Jacobin leader Maximilien ROBESPIERRE took advantage of invasion fears to seize power and have thousands of people put to death while hundreds of thousands more faced arrest for arbitrary and imaginary infractions against the new government.

With the French Revolution, the concept of revolution as a single cataclysmic political event reached its mature phase. However, during the 18th century other changes were under way in agriculture and industry that would enrich the modern view of revolution, making it less bound to a single political event or moment.

Agriculture in the 17th century was not much different from agriculture in the 14th century. In general, farms were organized on the two-field system, with one field being planted with grain and the other left fallow to regenerate. During the 18th century, however, particularly in the more advanced areas of England, farmers reorganized their fields and introduced new crops. First, farmers divided their fields into thirds, planting an alternative crop such as clover in the second field, while leaving the third field fallow. Second, the clover was used to feed cows and sheep, which provided manure for fertilizing the soil. Third, farmers planted new crops such as turnips, vetch, and clover. James "Turnip" Townsend became famous for advocating these new methods. These crops had the advantage that animals could eat them, producing yet more manure, while also fixing nitrogen directly in the soil. Moreover, crops that Europe's IMPERIALISM had brought back from the New World, such as the potato and maize, made it possible to feed even more people. Potatoes in particular grew well even in bad soil, providing the rural poor with an alternative food source.

Changes in agricultural methods first appeared in England around 1750 and then gradually moved eastward. The resulting increases in food production were impressive. In England, for example, production yields of seed increased during the 18th century from 4.5:1 to 10:1. This increase in productivity did not go unnoticed on the Continent, as monarchs such as FREDERICK II of Prussia and CATHERINE II of Russia actively sought to import English farming methods to their own kingdoms. The overall increase in the quantity of food also supported a larger population. More people could be fed, and with more people needing food, the demand for food increased, which set in motion an agricultural cycle that resulted in ever greater exploitation of the land, and ever more people eating the food it produced. Between 1800 and 1860 the amount of land under cultivation increased by 75 percent.

The agricultural revolution brought an end to subsistence farming in Europe and created a pool of available workers who built, perhaps, the 18th century's most profound revolution, the INDUSTRIAL REVOLUTION. Manufacturing before the Industrial Revolution was mostly craft-based. In the cities, individual shops led by a master would produce the shoes, cloth, barrels, and so on that a given area needed. These masters were organized into guilds, which protected the members from competition. This system was destroyed by the appearance of mechanized factory production. Beginning around 1750 in England and moving eastward for the next century, factories became the most productive centers of European society. Reorganizing work, capital structures, the nature of politics, and social relationships, the Industrial Revolution fundamentally altered the foundations of European society.

Between 1750 and 1850, huge productive centers, usually in cities, employing large numbers of people, were developed. Although these centers were few in number, by the 1820s social reformers had already begun to decry this form of capitalist production and were putting to work many of the notions of rights and rationality that the 18th century had produced. The English city of Manchester, for example, became a regular stop for social critics who wanted to reform the ills of this new system.

The Industrial Revolution had two phases: textiles, and coal and steel. The second stage was important to the 19th century. The first stage, however, was deeply embedded in the 18th century. As mechanized spinning began to increase after 1780, Europe and especially England produced so much cloth that the European market could not consume it all. The excess production was then distributed throughout Europe's empires.

The 18th-century period of the Industrial Revolution finished off what was left of the ANCIEN RÉGIME's economic structures. Guilds could not compete with the new ways and disappeared. Some craftsmen did well by serving the needs of the new factory-based system, but many were harmed by the changeover, as without guild protection workers lost all control over their work and were forced to live solely on their wages. Thus, to the end of the ancien régime and the reworking of scientific authority one can add the origins of a working class in the 18th century.

See also JACOBINS; WOMEN AND THE ENLIGHTENMENT.

Further reading: J. C. D. Clark, *Revolution and Rebellion: State and Society in England in the Seventeenth and Eighteenth Centuries* (New York: Cambridge University Press, 1986); Deborah Kennedy, *Helen Maria Williams and the Age of Revolution* (Lewisburg, Pa.: Bucknell University Press, 2002); Haydn T. Mason, ed., *The Darnton Debate: Books and Revolution in the Eighteenth Century* (Oxford: Voltaire Foundation, 1998); Timothy Morton and Nigel Smith, eds., *Radicalism in British Literary Culture, 1650–1830, from Revolution to Revolution* (New York: Cambridge University Press, 2002).

Reynolds, Joshua (1723–1792) *English portrait painter who was the chief rival of Thomas Gainsborough*

Reynolds contributed to AESTHETICS and moved in the LONDON literary and intellectual circle of Samuel JOHN-

Mrs. Siddons as the Tragic Muse, by Sir Joshua Reynolds. Reynolds participated in a circle of English intellectuals and artists that included the writer Samuel Johnson and the actor David Garrick. His portraits record his insights into the personalities of these figures. *(Courtesy Henry E. Huntington Library and Art Gallery, San Marino, California)*

SON. Reynolds stemmed from a family of clergymen and scholars, but he showed little inclination to follow in the footsteps of his father or forebears. He apprenticed himself in 1740 to Thomas Hudson, a portrait painter in Plymouth. In 1749, Reynolds embarked on an unusual GRAND TOUR of Europe and North Africa, sailing as a passenger on the ship of Commodore Augustus Keppel. Reynolds visited Lisbon, Cadiz, Algiers, and finally Minorca, where a fall from a horse resulted in a severe injury to his lip.

After his injury, Reynolds left Keppel's ship and traveled to ITALY. He remained in ROME for two years, mingling with the English artists who were residing in that city. On his return journey to ENGLAND, Reynolds visited Florence, Bologna, Modena, Mantua, VENICE, and PARIS, arriving in London in 1752.

With relative ease Reynolds established a reputation as an outstanding portrait artist. He lived comfortably on the earnings from his hundreds of private portrait commissions. His sitters included many prominent individuals and families, as well as King George III and Queen Charlotte. Among the intellectuals and artists whom he depicted were Horace WALPOLE, Samuel Johnson (five portraits), Laurence STERNE, David GARRICK, Oliver GOLDSMITH, Charles BURNEY, and Joseph BANKS. He also painted his beloved friend Angelica Kauffman and sat for portraits by her in return.

Reynolds was appointed the first president of the new Royal Academy of Arts established by King George III in 1768. Among his many academic duties was the delivery of an annual public address. In these speeches, Reynolds developed over the years his ideas on beauty, the imitation of NATURE, and other central themes of the ENLIGHTENMENT.

A lover of club life, Reynolds founded the famous Literary Club of London in order to give his friend Samuel Johnson a place to exercise his artful conversational skills. Original members besides Johnson and Reynolds included Oliver Goldsmith, Sir John Hawkins, Bennet Langton, Topham Beauclerk, Dr. Nugent, and Edmund BURKE. Later, David Garrick, James BOSWELL, and Charles Burney would also be accepted as members. Reynolds met Fanny BURNEY, the daughter of Charles Burney, in 1778. He also became a favorite with the "Bluestockings," a group of women writers that included Lady Mary MONTAGU, Mrs. Vesey, Mrs. Thrales, Mrs. Ord, Mrs. Walsingham, and Mrs. Cholmondeley.

Some of Reynolds's most important paintings were *Infant Samuel* (1776) and his masterpiece *Mrs. Siddons as the Tragic Muse* (1783). *The Witch Scene in Macbeth, The Death of Cardinal Beaufort,* and *Puck* were all painted for John Boydell's edition of Shakespeare's plays. Other paintings were *The Duchess of Devonshire Playing Hot Cockles with her Baby, Lady Smyth and her Children, Lord Heathfield,* and *Resignation* (dedicated to Oliver Goldsmith). In addition to his paintings, Reynolds left various essays and speeches about art and aesthetics.

Reynolds depicted his subjects in a manner that revealed the subtler aspects of their emotions and temperament. His paintings thus portray the intimate sides of personality and of daily life in a manner that sets them apart from the work of earlier portrait artists.

See also BLUESTOCKING; KAUFFMANN.

Richardson, Samuel (1689–1761) *English novelist and publisher*

Samuel Richardson's dual roles as publisher and best-selling author enabled him to exert great influence over English LITERATURE and middle-class public morality, and to obtain recognition throughout Europe. His hugely successful novels were important contributors to contemporary debates on women's EDUCATION and social and moral status.

Born in Derbyshire to a poor family, Richardson's earliest vocation was to enter the clergy, but his family could not finance the necessary schooling. When his father allowed him to select a trade, Richardson chose printing and was apprenticed in 1706 to John Wilde, later marrying his daughter Martha. In 1721, Richardson was able to establish his own press in LONDON, from which he printed speeches and records of the English House of Commons. Before beginning his own literary career, Richardson is believed to have revised in the 1730s two of Daniel DEFOE's works, *Complete English Tradesman* (1726) and *Tour Through the Whole Island of Great Britain* (1724–26).

It was this ongoing connection to PUBLISHING that ultimately brought Richardson his first literary success. Inspired by a book of sample letters that included a series of exchanges between a parson and his daughter who faced moral quandaries, Richardson turned his hand to writing with PAMELA, OR VIRTUE REWARDED (1740). The book was successful to the point of creating one of England's first examples of a runaway best seller. For months after it emerged, the public could talk of little else but Richardson's novel, and spent money on merchandise bearing images of the heroine.

With *Pamela* Richardson helped to develop and popularize what is termed the sentimental NOVEL. This new form was one of the major expressions of the culture of SENSIBILITY that dominated ENLIGHTENMENT ideas during the middle decades of the 18th century. Richardson's novels extolled simple virtue, particularly as exemplified by their female protagonists, who claimed to follow the impulses of their hearts and who frowned on sexual pleasures of the senses. These novels were filled with intimate descriptions of intense and private emotions. They also drew their heroes and heroines from the middle and lower classes, thereby putting forth the proposition that these classes rather than the aristocracy were the nurturing grounds for moral advancement. Middle-class moral-ity was based on piety, hard work, and, among women, modesty and abstinence from sex before marriage.

Richardson's first novel's immense success provoked a number of parodies that were also widely read. Henry FIELDING critiqued the morals of emerging sentimentalism, or sensibility, first in his NOVEL *An Apology for the Life of Mrs. Shamela Andrews,* which reversed Richardson's plot in its depiction of a sexually aggressive woman pretending to be naïve in order to trap an upper-class husband. In *Joseph Andrews,* Fielding expanded the satiric focus by depicting a virtuous young man beset by an older, sexually aggressive noblewoman. Others also joined in the attack against Richardson for various literary purposes, including the author Eliza HAYWOOD, whose *Anti-Pamela: Or, Feign'd Innocence Detected* (1742) is a darker satire than Fielding's. In her depiction of the antiheroine Syrena Tricksey, who uses sexuality as a means to manipulate men, Haywood engaged one of her continuing targets, the inequalities between men's and women's social status in England.

Richardson followed *Pamela* with CLARISSA, OR THE HISTORY OF A YOUNG LADY (1747–48), a novel that also attracted enthusiastic acclaim throughout Europe and helped to popularize SENTIMENTAL FICTION, contributing significantly to the spread of this genre and its associated views of humanity. A third novel, *The History of Sir Charles Grandison* (1753), presented Richardson's ideal Christian gentleman. In addition to these novels, Richardson left a large correspondence, much of it with women friends. His intimacy with the world of women is revealed throughout his novels, and his appreciation of their world is underscored in the high moral status assigned to it.

See also WOMEN AND THE ENLIGHTENMENT.

Further reading: Elizabeth Bergen Brophy, *Samuel Richardson* (Boston: Twayne, 1987); Ewha Chung, *Samuel Richardson's New Nation* (New York: Peter Lang, 1998); Carol Houlihan Flynn, *Samuel Richardson: A Man of Letters* (Princeton, N.J.: Princeton University Press, 1982); Mark Kinkead-Weekes, *Samuel Richardson: Dramatic Novelist* (Ithaca, N.Y.: Cornell University Press, 1973); Cynthia Griffin Wolff, *Samuel Richardson and the Eighteenth-Century Puritan Character* (Hamden, Conn.: Archon, 1972).

rights Privileges that belong to a person by nature or law. The idea of rights is a centuries-old concept that acquired significant new meaning during the ENLIGHTENMENT. During that era, it lost its association with corporate legal theories and moral theology, coming instead to denote a certain attribute of the individual. Throughout the 18th century there was talk of NATURAL RIGHTS and also of political rights. The two categories are not identical, although they are related. The first is all-inclusive (universal); the second is exclusive, reserved by law to the inhabitants of a specific nation at a given time in history. The concept of natural rights, newly framed as subjective individual rights, was enshrined in the revolutionary documents of the late 18th century, especially in the American DECLARATION OF INDEPENDENCE and in the French DECLARATION OF THE RIGHTS OF MAN AND CITIZEN. Meanwhile, specific political rights came to be separately recognized in the French declaration as well as in the UNITED STATES BILL OF RIGHTS.

The Concept of Natural Rights

Most rights theorists of the Enlightenment era believed that rights are "natural," related in some manner to an

Facsimile of the Bill of Rights, 1789, signed by John Adams *(Courtesy New York Public Library)*

unchanging foundation of universally recognizable principles presumed to operate in some way in and through human nature. Most writers of the era also believed that natural rights are "universal" and "individual," belonging not to legally distinct groups but to all individual men (though rights for women and people of color proved to be a thorny question), and that they constitute a form of PROPERTY, something possessed by individuals. Late in the 18th century, American writers such as Thomas JEFFERSON added two more basic attributes, thereafter widely accepted in enlightened circles: that rights are "inalienable," not removable by force or by decree, and "self-evident" because their existence is obvious to the human mind. Most writers also agreed that the primary natural right is the right to self-preservation, or life, but there the agreement ends.

The concept of rights is linked with ideas about REASON, JUSTICE AND THE LAW, NATURAL LAW, universalism, EQUALITY, and FREEDOM. Rights are also linked, less obviously, with UTILITY, HAPPINESS, VIRTUE, and the SOCIAL CONTRACT. The subject of rights during the Enlightenment was an integral part of two disciplines, MORAL PHILOSOPHY and jurisprudence, but the material for rights theories came not only from these mother disciplines but also from NATURAL PHILOSOPHY, MECHANICAL PHILOSOPHY, POLITICAL THEORY, and PSYCHOLOGY. Nuances in the treatments of the concept arise not only from different disciplinary origins but also from larger historical shifts of meaning during the 18th century.

The earliest enlightened writers on the subject drew their ideas from two primary sources: 17th-century natural law and the ancient Roman philosophies of stoicism and epicureanism. In the middle of the century, Scottish moral philosophers incorporated the Renaissance Machiavellian notion of civic virtue into their rights theories. Toward the end of the century, as the discourse of Enlightenment began giving birth to political calls for revolution, theories shifted once again, so that rights discussions referred to individual political rights.

Seventeenth-Century Natural Law

Natural law philosophers in the 17th century relied heavily on the belief that human nature partakes in the rational order of the universe, and on rational arguments, patterned after the deductive form of reasoning associated with geometry. Theories differed, however, in their explanations of the method by which the human mind acquires its basic ideas about rights; in their understanding of the relationship of rights to law, justice, and morality; in their definitions of the source of rights; and in their beliefs about how rights are legitimized and given compelling power to shape behavior.

The principal early writers in this tradition include the Dutch statesman Hugo Grotius, the Englishmen Thomas HOBBES and John LOCKE, the "Germans" Samuel PUFENDORF, Gottfried Wilhelm LEIBNIZ, and Christian THOMASIUS, and the Scottish Francis HUTCHESON. In the middle of the 18th century, two Swiss jurists, Jean-Jacques BURLAMAQUI and Emmerich de VATTEL, would rearticulate this tradition, applying it to a new set of problems. Even the eccentric and immensely important Genevan Jean-Jacques ROUSSEAU belongs in some ways to this tradition, although he ultimately turned it on its head.

Natural rights theory split very early into two schools, one that asserted that the idea of rights exists innately in the rational human mind, to be discovered by the simple application of unaided reason, and another that claimed that our ideas about rights are empirically derived in the processes by which the human mind constructs ideas from the raw materials provided by the senses. Of the early natural law writers, for whom this question was paramount, Grotius, Hobbes, Pufendorf, Leibniz, and Thomasius adopted the first line of argumentation, while Locke and Hutcheson championed the second. These writers also disagreed about whether law precedes rights in the order of the world, and about the relationship between rights and justice.

The concept of rights had long been linked to the idea that right and wrong, and good and evil have objective existence, but the task of proving this belief had taken on new urgency in the last half of the 17th century. Europeans were confronted at that time with the reality of a new international order, the product of the division of Western Christendom into competing branches (ROMAN CATHOLICISM and the various Protestant confessions). Furthermore, they were being introduced, through the many European VOYAGES OF DISCOVERY, to cultures organized on moral principles fundamentally different from the ones common in Europe. Both developments helped to undermine the idea that a God-given moral and social order rules everywhere in the universe, and seemed to open the door to moral relativism. The latter, however, was a repugnant idea, so philosophers set out to replace the old theological principles of good and evil with universal natural philosophical principles, which all people would recognize and accept. They hoped in this way to place the subject of morality beyond the reach of warring theologians and squabbling religious faiths. It is in this context that the subject of moral philosophy assumed its compelling prominence during the Enlightenment.

Discussions of rights were affected because, as the source of morality in the old order, God had also been the guarantor and enforcer of justice and human rights. Having posited a world in which God no longer directly exercised these roles, philosophers also began seeking to ground rights in the natural world. Grotius posited that an innate human "social appetite" leads individuals to gather into groups and allows them to recognize that their own behavior affects others beside themselves. Leibniz believed that "benevolence" operates in the universe to guarantee that our actions are beneficial not only to us but to others. Hobbes argued that two nonmoral principles, "necessity" and "utility," lead fundamentally selfish individuals to come together into communities governed by social contracts. These contracts require individuals to give up some of their natural liberty in exchange for the protections of society. Pufendorf asserted that "duty" and "sociality" are the source of a universal moral obligation to respect the dignity of all our fellow human beings.

For the Enlightenment, the notions of utility, duty, and equality would prove especially provocative and productive as writers reacted to their implications. In keeping with his empirical bent, Locke argued that human ideas about good and evil develop directly from experience. To elaborate, he adopted Hobbes's basic idea of utility but paired it with a psychological explanation of morality, which relied for its basic idea on ancient Epicurean writings. Underlying utility, Locke argued, is the pleasure-pain principle. We derive the idea "good" from the experience of pleasure and the idea "bad" from experiences of pain. The experience of pain produces a kind of psychological uneasiness that is unpleasant, and it is this discomfort and the desire for pleasure that cause humans to choose good and ultimately useful behavior.

Scottish Moral Philosophers

Toward the middle of the 18th century, logical and practical problems in these traditions moved younger writers, especially in SCOTLAND, to subject morality and rights to renewed scrutiny. David HUME, for example, applied skeptical, critical reason to the whole enlightened tradition of rights, showing that no valid proof can be given either for rational, a priori (theoretically deduced) forms of law and rights or for universal, empirical forms. He argued that human reason is entirely incapable of discerning moral principles or their derivative, natural rights. But, unwilling to abandon the world to moral neutrality, he asserted that ideas about morality still exist; they come, however, directly from the senses, specifically from a sixth moral sense that allows us to feel SYMPATHY with others. Hume borrowed the idea of a moral sense from Francis Hutcheson, the moral philosopher at the University of Glasgow who was Adam SMITH's teacher. But Hutcheson's moral sense operated in the Lockean manner to produce ideas about good and evil. Hume's innovation was the decision to make morality a matter of feeling and intuition.

Hume's ideas were greeted with outrage and fear by many people, but among those who looked on them positively were two men of great significance for rights theories of the later Enlightenment: Adam Smith in Scotland and Denis DIDEROT in FRANCE. Smith combined Hume's idea of sympathy with the utilitarian idea that pleasure motivates good behavior (articulated by Hutcheson as well as Locke) and with the Renaissance idea of civic virtue. The result was a persuasive alternative to Locke's vision of society, social good, and human rights. Whereas Locke had asserted that owning property (land, moveable goods, and ideas) is essential to the good of humankind, Smith posited the existence of a basic human need to engage in exchange, or commerce. It is from the act of exchanging money and things that moral good ("happiness" in Smith's language) is created. Smith gives happiness a decidedly social twist, since the happy man will not only seek money and property but will also work to advance knowledge and the arts and will participate fully in the civic life of the community. Smith thus argued, in essence, that a person cannot be happy or good unless he or she is thoroughly involved in all aspects of civil society. Thus, it followed that he also claimed that the pursuit of happiness through the medium of commerce and exchange is a basic human right.

Smith's ideas influenced Thomas Jefferson's assertion in the American Declaration of Independence that the pursuit of happiness numbers among the inalienable rights of man. But there are other, equally influential usages of this concept, most notably by Cesare BECCARIA, who argued against CAPITAL PUNISHMENt by pointing out that effective punishment must not infringe on the right of a person to live, and further argued that capital punishment works against utilitarian principles by allowing a criminal to escape the much greater pain of imprisonment. Meanwhile, the philosophe Diderot used the ideas of sympathy and utility to mount outspoken, though anonymous, attacks on SLAVERY and other oppressive forms of human domination.

Rights and the Individual

Toward the end of the 18th century, the concept of rights became part of reforming and revolutionary discourses alike. Specific formulations and applications of rights theory would be scrutinized and criticized as people reacted not only to oppression but also to the use of the language of rights to justify it. The subject of rights took on ever-greater importance, playing a major role in the well-known works of Jean-Jacques Rousseau and Immanuel KANT, and appearing in new form in works by radical thinkers such as Mary WOLLSTONECRAFT and her husband, William GODWIN. In the SOCIAL CONTRACT Rousseau overturned the idea that rights belong to individuals, locating them instead in the community. His goal was to transform the less-than-ideal natural world of individuals into an artificial society within which each person acquires individual rights by participating in a community. Rousseau also addressed the question of rights for women, a subject that received increasing attention toward the end of the century. All discussions of universal rights prior to this point used the term *men,* which could be used to refer to all humanity or to all members of the male gender. Rousseau, however, argued specifically against rights for women, drawing on the common notion, also deeply rooted in the Enlightenment, that women could not be given rights because they lacked the requisite capacity to reason. Rousseau stated a variant of this idea in ÉMILE, arguing that men and women are equal but different in a complementary way. Men are rational and thus have rights, and women are intuitive and lack rights. This natural fact meant that the world of active, civic, political life should be the preserve of men, while the world of home and family should be reserved for women. Rousseau went on to argue that men and women should have different educations to prepare them for their special roles.

The outspoken feminist Wollstonecraft argued against Rousseau that women and men are fully equal, and that women should have the same rights and education as men. Meanwhile, Godwin began articulating a primitive form of communism as he sought ways to guarantee equal rights and freedoms for all men and women.

Kant, seeking to synthesize all the traditions of the Enlightenment in their Scottish, English, French, and German garbs, once again separated rights and law from the order of nature. He argued that both rights and law are human creations, neither derived from nature nor learned from God's revelations. Moreover, they are not universal in scope. With this argument, Kant raised the problem of morality anew: If the principles and laws governing human relations were no longer rooted in nature or in God, then how were right and wrong and good and evil to be distinguished, and how could human societies ensure that right and good would have the upper hand. Kant's answer was that individual freedom must be protected at all costs, for unless people are free to choose one act over another, no morality can exist. He also elevated the so-called categorical imperative, a version of the biblical golden rule, to preeminence. Today, of course, the problem of rights, and of the relation between rights and what is right, remain central to political discourse.

See also COLONIALISM; EPICUREAN PHILOSOPHY; IMPERIALISM; TOLERATION.

Further reading: Stephen Buckle, *Natural Law and the Theory of Property. Grotius to Hume* (Oxford: Clarendon Press, 1991); Charles L. Griswold, Jr., *Adam Smith and the Virtues of Enlightenment* (Cambridge: Cambridge University Press, 1999); Anthony Pagden, *The Language of Political Theory in Early Modern Europe* (Cambridge: Cambridge University Press, 1987); Leo Strauss and Joseph Cropsey, *History of Political Philosophy,* 3rd ed. (Chicago: University of Chicago Press, 1987); R. Tuck, *Natural Rights Theories: Their Origin and Development* (Cambridge: Cambridge University Press, 1991).

Rights of Man, The   A two-part pamphlet (part one, 1791; part two, 1792) written by the radical English-American political philosopher and propagandist Thomas PAINE. *The Rights of Man* supported the FRENCH REVOLUTION and analyzed the social, economic, and political problems of 18th-century societies.

Paine wrote the first part of *The Rights of Man* as a response to *REFLECTIONS ON THE REVOLUTION IN FRANCE* by Edmund BURKE. Burke had criticized the French Revolution as a dangerous enterprise founded on abstract ideas rather than well-rooted in historical tradition. Paine rebutted Burke by criticizing the English institutions so cherished by Burke. Paine contrasted the limited suffrage and religious discrimination of ENGLAND with the universal suffrage and religious TOLERATION that had been established in revolutionary France. Paine based his arguments on the concepts of NATURAL RIGHTS and EQUALITY, both of which had entered the discourse of the ENLIGHTENMENT through the writings of John LOCKE.

Paine's pamphlet met with sensational success in Great Britain, the UNITED STATES, and France and made Paine one of the more controversial figures of the late 18th century.

In 1792, part two of *The Rights of Man* appeared. It explored the idea of a republic, linking it to progressive social policies designed to minimize the privileges of the rich and the oppression of the poor. Paine proposed a progressive tax on land and other forms of property that would fund a system of social security for older people and EDUCATION for poor children. He also proposed a system of public employment for the jobless, assistance for the poor, and housing for displaced people. He pointed out that despite these programs, taxes could still be reduced if only the government would stop spending money on useless wars and on pensions for aristocrats.

Paine then moved beyond proposing radical social and economic reforms by calling for political revolution. "From a small spark kindled in America, a flame had arisen not to be extinguished . . . If universal peace, civilization, and commerce are ever to be the happy lot of man, it cannot be accomplished but by a revolution in the systems of government."

An astounding 1.5 million copies of part two were sold in Great Britain alone—much to the alarm of the British government, which banned *The Rights of Man.* Officials feared the influence of the pamphlet on the artisans, unskilled workers, poor people, and small-business owners who did not possess the right to vote in Great Britain. The British government tried and convicted Paine for seditious libel, that is, for writing to incite violent change and rebellion against the government. Paine was declared an outlaw. Before the trial, however, Paine had fled to France, where he was greeted by enthusiastic crowds and, as an honorary French citizen, was elected to the National Convention.

See also POLITICAL THEORY.

Rittenhouse, David (1732–1796) *American astronomer, inventor, surveyor, and politician*
Rittenhouse was born near Germantown, Pennsylvania, and spent most of his life in the PHILADELPHIA area. He

was a clock maker by profession, who also built compasses, surveying devices, barometers, and several famous American telescopes and orreries. Rittenhouse introduced the practice of using spiderwebs as cross hairs in the eyepieces of telescopes.

Rittenhouse was an acquaintance of Benjamin FRANKLIN and other members of the AMERICAN PHILOSOPHICAL SOCIETY, to which he was elected as a member in 1768. Eventually, he succeeded Franklin as president of the American Philosophical Society, serving in that capacity from 1791 until 1796.

In 1769, Rittenhouse participated in the international scientific project of observing the TRANSIT OF VENUS and was one of the first astronomers to note that the planet Venus had an atmosphere. His skills at instrumental measurement also made him a valuable surveyor, and he helped to establish the legal boundaries of the states of Pennsylvania, Maryland, New York, New Jersey, and Massachusetts.

During the AMERICAN REVOLUTION, Rittenhouse served as a member of the Pennsylvania Assembly (1777–89), president of the Council of Safety (1777), and treasurer of Pennsylvania (1777–89). President George WASHINGTON appointed him as the first director of the United States Mint (1792–95). Thomas JEFFERSON praised Rittenhouse's talents, noting that "the world has but one Ryttenhouse [sic], and never had one before."

See also ASTRONOMY; BAROMETER; ORRERY; SCIENTIFIC ACADEMIES; TECHNOLOGY AND INSTRUMENTATION; TELESCOPE; UNITED STATES.

Rivals, The   Play by Richard Brinsley SHERIDAN, who claimed to have written it during a three-week period. He based several of the 1775 play's episodes on his own highly publicized courtship of and marriage to the famous singer Eliza Linley. While courting Linley, Sheridan had fought duels with another zealous admirer, Captain Matthews. Both the duels and the theme of courtship competition appeared in the play and contributed to its success in the fashionable society of LONDON and Bath.

The play's heroine is Lydia Languish, the young niece of Mrs. Malaprop, who must marry with her aunt's consent or lose half of her fortune. Lydia's reading in SENTIMENTAL FICTION has led her to expect that her own life will contain a high degree of excitement and emotion. She has decided that she, like the heroine of her favorite sentimental novel, will sacrifice the interests of money and family in order to marry for love. Aware of Lydia's determination to avoid an arranged marriage, a young aristocrat named Captain Absolute courts Lydia under the assumed identity of a penniless junior officer, Ensign Beverley.

Difficulties arise because Absolute's father, unaware of his son's activities, has independently decided to arrange with Mrs. Malaprop for Lydia and Captain Absolute to marry. Young Captain Absolute, alias Ensign Bev-

erley, fears that he will lose Lydia if he drops his disguise, and reveals that he is the man Mrs. Malaprop intends for her to marry. Hearing of Beverley's courtship, Bob Acres, another suitor for Lydia's hand, sends a challenge to the ensign, unaware that Beverley is actually his old friend, Captain Absolute. All the characters are trapped into a series of superficial and deceitful relationships on account of Lydia's rejection of arranged marriage and Captain Absolute's deceit.

Sheridan uses the devices of disguise and mistaken identity popular in the 18th century to satirize both the values espoused in sentimental novels and the culture of enlightened female intellectuals (BLUESTOCKINGS) led by Elizabeth MONTAGU. Sheridan mocks the shallow nature of sentimental concerns, makes a strong plea for genuine confrontation with the passions, and calls for a return to conventional forms of marriage. Like Oliver GOLDSMITH, he lamented the substitution of superficial comedy during the 18th century for the authentic "laughing comedy," which had been written by Shakespeare and playwrights of the 17th century.

With *The Rivals,* Sheridan revived the old comedy of manners that had been popular during the 17th-century Restoration. His work joined the chorus of voices calling for a rejection of the values of the culture of SENSIBILITY. By implication, it also criticized the general culture of the ENLIGHTENMENT, turning back to pre-enlightened eras for its inspiration. That impulse would grow stronger as the 18th century drew to a close, eventually producing the new era called ROMANTICISM.

Robertson, William (1721–1793)   *Scottish historian*
Robertson was one of the three great leaders of the Scottish ENLIGHTENMENT who, in an allusion to the ancient republic of ROME, were known as "the triumvirate." His partners in this position were Edward GIBBON and David HUME. These three men were the most widely read historians of their time. Robertson's work remained popular well into the 19th century.

Robertson was a Presbyterian minister, a member of the principals of Edinburgh University, and the moderator (head) of the Scottish Presbyterian Assembly. He was a member of the Select Society, a renowned group of enlightened laymen that included Henry Home (Lord Kames), David Hume, Adam SMITH, James Burnett (Lord Monboddo), Sir David Dalrymple (Lord Hailes), Adam FERGUSON, and other prominent intellectuals of EDINBURGH.

Robertson wrote in the historical style called "philosophical history." He believed that natural causes act in history and reveal the action of God's plan for humankind. Like many of his contemporaries, Robertson believed that all societies go through a universal series of developmental stages. If similarities exist between two different societies, it is because they stand at the same level of development, not because one has directly influenced or shaped the other. Robertson was particularly noted for his ability to generalize from particular historical observations to universal theories about the history of humanity.

His *History of the Reign of the Emperor Charles V* offered a pioneering attempt to combine an analysis of change over time with a portrayal of the internal relations and character of a specific period (where time is stopped). His portrait of European civilization during the era of Charles V inspired Gibbon's own descriptions of Rome and also served as a model for the great American historian William Prescott.

Robertson left four major historical works: *The History of Scotland* (1759); *The History of the Reign of the Emperor Charles V* (1769); *The History of America* (1777); and *Historical Disquisition concerning the Knowledge Which Ancients had of India* (1791).

See also HISTORY.

Robespierre, Maximilien François Isadore (1758–1794) *French lawyer, orator, statesman, and radical democrat, leader of the Mountain (a Jacobin faction) in the French Revolution*

Robespierre came from a family of lawyers and local notables in the city of Arras. His father, Maximilien Barthélémy François de Robespierre, worked as a lawyer for the Council of Artois. His mother was Jacqueline Marguerite Carraut. Young Maximilien had a brother, Augustin, who also participated in the revolution. His sister, Marguerite Charlotte, joined the two brothers in their political activities. Robespierre studied with the Oratorians at Arras, then with the JESUITS in PARIS at the prestigious Collège Louis-le-Grand. He distinguished himself as a student, showing special talent in rhetoric. His classes included the study of writers associated with the ENLIGHTENMENT: MONTESQUIEU, Abbé CONDILLAC, Gabriel Bonnot de Mably, John LOCKE, Anne-Robert-Jacques TURGOT, and Jean-Jacques ROUSSEAU.

Robespierre received a degree in law in 1781, entered the bar at Arras in 1782, and earned both professional and social recognition rather quickly. He became a member of the Academy of Arras in 1783 and won a seat representing the Third Estate (bourgeoisie) in the delegation from Arras to the 1789 Estates General meeting. He left Arras for Paris, returning only once, in 1791, to his native city.

In Paris, Robespierre joined the Club Breton (later called the JACOBIN Club), becoming its president in 1790. Robespierre also served between 1789 and 1791 as a representative to the Constituent Assembly. He played a minor role in the general exercise of power, but he stood out on account of his support for the abolition of capital punishment and for universal male voting rights. During the Legislative Assembly meetings (1791–92), he called for political democracy and opposed the declaration of war with Austria (April 1792).

With the opening of the National Convention, Robespierre became a leading member of the Mountain wing of the Jacobin party. As events unfolded, he increasingly opposed the policies of the moderate Girondin faction of the Jacobin party. Although he did not plan or participate in the insurrection of August 10, 1792, that brought the downfall of the Girondin leaders, he welcomed the ascendancy gained by the radical Mountain faction. He also supported the abolition of the French monarchy (September 1792) and voted for the condemnation and execution of King LOUIS XVI.

The Mountain leaders assumed control in the Convention at a point when anarchy and rebellion were becoming increasingly common in Paris and throughout FRANCE. In addition, the war in Europe was going poorly and one of the leading revolutionary generals, Dumouriez, had defected to the Austrians in early April. The Mountain leaders viewed the situation as a crisis. In order to reestablish government control and order, they set up the Committee of Public Safety with Robespierre as its head. He was joined by 11 other colleagues, including Louis-Antoine-Léon de SAINT-JUST. The Committee of Public Safety established judicial tribunals throughout France whose purpose was to wrest control of the prosecution of counter-revolutionary enemies from the hands of the mob. These tribunals backed the famed Reign of Terror (August 1793 to July 1794) in which thousands of people were executed and many thousands more imprisoned.

The downfall of Robespierre, commonly called 9 Thermidor in reference to its date on the revolutionary calendar, occurred in July 1794. The war in Europe had turned in favor of the French, thereby easing the sense of crisis and making people less willing to tolerate political terror. The Parisian working classes resented some of the economic regimentation that had been established on their behalf. Members of the Convention began to fear the actions of Robespierre after Danton was guillotined. Finally, a faction in the Convention succeeded in pushing through a decree that outlawed Robespierre, Saint-Just, and their associates and decreed their arrest. Robespierre was arrested on July 27, 1794 (9 Thermidor) and guillotined the next day.

Robespierre had built his political and economic program on the enlightened concepts of EQUALITY and the NATURAL RIGHTS of man, derived from Rousseau and Locke. Robespierre drew radical conclusions from the writings of these two men. He believed that the sovereignty of the nation resides in the people, not in the monarch or any constituted body. Principles of justice and humanity require the recognition of the equality of all citizens of a nation. This civic equality, in turn, requires equal political rights; thus, Robespierre always called for universal suffrage (males only), for the universal right to join the National Guard, and for universal access to public office. Robespierre viewed the

Constitution of France as an expression of the general will of the sovereign people.

From the concept of equality, Robespierre also derived the idea of the "right to exist." This right translated easily into economic policies designed to protect the basic subsistence of the working classes and the peasantry. As a result, Robespierre opposed liberal policies that deregulated business, trade, commerce, and capital investment. However, he also opposed the existence of any organization—whether guild, privileged owner, producer, or worker trade union—that served special economic interests.

Robespierre envisioned a day when the citizens of France would be enlightened enough to exercise all power themselves through local direct democracy and national representative institutions. But he did not believe that the people were yet capable of exercising such responsibility. Hence, he and the other members of the Committee of Public Safety would serve as custodians of the sovereign power of the people (a variation of Rousseau's "virtuous legislator"). To meet the goal of widespread enlightenment of French citizens, Robespierre instituted reforms of the system of EDUCATION.

Like most PHILOSOPHES, Robespierre believed that genuine enlightenment and the creation of modern civic virtue required shaping both the intellectual quality and moral character in a people. Consequently, he also supported the creation of a new secular cult, the Cult of the Supreme Being, to replace Christianity.

In the end, Robespierre's distrust of conservative and anarchical facets in human character and his impatience with the slow pace of change combined with domestic and international circumstances to lead him into the excesses of the Reign of Terror. After his era of ascendancy, the French Revolution began to move into more conservative phases. Robespierre's career thus stands as a testimonial to the Enlightenment, as an example of the political egalitarianism and humanitarian programs that it helped to nurture and as evidence of the difficulties and pitfalls that would face European political parties committed irrevocably to implementing them.

See also MORAL PHILOSOPHY; POLITICAL THEORY.

Further reading: C. B. A. Behrens, *Society, Government and the Enlightenment: The Experiences of Eighteenth-Century France and Prussia* (London: Thames & Hudson, 1985); Alfred Cobban, *A History of Modern France Vol. I: 1715–1799. Old Régime and Revolution*, 3rd ed. (Baltimore: Penguin Books, 1963); François Furet, *Interpreting the French Revolution,* tr. Elborg Forster (Cambridge: Cambridge University Press, 1981).

Robinson Crusoe Novel by Daniel DEFOE first published in 1719. The full title of the book is *The Life and Strange Surprising Adventures of Robinson Crusoe.*

Robinson Crusoe was inspired by several accounts of shipwrecked mariners that Defoe had read in contemporary periodicals. The most notable of these was the tale of Alexander Selkirk, a young sailor set ashore in 1714 on an uninhabited island off the coast of Chile. Selkirk remained on the island for more than four years before another ship discovered him and rescued him. During this time, he lived by fishing, gathering food, and domesticating a native breed of wild goats.

Defoe includes many of the details from Selkirk's story in *Robinson Crusoe.* Crusoe narrates, beginning his tale with an account of his original decision to go to sea. In doing so, he defies his father, who had wanted him to follow a solid, middle-class profession such as business or law. Crusoe dates the beginning of his misfortunes to this original sin of disobedience, which casts the novel in the form of a spiritual autobiography. Throughout the novel, the hero attempts to determine God's will by interpreting the "signs" he finds in the world around him.

As a sailor, Crusoe makes several voyages to the coast of Africa. He is on his way to Africa to trade for slaves when his ship is wrecked in a storm, and he swims to the shore of a nearby island. When he wakes up the next morning, he discovers that he is the only survivor of the wreck. A day later, he swims out to the ship and salvages useful materials such as clothing, tools, weapons, and gunpowder. These items represent the European technology that helps Crusoe to convert his island from an inhospitable wilderness into a productive kingdom.

After Crusoe has spent several years on the island, he sees a footprint on a beach not far from his own settlement. He discovers that a tribe of cannibals from a nearby island have been bringing their human sacrifices to his island. On one of these occasions, he manages to rescue a young native from the cannibals. The young man, whom Crusoe names Friday, becomes the hero's companion and slave. He teaches Friday to speak the English language and converts him to Christianity. Crusoe recognizes that his new "slave" is a better Christian and an inherently more noble human being than he is.

Crusoe's experience on the island serves as a general metaphor for the European colonization of the so-called New World. The character of Friday offers a vehicle for Defoe's criticisms of modern European civilization. Friday, a black man, represents a primitive, pristine, and highly moral alternative way of life. The concept of the NOBLE SAVAGE and the associated notion that primitive civilizations, whether ancient or modern, were superior to the 18th-century European culture, became widespread in the later years of the ENLIGHTENMENT.

In general, Defoe voiced several themes that were common to enlightened critical thinkers: distrust of RATIONALISM, criticism of the social ills associated with technological change, and rejection of the inhumane treatment of colonial peoples. His positions reveal that the rule of REASON and pursuit of PROGRESS associated with the Enlightenment did not, in the eyes of contemporaries, necessarily produce humanitarian results.

Robinson Crusoe was an enormous success throughout Europe. Jean-Jacques ROUSSEAU honored the book by declaring in his educational novel *ÉMILE* that Defoe's book should be the first book read by a developing child.

See also TRAVEL LITERATURE.

rococo   Term denoting the style in art and architecture that was closely allied with the culture of SENSIBILITY during the ENLIGHTENMENT. Recognizable elements of the rococo began to appear in FRANCE around 1700 and quickly spread throughout Europe. Until 1760, the style dominated the ART AND ARCHITECTURE in most European nations. The rococo had musical counterparts in the *STYLE GALANT* (gallant style) of France and the Italian peninsula.

As part of the culture of sensibility, rococo art tried to evoke pleasurable feelings rather than to create the awe, reverence, and contemplation desired by BAROQUE STYLE artists. It utilized the idea that the natural is simple and pleasant, that it brings forth feelings of delight and warmth.

Rococo was primarily an ornamental style, associated with interior decoration and art objects. In Bavaria, Swabia, AUSTRIA, and SWITZERLAND, however, where its various motifs were incorporated into the construction of

The Kaisersaal, Würzburg Residenz, Würzburg, designed by Balthasar Neumann. The Kaisersaal, one of the finest German rococo interiors, shows the treatment of natural light and the love of decoration that were hallmarks of the rococo style. *(Courtesy Photo-Verlag Gundermann, Würzbarg)*

palaces, theaters, and pilgrimage churches, rococo also had pronounced architectural impact.

Scholars disagree about the origins of the term *rococo*, but the most common etymology treats the word as a creation of late-18th-century AESTHETICS and art criticism. According to this interpretation, the term *rococo* combined the French word *rocaille* with the Portugese *barroco*. The first term denoted the "grotto" style with falling water, decorative shell motifs, scrollwork, and rocks. The second word, also often treated as the origin of the term *baroque,* denoted a rough, irregular pearl. The combination of the two words created the idea of an irregular, asymmetrical form elaborately decorated with playful curving shell and scroll motifs.

Whatever the origins of the term *rococo*, the style, known originally as *genre pittoresque* (PICTURESQUE genre), was fully described as early as 1734 in a book by the goldsmith Juste-Aurèle Meissonier. The title of the book—*Des fontaines, des cascades, des ruines, des rocailles et coquillages, des morceaux d'architecture qui font des effets bizarres, singuliers et pittoresques, par leurs formes piquantes et extraordinaires, dont souvent aucune partie ne répond à l'autre* (On fountains, waterfalls, ruins, grottoes, and shellwork, on the parts of architecture that produce bizarre, unusual or picturesque effects by means of their piquant and extraordinary forms whose parts often are unrelated)—actually lists the major rococo decorative motifs and the effects they wished to create. As the list reveals, the motifs are all drawn from the natural world. Whether in building interiors, decorative porcelains, or paintings, rococo embellished its subjects with these motifs.

But rococo was more than this list suggests. It extended and changed baroque architecture by increasing the use of curved components, by adapting the use of natural light sources to different effects, and by opening up interiors to create structures that almost seem to float.

The adoption of the S-curve as a primary form accomplished the goal of creating more motion. William HOGARTH, the English artist and critic, called the S-curve "the line of beauty" and, like many of his contemporaries, believed that it conveyed feminine qualities. In fact, the entire rococo style and the culture of sensibility were associated with the feminine in formal 18th-century aesthetic theory. Favorite rococo themes revealed how the feminine was perceived: Images of Venus and Cupid, or themes of love, and depictions of the aristocracy at play in the countryside abounded. NEOCLASSICISM, in contrast, depicted the activities of gods or kings in compositions organized symmetrically along straight lines; they were declared representative of the masculine.

Rococo concepts inspired buildings that seemed light, airy, almost ethereal in nature. This effect was produced by opening up interior structures. No better example exists than the open staircase by Balthasar NEUMANN at the Schönborn Residenz in Würzbürg. The structure seems to float despite its great width and height.

Finally, rococo architecture modified the typical baroque uses of natural light. No longer were light sources harnessed for the purpose of producing dramatic effect. Instead, light provided an element of play. Interior walls, sculptures, and plaster were embedded with tiny bits of glass to create a mosaic mirror. Sunlight streaming through glass windows reflected off the glass, creating surfaces that shimmered and sparkled, light that seemed to dance across rooms. The rococo adapted scientific optical discoveries, so central during the Enlightenment, to its goal of creating playful beauty. Rococo interiors used white and pastel marbles, plaster, and paint, rather than the primary colors and dark marbles favored by baroque architects.

Major rococo architects were Balthasar Neumann, Germain Boffrand, Juste-Aurèle Meissonier, Cosmas Damian ASAM, and his brother Egid Quirin ASAM, François de CUVILLIÉS, Johann Bernhard FISCHER VON ERLACH, Peter Thumb, Dominikus Zimmermann, Johann Michael Fischer, K. I. Dientzenhofer, and Bartolomeo RASTRELLI.

Notable structures were the Tsarskoe Seloe Palace outside SAINT PETERSBURG, Russia; the Schönborn Residenz and Hofkapelle of Würzburg, GERMANY; Pommersfelden in the countryside between Würzburg and Bamberg; the Nymphenburg Palace of MUNICH, Germany, with its outbuildings such as the Amalienburg Hunting Lodge, and the Chinese Pagodenburg; the Residenztheater in Munich; and the old Opera House in Bayreuth, Germany. In France, the leading rococo works were interiors. Outstanding examples in PARIS included the Hôtel de Soubise, now part of the Archives Nationales; the Petit Luxembourg Palace; and the many rooms that were decorated for Madame de POMPADOUR at Versailles.

In the realm of painting, rococo style manifested itself through shifts in subject matter, coloration, and compositional design. Gone were the serious subjects of the baroque drawn from mythology and religion. In their place, the rococo offered depictions of pastoral pleasures such as bathing in a stream or swinging; or they depicted simple daily activities. Subjects were usually aristocrats, but some painters like Jean-Baptiste-Siméon CHARDIN preferred bourgeois or peasant models as themes. Paintings generally explored pleasurable feelings. To capture this new set of thematic interests, rococo artists adopted a palette of pastel colors and increased the softness and fullness of figures. The paintings are filled with activity and motion, but seldom convey a sense of drama.

Rococo painting was more widely spread throughout Europe than was the associated architecture. It appeared not only in France, the HAPSBURG EMPIRE, and the HOLY ROMAN EMPIRE, but also in ENGLAND. Painters who sometimes used the style include Jean-Baptiste-Siméon Chardin, Jean Honoré FRAGONARD, François BOUCHER, Antoine WATTEAU, Joshua REYNOLDS, Thomas GAINSBOROUGH, and William Hogarth.

Rococo style also influenced the production of decorative objects and of landscaping. Eighteenth-century porcelains, with their characteristic decorative CHINOISERIE, emerged as a popular item in the rococo and proved enormously adapted to the style. Silver, gold, tapestry, and glass also proved amenable to the style. The passion for decorating produced fantastic table centerpieces, snuffboxes, scientific instruments, and musical instruments.

In landscaping, the rococo definition of the natural as curving and disorderly produced the beautiful new form called the ENGLISH GARDEN. Baroque classical geometric lines were replaced with gentle landscapes, meticulously planned and kept, but seeming to reflect the state of things in an untamed forest or streamside. Lord Burlington, William KENT, and the poet Alexander POPE all contributed to creating this new and immensely popular garden style.

In France, the birthplace of rococo, the style rather quickly gave way under the growing influence of neoclassicism. Other nations retained love for the rococo style for longer periods, but eventually neoclassicism assumed primary importance everywhere.

Further reading: Anthony Blunt, ed., *Baroque and Rococo Architecture and Decoration* (New York: Portland House, 1978); Emil Kaufmann, *Architecture in the Age of Reason: Baroque and Post-Baroque in England, Italy, France* (New York: Dover Publications, 1955); William Park, *The Idea of Rococo* (Newark: University of Delaware Press, 1992).

Roman Catholicism A major division of Christianity, with its central administration located in ROME. The Roman Christian church is headed by the bishop of Rome, who is called the pope. Roman Catholicism traces its roots in an unbroken line back to the earliest era of Christianity in the first century A.D. The original unity of Christianity disappeared with the schism (A.D. 1054) between western Christianity (the Roman Church) and eastern Christianity (Eastern Orthodoxy). Western Christendom remained formally monolithic until the 16th century, when the Reformation splintered the church into a branch governed from Rome by the pope and the various denominations of PROTESTANTISM. The Roman-led church became known as the Roman Catholic Church and has retained its international scope.

In the 18th century, Roman Catholicism dominated large geographical areas, particularly in southern and central Europe and in the Spanish and Portuguese colonies. Among the major Catholic states were FRANCE, AUSTRIA, the AUSTRIAN NETHERLANDS, SPAIN, the states of the Italian Peninsula, and PORTUGAL. Within the HOLY ROMAN EMPIRE, Bavaria was staunchly Catholic. Certain sovereign territories such as Würzburg, Mainz, Bamberg, and COLOGNE were actually ruled by Roman Catholic archbishops. The pope himself was a secular ruler in the Italian peninsula (the Papal States) as well as the spiritual head of the international Roman Catholic Church. Divisions between secular political affairs and sacred religious matters were unclear and provided one of the grounds for the intense conflicts in church-state relations.

Roman Catholicism differed from the various Protestant groups on several major issues of THEOLOGY. Disputes touched on the sources of divine revelation, the role of priests and saints, the list of official sacraments, and the specific interpretation of the sacrament called the Eucharist. The Catholic Church maintained that revelation from God is ongoing, contained not only in the Bible and the writings of the early church fathers but also in the doctrines formulated by leaders of the contemporary church. Consequently, it also placed heavy emphasis on the sanctity of its historical traditions. In contrast, Protestant groups tended to limit revelation to the Bible and a few of the earliest church fathers. They were seeking to recover the pristine early church and generally looked upon the traditions built up over the centuries as impure additions to the faith. The Catholic priest exercised an important role as a direct mediator between the faithful and God. Thus, his role in the sacraments was more than that of a mere teacher; without his actions, for example, the miracle of the Eucharist—the conversion of the bread and wine into the actual body and blood of Jesus Christ—could not occur. Saints also played mediating roles, facilitating communication between God and the faithful on Earth.

Protestants envisioned a much more direct relationship between God and the faithful that did not necessitate special action by priests and saints. The Catholic Church listed seven sacraments (baptism, confirmation, marriage, confession, the Eucharist, holy orders, and extreme unction) but Protestants generally retained only two (baptism and communion, the common Protestant term for the Catholic Eucharist). Furthermore, Catholics and the various Protestant groups quarreled sharply over the actual nature of the Eucharist or communion. At issue was the question of whether or not the bread and wine actually change their nature in a miraculous event associated with the ceremony of the Eucharist.

Roman Catholic polity was hierarchical and monarchical. The pope was the elected ruler of the church, chosen by the Sacred College of Cardinals. The pope functioned much like an elected king or emperor in the secular world. A council (curia) of cardinals (appointed heads of various churches in the city of Rome) advised him in matters of doctrine, church government, and political affairs. Papal courts (the feared courts of the Inquisition) existed in certain Catholic lands (Spain, the Italian states, and Portugal) but had been forbidden entry to powerful states such as France, Austria, and most regions of the Holy Roman Empire.

For administrative purposes, Catholic lands were divided into regions called dioceses and archdioceses, each of which possessed a cathedral. An archbishop or bishop served as head of the church in these regions. He owned lands and enjoyed the privileges of secular noble landholders as well as the various immunities accorded to clergymen. The archbishops and bishops, assisted by the canons of their cathedrals, were responsible for the pastoral care of Catholics living within their territories and for the education of priests. Priests and their assistants staffed the local parish churches, providing spiritual oversight to parishioners and services such as marriage and burial. Archbishops, bishops, and parish priests were called secular clergy. Their primary duty lay in serving the spiritual needs of the Catholic laity (the secular world). A parallel organization existed in the multitude of monastic religious orders of Catholicism. Individuals, both male and female, entered the religious orders sometimes freely, sometimes by familial coercion. They dedicated their lives to the service of God by withdrawal from ordinary life. Their activities included scholarly study, teaching, and charitable work. Monasteries and convents enjoyed special fiscal privileges and often were major landlords in local regions. Peasants worked their lands and owed certain goods and services to the abbot or abbess who headed the organization. Finally, the Roman Catholic Church sponsored certain religious orders such as the Society of Jesus (JESUITS) and the Oratorians whose structure was monastic but whose members remained actively involved in secular affairs.

To understand 18th-century Catholicism, it is critical to remember that the pope was not accepted as infallible, in spite of the fact that several popes had tried to make such claims and to impose them on the national Catholic churches. These popes, like their secular, monarchical counterparts, wished to enjoy absolute power. However, papal claims were constantly and successfully challenged throughout the 18th century. In fact, the infallibility of the pope in matters of faith and morals did not become formal Catholic doctrine until 1871.

Three major types of struggle occurred over the nature of Catholic polity. Each of these struggles had parallels in the secular debates over the nature of political power. One type of conflict pitted secular rulers (kings, emperors, and their ministers) against the pope. Arenas of conflict included church appointments (some secular rulers enjoyed limited rights to nominate bishops and archbishops), the acceptance and promulgation of papal decrees (bulls and letters), control over marriage and over educational institutions. French royal Gallicanism, JANSENISM, and JOSEPHINISM all were movements encompassing elements of this basic conflict over church-state relations in Catholic nations.

A second type of conflict involved disagreement over the internal structure of the Catholic Church and pitted bishops or archbishops against the pope. At issue was the nature of the monarchy within the church: Would it be absolute, with the pope as the undisputed leader, or would it be limited, with power shared by the higher clergy? French clerical Gallicanism and FEBRONIANISM were major examples of this mode of conflict. In both cases, Catholic clergy were demanding to share power with the pope.

A third type of conflict was also primarily internal. Local parish priests wanted greater independence in the exercise of their duties. They sought to establish a kind of presbyterian form of government in which parish control lay in the hands of local officials rather than in the hands of the higher clergy. This conflict is best known in its French version, Richerism. It was intertwined with Jansenism and with the opposition of the French PARLEMENTS to the centralizing, absolute claims of the Crown.

Roman Catholicism had experienced a strong, creative flowering in the 17th century. In part, the renewal was a response to Protestantism, but much ferment had appeared before Martin Luther initiated the Reformation. By the 18th century, the fortunes of Catholicism were waning at least among the intellectual classes of Catholic nations. Educated individuals were substituting various concepts of NATURAL RELIGION such as DEISM for orthodox Catholic belief. They no longer viewed religious confession as a central source of civic and social identity. Increasingly, religious belief was assigned to the realm of the private and removed from the purview of the public sphere. Therefore, interest in the political persecution of individuals on account of their religious beliefs was dying. The outrage expressed by VOLTAIRE and other PHILOSOPHES following the execution of Jean CALAS, disgust at the repression of the CAMISARDS, criticism of the luxurious lifestyles followed by the higher Catholic clergy, and feelings of horror at the spectacle of the persecution of the WALDENSIANS all helped to fuel strong ANTICLERICALISM in Catholic nations. All these phenomena also helped to popularize the enlightened ideal of religious TOLERATION in many European states.

Nevertheless, Catholic beliefs retained strength in many segments of the European population. The southern German-speaking lands, for example, experienced an enormous flowering of Catholic piety. Pilgrimages, various forms of public worship, the cult of the saints all flourished. ROCOCO and late BAROQUE STYLE pilgrimage churches constructed on sites associated with various miracles and saints dot the landscape throughout southern Germany, Austria, and central or eastern Switzerland, providing testimony to the intensity of Catholic sentiment. Catholic piety was strong enough in Austria that Joseph II felt compelled to try to control it by secular means. As a result, he instituted the rather harsh reforms of Josephinism.

Throughout the Catholic lands, the power of the pope was seen as a potential or actual threat to the power of the secular ruler. The Jesuits, whose religious vows included an oath of obedience to the pope, were suspected of seditious activities. Although accusations against the Jesuits were sometimes overblown or downright fictitious, secular rulers were correct in understanding that in the context of 18th-century politics, the Jesuit loyalty to the pope could be a source of political turmoil within their kingdoms. One by one the Catholic nations, beginning with Portugal, ousted the Jesuits from their territories. Finally, in 1773, Pope CLEMENT XIV reluctantly dissolved the order. It survived because the enlightened, non-Catholic rulers FREDERICK II (THE GREAT) and CATHERINE II (THE GREAT) refused to disband Jesuit houses in PRUSSIA and Russia. These two rulers, whose state policies were not intimately intertwined with those of the pope, felt that they could risk retaining the Jesuits within their states, in order to capitalize on their skill as educators and scholars.

The fortunes of Roman Catholicism reached a low point during the FRENCH REVOLUTION. Priests were forced to take an oath of allegiance to the secular state, monastery and church lands were confiscated, and a Cult of the Supreme Being was instituted as the official state religion of France. After the revolution, however, Catholicism was restored to its official status, but the bonds that had intertwined its fortunes with those of the secular rulers were loosened.

See also CLEMENT XII; ITALY; RELIGION.

Further reading: Gerald R. Cragg, *The Church and the Age of Reason, 1648–1789* (New York: Penguin Books, 1970); Henri Daniel-Rops, *The Church in the Eighteenth Century* (Garden City, N.Y.: Doubleday, 1964).

romanticism   A name generally given to the movement supposedly generated by opposition to the ENLIGHTENMENT. Romanticism is usually described as originating in GERMANY, whence it spread quickly to ENGLAND and later to FRANCE. Its major figures in Germany were Friedrich Wilhelm Joseph van Schelling, the brothers August Wilhelm von Schlegel and Friedrich von Schlegel, Georg Wilhelm Friedrich Hegel, Jakob Ludwig Carl Grimm and his brother Wilhelm Carl Grimm, Friedrich Ernst Daniel Schleiermacher, Ludwig van BEETHOVEN, Felix Mendelssohn, Robert Schuman, and a host of German poets. In England, Samuel Taylor Coleridge, William Wordsworth, George Gordon Byron (Lord Byron), Percy Bysshe Shelley, John Keats, William BLAKE, Edmund BURKE, and Thomas Carlyle are usually treated as romantics, while in France, the most prominent figures were Joseph De Maistre, Hector Berlioz, and François-Auguste-René de Chateaubriand.

Romanticism, like the Enlightenment, was a movement of disparate and sometimes contradictory elements, ranging from a celebration of the individual and irrational freedom to a stress on community and group cohesiveness. In most of its variations, however, it borrowed concepts from the Enlightenment, which it removed from their specific intellectual and historical context. In this process, the intellectual assumptions that had limited and shaped these concepts were removed, opening up the possibility for radical departures from their origins. For this reason, romanticism can be seen as both the logical heir to the Enlightenment and its antagonistic opposite.

Some order can be imposed on the ideas associated with romanticism by classifying according to the original enlightened concepts: community, uniqueness, development, INDIVIDUALISM, and INTUITION AND IMAGINATION.

The concept of community contained the notion that individual lives derive meaning only when lived within the context of an organic whole, the community. For romanticism, awareness of the significance of community translated into explorations of the distant historical past, especially the Middle Ages, and extolled the power of tradition as a source of human identity. In this realm, romanticism borrowed from the ideas of both MONTESQUIEU and Jean-Jacques ROUSSEAU but eliminated their sharp criticism of contemporary European society.

Romanticism maintained that all entities, whether the individual, a specific group, or a nation, were unique. Analytic methods, which dissected these entities and attempted to find underlying universality, were thus useless in many areas of investigation. In this realm, romanticism adopted the concerns of VITALISM with diversity but abandoned the search for the principles or mechanisms presumed to mediate between the general and the specific, the universal and the unique.

The romantics assumed that all phenomena exist in time and pass through developmental stages. In many senses, this concept was borrowed directly from the Enlightenment. During that earlier era, the novel idea that things change over time had been introduced, and the associated concept of HISTORY—whether of individuals, nations, religion, or the Earth itself—had assumed central importance in various intellectual schemes. In the hands of enlightened writers, however, the direction of development or history was not predetermined; some writers believed in upward PROGRESS, others believed that decay had marked most of human history, and still others believed that development was cyclical, marked by recurring phenomena. In romanticism, the variety of treatments given history during the Enlightenment disappeared, and the past was imbued with a kind of sentimental, nostalgic, and always positive quality.

The romantic era is well known for its struggling poetic and artistic giants, engaged in rebellion against the constraints of society. Here again, the debt to the Enlightenment in the form of the concept of the GENIUS, the emphasis on the individual, and the concern with the nature of artistic creativity, is apparent. In romanticism, the ambivalence of the Enlightenment toward unrestrained individualism and freedom disappears. The creative artist—whether painter, poet, or musician—became a new cultural hero, the link between ordinary humanity and the gods.

Romanticism is usually depicted as a movement in which irrationalism is glorified, but this generalization requires some fine tuning. Romantics indeed criticized REASON and RATIONALISM, continuing trends that had begun early in the Enlightenment. But in the place of reason, they raised the faculty of intuition to prominence. Human intuition, they believed, provided understanding that approached the kind of knowledge possessed by God. During the Enlightenment, attention had turned to intuition and imagination as alternatives to limited reason. Enlightened writers thus initiated the approaches to intuition that culminated in romanticism but generally hesitated to carry claims for its power as far as the romantic generations did. Similarly, although a role in human understanding was given by the Enlightenment to feeling and sentiment, the romantic fascination with powerful, uncontrollable passions explored new territory.

Because of its many variations, romanticism cannot be associated with any specific political ideology. It fed everything from extreme radical, secular, revolutionary individualism, as illustrated by Shelley, to conservative Christian communitarianism represented by De Maistre. Thus, like its progenitor, the Enlightenment, romanticism must be approached with an eye toward appreciating its nuances, the various shades of meaning and action that colored its canvas.

See also AESTHETICS.

Rome   Italian city, the ancient capital of the Roman Empire and seat of the pope of the Catholic Church. The city sits on seven hills above the Tiber River, not far from the western, Mediterranean coast of Italy. Archaeological ruins and artifacts suggest that the site has been settled since the 10th century B.C.

In the first century A.D., the early Christians made Rome their center. They experienced some persecution from Roman authorities until A.D. 313, when Emperor Constantine converted to Christianity and granted it official status within the empire. The Christian bishop of Rome, called the pope, enjoyed a certain primacy from the early years of Christian history on account of his alleged descent from the apostle Peter, but he did not become the undisputed head of the church until much later.

In the fifth century A.D., the Roman Empire experienced a severe decline caused by a combination of economic conditions, political crisis, and climate. The empire became vulnerable to the movements of "barbarian" tribes, and Rome was sacked in 410 A.D. The empire in western Europe ceased to exist as a political entity in A.D. 476.

The Christian papacy survived the downfall of the empire, however, and the pope began to function as both the secular ruler and the spiritual leader of Rome. He also controlled some central Italian territories called the Papal States. During the Middle Ages, the popes ruled over a Rome that was a mere vestige of its former self. The city experienced strife and difficulty, although for most of that period the papacy retained a respected position throughout the Latin Christian world. For several decades in the 14th century, however, the papacy was forcibly moved from Rome to Avignon. After 1378, two popes ruled, one in Rome and the other in Avignon. The return of the popes to Rome did not immediately ameliorate the situation in the city. A low point in the city's history was reached in 1415, when wolves were roaming freely through the cemetery of the papal residence (Vatican).

Revival in Rome began shortly afterward as the city began to benefit from the vigor and creativity of the Italian Renaissance. But dramatic changes waited until the beginning of the 16th century, when several popes sponsored impressive building projects. Prominent Roman families also contributed to the urban renewal by constructing large Renaissance palaces. The Vatican underwent renovation, the main streets of the city were straightened and rearranged, and new aqueducts were built to bring water into the city. Population rose from a few thousand in the late medieval period to 130,000 during the Renaissance, but it fell to 40,000 after the 16th-century sacking of Rome by Charles V, Emperor of the HOLY ROMAN EMPIRE. Population rose again to 100,000 by the end of the 16th century.

Rome began changing dramatically in the late 16th century as the Catholic Church responded to the challenge presented to its vision of Christianity by the Protestant Reformation. The BAROQUE STYLE in art and architecture developed in Rome as one manifestation of the Catholic response. The principles of this style not only served the propaganda needs of the Catholic Church, but also beautified the city with magnificent structures whose utilization of space and interior decoration all emphasized the extent of papal power. The great piazzas—the one fronting the Palazzo dei Barberini, the Piazza Navona, the Piazza San Pietro, the Piazza di Spagna and, of course, the marvelous Piazza of Bernini at the Vatican—all appeared during the 17th century. The baroque style continued through the 18th century and is represented by the Spanish Steps, the Trevi fountain, and the great facades of the Lateran, Santa Maria Maggiore, and Santa Croce churches. In the later decades of the 18th century, a neoclassical style also emerged as artists and architects reacted to the heavy, ornate qualities of the baroque.

As the center of the international Catholic Church, 18th-century Rome retained prominence in Europe, but the pope no longer played the great role in international diplomacy that had characterized his predecessors in earlier centuries. Instead, he was gradually yielding control over secular affairs to national rulers. Nevertheless, Rome continued to dominate the Italian Papal States and to defend them against encroachments by the kingdom of Naples to the south. Popes such as BENEDICT XIV improved the city with major public works projects and enhanced cultural life by supporting the museums and university.

During the ENLIGHTENMENT, Rome served as a major cultural center in Europe. In fact, the city that had once served as the capital of the great Roman Empire now fired imaginations intent on reviving the ideals of that ancient world. Artists, architects, writers, and musicians went to the city to study, and young wealthy Europeans nearly always included it on the itineraries of their GRAND TOURS. In short, the city exerted a spellbinding fascination on enlightened minds, serving as a symbol of both good and bad institutions and events and as a model—either positive or negative—for visionary reformers.

See also CLEMENT XII.

Romney, George (1734–1802) *English painter*

Son of a cabinetmaker of Lancashire, Romney studied portrait and genre painting with Christopher Steele, a traveling artist. Romney followed his teacher's footsteps, touring the northern parts of England and painting portraits for small sums. In this manner, he saved enough money to move to LONDON and establish himself as a successful painter. Romney traveled to PARIS several times and spent two years in ITALY.

After Joshua REYNOLDS and Thomas GAINSBOROUGH, Romney was the most popular portrait artist of his day. He and Reynolds had cool relations, due in part to the competition between them for dominance. Romney's strength lay in his mastery of form rather than in his color sense. Although Romney painted portraits just as his illustrious ROCOCO competitors Reynolds and Gainsborough, his treatment of his subjects owes more to NEOCLASSICISM than to rococo style.

Among his many works, the following must be noted: *Mrs. Yates and the Tragic Muse* (1771); *Mr. and Mrs. William Lindow* (1772); *Mrs. Carwardine and Son* (1775); *Sir Christopher and Lady Sykes* (1786); and *Warren Hastings* (1795). In addition, his many paintings of Lady Hamilton, his "dear Emma"—posed as Cassandra, Circe, Calypso, a Bacchante, Joan of Arc, and Mary Magdalene—display not only his fascination with his friend but also the appeal for him of female mythological and historical subjects.

Rosicrucians

A secret society whose name derived from a combination of two words: rose and cross. It was also known as the Rosy Cross.

Evidence for the possible existence of the Rosicrucians first appeared in Europe between 1614 and 1616 with the publication of three pamphlets, collectively known as the Rosicrucian manifestos. These works carried the titles: *Fama Fraternitatis dess [sic] Löblichen Ordens des Rosenkreutzes* (Report on the brothers of the praiseworthy Order of the Rosy Cross; 1614); *Confessio Fraternitatis* (Confession of the brothers; 1615); and *Chymische Hochzeit Christiani Rosenkreutz* (The chemical wedding of Christian Rosenkreutz; 1616). The alleged founder of the society was one Christian Rosenkreutz, an individual of unknown identity. Most scholars believe that Rosenkreutz was a mythological figure, perhaps the creation of the Lutheran theologian Johann Valentin Andreae.

The Rosicrucian manifestos spoke in millenarian terms about the coming of a new age of illumination (the 17th-century form of enlightenment) in which religious strife would come to an end and all men would be united in one brotherhood. Rosicrucian knowledge would assist in this process.

It is not known to this day whether the 17th-century Rosicrucian organization actually existed outside the imaginations of its founders. No concrete evidence has been found, and contemporaries of the period were uncertain about this question.

The appearance of the strange Rosicrucian manifestos between 1614 and 1616 provoked widespread interest and a variety of reactions ranging from fear to curiosity. In FRANCE, news of the Rosicrucians arrived during a politically unstable period and created a veritable panic. Many people, including the philosopher René DESCARTES, were suspected of Rosicrucian sympathies, and a barrage of works by Marin MERSENNE and other critics appeared in an effort to offset interest in the mysterious group.

The Rosicrucian phenomenon died out within a decade, a victim of the terrible upheavals in the HOLY ROMAN EMPIRE brought on by the Thirty Years' War (1618–48). By the beginning of the 18th century, however, the Rosicrucian brotherhood had reappeared in German territories as the Gold- und Rosenkreuz (Gold- and Rosy Cross). This renewed organization played a minor but important role in intellectual conflicts of the German ENLIGHTENMENT (*AUFKLÄRUNG*).

The Rosicrucians of the 18th century claimed to have access to secret knowledge that would empower men (no women were admitted to the membership) to dominate NATURE and would assist their attainment of perfection. This knowledge consisted of a blending of ALCHEMY, the ancient occult teachings of Egypt, and Renaissance Neoplatonism with Christian doctrine. Rosicrucians claimed to have the secrets that would allow the transmutation of metals into precious gold and the acquisition of "the philosopher's stone."

Rosicrucian knowledge provided an alternative to REASON as the path to wisdom and to perfection. It also provided a set of rituals and knowledge that could replace traditional Christianity. Thus, Rosicrucian doctrine shares with the Enlightenment belief in the PERFECTIBILITY of men and in the ability of the human intellect to acquire the wisdom of God. In fact, Rosicrucian rites and "degrees of knowledge" were incorporated by some lodges of the FREEMASONS into their own practices.

Unlike Freemasonry, however, Rosicrucian thought does not rely on reason as the means by which its lofty goals are to be reached. Rather, it seeks an alternative to reason, in the form of knowledge based on an intuitive understanding of the occult, hidden structures of the world. It rejects the atomistic, mechanical vision of the world embodied in the MECHANICAL PHILOSOPHY and in EPICUREAN PHILOSOPHY. Rosicrucian doctrine thus stands at the pole of enlightened thought that criticizes reason and that searches for alternative avenues to truth.

Within the German social and political context, Rosicrucian brotherhoods became gathering points for critics of the Enlightenment and for conservatives who desired to preserve the traditional social and political structures of the German states. They were strongly criticized by representatives of the radical, progressive Enlightenment such as the Bavarian ILLUMINATI for their reliance on alchemy as a path toward knowledge. The Rosicrucians, in turn, bitterly opposed the reforms advocated by the Illuminati and probably played a significant role in obtaining the 1785 suppression of that order.

Major Rosicrucian writers during the 18th century were Bernard Joseph Schleiss von Löwenfeld (pseudonym, Phoebron); Joseph Wilhelm Schröder (1733–78); Georg von Welling (pseudonym, Gregorius Anglus Sallwigt); Carl Wächter (pseudonym, Carl Hubert Lobreich von Plumenoek); and Joseph Friedrich Göhrung (pseudonym, Chrysophiron).

See also INTUITION AND IMAGINATION; SECRET SOCIETIES.

Rousseau, Jean-Jacques (1712–1778) *Swiss writer; one of the most original thinkers of the Enlightenment*

Possessed with a complex, sensitive, restless, and sometimes disturbed personality, Rousseau eventually quarreled with most of his supporters and enlightened colleagues. But even when they criticized his work, both friends and enemies recognized the originality and persuasiveness of his ideas. Rousseau's contributions to POLITICAL THEORY, to EDUCATION, and to LITERATURE are outstanding monuments to the ENLIGHTENMENT, revealing its potential, its dangers, and its limits.

A native of the Swiss republic of GENEVA, Rousseau grew up within the culture of CALVINISM. Since his mother died a few days after his birth, Rousseau was raised by his father Isaac Rousseau, a watchmaker and a rebel. Isaac introduced his son to reading and generally oversaw his early education. Trouble with the Genevan authorities resulted in the elder Rousseau's exile from the city; Jean-Jacques was 10 years old at the time.

By the age of 13, young Rousseau was apprenticed to an engraver. He seems to have experienced the usual troubles of apprenticeship, including harsh treatment and long hours of labor. In 1728, when he was 16 years old, a chance event changed the course of his life. He left Geneva for a Sunday walk, but returned to the city too late to gain admittance; the gates had already been closed for the evening. Rousseau reacted by leaving the city, making his way via Annecy to TURIN, the capital of the kingdom of Savoy.

It proved impossible to find work in Turin, and Rousseau, now converted to ROMAN CATHOLICISM, settled in Annecy in the house of Madame de Warens. There, he proceeded to educate himself and also to become the lover of his protectress. He left Savoy in 1742 but always looked back on the experience at the Warens house as the only period of real happiness in his life.

Rousseau arrived in PARIS in the fall of 1742, hoping to impress the FRENCH ACADEMY OF SCIENCES with his scheme for a simplified, easily comprehensible system of musical notation. The academy responded coolly, but Rousseau remained in Paris, entering the social world of the PHILOSOPHES and ENCYCLOPEDISTS.

By 1744, Rousseau had entered the relationship with Thérèse Levasseur that was to last throughout his lifetime. The couple produced several children whose upbringing they could not afford. Therefore, following the custom of the time, they abandoned them to be raised as orphans.

Between 1744 and 1751, under the patronage of the Dupin family, Rousseau worked as a secretary, tutor, and music copyist in Paris. His fortunes changed in 1750, when his *Discours sur les sciences et les arts* (Discourse on the sciences and arts) won the prize in an essay contest sponsored by the Academy of Dijon. Responding to the contest question, "Has the progress of the sciences and arts contributed to the purification of morals?" Rousseau revealed himself as a critic of the modern civilized society in which he lived. He contrasted the moral corruption of contemporary society with the natural goodness of simple human beings. This theme would reoccur throughout his subsequent work.

The success of the *Discours sur les sciences et les arts* was followed in 1752 by popular acclaim for his opera *Le devin du village* (The village fortune-teller) and by a second essay prize in 1755 for the *Discours sur l'origine de l'inégalité* (DISCOURSE ON THE ORIGINS OF INEQUALITY). This second discourse expanded Rousseau's critique of contemporary society to the political and general cultural realms, arguing that private PROPERTY and luxury lie at the base of political inequality and corruption.

During the early 1750s, Rousseau also wrote articles on music and on political economy for the ENCYCLOPÉDIE. The articles on music presented his notation system and argued that music should be immediately pleasurable to listeners. The article on political economy offered posi-

The Last Words of Jean-Jacques Rousseau, by Moreau le Jeune *(Courtesy New York Public Library)*

tive suggestions for government, public education, and state finance.

In 1754, Rousseau decided to return to Geneva. He resumed his citizenship rights, reconverting to his native religion of Calvinism. His sojourn in Geneva did not last long, for he was soon embroiled in quarrels with VOLTAIRE, who was residing nearby, and with the powerful Tronchin family. By 1756, he had once again left the city, taking up residence at L'Ermitage, an estate belonging to Madame D'EPINAY, located on the edge of the great Montmorency forest. An affair with Madame Sophie d'Houtetot, Madame d'Epinay's sister-in-law, complicated Rousseau's existence. Within a year, he was quarreling with his hostess and with Denis DIDEROT, whom he believed had shared confidential information about the affair. Rousseau left L'Ermitage, but settled in the nearby town of Montmorency, where he lived until 1762. He made a public declaration of the break with Diderot in his *Lettre à M. d'Alembert sur les spectacles* (Letter to M. d'Alembert on spectacles; 1758).

During the Montmorency years Rousseau wrote his most significant works: *LA NOUVELLE HÉLOISE* (1761), an immensely popular novel; *ÉMILE* (1762), his tract on edu cation; and *Le contrat social* (SOCIAL CONTRACT; 1762), h seminal treatise on the foundations of political socie The inclusion in *Émile* of the "Profession de foi du vicai savoyard" (Profession of faith of the Savoyard vica forced Rousseau to flee from FRANCE. The Parlement Paris condemned the DEISM of the "profession de foi" ar ordered the arrest of Rousseau. He avoided arrest by fle ing, intending to return to Geneva. But the Genev authorities also censored his works, condemning bo *Émile* and the *Social Contract* as destructive and dange ous. Rousseau responded by renouncing his Genevan c izenship in 1763.

Between 1762 and 1770, Rousseau moved sever times to avoid harassment by various civil authorities. I lived briefly in the Swiss canton of Neuchâtel and also the canton of Berne. David HUME, the Scottish philosophe, invited Rousseau to SCOTLAND, but the two men quickly quarreled. Rousseau then settled in ENGLAND for nearly a year and a half but returned in 1767 to France. Finally, in 1770, he received assurance that he could resettle in Paris without fear of prosecution.

These experiences produced an emotional crisis for Rousseau, accentuating his natural tendency to see conspiracy everywhere. He turned to self-examination in an effort both to understand and to justify his troublesome relationships with his world. The resulting CONFESSIONS and the dialogues entitled *Rousseau, juge de Jean-Jacques* (Rousseau, judge of Jean-Jacques) were not published until 1781 and 1788, after his death. The *Rêveries du promeneur solitaire* (Reveries of a solitary walker), his last work written after he had found inner peace, also appeared posthumously, in 1782.

Rousseau died suddenly in 1778, shortly after he had moved to Ermenonville at the invitation of the marquis de Girardin. His remains, first buried at Ermenonville, were transferred during the FRENCH REVOLUTION to the Panthéon in Paris.

In nearly all of his writings, Rousseau struggled with the problem of how to preserve individual FREEDOM within the confines of civilized society. This, of course, was a profoundly autobiographical theme, but also one of central importance to the Enlightenment. Rousseau extolled the virtues of natural man, but he realized that life in society was necessary in order for people to develop their moral nature and capacity to REASON. But society as it then existed did not assist this general PROGRESS of humankind; rather it corrupted people by pitting individuals against each other.

Rousseau was seeking a solution to this dilemma of modern man. Like most enlightened intellectuals, he believed that reforms in education and in the constitution of political society could resolve these problems. But Rousseau's specific solutions explored new territory and marked him as a radical thinker.

His educational ideas, spelled out in *Émile,* turned on his conviction that the child differs from the adult in a manner analogous to the relationship between primitive, natural man and civilized man. The child sees, feels, and thinks in unique ways. Proper education will not only recognize these differences but also tailor activities and curriculum to them. It will provide a universal kind of training applicable to any adult occupation that a young person might choose. It will also preserve the best facets of human nature, adapting them to the needs of civilization. It will allow a person to protect the individuality of his perceptions, while still living comfortably and productively in society.

Rousseau believed that the preservation of political liberty depended on the creation of a new society by means of a social contract. The idea of a social contract lying at the base of legitimate political society was not new, of course. But the common enlightened version of this theory derived from John LOCKE and Rousseau's creativeness lay in his radical departure from the Lockean vision. For Locke, liberty was protected by the preservation of specific individual rights such as freedom and property.

For Rousseau, these specific rights brought corruption and inequality. He believed that a social contract could preserve absolute EQUALITY. But in his social contract, people would necessarily relinquish their individual rights and submit to the general will, the guarantor of the social contract. The general will, a vaguely conceived entity, would then be translated into a set of positive laws by a virtuous legislator. These laws, which Rousseau conceived as absolute, would preserve absolute equality between people. If this equality were to be violated, then people retained the right to overthrow the political system.

Rousseau's theories were enthusiastically received by the generations of the late Enlightenment. His educational reforms were adopted by Johann Bernhard Basedow (1724–90) and Johann Heinrich PESTALOZZI. The STURM UND DRANG generation saw Rousseau as the champion of personal freedom against authority. And certain leaders of the French Revolution drew on the concept of the general will to justify both radical democracy and totalitarian control. Rousseau's ideas have subsequently been dissected and discussed by every generation, as people try to wrestle with the paradoxes they seem to contain.

See also MABLY; NOBLE SAVAGE; OPERA.

Further reading: Ernst Cassirer, *Rousseau, Kant, Goethe: Two Essays by Ernst Cassirer,* tr. James Gutmann, Paul Oskar Kristeller, and John Hermann Randall, Jr. (Princeton, N.J.: Princeton University Press, 1970); Elie Halévy, *The Growth of Philosophic Radicalism* (London: Faber & Faber, 1928); Jean-Jacques Rousseau, *The Social Contract and Discourses,* tr. and intro. G. D. H. Cole (London: Everyman's Library, 1973).

Rowlandson, Thomas (1756–1827) *artist who specialized in the portrayal of everyday life, politics, and society*
Born in July 1756 in LONDON, Rowlandson showed artistic talent from an early age, learning to draw before he could write. Rowlandson's father was a successful businessman who sent young Thomas to Eton as well as the Royal Academy. At 16 he left ENGLAND to study art in PARIS. Although he would be influenced by the French ROCOCO style, art historians identify his style with the English school.

Rowlandson began his career painting portraits and opened his own studio in 1777. However, his gambling addiction caused him to lose a great deal of money. He began to draw everyday scenes of the grim reality of life in lower-class London. The drawings met with success, and he was able to pay off his debts. They also brought him into contact with the leading caricaturists and lithographers of the day.

He began to critique English society and politics in his drawings and cartoons. Many considered them to be vulgar, but many others found them to be refreshingly realistic. Rowlandson contributed illustrations to some of the more radical of Smollett's works and was imprisoned for libel. However, he continued to produce political illustrations and lithographs into the 19th century. Rowlandson collaborated with Rudolph Ackerman on *The Microcosm of London* and William Combe on the *Dance of Life,* both of which studied everyday life in London.

Rowlandson's more well-known paintings include *Vauxhall Gardens* (1784); *The Comforts of Bath* series (1789); *Tour of Dr. Syntax* (1812–21); *Dance of Death* (1814–16); and *Dance of Life* (1822). After the government charged the people who had come to hear a speech on parliamentary reform in 1819, Rowlandson painted *Mounted Cavalry Charging a Crowd* (1819) in protest. His drawings can be found in the works of Henry FIELDING, Oliver GOLDSMITH, Laurence STERNE, and Tobias SMOLLETT. He is also known for his more traditional drawings and paintings of the Welsh countryside. Thomas Rowlandson died in 1827, but he left a wide-ranging legacy and a challenge for future political artists and social critics to depict political corruption and everyday social conditions realistically.

Further reading: Ronald Paulson, *Rowlandson: A New Interpretation.* New York: Oxford University Press, 1972.

Royal Society of Edinburgh

An 18th-century scientific society founded in EDINBURGH, SCOTLAND. It was one of the major institutional supports of the ENLIGHTENMENT in Scotland. The Royal Society was founded in 1783, largely as a result of the activities of William ROBERTSON, an eminent Scottish historian. Its model was certain foreign societies such as the BERLIN ACADEMY, whose activities were not limited strictly to scientific pursuits. Thus, the Royal Society of Edinburgh differed from its illustrious southern counterpart, the ROYAL SOCIETY OF LONDON. In the 1790s, however, the Edinburgh organization gradually transformed itself into a more narrowly circumscribed institution dedicated to the pursuit of the natural sciences. Members of the Royal Society of Edinburgh included Robertson, Adam FERGUSON, and Hugh Blair.

The Royal Society of Edinburgh was preceded in Edinburgh by two important societies—the Philosophical Society of Edinburgh and the Select Society—whose members were drawn from the leadership of the Scottish Enlightenment. The membership rosters included David HUME, William CULLEN, Joseph BLACK, and a host of less well known figures who helped to make the Scottish Enlightenment a particularly fecund intellectual movement.

Royal Society of London

Scientific society formally founded in 1660 and chartered in 1662 as the Royal Society of London for the Promotion of Natural Knowledge. The Royal Society was one of the major institutional centers for the 18th-century scientific community and, therefore, was also a major center of the ENLIGHTENMENT. Its members fostered the practice and dissemination of the scientific theories and experimental methods that had developed during the 17th-century SCIENTIFIC REVOLUTION. Although the Royal Society dominated the scientific life of 18th-century Great Britain, smaller and significant informal societies such as the LUNAR SOCIETY OF BIRMINGHAM, the MANCHESTER LITERARY AND PHILOSOPHICAL SOCIETY, the Philosophical Society of Edinburgh, the Select Society, and the ROYAL SOCIETY OF EDINBURGH also contributed to scientific life.

The Royal Society originated about 1648 as an informal club of astronomers, mathematicians, and physicists who lived in or near Gresham College. The club was consciously dedicated to the ideal program of knowledge acquisition and organization that had been advocated by Francis BACON in the *Advancement of Learning* (1605) and the *Novum Organum* (1620). Despite this lofty goal, the Royal Society was always loosely organized and lacked any official role as a government scientific agency. This character sharply distinguishes the Royal Society from the formal and official organizations of continental Europe such as the FRENCH ACADEMY OF SCIENCES, the BERLIN ACADEMY, or the SAINT PETERSBURG ACADEMY OF SCIENCES.

The Royal Society held regular meetings at which papers were read or scientific experiments demonstrated. It also sponsored public lectures and experimental demonstrations, thereby helping to spread knowledge of the new sciences to the educated, interested populace. Through its official journal, the *Philosophical Transactions of the Royal Society,* the papers reported at its meetings were spread throughout the European and American scientific worlds. Royal Society membership, which was achieved by election, was not restricted to professional scientists or to British subjects but also included amateur scientists, foreign correspondents, and other interested individuals. Election to the society was usually obtained through the patronage of a member and therefore depended to some extent on the social and professional connections of individuals. Prominent British members of the society included Robert Boyle, Isaac NEWTON, Joseph BLACK, William CULLEN, Edmond HALLEY, William HERSCHEL, Henry CAVENDISH, John DESAGULIERS, Joseph BANKS, and John PRINGLE.

Rumford, Benjamin Thompson, count (1753–1814)
United States–born physicist and Bavarian noble

Rumford was born Benjamin Thompson to a farming family in Massachusetts. Despite being mostly self-taught, young Benjamin became a schoolteacher when he was just 19 years old. After moving to Rumford, New Hampshire, he married a local widow. Politically, he supported the British against the American colonists, and in 1776 he left America and also parted ways with his wife. During the Revolutionary War, he returned to America to work as a spy for General Thomas Gage. In return for his service to the British, he was knighted by King George III, was granted the rank of lieutenant colonel, and was sent to New York.

After the war, he lived in exile on the Continent in both FRANCE and present-day GERMANY. Eventually, he settled in Bavaria and worked for the civil administration of the elector. He conducted extensive research on gunpowder, cannon, and other guns that was very beneficial to the Bavarian state. In recognition of his scientific work, he was made a member of the Bavarian Academy of Sciences and Humanities in 1785. Six years later, in recognition of his service to the state, the elector made Thompson a count of the HOLY ROMAN EMPIRE. Thompson then took the name Rumford in honor of the American town where he had lived. Returning to France, he married the chemist Antoine LAVOISIER's widow, but this second marriage, too, was unsuccessful. Rumford remained in France until his death in 1814.

Rumford's great contribution to SCIENCE came from a discovery he made in 1798 through his cannon research. At the time, heat was believed to be a fluid called CALORIC that was emitted by objects, in this case, from the cannon. Rumford's observations established that heat did not exist as caloric in the metal itself, but was generated by the friction involved in releasing the cannon ball from the cannon bore. This idea was seminal to later discoveries that showed that heat is a form of energy.

The percolator, photochemistry, the standard candle, and a standard for gunpowder were among Rumford's other scientific contributions. Rumford was keen to contribute to society in ways other than pure science. To promote science education, he founded the Royal Institution of Great Britain in LONDON in 1799 and established the Rumford chair at Harvard College in 1816, both of which still exist. He also helped people in more direct ways, establishing programs to help the needy. Rumford was the inventor of the soup kitchen. He also often employed beggars and unemployed soldiers in his government work, some of whom helped to create the Englischer Garten in MUNICH.

Rush, Benjamin (1746–1813) *American physician, educator, political leader, and philosophe*

Born near PHILADELPHIA, Rush studied at the College of New Jersey at Princeton. After graduating, he traveled to SCOTLAND, where he pursued a course in MEDICINE at the University of Edinburgh. There, he encountered the ideas of the ENLIGHTENMENT, especially as they were being formulated by Scottish intellectuals. Rush received his medi-

cal degree in 1768, returned to America, and began teaching chemistry at the College of Philadelphia in 1769. He published the first American textbook on chemistry, *Syllabus of a Course of Lectures on Chemistry,* in 1770. Rush taught chemistry and medicine at the College of Philadelphia until 1791. He also taught at the University of Pennsylvania and, at the same time, established himself as one of the most successful physicians in North America.

Rush shared many beliefs with the European PHILOSOPHES, including the enlightened faith that practical solutions could be found for various ethical and political problems. He was an early member of the AMERICAN PHILOSOPHICAL SOCIETY and an outspoken critic of SLAVERY who helped to found the first antislavery society in the British colonies. Rush also opposed CAPITAL PUNISHMENT and favored educating girls—at a time when most people regarded formal EDUCATION as a matter only for boys. He supported a curriculum model in which practical subjects such as agricultural techniques and botany would be given as much weight as classical Greek and Latin.

During the AMERICAN REVOLUTION Rush served in the Continental Congress and signed the DECLARATION OF INDEPENDENCE. He also supported Thomas PAINE, urging him to publish his essays as a collection under the title *COMMON SENSE.*

Rush held the post of surgeon general for the Continental Army but resigned that post in 1778 after a dispute with one of George WASHINGTON's military hospital administrators. Rush's subsequent criticism of Washington's military leadership has contributed to his neglect in American scholarship.

In 1778, Rush published *Directions for Preserving the Health of Soldiers,* a book that incorporated his experience during the Revolutionary War. He continued his medical practice and teaching after the conclusion of the war, and in 1786 founded the first free medical dispensary in the UNITED STATES. Physicians often turned to his *Medical Inquiries and Observations* (1789–98) for guidance. In 1812, he published *Medical Inquiries and Observations upon the Diseases of the Mind,* a book that, like the works of Philippe Pinel in FRANCE and Johann Christian REIL in GERMANY, treated mental disturbance as a disease rather than as a moral condition.

Rush rounded out his public life by serving as the treasurer of the United States Mint from 1797 until his death in 1813.

Russia See CATHERINE II (THE GREAT); MOSCOW; PETER I (THE GREAT); SAINT PETERSBURG; SAINT PETERSBURG ACADEMY OF SCIENCES.

S

Sade, marquis de (1740–1814) *French novelist*
Donatien-Alphonse-François, comte de Sade, or the marquis de Sade as he called himself, was related to the Condé branch of the French royal family. He grew up with the educational and career opportunities available to the aristocracy, attended the prestigious Jesuit Collège Louis-le-Grand, and then obtained an army commission. He abandoned his military career after the SEVEN YEARS' WAR.

The marquis de Sade embarked in the 1760s on a career of debauchery and sexual scandal that resulted in three imprisonments for sexual abuse offenses (1763, 1768, and 1777). The third imprisonment included a year at the Charenton insane asylum and lasted until April 1790. De Sade's release proved to be brief, for he was again arrested after helping some French nobles to escape the Terror. At the request of his wife and mother-in-law, who benefited by gaining his property, de Sade was officially declared insane and confined for his remaining years in Charenton. During his long years of incarceration, the marquis de Sade turned to writing pornographic novels that described all manner of sexual activity. They included *Les infortunes de la vertu* (The misfortunes of virtue; 1787); *Justine, ou les malheurs de la virtue* (Justine, or the unhappiness of virtue; 1791); and *Juliette, ou la suite de Justine* (Juliette, or the sequel of Justine; 1797). The word *sadism*, meaning sexuality in which gratification is obtained from the infliction of physical and mental pain, is derived from de Sade's name.

De Sade was a rebel whose works reveal a mind bent on pushing the darker sides of the ENLIGHTENMENT to extremes. He attacked all religious belief, declaring that if there is a God, people should hate him for creating such an evil world. De Sade questioned the Enlightenment assumption that human nature is essentially good, and he also rejected the common belief that true and universal moral standards exist. He argued that the decision to act according to society's standards should come out of naked SELF-INTEREST, rather than from any sense of ethical duty. In the place of a society bound by moral codes, he wished to construct a world based upon total human freedom. He also attacked the concept of PROPERTY, calling it nothing but theft. In short, de Sade turned major themes of the Enlightenment against the very values and goals they were intended to uphold. And underneath his dark vision, he placed a radical MATERIALISM built on a vision of the viciousness of NATURE.

This vision of de Sade, stark as it is, marks him as one of the individual rebels whose attitudes would eventually bring the period of the Enlightenment to a close. His positions would later serve the development of radical forms of ROMANTICISM. Although he was an extreme and disturbed individual, de Sade should not be dismissed as a mere aberration. His ideas have a direct logical connection with the Enlightenment. They illustrate with disturbing power the dark conclusions that were possible in the great century of light.

See also MORAL PHILOSOPHY; PORNOGRAPHY; RELIGION.

Saint-Germain, comte de (ca. 1707–1784) *Eighteenth-century adventurer and storyteller noted for his charm, prodigious memory, and knowledge of the world*
Saint-Germain's actual identity and the source of his wealth were mysterious during his lifetime and remain

unclear today. Some sources suggest that he was of Portuguese-Jewish origin; others, that he was the son of Marie-Anne of Neuburg, widow of Charles II of Spain. Some of Saint-Germain's contemporaries, including VOLTAIRE, insinuated that he was a secret agent in the service of the duc de CHOISEUL, Wenzel Anton von KAUNITZ, or William Pitt. Whatever the facts about these matters, the comte de Saint-Germain entertained and fascinated Parisians with his mysterious tales and bizarre personality.

Saint-Germain dipped into all the irrational aspects of knowledge. He claimed to be 2,000 years old, to be able to predict the future, to engage in astral projection, to possess the secret of the alchemical philosophers' stone, and even to have known Jesus Christ. The high society of PARIS proved curious and, in the opinion of some disgruntled contemporaries, gullible. Even LOUIS XV and Madame de POMPADOUR enjoyed spending evenings with him.

Saint-Germain lived in Paris from about 1748 to 1760. Having participated in some intrigues against Foreign Minister Choiseul, he was compelled to flee FRANCE. He settled first in LONDON where he was involved with the FREEMASONS, then appeared in SAINT PETERSBURG, in Hamburg, and again in Paris (1770–74). He ended his days in the employment of Landgrave Charles of Hesse-Kassel, a student of the occult and hermetic philosophies. When Saint-Germain died in 1784, the landgrave burned his papers and refused to reveal any information about his former employee and guest. The conte di CAGLIOSTRO later claimed to have been a student of Saint-Germain.

The phenomenon of the comte de Saint-Germain, in conjunction with the similar ones of Cagliostro and Giovanni Giacomo CASANOVA, illustrates an important facet of 18th-century culture. The emphasis on RATIONALISM and NATURAL LAW did not eliminate undercurrents of fascination with the irrational. As the century progressed, this undercurrent would swell with remarkable and significant results in art, SCIENCE, and LITERATURE.

Saint-Just, Louis-Antoine-Léon de (1767–1794) *French revolutionary democrat, one of the 12 leaders of the Comité de Salut Public (Committee on Public Health) during the Reign of Terror*

Saint-Just was called the "Angel of Death." He came from a military family. He lost his father, a cavalry captain, at the age of 10 and was subsequently raised by his mother and grandparents. He attended a school run by the Oratorians in Soissons. He was a gifted but unruly student who found the school atmosphere stifling. In 1786, after a squabble with his family, Saint-Just ran away to PARIS with some of the family silver. He sold the silver, spent the proceeds quickly, and soon was asking for more funds. His mother responded by obtaining one of the infamous *LETTRES DE CACHET* that were used by families to control their unruly children. As a result, Saint-Just was placed in

protective custody for six months. During that period, he wrote a scathing, pornographic satirical poem (*Organt*) about French political and religious institutions. Upon release from custody, he went to Reims to study law.

Saint-Just moved to Paris just before the outbreak of the FRENCH REVOLUTION. From the beginning, he allied himself with the cause of the lower classes, but he advocated gradual reform rather than violence. He served as a local representative to revolutionary assemblies in the province of Picardy. As the Revolution progressed, Saint-Just became impatient with the slow rate of change and the incomplete nature of the transformations that were occurring, and moved toward more radical positions, in which he advocated violence as a means to an end. Having been elected to the National Convention in September 1792, he attracted attention with his impassioned speeches. Saint-Just played a major role in securing the trial, condemnation, and execution of LOUIS XVI, and he also spent five months with the French army on the Rhine.

Saint-Just became a member of the Committee of Public Safety under direction of Maximilien ROBESPIERRE in June 1793. In this capacity, he participated in writing the new Constitution of France. His combination of idealism, youthful impatience, and rigid principle made him an enthusiastic participant in the executions of the Reign of Terror. He secured the deaths of political rivals, including not only the leaders of the Girondin wing (moderates) of the radical Jacobin Party but also the Dantonists (followers of Danton) and the Hébertists (followers of Hébert). Saint-Just was elected president of the National Convention, and in February and March 1794 he pushed through the so-called Ventôse decrees. These radical decrees declared that the property of the alleged enemies of the revolution (aristocrats, clergymen, and general critics) was to be confiscated and distributed to the poor. In June, he led the French forces to victory against the Austrians in the AUSTRIAN NETHERLANDS. By July, however, the political tide had turned against him and the other Jacobin leaders. On 9 Thermidor (July 27), Saint-Just, Robespierre, and other leaders of the Reign of Terror were arrested and the next day sent to the guillotine.

Besides the poem, *Organt*, Saint-Just left a thoughtful essay about revolution, *Esprit de la révolution et de la constitution de France* (Spirit of the revolution and of the constitution of France; 1791).

See also JACOBINS.

Saint-Martin, Louis-Claude de (1743–1803) *French mystic and writer, popularly known as "Le Philosophe Inconnu" (the Unknown Philosopher)*

Saint-Martin was a disciple of the early-17th-century German mystic Jakob Böhme (1575–1624). Böhme based his ideas and teachings on ALCHEMY and especially on the writings of the 16th-century physician Paracelsus. In addition to appealing to Saint-Martin, Böhme's writings influenced the Cambridge Platonists, the QUAKERS, the Pietists, Johann Wolfgang von GOETHE, and German ROMANTICISM. Through these avenues, his ideas entered the discourse of the late ENLIGHTENMENT. In general, the teachings of Saint-Martin, along with those of Emanuel SWEDENBORG, Johann LAVATER, Franz MESMER, and the comte de SAINT-GERMAIN, represent an important strand of mystical, irrational thought, sometimes called illuminism, that developed in that period. These approaches all sought wisdom not in the form of REASON, but rather looked for guidance from an inner light, a combination of irrational insight, intuition, and spiritual awareness.

Saint-Martin wrote several works of which the most important was *L'homme de désir* (Man of desires), published in 1790. He emerged as an early conservative critic of the FRENCH REVOLUTION, arguing that the revolution was a chastisement from God visited upon humankind. Implied in this position was a rejection of the secular RATIONALISM that characterized certain aspects of the Enlightenment. As a remedy to the ills of the revolution, Saint-Martin proposed the return of human existence to its allegedly idyllic and moral primitive state. This position identifies Saint-Martin as one of the many enlightened individuals—Jean-Jacques ROUSSEAU being the most prominent—who viewed the course of human HISTORY as one of degeneration.

Saint Matthew Passion   Grand choral work by Johann Sebastian BACH. Picander (the pseudonym of Christian Friedrich Henrici) wrote the text, drawing material from the New Testament Gospel of Saint Matthew and arranging it according to common practices of the era. The *Saint Matthew Passion* was first performed on April 15 (Good Friday), 1729, at the Thomaskirche in Leipzig. Although today the composition is recognized as a masterpiece, the culmination of the oratorio passion in BAROQUE STYLE MUSIC, it was rather poorly received by the residents of Leipzig. They much preferred the *Passion* by Gottfried Frober that was programmed on the same occasion at the rival Neuekirche.

An outstanding example of baroque oratorio writing, the *Saint Matthew Passion* also illustrates the baroque practices of tone painting (evoking images with sound) and numerical symbolism (structural reliance on numbers, which have symbolic meaning: the number three, for example). It also draws heavily on the late-baroque theory of the musical "affects." The composition is for double choirs and orchestras with the addition of one organ and a harpsichord. The two choirs engage each other in a dialogue—one choir representing Jesus, the "Daughter of Zion" (a favorite baroque character), and the Evangelist; and the second choir representing the Faithful. The two choirs sing together to symbolize the angry crowds at the trial of Jesus before Pontius Pilate.

The use of two choirs, which are physically separated in the church, emphasizes the dialogic nature of the text and provides an all-encompassing sound that places the listener in the middle of the action. This is an excellent example of baroque theatricality applied to the transmission of a sacred message.

Saint Petersburg   Russian city built at the beginning of the 18th century by PETER I (THE GREAT) as his new capital. Saint Petersburg provides an excellent example of the BAROQUE STYLE of architecture and its approach to the symbolic representation of central power in three-dimensional space. Today, it preserves aspects of its 18th-century appearance and allows visitors to see how the baroque and ROCOCO style AESTHETICS of the 18th century were transformed in the extreme northern region of Europe. Saint Petersburg differed markedly from the former Russian capital, MOSCOW, which had grown haphazardly over time and displayed a noticeable debt to Asian architectural styles.

The marshy site of Saint Petersburg, at the point where the Neva River meets the Baltic Sea, was uninhabited when Peter initiated his building project. Construction began in 1703, and the city became the official capital of Russia in 1712. It has been estimated that nearly 100,000 laborers lost their lives toiling on the project. Peter the Great intended the city to symbolize the new Russia he was trying to create. Its location on the Baltic emphasized the Western Orientation of Peter's policies; in fact, the city was often called Russia's "window on Europe." The city plan and architecture borrowed heavily from European capitals. Canals evoked Amsterdam and caused the city to be called "the Amsterdam of the North" by some visitors. Town houses and official state buildings reminiscent of contemporary European cities began to line the quays along the canals. Peter the Great's successors, Elizabeth and CATHERINE II (THE GREAT) continued the work of building Saint Petersburg.

The chief architects of the original baroque building phase were Domenico Trezzini and Andreas Schlüter. During Catherine the Great's reign, Bartolomeo RASTRELLI introduced elements of the rococo. Finally, Vallin de La Mothe and Antonio Rinaldi adorned the city with neoclassical monuments. Examples from this magnificent century of building still remain. They include the baroque style Church of the Fortress of Peter and Paul; the rococo Winter Palace, the Tsarskoe-Selo Palace, the Smolny Convent, and the Nevsky Prospect; and the neoclassical Hermitage Pavilion and Church of Saint Catherine.

See also NEOCLASSICISM.

Saint Petersburg Academy of Sciences   Institution founded in the 1720s by Czar PETER I (THE GREAT) of Russia. He designed the Saint Petersburg Academy after the BERLIN ACADEMY that had been inspired by Gottfried

Wilhelm LEIBNIZ. The primary purpose of the new Russian institution lay in overseeing the introduction of Russian intellectuals to European SCIENCE, but it also encouraged the gathering of knowledge about Russian HISTORY and natural history. The Academy did not begin operating until 1726, a year after Peter the Great's death.

Peter the Great imported a group of foreigners into Russia to people his new academy. Members included the prominent mathematicians Leonhard EULER and Daniel BERNOULLI, the historians August Ludwig von SCHLÖZER and Gerhard Müller, the geographer Joseph DELISLE, and the naturalist Johann Gmelin. Foreigners found life in Russia difficult at best, and by 1750 few prominent non-Russians resided at the academy.

From the beginning, the academy was set up to act not only as a place for meetings and reports by practicing research scientists but also to oversee the establishment of a new University of Saint Petersburg and a secondary school (gymnasium) on the German model. Both institutions developed slowly and required significant state backing to overcome the reluctance of Russian families to enroll their children.

The Saint Petersburg Academy served throughout the ENLIGHTENMENT as the primary channel through which enlightened ideas entered Russian thought.

See also SCIENTIFIC ACADEMIES.

Saint-Simon, Claude-Henri, de Rouvroy, comte de
(1760–1825) *French writer, sociologist, and economist*
Born in PARIS into a poor aristocratic family, Claude-Henri de Saint-Simon served with the French army in the AMERICAN REVOLUTION. He fought in the Battle of Yorktown in 1781. After a period of imprisonment in Jamaica and travel in Mexico, he returned to FRANCE. A believer in the FRENCH REVOLUTION, he cast off his noble title. He was not rewarded for his trouble, however, as he was imprisoned from 1793 until 1794 for being a noble by Maximilien ROBESPIERRE. After his release from prison, Saint-Simon improved his finances by speculating in the buying and selling of former aristocratic and church lands.

Financially secure, Saint-Simon turned his attention to intellectual matters. He wrote his first book on the reform of human society in 1802 after meeting Madame de STAËL in GENEVA. Saint-Simon produced several pamphlets that called for changes in human society. Sometimes this caused trouble for him with the authorities. He was tried for the revolutionary ideas advanced in his pamphlet "Parabole" in 1820. After a suicide attempt in 1823, he also explored religious means of changing society in *The New Christianity*, an 1825 selection of his work in English. He died in 1825, but his loyal followers, who had nursed him through his period of depression, carried on his work.

The hallmark of Saint-Simon's writings is the use of SCIENCE and NATURAL LAWS to study society and to over-come social disorganization and individualism. He believed that Europe was in a state of extreme disorganization and close to collapse. However, he believed that society could be rebuilt on scientific principles. The plan for his utopia is outlined in *Memoire sur la Science de l'Homme* (Memoir on the science of man; 1813), and *De la Réorganisation de la Société Européene* (On the reorganization of European society; 1814).

Saint-Simon also believed that a state-planned economy was necessary for the construction of his utopia. He wanted scientists, philosophers, and engineers to play a major role in the reconstruction of society. These intellectuals would lead government industrialization of society by advising government on planning, EDUCATION, building, and the allocation of capital resources. Due to the presence of such government control, Saint-Simon's works are sometimes linked to both communism and fascism. However, his economic ideas cannot be classified as truly communist because he recognized the importance of privately owned capital and entrepreneurship. Saint-Simon promoted industrialization as a new way to better all of society and eliminate unemployment.

Saint-Simon's ideas were further developed after 1825 by his followers, who published *An Explanation of the Doctrine of Saint-Simon* in 1830. Saint-Simonianism soon became synonymous with socialism, as his followers argued strongly for an equal redistribution of wealth. His ideas greatly influenced French thinkers such as Auguste Comte, and English writers such as Thomas Carlyle and John Stuart Mill.

See also UTILITY.

Further reading: Ghita Ionescu, *The Political Thought of Saint-Simon* (Oxford: Oxford University Press, 1989).

salons   *See* SOCIAL INSTITUTIONS OF THE ENLIGHTENMENT.

Sancho, Ignatius (1729–1780) *African-British man of letters*
Along with Olaudah EQUIANO, Phyllis Wheatley, and Quobna Ottobah Cugoano, Ignatius Sancho is one of the 18th century's most notable English-language writers of African descent. Sancho was born on a slave ship making its way from Guinea to the Spanish West Indies. He received his Christian name from the bishop at Cartagena in the Spanish colony of New Granada (Colombia). His parents died when he was young, his mother of illness and his father by suicide. His master brought him to ENGLAND and gave him to three sisters who reputedly treated him poorly. They gave him the surname "Sancho" because of his supposed resemblance to Sancho Panza, Don Quixote's squire in Cervantes's NOVEL.

Ignatius was a precocious child. John, the second duke of Montagu, befriended Sancho when he was young and instilled in him a love of books. When the duke died, Sancho fled to the duchess and went to work as her butler. Upon her death two years later, she left him £70 and an annuity of £30. However, Ignatius, who loved to gamble, soon dissipated his income. He returned to service with the chaplain of the Montagu household and, eventually, with the new duke. Sancho married Ann Osborne, a woman of West Indian origin, in 1758 and fathered six children. Suffering from intense attacks of the gout, he gave up service in 1773 and settled with Ann in a grocery shop.

Sancho became famous as a man of taste and letters. He is best known today for his florid letters, written at least in part in imitation of the English novelist Laurence STERNE. Sancho made Sterne's acquaintance in 1766, when he wrote a letter encouraging Sterne to continue speaking out against the evils of SLAVERY. Although he was a sentimentalist who extolled the virtues of commerce (and hence, by association, the slave trade), Sancho was also a lucid and occasionally trenchant commentator about the European treatment of Africans. For example, he defended the poet Phyllis Wheatley as having a genius superior to that of her master. He also wrote optimistically that commercial PROGRESS might one day unite humankind in bonds of brotherhood, freeing the slaves who were the victims of commercial progress in America during the 18th century.

Sancho's letters were published posthumously in 1782. Subsequent editions appeared in 1783, 1784, 1802, and 1803.

Further reading: Vincent Carretta, ed., *Genius in Bondage: Literature of the Early Black Atlantic* (Lexington, Ky.: University of Kentucky Press, 2001); Paul Edwards and Polly Rewt, eds., *The Letters of Ignatius Sancho* (Edinburgh: Edinburgh University Press, 1994).

Savoy French-speaking duchy lying on the western slope of the Alps. Today, the French *départements* of Savoie and Haut-Savoie contain most of the territory of the historic duchy. In the 18th century, Savoy was part of the Savoyard dynastic state, which had its political and economic center in TURIN, a city of the Italian PIEDMONT region. Savoy, which had dominated the state until 1560, was an administrative backwater in the 18th century, but it retained some economic importance because of the network of trade routes that crisscrossed its regions. Savoy also remained strategically important in 18th-century Europe because it contained major Alpine passes that allowed movement of troops and supplies between Italy and France. For this reason, its rulers, the dukes of Savoy, were able to drive skillful, daring diplomatic bargains with the major European powers.

The duchy itself gained little advantage from either the trade or military movement through its territories. The economy was stagnant, largely consisting of subsistence agriculture and pastoralism. Small industries produced some silks and iron nails. The population of the region was sparse and the terrain mountainous. The major city in Savoy was the Alpine town of Chambéry, which served as a local administrative center. Jean-Jacques ROUSSEAU, who was a native of GENEVA, spent several years in Savoy and immortalized the region in a famous chapter from *ÉMILE* entitled "Profession of Faith of the Vicar of Savoy."

The French annexed Savoy in 1792, during the wars associated with the FRENCH REVOLUTION. It was returned to the house of Savoy in 1815 but again became a part of FRANCE in 1860.

Scarlatti, Giuseppe Domenico (1685–1757) *Neapolitan composer, performer on keyboard instruments, and teacher*

Giuseppe Domenico Scarlatti, or Domenico Scarlatti as he is most commonly known, was a member of an illustrious musical family that produced prominent composers and performers for several generations. He was the sixth of the 10 children of Alessandro Scarlatti and Antonia Anzalone Scarlatti. Alessandro Scarlatti was a major composer and is often called the "father of Neapolitan opera." Very little is known about Domenico Scarlatti's early training, although it is possible that he had instruction from family members of the older generation as well as from the musicians and composers Francesco Gasparini, Bernardo Pasquini, and Gaetano Greco.

Scarlatti acquired his first positions through the auspices of his father, and his early career moves seem also to have been dictated by the elder Scarlatti. In 1701, the 16-year-old Domenico obtained a post as organist and composer of the Naples royal chapel where his father was the director of music. In the next three years Scarlatti moved with his father to Florence, and then, in 1705, was ordered by his father to travel with the castrato Nicolas Grimaldi to ROME, Florence, and VENICE. The younger Scarlatti was unable to free himself from domination by his father until early 1717, when he finally obtained legal documents guaranteeing his independence. Even after that date, however, Scarlatti had to fight his father's emotional hold on his life.

Scarlatti settled in Rome sometime before 1709 and in that year entered the service of the exiled Polish queen, Maria Casimira. In 1713, he became *maestro di capella* for the Basilica Giulia, and early in 1714, after Maria Casimira left Rome, he accepted employment in the service of the Portuguese ambassador to Rome, the marquês de Fontes. He also worked from 1714 to 1719 as musical director at Saint Peter's Basilica in the Vatican. In these positions Scarlatti wrote OPERAS, sacred MUSIC, and secular instrumental works. He began to frequent the weekly meetings of the Accademie Poeticomusicali at the residence of Cardinal Pietro Ottoboni, where he met the composers Arcangelo CORELLI and George Frederick HANDEL. At the academy meetings Scarlatti also met Thomas

Roseingrave, who later greatly facilitated the dissemination of his vocal and keyboard compositions in ENGLAND.

In 1719, Scarlatti moved to PORTUGAL and assumed duties as maestro for the chapel of the archbishop of Lisbon. He remained in Portugal until 1728. Few records exist of his activities during these years, and it is assumed that they were lost in the great LISBON EARTHQUAKE of November 1, 1755. It is known that Scarlatti was charged with teaching the Infanta Maria Bárbara, the talented daughter of King John V of Portugal. In 1728 Scarlatti followed Maria Bárbara to MADRID after she married the future king of Spain, Crown Prince Fernando. Scarlatti spent the remainder of his life performing, supervising theatrical music productions, teaching, and composing in relative obscurity. He became a knight of the Order of Santiago in 1738.

Scarlatti developed an idiosyncratic style, which is assumed to owe some debt to musical practices in the Iberian peninsula. The same lack of source material prevents knowledge of this matter and complicates any understanding of the events of Scarlatti's life. Scarlatti is best known for his many harpsichord sonatas (called *Essercizi,* exercises).

Scheele, Carl Wilhelm (1742–1786) *Swedish pharmacist and chemist who contributed to the Chemical Revolution of the late Enlightenment*

Scheele received a rudimentary EDUCATION that lacked the rigorous mathematical and linguistic instruction characteristic of the best 18th-century schools. Having developed an interest in pharmacy from his childhood, he apprenticed himself to the pharmacist Martin Bauch in Göteborg. He left Göteborg in 1756 and worked in various settings as a journeyman for the next 10 years. In Malmö, his laboratory skills were recognized and fostered. In 1768, Scheele moved to Stockholm and then in 1770 to Uppsala. In Uppsala he had access to a laboratory and met the prominent Swedish chemist Torbern BERGMAN, who assisted him with the dissemination of his experimental results. In 1775, Scheele became the pharmacist for the town of Köping, where he remained until his death in 1786. Scheele was elected to the Swedish Academy of Sciences in 1775 and was received in 1777 into the membership of the Royal Swedish Academy of Sciences.

Scheele was troubled by certain inconsistencies in the PHLOGISTON THEORY that provided the then standard chemical explanation of combustion, respiration, and calcination processes. He engaged in an intensive examination of past chemical experiments on fire and air in an effort to resolve the problems raised by phlogiston theory. He never completely abandoned the theory. In the course of these investigations, Scheele isolated oxygen gas sometime in the early months of 1774, apparently before either Joseph PRIESTLEY or Antoine LAVOISIER suc-

ceeded at the task. The dating is supported by the fact that Scheele reported his discovery to the chemist Torbern Bergman, who published a summary of the findings with a report on Scheele's related theory of heat in the *Nova Acta Regiae Societatis Scientarum Upsaliensis* (New acts of the Royal Society of Sciences of Uppsala). The notice appeared several months before Priestley announced his own discoveries in August 1774. Scheele sent Lavoisier a letter on September 30, 1774, in which he outlined his discovery of oxygen and provided detailed instructions on the process of making pure oxygen. He sent the information to Lavoisier in thanks for the receipt of the French chemist's *Opuscules physiques et chymiques* (Tracts on physics and chemistry). Lavoisier did not acknowledge Scheele in his own papers on the discovery of oxygen, although he carried out his oxygen isolation experiments only in early 1775. Scheele's letter to Lavoisier was not discovered in Lavoisier's manuscript papers until the late 19th century.

Even today, Scheele's contribution to the CHEMICAL REVOLUTION is not widely known, and the discovery of oxygen is usually treated as an example of simultaneous independent discovery. Certainly, the interests of chemists of the era, the problems posed by phlogiston theory, and the manner in which experiments were being framed, made the isolation of oxygen imminent. But the information about Scheele suggests that the process may have involved more dissemination of information between scientists than has normally been acknowledged.

Scheele made several additional discoveries of note. He isolated chlorine gas and noted its bleaching capabilities. He discovered several organic acids such as malic acid in apples, mucic acid, and oxalic acid. He also discovered glycerol and developed a method of preserving vinegar by heating it in a container immersed in a kettle of boiling water.

Scheele published the *Chemische Abhandlung von der Luft und dem Feuer* (Chemical treatise on air and fire; 1777). Many of his experimental findings were reported in the official journals of the two Swedish academies to which he belonged, and the remainder of his work is in manuscript form.

Schiller, Johann Christoph Friedrich (1759–1805) *German dramatist, poet, literary critic, and historian*

Friedrich Schiller, as he is better known, ranks with Johann Wolfgang von GOETHE as one of the greatest literary figures to have lived and worked in GERMANY. Schiller's plays and poetry have become worldwide symbols of the quest for human dignity and FREEDOM associated with the ENLIGHTENMENT, and they offer brilliant examples of both its passion and its commitment to the highest human ideals. His literary criticism, in turn, has served as a major force in defining modern ideas of AESTHETICS and culture.

Schiller's parents were not wealthy. His father was a soldier who worked his way up slowly to the rank of captain (1761) in the army of the duke of Württemberg, and his mother was the daughter of an impoverished innkeeper. Schiller himself was a sickly child, continually plagued by a host of ailments, which finally led to his early death. As a young man, Schiller was consumed by an enthusiastic concern for RELIGION. He wanted to enter the Lutheran clergy, but because he showed great promise, Duke Karl Eugen of Württemberg ordered him to attend the Karlsschule, a newly founded military academy bearing the duke's name. The Karlsschule was designed to train future bureaucrats and also to compete with the University of Tübingen for the best of Württemberg's talent. Discipline was harsh and the course of study highly organized. The students (called *Eleven* after the French word *élève*, meaning student) were required to wear uniforms and wigs. They were also subjected to constant supervision. This repressive regime helped to generate Schiller's lifelong commitment to freedom.

At first Schiller began studying the humanities and was not a very good student. It was only after he decided to switch to MEDICINE that his academic zeal began to appear. In addition to medical tomes, he read widely in Shakespeare and in 18th-century German works by Gotthold Ephraim LESSING, Christoph Martin WIELAND, and Albrecht von HALLER. Schiller was equally fascinated by the philosophy of the Enlightenment and read Christian GARVE, J. G. Sulzer, Moses MENDELSSOHN, Adam FERGUSON, and Johann Gottfried HERDER. But his main interest, at that time, was what he called "philosophical medicine," the study of the human body guided by the desire to understand its functions and its relation to spirit or mind. In short, Schiller's philosophical medicine probed two basic questions concerning human existence, the relationship between mind and body and the connection between freedom and necessity. These themes, expressed in various forms, run like a thread through all of his writings.

Schiller's first attempt to explicate these questions in his doctoral dissertation, *The Philosophy of Physiology* (1779), was rejected as too radical. Only in 1780, after two more attempts, was he finally granted a medical degree from the Karlsschule. He was then appointed as a regimental doctor with a very low salary.

Within two years after this appointment, Schiller achieved literary fame with the production of his play *Die Raüber* (The Robbers), which was one of the central pieces of the youthful STURM UND DRANG movement. The play was premiered outside the duchy of Württemberg, in more enlightened Mannheim and to wild applause. The play, which espoused an extreme form of INDIVIDUALISM, was interpreted as an attack on despotism, moral corruption, and narrow-minded thinking. The major figure in the play, Karl Moor, became, along with Goethe's Werther, a symbol for that restless *Sturm und Drang* gen-

Friedrich Schiller, sketch by Professor Weitsch. The poet and dramatist Friedrich Schiller championed human political freedom in his dramatization of the tale of Wilhelm Tell. *(Courtesy Staatlich Museum Berlin/Bildarchiv Preussischer Kulturbesitz)*

eration of gifted young German intellectuals who so resented the restrictions of society and the social dominance of an aristocracy they considered hopelessly out of date.

Duke Karl Eugen, who possessed the right to discipline his subjects, was extremely displeased with Schiller's play and ordered the rebellious young man to stay away from Mannheim. When Schiller returned to the city and its theater without permission, Karl Eugen condemned him to 14 days arrest and forbade him from writing anything but medical treatises. As a result, Schiller and his friend Andreas Streicher fled from the duchy of Württemberg, traveling under pseudonyms.

In 1783, Schiller was given a position as theater writer in Mannheim, where he was charged with writing three plays a year for production. He wrote *Fiesco, Luise Müllering,* and the highly successful *Kabale und Liebe*. In 1785, he moved to Leipzig and lived there until 1787. During this period, he wrote what probably is his most famous single work, the poem "An die Freude" (Ode to joy), which Ludwig van BEETHOVEN used in the final movement of his Ninth Symphony. Schiller also began delving into HISTORY and began work on the first of his famous historical plays, *Don Carlos*.

In 1787, Schiller moved to Weimar, where he spent the rest of his short life. He was given a position at the court, again with a low salary, and began to make friends with some of the luminaries at Weimar, especially Wieland and Herder. In 1789, the duke of Weimar appointed him professor of history at the University of Jena. Schiller's inaugural lecture, *Was heißt und zu welchem Ende studiert man Universalgeschichte* (What is and to what ends does one study universal history), was a great success. Following the ideas of August Ludwig von SCHLÖZER, Schiller presented a broad view of human development claiming that the study of history helps one to better understand the world and self, resulting in an intensification of positive personal qualities.

With his appointment to a chair in history, Schiller, for the first time in his life, was able to earn a decent salary and therefore to marry. But this secure existence was interrupted after only a short time by a serious illness (1791), which weakened him so much that he could not continue his teaching. Destitute, he was rescued by the prince of Schleswig-Holstein, who gave him a yearly grant of 1000 talers (half the amount of his university position) for five years.

At the same time, Schiller's interests were being expanded by his serious study of the philosophy of Immanuel KANT. In response to Kant, Schiller wrote two outstanding theoretical works, *Ueber die ästhetische Erziehung des Menschen in einer Reihe von Briefen* (On the aesthetic education of mankind in a series of letters; 1794) and *Ueber naive und sentimentalische Dichtung* (On naive and sentimental poetry; 1795). Both works, although stimulated by Kant's writings, drew heavily upon Schiller's earlier physiological studies. The first work, *On the Aesthetic Education of Mankind*, offered his attempt to find an intermediary between uncontrolled freedom and determinism in human activity. He suggested that the aesthetic realm—the world of beauty and art—provides the necessary link, because art is an activity in which true human freedom is expressed. In the second work, *On Naive and Sentimental Poetry*, Schiller continued his exploration of ways to avoid the extremes of chaos and control, of idealism and realism, of mind and body. Modern poetry, he argued, should seek to combine the natural feeling of the ancients (naive, because it was not conscious) with the rationality of the modern age (sentimental in the sense that it was derived from sensation). Rather than calling for a return to the classical past, Schiller, in the spirit of the Enlightenment, hoped that a new, higher form of poetry and human sensibility could be created.

As Schiller was writing these essays, he established closer contacts with a former antagonist, Goethe. Goethe did not like Schiller's work, considering it too emotional, and Schiller thought Goethe an overpaid upper-class snob. Their close relationship emerged through the medium of the natural sciences. They began by discussing the manner in which NATURE should be observed and then proceeded to questions of art and literature. Very quickly the relationship developed into an extremely intense one, becoming one of the most fruitful friendships in the history of LITERATURE. The two men exchanged works, criticized each other, made suggestions for new areas to be investigated, and attracted a group of extremely gifted young men to their circle, the most famous of whom were the two HUMBOLDT brothers, Wilhelm and Alexander.

Under the influence of Goethe, Schiller turned again to drama and, in the 10 years left to him, wrote his most famous dramatic works. They included the *Wallenstein* trilogy, *Maria Stuart*, *Die Jungfrau von Orleans* (The Maid of Orleans), and WILHELM TELL. As he worked on these historical plays, his researches also led him to write actual history, the *Geschichte des Abfalls der vereinigten Niederlande von der spanischen Regiurung* (History of the succession of the United Netherlands from Spain) and *Geschichte des dreißigjärigen Kriegs* (History of the Thirty Years' War). He also composed some of his most popular ballads and poems and founded a journal, entitled *Horen*, which he hoped would serve as the vehicle for a regeneration of German literature and letters. Although never a financial success, *Horen* was an outstanding contribution to German literary journalism.

Schiller's works, especially the plays, became part of Germany's liberal literary tradition, each one exploring in its own way the tension between freedom and duty, between the use of force and passive acceptance, between traditional and charismatic forms of rule, and employing a language that reflected Schiller's desire to mediate between extremes. Nowhere are these characteristics better illustrated than in his last play, *Wilhelm Tell*. Tell was conceived by Schiller as a naive thinker who was confronting a purely self-interested rational opponent. The famous scene in which Tell is required to shoot an apple from his son's head transforms Tell into both a self-conscious individual and a national leader. In the figure of Tell, Schiller thus presents his ideal of the harmonic union between the individual and the nation.

Although Schiller's last 10 years were the most fruitful and intensive years in his life, he was continually plagued by physical disabilities. He had written his four children in 1805 that he prayed that he could "live until he was fifty," but his wish was not granted. He died in 1805 at the age of 46. The autopsy revealed that his internal organs were so damaged that, as the doctor remarked, it was a miracle that he had lived so long. Goethe's reaction to Schiller's death sums up his importance. "His death marked the close of an epoch which will never reappear, but which will continually have an effect on the future."

See also Wilhelm von HUMBOLDT.

Further reading: W. H. Bruford, *Germany in the Eighteenth Century: The Social Background of the Literary Revival* (Cambridge: Cambridge University Press, 1971); Henri Brunschwig, *Enlightenment and Romanticism in Eighteenth-Century Prussia,* tr. Frank Jellinek (Chicago: University of Chicago Press, 1974); Kenneth Dewhurst and Nigel Reeves, *Friedrich Schiller: Medicine, Psychology, Literature* (Berkeley, Calif.: University of California Press, 1978).

Schlözer, August Ludwig von (1735–1809) *German historian, publicist, linguist, and political theorist*
Schlözer was a professor at the University of GÖTTINGEN and the teacher of Johannes von MÜLLER. The son of a clergyman, August Ludwig von Schlözer began his university education studying theology at Wittenberg. He transferred to the University of Göttingen, turning to philology, Oriental studies, and MEDICINE. After graduation, Schlözer spent several years in SWEDEN and in SAINT PETERSBURG, Russia, as a tutor and lecturer. He was a member of the SAINT PETERSBURG ACADEMY OF SCIENCES. Schlözer eventually moved back to Göttingen, where he spent most of his life as a professor of HISTORY and *Staatswissenschaft* (political science) at the university.

With his Göttingen colleague Johann Christoph GATTERER, Schlözer contributed substantially to the transformation of history into a critical science of the human past. This task was accomplished by adapting the intellectual tools and concepts of the ENLIGHTENMENT to historiography (the theory of history writing).

For Schlözer, history was a study not only of political events, but also of the cultural and social context in which these events occurred. He criticized traditional historiography as a mere collection (aggregate) of political facts. In its place, Schlözer wanted to see histories written in a systematic manner. By this, he meant that scholars should analyze events, placing them in their broad context, but then should explain the factors that cause events to unfold over time. In other words, individual events were to be placed together in a system that assumed these events were somehow related to one another. Schlözer believed that PROGRESS in history unfolds by means of a series of revolutions: fundamental changes in the political, social, cultural, technological, and economic organization of human societies.

Schlözer made important contributions toward developing a body of historical scholarship on Russia. He edited the chronicles of Nestor, a document that records early events in the history of Russia, and he also wrote *Nördische Geschichte* (Northern history; 1771). The *Noördische Geschichte* offers one example of Schlözer's research into the history of languages. He treated Russian and other northern languages as a family with a common background and set of origins. He applied the same approach to the languages of the Near East, coining the term *Semitic languages* in the process. Unlike some enlightened writers who stressed the uniqueness of the histories and cultures of specific peoples, Schlözer remained wedded to the ideal of writing a universal history of humankind. A book entitled *Vorstellung seiner Universalhistorie* (Idea of his universal history; 1772) presented his ideas, exploring in some depth the problems raised by disparities between biblical chronology and emerging theories of the Earth's natural history. It was sharply criticized by Johann HERDER, who was one of the early champions of the uniqueness of various peoples.

It was primarily through his political journals that Schlözer emerged as a central figure in the AUFKLÄRUNG (German Enlightenment). The *Briefwechsel* (Correspondence; 1776–82) and *Göttinger Staatsanzeigen* (Reports from the city of Göttingen; 1786–94) presented basic facts (statistics, according to Schlözer) about the various states of the region now called GERMANY, criticized various political abuses, and offered information about subjects ranging from the cultivation of the potato to the AMERICAN REVOLUTION. The *Göttinger Staatsanzeigen* also printed the first German translation of the French DECLARATION OF THE RIGHTS OF MAN AND CITIZEN in 1791. Its positive reports of the FRENCH REVOLUTION caused it to be censored in 1794.

In his many activities, from political essays to historical theorizing, Schlözer revealed himself as a man thoroughly imbued with ideals of the Enlightenment. Perhaps nowhere is this characteristic more clearly revealed, however, than in his treatment of his daughter. Schlözer personally supervised her EDUCATION, seeing that she was introduced from childhood to the works of the Enlightenment and thoroughly trained in general academic skills. As a result, Dorothea Schlözer became the first woman in Germany to receive a doctorate in philosophy from a university.

science The ENLIGHTENMENT coincided with a great 18th-century expansion of human knowledge about the natural world. This change was stimulated by shifts during the 17th century in philosophical conceptualizations about the physical world and about the limits of human knowledge. These philosophical shifts, in turn, produced changes in beliefs about the strucure of the universe, about the type of knowledge possible to the human mind, and about the proper methods for obtaining such knowledge. The whole complex of these changes is sometimes

Benjamin Thompson, count Rumford, engraving by Franz Xaver Muller after an unidentified artist. Scientists of the Enlightenment often held official government posts and pursued their scientific inquiries as an avocation. *(Courtesy Art Resource, New York; original in National Portrait Gallery, Smithsonian Institution, Washington, D.C.)*

called the SCIENTIFIC REVOLUTION. Whether or not the term *revolution* is justified—and the question is being debated by current scholars of the history of science—the face of science by the end of the 18th century was noticeably different in appearance from the one that existed in the early 17th century. Furthermore, the PHILOSOPHES of the 18th-century Enlightenment conceived of their era as one in which the great revolution of the 17th century was being completed. The mathematician Jean Le Rond d'ALEMBERT described the developments of his century in scientific realms as "a revolution," and the chemist Antoine LAVOISIER predicted in 1773 that his own experiments in chemistry and physics might provoke a CHEMICAL REVOLUTION.

From the 17th century, the Enlightenment inherited the notion that REASON, manifested as natural physical laws expressible in mathematical equations, informs and governs the whole structure of creation. It also inherited a new way of conceiving the activity of doing scientific research, the so-called SCIENTIFIC METHOD originally outlined by Isaac NEWTON. The relationships between the general ideas of the Enlightenment and significant developments in the natural sciences, however, was a compli-

cated one of reciprocal cause and effect. This situation derived from the fact that the seminal philosophical changes in the Scientific Revolution—shifts in the basic intellectual model used to describe the universe—also provided metaphors and methods that could be applied to human affairs. Thus, three central concepts of the Enlightenment—reason, NATURE, and NATURAL LAW—all had roots in the then contemporary scientific model of the world.

It is misleading as well as anachronistic to apply modern categories of science indiscriminately to the era. In fact, at the beginning of the century, the very term *science* was only occasionally used to describe the disciplines that studied the natural world. The more common rubric was NATURAL PHILOSOPHY, a category that betrayed the fact that the study of the natural world was conceived as an intellectual inquiry closely linked with investigations of MORAL PHILOSOPHY, EPISTEMOLOGY, and ontology. Furthermore, natural philosophy was closely related to concerns of THEOLOGY and RELIGION.

Specific subdisciplines also did not have definitions or content like those of our modern divisions. Physics, for example, was conceived at the beginning of the Enlightenment as a science that teaches the reasons and causes of all living and nonliving entities. Certain categories of modern physics, such as ASTRONOMY, optics, statics, hydraulics, geology, navigation, surveying, and fortification, were subsumed under the discipline of mixed mathematics. By the end of the century, however, experimental physics, the study by quantitative, experimental methods of the RELATIONS that govern the inorganic world, had begun to acquire a separate status. In conjunction with this development, the old concept of physics gradually disappeared. Similarly, during most of the 18th century, chemistry belonged to two realms: ALCHEMY and MEDICINE. Toward the end of the century, a dramatic change occurred in the concepts and methods of chemistry so that by the end of the century the newly rationalized discipline acquired a new status and identity. BIOLOGY also did not exist as a separate category but was rather studied as a facet of medicine, chemistry, or even physics. The term *biologie*, in fact, was not coined until 1802, when it was used by Jean de LAMARCK and Gottfried Reinhold Treverinus. The proper 18th-century term, when people wanted to differentiate the study of living matter from other subjects of investigation, was life sciences.

All these shifts in philosophical conceptualization, disciplinary structure, and scientific method were accompanied by significant changes in the manner in which the practice of science was organized. The individuals who pursued scientific studies in the early years of the Scientific Revolution were natural philosophers or mathematicians, employed either by wealthy patrons, royal bureaucracies, UNIVERSITIES, or the various Christian churches. In the 1660s, the first official academies devoted specifically and exclusively to the study of the natural sciences and mathematics were founded in ENGLAND and FRANCE. The academies varied in organization, degree of freedom, and type of membership from one country to another, but the overall effect of their activities was to stimulate the professionalization of science. Gradually, the serious business of science became limited to individuals for whom doing science was the major activity of their lives. Amateurs became increasingly excluded, although in certain areas of science and in certain countries (especially England), amateur science persisted well into the 19th century. Closely related to the process of professionalization in the sciences was the development of increasingly sophisticated and expensive TECHNOLOGY AND INSTRUMENTATION that both supported and stimulated scientific discovery.

The thought of the Enlightenment was intimately linked with science, for nature was one of its fundamental concepts. As definitions of nature and what was natural varied, so did outlooks on nearly every facet of human existence. During the years of the Enlightenment, several significant shifts in science altered common European conceptualizations of the universe. Within the physical sciences, the universe described by Isaac Newton gradually came to dominate both professional and lay visions. Several international scientific projects and discoveries offered verification for Newton's theory of universal gravitation, thereby creating a climate in which scientists began looking for other manifestations of Newtonian forces.

The process of mathematizing the natural laws operating in the physical world (that is, expressing its relations in mathematical terms) advanced considerably, especially under the stimulus provided by the powerful tools of mathematical calculus and PROBABILITY. These two creations made it possible to express motion in mathematical terms and to introduce some predictability into seemingly random, unrelated natural events. Mathematical probability also stimulated the development of various social sciences and demography, all of which tried to apply the model of the natural sciences to the study of human behavior. Closely related to the impulse to mathematize was the tendency to replace qualitative descriptions with quantitative methods. This approach yielded important results in chemistry, providing one of the bases for the Chemical Revolution.

In the life sciences, two extreme views of the organism competed throughout the century: the mechanical model derived from Cartesian MECHANICAL PHILOSOPHY and an organic model based on VITALISM. Physicians and researchers adopted many different variants of these two extremes, creating a wide array of theories about life. Generally, as the 18th century progressed, however, vitalistic elements were incorporated into theoretical explanations of life processes, yielding more complex models of life than those that had predominated at the beginning of the century.

The general tendency to mathematize and to quantify certain processes was matched by an equally powerful tendency to historicize the world; in other words, the important concept that structures and things change over time was introduced into nearly every realm of scientific thought. The Earth, therefore, acquired a geological history, embryos began to be described in terms of their development over time, and animal and plant species began to be conceived as having transformed in some manner from their original status at the time of the creation.

All these activities reflected a general impulse, begun during the Scientific Revolution and continued through the Enlightenment, to uncover the order that was presumed to govern the structure of the world. This impulse, in some cases, translated into efforts to impose categories on natural phenomena and led scientists into extended discussions about the best way to arrive at valid forms of organization and CLASSIFICATION. In the end, most scientists, whatever their specific orientations, believed that their successes would help to further the general cause of human progress and enlightenment, providing human beings with the intellectual tools to master the world.

See also AFFINITY CHEMISTRY; ANIMALCULISM; ANIMISM; ANTHROPOLOGY; BACON; BANKS; BAROMETER; BARTHÈZ; BERGMAN; BERLIN ACADEMY; BERNOULLI; BERTHOLLET; BICHAT; *BILDUNG*; BLACK; BLUMENBACH; BOERHAAVE; BONNET; BORDEU; BOSCOVICH; BUFFON; CABANIS; CALORIC; CAMPER; CASSINI; CAVENDISH; CLAIRAUT; COPERNICAN REVOLUTION; COPERNICUS; COULOMB; CULLEN; CUVIER; DARWIN; DAUBENTON; DEGENERATION; DELISLE; DESAGULIERS; DESCARTES; DESMAREST; DIDEROT; DU CHÂTELET; EMPIRICISM; EPIGENESIS; EULER; FAHRENHEIT; FONTENELLE; FOURIER; FRANKLIN; FRENCH ACADEMY OF SCIENCES; GALILEI; GALL; GALVANI; GASSEND; GENERATION; GEOCENTRIC; GOETHE; GRAVESANDE; GREAT CHAIN OF BEING; HALES; HALLER; HALLEY; HELIOCENTRIC; HOFFMANN; Alexander von HUMBOLDT; HUNTER (John and William); HUTTON; IATROCHEMISTRY; IATROMECHANICS; INGEN-HOUSZ; INOCULATION; JARDIN DES PLANTES; JENNER; KANT; KEPLER; LAGRANGE; LALANDE; LA METTRIE; LAPLACE; LAVATER; LEEUWENHOEK; LEIBNIZ; LINNAEUS; LONGITUDE; LUNAR SOCIETY OF BIRMINGHAM; MALEBRANCHE; MALTHUS; MANCHESTER LITERARY AND PHILOSOPHICAL SOCIETY; MARAT; MARGGRAF; MATERIALISM; MATHEMATICS AND MECHANICS; MERSENNE; MESMER; MICROSCOPE; MUSSCHENBROEK; ON THE REVOLUTIONS OF THE HEAVENLY SPHERES; ORRERY; PHYSICO-THEOLOGY; PREFORMATION THEORY; PRIESTLEY; PRINCIPIA MATHEMATICA; PRINGLE; PSYCHOLOGY; PYRRHONISM; RATIONALISM; REIL; RITTENHOUSE; ROYAL SOCIETY OF EDINBURGH; ROYAL SOCIETY OF LONDON; RUMFORD; RUSH; SAINT PETERSBURG ACADEMY OF SCIENCES; SCHEELE; SCIENCE OF MAN; SCIENTIFIC ACADEMIES; SKEPTICISM; SPALLANZANI; SPINOZA; STAHL; SUBTLE FLUIDS; SÜSSMILCH; SWIETEN, Gerard van; SYMPATHY; TELESCOPE; TRANSIT OF VENUS; TREMBLEY; WERNER; WHYTT; WOLFF.

Further reading: Christopher Fox et al., eds., *Inventing Human Science: Eighteenth-Century Domains* (Berkeley: University of California Press, 1995); Charles Coulston Gillispie, *The Edge of Objectivity: An Essay in the History of Scientific Ideas* (Princeton, N.J.: Princeton University Press, 1960); Roger Hahn, *The Anatomy of a Scientific Institution: The Paris Academy of Sciences (1666–1803)* (Berkeley: University of California Press, 1971); Thomas L. Hankins, *Science and the Enlightenment* (Cambridge: Cambridge University Press, 1985); A. E. Musson, *Science, Technology and Economic Growth in the Eighteenth Century* (London: Methuen, 1972); Aram Vartanian, *Science and Humanism in the French Enlightenment*, intro. Lester G. Crocker (Charlottesville, Va.: Rookwood Press, 1999).

science of man Knowledge or wisdom about humankind. The use of the concept "science of man" during the ENLIGHTENMENT underscored the prevalent belief that the study of basic human nature could provide the material for creating a systematic body of reliable knowledge about human behavior and character. The concept of a science of man also embodied the notion that the proper study of humankind should be separated from THEOLOGY, RELIGION, and metaphysics.

PHILOSOPHES began to use the term with these new meanings around the middle of the 18th century, especially after David HUME incorporated it in his TREATISE OF HUMAN NATURE. In the flush of OPTIMISM about the power of human REASON to uncover the lawful organization of the universe, some intellectuals, especially in SCOTLAND and FRANCE, dreamed of bringing even human behavior into the realm of mathematically expressed SCIENCE. The concept lay under the whole program of the IDÉOLOGUES during the FRENCH REVOLUTION. It also informed enlightened searches for natural foundations of morality, political action, and economic behavior.

This general belief that human existence could be studied as a science modeled after the natural sciences helped to stimulate the development of specific new disciplines during the Enlightenment. PSYCHOLOGY, for example, began to emerge as a discipline separate from EPISTEMOLOGY. ANTHROPOLOGY, as a cultural and physical study of humankind, also became a distinct subject. Elements of what would eventually become sociology appeared in the works of MONTESQUIEU and some historians, but the distinct discipline was a 19th-century creation.

See also AUTOMATA; CABANIS; CONDORCET; DESTUTT DE TRACY; ECONOMICS; FERGUSON; HELVÉTIUS; HISTORY; IDÉOLOGIE; MATHEMATICS AND MECHANICS; MILLAR; MORAL PHILOSOPHY; POLITICAL THEORY; SMITH.

scientific academies Formal institutions established to foster the pursuit of the natural sciences. The establishment of scientific academies was one facet of a general trend, begun in the late 16th-century Renaissance, toward creating institutions to foster activities in various intellectual and artistic fields. The SCIENTIFIC REVOLUTION of the 17th century provided a major impetus for the establishment of specific academies dedicated to science. Prior to that time, a few scientific academies enjoyed brief existence, but the 17th century saw the creation of permanent institutions. The era of the ENLIGHTENMENT continued the trend by overseeing the foundation of state-sponsored scientific academies in nearly every European state. This phenomenon was greatly stimulated by the writings and activities of the German philosopher Gottfried Wilhelm LEIBNIZ.

The new scientific academies provided institutional support for the adherents of the transformed science that was developing during the 17th and 18th centuries. At academy meetings, scientific papers were read and freely discussed. Some papers were also published in journals that enjoyed circulation throughout Europe. During the 18th century, certain academies aided in the development of the concept of the professional scientist as distinct from the educated, interested amateur. Except in the British Isles and the British North American colonies, most scientific academies in the 17th and 18th centuries were formal state organizations whose roles were intricately bound with the phenomenon of extension of central state control.

The 17th century saw the establishment of two prominent scientific academies. In FRANCE, the Académie Royale des Sciences (FRENCH ACADEMY OF SCIENCES) began in the 1630s as an informal private gathering of men such as Blaise Pascal, René DESCARTES, Pierre GASSEND, and Marin MERSENNE. In 1666, surviving members of this group received a royal charter incorporating their organization as an official arm of the emerging absolute French monarchy. The French Academy of Sciences always had two functions. On the one hand, it sponsored new scientific investigation stimulated by the evolving Scientific Revolution; on the other hand, it defined French science, an official science condoned by the state. In ENGLAND, the ROYAL SOCIETY OF LONDON developed along a different path. It *began* as a private gathering in 1645, but when it was incorporated in 1662, it remained a private organization. The Royal Society never played a formal official role and therefore enjoyed greater independence than did its counterpart in France.

Scientific academies founded during the 18th century included the Societät de Scienzen (founded in 1700 by Frederick III of Brandenburg), afterward called the Königliche Preussische Akademie der Wissenschaften and reorganized in 1744 by FREDERICK II (THE GREAT) in PRUSSIA; the Bayerische Akademie der Wissenschaften (founded in 1759 by Maximilien I) in MUNICH; the Akademie der Wissenschaften (1755) at Mannheim; Det Kongelige Danske Videnskabernes Selskab (founded in 1742 by King Christian VI) in Copenhagen, DENMARK; the Akademie der Wissenschaften (founded in 1751 by

Albrecht von HALLER) of Göttingen; the Prager Gelehrte Gesellschaft (founded in 1771 by Ignaz von Born), later the Societas Regia Scientarum Bohemica (1784) in Prague; Societá Reale (founded in 1761 by Cesare BECCARIA, Joseph LAGRANGE, and others), later the Regia Accademia delle Scienze (1783) in TURIN; Accademia delle Scienze e Belle Lettere (founded in 1779 by Bernardo TANUCCI) at Naples; the Accademia dei Ricovrati (1779) in VENICE; the Hollandsche Maatschappij der Wetenschappen (1752); the Academia Real das Ciências (1779) in PORTUGAL; the Academia Real (1774) in SPAIN; the Kungliga Svenska Vetenskapsakademien (founded in 1741 by Carolus LINNAEUS) in Stockholm, SWEDEN; and the ST. PETERSBURG ACADEMY OF SCIENCES (founded in 1724 by PETER I) in Russia. Private academies founded in the 18th century included the ROYAL SOCIETY OF EDINBURGH (1739); the Royal Dublin Society; the AMERICAN PHILOSOPHICAL SOCIETY (founded in 1743 by Benjamin FRANKLIN) in PHILADELPHIA; the American Academy of Arts and Sciences (1780) in Boston; the Kungliga Vetenskaps Societaten (founded in 1739 by Emanuel SWEDENBORG and others) in Uppsala, Sweden; and the Société pour l'Avancement des Arts (founded by H. B. Saussure and approved in 1776) in GENEVA.

See also BERLIN ACADEMY; SCIENCE; SOCIAL INSTITUTIONS OF THE ENLIGHTENMENT.

scientific method   The process by which valid knowledge is obtained about the natural world. In somewhat modified form, the system of scientific practices and assumptions that made up the scientific method of the ENLIGHTENMENT still governs our basic approach to SCIENCE in the modern world. The method consisted of a blending of EMPIRICISM, the MECHANICAL PHILOSOPHY, and mathematics that marked a significant change in the way that scientific problems were studied and solved.

The early decades of the 17th-century SCIENTIFIC REVOLUTION gave birth to this method in the work of Galileo GALILEI, René DESCARTES, Pierre GASSEND, and Marin MERSENNE. But it was Isaac NEWTON who provided the concise and clear statement of the method for the Enlightenment, and it is his name that is most often associated with it.

Any scientific method makes certain assumptions about the fundamental characteristics of NATURE. The Newtonian method used the new assumptions about nature that had been put forth by the creators of the Scientific Revolution. The view of nature contained in these assumptions, it should be noted, differed fundamentally from the vision that had prevailed in older forms of science, even though it was also partially derived from that older vision.

The assumptions underlying the Newtonian scientific method were the premise that nature does nothing in vain and, therefore, works in the most efficient possible ways; the idea that nature is simple; and the belief that a few basic laws, expressible as mathematical equations, govern the actions of the physical universe.

In the *Philosophiae naturalis principia mathematica* (Mathematical principles of natural philosophy), usually called PRINCIPIA MATHEMATICA, Newton developed four rules of method based on the above assumptions about nature. The first rule stated, "We are to admit no more causes of natural things than such as are both true and sufficient to explain their appearances." By following this rule, science abandoned the search for the ultimate or final causes of events in nature and concentrated on relations that were more directly accessible to human observation. It was assumed that final or ultimate causes were knowable only to God and that human reason, no matter how sharp, could not uncover them.

The second rule stated, "Therefore to the same natural effects we must as far as possible, assign the same causes." In other words, because nature is simple and economical in action, scientists should assume that similar phenomena have the same causes. For example, Newton believed that the light of both the sun and of earthly fires was the result of similar physical actions.

The third rule stated, "The qualities of bodies, which admit neither intensification nor remission of degrees, and which are found to belong to all bodies within the reach of our experiments, are to be esteemed the universal qualities of all bodies whatsoever." This rule set forth Newton's theory of matter, which was an elaboration of the mechanical philosophy. Characteristics of bodies (matter) that do not change as we observe them were considered the fundamental qualities of matter. Newton listed these qualities as extension (geometric form), hardness, impenetrability, mobility, and inertia (the tendency to continue in a state of motion). Any changing aspects of bodies—color or sound, for example—were to be considered secondary qualities; they were not part of the essence of matter.

Newton further elaborated on this theory by saying that, for the purposes of research, scientists could divide bodies into small parts and could assume that in making these divisions they were not changing the body in any significant way. This act of dividing (analyzing or resolving into parts) could be either real or only a mental experiment. It was analogous to mathematical calculus, a discipline that Newton, together with Gottfried Wilhelm LEIBNIZ, helped to create.

A close relationship existed between Newton's idea of physical matter and the mathematical discipline of calculus. This fact illustrates the general connection between the mechanical philosophy and the scientific ideal of quantifying or mathematizing the laws that govern natural phenomena. Both the mechanical philosophy of nature and calculus draw on the notion that analysis (breaking down) of problems yields true knowledge. Both also assume that, after analysis, a problem or physical body can be reassembled in an equally true or valid synthesis.

Finally, Newton's fourth rule asserted, "In experimental philosophy we are to look upon propositions inferred by general induction from phenomena as accurately or very nearly true, notwithstanding any contrary hypotheses that may be imagined, till such time as other phenomena occur by which they may either be made more accurate or liable to exceptions." This rule contains the elements that modern students usually associate with the scientific method. It asserts that from our observations and experiences of phenomena, we can develop general laws that we can accept as true, until new observations provide conflicting evidence. Often this rule of Newton's is called the experimental method and is praised for its empiricism. It is indeed empirical in the sense that experience and observation, rather than abstract reasoning, provide the material for statements about scientific laws. But Newton was not advocating controlled experiment as we know it today. He was simply saying that we must use our sensory experience as the primary source of information, that we must concentrate on aspects of nature that can be observed.

See also MATHEMATICS AND MECHANICS.

Scientific Revolution Term commonly used to describe the changes in the theory and practice of SCIENCE that took root in the early 17th century and paved the way for science as we know it today. The ideas, methods, and new institutions associated with the Scientific Revolution provided one basic set of ingredients for the construction of the thought of the ENLIGHTENMENT.

The Scientific Revolution created its new approaches, in part, by substituting neglected ancient Greek and Roman ideas for the dominant ideas of Aristotle and the medieval Scholastics. Of particular importance were the philosophies of Plato, Pythagoras, the Epicureans, and the Stoics. But the ideas of Aristotle were not completely rejected, especially in certain disciplines such as the life sciences and MEDICINE.

The Scientific Revolution grew initially out of changes in ASTRONOMY and physics, accompanied by mathematical inventions. These changes consisted of the creation of the MECHANICAL PHILOSOPHY and the adoption of mathematics (geometry and later calculus) as the proper and basic scientific language.

These two developments were intimately related. The mechanical philosophy contained a general theory of NATURE that encouraged the use of mathematics as a scientific tool. What were the basic elements of this theory? First, the operations of nature came to be conceived as regular, governed by REASON and by NATURAL LAW. It was argued that if reason governed nature, then the reason of human beings could uncover the operations of nature. Furthermore, since mathematics is a form of reason related to deductive logic, it could become the language of the scientific study of nature; for mathematical equations are nothing more than the numerical expression of regular, reasonable, lawful relations between a and b, or between one body and another. Second, the essential aspects of nature were defined so that they could be measured (quantified) and then translated into numbers to be manipulated by mathematical formulae. Third, the laws that operate in nature were assumed to be universal and few in number; they applied to events in the heavens as well as to those occurring on Earth. Finally, nature was viewed as economical and efficient in its actions. In general, the Scientific Revolution made mathematics the language of science and reason the formative attribute of the natural world.

The Scientific Revolution also produced specific theoretical innovations, which began in astronomy and mechanics (physics) but spread during the years of the Enlightenment, to spawn the new field of social sciences and to encompass all existing scientific disciplines.

In the realm of astronomy, early steps toward revolution had been taken in the 16th century by Nicolaus COPERNICUS. He developed the HELIOCENTRIC (sun-centered) theory of the universe that became a cornerstone of the revised scientific vision of the world.

Copernicus's ideas, though radical in their implications for world views, were largely unnoticed by his contemporaries. They became the center of controversy only in the late 16th and early 17th centuries, when the writings of Giordano Bruno, Tommaso Campanella, and Galileo GALILEI made them seem threatening to the leaders of ROMAN CATHOLICISM.

The gradual acceptance of Copernican theory despite theological opposition was one hallmark of the Scientific Revolution. The general popular acceptance of this theory, however, was slower in coming, reaching a full flowering only during the Enlightenment, after the positions of traditional Christianity had been weakened sufficiently to allow a competing vision of the world to exist.

In physics, an equally marked revolution, centered first in mechanics, radically altered the vision of the world. Many individuals contributed to this revolution, but Galileo, Christian Huygens, Blaise Pascal, Marin MERSENNE, Pierre GASSEND, Thomas HOBBES, and René DESCARTES must especially be noted. Their work provided the building blocks from which Isaac NEWTON and Gottfried Wilhelm LEIBNIZ fashioned the natural philosophies, mechanical theories, and mathematics that were directly inherited by the Enlightenment.

The fundamental shift in physics can be summarized as follows: All physical phenomena can be explained in terms of matter and its motion. This simple formulation encompassed a radical conceptual change. The old Aristotelian physics that dominated until the Scientific Revolution assumed that matter tends naturally to seek rest. Motion is an unnatural state of affairs. The new system assumed that motion is the natural state of the world, that the universe is a dynamic entity. Galileo's work on free fall and general mechanics provided the experimental evidence and mathematical equations for this new definition of matter and the universe. According to his vision, forces such as friction acting on matter cause it to come to rest; if friction ceased to exist, then bodies would move forever.

Aristotelian physics assumed that all bodies have unique sets of qualities that distinguish them from other bodies. These qualities make up their essence and define their nature. The new mechanical philosophy wiped out the idea that many unique qualities distinguish bodies from each other. Rather, it declared that all bodies are composed of particles of a universal substance (matter). All bodies are extended, that is, they have a recognizable geometric form and occupy space. Their differences can be explained in terms of shape, size, and a set of unessential qualities like color. René Descartes developed and popularized this idea, thereby providing the first systematic statement of the physical and mathematical assumptions that were being embraced by his contemporaries.

The Scientific Revolution developed as a response to a perceived crisis in the philosophical discipline of EPISTEMOLOGY. It seemed to early 17th-century thinkers that true and certain knowledge about the world was not available to human beings. The TELESCOPE and the MICROSCOPE had demonstrated that the senses can deceive. Discoveries in the so-called New World had shown that the truths of revealed religion (Christianity) were not universally recognized. And the division of Christianity into PROTESTANTISM and Roman Catholicism had plunged European states into long and bitter years of strife over religious dogma.

If sensory knowledge and revelation (the word of God) could not be trusted to provide truth, then what could? The Scientific Revolution provided one set of answers: reason and its daughter, mathematics, both of which could teach truths about the natural world and about human nature of sufficient certainty to be trusted.

Ultimately, this vision even seemed to provide a new justification for faith in God; the design of the universe and its lawful order suggested the existence of a higher wisdom and creative power. The form of NATURAL RELIGION called DEISM gave voice to these beliefs and helped to remove some fears that the new science would divorce people from belief in God.

The Enlightenment continued the work of the Scientific Revolution by extending its ideas to new disciplines such as demography, the SCIENCE OF MAN, and ANTHROPOLOGY; by transforming chemistry, the life sciences (BIOLOGY), and the study of electricity; and by vastly developing the power of mathematics as the language of science. Furthermore, the Enlightenment aided the transformation of the practice of science into an enterprise dominated by professionally trained men (and a few women) working together in SCIENTIFIC ACADEMIES and laboratories. Finally, certain intellectuals played significant roles in spreading the new philosophy and ideas of science to the general reading public. Without VOLTAIRE, Madame DU CHÂTELET, Pierre de MAUPERTUIS, John DESAGULIERS, Benjamin FRANKLIN, Abbé NOLLET, and Francesco ALGAROTTI, the new science might have remained an affair of specialists working and communicating among themselves. Instead, it moved into popular consciousness and provided the foundation for a new, increasingly secular vision of the natural world. Thus, although the Enlightenment did not create the Scientific Revolution, it definitely supported the new science and provided it with the institutional, cultural, and political bases that it needed to survive.

See also CHEMICAL REVOLUTION; MATHEMATICS AND MECHANICS.

Further reading: T. M. Devine, *The Scottish Nation: A History 1700–2000.* (New York: Penguin Books, 1999).

Scotland   A historic nation within the modern United Kingdom, with territory occupying the northern part of the island of Britain. Its inhabitants traditionally spoke various Gaelic dialects, but by the 18th century, educated people also spoke and read English. On its southern border, Scotland meets ENGLAND, and much of its history has been dominated by conflict with English governments.

Scotland has a long history dating back to prehistoric times. The first known Scottish kingdom appeared in the ninth century. The relationship between Scotland and its neighbor England proved difficult from the beginning, with numerous conflicts. Scotland enjoyed varying degrees of independence from England (and sometimes FRANCE) through the Middle Ages and early Renaissance. Its kings struggled like other European monarchs to extend control over both noble lords and the Catholic clergy. Evidence for the existence of a Scottish Parliament with rights to offer advice and to vote monies for the king dates from the early 14th century.

The Protestant Reformation combined with political events to bring substantial change to Scotland. Mary Stuart (1542–67) became queen of the Scots as an infant after the death of her father, King James V. This situation produced instability and uncertainty in Scotland. The English and the French began vying for control of the kingdom. Eventually, Mary became the wife of the future Francis II of France. With this marriage, the French seemed well situated to tighten their control over Scotland.

As a result, Scottish leaders opposed to French domination joined with preachers devoted to early PROTESTANTISM to create a movement against the Catholic Queen Mary. In 1560, the Parliament of Scotland abolished the authority of the pope, removing Scotland from the jurisdiction of ROMAN CATHOLICISM. In place of Catholicism, Parliament set up a new confession of faith that served as the foundation for the Scottish form of CALVINISM known as Presbyterianism. From that point, Scotland became one of the strongest centers of Calvinism in Europe.

Mary Stuart was eventually forced to abdicate her throne and flee to England. Her Catholic son, James VI, assumed the Scottish throne. Old dynastic ties also left him with a claim to the English throne. As a result, when Queen Elizabeth I died in 1603, James VI of Scotland also became James I of England. England and Scotland were united as a DYNASTIC STATE whose legitimacy lay in the person of a Stuart, King James.

This union between Scotland and England left Scottish political institutions intact: The Scottish Parliament and courts continued to exercise power over Scottish affairs. Full union, involving the creation of a single British government, did not occur until 1707, six years after the death of James VII (James II of England).

The 1707 union with England caused the Scottish Parliament to be abolished. In its place, the Westminster Parliament added 45 House seats and 16 Lords as Scottish representatives. The union produced eventual economic benefits for Scotland in the form of FREE TRADE privileges with England, but improvements were slow to manifest themselves.

At the time of the GLORIOUS REVOLUTION in England, James II (James VII in Scotland) had fled to France, where his personal safety was secure. He collected a group of loyal people around him. These JACOBITES, as they were called, represented the cause of both Roman Catholicism and monarchical ABSOLUTISM. Even after James's death and the union of Scotland with England, the Jacobites continued to support the claims of the Stuart heirs to the throne and to work for renewed Scottish independence. Their activities produced two abortive rebellions, the first in 1715 and the second in 1745.

A strong and unique center of the ENLIGHTENMENT developed in Scotland around EDINBURGH. Glasgow and Aberdeen were also important. Each of these cities possessed an outstanding university where the presentation of new ideas, so long as they did not seem to support ATHEISM, was encouraged. Edinburgh was also the home of the Philosophical Society of Edinburgh, the Select Society, the ROYAL SOCIETY OF EDINBURGH, and many clubs sponsoring a combination of intellectual and social activities.

Leaders in the Scottish Enlightenment—David HUME, Adam SMITH, Francis HUTCHESON, Thomas REID, and Henry Home, Lord Kames, for example—made especially significant contributions to PSYCHOLOGY, POLITICAL THEORY, MORAL PHILOSOPHY, and AESTHETICS. The theory and practice of MEDICINE shifted in the hands of expert physicians like Alexander MONRO Secundus, John HUNTER, William HUNTER, and Joseph BLACK. The INDUSTRIAL REVOLUTION received the steam engine from James WATT. And finally, the discipline of HISTORY developed greater sophistication as a result of the work of Adam FERGUSON, David Hume, John MILLAR, and William ROBERTSON.

From Scotland, the legacy of these intellectuals spread throughout Europe. Their works received special attention in the German states of the HOLY ROMAN EMPIRE and in the new UNITED STATES OF AMERICA. In short, the intellectual ferment of the Scottish Enlightenment served as a strong force in shaping the general movement of the Enlightenment on an international scale.

See also BURNS.

secret societies Political and occult organizations whose goals were variously to reform political and social institutions or to experience personal enlightenment. During the 18th century, the number of secret societies in Europe grew rapidly. These secret societies were founded both as a reaction to and a result of the period's emphasis on rationality.

Ritualistic and Mystical Secret Societies

Many secret societies were occult or mystical in nature. The 18th century saw the growth of groups devoted to the study and rituals of the texts of HERMETICISM, the Jewish kabbalah, and other ancient writings that had supposedly been "lost" to earlier generations. While the hermeticists maintained some practice of science in their societies, many of the esoteric 18th-century secret societies were more purely spiritual in nature and focused on arcane ritual rather than science. Many of these groups mingled ALCHEMY, astrology, and MAGIC together to in an attempt to attain higher knowledge of the self, God, and the universe. The purpose of the quasireligious secret societies was to help humankind achieve higher states of being and fulfill its full potential. Members were required to engage in numerous periods of study and pass through several stages of initiation. In most cases, the final level of initiation was believed to bring higher wisdom or divine knowledge. The ROSICRUCIANS and the Knights Templar are just two of many examples. Other major secret groups that arose at this time include the Bavarian ILLUMINATI, founded by Adam Weishaupt, and the FREEMASONS in FRANCE and Britain.

The Freemasons are perhaps the best-known secret society, whose formal organization in Europe began in the 18th century. The brotherhood of the Freemasons supposedly evolved from the guilds of stonemasons of the 15th century and, according to Masonic history, dates back to the construction of the Temple of Solomon in the Old Testament. In 1717, a grand lodge was formed in LONDON, uniting the various lodges in Britain. A similar lodge was founded in PARIS in 1725. Yet, despite its dependence on ritual and esoteric lore, Masonry was seen as a threat to the established order in France. LOUIS XV issued an edict in 1768 prohibiting membership in the Freemasons. Louis was threatened by the fact that many freethinkers and reformers were Freemasons.

Indeed, Freemasonry had a political dimension, and its members were free to discuss and disseminate radical ideas. One of the mottoes of the Masons was "liberty, equality, and fraternity." In the lodges, members were brothers, regardless of their social or economic background. Membership conferred a new identity, as the inducted were given new names.

After the founding of the grand lodge in London, Masonry spread swiftly across the Continent and through the colonies. Many of the American founding fathers belonged to Masonic lodges. Thomas JEFFERSON, George WASHINGTON, and Benjamin FRANKLIN all had connections to Masonic organizations. Likewise, many supporters of the FRENCH REVOLUTION, such as Thomas PAINE and VOLTAIRE, were also Masons. One reason for the strong connection between radicalism, independence movements, and the Masons is the Masonic belief that members who have reached advanced stages of study have the wisdom to create a utopia.

Political Secret Societies

Not all the secret societies in the 18th century were of an occult nature. There were many clubs whose political goals required that their membership be secret. The ILLU-MINATI, founded in Bavaria by Adam Weishaupt, sought to reform society and religion. Throughout the British Isles and the Continent, secret clubs of JACOBITES flourished. Their purpose was generally to support the restoration of the Stuart monarchy, but the specific goals of each club were as varied as their locations. Several were drinking clubs; others raised money and arms for rebellion; and still others in SCOTLAND, Ireland, and Wales were primarily concerned with resisting English Hanoverian rule and laws.

Secret political societies continued to proliferate in Ireland at the end of the 18th century and into the 19th century. In response to the Penal Laws and other strictures the English placed on the Irish, Catholics and Protestants alike joined secret resistance organizations. The Whiteboys were one such group. Their members were identified by their white shirts. They staged raids on the manor houses of wealthy people, tax collectors, and other supporters of English rule. Irish secret political societies included the Oakboys, the Defenders, and the United Irishmen. Several of these groups, led by the United Irishmen and the lawyer and reformer Theobald Wolfe Tone, staged a spectacular although fatal uprising against the English in 1798. Despite assistance from the French, Tone's men were outnumbered by the English five to one and lacked weapons. Up to 30,000 Irishmen alone died in the fighting.

In the British American colonies, the Sons of Liberty were a secret group who opposed the Stamp Act and called for an end to British rule. Similar secret political societies focused on independence were formed in several European countries in the 19th century. The Carbonari was formed in the 1820s in Naples, but as membership spread it contributed to uprisings in Naples, SPAIN, and northern ITALY. Whether they were merely quasireligious, ritualistic, or purely political in nature, the secret societies that flourished during the Enlightenment had a major impact on politics in the 18th and 19th centuries.

See also KINGDOM OF THE TWO SICILIES; RADICAL ENLIGHTENMENT.

Further reading: Margaret Jacob, *The Radical Enlightenment: Pantheists, Freemasons, and Republicans* (London: Allan & Unwin, 1981); Margaret Jacob, *Living the Enlightenment: Freemasonry and Politics in Eighteenth-Century Europe* (New York: Oxford University Press, 1991); Marie Roberts, Hugh Ormsby-Lennon, Mary Mulvey-Robert, and Michael Foot, eds., *Secret Texts: The Literature of Secret Societies* (New York: AMS Press, 1995); Jim Smyth, *The Men of No Property: Irish Radicals and Popular Politics in the Late Eighteenth Century* (Houndmill: Macmillan, 1992).

self-interest Concern with one's own preservation, interests, and advancement. Although the issues of personal interests and individual will within sociopolitical groups were matters of European intellectual debate from the 16th century onward, it is in the coalescence of ENLIGHTENMENT philosophy that they reach crucial significance in considerations of how society and government are to be structured using principles of REASON. Interpretations of self-interest shifted significantly between the 17th and 18th centuries. Originally seen as a negative assessment of human weakness, the concept gradually became accepted as a natural factor of human life and was even viewed as a positive good for society.

Thinkers of the 17th century placed self-interest in a Christian context, where it was seen as a flaw inherent in human nature. For the French mathematician and religious thinker Blaise Pascal, humans were a bundle of contradictions and weaknesses who needed to rely on divine grace for salvation. In his somber vision, Pascal described people as so weak and frivolous that they did not even have a consistent vision of their own self-interest. In his *Pensées* (Thoughts; published in 1670), he cited the example of a man who has lost his only son and who is troubled by legal problems. Grief-stricken in the morning, the man goes out hunting in the afternoon and becomes happy and excited while pursuing a boar in the woods. For Pascal, this is an example of human weakness and unreliability.

In his *Maximes* (1665), the French thinker La Rochefoucauld returned constantly to the theme of *amour-propre,* or self-love, which was closely related to the notion of self-interest. La Rochefoucauld attributed all human striving to this single force, describing the urge to attain glory, the desire to be seen as generous or virtuous, and even the search for love as ways in which humans try to gratify their own selfish needs. His maxims demean all human achievements by basing them on self-interest, and, although his book never proposes any solution to this unfortunate situation, it can be inferred that the only possible redemption for humans lies in the grace of God.

In the 18th century, this negative vision of self-interest would gradually give way to a positive interpretation as the concept was reevaluated. The year 1723 saw the publication of an anonymous satire titled *The Fable of the Bees: Or, Private Vices, Publick Benefits*. As in La Rochefoucauld's maxims, this work acknowledged that people are motivated by selfishness and affirmed that citizenship and public morality are merely illusions. Even so, the tract concluded that society functions excellently under such conditions because economic growth and increased interdependency create new social bonds that replace earlier religious models of behavior. The author, London doctor Bernard MANDEVILLE, became quickly infamous as theologians and government authorities attacked the book and called for its suppression grew. Such critiques were motivated in no small part by his ridicule of religious authorities who made claims to moral rectitude while surrounding themselves with opulence.

Later intellectual figures in the period debated Mandeville's position. The English author Henry FIELDING criticized Mandeville's doctrine of self-interest for ignoring the possibility of social interaction as a force for morality. Throughout his body of fiction, Fielding ridicules Mandeville's position by placing it in the mouths of obviously unsympathetic characters. The French philosopher Jean-Jaques ROUSSEAU established a distinction between *amour de soi* and *amour-propre,* which could both be translated as "self-love." For Rousseau, *amour de soi* represented the natural urge for self-preservation: All humans will instinctively take action to maintain their health or save their lives. Rousseau contrasted this positive quality with *amour-propre,* which was an exaggerated, egotistical love of oneself created by the conditions of civilization, such as Mandeville describes.

Mandeville's notion of self-interest is reflected in the Scottish philosopher Adam SMITH's treatise *WEALTH OF NATIONS* (1776). Smith systematically investigated the influence of self-interest in commerce and concluded that it has a positive effect on human societies. In this way, the new science of ECONOMICS removed the issue of self-interest from the realms of religion and morality. The Enlightenment emphasis on reason meant that humans were viewed as rational creatures who could shape their own destinies. By Smith's time, Christian critics who saw self-interest as a sin had begun to seem outdated. Although many questions remained as to how society should be organized and what kind of role commerce should play in a nation, it became an accepted notion to consider self-interest a basic human characteristic that could be controlled by social mechanisms, or, in Smith's

view, that could be trusted to make the social and economic order function efficiently.

See also FREE TRADE; UTILITY; VIRTUE.

Further reading: Albert O. Hirschman, *The Passions and the Interests: Political Arguments for Capitalism Before its Triumph* (Princeton, N.J.: Princeton University Press, 1996); E. G. Hundert, *The Enlightenment's Fable: Bernard Mandeville and the Discovery of Society* (New York: Cambridge University Press, 1994); A. J. Krailsheimer, *Studies in Self-Interest: From Descartes to La Bruyère* (New York: Oxford University Press, 1962); Richard K. Matthews, ed., *Virtue, Corruption, and Self-Interest: Political Values in the Eighteenth Century* (Bethlehem, Pa.: Lehigh University Press, 1994).

Semler, Johann Salomo (1725–1791) *German Lutheran theologian, one of the founders of a school of biblical criticism known as neology (new knowledge)*
Johann Salomo Semler was the son of a Lutheran pastor and grew up in an environment suffused with PIETISM. In his autobiography, *Johann Semlers Lebensbeschreibung von ihm selbst abgefasst* (Description of Johann Semler's life written by himself; 1781–82), Semler described the powerful effects of this home atmosphere on his and his brother's formative years. Semler developed a lasting distaste for unexamined Pietism, but his lifework betrayed its influence.

Semler studied THEOLOGY with Sigmund J. Baumgarten at the University of HALLE, a stronghold of Pietist thought. The university called him to a professorship in 1753, and in 1757 he succeeded his old teacher and mentor Baumgarten to the directorship of the theological faculty. Semler remained in Halle throughout his life. He published several books, the most significant of which were *Neuer Versuch die gemeinnüzige Auslesung und Anwendung des Neuen Testaments zu befördern* (New attempt to foster the beneficial reading and application of the New Testament; 1786) and *Zur Revision der kirchlichen Hermeneutik und Dogmatik* (Toward the revision of ecclesiastical hermeneutics and dogma; 1788).

As a scholar of the New Testament, Semler helped develop a school of theology known as neology. Together with his contemporary Johann August Ernesti, Semler created a method drawn from HISTORY and BIBLICAL CRITICISM that could not only challenge orthodox belief but also lead to deeper religious understanding. He supported the idea of studying the historical Jesus and of investigating the processes by which the Bible acquired its 18th-century form. His work directly inspired the research of Friedrich August WOLF and of the great 19th-century biblical scholar Friedrich Ernst Daniel Schleiermacher.

Semler believed that religions are constantly developing and that religious understanding at any given time is strongly colored by environmental and general cultural conditions. This holds true for the biblical era as well as for subsequent periods of Christian history. Authentic faith requires an understanding of the way that historical context has shaped religious ideas and a recognition of the fact that religions must grow and change over time.

Semler intended his work to assist faith in Christianity and did not deny that the Bible was divinely inspired. He simply believed, as did other influential writers of the AUFKLÄRUNG (German Enlightenment), that the specific forms of religious practice and dogma contained in the Bible reflected historical conditioning rather than absolute and unchangeable laws. He thought that knowledge of the historical aspects of Christianity would provide believers with a surer understanding of the universal essence that lies underneath the imperfect, changing facets of belief and practice. However, this position did not place Semler in the ranks of rational theologians. REASON alone, for Semler, could never be a sufficient support of religious belief, because not all religious understanding was accessible to reason. Belief also required acts of faith.

In this position, Semler differed radically from Hermann Samuel REIMARUS, who had adopted a rationalist position closer to DEISM. In his *Beantwortung der Fragment eines Ungennanten insbesondere vom Zweck Jesu und seine Jünger* (Response to the fragment of an unknown author especially on the purpose of Jesus and his disciples; 1779), Semler attacked the anonymous *Fragmente einer Ungennante* (Fragments from an unknown author; 1774–78), which had been published by Gotthold Ephraim LESSING and written (although only Lessing knew it) by Reimarus.

Semler distinguished between religion and theology, between external religious forms (institutions, dogma) and internal forms (spiritual understanding of the individual). He believed that both aspects of religion are necessary, that neither the external nor the internal form alone represents total religious experience. This position led him to stress the importance of practicing both public worship or ritual and private spiritual contemplation or devotion.

For Semler, as for many enlightened individuals of central European regions, the external practice of religion served the cause of public order. Therefore, it required certain regulation to prevent it from disrupting the internal peace of a state. This line of thought led Semler to support the Prussian *Religionsedikt*, a decree of 1788 that attempted to rid Prussian churches of various unsettling enlightened tendencies.

Semler provides an example of a man who used the tools of the ENLIGHTENMENT—reason, criticism, history—to investigate orthodox religion and to challenge some of its claims. Like most of his enlightened contemporaries, however, he retained elements of religious faith and attempted to integrate that faith into the new, more secular visions of the world.

sensibility The capacity to have sensations or feelings. One of the most popular concepts during the first decades of the ENLIGHTENMENT, the idea of sensibility appeared in discussions within SCIENCE, RELIGION, LITERATURE, art, and MUSIC.

Sensibility was a notion taken from physiology and PSYCHOLOGY. It combined observations from both disciplines into a complex notion with many shades of meaning. Students of the human nervous system had created the theory of nerve sensibility in an attempt to explain how and why nerves react to external stimuli and transmit these reactions (sensations) to the brain. John LOCKE had popularized the theory that all human ideas have their origins in experience. Experience, for him, was none other than a collection of sensations and resulting simple ideas. Thus sensation, one aspect of sensibility, lay at the base of all human understanding and consciousness.

MORAL PHILOSOPHY had added an additional layer of meaning to the concept of sensibility by suggesting that ideas of good and bad behavior derive from the sensations of pleasure or pain produced by specific behaviors. Both consciousness and conscience arose, according to

La Reveuse, by Jean-Baptiste Greuze. In the early years of the Enlightenment, the cult of sensibility emphasized delicate feeling and sensation, challenging the primacy of reason in human experience and understanding. *(Courtesy New York Public Library)*

this position, from physiological and psychological sensation. Since moral qualities of good and bad were closely linked to concepts of beauty and truth, the notion of sensibility also embraced aesthetic and spiritual dimensions. The groundwork was thus laid for the spread of the concept of sensibility into discussions far removed from its initial sources.

In the early 18th century, essayists responded to the implications of sensibility by creating a literature of sentiment or SENTIMENTAL FICTION aimed at drawing emotional responses from readers. Characters were portrayed so that readers would sympathize with their plights and draw certain moral lessons from them. Joseph ADDISON and Richard STEELE demonstrated both the UTILITY of sentimental fiction for social and moral reform and also its potential popularity. Sentimental novels widened the appeal of this type of literature. Samuel Richardson's PAMELA and CLARISSA were read and imitated not only in ENGLAND but also throughout Europe.

It became fashionable for both men and women to read, to display emotion, and to demonstrate sensitivity in action and attitude. Although strongly associated now with feminine culture, sentimental forms of expression were not so gender-bound in the early 18th century. Only later in the century did they become associated with values that placed their "feminine" qualities in strict opposition to "masculine" actions.

The taste for sentimental literature appeared in concert with the earliest manifestations of the ROCOCO style in ART AND ARCHITECTURE. Rococo works aimed at producing emotional responses, but these responses were not paired with moral notions as they were in sentimental literature. In art and architecture, artists tried simply to delight the feelings, to produce pleasing images, colors, forms, and compositions.

Music produced yet another variation on the theme of sensibility. The STYLE GALANT of ITALY and FRANCE translated the painter's goal of pleasing the eye into that of tickling the ear. Music of this style departed from its baroque heritage by seeking to evoke pleasurable responses rather than passionate ones. It offered highly ornamented melodies with simple accompaniment, suitable more for the pleasures of the salons than for the expression of religious awe.

The cultural roles played by enlightened ideas of sensibility varied in England and France. The English married sensibility with morality at an early date, tapping it as a tool for creating the morals and manners necessary to a successful, commercial society. The softening of male manners, for example, aided commercial transactions; while the emphasis on female sensibility served to reinforce domestic virtues. In France, sensibility began as a taste associated with the urban middle classes but soon entered the arena of the aristocracy. Although manners were modified under its influence, sensibility in France tended to lack the moralizing tone of its English counterpart. It became associated with aristocratic leisure, luxury, and idleness, thereby acquiring negative connotations for later enlightened generations.

The concept of sensibility carried with it certain revolutionary social implications: If ideas and morality are the product of sensations, and if all people are born with minds waiting to be shaped by experience, then all people, whatever their social status or gender, must be equal at birth. These egalitarian implications eventually spawned countertheories in which fundamental physiological, moral, and aesthetic differences between males and females were drawn. The nerves of women were delicate and easily moved, it was argued, and a woman's will exercised only weak control over her emotions. Men, in contrast, were goal-oriented, directed by REASON, and possessed of strong wills. The ideal personality and culture would combine these traits and harmonize them into a whole. Women would become more rational and men more sensitive.

While gendered theories of human behavior and nature undermined the earliest forms of culture associated with sensibility, they heightened the implied connections between concepts of the feminine and the idea of sensibility. As the Enlightenment moved into its twilight, feminine behavior and females were gradually removed from the public arena and consigned to the home. Thus, the radical potential of sensibility was transformed and placed in the service of 19th-century conservative ROMANTICISM.

See also SOCIAL INSTITUTIONS OF THE ENLIGHTENMENT; SYMPATHY; WOMEN AND THE ENLIGHTENMENT.

sentimental fiction A literary form that became popular in ENGLAND during the middle decades of the 18th century. It was particularly associated with a new emphasis on allegedly feminine traits such as feeling (the antithesis of REASON), vulnerability, and delicate, sensual beauty. This LITERATURE was particularly read by women, and many of the women writers of the century found success by producing novels of this type. Much of its popularity can be attributed to PAMELA (1740), the sensationally successful first novel by Samuel RICHARDSON. The intellectual and aesthetic currents that prepared this success, however, developed much earlier in the century.

The roots of sentimental literature lay in a philosophy that assumed the essential goodness of human nature. It maintained that the laws of nature that govern human action and development would produce moral, harmonious action, if not artificially restrained or contorted. It drew its inspiration from the PSYCHOLOGY of John LOCKE and a group of philosophers and theologians called the Cambridge Platonists, who had rejected the negative image of humankind contained in the well-known philosophy of Thomas HOBBES.

Anthony Ashley Cooper, third earl of SHAFTESBURY, a former student of John Locke, provided the earliest concise statement of sentimental AESTHETICS in his *Characteristicks of Men, Manners, Opinions, Times* (1711). The treatise also contained one of the earliest statements of DEISM and illustrated the close connections between sentimental aesthetics and that form of NATURAL RELIGION. Shaftesbury argued that the natural impulses of human beings lead to benevolent behavior and that the beauty of the world proclaims the existence of benevolence.

In the specific realm of literature, sentimental forms appeared in conjunction with the emergence of a new literature of middle-class morality, intimately associated with the work of Joseph ADDISON and Richard STEELE. The pages of THE SPECTATOR spelled out the new morality, and dramas such as Steele's *Conscious Lovers* (1722) presented the new values and aesthetic on stage. Plots of high moral tone, humorless but reflective, replaced the witty, sexually explicit comedies of the Restoration.

These works exercised the audience's capacity for feeling, frequently moving it to tears. They celebrated the virtues of friendship and benevolence, giving examples of such behavior for others to follow. Sentimental fiction thus served as the vehicle for moral PROGRESS and individual enlightenment (EDUCATION) that were favored by its creators. It posited a direct link between art and life, maintaining that art could shape the way people actually behave. In fact, sentimental fiction was one of the earliest literary forms of the new culture of the ENLIGHTENMENT.

Sentimental fiction quickly merged with the general culture of SENSIBILITY to produce shifts in literary themes and tone. Early sentimental fiction had been inspired by the belief that feelings influence reason through a process of moral reflection. The later form substituted the term *sensibility* for *sentiment*. A concept derived from physiology, sensibility denoted sensation and elevated basic sensory experience (feeling) to central importance.

The culture of sensibility developed this approach to feeling into an aesthetic emphasizing refined emotion and sensitivity to the suffering of others. Literary forms reflected this shift by intensifying the emotional plights of characters in order to draw forth sentimental responses from readers. But they retained the emphasis on morality and VIRTUE that had characterized the earliest sentimental writings.

Novels painted virtuous heroines (sometimes heroes) in distress. Conflict was resolved either through a happy marriage or the release and redemption of death. Protagonists were often too sensitive and benevolent to survive in the harsh, commercial world of contemporary Britain. This literary form, therefore, offered an implicit criticism of economic liberalism with its emphasis on capital accumulation and competitive relationships.

Popular novelists writing in this style were Henry MacKenzie (*Man of Feeling*); Samuel Richardson (*Pamela* and *CLARISSA, OR THE HISTORY OF A YOUNG LADY*); Sarah FIELDING; Charlotte LENNOX; and Fanny BURNEY.

Pierre Ambroise François Choderlos de LACLOS (*Dangerous Liaisons*) used the style, partly in order to satirize its image of the pious, upright female. And, of course, Henry FIELDING mocked the immensely popular *Pamela* in his burlesque, *An Apology for the Life of Mrs. Shamela Andrews,* better known as *Shamela*. Finally, Jane Austen, in *Sense and Sensibility* (1811), satirized the culture of sensibility that had been so popular in her youth, pointing out that the use of reason would serve women better than the expression of feeling in their struggle for dignity.

separation of church and state   The idea of preventing the mingling of religious doctrinal issues with activities of the secular state. Christian institutions had been intricately intertwined with state affairs for centuries in Europe. The precedent for this situation had been set during the ancient Roman Empire, when Emperor Constantine had converted to Christianity and granted it official status within the empire.

After the fall of the Roman Empire, the Christian Church supplied a form of loose unity to Europe and also assumed many secular functions. It owned land and serfs, collected taxes, administered justice, and generally behaved in these ways like any secular power in medieval Europe. Cathedrals and parishes also operated schools, preserved some of the ancient classical learning, and provided official recognition of births, marriages, and deaths.

Relations between monarchs and the pope, the head of the Christian Church, were complicated and often tense. The pope was both a secular and a sacred authority, and his interests embroiled the church in major political conflicts over the centuries. Monarchs tried to free themselves from papal control, but they seldom ever questioned the idea that their states should be officially Christian.

The complicated intertwining between church and state continued even after the unity of Christianity was broken during the Protestant Reformation. Much of the strife between Catholics and Protestants actually revolved around political issues. The assumption had always existed that uniformity in religious affairs was the natural state of affairs and necessary for security. This belief, of course, helped to create the periodic persecutions of Jews, Muslims, and anyone whose views caused Christians to label them as heretics.

The desire for religious TOLERATION grew out of experiences with the horrible consequences of religious persecution and warfare. Seventeenth-century Europe was torn by the Thirty Years' War (1618–48), a complicated international struggle based partly on quarrels over religious confessions. The German territories of the HOLY ROMAN EMPIRE lost one-third of their population to battle and to the disease that inevitably accompanied such warfare. The English had their Civil War and Puritan Revolution, another admixture of political and religious affairs. The French witnessed several civil wars with religious overtones, and later watched thousands of HUGUENOTS flee to safety in the UNITED PROVINCES OF THE NETHERLANDS after an overly zealous LOUIS XIV rescinded the Edict of Nantes. Witches, usually women who dared to question official doctrines or who challenged the established order in some other way, were burned and tortured throughout Europe.

Some people reacted to these events by asking whether or not religious uniformity was really important to a healthy state. John LOCKE, VOLTAIRE, Gotthold Ephraim LESSING, Moses MENDELSSOHN, FREDERICK II (THE GREAT), and JOSEPH II all championed the cause of toleration. In the meantime, POLITICAL THEORY, SCIENCE, and MORAL PHILOSOPHY were advancing ideas about the universe and God's relation to it that made doctrinal uniformity unnecessary. Religious dogmatism increasingly seemed to foster attitudes opposed to the enlightened ideals of criticism, reform, and intellectual PROGRESS.

In this atmosphere, it became possible to discuss the separation of church and state. Enlightened rulers realized that such policies would limit interference in secular affairs by church authorities. Secular control could be extended over EDUCATION and marriage, two areas in which states took increasing interest. Skilled citizens could be retained, no matter what their religious beliefs. In short, the pragmatic interests of state seemed to favor the dissolution of old bonds between the sacred and the secular.

In the meantime, political theorists asserted that separation of church and state was necessary if intellectual and personal FREEDOM were to be maintained. A healthy political sphere seemed to demand immunity from ecclesiastical interference.

All these factors influenced leaders in both the AMERICAN REVOLUTION and the FRENCH REVOLUTION to make separation of church and state a constitutional principle. Religious belief was transformed into a private matter, removed from the public realm. Reform in France, however, required attacking the entrenched material, political, and intellectual interests of ROMAN CATHOLICISM. This lasted only during the few revolutionary years before Napoleon assumed power. The American experiment, as formulated in the first amendment of the UNITED STATES CONSTITUTION, had greater success, although many issues were left unresolved.

The idea of separating church affairs from those of the secular state was one of the most striking innovations of the ENLIGHTENMENT. It represented one concrete form of expressing the commitment of that era to freedom, political EQUALITY, NATURAL LAW, and human progress.

See also RELIGION.

separation of powers A concept in POLITICAL THEORY that makes the division of sovereign power among various branches of government a necessary ingredient for the preservation of FREEDOM and political stability. The concept was articulated in *THE SPIRIT OF LAWS*, the immensely influential political and historical treatise by MONTESQUIEU. The separation of powers was closely intertwined with the idea of checks and balances in government.

Montesquieu had two sources of inspiration for his theory: the political system in ENGLAND and a theory from BIOLOGY called VITALISM. He had spent a few years in England directly observing the political life of that nation, and, like VOLTAIRE, he came away with great admiration for that nation. Montesquieu was especially impressed with the fact that the English monarchy was limited by the powers of Parliament. This division of sovereign power between monarch and Parliament had been written into the formal agreement signed by WILLIAM III AND MARY II after the GLORIOUS REVOLUTION of 1688. Through the terms of this agreement Parliament had extended its power to make law and to vote on fiscal matters.

As a professional lawyer, Montesquieu believed that the English system contained certain features that could prevent the kind of abuses suffered in France under the ABSOLUTISM of LOUIS XIV. The doctrine of the separation of powers provided a theoretical statement of his observations about England. He noted the division of power between the executive (the monarch) and the legislature (the Parliament), but he did not discuss the judiciary as a separate power. His treatment of the separation of powers also argued that the privileged aristocracy could serve as an intermediary balancing power capable of offsetting excesses on the part of the king (monarchy) or people (democracy). In France, this aristocracy happened to include the members of the PARLEMENTS (sovereign courts of law of which Montesquieu was a member), who aspired to assume the role and powers of the English Parliament.

During his professional years in the Parlement of Bordeaux, Montesquieu had participated in the activities of the Academy of Bordeaux. One of his chief interests lay in biology, and he was especially drawn to vitalism. This theory opposed the vision of life contained in the popular MECHANICAL PHILOSOPHY, by positing the existence of active, vital forces in living organisms. Vitalism conceived the organism not as a machine but rather as a constantly changing entity striving to maintain a state of dynamic equilibrium.

Montesquieu translated this concept of dynamic equilibrium into his political theory in the form of the idea of checks and balances. According to his ideal, the separate branches within a government should constantly exert a force on each other, producing a dynamic but balanced system. Vital, alive, and responsive to needs and pressures, the ideal system nevertheless retains a certain stability, and it produces a government far preferable to the rigid, paralyzed forms of French absolutism.

These twin notions, the separation of powers and the system of checks and balances, served as a model for the creators of the UNITED STATES CONSTITUTION. They also inspired the first constitutions written during the FRENCH REVOLUTION. In fact, Montesquieu's concepts are one of the lasting contributions of the ENLIGHTENMENT to modern political theory.

serfdom An inheritable legal status that applied primarily to peasants. Serfdom originated in the feudal manorial system of the Middle Ages. Land was owned by lords but worked by peasant serfs. These serfs were tied legally to the land and could not leave the land to move elsewhere without the express permission of the lord. But the lord could not, in theory, forcibly remove them from the land to which they were born, nor could he sell individuals as could masters in systems where SLAVERY existed. But if a lord sold his land, the serfs on that land were also transferred to the new owner.

Serfs possessed very few individual rights. They were obligated to work on the lands of their lords a certain number of days each week (forced labor, called the *robot* in Bohemia). Whatever time was left could be spent working their own small plots. They owed certain other forms of service and dues paid in kind. Serfs could not marry or learn a trade without the permission of the lord. Legal problems were settled in courts presided over by the lord. In most ways, therefore, peasant serfs were the subjects of their lords.

During the economic and social transformations of the Renaissance, serfdom began to disappear in western European lands. Peasants remained on the land, subject to the justice of the lord, but they were free to move if they wished. Labor obligations were transformed into money payments. In FRANCE during the 18th century, for example, peasants owed 10 days of labor per year (the hated corvée) to the lord. Lords retained certain (manorial) rights—hunting privileges; control of the village mill, wine press, and bakery—and were responsible for specific police and justice functions. All these rights and powers constituted part of the "feudal privileges" that were abolished in August 1789 by progressive aristocratic leaders of the FRENCH REVOLUTION.

In general, in western Europe (Europe west of the Elbe River) serfdom had completely disappeared by the end of the 16th century. But in eastern Europe, the opposite occurred. Peasants who had been free were subjected to serfdom in decrees passed in PRUSSIA (1412), Bohemia (1497), POLAND and HUNGARY (early 16th century), and Russia (1561). The 18th-century absolute monarchs and enlightened despots in Prussia and Russia actually tight-ened the hold of this system on their peasant subjects. In Russia, for example, CATHERINE II (THE GREAT) degraded the legal position of the serf, transforming it into a kind of slavery by allowing lords to sell their serfs and to use their forced labor in factories. This move was one of the concessions Catherine the Great made to the lords in return for their submission to central authority.

Criticism of the institution of serfdom can be found embedded in the broader critiques of feudalism and feudal privilege that appeared during the ENLIGHTENMENT. In general, critics of serfdom drew from the ideals of EQUALITY and FREEDOM or from humanitarian and utilitarian arguments for support of their positions. In the 1770s, for example, Voltaire engaged in a polemic aimed at obtaining freedom for the last French peasant serfs, tied to Catholic church lands. The Physiocrat Pierre-François Boncerf published a tract condemning the economic destructiveness of serfdom; the tract was ordered burned by the Parlement of Paris. Only the intervention of Anne-Robert-Jacques TURGOT, himself a follower of the PHYSIOCRATS, protected Boncerf. *Le Mariage de Figaro* (Marriage of Figaro), a play by Pierre de BEAUMARCHAIS, contained a scathing attack on feudal privileges, clothed, of course, in humor. It, too, was condemned in Paris, only to be greeted with great success after it was transformed into the opera LE NOZZE DI FIGARO by Wolfgang Amadeus MOZART. In Russia, Catherine the Great sent Alexander Radischev to prison in Siberia for writing an impassioned indictment of Russian serfdom.

Eighteenth-century efforts to minimize the negative consequences of serfdom or to abolish the institution had very little effect. In the HAPSBURG EMPIRE, MARIA THERESA instigated laws designed to protect the peasants from excessive forced labor demands (six days/week was a common obligation before her new laws). JOSEPH II, her son, abolished serfdom altogether in the Hapsburg-controlled lands. But reaction to Joseph's decree was negative. His successor and brother, the equally enlightened Leopold II, felt compelled to reinstitute aspects of the system. Serfs in the Hapsburg Empire would wait until 1848 to obtain their freedom. In that same year, Prussia abolished serfdom, and Russia followed suit in 1861.

See also POLITICAL THEORY.

Serva Padrona, La (**The Maid Mistress**) Italian *opera buffa* by Giovanni Battista PERGOLESI. It debuted in Naples at the Teatro di San Bartolomeo on August 28, 1733. The piece served as an intermezzo, a lighthearted, short, two-act work presented between the sections of its serious operatic companion, *Il prigioniero superbo* (The Proud Prisoner). *La serva padrona* was extremely successful and was produced even after the premature death of Pergolesi in 1736. It played in Dresden (1740), VIENNA (1746), and PARIS (1746). The Parisians responded coolly to the 1746 production. In 1752, however, when an

Italian OPERA company in Paris restaged the work, it was enthusiastically received and sparked the great dispute in the French critical press called the BATTLE OF THE BUFFOONS. That "battle" helped to create a revolution in French opera that not only produced the new French comic opera but also paved the way for the successes of Christoph Willibald GLUCK in Paris.

The text of *La serva padrona* contains biting observations about Neapolitan life. It reflects the egalitarianism of the ENLIGHTENMENT by presenting its two characters, the rich aristocratic master and his impertinent maid, as fundamentally alike. Pergolesi's work challenges the conventions of serious opera in a manner similar to John Gay's THE BEGGAR'S OPERA, and its portrayal of the maid as a heroine resembles Wolfgang Amadeus MOZART's treatment of the servants Figaro and Susanna in LE NOZZE DI FIGARO.

See also MUSIC.

Seven Years' War

A war fought between 1756 and 1763, in Europe, North America, and India. PRUSSIA and Great Britain emerged as the victors in this war, in spite of the enormous resources that were available to their enemies, FRANCE and AUSTRIA. The war broke out in Europe shortly after France and Austria signed the treaty that established the great reversal of alliances called the DIPLOMATIC REVOLUTION OF 1756. That agreement allied the Bourbons in France with the Hapsburgs in Austria, temporarily bringing their traditional enmity to an end.

The Seven Years' War began as a conflict between Prussia and Austria. MARIA THERESA wanted to recover Silesia, the territory she had lost to FREDERICK II (THE GREAT) in the Silesian campaigns of the WAR OF THE AUSTRIAN SUCCESSION. Another major impetus for war came from the desire of France and Russia to curtail the growing power and expansion of Prussia. In North America, British and French colonists had already begun fighting in 1754 and 1755, although no war had formally been declared. They battled in the Allegheny River region and in Quebec, Canada. In India, the British East India Company and the French East India Company squabbled over control of seacoast establishments.

The European war ended after seven years of fighting with the Treaty of Hubertusburg (1763). The North American conflict, known to historians as the French and Indian War, ceased with the Treaty of Paris (1763). The Hubertusburg settlement recognized Prussia as a major power and rewarded its tenacity during the war by validating Frederick's hold on Silesia. The Treaty of Paris stripped France of its North American continental colonies. Great Britain gained the French territories in Canada, while French territories west of the Mississippi River were ceded to SPAIN. Territories east of the Mississippi fell under British domination.

Even though France lost these colonies, it retained economically valuable lands in the West Indies. The negotiating skills of the duc de CHOISEUL, thus helped to protect France from the worst consequences of defeat. The Seven Years' War proved without a doubt that Prussia had become a major European power, and the Treaty of Hubertusburg formalized the new power balance in Europe.

The Seven Years' War wrought great destruction in central Europe. At its conclusion, Maria Theresa and Frederick the Great both turned their attention inward to relieving the devastation in their respective kingdoms. Nearly 30 years of peace followed until 1792, when the revolutionary French Republic, frightened by a new alliance between Prussia and Austria, declared war anew against Austria.

Sèvres

French porcelain manufactory that dominated the European ceramics market during the last half of the 18th century. The Sèvres factory, originally established by private citizens at Vincennes, initially produced soft porcelains and established the French as leaders in this branch of ceramics manufacture. In 1756, the factory was moved to Sèvres, near Versailles. It became a royal manufactory in 1760, receiving state direction and support from LOUIS XV.

Madame de POMPADOUR had been the primary supporter of the idea of establishing an outstanding royal porcelain factory. The delicate, sensual ROCOCO porcelains created at Sèvres partially reflect her stylistic tastes, although she died before actual production of hard porcelains began in 1769. The hard Sèvres porcelains soon captured the European market, replacing the products of the MEISSEN WORKS as the most popular porcelains of the era. Sèvres subjects were often pastoral, rendered in warm colors softened by glazing techniques. Artists who provided models for porcelain production included Claude-Thomas Duplessis, Étienne Maurice FALCONET, who was influenced by the style of François BOUCHER, Louis-Simon Boizot, and Jean Le Riche. Falconet and Boizot served successfully as superintendents of the Sèvres works. Under Boizot, production style shifted from the rococo to NEOCLASSICISM.

Shaftesbury, Anthony Ashley Cooper, third earl of

(1671–1713) *English writer, deist, moral philosopher, and early theorist of aesthetics*

Shaftesbury was the grandson of the earl of Shaftesbury, the great patron of John LOCKE. Locke tutored the young Shaftesbury during his early childhood.

The third earl of Shaftesbury served in the English Parliament, first in the House of Commons between 1695 and 1699, and, after inheriting the title of earl, as a member of the House of Lords from 1699 to 1702. On account of ill health, Shaftesbury left ENGLAND in 1709, settling for the remainder of his life in ITALY.

Skeptical of the received Christian view of the world, offended by religious ENTHUSIASM, and critical of the roles played by the institutionalized church in England, Shaftesbury, like many of his contemporaries, began searching for an alternative philosophical and practical position. He developed a general outlook, which equated NATURE and the natural with the divine and benevolent. This nature was pervaded with harmony, beauty, truth, and goodness, all qualities of the divine and accessible to human understanding through the exercise of a natural mental faculty called the moral sense. The moral sense yielded an intuitive rather than a rational knowledge of harmony, beauty, goodness, and truth. Thus, imagination rather than REASON or experience (sensation) acquired preeminence in fashioning perceptions of the world.

Because Shaftesbury equated truth, goodness, and beauty, he rather logically focused his attention on problems of AESTHETICS and MORAL PHILOSOPHY. He bequeathed to the ENLIGHTENMENT the first comprehensive doctrine of the beautiful, offering influential treatments not only of the quality of beauty but also of the act of creating. It was Shaftesbury who introduced into enlightened thought the concept of GENIUS. He also moved attention in aesthetic theory away from concern with beautiful objects or with the experience of perceiving beauty, stressing instead that artistic genius manifests itself primarily in the act of creating, in the process by which an individual engages intuitively with the beauty, harmony, truth, and goodness of nature.

Shaftesbury's ideas were enormously influential in GERMANY, where they stimulated the development of aesthetics as an independent branch of philosophy and helped intellectuals to focus on the roles played by INTUITION AND IMAGINATION in the production of human knowledge. In England and SCOTLAND, Shaftesbury's attitudes were embraced by Alexander POPE, and his ideas helped to shape the thought of Joseph BUTLER, Adam FERGUSON, Francis HUTCHESON, and Henry Home, Lord Kames. Shaftesbury's first major opponent was Bernard MANDEVILLE, who offered his doctrine of *self-interest* as the driving force behind human society, in conscious contrast to Shaftesbury's notion of "disinterested pleasure."

Shaftesbury's publications include a three-volume set of essays entitled *Characteristics of Men, Manners, Opinions, and Times* (1711); *Moralists* (1709); and *Soliloquy or Advice to an Author* (1710).

See also DEISM.

Sheridan, Richard Brinsley (1751–1816) *Irish dramatist and politician who lived and worked in England*

Sheridan, a native of Dublin, Ireland, was the son of the Irish actor and theater manager Thomas Sheridan. He grew up in the fashionable resort town of Bath, ENGLAND. He eloped to FRANCE with a singer named Elizabeth Ann Linley, and after marrying her, he settled with her in LONDON. Sheridan made a notable career as a playwright and as the manager of Drury Lane Theatre in London (from 1776). He also served as a member of the House of Com-

mons. In 1777, he was elected to membership in the Literary Club, a club founded by Joshua REYNOLDS for Samuel JOHNSON.

Sheridan wrote in reaction to the culture of SENSIBILITY that had dominated the middle years of the ENLIGHTENMENT. This culture had produced a SENTIMENTAL FICTION replete with weeping, sighing emotionality. Like his Literary Club friend Oliver GOLDSMITH, Sheridan resurrected the witty comedy of manners of the 17th-century English Restoration period. He drew on the example of William CONGREVE as well as on the great 17th-century French dramatist Molière. Sheridan used his comedies as vehicles for ridiculing the various social and intellectual pretensions of English high society.

Sheridan is renowned for the following plays: *The Rivals* (1775, containing the famous Mrs. Malaprop); *School for Scandal* (1777); and *The Critic* (1779). In addition, he wrote *Saint Patrick's Day* (1775), a farce; the libretto for *The Duenna* (1775), a comic OPERA; *A Trip to Scarborough* (1777), ridiculing the new fad of seaside bathing; and *Pizarro* (1799), a patriotic melodrama adapted from the work of the German dramatist August Friedrich Ferdinand von Kotzebue.

As a member of the Whig Party, Sheridan served in the House of Commons from 1780 until 1812. He was the political ally of James Fox. Sheridan served as undersecretary of foreign affairs (1782), secretary to the treasury (1783), and as confidential adviser to the Prince of Wales, the future George IV. Sheridan also served as treasurer of the navy (1806–07) and opposed the union of Ireland with Britain (1799). During the early years of the FRENCH REVOLUTION, Sheridan supported the right of the French to determine their form of domestic government without intervention from the outside. However, he opposed the exportation of revolution by war. In 1794, he made a dramatic statement of this position in a reply to a speech by the earl of Mornington. An edition of Sheridan's Parliament speeches was published in five volumes in 1798.

See also LITERATURE.

She Stoops to Conquer, or the Mistakes of Night

Play by Oliver GOLDSMITH. *She Stoops to Conquer* (1773) focuses on the relationship between Charles Marlow, a shy young man, and Kate Hardcastle, a clever and enterprising young woman. Sir Charles Marlow, young Marlow's father, has proposed a match between his son and Kate, the daughter of his oldest friend. Young Marlow sets out to meet his new bride but gets lost on the way, thereby setting up the action of the drama. He finds the Hardcastle house, but he mistakes it for an inn and decides to stay for the night.

When young Charles Marlow meets Kate Hardcastle at the "inn," he assumes that she is a servant and begins to make sexual advances to her. Kate, in the meantime, has learned from Charles's friend Hastings, who is in love with her cousin Miss Neville, that Charles is exceedingly shy with women of his own class. Armed with this knowledge she decides not to reveal her true identity to him but rather to allow him to continue his erroneous assumptions about her status. Finally, Marlow's father, Sir Charles Marlow, arrives and clears up the misunderstanding, paving the way for marriages between young Charles and Kate, Hastings and Miss Neville.

Oliver Goldsmith wrote *She Stoops to Conquer* as an example of "laughing comedy," a form he presented as an alternative to the weeping sentimental comedies that were so popular during the 18th century. Goldsmith's play was well received, and its popularity helped to stimulate a general revival of the comedy of manners. *She Stoops to Conquer* stands as a reaction against the middle-class characters, settings, and sentiments that commonly appeared in sentimental "bourgeois" drama. Goldsmith's attitude at least partly reflects the views of his circle, the group of writers, artists, and intellectuals associated with Samuel JOHNSON.

See also LITERATURE.

Siècle de Louis XIV (The Century of Louis XIV)

A critical history of the reign of the French monarch LOUIS XIV, published by VOLTAIRE in BERLIN in 1752. A pirated edition appeared in FRANCE in 1753, published by Laurent Angliviél La Beaumelle. Voltaire responded to this later edition with the 1753 *Supplément au Siècle de Louis XIV* (Supplement to the century of Louis XIV).

Voltaire's approach to the reign of Louis XIV marked a significant change in the way that HISTORY was conceived. The book presents a picture of French society, economy, law, political structure, and cultural institutions during the years of Louis's reign. It neither chronicles the great actions of the king nor concentrates in the style of Bishop BOSSUET on the reign as a realization of God's purpose in history.

Voltaire used his book as a forum for presenting his criticism of French institutions. He gave more weight to Louis's useful acts, such as the building of a canal in Languedoc, than he did to military exploits.

Whatever his criticisms of Louis XIV, Voltaire still believed at this time that ABSOLUTISM transformed by ENLIGHTENMENT into enlightened despotism (see DESPOTISM, ENLIGHTENED) could serve the cause of human PROGRESS. As he grew older, Voltaire tempered this view and relaxed his enthusiasm for enlightened despotism, having learned from his experiences in France, GENEVA, and PRUSSIA that the concentration of power in the hands of any single person or institution, no matter how enlightened, can lead to abuses.

See also POLITICAL THEORY.

siècle des lumières

The French term for the ENLIGHTENMENT, consciously used by the PHILOSOPHES to describe their century. The phrase *siècle des lumières* literally means "century of lights." Writers referring to their enlightened French colleagues called them *lumières*.

In adopting this language, the philosophes, borrowing from their predecessors of the SCIENTIFIC REVOLUTION, used the symbolic language of Neoplatonism that equated light with wisdom. They believed that their new philosophy was leading humanity toward greater wisdom and perfection, completing the great transformation of human knowledge commenced by their 17th-century forebears.

Sieyès, Emmanuel Joseph, Abbé (1748–1836) *prominent leader during all phases of the French Revolution except the Reign of Terror*

Sieyès, son of a minor official in the town of Fréjus, received his primary education from the JESUITS, took religious vows as a priest, and studied THEOLOGY at the Sorbonne. He earned his degree in theology and in 1775 became a cathedral canon for J. B. de Lubersac, Bishop of Tréguier. Sieyès also became the chaplain of Madame Sophie, an aunt of King LOUIS XVI. In 1780, Bishop Lubersac transferred to the bishopric of Chartres. Sieyès accompanied him as grand vicar, becoming a canon of the Chartres cathedral in 1783, and chancellor for Bishop Lubersac in 1788. Sieyès entered ecclesiastical politics, serving as a deputy from the clergy to the 1788 Provincial Assembly at Orléans. The provincial assemblies had been charged with the task of preparing *cahiers* (lists of grievances and topics of concern) for presentation to the Estates General meeting that had been called for May 1789.

Sieyès earned national recognition in 1788–89 with two pamphlets: *Vues sur les moyens d'exécution dont les représentants de la France pourront disposer en 1789* (Views on the means of action which the representatives of France will have at hand in 1789; November 1788); and the renowned *1) Qu'est ce que le Tiers Etat? Tout. 2) Qu'est-il jusqu'à maintenant dans l'ordre politique? Rien. 3) Que désire-t-il? Etre quelque chose* (What is the Third Estate? Everything; What has it been until now in the political order? Nothing; What does it wish? To be something; January 1789). The latter pamphlet established Sieyès, who as a priest was technically a member of the First Estate (clergy), as an ardent defender of the interests of the Third Estate (bourgeoisie) in its struggle against the political and social privileges of the nobility under the French ANCIEN RÉGIME. It resulted in his being elected to the 1789 meeting of the Estates General as a representative of the Parisian Third Estate.

Sieyès became a prominent leader of the early French Revolution and proved to be a skilled politician who was able to survive the political storms that followed. He served in both the National Assembly and the National Convention (1792–95). During the ascendancy of Maximilien ROBESPIERRE and the Reign of Terror, Sieyès wisely kept a low profile and even refrained from appearing in the National Convention. Sieyès resumed his political participation in November 1794, well after the fall of Robespierre, serving on the reformed Committee of Public Safety (1795), as president of the constitutional committee appointed in 1795, and as a member of the Council of Five Hundred (1795–99). He played a major organizing role in the coup d'état that brought Napoleon to power as first consul. Napoleon later appointed Sieyès to the Senate and rewarded him with the title of "Count of the Empire."

In addition to holding these many political posts, Sieyès served as ambassador to PRUSSIA (1798) and helped to negotiate the constitution of the revolutionary Batavian Republic in the territories of the UNITED PROVINCES OF THE NETHERLANDS. Sieyès was a member of the class of political and moral science in the Institut de France, the comprehensive institution that replaced the former royal academies. When the Institut was replaced in 1804 with a renewed FRENCH ACADEMY OF SCIENCES, he was received into the membership of the new organization. Expelled from France in 1816 after the Bourbon Restoration, Sieyès was allowed to return to France after the Revolution of 1830, and was elected in 1832 to the Academy of Moral Sciences. Sieyès was also active in the French FREEMASONS.

Sieyès acquired a reputation as a constitutional expert during the years of the French Revolution. In 1789, he adopted a constitutional position that favored the principle of EQUALITY of voting power (one vote for each man; none for women). From this principle he deduced that in France a bicameral legislature and an executive veto, such as existed in the new UNITED STATES OF AMERICA or ENGLAND, would only perpetuate the unjust political conditions of the ancien régime. In 1789, the French executive would necessarily have been the king who enjoyed his office as hereditary right. If he were given a constitutional right to an executive veto, he would retain the powers that had caused so much difficulty in prerevolutionary years. A bicameral legislature in France would have also perpetuated the division of society into legal social orders. The upper house would have consisted of a few aristocrats retaining the constitutional power to block the will of the larger lower house. This too, in Sieyès's opinion, would have simply perpetuated the traditional political arrangements in France. For these reasons, he supported a unicameral system without an executive.

After the fall of the French monarchy and the anarchy of the Reign of Terror, Sieyès began to favor the introduction of a weak executive into the French political system. It was this desire that led to his participation in the coup d'état that brought Napoleon Bonaparte to power under a new constitution. The same set of convictions contributed to Sieyès's decision to help draft the act of dethronement in 1814, which unseated Emperor Napoleon. In the aftermath of this act, Sieyès did not favor the return of the Bourbon monarchy. He therefore went into exile in BRUSSELS during the 15 years of the Bourbon monarchy's restoration. Sieyès returned to France only in 1830 after the new revolution of that year. He died at the age of 88 in PARIS.

See also POLITICAL THEORY.

Simon, Richard (1638–1712) *French priest of the Oratory, scholar of the ancient Hebrew language, and one of the founders of biblical criticism*

Richard Simon was the son of a blacksmith in Dieppe. He received his education from the Oratorians at Dieppe. Deciding to enter the Oratory, he went to PARIS as a novice. Simon briefly abandoned his plans for a clerical profession, but in 1662 he resumed his preparation for the priesthood. He was ordained in 1670. Simon studied Hebrew, read the Polyglot Bible, and digested critical biblical commentaries. In 1678, he published his *Histoire critique du Vieux Testament* (Critical history of the Old Testament). The book caused him to be expelled from the Oratory on May 21, 1678, and it was banned by the royal council. All copies were ordered impounded. In 1683, it was also placed on the official Index of Forbidden Books of the Catholic Church, but none of these actions prevented it from circulating in Paris or elsewhere. Simon republished the book in 1685 with a Dutch press. He followed that with additional critical studies of New Testament materials.

In 1702, Simon published the *Nouveau testament de N.-S. Jésus-Christ, traduit sur l'ancienne édition latine avec des remarques* (New Testament of Our Lord Jesus Christ, translated from the old Latin edition, with some remarks). He intended this work as a literal translation of the biblical text, stripped of accretions and interpretations that distorted its meaning. His translation was condemned along with his other works.

By using the tools of philology—the study of words, their origins, and their history—Simon analyzed the Old Testament of the Bible, to determine which of its writings were authentic. Simon was not the only scholar of his era to subject the Bible to criticism, for Benedict de SPINOZA was also exploring it as a document of human HISTORY. But Simon carried critical examinations further and established a rigorous method for approaching ancient texts. He also published his book in French so that it would be accessible to general readers. He was accused of heresy by the Catholic authorities in ROME, but he always insisted on the orthodoxy of his position and beliefs.

For Simon, the texts of the Bible were divinely inspired, even if it could be proved that they had been written and revised throughout history. Thus, he subjected the Bible to criticism not to destroy its authority, but to better understand its content. Simon also hoped that his critical activities would help to bring Protestants back into the fold of ROMAN CATHOLICISM. If it could be shown that the Bible was a historical product, changed over time, but still divinely inspired, then the same claim could be made for the writings of Catholic tradition. Simon hoped that this would convince the Protestants that they need not insist solely on consulting the Bible for theological truth. In the hope of persuading Protestants to return to the Catholic fold, Simon engaged in intense controversies with Isaac Vossius (a canon at Windsor) and Jacques Basnage (a Huguenot pastor at Rouen and Rotterdam).

Although a product of the Catholic fervor of the 17th century in FRANCE, Simon nevertheless embraced a set of attitudes that placed him at odds with the religion to which he was so committed. He took courageous steps into uncharted intellectual territory, helping to pave the way for the critical intellectual attitudes and methods that would become the hallmark of the ENLIGHTENMENT.

See also BIBLICAL CRITICISM; RELIGION.

skepticism Form of philosophical EPISTEMOLOGY that deals with the possibilities and limits of human knowledge. Skepticism originated in ancient Greek philosophy. It had two primary forms. Academic skepticism developed in the third century B.C. in the Platonic Academy. Its chief adherents were Carneades (ca. 213–129 B.C.) and Aresilas (ca. 315–241 B.C.) They had asserted positively that no knowledge is possible; or in other words, they believed that the only thing that can be known is that we cannot know anything. These arguments reached Renaissance Europe in the writings of Cicero, Diogenes Laertius, and Saint Augustine. Pyrrhonian skepticism allegedly was created by a legendary figure, Pyrrho of Elis (ca. 360–275 B.C.), and Timon (ca. 315–225 B.C.), his student. Pyrrhonist skepticism asserted that there is insufficient evidence to assert anything with certainty; therefore, the wisest stance for man is to suspend judgment on all matters of knowledge. Pyrrhonian skepticism reached Renaissance Europe in the fragmentary manuscripts by Sextus Empiricus (ca. A.D. 200). It was the Pyrrhonist stance that shaped the great outpouring of skeptical philosophy beginning with Michel de Montaigne in the late 16th century and continuing into the 17th century.

The original impetus for late-16th-century skeptical thought lay in the crises produced by the Protestant Reformation and by the subsequent schism within Western Christianity. Since tradition was no longer accepted as an infallible authority, it seemed imperative to find some way to ground spiritual beliefs in philosophical certainty. But this was impossible for the human mind. Belief therefore had to depend on an act of faith, not on the dictates of REASON. The appeal of skepticism received another stimulus at the beginning of the 17th century when new scientific instruments such as the TELESCOPE began to demonstrate that the senses were potentially fallible sources of knowledge.

The perceived crisis about knowledge and certainty also stimulated the development of 17th-century RATIONALISM, NATURAL LAW, and efforts at mathematizing the RELATIONS governing events in the natural world. In FRANCE, René DESCARTES, Pierre GASSEND, Blaise Pascal, and Marin MERSENNE all wrestled with the question of how to attain certainty. Each reached a unique solution, the outlines of which shaped much of late-17th-century and early-18th-century thought. Descartes developed his method of deductive reasoning as an answer to the problem. Gassend turned to empirical observation, Mersenne developed a compromise position based on the mathematical nature of the laws that govern the universe, and Pascal turned to the form of certainty offered by mathematical PROBABILITY and inner emotion. These solutions mitigated the intellectual crisis temporarily.

Toward the end of the 17th century, however, a new critical spirit began to question the reliability of reason and experience as sources of knowledge. Once again, it was asked whether or not human beings could know anything with certainty. The work of Pierre BAYLE epitomizes this critical spirit. His *HISTORICAL AND CRITICAL DICTIONARY* raised the method of criticism to new heights, using it to examine all received traditions, institutions, and beliefs. Later, in the 18th century, David HUME again revived the skeptical stance in his *ENQUIRY CONCERNING HUMAN UNDERSTANDING*. He was concerned to demonstrate the weaknesses in theories of knowledge based on rationalism (reason) and EMPIRICISM (experience). His ideas paved the way for the development of new forms of PSYCHOLOGY and epistemology, and helped to move the thought of the ENLIGHTENMENT in new directions. At the end of the Enlightenment, Immanuel KANT once again addressed the problem of skepticism and human knowledge, offering a new synthesis and treatment of received philosophical traditions.

See also PYRRHONISM.

slavery A legal institution that was used primarily to provide agricultural labor in the colonies of European nations. Slaves were taken into captivity and bought and sold like material possessions. They were deprived of all civil or legal rights and of personal FREEDOM, and they were completely subject to their masters or mistresses.

The institution of slavery had existed in antiquity but had largely disappeared from Europe after the fall of the Roman Empire. It had continued, however, in parts of the Byzantine Empire and in the lands under Islamic control. Slavery reappeared in central Europe in the eighth to 10th centuries, when Slavic captives (hence, the origin of the word *slave*) were taken to GERMANY and sold as forms of PROPERTY. The institution reappeared in western Europe with the beginning of the era of European colonization.

The Portuguese explorer Henry the Navigator brought the first African slaves to Europe in 1444; after that, the institution was established in European colonies in Asia, Africa, and the Americas. It provided a cheap and reliable pool of labor for working large estates, plantations, and mines. Slave trading was a common practice in ENGLAND, PORTUGAL, SPAIN, FRANCE, the UNITED PROVINCES OF THE NETHERLANDS, and the European settlements overseas.

During the 18th century, slavery was common in North America and South America. It also existed in African and Asian colonies. It was intimately connected with the growth of plantation economies. Estimates place the number of slaves traded in the various British colonies between 1650 and 1786 at more than 2,000,000 people.

The abolition movement first appeared in the last third of the 17th century in England. Among the early opponents of slavery were Robert Baxter, a Protestant Dissenter; Morgan Goodwyn, an Anglican; George Fox, the founder of the QUAKERS; John LOCKE, the great political theorist of the early ENLIGHTENMENT; and Aphra BEHN, a female novelist. Richard STEELE and Alexander POPE also condemned the institution.

The Quakers made abolition one of their central causes throughout the 18th century. In 1774, the British Quakers decided to expel any member who engaged in the slave trade. Slavery in the British colonies was finally abolished by a law passed in 1833 that set final emancipation in 1839.

In France, organizations such as the Société des Amis des Noirs (Society of Friends of the Blacks), established in 1788, and radical lodges of FREEMASONS attacked the evils of slavery. Writers such as Abbé RAYNAL, Denis DIDEROT, and the Abbé Grégoire condemned the institution of slave trading for humanitarian and practical economic reasons. In 1794, during the FRENCH REVOLUTION, the National Convention abolished slavery in Haiti, but the practice was restored by Napoleon in an effort to regain control of the island. Slavery in other French colonies lasted until 1848.

In Germany, outspoken critics of slavery—the historian August von SCHLÖZER, the writer Georg Christoph LICHTENBERG, and the anthropologist Johann BLUMENBACH—were located at the University of GÖTTINGEN.

Enlightened leaders in the UNITED STATES, men such as George WASHINGTON, Thomas JEFFERSON, and Benjamin FRANKLIN, also condemned slavery. States north of Maryland all abolished slavery between 1777 and 1804. The southern states resisted until their defeat in the Civil War forced them into compliance. The Emancipation Proclamation of 1863 and the Thirteenth Amendment to the Constitution (1865) provided the legal force for abolition.

The combined forces of RELIGION and the Enlightenment stimulated the original calls for the abolition of slavery. The institution was characterized as inhumane, flagrantly abusive, and opposed to all ideals of equality and brotherhood. In short, it violated all values espoused by enlightened individuals and by their counterparts in various religious groups.

See also COLONIALISM; EQUALITY; EQUIANO; GREGOIRE; HISTOIRE DESDEUX INDES; POLITICAL THEORY; SANCHO; SERFDOM; TOUSSAINT LOUVERTURE; WILBERFORCE.

Smith, Adam (1723–1790) *Scottish moral philosopher and political economist*

A native of Kirkcaldy, SCOTLAND, Adam Smith was raised without a father by his widowed mother. After studies at the University of Glasgow and at Oxford University, Smith returned home for a year before settling in 1748 in EDINBURGH. In 1751, he was elected professor of logic at the University of Glasgow, a post he exchanged in 1752 for the chair in MORAL PHILOSOPHY.

The publication in 1759 of the *Theory of Moral Sentiments* brought Smith widespread acclaim and resulted in an invitation to serve as a tutor, with a lifetime pension, to the young duke of Buccleuch. Smith resigned from his Glasgow professorship and embarked with his young charge on a GRAND TOUR of Europe that extended from 1764 to 1766. During these travels, Smith met Anne-Robert-Jacques TURGOT and other PHYSIOCRATS in PARIS and at Versailles. He also visited VOLTAIRE outside GENEVA.

Upon returning to Scotland, Smith retired to Kirkcaldy, where he wrote the *Inquiry into the Nature and Causes of the Wealth of Nations*, better known by its short title, WEALTH OF NATIONS. Published in 1776, *Wealth of Nations* offered a theory of economic structure and functions that is considered one of the foundations of modern liberal political economy.

Smith was a friend of David HUME, Adam FERGUSON, Henry Home, Lord Kames, and other members of the Royal Philosophical Society of Edinburgh. He was also a member of the Literary Club, a group of writers and artists organized in LONDON around Samuel JOHNSON. His friends in the latter organization included not only Johnson and James BOSWELL but also the actor David GARRICK and the political theorist Edmund BURKE.

Smith's *Theory of Moral Sentiments* grounded social behavior and ethics in the human capacity for SYMPATHY with others. According to Smith, we observe things happening to other people and are capable of feeling compassion, grief, or joy on their behalf. These feelings, rather than some natural law perceived by our REASON, provide the basis of our general notions of pleasure and pain, or of good and evil. Thus sensory experiences in the form of sympathy underlie our ideas of propriety and merit.

The emotional perception of the moral worth of actions grows from three underlying principles of virtue: the sense that an action represents a proper path for our

Portrait of Adam Smith. An important figure in the Scottish Enlightenment, Smith provided in his *Wealth of Nations* the theoretical foundation for liberal economic theory. *(Courtesy New York Public Library)*

feelings (propriety); the sense that an action involves a balanced exercise of self-interest (prudence); and the sense that the behavior will ensure the HAPPINESS of others (benevolence).

Although this description of virtue and sympathy might seem to resemble the moral sense theory proposed by Francis HUTCHESON and David Hume, Smith actually rejects their approaches, saying that it is not necessary to postulate the existence of such a moral sense in order to explain moral behavior.

Smith also left a legacy in political economy of major significance to the subsequent development of capitalist economic theory and practice. *Wealth of Nations* provided an alternative to the economic theory of MERCANTILISM. He defined wealth as economic productiveness rather than as the physical possession of large quantities of gold or silver. Smith's book offered a clear description of the actual working conditions in ENGLAND that were being produced by the INDUSTRIAL REVOLUTION. It sketched out theoretical framework that justified these historical developments in terms of the overall economic progress of society.

Wealth of Nations also contained a critique of the theories of the Physiocrats, theorists who had made agriculture the primary source of wealth in society. Smith praised the role played by commercial and industrial activities in creating British economic prosperity, and he argued for the importance of these activities in creating national wealth.

With his thorough grounding in the basic principles of enlightened moral philosophy, Smith recognized the potency of SELF-INTEREST in determining human behavior. He attempted to create theories of morality and ECONOMICS that would demonstrate how the pursuit of individual self-interest, tempered by enlightenment, could benefit the good of the community. For Smith, in the realm of morality, natural human benevolence and the faculty of sympathy provided needed protection against the potential harm that could result from the unrestrained pursuit of self-interest. In economic behavior, restraint was provided by the operations of the Hidden Hand, a metaphor for the laws and forces that would preserve equilibrium and the common good in unregulated capitalist market systems.

Smith's ideas thus provided a theoretical framework to support the emergence of a morally tempered INDIVIDUALISM and contributed to the new SCIENCE OF MAN that was one of the significant creations of the ENLIGHTENMENT.

See also CAPITALISM; FREE TRADE; RIGHTS.

Smollett, Tobias George (1721–1771) *Scottish novelist* Smollett trained as a physician at the University of Glasgow but left the university without his degree to seek his fortune in LONDON. He obtained a job as a shipboard surgeon on an expedition to the West Indies (1741–43). Smollett married a wealthy Jamaican woman, Nancy Lascelles, and then settled in London.

Smollett was a committed Tory, a strong Scottish nationalist, and the leader of a group of prominent Scots in London.

Smollett turned to a literary career after the success of his novels *The Adventures of Roderick Random* (1748) and *The Adventures of Peregrine Pickle* (1751) had suggested the feasibility of such a path. He wrote in many literary forms: novels, political essays, travel reports, and HISTORY. His opus includes the novel *Ferdinand Count Fathom* (1753); *A Complete History of England* (1757–58); *Travels Through France and Italy* (1766); the satire *Adventures of an Atom* (1769); and the novel *The Expedition of Humphry Clinker* (1771). Smollett edited both the Tory periodical *Critical Review* (1756) and *The Briton* (1762–63). He also translated the late 16th-century Spanish NOVEL *Don Quixote* and 38 volumes of the writings of VOLTAIRE into English.

Smollett was one of the many sharp social and political critics of the 18th century. His literary strength lay in writing picaresque novels. They contained detailed descriptions of various horrors drawn from his youth at Bath and his shipboard experience. He created masterly comic caricatures and colorful, roguish characters. Smollett hated Henry FIELDING, in part because Fielding was his chief competitor in the production of picaresque works.

Smollett's health failed during the intense labor he put into his *Complete History of England*. He never completely recovered, and retired as an invalid to ITALY in 1768. Smollett died in Livorno in 1771.

See also LITERATURE; NOVEL; ROWLANDSON.

Social Contract Treatise on POLITICAL THEORY by the Genevan philosophe Jean-Jacques ROUSSEAU. Both the *Social Contract* (*Le contrat social*) and Rousseau's educational novel *ÉMILE* appeared in 1762. They were condemned to be burned in GENEVA as threats to the religious and political order. The French censors forbade the distribution of the *Social Contract* in FRANCE, but they did not follow up with more severe measures.

Both the *Social Contract* and *Émile* address the problems of people in civilization. Each book contains an ideal prescription for correcting the ills of 18th-century society; the *Social Contract* focuses on curing political ills, while *Émile* tackles the problem of educating people for societal life.

Rousseau disliked the general process of civilization and the associated emphasis on individual rights, viewing both as corruptions of natural man, rather than as examples of human PROGRESS. In his vision, the course of HISTORY was not one of relentless upward progress, but rather of downward degradation—to the sad state of affairs represented by 18th-century Europe. Rousseau had already sketched the outlines of this bleak assessment of contemporary civilization in two earlier works, the *Discourse on the Sciences and the Arts* (1750) and *DISCOURSE ON THE ORIGINS OF INEQUALITY* (1755).

The *Social Contract* offered a model for a political society that could be consciously constructed to replace the existing corrupt order. This new order would substitute an artificial political virtue for the degraded natural virtue of the old order. The new society would have analogous relations to the lost primitive state, but it would rest on man-made rather than natural foundations.

Rousseau rejected both the liberal political vision associated with the theory of John LOCKE and the NATURAL LAW theories stimulated by the work of Thomas HOBBES and Samuel PUFENDORF. He did not believe that a unified society could appear from the simple pursuit of SELF-INTEREST, nor did he believe that laws, allegedly inscribed in NATURE could answer the problem of RELATIONS between individuals and the social order.

The heart of the difficulty in creating a genuine, virtuous political society lay, for Rousseau, in the challenge of creating a true unity (something without individual parts) from a collection of individuals. This statement of the problem was not unique to Rousseau: Gottfried Wilhelm LEIBNIZ, for example, had written his monadology 50 years earlier, seeking in its arguments to offer a philosophical solution to the problem. Rousseau, however, provided a restatement of the problem cast in the specific terms of political structure.

Rousseau suggested that the solution to the problem of creating a virtuous society lay in the formulation of a genuine social contract, which would be created when all people simultaneously agreed to join together as a political unit. Each individual would freely surrender all PROPERTY rights and other individual rights to the new unit. In the process, a General Will would emerge, which would represent the collective desires of the society and would provide legitimacy for the positive (human-made) laws of the society. Rousseau did not see this process as a surrender of individual liberty, because he defined liberty as the FREEDOM to live under self-imposed law. The process by which law would be created in his envisioned society would guarantee this kind of freedom.

According to Rousseau, once the social contract had established a society possessed of a collective General Will, this Will would need to be embodied in a set of positive laws. These positive laws would be created by a virtuous Legislator, an extremely perceptive man possessed of abilities both to understand the emotions of people and to rise above them. This Legislator would transform human passions into just laws.

The General Will was an abstract concept for Rousseau, one that he struggled to define clearly but that has served as a source of conflicting interpretations ever since the first publication of the *Social Contract*.

Rousseau believed that his ideal political society could be formed only when certain external conditions existed: People had to be already united by some common bond; they had to be free of SUPERSTITION, secure from invasion, and capable of subsisting without external assistance. Furthermore, a degree of economic EQUALITY had to exist, thereby eliminating the divisive conditions caused by extremes of wealth and poverty.

In 1762, when the *Social Contract* was published, Rousseau believed that the only nation where his ideal political society might be established was the island of Corsica. The Corsicans had recently revolted from their colonial overlords, the Genoans. For many enlightened intellectuals they served as a symbol of the potential for political reform and human progress. By 1770, Rousseau had come to believe that the kingdom of POLAND could also create his ideal new system. Instead, he lived to see the infamous PARTITIONS OF POLAND in which the kingdom was eventually totally swallowed up by PRUSSIA, Russia, and AUSTRIA.

The *Social Contract* generated extensive interest and commentary in the later ENLIGHTENMENT. Still a subject of controversy, it has been called both a blueprint for pure democracy and a plan for totalitarian government. Much of the controversy over its message has roots in the events of the FRENCH REVOLUTION. The book served as a major source of inspiration for Maximilien ROBESPIERRE and the JACOBINS. Because their period of leadership during the Revolution was marked by the emergence of the Reign of Terror, events seemed to underscore the tendency of the General Will and its representative Legislator to become totalitarian in spirit and practice.

Whatever the way in which its message was interpreted and translated into political practice, the *Social Contract* stands as one of the outstanding pieces of political theory created during the Enlightenment. Rousseau challenged the positive contributions of INDIVIDUALISM, criticized the idea that private property serves as a guarantor of freedom, and rejected the idea that desirable societies could be founded on traditional concepts of natural law. Thus, in the name of the enlightened ideals of liberty and progress, Rousseau offered a political vision that reversed the very models that had been created during the earlier years of that enlightened era.

See also CIVIL SOCIETY.

social institutions of the Enlightenment   A term designating the various sites and social organizations where ideas about the ENLIGHTENMENT were shared among friends and acquaintances. Although primarily an intellectual movement, in every nation the movement also had a strong social component that distinguished it from preceding eras. People committed to the cause of enlightenment tended to gather together to discuss their ideas in the context of other social activities. The social network that grew from these activities served as one of the primary paths for the spread of enlightened ideas within Europe and North America. Thus, the social institutions of the Enlightenment helped to shape the era as one marked by an explosion in the dissemination of knowledge throughout society.

Salons and coffeehouses provided the most popular meeting places where aristocrats could mingle openly with educated commoners. Salons took place in private homes where wealthy, powerful, and educated women usually presided as hostesses. These meetings served intellectuals by providing them with receptive yet critical audiences, but they also served as places for making important contacts. The Parisian salon hostesses intervened on behalf of several PHILOSOPHES to gain them academy chairs or other positions of stature. Parisian salons were the most famous in Europe, but counterparts existed throughout the Italian peninsula, the HOLY ROMAN EMPIRE, and ENGLAND.

The list of enlightened salons in Europe is much too long to be fully enumerated, but a few examples can be given. Notable and important salons were held in PARIS by Madame de LAMBERT, Madame de Tencin, Madame GEOFFRIN, Madame DU DEFFAND, Madesmoiselle LESPINASSE, and baron d'HOLBACH. Regular gatherings occurred at Ferney, the Swiss home of VOLTAIRE, and at Cirey, a residence owned by Madame DU CHÂTELET. In the German territories, late 18th-century BERLIN offered the salons of Henriette Herz and Rachel Varnhagen. Anne-Amélie, duchess of Saxe-Weimar, gathered people in her residence at Weimar. The social and intellectual elite of England gathered at the homes of Samuel JOHNSON, Charles BURNEY and his daughter Fanny BURNEY, Mary W. MONTAGU, Alexander POPE, and in the residences of a group of English upper-class women called the BLUESTOCKINGS.

Coffeehouses, those favored establishments where 18th-century people could indulge their desire for caffeine, provided public meeting places for people of enlightened persuasion. The first coffeehouse appeared in

British coffeehouse. Coffeehouses served as meeting places where people could exchange ideas, read the latest popular journals and newspapers, and generally partake of the sociability that was a central feature of the Enlightenment. *(Courtesy Bettmann Archive)*

LONDON in the middle of the 17th century and was prosecuted for causing a public nuisance. By 1715, however, London had more than 3,000 such establishments. Joseph ADDISON, who recognized that the coffeehouse was providing a place where the middle classes could acquire the virtues associated with lively, informed conversation, visited Button's regularly. Alexander Pope preferred Will's, and Samuel Johnson's famous Literary Club met in yet another establishment. In Paris, Voltaire could be found at the Café Procope. The ILLUMINISTI of MILAN gathered in a coffeehouse when not meeting at the home of Pietro VERRI, and they even immortalized the association of the Enlightenment with coffee by naming their short-lived progressive journal *Il Caffè*.

Reading clubs and lending libraries proliferated throughout Europe. At these clubs, members gathered to read and discuss enlightened books and clandestinely circulating manuscripts. As private institutions, these clubs thus provided a way for people to learn about ideas even when the books containing them had been officially censored.

These informal meetings tended sometimes to develop into formal organizations dedicated to some activity or goal, such as political reform, LITERACY, agriculture, MUSIC, art, THEATER, public health, abolition of SLAVERY, or SCIENCE. Other groups, such as SECRET SOCIETIES and a host of eating clubs, had more explicitly social purposes. Examples of these organizations include the Club de L'Entresol, a political society in Paris; the Helvetic Society, a cultural society in SWITZERLAND; the Société des Amis des Noirs, an abolitionist group in Paris; the Select Society, a general intellectual society in EDINBURGH; the Friends of Ancient Music in London; the Humane Society, a group dedicated to public health issues; Phi Beta Kappa, a society for outstanding university students; and the Junto, a debating society in PHILADELPHIA. Hundreds of additional examples could be listed drawn from nearly every 18th-century European city and town.

Complementing the activities of these groups were the formal fraternal organizations, whose members were striving to reach the highest possible levels of human knowledge. The most important of these institutions were the FREEMASONS, the Bavarian ILLUMINATI, and the ROSICRUCIANS. Certain lodges of the Freemasons and Illuminati were actively dedicated to radical political and social causes of the Enlightenment. The Rosicrucians and the Scottish Rites lodges of the Freemasons, however, generally tended to embrace a more conservative political program.

Other important formal institutions were the many SCIENTIFIC ACADEMIES—the BERLIN ACADEMY, the ROYAL SOCIETY OF LONDON, and the FRENCH ACADEMY OF SCIENCES being only the most powerful of such groups. UNIVERSITIES played a less important role, except in SCOTLAND, certain German principalities, and the Italian peninsula.

Primarily in England, but also in PRUSSIA and FRANCE, a less formal social phenomenon was the public pleasure garden. This public space permitted the enjoyment of the polite arts and social intermingling by all classes of visitors. Famous London gardens at Vauxhall, Marylebone, Ranelegh, and several other sites gratified the senses in an edifying environment. While they were not formal clubs or salons, they served a similar, if more egalitarian, purpose. The first of these fashionable gardens was Jonathan Tyers's New Spring Garden at Vauxhall (1728). It was an urban pastoral park, complete with orchestra and commissioned artworks where the public could appreciate at leisure the delights of nature, music, sculptures, fireworks, and light entertainment. The cost of admission was about the same as a theater ticket or mass-market book: just over a shilling. Ranelegh, more refined and boasting a rotunda underwritten by its aristocratic clientele, cost two shillings and sixpence. In its English form, the pleasure garden was a place for leisured community and the display or acquisition of refined tastes. These public gardens were described frequently in contemporary literature, journals, and letters. This popularity in both the private and public spheres illuminates the function of such gardens in the formation of a cross-class community of taste, a democratization of cultural knowledge. In Paris, too, the Palais Royal housed a substantial art collection, and the garden behind was a fashionable promenade for well-to-do people. Perhaps following the English example, the duke of Chatrres in 1781 embarked upon major site developments. He built upscale retail shops for rent and provided space for restaurants, theatrical troupes, and other entertainment on the grounds. Beyond the control of the Paris police, the site soon became more than a fashionable urban garden. Along with the aficionados of art, LANDSCAPES, and pleasure came radicals interested in debating revolutionary politics.

The existence of these various institutions owed much to the common 18th-century belief that human PROGRESS required the exchange of ideas. The act of association (that is, the formation of individuals into groups) was given a central role to play not only in the dissemination of the knowledge necessary for progress but also in the creation of the human sociability and civic virtue that were believed to be essential ingredients of just societies. Thus, the social institutions of the Enlightenment were viewed as leading actors in the drama that was being played out during the century of light.

See also BOSWELL; ENGLISH GARDEN; NOVEL; *THE SPECTATOR.*

Further reading: Jürgen Habermas, *Structural Transformation of the Public Sphere,* trans. Thomas Burger (New York: Cambridge University Press, 1981); Thomas Munck, *The Enlightenment: A Comparative Social History 1721–1794* (New York: Oxford University Press, 2000).

society, concept of *See* MANDEVILLE; MONTESQUIEU; POLITICAL THEORY; ROUSSEAU; SMITH.

sociology *See* HISTORY; IDÉOLOGIE; MONTESQUIEU; SCIENCE OF MAN.

Sonnenfels, Josef von (1733 or 1734–1817) *Austrian statesman and reformer*
Sonnenfels belonged to a Jewish family that may have been affiliated with the mystical Jewish sect called the Sabbatianer. His native town, Nikolsburg in the Südmähren region of the HAPSBURG EMPIRE, was a center for this group. Josef's father was Lipman Perlin. He moved his family away from Nikolsburg in 1733 after having entered the service of Prince Dietrichstein. Not long afterward, the family settled in VIENNA. Lipman Perlin converted to ROMAN CATHOLICISM and was raised to noble status.

Young Sonnenfels studied PHILOSOPHY and languages at the University of Vienna between 1745 and 1749. He served five years (1749–54) in the army, returning in 1754 to Vienna for law studies. His teachers included the two reformers Karl Anton von Martini and Paul Joseph von Riegger.

After obtaining his law degree, Sonnenfels entered the Hapsburg civil service, occupying a variety of posts. He also became a THEATER and MUSIC critic. Over the years his critical essays appeared in journals such as *Der Vertraute* (The confidant), *Der Mann ohne Vorurtheil* [sic] (The man without prejudice), and the *Wiener Realzeitung* (Viennese news). A champion of the refined CLASSICISM whose major German-language spokesman was Johann Christoph GOTTSCHED, Sonnenfels believed that clear, well-constructed language could serve as a vehicle for greater enlightenment.

In 1762, Sonnenfels received an appointment as professor of *Polizey- und Kameralwissenschaft* (public administration). He began serving as a formal adviser to the imperial council of the Hapsburg Empire in 1780. His special areas of concern were economic, educational, and legal reform.

Sonnenfels was a member of the FREEMASONS, belonging to the Viennese lodge "Zur wahren Eintracht." This lodge had incorporated the teachings and revolutionary aims of the Bavarian ILLUMINATI into its structure and programs.

As a devoted supporter of the theory of state known as CAMERALISM, Sonnenfels worked to make the goals of enlightened despotism (see DESPOTISM, ENLIGHTENED) a reality in the Hapsburg Empire. The purpose of the state lay in fostering the general welfare of its subjects by advancing their material, intellectual, and moral status. In line with these general ideals, Sonnenfels pressured Empress MARIA THERESA to abolish torture. He supported compulsory EDUCATION, stating that the government should have the right to place children in schools if their parents failed to procure an adequate education for them.

Sonnenfels tried to steer the Hapsburg government toward enlightened reform. Following the interpretation of law that had been outlined by MONTESQUIEU, he conceived of law as the embodiment of natural principles that could provide the fundamental framework for a new imperial constitution. Most of Sonnenfels's colleagues disapproved of his constitutionalism, but his other enlightened policies found support.

In all his activities, Sonnenfels's commitment to the ENLIGHTENMENT—in the special forms it acquired in central Europe—stands out clearly, and he is remembered in historiography as one of the great public officials to have worked in the 18th-century Hapsburg Empire.

Sorrows of Young Werther, The This short novel (*Die Leiden des jungen Werthers*, 1774), written by the 25-year old Johann Wolfgang von GOETHE, became one of the most controversial and widely read books in the last quarter of the 18th century. Its story was based upon a real incident. As Goethe was finishing his legal studies by attending the Imperial Court sessions at Wetzlar, an acquaintance, Karl Wilhelm Jerusalem, committed suicide out of frustrated love.

Goethe wove this incident into a beautifully crafted story of youthful innocence, infatuation, denial, and despair leading to self-inflicted death. The story was framed as an epistolary novel, a literary mode that brings the reader into close contact with the feelings of the protagonist by avoiding intrusions from an omniscient third-party narrator.

The plot was simple. The young Werther, filled with enthusiasm and a love for NATURE, sojourns in the countryside. He is attracted to and falls in love with Lotte, a woman engaged to a solid, bourgeois man named Albert. Clearly a close relationship between Lotte and Werther is established, but Lotte shows no desire to leave Albert for Werther. In an attempt to overcome his feelings of frustration, Werther leaves Lotte and tries to make a career at court. But the restrictions of court life, the strict hierarchies separating the classes, and the pettiness of peoples' reactions all combine to make Werther's experience there a complete failure. Defeated, Werther returns to Lotte and, in her presence, increasingly loses his self-control. The climax of the story occurs in a meeting between Lotte and Werther where it appears that Lotte does indeed love Werther but where she, nevertheless, persists in her refusal to give up Albert. Dejected and filled with despair, Werther takes his own life.

In weaving this plot, Goethe introduced basic questions central to the ENLIGHTENMENT and especially to his generation. The tension between social conformity and the free expression of individual creativity and desire lies at the core of the work. This theme is symbolized by Werther's close relationship to nature at the beginning of the work. But the original correspondence between natural freedom and productive nature was brought into question by the demands and restraints of society. The court scenes in which Werther is subjected to affront after affront based on traditional and unnatural concepts of privilege and social hierarchy, highlight this theme. And so does Lotte's refusal to betray social norms by abandoning her publicly acknowledged fiancé, making Werther a victim of social convention. Throughout the work, the sub-theme of suicide as an act against society, as an ultimate revolution against the prison in which all men live, is sounded. The final act, Werther's suicide from despair, raises the human dilemma in heightened form. Was his act justified or was it the response of an overly excited person who had lost his sense of reality and proportion?

For many who read the book—especially the people of Goethe's generation, who had been raised on the principles of the Enlightenment but felt themselves restricted by traditional society—the act seemed justified. Werther's act of defiance was reenacted by a number of young men suffering from unrequited love. A whole generation imitated Werther's form of free and casual dress—open-necked shirts, natural, loosely bound hair (no wigs), yellow vests, and blue jackets. They saw *Werther* as a monument to FREEDOM, creativity, individual liberty, and the creative forces of nature. This positive set of responses was greeted by a host of attacks and satires against the work, the most famous being *The Joys of Young Werther* by Christoph Friedrich NICOLAI.

On account of the storm of controversy generated by the work, Goethe felt compelled to write an explanation. He denied the assertion that he was advocating suicide as a responsible action in the face of emotional hardship. According to him, the story of Werther demonstrated the danger of allowing emotions to dictate actions. At the same time, the story also warned against basing life upon sterile speculations and unnatural traditions. In short, while Goethe was extremely critical of existing society and its conventions, he advocated working within society to reform it rather than rejecting it. In the end, human action should seek to harmonize relations between individual liberty and social responsibility.

See also AUFKLÄRUNG; LITERATURE; MORAL PHILOSOPHY.

Soufflot, Jacques Germain (1713–1780) *French neoclassical architect*

Soufflot studied law before turning to architecture. Once Soufflot had abandoned law, he traveled to ROME, where the French Academy in Rome admitted him to its training program.

Upon completing his courses at the French Academy, Soufflot moved to Lyons, where he was able to secure several important building commissions, including that for the new Hôtel-Dieu of Lyons. He also became a member of the Lyons Academy. His work came to the attention of the marquis de Marigny, brother of Madame de POMPADOUR. Marigny asked Soufflot to accompany him and Jean Bernard Leblanc and Charles Nicholas Cochin on a 1750 trip to ITALY. The foursome visited the new excavations at Herculaneum and the Doric temples at Paestum. Marigny provided Soufflot with important patronage that allowed the young architect to begin developing his ideas about what would become French NEOCLASSICISM.

Soufflot approached architectural design from a highly rational, theoretical point of view. This habit embroiled him in controversies with architects who designed according to experience and practical demands. Conflict of such a nature erupted with Pierre Patte over Soufflot's designs for the Church of Sainte Geneviève, the structure that was renamed the Panthéon during the FRENCH REVOLUTION. The Panthéon design was modeled after the ancient temple in Rome known as the Pantheon. Soufflot's structural supports for the dome of the church, conceived according to his theory rather than by applying experience to the problem, were inadequate for the load they had to carry. Changes were necessitated, and the stress caused by the resulting difficulties in completing the construction of the building were said to have caused Soufflot's death.

Besides the Hôtel-Dieu in Lyons and the Panthéon in PARIS, Soufflot's most significant buildings were the town and country homes that he designed for Marigny, one of which still survives at Ménars. Soufflot recorded his architectural theories in two works, *De l'architecture gothique* (On gothic architecture) and *Suite de plans de trois temples antiques à Pestum* (Plans of three ancient temples at Paestum). Soufflot's designs and publications helped to create the French appreciation of Roman antiquities.

South Sea Bubble

Name referring to the wave of financial speculation during 1720 in stocks of the SOUTH SEA COMPANY. The South Sea Bubble came about in response to the English government's attempts to finance its troublesome national debt. The South Sea Company had been established in 1711 to oversee commercial trade with South America. In 1720, the English treasury under First Lord of the Treasury Sunderland established a program to stabilize its financial situation by shrinking the total deficit and by slowly reducing the interest payable on outstanding debts. The South Sea Company offered to assume the government debt according to a schedule with steadily decreasing interest rates. It also proposed to pay off the many private individuals who held government securities by giving them South Sea Company stock. The rate of exchange would be fixed at the outset of the venture so that any increase in the value of South

Sea Company stock would allow the company to acquire government securities at a cheaper redemption rate. The English government guaranteed that its securities would be paid off at face value.

The South Sea Company proposal was made at a time when Europe was emerging from a depression and stock speculation was on the rise. When the English Parliament approved the South Sea Company scheme, company stocks rose rapidly to 10 times their face value. Parliament reacted by passing the Bubble Act forbidding the issue of transferable shares by new companies. The general mood of confidence rapidly disappeared, and a wave of stock sales followed. This threatened the financial soundness of the central government, since it had tied the financing of its debt to the fortunes of the South Sea Company. Sir Robert WALPOLE, the prominent Whig Party leader, was recalled to office in the crisis and instituted measures to reestablish confidence in the government. Walpole divided the national debt holdings of the South Sea Company equally between the Bank of ENGLAND and the EAST INDIA COMPANY.

The South Sea Bubble had both political and economic consequences for England. It consolidated Walpole's political position by undermining the power of his major opponents, the faction led by Sunderland. The Walpole government and associated political allies dominated the politics of 18th-century England for many years. The Bubble fiasco also retarded the development of joint-stock methods for financing commercial and industrial enterprises.

The South Sea Bubble had parallels in the 1720 MISSISSIPPI BUBBLE, which occurred during the brief ascendancy of John LAW in FRANCE. Both incidents arose from the financial environment and government fiscal practices of the early 18th century. At that time, orthodox mercantilist theories of wealth (accumulation of gold equals wealth) were being revised to allow schemes that emphasized the importance of currency circulation, credit, and volume of trade. Large amounts of wealth were being created and accumulated during the early 18th century by private individuals engaged in financial speculation. But central governments were unable to tax this wealth in order to fund their debts or to pay for various activities. The Bubble schemes grew out of attempts both to resolve government fiscal crises and to tap into the new private wealth.

See also MERCANTILISM.

South Sea Company British joint-stock company. The South Sea Company was created as a national venture in 1711, primarily as a means of easing the massive debt Britain had accumulated due to years of wars with FRANCE, the UNITED PROVINCES OF THE NETHERLANDS, and SPAIN. The concept behind its formation was that holders of the national debt would trade in their government securities in exchange for shares of the company, which was granted a virtual monopoly on British trade in South America. In principle, shareholders would receive a portion of the annuity granted to the company as well as the profits of the trade; the nation and private speculators would thus prosper together.

Things did not work out as well as many of its shareholders projected. In part, this was because the South Sea Company originated as the political vehicle of a Tory ministry, led by Robert Harley, that was battling the Whig strongholds of the Bank of England and the EAST INDIA COMPANY. These institutions threatened to force the government's hand on matters of policy through their power to diminish the nation's swelling debts. The South Sea Company circumvented these creditors, and yet, largely because of its political origins, the company never made good on its lavish promises. While the company appeared capable of extracting concessions from the Spaniards in matters of commerce in South America, it served instead to facilitate peace treaties closer to home. As a result, the company was forced to work within the parameters of compromise regarding its trade in South America, severely curtailing its returns. Much of the profit, in fact, resulted from the illicit trading of African slaves, enriching only those who took part in these secret deals. In order to maintain the illusion of profitability, the company took on more and more of the government's debt, lending the shareholders money based on the security (value) of their stock, and thus increasing the price of the stock.

This feat of speculative financing is what led to the famous SOUTH SEA BUBBLE of 1720. On the first of the year, stock was worth 128 pounds sterling. By July, it had risen almost 10 times. In September, the "bubble" burst, and the stock plummeted to its former worth. The financial ruin extended from individual stockholders to banks. At the time, it was the most calamitous market crash Britain had ever known. The South Sea Bubble became a cultural symbol of the dangers of speculation, credit, and paper currency. Its long-term effect was to slow, though certainly not stop, British financial speculation for roughly half a century.

Further reading: John Carswell, *The South Sea Bubble,* 3rd ed. (Dover, N.H.: Alan Sutton, 1993); Charles Poor Kindleberger, *Manias, Panics and Crashes: A History of Financial Crises,* 4th ed. (New York: Wiley, 2000).

Spain Dynastic state whose central lands lay in the Iberian peninsula. Early in the Middle Ages, the peninsula had fallen under Arab control. As a result, it became the site of a creative meeting of three religious cultures, that of Muslims, Jews, and Christians. The late medieval period brought a resurgence of Christian power, and the Arabs were driven out of most of the Iberian peninsula by the armies of several Christian princes. The marriage (1469) of King Ferdinand of Aragon and Queen Isabella of Castile produced in 1479 a dynastic state called Spain with its capital in MADRID.

In 1492, the year that Christopher Columbus landed in America on a VOYAGE OF DISCOVERY for the Spanish, Ferdinand and Isabella, devout Catholic rulers, issued a decree expelling the Jews from their lands. Spanish troops also conquered Granada, thereby driving the last Arab Islamic rulers from the Iberian peninsula.

The explorations of the 15th and 16th centuries made Spain the ruler of a vast colonial empire with lands in the Americas, the West Indies, and the Philippine Islands. During the 16th century, the political fortunes of Spain were joined to those of the Austrian Hapsburg emperors of the HOLY ROMAN EMPIRE, when Philip I, the son of the Austrian Hapsburg emperor Maximilian I, married Joanna of Spain, the daughter of Ferdinand and Isabella. Philip I and Joanna had a son, Charles I of Spain, who was elected Emperor Charles V of the Holy Roman Empire in 1520. During his rule, the Spanish Hapsburg family thus controlled the lands of Spain, AUSTRIA, the Low Countries (modern BELGIUM and the Netherlands), the Free County of Burgundy, Spanish America, Sardinia, Sicily, and the kingdom of Naples. This situation lasted until 1555, when Charles V ceded control of Spain, the Low Countries, Naples, and the Spanish colonies to his son Philip II. In 1556, Charles also ceded the crown of the Holy Roman Empire to his brother Ferdinand I. These acts permanently divided the Hapsburg family into Spanish and Austrian branches.

Silver and gold from the American colonies made Spain fantastically wealthy and powerful during the 16th century. Furthermore, it emerged as a bastion of ROMAN CATHOLICISM. Charles V allied the region staunchly with the pope during the Protestant Reformation and encouraged the activities of both the Inquisition (the ecclesiastical courts of the Catholic Church charged with combating heresy) and the JESUITS. Seventeenth-century Spain saw a flowering of culture associated with the so-called Catholic Counter-Reformation, and its monarchs continued supporting policies designed to secure Catholicism from encroachments by PROTESTANTISM.

In spite of the continued influence exerted by Spain in 17th-century diplomacy and international relations, the century also saw the beginning of a slow decline of Spanish economic and political fortunes. The northern maritime nations—the UNITED PROVINCES OF THE NETHERLANDS and ENGLAND—assumed dominance in European economic activities, while FRANCE, England, and the Austrian HAPSBURG EMPIRE slowly emerged as the major European political powers.

During the 18th century, the Spanish crown passed from the Spanish Hapsburgs to the Bourbons when a grandson of LOUIS XIV assumed the Spanish throne as Philip V. In the turmoil of the succession crisis (War of the Spanish Succession), Spain gave up some of her European holdings to the Austrian Hapsburgs. Thus, the Spanish Netherlands became the AUSTRIAN NETHERLANDS, and MILAN, Naples, and Sicily also passed to Austrian rule. Spain regained Naples in 1734.

The Bourbon kings of Spain, especially Philip V and CHARLES III, pursuing a course inspired by enlightened absolutism (see ABSOLUTISM, ENLIGHTENED), attempted to consolidate their power over local secular interests and the Catholic Church. Charles III eventually joined other European rulers in expelling the Jesuits from his territories. He also tried to reform certain religious practices and to restructure EDUCATION. Philip V and Charles III both tried to reform Spanish finances and to stimulate the economy through a combination of policies borrowed from the PHYSIOCRATS and from MERCANTILISM. In general intent, the policies of these 18th-century Spanish kings and their advisers resembled those of their enlightened counterparts throughout Europe. The activities of the periodical press, UNIVERSITIES, and economic clubs called Amigos del Pais (Friends of the Nation), for example, were encouraged by King Charles III as means by which certain ideas of the ENLIGHTENMENT could gain a Spanish audience. Spanish royal patronage also supported cultural activities in Madrid, where the composer Domenico SCARLATTI and the great painter Francisco de GOYA lived and worked.

If Spain was not noted as a center of the Enlightenment, it nevertheless harbored groups of intellectuals and political leaders who turned to that movement for inspiration and guidance. The works of Jean-Jacques ROUSSEAU, for example, enjoyed a wide following in spite of the fact that they had been placed on the Index of Forbidden Books by the Spanish Inquisition. Historical studies stimulated criticism of contemporary institutions, thereby helping to shape demands for reform. In general, however, the extent of enlightened reform in Spain remained limited, especially when compared with the notable changes that were occurring in PORTUGAL, PRUSSIA, or Austria.

See also COLONIALISM; DYNASTIC STATES; SOCIAL INSTITUTIONS OF THE ENLIGHTENMENT.

Spallanzani, Lazzaro (1729–1799) *Italian natural historian and physiologist*

Spallanzani was noted for the breadth of his education and for his contributions to the 18th-century scientific quarrel over the causes and processes of the GENERATION of life. Spallanzani was the son of a lawyer who lived in the Italian region of Emilia. He had many siblings, including a sister, Marianna, who became a naturalist. His paternal cousin Laura Bassi was a professor of physics and mathematics at the University of Bologna. Young Spallanzani studied in the Jesuit seminary of Reggio Emilia and then enrolled in the course of jurisprudence at the University of Bologna. With the encouragement of

Laura Bassi, he also followed courses in mathematics, physics, chemistry, and natural history. Professor Bassi and Antonio Vallisneri the Younger persuaded Spallanzani's father to approve his son's transfer from jurisprudence to NATURAL PHILOSOPHY. In 1753 or 1754, Spallanzani received a doctorate in philosophy. After some additional courses in THEOLOGY and metaphysics, he took minor orders in the Roman Catholic church. He was ordained a priest after a few years and was sent to Modena to assume ecclesiastical duties. He remained in the church throughout his life, although he seems to have performed priestly functions somewhat irregularly.

Spallanzani paired his clerical activities with teaching throughout his post-university career. He taught courses ranging from Greek, logic, and metaphysics, to philosophy, mathematics, and natural history. He began his career in Reggio Emilia, taught philosophy at Modena (1763–69), and then moved to Pavia (1769–99), where he assumed the chair of natural history at the University of Pavia.

Spallanzani's inquisitive mind roamed broadly over several research questions of central significance for his era. He was a skilled microscopist and a careful observer, who was also capable of close, logical deductive reasoning; all these abilities assisted him in his scientific disputes. He is most renowned for having refuted the theory of spontaneous generation proposed by another Catholic priest, John NEEDHAM. Spallanzani demonstrated that the alleged spontaneous generation of animalcules (microscopic organisms), which could be observed in flasks containing various organic infusions, actually occurred because the flasks were not properly sealed. He reported these findings in 1765 to the Bologna Academy of Sciences in a paper titled *Saggio di osservazioni microscopiche*. Spallanzani followed these experiments with contributions to the quarrel between preformationists and epigeneticists over reproduction. He especially focused on refuting the epigenetic views of the comte de BUFFON. Like his friend Charles BONNET, Spallanzani was committed to the theory of PREFORMATION and specifically to its ovist version. He believed that both sperm and egg were necessary for the reproductive process to occur, but he did not think that the sperm contributed any essential components to the embryo. Rather, the sperm merely activated the preformed individual contained within the egg. Spallanzani also studied the processes of regeneration in simple animals, greatly extended the knowledge about the potential for regeneration, and established that such potential declines as the age of an organism increases.

In addition to his work on the broad questions of generation, Spallanzani made contributions to the study of circulation and digestion. His circulation experiments aimed at resolving questions and problems raised by the German physiologist Albrecht von HALLER. The digestion studies yielded new insights into the role of the stomach in digestive processes. Spallanzani invented the name *hydrochloric acid* for stomach acid. He engaged in a brief polemic with John HUNTER over his findings.

Spallanzani was an avid traveler and collector of specimens for the Public Museum of Natural History at the University of Pavia. He also made contributions to the study of volcanoes, freshwater mountain springs, and bat navigation. He was an early convert to the chemical theories of gases proposed by chemists in SCOTLAND and ENGLAND.

Spallanzani died in 1799 of the complications caused by chronic bladder infection. He asked that his bladder be preserved as an exhibit in the Museum of Natural History at the University of Pavia.

The catalog of Spallanzani's works includes *De' fenomeni della circolazione* (On the phenomena of circulation; 1773); *Opuscoli di fisica, animale e vegetabile* (Works on animal and vegetable physics; 1776), the studies on spontaneous generation, translated during the 18th century into English and French; *Dissertazioni di fisica animale e vegetabile* (Dissertation on animal and vegetable physics; 1780), the digestion studies, also existing in 18th-century English and French translations; and *Viaggi alle due Sicilie e in alcune parti dell'Appennino* (Travels through the Two Sicilies and some parts of the Apennines; 1792 and 1797), with 18th-century translations into French, German, and English). Spallanzani translated Charles Bonnet's two-volume *Contemplation de la nature* (Contemplation of nature) into an Italian edition that went through several printings.

Spectator, The English periodical that appeared six times weekly; written and published (1711–12, 1714) by Joseph ADDISON and Richard STEELE. In general, a substantial reading public seems to have existed in the 18th century. LITERACY was fairly widespread, having been stimulated by the Protestant emphasis on Bible reading. During the ENLIGHTENMENT, the practice of reading secular LITERATURE spread, and numerous periodicals with varying foci appeared in all countries of Europe. *The Spectator* was one of the most influential periodicals of the early Enlightenment.

Addison and Steele used *The Spectator* as a vehicle for spreading their concepts of proper middle-class manners and morality. They also attempted to give substance to abstract concepts such as virtue, or the new notion of "goodness of heart." These concepts were illustrated by specific example in the activities of Mr. Spectator and his friends. In general, *The Spectator* articles aimed, in Addison's words, to bring "philosophy out of the closets and libraries, schools and colleges, to dwell in clubs and assemblies, at tea-tables and in coffee-houses."

The articles purport to be pages from the diary of a Mr. Spectator, who records the activities of his small club. The club members constitute a cross section of British society. Of all the characters drawn by Addison and

Steele, Sir Roger de Coverley, a country squire, is best known. Although publication of *The Spectator* lasted only for about two years, the journal contributed substantially to the development and popularization of the new periodical essay.

See also PUBLISHING; SOCIAL INSTITUTIONS OF THE ENLIGHTENMENT.

Spener, Philipp Jakob (1635–1705) *German theologian and founder of Pietism*

Philipp Jakob Spener brought about a religious revival in GERMANY in the late 17th century through his activities as a pastor and writer. He ensured that this revival, known as PIETISM, would have a lasting and far-reaching impact by helping to found the University of HALLE, which became the center of Pietism, and by passing his ideas on to an important group of followers, among them August Hermann FRANCKE.

Spener was born in Rappoltsweiler (Ribeauville), Alsace (today part of FRANCE). At 13, Philipp Jakob matriculated at the University of Strasbourg, where he studied HISTORY and PHILOSOPHY. Early influences included not only his Lutheran faith, but also both the mysticism prevalent at the end of the Thirty Years' War, whose ravages had led to an increased concern with death, and the neo-Stoic writings of Dutch thinker Justus Lipsius, who preached spiritual and temperamental constancy in the face of strife and upheaval. Spener received his master's degree in 1653 at the age of 18; his thesis was a critique of the thought of Thomas HOBBES from the orthodox Lutheran viewpoint. He continued his education in Strasbourg, studying theology, and taught philosophy and history. Beginning in 1659, Spener traveled to Basel and GENEVA, where he studied Hebrew and the Old Testament. In 1662, he arrived in Tübingen, in southwestern Germany, where he studied heraldry at the university and preached in the city's church. He received his doctorate in theology in 1664.

Spener went to FRANKFURT am Main in 1666 to serve as head pastor of the Lutheran congregation. In 1670, he took a decisive step, founding a Bible study group that met regularly and was open to all levels of society. This marked the beginning of a religious revival, and such *collegia pietatis* (spiritual meetings) or *collegia biblia* (Bible meetings) spread throughout the German-speaking lands and other parts of Europe. He also founded a workhouse on the English model in Frankfurt to provide unemployed or impoverished people with a new start. Workhouses and orphanages soon followed in other large German cities. Spener's *Pia desideria* (Pious desires; 1675), which criticized the orthodox Lutheran Church for ignoring social problems and emphasized the importance of study, prayer, and the cultivation of individual piety, reflected his experiences in Frankfurt.

Spener continued to publish works that were critical of Lutheran orthodoxy throughout the rest of the 1670s and the 1680s. His fame increased, and he was invited by Johann Georg III, the elector of Saxony, to come to Dresden as court chaplain, a post Spener assumed in 1686. He was highly controversial and soon ran afoul of the elector and his courtiers. In 1691, the Saxon ambassador to Brandenburg-Prussia convinced that court to offer him a position as rector of Berlin's St. Nicholas Church, and Spener accepted. In 1694, Spener helped to found the University of Halle, which became the center of Pietism. The next year, the theological faculty at the University of Wittenberg, the center of Lutheran orthodoxy, leveled charges against Spener, and he devoted much of the rest of his life to defending himself. He spent the final decade of his life in BERLIN, where, in 1699, he organized a printing of the Bible. The publication and dissemination of Bibles was an important aspect of Pietism's encouragement of individual piety and Bible study. His work was carried on after his death by his follower August Hermann Francke.

See also LUTHERANISM.

Further reading: F. Ernest Stoeffler, *The Rise of Evangelical Pietism* (Leiden: E. J. Brill, 1965).

spinning jenny A machine for spinning cotton thread invented by James HARGREAVES in 1764 or 1765. Hargreaves patented his machine in 1770. The spinning jenny greatly increased the production of cotton yarn. The machine drew and twisted yarn simultaneously just as a human spinner with a wheel would do. The early machine had eight spindles that could be hand-operated by one worker, but later models had as many as 80 spindles. In a given period the jenny could produce up to 24 times more cotton yarn than a spinning wheel. In addition, the jenny produced a higher and more consistent quality of yarn.

The invention of the spinning jenny raised the specter of unemployment for many spinners. The increased output of yarn also caused an oversupply that was later met by the invention of the POWER LOOM for weaving. The jenny, therefore, played a major role in stimulating the transformation of the British cloth industry. The adjustments it forced in English labor organization offered an early glimpse of the great social changes that would be provoked by the later INDUSTRIAL REVOLUTION. The jenny was eclipsed at the end of the 18th century by the more efficient SPINNING MULE.

spinning mule Power-driven machine for spinning cotton yarn that combined the principles of the SPINNING JENNY and the WATER FRAME. The spinning mule was invented in 1779 by Samuel CROMPTON and made a significant technological contribution to the transformation of the English cloth industry during the early INDUSTRIAL REVOLUTION. The mule was considerably more efficient than either the jenny or the water frame. Each machine had anywhere from 200 to 300 spindles.

Because it produced a fine, strong yarn, the mule doubled the number of hanks of yarn that could be spun from a pound of raw cotton. The mule thus helped to create the tremendous increase in yarn supply that ultimately stimulated Edmund CARTWRIGHT to invent a POWER LOOM for weaving.

Spinoza, Benedict de (1632–1677) *Dutch philosopher, one of the major systematic rationalist philosophers of the 17th century*

The works of Benedict de Spinoza (Hebrew: Baruch Spinoza; Latin: Benedictus de Spinoza) provoked strong reactions, both negative and positive, during his lifetime and throughout the years of the ENLIGHTENMENT. Spinoza, a native of AMSTERDAM, came from a family of Portuguese Jews that had immigrated to the UNITED PROVINCES OF THE NETHERLANDS at the end of the 16th century. He received a traditional Jewish rabbinical education with immersion in the study of the Torah (the first five books of the Old Testament of the Bible), Talmud, and medieval Jewish philosophy. He also studied mathematics and the philosophy of René DESCARTES under a private tutor, Francis Van den Ende. Spinoza's native language was Spanish, but he also spoke Portuguese, Dutch, and German; and could read French, Italian, Latin, Hebrew, and some ancient Greek.

Spinoza could not accept orthodox Jewish teaching, a fact that caused him to be excommunicated in 1656 from the Amsterdam Jewish community. He became a professional grinder of optical lenses, devoting his extra time to the study and writing of philosophy.

Spinoza resided in Amsterdam until 1660, near Leiden from 1660 until 1663, and thereafter in the Dutch capital, The Hague. He never held an academic position, although he did refuse a post at the German University of Heidelberg. He died in 1677 of consumption (tuberculosis).

Spinoza developed a highly original system of philosophy that covered metaphysics (God and his relation to the world), EPISTEMOLOGY (theory of knowledge), MORAL PHILOSOPHY (the philosophical grounds for ethics), BIBLICAL CRITICISM, and POLITICAL THEORY. He published only two works during his lifetime: *Renati des Cartes Principiorum philosophiae* (Principles of the philosophy of René Descartes; 1663) and *Tractatus theologico-politicus* (published anonymously, 1670). His remaining works appeared posthumously as *Opera posthuma* (Posthumous works) in 1677. This publication contained the *Tractatus de intellectus emendatione* (Treatise on the correction of the understanding), the *Ethica ordine geometrico demonstrata* (Ethics demonstrated according to the geometrical order), and the *Tractatus politicus* (Political treatise).

Spinoza built his system on a geometric model derived from the method of Descartes. The *Ethica*, his most important work, is divided into sections, each of which contains a general proposition followed by detailed logical proofs. The system begins with a general proposition about the whole system of the universe, from which it proceeds to derive philosophies of knowledge, ethics, and politics.

At the foundation of Spinoza's philosophy lay his philosophical monism, the assertion that the universe contains only one substance, the divine substance. This divine substance has an infinite number of attributes (characteristics or qualities), any of which may be given specific real form in the universe. For Spinoza, the dualist view of the universe that separates God from nature, or mind from body, is incorrect. God and nature are simply different forms of the divine substance; mind and body are likewise different manifestations of the one divine substance. Spinoza summed up this view in the famous phrase *Deus sive Natura* (God or Nature).

It was this view that caused Spinoza to be accused of ATHEISM or pantheism by Christian theologians and philosophers. The Christian vision of God made a clear distinction between God and nature, emphasizing that God had created nature, much as a man might create a work of art. The Spinozist position clashed fundamentally with such a vision, suggesting that God is nature and is everywhere in nature.

Spinoza built his system of knowledge and of the rational order of the world on his monism. According to his vision, the thorny problems of the relationship between mind and body, or between physical sense experience and ideas, disappeared. If both mind and body are expressions of the same substance, their corresponding experiences (sensory perception for the body and ideas for the mind) must, of necessity, be derived from the same underlying laws, and must therefore agree with each other. This is Spinoza's version of the law of psychophysical parallelism—the law that guarantees not only that our experience of the world and our ideas about the world are truly related to each other, but also that our ideas about the world are accurate.

The monist philosophy also made it possible for Spinoza to offer a completely natural philosophical base for ethics and morality as an alternative to ethical systems rooted in religious revelation. According to Spinoza, human nature, operating according to unchangeable natural laws, reacts to all experiences with passive natural emotions of pleasure or pain. Pleasurable experiences are defined as good, painful experiences as bad; thus moral concepts are rooted in naturally occurring responses to experience.

Moral advancement comes when people free themselves from automatically following the passions. They can attain this freedom by developing active emotions, emotions that for Spinoza are governed by the intellect or REASON. Such active emotions produce either acts of courage (aimed at promoting the good of the individual actor) or of nobility (aimed at securing the good of the community).

Spinoza was often accused by 17th-century and 18th-century critics of robbing humankind of personal FREE-

DOM. These critics believed that behavior in his system of moral philosophy was completely determined, that there was no room left for the exercise of the free will. This was the same criticism they threw at materialists such as Thomas HOBBES, Julien Offray de LA METTRIE, and Claude-Adrien HELVÉTIUS.

Spinoza believed strongly in the PERFECTIBILITY of human beings and in the possibility of individual PROGRESS toward perfection. His ideal human somewhat resembled that ideal of ancient Stoicism: a person who lives a life governed by reason and is thus freed from blind obedience to the passions. Reason, therefore, guarantees freedom from the determinism of the passions and allows human progress.

Spinoza continued to emphasize freedom and the rule of reason in his political theory. The *Tractatus theologico-politicus* makes an argument for the foundation of political society on a social compact or contract. Spinoza's vision of the conditions that led up to the formation of political society resembles that of Thomas Hobbes, whose *De Cive* (On the citizen) and *Leviathan* he had read. But the *Tractatus theologico-politicus* departs dramatically from Hobbes in its prescriptions for relations between church and state.

Both men hated wars and persecution motivated by RELIGION and both desired to see such practices eliminated. Hobbes believed that the solution lay in subjugating the church completely to the state. Spinoza, on the other hand, supported religious TOLERATION so long as the activities of a group did not threaten the good of the larger society. In fact, where Hobbes generally prescribed total state control of human institutions and expression (ABSOLUTISM), Spinoza believed that the maintenance of freedom was essential. His ideal state was a DEMOCRACY, a form of government he considered the most natural.

Spinoza embedded a radical approach to the Bible in his *Tractatus theologico-politicus*. He treated the Old Testament simply as a HISTORY of the ancient Jewish people. The compact between the Jews and God was relevant to that ancient era but not to the modern era. Spinoza's use of the Bible as a history book offended and troubled his contemporaries, for he was violating, it seemed, the vision of the Bible as a revelation from God of universal, eternal truths. His approach, however, would be picked up in the 18th century by both critics of revealed religion and devout biblical scholars.

The reception of Spinozist philosophy in Europe was largely hostile until the second half of the 18th century. In fact, the term *Spinozist* was often used in a pejorative sense to smear a person with the taint of atheism and materialism. This negative tradition began with Pierre BAYLE, whose *HISTORICAL AND CRITICAL DICTIONARY* attacked Spinoza's system. Bayle's assessment was continued by the French PHILOSOPHES who generally rejected Spinoza's system even when they admired his originality. The ENCYCLOPÉDIE contained a negative article on Spinozism by Denis DIDEROT that essentially repeated Bayle's viewpoint. VOLTAIRE, who admired aspects of Spinoza's political theory, nevertheless ridiculed him as "the dupe of his geometrical spirit."

In GERMANY, Gottfried Wilhelm LEIBNIZ was impressed with Spinoza's intellect but disturbed by the implicit determinism in his philosophy. Leibniz tried to develop a system of philosophy that would utilize certain strengths of the Spinozist vision, while avoiding its alleged determinism and materialism. A fresh assessment of Spinoza emerged about 1780 among German intellectuals, when a quarrel known as the *Pantheismusstreit* (Pantheism Quarrel) broke out between Friedrich Heinrich JACOBI and Moses MENDELSSOHN. Jacobi had accused Gotthold Ephraim LESSING of pantheism and Spinozism, a charge that Mendelssohn wished to dispute. In the process, the contents of Spinozism were discussed, allowing young German intellectuals to gain knowledge of the system. Johann Wolfgang von GOETHE and Johann Gottfried HERDER became avid fans of Spinoza as a result, and Spinozism provided important intellectual foundations for the later innovations of German *Naturphilosophie* (nature philosophy) during the era of romanticism.

See also MATHEMATICS AND MECHANICS; PSYCHOLOGY; RADICAL ENLIGHTENMENT; RATIONALISM.

Further reading: Benedict de Spinoza, *On the Improvement of the Understanding, The Ethics, and The Correspondence,* tr. R. H. M. Elwes (New York: Dover Publications, 1951); Benedict de Spinoza, *A Theologico-Political Treatise and A Political Treatise,* tr. R. H. M. Elwes (New York: Dover Publications, 1951).

Spirit of Laws, The Book on POLITICAL THEORY by Charles-Louis de Secondat, baron de MONTESQUIEU; first published in GENEVA in 1748. Unlike the *PERSIAN LETTERS,* *The Spirit of Laws* (original French title: *L'Esprit des Lois*) was freely distributed in FRANCE, even though the censors never gave it official approval. An immediate success, it sold out 22 editions in two years but also earned a spot on the Catholic Index of Forbidden Books.

A large and seemingly disorganized volume consisting of 31 sections, *The Spirit of Laws* represents Montesquieu's attempt to write a natural HISTORY of political society. Montesquieu modeled his investigation on the idea of natural history spelled out by Francis BACON. He collected facts about human existence and described elements of political, social, and economic organization in various states across the whole of time. From this collection of facts, Montesquieu derived certain principles whose action, he believed, had shaped the course of events in history. This endeavor served as an example of the scientific, experimental, inductive method at its best, but applied to the study of people rather than to natural phenomena.

Montesquieu intended to criticize several popular approaches to the analysis of political society: the universal history of Jacques-Bénigne BOSSUET; the rational histories based in NATURAL LAW by Thomas HOBBES and Samuel PUFENDORF; the liberal theory rooted in the concept of PROPERTY by John LOCKE; all forms of social contract theory; and the standard empirical histories, which, using the criterion of utility, judged the value of a political order only according to how well it worked.

From his vast collection of observations, Montesquieu derived a scheme of distinct forms of government: republics, monarchies, and despotisms. Republics could be either democratic (rule by many) or aristocratic (rule by the few); monarchies had one ruler whose powers were limited by laws; despotisms consisted of rule by one individual who was unrestrained by law or any other human institution. To each form of government, Montesquieu also assigned an underlying animating principle that rules its actions much as the soul or will operates in the human body. Virtue animates republics; honor rules monarchies; and fear rules in despotisms.

With this typology, Montesquieu was trying to illustrate the relationships between the character of a people (formed partly by environment and climate) and its form of government. He believed that this character not only demands certain forms of government but also shapes the specific nature of the positive laws of societies.

The question of FREEDOM—how it is expressed and how it is maintained—informed much of Montesquieu's work. He believed that certain environmental conditions—rugged mountains for instance—make it easier for human beings to protect their liberties. But he also believed that the form of laws and political structure can either help or hinder the expression of individual liberty.

One of his aims was to illustrate that in France and other large states the republic was not a viable form of government. Republics had flourished best in simple societies lacking multiple social and economic divisions. France, in contrast, was a complex society marked by the coexistence of agrarian, commercial, and other interests. The motives behind action in France were dominated by perceptions of SELF-INTEREST, a situation that would not support traditional republican virtues. The problem for Montesquieu was to identify a government form that could create an artificial form of civic virtue based on the operation of self-interest. The same problem preoccupied political theorists such as John Locke, Adam SMITH, and Bernard MANDEVILLE.

In fact, Montesquieu believed that the best form of government for a large nation was a limited monarchy of the type he had observed in ENGLAND. Such a government consisted of a ruler (king) whose power was limited (mediated) by an intermediary body. Montesquieu believed that in France, the aristocracy of the robe (the ennobled lawyers, judges, and officials) could serve as this intermediary body. They would stand between the king and the rest of his subjects, making laws that would balance the interests of all in the society. Their sense of honor would ensure that they would tailor their concepts of self-interest to fit those of the nation.

In describing the system of England, Montesquieu spelled out the concept of the SEPARATION OF POWERS, a system in which executive and legislative duties are assigned to different individuals or groups. He believed that such a separation of powers preserves freedom by setting up a system of checks and balances, which in turn creates a dynamic equilibrium capable of minimizing abuses of authority.

Certain of Montesquieu's contemporaries believed that he was simply offering an apology for the claims of his own class (he was a member of the robe aristocracy). But this criticism did not prevent his ideas from exercising a strong influence on the political theory of the ENLIGHTENMENT. Liberal reformers throughout Europe turned to *The Spirit of Laws* for inspiration. Both the American rebels and the French revolutionaries derived ideas from Montesquieu, and the UNITED STATES CONSTITUTION made the principle of the separation of powers the foundation of the new nation's political structure.

Staël, Anne-Louise-Germaine Necker, Madame de
(1766–1817) *French salon hostess, government critic, and writer*

The daughter of Jacques NECKER, a Swiss banker who became director general of finance in FRANCE, and of Suzanne Curchod NECKER, Anne-Louise-Germaine Necker grew up frequenting the enlightened salons hosted by her parents in PARIS and outside GENEVA. At the age of 20 (1786), she was married to a Swedish baron, Erik Magnus de Staël-Holstein, who was the Swedish ambassador in Paris. The marriage lasted until 1797.

Madame de Staël (as she was commonly called) was committed to the ideals of FREEDOM, human PROGRESS, and liberal political reform. Her major source of inspiration was Jean-Jacques ROUSSEAU, whose image of authentic religious expression she especially admired.

These commitments were reflected in her actions during the FRENCH REVOLUTION. Using her protected status as an ambassador's wife, she sheltered French intellectuals and friends from imprisonment until the intensification of political crisis during the Reign of Terror forced her to flee from Paris. She returned to France in 1794 after the downfall of Maximilien ROBESPIERRE and operated a salon where major intellectual figures gathered. She also entered into a stormy love affair with Benjamin Constant (1767–1830), an influential writer, political theorist, and politician. Madame de Staël spoke out openly against Napoleon Bonaparte after he started gathering all French power into his own hands. She was exiled from France in 1802 for having advocated constitutional monarchy and representative political forms.

A writer of novels and of cultural criticism, Madame de Staël left works in both realms that provide insight into her particular understanding of the ideals of the ENLIGHTENMENT. Her influential book, *De l'Allemagne* (On Germany; 1810–13), used the concept of an environmentally and socially conditioned national character to highlight differences between the French and Germans. The theme of national character had found its most powerful enlightened expression in THE SPIRIT OF LAWS by MONTESQUIEU, and had been developed along radically different lines by Johann Gottfried HERDER. Madame de Staël's book introduced French readers to the ideas of Immanuel KANT, Johann Gottlieb Fichte (1762–1814), Friedrich Wilhelm Joseph von Schelling (1775–1854), and Friedrich von Schlegel (1772–1829).

An earlier work by Madame de Staël, *De la littérature considérée dans ses rapports avec les institutions sociales* (On literature considered in its relations to social institutions; 1800), investigated the reciprocal RELATIONS between LITERATURE and the institutions of RELIGION, morals, and law.

Madame de Staël's novels include *Delphine* (1802) and *Corinne* (1807). In addition, she wrote *Lettres sur le caractère et les écrits de J. J. Rousseau* (Letters on the character and writings of J. J. Rousseau; 1788); *De l'influence des passions sur le bonheur des individus et des nations* (On the influence of the passions on the happiness of individuals and of nations; 1796); and *Dix années d'exil* (Ten years in exile; 1821).

See also AESTHETICS; HAPPINESS; MORAL PHILOSOPHY; POLITICAL THEORY; SOCIAL INSTITUTIONS OF THE ENLIGHTENMENT.

Stahl, Georg Ernst (1659 or 1660–1734) *German chemist and physician, who provided theories of central concern for scientists of the late Enlightenment*

His PHLOGISTON THEORY dominated late-18th-century chemistry until it was displaced by theories associated with the CHEMICAL REVOLUTION. In theoretical treatments of living organisms, Stahl's ANIMISM helped to create alternatives to the influential MECHANICAL PHILOSOPHY.

Stahl's early life remains shrouded in mystery. Even the date of his birth is a matter disputed by scholars. Stahl studied MEDICINE at the University of Jena, received his degree in 1684, and accepted an invitation to Weimar as court physician in 1687. He remained at Weimar for seven years, then moved to the newly established University of HALLE, where, from 1694 until 1715, he lectured on the theories of medicine and chemistry. In 1715, Stahl moved to BERLIN, where he served as court physician to King Frederick William I of PRUSSIA. Stahl remained in Berlin until his death in 1734.

Stahl was a devout believer in PIETISM, and some scholars assume that this religious background helped to shape his scientific theories. Stahl never presented his theories systematically; rather, they must be pieced together from his complex and copious writings. Stahl

insisted that a fundamental difference exists between inanimate matter and living organisms. He asserted that living beings are organized in a holistic system of synergies, that is, in organic relations in which the various unique parts of a body are interrelated. According to this viewpoint, a change in one part of the body affects all other parts. Stahl also insisted that mind must be distinguished from matter: Mind is immaterial whereas matter occupies space (is extended). In opposition to Gottfried Wilhelm LEIBNIZ's theory of preestablished harmony, which denied the ability of mind to influence matter, Stahl argued that mind could act directly on matter. Mind manifests itself primarily as *anima*, an immaterial entity that directs all activities of the organism toward certain goals. Stahl contrasted this type of organization from that of dead matter in which parts are independent and related only through simple mechanical laws.

Armed with this theory, Stahl developed medical approaches that countered the tendencies of IATROCHEMISTRY and IATROMECHANICS to reduce medical phenomena to chemical principles or to mechanical laws. He stressed the complexity of states of health and illness, and he suggested that the maintenance of circulation, secretion, and excretion play an important role in ensuring the preservation of health. Stahl also asserted that the human will can play a role in curing disease, a position that grew directly from his insistence that spirit or mind influences matter. Hence, he considered the patient's mental state to be as important to the healing process as any medication or surgical procedure. He opposed the practices of bloodletting and of extreme purges, and rejected the use of drugs such as opium.

Stahl believed that the atomistic (corpuscular) vision of chemical reactions supported by the mechanical philosophy was wrong. In its place, he sought to create a chemistry from the combination of two traditional qualitative chemical concepts: the concept of elements and the concept of active chemical principles. Stahl followed an earlier German chemist, J. J. Becher, in speaking of three elements: earth, water, and air. Earth, however, existed in three different forms that provided substances with the different characteristics of volatility, oiliness or solidity. These three forms of earth each embodied one of the three active chemical principles. The second form of earth, the one that provided moistness and oiliness, embodied the principle traditionally called sulfur. Stahl called it "phlogiston". Phlogiston could be separated from the bodies in which it existed, and it was the chief "actor" in combustion processes.

By the end of the 18th century, most European scientists had abandoned Stahl's chemical theories. The discovery of oxygen by Joseph PRIESTLEY, Carl SCHEELE, and Antoine LAVOISIER laid the ground for the modern oxygen theories of combustion that replaced phlogiston theory. Also, during the latter part of the 18th century, the medical theory of VITALISM generally discredited animism even while it retained some of the Stahlian emphasis on holistic life principles. Despite these developments, many medical writers at the end of the century still considered Stahl one of the greatest physicians ever to have lived.

Although often slighted by modern historians of science as an example of misdirected scientific spirit, Stahl, in fact, was one of the most influential figures in 18th-century chemistry and life sciences.

Important published works by Stahl include *Theoria medica vera, physiologiam et pathologiam . . . sistens* (True medical theory . . . causing physiology and pathology; 1708); *Zymotechnia fundamentalis* (1697); *Specimen Beccherianum* (The Becherian model, published in Becher's *Physica subterranea* [Subterranean physics]; 1703); and *Zufällige Gedancken . . . über den Streit von den sogennanten Sulphure* (Chance thoughts . . . on the dispute over so-called sulphur; 1718). The latter work was translated by Baron d'HOLBACH into French as *Traité du soufre* (Treatise on sulfur, 1766). A composite work written by Stahl's pupils, *Fundamenta chymiae dogmaticae et experimentalis* (Foundations of dogmatic and experimental chemistry; 1723), was translated into English and published as the *Philosophical Principles of Universal Chemistry* by Peter Shaw in 1730.

Stamitz, Carl (1745–1801) *German composer and performer*

Carl Stamitz was a leading member of the MANNHEIM SCHOOL of composers and performers. His symphonies, *symphonies concertantes* (works for orchestra and two or more solo instruments), and concertos defined the musical style of the Mannheim school during the last third of the 18th century.

Stamitz was born in Mannheim, in what is now GERMANY. His father, Johann, composed some of the most important early symphonies and helped turn Mannheim into a center for groundbreaking music and renowned orchestral performances. Carl studied first with his father, who died when he was 11, and then with other important members of the Mannheim musical establishment from his father's generation. Stamitz thus received solid training both as a composer as well as a performer on the violin, VIOLA, and viola d'amore.

In 1770, Stamitz went to PARIS, and within a year he had secured a position as composer and conductor to Duke Louis de Noailles. In this capacity, Stamitz traveled extensively, and he also performed regularly at the *Concert spirituel* in Paris. In 1777, Stamitz left Paris and began a career as a traveling virtuoso, playing in cities such as LONDON, The Hague, Hamburg, BERLIN (where he was the concertmaster in a massive performance of George Frederick HANDEL's *Messiah* in 1786), Dresden, Prague, and Kassel (where he directed a series of concerts in 1789 and 1790). In 1795, he visited Mannheim before

settling in Jena, where he had accepted a post teaching music at the university. He died there in 1801.

Stamitz's importance for 18th-century music is twofold. First, he was part of a generation of composers and performers who left the relative security of a steady position at a princely court to pursue careers as traveling virtuosos or freelance composers. (The best-known of these musicians is Wolfgang Amadeus MOZART.) Second, Stamitz composed nearly 150 orchestral works that played an important part in shaping the classical symphony and concerto. As a result of his travels, his music circulated widely and influenced composers in many of Europe's larger cities.

See also CLASSICISM, MUSIC; SYMPHONY ORCHESTRA.

statistics   The science of numerical analysis, intended to find patterns of occurrence and predictable trends. The drive among ENLIGHTENMENT philosophers to catalog and understand the rational principles that lay behind natural phenomena led to the development of analytical tools, among them statistics, that sought to analyze volumes of information, such as population figures, to determine present patterns and predict future phenomena.

Two precursors of the modern field of statistics were developed during the 17th and 18th centuries: the political arithmetic of English researchers, and the descriptive statistics arising in GERMANY. The former is often recognized as closer to modern statistical analysis because of its emphasis on mathematical manipulation of focused selections of data, such as birth and death rates. Researchers advocated the meticulous gathering of demographic information, driven by the developing governmental trend of record keeping intended to quantify and fix the information available for individual citizens. This data was then classified into standardized categories and analyzed in comparisons designed to show a range of relationships, such as changes in birth rates over time in a particular city. Although population growth was an important theme, it should also be noted that contemporaries applied these methods to public finances, economic developments, religious affiliations, and military topics, among many other things.

The German model, while lacking the other's analytical force, provided an alternative but important emphasis on the exhaustive study of the qualities of a group of people by gathering as wide a range of descriptive information as possible, such as birthplaces and religious affiliations. This was a product of the German CAMERALIST tradition of *Polizeiwissenschaft*, which saw statistics as the orderly presentation of information relevant to the state. These approaches to population description were well established in the 18th century at colleges such as the University of GÖTTINGEN, which was the first to possess a defined school of statistics. Significantly, as part of the kingdom of Hanover, Göttin-

Mathematician Karl Gauss (1777–1855) on the terrace of the Göttingen Observatory with the heliotrope instrument that he invented *(Courtesy New York Public Library)*

gen was also a possession of Britain's Hanoverian dynasty, which made it a key point for importing English ideas. Thus, as this branch of statistics developed in the early 1800s it began to take on aspects of English political arithmetic as researchers increasingly sought cross-sectional analyses (comparisons of data from the same time period) of the descriptive information they had gathered.

Other European powers developed statistical methods that illustrated aspects of both schools. Attempts in FRANCE in the 18th century to codify physical information about the country's geographical qualities (size and physical features, including rivers and mineral deposits) and boundaries were joined to attempts to quantify population information, such as the number of residents in cities and towns. Both these projects grew from the monarchy's desire to measure the nation's economic potential and improve it by cataloging accurate data and using such information to solve problems and improve economic development. Statistics also addressed the need for accurate population and economic information to aid the monarchy's response to national disasters, such as the Marseilles epidemic of 1720.

Government classification of populations was not always readily accepted. One of the greatest outcries against such research occurred in 1753, when the English government considered taking a general census of the nation; the Whigs mobilized political opposition to what was seen as an infringement on liberties as well as a French idea, so that the development of the field of statistics in England suffered for decades afterward.

See also DEMOGRAPHY; EDUCATION; MATHEMATICS AND MECHANICS.

Further reading: Alain Desrosiers, *The Politics of Large Numbers: A History of Statistical Reasoning* tr. Camille Naish (Cambridge, Mass.: Harvard University Press, 1998); D. V. Glass, *Numbering the People: The Great Demography Controversy* (New York: Gordon & Cremonesi, 1973); Helen M. Walker, *Studies in the History of Statistical Methods* (Baltimore: Williams & Wilkins, 1929); Harald Westergaard, *Contributions to the History of Statistics* (New York: Agathon Press, 1968).

steam engine A seminal technological invention of the British INDUSTRIAL REVOLUTION. Historians of technology consider the primitive steam engine invented by Thomas NEWCOMEN in 1705 to be the first viable modern engine. It harnessed an entirely new source of inanimate power and transferred that power into mechanical action. The power provided by steam far surpassed what had been provided by wind, running water, human beings, or horses.

The Newcomen steam engine worked by creating a vacuum behind a piston. The piston was activated by atmospheric pressure moving to fill the vacuum. Experimental devices that operated on these principles had been created by Otto von Guericke, Christian Huyghens, and Denis Papin in the 17th century. But Newcomen's engine was the first steam engine that was a usable engine. The first known installation of a Newcomen engine occurred in 1712 at a coal mine near Wolverhampton, England.

The Newcomen engine dominated 18th-century manufacturing even after the invention by James WATT of a more efficient two-cylinder engine.

See also TECHNOLOGY AND INSTRUMENTATION.

Steele, Richard (1672–1729) *Irish-born essayist, dramatist, and publisher, with Joseph Addison, of the influential journal called* The Spectator

Steele played a primary role in developing a new literary form, the periodical essay. His work contributed significantly to the creation of a new literary sensibility opposed to the aristocratic values of Restoration-period LITERATURE. The new form espoused the ideals, values, and lifestyles that were developing in the English middle classes.

Richard Steele, born in Dublin, Ireland, and fatherless after 1676, was raised under the guardianship of an uncle, Henry Gascoigne. Gascoigne had Steele educated at the Charterhouse School and at Oxford University. Steele met Joseph ADDISON during his school years, and the two became fast friends. Steele left Oxford without a degree, served in the army (1692–1705), and then settled in LONDON where he launched a career in periodical writing and publishing.

In 1709, he began publishing *The Tatler,* a journal devoted to teaching manners and morals to the English reading public. *The Tatler* purported to be written from different London coffeehouses and to be reporting on the social and intellectual life of these popular social institutions of the ENLIGHTENMENT. Steele's essays appeared under the name of Isaac Bickerstaff, who was a character in an earlier satirical piece by Jonathan SWIFT. Addison began contributing articles in the 18th issue of the journal. Despite its success, Steele was pressured to cease publication of *The Tatler* in 1710 when the Tory Party resumed power in ENGLAND.

In 1711, Steele and Addison began producing THE SPECTATOR (1711–12, 1714). It was an immediate success, popular among English-reading audiences throughout Europe.

Steele continued producing journals after the demise of *The Spectator.* Their number includes *The Guardian* (1713), *The Englishman* (1713–14, 1715), *The Lover* (1714), *The Reader* (1714), *Town-Talk* (1715–16), and *The Theatre* (1720).

Steele entered politics in 1713 as a Whig Party member of the House of Commons. By 1714, he was pressured to resign on account of his unpopular support for the idea of the Hanoverian succession. After Queen Anne died in late 1714 and the Hanoverian George I actually assumed the throne, Steele was able to revive his political career, and he served in Parliament from 1715 until 1724. He also received the directorship of the Drury Lane Theatre in 1714.

In addition to his journalistic essays, Steele's writings include three comedies, *The Funeral* (1701), *The Lying Lover* (1703), and *The Tender Husband* (1705) and a serious drama, *Conscious Lovers* (1722). He also wrote a devotional manual called *The Christian Hero* (1701).

Steele's early existence was constantly troubled by shortages of money. The death of his first wife, Margaret Stretch, in 1705 provided him with an annuity of £850 per year. His subsequent literary successes helped to secure him financially. His second marriage, to Mary Scurlock, the "dear Prue" of his correspondence, brought four children, only one of whom survived him.

See also PUBLISHING; SOCIAL INSTITUTIONS OF THE ENLIGHTENMENT.

Sterne, Laurence (1713–1768) *Irish-born novelist*

As a member of the Anglican clergy, Sterne was the vicar of the parish Sutton-in-the-Forest. He turned to writing later in life, using his experiences in the church as material for his literary creations. Sterne wrote in a critical vein, veiling his pointed observations in humor. He especially questioned the faith in REASON and an ordered NATURE that had dominated the early ENLIGHTENMENT. Sterne emphasized the positive roles that spontaneous feeling, benevolence, and SYMPATHY play in cementing human relations. He opposed a world wedded rigorously to cold reason or to its clerical counterpart, theological dogma. He also questioned standard ideas about childhood, EDUCATION, conception, birth, maturity, and death. Thus, Sterne acted as an important social critic who did not hesitate to explore fundamental questions about human life and destiny.

Sterne elaborated these views in his multivolumed novel, *The Life and Opinions of Tristram Shandy, Gentleman* (1759–67). The book enjoyed sensational success and was widely imitated in Europe. In addition to TRIS-

TRAM SHANDY, Sterne produced *A Sentimental Journey through France and Italy* (1768), an exploration of the experiences of a GRAND TOUR of the European continent; *Sermons of Mr. Yorick* (1760–66); and *Letters of Yorick to Eliza* (1766–67).

See also ANGLICANS; LITERATURE; RELIGION; ROWLANDSON; SANCHO.

Stowe English house and grounds of Sir Richard Temple, viscount Cobham, that came to represent the 18th-century taste for the neoclassical ideal. Cobham was an army officer and political figure in the 18th century during the administration of Robert WALPOLE. He was in and out of favor over the years with both the king and the prince of Wales.

When Cobham was not engaging in war or politics, he devoted himself to his lands. He inherited and renovated Stowe House in 1697 and continued to renovate into the 1740s. He also made extensive changes to the grounds by hiring artists to create its large and impressive gardens and fill them with temples and statues of ancient Greek and Roman intellectuals.

Many literary figures, such as Alexander POPE and Jonathon SWIFT, were visitors at Stowe. William CONGREVE was another frequent guest, and there is a funerary monument in his honor on the grounds. Stowe itself is lauded in the works of Pope, Congreve, and the writer Gilbert West, among others. Many parliamentary ministers were also received at Stowe, and Cobham's nephews, including William Pitt, all trained there for their political careers.

The most remarkable features of Stowe are its 400 acres of landscaped gardens. Cobham hired the best artists of the time to transform the LANDSCAPE of Stowe. Capability BROWN designed several of the gardens, which contain ornamental temples and statuary by William KENT.

Despite his dedication to his gardens, Cobham did not abandon politics. In the gardens of Stowe visitors could view political symbols critical of the corruption of the Walpole administration. For example, the Temple of Ancient Virtue, designed by Kent, was in perfect condition, reflecting the good of ancient politics. Meanwhile, the Temple of Modern Virtue, by the architect James Gibbs, was built as a ruin to critique the failures of the Walpole administration.

The gardens at Stowe are an ideal example of the 18th-century English landscaped garden. The house and gardens also provide examples of 18th-century English neoclassical ART AND ARCHITECTURE. With more than 40 features of interest, the Stowe estate, which now also includes a school, is open to the public and continues to be a source of inspiration today.

See also NATURE.

Struensee, Johann Friedrich, count von (1737–1772) *court physician who became chief councillor to Christian VII of Denmark and Norway and the acknowledged lover of the queen*

CHRISTIAN VII was mentally unstable, and Struensee, as chief councillor, virtually usurped absolute power between March 1771 and January 1772. Struensee instigated a series of reforms, characteristic of enlightened despotism (see DESPOTISM, ENLIGHTENED), which embodied some of the major goals of enlightened POLITICAL THEORY. He attacked the royal budget by introducing a series of stringent economizing measures and therefore putting a large number of officials out of work. These men became one source of the protest that eventually proved his undoing. Struensee revised the legal system in DENMARK, abolished torture, and revised the penal code. He promised all subjects EQUALITY before the law, advancement in government service based on merit rather than status, and religious TOLERATION. He began to dismantle the long-standing regulations that governed labor and trade. He also created a public hygiene and sanitation system that was unique in the 18th century.

Struensee carried out his reforms with thoroughness, ruthlessness, and complete disregard for the interests of those whose privileges and livelihood were being so radically altered. His political enemies succeeded in convincing the incapable Christian VII that his minister had overstepped the proper bounds of power. Using the pretext of Struensee's affair with his queen, Christian VII signed an order for his powerful minister's arrest in January 1772. The Struensee experiments came to an end with the public execution of their creator two months later.

Stubbs, George (1724–1806) *English painter*
Son of a Liverpool tanner, Stubbs studied painting as an apprentice to Hamlet Winstanley for a few weeks and thereafter developed his talent independently. He became an outstanding painter of animals, especially noted for his powerful depictions of horses. Stubbs relied both on natural observation of living animals and on detailed study of animal anatomy through the activity of laboratory dissections. Besides his animal paintings and anatomical studies, other notable pictures depict ordinary countryside activities. He also attempted without much success to paint narrative historical subjects.

As the years passed, Stubbs's depiction of NATURE began to change. His earlier paintings such as *Mare and Foals in a Country Landscape* (ca. 1660) show the idyllic, benign side of nature in a manner consistent with ROCOCO style. His later paintings, however, such as *Lion Attacking a Horse* (1770), portray the violent and stormy side of nature in a manner that suggests that Stubbs was making a transition toward the more complex moral conception of nature that characterized the late ENLIGHTENMENT.

In addition to paintings, Stubbs created etchings and prints for book illustrations. He contributed 18 plates for *An Essay Towards a Complete New System of Midwifery* (1751) by Dr. John Burton. He also produced etchings for and published *The Anatomy of the Horse* (1766), a major reference for scientists and artists. Toward the end of his life, Stubbs worked on drawings and engravings for *A Comparative Anatomical Exposition of the Structure of the Human Body, with that of a Tiger and Common Fowl.* His death in 1806 prevented completion of the project.

Sturm und Drang A literary movement of the late ENLIGHTENMENT decades of the 1770s and 1780s. It occurred primarily in German territories such as PRUSSIA, Weimar, and Saxony. The name *Sturm und Drang* (storm and stress) was taken directly from *Der Wirrwarr, oder Sturm und Drang* (Chaos, or storm and stress; 1776), a play by Friedrich Maximilian von Klinger (1752–1831) in which the action occurred in the AMERICAN REVOLUTION.

The *Sturm und Drang* movement had its roots in the rebellion by a group of young German writers and intellectuals against the concept of an ordered, harmonious NATURE. Restraints of any kind—whether imposed by rules in AESTHETICS, by NATURAL LAW, by social convention, or by political authorities—were rejected. *Sturm und Drang* adherents carried the aesthetic ideas of Moses MENDELSSOHN and Friedrich LESSING to extremes, transforming them into impassioned defenses of human creative FREEDOM. In addition to stressing freedom and INDIVIDUALISM, *Sturm und Drang* writers emphasized the role played by creative GENIUS in literary productions. They conceived of themselves as geniuses, closer to the gods than to mortal men.

The primary creators of this movement were Johann Wolfgang von GOETHE, Friedrich SCHILLER, and Johann Gottfried HERDER. Goethe wrote his play *Goetz von Berlichingen* (Goetz of Berlichingen; 1773) as a protest against the forms and rules imposed by NEOCLASSICISM. But it was his novel *Die Leiden des jungen Werthers* (THE SORROWS OF YOUNG WERTHER; 1774) that bequeathed a central hero and model to the discontented *Sturm und Drang* generation. The influence of Goethe's protagonist Werther was matched by that of the characters in Schiller's play, *Die Räuber* (The Robbers). Other participants in the *Sturm und Drang* movement were a group of lesser-known writers such as H. L. Wagner, M. R. Lenz, Wilhelm Heinse, and the members of the Göttingen poetic circle called *Der Hain* (The Grove).

Some historians maintain that *Sturm und Drang* had a musical counterpart in the musical EMPFINDSAMER STIL. This style consciously sought to depict human emotions and to break conventional rules of composition in a manner suggestive of the rebellion associated with *Sturm und Drang* writers.

See also LITERATURE; ROMANTICISM.

style galant French term for gallant style, a musical style sometimes also called ROCOCO that emerged in ITALY and FRANCE after 1720. The term *galant* was commonly used to refer to chic, pleasing modes of behavior. The *style galant* gave musical form to the ideals of the culture of SENSIBILITY, that aspect of the ENLIGHTENMENT that helped give birth to the rococo aesthetic. *Style galant* MUSIC aimed at expressing sentiment and feeling, rejecting the so-called learned music of the baroque era. It is usually distinguished also from its slightly later 18th-century musical cousin, EMPFINDSAMER STIL.

To accomplish its goals, *style galant* music relied on the copious ornamentation of simple melodies. The ornaments imparted a lighthearted nature to this music that made it a natural companion to the activities of enlightened salons. *Style galant* music was meant to be played in intimate settings rather than in grand structures such as churches or royal palaces. To critics, this music was supple and delightful but empty; it did nothing but "tickle" the ear.

Outstanding examples of *style galant* music can be heard in the compositions of Baldassare Galuppi (1706–85), Georg Philipp TELEMANN, and Johann Joachim Quantz (1697–1773).

See also SOCIAL INSTITUTIONS OF THE ENLIGHTENMENT.

sublime A term capturing the experience of exalted, lofty, intense emotions often associated with danger or passionate sexuality. The concept of the sublime as a distinct form of artistic representation and experience began to appear in theories of AESTHETICS after 1750. With the emergence of this new theory, the aesthetics of the ENLIGHTENMENT entered a new era.

Prior to the 1750s, discussions about artistic truths and values had focused primarily on the concept of beauty. Beauty had been associated with various forms, regular or irregular, straight or curving, depending on whether a theorist favored neoclassical or ROCOCO styles. In both cases, the expression of beauty was separated from strong emotion. If feelings were evoked at all, they were the delicate ones of delight rather than the raging ones of passion.

With the concept of the sublime, the passions—violent emotions of love, hate, awe, and fear—were readmitted to the arts and assigned a special creative value. Representations of NATURE, whether in painting, poetry, or music, began to emphasize its violent, chaotic, and frightening elements.

The first formulation of a theory of the sublime appeared in a work by Edmund BURKE entitled *Philosophical Inquiry into the Origin of Our Ideas on the Sublime and the Beautiful* (1757). Burke separated the sublime from the beautiful and linked their differences to their specific physiological effects. The beautiful causes the solid parts of the body to relax, while the sublime produces tension. The sublime emphasizes the isolation and individuality of human experience, whereas the beautiful urges people toward a refined life within civilized society.

Burke's ideas were transmitted to the *AUFKLÄRUNG* (German Enlightenment) through a translation by Moses MENDELSSOHN. Before he translated Burke, Mendelssohn had written his *Betrachtungen über das Erhabene und das Naive in den schönen Wissenschaften* (Contemplations on the sublime and the naive in the fine arts; 1757). The work contained a distinction between the sublime and the naive (the simple and graceful), which Mendelssohn had derived from the works of Anthony Ashley Cooper, third earl of SHAFTESBURY. The sublime became a central concept for the later generations of enlightened German writers, receiving theoretical treatment from Johann Georg HAMANN and Johann Gottfried HERDER. The young Immanuel KANT also addressed the concept in a work entitled *Observations on the Feeling of the Beautiful and the Sublime* (1763).

In the meantime, painters, writers, dramatists, and some composers were trying to represent the sublime in their works. Paintings tended to represent the violent aspects of nature and the irrational expressions of the human psyche. Examples from painting include *Lion Attacking a Horse* by George STUBBS, *The Nightmare* by John Henry FUSELI, and *The Bard* by John Martin. LITERATURE concentrated on forms such as the GOTHIC ROMANCE, on dramatic elegies, and ballads.

The sublime exercised an important influence on the artistic expressions of ROMANTICISM and is often associated exclusively with that post-Enlightenment movement. However, the concept is actually a creation of the Enlightenment that developed out of efforts to deal with the role of the passions in human nature. It thus can be treated as one of those concepts whose content was ambivalent: Although born in the context of the Enlightenment, it was capable of translating into a different intellectual and aesthetic era.

subtle fluids   One of the primary physical theories in 18th-century science. The theory was developed from Isaac NEWTON's notion of "ether," a concept that he used in his private manuscripts but never published during his lifetime. Ether was a fluid substance that consisted of minute particles and allegedly filled all spaces between tangible matter. The ether fluid was weightless, or at least could not be weighed because of the tiny size of its particles. The ether theory allowed Newton to avoid positing the existence of empty spaces (vacuum) in NATURE and provided a mechanical explanation for the action of gravity in the solar system. It thus protected Newton from being accused of supporting the idea of physical action across distances, a notion that was suspect because of its ties with natural magic. Subtle-fluid theories served similar purposes in describing and explaining actions between the atoms of matter in terrestrial bodies.

Eighteenth-century scientists began developing various subtle-fluid theories in the 1740s when Newton's ideas about ether were first published. Subtle fluids were enlisted to explain phenomena such as heat, temperature, electrical charge, electrical tension, and heat capacity—all phenomena that were associated with the troublesome Aristotelian elements called fire and air.

Eighteenth-century subtle fluids retained all the characteristics of Newton's ether: They were fluid matter composed of tiny particles that escaped detection through weighing, and thus they were treated as weightless. It was also assumed that the particles of subtle fluid were self-repulsive, causing the fluid to expand indefinitely if unrestrained.

The theory of subtle fluids actually aided early processes of quantification in chemistry and physics. The CALORIC theory of heat developed by Antoine LAVOISIER was a subtle-fluid theory, as was the electrical one-fluid theory advanced by Benjamin FRANKLIN.

See also SCIENCE.

superstition   In modern usage, beliefs and ritual practices resulting from ignorance, fear of the unknown, or trust in MAGIC and chance. During the ENLIGHTENMENT, radical critics of RELIGION called any belief in miracles, revelation, magic, or the supernatural, a superstition. They often equated most Christian doctrine with superstition.

During the 17th century, a campaign had been mounted by orthodox Christian theologians, both Catholic and Protestant, against the practice of magic. These undesirable practices were labeled superstition, and practitioners of magic were persecuted as heretics. Enlightened 18th-century critics of religion spelled out the similarities between heretical superstitions and orthodox beliefs, underscoring the fact that all miracles, for example, were unnatural events that disobeyed the normal laws operating in the universe. They particularly attacked the traditions surrounding the miracles of Jesus Christ and the saints. By equating all Christian beliefs except those accessible to unaided REASON with superstition, these critics of religion succeeded in turning the 17th-century Christian campaign against magic and superstition into a campaign against Christianity itself.

The pairing of Christianity with superstition often contained implicit attacks on religious ENTHUSIASM, on intolerance, and on closely intertwined relations of power between church and state. Prominent enlightened writers associated with the attack on superstition were Pierre BAYLE, David HUME, and VOLTAIRE.

See also SEPARATION OF CHURCH AND STATE; TOLERATION.

Süssmilch, Johann Peter (1707–1767) *German population theorist*
A native of the Prussian capital BERLIN, Süssmilch was sent by his parents to study Latin and law at the University of

HALLE. He decided to enter the ministry, supplementing training in Protestant theology with courses in philosophy, mathematics, and physics at the University of Jena.

Süssmilch acquired his first position in 1736 as a chaplain in the Prussian army. He served in the first of the Silesian Wars perpetrated by FREDERICK II (THE GREAT). After the war, Süssmilch settled in Berlin, where, he served as a pastor and pursued his interest in the theory of population. The BERLIN ACADEMY elected him to its membership in 1745.

Süssmilch wrote the first systematic and comprehensive treatise on the subject of population, *Die göttliche Ordnung in den Veränderungen des menschlichen Geschlechts, aus der Geburt, dem Tod und der Fortpflanzung desselben erwiesen* (The divine order in the changes of the human race . . .). First published in 1741, the book went through four subsequent 18th-century German editions and was reprinted until 1798.

Süssmilch believed that the study of population trends could yield valuable information for planning state economic and social policies. He accepted the belief, common to economic MERCANTILISM, that a growing population provides one of the best guarantees of prosperity. He also believed that state policies designed by enlightened monarchs (see MONARCHS, ENLIGHTENED) should aim at promoting population growth.

Although Süssmilch used mathematical statistics to analyze population data from Prussian Protestant church registers, he was mostly interested in the theoretical consequences that could be drawn from his analyses. Borrowing concepts from PHYSICO-THEOLOGY and from the MECHANICAL PHILOSOPHY, he elaborated a vision of how the laws of God operate on human populations. The laws of God resemble those of mathematics and operate according to the dynamic mechanical principle of balance between forces. God has established a balance between the size of population and the food supply. This balance determines the ratio between live births and deaths, and it also controls the fertility of a population.

Süssmilch believed that certain natural and human catastrophes—famine, sickness, and warfare—could upset the operation of these laws. He criticized urbanization, asserting that the movement of people to cities actually hindered population growth.

Süssmilch's treatise had a wide readership in German states, but it did not translate across international boundaries. His theories were eclipsed in ENGLAND, the UNITED PROVINCES OF THE NETHERLANDS, and FRANCE by the pessimistic vision of Thomas Robert MALTHUS. Nevertheless, his work is significant for the history of the ENLIGHTENMENT as an early example of the application of statistical mathematical techniques to human problems.

See also CAMERALISM; MATHEMATICS AND MECHANICS.

Sweden A predominantly Lutheran, Scandinavian kingdom lying on the Baltic Sea across from the Jutland peninsula. In the 18th century, the kingdom included modern Sweden and Finland. Before the 1721 treaty that ended the Northern Wars, Sweden had held vastly more extended territories. It relinquished lands on the southern shores of the Baltic Sea to PETER I (THE GREAT) and slipped into second-class status on the European diplomatic scene. For the remainder of the century, Sweden enjoyed peace.

The period from 1718 to 1772 is called the Frihetstiden (the Age of Freedom) in Swedish histories. It began with a dynastic crisis when King Charles XII died without immediate heirs and without having named a successor. The Swedish monarch was officially elected by a representative body called the Diet, but it usually respected the wishes of the former monarch and elected one of his or her direct heirs. Since Charles XII had left no specific wishes or instructions, the Diet was free to elect whomever it pleased. From 1718 to 1720, the crown was in the hands of Ulrica Eleanora, Charles XII's sister. She abdicated in 1720 in favor of her husband, Frederick I, and the Diet chose that moment to impose a constitution, placing strict limitations on monarchical power. According to the new constitution, the Diet was granted broad legislative and executive powers that made it actually more powerful than the monarch. Two major political parties—the Hats and the Caps—controlled elections to the Diet. The half century during which they dominated Sweden was marked by political squabbling and a resultant paralysis in the government.

In spite of the difficulties, the Age of Freedom did see some major reforms. Swedish peasants, until then tied legally to the land in a form of SERFDOM, were granted an opportunity to buy their freedom and to become regular, tax-paying citizens. This gave them higher status and more power, but it scarcely improved their economic situation. Agriculture received official encouragement. The noted natural scientist Carolus LINNAEUS, for example, undertook a tour throughout Swedish lands to provide advice on agricultural reform. The Swedish government also established a statistical office, the first of its kind in Europe, in 1749.

The political situation in Sweden changed dramatically in 1772, when GUSTAV III, a direct descendant of Charles XII, was elected to the throne. He assumed power in a bloodless coup d'état wherein he reversed the political order, subjugated the Diet to the king and reestablished monarchical ABSOLUTISM in the kingdom. Gustavus III ruled Sweden as an enlightened despot for the next 20 years. In spite of opposition within the kingdom, he managed to protect and to extend his absolute powers through 1790. In 1792, he was assassinated at a masked ball at the Opera House in Stockholm.

See also ABSOLUTISM, ENLIGHTENED; POLITICAL THEORY.

Swedenborg, Emanuel (1688–1772) *Swedish scientist, philosopher, mystic, and theologian*

A native of Stockholm, Swedenborg was the son of Jesper Swedberg, a Lutheran pastor who ultimately became a bishop in that church. The family received noble status in 1719 at which time it adopted the name Swedenborg. Emanuel Swedenborg studied at the University of Uppsala, acquiring a foundation in CARTESIANISM, classics, natural science, and mathematics. From 1710 until 1714, he pursued his intellectual interests in ENGLAND, Holland, FRANCE, and GERMANY. He acquired knowledge of the NATURAL PHILOSOPHY of Isaac NEWTON, of the PSYCHOLOGY of John LOCKE, and of the rational philosophies of Gottfried Wilhelm LEIBNIZ and Christian WOLFF. Upon returning to his native land, Swedenborg obtained an appointment from King Charles XII as an assessor to the Royal Board of Mines.

Swedenborg's life is traditionally divided into two major periods defined by a great mystical and visionary religious experience that occurred in 1747: the years of scientific pursuit before 1747 and those of religious inquiry and activity after 1747. In reality, these periods displayed great continuity and unity with respect to questions, themes, and philosophy. Swedenborg was particularly interested in the relationships between mind and body and between spiritual and earthly existence. He tried throughout his life to create a philosophical synthesis of Christian THEOLOGY, ancient forms of wisdom, 17th-century RATIONALISM, and modern empirical SCIENCE.

Swedenborg first developed his ideas in the context of scientific and philosophical inquiry into the relationship between physical matter and mind or spirit. He believed that mathematical points provided the link between these two worlds. In mathematics, points lack extension, that is, they do not take up space in the way that regular objects do. But points moving through space create lines, and lines moving through space form flat surfaces. Swedenborg translated these ideas from geometry into physics and theology. He treated points as something resembling mind or spirit and postulated that the motion of points actually creates physical matter or bodies.

Swedenborg applied this theory to human physiology, postulating that pure tiny parts in the blood were the equivalent of mathematical points in his theory and that these parts provided the actual link between mind and body in human existence. He also applied the theory to PHILOSOPHY and to RELIGION, creating an elaborate theory of the creation of the universe.

Swedenborg developed a second central theory, the doctrine of correspondences. This doctrine, a synthesis of elements from Renaissance Neoplatonism and the monadology of Leibniz, rested on two central beliefs: that everything in the universe, whether spirit or matter, acts in harmony; and that all levels of existence, whether vegetable, animal, mineral, human, or spirit, are linked in one unbroken GREAT CHAIN OF BEING. Existence on Earth has harmonious parallels in the world of spirit, a fact that Swedenborg believed could be verified through the study of words and their meanings.

After 1747, Swedenborg turned away from science toward theology, adapting his philosophy accordingly. Like many of his contemporaries, Swedenborg believed that Christian theology represented a corruption of an ancient, universal, pure religion. Although this ancient religious knowledge had been lost, Swedenborg and his like-minded contemporaries believed that it could be regained by enlightened individuals through proper contemplation. Swedenborg believed that his particular philosophy provided the key for recovering ancient, pristine wisdom so that it could once again govern human existence.

Works by Swedenborg include *Opera Philosophica et Mineralia* (Works of philosophy and mineralogy; 1734); *De Cultu et Amore dei* (On reverence and love of God; 1745); *Oeconomia regni Animalis* (Economy of the animal kingdom; 1740–41); and *Regnum Animale* (Animal kingdom; 1744–45). *Clavis Hieroglyphica* (Hieroglyphic key; 1784) presents Swedenborg's LANGUAGE theory, and *Arcana Coelestia quaue in Genesis et Exodo sunt detecta* (Heavenly secrets detectable in Genesis and Exodus; 1749–56) outlines his new theology.

Swedenborg is often treated as an eccentric or insane man. His philosophy, however, clearly represents major strands of intellectual inquiry and theory characteristic of the late ENLIGHTENMENT. His cosmogony (theory of the birth of the universe) resembles the theories of the marquis de LAPLACE, Immanuel KANT, and the comte de BUFFON. The belief in an ancient pure religion, accessible to modern man through the exercise of reason, was shared by FREEMASONS, ROSICRUCIANS, and followers of DEISM. In addition, many enlightened intellectuals, especially in German lands, shared the desire of synthesizing old and new forms of knowledge into a modern system. Swedenborg, then, is a colorful but nevertheless serious representative of the late Enlightenment, whose philosophy can shed light on the range of creative possibilities contained in that era.

See also MATHEMATICS AND MECHANICS.

Swieten, Gerard van (1700–1772) *Dutch physician who immigrated to Vienna*

As a member of a Catholic noble family in the Calvinist UNITED PROVINCES OF THE NETHERLANDS, Gerard van Swieten grew up faced with legal professional obstacles and liabilities. He attended the Catholic University of Louvain and later matriculated with the medical faculty of the renowned University of Leiden.

A devoted student of Hermann BOERHAAVE, van Swieten regularly attended the illustrious teacher's lectures even after he had received his medical degree. Van Swieten accumulated notes from these lectures over a period of 21 years.

Boerhaave admired the young man and considered him a possible successor to his professorship at Leiden. However, the fact of Van Swieten's Catholic faith was a liability, for Leiden was a staunchly Protestant institution. As a result, when van Swieten received an invitation (his second) to become court physician for the Hapsburg empress MARIA THERESA, he accepted readily, moving to VIENNA in 1745.

Van Swieten soon assumed the task of reforming the medical faculty of the University of Vienna. Under his direction, the medical school adopted the organizational model of Leiden, established botanical gardens and a chemistry lab, and began a rise to preeminence.

As a practicing physician, van Swieten developed a new treatment for venereal disease, and supported Jan INGENHOUZS in efforts to persuade Viennese physicians to accept INOCULATION as a preventive for smallpox.

Van Swieten assisted in the dissemination of Boerhaave's teachings throughout Europe by publishing his notes from Boerhaave's lectures together with his own commentaries as *Commentaria in Hermanni Boerhaave Aphorismos de cognoscendis et curandis morbis* (5 vols., 1742–72). These volumes were translated quickly into Dutch, German, French, and English.

Boerhaave's work provided one of the foundations for medicine during the ENLIGHTENMENT. Van Swieten, through his loyalty to Boerhaave's approach, his institutional activities, and his *Commentaries* greatly facilitated the spread of his teacher's ideas, thereby helping to shape the theory, practice, and teaching of MEDICINE during the 18th century.

Swieten, Gottfried Bernhard, baron van (1733–1803) *Austrian official, major patron of music, and opera librettist*

Gottfried van Swieten was born in Leiden in the UNITED PROVINCES OF THE NETHERLANDS. His father, Gerard van SWIETEN, was a distinguished doctor of MEDICINE who became one of MARIA THERESA's advisers on reform and her court physician. Gerard van Swieten moved his family to AUSTRIA because, as a Catholic in the Calvinist Netherlands, certain occupations and activities were closed to him. Young Gottfried received his education at the Theresianum, the Jesuit school in VIENNA. After a short term in the Austrian civil service, he entered the diplomatic service. He held posts in BRUSSELS (1755–57), PARIS (1760–63), Warsaw (1763–64), and ENGLAND (1769). As ambassador from Austria, he lived in BERLIN for seven years (1770–77) and directed the Austrian negotiations with PRUSSIA and Russia concerning the First Partition of Poland.

Van Swieten was called back to Vienna to assume responsibilities in the joint government of Maria Theresa and her son JOSEPH II. He served as the president of the Court Commission on Education and Censorship, working to implement the radical educational and censorship reforms favored by Joseph II. He tried to persuade Joseph II in 1784 to pass a copyright law making pirated editions of books illegal, but Joseph refused on the grounds that this would interfere with commercial prosperity. In general, van Swieten was considered an outspoken advocate of the ideals of the ENLIGHTENMENT. As Joseph II grew more conservative, friction existed between the emperor and his official, but it was left to Joseph's successor, the once progressive Leopold II, to remove van Swieten from office in 1791.

Throughout his life, van Swieten provided important patronage to MUSIC. Johann Sebastian BACH, C. P. E. BACH, George Frederick HANDEL, Franz Joseph HAYDN, and Wolfgang Amadeus MOZART all benefited from his assistance and interest. Van Swieten commissioned C. P. E. Bach's *Six Symphonies for Strings* (w 182) in 1773. In Vienna, during the 1780s, van Swieten organized a circle of aristocratic patrons, the Gesellschaft der Associierten [sic]. These wealthy men sponsored private performances. Under their auspices, Mozart arranged for the production of Handel's *Messiah, Acis and Galatea*, the *Ode for St. Cecilia's Day*, and *Alexander's Feast*. Haydn's oratorios *The Seven Last Words, The Creation*, and *The Seasons* also premiered under the auspices of the Gesellschaft. Van Swieten assisted in writing the libretti (word texts) for these Haydn masterpieces and also helped Haydn in his dealings with music publishers. The young Ludwig van BEETHOVEN also received his patronage. Van Swieten even tried his own hand at composing, for, in common 18th-century style, he was an active amateur musician. He is known to have written three comic operas and 10 symphonies. Three of his symphonies were originally published over Haydn's name. Johann Nikolaus Forkel, the first biographer of Johann Sebastian Bach, dedicated his book to van Swieten in recognition of outstanding services as a protector of music and musicians.

Swift, Jonathan (1667–1745) *Irish-born writer, clergyman; the outstanding master of satire in English literary history*

Satire became a favorite and influential vehicle for political and social criticism during the ENLIGHTENMENT. A controversial literary figure in his own era, Swift presents a complex character whose life still generates academic dispute.

Jonathan Swift was born after his father's premature death and was, therefore, raised by his uncles. He was the cousin of the poet John DRYDEN. During his student years at Trinity College, Dublin, Swift established a solid friendship with William CONGREVE that lasted a lifetime. In 1688 Swift went to ENGLAND, where he worked as secretary to Sir William Temple. He returned to Ireland in 1694, took ecclesiastical vows, and accepted an appointment as vicar (pastor) of a parish near Belfast. In 1696, Swift returned to Surrey, England, to resume his employment with Sir William Temple. After Temple's death in 1699, he again went to Ireland, where he accepted some official posts in the Church of Ireland, the Irish branch of the Anglican Church. However, he traveled regularly between Ireland and LONDON where his literary career was blooming.

During the first decade of the 18th century, Swift associated with writers of Whig Party sympathies such as Joseph ADDISON and Richard STEELE. He was also allied with Charles Montagu, first earl of Halifax. In 1701, he published a clear and persuasive statement of Whig principles, *A Discourse of the Contests and Dissentions . . . between the Nobles and Commoners in Athens and Rome.* By 1710, Swift had become disenchanted with Whig Party policies and moved into the Tory camp. This political shift was motivated largely by his devotion to the church.

Swift became the chief literary spokesman for the Tories. In addition to editing their party journal, *The Examiner,* he wrote political pamphlets for the periodicals that were coming from the GRUB STREET presses. He left England when the Whigs resumed power, returning permanently to Ireland, where he took up the political defense of Ireland against England. Major works from this period include *Drapier's Letters* (1724), a biting tract that forced the Whig minister Robert WALPOLE to rescind plans for issuing a new coinage in Ireland; *GULLIVER'S TRAVELS* (1726), the story of the perils that beset a normal, decent human being and of his success at transcend-

ing them; and *A Modest Proposal* (1729), a famous condemnation of the effects of English economic policy in Ireland. Swift served as dean of Saint Patrick's Cathedral in Dublin from 1713 until 1745.

Swift contributed political and satirical essays not only to the Tory *Examiner* but also to periodicals such as *The Tatler,* THE SPECTATOR, and *The Intelligencer.* Together with Alexander POPE, John GAY, and John Arbuthnot, he formed the noted literary group called the Scriblerus Club. Swift and other club members collaborated to produce *The Memoirs of Martin Scriblerus.* Swift also wrote the *Miscellaneous Works, Comical and Diverting* (1720) that contained *The Tale of the Tub, The Battle of the Books,* and *Discourse Concerning the Mechanical Operations of the Spirit.* His *Journal to Stella* (1710–13) was addressed to his dear friend Esther Johnson. Among his many political tracts, *The Conduct of the Allies* and *The Public Spirit of the Whigs* should also be noted.

Swift is best known for his biting observations and satire about English life. These were rooted in his turn to the conservative Tory Party and in his related opposition to the political, social, and economic changes that were being brought to England by Whig-supported liberal policies. His beliefs were thoroughly rooted in RATIONALISM, but in a rationalism defined by the notion of common sense.

Swift died in 1745 after three years of physical debilitation during which a guardian attended to his clerical and economic affairs. He was buried in Saint Patrick's Cathedral in Dublin next to Stella.

See also LITERATURE.

Illustration from *Gulliver's Travels.* The Irish-born churchman and satirist Jonathan Swift wrote critical political commentary on both Whig and Tory policies in England. *(Courtesy New York Public Library)*

Switzerland Small central European nation straddling the Alps; bounded in the 18th century by FRANCE, Bavaria, AUSTRIA, the kingdom of SAVOY, the republic of GENEVA, and the duchy of MILAN. Switzerland was a loose confederation of 13 sovereign cantons linked together by a common oath for the purpose of self-defense. Its chief cities were Zürich, Basle, and Bern. GENEVA stood outside the confederation. The Swiss Confederation (Schweizerische Eidgenossenschaft) dated back to 1291, when the three mountainous cantons, Uri, Schwyz, and Unterwalden, successfully threw off Hapsburg domination. Each canton maintained a high degree of independence and operated with its particular constitution. For 18th-century observers, the Swiss Confederation offered a laboratory for the firsthand study of various government forms such as DEMOCRACY, urban aristocracy, and oligarchy.

The Swiss Confederation established its neutrality in the 17th century in an effort to avoid constant warfare on account of its strategically located valleys and Alpine passes. This neutrality was fully respected from 1712 until 1798, when the revolutionary French, in conjunction with Swiss reformers, set up the brief-lived Helvetic Republic.

The major Swiss cities were Protestant, but the eastern and central, rural, mountainous cantons remained mostly Catholic. Several urban commercial centers existed, but even with these cities the country could not support its population. Therefore, young Swiss men routinely entered foreign armies as mercenary soldiers. Swiss guards provided personal protection for French kings, the pope, and other European rulers.

The history and legend of the Swiss struggle for political autonomy fired the imaginations of enlightened Europeans. Friedrich SCHILLER immortalized the Swiss struggle for freedom in his drama, *WILHELM TELL* (*The Legend of William Tell*). Switzerland produced a unique, highly creative species of the ENLIGHTENMENT, contributing especially to developments in EDUCATION, mathematics, AESTHETICS, the natural sciences, and the social sciences. Native Swiss, such as the members of the BERNOULLI family, Leonhard EULER, Johann Heinrich PESTALOZZI, Johann Jakob BODMER, Johann Jakob BREITINGER, Albrecht von HALLER, Johann Christoph GOTTSCHED, and Johannes von MÜLLER made the cities of Bern, Basle, Zürich, and Lausanne important centers for certain enlightened intellectual activities.

See also MATHEMATICS AND MECHANICS; PROTESTANTISM.

sympathy A feeling that is shared or experienced in common. The word derives from the Greek *sympatheia*. During the ENLIGHTENMENT, the concept of sympathy played an important role in two intellectual realms: VITALISM and MORAL PHILOSOPHY.

Wherever sympathy appeared as an explanatory concept, it was associated with a vision of NATURE built on the phenomenon of sympathetic vibration in acoustics. The vibration of one string on a violin can set the others in motion without any direct contact.

Sympathetic vibration provided a metaphor for vitalists and moral philosophers who were trying to explain certain biological and ethical phenomena. In particular, they applied the concept to general problems concerning the RELATION between individuals (bodily parts or human beings) and greater wholes (the organism or human society). The metaphor of sympathetic vibration particularly pleased people who were committed to a view of nature based on harmony and organic unity. It emphasized that the individual parts constituting any whole, whether a body or society, unite to create an entity that is greater than the simple sum of its parts.

This vision, though partly derived from the mechanical laws governing sound, departed from the concept of the whole as a sum of the parts typically espoused in the MECHANICAL PHILOSOPHY. Those who used the notion of sympathy generally were offering scientific and ethical theories critical of mechanical metaphors.

The Scottish school of moral philosophy represented in part by David HUME and Adam SMITH enlisted the concept of sympathy to explain how individual moral behavior produces similarly moral responses in other human beings. When one person observes another person experiencing emotional or physical pain, the observation calls forth a set of memories that elicit similar painful feelings in that observer. This causes the observer to feel compassion for his or her fellow human being, and to pass judgment on the UTILITY and goodness of the behavior that caused the pain. This entire chain of events represents sympathy in action; sympathy, therefore, provides a way for individuals to place behavior into a broader social and moral context.

Vitalists applied the concept of sympathy in a related but slightly different way. They spoke of the sympathetic vibrations assumed to occur in nerve fibers in response to certain types of sensation. These sympathetic vibrations called up earlier memories and associations from the brain fibers, thereby creating a historical context in which a specific experience could be evaluated. Denis DIDEROT adopted this model of mental activity and provided a clear description of it in his novel *D'Alembert's Dream*.

The appearance of the concept of sympathy in SCIENCE and moral philosophy serves as one of the indicators of the transition that occurred in enlightened conceptions of natural action after the middle of the 18th century.

symphony orchestra A large ensemble of instrumental musicians who play together to perform a musical composition. The orchestra as we know it today developed in the course of the 18th century, although, at its largest, it never approached the size of modern orchestras. The origins of this performing institution lie in the

court bands of baroque-era rulers. These bands were small ensembles, containing at most eight to 12 string players, a pair of players who doubled on recorders and oboes, a pair of bassoonists, valveless horns, perhaps one valveless trumpet, a harpsichordist, and, when needed, a percussionist. The harpsichordist led the group from his seated position at his instrument. As the 18th century progressed and musical CLASSICISM emerged as a distinct style, the orchestra increased in size and musical importance, while the composition of the ensemble changed markedly. The number of string players expanded; at Mannheim, which had one of the largest 18th-century orchestras, there were 20 players. One-keyed or two-keyed transverse flutes replaced recorders, oboes remained in pairs, CLARINETS became regular members, and the practice of doubling (playing more than one instrument as needed) receded. In general, orchestras remained small; they were rarely larger than 25 to 30 players. The harpsichord disappeared from the orchestra toward the end of the century, and the job of leading went to the first violinist. Only rarely did a conductor stand before the group with a baton. Large works written for orchestra, such as symphonies, concerti for soloist and orchestra, or oratorio accompaniments, became extremely popular during the classical era and have remained popular to our day. Franz Joseph HAYDN, Wolfgang Amadeus MOZART, and Ludwig van BEETHOVEN are the most renowned 18th-century composers of orchestral pieces, but many others made significant contributions: Arcangelo CORELLI, Antonio VIVALDI, Johann Wenzel Anton Stamitz, Johann Christian BACH, C. P. E. BACH, and Franz Xaver Richter.

The 18th century also produced a musical form, the symphony, which was none other than a large composition for the symphony orchestra. Compositions of this type contain three or four movements of varying mood and tempo. Symphonic form developed during the 18th century from the Italian opera overture form called *sinfonia*. These overtures were often played as independent concert pieces; around 1730, Italian composers began creating separate compositions following their form (three movements in fast-slow-fast order). Giovanni Battista Sammartini in MILAN, Baldassare Galuppi, Rinaldo di Capua, and Niccolò Jommelli were especially important in these early Italian efforts. The new form was developed at Mannheim by Stamitz and Richter, and by J. C. Bach in LONDON. Toward the end of the century, the form had matured so that it usually contained four movements. It was, of course, used brilliantly by the great composers Haydn, Mozart, and Beethoven, and it has continued to provide a richly creative musical medium ever since.

See also BAROQUE STYLE; MUSIC; OPERA; STAMITZ.

synergy Theological view of the world that posits both human and divine efforts as crucial to ultimate salvation. The concept of free will has complicated all of Christianity's debates over the roles that individual people will or can play in the healing of sin and corruption in the world. The discussion ranges from positions such as Pelagianism, which asserts that individuals can use free will to bring about their own salvation, to Calvinism, which asserts that salvation is predetermined by divine will. Synergy, also known as synergism, negotiates a middle ground between these two positions, asserting a crucial interaction between divine and human will that enables an individual to gain salvation.

This idea reached prominence in theological debates of the 16th century with the support of Philipp Melanchthon, a German religious reformer and professor at Wittenberg of Greek studies. He worked there with Martin Luther to refine and codify the ideas of LUTHERANISM. In 1521, Melanchthon published his *Loci communes* (Commonplaces of theology). It asserts Luther's doctrine of justification, that human salvation results from the cooperation of the Holy Spirit with individuals' free will, strengthened by the power of the Scriptures. He played a major role in the ensuing debates of Protestant theology for the remainder of his life. The concept of synergism continued through Lutheran theological debates of the 17th and 18th century, such as those concerning the followers of PIETISM, which was a reaction against Orthodox Lutheranism calling for greater focus on the individual's spiritual development.

See also DEISM.

Further reading: Peter L. Thorslev, Jr., *Romantic Contraries: Freedom versus Destiny* (New Haven, Conn.: Yale University Press, 1984).

T

Tahiti (Otaheiti) Island in the South Pacific. Tahiti entered European consciousness in 1767, when it was sighted and explored by the British commander Samuel Wallis. The French explorer Louis Antoine de BOUGAINVILLE "discovered" it less than a year later, in 1768, and James COOK touched ground on the first of his three voyages to Tahiti in 1769. These and other explorers wrote ethnographic accounts of the island and its inhabitants, igniting imaginations back home and spawning other, imaginative accounts such as Denis DIDEROT's *Supplément au Voyage de Bougainville.*

The island quickly became a European emblem of pristine, primeval simplicity. For some observers and their readers, native islanders exemplified the ideal of the NOBLE SAVAGE, a cultural conceit that attributed to indigenous and colonized peoples characteristics that evoked the Judeo-Christian ideas of Eden. The noble savage carried contradictory connotations: On the one hand, such savages were extolled for their purity, which contrasted with the supposed corruption of European civilization; on the other hand, the simplicity of these savages rendered them innately inferior to Europeans, who were the exponents of PROGRESS. Noble savages were also associated in Europe with sexual fertility, something that both attracted and repulsed European visitors and readers. One manifestation of European ambivalence in ethnographic accounts of Tahiti during the 18th century was the depiction of the islanders' skin color. Generally, it was depicted as dark, which was perceived as inferior to light skin, but still agreeable, although some Tahitians were described as being quite fair, with blue eyes and reddish or even blond hair.

From 1767 through the end of the century, explorers and settlers seemed fairly content to commingle with Tahitians, offering goods in trade (e.g., livestock and tailored clothing for tapa cloth, beads, and the like) but seeming content to let the island continue in its state of noble savagery. However, after 1797, when the British commander James Wilson brought missionaries to the island, a process of more aggressive acculturation began. Land was granted to the missionaries, schools were instituted, settlements increased in size, and Tahitian customs (such as the topless dress of women) were brought into conformity with European mores.

Further reading: Edwin N. Ferdon, *Early Tahiti as the Explorers Saw It, 1767–1797* (Tucson: University of Arizona Press, 1981).

Tanucci, Bernardo, marchese (1698–1783) *lawyer from Tuscany; a champion of enlightened reform from above who served as a statesman in the kingdom of Naples*
Tanucci served as chief adviser to CHARLES III during his years as king of Naples and Sicily (1734–59). When Charles III assumed his throne in SPAIN, ceding Naples and Sicily to his minor son, Ferdinand, Tanucci remained behind. From 1759 to 1767, Tanucci dominated the government as one of its regents. In 1768, Ferdinand appointed Tanucci first secretary of state.

The kingdom of Naples offered formidable challenges to anyone dedicated to political, social, or economic reform. The Catholic Church and a nobility structured along feudal lines controlled the Neapolitan state. Tanucci succeeded in imposing taxes on the wealth of the churches and in reducing the number of clergy by 20 percent. He also reformed the legal system, reducing the brutality of punishments and restricting the legal jurisdiction of feudal nobles over the peasants who lived on their lands. He did not succeed in establishing a uniform law code, and the kingdom of Naples remained subject to 11 different legal systems. Tanucci managed to introduce uniform land taxes and to secure better central control over tax collection. But the extent of reform possibilities remained small because of both the poverty endemic in the kingdom of Naples and the persistent feudal organization of the land.

Even in the 1760s, the limits of Tanucci's approach to reform had already begun to be apparent. As his time in office grew longer and as the nature of his reforms became more radical, Tanucci encountered increasingly determined opposition. He was finally forced to resign in 1776 on account of opposition from Queen Maria Carolina and a party of nobles.

The plight of Tanucci and the ultimate shipwreck of his programs stimulated many young thinkers and reformers of the Neapolitan ENLIGHTENMENT, such as Ferdinando GALIANI, Gaetano FILANGIERI, and Antonio GENOVESI, to develop new ideas and methods for combating the limits on change posed by Neapolitan social, economic, and political structures.

Taylor, Brook (1685–1731) *English mathematician*

Taylor, a graduate of Cambridge University, was elected to the ROYAL SOCIETY OF LONDON in 1712. His mathematics centered not only on problems of mechanics, but also on musical acoustics (string vibrations) and linear perspective. He is best known in mathematics for the Taylor theorem that expands functions into infinite series.

Taylor wrote two important mathematical books: *Methodus incrementorum directa et inversa* (1715), dealing with the calculus of finite differences; and *Linear Perspective* (1715), a book that systematically and mathematically explains the practice of using vanishing points in perspective.

As a young man Taylor had planned to write a book with Isaac NEWTON on MUSIC, but the two men never brought their ideas to fruition. In his later years, Taylor turned to philosophical and religious themes, writing a work entitled *Contemplatio philosophica* (published posthumously, 1793).

Taylor's work advanced the ability of mathematics to provide solutions and insight into practical scientific problems. His specific activities complemented and sometimes overlapped the work of major continental mathematicians such as Johann I BERNOULLI and Jean Le Rond d'ALEMBERT.

See also MATHEMATICS AND MECHANICS.

technology and instrumentation Term referring to the methods and precision tools that were used in the production of scientific knowledge and the practical application of such knowledge to human problems. In the course of the SCIENTIFIC REVOLUTION and ENLIGHTENMENT developments in scientific theory were closely connected with innovations in technology and with the production of new precision instruments for making experimental measurements. Causal relationships were reciprocal: Theory sometimes stimulated the development of instruments, but often it was the invention of a new instrument or the creation of a new practical method for addressing a problem that stimulated new scientific ideas.

"Agriculture, Ploughing," engraving from the *Encyclopédie*. The *Encyclopédie* included several volumes of plates illustrating the various technological tools and machines that were contributing to the material progress of humanity. *(Courtesy New York Public Library)*

The Scientific Revolution of the 17th century saw the creation of several significant new instruments, which, in turn, helped to advance theoretical knowledge. Instruments that played such roles were the TELESCOPE and the MICROSCOPE, each of which opened new arenas for scientific investigation. Instruments for the precise measurement of natural phenomena also appeared as scientists sought to collect adequate data for use in mathematical equations. The thermometer and BAROMETER were two instruments developed in response to these demands of experimental science.

The relationship between theory and experience in stimulating technological innovation varied according to the manner in which scientific and technological pursuits were organized. In FRANCE, theory tended to predominate, stimulating, for example, technological innovations in thermodynamics. In ENGLAND and SCOTLAND, however, the opposite causal relationship tended to hold. British inventors, who were usually craftsmen, manufacturers, or instrument makers rather than theoretical scientists, created many new industrial and public health technologies—the FLYING SHUTTLE, POWER LOOM, and water closet, for example—in response to practical needs or problems. The dilemmas posed by theory played relatively minimal roles in these advances.

The invention of scientific instruments introduced a new element into experimental science, since instruments represented an intermediate element between the observer and actual phenomena. Conflicts and problems developed around the question of how to interpret the information yielded by an instrument. Disputes of this nature occurred, for example, with data gathered by the telescope and the microscope. Robert Boyle's pressure pump also generated a famous dispute between Boyle and Thomas HOBBES over the correct interpretation of data.

Like their counterparts in the early Scientific Revolution, enlightened thinkers believed that technology provided one key to future human HAPPINESS. Therefore, many of them espoused technological solutions to problems that slowed the pace of human PROGRESS. Instruments and technology were treated as aids in the battle to conquer nature through art (artifice).

The creators of the French ENCYCLOPÉDIE, who believed in the power and utility of practical knowledge, set as one of their goals the collection and presentation of all knowledge about instruments and technology. Not only did they include large numbers of articles on practical technologies and scientific instruments, but they also devoted 10 volumes of the original edition (vols. 18–28) to a collection of engravings depicting various technologies in the sciences, arts and crafts, and practical mechanical arts. Consequently, the *Encyclopédie* is a rich source for information about the methods and instruments commonly used during the Enlightenment.

See also ARKWRIGHT; ASTRONOMY; BACON; BOULTON; BRAMAH; CARTWRIGHT; CHEMICAL REVOLUTION; CORT; CROMPTON; DALE; FAHRENHEIT; FRANKLIN; GALILEI; HADLEY; HALLEY; HARGREAVES; HERSCHEL; JEFFERSON; KAY; LAVOISIER; LONGITUDE; MARGGRAF; SPINNING JENNY; SPINNING MULE; STEAM ENGINE; TULL; VOYAGES OF DISCOVERY; WATER FRAME; WATT; WEDGWOOD.

Telemann, Georg Philipp (1681–1767) *German composer strongly associated with the development of the* style galant *and considered by his contemporaries as the outstanding German composer of his time*

Telemann was born into a family that had a strong tradition of service in the clergy. His father was a Protestant minister, and the son was expected to follow in his footsteps. Historical tradition maintains that young Telemann was forbidden to study MUSIC. He was educated in Magdeburg at the Altstädtisches Gymnasium and at the Domschule.

In the fall of 1693 or early 1694, Telemann's widowed mother sent him to school at Zellerfeld, where it was hoped that a change of surroundings would further discourage the young man from pursuing his love of music. However, Caspar Calvoer, with whom Telemann resided in Zellerfeld, allowed Telemann to study music theory and the relationships between mathematics and music, thereby providing Telemann with an avenue for pursuing his musical interests. Four years of study at Zellerfeld were followed by attendance at the Gymnasium Andreanum (high school and early college) in Hildesheim. During the Hildesheim years, Telemann composed songs and visited the towns of Hanover and Braunschweig (Brunswick) where he became acquainted with both French instrumental music and Italian OPERA.

Telemann completed his formal education at the university in Leipzig. Though intending to study law, he rapidly became involved in student musical activities and founded a *collegium musicum* (a student musical society) at the university in 1702. He became director of the Leipzig Opera in the same year, and he also began composing cantatas for biweekly performances at the Thomaskirche (Church of St. Thomas). Telemann worked in Leipzig until 1705, when he accepted an appointment as kapellmeister at the court of Count Erdmann II of Promnitz at Sorau, in Lower Lusatia (modern POLAND). Late in 1708, Telemann was appointed to a new post as director of musical activities at the court of Eisenach. There, he must have met Johann Sebastian BACH, because Bach later asked Telemann to stand as godfather for Carl Philipp Emanuel BACH. Since the role of godfather entailed certain financial and spiritual obligations to the godchild, it was usually offered to a person in a position of power. In the case of Telemann and J. S. Bach, the fact that Bach asked the younger Telemann to play this role underscores that Telemann was, during his lifetime, the more powerful and successful of the two illustrious musicians.

In 1712, Telemann accepted a summons to become director of music for the city of FRANKFURT am Main. He remained in Frankfurt until 1721, when he assumed new responsibilities as director of music in the five main churches of the city of Hamburg. In 1722, he also became director of the Hamburg Opera. Telemann remained in Hamburg for the rest of his life, departing only for a few months in 1737 and 1738 to produce concerts in PARIS. Telemann died in Hamburg in 1767. His position as director of the Hamburg Opera went to his godson, Carl Philipp Emanuel Bach.

Telemann was one of the most prolific German composers of the 18th century. His various appointments required the regular composition—a normal set of demands for the 18th century—of vocal cantatas and instrumental music. Telemann was particularly interested in producing concerts for public attendance. Even as a student in Leipzig, he had the *collegium musicum* play regular public performances. He continued these activities in Frankfurt by writing chamber music, orchestral music, and oratorios for the weekly concerts put on by the Frauenstein Society. In Hamburg, Telemann also presented public concerts as well as the operas for whose production he was officially responsible. Telemann supplemented these activities by writing music that could be played by trained amateurs and by publishing extensively. He consciously strove to avoid writing structurally complex "learned music" like the BAROQUE STYLE works by his predecessors. Much of his music has simple melodic lines and easily discernible structure with clearly subordinate accompaniments, traits that were characteristics of the early 18th-century *STYLE GALANT*.

In addition to composing, Telemann devoted himself to theoretical problems of music and tackled the challenge of making both performance practices and compositional techniques accessible to amateurs by publishing methodical treatises. They included the *Sonate methodice* (Methodical sonatas for flute or violin and continuo), the *Neues musikalisches System* (New musical system), and the *Singe-, Spiel-und Generalbass-Uebungen* (Exercises for singing, playing, and continuo).

The catalog of compositions by Telemann contains some 40 operas, 12 complete cantata cycles (over 3,000 pieces), 44 choral passions, numerous oratorios, and hundreds of orchestral and chamber works. Many of his opera scores have been lost. Among his many works are *Tafelmusik* (Music for dining), the *Sonates Corellisantes* (Sonatas in the style of Corelli), and *12 Fantaisies* (12 fantasias).

See also MATHEMATICS AND MECHANICS.

telescope Instrument used in ASTRONOMY consisting of a system of large optical lenses to bring distant objects closer for observation. The earliest telescopes were built at the end of the 16th century, but their revolutionary potential for astronomy was revealed only in 1609, when Galileo GALILEI first turned his crude instrument toward the Moon and planets. Galileo's claim that the surface of the Moon was irregular rather than perfectly smooth upset the ancient and long-held belief in the absolute perfection of the celestial bodies. His later discovery of the phases of the planet Venus helped to provide support for the HELIOCENTRIC (sun-centered) view of the universe. The shift from conceptualizing the universe as Earth-centered (GEOCENTRIC) to Sun-centered was an important element in the 17th-century transformation of the natural sciences called the SCIENTIFIC REVOLUTION. In part, this revolution occurred because of the discoveries made with the telescope and the new problems they posed for scientists and philosophers. The telescope therefore provides a good example of the interaction between developments in scientific theory, experimental practices, and available instrumentation.

The telescope supported much astronomical research during the 17th and 18th centuries as people tried to chart the heavens, to explain the observed motions of celestial bodies, and to reformulate models for the structure of the universe. Astronomers, physicists, and mathematicians raised questions requiring more powerful instruments. Larger telescopes were built, which aided observers such as William HERSCHEL in distinguishing double stars, star clusters, and nebulae from other celestial bodies.

Herschel built a 40-foot reflecting telescope, but it proved too awkward for regular use and its large mirror produced distorted images. Telescope technology did not extend beyond that point during the 18th century.

See also COPERNICAN REVOLUTION; CORELLI; SCIENCE; TECHNOLOGY AND INSTRUMENTATION.

Temple, William (1628–1699) *English statesman, diplomat, and man of letters*
William Temple was born into an old English family that had settled in Ireland. He attended Cambridge, but in 1647 he left school without taking his degree in order to travel. While on the Isle of Wight, he made the acquaintance of Dorothy Osborne, with whom he fell in love. Her love letters to him have become the stuff of legend. However, only one of his letters to her survives. Her parents were staunch supporters of the exiled Stuart dynastic family. Temple's father, meanwhile, had embraced the cause of the Commonwealth and served for a time in the Long Parliament—the body established to govern ENGLAND in the absence of a monarch. As a result, Osborne's parents initially objected to a marriage between Temple and their daughter. Seven years later, however, in 1654, after a lengthy love affair and Osborne's survival of smallpox, the two were married.

Temple's reputation derives mainly from his capable work as a diplomat in the tense international climate of the 1660s and 1670s. He is most famous for helping to negotiate the Triple Alliance in 1668, a treaty that joined England with SWEDEN and the UNITED PROVINCES OF THE NETHERLANDS in halting the territorial encroachments of FRANCE. Charles II reversed the treaty two years later, but Temple had already achieved his fame. He later helped to effectuate the Treaty of Westminster of 1674 (putting an end to England's war with the United Provinces of the Netherlands) and to bring about the marriage of William and Mary, an event that would prove instrumental in removing the Stuart family from the throne. Temple served as ambassador to The Hague as well as to SPAIN, and declined the secretaryship of state on three separate occasions.

Temple wrote a number of respected political essays, as well as essays on other subjects (e.g., gardening) and some poetry. He may be best remembered for his "Essay upon Ancient and Modern Learning" (1690), which rehearsed in gentle, eloquent form the familiar argument that the ancients (the writers of classical Greece and ROME) were wiser than the moderns. This essay elicited the ire of William Wotton and Richard Bentley, who refuted it spiritedly in print. This, in turn, provoked Jonathan SWIFT, whose patron was Temple, to satirize Bentley in Temple's defense in *The Battle of the Books* (1704).

See also QUARREL BETWEEN THE ANCIENTS AND THE MODERNS; WILLIAM III AND MARY II.

Further reading: Richard Faber, *The Brave Courtier: Sir William Temple* (London: Faber & Faber, 1983); Joseph M. Levine, *The Battle of the Books: History and Literature in the Augustan Age* (Ithaca, N.Y.: Cornell University Press, 1991).

theater   Stage performances, including, but not limited to, drama, comedy, ballet, and OPERA. During the 18th century, theater in Europe developed forms common to or invented during the 17th century (French tragedy, Italian opera), and assumed many of its modern characteristics. Theater played an important political and social role during this period.

The two most important theatrical genres in continental Europe during the 18th century were the French tragedy and the Italian opera, sometimes called the *opera seria* (serious opera) or, more correctly, the *dramma per musica* (music drama). In many places, including PARIS and the court cities of GERMANY, French plays from the 17th century by authors such as Jean Racine and Pierre and Thomas Corneille were staged alongside 18th-century works by writers such as VOLTAIRE. Popular operatic works included George Frederick HANDEL's *Giulio Cesare in Egitto* (Julius Caesar in Egypt; 1724), Johann Adolf Hasse's *Artaserse* (Artaxerxes; 1731), and, later, Wolfgang

Engraving made from a print, 1749, of James Quin as Coriolanus in William Shakespeare's play of the same name *(Courtesy New York Public Library)*

Amadeus MOZART's *LE NOZZE DI FIGARO* (The marriage of Figaro; 1786) and *DON GIOVANNI* (1787).

Italian opera was prevalent not only in ITALY, but also in LONDON, in many of the wealthier court cities of Germany (such as MUNICH, BERLIN, and Dresden), and in other European capitals (such as Warsaw and SAINT PETERSBURG). Because of the great expense involved in producing operas, many smaller court cities relied on French tragedy instead. Paris also had opera, but the texts were in French. Opera singers were paid huge salaries, and the best were idolized. The most famous example was the castrato Carlo Broschi, known as Farinelli, who triumphed on the stages of Europe before retiring to SPAIN, where he occupied a socially prominent position at the court of King Ferdinand IV. Ballets and Italian comic operas were often performed between the acts of the serious operas, resulting in an entertainment that sometimes lasted six hours.

Both French tragedy and Italian opera relied on stories from Greek and Roman antiquity for their plots. The creators of these tragedies and operas used all the means at their disposal to reflect the political and social order in their works. The tragic heroes of the French works were meant to reflect the glories of the monarch, and the allocation of scenes and arias in an Italian opera precisely delineated the social and political status of each of the characters.

Many other types of theater were popular on the European continent as well. In France, the *comédie*, with roots in the 17th century, met the demand for lighter entertainment. Comedies by writers such as Voltaire, Caron de BEAUMARCHAIS, and Pierre Marivaux joined works by Molière in the repertory of the Comédie Française in Paris and in those of troupes located in cities throughout German-speaking Europe. The Italian counterparts to these witty, urbane comedies included the plays of Carlo GOLDONI and the fairy tales of Carlo Gozzi, among them *The Love for Three Oranges* (1761) and *Turandot* (1762).

Popular theater had many manifestations during the 18th century. In Italy, commedia dell' arte, a kind of farce that relied on stock characters (the master, his maid, Harlequin, etc.), was popular. Variants on this type of entertainment were found in other places as well. For example, the German Hanswurst (John Sausage) farces were directly indebted to commedia dell' arte. Performances in public places such as markets, squares, fairgrounds, and streets featured stock characters such as Harlequin and Hanswurst; these popular performances also included puppet shows and dumb shows.

In England, in addition to Italian opera performed in London during the first four decades of the 18th century, there were other popular genres. During the first decade of the century, Restoration theater produced its final comedic masterworks, including William Congreve's *The Way of the World* (1700) and George Farquhar's *The Recruiting Officer* (1706) and *The Beaux' Stratagem* (1707). This style of comedy was supplanted by the ballad operas of the 1720s and 1730s that satirized social mores and mocked the conventions of Italian opera. The most famous example of these was John GAY's *The Beggar's Opera* (1728). English comedy saw a renaissance of sorts in the 1770s with works such as Oliver GOLDSMITH's SHE STOOPS TO CONQUER (1773) and with the emergence of Richard SHERIDAN, whose plays included *The Rivals* (1775), *The School for Scandal* (1776), and *The Critic* (1779).

The works of William Shakespeare and his contemporaries continued to form the core of the English theater's tragic repertory during the 18th century. These were joined by later 17th-century works and by 18th-century successes such as Samuel JOHNSON's *Irene* (1736), Edward Moore's *The Gamester* (1753), and Horace WALPOLE's *The Mysterious Mother* (1768).

Institutionally, theater underwent a series of fundamental changes during the 18th century. First, famous actors and actresses improved the social status of all actors. At the beginning of the century, performers were considered the equivalent of prostitutes and criminals, but, 100 years later, they had gained respectability and were counted alongside men and women of letters as members of the middle class. Those responsible for the change included Marie-Justine Favart and Henri-Louis Kain (known as Lekain) in France, David GARRICK and Sarah Siddons in London, and Conrad Ekhof in German-speaking central Europe. (Ekhof wrote eloquently on the subject of the social status of actors in the famous *Gotha Theater Calendar*, published between 1775 and 1800).

Second, the social makeup and arrangement of audiences changed. At the beginning of the period, people attending the theater were placed in the auditorium according to their social rank, with non-nobles separated from nobles in theaters where the two groups comingled, and according to the strictures of courtly etiquette. By the end of the century, audience members bought tickets that were more or less expensive and were thus seated according to personal means and not social class. Finally, audiences became increasingly silent and attentive over the course of the 18th century; the increasing respect for their work reflected the increase in the status and respectability of the actors and actresses on the stage.

Further reading: Marvin Carlson, *Voltaire and the Theatre of the Eighteenth Century* (Westport, Conn.: Greenwood Press, 1998); A. M. Nagler, ed., *A Source Book in Theatrical History* (New York: Dover, 1959); Reinhard Strohm, *Dramma per Musica: Italian Opera in the Eighteenth Century* (New Haven, Conn.: Yale University Press, 1997.

theology The discipline that yields knowledge of God.
See also EPISTEMOLOGY; MORAL PHILOSOPHY; RELIGION.

Thomasius, Christian (1655–1728) *German philosopher, lawyer, and pedagogue*
Thomasius is considered with Christian WOLFF to be one of the founders of the AUFKLÄRUNG (ENLIGHTENMENT) in the German territories of the HOLY ROMAN EMPIRE. Thomasius was a native of Leipzig, the son of a law professor at the University of Leipzig. Young Thomasius attended the university at Frankfort an der Oder, receiving a law degree in 1679. Contact with the NATURAL LAW theories of Samuel PUFENDORF dramatically affected Thomasius's perspectives on law and society, causing him to turn away from the Lutheran orthodoxy that was his heritage.

In 1682, Thomasius began lecturing at the University of Leipzig. He openly defied university tradition in 1688 by offering his lectures in German rather than in the customary Latin, and in 1689 he began publishing the first monthly literary journal in German.

Thomasius openly demonstrated his new philosophical orientation in 1688, when he published *Institutiones iurisprudentiae divinae* (Institutes of divine jurisprudence) and *Philosophia aulica* (Introduction to court philosophy). Under the influence of Pufendorf's ideas, Thomasius asserted in the *Institutiones iurisprudentiae divinae* that knowledge of law comes from the exercise of human REASON and the accumulation of experience rather than through revelations from God. God remains the ultimate source of natural laws, but he does not communicate them directly to humanity. *Philosophia aulica* offered a novel conception of the role of philosophy in human EDUCATION, suggesting that the truths uncovered by philosophy were less important than its general function as a mode of human discovery. Philosophy students, Thomasius argued, should be men destined for action in the world, rather than theologians or academics who would remain aloof from worldly activities. He elaborated this position by calling for pedagogical approaches that would produce students freed from narrow dogmatic thinking, possessed, instead, with openness of mind and an eclectic point of view.

Thomasius's activities and ideas offended the authorities in Leipzig, who in 1690 forbade him to teach or to write. He avoided arrest by fleeing to BERLIN, where he was welcomed by Elector Frederick I of PRUSSIA and awarded an appointment at the Ritters Akademie in Halle. In 1694, the Ritters Akademie became the new University of HALLE, whose express purpose was to train officials for the Prussian civilian and military bureaucracy. Thomasius became the first rector of the university and a professor of law.

Between 1691 and 1694, Thomasius wrote four treatises on logic and ethics. The first three continued his optimistic exploration of alternatives to traditional philosophy. These books were the *Einleitung zu der Vernunfte-Lehre* (Introduction to logic; 1691), *Ausübung der Vernunfte-Lehre* (Exercises in logic; 1691) and *Einleitung zur Sitten-Lehre* (*Introduction to ethics*; 1692). The practical uses of philosophy for life and the sources of human error occupied center stage in these works. Thomasius began to emphasize that both societies and individuals produce human error. Society supports prejudices that distort understanding and interpretation, while individuals devote themselves stubbornly to the unreasonable love—that is, desire for approval—of others. The same sources that create intellectual error also create evil in the world.

As an antidote to evil, Thomasius proposed the accumulation of practical knowledge. Skills obtained through social interaction and through the exploration of HISTORY or LITERATURE will provide the foundations that will enable people to control their personal, rational, and emotional weaknesses.

Thomasius lived his commitment to openmindedness by supporting the then unpopular idea of religious TOLERATION. He was one of the primary opponents of the persecution of so-called witches. By questioning the very possibility that such practices could have any effect on people or nature, he not only discredited beliefs in such practices but also helped to dissuade German authorities and people from reporting and prosecuting alleged witches.

In 1694, while writing the treatise titled *Ausübung der Sitten-Lehre* (Exercises of ethics; 1694), Thomasius experienced a conversion to an extreme form of PIETISM. He began to doubt the ability of human reason to overcome flaws (sin), and he began to discuss these issues in lectures. A mystical element derived from the earlier teachings of Jakob Böhme and Sebastian Franck entered his thought. The 1699 *Versuch von Wesen des Geistes oder Grund-Lehren sowohl der natürlichen Wissenschaft als der Sitten-Lehre* (Essay on the essence of spirit, or fundamental theory of both natural science and ethics) illustrated this change of heart.

Thomasius's form of Pietism actually entailed a stringent criticism of its normal practices. As a result, he encountered difficulties with the authorities in Pietist Halle. Thomasius was especially critical of current educational practices as they were institutionalized in the curriculum of the Halle Orphanage. He had actually helped to establish the orphanage with his friend August Hermann FRANCKE, but he believed that it had become a place of pedagogical rigidity, producing narrow-minded, obstinate, and intolerant people. Thomasius and Francke parted ways in a bitter public quarrel, and Thomasius was ordered to stop discussing education.

In his later years, Thomasius returned to the subject of law, writing his *Fundamentum iuris naturae et gentium ex sensu communi deducta* (Foundation of the law of nature and nations, deduced from common sense; 1705). This book argued for the complete separation between God and natural law, claiming that God was neither the author of natural laws, nor the source of their authority. It laid the groundwork for a thoroughly secular version of law, founded in MORAL PHILOSOPHY rather than in theology.

Between 1710 and 1750, a small group of professors at Halle and Leipzig followed Thomasius's ideas and principles. But his importance for the *Aufklärung* became apparent only after 1740, when his ideas were adopted by the so-called popular philosophers in Berlin and Göttingen.

threshing machine A machine invented in 1732 by Michael Menzies. It mechanized the process of separating grain seeds from harvested plants, a process called threshing that had been traditionally carried out by painstaking hand labor.

The introduction of the threshing machine helped to make practical the possibility of enclosure, whereby the old common lands in Britain were fenced and reserved for the private agricultural use of lords. In effect, the threshing machine reduced the need of a lord for the physical labor of many peasants and, at the same time, allowed production levels to increase. The enclosure process brought serious social upheaval in its wake as tenant farmers were forced to leave the land.

Enclosure was one of several innovations in agricultural organization and practice that not only revolutionized the English countryside but also created large pools of cheap labor to be tapped by enterprising factory owners. The events of the so-called Agricultural Revolution thus became thoroughly intertwined with the emergence of the INDUSTRIAL REVOLUTION. Both phenomena acted together to make the 18th century one of major change in the social and economic structures of Great Britain.

Tiepolo, Giovanni Battista (Giambattista) (1696–1770) *Italian fresco painter*

Tiepolo was born in VENICE, the son of a merchant and ship owner. He apprenticed as a young boy in the workshop of the painter Gregorio Lazzarini. By 1717, Tiepolo had become a member of the painters' confraternity in Venice. He married Maria Cecilia Guardi, sister of the painter Francesco GUARDI, in 1719. Of their nine children, two sons, Giovanni Domenico and Lorenzo Baldissera, worked with their father as assistants and later pursued their own artistic careers.

Tiepolo worked in Venice until about 1725, when he received a commission from the archbishop of Udine to decorate the archbishop's palace with frescoes. Afterward, Tiepolo began to receive many commissions from other Italian cities such as MILAN, Bergamo, and Vicenza.

In 1750, the bishop of Würzburg called Tiepolo to that city to decorate the rooms of his new Residenz. Tiepolo decorated the huge vault over the staircase designed by Balthasar NEUMANN with a magnificent fresco entitled *The Four Corners of the World.* He also decorated the Kaiserssaal in the Residenz. This room, with its plaster work and ceiling fresco called *Wedding Allegory,* is considered one of the most outstanding ROCOCO rooms in southern GERMANY and AUSTRIA. Tiepolo's work became a model for rococo painters throughout Catholic Germany and Austria. Tiepolo returned to Italy in 1753, where he continued to provide frescoes for various palaces in the north.

In 1761, King CHARLES III OF SPAIN invited Tiepolo to MADRID. Having arrived in 1762, Tiepolo decorated the Throne Room of the Royal Palace with a vast allegorical and symbolic work, *Apotheosis of the Spanish Monarchy.* Tiepolo lived his remaining years in Madrid, where he worked continually but was largely unappreciated. Stylistic taste was changing, and Anton Rafael MENGS,

The Capture of Carthage, by Giovanni Battista Tiepolo. The rococo master Tiepolo not only created canvases depicting scenes from antiquity but also decorated rococo buildings with magnificent frescos. *(Courtesy Metropolitan Museum of Art, Rogers Fund, 1965)*

the German neoclassicist also living in Madrid, was gaining influence with wealthy patrons. Tiepolo died March 27, 1770, while he was working at his painting easel.

Tiepolo was considered, in his own time, one of the greatest European painters. His style contained elements of BAROQUE STYLE theatricality and grandeur: allegorical themes and a masterly, dramatic use of light to accentuate. His work also incorporated elements associated with rococo sensibility, especially in its palette of lighter pigments and its playful, imaginary applications of stucco work.

Tiepolo's catalog of works is filled with items ranging from magnificent decorative frescoes, to ordinary canvases and engravings. Of particular note are the following surviving frescoes: *Fall of the Rebel Angels, Rachel Hiding the Idols,* and *Judgment of Solomon,* all in the Palace of the Archbishop at Udine; *Saint Dominic Instituting the Rosary, Saint Dominic in Glory,* and *The Virgin Hearing the Saint's Prayers,* all in the Church of the Jesuits in Venice; *The Banquet of Anthony and Cleopatra* at the Palazzo Labia; the *Four Corners of the World* in Würzburg; *Triumph of Hercules* in the Palazzo Canossa in Verona; and the *Apotheosis of the Spanish Monarchy* in Madrid. Several important Tiepolo frescoes were destroyed during World War II. Tiepolo produced many easel canvases. The series commissioned by Count Francesco ALGAROTTI for Augustus III, elector of Saxony, deserves mention. It includes the *Rape of Europa* and *The Triumph of Flora.* Tiepolo also left portraits and drawings, many of which have been destroyed.

Tillotson, John (1630–1694) *English theologian*

John Tillotson served as archbishop of Canterbury, the chief post within the Anglican Church, from 1691 until his death in 1694. Prior to that he served as chaplain to Charles II, as dean of Canterbury, and as canon and dean of Saint Paul's Cathedral in LONDON.

Tillotson avidly defended the THEOLOGY and practices of the ANGLICANS against criticisms from ROMAN CATHOLICISM. But he used arguments based on universal human REASON to counter Catholic appeals to tradition and to authority. Critics of Tillotson rightly recognized that his arguments could be turned against all Christian belief. English deists such as Anthony COLLINS often borrowed the cloak of authority from Tillotson's arguments by capitalizing on his appeals to reason and RATIONALISM in their own criticisms of established Christianity. Furthermore, David HUME openly acknowledged the debt of his own essay "On Miracles" to Tillotson's arguments against the Catholic interpretation of the sacrament of the Eucharist.

Tillotson's published works include his *Sermons, preach'd upon several occasions* (1671, 1688) and essays such as the "Rule of Faith," which was also used by Hume.

See also DEISM; RELIGION.

Tindal, Matthew (ca. 1657–1733) *English lawyer and proponent of Christian deism*

Tindal taught law at All Souls College, Oxford University, and practiced law at Doctor's Commons.

Tindal wrote a deistic treatise aimed at defending the truth of Christianity. It tried to root legitimate belief in REASON and in the innate ideas possessed by people before they begin acquiring knowledge through experience. Tindal believed that the nature and characteristics of God could be determined through the exercise of human reason and that, from a few rationally derived ideas, a whole system of religious truth could be constructed. Special revelations from God were not necessary to this process. Furthermore, historical tradition was useless, since it could be used by believers in any religion to bolster their claims to truth.

Tindal published his ideas in *Christianity as Old as the Creation: Or, The Gospel A Republication of the Religion of Nature* (1730). His book forced critics of DEISM to abandon any appeals of their own to reason and to search for support from other arenas. Of the many impassioned responses to Tindal's book, *The Analogy of Religion* by Bishop Joseph BUTLER was particularly powerful.

Tindal's work illustrates how the enlightened belief in reason as the path that leads to truth could be used to bolster Christianity in the face of criticism by its detractors. It shows that enlightened discourse based on rationalism was the exclusive preserve neither of critics of religion, nor of religion's orthodox defenders, but could be adapted to many forms of argument on both sides of an issue. Reason was showing itself, therefore, to be less than invincible as a source of unchallengeable truth. At least in the realm of religion, Tindal's demonstrations helped to stimulate a turning away from reason toward HISTORY and feeling as alternative sources of truth.

See also NATURAL RELIGION.

Tissot, Samuel-Auguste-André-David (1728–1797) *Swiss doctor and writer of medical treatises*

Tissot played an important role in disseminating medical information to the public. He was best known for his book on the dangers of masturbation. First published in Latin in 1758, it became available to a general readership when Tissot published a French version in 1760 titled *L'Onanisme: Dissertation sur les maladies produites par la masturbation* (Onanism: A study of the illnesses produced by masturbation). This book was very widely read and soon translated into English. It helped make masturbation a major concern, influencing moral precepts and educational practices. Indeed, Tissot's views on the subject, although they are outdated today, were still influential in the early 20th century.

Tissot's discussion of masturbation marked the first time the subject was presented to the public in the context of medical thought. The philosophy of nature that informed his thinking on this issue corresponded to a Christian moral framework, but it was significant that Tissot saw nature rather than God as the source of laws against which individuals must not rebel. His rational approach warned of bodily ills instead of invoking moral or religious prohibitions. This thinking was based on the scientific theory that the body loses vital forces when its fluids are depleted. According to Tissot, the negative consequences of masturbation included acne, feebleness, convulsions, impotence, dizziness, imbecility, memory loss, and early death, either by suicide or by diseases such as gonorrhea and syphilis. He advised fathers to investigate their households scrupulously to discover whether masturbation was taking place, a dictum quickly adopted by new theories of EDUCATION.

His subsequent book *L'avis au peuple sur sa santé ou traité des maladies les plus fréquentes* (Recommendations to the people on health, or treatise on the most common illnesses; 1761) was a forerunner of today's medical encyclopedias for home use, describing illnesses and the treatments they require. Tissot also published a work titled *De la santé des gens de lettres* (On the health of writers; 1766), in which he expressed concern that the sedentary lifestyle of intellectuals led to medical problems. Resolutely oppposed to any excess—whether involving masturbation or mental activity—Tissot recommended clean living that included a balance of rest, exercise outdoors, and social interaction.

See also MEDICINE.

Further reading: Antoinette Emch-Dériaz, *Tissot, Physician of the Enlightenment* (New York: Peter Lang, 1992); Anne Vila, *Enlightenment and Pathology: Sensibility in the Literature and Medicine of Eighteenth-Century France* (Baltimore: Johns Hopkins University Press, 1998).

Toland, John (1670–1722) *British philosopher and freethinker, a major contributor to the development of deism in England*
A native of Ireland raised as a Catholic, Toland converted to PROTESTANTISM sometime between 1687 and 1695. He attended universities at Leiden in the UNITED PROVINCES OF THE NETHERLANDS, at EDINBURGH and Glasgow in SCOTLAND, and at Oxford in ENGLAND.

Toland attacked beliefs in miracles and supernatural events whether they came from Christian or pagan traditions. He earned early notoriety when he published *Christianity Not Mysterious* (1696), a book arguing that all Christian doctrines, miracles, and revelations can be explained in rational terms and can, therefore, be made intelligible to the human mind. The *Life of Milton* published in 1701 called attention to the many books that posed as works of Jesus Christ or of his disciples. *Amyntor, or a Defence of Milton's Life* (1699) drew attention to the claim that the Bible was a historical creation in which councils of church authorities had decided whether or not to include or to exclude certain books. *Socinianism Truly Stated* (1705) argued on behalf of Socinianism, the movement from the 16th and 17th centuries out of which Unitarianism eventually developed. Socinians denied the divinity of Jesus Christ and rejected the Christian doctrine of the Holy Trinity, arguing, instead, that Jesus of Nazareth was simply a wise teacher. Toland's book defended this position by exposing weaknesses in the arguments of its enemies. The book introduced the concept of pantheism into the discourse of the ENLIGHTENMENT. *Tetradymus* (1720) provided natural explanations for Old Testament miracles.

Toland used not only REASON and concepts of NATURAL LAW but also the tools of BIBLICAL CRITICISM and HISTORY to undermine the truth claims of Christianity. *Adeisidaemon* (The unsuperstitious man; 1709) pointed to the many miraculous events reported by the pagan Roman historian Livy in order to show that miracles did not occur exclusively in Christian contexts. His *Origines Judaicae* (Origins of Judaism; 1709) challenged biblical accounts of Jewish history by arguing that the Jews were originally an Egyptian people. *Nazarenus: Jewish, Gentile, and Mahometan Christianity* (1718) called attention to the role played by the Ebionites in the development of early Christianity.

In attacking Christianity, Toland was trying to establish grounds for a universal NATURAL RELIGION based on reason and natural law. It is this aspect of his work that causes scholars to call him a deist. Toland was committed to the principle of religious TOLERATION. His ideas, however, were too extreme for many of his contemporaries. Even John LOCKE, the great champion of tolerance, tried to distance his positions from those of Toland.

Toland supported the claims of the electors of Hanover to the English throne. He spent some years in Hanover and BERLIN, recording his experiences and observations in the *Account of the Courts of Prussia and Hanover* (1705) and *Letters to Serena* (1704). The latter were addressed to Sophia Charlotte of Hanover, wife of the elector of BRANDENBURG. They contained materials that contributed to the development of 18th-century philosophies of MATERIALISM.

Toland's work demonstrates the manner in which the Enlightenment supported the application of critical reason to RELIGION but also turned to reason and the presumed lawful order of the universe to provide arguments in favor of a belief in God. His interest in demonstrating the universal rational basis for religion would be picked up by deists and by radical freethinkers such as the FREEMASONS.

toleration Policy that permits individuals to choose their forms of religious worship even if those forms are not the official ones endorsed by the state. The ENLIGHTENMENT was marked by widespread calls for religious toleration and by the development of political theories of the state that would support such reforms. The campaigns for such reforms were successful to varying degrees. By the end of the Enlightenment, official toleration policies existed in all major European nations and in the new UNITED STATES OF AMERICA. One of the great achievements of the Enlightenment, therefore, was the creation of a POLITICAL THEORY and associated vision of humanity that made it possible for states to abandon religious persecution as a means for controlling citizens' behavior.

As the era of the Enlightenment began to unfold, the religious organization of Europe mostly revealed close relationships between church and state. Rulers generally tried to ensure that their subjects belonged to one faith, either ROMAN CATHOLICISM or one of the various forms of PROTESTANTISM. The choice of religious belief defined individual identity and carried political meaning that rulers believed could not be ignored. People who refused to conform, whether Jews or adherents of some unfavored form of Christianity, often found themselves persecuted.

In FRANCE, for example, marriages between HUGUENOTS, as French Calvinists were called, were sometimes invalidated and the children of such unions deprived of inheritances. Huguenot pastors could be put to death, and ordinary believers could be imprisoned or sent for life to the galleys. In SPAIN, PORTUGAL, and ITALY, the Roman Inquisition persecuted non-Catholics. Within the HAPSBURG EMPIRE, the Protestants of HUNGARY and other regions were pressured to convert to Catholicism. The Polish government was actively trying to force its Protestants back into the Catholic fold. Even in countries like ENGLAND, the UNITED PROVINCES OF THE NETHERLANDS, and GENEVA, where limited religious toleration existed, members of minority religions suffered under civic discrimination. Thus, in England, Catholics, Jews, and Protestant DISSENTERS lacked certain political and civic rights that were guaranteed to Anglicans. They were barred from attending prestigious UNIVERSITIES, forbidden from appointive offices, and excluded from the local municipal corporations that were the foundation of English political life. Geneva refused not only citizenship but sometimes also residency to non-Calvinists. Policies of genuine toleration existed only in BRANDENBURG, where the Calvinist Hohenzollerns ruled Lutheran subjects and decided, for practical reasons, to establish official toleration as a state policy.

An intimate relationship links early enlightened political theory with the issue of toleration, for the era opened on the heels of an era of religious turmoil and persecution. In England, the birthplace of the early Enlightenment, John LOCKE wrote the LETTERS ON TOLERATION in reaction to the political and social upheavals caused by religious quarrels. His famous contract theory of the state was intimately linked to the desire for religious peace. At the same time, early theorists of DEISM were developing their rational form of NATURAL RELIGION in an effort to provide an alternative to religious dogmatism. The resulting critique of ENTHUSIASM often blended with toleration issues in the thought of later enlightened writers.

These early English intellectual ventures into toleration were accompanied by a limited Act of Toleration passed in 1689 as part of the settlement of the GLORIOUS REVOLUTION. This act allowed non-Anglican Protestants (Dissenters) to worship, but it did not remove other limitations on their existence. Full religious toleration accompanied by the removal of civic liabilities would not come to England until the 19th century.

The issue of toleration in France came to the forefront during the later years of the reign of LOUIS XIV. He had decided that the presence of religious divisions within his kingdom threatened royal ABSOLUTISM. To remedy the situation, Louis ordered the revocation of the Edict of Nantes and thus deprived French Calvinists of the limited tolerance they had enjoyed since 1598. Huguenots were ordered to convert to Roman Catholicism. Many obeyed, but thousands fled to the safety of the United Provinces of the Netherlands, BERLIN, or England.

The death of Louis XIV was followed by a dramatic loosening of central control over French life and thought. In this atmosphere, the early PHILOSOPHES began to discuss toleration. As the 18th century progressed, the campaign for toleration gathered momentum, easily reinforced by the ANTICLERICALISM, calls for reform, and criticism of religious belief that were prominent components of the French Enlightenment. The name of VOLTAIRE is commonly associated with the toleration issue, but the PHYSIOCRATS and their adherents such as Anne-Robert-Jacques TURGOT also supported the idea. The movement for toleration finally achieved official recognition in the critical years that led to the FRENCH REVOLUTION. An Edict of Toleration decreed in 1787 granted civil rights to French Protestants and removed the prohibition against their marriages. French Jews benefited in 1784 from an edict that eliminated the special personal taxes they had been required to pay.

The French Revolution finally eliminated the links between Roman Catholicism and the secular state that had hindered the cause of official toleration. However, in its most radical phases, leaders substituted total secularization and the Cult of the Supreme Being—an artificial rational religion of state—for traditional religious forms. They thus fostered intolerance of all traditional religious creeds in the name of REASON and human PROGRESS.

The German-speaking regions of central Europe presented a variety of official responses to the problem of religious diversity at the beginning of the Enlightenment.

Most states, with the exception of PRUSSIA were aiming for religious conformity. As the Enlightenment developed, the example of Prussia began to demonstrate that religious conformity was not necessary in order to secure tight control of a state. Toleration seemed to have some practical utility for central administration. Concomitantly, German writers such as Gotthold Ephraim LESSING and Moses MENDELSSOHN were calling for toleration on moral and rational grounds. The FREEMASONS, whose lodges flourished in German lands, emphasized the universal brotherhood of mankind, thereby supplying a philosophical support for toleration.

These movements bore fruit in AUSTRIA in 1781, when the Hapsburg emperor JOSEPH II passed an Edict of Toleration granting full citizenship rights to all non-Catholics. The provisions of the edict affected Protestants and Jews. The latter group was freed from clothing restrictions and from the requirement that they live in ghettos.

With the founding of the United States, religious toleration and the associated principle of the SEPARATION OF CHURCH AND STATE were written into the federal UNITED STATES CONSTITUTION and UNITED STATES BILL OF RIGHTS. Individual states made independent decisions about whether to support an official church, but by 1833, all of them had also chosen the principle of separation.

The Enlightenment produced outstanding literature calling for toleration in the *DICTIONNAIRE PHILOSOPHIQUE* by Voltaire, *Nathan der Weise* (*NATHAN THE WISE*) by Lessing, and the Letters on Toleration by Locke. New political theory and MORAL PHILOSOPHY provided theoretical foundations for major shifts in church and state relations. The language of universal human rights helped to create a sense of moral urgency to reform, and practical considerations of economic prosperity and stability also seemed to support the wisdom of toleration. Together, these factors helped to make the Enlightenment an era of radical change in which religious diversity could be accepted as a natural factor in human existence.

See also COSMOPOLITANISM.

Further reading: C. J. Betts, *Early Deism in France: From the So-Called Déistes of Lyon (1564) to Voltaire's Lettres philosophiques (1734)* (The Hague: Martinus Nijhoff, 1984); Margaret C. Jacob, *The Radical Enlightenment: Pantheist, Freemasons, and Republicans* (London: George Allen & Unwin, 1981); Charles Alan Kors, *Atheism in France, 1650–1729*, vol. 1 of The Orthodox Sources of Disbelief (Princeton, N.J.: Princeton University Press, 1990).

Tom Jones NOVEL published in 1749 by Henry FIELDING. The complete title is *The History of Tom Jones, A Foundling*. This novel was even more successful than Fielding's previous novel, *Joseph Andrews* (1742). Fielding disliked the epistolary novel form that was then the rage in ENGLAND, and consciously set about creating a new form. His novel used an omniscient narrator to relate the plot and to comment on the actions, motivations, and fates of the characters. Through this narrator, Fielding also offered opinions about philosophical issues, contemporary politics, and aesthetic theories.

The narrative begins when a benevolent gentleman, Squire Allworthy, finds an infant in his bed. A widower, the squire decides to raise the child, whom he names Tom Jones after Jenny Jones, a woman whom he supposes to be the child's mother. Later, the squire's sister Bridget Allworthy marries and has a child, Master Blifil. The two boys are educated together, but while Tom grows up to become an openhearted, benevolent young man, Blifil grows into a mean-spirited and pedantic scholar, jealous of any attention given to his foster brother.

Tom becomes a favorite with Squire Western, who owns the neighboring estate. Western is a parody of the rustic, fox-hunting gentry who lived in rural England during the 18th century. He admires young Tom's ability to manage a horse and shoot a gun, and after Tom breaks his arm while rescuing the squire's daughter, Sophia, from a runaway horse, he insists that Tom remain in his house as his guest. However, when his daughter falls in love with Tom, Western banishes the young man from his estate.

Although Squire Western admires Tom, he wants Sophia to marry Blifil, who will inherit the bulk of the Allworthy estate. To escape the wishes of her family, Sophia runs away to LONDON. Tom follows the same road to London after being turned out of the Allworthy house because of the machinations of Blifil and his tutor.

On his journey to London, Tom provides assistance to a Mrs. Waters, who is none other than Jenny Jones, the woman his foster father had assumed was his mother. She provides Squire Allworthy with information that clears Tom's name and implicates Blifil in the various happenings at the estate. Through Mrs. Waters, Allworthy discovers that Tom is actually the eldest son of his sister Bridget and thus his natural nephew. Allworthy then acknowledges Tom as his heir, and Squire Western removes his objections to a marriage between Sophia and Tom.

Samuel Taylor COLERIDGE called the action in *Tom Jones* one of the three greatest plots of all literature. The highly complex story reflected Fielding's belief that despite the apparent randomness of existence, life is actually ordered by a divine creator. He wished to present the reality of life and human nature in all its complexity: good, evil, ugly, and beautiful. He did not, however, dwell on the kind of minute detail that filled the novels of Samuel RICHARDSON and Daniel DEFOE, but rather illustrated more general truths. This characteristic brings Fielding's fiction close to the neoclassical literary aesthetic articulated by Alexander POPE in *An Essay on Criticism* and by Samuel JOHNSON in *Rasselas*.

See also LITERATURE.

Tooke, John Horne (1736–1812) *English political radical, reformer, and linguist*

John Horne was born in LONDON. He adopted the surname Tooke in 1782 when his wealthy friend William Tooke left him his estate. Despite having little wealth, his father was respected in his poultry trade and was able to provide his seven children with a good EDUCATION. John Horne Tooke attended Westminster School and Eton before starting college at Cambridge University in 1754.

In 1760, Tooke became an Anglican minister. A believer in equality of opportunity and justice for all, Tooke became politically active. With John WILKES he founded the Society of Supporters of the Bill of Rights in London in 1769 to promote parliamentary reform and increased rights for the British people. In 1771, he started the Constitutional Society to advocate both parliamentary reform and increased freedom for the American colonies.

Tooke was often in trouble with the British authorities for his involvement in radical activities. He was sent to prison in 1778 for trying to raise money for Americans who were injured in the Battle of Lexington and Concord. In 1794, he was tried for treason but was later acquitted. Although he had been elected to Parliament in 1801, members of the House of Commons purposely passed legislation barring clergymen from sitting in Parliament.

Tooke was an avid supporter of the FRENCH REVOLUTION as well as the American. Among his friends and compatriots were other political radicals. These included William GODWIN, Mary WOLLSTONECRAFT, and Thomas PAINE. He was also the sole Englishman to be put in prison for supporting the AMERICAN REVOLUTION.

Apart from politics, Tooke had a lifelong interest in the study of LANGUAGE. He began his major work, *The Diversions of Purley*, while he was in prison in 1778, and wrote the remainder at William Tooke's estate of Purley. The first volume appeared in 1786, with a second edition in 1798. The *Diversions* is an attempt to study language scientifically. In the three-volume work he uses his method to derive the Anglo-Saxon origins of more than 2,000 words. The study was also political, as Horne Tooke believed that he had been imprisoned due to a misinterpretation of his language and writing. He also attempted to show that English had developed in a way that supported state power. Ever the reformer, Tooke also hoped that the book would make the study of language more accessible to all people. James Mill and other English utilitarians praised the book for its use of philosophy in the study of grammar and language. Despite its complexity, the book was popular. Tooke wrote an equally well received second volume in 1806 during his retirement at Purley.

Toussaint Louverture, François-Dominique (1743–1803) *leader of the Haitian slave revolt*

François-Dominique Toussaint Louverture was the key leader of the Haitian slave revolt (1791–1804) that ended SLAVERY in the French colony of Saint-Domingue (Haiti) and brought about Haiti's independence from France. Toussaint was born on the Bréda plantation near the city of Le Cap in northern Haiti. His father had been born in Africa and told his son about life there; his mother had been born in Saint-Domingue. From an early age, Toussaint stood out among the slaves who worked in the stable. His master made him a coachman, which gave Toussaint enough free time to teach himself to read and write. He read widely and was especially influenced by the literature of the French ENLIGHTENMENT, with its emphasis on the rights of man.

Toussaint was nearly 50 when the slave revolt broke out in Saint-Domingue in 1791. The National Assembly in PARIS had sided with planters and merchants, denying free people of color in the colonies the right to vote in an attempt to preserve slavery. Freemen in Saint-Domingue revolted, and, although their brief uprising failed, it incited slaves to join the revolution. Toussaint had been a slave his whole life and did not immediately join the revolt. Encouraged by Abbé RAYNAL's prediction that a chief would rise up to lead the slaves to freedom in the *HISTOIRE DES DEUX INDES* (History of the two Indies) and fired by the ideals espoused by the FRENCH REVOLUTION, Toussaint joined the revolt near the end of 1791. He immediately distinguished himself, and by the end of December of that year, Toussaint was a high officer, acting as counselor to the slave leader Jean-François.

When war between FRANCE and SPAIN broke out in 1793, Toussaint threw in his lot with the Spanish. By this point, he was the commander of a well-armed, highly disciplined contingent of 600 black revolutionaries. The men were trained by French officers who deserted and joined the slaves after the destruction of their fortifications at Le Cap. He no longer reported to Jean-Frangois, but directly to the Spanish general. Victories on the battlefield brought more men to him, and by the spring of 1794, Toussaint commanded more than 4,000 troops.

The National Convention abolished slavery in its colonies in February 1794. When news of this reached Haiti in April, Toussaint and his men switched sides, massacring the Spanish soldiers under his command and moving into French-held territory. The ensuing chaos among the Spanish forces allowed Toussaint to move against the English, who were anxious about unrest spreading to their Caribbean possessions and wanted to crush the slave revolt at its source, in Saint-Domingue.

The British had landed in Saint-Domingue in 1793 and captured Port-au-Prince, but were paralyzed by yellow fever. The struggle with the British went back and forth, with Toussaint and his forces in the north and other revolutionary forces in the south unable to defeat them decisively. The Spanish, however, were kept on the defensive as a result of Toussaint's military acumen, and in September 1795, they made peace with France, which received Spain's part of Saint-Domingue in the settlement. In October, 7,000 fresh English troops arrived, but Toussaint and his fellow revolutionaries in the south were able to defeat them with minimal losses. The British finally withdrew in 1798, having sustained 13,000 casualties.

With the Spanish defeated and the British on the defensive, Toussaint began to consolidate his power. Jean-François had retired to Spain after the conclusion of the peace, removing one of Toussaint's rivals for leadership in Saint-Domingue. Toussaint now turned his attention to limiting the power of the mulattoes on the island. Le Cap had been controlled by a mulatto officer since the withdrawal of French troops in the autumn of 1793, and the city had become the center of mulatto activity in the north. The mulattoes had been allied with the white planters and the French against the slaves since the revolt had broken out. On March 20, 1796, Toussaint entered Le Cap with 10,000 men, forcing the mulattoes from the town and securing his power. By April, he ruled Saint-Domingue with the consent of the French governor.

The country prospered under Toussaint's rule, but his position depended partly on France's inability to access any of its colonies because of the English naval blockade. The Peace of Amiens between Britain and France in 1802 lifted the blockade, allowing Napoleon to reassert control over Saint-Domingue. Toussaint was arrested on Napoleon's secret orders and sent to France. He died of starvation and exposure in the Fort-de-Joux prison in the Jura mountains on April 7, 1803. On January 1, 1804, protected again by the reinstated blockade, Haiti declared its independence. Two of Toussaint's lieutenants drove out the French troops sent by Napoleon, and slavery never returned to Haiti.

See also HAITIAN REVOLUTION; NATURAL RIGHTS.

Further reading: C. L. R. James, *The Black Jacobins* (New York: Vintage Books, 1963).

transit of Venus An apparent phenomenon observed in the heavens that occurs when the orbit of the planet Venus causes it to pass across the face of the Sun when viewed from the Earth. In the 18th century two transits of Venus occurred, one in 1761 and the second in 1769. Edmond HALLEY, who died in 1743, had predicted that measurements made of the transit of Venus from different spots on the Earth would allow the accurate calculation of the distance between the Earth and the Sun. The French astronomer Joseph DELISLE had discussed these ideas with Halley and made arrangements to observe the transit of Venus in 1761. British astronomers entered the enterprise when they heard of Delisle's plans. Ultimately, astronomers at more than 60 locations made observations and positional measurements in both 1761 and 1769. From these observations, the distance between Earth and Sun was calculated at 95 million miles, the most accurate figure that had been produced up until that time.

See also ASTRONOMY; SCIENCE; TECHNOLOGY AND INSTRUMENTATION.

David Rittenhouse. The American statesman and astronomer David Rittenhouse participated in the international cooperative scientific project to observe the 1769 transit of Venus. *(Courtesy Independence National Historical Park)*

travel literature A literary form that reported about exotic, foreign cultures. The global explorations begun by Europeans in the late 15th century were still producing new discoveries during the 18th century. Travelers such as Captain James COOK, Johann Georg Adam FORSTER, Johann Reinhold FORSTER, Louis de BOUGAINVILLE, Baron Lahontan, and Michel de CRÈVECOEUR, found the European reading public eager for their memoirs about travel in exotic lands, and the publication of such books provided a reliable source of income. Other travelers, such as Charles BURNEY, Alexander Radischev, Arthur YOUNG, Samuel JOHNSON, J. G. A. Forster, and James BOSWELL, used the travel memoir as a vehicle for expressing views about various facets of European culture.

Travel literature, however, was not limited to descriptions of personal experience. In fact, much of the 18th-century literature is fictional, either covertly or overtly. In this category, one can place the novels of Daniel DEFOE and Jonathan SWIFT, both of whom used the backdrop of exotic lands as a vehicle for cultural and political criticism. Perhaps the major work in this category, the *PERSIAN LETTERS* by MONTESQUIEU, used the travel commentary as a means of writing critically about contemporary culture while avoiding difficulties with

Noble Savage, portrait of Stalking Turkey, chief of the Cherokee Indians. Some enlightened writers imagined that the culture of the Native American peoples represented the simple, honest virtues of humanity, untainted by the corruptions of civilization. *(Courtesy Smithsonian Institution, Washington, D.C.)*

thus provided materials that were readily adapted to the activity of general cultural, religious, and political criticism that was central to the ENLIGHTENMENT.

See also AESTHETICS; COSMOPOLITANISM; HISTORY; LITERATURE; MORAL PHILOSOPHY; PARK; POLITICAL THEORY; VOYAGES OF DISCOVERY.

Treatise of Human Nature, A   Book by the Scottish philosopher David HUME, written in FRANCE between 1734 and 1737 and published in three volumes in 1739 and 1740. The *Treatise* presented Hume's attempt to "introduce the experimental method of reasoning into moral subjects."

Hume wanted to build a science of human behavior that would have the certainty and utility of Newtonian physics. To attain this end, he proposed reexamining the basic facts of human behavior and identifying the major principles that shape it. Isaac NEWTON had identified three principles or laws of motion from which he had built a complete system of terrestrial and celestial mechanics. Following Newton's model, Hume described three laws of mental association—resemblance, contiguity, and cause and effect—that he believed determine the structure of all human understanding and knowledge. This knowledge, in turn, shapes human responses to the environment and provides the foundation on which ethical systems are constructed.

Hume intended his theory to provide a comprehensive vision of human sciences that would avoid the weaknesses contained in earlier formulations. He used materials from John LOCKE, George BERKELEY, René DESCARTES, and Benedict de SPINOZA, but his examination tended to undermine the EMPIRICISM, idealism, and RATIONALISM that had informed their respective approaches.

The publication of *A Treatise of Human Nature* did not bring the response that Hume had desired. It was largely ignored in both ENGLAND and France; and where noticed it was criticized for its alleged ATHEISM and SKEPTICISM. Hume himself remarked that the *Treatise* "fell dead-born from the press."

Disappointed with the reception of his *Treatise,* Hume devoted several years to revising it, paring its length, and reformulating some positions. The revised version appeared in 1758 as AN ENQUIRY CONCERNING HUMAN UNDERSTANDING. Unlike its parent treatise, the *Enquiry* was widely read and enormously influential throughout enlightened Europe.

As Hume matured, his status as a philosopher increased. As a result, the *Treatise* began to receive more attention, eventually coming to be recognized as a revolutionary and highly significant milestone in the ENLIGHTENMENT. Its analyses of the limits of human knowledge provided major foundations for modern empirical PSYCHOLOGY. Furthermore, his laws of association were

censors. Works by Abbé RAYNAL and Denis DIDEROT also fall into this category.

Genuine travel literature helped to create an avid interest in so-called primitive cultures. In the hands of anthropologists, general writers, and reformers, travel accounts stimulated cultural criticism and speculations about the essentials of human NATURE. These accounts provided materials from many different cultures to support arguments for or against the existence of universal and natural forms of RELIGION, THEOLOGY, human knowledge, and morality. In the hands of some writers such as Raynal, the encounter with so-called primitive peoples also helped to bolster arguments against SLAVERY.

Travel literature stimulated the comparative study of human societies and the development of ANTHROPOLOGY. It also helped to create an awareness that factors such as environment, climate, and general culture play a role in shaping human moral, social, and political character. It developed by David HARTLEY into a comprehensive and influential association psychology.

Trembley, Abraham (1710–1784) *Genevan zoologist and writer*

Trembley, son of an officer in the Genevan army, attended the Academy of GENEVA for his higher education and then moved to Holland, where he became tutor to the son of Count Bentinck. In 1756, Trembley received a large sum of money from another student, the young duke of Richmond. This largesse allowed Trembley to retire for the rest of his life on an estate, Petit Sacconex, near Geneva and to pursue his scientific and other intellectual interests at leisure.

While in Holland, Trembley established connections with noted scientists at the University of Leiden and carried out his famous experiments on regeneration in the simple animal called the hydra. Having cut a hydra into pieces, Trembley noted that each piece regenerated to create a whole organism. He was not sure whether the hydra was a plant or an animal, but eventually he assigned it to the animal kingdom.

Count Bentinck and the duke of Richmond forwarded Trembley's findings to the ROYAL SOCIETY OF LONDON, where they caused a sensation. VOLTAIRE refused for years to believe the reports. But the findings were convincing enough for the members of the Royal Society that they elected Trembley to their group in 1743.

In the meantime, Trembley had continued his hydra experiments, producing a graft between two animals to form a single organism and also regenerating a normal hydra from a specimen that he had turned inside out. Trembley corresponded with the French naturalist René-Antoine Ferchault de RÉAUMUR (1683–1757) about his experiments and also discussed them with his friend and fellow Genevan, Charles BONNET. Bonnet undertook his own experiments with the rainwater worm and produced similar phenomena. All these experiments on regeneration helped to strengthen, if only temporarily, the explanations of GENERATION (reproduction) supported by PREFORMATION THEORY.

Trembley published his experimental findings in an illustrated volume called *Mémoires, pour servir à l'histoire d'un genre de polypes d'eau douce, à bras en forme de cornes* (Memoirs on the history of a kind of freshwater polyp with arms shaped like horns; 1744).

Trimmer, Sarah (1741–1810) *English reviewer and author of children's books*

Sarah Trimmer was born Sarah Kirby, the daughter of John Kirby, an engraver and artist. The family settled in LONDON in 1755, and their friends included the artist William HOGARTH and the writer Samuel JOHNSON. Sarah's marriage to James Trimmer in 1762 resulted in six daughters and six sons. Trimmer became interested in EDUCATION, and in 1786 she founded her own church school in her hometown of Brentford. She became known as an expert on Sunday schools; her treatise on the subject, *The Oeconomy of Charity* (1786), stresses the importance of making basic knowledge of RELIGION, but also of home economics, available to all classes in order that each person should make the most of his or her given station in life.

She had published her first book, *An Easy Introduction to the Knowledge of Nature and Reading the Holy Scriptures, Adapted to the Capacities of Children,* in 1780. The goal of this work was to lead children, through the study of nature, to an understanding of God. In 1786, she followed it with *A Description of a Set of Prints of Scripture History,* dedicated to Félicité de GENLIS; the little prints it described (three inches square) were sold separately, either as a book or in a format suitable for hanging on the wall of a child's room. Over the next two decades she issued several similar sets, including *The New Testament, Ancient History,* and *British History.*

Also in 1786, she published a work that became a classic of children's literature: *Fabulous Histories: Designed for the Instruction of Children, Respecting Their Treatment of Animals,* better known as *The History of the Robins.* Although Trimmer's purpose in writing the book was strictly didactic—to show her young readers the proper behavior of the members of a family—the baby robins (Pecksy, Flapsy, Robin, and Dick) who stand in for children in the book became beloved characters for generations of children.

From 1788 to 1789, Trimmer edited *The Family Magazine.* She then founded the grand project that addressed her principal concerns, the periodical *Guardian of Education,* published from 1802 to 1806. Trimmer was deeply concerned that dangerous ideas, especially ideas imported from revolutionary FRANCE—excessive rationalism, ATHEISM, and egalitarianism—could seep into British children's minds through the books they were given to read. In the *Guardian* she provided guidance for parents to help them choose books for their children that would preserve and promote VIRTUE and religion. She was not above recommending the use of scissors to improve a book that contained dangerous passages. Nonetheless, the *Guardian* is recognized as the first publication to treat children's literature seriously and review it in a systematic way.

In the last years of her life Trimmer became involved in a controversy about the mutual instruction method advocated by Doctor Andrew Bell, in which students participated in their own education by teaching their peers. Bell's method was first published in 1797 as *Experiment in Education.* Joseph Lancaster, a Quaker educator, founded a school based on his understanding of Bell's ideas and published a treatise, *Improvements in Education,* in 1803.

Trimmer attacked Lancaster's work in *A Comparative View* (1805) for failing to make Anglican Christianity the center of its system; without the commitment to established religion, she felt, Lancaster's monitors could be seduced by the power the system gave them and become rebellious. Bell and Trimmer united against Lancaster, and Bell's and Lancaster's rival systems became a subject of hot debate all over the country. Out of this conflict was born the National Society for Promoting the Education of the Children of the Poor in the Principles of the Established Church, which, using Bell's system, laid the foundation of elementary public education in Britain. Because of Trimmer's reputation as an author for children and as an expert on what children should read, her advocacy of Bell had a lasting influence.

See also WOMEN AND THE ENLIGHTENMENT.

Further reading: Peter Hunt, *Children's Literature* (Malden, Mass.: Blackwell, 2001); Andrea Immel, *Revolutionary Reviewing: Sarah Trimmer's Guardian of Education and the Cultural Politics of Juvenile Literature* (Los Angeles: Department of Special Collections, University Research Library, University of California, Los Angeles, 1990); Cornelia Meigs et al., *A Critical History of Children's Literature: A Survey of Children's Books in English* (New York: Macmillan, 1969); Eric Quayle, *Early Children's Books: A Collector's Guide* (Lanham, Md.: Rowman & Littlefield, 1983); Karen Patricia Smith, *The Fabulous Realm: A Literary-Historical Approach to British Fantasy, 1780–1990* (Lanham, Md.: Scarecrow Press, 1993).

Tristram Shandy   A nine-volume NOVEL by Laurence STERNE published between 1759 and 1767. The first two books were rejected by a publisher in LONDON and printed instead at York. When they appeared in London, they enjoyed great success. The last volume appeared just one year before Sterne's death, and critics have debated whether or not he actually completed what he had planned.

Tristram Shandy poses as an autobiography of its main character, a form that became popular during the ENLIGHTENMENT. It begins with the moment of Tristram's conception and proceeds by a long and convoluted path to relate the development of his consciousness and life.

Sterne admired the *Essay on Human Understanding* by John LOCKE, and he used its portrayal of the development of human consciousness as the background for his presentation of Tristram's life.

Aside from the narrator, the most memorable character in the novel is Tristram's Uncle Toby, who is a former soldier and a man of so much benevolence that he refuses to kill a fly. In Toby's character, Sterne both celebrates and mocks SENTIMENTAL FICTION. A major portion of *Tristram Shandy* focuses on Toby's courtship of the beautiful widow, Mrs. Wadman, who desires to know the exact location of the wound Toby received in the groin during one of his most memorable campaigns. When she asks her question, Toby draws a map of the geographical location of the wound, constantly failing to satisfy the widow's real curiosity about his anatomy. The novel is full of comic misunderstandings like this one, which convey Sterne's awareness that written and spoken language can fail to serve our needs for communication with each other. The novel suggests that the languages of emotion and of physical gesture are more genuine and reliable.

See also BILDUNG; LITERATURE; PSYCHOLOGY.

Trotter, Catharine (1679–1749) *English playwright and philosophical writer*
As well known by her married name of Catharine Cockburn, Trotter was born in LONDON. Her father, a naval commander, died shortly thereafter, leaving her mother, who was connected to the Scottish nobility, to raise two daughters. Trotter was precocious. A short NOVEL first published in 1693, later reprinted under the title *Olinda's Adventures: Or the Amours of a Young Lady* (1718), has been widely attributed to Trotter. Her first play, *Agnes de Castro* (1695), was a tragedy based on a story by Aphra BEHN. The play was produced in London when she was 15, and this success was followed by *The Fatal Friendship* in 1698. She wrote five plays in all, the last one titled *The Revolution of Sweden* (1706). Trotter's influential social network ensured that her drama was produced on stage, but after their initial performances her plays were not revived. Her feminist exposition of women's intellect and strong moral sense in fairly static plots devoid of the usual scandalous intrigue and violence appear to have been relatively unpopular with audiences.

Despite her dramatic focus on women's morality and good sense, Trotter's reputation for moral behavior and intellectual range was not entirely positive in her own age. She was a celebrated beauty in the theatrical environment and subject to gossip. Like her contemporaries Mary PIX and Delariviere Manley, she is travestied in the satirical play *The Female Wits* (1696). Trotter becomes Calista, who is listed in the dramatis personae as a proud, vain lady pretending to great intellectual powers. Her intellectual range and talent were often ridiculed in the popular press.

Following her theatrical career, she participated in the public debate about philosophical and ethical issues. She published several philosophical treatises in defense of the principles of John LOCKE and, later, Samuel CLARKE. Modern feminists have been considerably kinder than were her contemporary critics, perceiving in Trotter's rigorous debating style and philosophical sophistication a strong intellectual role model for other 18th-century women. Indeed, she is now considered a philosopher in her own right.

Trotter's engaging idiosyncrasies included two religious conversions and her determination to marry an

Anglican curate named Patrick Cockburn despite his initial resistance and relative poverty. An early convert to Catholicism, she returned to the Church of England in 1707 under the influence of John Locke and Bishop Burne. The following year, she married Cockburn. Because he would not agree to swear the Oath of Allegiance to George I (1714), he languished as a poorly paid teacher until 1726, when he overcame his scruples and was reinstated in the church. During that difficult period, Trotter remained a devoted wife and mother, intellectually active until her death.

See also MORAL PHILOSOPHY.

Further reading: Kathryn J. Ready, "Damaris Cudworth Masham, Catharine Trotter Cockburn, and the Feminist Legacy of Locke's Theory of Personal Identity," *18th-Century Studies* 35:4 (summer 2002) 563–76.

Tull, Jethro (1674–1741) *English agriculturalist and inventor*

Jethro Tull was born into a farming family in Berkshire, ENGLAND. Originally he had no interest in farming. He studied law at Oxford University to prepare for a career in politics. However, after marriage in 1699, he had a series of health and financial problems. Unable to continue to pursue his legal and political career, he returned to his family's farm.

By 1700, Tull was frustrated with the labor and costs of the farming life. He was interested in both increasing production and lowering the amount of manual labor required to farm successfully. In addition, he wanted to lower farming costs by reducing the number of workers on his farm, thus lowering the amount of money he paid in wages. Eliminating hard labor would reduce the need to pay higher wages. As his costs and frustrations began to increase, Tull began to explore alternatives in 1701.

He traveled to Europe and other parts of England in order to improve his health and to observe various farming methods. Tull invented a mechanical drill for sowing seeds. This was a great improvement over planting seeds by hand. The drill allowed seeds to be planted more deeply in the soil and to be spaced a precise distance apart. It also made it possible to plant three seeds at once. Shortly thereafter, he invented a horse-drawn hoe to remove weeds from fields. After keeping his own fields productive and weed-free for 13 years, in 1714 he marketed his machines in England and on the Continent.

Tull presented his ideas on agricultural reform in *The New Horse-Hoeing Husbandry* in 1731, which was criticized because its recommendations were seen as opposing the contemporary movement that favored the idea of old Roman, rural simplicity. Wealthier landowners with a great deal to gain were more willing to experiment with his methods. Although the benefits of Tull's seed drill and his ideas on manure fertilizer, crop rotation, and hoeing took time to prove themselves, once crop yields began to

increase, Tull's inventions and ideas sparked a revolution in the agricultural industry. The Agricultural Revolution was as important to the development of modern capitalism as was the INDUSTRIAL REVOLUTION. Tull played a major role in this momentous transformation, which marked the beginnings of the modern farming industry.

Turgot, Anne-Robert-Jacques, baron de l'Aulne (1727–1781) *French statesman and disciple of the Physiocrats*

Turgot received his education at the Jesuit Collège Louis-le-Grand. He began theology studies at the Sorbonne, intending to become a Catholic clergyman. At the Sorbonne, he became closely linked to the writer André Morellet (1727–1819). In 1751, Turgot graduated but abandoned his plans for an ecclesiastical career to pursue the study of law. By 1752 he had purchased an office as a legal councillor in the Parlement of Paris (sovereign law court). In 1753, when the *parlement* rebelled against LOUIS XV and refused to administer justice, Turgot sided with the king. He believed that the *parlement* had

Anne-Robert-Jacques Turgot. As controller general of finance in France, Turgot, a student of the Physiocrats and friend of the philosophes, attempted to introduce a series of government reforms inspired by enlightened principles. *(Courtesy New York Public Library)*

exceeded its legal authority and viewed the members of French *PARLEMENTS* as little more than defenders of their narrow personal interests and privileges.

Turgot desired to obtain a high government post. In 1761, he was appointed superintendent of the Limoges district. He retained his office in the Parlement of Paris and sat in the court when it reopened the case of Jean CALAS. Turgot made an impassioned appeal for the rehabilitation of the reputation of Calas and of his family.

During these years, Turgot became acquainted with both François QUESNAY and Jean-Claude GOURNAY, the founders of Physiocratic economic theory. He recognized the underlying similarities in their different approaches to ECONOMICS and proceeded to meld their ideas into a uniform theory. Seeing a supporter of the Enlightenment in Turgot, the PHILOSOPHES began using their publications to call for his appointment to the royal ministry. Jean Le Rond d'ALEMBERT, Marie-Jean de CONDORCET, Jean-François MARMONTEL, Étienne Bonnot de CONDILLAC and Morellet all characterized Turgot as the only man who could rescue FRANCE from its political and fiscal impasse. Turgot eventually received a position in the naval administration, and he acquired the powerful post of general controller in 1774. As general controller he proceeded to institute a program of ambitious economic reform guided by the teachings of the PHYSIOCRATS. He guaranteed FREE TRADE in the grain market, suppressed the corvée (forced peasant labor on roads), abolished the guilds that restricted entry into certain crafts and industries, and instituted a universal property tax to fund the maintenance of roads. He proposed establishing a universal, uniform civil law code in France, guaranteeing religious TOLERATION, suppressing the worst abuses of the still-existing feudal manorial system, and taxing the clergy. The *parlements* of the various French provinces refused to register his decrees, and the king had to force the Parlement of Paris to register the decree by holding a special session called a *lit de justice*. Adversaries in the royal government succeeded in turning LOUIS XVI against Turgot, who was dismissed from office in May 1776. Turgot died in 1781 from complications associated with gout.

Turgot had prodigious intellectual interests covering SCIENCE, mathematics, PHILOSOPHY, and the liberal arts. He translated the Swiss poet Salomon Gessner (1730–88) and the German poet Friedrich Gottlieb KLOPSTOCK into French. He also translated the ballads of Ossian from English into French. Turgot left several essays refuting certain scientific theories proposed by Georges Louis de BUFFON and Pierre Louis de MAUPERTUIS. He also contributed articles on various economic issues to the ENCYCLOPÉDIE. Pierre-Samuel DU PONT DE NEMOURS published Turgot's collected writings in 1782.

See also ANCIEN RÉGIME; MATHEMATICS AND MECHANICS.

Turin Italian city lying on the PIEDMONT plain along the banks of the upper Po River. Turin was the capital and largest city of the kingdom of SAVOY, a dynastic state whose rulers sometimes played an important role in European international relations.

Turin had served as the Italian center of Savoyard strength since the 13th century but did not become the capital of the kingdom until 1563. During the 17th and 18th centuries, the city grew under the patronage of Victor Amadeus II (ruler from 1675 to 1730) and his 18th-century successors. It also acquired progressively stronger fortifications so that by the early 18th century, it was one of the best-defended cities in Europe. The city population doubled during the 18th century.

The gridlike layout of the city betrays its roots in the rational urban planning characteristic of the baroque era. The many surviving monuments from the period offer an outstanding example of the baroque tendency to adapt urban planning to propagandistic purposes. Victor Amadeus II, for example, had certain buildings located so that they suggested themes of power and grandeur, either through their impressive presence in the city or because of the views they offered over the surrounding Savoyard-ruled countryside. Turin contains notable examples of baroque architecture in its various aristocratic palaces, the royal palace, the Chapel of the Holy Shroud by Guarino Guarini, and the Basilica of Superga.

Turin possessed a small industrial economy based on the manufacture of silks and other luxuries. Metal manufactures grew up in response to the demand for military goods. These industries were aided by the existence of a series of canals outside the city that provided water and power to operate machinery. The city had a significant Jewish minority for the era—about 1.8 percent of the population in the early 18th century—most of whom were artisans or small businessmen. A few were prosperous through banking or large-scale commercial ventures.

See also BAROQUE STYLE.

Two Treatises of Government Book by John LOCKE containing his POLITICAL THEORY, first published in 1690, one of the major sources of inspiration and ideas for the political theories of the ENLIGHTENMENT. *Two Treatises* went through five English editions before 1789: 1690, 1694, 1698, 1713, and 1764. Moreover, between 1713 and 1764, it was reprinted approximately every five years. The 1764 edition was intended to correct the many errors that had crept into the text during these reprints.

A French translation by the Huguenot refugee David Mazel appeared in 1691 in Holland just 18 months after the first publication. This edition was a much modified version of the original work. The entire *First Treatise* was missing, as well as the "Preface" and "Chapter I" of the *Second Treatise*. The book was entitled *Du gouvernement civil* (Of civil government) and contained subtle changes that stressed the right of a people to revolt against their sovereign. It was this French text that was read throughout continental Europe and that provoked both admiration and criticism from PHILOSOPHES such as VOLTAIRE, MONTESQUIEU, and Jean-Jacques ROUSSEAU. The book went through 12 reprints in the 18th century. Locke possessed a copy of it and may have known about the planned alterations.

Locke prepared the *Two Treatises* in response to the *Patriarcha* by Robert Filmer and to certain arguments contained in the *Leviathan* by Thomas HOBBES. Filmer's book had appeared in 1680, as an apology for absolute monarchy. It was highly regarded by the Stuart monarchs and their Tory party supporters. Locke, a Whig party sympathizer, probably wrote the *Second Treatise* between 1679 and 1681, not in 1688 as has long been maintained. The *First Treatise* was written in 1683 after Locke had encountered Filmer's book. The whole work was not published until 1690, when it certainly acted as a theoretical justification for the GLORIOUS REVOLUTION of 1688.

The *First Treatise* contains a detailed refutation of Filmer's book. Filmer had argued that patriarchy and, by extension, ABSOLUTISM, are founded in the teachings of the Bible and therefore divinely decreed. The first man, Adam, had been appointed monarch over the whole world and patriarch over all his descendants. Filmer had tried to legitimize the claims of 17th-century absolute monarchs by this appeal to biblical, historical tradition. Locke's arguments drew from the Bible just as Filmer had done but used the scriptural material to demolish Filmer's claims.

The *Second Treatise,* the one that was of significance for the Enlightenment, contained the heart of Locke's political theory. It began with the assertion that men are all free (of each other) and equal (to each other). This condition had been decreed by God at the beginning of HISTORY. FREEDOM, however, consists not of the right to do whatever one wishes, but of choosing by an act of will based on REASON to live within the bounds of the God-given laws of nature (NATURAL LAW).

In the natural state then, every individual possesses the executive power of the law of nature. Locke means by this, that every man has the right to enforce the laws of nature against those who disobey.

This vision of Locke might seem to imply that people would constantly be warring and quarreling with one another (Hobbes's view), but Locke believed that natural men also possess a tendency to help each other and to work for peace. He consciously used an analogy between the natural man at the beginning of history and the Native American Indians of the American colonies.

Locke's depiction of the natural state of humanity is idyllic. What then would motivate people to give up this state in order to create a society and government? Locke offered a startling new answer: The need to protect PROPERTY motivated people to give up their natural state.

Locke's concept of property is sometimes misrepresented to mean only material possessions such as land and movable goods. He caused some of this confusion himself by treating property from this material perspective in a specific chapter on the subject.

But when he introduced property as the motive for the formation of societies, Locke had a much broader definition in mind. He specifically wrote that "every Man has Property in his own Person so that the Labour of his Body, and the Work of his Hands are his." He expanded this idea by referring to the property of an individual as life, liberty, and estate (status). The protection of property thus meant the protection of life, liberty, estate, and material possessions.

Recognizing the need for some form of society, people met together and agreed to grant some power to specifically designated authorities. This agreement was the social contract, and it was accompanied by a constitution that outlined the formal structure of power. If, at any time, delegated leaders abused power, the people, in whom the absolute sovereignty of the state always resided, could throw them out by means of a revolution.

Having described this social contract theory of government by consent, Locke elaborated on its form. His ideal was a government in which executive and legislative powers are divided. According to Locke, the legislative power is supreme and should be exercised by representatives taken directly from the citizenry. Locke hinted at the theory of the SEPARATION OF POWERS and at the idea of checks and balances, but these ideas were developed much more explicitly and completely in the later work of Montesquieu.

Locke's theory contains the essential elements of English liberal political theory and certainly offered a theoretical justification for the Glorious Revolution. It entered into the mainstream of the Enlightenment, providing the foundations for political reforms based on representative government, on constitutions, and on the rule of positive law. The ideas of the *Two Treatises* joined with those of Montesquieu to supply the theoretical underpinnings for the AMERICAN REVOLUTION and for the moderate stages of the FRENCH REVOLUTION.

Further reading: Richard Ashcraft, *Revolutionary Politics and Locke's "Two Treatises of Government"* (Princeton, N.J.: Princeton University Press, 1986); John Locke, *Two Treatises of Government,* intro. and notes Peter Laslett (New York: New American Library, 1965).

U

United Provinces of the Netherlands   Nation located on the North Sea, composed of the seven Dutch-speaking provinces of Holland, Utrecht, Zeeland, Overyssel, Gelderland, Friesland, and Groningen. Its capital was The Hague, and AMSTERDAM was the chief commercial city. The geographic extent of the United Provinces (also called the Dutch Republic) was so limited that one 18th-century visitor claimed it was possible to see the entire country from the tower of the Utrecht Cathedral.

Commerce, shipping, and banking provided the basis for the remarkable wealth of the Dutch during the 17th and 18th centuries. The Dutch East India Company and the Dutch West India Company controlled important colonies and commerce on the high seas. However, by 1740 they had lost their preeminence in trade to English companies. In spite of this setback, prosperous colonies in the West Indies, Cape of Good Hope, Java, and Ceylon, and a trade monopoly with Japan ensured a continual supply of goods and money. Dutch capital financed the activities of many nations, but relations with the British were particularly strong. As a result, Dutch and English foreign policy were closely intertwined, although war between the countries did break out in the 18th century.

The United Provinces of the Netherlands and the provinces of modern BELGIUM were ruled as one territory called the Spanish Netherlands by the Spanish Hapsburgs until the end of the 16th century. In 1579, the provinces of the future United Provinces of the Netherlands formed the Union of Utrecht and in 1581 had declared their independence from Spanish control. Their claim was recognized in 1609, when the Twelve Years' Truce officially divided the seven Dutch provinces (the United Provinces) from the 10 provinces of the Spanish Nether-

lands. Most European nations formally recognized Dutch independence in 1648 at the conclusion of the Thirty Years' War.

The strongest princes in the new United Provinces of the Netherlands were the princes of Orange, who transformed the tiny new state into a bastion of CALVINISM. In the 18th century, the Calvinist Dutch Reformed Church remained the official state church, but other religious groups enjoyed de facto TOLERATION. Formal guarantees of religious FREEDOM, however, were not established until 1795. Approximately one-third of the population was Catholic and another one-tenth was Jewish during the 18th century.

The United Provinces of the Netherlands was structured politically as a republic in which the Estates General (representative assembly) held supreme power. The leading prince (prince of Orange) was called the Stadtholder and was charged with duties as the chief government official and as commander of the military. In the towns, councils of citizens controlled affairs. As happened in the republics of VENICE and GENEVA, the Dutch town governments in practice acted as a species of aristocratic oligarchy: A few families dominated the town councils so thoroughly that the positions were nearly hereditary.

Enlightened Frenchmen were ambivalent about the Dutch Republic. On the one hand they regarded it as an example of republican civic virtue, placing it in a lineage with the Athens of Socrates, republican ROME, PHILADELPHIA, or the Geneva described by the young Jean-Jacques ROUSSEAU. Writers such as the marquis d'ARGENS, Denis DIDEROT, and VOLTAIRE praised the country as a cradle of toleration, guardian of liberty, and protector of rule by law. The image they created was almost mythical and reveals as much about the ideals of the PHILOSOPHES as it does about reality in the United Provinces. Unfortunately, when the philosophes encountered the Dutch firsthand, their mythical image shattered and was replaced by a cynical vision. Voltaire and MONTESQUIEU, for example, complained bitterly about what they saw as the degenerate mercantile values of the Dutch, their emphasis on profit rather than quality of production, their habit of extorting foreigners, their unimaginative, stifling industriousness, and their unrefined manners.

Evidence of a specifically Dutch form of the ENLIGHTENMENT exists in both thought and practice. Religious concerns were central and writers turned to both natural theology and the PHILOSOPHY of Christian WOLFF and other early German *Aufklärer* (enlightened intellectuals) for inspiration. The rational, secular forms of the Enlightenment are barely represented. Social institutions associated with the Enlightenment—especially reading clubs, political clubs, and the periodical press—existed in Dutch towns just as elsewhere in Europe. Dutch book publishers played a seminal role in diffusing the ideas of the Enlightenment throughout Europe.

Censorship in the United Provinces was relatively lax in comparison to other nations, and it was possible to publish works there that were forbidden elsewhere. Books judged dangerous to RELIGION or to the nation's internal peace could, nevertheless, be banned. Rousseau's *SOCIAL CONTRACT*, Thomas HOBBES'S *Leviathan,* Julien Offray de LA METTRIE's *L'Homme machine* (Man, a machine), and Diderot's *Pensées philosophiques* (Philosophical thoughts) all were confiscated and burned by the public hangman.

Discussions about the form of government and the nature of law occupied Dutch thinkers. The AMERICAN REVOLUTION excited and inspired many reformers and helped to bring about the abortive rebellion known as the Patriot movement. The two words, *democrat* and *aristocrat,* were coined during the revolutionary upheavals that marked the 1780s in the United Provinces.

See also COLONIALISM.

Further reading: Simon Schama, *Patriots and Liberators: Revolution in the Netherlands, 1780–1813,* 2nd rev. ed. (London: Fontana Press, 1992).

United States Bill of Rights The first 10 amendments of the UNITED STATES CONSTITUTION, enacted into law in 1791. When the Constitutional Convention, meeting in PHILADELPHIA in 1787, drafted the Constitution, that document did not specify the specific political rights of American citizens. Most delegates believed that their individual states could adequately guarantee rights in their state constitutions. Some states, however, agreed to ratify the Constitution only if they were assured that a specific bill of rights would be added later.

When the new United States federal government began to function in 1789, one of the first actions of Congress was to amend the Constitution so that it would include a list of the inviolable rights of U.S. citizens. The government was forbidden to interfere with those rights. James MADISON, who had initially been reluctant to press for such amendments at the federal level of government, became the leader in the process of drafting and promoting the approval of the proposed list. This list, the Bill of Rights, was approved by Congress in 1789 and then was sent to the individual states for ratification. Madison led the campaign to assure that the necessary number of states gave their approval so that the Bill of Rights could become part of the Constitution.

In formulating the various concepts of rights for the American document, Madison and other framers drew on the centuries-old tradition of the "rights of Englishmen," which had derived originally from the Magna Carta and had been expanded in the Petition of Right of 1628 and the Bill of Rights of 1689. But they also drew on the theory of NATURAL RIGHTS associated with the ENLIGHTENMENT. This tradition, in the form given it by John LOCKE in his *TWO TREATISES OF GOVERNMENT,* had provided the language of the American DECLARATION OF INDEPENDENCE about the EQUALITY of people at birth and about their rights to life and LIBERTY. The American claim to the right of "the pursuit of HAPPINESS," however, departed from Locke, who had made right of PROPERTY central to his whole contractual theory of government.

The American Bill of Rights tried to translate the abstract concepts of the Declaration of Independence into concrete political rights. Some of the rights specifically protected are the freedoms of RELIGION, speech, and the press; the right to assemble peacefully; and the right to petition the government. Individuals are protected against unreasonable searches and seizures, double jeopardy, and cruel or unusual punishments. The rights to trial by jury and to due process of law are also guaranteed.

See also BECCARIA; *ESSAY ON CRIMES AND PUNISHMENTS;* FREEDOM; JUSTICE AND THE LAW; POLITICAL THEORY; RIGHTS.

United States Constitution The second constitution written for the UNITED STATES OF AMERICA, ratified in 1788. During the AMERICAN REVOLUTION, the national government had operated according to the Articles of Confederation, which Congress had passed in 1777 and which had finally received the necessary number of state ratifications in 1781. The Articles of Confederation had provided for a weak central government.

Congress called for the meeting of a Constitutional Convention in PHILADELPHIA in 1787 to revise the already obvious defects of the Articles of Confederation. Instead, the delegates to the Convention decided to write a new constitution, which was approved by 39 of them in 1787.

James MADISON and other framers of the new document hoped to provide the foundations for a strong central government while protecting the rights of citizens. Ratification by at least nine states was required for the document to become legal. The nationwide debates over ratification were bitter. To defend the document, Madison, Alexander HAMILTON, and John JAY wrote a series of 85 essays, which they published as *The Federalist Papers* (1787–88). These essays are regarded as a classic of the POLITICAL THEORY of the ENLIGHTENMENT. They helped to secure the state ratifications that were needed for the Constitution to take effect.

The Constitution established a federated republic in the United States, which was structured according to the principle of the SEPARATION OF POWERS. Each branch of the government—whether the executive, legislative, or judicial branch—was provided with specific duties and with powers consciously intended to balance the powers of the other two branches. The federal government was furthermore limited by certain powers reserved for the states. The whole system consisted of a series of checks and balances designed to create flexibility while still preserving a state of dynamic equilibrium within the political structures of the nation. Like the other documents produced during the creation of the United States, the 1787 Constitution drew on concepts—LIBERTY, justice, the rule of law, the separation of powers, checks and balances, and the common welfare—that had been given specific content and emphasis during the Enlightenment. The new American nation was, and still is, rooted in the most intimate fashion in that great European 18th-century movement.

See also MABLY; MONTESQUIEU; *THE SPIRIT OF LAWS*.

United States of America

The new nation formed when 13 British colonies in North America issued their DECLARATION OF INDEPENDENCE in 1776. The process of declaring and securing independence is called the AMERICAN REVOLUTION. Major cities of the 18th-century United States were PHILADELPHIA, New York, Boston, Charleston, and Savannah. Of these cities, Philadelphia offered the environment most compatible with the cultural and intellectual climate of the ENLIGHTENMENT in Europe.

Most of the Founding Fathers of the United States— John ADAMS, James MADISON, and Thomas JEFFERSON, for example—had classical educations in which the study of ancient Greek and Roman literature had been mixed with exploration of modern treatises by Isaac NEWTON, MONTESQUIEU, and John LOCKE.

In the process of creating the new nation, enlightened American leaders had an unprecedented opportunity to put their enlightened ideas into action. They constructed their new government on a foundation provided by such concepts as NATURAL RIGHTS, EQUALITY, HAPPINESS, TOLERATION, SEPARATION OF POWERS, FREEDOM,

and SEPARATION OF CHURCH AND STATE,—all central ideas in the POLITICAL THEORY of the Enlightenment in Europe.

For enlightened Europeans, the events that unfolded in North America raised hopes that fundamental changes could indeed occur in human society. It provided models of revolution and of constitutions that were influential not only in the early FRENCH REVOLUTION but also in the abortive reforms attempted by the Dutch Patriots in the UNITED PROVINCES OF THE NETHERLANDS. The United States also served as a kind of laboratory for testing conflicting ideas about how best to realize enlightened principles. As such, it was both praised and criticized in Europe.

Today, the legacy of the Enlightenment still informs the constitutional questions that face the United States, providing the framework for contemporary discussions of the role of government; of church-state relations; of the proper balance among the executive, legislative, and judicial branches; and of a host of other problems.

See also COLONIALISM; DU PONT DE NEMOURS; HAMILTON; JAY; PAINE; PRIESTLEY; RITTENHOUSE; RUSH; SLAVERY; UNITED STATES BILL OF RIGHTS; UNITED STATES CONSTITUTION; WASHINGTON; WESLEY.

universities   Institutions of higher learning. The first European university came into existence in the late 12th century in the Italian city of Bologna. It appeared when Italian students in professional schools of law, MEDICINE, and notarial work organized themselves into a formal guild. Other European cities quickly imitated the experiment in Bologna, setting up universities as privileged guilds or corporations of masters and students. The word *university* actually stems from the medieval Latin word for guild, *universitas*. In northern Europe, universities developed somewhat differently, as guilds of masters associated with the older cathedral schools. The University of Paris was incorporated in this manner about the year 1200.

Medieval universities offered training in four areas: theology, law, medicine, and the liberal arts. Instruction was in Latin. During the Renaissance, curricula offerings changed to incorporate newly created disciplines and shifts in conceptualization. Universities remained wedded, however, to official churches—Roman Catholic, Anglican, Lutheran, and Calvinist—and to producing practitioners of the major professions. They trained not only doctors and lawyers, but also theologians. Furthermore, in some regions they acted as official censors of the press; the Sorbonne, for example, which was the faculty of theology of the University of Paris, carried out censorship duties in FRANCE.

Universities continued to fulfill these functions during the ENLIGHTENMENT, and perhaps, largely for this reason, their intellectual leadership in France and ENGLAND was eclipsed or challenged during that era. Nevertheless, in the German states of the HOLY ROMAN EMPIRE, in SCOT-LAND, in the UNITED PROVINCES OF THE NETHERLANDS, in some states of the Italian peninsula, and in disciplines such as medicine, universities continued to play a role as leaders in developing or disseminating enlightened ideas.

A few examples will illustrate this situation. The University of Louvain, once a leading center of innovative study, remained under the control of the JESUITS, who refused to allow enlightened ideas or approaches into courses. But the University of Leiden, home of the great professor Hermann BOERHAAVE, served as a prominent center for the study of new ideas in PHILOSOPHY and medicine. France had 18 fully developed universities in the 18th century. Only one, however, the University of Montpellier, played an important role in the Enlightenment; it was the primary center for VITALISM, an approach to medicine that helped to transform the life sciences in the last half of the century. The University of Paris, once a leader in French intellectual life, stubbornly resisted the infiltration of new ideas, thus creating a situation that caused enlightened individuals to seek other institutional bases.

Established universities in England—Oxford and Cambridge—trained and employed some of the founders of the Enlightenment, such as Isaac NEWTON, John LOCKE, the deists, and the Cambridge Platonists. These two institutions, however, stepped into the background as the Enlightenment progressed, to be superseded by the academies of the Protestant DISSENTERS—Warrington, Northampton, and Hackney.

In some countries, however, existing universities were reformed to become centers of enlightened thought. The two established universities in Scotland, at EDINBURGH and Glasgow, contributed significantly to reforms in the disciplines of medicine, MORAL PHILOSOPHY, PSYCHOLOGY, chemistry, HISTORY, and ECONOMICS. In the Italian peninsula, the University of Pavia was reorganized during the years of Hapsburg domination so that some new disciplines could be taught. Universities at Naples and Bologna also provided support to enlightened intellectuals. Furthermore, under leadership provided by Gerard van SWIETEN, the University of VIENNA became a strong center for professional medical training.

In central and eastern Europe new universities became major promoters of the Enlightenment. In the Holy Roman Empire, for example, the University of GÖTTINGEN, founded in 1734 in the electorate of Hanover, and the University of HALLE, founded in 1694 in PRUSSIA, fostered the development of history, SCIENCES, ANTHROPOLOGY, pedagogy, jurisprudence, and medicine. In 1810, the University of BERLIN was completely reorganized according to enlightened principles under the leadership of Wilhelm von Humboldt. German universities worked in conjunction with various SCIENTIFIC ACADEMIES and societies on behalf of enlightened ideas. A similar situation existed in Russia, where the new universities in SAINT PETERSBURG (1747) and MOSCOW (1755) offered an institutional base for new ideas.

See also SOCIAL INSTITUTIONS OF THE ENLIGHTENMENT.

utility The idea that advances in knowledge and technology should bring benefits to society as a whole. This was a key concept in the ENLIGHTENMENT; it was generally felt that all human endeavors could be judged as valuable if they proved to be useful. René DESCARTES discussed utility as the goal of science in his *Discours de la méthode* (DISCOURSE ON METHOD; 1637), and advances in scientific knowledge confirmed the belief that SCIENCE could benefit society and even the human race as a whole.

Utility was closely connected to the notion of PROGRESS. Enlightenment thinkers felt that they were living in an era of unparalleled progress, as the secrets of NATURE were revealed to tireless scientists while the arts and crafts experienced improvements in technology. In his editorship of the ENCYCLOPÉDIE (1751–72), Denis DIDEROT investigated the practice of crafts and trades in FRANCE, such as stocking-making and the printing industry. He promoted the notion that the work of tradespeople and the mechanical inventions designed to make them more productive were sources of strength and happiness for the nation as a whole.

The 18th century also saw the development of useful inventions that depended on new scientific understanding. Benjamin FRANKLIN invented the wood-burning stove, and his investigations of electricity led him to design the lightning rod, an important safety device for preventing fires caused by lightning storms. Franklin's approach to work and life in general was closely tied to the notion of utility. The sayings of his *Poor Richard's Almanack* (1733–58), for example, are based on a common sense concern for maximizing safety and financial security.

Utility was even seen as a criterion for literary production. Novelists claimed to bring together the "useful and the agreeable," setting two separate goals for their work. Naturally, fiction was supposed to be entertaining or enjoyable, but at this time it was also felt that it should be useful in some moral sense. Depictions of characters' sufferings should inspire virtuous sympathy in readers; tragic events should serve to warn readers away from making the same mistakes that the characters made.

The emphasis on utility can be seen as part of the secular nature of the Enlightenment. Relegating religious concerns to the background, Enlightenment thinkers focused on human existence in the here and now. The PHILOSOPHES affirmed that philosophy could help people to lead more meaningful, happier lives. They removed concepts such as VIRTUE from a religious context and saw them as socially useful. They emphasized that people perform virtuous actions for others because they hope that in their time of need they can also benefit from the support of their fellow citizens. In this way, the notion of utility was tied not only to a belief in the power of science, but to a vision of the workings of society.

See also MATHEMATICS AND MECHANICS; NOVEL; SELF-INTEREST.

Further reading: Charles Frankel, *The Faith of Reason: The Idea of Progress in the French Enlightenment* (New York: Octagon Books, 1969); Thomas A. Horne, *The Social Thought of Bernard Mandeville* (New York: Columbia University Press, 1978); E. G. Hundert, *The Enlightenment's Fable: Bernard Mandeville and the Discovery of Society* (New York: Cambridge University Press, 1994); John C. McCarthy, ed., *Modern Enlightenment and the Rule of Reason* (Washington, D.C.: Catholic University of America Press, 1998).

V

Van der Kemp, Francis Adrian (1752–1829) *Mennonite pastor in the United Provinces of the Netherlands and one of the leaders of the Dutch revolutionary movement known as the Dutch Patriots*

Van der Kemp was born at Kampen into a family of Dutch Calvinists and originally prepared for a military career. He studied at the University of Groningen (1770–73), then, departing from parental expectations, entered the Mennonite Church seminary in AMSTERDAM. He joined that church in 1774, serving as a pastor at Huizen (1775–77) and Leiden (1777–87). Van der Kemp involved himself increasingly in politics and became an ardent member of the Dutch Patriots. He engaged in a literary propaganda campaign aimed at creating enthusiasm among the Dutch for the AMERICAN REVOLUTION and he also became a close friend of John ADAMS, who was serving in Holland as an American liaison. Van der Kemp published a collection of American public documents that included the constitution of Massachusetts. It is most likely that he received these documents from Adams.

The Dutch Patriots consisted of an unstable alliance of various groups critical of Dutch political structures and government policies. Its program called for elective assemblies, the arming of citizens, and reductions in the powers of the stadtholder. Although the Dutch practiced TOLERATION of dissident religious minorities, state offices and other positions of power were restricted to members of the Calvinist Dutch Reformed Church. The Patriots wished to open public office to members of minority sects. A man like Van der Kemp, who was a Mennonite pastor, could then have played a formal political role in the nation's affairs.

Van der Kemp organized groups of men to distribute pamphlets in the cities of the United Provinces. He joined the militia (Free Corps), the center of the most radical, democratic wing of the Patriot Party. After the quick repression of the 1787 Patriots Rebellion by FREDERICK II (THE GREAT), Van der Kemp was imprisoned. He was released in November 1787 on the condition that he leave the UNITED PROVINCES OF THE NETHERLANDS. Like many of his fellow Patriots, he went to the United States, where he took up farming and became an American citizen. He devoted himself for the rest of his life to Mennonite Church activities in upstate New York and to publishing theological and devotional essays.

Vattel, Emmerich de (1714–1767) *Swiss jurist*

Vattel left SWITZERLAND in 1743 to join the civil service of the elector of Saxony at Dresden. His legal treatise, *Le droit des gens ou principes de la loi naturelle, appliqués à la conduite et aux affaires des nations et des souverains* (Human law or principles of natural law applied to the conduct and to the affairs of nations and sovereigns; 1758), built a system of international law by combining NATURAL LAW with the principle of the balance of power. Only the pioneering international law theory of Hugo Grotius (1583–1645), contained in *De jure bellis ac pacis* (On the law of war and peace), was better known in enlightened Europe.

Vattel rejected the idea that international law is based on agreement (consensus) between nations about the validity of customary rules or laws. He argued, instead, that international law has its source in the nature of political states. These states are built according to general natural law, a fact that guarantees their equality with one another and their rights to independent existence. But states must, nevertheless, coexist with each other as if they were the components of a republic, bound together to preserve the common interest and mutual liberty. Thus, in international law, the goal must be to maintain a balance of power between states so that no single state can dominate the affairs of the others.

Vattel started with two assumptions: All people are naturally equal, and the actions of individual self-consciousness ultimately create natural law. He believed these assumptions were valid whether they were applied to people or to states (conceived as individuals). In all cases, the individual rather than the community was the fundamental, universally valid unit in nature. This stress on the individual tended to undermine the strong community orientation of the original German formulations of natural law by Samuel PUFENDORF, Gottfried Wilhelm LEIBNIZ, and Christian WOLFF.

Vattel derived his ideas from the philosophy of Christian Wolff. Like Wolff, he stressed that individuals have moral and ethical duties to self; that is, they are obligated to develop themselves according to their natural talents. But at this point a paradox appears; for one way of fulfilling the duty to self lies in recognizing the RIGHTS of other individuals. In other words, self is fulfilled by means of some self-denial, in the interest of others.

This paradox provides the mechanism that allows the rights of the individual to serve the interests of the larger group. It functions like a mechanical balance moving constantly around a point of equilibrium. For communities of individuals, and for international communities of nation-states, it balances individual needs against each other to preserve harmony and peace.

See also EQUALITY; INDIVIDUALISM; NATURAL RIGHTS; MORAL PHILOSOPHY.

Vaucanson, Jacques de (1709–1782) *French engineer and inventor of automata*

The ENLIGHTENMENT saw the development of a great interest in mechanics and mechanical inventions, and Vaucanson was among the most accomplished inventors working in this area. He used rubber to create mechanical figures with flexible bodies that were known for their lifelike quality and their range of movements. His most famous creation was a mechanical flute player exhibited in 1738 that played songs. It was mentioned with admiration by the philosopher Julian Offray de LA METTRIE in his *L'homme-machine* (Man, a machine; 1747). In 1741, Vaucanson displayed to the public a mechanical duck that imitated ingestion and digestion: It moved its neck to take seeds from an outstretched hand, swallowed them, and eventually evacuated them in digested form. It could also drink, play in water, and make quacking noises.

Vaucanson was admitted to the FRENCH ACADEMY OF SCIENCES, and his inventions not only stimulated the curiosity of a large public, but also intrigued the scientific community, whose interest in machines reflected not only a belief in scientific PROGRESS, but also an intellectual exploration of the nature of the human being, the body, and the soul.

See also AUTOMATA; SCIENTIFIC REVOLUTION.

Further reading: Catherine Liu, *Copying Machines: Taking Notes for the Automaton* (Minneapolis: University of Minnesota Press, 2000).

Venice Italian city located on a group of islands in a large lagoon of the Adriatic Sea. In the 18th century, the city remained the center of the Venetian Republic, but that formerly great state had slipped into the political background. Venice was, nevertheless, a thriving center of MUSIC and the arts, and, as a political and cultural symbol, the grip of the city on the imagination of European visitors had scarcely slipped.

In the early fifth century, the islands in the Venetian lagoon began serving as a temporary refuge for Italian mainlanders fleeing the barbarian invasions of the Roman Empire. The continuous history of Venice, however, began only with the Lombard invasions of Italy in A.D. 568. As wave after wave of invaders sacked the mainland cities, some hardy souls fled again to the safety of the offshore islands. They never returned to their homes, but instead set about building a viable permanent settlement in the safety of the lagoon. The nominal overlord of this new town of Venice was the Byzantine emperor. Within the city, an elected leader, the Doge, ruled with monarchical powers. By the 12th century, the office had yielded nearly all its political and administrative powers to a set of ruling councils, whose members were elected from the Venetian citizenry. The city had thus developed into a republic.

During the Italian Renaissance (especially the 14th and 15th centuries), the republic of Venice ruled the eastern Mediterranean as one of the greatest European powers. Its success rested on trade and related commercial ventures for which its position on the Adriatic Sea made it well suited. The opening of the New World in the late 15th and early 16th centuries brought a shift of commercial activity from the Mediterranean to the Atlantic. Venice could not compete with SPAIN and the other Atlantic trading nations. At the same time, the Ottoman Empire was emerging as a formidable power in the eastern Mediterranean. Venice lost lands to the Turks and its eastern trade routes shrank. The 16th century witnessed the beginning of a decline from which the city never recovered.

By the 18th century, Venice seemed a shadow of its former self. Nevertheless, anyone on a GRAND TOUR visited the city to marvel at its canals, beautiful architecture, and fine arts. The gaiety of the Venetian pre-Lenten carnival was renowned throughout Europe. But some observers, like MONTESQUIEU, judged the political culture of the city harshly, noting the corruption of the republic into a decadent, tyrannical oligarchy.

Whatever its decay in the political realm, Venice remained culturally vibrant. The great Venetian frescoist Giovanni Battista TIEPOLO decorated palaces throughout Europe. CANALETTO and Francesco GUARDI painted canvases that captured the moods and symbolism of the city. Young composers and musicians such as George Frederick HANDEL went to the city to study and to seek patronage. Antonio VIVALDI was producing his enormous opus of compositions, and Venetian OPERA was thriving. Traveling observers such as Charles BURNEY noted the manner in which music permeated every aspect of culture, from canals to cathedrals. In addition, a small group of intellectuals centered on Carlo GOLDONI and Francesco ALGAROTTI struggled to bring contemporary ideas to the city. Thus, the city experienced in its own way, the various innovations that were associated with the ENLIGHTENMENT.

See also BAROQUE STYLE; ITALY; POLITICAL THEORY; ROCOCO.

Verri, Alessandro, count (1741–1816) *Milanese novelist and reformer*

Alessandro Verri was the younger brother of Count Pietro VERRI. Alessandro assisted with the publication of the journal *Il Caffe* during the 1760s and helped his brother to establish the Società dei Pugni (Society of Fists) in MILAN. He then moved to ROME, which served as his home for the rest of his life.

Alessandro wrote the novels *Le avventure di Saffo poetessa di Mitilene* (The adventures of Sappho; 1780); *Vita di Erostrato* (The life of Erostrato; 1793); and *Le notti romane al sepolcro degli Scipioni* (Roman nights at the grave of the Scipions; 1792–1804). He translated the works of Shakespeare into Italian and also produced an Italian version of the ancient Homeric epic *The Iliad*. Alessandro Verri assisted his brother Pietro in writing *Reply to a Document entitled Notes and Observations on the Book Of Crimes and Punishments*, a work designed to defend the *ESSAY ON CRIMES AND PUNISHMENTS* by Cesare BECCARIA from vitriolic attacks by Ferdinando Facchinei.

See also ILLUMINISTI; ITALY.

Verri, Pietro, count (1728–1797) *Milanese (Italian) political economist, writer, and reformer*

Count Pietro Verri was born in MILAN and, after a brief period of military service during the SEVEN YEARS' WAR, entered the public civil service in his native city. In 1761, with assistance from his brother Alessandro VERRI, Pietro Verri founded an informal intellectual club called the Società dei Pugni (Society of Fists). Modeled on the social and intellectual world of the French ENCYCLOPEDISTS, the Società dei Pugni became a major center of the ENLIGHTENMENT in the Italian peninsula. From 1764 to 1766, the society sponsored a journal, *Il Caffe,* so-named because the group held its meetings in a Milanese coffeehouse.

Pietro Verri published his *Sull'economia politica* (Meditations on political economy) in 1771. The book wrestled with the tensions between state-directed reform and individual FREEDOM. Milan had experienced a period of active state reform after the Austrian Hapsburgs assumed the overlordship of the city and surrounding duchy.

Other publications by Verri dealt with political economy, legal reform, and Italian history. Titles included *Sulle leggi vincolanti il commercio dei grani* (On the laws limiting trade in grains; 1769); *Discorso sull'indole del oiacere e del dolore* (Discourse on nature of pleasure and pain; 1773); *Osservazioni sulla tortura* (Observations on torture; 1777); and *Storia di Milano* (History of Milan; 1783–99). His articles for *Il Caffe* included "Pensieri sullo spirito della letteratura d'Italia" (Thoughts on the spirit of Italian literature), "Il tempio dell'ignoranza" (The temple of ignorance) and "La coltivazione del lino" (The cultivation of flax). He left a correspondence rich with materials for the study of the Italian Enlightenment.

Pietro Verri played a significant role in persuading Cesare BECCARIA to write his renowned book *ESSAY ON CRIMES AND PUNISHMENTS*. Beccaria was a member of the Società dei Pugni and had developed his opinions in the course of discussions at society meetings. Verri facilitated the publication and dissemination of the book in ITALY and FRANCE.

See also ILLUMINISTI; MORAL PHILOSOPHY; POLITICAL THEORY, SOCIAL INSTITUTIONS OF THE ENLIGHTENMENT.

Vicar of Wakefield, The

Novel by the English writer Oliver GOLDSMITH; first published in 1766 through the agency of Goldsmith's close friend Samuel JOHNSON.

The Vicar of Wakefield focuses on the character of Dr. Primrose, a clergyman who lives in the country with his wife and six children. The novel begins by presenting the idyllic nature of rural life. But everything changes when the merchant with whom the Primroses have invested their money goes bankrupt, leaving them destitute.

The Primroses move to a poor parish on the estate of Squire Thornhill, who stages a fake marriage ceremony with the vicar's daughter Olivia, whom he quickly abandons. The family's fortunes sink still lower when the wicked squire sends the vicar to debtors' prison for failing to pay his rent.

In prison, however, the vicar's benevolence and rational piety inspire the other prisoners to reform, and the family fortunes begin to rebound. In the end, Sir William Thornhill, the virtuous uncle of the wicked squire, marries Sophia, the vicar's second daughter, and it is learned that Squire Thornhill's mock marriage to Olivia was really a legal marriage. On this happy note, the novel ends.

The Vicar of Wakefield follows the conventions of the SENTIMENTAL FICTION that was so popular in the last half of the 18th century. It appeals to the emotions of its readers, attempting to move them by depicting the plight of various characters. In this manner, the author hopes to inspire readers to reach for loftier goals in their own lives. The book illustrates the beliefs in the inherent goodness of human NATURE and in the possibility of moral PROGRESS that were associated with the ENLIGHTENMENT. Sentimental fiction was designed to capitalize on these qualities and to facilitate their existence.

See also LITERATURE.

Vico, Giovan Battista (Giambattista Vico) (1668–1744) *Neapolitan historian, philosopher, and jurist*

Although celebrated today for his contributions to modern historical methodology, Giambattista Vico was scarcely known outside ITALY during the ENLIGHTENMENT. He was born and lived nearly all his life in Naples. Son of a modest bookseller, he acquired a basic education from the JESUITS and a higher education at the University of Naples. Although he occupied the chair of eloquence and elocution at the University of Naples from 1699 until 1742, he always lived close to poverty. He worked in relative isolation in Naples, although his work was appreciated by Italian contemporaries such as the historian and legal scholar Ludovico Antonio MURATORI and the jurist G. V. Gravina. Nevertheless, Vico expressed disappointment that his work did not reach a wider European audience.

As a young man, Vico began to explore the world of ideas beyond the boundaries of his rather narrow education. He acknowledged Plato, Tacitus, Francis BACON, and the Dutch legal theorist Hugo Grotius as his major sources of inspiration.

The problem of the truth of historical knowledge proved especially fascinating to Vico. Both his research methods and his theory of HISTORY represented efforts to solve this epistemological problem. He distrusted knowledge based on abstract applications of REASON (RATIONALISM), preferring knowledge acquired through experience (EMPIRICISM). Vico believed that the only things that humans can know about with certainty are the things that they do or make (*verum est factum*). All other human knowledge, especially that concerning the gods, is a myth created by projecting aspects of the human mind out into the universe. In essence, Vico was arguing that human culture and stories about past events are the product of human PSYCHOLOGY rather than objective truths. He thus linked the human capacity to invent histories with the normal operations of the mind.

Vico believed that human minds have developed over time, passing through a series of stages that have produced unique and characteristic forms of civilization (languages, modes of expression, social institutions, RELIGION, PHILOSOPHY, and governments). Each stage in history corresponds to a specific type of mental functioning and yields unique forms of human knowledge about the world. The first stage of history, the age of the gods, was dominated by sensory experience; the second stage, the age of heroes, was ruled by imagination and fantasy; while the third stage, the age of the people, was dominated by intellect and reason.

Sculpture of Giovan Battista Vico at the Palazzo di Giustizia, Rome. Although Vico was scarcely known outside Italy during the Enlightenment, today his philosophy of history receives accolades for its creative approach to materials from the past. *(Courtesy Alinari/Art Resource, New York)*

Unlike many enlightened thinkers who believed that historical development was a matter of continual PROGRESS, Vico believed that civilizations change without any guarantee of upward advancement. He tended to view history as a circular process (*corsi e ricorsi*), somewhat like the organic processes of growth, maturity, decay, and regeneration.

In history, civilizations develop through the three "ages," progressing until they reach some limit prescribed by the tension between FREEDOM and limits imposed by reason. Times of trouble or crisis set in, and finally the civilization begins to decay and to degenerate. The stage of degeneration slowly transforms itself, however, into renewed growth, and the historical cycle begins anew.

Vico's writings include his outstanding *Principi di una scienza nuova dintorno alla natura delle nazioni, per la quale si ritruovano i principi di altro sistema del diritto naturale delle genti* (Principles of a new science . . . ; three editions, 1725, 1729, 1744); *De rebus gestis Antonii caraphei* (1716); and the essays *De nostri temporis studiorum ratione* (1709) and *De antiquissima italorum sapientia* (On the oldest wisdom of the Italians; 1710).

Because his work was largely ignored during the Enlightenment, Vico is often treated as a kind of GENIUS, a "man ahead of his times." His themes, however, reflect the general intellectual concerns of the era: inquiries into the foundations of knowledge (EPISTEMOLOGY); attempts to provide philosophical validity for empirical (factual) data; the introduction of concepts of change over time (i.e., the historicization of the natural world, of civilization, of the human mind, and of religion); contemplations about the direction of development (the possibility of progress); the concept of the spirit of a nation or civilization.

Parallels to the Vichian treatment of primitive mentality and religion can be found in Bernard de FONTENELLE, Charles de BROSSES, Nicolas BOULANGER, David HUME, Pierre BAYLE, and the baron d'HOLBACH. Vico's insistence that history examine the total context of a specific era or civilization was shared by historians such as MONTESQUIEU, VOLTAIRE, Johann Christoph GATTERER, and August von SCHLÖZER. Nevertheless, Vico remained an original, inventive figure whose vision of the sharp differences and utter incommensurability between civilizations was extreme for his time. This version was matched only by Jean-Jacques ROUSSEAU and Johann Gottfried HERDER, both working in the later years of the Enlightenment.

Vienna   Austrian city located on the Danube River. Ancient Celts and Romans occupied the site, but the modern history of the city dates from its medieval charter of 1147. The Hapsburg family made Vienna (German: Wien) its dynastic seat after being elected in 1278 to the throne of the HOLY ROMAN EMPIRE. The city received official status as the capital of the Holy Roman Empire in 1558. Vienna's importance as a stronghold of ROMAN CATHOLICISM was underlined by the permanent presence of a papal nuncio (diplomat).

Vienna flourished in the 18th century as a great cosmopolitan center that reflected the complex cultural and linguistic structure of the Hapsburg lands. The Turkish presence no longer threatened its security. Population grew from roughly 100,000 in 1700, to over 200,000 by 1800, making the city the largest in eastern Europe. As a result of a Hapsburg program of building, Vienna also became an outstanding example of the late-BAROQUE STYLE architecture. The architects Johann Bernhard FISCHER VON ERLACH and Johann Lukas von HILDEBRANDT built magnificent palaces such as Schönbrunn for MARIA THERESA and the Belvedere for Prince EUGÈNE OF SAVOY. Other outstanding baroque constructions included the beautiful Church of Saint Charles dedicated to the principal saint of the Catholic Reformation, Charles Borromeo; the Kinsky, Schwarzenberg, and Schönborn palaces; the Bohemian chancellery; and the Palace of the Sciences. Toward the mid-18th century, Vienna also emerged as a principal MUSIC center in Europe. The great classical composers Wolfgang Amadeus MOZART, Christoph Willibald GLUCK, Franz Joseph HAYDN, and the young Ludwig van BEETHOVEN all worked in the city. Vienna had a vibrant and highly influential group of FREEMASONS, dedicated to spreading the ENLIGHTENMENT. The organization claimed many Viennese statesmen, intellectuals, artists, and musicians as members.

See also AUSTRIA; HAPSBURG EMPIRE; INGEN-HOUSZ; JOSEPH II; KAUNITZ; MESMER; Gerard van SWIETEN; Gottfried van SWIETEN.

Vigée Lebrun, Élisabeth-Louise (1755–1842) *French artist*

The daughter of painter Louis Vigée, Élisabeth was born in PARIS. She spent the first five years of her life on a farm outside Épernon, and then went to a convent for schooling. At the age of 11, she returned to Paris to live with her parents and began to study drawing with her father. He died in May 1767, soon after her return, but she continued to refine her skills by copying paintings and drawing family members.

Largely self-taught, Élisabeth began painting portraits professionally by the time she was 15. Her first exhibit, at the salon of the Académie de Saint-Luc in 1774, established her as a legitimate artist. In 1776, the 20-year-old Elisabeth married painter and art dealer Jean-Baptiste Lebrun, who was also her family's landlord.

Élisabeth's growing reputation as a portraitist gained her clients at court, including the queen, MARIE-ANTOINETTE, whose portrait she painted in 1778. With Marie-Antoinette's support, Vigée Lebrun gained entry into France's Royal Academy of Painting and Sculpture. A tour of the Low Countries in 1781 introduced Vigée Lebrun to the works of 17th-century Dutch master Peter Paul Rubens, whose techniques for creating a sense of light and depth she emulated in her portraits. After her admission to the Royal Academy in 1783, several people of rank sat for Vigée Lebrun. These included the queen and her two children (1787), the marqise de Peze (1787), and the marquise de Fresne d'Aguesseau (1789).

The outbreak of the FRENCH REVOLUTION forced Vigée Lebrun to flee to ROME after Versailles fell in October 1789. She spent the next 12 years in exile, traveling with her daughter Julie (1780–1819) to several European capitals, including SAINT PETERSBURG, where Empress CATHERINE II became her patron. In 1793, her brother and husband, who were still in Paris, were both imprisoned. When Marie-Antoinette was tried and executed, Vigée Lebrun's husband, fearful of his wife's close association with the queen, divorced her in 1794.

Vigée Lebrun returned to Paris in 1801, painting and traveling until her ex-husband Jean-Baptiste's death on August 7, 1813. From that date, she remained in Paris until her own death nearly three decades later. She painted until a stroke in the final year of her life incapacitated her. Her *Mémoirs* were published in 1835.

Vigée Lebrun painted many of the late 18th and early 19th century's prominent figures. Her reputation rests on her numerous portraits of women and children, which are filled with emotion. She idealized her subjects, bringing out their best qualities, as in her portrait of Marie-Antoinette with her children (see page 372), and often used allegory to highlight the characteristics of the people she painted, as in her portrait of Madame de STÄEL as Corinne (1808). Her paintings are an expression of the current of sentimentality running through much art and literature of the last decades of the 18th century prior to the French Revolution.

See also WOMEN AND THE ENLIGHTENMENT.

Further reading: Mary D. Sheriff, *The Exceptional Woman: Elisabeth Vigée Le Brun and the Cultural Politics of Art* (Chicago: University of Chicago Press, 1996).

Vindication of the Rights of Woman, A   A polemical tract published by Mary WOLLSTONECRAFT in 1792 as a companion for her earlier *A Vindication of the Rights of Man* (1790). The latter essay had been written as a rebuttal to the REFLECTIONS ON THE REVOLUTION IN FRANCE (1790) by Edmund BURKE, and may have given Thomas PAINE ideas for his THE RIGHTS OF MAN, which followed several months later. *A Vindication of the Rights of Man* drew on Jean-Jacques ROUSSEAU's arguments in favor of the innate goodness of people and the consequent need for LIBERTY. However, in *A Vindication of the Rights of Woman*, Wollstonecraft directly attacked Rousseau's vision of gender difference expressed in his popular work *ÉMILE*.

Rousseau's *Émile* (1762) describes the ideal education of the imaginary boy of the title. It includes a chapter describing the corresponding ideal education for Sophie, Émile's female counterpart. Sophie is to be raised entirely for the purpose of pleasing Émile, learning primarily the domestic arts of cooking and sewing, and relying for moral guidance on her instinctive virtue; reasoning, in Rousseau's view, is foreign to and inappropriate for women. Wollstonecraft expresses rage at Rousseau's view of women's capabilities. She argues that women are born with the same capacity to REASON as are men and attributes the differences between the sexes to parental influence and EDUCATION. Reason is, for Wollstonecraft as for many writers of the ENLIGHTENMENT, the foundation of humanity and VIRTUE. The purpose of education, in her view, is to promote physical and moral fitness through the exercise of rational understanding. She points out that this is the same ideal that Rousseau promotes for men; her only difference from him is to extend it to women.

Wollstonecraft thus believed in the fundamental equality of all human beings, an idea derived from John LOCKE. Enlightenment writers commonly spoke of equality, but they often limited the concept to men. Wollstonecraft was one of a few radicals who called for the extension of the concept to women.

Wollestonecraft's beliefs were not just theoretical; *A Vindication of the Rights of Woman* contains passionately argued passages about the disastrous practical consequences for women of the limited educational and professional opportunities available to them. Without the possibility of independence, marriage becomes for women, in Wollstonecraft's words, "legal prostitution." Dependence, she says, is as harmful for women as for men, depriving them of a sense of purpose and accomplishment. Without access to meaningful education, women are condemned to a life of drudgery, or if they are well to do, to being frivolous, shallow, and hopelessly caught up in the seductions of romance. The social system that stunts women's intellectual and moral growth harms everyone. The opportunities that would make women better citizens would also make them better wives, daughters, and mothers.

See also WOMEN AND THE ENLIGHTENMENT.

Further reading: Catriona Mackenzie, "Reason and Sensibility: The Ideal of Women's Self-governance in the Writings of Mary Wollstonecraft," *Hypatia's Daughters: 1500 Years of Women Philosophers,* ed. Linda L. MacAlister (Bloomington: Indiana University Press, 1996); Janet M. Todd, *Mary Wollstonecraft: A Revolutionary Life.* (New York: Columbia University Press, 2000).

viola   Stringed instrument of the violin family, the intermediate between the violin and violoncello. Its four strings are tuned a fifth below those of the violin. The instruments of the violin family had begun to replace the older fretted stringed instruments called viols during the baroque era. By the 18th century, violins, violas, violoncellos, and stringed basses provided the backbone of the SYMPHONY ORCHESTRA.

Before the development of musical CLASSICISM, the viola usually played the same lines as the violin, thereby adding a certain darkness of color to the line that violins alone could not create. Franz Joseph HAYDN, Wolfgang Amadeus MOZART, and Christoph Willibald GLUCK, however, recognized the unique qualities and potential of the viola and began to exploit its capabilities in their orchestral compositions.

virtue   Moral excellence as demonstrated by beliefs or actions. The ENLIGHTENMENT attempt to remake the world according to rational principles during the 18th century took an increasing interest in the sphere of human morality and the ways it might be strengthened or corrected in people showing corrupt behavior. Philosophers such as ENGLAND's Anthony Ashley Cooper, the third earl of SHAFTESBURY, developed systems to explain and codify human morality. Shaftesbury's system was firmly grounded in a sense of the universe as powerfully ordered and ruled by harmony; human beings could gain their best happiness in pursuit of virtue. His position rejected earlier theories of society such as Thomas HOBBES's *Leviathan,* (1660) which reduced human motivation to self-centered impulses.

The link between virtue and happiness was very important for the PHILOSOPHES, who maintained virtue as an essential value while seeking to remove it from the religious sphere. They demonstrated that RELIGION did not have a monopoly on virtue, citing examples of pagans from antiquity who led upstanding moral lives, such as Socrates.

The philosophes hoped to ground moral behavior in an analysis of society: They saw SELF-INTEREST and virtue as linked. Since people depended on others in society, it was in their own interest to engage in virtuous behavior, in order to maintain the good will of their fellow citizens.

Another way in which virtue was conceptualized during the period was as an impulse of the heart. This vision of virtue was particularly prominent in SENTIMEN-TAL FICTION. In Samuel RICHARDSON's novel PAMELA, OR VIRTUE REWARDED (1740), the heroine follows her natural impulse toward morality as she resists the sexual threats of her employer. The transformative power of virtue in civilization is played out within the microcosm of Mr. B.'s household, as Pamela teaches him better behavior even as she continues to rebuff his advances. Her influence ultimately transforms the entire household. Richardson thus illustrates the practice of virtue as bringing harmony to all levels of society.

Richardson's works also exemplify Enlightenment notions of virtue in that it was frequently assumed to be a female responsibility. Women were seen as the moral caretakers of both their families and the wider community of the nation, and those who were unfortunate enough to gain an unvirtuous reputation, whether deserved or mistaken, could find themselves rejected by families and social contacts and even without any means of support.

Enlightenment thinkers recognized that virtue could be a thorny issue. Ideally, they hoped that it was a powerful factor in human behavior, whether it was inspired by self-interest and an urge for social acceptance, or whether it stemmed naturally from the human heart. Yet they realized that self-interest could lead people to reject virtuous behavior. Denis DIDEROT explored this issue in his dialogue Le Neveu de Rameau (Rameau's nephew; 1761). In this work, Diderot's character finds virtue beautiful and moving, but the character of Rameau's nephew is more concerned with his financial and physical well-being, maintaining that it is foolish to aspire to be virtuous in a corrupt world. Diderot never published this audacious work.

In the fiction of the marquis de SADE, virtue is entirely rejected by characters whose self-interest leads them to abuse and exploit others. In many ways, Sade's work can be seen as the worst nightmare of the philosophes: They had always maintained that philosophy and virtue were sisters. Sade's view of philosophy seemed to justify the opinions of the critics of Enlightenment, who claimed that the move from religion to philosophy would bring moral corruption. Certainly, by the end of the 18th century, it began to seem naïve to expect humans to be motivated by virtue. The violence of the Reign of Terror during the FRENCH REVOLUTION made the darker side of human nature impossible to overlook. Furthermore, analysis of human behavior in society had become more complex, with notions of self-interest, politics, and class playing a major role in understanding how human beings operate.

See also FREE TRADE; UTILITY; WOMEN AND THE ENLIGHTENMENT.

Further reading: Ruth H. Bloch, *Gender and Morality in Anglo-American Culture, 1650–1800* (Berkeley, Calif.: University of California Press, 2003); Richard K. Matthews, ed., *Virtue, Corruption, and Self-Interest: Political Values in the Eighteenth Century* (Bethlehem, Pa.: Lehigh University Press, 1994); Christine Roulston, *Virtue, Gender, and the Authentic Self in Eighteenth-Century Fiction: Richardson, Rousseau, and Laclos* (Gainesville: University Press of Florida, 1998).

vitalism   A theory about living organisms ("organized matter") that developed in the 1740s. Unlike the theories of life derived from the MECHANICAL PHILOSOPHY, vitalist theory asserted that essential differences, inexplicable in mechanical terms, divide the living matter of organisms from the dead matter of inanimate objects. But vitalists rejected the belief that the body is ruled by anima (spirit), thereby also distinguishing their theory from ANIMISM. Vitalism developed as an attempt to mediate between the opposing theories of mechanical philosophy (especially IATROMECHANICS) and animism. Both theories reduced life to a simple set of principles. For the mechanical philosophers, both living and nonliving entities could be explained in terms of matter (i.e., size and shape) and motion (i.e., direction and velocity). They stripped NATURE of any animating spirits or principles and tried to describe all life phenomena in terms of mechanical actions. The animists, in contrast, described life phenomena in terms of the actions of a ruling animated spirit or soul.

Animism had been discredited in the early 17th century for theological reasons, and its practitioners, whether Catholic or Protestant, had been frequently accused of heresy. The mechanical philosophy had appeared in part as a response to animism; it had attempted to eliminate the hold of the animist vision on human thought, and by the last third of the 17th century had succeeded in dominating European MEDICINE and physiology. Animist thought, however, never completely disappeared; in fact, in the early 18th century, it was revived by the German chemist and physician Georg STAHL.

The vitalists, attempting to create a compromise between these two extremes, attacked the principles of mechanical natural philosophy, substituting for its "dead" nature a nature filled with active forces. They posited a thorough distinction between living matter, imbued with active vital forces linked by RELATIONS of SYMPATHY, and nonliving matter. Vitalists nevertheless refused to see spirit as the ruling entity in living organisms. Instead, vitalists offered a unique, intermediary vision of living matter, human understanding, and nature, all organized around a new definition of the old metaphor of harmony.

The vitalist vision can be characterized by the following points:

a. The living body was redefined so that it was no longer conceived as a simple aggregate (sum) of parts, but rather as a complex union of highly inter-related parts. The idea of relation replaced aggregation as one of the defining principles of matter.

b. Living matter took precedence over "dead" matter as an object of research.

c. The process of GENERATION (reproduction) assumed major importance as a clue to understanding life processes and origins.

d. Vitalism defined the concept *scientific system* in terms analogous to its vision of relations in organic beings. In the "natural system" of science, symbiotic relations linked the constituting elements to each other and also to the environment in which they were embedded.

e. Vitalism expanded the definition of the concept of "forces" by introducing goal-directed (teleological), active or self-activating forces into their model of living organisms. It claimed that living matter contained a principle of self-movement stemming from the active powers residing within it. The most famous of the vitalist active forces was the *Bildungstrieb* (formative drive) of Johann Friedrich BLUMENBACH, but the young Friedrich SCHILLER also used the notion in his concepts *Stofftrieb* (material force) and *Formtrieb* (formal drive).

f. Nature was given a HISTORY (historicized) and thus was conceived as changing in a perceptible direction over time, but this "progression" did not necessarily occur in an unbroken line. Rather, it proceeded by alternation between drastic changes and gradual developments that entailed a constant interplay between free creation and regular orderly development. This 18th-century historicization of nature marked a radical departure from previous conceptions of the world.

g. Vitalism called for a type of understanding that could combine individual ideas into harmonious wholes without destroying either the unity or diversity of nature. The methods adopted to implement this program were comparative analysis of organic functions and reasoning by analogy.

h. Vitalism called for combining experimental investigation of empirical phenomena with creative scientific imagination. This method mediated between simple EMPIRICISM and abstract reasoning.

i. Vitalists believed that when the understanding moved between reason and empiricism, it passed through a middle, hidden realm; the actual ground upon which all reality rested, and the place where the inherent tensions between reason and empirical observation could be harmonized or resolved. Vitalists had different words for this middle concept: "internal mold" (Comte de BUFFON); "prototype" (Jean-Baptiste René Robinet); "*Urtyp*" (Johann Wolfgang von GOETHE); "*schemata*"

(Immanuel KANT); "*Haupttypus*" (Johann Gottfried HERDER); and "*Mittelkraft*" (Schiller).

j. Vitalists often used the political language of representative government ("assemblies" of independent forces working together to control and govern) to explain their vision of the harmony that exists in living bodies. They contrasted their vision to the one favored by animists in which an organism is subject to the monarchical rule of a single vital principle or force.

The universities at Montpellier, EDINBURGH, and GÖTTINGEN became leading centers of vitalism. Groups in PARIS, BERLIN, GENEVA, Jena, SAINT PETERSBURG, Königsberg, and Bologna also espoused the theory. The ranks of vitalists included major physiologists, natural historians, PHILOSOPHES, and physicians such as Paul-Joseph BARTHEZ, Théophile de BORDEU, Buffon, Denis DIDEROT, Abraham TREMBLEY, Charles BONNET, Caspar Friedrich Wolff, Blumenbach, Marie-François-Xavier BICHAT, William CULLEN, Robert WHYTT, Joseph BLACK, John PRINGLE, Alexander MONRO SECUNDUS, the young Schiller, and the brothers William and John HUNTER.

See also BIOLOGY; MONTESQUIEU; SCIENCE.

Vivaldi, Antonio (1678–1741) *Venetian composer, conductor and music teacher, known as* il prete rosso *(the red-headed priest)*

Vivaldi was the son of one of the leading violinists at St. Mark's Chapel in VENICE. He prepared for two careers, one in the Catholic priesthood and the second in MUSIC. He served one year (1703) in the active priesthood, but ill health necessitated his release from his duties, and thenceforth he pursued music.

Vivaldi worked in Venice as a composer, violinist, musical conductor, and superintendent of the city orphanage for girls (the conservatory of the Pietà). The conservatory incorporated a strong program of music instruction into the training of its young charges. The southern Italian city of Naples had a similar institution with an excellent music program. Vivaldi wrote musical compositions for the various public performances by the orphanage residents. He also wrote operas on commission, which were produced not only in Venice but also in ROME, Florence, and Verona.

Vivaldi's style is usually interpreted as transitional between the late-18th-century Italian BAROQUE STYLE forms and the earliest forms of musical CLASSICISM. Vigorous rhythms, idiomatic writing for solo instruments, and strong programmatic elements stand out in his music. It tends toward a homophonic treatment of melody and harmony (a characteristic of classicism) but retains incidental elements of baroque contrapuntal structure. Vivaldi was the first composer to weight the middle, slow movement of a solo concerto equally with the two faster, outer movements.

The catalog of Vivaldi's works includes 49 operas, 450 concertos for solo instrument and orchestra accompaniment, 23 sinfonias (an early form of the symphony), 75 solo or trio sonatas, and numerous vocal cantatas, motets, and oratorios. Perhaps his most famous work is the set of four concerti for string orchestra known as THE FOUR SEASONS (opus 8, no. 1–4).

See also OPERA; SYMPHONY ORCHESTRA.

Volney, Constantin François Chasseboeuf, comte de (1757–1820) *French cultural geographer, historian, linguist, social scientist, and politician*

While studying in PARIS, Volney was a regular guest at the salons hosted by Baron d'HOLBACH and Madame HELVÉTIUS. From his encounters, he learned about the principles, beliefs, and goals of the IDÉOLOGUES. They provided his basic source of intellectual inspiration throughout his life.

After completing his university education, Chasseboeuf traveled to Egypt and Syria (1782–85). Upon returning to FRANCE he entered the world of political journalism, founding and editing the Breton-based republican periodical *La sentinelle du peuple* (People's sentinel). During the early years of the FRENCH REVOLUTION, this journal became an organ of the Girondin Party. Chasseboeuf served in the Estates General and the Constituent Assembly during the Revolution. As a Girondin he was imprisoned during the Reign of Terror directed by Maximilien ROBESPIERRE, but he was not executed. In 1794, having regained his freedom after the downfall of Robespierre, Chasseboeuf became a professor of HISTORY at the new École normale. He moved to the UNITED STATES in 1795 and remained there until expelled in 1798 as an agent for the French government.

At first a supporter of Napoleon, whom he had known during a period of residency in Corsica, Chasseboeuf later became a critic of Napoleon's dictatorial tendencies and of the Napoleonic Empire. However, his views did not hinder his political career. He served in the French Senate and was awarded the title Count of Volney in 1808. He was elevated to the French peerage in 1814.

Chasseboeuf left publications in geography, linguistics, and social sciences, all of which reflect the penchant of the Idéologues for creating rational, systematic human sciences to assist the enlightenment and ultimate liberation of humanity. Chasseboeuf first gained literary prominence in 1781 with a work entitled *Sur la chronologie d'Hérodote* (On the chronology of Herodotus), an historical investigation of texts by the ancient Greek writer Herodotus. His record of his travels in the Levant, *Voyage en Egypte et en Syrie* (Travels in Egypt and Syria; 1787), is a pioneer in the discipline of geography. It reports systematically on social, political, and environmental facets of these nations and differs in this respect from the narrative TRAVEL LITERATURE of earlier decades. A later work, *Tableau du climat et du sol des États-Unis d'Amérique* (Description of the climate and soil of the United States of America; 1803) presents similar information about the United States. Chasseboeuf also published *Précis de l'état actuel de la Corse* (Summary of the present state of Corsica; 1793).

During the French Revolution, Chasseboeuf wrote a critical work entitled *Les ruines, ou méditations sur les révolutions des empires* (Ruins, or meditations on the revolutions of empires; 1791). In his last years, he turned to the task of creating a universal alphabet, in an effort to systematize the representation of human languages. He published three separate works on this subject: *Simplification des langues orientales* (Simplification of Oriental languages; 1795); *L'alphabet européen appliqué aux langues asiatiques* (The European alphabet applied to Asian languages; 1819); and *L'hebreu simplifié* (Hebrew simplified; 1820). His will established a cash prize to be awarded for work in the field of universal LANGUAGE.

See also SOCIAL INSTITUTIONS OF THE ENLIGHTENMENT.

Volta, Alessandro Giuseppe Antonio Anastasio (1745–1827) *Italian physicist and chemist, the inventor of the first electric battery (the Voltaic pile)*

Alessandro Volta was a member of a family with a strong tradition of service in the Catholic priesthood and was pressured by his parents to join the JESUITS. He refused, although he remained intensely devout and surrounded himself with clerical friends. A close working relationship developed between the young Volta and Giulio Cesare Gattoni (1741–1809). Gattoni provided Volta with space for a laboratory, books, instruments, and access to his private cabinet of curiosities. The two men also carried out some joint experiments.

Volta began teaching in 1774 at the new state gymnasium, a secondary school that prepared students for university education, which had been established in Como by the Austrian Hapsburg rulers of the duchy of Milan. In 1777, the Hapsburg minister, Count Carlo di Firmian, hired Volta to assume the professorship of experimental physics at the reorganized University of Pavia. Volta remained in that post for nearly 40 years. He was such a popular teacher that a new lecture hall was built to accommodate his many students. The university acquired many scientific instruments for use in his courses and laboratory. In 1815, Volta became director of the faculty of philosophy at Pavia.

After Napoleon captured the province of Lombardy, he elevated Volta (1801) to the status of count and senator of the new kingdom of Lombardy. Volta was honored professionally by reception into the ROYAL SOCIETY OF LONDON (1791), the BERLIN ACADEMY (1786), and the FRENCH ACADEMY OF SCIENCES (1803, corresponding member). The Royal Society awarded him the prestigious Copley Medal after his debates with Luigi GALVANI over animal electricity.

Volta devoted his primary scientific research to the thorny but popular problems of electrical phenomena. His discoveries of the electrophore (1775) and of atmospheric electricity, and his invention of the voltaic pile or battery (1800), all helped to foster basic changes in the conceptualization of electrical phenomena during the late ENLIGHTENMENT.

The exploration of inflammable gases (pneumatic chemistry), a fashionable subject that was fruitfully pursued by Antoine LAVOISIER, Joseph PRIESTLEY, and Carl SCHEELE, also captured Volta's imagination. Like Priestley and Scheele, Volta believed in the PHLOGISTON THEORY of chemistry and rejected Lavoisier's alternative theory until after the turn of the century. In 1776, while investigating the composition of marsh gas, Volta isolated methane. He also experimented with methods for mixing gases in laboratories and succeeded in producing water by sparking hydrogen and oxygen over mercury. His technique was repeated successfully by Lavoisier, Pierre-Simon de LAPLACE, and Gaspard Monge working together in PARIS.

Volta was a careful experimental scientist, committed to the idea of measuring chemical and electrical phenomena, but nevertheless loyal to existing theories. He exploited the utility of scientific instruments for experiment by developing or improving several important and imaginative devices: the electrophore, the voltaic pile; a carefully calibrated, improved electrometer; and a refined eudiometer.

See also CHEMICAL REVOLUTION; TECHNOLOGY AND INSTRUMENTATION; SCIENCE.

Voltaire (François-Marie Arouet) (1694–1778) *French philosophe and writer, one of the "fathers" of the Enlightenment in France*

Voltaire, or François-Marie Arouet, was the son of François Arouet, a notary and royal official at the Cour des Comptes. The abbé de Chateauneuf, a Parisian freethinker, stood as his godfather. The official record of Arouet's birth lists November 21, 1694, as his birth date; Arouet, however, always claimed that his actual birth date was February 20, 1694, and that his father was a Parisian poet and songwriter named Rochebrune.

As a youngster, Arouet attached himself to his godfather, who introduced him into the progressive, freethinking social circles of the French capital. He attended the prestigious Collège Louis-le-Grand, run by the JESUITS. Among his schoolmates was the future marquis d'ARGENSON, who became a lifelong friend and protector. Arouet graduated in 1711 with a degree in PHILOSOPHY.

Arouet quickly decided to pursue a literary career, although he was formally enrolled for law studies. He frequented literary salons, spent four months as secretary to M. de Chateauneuf (the brother of his godfather) in the French embassy at The Hague, and resettled in PARIS in 1713.

Several unpleasant encounters with the French system of justice marked Arouet's youthful years. An infatuation during his time at The Hague with the Huguenot Mademoiselle Du Noyer, for example, brought release from his secretarial position and threats of disinheritance from his father. Satirical poems ridiculing the incestuous love affairs of the new French regent, Philippe II, duke of Orléans, caused Arouet to be exiled in 1715 to Sully-sur-Loire. Renewed literary attacks against the regent in 1717, brought arrest, an 11-month imprisonment in the Bastille, and a second exile to Chatenay.

A period of notable success followed immediately on the heels of these years of tumult. Initiated by the 1718 staging of Arouet's *Oedipe* (Oedipus), this period saw Arouet assume the pen name of Voltaire, receive public recognition, and acquire a pension as a court poet under the protection of Queen Marie Leszczynska. Voltaire, as he now was called, circulated successfully in the Parisian salons; visited Lord BOLINGBROKE at his French residence-in-exile, La Source; and began studying the English language in order to read the works of John LOCKE.

Another encounter with French law, this time after a fight with a servant of the chevalier de Rohan, brought exile from FRANCE. As a result, Voltaire spent the years between 1726 and early 1729 in ENGLAND. The experience produced the first turning point in his career by bringing him into personal contact with English EMPIRICISM, religious diversity, freedom of thought, commerce, LITERATURE, and political structures. He read John Locke and Isaac NEWTON; met Alexander POPE, Jonathan SWIFT, George BERKELEY, and Samuel CLARKE; attended performances of Shakespeare plays; learned of English DEISM; and even witnessed Newton's funeral in 1727 at Westminster Abbey.

In Voltaire's eyes, English thought and institutions represented the highest point of development in human history. He decided, upon returning to France in 1729, to devote himself to introducing English ways into France. His activities had three specific foci: the reintroduction of tragedy to the French stage, the writing of philosophical HISTORY, and the presentation of various facets of the liberal English political system.

Voltaire's first efforts, a series of tragedies modeled after Shakespeare, flopped. But in 1732, *Zaire* brought great success. The 1731 publication of the *Histoire de Charles XII* (History of Charles XII) established Voltaire as an innovative historian, and the *Lettres philosophiques ou Lettres anglaises* (English or philosophical letters; 1734) brought both fame and notoriety. Incensed by the *Lettres philosophiques,* French authorities issued a warrant for Voltaire's arrest in May 1734. As a result, he fled to the Château de Cirey in Champagne, in the company of his friend and mistress, Madame Émilie du CHÂTELET.

The 15 years that Voltaire spent in the company and protection of Madame du Châtelet proved enormously stimulating and productive. Madame du Châtelet possessed a sharp intellect, an unusual degree of EDUCATION for a woman of the era, and great curiosity about intellectual matters. Even after their passion cooled, Voltaire and Madame du Châtelet worked together. At Cirey, Voltaire prepared the *Éléments de la philosophie de Newton* (Elements of the philosophy of Newton) and began writing two historical works, the *SIÈCLE DE LOUIS XIV* (The century of Louis XIV) and *L'essai sur les moeurs* (Essay on customs). He assisted Madame du Châtelet with her French translation of Newton's PRINCIPIA MATHEMATICA (Mathematical principles) and collaborated with her on a critical examination of Genesis, the first book in the Old Testament of the Bible.

Madame du Châtelet and Voltaire divided their time among BRUSSELS, Cirey, and Paris. In Paris, Voltaire acquired a substantial fortune through careful speculations in the French financial markets, and his literary career flowered under the influential patronage of Madame de POMPADOUR, mistress to King LOUIS XV. He produced two acclaimed plays, *Mahomet* (1741) and *Mérope* (1743). A poem celebrating the 1745 French military victory at Fontenoy brought rewards in the form of appointments as royal historiographer, gentleman of the king's chamber, and member of the French Academy.

Whatever his successes, Voltaire still had powerful enemies in the person of King Louis XV and the party of the devout at the court. In 1747, he and Madame du Châtelet were forced to flee from Paris in order to escape renewed prosecution. In hiding at the Château de Sceaux, Voltaire turned to writing stories. Between 1747 and 1749, he produced some of his most highly regarded tales: "Zadig," "Vision de Babouc," "Memnon," and possibly "Micromegas" (some scholars believe this story was written in 1739, although not published until 1752).

In 1748, Voltaire settled with Madame du Châtelet in Commercy at the court of Stanislaw, the former king of POLAND. There, Voltaire experienced the greatest tragedy of his life, when his beloved companion died of childbed fever (September 1749), shortly after delivering the infant of her new lover, the young military adventurer Saint-Lambert. Grieving, Voltaire returned to the Paris house they had shared.

At this critical point in his life, Voltaire finally accepted the longstanding invitation of FREDERICK II (THE GREAT) to move to BERLIN. He departed Paris in 1750. At first, Voltaire enjoyed Berlin, for he was well received at Frederick's court. He finally completed the *Siècle de Louis XIV,* his important examination of ABSOLUTISM under King LOUIS XIV. By 1752, however, Voltaire's disputatious manner had caused a number of conflicts, the most significant of which centered on the ideas of Pierre de MAUPERTUIS, the president of the BERLIN ACADEMY and Voltaire's old friend.

One of the earliest champions of Isaac Newton's physics, Maupertuis had also incorporated some ideas from the German philosopher Gottfried Wilhelm LEIBNIZ into his physical theories. Voltaire ridiculed Maupertuis in a satirical pamphlet entitled *Diatribe du docteur Akakis* (Diatribe of Dr. Akakis; 1752). Frederick the Great, incensed at this insult to his leading academician, ordered the pamphlet publicly burned and personally reprimanded Voltaire.

Portrait of Voltaire by an unknown artist after a portrait by Nicholas de Largillière, 1718. The brilliant, impassioned literary and political works of Voltaire, coupled with the tumultuous events of his private life, preserve a place for him as one of the outstanding figures of the French Enlightenment. *(Courtesy Musée Versailles, Versailles, France)*

Voltaire responded by leaving Berlin, but Frederick succeeded in having him placed under house arrest in FRANKFURT. Voltaire had nowhere to turn. Louis XV prohibited his return to France, and no other ruler was offering protection. The town of Colmar in Alsace provided a residence for one year; and finally, in 1755, Voltaire received permission to settle in GENEVA.

At his Genevan home, Les Délices, Voltaire established a popular salon that was attended by progressive Genevan pastors, women, and young people. He enjoyed patronage from the powerful Tronchin family. Voltaire privately produced plays at Les Délices and completed work on his history of the world, *L'Essai sur les moeurs* (1756).

By 1757, however, troubles with authorities—this time in Geneva—caused Voltaire to move once again. The problems centered on Voltaire's private theater presentations; The Genevan authorities tried to stop them but also refused to establish a public theater in the city. Tensions exploded late in 1757 when the seventh volume of the *ENCYCLOPÉDIE* appeared with its critical article "Genève" (Geneva) by Jean Le Rond d'ALEMBERT. Voltaire, of course, had inspired the article. Jean-Jacques ROUSSEAU jumped into the fray, defending his native Geneva and attacking Voltaire. As a result, the friendship between these two men was permanently ruptured. In the end,

Voltaire left Geneva, settling at the estate of Ferney, near the border with France. He also bought Tourney, an estate just inside the French border. In this manner, he could move between the two countries whenever it seemed prudent or necessary.

CANDIDE, Voltaire's most famous NOVEL, was written in 1758 and reflects Voltaire's many disillusioning experiences. Candide's prescription against metaphysical anguish and worldly troubles—withdrawal from the world in order to cultivate his garden in the company of friends—also proved to be Voltaire's solution to his personal situation. During the 20 years he lived at Ferney, he received an endless stream of visitors, corresponded with friends and intellectual acquaintances, and continued his activities on behalf of reform, PROGRESS, and TOLERATION.

These years produced Voltaire's impassioned interventions to secure judicial review in the cases of Jean CALAS (1762) and the chevalier de La Barre (1766). They also witnessed the intensification of the campaign against ROMAN CATHOLICISM and any form of intolerance based on religious SUPERSTITION or dogma (all signified in the term *l'infame*). Finally, these years produced the DICTIONNAIRE PHILOSOPHIQUE (Philosophical Dictionary; 1764); stories such as "La Princesse de Babylon" and "Le Taureau blanc"; examinations of the philosophies of Benedict de SPINOZA and Nicolas de MALEBRANCHE entitled *Le philosophe ignorant* (The ignorant philosopher; 1766) and *Tout en Dieu* (Everything in God; 1769); and the play *Tancrède* (1760).

Early in 1778, 28 years after he had left Paris, Voltaire returned to the French capital in order to direct rehearsals of his play *Irène*. He was welcomed as a hero, receiving 300 callers in his first day of open house. Kidney disease struck him on May 18 and by May 30, the great spokesman of the French Enlightenment was dead. Christian burial was accomplished secretly and in haste at the Abbey of Scellières; the decree prohibiting such burial arrived just after the inhumation had been completed. During the FRENCH REVOLUTION, however, Voltaire's remains were reburied with honor in the Panthéon of Paris.

Without a doubt, Voltaire was one of the greatest figures of the French ENLIGHTENMENT. An intense commitment to FREEDOM of thought, to religious toleration, to scientific and artistic progress, to the reform of justice, and to EMPIRICISM guided his activities throughout his life. With his contemporary MONTESQUIEU, Voltaire helped to shape the first half of the Enlightenment according to English models. It was Voltaire, for example, who first introduced French literate society to English institutions and ideas in his highly readable *Lettres philosophiques*. He performed a similar service for Newton, offering in his *Elements de la philosophie de Newton,* an interpretative distillation of the Englishman's NATURAL PHILOSOPHY. If the scientific community drew directly from the *Principia mathematica,* the general enlightened public drew its ideas from Voltaire.

As a historian, Voltaire helped to create a new way of examining the past. He was interested not in the activities of great men, but in the broader cultural, social, and political history of nations.

As a polemicist, Voltaire had no equal. His brilliant and caustic wit, his ability to distill a philosophical meaning from an event and to provide it with vibrancy through his mastery of language, remain impressive to this day. Possessed of uncommon vitality and intensity, of impressive social skills wedded with prickly combativeness, of sharp and wide-ranging intelligence, Voltaire provided a model of the enlightened philosophe that persists to this day.

See also OPERA; PORNOGRAPHY; SOCIAL INSTITUTIONS OF THE ENLIGHTENMENT.

Further reading: C. J. Betts, *Early Deism in France: From the So-Called Déistes of Lyon (1564) to Voltaire's Lettres philosophiques (1734)* (The Hague: Martinus Nijhoff, 1984); Voltaire, *Candide and Other Stories,* ed. and tr. Roger Pearson (New York: Oxford University Press, 1990); Voltaire, *The Portable Voltaire,* ed. Ben Ray Redman (New York: Viking Press, 1963).

voyages of discovery Naval expeditions with the primary purpose of advancing scientific knowledge. Early modern European voyagers had opened up sea routes to the Americas, around Africa, and into the East as far as the Philippines, Indonesia, Japan, and CHINA. The established imperial states of SPAIN and PORTUGAL (in Iberia), funded by New World gold and silver bullion, were successfully challenged at sea and on land during the 17th century by ENGLAND, FRANCE, and the UNITED PROVINCES OF THE NETHERLANDS. England, France, and Spain were the primary sponsors of scientific voyages during the ENLIGHTENMENT, but Russia and GERMANY made significant contributions.

Most 18th-century voyages were motivated by mercantile ambition, but this was the era of travel for the sake of knowledge as well as commercial gain. The two maritime puzzles that nations competed to resolve were whether there existed a Northwest Passage that would allow shipping a direct route across North America from the Atlantic to the Pacific Ocean, and whether the Southern Hemisphere contained a continent equivalent to the landmass in the Northern Hemisphere. Thus, 18th-century voyages of discovery focused on the unexplored reaches of the Pacific Ocean.

By 1623, the Dutch had claimed parts of Indonesia, and by 1642, the explorer Abel Janszoon Tasman had explored coastal areas of New Zealand and Australia, then named New Holland. In 1700, the English acquired two previously unknown Pacific islands when William Dampier, a former pirate, followed Sir Francis Drake's familiar route to New Guinea and named these islands New Britain and New Ireland. By the mid-18th century, European explorers were searching for the mysterious continent believed to lie in the South Pacific.

"An offering before Captain Cook in the Sandwich Islands," 1779 *(Courtesy New York Public Library)*

The English captain James COOK was commissioned on his first voyage of discovery to investigate the astronomical phenomenon named the TRANSIT OF VENUS from a suitable location in the Southern Hemisphere. He found an apt spot in TAHITI for this observation that permitted the calculation of the distance between the Sun and the Earth. On this voyage with Joseph BANKS, the English naturalist, Cook navigated throughout the region, even tracing the eastern coast of Australia along the Great Barrier Reef. They encountered Tahitians and various groups of Australasian aborigines, and Banks studied the unusual flora and fauna. (Banks's experience led him some time later to champion the establishment of an English penal colony at Botany Bay, Australia.) The same points visited by Banks and Cook on their voyage were discovered almost concurrently by Louis-Antoine de BOUGAINVILLE, a French navigator who had the advantage of first reporting these finds in Europe.

In 1772, on his second major voyage, Cook sailed as far south into the Antarctic as has anyone since and surmised that there was no land lying beyond the huge ice fields unless it was near the pole and out of the reach of navigation. His next mission was the exploration of the North Pacific in search of the elusive Northwest Passage. On his return from a detailed mapping of the Alaskan coastline, he stopped in Hawaii. After a lengthy period of mutual amity between the native Hawaiians and the English, he shot some Hawaiians in the aftermath of a theft and was killed in retaliatory mob violence in 1779.

Cook's skepticism about the existence of the Northwest Passage was confirmed on a later voyage by one of his former officers, George Vancouver. Vancouver had sailed with Cook on two expeditions, and he resumed charting the Alaskan coast to confirm that no Northwest Passage existed. His account, *A Voyage of Discovery to the North Pacific Ocean and Round the World, 1790–1795,* was published in 1798, shortly after he died.

North Pacific explorations by other countries also centered on Alaska. Russia was the first nation to explore this part of the American coastline, beginning in the early 17th century. The Second Kamchatka Expedition under Vitus Bering, a Dane employed by Russia, and his deputy, Alexsei Chirikov, was launched in 1740, years before Cook's commission and relying upon far less precise navigational tools than Cook had available. The Russian ships crossed the North Pacific, now called the Bering Strait, to discover Alaska and the Aleutian Islands. Russia's first landing, on Kayak Island in 1741, accorded Russia a colonial stake in Alaskan territories. The landing was also a significant scientific event in natural history discoveries and for the theory proposed by the expedition's scientist, Georg Wilhelm Steller (1709–46), that the ancestors of Native Americans crossed the Bering Strait from Asia to America.

Spain and France were equally keen on Alaskan exploration. Spain was determined to protect its interests on the West Coast of America, where it already had colonial possession of California. In part to counter Russian advance into California and in part to challenge Cook's successful voyage to Alaska, CHARLES III dispatched Alejandro Malaspina to claim the territory for Spain in 1789. The attempt failed. At the time, Charles encouraged Spanish naturalists to identify the resources—botanical, zoological, and mineralogical—of North and South America. He sponsored several voyages, including a royal scientific expedition in 1787 to establish a botanical garden in Mexico City and oversee studies of the native flora. But, by the end of the century, this project, too, had floundered.

The French fared better with Jean-François de Galaup, comte de La Pérouse. He cooperated with the Russians, who were vitally interested in the Alaskan fur trade, and transported secret documents from a Pacific Russian outpost to France, but La Pérouse believed that navigators' principal duties were to complete the survey of the globe. Another French navigator, Charles-Pierre Claret, comte de Fleurieu, in 1784 embarked on a mission to begin a systematic natural history collection for the Musée d'Histoire Naturelle in PARIS. Scientists always accompanied the French explorers, but France's primary interest in Alaska appears to have been the fur trade.

Without the mercantile or colonial aims of most European explorers, Alexander von HUMBOLDT (1769–1859) set off in 1799 for a five-year trip to South and Central America with the grand design of organizing the earth's physical laws so as to reveal the unity of nature. Dedicated to EMPIRICISM, this Prussian mine engineer carried with him a vast array of instruments to measure atmospheric oxygen, temperature, humidity, elasticity, electrical charge, and magnetism, others to assess altitude and angles, and still others to navigate with precision. His tables of readings reveal a "physics of the earth," the organic unity of physical forces. His innovations included the use of isotherms (lines connecting points of equal temperature) in mapmaking and what he called the geography of plants, a global law of physics based on organic matter, comparable to the laws governing magnetism and heat.

Numerous developments of the period vastly improved sea travel. These included the re-engineering of sailing ships for optimum capability and stability and experiments in improving the habits and health of mariners. Captain Cook was instrumental in establishing cleanliness and discipline in the English Navy. He also experimented with different kinds of foods in order to reduce losses from the dread disease scurvy, which killed thousands of sailors deprived of vitamin C on long voyages. His efforts at preventive MEDICINE by providing citrus juices, sauerkraut, a portable soup (a dehydrated soup stock), and fresh greens collected on shore essentially eliminated the incidence of scurvy.

Sea travel was also improved by accurate new maps and methods for determining latitude and LONGITUDE. The conjunction of the empirical method and new inventions was key. Newly discovered lands could not be mapped without data, and data was collected by sailors in repeated measurements of water temperature, barometric pressure, tidal flow, shoal formation, and currents. The earlier invention and development of the quadrant and, by the middle of the 18th century, the sextant had permitted a fairly accurate assessment of latitudes, but longitudes remained problematic until the invention of the chronometer by John HARRISON. Cook tested Harrison's invention in 1772, and on his Alaskan voyage in 1791, Vancouver confirmed the reliability of the instrument. It was a highly accurate timepiece that, when used in conjunction with the empirical data he collected and collated, enabled him to deduce longitude with relative ease and accurately enough for navigational purposes.

Europeans also carried problems to the lands they visited. They spread smallpox and syphilis, creating havoc in local populations. The sailors, in turn, often succumbed to tropical diseases such as malaria and parasitic infections. Cross-cultural disputes with native peoples, especially over theft, frequently led to violence. Naturally, the advantage always lay with the Europeans, who carried guns to kill or intimidate their hosts. Recent historical research has emphasized the negative effects of colonization during this era of exploration—the physical oppression and cultural coercion of local populations and the growth of racism, problems that continue to affect minority groups today.

At the same time, Europe and its New World colonies were beset by riots, wars, and revolutions, including the AMERICAN REVOLUTION (1776) and the FRENCH REVOLUTION (1789). Europeans appropriated newly discovered territories on a first-come, first-served basis, routinely warred with one another, and exploited the peoples and resources of their colonies. Nevertheless, the scientific projects undertaken during the voyages of discovery fostered a spirit of cooperation, and the knowledge arising from empirical science enhanced navigational technology and maritime health, changes that ultimately benefited all people.

See also ANTHROPOLOGY; BIOLOGY; CARTOGRAPHY; COLONIALISM; JARDIN DE PLANTES; MUSEUMS; NATURE; RACE; ROYAL SOCIETY OF LONDON; SCIENTIFIC METHOD; TECHNOLOGY AND INSTRUMENTATION; TRAVEL LITERATURE.

Further reading: Margarette Lincoln, ed., *Science and Exploration in the Pacific Oceans in the 18th Century* (Rochester, N.Y.: Boydell Press, 1998); Lynne Withey, *Voyages of Discovery: Captain Cook and the Exploration of the Pacific* (New York: William Morrow, 1987); O. W. Frost, ed., *Bering and Chirikov: The American Voyages and Their Impact* (Anchorage: Alaska Historical Society, 1992).

W

Waldensians Followers of a Christian sect that originated in 12th-century southern France and adopted CALVINISM in the 16th century. In the 18th century, most of the members of this group lived in certain mountainous valleys of the PIEDMONT. This region was part of the kingdom of SAVOY, whose ruler Victor Amadeus II (1675–1730), in order to preserve his kingdom, often allied himself with the powerful LOUIS XIV of FRANCE.

In 1685, Louis XIV ordered the revocation of the Edict of Nantes, thus ending a century of TOLERATION for French Calvinists, the so-called HUGUENOTS. Huguenots were faced with the choice of fleeing France or of converting, at least publicly, to ROMAN CATHOLICISM. Louis XIV forced Victor Amadeus to follow the same policy with the Waldensians.

The Waldensians refused to convert willingly and openly resisted. Louis XIV sent an army into the Piedmont and brutally suppressed the revolt. The Waldensians—men, women, and children—were rounded up and imprisoned. Out of a total number of 12,000 people, more than 8,000 died as a result of imprisonment and disease. The remainder were released and sent to Calvinist GENEVA in 1686.

The actions of Louis XIV outraged Protestant Europe. After the GLORIOUS REVOLUTION OF 1688 secured the English throne for the Protestant rulers WILLIAM III AND MARY II, the Waldensians in Geneva began to receive active English support designed to facilitate their return to the Piedmont. In August 1689, they invaded their former home valleys. Finally, in June 1690, when it seemed they were about to be defeated, Victor Amadeus reached an agreement with them. He had secretly decided to abandon his alliance with Louis XIV and to align himself with Louis's enemies. He assured the Waldensians that they could resume living peacefully in the Piedmont if they would join him in fighting against Louis XIV. This agreement ended the Waldensian persecutions and related rebellions.

For the PHILOSOPHES of the ENLIGHTENMENT, the persecution of the Waldensians stood as a chilling example of the horrors caused by religious fanaticism and provided one of the more recent historical experiences that fueled calls for religious toleration.

Walpole, Horace, fourth earl of Orford (1717–1797) *English man of letters, one of the founders of the English Gothic revival in architecture and literature*
Horace Walpole, fourth son of Sir Robert WALPOLE, attended school at the elite Eton College and at Kings College, Cambridge. Between 1739 and 1741, he made a GRAND TOUR of the European continent in the company of his friend, the poet Thomas GRAY. Upon returning to England, he served as a member of Parliament for Callington, Castle Rising, and Lynn. In 1765, on a second trip to FRANCE, Walpole became a frequent guest at the salon of Madame du DEFFAND, where he mingled with prominent leaders of the ENLIGHTENMENT.

In 1747, Walpole bought the estate called Strawberry Hill near Twickenham, which he remodeled using motifs drawn from medieval Gothic architecture. Renewed interest in the Gothic aesthetic was one manifestation of the distinct shift in the cultural sensibilities of the Enlightenment that occurred in the mid-18th century. Strawberry Hill became a symbol of this shift and a gathering point for English artists and writers of the period.

Walpole installed a printing press at Strawberry Hill, which he used between 1757 and 1789 to produce his own novels, antiquarian works, and histories and the poems of Thomas Gray. Walpole created the first GOTHIC ROMANCE novel when he wrote *The Castle of Otranto* (1764). His other works included *Historic Doubts on the Life and Reign of Richard III* (1768) and *Anecdotes of Painting in England* (1762–71). He owes much of his literary reputation to his witty letters. In the 19th century, two of his memoirs on the political events of his era were finally published.

See also BLUESTOCKING; GOTHIC REVIVAL.

Walpole, Robert (1676–1745) *British statesman*

Walpole was born into a family of wealthy Whig politicians. He attended Eton and then Cambridge University, where he prepared for a career in the Church of England. He left Cambridge in 1698 when the death of his elder brother made him the heir to his father's estates. In 1701, he entered Parliament, where his friendship with Sara Churchill, the wife of John Churchill, later the duke of Marlborough, led to his rapid rise in Whig Party ranks.

Walpole rose to power shortly after the first Hanoverian king, George I, assumed the British throne (1714). Walpole led the impeachment process against the Tory leader, Lord BOLINGBROKE, in 1715.

During this period, the British monarchy lost most of its effective political power to the Parliament, and Walpole played the major role in this development. A brilliant politician, Walpole was known for his willingness to compromise, and he argued for the principle of majority rule. Under his ministry, the House of Commons became more powerful than the House of Lords. Walpole refused a royal nomination to the English peerage in 1723, recognizing that he did not need this special title in order to exercise power.

The principles of MERCANTILISM still controlled British commerce and finance when Walpole came to power, determined to introduce FREE TRADE and to reform British finances. He strengthened the economic position of Britain's overseas colonies, arguing that the colonies were key to Britain's own wealth and power. But his attempts to reform Britain's tax system gained him many enemies in several different quarters.

Walpole's friends and allies included British writers such as Joseph ADDISON, Richard STEELE, and the playwright William CONGREVE. However, writers such as John GAY, Henry FIELDING, and Daniel DEFOE, angered by his pragmatic approach to government and by his use of corruption and bribery to maintain power, published satirical attacks on his character. Walpole and his government figure prominently in Gay's BEGGAR'S OPERA (1728). Attacks on Walpole's government by Henry Fielding prompted Walpole to pass the Licensing Act of 1737, which established a system of theatrical censorship in England that lasted until the 20th century.

See also LANDSCAPE; PICTURESQUE; PUBLISHING; SEPARATION OF POWERS.

War of the Austrian Succession

European war that broke out in 1740 upon the accession of a woman, MARIA THERESA OF AUSTRIA, to the throne of the HAPSBURG EMPIRE. By law the Hapsburg succession passed only through the male line, but Maria Theresa's father, Emperor Charles VI, had no male heirs. He attempted to stave off a succession crisis by decreeing and obtaining the Diet's approval of the Pragmatic Sanction, a document granting Maria Theresa the right to assume the throne. Although the Pragmatic Sanction was approved, her rights were, nevertheless, challenged by her male relatives.

FREDERICK II (THE GREAT), who had succeeded to the throne of PRUSSIA about five months earlier than Maria Theresa had succeeded to the Hapsburg throne, precipitated the actual hostilities by moving with sudden, astonishing speed into the Austrian territory of Silesia and annexing it to Prussia. His action shocked European sensibilities because it represented a blatant violation of existing treaties and diplomatic practices. The fighting spread quickly to become a general war involving the major nations of Europe. In the course of this war, which lasted until 1748, Maria Theresa demonstrated that she could hold her own in European conflicts; her legitimacy as the Hapsburg successor was recognized. However, she lost Silesia to Prussia.

The War of the Austrian Succession revealed the Machiavellian nature of Frederick the Great's vision of foreign policy and demonstrated that Prussia had become a major power. French and Austrian reactions to this new player on the international scene ultimately produced the great DIPLOMATIC REVOLUTION OF 1756 and dramatically restructured the European balance of power.

Washington, George (1732–1799) *founding father, military leader, and first president of the United States of America*

George Washington was born in Virginia to Augustine and Mary Ball Washington, a prosperous family of planters. His parents provided him with a gentleman's education. An able mathematician, at age 16 Washington went to work as a surveyor for the great Virginia landowner Lord Fairfax. In 1752, he inherited the estate of Mount Vernon and began to farm there.

In 1754, he received a commission as lieutenant colonel in the colonial army, and later fought with distinction with the British army in the French and Indian War, known in Europe as the SEVEN YEARS' WAR. He came to be known for his bravery and intelligence and rose to the rank of brigadier general. However, he felt that the British military's discrimination against colonial soldiers was unjust, and he resigned from the army in 1758.

After his army resignation, Washington served in the Virginia House of Burgesses. In 1759, he married Martha

Dandridge Custis, a young widow. He returned to his home at Mount Vernon in Virginia and devoted himself to farming and family life. He also continued to serve in the House of Burgesses.

During this time, Washington displayed various characteristics that were upheld as enlightened ideals. Due to his dedication to his various roles as farmer, statesman, and soldier, Washington was seen as a modern Cincinnatus. Cincinnatus, an ancient Roman farmer called to public service, was a hero to followers of the NEOCLASSICAL movement in art, LITERATURE, and political thought. Various contemporary writers, such as Jean-Jacques ROUSSEAU, painters, such as John Trumbull, and poets, such as Lord BYRON, represented Washington as Cincinnatus. Politically, while serving in the Burgesses, Washington also defended the ENLIGHTENMENT ideals of democracy and the RIGHTS of citizens. He believed that the taxes and regulations the British imposed on the American colonies were unfair. In his view, the British were trampling on the rights of colonists and jeopardizing their lives, LIBERTY, and PROPERTY.

Washington's dedication to the Enlightenment virtue of public service deepened as the conflict with Britain worsened. In 1775, Washington was elected as a delegate from Virginia to the Second Continental Congress in PHILADELPHIA, where he was voted commander in chief of the Continental Army. In July 1775, he began to train his troops for the coming struggle. Knowing that the colonial army could not outfight the British, he expected to use guerrilla tactics against the more traditional British Army. This prompted criticism that he was avoiding large-scale battles.

In truth, Washington seized opportunities as they appeared. His military abilities became legendary in 1776. On a bitterly cold December night, he led his ill-provisioned troops across the Delaware River from Pennsylvania in a successful surprise attack on British forces in Trenton, New Jersey. He followed this victory with a second in Princeton, New Jersey. In 1781, Washington forced Lord Charles Cornwallis to surrender at the Battle of Yorktown, ending the war.

To the astonishment and admiration of many in Europe and the New World, Washington resigned his command of the army in December 1783. By giving up power when he could have become the most powerful man in the new nation, Washington demonstrated how the Enlightenment republican ideals of holding moderate power and surrendering that power when it is no longer necessary should work.

After independence, Washington was among those who believed that the Articles of Confederation used to govern the states needed to be replaced. He supported the call for a convention of state delegates to meet in Philadelphia in 1787 to write a new constitution for the infant country. Among those present were Benjamin FRANKLIN, James MADISON, and Alexander HAMILTON. The delegates wrote the UNITED STATES CONSTITUTION, which specified the rights of the states and the federal government and is a landmark enlightened political document.

In 1789, Washington was elected to be the first president of the UNITED STATES OF AMERICA. He took the oath of office on April 30 in New York City at the age of 57. As a sign that he represented the entire country, he toured both the northern and southern states. Washington set many precedents. He affirmed the supremacy of the federal government by supporting the creation of a national bank and ending the Whiskey Rebellion, among other measures. He also appointed a highly capable first cabinet, including Thomas JEFFERSON as secretary of state and Hamilton as secretary of the treasury.

These two appointments caused problems for Washington once the FRENCH REVOLUTION began in 1789 and ENGLAND and FRANCE went to war. Due to his belief in the Enlightenment virtues of political independence and financial self-sufficiency, Washington wanted the United States to remain neutral and free of European influence. However, he wanted to maintain economic ties with Britain and to keep the weak United States out of the war. Jefferson, who was pro-French, and Hamilton, who was pro-British, disagreed bitterly over policy.

Their allies in Congress joined the dispute. The Hamiltonians, or Federalists, supported Washington's economic and foreign policies. Jefferson's Democratic-Republicans were critical of Washington's excise tax, lack of support for France, and conciliatory attitude toward Britain.

By 1796, wearied of politics, Washington refused to serve a third term. In his farewell address, Washington warned his fellow citizens against political and regional divisions, and advised them to avoid alliances with other nations that could ensnare the United States in their problems and threaten the country's self-sufficiency.

Vice president John ADAMS became president in 1797. Washington retired to Mount Vernon. It was not long, however, before he was asked to serve his country once more. In 1798, when war with France seemed imminent, Adams asked Washington to assume command of the army. Although he accepted, Washington kept his activities to a minimum and remained at Mount Vernon. In December 1799, he contracted a case of laryngitis that quickly developed into a more severe infection. Washington died of his illness on December 14, 1799, at the age of 67.

Washington's legacy is inestimable. In his policies and his life he advocated the most beneficial ideas of the Enlightenment. A promoter of EDUCATION, he wanted to found a national university. He also encouraged religious tolerance when he was commander of the army, and opposed the idea of a state RELIGION when he was president. On his own lands, he practiced the same prudence and frugality with which he governed the nation. Washington made agricultural improvements and ran the farms of Mount Vernon so efficiently that, on his death, his estate was able to provide a fund for his newly freed slaves. A man of vision and integrity, not only did Washington's military and political efforts help make the United States possible, but his dedication to the Enlightenment ideals of democratic and just leadership also provided the country with a stable beginning.

See also AMERICAN REVOLUTION; UNITED STATES BILL OF RIGHTS.

Further reading: Richard Brookhiser, *Founding Father: Rediscovering George Washington* (New York: Free Press, 1996); James Thomas Flexner, *George Washington: The Indispensable Man* (New York: Little, Brown, 1994); Gary Wills, *Cincinnatus: George Washington and the Enlightenment* (New York: Doubleday, 1984).

water frame   Machine for spinning cotton yarn that was operated by water power. It was invented by Richard ARKWRIGHT in 1769. The water frame worked on a different principle from the SPINNING JENNY. It drew the threads of cotton out and then twisted them to make yarn, whereas the jenny and the SPINNING MULE performed both operations simultaneously. The water frame produced a coarse thread suitable primarily for the warp in woven cloth. It fell into disuse around 1800, but then reappeared in the 1820s and 1830s when the general use of the POWER LOOM created a demand for strong warp yarns.

See also INDUSTRIAL REVOLUTION.

Watt, James (1736–1819) *Scottish inventor and engineer who patented several important improvements to the Newcomen steam engine that effectively transformed the early engine into a new machine*
James Watt thus played a significant role in the 18th-century INDUSTRIAL REVOLUTION. His role in the harnessing of power for industrial use was honored by giving his name, *watt*, to the unit of power in physics.

James Watt had a father and an uncle whose work involved the occasional production of precision instruments. After gaining some apprenticeship experience, Watt set himself up in Glasgow, SCOTLAND, as an instrument maker. He soon acquired contracts with the University of Glasgow for instrument repairs. In this capacity, he worked on a Newcomen STEAM ENGINE. After 1764, he concentrated primarily on repairing, on improving, and finally on manufacturing steam engines.

In 1765, Watt added a second cylinder to the Newcomen steam engine that greatly increased its fuel efficiency. He patented his invention in 1769. This improvement helped to make the steam engine an affordable technology and thereby enhanced its diffusion throughout the industrial world. Watt continued to work on steam engines, inventing the double-acting engine and various methods for converting reciprocal motion into rotary motion.

With Matthew BOULTON, Watt began manufacturing steam engines in 1774 at the Soho Engineering Works in Birmingham. The two men coined the term *horsepower* as a measure of the power of their machines.

See also LUNAR SOCIETY OF BIRMINGHAM.

Watteau, Jean Antoine (1684–1721) *French painter; led the transformation of French art from baroque to rococo style at the beginning of the 18th century*
Watteau abandoned the grandiose themes of baroque art and turned to subjects with more obvious human dimensions and emotional appeal. He mastered the delicate gracefulness necessary for CHINOISERIE. Watteau was a great technician, influenced by the outstanding baroque colorist, Peter-Paul Rubens, whose series on Marie de Medici he studied at the Luxembourg Palace in PARIS. Watteau adapted Rubens's techniques and masterly use of color to meet the demands of his own new style. His admittance to the Academy of Painting was a major vic-

Gilles, by Jean Antoine Watteau. Watteau wove theater and real life together in a series of enchanting paintings that captured the rococo love of play and illusion. *(Courtesy New York Public Library)*

tory for the French Rubenistes (colorists who insisted painting should appeal to the senses and the emotions) in their battle against the Poussainistes (artists who placed the intellectual, rational content of works above their sensual appeal in a scale of values).

Watteau's family lived in frugal circumstances supported by the father's earnings as a roof tiler. Watteau was apprenticed to a painter in his hometown of Valenciennes. In 1702, he journeyed to Paris, where he obtained work producing devotional pictures for a wholesale shop. Claude Gillot, an artist who specialized in painting theater scenery, accepted him as an apprentice in 1704. The experience gained under Gillot's tutelage left Watteau with a lifelong fascination for actors, actresses, and the THEATER. In 1708, Watteau transferred to Claude Audran's studio at the Luxembourg Palace. He tried unsuccessfully in 1709 to win the Prix de Rome awarded by the Academy of Painting. In 1712, however, his painting *Les Jaloux* brought him an associate membership in that prestigious organization. A diploma came in 1717, awarded for the painting *The Embarkation for Cythera*. The academy created a new category for Watteau's painting, that of *fêtes galantes,* or scenes of gallant merrymaking.

In 1715, Watteau established contact with the financier, art connoisseur, and patron Pierre Crozat. This new association provided Watteau with opportunities to study firsthand the many Italian and Flemish drawings in Crozat's rich collections. Watteau traveled to ENGLAND in 1719, returning to Paris in 1720 for the wedding of a friend and patron, Jean de Jullienne, who eventually published the *Recueil Julliene,* a collection of Watteau's engravings after drawings and paintings by outstanding European artists. This collection served as an important source for artists in Europe interested in digesting the styles of their predecessors. Watteau died from tuberculosis in Paris in 1721.

Watteau's various *fêtes galantes* pieces captured the playful spirit that reigned among the members of the French aristocracy during the Regency (1715–23). They also illustrated one way in which the emerging culture of SENSIBILITY could be translated into the visual arts.

See also ROCOCO.

Wealth of Nations

Wealth of Nations   Treatise on political economy published in 1776 by Adam SMITH. The complete title was *An Inquiry into the Nature and Causes of the Wealth of Nations.*

Borrowing from the life sciences, Smith assumed that NATURE is a dynamic but self-regulating entity. He believed that some power—God or NATURAL LAW—was operating behind the seeming chaos of everyday life to create a genuinely benevolent order in this world.

Smith received this model from his teacher Francis HUTCHESON, but it was common throughout Europe during the ENLIGHTENMENT. Smith adapted the model to ECO-NOMICS, using it to develop a theoretical foundation for the FREE TRADE policies and capitalistic structures associated with 18th-century British economic liberalism.

In writing *Wealth of Nations,* Smith also drew heavily from the theories of his friends, the French PHYSIOCRATS. But, because the Physiocrats had envisioned an economy dominated by agriculture, Smith adapted their theory to make it relevant to the needs of an economy driven by commerce and industry.

Smith argued that the free exercise of economic SELF-INTEREST would create the greatest prosperity for a nation. Thus, he maintained that regulations limiting freedom in the economic sphere should be abolished. He further argued that productivity could be increased by analyzing the activities associated with creating a given product and by then breaking up the job into unit tasks. This division of labor, in which one person performed the same task repeatedly rather than carrying out all the different tasks needed to make something, would speed up production and therefore reduce costs.

Smith described and analyzed conditions in the British Isles in an effort to demonstrate why British investors were making the choice to underwrite trading ventures rather than agricultural operations. He proposed removing restrictions against the free sale and use of land, promoting internal free trade, and abolishing restrictions on the free choice of occupation and the movement of labor.

Smith intended his new economic theory as a substitute for MERCANTILISM, a set of economic principles and practices that had developed in the context of monarchical ABSOLUTISM and colonial expansion during the 17th century. Mercantilism defined wealth in terms of the amount of gold or silver coin possessed by a nation. It tended to discourage the circulation of money in exchange for goods, and also promoted the regulation of trade and industry.

Smith believed that the general welfare of society would be preserved if people were free to pursue their self-interest without interference from the government. In his vision, self-interest motivates economic activity, encouraging people to be industrious and creative. It serves the common good, because the capitalist, desiring to make a profit, will be motivated to produce the goods demanded by the greatest number of people. In pursuing his own self-gain, the capitalist will then inevitably promote the common good. The whole system is guaranteed by the Hidden Hand, Adam Smith's version of the benevolent power or principle that ensures harmonious relations between expressions of self-interest and the social good.

Smith's theory is well known to students because of its close links with modern liberal economics. But in the 18th century, it had a number of competitors in the writings of François QUESNAY, Jean-Claude de GOURNAY, and Anne-Robert-Jacques TURGOT, all associated with the

Physiocrats; in Ferdinando GALIANI, the opponent of the Physiocrats; and in the school of CAMERALISM, associated with enlightened despotism (see DESPOTISM, ENLIGHTENED) in central European states such as the HAPSBURG EMPIRE or PRUSSIA. Each of these theoretical approaches built on ideas central to the Enlightenment, drawing different conclusions and developing implications along conflicting lines. Together, they reveal the complexity contained in enlightened views when they were applied to the problem of guaranteeing the material welfare of human beings.

See also INDIVIDUALISM; MORAL PHILOSOPHY; SYMPATHY.

Wedgwood, Josiah (1730–1795) *English pottery and ceramics designer and manufacturer*

The Wedgwood family had worked as potters since the 17th century. Josiah, who as a nine-year-old began learning the craft, demonstrated marked skill at the potter's wheel. An attack of smallpox imposed a long period of inactivity on the young man, but he utilized the time to study the theoretical scientific aspects of his craft. Consequently, he acquired the skills and knowledge necessary to allow him to make practical changes in the technology of pottery production. It was especially significant for the advancement of the business and the expansion of consumer markets that Wedgwood found a way to harness steam as the source of energy for driving potter's wheels and grinding machinery. Furthermore, even in the many production tasks that continued to require hand labor, Wedgwood innovated by applying the concept of the division of labor to the organization of his factories. Wedgwood's many innovations, and his expertise at translating theoretical knowledge into practice, made him one of the major figures in the 18th-century British INDUSTRIAL REVOLUTION. The result was high-quality hard, fire-resistant ceramics, appropriate for normal domestic use and affordable by wide cross sections of society.

In 1754, Wedgwood established a partnership with Thomas Whieldon, the leading pottery maker of the era. Out of this joint venture came Wedgwood's ivory creamware, also called "Queen's ware," in honor of the patronage provided by Queen Charlotte. This pottery, designed for ordinary domestic use, sold throughout the world. In 1768, Wedgwood established a second business venture with the Liverpool merchant Thomas Bentley. The two men built the ETRURIA WORKS for the production of ornamental ceramics. At Etruria, Wedgwood produced black basalt and jasperware pieces in neoclassical style decorated with ancient Greek and Roman motifs. About 1771, the original "Queen's ware" factory moved also to Etruria.

Wedgwood was not only an industrial innovator, but also a committed opponent of SLAVERY. He was a major figure in 18th-century English movements calling for abolition.

"Portland vase," a jasper dip by Josiah Wedgwood, 1790. Wedgwood produced his jasperware at the Etruria works factory, decorating the pieces with classical motifs taken from ancient Roman and Greek sources. *(Courtesy New York Public Library)*

See also NEOCLASSICISM; TECHNOLOGY AND INSTRUMENTATION.

Werner, Abraham Gottlob (1749–1817) *German geologist*

Werner was born in Upper Lusatia, then part of Saxony and now part of POLAND. His family had long been associated with various ironworks, and Werner followed the family tradition by apprenticing in the field. He also enrolled in the newly established *Bergakademie* in Freiberg where he ultimately spent 42 years as a professor.

Werner was one of the most influential geologists of his era. Werner's theory of the formation of the Earth was enormously popular and served as one pole of geological debate well into the 19th century. His theory stressed the role played by the deposit of sediments in the ocean (Neptune theory). According to Werner, the history of the formation of the Earth could be divided into four long periods, alternating between calm and stormy. In each period, a specific type of rock was formed from the oceans.

Werner also developed a systematic classification of minerals based partly on their external appearance and partly on their chemical composition. He started the great "basalt controversy" of the 18th century when he stated that basalt is a rock that originated in the ocean. His opponents believed it was formed by the action of volcanoes.

In a manner typical of the ENLIGHTENMENT, Werner ignored the biblical account of creation in developing his theories and thus managed to avoid the religious controversies that were swirling around geological theories about the history of the Earth. Nevertheless, his theory implicitly negated Christian interpretations of the Earth's history by suggesting that a much greater period of time had elapsed since the original creation than the 4,004 years allegedly supported by biblical narratives.

Werner was in close contact with most of the leaders of the German Enlightenment (AUFKLÄRUNG). He corresponded with Johann Wolfgang von GOETHE and, at the Bergakademie, taught such figures as Alexander von HUMBOLDT, Franz von Baader, and the German romantic poet Novalis. Werner also had close professional relations with the great Swiss natural historian Horace-Bénédict de Saussure.

See also RELIGION; SCIENCE.

Wesley, Charles (1707–1788) *cofounder of Methodism; hymnodist*

Charles was his mother's 18th child and the younger brother of John WESLEY, the more dynamic and famous cofounder of METHODISM. Certain biographers have referred to Charles as the "first Methodist" because it was he who, while a student at Christ Church College, Oxford, persuaded a small group of friends to follow the method of strict religious study prescribed by the university. John soon became a leader of the group, which went by the name of the Holy Club.

John and Charles were ordained deacons in the Church of England and, not long after, were sent on evangelical missions to Georgia in colonial America. They arrived in March 1736. Soon after, Charles fell ill and into a depression, and he returned to ENGLAND later that year. In 1738, he experienced what he felt to be a true conversion; John followed suit. The two became highly successful field preachers, along with their friend George Whitefield. Charles settled first in Bristol in 1739. He married Sarah Gwynne in 1749, and later settled in LONDON, where he eventually died.

Charles was known as the more sensitive of the Wesley brothers. John referred to himself as the "head" and Charles the "heart" of their joint ministry. While Charles often yielded the authority to his brother, he could stand firm when moved by the spirit to do so. For instance, unlike his brother, he ardently resisted separating from the Church of England, desiring only to practice a more purified form of that religion.

Charles is perhaps best known today as a writer of hymns. Legend has it that he composed no less than 9,000 hymns. This is an inflated number, but not by much: Scholars estimate that he wrote as many as 7,300, many of which are still sung regularly in congregations throughout Christendom. There is a striking variety to these hymns. They are written on conventional subjects of worship as well as on everyday matters, and many of them reflect the melancholy characteristics of mid-18th-century English poetry found in the works of Mark Akenside, Thomas GRAY, Edward Young, and others.

After settling in London in 1771, Wesley devoted most of his attention to overseeing the London Methodists. He remained a devout hymnist until the end of his life. The "heart" of Methodism suffered from poor health seemingly from birth, but he lived until he was 80.

Further reading: Frederick C. Gill, *Charles Wesley: The First Methodist* (New York: Abingdon, 1964); John R. Tyson, ed., *Charles Wesley: A Reader* (New York: Oxford University Press, 1989).

Wesley, John (1703–1791) *English lay preacher; the founder of the Protestant sect of Methodism*

John Wesley and his younger brother Charles WESLEY grew up in a strict Christian home. Their father, Samuel Wesley, was a clergyman who had once been part of a sect of DISSENTERS but had returned to the Church of England. Their mother, Susannah Wesley, the daughter of a Dissenting minister, instilled in her two sons the Puritan values of prayer and hard work.

John Wesley studied at Oxford University and spent three years assisting his father at the parishes of Epworth and Wroot. He was ordained in the Church of England in 1728.

In 1729, he returned to Oxford and joined the Holy Club, a group founded by his brother Charles. Club members met for Bible study and devotions. They practiced self-denial and committed themselves to doing good works by visiting prisons, teaching prisoners to read, and helping them to find outside work. They also visited poorhouses, where they ran a school and distributed necessary items such as food and clothing. The Holy Club earned the derisive name of "Methodists" and was strongly criticized when one of its members died either from his austere religious practices or from disease contracted in his charity work.

Despite his dedication to the activities of the Holy Club, John Wesley found no inner peace. Disillusioned with good works, self-examination, and study as avenues to salvation, and desiring a release from the Oxford intellectual world, he embarked on a missionary journey to the Native Americans in the British North American colony of Georgia. Wesley fell in love while in Georgia and found himself unable to maintain self-control or any balanced perspective. His behavior caused him to be driven out of Georgia.

The Georgia trip, however, had lasting effects on Wesley. Not only did it force him to confront the passionate side of his nature, but it also provided him with his first contact with the Pietist Moravian Brethren. After returning to LONDON, Wesley attended Moravian meetings and on May 24, 1738, had a mystical experience that changed his life. He felt a sudden strange warming of his heart, followed by a calm awareness of personal salvation.

Energized and driven by the wonder of this experience, Wesley set out to share it with other people. He began preaching in the open air since no Anglican church welcomed him. He traveled throughout ENGLAND and America. In the course of his activities, he developed the religious practices and teachings that came to be called METHODISM. Both Charles Wesley and Susannah Wesley actively helped to shape the new organization.

Wesley never intended to separate from the Church of England but hoped to have his Methodist practices serve as a supplement to Anglican worship. The ANGLICANS, however, refused to accept his ideas or to ordain preachers of Methodist persuasion. As a result, in 1784 Wesley broke with the Church of England.

By creating Methodism, Wesley placed himself in the ranks of the great enlightened interpreters of religion. His message reflected the branch of the ENLIGHTENMENT that was trying to find what it considered an honorable role for human emotion in knowledge and life. This branch reacted negatively to the disproportionate weight given to REASON as a means for securing PROGRESS and human perfection. Wesley's Methodism, a manifestation of religious ENTHUSIASM, placed the emotional expression of religious experience at the center of worship. In its reliance on feeling and sentiment as the avenues that best bring people to God, Wesley's Methodism resembled PIETISM and Quakerism, both of which played major roles in the Christian world of the Enlightenment.

At the time of Wesley's death in 1791, Methodism claimed 300 itinerant preachers, 72,000 members, and about 500,000 followers in Great Britain. The UNITED STATES OF AMERICA had about two-thirds as many participants and proved a fertile ground for later Methodist expansion. Besides the religious organization of Methodism, Wesley left a legacy of published sermons, the *Rules* (1743) for Methodist societies, and a book called *Primitive Physic*. He also compiled a 50-volume *Christian Library* of translated Christian writings, founded a monthly Methodist periodical in 1778, and wrote a *Journal* that was eventually published. The great hymns composed by John Wesley and his brother Charles continue to be treasured today in Protestant circles.

See also EPISTEMOLOGY; PSYCHOLOGY; QUAKERS; RELIGION; SENSIBILITY; Charles WESLEY.

Whytt, Robert (1714–1766) *Scottish physician and neurologist*

Whytt carried out medical experiments on the use of quicklime and soap to dissolve urinary tract stones. These experiments stimulated the important research of Joseph BLACK. Whytt also was a major participant, with Albrecht von HALLER, in the debates over irritability and sensibility that occupied physiologists during the 1750s. He explored reflex action in the spinal cord and was the first to localize a specific reflex (pupillary dilation) in a nerve.

Robert Whytt, who was the son of a lawyer, became an orphan at the age of six. He inherited the family estate so that his education was secure. He spent four years at St. Andrews University, receiving a degree in liberal arts in 1730, then matriculated at the University of EDINBURGH in the newly organized medical faculty. After four years at Edinburgh, Whytt went to LONDON and PARIS, where he gained clinical hospital experience. He then traveled to Leiden to study with Hermann BOERHAAVE. Whytt obtained medical degrees from the University of Rheims in France and Saint Andrews University in SCOTLAND. The Royal College of Physicians of Edinburgh received him as a member in 1737.

Whytt lectured and carried out research at the Royal Infirmary of Edinburgh and in 1747 received two appointments in the medical school at Edinburgh. He was elected to the ROYAL SOCIETY OF LONDON in 1752 on the recommendation of his friend John PRINGLE. In 1761, he was appointed physician to the king in Scotland and was elected president of the Royal College of Physicians in Edinburgh in 1763.

Whytt made important contributions to the study of nerve functions. His theoretical conceptualization of living organisms occupied an intermediate realm between ANIMISM and emerging VITALISM. Whytt did not accept the animist notion put forth by Georg Ernst STAHL that a conscious soul directs bodily activity, but he spoke of a sentient principle upon which stimuli act. He equated this sentient principle with the soul of man, but tended to locate it in the actual nerve fibers.

Whytt's major publications include *The Vital and Other Involuntary Motions of Animals* (1751) and *Physiological Essays* (1755), both important to the sensibility-irritability debates. His "Essay on the Virtues of Lime-Water and Soap in the Cure of Stone" was published in the *Observations and Essays in Medicine by a Society in Edinburgh* (1743). His "Observations on the Nature, Causes and Cure of those Diseases Which Are Commonly Called Nervous, Hypochondriac or Hysteric" (1764) is an important early English-language contribution to neurology. Two editions of collected works, *Works by Robert Whytt* (1768) and *Collected Works Relating to Theoretical Medicine* (1790), were translated into German before the end of the 18th century.

See also BIOLOGY; SCIENCE.

Wieland, Christoph Martin (1733–1813) *German poet, novelist, essayist, publicist, and translator*

Wieland was considered the greatest poet of his age in GERMANY and was one of its most important publicists, producing and editing two highly significant journals, *Der Teutsche Merkur* (The German messenger, modeled after the *Mercure de France*) and *Attischen Museum* (Attic museum). Like many leading German figures of the ENLIGHTENMENT, Wieland was the son of a Protestant pastor. Originally destined to follow in his father's footsteps, he abandoned THEOLOGY after reading the *Dictionnaire historique et critique* (*HISTORICAL AND CRITICAL DICTIONARY*) by Pierre BAYLE, the PHILOSOPHY of Christian WOLFF, and the writings of VOLTAIRE. Wieland also became a convinced follower of the aesthetic theories being taught by Johann Jakob BODMER and Johann Jakob BREITINGER. He spent several years studying with the latter two men in Zürich, SWITZERLAND.

After struggling as an independent professor for several years, Wieland was appointed professor of philosophy at the University of Erfurt in 1769. Later (1775) he was offered the position of tutor to the children of the duke of Weimar, with a lifetime pension. At the time Weimar was emerging as one of the cultural centers of the Enlightenment in Germany. Wieland's renown helped the duke and duchess of Weimar to induce Johann Wolfgang GOETHE, Friedrich SCHILLER, and Johann Gottfried HERDER to move to the principality. The articles of Wieland's *Der Teutsche Merkur* announced the emergence of Weimar as a major center of the broader German literary scene.

Wieland's poetry and novels combined explorations of Greek philosophy and poetry, modern philosophy, liberal enlightened ideas, and patriotic concern with a strong dose of sentimental eroticism. His favorite authors were Plato, Horace, the earl of SHAFTESBURY, William Shakespeare, Sophocles, and Miguel de Cervantes. The scope of his writings was immense; his collected works, published during his lifetime and edited by him, reached 42 volumes, excluding his major translations, his later novels, and some very important political essays. Among his most important works were the novel *Geschichte des Agathon* (History of Agathon); a German translation (the first) of Shakespeare's dramas; the novel *Der goldene Spiegel* (The golden mirror); the collection of fairy tales entitled *Dschinnistan oder auserlesene Feen- und Geister Märchen* (Dschinnistan or selected fairy and ghost tales; 1786–89), the book from which Emanuel Schikaneder drew the story for the libretto of Wolfgang Amadeus MOZART's opera, *THE MAGIC FLUTE*; the political essay *Das Gehiemniß des Kosmopoliten Ordens* (The secret of cosmopolitan order); the Singspiel *Alceste;* the novel *Aristipp*; and a superlative translation of Horace.

In all of these works, Wieland pleaded for a return to the spirit of ancient Greece, not in terms of imitating the Greeks, but rather with the intent of using their wisdom to create a synthesis of modern and classical spirits. In this sense, Wieland can be considered one of the founders of German "classicism" (a form of NEOCLASSICISM), which reached its pinnacle in the writings of Goethe and Schiller.

Wieland remained loyal to the ideals of Bodmer and Breitinger, who had proposed that the cultivation of national poetic traditions could bring about national regeneration and a general elevation of German culture. Wieland's program of regeneration and perfection, however, avoided a narrow nationalism. Rather, it was embedded in the commitment to a liberal cosmopolitan world where friendship and REASON would limit the expression of narrowly defined SELF-INTEREST.

This world of friendship tempered by reason was theoretically inhabitable by both men and women. Throughout his life, Wieland was a supporter of women's RIGHTS. He helped to advance the careers of women writers and was closely in touch with some of the more prominent German women intellectuals of the period.

Wieland's activities as publisher and editor certainly contributed greatly to the flowering of LITERATURE and letters during the Enlightenment in Germany. *Der Teutsche Merkur* published works by Goethe and Schiller, the novels of Sophie La Roche, and numerous reviews of the most important contemporary books.

Wieland participated in the wave of sentimental-erotic feeling that characterized the period, engaging in several love affairs that helped shape his literary output. He always, however, combined these feelings with a strong realistic and practical sense. When he finally married, he took his parental duties seriously and spent a great deal of time with his wife and their 14 children. In marriage, as in his works, Wieland's commitment to the general advancement of humankind was evident.

Because of his cosmopolitan humanism, his desire to combine clarity with controlled emotion, and his important position as a public spokesperson for the ideals of the Enlightenment, Wieland became a perfect target for the young German romantics, led by the Schlegel brothers. They launched one of the most vicious attacks in the history of German literature against Wieland. In many ways they were successful. Wieland's name faded quickly from the ranks of "canonized" German writers. Nietzsche's comments on Wieland were typical: Wieland, he said, "wrote German better than anyone, but his thoughts don't give us anything more to think about." Today, Wieland's reputation has been refurbished as scholars realize that his vision of enlightened humanism has much still to offer the modern world.

See also AESTHETICS; ROMANTICISM.

Wilberforce, William (1759–1833) *English member of Parliament, philanthropist, and abolitionist*

Born into a wealthy mercantile family in Hull, ENGLAND, Wilberforce enjoyed a privileged life. He acquired influential friends at Cambridge University, including William Pitt the Younger, and was elected to the House of Commons in 1780 when he was only 21 years old. Although slightly built, weak of sight, and somewhat frail—to the point, indeed, that he took opium as a daily tonic under his physician's care—his personal attributes attracted a wide circle of friends.

Wilberforce possessed a much-admired singing voice, a kindly disposition, and a keen interest in philanthropic action. In fact, he was highly respected and admired by contemporaries for his reformist and philanthropic work. His dedication to the abolition of the slave trade and SLAVERY; his interest in mitigating the horrors of the British penal system; his charitable contributions to many causes and people, including Hannah MORE; his support of electoral reform (his own elections routinely cost in the region of £8,000 in bribes to the voting freeholders); and his commitment to the reformation of manners all helped mold his admirable reputation.

In Parliament, Wilberforce doggedly pursued the abolition of the slave trade despite many setbacks. From the time he first met Charles Middleton and his wife, who were the driving force behind the establishment of English abolitionist activism, Wilberforce strove to improve the lot of suffering humanity—not only slaves, but also the laboring poor in his country. He was a major shareholder in the ill-conceived Sierra Leone project organized by Granville Sharp to repatriate former slaves and improve economic conditions in Africa.

Married to Barbara Spooner in 1797 and a devoted father of several children, Wilberforce led an exemplary political and moral life. As a young man, he had been a happy slacker; indeed, he never acquired the discipline characteristic of many great figures. Yet, once he was converted to evangelical Christianity under the influence of clergyman Isaac Milner, Wilberforce took seriously a spiritual mission to do God's work. Several Christian sects, including QUAKERS, Methodists, and evangelical ANGLICANS were instrumental in promoting charitable works and social reform during the ENLIGHTENMENT. Wilberforce's published works include *A Practical View of the Prevailing Religious System of Professed Christians . . .* (1797) and various appeals on the topic of slavery.

Further reading: Roger Anstey, *The Atlantic Slave Trade and British Abolition, 1760–1807* (London: Macmillan, 1975); John R. Oldfield, *Popular Politics and British Anti-Slavery* (Manchester: Manchester University Press, 1995).

Wilhelm Tell   A drama by Friedrich SCHILLER. Schiller's Wilhelm Tell (1804) is the story of one man's struggle to maintain his personal FREEDOM and integrity in the face of political oppression. It takes place in 14th-century SWITZERLAND during the period when the Swiss cantons were still ruled by the Austrian Hapsburgs. The story of

Wilhelm Tell was originally recorded by the Swiss historian Aegidius Tschudi (1505–72), who included it in his *Chronicum Helveticum*. Although written in the 16th century, this chronicle was first published between 1734 and 1736.

Schiller transformed the story into a vehicle for presenting themes of the ENLIGHTENMENT. It illustrates the commitment to LIBERTY, justice, and human PROGRESS toward perfection that preoccupied later generations of enlightened Germans. Underlying the plot is Schiller's conviction that people must devote both their natural hatred for oppression and their individual sense of moral duty to the cause of rising to higher levels of consciousness. He believed that the needs of individuals could be harmonized with those of the general community in a manner that would preserve both.

The action in Schiller's play begins when the archer, Tell, expressing his hatred of tyranny, refuses to salute the hat of the Austrian overlord, Gessler. The hat symbolizes oppression. In revenge for Tell's insubordination, Gessler requires Tell to shoot his bow at an apple placed on the head of his (Tell's) son. Tell is thus faced with the unpalatable choice of surrendering to Gessler's demands for political subordination or of risking his son's life. This predicament moves Tell to a second level of consciousness, the so-called moral stage. Generalizing from his own experience to that of his people, Tell decides to lead a revolution against the system for which Gessler is a spokesman and symbol. With this act, Tell reaches a third stage of consciousness, the aesthetic stage, which is the highest stage accessible to human beings. In an act that defies ordinary human limits, Tell kills Gessler and thus frees Switzerland from its oppressors.

Wilhelm Tell presents the argument that the duty to fight for liberty and justice demands human action even when the consequences may be painful for individuals. Together with NATHAN THE WISE by Gotthold Ephraim LESSING, Schiller's play represents a pinnacle in the expression of the ideals of the AUFKLÄRUNG (German Enlightenment).

See also AESTHETICS; INTUITION AND IMAGINATION.

Wilkes, John (1725–1797) *Radical English journalist and politician*

Wilkes was the son of a wealthy distiller; his father married him to a rich, older widow. Wilkes possessed a sharp wit, a rebellious temperament, and a reputation for libertinism. As a member of the House of Commons, he supported the Whig Party and William Pitt until the accession of King George III resulted in the Whigs' loss of power. In 1762, Wilkes founded the liberal journal *The North Briton*, which served as an organ of intense political criticism. After he published a harsh attack on a 1763 speech by George III, Wilkes was arrested along with 48 other men on a general warrant, an order authorizing the arrest of authors, publishers, and printers of so-called obscene or seditious libels. The general warrant did not specifically name the people to be arrested and thus could be used to bring in anyone suspected of these activities. Wilkes went to prison in the Tower of London but was soon released. Police ransacked his house and confiscated his papers. From Wilkes's confiscated papers, his enemies extracted an obscene poem, "An Essay on Women." These incidents coupled with Wilkes's participation in an illegal duel left him in a politically vulnerable situation. To escape prosecution, he fled to FRANCE. Four weeks later, the English Parliament expelled Wilkes from its chambers at King George's request.

Wilkes lived in PARIS for four years, where he was welcomed as a defender of liberty against tyranny. The Parlement of Paris (court of justice) especially praised him, as it was, at that time, struggling to defend its corporate rights against encroachments by King LOUIS XV and his ministers. Handkerchiefs embroidered with the letter "W" became highly fashionable in Parisian circles.

Wilkes returned to LONDON in 1768, and, before he could be arrested, he was elected to the House of Commons by the county of Middlesex. In 1769, however, having again been arrested on charges of seditious libel, he was expelled from Parliament. He was then reelected three times, but King George and his party persuade Parliament to refuse to seat him. In the meantime, the English courts had ruled on the legality of the general arrest warrant that had started Wilkes's troubles. They found the practice of issuing general warrants illegal, thereby establishing important protection for individual FREEDOM of speech and security against sweeping arrests.

Wilkes was becoming a popular hero, supported by crowds and political placards carrying slogans such as "Wilkes and Liberty." King George reacted to the situation by trying to suppress popular enthusiasm and defuse Wilkes's power. Through a combination of political machinations in Parliament and outright distortions of justice, the King managed to get Wilkes imprisoned for 22 months.

In response, Wilkes's supporters founded a society of Supporters for the Defence of a Bill of Rights in 1769. They began demanding parliamentary reforms, such as more frequent elections, fewer property qualifications for suffrage, and an end to the practice of setting up election districts controllable by a handful of local aristocrats. They gathered 60,000 signatures on a petition requesting the reinstatement of Wilkes. Wilkes also gained significant financial backing. In 1771, again free, Wilkes won election as lord mayor of London. He and his supporters won the right to publish the Parliament debates in London journals; as a result, Parliament business became a public affair in a significant new way.

Shortly after his election as mayor of London, Wilkes again won a seat in the House of Commons, and this time the Commons seated him. He introduced a Parliament reform bill in 1776, but he failed to secure its passage. The bill not only called for reform in order to make the Parliament more representative of British subjects, but it also explicitly blamed recalcitrant Parliament members for the AMERICAN REVOLUTION. Wilkes had many admirers in the American colonies and corresponded with discontented American leaders.

Wilkes's personal history and the causes he supported dramatically illustrate that individual human rights lacked protection under the old English system. But it also shows how the activities of the press could assist in whipping up public sentiment for a political figure and thus help to create a political crisis. Wilkes's calls for reform were received enthusiastically by radical reformers such as Joseph PRIESTLEY and Richard PRICE, even though both men disliked his personal morality. His political successes thus demonstrate how the POLITICAL THEORY of the ENLIGHTENMENT combined with social and economic restructuring toward the end of the 18th century to force European political systems to confront demands for substantial reform.

See also ENGLAND; INDIVIDUALISM; PUBLISHING; TOOKE.

William III and Mary II *William III (1650–1702), prince of Orange, Dutch Protestant nobleman, son of William II, prince of Orange and stadtholder; Mary II (1662–94), also Protestant, wife of William III and daughter of staunchly Catholic King James II of England*
William III served as stadtholder of the UNITED PROVINCES OF THE NETHERLANDS from 1672 until 1702. William and Mary ruled ENGLAND and Ireland as joint sovereigns after the GLORIOUS REVOLUTION of 1688.

After the death of William II in 1650, the Dutch declined to appoint another individual as stadtholder. The office had been traditionally occupied by the princes of Orange and had served as a symbol of aristocratic, quasi-royal power in the Dutch government. From 1650 until 1672, the Dutch Republic functioned as a true republic without a chief leader. But in 1672, LOUIS XIV of FRANCE attacked the Netherlands, and the Dutch government, responding to popular outcry, decided to reinstate the office of stadtholder.

William III, who had inherited the title Prince of Orange from William II, was installed as stadtholder and also given the office of captain general of the Dutch armies. In these capacities, he succeeded in bringing AUSTRIA, SPAIN, DENMARK, and BRANDENBURG into an alliance against Louis XIV. William III led the Dutch forces against France in the Dutch War (1672–78) that ended with the Treaty of Nijmegen in 1678. During his tenure as stadtholder (1672–1702), William attempted with varying degrees of success to centralize the Dutch government, to suppress certain liberties in the provinces, and generally, to secure the stadtholder's power according to the model of ABSOLUTISM.

In 1688, the fortunes of William III took a significant turn and threw him into a role of great importance for the future of political practices and theory in England. William and Mary were invited by a coalition of Tories and Whigs to assume the throne of England during the rebellion known to history as the Glorious Revolution of 1688. In that rebellion, King James II fled from England, an act that was interpreted as abdication by his enemies. Early in 1689, William and Mary occupied the vacant English throne as joint sovereigns after making significant concessions to the English Parliament. The outlines of the agreement were spelled out in the Declaration of Rights (1689), the Act of Toleration (1689), and the later Act of Settlement (1701). William secured his position militarily by defeating James II at the battle of the Boyne in 1690.

By signing the agreement with Parliament, William and Mary accepted substantial limitations on royal power. They held their power by contract with the Parliament and by implication could be overthrown if they failed to honor the terms of their agreement. William and Mary accepted the limits on English royal authority as a matter of pragmatism. They did not oppose the exclusion of Catholics from the English throne (codified in the 1701 Act of Settlement), but they did insist on religious TOLERATION for non-Anglican Protestants.

The reign of William and Mary assumed great symbolic power as an example of government by contract. It revived discussion of earlier contractual theories of kingship and also stimulated the development of new theories. In this manner the legacy of the Glorious Revolution and of William and Mary helped to shape aspects of the POLITICAL THEORY of the ENLIGHTENMENT.

See also JACOBITES; LOCKE; TEMPLE; *TWO TREATISES OF GOVERNMENT*.

Winckelmann, Johann Joachim (1717–1768) *German archaeologist, art historian, and theorist of the aesthetics of neoclassicism*

Winckelmann was born in Stendal, Brandenburg, the son of a poor cobbler. He studied THEOLOGY at the University of HALLE (1738–40) and MEDICINE at Jena (1741–42) before becoming librarian for Count Heinrich von Bünau at his estate near Dresden.

Winckelmann developed an intense interest in antiquity and championed the idea of imitating the aesthetic principles embodied in the art and architecture of ancient Greece and ROME. In 1754, he converted to ROMAN CATHOLICISM and in 1755 moved to Rome, where he spent the remainder of his life. He studied the antiquities of Florence, Pompeii, Naples, and other places in the Italian peninsula. In the 1760s, Winckelmann became head of antiquities and librarian at the Vatican.

Winckelmann's first treatise, *Gedanken über die Nachahmung der griechischen Werke in der Malerei und Bildhauerkunst* (Reflections on the imitation of Greek painting and sculpture; 1755), appeared before he had visited either Greece or Rome. His monumental *Geschichte der Kunst des Altertums* (History of the art of antiquity) appeared in 1764 in German and then was translated into French (1766), Italian (1779, 1783), and English (1850). Winckelmann died in Trieste in 1768, of stab wounds acquired during a robbery.

Winckelmann spelled out the ideals of NEOCLASSICISM clearly in his *History of the Art of Antiquity*. In particular, he advocated simplicity and calm grandeur, two ideals starkly opposed to the intensely passionate grandeur evoked in BAROQUE STYLE works. Winckelmann derived his neoclassical ideals from his own observations and from his reading of ancient Greek literature. He worked with a group of like-minded artists in Rome that included Anton Raphael MENGS. The latter received high praise from Winckelmann as the best artist produced by Europe in two centuries. Winckelmann's work was read and admired in GERMANY by writers such as Gotthold Ephraim LESSING and Johann Wolfgang von GOETHE, both of whom helped to popularize his aesthetic ideals through their own publications.

See also AESTHETICS; HAMILTON, SIR WILLIAM; KAUFFMANN; POMPEII.

Wolf, Friedrich August (1759–1824) *German scholar who was one of the founders of modern classical philology*

Wolf was educated at the University of GÖTTINGEN, where he studied with Christian Gottlob Heyne. Wolf was appointed professor of philology and pedagogy at the University of HALLE in 1783 and began working on the problem of the origin of the ancient Greek classics ascribed to Homer. He published the results of his research as *Prolegomena ad Homerum sive de Operum Homericorum Prisca et Genuina Forma Variisque Mutationibus et Probabili Ratione Emendandi* (Prolegomenon to Homer; 1795).

The *Prolegomenon* argued that the Homeric epics were not composed by a single person, but rather that they represented a rich mythic tradition that had been part of an ancient oral culture. The biblical critic Johann Gottfried Eichhorn (1752–1827), who had interpreted the Old Testament as sacred poetry combining a number of oral traditions, had established a precedent for treating ancient texts in this fashion. Wolf tried to show that the epics associated with Homer had to be older than written culture, that they contained several separate, competing story lines, and that they embodied different poetic traditions. In Wolf's interpretation, Homer emerged as a gifted collector rather than creator, someone who combined various oral traditions into a whole. From the very beginning Wolf's thesis created a stir, and the controversy concerning the identity of Homer and the composition of Homeric texts still rages today.

Wolf was appointed to the newly founded University of BERLIN in 1810 and helped it to emerge as one of the leading centers in the 19th century for the study of historical classical philology. Although Wolf's interpretation of Homer seemed radical to his contemporaries, his method was founded upon theories evolved during the ENLIGHTENMENT by people such as Heyne, Johann Salomo SEMLER, and Johann August Ernesti (1707–81). Like many enlightened thinkers, Wolf turned to popular literature, oral traditions, and to a reevaluation of poetry and mythic traditions. Wolf's achievement attests to the important role played by the Enlightenment in shaping modern conceptions of HISTORY and antiquity.

Wolff, Christian (1679–1754) *German philosopher and mathematician, one of the founders of the early Enlightenment in German territories*

A native of Breslau in Silesia, Wolff studied both PHILOSOPHY and mathematics at the universities in Jena and Leipzig. After earning a master's degree in 1702, he assumed responsibilities in 1706 as a professor of mathematics and NATURAL PHILOSOPHY at the University of HALLE.

Wolff acquired the Halle position on the strength of a recommendation from Gottfried Wilhelm LEIBNIZ. The two men had been corresponding for several years. Wolff eventually developed a modified Leibnizian philosophy that served as the medium through which Germans learned about the work of their illustrious 17th-century forebear.

As supplements for his lectures, Wolff wrote three textbook treatises in the German language (Latin was the norm). As he struggled to translate Latin concepts into German, Wolff developed a philosophical vocabulary for the German language. Through the medium of the German language, philosophical questions reached a broader audience than had been possible when all discussion occurred in Latin.

The Leibnizian philosophy that Wolff favored contained certain tendencies toward determinism in matters regarding human behavior. For this reason, Wolff earned the disapproval of authorities in Halle. He was dismissed from his university post in 1723, after which he assumed a post at the Calvinist University of Marburg. He eventually returned to Halle, where he remained for the rest of his life.

Wolff's philosophical system consisted of an eclectic mix of concepts drawn from Scholastic philosophy, from Leibniz, and from modern mathematics and SCIENCE. Wolff struggled with the Leibnizian distinction between truths of reason and truths of fact. He attempted to give truths of fact a greater philosophical certainty by showing how their underlying philosophical principle (derived from Leibniz) was actually connected to the principle that creates truths of reason. Wolff's universe, as a result,

Christian Wolff, engraving by J. M. Bernigeroth, 1755. Wolff interpreted the philosophy of Gottfried Wilhelm Leibniz and transmitted it to the earliest generations of enlightened German intellectuals. *(Courtesy Archiv für Kunst und Geschichte, Berlin)*

was more tightly determined by logical laws than Leibniz's universe had been. Wolff also raised Leibniz's principle of sufficient reason, which was later vulgarized by Voltaire in CANDIDE as Pangloss's insistence that this is "the best of all possible worlds," to central importance. In emphasizing the principle of sufficient reason, Wolff concomitantly minimized the importance of Leibniz's complex and controversial concept of the monad (the basic building block of the world, consisting of active perception rather than material substance). Wolff also opened new ways of exploring AESTHETICS by introducing the concept of mixed feelings, that is, of perceptions in which reason and emotion were joined. The forms in which Wolffian philosophy posed questions dominated German philosophical discussions until Immanuel KANT finally replaced them with a new language and conceptual scheme.

Wolff's major German works include *Vernünftige Gedanken von den Kräften des menschlichen Verstandes* (Rational thoughts on the powers of human understanding; 1713); *Auszug aus den Anfangsgründen aller mathematischen Wissenchaften* (Summary of the foundations of all mathematical sciences; 1717); *Vernünftige Gedanken von Gott, der Welt, und der Seele der menschen . . .* (Rational thoughts on God, the world, and the human soul . . . ; 1729); *Vernünftige Gedanken von der Wirkungen der*

Natur (Rational thoughts on the effects of nature; 1723); *Vernünftige Gedanken von den Absichten der natürlichen Dinge* (Rational thoughts on the purpose of natural things; 1724); and *Vernünftige Gedanken von dem Gebrauch der Theile in Menschen, Tieren und Pflanzen* (Rational thoughts on the use of parts in men, animals, and plants; 1725). Latin works were *Philosophia rationalis sive logica* (Rational philosophy, or logic; 1728); *Philosophia prima, sive ontologia* (First philosophy, or ontology; 1729); and *Cosmologia generalis* (General cosmology; 1731).

See also MATHEMATICS AND MECHANICS; RATIONALISM.

Wollstonecraft, Mary (1759–1797) *British novelist, journalist, and polemical writer*
Wollstonecraft's father was the son of a successful weaver, who left him enough money to live as a gentleman farmer. He was unsuccessful and lost most of his family's money. Mary educated herself at home and expressed bitterness over the resources spent on the EDUCATION of her eldest brother.

At age 19, Wollstonecraft escaped from her family by becoming a companion to a wealthy widow in Bath. After returning to her family to nurse her mother through a final illness, she founded a school with her sister and her friend Fanny Blood in 1784. After the school failed in 1786, Wollstonecraft became a governess for one year in the family of Lord Kingsborough in Ireland.

While in Ireland, Wollstonecraft completed her first novel, *Mary, A Fiction* (1787). This largely autobiographical account of her own life was followed by two educational books for children, *Original Stories from Real Life* (1791) and *The Female Reader* (1790).

Having moved to LONDON, Wollstonecraft worked as a journalist and assistant on the *Analytical Review*. Her political and social views gradually became more radical during this period. In 1792, she published *A Vindication of the Rights of Man*, in which she attacked the REFLECTIONS ON THE REVOLUTION IN FRANCE by Edmund BURKE. Later that year, she published her most famous work, *A VINDICATION OF THE RIGHTS OF WOMAN*.

Wollstonecraft's enthusiasm for the FRENCH REVOLUTION led her to FRANCE in 1792, where she arrived in time to see King LOUIS XVI pass by on his way to his trial. While in France, she wrote a history of the revolution, *An Historical and Moral View of the Origin and Progress of the French Revolution* (1794), which criticized the violent direction the revolution had taken while still praising its underlying ideals of EQUALITY and FREEDOM. In FRANCE, Wollstonecraft met an American businessman, Gilbert Imlay, with whom she had a child.

After her return to LONDON, Wollstonecraft entered into a relationship with the radical liberal philosopher William GODWIN, whom she later married. She died 11

Portrait of Mary Wollstonecraft Godwin, by John Opie. An outspoken defender of women's rights, Mary Wollstonecraft and her husband, William Godwin, championed the most radical social causes of the Enlightenment. *(Courtesy New York Public Library)*

days after giving birth to her second daughter, Mary Wollstonecraft Godwin, who later married the British romantic poet Percy Bysshe Shelley.

Godwin published a memoir of his wife in which he included her love letters to Gilbert Imlay. The scandal caused by this memoir, with its open acknowledgment of Wollstonecraft's sexual behavior, tarnished her reputation during the reactionary years immediately following the French Revolution.

The ideas of Mary Wollstonecraft extended the basic principles of the ENLIGHTENMENT—EQUALITY, FREEDOM, justice—to their logical conclusions by applying them to all human beings whatever their gender. Her unconventional behavior underlined the socially revolutionary implications of this logical extension. Mary Wollstonecraft, like other radical thinkers at the end of the Enlightenment, presented a vision of society that many people wished to avoid. Their reactions against her positions provided one of the strands that fed into the web of 19th-century ROMANTICISM and middle-class culture.

See also BLUESTOCKING; PROSTITUTION; RADICAL ENLIGHTENMENT; WOMEN AND THE ENLIGHTENMENT.

women and the Enlightenment Perspectives on the nature of women and their roles in 18th-century culture. Several developments occurred at this time in Europe to create the means for public debate about the nature of women and their intellectual potential. These developments included a marked increase in literacy for both men and women, the burgeoning of the print industry, and the rise of the bourgeoisie (the middle class), all of which tended to facilitate ordinary women's participation in public discussions.

For centuries, most male philosophers had agreed with biblical injunctions against women's empowerment and relegated women to the traditional domestic roles of wife, mother, daughter, and sister. Of course, throughout Europe many women controlled family estates or worked, whether by necessity or choice, in agriculture, manufacture, or trade, and some enjoyed a high degree of economic independence. Their social and political influence was, however, severely limited unless they were high-ranking women, possessing intelligence and wit, who were members of princely courts. These women were often deeply implicated in political currents and patronage. On the whole, however, lip service was paid to the notion of EQUALITY.

Even in the age of the ENLIGHTENMENT, few men advocated EDUCATION or professional and political status for women. Women were the object of male attention, evaluated and categorized as inferior in several important ways. Although women possessed beauty, beauty was considered irreconcilable with REASON—the ability most valued by enlightenment thinkers. Considered alternate versions of men, incomplete men as it were, women were depreciated as creatures of nature rather than rational beings. Jean-Jacques ROUSSEAU, the baron de MONTESQUIEU, and Immanuel KANT conceived of women as morally weak, lacking in inventive imagination or genius, and submissive. David HUME was astute enough to recognize that what human beings called NATURE was a collection of customary roles and behaviors that had become gender specific over a long period of time. The marquis de CONDORCET went further in championing women (and Africans). He insisted in various tracts that women were equal to men and as capable as men of benefiting from education and political involvement. He endorsed women's education and their right to full citizenship.

Contemporary religious thought tended to work against women's intellectual or political empowerment. The traditional role for women repudiating marriage or failing to make an appropriate match in Roman Catholic countries was life as a nun, which could be intellectually stimulating and publicly useful. In the anticlerical environment of the Enlightenment, that avenue of piety or intellectualism was begrudged women. Paradoxically, PROTESTANTISM in ENGLAND and the UNITED PROVINCES OF THE NETHERLANDS promoted equality and mutual affection in marriage, to the extent that female domesticity was elevated to piety, a virtue far above intellectual achievement. At the same time, there were innumerable instances of 17th- and 18th-century women's involvement in preaching and good works.

Despite entrenched male resistance, the 18th-century public sphere opened up new avenues to women in western Europe. Women's influence was increased through the establishment of the salon; the professionalization of women writers; the availability of educational opportunities for girls; and the beginning of bourgeois women's public activism—in charitable works, in political action, and in philosophical and scientific debates.

Salons were hosted by wealthy, literary women who influenced matters of taste and pleasure but primarily served to facilitate discussion of philosophical, literary, and scientific issues of the day. Often writers themselves, the hostesses nurtured, encouraged, and culled homage from men who rose to cultural prominence. In the FRANCE of the ANCIEN RÉGIME, women of letters such as Mademoiselle de Scudéry and Madame de Sévigné aired their views about female education. In ENGLAND, Elizabeth MONTAGU hosted the BLUESTOCKING circle, a sober group of intellectuals that included Hannah MORE, Horace WALPOLE, Fanny BURNEY, and Richard PRICE. Salon life also flourished in GERMANY. For example, in BERLIN, the German-Jewish Rahel Levin (1771–1833), who was married to the writer Karl August Varnhagen von Ense, presided over important, early-19th-century literary salons. Her writings were collected by her husband in a volume entitled *Rahel: Ein Buch des Andenkens für ihre Freunde* (Rahel: A book of memories for her friends; 1834).

Women writers—dramatists, novelists, poets, advocates, scientists, and philosophers—came into the foreground in the 18th century in large part because the PUBLISHING industry had become central to the public sphere but also because the traditional equation of public women and immorality had subsided. Women were sometimes able to earn their living entirely by writing: Two early but notable English examples are Aphra BEHN and Mary PIX.

Another Englishwoman of note, Mary WOLLSTONECRAFT, was an important voice in promoting female education. She believed that education would overcome the inadequacies attributed to contemporary women. Her first published work was *On the Education of Daughters* (1786). Later, her VINDICATION OF THE RIGHTS OF WOMAN (1792) made a vital contribution to the understanding of women's oppression. Her critique focused on the deficiencies in women's education but also discounted the traditional dichotomy between women as passionate and men as reasonable, arguing that passion and rationality in combination created the most persuasive effect.

Progressive 18th-century attitudes toward women's intellectual competence and moral worth tended to validate women's political involvement. This involvement was usually indirect, but it became a potent force for social change. Hannah More was a prolific activist, writing extensively on numerous topics and campaigning on behalf of miners, the uneducated poor, prostitutes, and slaves. She was, like many Britons, vehemently opposed to the FRENCH REVOLUTION. Wollstonecraft and Helen Maria Williams visited France following the revolution; in their works they imagined that women might transform the state. The French writer Louise de Kéralio (1752–1822) published histories about female power, and, in line with much postrevolutionary rhetoric, represented women as masculinized, capable of leading armies, engaging in politics, and participating fully in civic life. The Swiss aristocrat Madame de STAËL was central to Parisian political and literary culture. Indeed, the first republican constitution was debated in her drawing room.

Of less practical value to women, but no less important in shaping women's lives, were the culture of SENSIBILITY that promoted new ideals of female VIRTUE and the sentimentalization of the family that cast wives as the moral and religious guardians of errant men. The culture of sensibility that arose in the second half of the 18th century mitigated the force of the gender-biased focus on reason characteristic of the early enlightenment, but it proved almost as repressive as earlier notions of female virtue that advocated chastity, silence, and obedience. The widespread sentimental approval of women vitally concerned with their domestic roles continues unabated today. Women's voices were heard in public debates about RELIGION, SCIENCE, LITERATURE, and social justice throughout the 18th century, but political pressure for women's civil RIGHTS failed to emerge until the 19th century.

See also SOCIAL INSTITUTIONS OF THE ENLIGHTENMENT.

Further reading: Mary Wollstonecraft, *A Vindication of the Rights of Woman* (Mineola, N.Y.: Dover, 1996); Natalie Zemon Davis and Arlette Farge, eds. *A History of Women in the West; Volume 3, Renaissance and Enlightenment Paradoxes* (Cambridge, Mass.: Belknap Press of Harvard University Press, 1993).

Woolston, Thomas (1670–1731) *English freethinker and deist; a disciple of Anthony Collins*
Woolston was one of the more notorious supporters of DEISM in the early years of the ENLIGHTENMENT. A graduate of Cambridge University and fellow at Sidney Sussex College of Cambridge, Woolston used his critical skills to attack belief in miracles and to expose alleged corruptions in the clergy. These attacks against Christianity offended his colleagues at Sidney Sussex College, who took away his fellowship at the school.

Woolston spelled out his ANTICLERICALISM in *Moderator between an Infidel and an Apostate* (1721) and *Free Gifts to the Clergy* (1723–24). His chief polemic against miracles was contained in *The Old Apology for the Truth of the Christian Religion against the Jews and Gentiles Revived* (1705) and in the *Discourses on Miracles* (1727–30). He claimed that the chief Christian miracle, the Resurrection of Jesus, was a hoax and that miracles were inspired by the devil. Treatises on RELIGION were still subject to censorship in England. Consequently, the publication of *Discourses on Miracles* caused Woolston to be convicted of blasphemy by the English courts in 1729, fined, and imprisoned. He died in prison in 1731.

See also COLLINS.

Wren, Sir Christopher (1632–1723) *English architect and scientist*
Wren, the son of a clergyman, was born in Wiltshire, ENGLAND, and educated in LONDON at the Westminster School. He attended Oxford University, where he studied ASTRONOMY. He served as professor of astronomy at Gresham College until 1661, when he assumed a similar title at Oxford. Wren studied comets, eclipses, and the ringed planet, Saturn. He was one of the founders of the ROYAL SOCIETY OF LONDON and served as its president between 1681 and 1683. Wren was twice elected to the House of Commons in the English Parliament and was a member of the governing council of the Hudson's Bay Company. He reportedly was also a member of a lodge of FREEMASONS.

Wren began his architectural career by designing the chapel of Pembroke College at Cambridge University (1663–65). He followed this with a theater at Oxford (1664–69). Both buildings were classical in style. Wren visited PARIS in 1665 to study astronomy and architecture. The French "classical" (BAROQUE STYLE) buildings commissioned by LOUIS XIV produced a lasting impression.

London, hard hit by the Black Plague in 1665, was devastated by fire in 1666. Wren became a member of the commission charged with redesigning and building the city. In 1669, he was appointed to the post of surveyor of works for King Charles II.

Wren designed St. Paul's Cathedral as well as more than 50 city parish churches. The plans for St. Paul's went through many drafts before a final design, adhering to the conventions of English PALLADIAN STYLE, was approved in 1675. St. Paul's Cathedral was not completed until 1711. Wren designed many other buildings for the English Crown, for UNIVERSITIES, and for private individuals. Most prominent of these creations include the library at Trinity College, Cambridge; Chelsea Hospital; additions to Hampton Court; and Kensington Palace. The dome of St. Paul's and the steeples on his many church buildings earned Wren international recognition.

Wright, Joseph (1734–1797) *English painter, one of the first artists to turn to the Industrial Revolution for subject matter*
Wright, known as Joseph Wright of Derby, was born in Derby and chose to remain there rather than to move to LONDON to establish a painting career. He lived in one of

the regions of ENGLAND that was being transformed by the early stages of the INDUSTRIAL REVOLUTION. He produced images of the industrial landscape that contrasted sharply with the natural world and with other facets of the human-made world. He also depicted scientific instruments in works such as *The Air Pump* (1768) and *The Orrery* (1763–65). His style presents a blending of realist depiction with romantic imagination.

Wright spent two years in ITALY from 1773 to 1775, much of it in ROME. He also visited Naples and witnessed an eruption of Mt. Vesuvius that greatly fascinated him. Besides his industrial and technological pictures, Wright produced imaginative LANDSCAPES and paintings on mythological themes. Certain great industrial and scientific figures of the era served as his subjects. Among them were Richard ARKWRIGHT and Erasmus DARWIN. Josiah WEDGWOOD, creator of the neoclassic style of Wedgwood jasperware, commissioned many pictures from Wright on themes from classical fable and myth.

Y

Young, Arthur (1741–1820) *British writer and agricultural scientist*

Young was born into a prosperous family of rural Suffolk. His parents sent him to a local grammar school and then apprenticed him to a merchant. Young would have preferred being sent to university.

At 17, Young began to write, giving his manuscripts to publishers in exchange for printed books. For a while, he could not decide between a career in literature or agriculture. At 22, he leased a farm on his mother's estate in Bradfield, which he inherited at her death in 1788.

On this and other farms, Young conducted experiments in which he developed new scientific techniques to increase agricultural production, thereby helping to bring about the 18th-century changes often called the Agricultural Revolution. The improvements in agricultural production made by Young and his followers enabled Britain to produce more food with fewer laborers.

As a result, many English gentlemen farmers began enclosing the land on their estates that had traditionally been available for communal use. They backed up these activities by forcing the Enclosure Acts, designed to legalize their activities, through Parliament. Peasant farmers were forced to leave the land and began moving into cities, providing a cheap labor force for the INDUSTRIAL REVOLUTION. The immediate social costs of enclosure were severe, producing disruptions in traditional living patterns, family relationships, and occupations.

By his 30th birthday, Young had published seven major books on farming, including *The Farmer's Letters* (1767). He founded the journal *The Annals of Agriculture* in 1784 and continued as its editor until his death, contributing more than 400 articles to its various issues. Young became a fellow of the ROYAL SOCIETY OF LONDON and served the British government as the secretary of the first government agency for agricultural development. He also traveled widely and communicated with leading agriculturalists in FRANCE, SWITZERLAND, GERMANY, Russia, and the American colonies.

Young traveled throughout ENGLAND, Ireland, and France, recording his observations of political and social conditions. His *Six Months' Tour through the North of England* (1770), *Farmer's Tour through the East of England* (1771), *Tour in Ireland* (1780), and *Travels in France* (1792) reported his findings and increased the awareness of urban readers about rural conditions. Young also published a book on political economy called *Political Arithmetic* (1774).

Young's activities provide an excellent example of the manner in which the ENLIGHTENMENT fostered the application of SCIENCE to practical problems of existence. But his commitment to agricultural reform illustrates the paradoxes contained within the reforming goals of the Enlightenment. On the one hand, Young's technical innovations increased crop yields and helped to create a more secure food supply for Britain, thereby contributing to overall PROGRESS. On the other hand, his innovations created social disruption and suffering by stimulating the enclosure process, by displacing farmers of the lower classes, and by allowing English aristocrats to reserve the profits from the Agricultural Revolution for themselves.

Z

Zimmermann, Johann Georg (1728–1795) *Swiss philosopher, writer, and physician*

Johann Zimmermann was born in Brugg in the Swiss canton of Bern. His father was German Swiss and his mother French Swiss, and Zimmermann spoke both languages fluently. While not wealthy, Zimmermann's father was a well-respected member of the town council. Zimmermann studied MEDICINE at the University of GÖTTINGEN under the famed Albrecht von HALLER, who took an interest in the talented young man and directed his dissertation, *De Irritabilitate* (On irritability; 1751). The dissertation explored the theory of the irritation of tissues as a cause of illness.

After earning his degree, Zimmermann traveled throughout FRANCE, ENGLAND, ITALY, and the Netherlands. He returned to Bern and set up his medical practice. In 1752, his mentor Haller also retired to Bern and sent Zimmermann to bring his family from Göttingen. When he returned to Bern, Zimmermann also brought a wife of his own. He wrote a biography of Haller in 1755. He gained much fame in Europe with his next book, *Über die Einsamkeit* (On solitude; 1756), which explored themes of loneliness and physical suffering. The work was written after the recent death of his young daughter. It contained reflections on the isolating and meditative effects of illness and the deaths of loved ones, as well as the grief of seeing the suffering of his patients. Another work, *Vom Nationalstolz* (On national pride), followed in 1758, exploring the ways in which pride and patriotism can be used to both help and hurt a nation's welfare. Zimmermann discussed his experience with medical methodology in *Von der Erfahrung in der Arzneiwissenschaft* (On medical practice) in 1764. The books won him acclaim throughout Europe and were translated from German into English and French.

His writings brought Zimmermann invitations to visit several courts in Germany and abroad. In 1768, he was appointed the official court physician of King George III of England. He was unhappy there because George's German court did not accept him, his health continued to suffer, and his wife died. A new work on loneliness followed in 1773. After another bout with depression, Zimmermann went to a doctor in BERLIN.

Zimmermann declined an invitation from CATHERINE II (THE GREAT) of Russia to be her court physician. However, he did accept an appointment to be physician to FREDERICK II (THE GREAT) in his last years. Zimmermann continued to write and produced books about his years in Frederick's court in 1788 and 1790.

Ironically, for a talented physician, Zimmermann suffered from physical and emotional problems throughout his life. He suffered from severe depression, which is sometimes reflected in his writings, and which contributed to his struggles with hypochondria throughout his life.

As a physician and a writer, Zimmermann was a success. His practice in Bern lasted more than 16 years, and he was in demand at several royal courts in Europe. As well as having many friends, Zimmermann was also highly respected in intellectual circles. He died at Hanover on October 7, 1795.

See also UNITED PROVINCES OF THE NETHERLANDS.

Zinzendorf, Nicolaus Ludwig, count von (1700–1760) *German religious reformer*

Nicolaus von Zinzendorf played an important role in 18th-century PROTESTANTISM. His critical views of LUTHERANISM and PIETISM led to his support of the MORAVIAN BRETHREN and to an original set of religious ideas.

Zinzendorf was born in Dresden, which was then the capital of the German kingdom of Saxony. His parents were both Pietists, and the prominent Pietist leader and theologian Philipp Jakob SPENER was his godfather. Zinzendorf studied at HALLE and attended the University of Wittenberg, where he pursued a law degree in hopes of having a career as a diplomat. After taking the GRAND TOUR, Zinzendorf stayed with his aunt's family, where he fell in love with a cousin. Her mother refused to allow the marriage, and Zinzendorf returned to Dresden, where he worked in the court of August the Strong and married a sister of the man his cousin had wed.

In 1722, Zinzendorf agreed to allow a group of persecuted Protestants from Moravia to settle on his lands. Five years later, he retired from court and devoted his energies to leading the Moravians. In 1731, Zinzendorf attended the coronation of Christian VI of DENMARK, where he met a slave from the West Indies. Based on the slave's description of conditions on the sugar plantations there, Zinzendorf organized the first Protestant mission, sending two men to the West Indies. Missions to Greenland and North America followed, and, by the time of Zinzendorf's death, missions had been established in eastern Europe, North Carolina, Suriname, the East Indies, Egypt, and South Africa. Zinzendorf traveled as well, visiting Saint Thomas in the West Indies as well as Pennsylvania, where he founded the town of Bethlehem and his daughter laid the groundwork for Moravian College. He died at Herrenhut, the settlement of the Moravian Brethren on his lands, in 1760.

During his lifetime, Zinzendorf came into conflict with both orthodox Lutherans and Pietists. The Saxon monarch banished him from the kingdom between 1736 and 1749 because of his religious stance. Zinzendorf criticized Lutheran orthodoxy for its hollow intellectualism and broke with Spener and the Pietists over Spener's refusal to separate from the Lutheran Church. Zinzendorf instead encouraged his followers to cultivate an intense, personal connection to Christ. Under his leadership, the Moravian Brethren also took a progressive stance with respect to women, who could hold leadership positions in the church, including those requiring ordination. Zinzendorf wrote several hymns, and 10 volumes of his sermons were published.

Like Jean-Jacques ROUSSEAU, Zinzendorf believed that people were inherently good—which meant a rejection of Martin Luther and Jean Calvin's notion of original sin—and that through spiritual contemplation, they could lead pure lives. His support and leadership of the Moravian Bretheren, with its emphasis on the individual's relationship with Jesus Christ, was an expression of the ENLIGHTENMENT critique of religious orthodoxy.

Further reading: Nicolaus Ludwig von Zinzendorf, *Nine Public Lectures on Important Subjects in Religion, Preached in Fetter Lane Chapel in London in the Year 1746* (Iowa City: University of Iowa Press, 1973).

SELECTED BIBLIOGRAPHY

Abrams, M. H., ed. *The Norton Anthology of English Literature,* 6th ed., Vols. 1 and 2. New York: Norton, 1993.

Adorno, Theodor W., and Horkheimer, Max. *Dialectic of Enlightenment.* New York: Herder and Herder, 1972.

Agethen, Manfred. *Geheimbund und Utopie: Illuminaten, Freimauer und deutsche Spätaufklärung* [Secret Society and Utopia: The Illuminati, Freemasons, and the German Late-Enlightenment]. Munich: R. Oldenbourg Verlag, 1984.

Alembert, Jean Le Rond d'. *Preliminary Discourse to the Encyclopedia of Diderot,* trans. and ed., Richard N. Schwab. Indianapolis: Bobbs-Merrill, 1963.

Anchor, Robert. *The Enlightenment Tradition.* Berkeley: University of California Press, 1967.

Andrews, Alexander. *The Eighteenth Century.* London: Chapman & Hall, 1856.

Apel, Willi. *The New Harvard Dictionary of Music.* Revised edition, Randel, Don Michael, ed. Cambridge: Harvard University Press, 1986; first published 1944.

Appleby, Joyce Oldham. *Capitalism and A New Social Order: The Republican Vision of the 1790s.* New York: New York University Press, 1984.

———. *Liberalism and Republicanism in the Historical Imagination.* Cambridge, Mass.: Harvard University Press, 1992.

Baker, Keith Michael. *Condorcet: From Natural Philosophy to Social Mathematics.* Chicago: University of Chicago Press, 1975.

Baker, Keith, and Reill, Peter Hanns. *What's Left of the Enlightenment? A Postmodern Question.* Stanford, Calif.: Stanford University Press, 2001.

Balteau, J., et al., eds. *Dictionnaire de biographie française,* 18 vols. Paris: Librairie Letouzey et Ané, 1933–1989.

Barker-Benfield, G. J. *The Culture of Sensibility. Sex and Society in Eighteenth-Century Britain.* Chicago: University of Chicago Press, 1992.

Bayle, Pierre. *Historical and Critical Dictionary, Selections.* Indianapolis: Bobbs-Merrill, 1965.

Beck, Lewis White. *Early German Philosophy: Kant and His Predecessors.* Cambridge, Mass.: Belknap Press of Harvard University Press, 1969.

Beck, Lewis White, ed. *Immanuel Kant, On History.* Indianapolis: Bobbs-Merrill, 1963.

Becker, Carl L. *The Heavenly City of the Eighteenth-Century Philosophers.* New Haven, Conn.: Yale University Press, 1959.

Behrens, C. B. A. *Society, Government and the Enlightenment: The Experiences of Eighteenth-Century France and Prussia.* London: Thames & Hudson, 1985.

Bergin, Thomas G., and Speake, Jennifer. *The Encyclopedia of the Renaissance.* New York: Facts On File, 1987.

Berlin, Isaiah. *Vico and Herder. Two Studies in the History of Ideas.* New York: Viking Press, 1976.

Berry, Christopher J. *Social Theory of the Scottish Enlightenment.* Edinburgh: Edinburgh University Press, 1997.

Biagioli, Mario. *Galileo, Courtier: The Practice of Science in the Culture of Absolutism.* Chicago: University of Chicago Press, 1993.

Boia, Lucian, ed. *Great Historians from Antiquity to 1800, An International Dictionary.* Westport, Conn.: Greenwood Press, 1989.

Brewer, John. *The Pleasures of the Imagination: English Culture in the Eighteenth Century.* Chicago: Chicago University Press, 2000.

Bromley, J. S., ed. *The Rise of Great Britain and Russia, 1688–1725,* vol. 6 of New Cambridge Modern History. Cambridge: Cambridge University Press, 1971.

Brown, S. C., ed. *Philosophers of the Enlightenment.* Brighton, England: Harvester Press, 1979.

Browning, J. D., ed. *Education in the Eighteenth Century.* New York: Garland Publishing, 1979.

Bruford, W. H. *Germany in the Eighteenth Century. The Social Background of the Literary Revival.* Cambridge: Cambridge University Press, 1971.

Brunn, Geoffrey. *The Enlightened Despots,* 2nd ed. New York: Holt, Rinehart and Winston, 1967.

Brunschwig, Henri. *Enlightenment and Romanticism in Eighteenth-Century Prussia,* trans. Frank Jellinek. Chicago: University of Chicago Press, 1974.

Burke, John G. *The Uses of Science in the Age of Newton.* Los Angeles: William Andrews Clark Library, UCLA, 1983.

Burney, Charles. *A General History of Music from the Earliest Age to the Present Period,* 2 vols. New York: Dover Publications, 1957.

Cassirer, Ernst. *Kant's Life and Thought,* trans. James Haden, intro. Stephen Körner. New Haven, Conn.: Yale University Press, 1981.

———. *The Philosophy of the Enlightenment,* trans. Fritz C. A. Koelin and James P. Pettegrove. Princeton, N.J.: Princeton University Press, 1979.

Chamberlain, M. E. *Decolonization: the Fall of the European Empires.* New York: Basil Blackwell, 1985.

Chartier, Roger. *Cultural History, Between Practices and Representations.* Ithaca, N.Y.: Cornell University Press, 1988.

———. *The Cultural Origins of the French Revolution,* tr. Lydia G. Cochrane. Durham, N.C.: Duke University Press, 1991.

Chaunu, Pierre. *La Civilisation de L'Europe des Lumières.* Paris: Arthaud, 1971.

Chisick, Harvey. *The Limits of Reform in the Enlightenment: Attitudes toward the Education of the Lower Classes in Eighteenth-Century France.* Princeton, N.J.: Princeton University Press, 1981.

Clark, Kenneth. *The Gothic Revival, An Essay in the History of Taste.* Harmondsworth, England: Penguin Books, 1962.

Clark, William, Golinski, Jan and Schaffer, Simon, eds. *The Sciences in Enlightened Europe.* Chicago: University of Chicago Press, 1999.

Cobban, Alfred. *A History of Modern France, Vol. I: 1715–1799. Old Régime and Revolution.* Baltimore: Penguin Books, 1963; 3rd ed.

Colley, Linda. *Captives: Britain, Empire, and the World, 1600–1850.* New York: Pantheon Books, 2002.

Copleston, Frederick, S. J. *A History of Philosophy,* vols. 4, 5 and 6. Garden City, N.Y.: Image Books, 1964.

Cragg, Gerald R. *The Church and the Age of Reason, 1648–1789.* New York: Penguin Books, 1970.

Crocker, Lester G. *An Age of Crisis. Man and World in Eighteenth-Century French Thought.* Baltimore: Johns Hopkins Press, 1959.

Daniel-Rops, Henri. *The Church in the Eighteenth Century.* Garden City, N.Y.: Doubleday (Image Books), 1964.

Darnton, Robert. *The Business of Enlightenment. A Publishing History of the Encyclopédie, 1775–1800.* Cambridge, Mass.: Harvard University Press, 1979.

———. *George Washington's False Teeth: An Unconventional Guide to the Eighteenth Century.* New York: Norton, 2003.

———. *Mesmerism and the End of the Enlightenment in France.* Cambridge, Mass.: Harvard University Press, 1968.

Davies, Norman. *Europe: A History.* New York: Oxford University Press, 1996.

Davis, Natalie Zemon, and Arlette, Farge, eds. *Renaissance and Enlightenment Paradoxes,* vol. 3 of *A History of Women in the West.* Cambridge, Mass.: Harvard University Press, 1993.

Diderot, Denis, and Jean Le Rond, d'Alembert, eds. *L'Encyclopédie ou Dictionnnaire raisoné des sciences des arts et des métiers.* 18 vols. New York: Elsevier Science, 1979.

Drabble, Margaret, ed. *The Oxford Companion to English Literature.* Oxford: Oxford University Press, 1985; 5th ed.

Edwards, Paul, editor in chief. *The Encyclopedia of Philosophy,* 8 vols. New York: Macmillan and the Free Press, 1967.

Encyclopaedia Britannica, 32 vols. Chicago: Encyclopaedia Britannica, 2003.

Encyclopedia of World Art, 17 vols. New York: McGraw-Hill, 1959–1987.

Fäy, Bernard. *Revolution and Freemasonry, 1680–1800.* Boston: Little, Brown, 1935.

Ferguson, Robert. *The American Enlightenment, 1750–1820.* Cambridge, Mass.: Harvard University Press, 1997.

Foucault, Michel. *The Order of Things, An Archaeology of the Human Sciences* [les Mots et les Choses]. New York: Vintage Books (Random House), 1970.

Furet, François. *Interpreting the French Revolution,* tr. Elborg Forster. Cambridge: Cambridge University Press, 1981.

Gay, Peter. *The Enlightenment: An Interpretation. The Rise of Modern Paganism.* New York: Vintage Books, 1966.

———. *The Party of Humanity, Essays in the French Enlightenment.* New York: Alfred A. Knopf, 1964.

Gay, Peter, and the Editors of Time-Life Books. *Age of Enlightenment.* New York: Time Incorporated, 1966.

Gillispie, Charles Coulston. *The Edge of Objectivity. An Essay in the History of Scientific Ideas.* Princeton, N.J.: Princeton University Press, 1960.

Goodwin, A., ed. *The American and French Revolutions, 1763–93,* vol. 8 of New Cambridge Modern History. Cambridge: Cambridge University Press, 1968.

Gordon, Daniel. *Postmodernism and the Enlightenment: Theory and Practice in the Study of Eighteenth-Century French History.* London: Routledge, 2000.

Green, Jack P., and Pole, J. R., eds. *The Blackwell Encyclopedia of the American Revolution.* Cambridge, Mass.: Blackwell Publishers, 1991.

Gregory, Jeremy, and Stevenson, John, eds. *Longman Companion to Britain in the 18th Century, 1688–1820.* New York: Longman, 2000.

Griswold, Charles L., Jr. *Adam Smith and the Virtues of Enlightenment.* Cambridge: Cambridge University Press, 1999.

Grout, Donald Jay. *A History of Western Music,* rev. ed. New York: W. W. Norton, 1973.

Hampson, Norman. *The Enlightenment,* vol. 4 of the Pelican History of Human Thought. Baltimore: Penguin Books, 1968.

Hankins, Thomas L. *Science and the Enlightenment.* Cambridge: Cambridge University Press, 1985.

Haycox, Stephen, James Barnett, and Caedmon, Liburd. eds. *Enlightenment and Exploration in the North Pacific, 1741–1805.* Seattle: University of Washington Press, 1997.

Hazard, Paul. *European Thought in the Eighteenth Century from Montesquieu to Lessing,* tr. J. Lewis May. Cleveland: Meridian/World, 1963.

Herr, Richard. *The Eighteenth-Century Revolution in Spain.* Princeton, N.J.: Princeton University Press, 1958.

Holborn, Hajo. *A History of Modern Germany (1648–1840).* New York: Alfred A. Knopf, 1967.

Honour, Hugh. *Romanticism*. New York: Harper and Row, 1979.

Houston, R. A. *Literacy in Early Modern Europe. Culture and Education, 1500–1800*. London: Longman, 1988.

Hunt, Margaret, et al., eds. *Women and the Enlightenment*. New York: Haworth Press, 1984.

Hunter, Michael, and Wooton, David, eds. *Atheism from the Reformation to the Enlightenment*. Oxford: Clarendon Press, 1992.

Hutchinson Dictionary of Scientific Biography. New York: Helicon Publishing, 1999.

Israel, Jonathan. *Radical Enlightenment: Philosophy and the Making of Modernity 1650–1750*. Oxford: Oxford University Press, 2002.

Jacob, Margaret C. *Living the Enlightenment, Freemasonry and Politics in Eighteenth-Century Europe*. New York: Oxford University Press, 1991.

———. *The Radical Enlightenment: Pantheists, Freemasons, and Republicans*. London: George Allen & Unwin, 1981.

Janson, Horst Woldemar. *History of Art: A Survey of the Major Visual Arts from the Dawn of History to the Present Day*. New York: Abrams/Englewood Cliffs, N.J.: Prentice-Hall, 1964.

Keohane, Nannerl O. *Philosophy and State in France, The Renaissance to the Enlightenment*. Princeton, N.J.: Princeton University Press, 1980.

King, Lester. *The Philosophy of Medicine: The Early Eighteenth Century*. Cambridge, Mass.: Harvard University Press, 1978.

Klein, Lawrence E., and Anthony La Vopa, eds. *Enthusiasm and Enlightenment Europe, 1650–1850*. San Marino, Calif.: Huntington Library, 1998.

Krieger, Leonard. *An Essay on the Theory of Enlightened Despotism*. Chicago: University of Chicago Press, 1975.

———. *The German Idea of Freedom, A History of a Political Tradition from the Reformation to 1871*. Chicago: University of Chicago Press, 1957.

———. *Kings and Philosophers, 1689–1789*. New York: W. W. Norton, 1970.

Kuhn, Thomas S. *The Copernican Revolution: Planetary Astronomy in the Development of Western Thought*. Cambridge, Mass.: Harvard University Press, 1957.

Landes, David. *The Unbound Prometheus: Technological Change and Industrial Development in Western Europe from 1750 to the Present*. Cambridge: Cambridge University Press, 1969.

Lavoisier, Antoine. *Elements of Chemistry in a New Systematic Order Containing All the Modern Discoveries*, tr. Robert Kerr. New York: Dover Publications, 1965.

Louis, William Roger, ed. *The Oxford History of the British Empire: The 18th Century*. Oxford: Oxford University Press, 1998.

McManners, J. *Death and the Enlightenment: Changing Attitudes to Death Among Christians and Unbelievers in Eighteenth-century France*. Oxford: Clarendon Press, 1981.

Manuel, Frank E. *The Age of Reason*. Ithaca, N.Y.: Cornell University Press, 1951.

———. *The Eighteenth Century Confronts the Gods*. New York: Atherton, 1967.

May, Henry F. *The Enlightenment in America*. New York: Oxford University Press, 1976.

Merriam-Webster, Editors of. *Webster's New Biographical Dictionary*. Springfield, Mass.: Merriam-Webster, 1983.

Milic, Louis T., ed. *The Modernity of the Eighteenth Century*. Cleveland: Press of Case Western Reserve University, 1971.

Musson, A. E. *Science, Technology and Economic Growth in the Eighteenth Century*. London: Methuen, 1972.

Neill, Anna. *British Discovery Literature and the Rise of Global Commerce*. London: Palgrave, 2003.

New Schaff-Herzog Encyclopedia of Religious Knowledge, 13 vols. Grand Rapids, Mich.: Baker House, 1951–1954.

Newton, Sir Isaac. *Sir Isaac Newton's Mathematical Principles of Natural Philosophy and His System of the World*, tr. Andrew Motte, ed. Florian Cajori. Berkeley: University of California Press, 1962.

Nussbaum, Felicity, ed. *The Global Eighteenth Century*. Baltimore: Johns Hopkins University Press, 2003.

Pacey, Arnold. *The Maze of Ingenuity: Ideas and Idealism in the Development of Technology*. Cambridge, Mass.: M.I.T. Press, 1985.

Palmer, Robert R. *Catholics and Unbelievers in Eighteenth-Century France*. New York: Cooper Square, 1961.

———. *The Improvement of Humanity: Education and the French Revolution*. Princeton, N.J.: Princeton University Press, 1985.

———. *The Age of Democratic Revolution: A Political History of Europe and America, 1760–1800*, 2 vols. Princeton, N.J.: Princeton University Press, 1959 and 1964.

Palmer, Robert R., and Joel Colton. *A History of the Modern World*. New York: Alfred A. Knopf, 1984.

Plumb, J. H. *England in the Eighteenth Century (1714–1815)*. Baltimore: Penguin Books, 1950.

Pocock, J. G. A. *The Machiavellian Moment: Florentine Political Thought and the Atlantic Republican Tradition*. Princeton, N.J.: Princeton University Press, 1975.

———. *Virtue, Commerce, and History: Essays on Political Thought and History, Chiefly in the Eighteenth Century*. Cambridge: Cambridge University Press, 1985.

Popkin, Richard H. *The History of Skepticism*. Berkeley: University of California Press, 1979.

Porter, Roy. *The Creation of the Modern World: The Untold Story of the British Enlightenment*. New York: Norton, 2001.

———. *Enlightenment*, 2nd ed. New York: Palgrave, 2001.

Porter, Roy, ed. *The Cambridge History of Science, Volume 4: The Eighteenth Century*. Cambridge: Cambridge University Press, 2002.

Porter, Roy, ed. *The Cambridge Illustrated History of Medicine*. Cambridge: Cambridge University Press, 2000.

Porter, Roy, and George Rousseau, eds. *The Ferment of Knowledge: Studies in the Historiography of Eighteenth-Century Science.* Cambridge: Cambridge University Press, 1980.

Porter, Roy, and Mikulas Teich. *The Enlightenment in National Context.* Cambridge: Cambridge University Press, 1981.

Raeff, Marc. *The Well-Ordered Police State: Social and Institutional Change Through Law in the Germanies and Russia, 1600–1800.* New Haven, Conn.: Yale University Press, 1984.

Reill, Peter Hanns. *The German Enlightenment and the Rise of Historicism.* Berkeley: University of California Press, 1975.

Roche, Daniel. *France in the Enlightenment.* Cambridge, Mass.: Harvard University Press, 2000.

———. *Vitalizing Nature in the Enlightenment.* Berkeley: University of California Press, 2005.

Roger, Jacques. *Les sciences de la vie dans la pensée française du XVIIIe siècle.* Paris: Armand Colin, 1971.

Rossi, P. *The Dark Abyss of Time: The History of the Earth and the History of Nations from Hooke to Vico.* Chicago: University of Chicago Press, 1984.

Sambrook, James. *The Eighteenth Century: The Intellectual and Cultural Context of English Literature, 1700–1789.* London: Longman Group, 1993.

Schama, Simon. *Citizen: A Chronicle of the French Revolution.* New York: Knopf, 1989.

Schofield, Robert E. *Mechanism and Materialism: British Natural Philosophy in the Age of Reason.* Princeton, N.J.: Princeton University Press, 1970.

Smith, Roger. *The Norton History of the Human Sciences.* New York: W. W. Norton, 1997.

Stephen, Sir Leslie. *History of English Thought in the Eighteenth Century,* 2 vols. New York: Harcourt, Brace and World, Inc. (Harbinger Books), 1962.

Stephen, Sir Leslie, and Sir Sidney Lee. *The Dictionary of National Biography,* 22 vols. Oxford: Oxford University Press, 1937–[ongoing].

Stewart, Larry. *The Rise of Public Science: Rhetoric, Technology, and Natural Philosophy in Newtonian Britain, 1660–1750.* Cambridge: Cambridge University Press, 1993.

Terrall, Mary. *The Man Who Flattened the Earth: Maupertius and the Sciences of the Enlightenment.* Chicago: The University of Chicago Press, 2002.

Turberville, A. S. *English Men and Manners in the Eighteenth Century.* New York: Oxford University Press, 1957.

Vartanian, Aram. *Diderot and Descartes: A Study of Scientific Naturalism in the Enlightenment.* Princeton: Princeton, N. J. University Press, 1953.

Venturi, Franco. *The End of the Old Regime in Europe, 1768–76: The First Crisis,* tr. R. Burr Litchfield. Princeton: Princeton University Press, 1989.

———. *Italy and the Enlightenment: Studies in a Cosmopolitan Century,* tr. Susan Corsi. New York: New York University Press, 1972.

———. *Utopia and Reform in the Enlightenment.* Cambridge: Cambridge University Press, 1971.

Wade, Ira O. *The Clandestine Organization and Diffusion of Philosophic Ideas in France, 1700–1750.* Princeton, N.J.: Princeton University Press, 1967.

———. *The Structure and Form of the French Enlightenment,* 2 vols. Princeton, N.J.: Princeton University Press, 1977.

Walker, Ralph, C. S. *Kant: The Arguments of the Philosophers.* Boston: Routledge and Kegan Paul, 1978.

Wangermann, Ernst. *The Austrian Achievement, 1700–1800.* London: Thames & Hudson, 1973.

Westfall, Richard S. *The Construction of Modern Science: Mechanisms and Mechanics.* Cambridge: Cambridge University Press, 1977.

Wiener, Philip P., editor in chief. *Dictionary of the History of Ideas: Studies of Selected Pivotal Ideas,* 5 vols. New York: Scribner's, 1968, 1973, and 1974.

INDEX

Page numbers in **boldface** indicate extensive treatment of a topic. Numbers followed by c refer to topics in the chronology; *italic* numbers indicate illustrations.

A

Abel, Karl Friedrich **1**, 33, 352, 410
absolutism **1–3**, *2*. *See also* absolutism, enlightened; *specific headings, e.g.:* Louis XIV of France
 aesthetics 7
 ancien régime 15
 Austrian Netherlands 29
 baroque style 38
 Aphra Behn 48
 Jacques-Bénigne Bossuet 67
 bureaucracy 76
 Calvinism 86
 Étienne-François Choiseul 110
 classicism 115
 Robert-François Damiens 138
 Declaration of the Rights of Man 143
 Denmark 151
 Jean-Baptiste Du Bos 165
 dynastic states 166, 167
 England 178
 enlightened despotism 155
 enlightened monarchs 395
 equality 186
 François Fénelon 195
 France 203
 French Revolution 215
 Glorious Revolution 232
 Gustav III of Sweden 250
 history 272
 Thomas Hobbes 274
 Friedrich Heinrich Jacobi 303
 John Locke 349
 Gabriel Bonnot de Mably 361
 René-Nicolas-Charles-Augustin de Maupeou 377
 mercantilism 387
 Louis Sébastien Mercier 388
 Montesquieu 398
 Paris 446
 parlements 446
 political theory 461
 religion 502
 Royal Palace at Versailles *4*
 Scotland 544
 separation of powers 550
 Siècle de Louis XIV 554
 Benedict de Spinoza 569
 Sweden 578
 toleration 594
 Two Treatises of Government 603
 Voltaire 619
 Wealth of Nations 627
 William III and Mary II 633
absolutism, enlightened **3–4**, 268, 300, 314, 366, 378
Adam, Robert and James *4*, 109, 170, 421

Adams, John **4–6**, *5*, 14, 141, 259, 308, 361, 456, 506, 606, 608, 625
Addison, Joseph xiv c, **6**
 Johann Jakob Bodmer 62
 Johann Jakob Breitinger 72
 Benjamin Franklin 205
 Grub Street 248
 Alexander Hamilton 258
 literature 348
 magic 364
 Pierre de Marivaux 373
 Antoine-François Prévost 470
 sensibility 548
 sentimental fiction 549
 social institutions 561
 The Spectator 566
 Richard Steele 574
 Jonathan Swift 581
 Robert Walpole 624
 Mary Wortley 397
Adelung, Johan Christoph 6
aesthetics x, **6–9**
 Gottfried Arnold 24
 Aufklärung 27
 baroque style 38
 Battle of the Buffoons 42
 Alexander Gottlieb Baumgarten **43–44**
 Johann Jakob Bodmer 62
 Johann Jakob Breitinger 72
 Edmund Burke 78
 Denis Diderot 158
 Jean-Baptiste Du Bos 165
 epistemology 185
 Étienne-Maurice Falconet 192
 Henry Fielding 196
 Johann Georg Adam Forster 199
 Jean-Honoré Fragonard 201
 August Hermann Francke 204
 Henry Fuseli 217
 genius 226
 Johann Wolfgang von Goethe 236
 Gothic revival 239
 Johann Georg Hamann 257
 Johann Gottfried Herder 268
 intuition and imagination 299
 Immanuel Kant 317
 Laokoon 333
 Gotthold Ephraim Lessing 342
 literature 348
 Louis XIV of France 355
 Moses Mendelssohn 384, 385
 Anton Raphael Mengs 386, 387
 Louis Sébastien Mercier 388
 Abbé Morelly 404
 piano 454
 psychology 480
 Quakers 489
 Quarrel between the Ancients and the Moderns 489
 Joshua Reynolds 508
 rococo 518
 Saint Petersburg 531
 Johann Friedrich Schiller 534
 Scotland 544
 sentimental fiction 549
 earl of Shaftesbury 553

 Sturm und Drang 576
 sublime 576
 Switzerland 582
 Christian Wolff 635
affinity chemistry 9, 50, 54, 58, 159, 237, 379, 380
Age of Reason, The (Thomas Paine) **9–10**, 38, 148, 442, 494
alchemy 10. *See also* magic
 Johann Friedrich Böttger 68
 Alessandro Cagliostro 83
 Chemical Revolution 103
 Faust 193
 hermeticism 269
 iatrochemistry 291
 mechanical philosophy 380
 natural philosophy 414
 nature 416
 Isaac Newton 424, 425
 Rosicrucians 523
 Louis-Claude de Saint-Martin 530
 science 538
 secret societies 544
Alembert, Jean Le Rond d' xv c, **10–12**, *11*
 Marc-Pierre de Voyer Argenson 21
 Paul-Joseph Barthez 41
 Cesare Beccaria 46
 Berlin Academy 52
 Louis-Antoine de Bougainville 69
 capital punishment 94
 Catherine II 98
 Clement XIII 118
 Marie Condorcet 124
 Marie de Vichy-Chamrond Deffand 144
 Denis Diderot 158
 Encyclopédie 175–177
 encyclopedists 177
 Louise-Florence-Pétronville de la Live Épinay 184
 Leonhard Euler 191
 François Fénelon 195
 French Academy of Sciences 212
 Élie-Cathérine Fréron 216
 Geneva 226
 Marie-Thérèse Rodet Geoffrin 230
 Friedrich Melchior Grimm 247
 Anne-Cathérine Helvétius 266
 inoculation 299
 Kingdom of the Two Sicilies 324
 Joseph-Louis Lagrange 327
 Joseph de Lalande 328
 Pierre-Simon Laplace 334
 Maurice-Quentin de La Tour 335
 Gottfried Wilhelm Leibniz 340
 Julie-Jeanne-Eléonore de Lespinasse 341, 342
 Pierre de Marivaux 373
 Jean-François Marmontel 373
 Montesquieu 399
 philosopher-king 451
 Physiocrats 454
 marquise de Pompadour 465

 Jean-Philippe Rameau 495
 revolution 506
 science 538
 Brook Taylor 585
 Anne-Robert-Jacques Turgot 602
 Voltaire 619
Algarotti, Francesco **12–13**, 102, 424, 472, 543, 592, 611
American Philosophical Society **13**, 61, 205, 288, 408, 451, 514, 528, 541
American Revolution x, xvi c, *13*, **13–14**
 John Adams 5
 Joel Barlow 37
 Pierre-Augustin Caron de Beaumarchais 45
 Louis-Antoine de Bougainville 69
 Edmund Burke 78
 class and rank 115
 colonialism 122
 Common Sense 122
 Michel de Crèvecoeur 134
 Declaration of Independence 141
 Declaration of the Rights of Man 143
 deism 148
 democracy 149
 Maria Edgeworth 169
 Benjamin Franklin 205
 freedom 209
 Freemasons 211
 free trade 211
 French Revolution 216
 George III *13*
 Alexander Hamilton 258–259
 Sir William Hamilton 259
 John Jay 306
 Immanuel Kant 318
 literacy 347
 James Madison 362
 Thomas Paine 442, 443
 Philadelphia 451
 picturesque 456
 political theory 463
 Richard Price 470
 Reflections on the Revolution in France 499
 revolution 506
 David Rittenhouse 514
 Benjamin Rush 528
 Claude-Henri de Saint-Simon 532
 August Ludwig von Schlözer 537
 Sturm und Drang 576
 John Horne Tooke 596
 Two Treatises of Government 603
 United Provinces of Netherlands 605
 United States Constitution 605
 United States of America 606
 Francis Adrian Van der Kemp 608
 voyages of discovery 622
 John Wilkes 633
Amsterdam **14–15**

ancien régime **15–16**. *See also specific headings, e.g.:* Louis XIV of France
 John Adams 5
 Marc-Pierre de Voyer Argenson 21
 aristocratic resurgence 22
 Benedict XIV 49
 bureaucracy 76
 Jean Calas 83
 Charles-Alexandre de Calonne 84
 class and rank 114
 Declaration of the Rights of Man 143
 Antoine-Louis-Claude Destutt de Tracy 156
 Pierre-Samuel Dupont de Nemours 166
 France 202
 French Academy of Sciences 212
 French Revolution 213
 Marie-Thérèse Rodet Geoffrin 230
 Gobelins tapestry 234
 Jacques-Claude-Marie-Vincent de Gournay 241
 Mississippi Bubble 394
 Paris 445, 446
 parlements 446
 Physiocrats 453
 marquise de Pompadour 465
 property 476
 Reflections on the Revolution in France 499
 revolution 507
 Emmanuel-Joseph Sieyès 554
 women and the Enlightenment 637
Anglicans **16–18**, *17*
 association movement 24
 Calvinism 86
 Dissenters 163
 England 177
 freedom 208
 justice and the law 316
 John Locke 350
 Joseph Priestley 471
 Protestantism 478
 John Tillotson 592
 William Wilberforce 632
animalculism 18, 184, 391, 419, 469
animism **18–19**, x
 Paul-Joseph Barthez 41
 Marie-François-Xavier Bichat 55
 Hermann Boerhaave 63
 Théophile de Bordeu 66
 Albrecht von Haller 255
 iatromechanics 291
 medicine 382
 preformation theory 469
 Georg Ernst Stahl 571
 vitalism 615
 Robert Whytt 630
anthropology **19–20**
anticlericalism 20
 Aufklärung 27
 Marie Condorcet 124

deism 148
pornography 468
religion 504
Roman Catholicism 520
toleration 594
Thomas Woolston 638
Argens, Jean-Baptiste de Boyer, marquis d' 20–21, 52, 239, 267, 328, 384, 604
Argenson, Marc-Pierre de Voyer, comte de Weil d' 21, 21, 138, 175
Argenson, René-Lous de Voyer de Paulmy, marquis d' 21, 21–22, 64, 149, 155, 329, 618
aristocratic resurgence 3, 22–23, 64, 70, 114, 195, 203
Arkwright, Sir Richard 23, 138, 422, 626, 639
Arnold, Gottfried 23–24, 457
art vii. See also specific artists, e.g.: Cruikshank, George; specific styles, e.g.: rococo
baroque style 39–40
William Blake 60
Catherine II 98
Anne-Claude-Philippe de Levis Caylus 99
ceramic arts 99–100
Illuministi 294
neoclassicism 420
paganism 442
marquise de Pompadour 465
Rake's Progress 495
rococo 517–519
sensibility 547, 548
social institutions 561
Stowe 575
Asam, Cosmas Damian 24, 24, 407, 518
Asam, Egid Quirin 24, 24, 407, 518
association movement 24–25
astronomy 25, 25–26. See also specific astronomers, e.g.: Copernicus, Nicolaus
Daniel Bernoulli 53
Jakob I and Johann I Bernoulli 54
biology 56
Alexis-Claude Clairaut 112
Copernican Revolution 127–129
Joseph-Nicolas Delisle 149
Leonhard Euler 190
Galileo Galilei 219–221
Pierre Gassend 224
geocentric 228–229
Willem Jacob's Gravesande 243
John Hadley 252
heliocentric 266
hermeticism 270
Alexander von Humboldt 282
Immanuel Kant 319
Pierre-Simon Laplace 335
John Locke 351
longitude 353
natural philosophy 414
On the Revolutions of the Heavenly Spheres 433–435
orrery 440
David Rittenhouse 514
science 538
Scientific Revolution 542
telescope 587
transit of Venus 597
Sir Christopher Wren 638
atheism 26–27
The Age of Reason 10
Nicolas-Antoine Boulanger 71
China 108
Ralph Cudworth 135
deism 147
Denis Diderot 158
Freemasons 211

Johann Georg Hamann 257
Claude-Adrien Helvétius 267
Johann Gottfried Herder 269
Julien Offray de La Mettrie 330
Johann Kaspar Lavater 335
Gotthold Ephraim Lessing 342–343
Letters on Toleration 343
Mikhail Vasilivich Lomonosov 351
materialism 375
mechanical philosophy 380
medicine 382
Marin Mersenne 388
Montesquieu 399
moral philosophy 401
John Turberville Needham 419
La Nouvelle Héloïse 429
religion 503
Scotland 544
Benedict de Spinoza 568
A Treatise of Human Nature 598
Sarah Trimmer 599
Aufklärung (German Enlightenment) xi, 27–28. See also Enlightenment
Johan Christoph Adelung 6
Gottfried Arnold 24
Berlin Academy 52
Bildung 56
Johann Jakob Bodmer 62
deism 148
Denis Diderot 160
Faust 193
August Hermann Francke 204
Johann Christoph Gatterer 224
Germany 230
Johann Georg Hamann 257
David Hume 286
Bavarian Illuminati 292
Illuministi 293
Friedrich Heinrich Jacobi 302
Karl Wilhelm Ferdinand 321
Friedrich Gottlieb Klopstock 324
Laokoon 334
Gottfried Wilhelm Leibniz 340
Gotthold Ephraim Lessing 342
Moses Mendelssohn 385
Justus Möser 405
Christoph Friedrich Nicolai 426
paganism 442
Pietism 457
psychology 480
Rosicrucians 523
August Ludwig von Schlözer 537
Johann Salomo Semler 547
sublime 577
Christian Thomasius 589
University of Göttingen 240
University of Halle 255
Abraham Gottlob Werner 629
Aulnoy, Marie-Catherine d' 28
Austria. See also Vienna
Cosmas Damian Asam 24
Marie-Antoinette 371
Catherine II 97
Étienne-François Choiseul 110
Diplomatic Revolution of 1756 160
dynastic states 166
enlightened despotism 155
France 203
Frederick II 207
Freemasons 210
Germany 230
Haitian Revolution 254
Hapsburg Empire 261
Haskalah 263

Johann Lukas von Hildebrandt 270
Holy Roman Empire 278
Wilhelm von Humboldt 283
Hungary 287
Bavarian Illuminati 293
Illuministi 293
inoculation 299
Jews and Judaism 312
Joseph II of Austria 313–314
Josephinism 314–315
Wenzel Anton von Kaunitz 322
Johannes Kepler 323
Louis XVI of France 357
Maria Theresa of Austria 370–371
Jean-François Marmontel 374
Milan 392
Montesquieu 398
partitions of Poland 447
philosopher-king 452
Poland 460
political theory 463
Stanislaw Augustus Poniatowski 466
Jakob Prandtauer 469
Protestantism 478
religion 502
rococo 517
Roman Catholicism 519
Seven Years' War 552
Social Contract 559
Spain 565
Gottfried Bernhard Swieten 580
Switzerland 582
Giovanni Battista Tiepolo 591
toleration 595
University of Göttingen 240
War of the Austrian Succession 624
William III and Mary II 633
Austrian Netherlands 29
Belgium 48
Brussels 74
Charles Burney 79
Anne-Claude-Philippe de Levis Caylus 99
China 108
Robert-François Damiens 138
democracy 149
Eugène of Savoy 190
France 201
Hapsburg Empire 261
Joseph II of Austria 313
Roman Catholicism 519
Louis-Antoine-Léon de Saint-Just 530
Spain 565
automata 29–30, 610

B

Babeuf, François-Noel 31–32, 149, 186
Bach, Carl Philipp Emanuel 32–33, 33, 34, 174, 207, 230, 368, 410, 455, 580, 583, 586
Bach, Johann Christian 1, 32–34, 33, 241, 352, 392, 406, 410, 583
Bach, Johann Sebastian xiv c, xv c, 33–35, 34
Carl Philipp Emanuel Bach 32
Johann Christian Bach 33
Wilhelm Friedemann Bach 35
baroque style 40
Brandenburg Concertos 72
Frederick II 207
Germany 230
Mass in B Minor 374
Wolfgang Amadeus Mozart 406
music 408
Saint Matthew Passion 531

Gottfried Bernhard Swieten 580
Georg Philipp Telemann 586
Bach, Wilhelm Friedemann 32–34, 35–36, 174, 457
Bacon, Francis (baron of Verulam) 36
aesthetics 7
Jean Le Rond d'Alembert 11
education 170
empiricism 175
Encyclopédie 175
England 178
epistemology 184
David Hume 285
Gottfried Wilhelm Leibniz 339
John Locke 350
Isaac Newton 423
progress 475
reason 498
Royal Society of London 527
The Spirit of Laws 569
Bahrdt, Carl Friedrich 36–37
banking system 336–337
Banks, Joseph 37, 109, 126, 316, 446, 508, 527, 621
Barlow, Joel 9, 14, 37–38
barometer 38, 586
baroque style 38–41
Karl Friedrich Abel 1
Austria 29
Carl Philipp Emanuel Bach 32
Johann Sebastian Bach 35
Wilhelm Friedemann Bach 36
Budapest 74
Ranieri de'Calzabigi 87
classicism 115
François Couperin 133
empfindsamer Stil 174
Miklós József Esterházy 189
Eugène of Savoy 190
Johann Bernhard Fischer von Erlach 197, 198
John Gay 224
Franz Joseph Haydn 265
Johann Lukas von Hildebrandt 270
William Hogarth 275
Italy 301
Pietro Longhi 353
Louis XIV of France 355
Madrid 363
Mannheim school 368
Mass in B Minor 374
Munich 407
music 408
neoclassicism 420
Balthasar Neumann 422
Palladian style 444
piano 455
Giovanni Battista Piranesi 457
Portugal 468
Jakob Prandtauer 469
Jean-Philippe Rameau 495
Bartolomeo Rastrelli 496
rococo 517
Roman Catholicism 520
Rome 522
Saint Matthew Passion 531
Saint Petersburg 531
Georg Philipp Telemann 587
Giovanni Battista Tiepolo 592
Vienna 613
Antonio Vivaldi 616
Johann Joachim Winckelmann 634
Sir Christopher Wren 638
Barry, Jeanne Bécu, comtesse du 42, 66, 110, 200, 356, 371, 465
Barthélemy, Jean-Jacques 41
Barthez, Paul-Joseph 41–42, 57, 176, 177, 184, 212, 382, 616
Batteux, Charles 42
Battle of the Buffoons 42–43
anthropology 19
Ranieri de'Calzabigi 87

Christoph Willibald Gluck 233
Friedrich Melchior Grimm 247
music 409
opera 436
Giovanni Battista Pergolesi 448
Jean-Philippe Rameau 495
La Serva Padrona 552
Baumgarten, Alexander Gottlieb 7, 43–44, 52, 257, 300
Bayle, Pierre xiv c, 44–45
anthropology 19
Jean-Baptiste de Boyer Argens 21
Calvinism 87
Catherine II 97
China 108
cosmopolitanism 131
deism 147
Dialogues Concerning Natural Religion 157
Jean-Baptiste Du Bos 165
An Enquiry Concerning Human Understanding 182
enthusiasm 183
epistemology 185
Gulliver's Travels 250
Historical and Critical Dictionary 271
David Hume 285
libertine 344
publishing 486
pyrrhonism 487
rationalism 497
reason 498
Republic of Letters 505
skepticism 556
Benedict de Spinoza 569
superstition 577
Giovan Battista Vico 613
Christoph Martin Wieland 631
Beaumarchais, Pierre-Augustin Caron de xvi c, 45, 412, 432, 437, 551, 588
Beaumont, Jeanne Le Prince de 45
Beccaria, Cesare Bonesana, marchese di ix, x, xvi c, 45–46
Jeremy Bentham 50
capital punishment 94
cosmopolitanism 130
Robert-François Damiens 138
Essays on Crimes and Punishments 188–189
Gaetano Filangieri 197
Illuministi 293
Italy 300
justice and the law 315
Milan 392
political theory 462
rights 512
scientific academies 541
Alessandro Verri 611
Pietro Verri 611
Beethoven, Ludwig van 46–47, 118, 119, 174, 199, 230, 409, 421, 437, 521, 536, 580, 583
Beggar's Opera, The (John Gay) 47, 225, 437, 552, 624
Behn, Aphra 47–48, 344, 458, 486, 637
Belgium 48
Austrian Netherlands 29
Brussels 74
colonialism 122
François de Cuvilliés 137
France 201
Gobelins tapestry 234
Holy Roman Empire 278
justice and the law 315
Karl-August 321
Louis XIV of France 354
Spain 565
United Provinces of Netherlands 604

Bellotto, Bernardo **48**, 89, 293
Benedict XIV (pope) 3, **49**, 110, 117, 219, 523
Bentham, Jeremy xvi c, xvii c, 49, **49–50**, 94, 316, 423, 462, 482
Bergman, Torbern Olof 9, **50–51**, 103, 115, 452
Berkeley, George xiv c, **51**, 351, 482, 598, 618
Berlin **51–52**
Berlin Academy **52**
  Jean Le Rond d'Alembert 11
  Jean-Baptiste de Boyer Argens 21
  Berlin 52
  Johann Friedrich Blumenbach 61
  Georges-Louis Leclerc Buffon 75
  Denis Diderot 159
  Leonhard Euler 190
  Adam Ferguson 195
  Frederick II 207
  Caspar David Friedrich 217
  Joseph-Louis Lagrange 327
  Joseph de Lalande 328
  Julien Offray de La Mettrie 330
  Gottfried Wilhelm Leibniz 338
  Thomas Robert Malthus 367
  Pierre-Louis Moreau de Maupertuis 379
  Moses Mendelssohn 385
  Montesquieu 399
  Johannes von Müller 406
  Royal Society of Edinburgh 527
  Royal Society of London 527
  Saint Petersburg Academy of Sciences 531
  social institutions 561
  Johann Peter Süssmilch 578
  Alessandro Giuseppe Antonio Anastasio Volta 617
  Voltaire 619
Bernardin de Saint-Pierre, Jacques-Henri **52–53**, 342, xvi c
Bernoulli, Daniel 52, **53**, 54, 190, 299, 532, 582
Bernoulli, Jakob I and Johann I 53, **53–54**, 190, 376, 379, 473, 582, 585
Berthollet, Claude-Louis 9, **54**, 105, 212, 334
biblical criticism **54–55**
  Jacques-Bénigne Bossuet 67
  Antoine Calmet 84
  deism 146
  Moses Mendelssohn 385
  Johann David Michaelis 390–391
  Isaac Newton 424
  Protestantism 478
  reason 499
  religion 503
  Johann Salomo Semler 546
  Richard Simon 555–556
  Benedict de Spinoza 568
  John Toland 593
Bichat, Marie-François-Xavier **55–56**, 57, 382, 616
Bildung (formation) 28, 56, 431
biology **56–57**. *See also* vitalism
Black, Joseph 57, **57–58**, 103, 136, 170, 195, 255, 452, 527, 544, 616, 630
Blackstone, Sir William xvi c, **58**, **58–59**, 94, 98, 142, 316, 472
Blackwell, Thomas 59, 226
Blake, William **59–60**, 217, 270, 521, xvii c
Blanchard, Jean-Pierre-François **60**
Bluestocking **60–61**, 197, 403, 514, 560, 637

Blumenbach, Johann Friedrich 20, 56, **61–62**, 240, 282, 300, 382, 492, 557, 616, xvi c
Bodmer, Johann Jakob xv c, 8, **62**, 72, 217, 240, 300, 406, 582, 631
Boerhaave, Hermann **62–63**
  Paul-Joseph Barthez 41
  Marie-François-Xavier Bichat 55
  biology 57
  Chemical Revolution 103
  Daniel Gabriel Fahrenheit 192
  Willem Jacob's Gravesande 243
  Albrecht von Haller 255
  Friedrich Hoffmann 275
  iatrochemistry 291
  iatromechanics 291
  Julien Offray de La Mettrie 330
  Carolus Linnaeus 345
  medicine 380, 381
  Gerard van Swieten 579
  universities 607
  Robert Whytt 630
Bolingbroke, Henry St. John, viscount 22, **63–64**, 144, 147, 250, 467, 618, 624
Bonnet, Charles **64–65**
  animalculism 18
  biology 57
  Johann Friedrich Blumenbach 61
  generation 225
  Geneva 226
  great chain of being 244
  Friedrich Heinrich Jacobi 302
  Johann Kaspar Lavater 335
  Montesquieu 399
  John Turberville Needham 419
  preformation theory 469
  Lazzaro Spallanzani 566
  Abraham Trembley 599
  vitalism 616
Bordeu, Théophile de 57, **65–66**, 159, 176, 184, 382, 616
Boscovich, Ruggiero Giuseppe **66–67**, 290, 309, 472
Bossuet, Jacques-Bénigne 2, **67–68**, 86, 163, 194, 271, 340, 355, 365, 399, 569
Boswell, James 68, 312, 477, 505, 508, 557, 597
Böttger, Johann Friedrich **68**, 100, 108, xiv c
Boucher, François **68–69**, 109, 200, 230, 234, 384, 440, 465, 518, 552
Bougainville, Louis-Antoine de **69**, 212, 442, 584, 597, 621
Boulainvilliers, Henri de **70**, 148, 165
Boulanger, Nicolas-Antoine 19, 26, **70–71**, 157, 176, 177, 277, 504, 613
Boulogne, Joseph, chevalier de Saint-Georges **71**
Boulton, Matthew **71**, 358, 471, 626
Bradley, James **71–72**, 252
Bramah, Joseph **72**
Brandenburg **72**
  Berlin 51
  Brandenburg Concertos 72
  Friedrich Rudolf Ludwig Canitz 90
  dynastic states 166
  August Hermann Francke 204
  Frederick II 207
  Gottfried Wilhelm Leibniz 338
  Jacques Necker 418
  Pietism 457
  Prussia 479
  John Toland 593

toleration 594
  University of Halle 255
  William III and Mary II 633
Brandenburg Concertos (Johann Sebastian Bach) 35, 72
Breitinger, Johann Jakob xv c, 8, 62, **72–73**, 240, 300, 582
Brosses, Charles de xv c, 19, 70, **73**, 613
Brown, Lancelot "Capability" **73–74**, 331, 455–456
Brussels **74**
  Belgium 48
  Jacques-Louis David 141
  Hapsburg Empire 261
  Wenzel Anton von Kaunitz 322
  John Law 337
  John Turberville Needham 419
  Gottfried Bernhard Swieten 580
  Voltaire 619
Budapest **74**, 261, 287
Buffon, Georges-Louis Leclerc, comte de xv c, **74–76**, 75
  anthropology 19
  marchese di Beccaria 46
  Berlin Academy 52
  biology 57
  capital punishment 94
  Louis-Jean-Marie Daubenton 139
  degeneration 146
  Denis Diderot 159
  epigenesis 184
  French Academy of Sciences 212
  generation 225
  Anne-Catherine Helvétius 266
  intuition and imagination 300
  Jardin des Plantes 306
  Jean-Baptiste-Pierre-Antoine de Monet de Lamarck 328
  Carolus Linnaeus 345
  Suzanne Necker 419
  John Turberville Needham 419
  Lazzaro Spallanzani 566
  Emanuel Swedenborg 579
  Anne-Robert-Jacques Turgot 602
  vitalism 616
bureaucracy **76–77**, 106, 155, 207, 287, 314, 450, 479
Burke, Edmund xv c, xvii c, **77–78**, 78
  aesthetics 8
  American Revolution 14
  Joel Barlow 37
  Charles Burney 79
  Confessions 126
  Christian Garve 223
  Félicité de Genlis 228
  Oliver Goldsmith 238
  Warren Hastings 264
  John Jay 306
  Samuel Johnson 313
  literature 348
  Elizabeth Montagu 396
  Thomas Paine 443
  picturesque 455–456
  Richard Price 471
  Reflections on the Revolution in France 499
  Joshua Reynolds 508
  The Rights of Man 513
  romanticism 521
  Adam Smith 557
  sublime 576–577
  Mary Wollstonecraft 636
Burlamaqui, Jean-Jacques 14, **78–79**, 414, 511
Burney, Charles 1, 79, 79, 233, 238, 241, 313, 508, 549, 560, 597, 611

Burney, Fanny 79, 79, 228, 266, 396, 560, 637
Burns, Robert **80**
Butler, Joseph **80–81**, 402, 553, 592
Byron, George Gordon, sixth baron **81**, 625

C

Cabanis, Pierre-Jean-Georges 55, 57, **82–83**, 170, 266, 292, 329, 335, 382, 480, 481
Cagliostro, Alessandro, conte di 10, **83**, 530
Calas, Jean **83**, 87, 88, 109, 502, 520, 602, 620, xvi c
Calmet, Antoine **83–84**
Calonne, Charles-Alexandre de 22–23, **84–85**, 166, 203, 357, 418
caloric **85**, 336, 528, 577
Calvinism **85–87**
  ancien régime 15
  Anglicans 16
  Pierre Bayle 44
  Berlin 51
  Camisards 88
  Marie Condorcet 124
  deism 147
  Jonathan Edwards 171
  England 177
  François Fénelon 194
  freedom 208
  Geneva 225
  Huguenots **281–282**
  Industrial Revolution 297
  Jansenism 305
  Gottfried Wilhelm Leibniz 340
  Jean-Paul Marat 368
  Protestantism 478
  On the Revolutions of the Heavenly Spheres 434
  Jean-Jacques Rousseau 524, 525
  Scotland 543
  United Provinces of Netherlands 604
  University of Göttingen 240
  Waldensians 623
Calzabigi, Ranieri Simone Francesco Maria de' **87**, 233, 438
cameralism **87–88**
  Aufklärung 27
  Catherine II 98
  enlightened absolutism 3
  enlightened despotism 155
  free trade 211
  Industrial Revolution 298
  Joseph II of Austria 313
  mercantilism 387
  political theory 462
  Josef von Sonnenfels 562
  statistics 572
  Wealth of Nations 628
Camisards xiv c, **88**, 282, 355, 502, 520
Camper, Pieter 57, 61, **88–89**
Canaletto 48, **89**, 250, 293, 611
Candide (Voltaire) **90**, 130, 340, 347, 385, 438, 620, 635
Canitz, Friedrich Rudolf Ludwig, freiherr (baron) von **90**
Canova, Antonio **90–91**, 421
capitalism **91–93**, 92, 107, 120
capital punishment **93–94**, 138, 188, 279, 315, 316, 512, 515, 528
Carnot, Lazare **94–95**, 327
Cartesianism x, 162, 191, 378, 428, 480, 486, 579
cartography **95**, 96. *See also* longitude
Cartwright, Edmund **95–96**, 298, 469, 568

Casanova, Giovanni Giacomo 10, 87, **96**, 344, 364, 505, 530
Cassini de Thury, César-François 26, **96**, 212
Catherine II (the Great) xvi c, **96–98**, 97
  absolutism 3
  Jean Le Rond d'Alembert 12
  automata 30
  capital punishment 94
  Jean-Baptiste-Siméon Chardin 101
  Charles III of Spain 101
  class and rank 114
  Clement XIV 118
  Denis Diderot 159
  enlightened absolutism 3
  enlightened despotism 155
  enlightened monarchs 395
  Étienne-Maurice Falconet 192
  Friedrich Melchior Grimm 247
  Haskalah 263
  Jean-Antoine Houdon 280
  Jesuits 310
  Jews and Judaism 312
  Jean-François Marmontel 374
  Louis Sébastien Mercier 388
  neoclassicism 421
  partitions of Poland 447
  Peter I 450
  philosopher-king 452
  Physiocrats 454
  Poland 460
  Stanislaw Augustus Poniatowski 466
  progress 476
  Bartolomeo Rastrelli 496
  revolution 507
  Roman Catholicism 521
  Saint Petersburg 531
  serfdom 551
  Élisabeth-Louise Vigée Lebrun 613
  Johann Georg Zimmermann 641
Cavendish, Henry 99, 103, 452, 527
Caylus, Anne-Claude-Philippe de Tubières de Grimoard de Pestel de Levis, comte de 41, **99**, 230
century of Louis XIV, The. *See Siècle de Louis XIV*
ceramic arts **99–100**, 108, 189. *See also* porcelain
Chamfort, Sébastien-Roch-Nicholas **100**, 144, 211
Chardin, Jean-Baptiste-Siméon **100–101**, 160, 200, 518
Charles III of Spain xvi c, 3, **101–102**, 117, 323–324, 363, 387, 395, 565, 584, 591, 622
Châtelet, Gabrielle-Émilie Le Tonnelier de Breteuil, marquise du xv c, **102**, **102–103**, 112, 379, 472, 543, 560, 618
Chemical Revolution **103–106**, 104, 105
  affinity chemistry 9
  Joseph Black 58
  Hermann Boerhaave 63
  Henry Cavendish 99
  William Cullen 136
  Antoine-Laurent Lavoisier 335, 336
  phlogiston theory 452
  Joseph Priestley 472
  Carl Wilhelm Scheele 534
  science 538, 539
  Georg Ernst Stahl 571
Chesterfield, Philip Dormer Stanhope, fourth earl of **106**, 113, 313
China 99, **106–109**, 107, 109, 439, 440, 465, 620. *See also* orientalism

chinoiserie 68, 109, 109, 383, 439, 519, 626
Chippendale, Thomas 109–110
Chodowiecki, Daniel Niklaus 110
Choiseul, Étienne-François, comte de Stainville, duc de 41, 42, 83, 98, 110, 138, 270, 310, 356, 378, 418, 465, 530, 552
Christian VII of Denmark and Norway 110–111, 151, 325, 575
civil society 111–112, 246
Clairaut, Alexis-Claude 26, 96, 102, 112, 191, 212, 328
clarinet 33, 112, 409, 435, 454, 583
Clarissa, or The History of a Young Lady (Samuel Richardson) 112–113, 326, 344, 373, 473, 509, 548, 549
Clarke, Samuel 81, 113–114, 147, 289, 366, 401–402, 600, 618
class and rank in the 18th century 114–115, 115
classicism 115. See also neoclassicism
    aesthetics 7
    baroque style 39, 40
    Battle of the Buffoons 43
    Johann Jakob Bodmer 62
    Johann Jakob Breitinger 72
    John Dryden 165
    empfindsamer Stil 174
    genius 226
    Christoph Willibald Gluck 233
    Johann Wolfgang von Goethe 236
    Johann Christoph Gottsched 240
    Johann Georg Hamann 257
    Franz Joseph Haydn 264
    Laokoon 334
    Gotthold Ephraim Lessing 342
    literature 348
    Louis XIV of France 355
    Mannheim school 368
    Louis-Sébastien Mercier 388
    Moscow 405
    music 408
    neoclassicism 420
    Palladian style 444
    piano 455
    Alexander Pope 467
    Quarrel between the Ancients and the Moderns 489
    Jean-Philippe Rameau 496
    Josef von Sonnenfels 562
    symphony orchestra 583
    viola 614
    Antonio Vivaldi 616
classification 115, 116
    aesthetics 9
    Francis Bacon 36
    Torbern Olof Bergman 50
    biology 56
    Hermann Boerhaave 63
    Georges-Louis Leclerc Buffon 75
    cosmopolitanism 131
    William Cullen 136
    Georges Cuvier 136–137
    Erasmus Darwin 139
    Denis Diderot 159
    Jardin des Plantes 306
    Jean-Baptiste-Pierre-Antoine de Monet de Lamarck 329
    Carolus Linnaeus 345
    medicine 382
    progress 475
    reason 499
    science 539
Cleland, John 115–117, 468
Clementi, Muzio 118–119

Clement XIII (pope) 90, 117–118, 457
Clement XII (pope) 117, 118
Clement XIV (pope) 20, 66, 90, 118, 171, 310, 387, 457, 464, 521
coffeehouses 27, 131. See also social institutions of the Enlightenment
Coleridge, Samuel Taylor 119, 134, 270, 595
Collins, Anthony 55, 113, 119–120, 147, 267, 277, 592
Cologne 120, 137, 519
colonialism 120–122, 121, 179, 332
Common Sense (Thomas Paine) 122–123, 141, 442, 443, 528
Condillac, Étienne Bonnot de ix, xv c, 123, 123–124
    Jean Le Rond d'Alembert 11
    Georges-Louis Leclerc Buffon 76
    Chemical Revolution 104–105
    Antoine-Louis-Claude Destutt de Tracy 156
    Denis Diderot 158, 160
    education 170
    empiricism 174
    Franz Joseph Gall 221
    Gothic romance 239
    Anne-Catherine Helvétius 266
    Claude-Adrien Helvétius 267
    Idéologie 292
    Idéologues 292
    language 332, 333
    Julie-Jeanne-Eléonore de Lespinasse 342
    John Locke 351
    Gabriel Bonnot de Mably 361
    perfectibility 447
    Maximilien Robespierre 515
    Anne-Robert-Jacques Turgot 602
Condorcet, Marie-Jean-Antoine-Nicolas Caritat, marquis de xvii c, 124–125, 125
    Jean Le Rond d'Alembert 10
    American Revolution 14
    Joel Barlow 37
    Pierre-Jean-Georges Cabanis 82
    cosmopolitanism 130
    education 170
    Encyclopédie 176
    Freemasons 211
    French Academy of Sciences 212
    French Revolution 216
    Guadeloupe 249
    history 272
    Idéologie 292
    Idéologues 292
    Joseph-Louis Lagrange 327
    Pierre-Simon Laplace 334
    Julie-Jeanne-Eléonore de Lespinasse 342
    Thomas Robert Malthus 367
    Montesquieu 399
    perfectibility 447
    reason 498
    Anne-Robert-Jacques Turgot 602
    women and the Enlightenment 637
Confessions (Jean-Jacques Rousseau) 125–126, 526
Congreve, William xiv c, 6, 126–127, 458, 486, 553, 575, 580, 624
Cook, James xvi c, 79, 127, 199, 282, 353, 427, 446, 476, 584, 597, 621, 622
Copernican Revolution 38, 127–129, 128, 129, 228, 266, 319, 323, 433

Copernicus, Nicolaus 129
    astronomy 25
    James Bradley 71
    Copernican Revolution 127
    deism 146
    Bernard Le Bovier de Fontenelle 198
    Galileo Galilei 220
    heliocentric 266
    hermeticism 269
    Immanuel Kant 319
    Johannes Kepler 323
    orrery 440
    Poland 459
    religion 502
    On the Revolutions of the Heavenly Spheres 433–435
    Scientific Revolution 542
Corelli, Arcangelo 1, 129–130, 410, 533, 583
Cort, Henry 130, 298
Così fan Tutte (Wolfgang Amadeus Mozart) 130, 389, 406, 437
cosmopolitanism 130–131, 408, 493
Cottin, Sophie 131–132, 431
Coudary, Angélique-Marguérite Le Boursier du 132, 391
Coulomb, Charles-Augustin de 132–133, 212
Couperin, François 40, 130, 133
Cowley, Hannah 133
Cowper, William 134
Creation, The (Joseph Haydn) 134, 265
Crèvecoeur, Michel-Guillaume-Saint-Jean de 134, 597
Crompton, Samuel 134–135, 567
Cruikshank, George 135
Cudworth, Ralph 135, 147, 350, 401, 405, 471
Cullen, William 57, 103, 135–136, 170, 288, 298, 382, 527, 616
Cuvier, Georges 57, 136–137, 212, 306, 453, 493
Cuvilliés, François de (The Elder) 120, 137, 137, 407, 518

D

Dale, David 138, 422
Damiens, Robert-François xv c, 138, 310, 378
Darby, Abraham 138, 298
Darwin, Erasmus 139, 169, 263, 358, 471, 639
Daubenton, Louis-Jean-Marie 57, 75, 89, 139–140, 159, 212, 306
David, Jacques-Louis xvii c, 99, 140, 140–141, 200, 299, 370, 421
Declaration of Independence ix, xvi c, 141–143, 142
    John Adams 5
    American Revolution 14
    Common Sense 122
    Declaration of the Rights of Man 143
    Benjamin Franklin 205
    happiness 261
    Thomas Jefferson 307
    natural law 414
    natural rights 416
    Philadelphia 451
    publishing 486
    race 493
    revolution 506
    rights 510
    Benjamin Rush 528
    United States Bill of Rights 605
    United States of America 606

Declaration of the Rights of Man and Citizen ix, xvii c, 143–144
    Declaration of Independence 143
    French Revolution 213
    Haitian Revolution 253
    natural law 414
    natural rights 416
    Paris 446
    property 476
    rights 510
    August Ludwig von Schlözer 537
Deffand, Marie de Vichy-Chamrond, marquise du xv c, 11, 144–145, 145, 184, 341, 398, 560, 623
Defoe, Daniel xiv c, 145–146, 163, 248, 331, 364, 429, 473, 516, 517, 595, 597, 624
degeneration 56, 75, 146, 306
deism 146–148
    anticlericalism 20
    atheism 26
    William Blake 59
    Henry St. John Bolingbroke 64
    Henri de Boulainvilliers 70
    Joseph Butler 80
    China 108
    Anthony Collins 119–120
    The Creation 134
    Ralph Cudworth 135
    Erasmus Darwin 139
    Declaration of Independence 142
    René Descartes 154
    Dictionnaire philosophique 158
    Denis Diderot 159
    Émile 172
    England 178
    enthusiasm 182
    Freemasons 209
    Edward Gibbon 232
    Johann Georg Hamann 257
    David Hume 285
    James Hutton 290
    Jews and Judaism 310
    Joseph II of Austria 314
    Johann Kaspar Lavater 335
    Gotthold Ephraim Lessing 342
    John Turberville Needham 419
    La Nouvelle Héloïse 429
    Thomas Paine 443
    physico-theology 453
    Hermann Samuel Reimarus 501
    religion 503
    Roman Catholicism 520
    Jean-Jacques Rousseau 525
    Scientific Revolution 543
    Johann Salomo Semler 547
    Matthew Tindal 592
    John Toland 593
    toleration 594
    Voltaire 618
    Thomas Woolston 638
Delille, Jacques 148
Delisle, Joseph-Nicolas 149, 190, 212, 328, 532, 597
democracy 149, 155, 298, 466, 569, 582
demography 149–150, 367, 376. See also Malthus, Thomas Robert
Denmark 150–151
    Christian VII of Denmark and Norway 110–111
    Germany 230
    Holy Roman Empire 278
    Friedrich Gottlieb Klopstock 325
    literature 348
    Lutheranism 358, 359
    Protestantism 479
    Samuel Pufendorf 487

scientific academies 540
Johann Friedrich Struensee 575
William III and Mary II 633
Nicolaus Ludwig Zinzendor 642
De Revolutionibus Orbium Coelestium. See On the Revolutions of the Heavenly Spheres
Desaguliers, John Theophilus 96, 151, 209, 243, 424, 428, 527, 543
Descartes, René 151–155, 152. See also Cartesianism
    Aufklärung 27
    automata 29
    Francis Bacon 36
    Jacques-Bénigne Bossuet 67
    César-François Cassini de Thury 96
    classicism 115
    Étienne Bonnot de Condillac 123
    Confessions 126
    Copernican Revolution 128
    Dialogues Concerning Natural Religion 157
    Discourse on Method 161–162
    empiricism 174
    epistemology 184
    Essays on Crimes and Punishments 188
    Bernard Le Bovier de Fontenelle 198
    Jean-Baptiste-Joseph Fourier 200
    France 201
    Galileo Galilei 220
    Pierre Gassend 224
    Willem Jacob's Gravesande 243
    Friedrich Hoffmann 275
    David Hume 286
    iatromechanics 291
    Julien Offray de La Mettrie 330
    Gottfried Wilhelm Leibniz 339
    John Locke 350
    Louis XIV of France 355
    Nicolas de Malebranche 365
    mathematics and mechanics 375
    mechanical philosophy 380
    Moses Mendelssohn 385
    Marin Mersenne 389
    nature 416
    Isaac Newton 423
    probability 473
    progress 475
    psychology 480, 481
    pyrrhonism 488
    rationalism 496
    reason 498
    Republic of Letters 505
    Rosicrucians 523
    scientific academies 540
    scientific method 541
    Scientific Revolution 542, 543
    skepticism 556
    Benedict de Spinoza 568
    A Treatise of Human Nature 598
    utility 607
Desmarest, Nicolas 155, 176, 177, 212
despotism, enlightened 155–156
    absolutism 3
    Aufklärung 27
    Charles III of Spain 101
    China 106
    Christian VII of Denmark and Norway 110–111
    Denmark 151
    enlightened absolutism 3
    enlightened monarchs 395

Frederick II 206
French Revolution 216
Bavarian Illuminati 292
literacy 347
Maria Theresa of Austria 370
medicine 383
Louis-Sébastien Mercier 388
Milan 392
natural rights 416
perfectibility 448
philosopher-king 452
political theory 462
Sebastiano José de Carvalho e
  Mello Pombal 464
Portugal 468
Siècle de Louis XIV 554
Josef von Sonnenfels 562
Johann Friedrich Struensee
  575
Wealth of Nations 628
Destutt de Tracy, Antoine-Louis-
  Claude, comte 156, 170, 266,
  292, 399
Dialogues Concerning Natural
  Religion (David Hume) 130,
  156–157, 285
diamond necklace scandal 42,
  83, 157, 357, 371
Dictionnaire philosophique
  (Voltaire) 84, 148, 157–158,
  595, 620
Diderot, Denis x, xv c, xvi c,
  158–160, 159
  aesthetics 8, 9
  American Revolution 14
  anthropology 20
  Marc-Pierre de Voyer
    Argenson 21
  atheism 26
  Francis Bacon 36
  marchese di Beccaria 46
  Marie-François-Xavier Bichat
    55
  biology 57
  Théophile de Bordeu 66
  François Boucher 69
  Louis-Antoine de Bougainville
    69
  Anne-Claude-Philippe de Levis
    Caylus 99
  Clement XIII 118
  Confessions 126
  cosmopolitanism 130
  Encyclopédie 175–177
  encyclopedists 177
  enlightened despotism 155
  Louise-Florence-Pétronville de
    la Live Épinay 184
  Étienne-Maurice Falconet 192
  France 201
  freedom 209
  Élie-Cathérine Fréron 216
  Ferdinando Galiani 219
  genius 226
  Marie-Thérèse Rodet Geoffrin
    230
  Jean-Baptiste Greuze 246
  Friedrich Melchior Grimm 247
  Haitian Revolution 253
  Johann Georg Hamann 258
  Anne-Cathérine Helvétius 266
  Claude-Adrien Helvétius 267
  Histoire des deux Indes 270
  Historical and Critical
    Dictionary 271
  Jean-Antoine Houdon 280
  Friedrich Heinrich Jacobi 302
  Kingdom of the Two Sicilies
    324
  Julie-Jeanne-Eléonore de
    Lespinasse 342
  libertine 344
  Jean-François Marmontel 373
  materialism 375
  moral philosophy 402
  Abbé Morelly 404

museums 408
novel 429
orientalism 439
paganism 442
philosophes 452
Physiocrats 454
politeness 460
political theory 462
pornography 468
progress 475
psychology 480
radical Enlightenment 494
Jean-Philippe Rameau 495
Guillaume-Thomas-François
  de Raynal 497
religion 504
Republic of Letters 505
revolution 506
rights 512
Jean-Jacques Rousseau 525
slavery 557
Benedict de Spinoza 569
sympathy 582
travel literature 598
United Provinces of
  Netherlands 604, 605
utility 607
virtue 615
vitalism 616
Diplomatic Revolution of 1756
  xv c, 160–161
Étienne-François Choiseul
  110
Frederick II 207
Hapsburg Empire 261
Italy 300
Wenzel Anton von Kaunitz
  322
Louis XV of France 356
Maria Theresa of Austria 371
marquise de Pompadour 465
Prussia 479
Seven Years' War 552
War of the Austrian Succession
  624
Discourse on Method (René
  Descartes) 152, 161–162, 291,
  375, 488, 607
Discourse on the Origins of
  Inequality (Jean-Jacques
  Rousseau) 162–163, 186, 476,
  524, 559
Dissenters 163
  American Revolution 14
  Anglicans 16
  association movement 24
  Sir William Blackstone 59
  Henry St. John Bolingbroke 63
  Joseph Butler 80
  Calvinism 85
  Declaration of Independence
    141
  Daniel Defoe 145
  education 171
  England 178
  freedom 208
  Glorious Revolution 232
  Francis Hutcheson 289
  John Locke 350
  Lunar Society of Birmingham
    358
  Thomas Robert Malthus 367
  Richard Price 470
  Joseph Priestley 471
  Protestantism 478
  toleration 594
  universities 607
  John Wesley 629
divine right of kings 2, 15, 48,
  67, 106, 163–164, 274, 399
Dobrovský, Josef 164
Don Giovanni (Wolfgang
  Amadeus Mozart) 164, 437,
  588
Dryden, John 6, 47, 164–165,
  580

Du Bos, Jean-Baptiste, Abbé 8,
  165
Duclos, Charles-Pinot 165–166,
  176, 184, 342, 374
Dupont de Nemours, Pierre-
  Samuel 166, 328, 394, 453,
  602
dynastic states 166–167,
  261–262, 456, 479, 544

E

East India Company 168,
  168–169
  American Revolution 13
  capitalism 93
  China 108
  chinoiserie 109
  John Cleland 115
  colonialism 121
  Hannah Cowley 133
  Warren Hastings 263
  Thomas Robert Malthus 367
  South Sea Bubble 564
  South Sea Company 564
economics ix
  cameralism 87–88
  capitalism 91–93
  colonialism 120
  Dissenters 163
  England 178
  Adam Ferguson 196
  Gaetano Filangieri 197, 197
  France 201–202
  free trade 211–212
  Ferdinando Galiani 219
  Antonio Genovesi 228
  Francis Hutcheson 289
  James Hutton 289
  individualism 296
  Italy 300
  Kingdom of the Two Sicilies
    324
  laissez-faire 328
  Gabriel Bonnot de Mably 361
  mercantilism 387
  self-interest 546
  Adam Smith 557–556
  Anne-Robert-Jacques Turgot
    602
  universities 607
  Wealth of Nations 627
Edgeworth, Maria 169
Edinburgh 169–170
  biology 57
  Joseph Black 57
  Hermann Boerhaave 63
  James Boswell 68
  Robert Burns 80
  civil society 111
  Freemasons 209
  David Hume 286
  Jacobites 304
  Thomas Jefferson 307
  John Law 336
  James Macpherson 362
  Jean-Paul Marat 368
  medicine 382
  Alexander Monro 395
  Mungo Park 446
  John Pringle 472
  Thomas Reid 500
  Republic of Letters 505
  William Robertson 514
  Royal Society of Edinburgh
    527
  Scotland 544
  Adam Smith 557
  social institutions 561
  John Toland 593
  universities 607
  vitalism 616
  Robert Whytt 630
education 170–171
  aesthetics 8
  ancien régime 15
  Aufklärung 28

Pierre-Jean-Georges Cabanis
  82
Marie Condorcet 124
Confessions 126
Antoine-Louis-Claude Destutt
  de Tracy 156
Denis Diderot 160
empiricism 174
England 179
Essays on Crimes and
  Punishments 188
August Hermann Francke 204
French Revolution 216
Félicité de Genlis 228
grand tour 241
Henri Gregoire 245
Gustav III of Sweden 250
Hapsburg Empire 261
Haskalah 263
Eliza Haywood 266
Claude-Adrien Helvétius 267
history 271
Wilhelm von Humboldt 283
Idéologie 292
Idéologues 292
Elizabeth Inchbald 296
individualism 296
Thomas Jefferson 308
Jesuits 309
Jews and Judaism 312
Joseph II of Austria 313
Anne-Thérèse de Marguenat de
  Courcelles Lambert 329
literacy 347
literature 348
John Locke 351
Mikhail Vasilivich Lomonosov
  351
Maria Theresa of Austria 371
Abbé Morelly 404
Moscow 405
natural religion 414
New Lanark 423
Pamela 445
perfectibility 448
Johann Heinrich Pestalozzi 449
Pietism 457
political theory 463
marquise de Pompadour 464
Richard Price 471
Joseph Priestley 472
progress 475
Quakers 489
radical Enlightenment 494
Johann Christian Reil 500
Republic of Letters 505
Samuel Richardson 509
The Rights of Man 513
Maximilien Robespierre 516
Jean-Jacques Rousseau 524
Benjamin Rush 528
Claude-Henri de Saint-Simon
  532
Carl Wilhelm Scheele 534
August Ludwig von Schlözer
  537
sentimental fiction 549
separation of church and state
  550
Josef von Sonnenfels 562
Spain 565
Laurence Sterne 574
Switzerland 582
Christian Thomasius 589
Samuel-Auguste-André-David
  Tissot 593
John Horne Tooke 596
Sarah Trimmer 599, 600
universities 606–607
A Vindication of the Rights of
  Woman 614
George Washington 625
Mary Wollstonecraft 636
women and the Enlightenment
  637

Edwards, Jonathan 171–172,
  244, 393
Émile (Jean-Jacques Rousseau)
  172–173, 173
  Clement XIII 118
  Confessions 126
  Discourse on the Origins of
    Inequality 163
  Maria Edgeworth 169
  education 170
  Claude-Adrien Helvétius 267
  Johann Heinrich Pestalozzi
    449
  rights 513
  Robinson Crusoe 517
  Jean-Jacques Rousseau 525
  Social Contract 559
  A Vindication of the Rights of
    Woman 614
empfindsamer Stil (sensitive) 32,
  36, 174, 265, 408, 409, 455, 576
empiricism 174–175
  Aufklärung 27
  George Berkeley 51
  Nicolas-Antoine Boulanger 70
  Dialogues Concerning Natural
    Religion 156
  Dictionnaire philosophique 158
  Encyclopédie 176
  England 178
  epistemology 184
  Christian Garve 223
  Antonio Genovesi 228
  Willem Jacob's Gravesande
    243
  David Hartley 262
  Thomas Hobbes 274
  David Hume 284
  James Hutton 290
  Immanuel Kant 318
  Joseph-Louis Lagrange 327
  John Locke 350
  moral philosophy 402
  Isaac Newton 423
  Joseph Priestley 471
  progress 475
  psychology 480
  rationalism 496
  reason 498
  scientific method 541
  skepticism 556
  A Treatise of Human Nature
    598
  Giovan Battista Vico 612
  vitalism 616
  Voltaire 618, 620
Encyclopédie 175, 175–177, 176
  Jean Le Rond d'Alembert 11,
    12
  anticlericalism 20
  Marc-Pierre de Voyer
    Argenson 21
  Francis Bacon 36
  Paul-Joseph Barthez 41
  Battle of the Buffoons 43
  Théophile de Bordeu 66
  Nicolas-Antoine Boulanger 70
  Charles de Brosses 73
  Ranieri de'Calzabigi 87
  Catherine II 97
  Chemical Revolution 103
  Étienne-François Choiseul
    110
  Clement XIII 118
  Nicolas Desmarest 155
  Denis Diderot 158
  Charles-Pinot Duclos 166
  encyclopedists 177
  France 201, 202
  Élie-Cathérine Fréron 216
  Christian Garve 223
  Geneva 226
  Marie-Thérèse Rodet Geoffrin
    230
  Nicolas-Joseph-Laurent Gilbert
    232

Claude-Adrien Helvétius 267
Johann Gottfried Herder 269
Paul-Henri Thiry d'Holbach 276
Idéologie 292
Kingdom of the Two Sicilies 324
Joseph de Lalande 328
literature 348
Chrétien-Guillaume de Malesherbes 366
Jean-François Marmontel 373, 374
moral philosophy 402
museums 408
orientalism 439
perfectibility 448
Physiocrats 453–454
marquise de Pompadour 465
François Quesnay 490
race 493
religion 504
Jean-Jacques Rousseau 524, 525
Benedict de Spinoza 569
technology and instrumentation 586
Anne-Robert-Jacques Turgot 602
utility 607
Voltaire 619
encyclopedists 177
anticlericalism 20
Anne-Claude-Philippe de Levis Caylus 99
Declaration of the Rights of Man 143
Mme du Deffand 145
generation 225
Haitian Revolution 253
John Locke 351
philosophes 452
radical Enlightenment 494
Jean-Philippe Rameau 495
Jean-Jacques Rousseau 524
Pietro Verri 611
England x, xiv c, 177–179. See also specific headings, e.g.:
William III and Mary II
absolutism 2
The Age of Reason 10
anticlericalism 20
Aufklärung 27
Francis Bacon 36
baroque style 40
comtesse du Barry 42
Aphra Behn 47
Jeremy Bentham 50
Jakob I and Johann I Bernoulli 54
biology 56
Lord Byron 81
Calvinism 85
Camisards 88
Canaletto 89
Friedrich Rudolf Ludwig Canitz 90
capitalism 92–93
capital punishment 93
cartography 95
Anne-Claude-Philippe de Levis Caylus 99
China 106
chinoiserie 109
Thomas Chippendale 109
civil society 111
Clarissa 113
classicism 115
John Cleland 115
Muzio Clementi 118
Samuel Taylor Coleridge 119
colonialism 121
Common Sense 122
William Congreve 126
cosmopolitanism 130
Sophie Cottin 131

Hannah Cowley 133
Ralph Cudworth 135
Declaration of Independence 141
Daniel Defoe 145
deism 146
Jacques Delille 148
Joseph-Nicolas Delisle 149
democracy 149
John Theophilus Desaguliers 151
René Descartes 154
diamond necklace scandal 157
Dissenters 163
dynastic states 166
East India Company 168
Edinburgh 169
education 171
enthusiasm 182
Epicurean philosophy 183
epistemology 184
Olaudah Equiano 187
Johann Georg Adam Forster 199
France 202
Benjamin Franklin 206
Frederick II 207
freedom 208
Freemasons 209
French Revolution 215
Henry Fuseli 217
Pierre Gassend 224
Antonio Genovesi 228
Edward Gibbon 231
Christoph Willibald Gluck 233
Gothic revival 239
Willem Jacob's Gravesande 243
Thomas Gray 243
Gulliver's Travels 250
Stephen Hales 254–255
George Frederick Handel 260
James Hargreaves 262
Warren Hastings 264
Eliza Haywood 265
Claude-Adrien Helvétius 267
hermeticism 269
William Herschel 270
Thomas Hobbes 273
William Hogarth 275–276
Paul-Henri Thiry d'Holbach 277
homosexuality 279
Huguenots 282
David Hume 286
James Hutton 290
imperialism 295
Elizabeth Inchbald 296
Industrial Revolution 296–298
Jacobins 304
John Jay 306
Thomas Jefferson 307
Jews and Judaism 312
Samuel Johnson 313
justice and the law 315, 316
language 332
Antoine-Laurent Lavoisier 336
Antoni van Leeuwenhoek 337
Gottfried Wilhelm Leibniz 339
Charlotte Ramsay Lennox 341
libertine 344
literacy 347
literature 348
John Locke 349–351
longitude 353
Louis XIV of France 355
Louis XVI of France 357
magic 364
Thomas Robert Malthus 367
Bernard Mandeville 367
John Loudon McAdam 379
Moses Mendelssohn 386
mercantilism 387
Methodism 390
Johann David Michaelis 390

midwifery 391
millenarianism 393
Elizabeth Montagu 396
Montesquieu 398
moral philosophy 402
Moravian Brethren 403
Hannah More 403
Johann Lorenz von Mosheim 405
neoclassicism 421
novel 431
opera 437
orrery 440
Thomas Paine 442, 443
Palladian style 444
Pamela 445
Mungo Park 446
Persian Letters 449
Peter I 450
Philadelphia 451
phlogiston theory 452
Physiocrats 454
Pietism 457
Mary Pix 458
politeness 460
political theory 461
Sebastiano José de Carvalho e Mello Pombal 464
Stanislaw Augustus Poniatowski 466
pornography 467
power loom 469
Antoine-François Prévost 348
probability 473
prostitution 476–477
Protestantism 478
psychology 480
public health 482
publishing 484
Quakers 489
race 493
Rake's Progress 495
reason 498
Reflections on the Revolution in France 499
religion 502
Republic of Letters 505
revolution 506
Joshua Reynolds 508
Samuel Richardson 509
The Rights of Man 513
Victor de Riqueti 394
rococo 518
romanticism 521
Jean-Jacques Rousseau 525
Thomas Rowlandson 526
Ignatius Sancho 532
Giuseppe Domenico Scarlatti 534
science 539
scientific academies 540
Scotland 543
secret societies 545
sentimental fiction 548
separation of powers 550
earl of Shaftesbury 552, 553
Richard Brinsley Sheridan 553
Emmanuel-Joseph Sieyès 555
slavery 557
Adam Smith 558
social institutions 560
South Sea Bubble 564
Spain 565
Lazzaro Spallanzani 566
The Spirit of Laws 570
Richard Steele 574
Johann Peter Süssmilch 578
Emanuel Swedenborg 579
Gottfried Bernhard Swieten 580
Jonathan Swift 580
technology and instrumentation 586
William Temple 587–588
John Toland 593
toleration 594

Tom Jones 595
A Treatise of Human Nature 598
Jethro Tull 601
universities 606
University of Göttingen 240
virtue 614
Voltaire 618
voyages of discovery 620
George Washington 625
Jean-Antoine Watteau 627
Charles Wesley 629
John Wesley 630
William Wilberforce 631–632
John Wilkes 632–633
William III and Mary II 633–634
women and the Enlightenment 637
Mary Wortley 397
Sir Christopher Wren 638
Joseph Wright 639
Arthur Young 640
Johann Georg Zimmermann 641
English garden 179, xv c
Lancelot "Capability" Brown 73–74
Gothic revival 239
William Kent 323
landscapes 331
Munich 407
Palladian style 444
picturesque 455–456
Alexander Pope 467
rococo 519
social institutions 561
Enlightenment, the 179–182. See also Aufklärung; Haskalah; specific topics, e.g.: social institutions of the Enlightenment
Enquiry Concerning Human Understanding, An (David Hume) 156, 182, 185, 284, 500, 556, 598
enthusiasm 182–183
Dialogues Concerning Natural Religion 157
Dictionnaire philosophique 158
Denis Diderot 160
genius 227
Paul-Henri Thiry d'Holbach 278
natural religion 415
reason 498
religion 503, 504
earl of Shaftesbury 552
superstition 577
toleration 594
John Wesley 630
Epicurean philosophy 183
atheism 26
Declaration of Independence 143
Pierre Gassend 223
Thomas Hobbes 273
Paul-Henri Thiry d'Holbach 278
Julien Offray de La Mettrie 330
John Locke 349
Rosicrucians 524
epigenesis 183–184
Johann Friedrich Blumenbach 62
Charles Bonnet 65
generation 225
Albrecht von Haller 255
Pierre-Louis Moreau de Maupertuis 379
microscope 391
John Turberville Needham 419
preformation theory 469
Épinay, Louise-Florence-Pétronville de la Live, Madame d' 126, 159, 184, 247, 525

epistemology 184–185
Jean Le Rond d'Alembert 12
Confessions 126
René Descartes 152
Dialogues Concerning Natural Religion 156
Encyclopédie 176
England 178
Epicurean philosophy 183
August Hermann Francke 204
Franz Joseph Gall 221
Pierre Gassend 224
Johann Christoph Gatterer 224
David Hartley 262
David Hume 284
intuition and imagination 299, 300
Friedrich Heinrich Jacobi 303
Immanuel Kant 319
Gottfried Wilhelm Leibniz 339
Georg Christoph Lichtenberg 345
John Locke 350
Nicolas de Malebranche 366
Moses Mendelssohn 386
moral philosophy 402
Isaac Newton 423
psychology 479
pyrrhonism 487
rationalism 496–497
reason 499
science 538
science of man 540
Scientific Revolution 543
skepticism 556
Benedict de Spinoza 568
Giovan Battista Vico 613
equality 185–187
ancien régime 15
René-Lous de Voyer de Paulmy Argenson 22
association movement 25
Aufklärung 28
François-Noel Babeuf 32
Joel Barlow 37
capital punishment 94
Mme du Châtelet 103
civil society 111
Declaration of the Rights of Man 143
Discourse on the Origins of Inequality 162
divine right of kings 163
education 171
England 179
Johann Georg Adam Forster 199
freedom 208, 209
French Revolution 215
Haitian Revolution 253
Haskalah 263
honor 280
individualism 296
Thomas Jefferson 308
Joseph II of Austria 313
Louis XVI of France 357
Gabriel Bonnot de Mably 361
Methodism 390
natural law 414
natural rights 415
Pamela 445
parlements 446
political theory 463
Pompeii 466
Richard Price 471
property 476
radical Enlightenment 494
Reflections on the Revolution in France 499
rights 511
The Rights of Man 513
Maximilien Robespierre 515
Jean-Jacques Rousseau 526
separation of church and state 550

serfdom 551
Emmanuel-Joseph Sieyès 555
Social Contract 559
Johann Friedrich Struensee 575
United States Bill of Rights 605
United States of America 606
Mary Wollstonecraft 636
women and the Enlightenment 637
Equiano, Olaudah 187, 187–188, 532
Essays on Crimes and Punishments (Beccaria) ix, 45, 46, 94, 138, 188–189, 197, 293, 392, 611
Esterházy, Miklós József 189, 264
Etruria works 100, 189, 628
Eugène of Savoy, Prince 189–190, 197, 270, 339, 613
Euler, Leonhard xv c, 52, 53, 102, 149, 150, 190–191, 327, 328, 334, 376, 532, 582
explorers. See voyages of discovery

F

Fahrenheit, Daniel Gabriel xiv c, 192
Falconet, Étienne-Maurice 192, 552
Faust (Johann Wolfgang von Goethe) 192–193
Favart, Charles-Simon 193
Febronianism 28, 118, 194, 306, 314, 464, 504
Fénelon, François de Salignac de la Mothe 67, 70, 194–195, 329, 355, 365
Ferguson, Adam 195–196
  aesthetics 7
  American Revolution 14
  Joseph Black 57
  civil society 111
  Edinburgh 170
  freedom 209
  Christian Garve 223
  history 272
  James Hutton 289
  psychology 480
  race 492
  William Robertson 51
  earl of Shaftesbury 553
  Royal Society of Edinburgh 527
  Johann Friedrich Schiller 535
  Scotland 544
  Adam Smith 557
Fielding, Henry 47, 196, 196, 266, 341, 445, 527, 516, 558, 595, 624
Fielding, Sarah 196–197, 549
Filangieri, Gaetano 197, 301, 324, 585
financial speculation. See Mississippi Bubble; South Sea Bubble; South Sea Company
Fischer von Erlach, Johann Bernhard xiv c, 39, 190, 197–198, 270, 422, 444, 518, 613
flying shuttle 198, 322, 586
Fontenelle, Bernard Le Bovier de 19, 47, 52, 65, 144, 157, 198–199, 212, 230, 266, 329, 355, 489, 613, xiv c
Forster, Johann Georg Adam 199, 199, 240, 282, 302, 597
Forster, Johann Reinhold 199, 199, 597
Fourier, Jean-Baptiste-Joseph 200
Four Seasons, The (Antonio Vivaldi) 199–200, 617
Fragonard, Jean-Honoré xvi c, 200–201, 201, 518

France ix, x, 201–204. See also specific headings, e.g.: French Revolution
absolutism 3
John Adams 5
The Age of Reason 10
American Revolution 13
Amsterdam 14
anticlericalism 20
Jean-Baptiste de Boyer Argens 20
René-Lous de Voyer de Paulmy Argenson 21
aristocratic resurgence 22–23
association movement 25
Aufklärung 27
Austrian Netherlands 29
François-Noel Babeuf 31
Francis Bacon 36
baroque style 39
comtesse du Barry 42
Pierre Bayle 44
Benedict XIV 49
Jeremy Bentham 50
Berlin 51
Jacques-Henri Bernardin de Saint-Pierre 52
Jakob I and Johann I Bernoulli 54
biology 56
Joseph Black 57
James Boswell 68
François Boucher 68
Henri de Boulainvilliers 70
Charles de Brosses 73
Georges-Louis Leclerc Buffon 75
bureaucracy 76
Pierre-Jean-Georges Cabanis 82
Alessandro Cagliostro 83
Jean Calas 83
Antoine Calmet 84
Charles-Alexandre de Calonne 84
Calvinism 85
Ranieri de'Calzabigi 87
Camisards 88
Friedrich Rudolf Ludwig Canitz 90
capitalism 93
Lazare Carnot 94
cartography 95
Giovanni Giacomo Casanova 96
Henry Cavendish 99
Charles III of Spain 101
Chemical Revolution 103
China 106
chinoiserie 109
Étienne-François Choiseul 110
civil society 111
class and rank 114
classicism 115
John Cleland 117
Muzio Clementi 118
Clement XIII 117
Clement XIV 118
colonialism 120
Marie Condorcet 124
Confessions 126
cosmopolitanism 130
Sophie Cottin 131
Angélique-Marguérite du Coudary 132
Charles-Augustin de Coulomb 132
Michel de Crèvecoeur 134
Robert-François Damiens 138
Jacques-Louis David 141
Declaration of Independence 143
deism 146
Joseph-Nicolas Delisle 149
democracy 149

René Descartes 152
Antoine-Louis-Claude Destutt de Tracy 156
Dictionnaire philosophique 158
Diplomatic Revolution of 1756 160
Jean-Baptiste Du Bos 165
Pierre-Samuel Dupont de Nemours 166
dynastic states 166
Maria Edgeworth 169
education 171
Encyclopédie 175, 176
England 178
enlightened absolutism 3
enthusiasm 183
Epicurean philosophy 183
Eugène of Savoy 189
Charles-Simon Favart 193
François Fénelon 194
Johann Georg Adam Forster 199
Jean-Honoré Fragonard 200
Benjamin Franklin 205, 206
freedom 208
Freemasons 209, 210
Élie-Catherine Fréron 216
Gallicanism 222
David Garrick 223
Pierre Gassend 223
Félicité de Genlis 228
Antonio Genovesi 228
Marie-Thérèse Rodet Geoffrin 229–230
Germany 230
Edward Gibbon 231
Nicolas-Joseph-Laurent Gilbert 232
Johann Wolfgang von Goethe 237
Carlo Goldoni 238
grand tour 241
Thomas Gray 243
Henri Gregoire 245
Jean-Baptiste Greuze 246
Guadeloupe 248–249
Gulliver's Travels 250
Haitian Revolution 254
Johann Georg Hamann 257
Alexander Hamilton 259
Anne-Catherine Helvétius 266
Claude-Adrien Helvétius 266, 267
Histoire des deux Indes 271
Thomas Hobbes 273
William Hogarth 276
Paul-Henri Thiry d'Holbach 276–278
Holy Roman Empire 278
homosexuality 279
Wilhelm von Humboldt 283
David Hume 286
James Hutton 290
Idéologie 292
Idéologues 292
Bavarian Illuminati 293
Illuministi 293
imperialism 295
Jacobites 304
Jansenism 305
Thomas Jefferson 308
Jews and Judaism 310
justice and the law 315, 316
Joseph-Louis Lagrange 327
laissez-faire 328
Julien Offray de La Mettrie 330
John Law 336–337
lettres de cachet 343
libertine 344
Carolus Linnaeus 345
Lisbon earthquake 347
literacy 347
literature 348
John Locke 349
London 352

London Corresponding Society 352
Gabriel Bonnot de Mably 361
James Madison 362
magic 364
Manchester Literary and Philosophical Society 367
Maria Theresa of Austria 371
Jean-François Marmontel 373
materialism 375
Pierre-Louis Moreau de Maupertuis 378
mechanical philosophy 380
medicine 382
mercantilism 387
Louis-Sébastien Mercier 387–388
Marin Mersenne 388, 389
millenarianism 393
Mississippi Bubble 394, 395
Montesquieu 397, 399
Jacque-Étienne and Michel-Joseph Montgolfier 400
Abbé Morelly 404
Moscow 404
museums 408
Pieter van Musschenbroek 411
natural rights 416
Jacques Necker 418, 419
Suzanne Necker 419
novel 431
opera 436, 437
Thomas Paine 442, 443
partitions of Poland 447
Persian Letters 448, 449
phlogiston theory 452
Physiocrats 453, 454
Piedmont 456
François-André-Adrien Pluquet 459
politeness 460
political theory 461
marquise de Pompadour 464
pornography 467, 468
Richard Price 471
property 476
prostitution 477
Protestantism 478
Prussia 479
psychology 480
public health 483
publishing 484
race 493
radical Enlightenment 494
rationalism 496
Guillaume-Thomas-François de Raynal 497
reason 498
René-Antoine Ferchault de Réaumur 499
Johann Christian Reil 501
religion 502
Republic of Letters 505
revolution 506, 507
rights 512
Victor de Riqueti 394
Maximilien Robespierre 515–516
rococo 517
Roman Catholicism 519, 521
romanticism 521
Rosicrucians 523
Jean-Jacques Rousseau 525
Benjamin Rush 528
Saint-Germain 530
Louis-Antoine-Léon de Saint-Just 530
Claude-Henri de Saint-Simon 532
Savoy 533
science 539
scientific academies 540
Scotland 543
secret societies 544
sensibility 548
serfdom 551

Seven Years' War 552
Sèvres 552
Richard Brinsley Sheridan 553
Siècle de Louis XIV 554
siècle des lumières 554
Richard Simon 556
slavery 557
Social Contract 559
social institutions 561
Jacques-Germain Soufflot 563
South Sea Bubble 564
South Sea Company 564
Spain 565
Philipp Jakob Spener 567
The Spirit of Laws 569
Madame de Staël 570
statistics 573
style galant 576
Johann Peter Süssmilch 578
Emanuel Swedenborg 579
Switzerland 582
technology and instrumentation 586
Benjamin Thompson 528
toleration 594
Toussaint Louverture 596, 597
A Treatise of Human Nature 598
Sarah Trimmer 599
universities 606
utility 607
Pietro Verri 611
Constantin François Chasseboeuf Volney 617
Voltaire 618
voyages of discovery 620, 622
Horace Walpole 623
George Washington 625
John Wilkes 633
Mary Wollstonecraft 636
women and the Enlightenment 637
Arthur Young 640
Johann Georg Zimmermann 641
Francke, August Hermann 170, 204, 255, 457, 567, 590
Frankfurt 204
Johann Wolfgang von Goethe 235
Friedrich Heinrich Jacobi 302
Jews and Judaism 310
Lutheranism 359
Le Nozze di Figaro 432
Pietism 456
publishing 485
Philipp Jakob Spener 567
Georg Philipp Telemann 587
Voltaire 619
Franklin, Benjamin xv c, 204–206, 205
John Adams 5
American Philosophical Society 13
American Revolution 14
automata 30
Torbern Olof Bergman 50
Jean-Pierre-François Blanchard 60
cosmopolitanism 130
Declaration of Independence 141
deism 148
Gaetano Filangieri 197
Freemasons 211
Anne-Catherine Helvétius 266
Historical and Critical Dictionary 271
Jan Ingen-Housz 298, 299
John Jay 307
Lunar Society of Birmingham 358
Gabriel Bonnot de Mably 361
Madrid 363
Cotton Mather 377
Franz Anton Mesmer 389

Jean-Antoine Nollet 428
Thomas Paine 442
Philadelphia 451
Richard Price 470
Republic of Letters 505
revolution 506
David Rittenhouse 514
scientific academies 541
Scientific Revolution 543
secret societies 545
subtle fluids 577
utility 607
George Washington 625
Frederick II (the Great) of
   Prussia xv c, 206–208
   absolutism 3
   Jean Le Rond d'Alembert 12
   Francesco Algarotti 12
   Jean-Baptiste de Boyer Argens
     21
   René-Lous de Voyer de Paulmy
     Argenson 21
   Carl Philipp Emanuel Bach 32
   Johann Sebastian Bach 35
   Torbern Olof Bergman 51
   Berlin 52
   Berlin Academy 52
   Brandenburg 72
   bureaucracy 77
   cameralism 87
   Candide 89
   capital punishment 94
   Giovanni Giacomo Casanova
     96
   Catherine II 96
   Charles III of Spain 101
   class and rank 114
   Clement XIV 118
   Diplomatic Revolution of 1756
     160, 161
   education 171
   enlightened despotism 155
   enlightened monarchs 395
   Eugène of Savoy 189
   Leonhard Euler 190
   August Hermann Francke 204
   Freemasons 210
   Élie-Cathérine Fréron 216
   Gustav III of Sweden 250
   Johann Georg Hamann 257
   Hapsburg Empire 262
   Haskalah 263
   Claude-Adrien Helvétius 267
   Historical and Critical
     Dictionary 271
   Jesuits 310
   Joseph II of Austria 313, 314
   Immanuel Kant 318
   Karl-August 320
   Karl Wilhelm Ferdinand 321
   Friedrich Gottlieb Klopstock
     325
   Julien Offray de La Mettrie
     330
   Louis XV of France 356
   Maria Theresa of Austria 371
   materialism 375
   Pierre-Louis Moreau de
     Maupertuis 379
   Meissen works 384
   Moses Mendelssohn 384
   neoclassicism 421
   partitions of Poland 447
   philosopher-king 451,
     451–452
   Physiocrats 454
   piano 455
   Pietism 457
   progress 476
   Prussia 479, 480
   Guillaume-Thomas-François
     de Raynal 497
   religion 504
   Republic of Letters 505
   revolution 507
   Roman Catholicism 521

scientific academies 540
separation of church and state
   550
Seven Years' War 552
Johann Peter Süssmilch 578
University of Halle 255
Francis Adrian Van der Kemp
   608
Voltaire 619
War of the Austrian Succession
   624
Johann Georg Zimmermann
   641
freedom 208–209
   aesthetics 8
   Aufklärung 28
   capital punishment 94
   civil society 111
   Samuel Clarke 113
   Declaration of the Rights of
     Man 143
   Dictionnaire philosophique 158
   England 178
   Johann Georg Adam Forster
     199
   genius 226
   Edward Gibbon 232
   William Godwin 235
   Johann Wolfgang von Goethe
     236
   David Hartley 263
   Johann Gottfried Herder 268
   The History of the Decline and
     Fall of the Roman Empire 144
   individualism 296
   Friedrich Heinrich Jacobi 303
   Jansenism 305
   Thomas Jefferson 308
   Immanuel Kant 318
   Laokoon 334
   Gottfried Wilhelm Leibniz 340
   Letters on Toleration 343
   literature 348
   John Locke 350
   Louis XVI of France 357
   Lutheranism 359
   Nicolas de Malebranche 366
   Montesquieu 398
   moral philosophy 400
   Justus Möser 405
   Johannes von Müller 406
   natural law 414
   natural rights 415
   nature 418
   political theory 461
   Richard Price 470
   progress 476
   religion 504
   rights 511
   Jean-Jacques Rousseau 526
   Johann Friedrich Schiller 534
   separation of church and state
     550
   separation of powers 550
   serfdom 551
   slavery 556
   Social Contract 559
   The Sorrows of Young Werther
     563
   Benedict de Spinoza 568–569
   The Spirit of Laws 570
   Madame de Staël 570
   Sturm und Drang 576
   Two Treatises of Government
     603
   United Provinces of
     Netherlands 604
   United States of America 606
   Giovan Battista Vico 612
   Voltaire 620
   Wilhelm Tell 632
   John Wilkes 633
   Mary Wollstonecraft 636
Freemasons 209–211, 210
   American Revolution 14
   Aufklärung 27

Austria 29
   Carl Friedrich Bahrdt 37
   Jean-Pierre-François Blanchard
     60
   Alessandro Cagliostro 83
   Giovanni Giacomo Casanova
     96
   Catherine II 98
   deism 148
   John Theophilus Desaguliers
     151
   education 170
   Benjamin Franklin 206
   Claude-Adrien Helvétius 267
   Bavarian Illuminati 292
   Jacobins 303
   Joseph II of Austria 314
   Joseph de Lalande 328
   Gotthold Ephraim Lessing 342
   The Magic Flute 365
   Franz Anton Mesmer 389
   Montesquieu 398
   Wolfgang Amadeus Mozart
     406
   perfectibility 447
   physico-theology 453
   reason 499
   Rosicrucians 524
   comte de Saint-Germain 530
   secret societies 544
   Emmanuel-Joseph Sieyès 555
   slavery 557
   social institutions 561
   Josef von Sonnenfels 562
   Emanuel Swedenborg 579
   John Toland 593
   toleration 595
   Vienna 613
   Sir Christopher Wren 638
free trade 115, 131, 211–212,
   298, 453, 602, 624, 627
French Academy of Sciences
   212–213
   Marc-Pierre de Voyer
     Argenson 21
   Daniel Bernoulli 53
   biology 56
   Johann Friedrich Blumenbach
     61
   Hermann Boerhaave 63
   Charles Bonnet 65
   Théophile de Bordeu 66
   Louis-Antoine de Bougainville
     69
   Georges-Louis Leclerc Buffon
     75
   cartography 95
   Marie Condorcet 124
   Charles-Augustin de Coulomb
     132
   Michel de Crèvecoeur 134
   Louis-Jean-Marie Daubenton
     140
   Joseph-Nicolas Delisle 149
   Nicolas Desmarest 155
   England 178
   Bernard Le Bovier de
     Fontenelle 198
   Jean-Baptiste-Joseph Fourier
     200
   Franz Joseph Gall 221
   Stephen Hales 255
   Edmond Halley 256
   Joseph-Louis Lagrange 327
   Joseph de Lalande 328
   Jean-Baptiste-Pierre-Antoine de
     Monet de Lamarck 328
   Pierre-Simon Laplace 334
   Antoine-Laurent Lavoisier 335
   Antoni van Leeuwenhoek 337
   Carolus Linnaeus 346
   Pierre-Louis Moreau de
     Maupertuis 378
   Montesquieu 399
   Jacques-Étienne and Michel-
     Joseph Montgolfier 400

Pieter van Musschenbroek 411
Jean-Antoine Nollet 428
phrenology 453
Jean-Jacques Rousseau 524
Royal Society of London 527
scientific academies 540
Emmanuel-Joseph Sieyès 555
social institutions 561
Jacques de Vaucanson 610
Alessandro Giuseppe Antonio
   Anastasio Volta 617
French Revolution x, xvii c,213,
   213–216, 214
   absolutism 3
   The Age of Reason 9
   American Revolution 14
   ancien régime 15
   aristocratic resurgence 22
   association movement 24
   Austrian Netherlands 29
   Marie-Antoinette 371–373
   François-Noel Babeuf 31
   Carl Friedrich Bahrdt 37
   Joseph Banks 37
   Joel Barlow 37
   Jean-Jacques Barthélemy 41
   Paul-Joseph Barthez 41
   Ludwig van Beethoven 46
   Belgium 48
   Claude-Louis Berthollet 54
   Jean-Pierre-François Blanchard
     60
   Bluestocking 61
   Louis-Antoine de Bougainville
     69
   Joseph Boulogne 71
   bureaucracy 77
   Edmund Burke 78
   Robert Burns 80
   Pierre-Jean-Georges Cabanis
     82
   Charles-Alexandre de Calonne
     85
   Calvinism 86
   Antonio Canova 90
   capital punishment 94
   Lazare Carnot 94
   Catherine II 98
   ceramic arts 100
   Sébastien-Roch-Nicholas
     Chamfort 100
   class and rank 115
   Marie Condorcet 124
   Sophie Cottin 131
   Charles-Augustin de Coulomb
     132
   Georges Cuvier 136
   Louis-Jean-Marie Daubenton
     139
   Jacques-Louis David 141
   Declaration of the Rights of
     Man 143
   Jacques Delille 148
   democracy 149
   Nicolas Desmarest 155
   diamond necklace scandal
     157
   Denis Diderot 158
   Diplomatic Revolution of 1756
     161
   Pierre-Samuel Dupont de
     Nemours 166
   Maria Edgeworth 169
   education 171
   England 179
   equality 186
   Gaetano Filangieri 197
   Johann Reinhold Forster 199
   Jean-Baptiste-Joseph Fourier
     200
   Jean-Honoré Fragonard 200
   freedom 209
   Freemasons 211
   French Academy of Sciences
     212
   Franz Joseph Gall 221

Gallicanism 222
Félicité de Genlis 228
Germany 230
Gobelins tapestry 234
Johann Wolfgang von Goethe
   237
grand tour 241
Henri Gregoire 245
Friedrich Melchior Grimm
   247
Guadeloupe 248
Haitian Revolution 252
Hapsburg Empire 262
Anne-Cathérine Helvétius 266
Johann Gottfried Herder
   268–269
honor 280
Jean-Antoine Houdon 280
Idéologie 292
Idéologues 292
Jan Ingen-Housz 299
Jacobins 303
Jardin des Plantes 306
Thomas Jefferson 308
Jews and Judaism 312
justice and the law 315
Immanuel Kant 317
Karl-August 321
Karl Wilhelm Ferdinand 321
Angelica Kauffman 322
Friedrich Gottlieb Klopstock
   325
Pierre de Laclos 326
Joseph-Louis Lagrange 327
Joseph de Lalande 328
Pierre-Simon Laplace 334
Antoine-Laurent Lavoisier 336
literacy 347
Louis XIV of France 355
Louis XVI of France 357–358
Lunar Society of Birmingham
   358
Gabriel Bonnot de Mably 361
Jean-Paul Marat 368–370
Maria Theresa of Austria 371
Jean-François Marmontel 374
Louis-Sébastien Mercier 387,
   388
millenarianism 393
Montesquieu 399
Johannes von Müller 406
museums 408
Jacques Necker 418
Le Nozze di Figaro 432
opera 437
Thomas Paine 443
Paris 445, 446
parlements 446, 447
Johann Heinrich Pestalozzi
   449
Poland 460
political theory 463
pornography 468
Richard Price 470
Joseph Priestley 471
property 476
prostitution 477
publishing 485–486
radical Enlightenment 494
René-Antoine Ferchault de
   Réaumur 499
Reflections on the Revolution in
   France 499
revolution 507
The Rights of Man 513
Roman Catholicism 521
Jean-Jacques Rousseau 526
Louis-Antoine-Léon de Saint-
   Just 530
Louis-Claude de Saint-Martin
   531
Claude-Henri de Saint-Simon
   532
Savoy 533
August Ludwig von Schlözer
   537

science of man 540
secret societies 545
separation of church and state 550
serfdom 551
Richard Brinsley Sheridan 553
Emmanuel-Joseph Sieyès 554–555
slavery 557
Social Contract 559
Jacques-Germain Soufflot 563
Mme de Staël 570
toleration 594
John Horne Tooke 596
Toussaint Louverture 596
Two Treatises of Government 603
United States of America 606
Élisabeth-Louise Vigée Lebrun 613
virtue 615
Constantin-François Chasseboeuf Volney 617
Voltaire 620
voyages of discovery 622
George Washington 625
Mary Wollstonecraft 636
women and the Enlightenment 638
Fréron, Élie-Catherine 216–217
Friedrich, Caspar David 217
Fuseli, Henry 60, 62, 217, 321, 577

G

Gainsborough, Thomas xv c, xvi c, 1, 218, 218–219, 223, 518, 523
Galiani, Ferdinando 101, 219, 219, 230, 293, 298, 300, 324, 373, 388, 585, 628, xvi c
Galilei, Galileo 219–221
  astronomy 25
  baroque style 38
  Copernican Revolution 128
  René Descartes 152
  Pierre Gassend 224
  hermeticism 269
  Thomas Hobbes 273
  Johannes Kepler 323
  Gottfried Wilhelm Leibniz 339
  mathematics and mechanics 375, 376
  mechanical philosophy 380
  medicine 381
  Marin Mersenne 388, 389
  microscope 391
  Principia mathematica 472
  religion 502
  revolution 506
  On the Revolutions of the Heavenly Spheres 435
  scientific method 541
  Scientific Revolution 542–543
Gall, Franz Joseph 29, 57, 221–222, 452–453
Gallicanism 222
Galvani, Luigi 222, 222–223, 617
gardens 306. *See also* English garden
Garrick, David 79, 133, 223, 238, 312, 345, 403, 477, 508, 557, 589
Garve, Christian 196, 223, 386, 535
Gassend, Pierre 223–224
  Epicurean philosophy 183
  Galileo Galilei 220
  Thomas Hobbes 273
  Gottfried Wilhelm Leibniz 339
  John Locke 349
  Louis XIV of France 355
  mathematics and mechanics 376

mechanical philosophy 380
pyrrhonism 488
scientific academies 540
scientific method 541
Scientific Revolution 542
skepticism 556
Gatterer, Johann Christoph 224, 240, 268, 272, 537, 613
Gay, John 47, 126, 224–225, 250, 313, 437, 467, 589, 624
generation 225. *See also* preformation theory
  animalculism 18
  biology 56
  Johann Friedrich Blumenbach 62
  Charles Bonnet 64
  Georges-Louis Leclerc Buffon 75
  epigenesis 183–184
  Albrecht von Haller 255
  Jardin des Plantes 306
  Antoni van Leeuwenhoek 337
  Pierre-Louis Moreau de Maupertuis 379
  microscope 391
  Alexander Monro 396
  John Turberville Needham 419
  preformation theory 469–470
  Lazzaro Spallanzani 565, 566
  Abraham Trembley 599
  vitalism 616
Geneva 225–226
genius 226–228, 227
  aesthetics 7
  William Blake 60
  Denis Diderot 160
  enthusiasm 183
  epistemology 185
  Faust 193
  Johann Wolfgang von Goethe 235, 236
  Johann Gottfried Herder 268
  intuition and imagination 300
  Friedrich Heinrich Jacobi 302
  literature 348
  Nicolas de Malebranche 366
  Wolfgang Amadeus Mozart 406
  progress 475
  pyrrhonism 488
  Quakers 489
  romanticism 521
  earl of Shaftesbury 553
  Sturm und Drang 576
  Giovan Battista Vico 612
Genlis, Félicité de 228, 599
Genovesi, Antonio 101, 219, 228, 300, 324, 585
geocentric 146, 198, 228–229, 266, 587
Geoffrin, Marie-Thérèse Rodet, Madame 52, 99, 144, 184, 198, 229, 229–230, 342, 373, 466, 505, 560
Germany x, 230
  Berlin 51–52
  Berlin Academy 52
  biology 56
  Giovanni Giacomo Casanova 96
  China 108
  chinoiserie 109
  civil society 111
  classicism 115
  Cologne 120
  colonialism 122
  cosmopolitanism 130
  Michel de Crèvecoeur 134
  demography 150
  René Descartes 152
  Daniel Gabriel Fahrenheit 192
  Faust 193
  Adam Ferguson 196
  Johann Reinhold Forster 199

August Hermann Francke 204
Frankfurt 204
Caspar David Friedrich 217
Christian Garve 223
genius 226
Gobelins tapestry 234
Johann Wolfgang von Goethe 235–238
Johann Christoph Gottsched 240–241
Friedrich Melchior Grimm 247
Albrecht von Haller 256
Johann Gottfried Herder 267
Holy Roman Empire 278
Jean-Antoine Houdon 280
David Hume 286
Illuministi 293
Friedrich Heinrich Jacobi 303
Jansenism 305
Jews and Judaism 310
Immanuel Kant 317
Johannes Kepler 323
Friedrich Gottlieb Klopstock 324, 325
landscapes 331
Gotthold Ephraim Lessing 343
Georg Christoph Lichtenberg 345
Mikhail Vasilivich Lomonosov 351
Lutheranism 358, 359
Mannheim school 368
Meissen works 383–384
Moses Mendelssohn 384–386
Franz Anton Mesmer 389
millenarianism 393
Montesquieu 399
Justus Möser 405
Johann Lorenz von Mosheim 405
Munich 407
Balthasar Neumann 422
Christoph Friedrich Nicolai 426
Carsten Niebuhr 427
novel 431
perfectibility 448
Philadelphia 451
publishing 484
race 492
Johann Christian Reil 501
Republic of Letters 505
rococo 518
romanticism 521
Benjamin Rush 528
Johann Friedrich Schiller 534
August Ludwig von Schlözer 537
earl of Shaftesbury 553
slavery 556
Philipp Jakob Spener 567
Benedict de Spinoza 569
Carl Stamitz 572
statistics 572
Emanuel Swedenborg 579
theater 588
Benjamin Thompson 528
Giovanni Battista Tiepolo 591
voyages of discovery 620
Christoph Martin Wieland 631
Johann Joachim Winckelmann 634
women and the Enlightenment 637
Arthur Young 640
Giannone, Pietro 111, 230–231, 301, 398
Gibbon, Edward xvi c, 24, 130, 144, 195, 209, 231, 231–232, 271, 272, 348, 398, 442
Gilbert, Nicolas-Joseph-Laurent 232
Glorious Revolution x, xiv c, 232
  Anglicans 17
  Aphra Behn 48

Sir William Blackstone 58
Edmund Burke 78
capitalism 93
Daniel Defoe 145
John Dryden 165
England 178
David Hume 286
Jacobites 304
Jews and Judaism 312
John Locke 349
political theory 462
Richard Price 471
radical Enlightenment 494
Reflections on the Revolution in France 499
religion 502
Scotland 544
separation of powers 550
toleration 594
Two Treatises of Government 603
Waldensians 623
William III and Mary II 633
Gluck, Christoph Willibald xvi c, 232–233
  Austria 29
  Marie-Antoinette d'Autriche 371
  Battle of the Buffoons 43
  Ranieri de'Calzabigi 87
  clarinet 112
  empfindsamer Stil 174
  Jean-Antoine Houdon 280
  Jean-François Marmontel 374
  Milan 392
  music 410
  neoclassicism 421
  opera 437
  Orfeo ed Eurydice 438–439
  Vienna 613
  viola 614
Gobelins tapestry 54, 68, 233–234, 440
Godwin, William xvi c, 60, 169, 209, 234–235, 263, 367, 494, 512, 513, 596
Goethe, Johann Wolfgang von xvi c, xvii c, 235, 235–238
  affinity chemistry 9
  alchemy 10
  Gottfried Arnold 24
  Aufklärung 28
  Johann Sebastian Bach 35
  Bildung 56
  George Gordon Byron 81
  Daniel Niklaus Chodowiecki 109
  Confessions 126
  Faust 192–193
  Johann Georg Adam Forster 199
  Frankfurt 204
  freedom 209
  Caspar David Friedrich 217
  genius 226
  Germany 230
  Johann Georg Hamann 256
  hermeticism 270
  Wilhelm von Humboldt 283
  Bavarian Illuminati 293
  Friedrich Heinrich Jacobi 302
  Karl-August 320
  Angelica Kauffman 322
  Friedrich Gottlieb Klopstock 325
  landscapes 331
  Laokoon 334
  literature 348
  Lutheranism 359
  James Macpherson 362
  Justus Möser 405
  neoclassicism 421
  Christoph Friedrich Nicolai 426
  novel 431
  perfectibility 448

progress 475
Louis-Claude de Saint-Martin 531
Johann Friedrich Schiller 534
The Sorrows of Young Werther 562–563
Benedict de Spinoza 569
Sturm und Drang 576
vitalism 616
Abraham Gottlob Werner 629
Christoph Martin Wieland 631
Johann Joachim Winckelmann 634
Goldoni, Carlo 238, 301, 353, 589, 611
Goldsmith, Oliver xvi c, 238–239, 248, 313, 341, 508, 514, 527, 553–554, 589, 611
Gothic revival 134, 239, 239, 243
Gothic romance 239, 239–240, 348, 470, 577, 624
Göttingen, University of 240
  Aufklärung 27
  biology 57
  Johann Friedrich Blumenbach 61
  Hermann Boerhaave 63
  Johann Christoph Gatterer 224
  Johann Wolfgang von Goethe 235
  Albrecht von Haller 256
  history 272
  Alexander von Humboldt 282
  Wilhelm von Humboldt 283
  Bavarian Illuminati 293
  Georg Christoph Lichtenberg 344
  medicine 382, 383
  Johann David Michaelis 390
  Johann Lorenz von Mosheim 405
  Johannes von Müller 406
  Carsten Niebuhr 427
  Johann Christian Reil 500
  Republic of Letters 505
  August Ludwig von Schlözer 537
  slavery 557
  universities 607
  University of Halle 255
  vitalism 616
  Friedrich August Wolf 634
  Johann Georg Zimmermann 641
Gottsched, Johann Christoph 8, 52, 62, 72, 115, 240–241, 247, 271, 348, 562, 582
Gournay, Jacques-Claude-Marie-Vincent de 241, 453, 490, 602, 627
Goya y Lucientes, Francisco José de xvii c, 102, 241–242, 363, 565
grand tour 242–243
Henry St. John Bolingbroke 63
James Boswell 68
Georges-Louis Leclerc Buffon 75
Charles Burney 79
George Gordon Byron 81
Friedrich Rudolf Ludwig Canitz 90
Catherine II 98
Edward Gibbon 231
Johann Wolfgang von Goethe 236
Oliver Goldsmith 238
Thomas Gray 243
George Frederick Handel 260
Illuministi 294
Italy 301
Wenzel Anton von Kaunitz 322

Alexander Monro 396
John Turberville Needham
419
La Nouvelle Héloïse 429
Peter I 450
picturesque 455–456
Republic of Letters 504
Joshua Reynolds 508
Rome 523
Adam Smith 557
Venice 610
Horace Walpole 623
Nicolaus Ludwig Zinzendorf
642
Gravesande, Willem Jacob's 88,
151, 192, **243**, 428
Gray, Thomas 60, 226, 239,
243–244, 623, 629
Great Awakening 171–172, **244**,
393, 504
great chain of being **244**
Johann Friedrich Blumenbach
61–62
Charles Bonnet 65
Georges Cuvier 136
degeneration 146
Dictionnaire philosophique 158
Gottfried Wilhelm Leibniz
339
microscope 391
John Turberville Needham
420
race 492
Emanuel Swedenborg 579
Gregoire, Henri Abbé *245*,
245–246, 494
Greuze, Jean-Baptiste xv c, 160,
230, *246–247*, *247*, 276, 547
Grimm, Friedrich Melchior,
baron von 126, 155, 157, 159,
184, **247**, 266, 342, 373, 505
Grub Street 78, 238, **248**, 313,
581
Guadeloupe 71, **248–249**, *249*,
254
Guardi, Francesco 89, *249–250*,
591, 611
Gulliver's Travels (Jonathan
Swift) *250*, 348, 430, 581
Gustav III of Sweden 230,
250–251, 374, 395, 578

H

Hadley, John **252**
Haitian Revolution xvii c, 71,
252–254, *253*, 596–597
Hales, Stephen 57, 103,
254–255
Halle, University of **255**
Johan Christoph Adelung 6
Aufklärung 27
Carl Friedrich Bahrdt 37
biology 57
cameralism 87
Christian Garve 223
George Frederick Handel 259
Friedrich Hoffmann 275
medicine 380
Johann David Michaelis 390
Friedrich Christoph Oetinger
433
Pietism 457
Johann Christian Reil 500
Hermann Samuel Reimarus
501
Johann Salomo Semler 546
Philipp Jakob Spener 567
Georg Ernst Stahl 571
Johann Peter Süssmilch
577–578
Christian Thomasius 590
universities 607
University of Göttingen 240
Johann Joachim Winckelmann
634
Friedrich August Wolf 634

Christian Wolff 635
Nicolaus Ludwig Zinzendor
642
Haller, Albrecht von xv c,
255–256
Paul-Joseph Barthez 42
Johann Friedrich Blumenbach
61
Hermann Boerhaave 63
Théophile de Bordeu 66
Denis Diderot 159
epigenesis 184
generation 225
Julien Offray de La Mettrie
330
Carolus Linnaeus 345
medicine 380, 382
preformation theory 469
Republic of Letters 505
Johann Friedrich Schiller 535
scientific academies 541
Lazzaro Spallanzani 566
Switzerland 582
University of Göttingen 240
Robert Whytt 630
Johann Georg Zimmermann
641
Halley, Edmond xiv c, 26, 71,
149, **256**, 425, 472, 527, 597
Hamann, Johann Georg
256–258, 267, 302, 386, 577
Hamilton, Alexander ix, 5,
258–259, 307, 308, 363, 399,
606, 625
Hamilton, Sir William **259**, 359,
360
Handel, George Frederick xiv c,
xv c, **259–260**, *260*
Karl Friedrich Abel 1
Wilhelm Friedemann Bach 35
baroque style 40
Arcangelo Corelli 130
Germany 230
Christoph Willibald Gluck
233
Franz Joseph Haydn 265
London 352
music 408
prostitution 477
Giuseppe Domenico Scarlatti
533
Carl Stamitz 572
Gottfried Bernhard Swieten
580
theater 588
Venice 611
happiness **261**
Declaration of Independence
142
Epicurean philosophy 183
Pierre Gassend 224
Thomas Jefferson 308
Immanuel Kant 319
moral philosophy 403
Lodovico Antonio Muratori
408
natural law 414
natural rights 415
nature 418
politeness 460
political theory 462
rights 511
Adam Smith 558
technology and instrumentation 586
United States Bill of Rights
605
United States of America 606
Hapsburg Empire xv c, xvi c,
261–262
anticlericalism 20
Austria 28
baroque style 39
Ludwig van Beethoven 46
Budapest 74
bureaucracy 76

dynastic states 166
education 171
enlightened absolutism 3
Miklós József Esterházy 189
Eugène of Savoy 190
Frederick II 207
French Revolution 213
Germany 230
Haskalah 263
Johann Gottfried Herder 268
Holy Roman Empire 278
Hungary 287
Italy 301
Joseph II of Austria 313
literacy 347
Maria Theresa of Austria
370–371
medicine 383
mercantilism 387
Montesquieu 398
Johannes von Müller 406
Peter I 450
Pietism 457
Prussia 479
religion 502
rococo 518
serfdom 551
Josef von Sonnenfels 562
Spain 565
toleration 594
War of the Austrian Succession
624
Wealth of Nations 628
Hargreaves, James xvi c, **262**,
298
Harrison, John 95, **262**, 353, 622
Hartley, David 157, 182,
262–263, 284, 351, 402, 472,
480, 481, 599
Haskalah (Jewish
Enlightenment) **263**, 310–312,
385, 413, 503. *See also*
Enlightenment
Hastings, Warren **263–264**
Haydn, Franz Joseph xvii, c,
264–265
Austria 29
Carl Philipp Emanuel Bach 32
Ludwig van Beethoven 46
Joseph Boulogne 71
Muzio Clementi 119
The Creation 134
empfindsamer Stil 174
Miklós József Esterházy 189
Freemasons 210
Mannheim school 368
music 409
neoclassicism 421
piano 455
Gottfried Bernhard Swieten
580
symphony orchestra 583
Vienna 613
viola 614
Haywood, Eliza xiv c, **265–266**,
280, 430, 509
heliocentric **266**
astronomy 25
Copernican Revolution
127–128
Nicolaus Copernicus 129
deism 146
John Theophilus Desaguliers
151
Bernard Le Bovier de
Fontenelle 198
Galileo Galilei 219
Pierre Gassend 224
geocentric 229
John Hadley 252
Johannes Kepler 323
orrery 440
*On the Revolutions of the
Heavenly Spheres* 433, 434
Scientific Revolution 542
telescope 587

Helvétius, Anne-Cathérine de
Ligniville D'Autricourt,
Madame 82, 100, **266**,
266–267, 617
Helvétius, Claude-Adrien xv c,
266–267
aesthetics 8
atheism 26
marchese di Beccaria 46
Berlin Academy 52
Nicolas-Antoine Boulanger 70
capital punishment 94
Clement XIII 118
democracy 149
education 170
Encyclopédie 176
enlightened despotism 155
enthusiasm 183
Epicurean philosophy 183
freedom 209
French Academy of Sciences
212
genius 227
Marie-Thérèse Rodet Geoffrin
230
Anne-Cathérine Helvétius 266
Bavarian Illuminati 293
Joseph de Lalande 328
Pierre de Marivaux 373
materialism 375
Montesquieu 399
moral philosophy 402
orientalism 439
perfectibility 447, 448
political theory 462
progress 475
psychology 480, 481
radical Enlightenment 494
Guillaume-Thomas-François
de Raynal 497
religion 502
Benedict de Spinoza 569
Herder, Johann Gottfried xvi c,
267–269, *268*
aesthetics 7
Nicolas-Antoine Boulanger 70
Josef Dobrovský 164
Adam Ferguson 196
freedom 209
Germany 230
Johann Wolfgang von Goethe
235
Johann Georg Hamann 256
history 272
Bavarian Illuminati 293
intuition and imagination 300
Friedrich Heinrich Jacobi 302
Karl-August 320
language 332, 333
Moses Mendelssohn 386
Johann David Michaelis 390
Montesquieu 399
Justus Möser 405
race 492
Johann Friedrich Schiller 535
August Ludwig von Schlözer
537
Benedict de Spinoza 569
Madame de Staël 571
Sturm und Drang 576
sublime 577
Giovan Battista Vico 613
vitalism 616
Christoph Martin Wieland 631
hermeticism **269–270**, 544
Herschel, William 26, **270**, 358,
527, 587
Hildebrandt, Johann Lukas von
190, **270**, 422, 613
Histoire des deux Indes
(Guillaume Raynal) 159, 253,
270–271, 596
Historical and Critical Dictionary
(Pierre Bayle) 44, 87, 147, 182,
250, **271**, 285, 426, 487, 556,
569, 631

history 271–273
anthropology 19
Gottfried Arnold 24
biblical criticism 54
Bildung 56
Johann Friedrich Blumenbach
62
Henry St. John Bolingbroke 64
Charles Bonnet 65
Jacques-Bénigne Bossuet 68
Charles Burney 79
degeneration 146
*Discourse on the Origins of
Inequality* 162
Dissenters 163
Jean-Baptiste Du Bos 165
empiricism 174
Faust 193
Adam Ferguson 196
Bernard Le Bovier de
Fontenelle 198
Johann Christoph Gatterer 224
Pietro Giannone 231
Edward Gibbon 231–232
Gothic revival 239
Johann Georg Hamann 257
Johann Gottfried Herder 267,
268
*The History of the Decline and
Fall of the Roman Empire* 144
David Hume 285
Illuministi 293
Jan Ingen-Housz 298
Jean-Auguste-Dominique
Ingres 299
intuition and imagination 299,
300
Italy 300
Immanuel Kant 320
Angelica Kauffman 321
Gottfried Wilhelm Leibniz 339
Gabriel Bonnot de Mably 361
James Madison 362
Thomas Robert Malthus 367
Milan 392
John Millar 392
Montesquieu 397
Johannes von Müller 406
Lodovico Antonio Muratori
408
John Turberville Needham 420
Isaac Newton 425
François-André-Adrien
Pluquet 459
Antoine-François Prévost 470
Joseph Priestley 472
progress 474
Protestantism 478
relations 502
William Robertson **514–515**
romanticism 521
Scotland 544
Johann Salomo Semler 546
Siècle de Louis XIV 554
Richard Simon 555
Philipp Jakob Spener 567
Benedict de Spinoza 569
The Spirit of Laws 569
John Toland 593
Two Treatises of Government
603
universities 607
University of Göttingen 240
Giovan Battista Vico 612
vitalism 616
Constantin-François
Chasseboeuf Volney 617
Voltaire 618
Friedrich August Wolf 635
*History of the Decline and Fall of
the Roman Empire, The* (Edward
Gibbon) 144, 231, 398
Hobbes, Thomas 273, **273–275**
aesthetics 7
Aphra Behn 47
civil society 111

Declaration of Independence 142

deism 147

England 178

Epicurean philosophy 183

equality 186

freedom 209

Pierre Gassend 223

Claude-Adrien Helvétius 267

John Jay 306

Gottfried Wilhelm Leibniz 339

John Locke 350

moral philosophy 401, 402

natural rights 416

noble savage 428

political theory 461, 462

Samuel Pufendorf 487

radical Enlightenment 494

rights 511, 512

Scientific Revolution 542

sentimental fiction 548

Social Contract 559

Philipp Jakob Spener 567

Benedict de Spinoza 569

The Spirit of Laws 570

technology and instrumentation 586

Two Treatises of Government 603

United Provinces of Netherlands 605

virtue 614

Hoffmann, Friedrich 63, **275**, 291, 380, 452

Hogarth, William xv *c*, 47, 109, 135, 164, 183, 223, 246, **275–276**, *276*, 345, 353, 477, 495, 518, 599

Holbach, Paul-Henri Thiry d' xvi *c*, **276–278**, *277*

anthropology 19

atheism 26

Berlin Academy 52

Nicolas-Antoine Boulanger 70

capital punishment 94

cosmopolitanism 130

deism 148

Dialogues Concerning Natural Religion 157

Denis Diderot 159

encyclopedists 177

enlightened despotism 155

enthusiasm 183

Adam Ferguson 196

Marie-Thérèse Rodet Geoffrin 230

Friedrich Melchior Grimm 247

Anne-Cathérine Helvétius 266

Bavarian Illuminati 293

Julie-Jeanne-Eléonore de Lespinasse 342

Pierre de Marivaux 373

materialism 375

moral philosophy 402

radical Enlightenment 494

Guillaume Thomas-François de Raynal 497

Republic of Letters 505

social institutions 560

Giovan Battista Vico 613

Constantin François Chasseboeuf Volney 617

Holy Roman Empire **278**

Aufklärung 27

Bernardo Bellotto 48

Brandenburg 72

Calvinism 85

Camisards 88

class and rank 114

Cologne 120

democracy 149

Denmark 150

education 171

France 201

Frankfurt 204

French Revolution 215

Germany 230

Johann Wolfgang von Goethe 235

Jacques-Claude-Marie-Vincent de Gournay 241

grand tour 241

Friedrich Melchior Grimm 247

Hapsburg Empire 261

Haskalah 263

Jansenism 306

Joseph II of Austria 313

justice and the law 315

Karl-August 320

Johannes Kepler 323

Gottfried Wilhelm Leibniz 338

literature 348

Louis XIV of France 354

Lutheranism 358

Maria Theresa of Austria 370

Milan 392

Montesquieu 398

moral philosophy 402

Johannes von Müller 406

Pieter van Musschenbroek 411

Balthasar Neumann 422

phlogiston theory 452

Poland 459

political theory 461

Protestantism 478

Prussia 479

Samuel Pufendorf 487

religion 502

rococo 518

Roman Catholicism 519

Rome 522

Rosicrucians 523

Scotland 544

separation of church and state 549–550

social institutions 560

Spain 565

Christian Thomasius 589

Benjamin Thompson 528

universities 607

University of Göttingen 240

Vienna 613

homosexuality 211, **278–279**

honor 279–280

Houdon, Jean-Antoine xvi *c*, 211, 266, 280–281, *281*, 421

Huguenots xiv *c*, 281–282

Amsterdam 14

Pierre Bayle 44

Berlin 51

Calvinism 85

Camisards 88

Marie Condorcet 124

John Theophilus Desaguliers 151

François Fénelon 194

France 201

freedom 208

David Garrick 223

Geneva 225

Louis XIV of France 355

Montesquieu 398

Persian Letters 449

Protestantism 478

religion 502

separation of church and state 550

toleration 594

human nature ix

Candide 89

civil society 111

education 170

An Enquiry Concerning Human Understanding 182

Johann Georg Hamann 257

Thomas Hobbes 274

Bernard Mandeville 367

paganism 441

Humboldt, Alexander von 240, **282–283**, 283, 302, 344, 500, 536, 622

Humboldt, Wilhelm von 164, 282, **283–284**, 302, 389, 536

Hume, David ix, x, xv *c*, xvi *c*, *284*, **284–287**

John Adams 5

aesthetics 7, 9

American Revolution 14

anthropology 19

marchese di Beccaria 46

Jeremy Bentham 49, 50

Joseph Black 57

Nicolas-Antoine Boulanger 70

Charles de Brosses 73

Charles Burney 79

civil society 111

Confessions 126

cosmopolitanism 130

René Descartes 154

Dialogues Concerning Natural Religion 156–157

Dictionnaire philosophique 158

Edinburgh 170

An Enquiry Concerning Human Understanding **182**

enthusiasm 182–183

epistemology 185

freedom 209

free trade 211

Marie-Thérèse Rodet Geoffrin 230

Edward Gibbon 231

Johann Gottfried Herder 268

Historical and Critical Dictionary 271

history 272

The History of the Decline and Fall of the Roman Empire 144

Paul-Henri Thiry d'Holbach 277

John Jay 306

justice and the law 315

Immanuel Kant 318

landscapes 330

language 332

John Locke 351

James Macpherson 362

Pierre de Marivaux 373

Moses Mendelssohn 386

John Millar 392

moral philosophy 402

optimism 438

paganism 442

progress 475

psychology 480

pyrrhonism 487, 488

race 492

reason 498

Thomas Reid 500

Republic of Letters 505

rights 512

Jean-Jacques Rousseau 525

Royal Society of Edinburgh 527

science of man 540

Scotland 544

skepticism 556

Adam Smith 557, 558

superstition 577

sympathy 582

John Tillotson 592

A Treatise of Human Nature **598–599**

Giovan Battista Vico 613

Hungary **287**

Austria 29

Budapest 74

Calvinism 85

dynastic states 166

Miklós József Esterházy 189

Hapsburg Empire 261

Jews and Judaism 312

Montesquieu 398

Poland 459

serfdom 551

Hunter, John 57, 89, 184, **287–288**, 288, 298, 309, 382, 395–396, 544, 566

Hunter, William 139, 184, 287, **288**, 298

Huntsman, Benjamin 288

Hutcheson, Francis 7, 14, 111, 284, **288–289**, *289*, 402, 448, 511, 544, 558, 627

Hutton, James 57, 170, **289–290**

I

iatrochemistry 10, 56, 63, 275, 288, 291, **291**, 571

iatromechanics 56, 63, 255, 275, **291**, 419, 571, 615

Idéologie 156, **292**

Idéologues **292**

Pierre-Jean-Georges Cabanis 82

Marie Condorcet 125

Antoine-Louis-Claude Destutt de Tracy 156

education 170

empiricism 174

French Academy of Sciences 213

Franz Joseph Gall 221

Idéologie 292

Montesquieu 399

perfectibility 448

progress 475

reason 498

science of man 540

Constantin-François Chasseboeuf Volney 617

Illuminati, Bavarian **292–293**

Aufklärung 27

Austria 29

Carl Friedrich Bahrdt 37

Freemasons 210

Joseph II of Austria 314

perfectibility 448

reason 499

Rosicrucians 524

secret societies 544, 545

social institutions 561

Josef von Sonnenfels 562

Illuministi 28, 197, **293–294**, 561

imperialism *294*, **294–296**, 507

Inchbald, Elizabeth 296

individualism 296

cosmopolitanism 131

René Descartes 153

Johann Georg Hamann 257

Industrial Revolution 298

John Locke 350

music 408

natural rights 415

political theory 462

romanticism 521

Adam Smith 558

Social Contract 560

Sturm und Drang 576

Industrial Revolution **296–298**, *297*

Matthew Boulton 71

civil society 111

Henry Cort 130

Abraham Darby 138

England 178

James Hargreaves 262

Methodism 390

Thomas Newcomen 422

New Lanark 422

power loom **469**

revolution 507

Scotland 544

Adam Smith 558

spinning jenny 567

spinning mule **567–568**

steam engine 574

threshing machine 590, **591**

Jethro Tull 601

James Watt **626**

Josiah Wedgwood 628

Joseph Wright 639

Arthur Young 640

Ingen-Housz, Jan **298–299**, 299, 309, 580

Ingres, Jean-Auguste-Dominique 141, **299**, 421

inoculation 299

Jean Le Rond d'Alembert 12

Jan Ingen-Housz 298

Edward Jenner 309

Cotton Mather 377

medicine 383

public health 482

Gerard van Swieten 580

Mary Wortley 397

intuition and imagination **299–300**

aesthetics 7

Aufklärung 27

enthusiasm 183

epistemology 185

genius 226

Johann Christoph Gottsched 241

Johann Georg Hamann 257

Johann Gottfried Herder 268

literature 348

progress 475

psychology 480

pyrrhonism 488

reason 498

romanticism 521

earl of Shaftesbury 553

Italy x, **300–301**. *See also* specific headings, e.g.: Milan

biology 56

Charles de Brosses 73

Georges-Louis Leclerc Buffon 75

Friedrich Rudolf Ludwig Canitz 90

cartography 95

Anne-Claude-Philippe de Levis Caylus 99

Clement XIV 118

colonialism 122

Nicolaus Copernicus 129

cosmopolitanism 130

Charles-Pinot Duclos 166

Jean-Honoré Fragonard 200

Henry Fuseli 217

Pietro Giannone 230

Edward Gibbon 231

Gobelins tapestry 234

Carlo Goldoni 238

grand tour 241

Thomas Gray 243

Jean-Baptiste Greuze 246

George Frederick Handel 260

Hapsburg Empire 261

Holy Roman Empire 278

Illuministi 293

Jansenism 305

Jews and Judaism 310

justice and the law 315

Angelica Kauffman 321

Pierre de Laclos 326

literacy 347

Montesquieu 398

Lodovico Antonio Muratori 408

neoclassicism 421

opera 435–437

Palladian style 444

Peter I 450

picturesque 455–456

Piedmont 456

Poland 460

Protestantism 478

public health 482, 483

publishing 484, 485

Jean-Philippe Rameau 495

Joshua Reynolds 508

George Romney 523

secret societies 545

sensibility 552

earl of Shaftesbury 552

Jacques-Germain Soufflot 563

style galant 576
theater 588
toleration 594
Turin 602
Pietro Verri 611
Giovan Battista Vico 612
Mary Wortley 397
Joseph Wright 639
Johann Georg Zimmermann
641

J

Jacobi, Friedrich Heinrich x, xvi
c, xvii c, 196, 235, 256, 269,
293, 300, 302–303, 343, 386,
569
Jacobins 269, 303–304, 494,
515, 559
Jacobites 209, 304–305, 544,
545
Jansenism 305–306
anticlericalism 20
Aufklärung 28
Étienne-François Choiseul
110
Clement XII 117
Robert-François Damiens 138
Encyclopédie 176
Eugène of Savoy 190
Febronianism 194
François Fénelon 195
Jesuits 310
Julien Offray de La Mettrie
329
Gottfried Wilhelm Leibniz 338
Louis XIV of France 355
Nicolas de Malebranche 365
Sebastiano José de Carvalho e
Mello Pombal 464
Quarrel between the Ancients
and the Moderns 490
Roman Catholicism 520
Jardin des Plantes 140, 306, 329,
335, 408
Jay, John ix, 14, 258, 306–307,
363, 399, 606
John Adams 5
Jefferson, Thomas ix, xvi c, 307,
307–309
John Adams 5
American Philosophical
Society 13
American Revolution 14
Joel Barlow 38
colonialism 122
Common Sense 122
Declaration of Independence
141, 142
deism 148
Antoine-Louis-Claude Destutt
de Tracy 156
Pierre-Samuel Dupont de
Nemours 166
Benjamin Franklin 205
freedom 209
Henri Gregoire 246
Alexander Hamilton 259
Anne-Cathérine Helvétius 266
Historical and Critical
Dictionary 271
Jean-Antoine Houdon 280
Francis Hutcheson 289
Jardin des Plantes 306
Gabriel Bonnot de Mably 361
James Madison 362
optimism 438
Thomas Paine 443
picturesque 456
Joseph Priestley 471
publishing 486
race 493
revolution 506
rights 511
David Rittenhouse 514
secret societies 545
slavery 557

United States of America 606
George Washington 625
Jenner, Edward xvii c, 298, 299,
309, 482
Jesuits xvi c, 309–310
Jean Le Rond d'Alembert 10
ancien régime 15
anticlericalism 20
René-Lous de Voyer de Paulmy
Argenson 22
Aufklärung 28
Pierre Bayle 44
Jacques-Bénigne Bossuet 67
Antoine Calmet 84
Candide 89
Charles III of Spain 101
China 106
Étienne-François Choiseul
110
Clement XIII 117
Clement XIV 118
Marie Condorcet 124
René Descartes 151
Denis Diderot 158
education 171
Bernard Le Bovier de
Fontenelle 198
Élie-Cathérine Fréron 216
Henri Gregoire 245
Historical and Critical
Dictionary 271
Bavarian Illuminati 293
Jansenism 305
Joseph de Lalande 328
Gabriel Bonnot de Mably 361
Maria Theresa of Austria 371
Jean-François Marmontel 373
Franz Anton Mesmer 389
Montesquieu 399
Lodovico Antonio Muratori
407
orientalism 439
Sebastiano José de Carvalho e
Mello Pombal 464
marquise de Pompadour 465
Portugal 468
Antoine-François Prévost 470
Guillaume-Thomas-François
de Raynal 497
religion 504
Maximilien Robespierre 515
Roman Catholicism 520, 521
Emmanuel-Joseph Sieyès 554
Spain 565
universities 607
Alessandro Volta 617
Voltaire 618
Jews and Judaism 310–312, 311
Aufklärung 27
Henri Gregoire 246
Haskalah 263
Joseph II of Austria 314
Moses Mendelssohn 384–386
millenarianism 393
religion 504
Josef von Sonnenfels 562
Benedict de Spinoza 568–569
University of Göttingen 240
Johnson, Samuel xv c, 312–313
Bluestocking 61
Edmund Burke 77
Charles Burney 79
Fanny Burney 79
David Garrick 223
Oliver Goldsmith 238
Thomas Gray 243
Grub Street 248
Charlotte Ramsay Lennox 341
James Macpherson 362
Elizabeth Montagu 396
Hannah More 403
novel 431
probability 473
prostitution 477
Joshua Reynolds 508
Richard Brinsley Sheridan 553

She Stoops to Conquer 554
Adam Smith 557
social institutions 560
theater 589
Tom Jones 595
travel literature 597
Sarah Trimmer 599
The Vicar of Wakefield 611
Joseph II of Austria 313–314,
xvi c
absolutism 3
Austria 29
Belgium 48
Catherine II 98
Cologne 120
Così fan Tutte 130
education 171
enlightened absolutism 3
enlightened despotism 155
enlightened monarchs 395
Febronianism 194
Frankfurt 204
Hapsburg Empire 261, 262
Haskalah 263
Hungary 287
Bavarian Illuminati 293
Jews and Judaism 312
Josephinism 314–315
Wenzel Anton von Kaunitz
322
Louis XVI of France 357
The Magic Flute 365
Maria Theresa of Austria 370
Milan 392
Le Nozze di Figaro 432
philosopher-king 452
Sebastiano José de Carvalho e
Mello Pombal 464
progress 476
religion 504
separation of church and state
550
serfdom 551
Gottfried Bernhard Swieten
580
toleration 595
Josephinism 29, 194, 314,
314–315, 520
justice and the law ix, 315–316
Sir William Blackstone 58–59
capital punishment 93–94
civil society 111
colonialism 120
Essays on Crimes and
Punishments 188–189
France 203
Pietro Giannone 230–231
lettres de cachet 343
parlements 446–447
Peter I 450
Joseph Priestley 472
publishing 486
rights 511
United States Bill of Rights 605
United States Constitution
605–606

K

Kant, Immanuel ix, xi, xvi c, xvii
c, 317–320, 318
aesthetics 7, 9
anthropology 20
Aufklärung 27
Alexander Gottlieb
Baumgarten 43
Ruggiero Giuseppe Boscovich
66
cosmopolitanism 130
deism 148
René Descartes 154
Dialogues Concerning Natural
Religion 157
education 170
epistemology 185
Johann Georg Adam Forster
199

freedom 209
Christian Garve 223
Germany 230
Johann Georg Hamann 257
Johann Gottfried Herder 269
William Hogarth 276
David Hume 286
intuition and imagination 300
Friedrich Heinrich Jacobi 303
Heinrich von Kleist 324
Friedrich Gottlieb Klopstock
325
Gottfried Wilhelm Leibniz 340
Lutheranism 359
Moses Mendelssohn 385, 386
moral philosophy 403
natural law 414
Christoph Friedrich Nicolai
426
perfectibility 448
physico-theology 453
progress 475
psychology 480, 481
race 492
reason 498–499
rights 512, 513
Johann Friedrich Schiller 536
skepticism 556
Mme de Staël 571
sublime 577
Emanuel Swedenborg 579
vitalism 616
Christian Wolff 635
women and the Enlightenment
637
Karl-August, duke of Weimar
267, 293, 320–321
Karl Wilhelm Ferdinand, duke of
Braunschweig-Wolfenbüttel
321, 412
Kauffman, Angelica 321–322
Kaunitz, Wenzel Anton von,
Prince von Kaunitz-Rietberg
xv c, 4, 161, 194, 233, 261, 314,
322, 371, 392, 438, 530
Kay, John 198, 298, 322
Kent, William 73, 179,
322–323, 331, 444, 455–456,
519
Kepler, Johannes 128, 220, 269,
323, 339, 375, 506
Kingdom of the Two Sicilies
101, 259, 298, 323–324, 359,
395
Kleist, Heinrich von 217, 324,
348
Klopstock, Friedrich Gottlieb
233, 324–325, 362, 602

L

Laclos, Pierre-Ambroise-François
Choderlos de xvi c, 326–327,
344, 348, 430
Lagrange, Joseph-Louis xvii c,
11, 26, 52, 175, 191, 200, 212,
327, 334, 376, 541
laissez-faire 22, 108, 219, 298,
328, 453
Lalande, Joseph-Jérôme Le
Français de 26, 166, 211, 212,
328
Lamarck, Jean-Baptiste-Pierre-
Antoine de Monet de xvii c, 56,
57, 65, 124, 136, 146, 328–329,
491, 538
Lambert, Anne-Thérèse de
Marguenat de Courcelles, marquise de 198, 329, 373, 489,
560
La Mettrie, Julien Offray de
329–330
atheism 26
automata 29
Berlin Academy 52
Clement XIV 118
enthusiasm 183

Frederick II 207
freedom 209
Claude-Adrien Helvétius 267
materialism 375
psychology 480, 481
publishing 485
radical Enlightenment 494
religion 504
Benedict de Spinoza 569
United Provinces of
Netherlands 605
Jacques de Vaucanson 610
Lancret, Nicolas 330, 353
landscapes 330–332, 455, 575,
639
language 332–333
Georges-Louis Leclerc Buffon
76
Chemical Revolution 104
Étienne Bonnot de Condillac
123
Antoine-Louis-Claude Destutt
de Tracy 156
Josef Dobrovský 164
Émile 173
Johann Gottfried Herder 268
Wilhelm von Humboldt 283
Idéologie 292
Mikhail Vasilivich Lomonosov
351
Joseph Priestley 472
progress 475
Emanuel Swedenborg 579
John Horne Tooke 596
Constantin-François
Chasseboeuf Volney 617
Laokoon (Gotthold Ephraim
Lessing) 9, 333, 333–334, 342,
421
Laplace, Pierre-Simon, marquis
de xvii c, 334–335
Jean Le Rond d'Alembert 11
astronomy 26
Claude-Louis Berthollet 54
Chemical Revolution 106
Marie Condorcet 125
empiricism 175
Leonhard Euler 190
Jean-Baptiste-Joseph Fourier
200
French Academy of Sciences
212
James Hutton 290
Joseph-Louis Lagrange 327
mathematics and mechanics
376
Emanuel Swedenborg 579
Alessandro Giuseppe Antonio
Anastasio Volta 618
La Serva Padrona (Giovanni
Battista Pergolesi) 448
La Tour, Maurice-Quentin de
230, 335
Lavater, Johann Kaspar 57, 62,
89, 109, 217, 256, 335, 345,
531
Lavoisier, Antoine-Laurent xvii
c, 335–336
affinity chemistry 9
ancien régime 15
Torbern Olof Bergman 50
Claude-Louis Berthollet 54
Joseph Black 57
caloric 85
Chemical Revolution 103,
106
classification 115
Étienne Bonnot de Condillac
124
Jacques-Louis David 141
French Academy of Sciences
212
Stephen Hales 255
Pierre-Simon Laplace 334
Franz Anton Mesmer 389
phlogiston theory 452

Joseph Priestley 471
science 538
Georg Ernst Stahl 571
subtle fluids 577
Benjamin Thompson 528
Alessandro Giuseppe Antonio
Anastasio Volta 618
Law, John 336–337, 394, 395,
395, 564
Leeuwenhoek, Antoni van 18,
57, 225, 337, 391, 469
Leibniz, Gottfried Wilhelm x,
xiv c, xvi c, 337–341, 338
aesthetics 8
alchemy 10
Aufklärung 27
Battle of the Buffoons 43
Alexander Gottlieb
Baumgarten 43
Berlin 52
Berlin Academy 52
Daniel Bernoulli 53
Johann Jakob Bodmer 62
Charles Bonnet 65
Ruggiero Giuseppe Boscovich
66
Jacques-Bénigne Bossuet 67
Calvinism 86
Candide 89
cartography 95
Mme du Châtelet 102
China 108
Samuel Clarke 113
Anthony Collins 119
cosmopolitanism 131
René Descartes 152
epistemology 184
Eugène of Savoy 190
Leonhard Euler 191
freedom 209
French Academy of Sciences
212
Antonio Genovesi 228
Germany 230
great chain of being 244
Edmond Halley 256
Johann Gottfried Herder 267
Friedrich Hoffmann 275
Jan Ingen-Housz 299
Immanuel Kant 317
Karl Wilhelm Ferdinand 321
Joseph-Louis Lagrange 327
Lutheranism 359
Nicolas de Malebranche 366
mathematics and mechanics
376
Pierre-Louis Moreau de
Maupertuis 379
mechanical philosophy 380
Moses Mendelssohn 384
moral philosophy 401, 402
Lodovico Antonio Muratori
408
natural law 413
Isaac Newton 424
Friedrich Christoph Oetinger
433
optimism 438
orientalism 439
perfectibility 448
political theory 461
preformation theory 469
probability 473
progress 475
psychology 480, 481
rationalism 496
Republic of Letters 505
rights 511
scientific academies 540
scientific method 541
Scientific Revolution 542
Social Contract 559
Benedict de Spinoza 569
Georg Ernst Stahl 571
Emanuel Swedenborg 579
Emmerich de Vattel 610

Voltaire 619
Christian Wolff 635
lending libraries. See social insti-
tutions of the Enlightenment
Lennox, Charlotte Ramsay xv c,
266, 280, 341, 430, 549
Lespinasse, Julie-Jeanne-
Eléonore de 11, 52, 123, 144,
341, 341–342, 505, 560
Lessing, Gotthold Ephraim x,
xvi c, 342–343
aesthetics 7–9
Aufklärung 28
biblical criticism 55
Daniel Niklaus Chodowiecki
109
freedom 209
Freemasons 210
Germany 230
Johann Christoph Gottsched
241
Johann Georg Hamann 257
Johann Gottfried Herder 267
William Hogarth 276
Bavarian Illuminati 293
intuition and imagination 300
Friedrich Heinrich Jacobi 303
Karl Wilhelm Ferdinand 321
Laokoon 333–334
literature 348
Lutheranism 359
Moses Mendelssohn 384, 386
Nathan the Wise 412–413
neoclassicism 421
Christoph Friedrich Nicolai
426
paganism 442
race 493
Hermann Samuel Reimarus
501
religion 504
Johann Friedrich Schiller 535
Johann Salomo Semler 547
separation of church and state
550
Benedict de Spinoza 569
Sturm und Drang 576
toleration 595
Wilhelm Tell 632
Johann Joachim Winckelmann
634
Letters on Toleration (John
Locke) 343, 349, 351, 594
lettres de cachet (sealed letters)
343, 378, 394, 530
libertine 117, 144, 279, 280,
344, 431, 444, 468, 495. See
also pornography
liberty
Samuel Clarke 113
freedom 209
free trade 212
French Revolution 215
homosexuality 279
Thomas Jefferson 308
Joseph II of Austria 314
radical Enlightenment 494
Reflections on the Revolution in
France 499
United States Bill of Rights
605
United States Constitution
606
A Vindication of the Rights of
Woman 614
Wilhelm Tell 632
Lichtenberg, Georg Christoph
240, 276, 344–345, 557
Linnaeus, Carolus (Carol von
Linné) xv c, 37, 50, 57, 63, 75,
115, 124, 139, 345–346, 491,
541, 578
Lisbon earthquake xv c,
346–347
Marie-Antoinette 371
Candide 89

Nicolas Desmarest 155
nature 416
optimism 438
Sebastiano José de Carvalho e
Mello Pombal 464
Portugal 468
Giuseppe Domenico Scarlatti
534
literacy 346, 347
Common Sense 123
Grub Street 248
literature 348
Methodism 390
museums 408
Paris 446
Pietism 457
Protestantism 478
publishing 485
social institutions 561
The Spectator 566
literature 347–349. See also
novel; poetry; sentimental fic-
tion; travel literature; specific
authors, e.g.: Blake, William
aesthetics 8
Jean Le Rond d'Alembert 12
Battle of the Buffoons 43
Jeanne Le Prince de Beaumont
45
Aphra Behn 47–48
Sébastien-Roch-Nicholas
Chamfort 100
classicism 115
Confessions 126
William Congreve 126
John Dryden 164–165
genius 226
Gothic revival 239
Gothic romance 239–240
Grub Street 248
Franz Joseph Haydn 265
Samuel Johnson 312
Georg Christoph Lichtenberg
345
music 409
nature 416
Jacques Necker 418
neoclassicism 420
paganism 442
Persian Letters 448–449
politeness 460
political theory 463
publishing 484–486
Jean-Jacques Rousseau 524
Louis-Claude de Saint-Martin
530–531
Claude-Henri de Saint-Simon
532
Johann Friedrich Schiller
534–536
sensibility 547
sentimental fiction 548–549
Richard Brinsley Sheridan 553
She Stoops to Conquer
553–554
The Spectator 566
Mme de Staël 571
Philip Dormer Stanhope 106
Richard Steele 574
Sturm und Drang 576
sublime 577
Christian Thomasius 590
travel literature 597–598
Voltaire 618
George Washington 625
Christoph Martin Wieland
631
women and the Enlightenment
638
Locke, John ix, xiv c, 349–351
absolutism 2
John Adams 5
Joseph Addison 6
aesthetics 7
Jean Le Rond d'Alembert 11
American Revolution 14

Anglicans 18
Francis Bacon 36
Jeremy Bentham 49
George Berkeley 51
Sir William Blackstone 58
Georges-Louis Leclerc Buffon
76
civil society 111
class and rank 115
Anthony Collins 119
colonialism 122
Étienne Bonnot de Condillac
123
cosmopolitanism 131
Declaration of Independence
141, 142
deism 147
René Descartes 154
Antoine-Louis-Claude Destutt
de Tracy 156
Dictionnaire philosophique 158
Denis Diderot 160
Discourse on the Origins of
Inequality 162–163
education 170
Jonathan Edwards 172
empiricism 174
Encyclopédie 176
England 178
Epicurean philosophy 183
epistemology 184
equality 186
Essays on Crimes and
Punishments 188
Gaetano Filangieri 197
freedom 209
Antonio Genovesi 228
Glorious Revolution 232
Johann Georg Hamann 257
Alexander Hamilton 258
David Hartley 262
Claude-Adrien Helvétius 267
Thomas Hobbes 274
David Hume 284
Idéologie 292
Idéologues 292
individualism 296
John Jay 306
Jews and Judaism 311
Samuel Johnson 312
Immanuel Kant 318
language 332
Letters on Toleration 343
literacy 347
Louis XIV of France 356
Nicolas de Malebranche 366
medicine 380
Moses Mendelssohn 385
moral philosophy 402
natural law 414
natural rights 416
Isaac Newton 424
Pamela 445
perfectibility 447
political theory 461, 462
Joseph Priestley 471
Principia mathematica 472
progress 475
property 476
psychology 480, 481
reason 498
religion 502–504
revolution 506
rights 511, 512
The Rights of Man 513
Maximilien Robespierre 515
Jean-Jacques Rousseau 526
sensibility 547
sentimental fiction 548
separation of church and state
550
earl of Shaftesbury 552
slavery 557
Social Contract 559
The Spirit of Laws 570

John Toland 593
toleration 594
A Treatise of Human Nature
598
Tristram Shandy 600
Catharine Trotter 600
Two Treatises of Government
602–603
United States Bill of Rights 605
United States of America 606
universities 607
A Vindication of the Rights of
Woman 614
Voltaire 618
Lomonosov, Mikhail Vasilivich
351–352
London 352
London Corresponding Society
352–353
Longhi, Pietro 293, 353
longitude 95, 149, 353
Louis XIV of France (1638–1715)
xiv c, 354, 354–356, 484
absolutism 2
aesthetics 7
Amsterdam 14
ancien régime 15
René-Louis de Voyer de Paulmy
Argenson 21
aristocratic resurgence 22
baroque style 39
Pierre Bayle 44
Henry St. John Bolingbroke 64
Jacques-Bénigne Bossuet 67
Henri de Boulainvilliers 70
bureaucracy 77
Calvinism 86
Camisards 88
capitalism 93
cartography 95
Anne-Claude-Philippe de Levis
Caylus 99
Charles III of Spain 101
class and rank 114
classicism 115
Marie Condorcet 124
François Couperin 133
John Theophilus Desaguliers
151
divine right of kings 163
England 178
Eugène of Savoy 189
François Fénelon 194
France 201, 203
French Academy of Sciences
212
Gallicanism 222
David Garrick 223
Geneva 225
Félicité de Genlis 228
Gobelins tapestry 233
history 272
Huguenots 282
Jansenism 305
Jardin des Plantes 306
John Law 337
Gottfried Wilhelm Leibniz 338
libertine 344
Pierre de Marivaux 373
René-Nicolas-Charles-
Augustin de Maupeou 377
mercantilism 387
Mississippi Bubble 394
Montesquieu 398, 399
Moscow 404
Suzanne Necker 419
Paris 445
parlements 446, 447
Persian Letters 449
political theory 462
pornography 468
Protestantism 478
religion 502
Royal Palace at Versailles 2
separation of church and state
550

separation of powers 550
Siècle de Louis XIV 554
Spain 565
toleration 594
Voltaire 619
Waldensians 623
William III and Mary II 633
Sir Christopher Wren 638
Louis XVI of France (1754–93)
xvii c, 357, 357–358
ancien régime 15
aristocratic resurgence 22
Austrian Netherlands 29
comtesse du Barry 42
Charles-Alexandre de Calonne
84
Étienne-François Choiseul
110
class and rank 114
Marie Condorcet 124
diamond necklace scandal 157
François Fénelon 195
France 203
French Revolution 213
Nicolas-Joseph-Laurent Gilbert
232
Haitian Revolution 254
Johann Gottfried Herder 269
Jacobins 304
Pierre de Laclos 326
Louis XV of France 356
Chrétien-Guillaume de
Malesherbes 366
Marie-Antoinette 371–373
Jacques Necker 418
Thomas Paine 443
Maximilien Robespierre 515
Louis-Antoine-Léon de Saint-
Just 530
Emmanuel-Joseph Sieyès 554
Anne-Robert-Jacques Turgot
602
Mary Wollstonecraft 636
Louis XV of France (ca.
1700–74) xiv c, 356
ancien régime 15
Marc-Pierre de Voyer
Argenson 21
René-Lous de Voyer de Paulmy
Argenson 21
comtesse du Barry 42
Benedict XIV 49
Claude-Louis Berthollet 54
Théophile de Bordeu 66
François Boucher 68
Charles de Brosses 73
Jean Calas 83
Charles-Alexandre de Calonne
84
class and rank 114
Angélique-Marguérite du
Coudary 132
Robert-François Damiens
138
Encyclopédie 176
enlightened absolutism 3
enlightened monarchs 395
Jean-Honoré Fragonard 200
France 203
Gobelins tapestry 234
Carlo Goldoni 238
Histoire des deux Indes 270
Jesuits 310
John Law 336
Chrétien-Guillaume de
Malesherbes 366
Marie-Antoinette 371
Jean-François Marmontel
373
René-Nicolas-Charles-
Augustin de Maupeou 377,
378
Mississippi Bubble 394
Jeanne-Antoinette Pompadour
464
pornography 468

François Quesnay 490
Victor de Riqueti 394
comte de Saint-Germain 530
secret societies 544
Sèvres 552
Anne-Robert-Jacques Turgot
601
Voltaire 619
Lunar Society of Birmingham
71, 139, 358, 471, 527
Lutheranism 358–359
Anglicans 16
Johann Christian Bach 33
Immanuel Kant 317
Gottfried Wilhelm Leibniz 340
Johann Lorenz von Mosheim
405
Pietism 456
Protestantism 478, 479
Hermann Samuel Reimarus
501
*On the Revolutions of the
Heavenly Spheres* 434
synergy 583
Nicolaus Ludwig Zinzendor
642
Lyon, Emma (Lady Hamilton)
259, 359–360

M

Mably, Gabriel Bonnot de, Abbé
361, 404
Macpherson, James xvi c, 59,
243, 348, 362
Madison, James ix, xvii c, 5, 38,
258, 307, 362–363, 399, 443,
605, 606, 625
Madrid 234, 282, 363, 473, 534,
565
magic 270, 363–364, 390, 544,
577. *See also* paganism
Magic Flute, The (Wolfgang
Amadeus Mozart) 314,
364–365, 406, 631
Magnasco, Alessandro 365
magnetism 389
*Maid Mistress, The. See Serva
Padrona, La*
Malebranche, Nicolas de xiv c,
67, 154, 340, 365–366, 401,
420, 470, 620
Malesherbes, Chrétien-
Guillaume de 176, 366, 378,
484
Malthus, Thomas Robert xvii c,
91, 92, 150, 367, 578
Manchester Literacy and
Philosophical Society 367, 527
Mandeville, Bernard xiv c, 111,
147, 212, 267, 367–368, 399,
402, 459, 553, 570
Mannheim school 112, 368,
410, 572
Marat, Jean-Paul 368–370, 369,
375
Marggraf, Andreas Sigismund
370, 452
Maria Theresa of Austria xv c,
370, 370–371
René-Lous Argenson 21
Austria 29
cameralism 87
capital punishment 94
Charles III of Spain 101
Étienne-François Choiseul
110
Cologne 120
education 171
enlightened absolutism 3
Freemasons 211
Christoph Gluck 233
Hapsburg Empire 261
Hungary 287
Bavarian Illuminati 293
Jan Ingen-Housz 298
inoculation 299

Jesuits 310
Joseph II of Austria 313
Josephinism 314
Wenzel von Kaunitz 322
Louis XVI of France 357
The Magic Flute 365
Milan 392
Balthasar Neumann 422
partitions of Poland 447
Peter I 450
Pietism 457
serfdom 551
Seven Years' War 552
Josef von Sonnenfels 562
Gerard van Swieten 580
Gottfried Bernhard Swieten
580
Vienna 613
War of the Austrian Succession
624
Marie-Antoinette-Joséphine-
Jeanne d'Autriche 42, 83, 110,
157, 233, 357, 358, 371–373,
372, 465, 468, 613
Marivaux, Pierre Carlet de
Chamblain de xv c, 230, 239,
329, 373
Marmontel, Jean-François 41,
176, 177, 216, 230, 266, 342,
373, 373–374, 419, 602
*Marriage of Figaro, The. See
Nozze di Figaro, Le*
Mass in B Minor (Johann
Sebastian Bach) 35, 374
materialism 374–375
mathematics and mechanics
375–376
Jean d'Alembert 10–11
Daniel Bernoulli 53
Jakob I and Johann I Bernoulli
54–55
China 108
Samuel Clarke 113
René Descartes 151–155
Leonhard Euler 190–191
Jean-Baptiste Fourier 200
Galileo Galilei 219–221
Willem Jacob's Gravesande
243
hermeticism 270
Thomas Jefferson 307
Immanuel Kant 319
Joseph-Louis Lagrange 327
Pierre-Simon Laplace 334–335
Gottfried Leibniz 339
Thomas Malthus 367
Pierre de Maupertuis 378–379
mechanical philosophy 379
Isaac Newton 423–425
Principia mathematica 472
probability 473–474
science 539
statistics 572–573
Brook Taylor 585
Mather, Cotton 204, 376–377
Maupeou, René-Nicolas-Charles-
Augustin de 42, 343, 356,
377–378
Maupertuis, Pierre-Louis Moreau
de 378–379
astronomy 26
Battle of the Buffoons 43
Berlin Academy 52
biology 57
César-François Cassini de
Thury 96
Mme du Deffand 144
Denis Diderot 159
epigenesis 184
Leonhard Euler 190
Frederick II 207
French Academy of Sciences
212
generation 225
Joseph de Lalande 328
language 332

Mme du Châtelet 102
Montesquieu 399
philosopher-king 451
Scientific Revolution 543
Anne-Robert-Jacques Turgot
602
Voltaire 619
McAdam, John Loudon 379
mechanical philosophy 379–380
absolutism 2
animism 19
atheism 26
Aufklärung 27
Francis Bacon 36
barometer 38
Paul-Joseph Barthez 41
Daniel Bernoulli 53
Marie-François-Xavier Bichat
55
biology 57
Hermann Boerhaave 63
Calvinism 87
Chemical Revolution 103
Étienne Bonnot de Condillac
123–124
Copernican Revolution 128
Ralph Cudworth 135
William Cullen 136
René Descartes 154
Denis Diderot 159
Freemasons 209
French Academy of Sciences
212
Galileo Galilei 221
Pierre Gassend 224
Johann Wolfgang von Goethe
237
David Hartley 263
Thomas Hobbes 273
Friedrich Hoffmann 275
John Hunter 288
iatrochemistry 291
iatromechanics 291
individualism 296
Immanuel Kant 318–319
Julien Offray de La Mettrie
330
Gottfried Wilhelm Leibniz 339
Louis XIV of France 355
Nicolas de Malebranche 365
materialism 374–375
mathematics and mechanics
376
medicine 380
Marin Mersenne 388
moral philosophy 401, 402
nature 416
Isaac Newton 423
Jean-Antoine Nollet 428
political theory 461
preformation theory 469
Principia mathematica 472
psychology 481
rationalism 496
rights 511
Rosicrucians 524
science 539
scientific method 541
Scientific Revolution 542
separation of powers 550
Georg Ernst Stahl 571
Johann Peter Süssmilch 578
sympathy 582
vitalism 615
medicine 380–383, 381. *See also*
inoculation; midwifery; *specific
individuals, e.g.:* Reil, Johann
Christian
anthropology 19
Paul-Joseph Barthez 41
Marie-François-Xavier Bichat
55
Hermann Boerhaave 63
Pieter Camper 88
Chemical Revolution 103
William Cullen 135

Erasmus Darwin 139
René Descartes 154
Encyclopédie 176
Franz Joseph Gall 221–222
Luigi Galvani 222–223
Oliver Goldsmith 238
Albrecht von Haller 256
David Hartley 262
hermeticism 270
iatrochemistry 291
iatromechanics 291
Idéologie 292
Jan Ingen-Housz 298
Jews and Judaism 311
Samuel Johnson 313
Jean de Lamarck 328
Julien Offray de La Mettrie
329
Carolus Linnaeus 345
Jean-Paul Marat 368
Cotton Mather 377
Alexander Monro 396
Moscow 405
Pieter van Musschenbroek 411
natural philosophy 414
psychology 480
public health 482–483
François Quesnay 490
rationalism 496
Benjamin Rush 528
Johann Friedrich Schiller 535
August Ludwig von Schlözer
537
science 538
Scientific Revolution 542
Georg Ernst Stahl 571
Gottfried Bernhard Swieten
580
universities 606, 607
University of Göttingen 240
University of Halle 255
vitalism 615
voyages of discovery 622
Johann Joachim Winckelmann
634
Meissen works 383–384, 465,
552
Mendelssohn, Moses x, xv c, xvi
c, xvii c, 384, 384–386
Aufklärung 27
deism 148
freedom 209
genius 227
Germany 230
Johann Christoph Gottsched
241
Johann Georg Hamann 257
Haskalah 263
Friedrich Heinrich Jacobi 302,
303
Jews and Judaism 311
Immanuel Kant 320
Johann Kaspar Lavater 335
Gotthold Ephraim Lessing 342
Nathan the Wise 413
Christoph Friedrich Nicolai
426
paganism 442
psychology 481
religion 504
Johann Friedrich Schiller 535
separation of church and state
550
Benedict de Spinoza 569
Sturm und Drang 576
sublime 577
toleration 595
Mengs, Anton Raphael 102, 118,
141, 241, 363, 386–387, 421,
591–592, 634
mercantilism 387
cameralism 88
capitalism 91
China 107
colonialism 120
Denmark 151

enlightened absolutism 3
France 202
free trade 211
Antonio Genovesi 228
Alexander Hamilton 258
Illuministi 294
Industrial Revolution 298
laissez-faire 328
Jacques Necker 418
Physiocrats 453–454
Adam Smith 558
South Sea Bubble 564
Spain 565
Johann Peter Süssmilch 578
Robert Walpole 624
Wealth of Nations 627
Mercier, Louis-Sébastien 31,
150, **387–388**
Mercier de la Rivière, Paul-Pierre
155, **388**, 453, 490
Mersenne, Marin **388–389**
René Descartes 152
epistemology 184
Galileo Galilei 220
Pierre Gassend 224
Thomas Hobbes 273
Louis XIV of France 355
mechanical philosophy 380
pyrrhonism 488
Rosicrucians 523
scientific academies 540
scientific method 541
Scientific Revolution 542
skepticism 556
Mesmer, Franz Anton 60, 83,
335, **389–390**, 453, 531
Methodism 59, 88, 172, 178,
182, 364, 390, 448, 457, 499,
503. *See also* Wesley, Charles;
Wesley, John
Michaelis, Johann David
390–391, 427
microscope 183, 225, 337, 370,
391, 543, 586
midwifery 89, 132, **391**
Milan **391–392**
Millar, John 111, 209, 272,
392–393, 544
millenarianism **393–394**
Mirabeau, Victor de Riqueti,
marquis de 155, 166, 386, *394*,
394, 453, 490
Mississippi Bubble 337,
394–395, *395*, 564
monarchs, enlightened 3,
155–156, **395**. *See also specific
monarchs, e.g.*: Charles III of
Spain; *specific types of monarchs,
e.g.*: absolutism
Monro, Alexander (Secundus)
57, 298, 382, 395–396, 544,
616
Montagu, Elizabeth [Robinson]
60, 241, 299, **396**, 467, 508,
514, 637
Montagu, Lady Mary Wortley
396, **396–397**, 560
Montesquieu, Charles-Louis de
Secondat, baron de La Brède et
de x, xiv *c*, xv *c*, *397*, **397–400**
absolutism 2
John Adams 5
American Revolution 14
René-Lous Argenson 22
marchese di Beccaria 46
Benedict XIV 49
Henry St. John Bolingbroke 64
Nicolas-Antoine Boulanger 70
Catherine II 97
China 106
civil society 111
Mme du Deffand 144
deism 147
Antoine Destutt de Tracy 156
Denis Diderot 158
Jean-Baptiste Du Bos 165

England 178
enlightened despotism 155
equality 187
Adam Ferguson 196
Gaetano Filangieri 197
France 201
freedom 209
Freemasons 211
French Revolution 216
Marie-Thérèse Rodet Geoffrin
230
Glorious Revolution 232
Oliver Goldsmith 239
Alexander Hamilton 258
Johann Gottfried Herder 268
history 272
Thomas Hobbes 274
honor 280
John Jay 306
Jews and Judaism 311
justice and the law 315
Anne-Thérèse Lambert 329
literature 348
James Madison 362
Louis-Sébastien Mercier 388
Abbé Morelly 404
Justus Möser 405
Johannes von Müller 406
natural law 414
orientalism 439
paganism 442
Persian Letters **448–449**
political theory 462
pornography 468
property 476
Guillaume-Thomas-François
de Raynal 497
Maximilien Robespierre 515
romanticism 521
science of man 540
separation of powers 550–551
Josef von Sonnenfels 562
The Spirit of Laws **569–570**
Madame de Staël 571
travel literature 597
Two Treatises of Government
603
United Provinces of
Netherlands 605
United States of America 606
Venice 610
Giovan Battista Vico 613
Voltaire 620
women and the Enlightenment
637
Montgolfier, Jacque-Étienne and
Michel-Joseph xvi *c*, **400**, *401*
Monticello (Virginia) *444*
moral philosophy **400–403**
aesthetics 7
Joseph Butler 81
capital punishment 94
Étienne Bonnot de Condillac
124
cosmopolitanism 130
Ralph Cudworth 135
René Descartes 152
*Dialogues Concerning Natural
Religion* 156
Denis Diderot 160
education 170
England 178
*An Enquiry Concerning Human
Understanding* 182
Epicurean philosophy 183
Adam Ferguson 195
Frederick II 208
genius 226
Johann Georg Hamann 257
happiness 261
Thomas Hobbes 274
David Hume 284
Francis Hutcheson 289
individualism 296
Thomas Jefferson 308
Immanuel Kant 317

Gottfried Wilhelm Leibniz
337
Bernard Mandeville 367–368
materialism 374
natural law 413
natural religion 415
perfectibility 448
François-André-Adrien
Pluquet 459
political theory 461
Richard Price 470
John Pringle 473
psychology 479
rationalism 496
Thomas Reid 500
relations 502
religion 503
rights 511
science 538
Scotland 544
sensibility 547–548
separation of church and state
550
earl of Shaftesbury 553
Adam Smith 557
Benedict de Spinoza 568
sympathy 582
Christian Thomasius 590
toleration 595
universities 607
Moravian Brethren xv *c*, **403**,
433, 456–457, 478, 642
More, Hannah 133, 396,
403–404, 477, 485, 637
Morelly, Abbé 361, **404**
Moscow 38, **404–405**, 450, 531,
607
Möser, Justus **405**
Mosheim, Johann Lorenz von
405–406
Mozart, Wolfgang Amadeus xvii
c, *406*, **406–407**
Austria 29
Johann Christian Bach 33
Pierre-Augustin Beaumarchais
45
Ludwig van Beethoven 46
Joseph Boulogne 71
Clement XIV 118
Così fan Tutte **130**
Don Giovanni **164**
empfindsamer Stil 174
Miklós József Esterházy 189
Charles-Simon Favart 193
Freemasons 210
Christoph Willibald Gluck
233
grand tour 241
Franz Joseph Haydn 264
Joseph II of Austria 314
The Magic Flute **364–365**
Mannheim school 368
Franz Anton Mesmer 389
music 409
neoclassicism 421
Le Nozze di Figaro **432**
opera 437
Giuseppe Parini 445
piano 455
serfdom 551
La Serva Padrona 552
Carl Stamitz 572
Gottfried Bernhard Swieten
580
symphony orchestra 583
theater 588
Vienna 613
viola 614
Christoph Martin Wieland
631
Müller, Johannes von 240, 407,
537
Munich 407
Muratori, Lodovico Antonio
300, 392, 398, **407–408**, 612
museums **408**

music **408–411**, *409*. *See also*
opera; *specific composers, e.g.*:
Bach, Johann Sebastian; *specific
compositions, e.g.*: The Magic
Flute
aesthetics 8
Jean Le Rond d'Alembert 12
baroque style 40
Catherine II 98
clarinet 112
empfindsamer Stil 174
Encyclopédie 176
Galileo Galilei 220
Germany 230
Italy 301
Angelica Kauffman 321
Nicolas Lancret 330
John Locke 351
London 352
Louis XIV of France 354
Louis XV of France 356
Mannheim school 368
Pierre-Louis Moreau de
Maupertuis 378
Milan 392
nature 416
neoclassicism 420
New Lanark 423
paganism 442
Paris 445
Johann Heinrich Pestalozzi
449
piano **454–455**
politeness 460
political theory 463
marquise de Pompadour 465
sensibility 547
social institutions 561
Josef von Sonnenfels 562
style galant 576
symphony orchestra **582–583**
Brook Taylor 585
viola **614**
Musschenbroek, Pieter van 57,
88, 102, 192, 243, 298, 411

N

Nathan the Wise (Gotthold
Ephraim Lessing) 342, 384,
412–413, 595, 632
natural history 139–140, **413**
natural law 413–414
anthropology 19
Jean-Jacques Burlamaqui 79
civil society 111
Ralph Cudworth 135
divine right of kings 164
enlightened absolutism 3
enlightened despotism 155
equality 186
Frederick II 208
Haitian Revolution 253
Johann Georg Hamann 257
Histoire des deux Indes 271
justice and the law 315
Lisbon earthquake 347
John Locke 350
Gabriel Bonnot de Mably 361
Louis-Sébastien Mercier 388
John Millar 392
moral philosophy 400
Abbé Morelly 404
natural rights 415
*On the Revolutions of the
Heavenly Spheres* 433
Physiocrats 453
political theory 461, 462
progress 474
Samuel Pufendorf 487
pyrrhonism 488
rationalism 496
reason 498
rights 511
comte de Saint-Germain 530
Claude-Henri de Saint-Simon
532

science 538, 539
Scientific Revolution 542
separation of church and state
550
skepticism 556
Social Contract 559
The Spirit of Laws 570
Sturm und Drang 576
Christian Thomasius 589
John Toland 593
Two Treatises of Government
603
Emmerich de Vattel 608
Wealth of Nations 627
natural philosophy x, **414**
Samuel Clarke 113
Anthony Collins 119
Nicolaus Copernicus 129
René Descartes 152
Jonathan Edwards 172
empiricism 174
Encyclopédie 176
Epicurean philosophy 183
Adam Ferguson 195
Galileo Galilei 221
Pierre Gassend 224
Willem Jacob's Gravesande
243
Thomas Hobbes 273
Alexander von Humboldt 283
David Hume 284
Jesuits 309
Immanuel Kant 317
Julien Offray de La Mettrie
329
Madame du Châtelet 102
Isaac Newton 425
Carsten Niebuhr 427
physico-theology 453
pornography 467
Joseph Priestley 471
rationalism 496
rights 511
science 538
Lazzaro Spallanzani 566
Emanuel Swedenborg 579
Voltaire 620
Christian Wolff 635
natural religion **414–415**
The Age of Reason 9
Anglicans 18
anthropology 20
William Blake 59
Joseph Butler 81
China 108
Samuel Clarke 113
deism 146–148
René Descartes 152
*Dialogues Concerning Natural
Religion* 156–157
enthusiasm 182
Freemasons 209
Histoire des deux Indes 271
Hermann Samuel Reimarus
501
religion 503
*On the Revolutions of the
Heavenly Spheres* 433
Roman Catholicism 520
Scientific Revolution 543
John Toland 593
toleration 594
natural rights *415*, **415–416**
American Revolution 14
aristocratic resurgence 22
association movement 25
François-Noel Babeuf 32
Jeremy Bentham 50
Marie Condorcet 124
cosmopolitanism 131
Declaration of the Rights of
Man 143
Thomas Jefferson 308
John Locke 350
natural law 414
opera 437

Thomas Paine 443
Richard Price 470
Samuel Pufendorf 487
rights 509
The Rights of Man 513
Maximilien Robespierre 515
United States Bill of Rights 605
United States of America 606
nature x, 416–418, *417*
Jacques-Henri Bernardin de
Saint-Pierre 53
biology 56
Johann Friedrich Blumenbach
62
Ruggiero Giuseppe Boscovich
67
Joseph Butler 81
Chemical Revolution 103
classicism 115
Copernican Revolution 128
*Discourse on the Origins of
Inequality* 162
English garden 179
Ferdinando Galiani 219
Johann Wolfgang von Goethe
236
Gothic romance 239
Francisco José de Goya y
Lucientes 241
grand tour 241
Willem Jacob's Gravesande
243
Thomas Gray 244
great chain of being 244
Eliza Haywood 265
Johann Gottfried Herder 268
history 271
Alexander von Humboldt 283
Gottfried Wilhelm Leibniz 339
Lisbon earthquake 347
Cotton Mather 377
natural law 413
natural rights 415
neoclassicism 420
Isaac Newton 423
optimism 438
orientalism 439
Palladian style 444
perfectibility 448
Johann Heinrich Pestalozzi
449
physico-theology 453
political theory 461
radical Enlightenment 494
Jean-Philippe Rameau 495
*On the Revolutions of the
Heavenly Spheres* 433
Joshua Reynolds 508
Rosicrucians 523
marquis de Sade 529
Johann Friedrich Schiller 536
science 538
scientific method 541
earl of Shaftesbury 553
Social Contract 559
The Sorrows of Young Werther
562
George Stubbs 575
Sturm und Drang 576
sublime 576
subtle fluids 577
sympathy 582
travel literature 598
utility 607
The Vicar of Wakefield 612
vitalism 615
women and the Enlightenment
637
Necker, Jacques 3, 22, 84, 114,
176, 280, 357, 418–419, *419*,
570
Necker, Suzanne Curchon de
Nasse 159, 231, 418, **419**, 570
Needham, John Turberville,
Abbé xv *c*, 57, 184, 225,
419–420, 566

Nelson, Admiral Horatio
359–360
neoclassicism **420–422**, *421. See
also* classicism
aesthetics 7
baroque style 38
Berlin 52
François Boucher 69
Edmund Burke 78
Jacques-Louis David 141
Gobelins tapestry 234
Johann Georg Hamann 257
Laokoon 334
Gotthold Ephraim Lessing 342
Anton Raphael Mengs 387
music 409
Pompeii 466
rococo 518
George Romney 523
Sèvres 552
Jacques-Germain Soufflot 563
Sturm und Drang 576
George Washington 625
Christoph Martin Wieland
631
Johann Joachim Winckelmann
634
Neumann, Balthasar xiv *c*, 120,
137, **422**, 518, 591
Newcomen, Thomas 298, **422**,
574
New Eloise, The. *See Nouvelle
Héloise, La*
New Lanark **422–423**
Newton, Isaac x, xiv *c*, **423–425**,
424
alchemy 10
atheism 26
Aufklärung 27
Francis Bacon 36
Daniel Bernoulli 53
Charles Burney 79
cartography 95
César-François Cassini de
Thury 96
Henry Cavendish 99
Mme du Châtelet 102
Samuel Clarke 113
Anthony Collins 119
Étienne Bonnot de Condillac
123
Copernican Revolution 128
cosmopolitanism 131
deism 146
Joseph-Nicolas Delisle 149
John Theophilus Desaguliers
151
René Descartes 154
*Dialogues Concerning Natural
Religion* 157
Dictionnaire philosophique 158
Discourse on Method 162
empiricism 175
Epicurean philosophy 183
epistemology 184
Benjamin Franklin 206
Freemasons 209
free trade 212
Pierre Gassend 224
Antonio Genovesi 228
Willem Jacob's Gravesande
243
Edmond Halley 256
hermeticism 269
Jan Ingen-Housz 299
Immanuel Kant 319
Pierre-Simon Laplace 334
Gottfried Wilhelm Leibniz 338
longitude 353
Louis XIV of France 356
Nicolas de Malebranche 366
Jean-Paul Marat 368
mathematics and mechanics
375, 376
Pierre-Louis Moreau de
Maupertuis 378

mechanical philosophy 380
millenarianism 393
Montesquieu 399
Jean-Antoine Nollet 428
physico-theology 453
Joseph Priestley 471
probability 473
reason 498
religion 502
Republic of Letters 505
revolution 506
Royal Society of London 527
science 538, 539
scientific method 541–542
Scientific Revolution 542
subtle fluids 577
Brook Taylor 585
A Treatise of Human Nature 598
United States of America 606
universities 607
Voltaire 618
Nicolai, Christoph Friedrich
223, 227, 235, 257, 335, 342,
384, **425–427**, 563
Niebuhr, Carsten **427**
noble savage **427–428**, 516, 584,
598
Nollet, Jean-Antoine, Abbé 60,
103, 136, 212, 411, **428–429**,
543
Nouvelle Héloise, La (Jean-
Jacques Rousseau) 184, **429**,
431
novel **429–431**, *430. See also
specific novelists; specific novels*
Nozze di Figaro, Le (Wolfgang
Amadeus Mozart) 45, 130, 164,
406, 432, 437, 551, 552, 588

O

Oetinger, Friedrich Christoph
10, **433**
*On the Revolutions of the Heavenly
Spheres* (Nicolaus Copernicus)
25, 127, 129, 220, **433–435**
opera *435*, **435–438**
The Beggar's Opera 47
Joseph Boulogne 71
Ranieri de'Calzabigi 87
Canaletto 89
Così fan Tutte **130**
Sophie Cottin 132
Don Giovanni **164**
Miklós József Esterházy 189
Frederick II 207
John Gay **224–225**
Christoph Willibald Gluck
233
Carlo Goldoni 238
George Frederick Handel 260
Franz Joseph Haydn 264
Illuministi 294
Italy 301
Louis XIV of France 355
The Magic Flute **364–365**
Mannheim school 368
Milan 392
music 409
Le Nozze di Figaro **432**
Orfeo ed Eurydice **438–439**
Paris 445
marquise de Pompadour 465
Antoine-François Prévost 470
Jean-Philippe Rameau 495
Giuseppe Domenico Scarlatti
533
La Serva Padrona **551–552**
Richard Brinsley Sheridan 553
Georg Philipp Telemann 586,
587
theater 588
Venice 611
optimism **438**, 498, 540
Orfeo ed Eurydice (Christoph
Willibald Gluck) 112, 437,
438–439

orientalism **439–440**. *See also*
China
orrery 440
Oudry, Jean-Baptiste 440

P

paganism 27, **441–442**, 503. *See
also* magic
Paine, Thomas xvi *c*, xvii *c*, *442*,
442–443
The Age of Reason **9–10**
American Revolution 14
Joel Barlow 37, 38
William Blake 60
Common Sense **122–123**
cosmopolitanism 130
Declaration of Independence
141
deism 148
radical Enlightenment 494
The Rights of Man 513
Benjamin Rush 528
secret societies 545
John Horne Tooke 596
*A Vindication of the Rights of
Woman* 614
Palladian style 4, 98, 197, 239,
307, 323, 443–444, *444*, 638
Pamela, or Virtue Rewarded
(Samuel Richardson) 196, 266,
373, 444–445, 468, 509, 548,
615
Parini, Giuseppe 445
Paris **445–446**
Park, Mungo 446
parlements (French royal courts
of law) **446–447**
absolutism 3
ancien régime 15
anticlericalism 20
aristocratic resurgence 22
Belgium 48
Benedict XIV 49
Jacques-Bénigne Bossuet 67
bureaucracy 76
Charles-Alexandre de Calonne
84
Étienne-François Choiseul 110
class and rank 114
Clement XIII 117
Robert-François Damiens 138
France 202, 203
Jansenism 305
Jesuits 310
lettres de cachet 343
Louis XIV of France 354
Louis XVI of France 357
Louis XV of France 356
René de Maupeou 377, 378
Montesquieu 398
political theory 462–463
publishing 485
religion 504
Roman Catholicism 520
Anne-Robert-Jacques Turgot
601–602
partitions of Poland 261, 447,
460, 466, 559
perfectibility **447–448**
Edmund Burke 78
Marie Condorcet 124
*Discourse on the Origins of
Inequality* 162
Encyclopédie 176
Freemasons 209
genius 227
William Godwin 234
Claude-Adrien Helvétius 267
Thomas Jefferson 308
Thomas Robert Malthus 367
moral philosophy 402
nature 418
Pompeii 466
progress 474
Rosicrucians 524
Benedict de Spinoza 569

Pergolesi, Giovanni Battista 40,
43, 293, 410, 448, 551–552, xv
c
Persian Letters (Montesquieu)
147, 329, 348, 397, 448–449,
569, 597
Peter I (the Great) xiv *c*, **450**
Catherine II 96
class and rank 114
Joseph-Nicolas Delisle 149
Étienne-Maurice Falconet 192
Josephinism 314
Antoni van Leeuwenhoek 337
Gottfried Wilhelm Leibniz 338
Mikhail Vasilivich Lomonosov
351
Moscow 404
Jean-Baptiste Oudry 440
Bartolomeo Rastrelli 496
Saint Petersburg 531
Saint Petersburg Academy of
Sciences 531
scientific academies 541
Sweden 578
Philadelphia **450–451**
American Philosophical
Society 13
Joel Barlow 37
Common Sense 122
Declaration of Independence
141
Olaudah Equiano 187
Benjamin Franklin 205
French Revolution 214
Great Awakening 244
Alexander Hamilton 258
John Jay 306
James Madison 362
museums 408
Quakers 489
David Rittenhouse 513
Benjamin Rush 528
scientific academies 541
social institutions 561
United Provinces of
Netherlands 604
United States Constitution 605
United States of America 606
George Washington 625
philosopher-king 206, 250, 387,
451, **451–452**
philosophes (philosophers) **452**,
484
absolutism 3
American Revolution 14
ancien régime 15
anticlericalism 20
Marc-Pierre de Voyer
Argenson 21
atheism 26
Aufklärung 27
Battle of the Buffoons 43
Jeremy Bentham 49
Jacques-Henri Bernardin de
Saint-Pierre 52
Nicolas-Antoine Boulanger 71
Camisards 88
capital punishment 94
Sébastien-Roch-Nicholas
Chamfort 100
Chemical Revolution 103
Étienne-François Choiseul
110
Copernican Revolution 128
Declaration of the Rights of
Man 143
deism 148
democracy 149
Denis Diderot 158
Encyclopédie 176
enthusiasm 182, 183
*Essays on Crimes and
Punishments* 188
François Fénelon 194
Adam Ferguson 196
France 201

Benjamin Franklin 206
freedom 208
Freemasons 211
Ferdinando Galiani 219
Geneva 225
Glorious Revolution 232
Friedrich Melchior Grimm 247
Anne-Cathérine Helvétius 266
Claude-Adrien Helvétius 267
history 272
Huguenots 282
David Hume 286
Italy 300
Thomas Jefferson 308
Karl Wilhelm Ferdinand 321
Wenzel Anton von Kaunitz 322
Joseph de Lalande 328
Maurice-Quentin de La Tour 335
Julie-Jeanne-Eléonore de Lespinasse 341
Louis XV of France 356
Chrétien-Guillaume de Malesherbes 366
Jean-François Marmontel 373
John Turberville Needham 419
Paris 445
parlements 446
philosopher-king 451
pornography 468
publishing 484
pyrrhonism 488
radical Enlightenment 494
Guillaume-Thomas-François de Raynal 497
religion 503
Republic of Letters 505
Maximilien Robespierre 516
Roman Catholicism 520
Jean-Jacques Rousseau 524
Benjamin Rush 528
science 538
science of man 540
siècle des lumières 554
social institutions 560
Benedict de Spinoza 569
toleration 594
Anne-Robert-Jacques Turgot 602
Two Treatises of Government 603
United Provinces of Netherlands 605
utility 607
virtue 614, 615
vitalism 616
Waldensians 623
philosophy. See specific disciplines, e.g.: aesthetics; specific philosophers, e.g.: Hobbes, Thomas
phlogiston theory 452
Torbern Olof Bergman 50
Claude-Louis Berthollet 54
Joseph Black 57
Henry Cavendish 99
Chemical Revolution 103, 104
Friedrich Hoffmann 275
James Hutton 290
Antoine-Laurent Lavoisier 336
Andreas Sigismund Marggraf 370
Joseph Priestley 472
Carl Wilhelm Scheele 534
Georg Ernst Stahl 571
Alessandro Volta 618
phrenology 221, 452-453, 500
physico-theology 56, 285, 453, 458, 499, 578
Physiocrats 453-455, 454
Pierre-Jean-Georges Cabanis 82
Charles-Alexandre de Calonne 84

Catherine II 97
China 108
Declaration of the Rights of Man 143
Denmark 151
Pierre-Samuel Dupont de Nemours 166
François Fénelon 195
Gaetano Filangieri 197
France 201
freedom 208
Ferdinando Galiani 219
Antonio Genovesi 228
Jacques de Gournay 241
Illuministi 294
Karl-August 320
laissez-faire 328
Gabriel Bonnot de Mably 361
mercantilism 387
Louis-Sébastien Mercier 388
Jacques Necker 418
perfectibility 448
Victor de Riqueti 394
serfdom 551
Adam Smith 557
Spain 565
toleration 594
Anne-Robert-Jacques Turgot 602
Wealth of Nations 627, 628
piano 409, 454-455
picturesque 331, 455-456, 518
Piedmont 201, 270, 300, 456, 602, 623
Pietism 456-457
Gottfried Arnold 23
Aufklärung 27
William Blake 59
Denmark 151
August Hermann Francke 204
Friedrich Heinrich Jacobi 302
Immanuel Kant 319
Johann Kaspar Lavater 335
Letters on Toleration 343
literacy 347
Moravian Brethren 403
Friedrich Christoph Oetinger 433
perfectibility 448
Protestantism 478
Quakers 489
reason 499
Hermann Samuel Reimarus 501
religion 503
Johann Salomo Semler 546
Philipp Jakob Spener 567
Georg Ernst Stahl 571
synergy 583
Christian Thomasius 590
University of Halle 255
John Wesley 630
Nicolaus Ludwig Zinzendor 642
Piranesi, Giovanni Battista 118, 293, 457
Pius VI (pope) 457-458
Pix, Mary 458, 637
Pluche, Noël-Antoine 458-459
Pluquet, François-André-Adrien xvii c, 459
poetry 6, 37, 90, 119, 342, 373, 374, 403, 404. See also specific poets, e.g.: Pope, Alexander
Poland 459-460
Joel Barlow 38
Bernardo Bellotto 48
Jacques-Henri Bernardin de Saint-Pierre 52
Brandenburg 72
Calvinism 85
Catherine II 97
ceramic arts 100
China 108
Daniel Niklaus Chodowiecki 109

Clement XIV 118
Nicolaus Copernicus 129
enlightened monarchs 395
Freemasons 210
Élie-Cathérine Fréron 216
Germany 230
Holy Roman Empire 278
Hungary 287
Madame du Châtelet 102
Mass in B Minor 374
neoclassicism 421
partitions of Poland 447
Stanislaw Augustus Poniatowski 466-467
Protestantism 478
On the Revolutions of the Heavenly Spheres 433
serfdom 551
Social Contract 559
Georg Philipp Telemann 586
Voltaire 619
Abraham Gottlob Werner 628
politeness 460-461
political theory ix, 461-464. See also specific headings, e.g.:
Locke, John
absolutism 1
John Adams 4-6
ancien régime 15
anthropology 19
René-Lous Argenson 22
association movement 25
Aufklärung 27
Jeremy Bentham 49-50
Edmund Burke 78
capital punishment 94
class and rank 114
colonialism 120
democracy 149
Denis Diderot 158
Émile 172
England 178
Epicurean philosophy 183
equality 186
Essays on Crimes and Punishments 188
Frederick II 208
French Revolution 216
William Godwin 234
Johann Wolfgang von Goethe 238
Alexander Hamilton 258
happiness 261
Thomas Hobbes 273
David Hume 286
Francis Hutcheson 289
Illuministi 293
individualism 296
Italy 300
Thomas Jefferson 308
Immanuel Kant 319
Letters on Toleration 343
literacy 347
John Locke 349-351
Gabriel Bonnot de Mably 361
James Madison 362-363
Montesquieu 397-400
Abbé Morelly 404
Thomas Paine 442-443
Richard Price 470
property 476
religion 504
rights 511
The Rights of Man 513
Jean-Jacques Rousseau 524
August Ludwig von Schlözer 537
Scotland 544
separation of church and state 550
separation of powers 550-551
Social Contract 559-560
Benedict de Spinoza 568
The Spirit of Laws 569-570
Johann Friedrich Struensee 575

toleration 594
Two Treatises of Government 602-603
United States Constitution 606
United States of America 606
John Wilkes 633
William III and Mary II 634
Pombal, Sebastiano José de Carvalho e Mello, marquês de xv c, 117, 395, 464, 468
Pompadour, Jeanne-Antoinette Poisson, marquise de xv c, 464-465, 465
Marc-Pierre de Voyer Argenson 21
François Boucher 68
Jean Calas 83
ceramic arts 100
Jean-Baptiste-Siméon Chardin 101
Étienne-François Choiseul 110
Robert-François Damiens 138
Étienne-Maurice Falconet 192
Jean-Honoré Fragonard 200
Élie-Cathérine Fréron 216
Marie-Thérèse Rodet Geoffrin 230
Jesuits 310
Louis XV of France 356
Jean-François Marmontel 373
rococo 518
Saint-Germain 530
Sèvres 552
Jacques-Germain Soufflot 563
Voltaire 619
Pompeii 90, 465-466
Poniatowski, Stanislaw Augustus 48, 97, 216, 230, 395, 460, 466-467
Pope, Alexander x, xv c, 467, 553
Henry St. John Bolingbroke 64
William Congreve 126
John Gay 225
Gulliver's Travels 250
Stephen Hales 255
Eliza Haywood 265
homosexuality 279
landscapes 331
literature 348
Moses Mendelssohn 385
Isaac Newton 424
physico-theology 453
rococo 519
social institutions 560
Philip Dormer Stanhope 106
Stowe 575
Tom Jones 595
Voltaire 618
porcelain xiv c, 383-384. See also Meissen works; Sèvres
pornography 467-468, 476, 529. See also libertine; Sade, marquis de
Portugal 468
absolutism 3
anticlericalism 20
George Gordon Byron 81
Clement XIII 117
Clement XIV 118
colonialism 120
East India Company 169
John Hunter 287
Jesuits 310
justice and the law 315
Lisbon earthquake 346
John Turberville Needham 419
Sebastiano Pombal 464
Protestantism 478
publishing 485
Roman Catholicism 519
Giuseppe Domenico Scarlatti 534
scientific academies 541

slavery 557
Spain 565
toleration 594
voyages of discovery 620
power loom 23, 96, 298, 469, 568, 586, 626
Prandtauer, Jakob 39, 469
preformation theory 62, 65, 183, 225, 255, 379, 391, 396, 419, 469-470, 566, 599
Prévost, Antoine-François 348, 470
Price, Richard 14, 163, 286, 470-471, 494, 633, 637
Priestley, Joseph xvi c, 471, 471-472
American Revolution 14
biology 57
Sir William Blackstone 59
William Blake 60
Henry Cavendish 99
Chemical Revolution 103
cosmopolitanism 130
Declaration of Independence 141
Dissenters 163
Stephen Hales 255
David Hartley 263
Jan Ingen-Housz 298
Antoine-Laurent Lavoisier 336
Lunar Society of Birmingham 358
phlogiston theory 452
radical Enlightenment 494
Thomas Reid 500
Carl Wilhelm Scheele 534
Georg Ernst Stahl 571
Alessandro Volta 618
John Wilkes 633
Principia mathematica (Isaac Newton) x, 102, 112, 113, 256, 425, 472, 541, 619
Pringle, John 57, 298, 472-473, 527, 616, 630
probability 334-335, 470, 473-474, 488, 498, 539
progress 474, 474-476, 475
property 476-477
prostitution 279, 476-477
Protestantism 477-479
Anglicans 16
Aufklärung 28
baroque style 38
Pierre Bayle 44
Dialogues Concerning Natural Religion 157
Dissenters 163
England 177
Gallicanism 222
Huguenots 281
Jansenism 306
Gottfried Wilhelm Leibniz 340
Letters on Toleration 343
literacy 347
Lutheranism 358-359
Methodism 390
religion 502
On the Revolutions of the Heavenly Spheres 434
Roman Catholicism 519
Scientific Revolution 543
Scotland 543
separation of church and state 549
Spain 565
John Toland 593
toleration 594
women and the Enlightenment 637
Nicolaus Ludwig Zinzendor 642
Prussia 479
Carl Philipp Emanuel Bach 32
Berlin 51
Brandenburg 72
bureaucracy 76

Catherine II 97
Daniel Niklaus Chodowiecki 109
Étienne-François Choiseul 110
class and rank 114
Clement XIV 118
Diplomatic Revolution of 1756 160
dynastic states 166
enlightened despotism 155
France 203
Frederick II 206–208
French Revolution 215
Johann Wolfgang von Goethe 237
Haitian Revolution 254
Haskalah 263
Holy Roman Empire 278
Huguenots 282
Wilhelm von Humboldt 283
Italy 301
Jews and Judaism 312
Immanuel Kant 317
Karl-August 320
Karl Wilhelm Ferdinand 321
Wenzel Anton von Kaunitz 322
Heinrich von Kleist 324
Friedrich Gottlieb Klopstock 325
Julien Offray de La Mettrie 330
literacy 347
Louis XIV of France 355
Louis XV of France 356
Maria Theresa of Austria 371
Jean-François Marmontel 374
materialism 375
Pierre-Louis Moreau de Maupertuis 379
Moses Mendelssohn 384
mercantilism 387
partitions of Poland 447
Peter I 450
philosopher-king 452
Pietism 457
Poland 460
political theory 463
Stanislaw Augustus Poniatowski 466
Protestantism 479
publishing 485
Samuel Pufendorf 487
Guillaume-Thomas-François de Raynal 497
Johann Christian Reil 500
religion 504
Republic of Letters 505
Roman Catholicism 521
scientific academies 540
serfdom 551
Seven Years' War 552
Siècle de Louis XIV 554
Emmanuel-Joseph Sieyès 555
Social Contract 559
social institutions 561
Spain 565
Georg Ernst Stahl 571
Sturm und Drang 576
Gottfried Bernhard Swieten 580
Christian Thomasius 590
toleration 595
universities 607
University of Halle 255
War of the Austrian Succession 624
Wealth of Nations 628
psychology 479–482
  aesthetics 7
  Jean Le Rond d'Alembert 11
  Aufklärung 27
  biblical criticism 54
  Charles Bonnet 65
  Pierre-Jean-Georges Cabanis 82–83

capital punishment 94
Anthony Collins 120
Étienne Bonnot de Condillac 123
Ralph Cudworth 135
René Descartes 152
Dialogues Concerning Natural Religion 157
Denis Diderot 159
Jean-Baptiste Du Bos 165
education 170
Jonathan Edwards 172
empiricism 174, 175
England 178
epistemology 184
equality 186
Essays on Crimes and Punishments 188
Adam Ferguson 196
Bernard Le Bovier de Fontenelle 198
Galileo Galilei 220
Franz Joseph Gall 221
Johann Christoph Gatterer 224
Gothic romance 239
Johann Georg Hamann 257
happiness 261
David Hartley 262–263
Claude-Adrien Helvétius 267
history 271
Thomas Hobbes 274
David Hume 284
Francis Hutcheson 289
Idéologie 292
Idéologues 292
individualism 296
intuition and imagination 299
Thomas Jefferson 308
Immanuel Kant 318
Georg Christoph Lichtenberg 345
John Locke 349–351
materialism 374
medicine 380
Moses Mendelssohn 386
moral philosophy 402
nature 416
perfectibility 447
phrenology 452–453
Pietism 457
Joseph Priestley 472
rationalism 496
reason 499
relations 502
religion 502
rights 511
science of man 540
Scotland 544
sensibility 547
sentimental fiction 548
skepticism 556
A Treatise of Human Nature 598
universities 607
Giovan Battista Vico 612
public health 474, 482–483, 483
publishing 42, 484, 484–486, 505, 566–567, 574, 637
Pufendorf, Samuel 486–487
  American Revolution 14
  civil society 111
  Declaration of Independence 142
  Germany 230
  Johann Gottfried Herder 268
  history 272
  Thomas Hobbes 274
  natural law 413
  political theory 461
  rights 511
  Social Contract 559
  The Spirit of Laws 570
  Christian Thomasius 589
  Emmerich de Vattel 610
pyrrhonism 271, 487–488

Q

Quakers 59, 77, 187, 343, 448, 451, 489, 499, 503, 531, 557, 632
Quarrel between the Ancients and the Moderns 7, 19, 43, 115, 195, 199, 329, 355, 489–490, xiv c
Quesnay, François xv c, xvi c, 91, 166, 176, 212, 241, 388, 394, 453, 490, 602, 627

R

race vii, 62, 120, 142, 246, 491, 491–494
radical Enlightenment 439, 494–495
Rake's Progress (William Hogarth) 495
Rameau, Jean-Philippe xv c, 12, 40, 43, 69, 87, 329, 374, 410, 436, 495–496
Rastrelli, Bartolomo 496, 518, 531
rationalism 496–497
  aesthetics 7
  Gottfried Arnold 24
  Aufklärung 27
  Alexander Gottlieb Baumgarten 44
  classification 115
  Samuel Taylor Coleridge 119
  Étienne Bonnot de Condillac 123
  deism 146
  René Descartes 152
  Dialogues Concerning Natural Religion 156
  empiricism 174
  enlightened monarchs 395
  An Enquiry Concerning Human Understanding 182
  epistemology 184
  equality 186
  August Hermann Francke 204
  Frederick II 208
  Antonio Genovesi 228
  Johann Georg Hamann 257
  Johann Gottfried Herder 269
  David Hume 284
  Immanuel Kant 318
  Gottfried Wilhelm Leibniz 339
  Gotthold Ephraim Lessing 342
  Moses Mendelssohn 385
  moral philosophy 401
  natural law 413
  natural religion 415
  Isaac Newton 423
  On the Revolutions of the Heavenly Spheres 433
  progress 475
  psychology 480
  pyrrhonism 488
  reason 499
  Robinson Crusoe 516
  romanticism 522
  comte de Saint-Germain 530
  Louis-Claude de Saint-Martin 531
  skepticism 556
  Benedict de Spinoza 568–569
  Emanuel Swedenborg 579
  Jonathan Swift 581
  John Tillotson 592
  A Treatise of Human Nature 598
  University of Halle 255
  Giovan Battista Vico 612
Raynal, Guillaume-Thomas-François de (Abbé) xvi c, 497–498
  anthropology 20
  demography 150
  Denis Diderot 159
  enlightened despotism 155
  Marie-Thérèse Rodet Geoffrin 230

Haitian Revolution 253
Histoire des deux Indes 270, 271
Industrial Revolution 298
Julie-Jeanne-Eléonore de Lespinasse 342
slavery 557
Toussaint Louverture 596
travel literature 598
reading clubs. See social institutions of the Enlightenment
reason ix, 498–499
  aesthetics 7
  The Age of Reason 10
  Jean Le Rond d'Alembert 12
  anthropology 19
  anticlericalism 20
  René-Lous Argenson 22
  Aufklärung 27
  Alexander Gottlieb Baumgarten 43
  Pierre Bayle 44
  Jeremy Bentham 49
  Jacques-Henri Bernardin de Saint-Pierre 53
  William Blake 59
  Johann Jakob Bodmer 62
  Johann Jakob Breitinger 72
  Georges-Louis Leclerc Buffon 76
  bureaucracy 76
  Pierre-Jean-Georges Cabanis 82
  Calvinism 87
  Samuel Clarke 113
  classicism 115
  Samuel Taylor Coleridge 119
  Anthony Collins 120
  Marie Condorcet 124
  Così fan Tutte 130
  Ralph Cudworth 135
  deism 146
  Dialogues Concerning Natural Religion 157
  Denis Diderot 160
  divine right of kings 163
  education 170
  Émile 172
  empiricism 174
  English garden 179
  An Enquiry Concerning Human Understanding 182
  enthusiasm 182
  epistemology 184
  Faust 193
  Bernard Le Bovier de Fontenelle 198
  Benjamin Franklin 206
  Freemasons 209
  French Revolution 214, 216
  Johann Christoph Gatterer 224
  genius 226
  Edward Gibbon 232
  Gothic revival 239
  Gothic romance 239
  Johann Christoph Gottsched 241
  Gulliver's Travels 250
  Johann Georg Hamann 257
  Eliza Haywood 265
  Claude-Adrien Helvétius 267
  Johann Gottfried Herder 267
  Historical and Critical Dictionary 271
  history 272
  David Hume 285
  Francis Hutcheson 289
  Industrial Revolution 298
  intuition and imagination 299
  Jansenism 306
  Thomas Jefferson 308
  Immanuel Kant 317
  Pierre de Laclos 326
  language 332
  Gottfried Wilhelm Leibniz 339

Gotthold Ephraim Lessing 342
libertine 344
John Locke 350
The Magic Flute 364
Nicolas de Malebranche 365
mathematics and mechanics 375
Methodism 390
Montesquieu 398
moral philosophy 400, 403
Justus Möser 405
natural law 413
natural religion 415
nature 416
neoclassicism 420
Isaac Newton 423
La Nouvelle Héloïse 429
optimism 438
paganism 441
Palladian style 443
perfectibility 447
Persian Letters 449
phrenology 453
Physiocrats 453
Pompeii 466
Richard Price 470
progress 474
Samuel Pufendorf 487
pyrrhonism 488
radical Enlightenment 494
rationalism 496
religion 503
rights 511
Robinson Crusoe 517
romanticism 522
Rosicrucians 523
Jean-Jacques Rousseau 526
Louis-Claude de Saint-Martin 531
science 538
science of man 540
Scientific Revolution 542
self-interest 545
Johann Salomo Semler 547
sensibility 548
sentimental fiction 548
earl of Shaftesbury 553
skepticism 556
Adam Smith 557
Benedict de Spinoza 568
Laurence Sterne 574
superstition 577
Christian Thomasius 589
John Tillotson 592
Matthew Tindal 592
John Toland 593
toleration 594
Two Treatises of Government 603
Giovan Battista Vico 612
A Vindication of the Rights of Woman 614
John Wesley 630
Christoph Martin Wieland 631
women and the Enlightenment 637
Réaumur, René-Antoine Ferchault de 428, 469, 499, 599
Reflections on the Revolution in France (Edmund Burke) 78, 443, 471, 499, 513, 614, 636
Reid, Thomas ix, x, 14, 286, 402, 453, 472, 480, 499–500, 544
Reil, Johann Christian 28, 57, 240, 382, 482, 500–501, 528
Reimarus, Hermann Samuel 148, 359, 501, 547
relations 501–502
religion vii, 502–504. See also theology; specific types of religion, e.g.: Roman Catholicism
  The Age of Reason 9–10
  anthropology 19

anticlericalism 20
Jean-Baptiste de Boyer Argens 20
Gottfried Arnold 24
atheism 27
Henry St. John Bolingbroke 64
Jacques-Bénigne Bossuet 67–68
Henri de Boulainvilliers 70
Nicolas-Antoine Boulanger 70
Charles de Brosses 73
Robert Burns 80
Antoine Calmet 83–84
Camisards 88
China 106, 107
Samuel Clarke 113
Clement XII 117
colonialism 120
James Cook 126
Nicolaus Copernicus 129
deism 146
Dialogues Concerning Natural Religion 156–157
Adam Ferguson 196
Bernard Le Bovier de Fontenelle 198
France 202
freedom 208
Gallicanism 222
Félicité de Genlis 228
Johann Wolfgang von Goethe 235
Great Awakening 244
great chain of being 244
Johann Georg Hamann 257
hermeticism 269–270
history 271
The History of the Decline and Fall of the Roman Empire 144
Thomas Hobbes 274
Paul-Henri Thiry d'Holbach 277–278
Friedrich Heinrich Jacobi 302
Jews and Judaism 310, 312
Joseph II of Austria 314
Josephinism 314–315
Immanuel Kant 318, 319
Friedrich Gottlieb Klopstock 324
Johann Kaspar Lavater 335
Gotthold Ephraim Lessing 342
Letters on Toleration 343
libertine 344
John Locke 350, 351
Louis XIV of France 355
Cotton Mather 376–377
medicine 382
Moses Mendelssohn 386
millenarianism 393–394
Moravian Brethren 403
natural religion 414–415
Suzanne Necker 419
Friedrich Christoph Oetinger 433
optimism 438
paganism 441–442
physico-theology 453
Pius VI 457–458
Noël-Antoine Pluche 458–459
political theory 463
Joseph Priestley 472
progress 476
Protestantism 477–479
psychology 479
pyrrhonism 487
François Quesnay 490
radical Enlightenment 494
reason 499
Hermann Samuel Reimarus 501
Republic of Letters 504
Johann Friedrich Schiller 535
science 538
science of man 540
sensibility 547

separation of church and state 549–550
slavery 557
Benedict de Spinoza 569
Mme de Staël 571
superstition 577
Emanuel Swedenborg 579
John Toland 593
travel literature 598
Sarah Trimmer 599, 600
United Provinces of Netherlands 605
United States Bill of Rights 605
virtue 614
George Washington 625
women and the Enlightenment 638
Thomas Woolston 638
Republic of Letters 153, 338, 504–506
revolution 506, 506–508. See also American Revolution; French Revolution
Reynolds, Joshua xvi c, 508, 508–509
James Boswell 68
Edmund Burke 77
Charles Burney 79
Henry Fuseli 217
David Garrick 223
Oliver Goldsmith 238
William Hunter 288
Samuel Johnson 313
Angelica Kauffman 321
Elizabeth Montagu 396
neoclassicism 421
rococo 518
George Romney 523
Richard Brinsley Sheridan 553
Richardson, Samuel xv c, 509
Clarissa 112–113
Henry Fielding 196
Sarah Fielding 197
Pierre de Laclos 326
Charlotte Ramsay Lennox 341
libertine 344
literature 348
Pierre de Marivaux 373
Pamela 444–445
pornography 468
probability 473
sentimental fiction 548
Tom Jones 595
virtue 615
rights vii, 415–416, 509–513, 510
Rights of Man, The (Thomas Paine) 130, 442, 443, 494, 513, 614
Rittenhouse, David 13, 451, 513–514
Rivals, The (Richard Brinsley) 514
Robertson, William 111, 144, 170, 195, 231, 272, 514–515, 527, 544
Robespierre, Maximilien François Isadore 515–516
François-Noel Babeuf 31
Louis-Antoine de Bougainville 69
Lazare Carnot 94
Jacques-Louis David 141
democracy 149
Antoine Destutt de Tracy 156
equality 186
Jean-Baptiste-Joseph Fourier 200
French Academy of Sciences 213
French Revolution 214
Idéologie 292
Jacobins 304
Pierre de Laclos 326
Joseph de Lalande 328

revolution 507
Louis-Antoine-Léon de Saint-Just 530
Claude-Henri de Saint-Simon 532
Emmanuel-Joseph Sieyès 554, 555
Social Contract 559
Mme de Staël 570
Constantin Volney 617
Robinson Crusoe (Daniel Dafoe) 429, 473, 516–517
rococo 517, 517–519
Robert and James Adam 4
aesthetics 8
Cosmas Damian Asam 24
Egid Quirin Asam 24
Austria 29
Johann Sebastian Bach 35
baroque style 38
Berlin 52
François Boucher 68
ceramic arts 99
chinoiserie 109
Thomas Chippendale 109
Cologne 120
François Couperin 133
François de Cuvilliés 137
English garden 179
Étienne-Maurice Falconet 192
Jean-Honoré Fragonard 201
Thomas Gainsborough 218
Germany 230
Gobelins tapestry 234
Francisco José de Goya y Lucientes 241
Johann Lukas von Hildebrandt 270
William Hogarth 275
Jean-Antoine Houdon 280
Illuministi 294
Nicolas Lancret 330
Maurice-Quentin de La Tour 335
Pietro Longhi 353
Louis XV of France 356
Pierre de Marivaux 373
Meissen works 384
Milan 392
music 408, 409
neoclassicism 420
Balthasar Neumann 422
Jean-Baptiste Oudry 440
Paris 446
marquise de Pompadour 465
Roman Catholicism 520
George Romney 523
Thomas Rowlandson 526
Saint Petersburg 531
sensibility 548
Sèvres 552
George Stubbs 575
style galant 576
sublime 576
Giovanni Battista Tiepolo 591
Roman Catholicism 519–521
The Age of Reason 10
ancien régime 15
Anglicans 16, 17
Gottfried Arnold 24
Johann Christian Bach 33
baroque style 38
comtesse du Barry 42
Pierre Bayle 44
Benedict XIV 49
Henri de Boulainvilliers 70
Jean Calas 83
Calvinism 85
Camisards 88
Candide 89
China 106
Clement XII 117
Clement XIII 117–118
Clement XIV 118
Cologne 120
Marie Condorcet 124

deism 147, 148
Dialogues Concerning Natural Religion 157
Dictionnaire philosophique 158
John Dryden 164
England 177, 178
Febronianism 194
François Fénelon 194–195
French Revolution 215
Gallicanism 222
Pierre Gassend 224
Edward Gibbon 231
history 272
Huguenots 281
Illuministi 293
Jansenism 305–306
Jesuits 309–310
Josephinism 314
Kingdom of the Two Sicilies 324
Letters on Toleration 343
Louis XIV of France 355
Lutheranism 358, 359
The Magic Flute 365
Jean-Paul Marat 368
Montesquieu 397
moral philosophy 402
Lodovico Antonio Muratori 408
John Turberville Needham 419
Pius VI 457–458
Alexander Pope 467
Protestantism 477, 478
publishing 485
Guillaume-Thomas-François de Raynal 497
religion 502
rights 511
Rome 522–523
Jean-Jacques Rousseau 524
Scientific Revolution 542
Scotland 543
separation of church and state 549, 550
Richard Simon 556
Josef von Sonnenfels 562
Spain 565
John Tillotson 592
toleration 594
University of Göttingen 240
Voltaire 620
Waldensians 623
Johann Joachim Winckelmann 634
romanticism x, 521–522
aesthetics 9
Aufklärung 28
Carl Philipp Emanuel Bach 32
Ludwig van Beethoven 46
Jacques-Henri Bernardin de Saint-Pierre 53
William Blake 59
Edmund Burke 78
George Gordon Byron 81
Samuel Taylor Coleridge 119
William Cowper 134
epistemology 185
Faust 193
Caspar David Friedrich 217
Henry Fuseli 217
Johann Wolfgang von Goethe 236
Gothic romance 239
Francisco José de Goya y Lucientes 241
Thomas Gray 243
Johann Georg Hamann 258
Johann Gottfried Herder 269
Jean-Auguste-Dominique Ingres 299
Immanuel Kant 320
Heinrich von Kleist 324
Laokoon 334
music 410
nature 416

John Turberville Needham 420
neoclassicism 422
paganism 442
perfectibility 448
reason 499
The Rivals 514
marquis de Sade 529
Louis-Claude de Saint-Martin 531
sensibility 548
sublime 577
Mary Wollstonecraft 636
Rome 522–523
Robert and James Adam 4
Francesco Algarotti 12
baroque style 38
Jean-Jacques Barthélemy 41
Bernardo Bellotto 48
Benedict XIV 49
Ruggiero Giuseppe Boscovich 66
François Boucher 68
Charles Burney 79
Alessandro Cagliostro 83
Canaletto 89
Antonio Canova 90
Giovanni Giacomo Casanova 96
Étienne-François Choiseul 110
Muzio Clementi 118
Clement XII 117
Clement XIV 118
Arcangelo Corelli 129
Jacques-Louis David 141
Dictionnaire philosophique 158
enlightened absolutism 3
Étienne-Maurice Falconet 192
Johann Bernhard Fischer von Erlach 197
Jean-Honoré Fragonard 200
France 203
Henry Fuseli 217
Gallicanism 222
Edward Gibbon 231
Francisco José de Goya y Lucientes 241
grand tour 241
Huguenots 281
Wilhelm von Humboldt 283
Bavarian Illuminati 293
Jean-Auguste-Dominique Ingres 299
Jesuits 310
Jews and Judaism 310
Joseph II of Austria 314
Angelica Kauffman 321
Wenzel Anton von Kaunitz 322
William Kent 322
Lutheranism 358
Anton Raphael Mengs 386
Montesquieu 398
neoclassicism 421
Giovanni Battista Piranesi 457
Protestantism 478
Joshua Reynolds 508
William Robertson 514
Giuseppe Domenico Scarlatti 533
Richard Simon 555
Jacques-Germain Soufflot 563
United Provinces of Netherlands 604
Antonio Vivaldi 616
Johann Joachim Winckelmann 634
Joseph Wright 639
Romney, George 523
Rosicrucians 98, 152, 210, 293, 338, 447, 523–524, 544, 561, 579
Rousseau, Jean-Jacques ix, x, xv c, xvi c, 524–526, 525
American Revolution 14
anthropology 20

Gottfried Arnold 24
François-Noel Babeuf 31
Battle of the Buffoons 43
Jacques-Henri Bernardin de
    Saint-Pierre 52
James Boswell 68
Jean-Jacques Burlamaqui 79
Ranieri de'Calzabigi 87
civil society 111
Clement XIII 118
Étienne Bonnot de Condillac
    123
Confessions **125–126**
Sophie Cottin 132
Declaration of Independence
    142
deism 148
*Discourse on the Origins of
    Inequality* **162–163**
Maria Edgeworth 169
education 170
Émile **172–173**
Encyclopédie 176
encyclopedists 177
Louise d'Épinay 184
equality 186
Charles-Simon Favart 193
freedom 209
French Revolution 216
Geneva 226
Friedrich Melchior Grimm
    247
Haitian Revolution 253
Johann Georg Hamann 258
Claude-Adrien Helvétius 267
*Historical and Critical
    Dictionary* 271
history 272
Thomas Hobbes 274
honor 280
Jean-Antoine Houdon 281
David Hume 286
Bavarian Illuminati 293
Elizabeth Inchbald 296
intuition and imagination 300
Friedrich Heinrich Jacobi 302
justice and the law 315
Immanuel Kant 317
Maurice-Quentin de La Tour
    335
Gabriel Bonnot de Mably 361
Chrétien-Guillaume de
    Malesherbes 366
Montesquieu 399
Abbé Morelly 404
Johannes von Müller 406
music 410
natural law 414
natural rights 416
noble savage 427–428
La Nouvelle Héloïse **429**
novel 431
paganism 442
perfectibility 448
Johann Heinrich Pestalozzi 449
philosophes 452
physico-theology 453
Poland 460
politeness 460
political theory 461
progress 475
property 476
Jean-Philippe Rameau 495
Republic of Letters 505
rights 511–513
Maximilien Robespierre 515
Robinson Crusoe 517
romanticism 521
Louis-Claude de Saint-Martin
    531
Savoy 533
self-interest 546
Social Contract **559–560**
Mme de Staël 570
Two Treatises of Government
    603

Giovan Battista Vico 613
*A Vindication of the Rights of
    Woman* 614
Voltaire 619
George Washington 625
women and the Enlightenment
    637
Nicolaus Ludwig Zinzendor
    642
Rowlandson, Thomas 526–527
Royal Society of Edinburgh 57,
    136, 170, 195, 289, 396, 527,
    541, 544
Royal Society of London 527
Francis Bacon 36
Joseph Banks 37
Johann Friedrich Blumenbach
    61
Hermann Boerhaave 63
Louis-Antoine de Bougainville
    69
Georges-Louis Leclerc de
    Buffon 75
Henry Cavendish 99
China 108
Samuel Clarke 113
James Cook 126
William Cullen 136
Erasmus Darwin 139
Joseph-Nicolas Delisle 149
England 178
epistemology 184
Daniel Gabriel Fahrenheit 192
Jean-Baptiste-Joseph Fourier
    200
Benjamin Franklin 206
Freemasons 209
Willem Jacob's Gravesande 243
John Hadley 252
Stephen Hales 255
Edmond Halley 256
Sir William Hamilton 259
William Herschel 270
John Hunter 288
William Hunter 288
Pierre-Simon Laplace 334
Antoni van Leeuwenhoek 337
Gottfried Wilhelm Leibniz 338
John Locke 349
London 352
Thomas Robert Malthus 367
Cotton Mather 377
Montesquieu 398
John Turberville Needham
    419
Isaac Newton 424
Richard Price 471
John Pringle 473
progress 475
Royal Society of Edinburgh
    527
scientific academies 540
social institutions 561
Brook Taylor 585
Abraham Trembley 599
Alessandro Volta 617
Robert Whytt 630
Sir Christopher Wren 638
Arthur Young 640
Rumford, Benjamin Thompson,
    count von 483, **527–528**, *538*
Rush, Benjamin 443, **528**
Russia. *See also specific headings,
    e.g.:* Catherine II
    bureaucracy 76
    class and rank 114
    Clement XIII 118
    colonialism 120, 121
    Denmark 150
    enlightened despotism 155
    Johann Georg Adam Forster
        199
    Germany 230
    Haskalah 263
    Wilhelm von Humboldt 283
    Jews and Judaism 310

Mikhail Vasilivich Lomonosov
    351
partitions of Poland 447
Poland 459
Stanislaw Augustus
    Poniatowski 466
serfdom 551

S

Sade, marquis de (Donatien-
    Alphonse-François) 344, 348,
    431, **529**, 615
Saint-Germain, comte de 10, 83,
    210, 448, **529–530**, 531
Saint-Just, Louis-Antoine-Léon
    de 214, 304, 515, **530**
Saint-Martin, Louis-Claude de
    10, 210, 448, 503, **530–531**
Saint Matthew Passion (Johann
    Sebastian Bach) (choral work)
    35, **531**
Saint Petersburg xiv *c*, **531**
Jean Le Rond d'Alembert 12
Francesco Algarotti 12
Berlin 52
Johann Friedrich Blumenbach
    61
François Boucher 68
Catherine II 98
Denis Diderot 159
Leonhard Euler 190
Étienne-Maurice Falconet 192
Friedrich Melchior Grimm
    247
Gottfried Wilhelm Leibniz 338
Mikhail Vasilivich Lomonosov
    351
medicine 383
Moscow 404
opera 437
Orfeo ed Eurydice **439**
Peter I 450
John Pringle 473
rococo 518
Saint-Germain 530
August Ludwig von Schlözer
    537
theater 588
universities 607
Élisabeth-Louise Vigée Lebrun
    613
vitalism 616
Saint Petersburg Academy of
    Sciences xv *c*, 53, 75, 112, 149,
    190, 527, **531–532**, 537, 541
Saint-Simon, Claude-Henri, de
    Rouvroy, comte de **532**
salons. *See also* social institutions
    of the Enlightenment
    Mme du Châtelet 102
    Marie Deffand **144–145**
    Louise Épinay 184
    Anne Helvétius 266
    Paul d'Holbach 277
    Anne-Thérèse Lambert 329
    Julie de Lespinasse **341–342**
    Marie-Thérèse Rodet **229–230**
    Elizabeth Montagu 396
    Suzanne Necker **419**
Sancho, Ignatius **532–533**
Savoy **533**
    Giovanni Giacomo Casanova
        96
    France 201
    Pietro Giannone 231
    Huguenots 282
    Italy 300
    Kingdom of the Two Sicilies
        323
    Joseph-Louis Lagrange 327
    Piedmont 456
    Switzerland 582
    Turin 602
Scarlatti, Giuseppe Domenico
    40, 293, 363, 410, **533–534**,
    565

Scheele, Carl Wilhelm 9, 103,
    336, 452, **534**, 571, 618
Schiller, Johann Christoph
    Friedrich xvi *c*, xvii *c*,
    534–537, *535*
Ludwig van Beethoven 46
Confessions 126
Adam Ferguson 196
Johann Georg Adam Forster
    199
freedom 209
Germany 230
Johann Wolfgang von Goethe
    236
Wilhelm von Humboldt 283
Karl-August 320
Friedrich Gottlieb Klopstock
    325
landscapes 331
literature 348
James Macpherson 362
Johannes von Müller 406
neoclassicism 421
Sturm und Drang 576
Switzerland 582
vitalism 616
Christoph Martin Wieland
    631
Wilhelm Tell **632**
Schlözer, August Ludwig von
    537
    enlightened despotism 155
    Johann Christoph Gatterer
        224
    Johann Gottfried Herder 268
    intuition and imagination 300
    Johannes von Müller 406
    perfectibility 448
    Saint Petersburg Academy of
        Sciences 532
    Johann Friedrich Schiller 536
    slavery 557
    University of Göttingen 240
    Giovan Battista Vico 613
science x, **537–540**, *538*, *vii*. *See
    also specific types of science, e.g.:*
    astronomy
    alchemy 10
    animalculism 19
    animism 19–20
    Aufklärung 27
    Francis Bacon 36
    Battle of the Buffoons 43
    Berlin Academy 52
    Georges-Louis Leclerc de
        Buffon **74–76**
    Henry Cavendish 99
    China 108
    Samuel Clarke 113
    Copernican Revolution 128
    Charles-Augustin de Coulomb
        132–133
    Ralph Cudworth 135
    deism 147
    John Theophilus Desaguliers
        151
    René Descartes **151–155**
    Denis Diderot 158
    Dissenters 163
    Maria Edgeworth 169
    education 170
    empiricism 174
    England 178
    epistemology 184
    Leonhard Euler 191
    Daniel Gabriel Fahrenheit **192**
    Bernard Le Bovier de
        Fontenelle 198
    Johann Georg Adam Forster
        199
    Benjamin Franklin 206
    French Academy of Sciences
        212–213
    Galileo Galilei **219–221**
    Luigi Galvani **222–223**
    Pierre Gassend 224

geocentric 228–229
Gothic revival 239
Willem Jacob's Gravesande
    243
Johann Gottfried Herder 268
hermeticism 269
history 271
Paul-Henri Thiry d'Holbach
    278
Alexander von Humboldt
    282–283
James Hutton 290
iatrochemistry **291**
iatromechanics **291**
Idéologues 292
Industrial Revolution 298
intuition and imagination 299
Jansenism 306
Thomas Jefferson 308
Immanuel Kant 318
Pierre-Simon Laplace **334–335**
Antoine-Laurent Lavoisier
    335–336
Gottfried Wilhelm Leibniz 339
literature 348
London 352
Louis XIV of France 354
Lunar Society of Birmingham
    358
James Madison 362
Manchester Literacy and
    Philosophical Society **367**
materialism 374–375
mathematics and mechanics
    376
Pierre-Louis Moreau de
    Maupertuis **378–379**
medicine 381
Marin Mersenne 388, 389
Moscow 405
nature 416
Isaac Newton **423–425**
Jean-Antoine Nollet **428–429**
Thomas Paine 443
phlogiston theory 452
Noël-Antoine Pluche **458–459**
radical Enlightenment 494
rationalism 496
reason 499
René-Antoine Ferchault de
    Réaumur 499
relations 502
Royal Society of Edinburgh
    527
Royal Society of London 527
Saint Petersburg Academy of
    Sciences **531–532**
Claude-Henri de Saint-Simon
    532
Carl Wilhelm Scheele **534**
science of man 540
scientific method **541–542**
Scientific Revolution **542–543**
sensibility 547
separation of church and state
    550
social institutions 561
subtle fluids 577
Emanuel Swedenborg 579
sympathy 582
Benjamin Thompson 528
Abraham Trembley 599
Anne-Robert-Jacques Turgot
    602
universities 607
utility 607
Alessandro Volta **618–619**
Abraham Gottlob Werner
    628–629
Robert Whytt **630**
Christian Wolff 635
women and the Enlightenment
    638
Arthur Young 640
science of man 286, 292, 335,
    448, 482, 540, 543, 558

scientific academies 531–532, 540–541. *See also specific academies, e.g.:* Saint Petersburg Academy of Sciences
scientific method 541–542
Scientific Revolution 542–543
  astronomy 25
  atheism 26
  barometer 38
  baroque style 38
  biology 56
  James Bradley 72
  caloric 85
  Samuel Clarke 113
  classification 115
  Copernican Revolution 127
  deism 146
  René Descartes 152
  Bernard Le Bovier de Fontenelle 198
  Galileo Galilei 221
  Pierre Gassend 224
  David Hartley 263
  Thomas Hobbes 273
  Bavarian Illuminati 293
  Industrial Revolution 297
  Johannes Kepler 323
  libertine 344
  mathematics and mechanics 375
  mechanical philosophy 379
  medicine 381
  Marin Mersenne 388
  moral philosophy 400
  natural philosophy 414
  nature 416
  physico-theology 453
  political theory 461
  progress 475
  religion 502
  revolution 506
  On the Revolutions of the Heavenly Spheres 433
  Royal Society of London 527
  science 538
  scientific academies 540
  scientific method 541
  siècle des lumières 554
  technology and instrumentation 585
  telescope 587
Scotland x, xiv c, 543–544
  biology 56
  Thomas Blackwell 59
  James Boswell 68
  Robert Burns 80
  George Gordon Byron 81
  Calvinism 85
  civil society 111
  colonialism 121
  Anthony Cooper 553
  David Dale 138
  democracy 149
  dynastic states 166
  Edinburgh 169–170
  Adam Ferguson 195
  Freemasons 209
  Sir William Hamilton 259
  David Hume 286
  James Hutton 290
  Industrial Revolution 296
  Friedrich Heinrich Jacobi 302
  Thomas Jefferson 307
  Samuel Johnson 312
  justice and the law 315
  language 333
  literacy 347
  James Macpherson 362
  John Loudon McAdam 379
  John Millar 392
  moral philosophy 402
  neoclassicism 421
  New Lanark 422–423
  Mungo Park 446
  Philadelphia 451
  John Pringle 472–473

psychology 480
publishing 485
Republic of Letters 505
rights 512
William Robertson 514
Jean-Jacques Rousseau 525
Royal Society of Edinburgh 527
Benjamin Rush 528
science of man 540
Adam Smith 557
social institutions 561
Lazzaro Spallanzani 566
technology and instrumentation 586
John Toland 593
universities 607
James Watt 626
Robert Whytt 630
secret societies 269, 303, 544–545, 561. *See also* Freemasons; Illuminati, Bavarian; Rosicrucians
self-interest 545–546
  civil society 111
  Anthony Cooper 553
  Discourse on the Origins of Inequality 162
  divine right of kings 163
  equality 186
  David Hartley 263
  Claude-Adrien Helvétius 267
  David Hume 285
  moral philosophy 401
  partitions of Poland 447
  marquis de Sade 529
  Adam Smith 558
  Social Contract 559
  The Spirit of Laws 570
  virtue 615
  Wealth of Nations 627
  Christoph Martin Wieland 631
Semler, Johann Salomo 10, 55, 270, 546–547, 635
sensibility 547, 547–548
sentimental fiction 548–549
  Clarissa 112–113
  John Cleland 117, 468
  literature 348
  Pierre de Marivaux 373
  music 409
  La Nouvelle Héloïse 429
  novel 430
  Pamela 444–445
  pornography 468
  Antoine-François Prévost 470
  Samuel Richardson 509
  The Rivals 514
  sensibility 548
  Richard Brinsley Sheridan 553
  Tristram Shandy 600
  The Vicar of Wakefield 611
  virtue 615
separation of church and state 549–550
  American Revolution 14
  ancien régime 16
  Joel Barlow 37
  capital punishment 93
  deism 148
  enlightened absolutism 3
  France 201
  French Revolution 216
  John Locke 350
  James Madison 362
  political theory 463
  religion 503, 504
  toleration 595
  United States of America 606
separation of powers 550–551
  John Adams 5
  American Revolution 14
  Declaration of the Rights of Man 143
  Essays on Crimes and Punishments 188

France 202
French Revolution 213
James Madison 362
Montesquieu 398
nature 418
political theory 462
The Spirit of Laws 570
Two Treatises of Government 603
United States Constitution 606
United States of America 606
serfdom xvi c, 151, 207, 450, 479, 551, 578
Serva Padrona, La (Giovanni Battista Pergolesi) 43, 551–552
Seven Years' War xv c, 552
  Austria 29
  Jacques-Henri Bernardin de Saint-Pierre 52
  Étienne-François Choiseul 110
  Michel de Crèvecoeur 134
  Diplomatic Revolution of 1756 161
  France 203
  Frederick II 207
  Edward Gibbon 231
  Guadeloupe 248
  Hapsburg Empire 261
  John Hunter 287
  imperialism 295
  Jean de Lamarck 328
  Julien Offray de La Mettrie 330
  Louis XV of France 356
  marquis de Sade 529
  Pietro Verri 611
  George Washington 624
Sèvres 100, 383, 552
Shaftesbury, Anthony Ashley Cooper, third earl of xiv c, 552–553
  aesthetics 7
  Joseph Butler 81
  deism 147
  Dialogues Concerning Natural Religion 157
  Denis Diderot 158
  enthusiasm 182
  David Hume 284
  Francis Hutcheson 289
  intuition and imagination 300
  John Locke 350
  Bernard Mandeville 367
  moral philosophy 402
  perfectibility 448
  sentimental fiction 549
  sublime 577
  virtue 614
  Christoph Martin Wieland 631
Sheridan, Richard Brinsley 238, 514, 553, 589
She Stoops to Conquer, or the Mistakes of Night (Oliver Goldsmith) 553–554
Siècle de Louis XIV (Voltaire) 3, 341, 554, 619
siècle des lumières (Enlightenment) 554
Sieyès, Emmanuel-Joseph, Abbé 211, 228, 249, 399, 554–555
Simon, Richard xiv c, 55, 555–556
skepticism 556
  Jean Le Rond d'Alembert 12
  Jean-Baptiste de Boyer Argens 20
  atheism 26
  Pierre Bayle 44–45
  Aphra Behn 47
  George Berkeley 51
  René Descartes 152–153
  John Dryden 164
  An Enquiry Concerning Human Understanding 182

Epicurean philosophy 183
epistemology 184
Historical and Critical Dictionary 271
David Hume 284
libertine 344
John Locke 351
Nicolas de Malebranche 366
Moses Mendelssohn 386
natural religion 414
psychology 481
pyrrhonism 487–488
rationalism 496
Thomas Reid 500
religion 503
A Treatise of Human Nature 598
slavery xvii c, 556–557
  colonialism 120, 122
  Declaration of Independence 142
  Olaudah Equiano 187, 188
  Benjamin Franklin 206
  Freemasons 211
  Henri Gregoire 245
  Guadeloupe 248
  Haitian Revolution 252–254
  Alexander Hamilton 258
  Histoire des deux Indes 271
  Industrial Revolution 298
  John Jay 307
  Thomas Jefferson 308
  Hannah More 403
  prostitution 477
  Quakers 489
  race 491
  radical Enlightenment 494
  Guillaume-Thomas-François de Raynal 497
  rights 512
  Benjamin Rush 528
  Ignatius Sancho 533
  serfdom 551
  social institutions 561
  South Sea Company 564
  Toussaint Louverture 596
  travel literature 598
  Josiah Wedgwood 628
  William Wilberforce 632
Smith, Adam ix, xvi c, 557–558, 558
  American Revolution 14
  Joseph Black 57
  capitalism 91
  civil society 111
  class and rank 115
  cosmopolitanism 130
  Edinburgh 170
  Adam Ferguson 195
  freedom 209
  free trade 212
  Christian Garve 223
  happiness 261
  David Hume 286
  James Hutton 289
  Illuminati 294
  Industrial Revolution 298
  Gabriel Bonnot de Mably 361
  James Macpherson 362
  Thomas Robert Malthus 363
  Bernard Mandeville 367
  mercantilism 387
  moral philosophy 402
  New Lanark 423
  optimism 438
  Physiocrats 454
  political theory 462
  Thomas Reid 500
  rights 512
  William Robertson 514
  Scotland 544
  self-interest 546
  The Spirit of Laws 570
  sympathy 582
  Wealth of Nations 627–628
Smollett, Tobias George 527, 558–559

Social Contract (Jean-Jacques Rousseau) 156, 163, 172–173, 186, 209, 216, 317, 476, 512, 525, 559–560, 605
social institutions of the Enlightenment 229–230, 266, 460–461, 560, 560–561, 570–571. *See also* coffeehouses; salons
social science 124–125
Sonnenfels, Josef von 3, 29, 87, 210, 233, 293, 371, 476, 562
Sorrows of Young Werther, The (Johann Wolfgang von Goethe) 235, 302, 426, 431, 562–563, 576
Soufflot, Jacques-Germain xv c, 230, 234, 400, 421, 563
South Sea Bubble 93, 337, 394, 563–564, 564
South Sea Company 93, 563, 564
Spain 564–565
  American Revolution 13
  anticlericalism 20
  Austrian Netherlands 29
  baroque style 40
  Lord Byron 81
  Charles III of Spain 101–102
  Clement XIV 118
  colonialism 120
  Sophie Cottin 131
  East India Company 169
  enlightened absolutism 3
  France 201
  Gobelins tapestry 234
  Jacques de Gournay 241
  Francisco José de Goya y Lucientes 241
  Haitian Revolution 254
  Huguenots 281
  Wilhelm von Humboldt 283
  imperialism 294
  Jesuits 309
  justice and the law 315
  Madrid 363
  Maria Theresa of Austria 371
  Milan 392
  Portugal 468
  Protestantism 478
  publishing 485
  Roman Catholicism 519
  secret societies 545
  Seven Years' War 552
  slavery 557
  Bernardo Tanucci 584
  William Temple 588
  theater 588
  toleration 594
  Toussaint Louverture 596, 597
  voyages of discovery 620, 622
  William III and Mary II 633
Spallanzani, Lazzaro 57, 225, 293, 382, 420, 469, 565–566
Spectator, The (Joseph Addison and Richard Steele) 566–567
  Joseph Addison 6
  Johann Jakob Bodmer 62
  Johann Jakob Breitinger 72
  Benjamin Franklin 205
  Alexander Hamilton 258
  Eliza Haywood 266
  magic 364
  Pierre de Marivaux 373
  Antoine-François Prévost 469
  publishing 486
  sentimental fiction 549
  Philip Dormer Stanhope 106
  Richard Steele 574
  Jonathan Swift 581
Spener, Philipp Jakob 456, 567, 642
spinning jenny 23, 198, 262, 298, 322, 567, 567, 626
spinning mule 134–135, 198, 322, 567, 567–568, 626

Spinoza, Benedict de xiv c, 568–569
Jacques-Bénigne Bossuet 67
deism 147
René Descartes 152
epistemology 184
freedom 209
Claude-Adrien Helvétius 267
Johann Gottfried Herder 267
Historical and Critical Dictionary 271
Friedrich Heinrich Jacobi 303
Gottfried Wilhelm Leibniz 338
Gotthold Ephraim Lessing 342–343
Georg Christoph Lichtenberg 345
Moses Mendelssohn 385, 386
Montesquieu 399
moral philosophy 401, 402
Nathan the Wise 413
natural law 413
paganism 442
perfectibility 448
psychology 481–482
pyrrhonism 487
radical Enlightenment 494
reason 498
Richard Simon 555
A Treatise of Human Nature 598
Voltaire 620
Spirit of Laws, The (Montesquieu) 569–570
Nicolas-Antoine Boulanger 70
Antoine Destutt de Tracy 156
Jean-Baptiste Du Bos 165
enlightened despotism 155
Adam Ferguson 196
French Revolution 216
Glorious Revolution 232
Louis-Sébastien Mercier 388
Montesquieu 397
Persian Letters 449
political theory 463
pornography 468
separation of powers 550
Mme de Staël 571
Staël, Anne-Louise-Germaine Necker, Madame de 166, 226, 418, 431, 532, 570–571, 614, 638
Stahl, Georg Ernst 571–572
alchemy 10
animism 18, 19
Paul-Joseph Barthez 41
Torbern Olof Bergman 50
Marie-François-Xavier Bichat 55
Hermann Boerhaave 63
Théophile de Bordeu 66
Chemical Revolution 104
René Descartes 154
Albrecht von Haller 255
Friedrich Hoffmann 275
medicine 380
phlogiston theory 452
vitalism 615
Robert Whytt 630
Stamitz, Carl 572
statistics 335, 473, 572–573, 573
steam engine 71, 138, 298, 422, 574, 626
Steele, Richard xiv c, 574
Joseph Addison 6
Johann Jakob Bodmer 62
Johann Jakob Breitinger 72
William Congreve 126
Benjamin Franklin 205
Grub Street 248
Alexander Hamilton 258
literature 348
Pierre de Marivaux 373
Alexander Pope 467
Antoine-François Prévost 470

publishing 486
sensibility 548
sentimental fiction 549
slavery 557
The Spectator 566
Jonathan Swift 581
Robert Walpole 624
Mary Wortley 397
Sterne, Laurence xvi c, 109, 257, 508, 527, 574–575, 600
Stowe 74, 323, 331, 575
Struensee, Johann Friedrich, graf von 110, 151, 395, 575
Stubbs, George 575–576, 577
Sturm und Drang (literary movement) 576
Aufklärung 28
Carl Philipp Emanuel Bach 32
Ludwig van Beethoven 47
empfindsamer Stil 174
freedom 209
genius 226
Franz Joseph Haydn 265
Johann Gottfried Herder 269
Georg Christoph Lichtenberg 345
literature 348
Wolfgang Amadeus Mozart 406
Jean-Jacques Rousseau 526
Johann Friedrich Schiller 535
style galant 576
Carl Philipp Emanuel Bach 32
Johann Christian Bach 33
baroque style 40
François Couperin 133
empfindsamer Stil 174
Franz Joseph Haydn 265
Nicolas Lancret 330
Mannheim school 368
music 408, 409
piano 455
rococo 517
sensibility 548
Georg Philipp Telemann 587
sublime ix, 7, 78, 183, 193, 239, 241, 256, 331, 348, 416, 455–456, 576–577
subtle fluids 85, 206, 577
superstition 158, 232, 274, 278, 476, 559, 577, 620
Süssmilch, Johann Peter 150, 332, 577–578
Sweden 578
China 108
colonialism 120
Denmark 150
René Descartes 152
Freemasons 210
Marie-Thérèse Rodet Geoffrin 230
Gustav III of Sweden 250–251
Antoine-Laurent Lavoisier 336
Carolus Linnaeus 346
Lutheranism 358, 359
Jean-François Marmontel 374
Peter I 450
phlogiston theory 452
Protestantism 479
Samuel Pufendorf 487
race 491
Republic of Letters 505
August Ludwig von Schlözer 537
William Temple 588
Swedenborg, Emanuel xv c, 59, 66, 210, 433, 503, 531, 541, 579
Swieten, Gerard van 579–580
Austria 29
Carl Philipp Emanuel Bach 33
Johann Sebastian Bach 35
Hermann Boerhaave 63
Pierre-Jean-Georges Cabanis 82
The Creation 134

Freemasons 211
Jan Ingen-Housz 298
Wenzel Anton von Kaunitz 322
Maria Theresa of Austria 371
medicine 383
Wolfgang Amadeus Mozart 406
progress 476
Gottfried Bernhard Swieten 580
universities 607
Swieten, Gottfried Bernhard, baron van 265, 580
Swift, Jonathan xv c, 580–581, 581
George Berkeley 51
Henry St. John Bolingbroke 64
William Congreve 126
John Dryden 164
Gulliver's Travels 250
Eliza Haywood 265
literature 348
novel 430
Alexander Pope 467
Philip Dormer Stanhope 106
Richard Steele 574
Stowe 575
William Temple 588
travel literature 597
Voltaire 618
Mary Wortley 397
Switzerland x, 582
Anglicans 16
Cosmas Damian Asam 24
Jakob I and Johann I Bernoulli 54
Johann Jakob Bodmer 62
James Boswell 68
Nicolas-Antoine Boulanger 70
Antoine Calmet 84
Lazare Carnot 94
Giovanni Giacomo Casanova 96
cosmopolitanism 130
democracy 149
education 170
Leonhard Euler 190
France 201
Geneva 225
Germany 230
Edward Gibbon 231
grand tour 241
Holy Roman Empire 278
Wilhelm von Humboldt 283
Friedrich Gottlieb Klopstock 325
Johann Kaspar Lavater 335
Jean-Paul Marat 368
Franz Anton Mesmer 389
Milan 392
Johannes von Müller 406
Suzanne Necker 419
Johann Heinrich Pestalozzi 449
Protestantism 479
publishing 485
Guillaume-Thomas-François de Raynal 497
Republic of Letters 505
rococo 517
Jean-Jacques Rousseau 524
social institutions 561
University of Göttingen 240
Emmerich de Vattel 608
Christoph Martin Wieland 631
Wilhelm Tell 632
Mary Wortley 397
Arthur Young 640
sympathy 582
Paul-Joseph Barthez 41
William Blake 60
civil society 111
Denis Diderot 160
Discourse on the Origins of Inequality 162

happiness 261
David Hartley 263
history 272
Friedrich Hoffmann 275
David Hume 285
Illuministi 294
moral philosophy 402
nature 418
rights 512
Adam Smith 557
Laurence Sterne 574
vitalism 615
symphony orchestra 112, 582–583, 614
synergy 583

T

Tahiti 476, 584, 621
Tanucci, Bernardo, marchese 101, 219, 228, 301, 324, 395, 541, 584–585
Taylor, Brook 210, 585
technology and instrumentation 585, 585–586
Sir Richard Arkwright 23
automata 29–30
barometer 38
Charles-Augustin de Coulomb 133
Samuel Crompton 134–135
Daniel Gabriel Fahrenheit 192
flying shuttle 198
John Hadley 252
John Harrison 262
William Herschel 270
Benjamin Huntsman 288
Antoni van Leeuwenhoek 337
longitude 353
Lunar Society of Birmingham 358
microscope 391
orrery 440
David Rittenhouse 514
science 539
telescope 587
Telemann, Georg Philipp 32, 40, 130, 230, 437, 576, 586–587
telescope 587
astronomy 26
Copernican Revolution 128
Galileo Galilei 220
John Hadley 252
William Herschel 270
Johannes Kepler 323
microscope 391
On the Revolutions of the Heavenly Spheres 435
Scientific Revolution 543
skepticism 556
technology and instrumentation 586
Temple, William 587–588
theater 588, 588–589
Pierre de Beaumarchais 45
François Boucher 69
Catherine II 98
William Congreve 126
Hannah Cowley 133
Charles-Simon Favart 193
Henry Fielding 196
David Garrick 223
Carlo Goldoni 238
Eliza Haywood 266
homosexuality 279
Elizabeth Inchbald 296
Louis XIV of France 355
Louis XV of France 356
Mannheim school 368
Louis-Sébastien Mercier 387
millenarianism 393
Paris 445
political theory 463
marquise de Pompadour 465
The Rivals 514
She Stoops to Conquer 553–554

social institutions 561
Josef von Sonnenfels 562
Catharine Trotter 600
Jean-Antoine Watteau 627
theology 589
Carl Friedrich Bahrdt 36–37
Calvinism 85
Samuel Clarke 113, 114
Clement XIII 117
Clement XIV 118
Copernican Revolution 127
enthusiasm 182
generation 225
Edward Gibbon 231
Johann Georg Hamann 257
heliocentric 266
hermeticism 269
history 271
Huguenots 281
Jansenism 305
Kingdom of the Two Sicilies 323
Gottfried Wilhelm Leibniz 339
Cotton Mather 377
Marin Mersenne 388
Johann Lorenz von Mosheim 405
natural philosophy 414
John Turberville Needham 419
Isaac Newton 424
Jean-Antoine Nollet 428
Johann Heinrich Pestalozzi 449
physico-theology 453
Pietism 456
Noël-Antoine Pluche 459
François-André-Adrien Pluquet 459
Joseph Priestley 471–472
Protestantism 478
psychology 482
religion 503
Roman Catholicism 519
science 538
science of man 540
Johann Salomo Semler 546–547
Emmanuel-Joseph Sieyès 554
Lazzaro Spallanzani 566
Emanuel Swedenborg 579
John Tillotson 592
travel literature 598
University of Göttingen 240
Christoph Martin Wieland 631
Johann Joachim Winckelmann 634
Thomasius, Christian 170, 204, 255, 268, 359, 457, 511, 589–590
threshing machine 590, 591
Tiepolo, Giovanni Battista xv c, 102, 241, 249, 293, 353, 363, 591, 591–592, 611
Tillotson, John 393, 592
Tindal, Matthew 20, 147, 592
Tissot, Samuel-Auguste-André-David 592–593
Toland, John 147, 210, 228, 277, 593
toleration xvi c, 593–595
The Age of Reason 10
American Revolution 14
Amsterdam 14
ancien régime 16
Anglicans 17
association movement 24
Aufklärung 27
Pierre Bayle 45
Belgium 48
Berlin 51
Edmund Burke 78
Calvinism 87
Camisards 88
Candide 89

capital punishment 93
Catherine II 97
Ralph Cudworth 135
Daniel Defoe 145
deism 147
Dictionnaire philosophique 158
England 177
enlightened absolutism 3
François Fénelon 195
Johann Georg Adam Forster
199
France 201
Frederick II 207
freedom 209
Freemasons 209
Germany 230
Gustav III of Sweden 251
*The History of the Decline and
Fall of the Roman Empire* 144
homosexuality 279
Huguenots 282
Thomas Jefferson 308
Jews and Judaism 311
Joseph II of Austria 313
Josephinism 314
Karl Wilhelm Ferdinand 321
Gotthold Ephraim Lessing 342
John Locke 350
Jean-François Marmontel 374
Moses Mendelssohn 385
Montesquieu 398
Nathan the Wise 412, 413
natural religion 415
Suzanne Necker 419
paganism 441
Philadelphia 451
political theory 463
Protestantism 478
Quakers 489
religion 502
The Rights of Man 513
Roman Catholicism 520
separation of church and state
549
Benedict de Spinoza 569
Johann Friedrich Struensee
575
Christian Thomasius 590
John Toland 593
Anne-Robert-Jacques Turgot
602
United Provinces of
Netherlands 604
United States of America 606
University of Göttingen 240
Francis Adrian Van der Kemp
608
Voltaire 620
Waldensians 623
William III and Mary II 634
Tom Jones (Henry Fielding) **595**
Tooke, John Horne 353, **596**
Toussaint Louverture, François-
Dominique xvii *c*, 253, 254,
596–597
transit of Venus 26, 50, 126,
149, 256, 328, 514, 597, *597*,
621
travel literature 19, 73, 179, 198,
199, 348, 448–449, 597–598,
617
Treatise of Human Nature, A
(David Hume) 156, 182, 185,
284, 500, 540, **598–599**
Trembley, Abraham 57, 225,
226, 469, 599, 616
Trimmer, Sarah **599–600**
Tristram Shandy (Laurence
Sterne) 574–575, **600**
Trotter, Catharine 458, **600–601**
Tull, Jethro **601**
Turgot, Anne-Robert-Jacques,
baron de l'Aulne xvi *c*,
601–602
John Adams 5
Charles de Brosses 73

Pierre-Jean-Georges Cabanis
82
Chemical Revolution 103
class and rank 114
Marie Caritat Condorcet 124
Mme du Deffand 144
Pierre-Samuel Dupont de
Nemours 166
education 170
encyclopedists 177
enlightened despotism 155
Ferdinando Galiani 219
Marie-Thérèse Rodet Geoffrin
230
Jacques de Gournay 241
Anne Helvétius 266
Claude-Adrien Helvétius 267
Julie-Jeanne-Eléonore de
Lespinasse 342
Louis XVI of France 357
Chrétien-Guillaume de
Malesherbes 366
Louis-Sébastien Mercier 388
Jacques Necker 418
Physiocrats 453
progress 476
François Quesnay 490
Maximilien Robespierre 515
serfdom 551
toleration 594
Wealth of Nations 627
Turin **602**
Bernardo Bellotto 48
Daniel Bernoulli 53
Charles Burney 79
Pietro Giannone 231
Gobelins tapestry 234
Illuministi 293
Wenzel Anton von Kaunitz
322
Joseph-Louis Lagrange 327
opera 436
Piedmont 456
Jean-Jacques Rousseau 524
scientific academies 541
Two Treatises of Government
(John Locke) 18, 178, 186,
232, 349, 462, **602–603**, 605

U

United Provinces of Netherlands
604–605
John Adams 5
American Revolution 13
Amsterdam **14–15**
Austrian Netherlands 29
Francis Bacon 36
baroque style 40
Pierre Bayle 44
Jakob I and Johann I Bernoulli
54
Charles Burney 79
Calvinism 85
Ranieri de'Calzabigi 87
Camisards 88
Pieter Camper 89
Friedrich Rudolf Ludwig
Canitz 90
capitalism 93
China 108
colonialism 120
René Descartes 152
Daniel Gabriel Fahrenheit 192
France 202
Galileo Galilei 220
grand tour 241
Albrecht von Haller 256
*Historical and Critical
Dictionary* 271
Paul-Henri Thiry d'Holbach
276
Huguenots 282
imperialism 295
Jews and Judaism 310
justice and the law 315
Karl-August 321

Wenzel Anton von Kaunitz
322
Julien Offray de La Mettrie
330
Carolus Linnaeus 345
literature 348
Louis XIV of France 355
Bernard Mandeville 367–368
materialism 375
mercantilism 387
Jean-Antoine Nollet 428
political theory 461
John Pringle 473
publishing 485
radical Enlightenment 494
religion 502
Republic of Letters 505
separation of church and state
550
Emmanuel-Joseph Sieyès 555
slavery 557
South Sea Company 564
Spain 565
Benedict de Spinoza 568
Johann Peter Süssmilch 578
Gerard van Swieten 579
Gottfried Bernhard Swieten
580
William Temple 588
John Toland 593
toleration 594
United States of America 606
universities 607
Francis Adrian Van der Kemp
608
voyages of discovery 620
William III and Mary II 633
women and the Enlightenment
637
United States Bill of Rights xvii
c, 308, 363, 414, 416, 451, 476,
510, *510*, 595, **605**
United States Constitution
605–606
American Revolution 14
Declaration of Independence
143
Benjamin Franklin 206
Alexander Hamilton 258
John Jay 307
James Madison 362–363
Philadelphia 451
separation of church and state
550
separation of powers 551
The Spirit of Laws 570
toleration 595
United States Bill of Rights
605
George Washington 625
United States of America ix, x,
606. *See also specific headings,
e.g.:* Philadelphia
John Adams 4–6
The Age of Reason 10
American Philosophical
Society 13
American Revolution **13–14**
colonialism 121
Michel de Crèvecoeur 134
Declaration of Independence
141, **141–143**
Antoine Destutt de Tracy 156
Pierre-Samuel Dupont de
Nemours 166
Benjamin Franklin **204–206**
Guadeloupe 248
Haitian Revolution 252, 253
Alexander Hamilton 258–259
imperialism 295
John Jay 307
justice and the law 316
Gabriel Bonnot de Mably 361
James Madison 362–363
Montesquieu 399

natural rights 416
Thomas Paine 442, 443
Pietism 457
Joseph Priestley 471
race 493
The Rights of Man 513
Benjamin Rush 528
Scotland 544
Emmanuel-Joseph Sieyès 555
slavery 557
toleration 594
United States Bill of Rights 605
United States Constitution
605–606
University of Göttingen 240
Constantin Volney 617
George Washington **624–626**
John Wesley 630
universities **606–607**. *See also
specific universities*
utility **607–608**
Jeremy Bentham 50
capital punishment 94
Declaration of the Rights of
Man 143
Epicurean philosophy 183
*Essays on Crimes and
Punishments* 189
French Academy of Sciences
212
Wilhelm von Humboldt 283
David Hume 285
materialism 375
moral philosophy 402
political theory 462
pyrrhonism 488
rights 511
sensibility 548
sympathy 582

V

Van der Kemp, Francis Adrian
609
Vattel, Emmerich de 14, 511,
609–610
Vaucanson, Jacques de **610**
Venice **610–611**
Francesco Algarotti 12
baroque style 39
Bernardo Bellotto 48
Daniel Bernoulli 53
Charles de Brosses 73
Charles Burney 79
Canaletto 89
Candide 89
Antonio Canova 90
Giovanni Giacomo Casanova
96
ceramic arts 100
Charles III of Spain 101
Clement XIII 117
Jean-Honoré Fragonard 200
Henry Fuseli 217
Pietro Giannone 231
Carlo Goldoni 238
grand tour 241
Francesco Guardi 249, 250
Illuministi 293
Italy 300
Jews and Judaism 310
John Law 337
Pietro Longhi 353
music 410
opera 436
Palladian style 444
publishing 484
Joshua Reynolds 508
Giuseppe Domenico Scarlatti
533
scientific academies 541
Giovanni Battista Tiepolo 591
United Provinces of
Netherlands 604
Antonio Vivaldi 616
Verri, Alessandro, count 46,
188, 301, 392, 611, **611**

Verri, Pietro, count 46, 188,
301, 392, 611, **611**
Vicar of Wakefield, The (Oliver
Goldsmith) **611–612**
Vico, Giovan Battista
(Giambattista) xv *c*, 19, 70,
111, 267, 272, 293, 300, 475,
612, **612–613**
Vienna **613**
Austria 28
Ludwig van Beethoven 46
Bernardo Bellotto 48
Jean-Pierre-François Blanchard
60
Hermann Boerhaave 63
Charles Burney 79
Ranieri de'Calzabigi 87
Friedrich Rudolf Ludwig
Canitz 90
Antonio Canova 90
Giovanni Giacomo Casanova
96
ceramic arts 100
Étienne-François Choiseul 110
Muzio Clementi 118
Clement XII 117
Così fan Tutte 130
Eugène of Savoy 189
Johann Bernhard Fischer von
Erlach 197
Jean-Honoré Fragonard 200
Frankfurt 204
Franz Joseph Gall 221
Germany 230
Pietro Giannone 231
Christoph Willibald Gluck
233
Hapsburg Empire 261
Franz Joseph Haydn 264
Johann Lukas von Hildebrandt
270
Wilhelm von Humboldt 283
Bavarian Illuminati 293
Jan Ingen-Housz 298
Jews and Judaism 311
Wenzel Anton von Kaunitz
322
Gottfried Wilhelm Leibniz 338
The Magic Flute 364
medicine 382
Franz Anton Mesmer 389
Wolfgang Amadeus Mozart
406
museums 408
music 410
neoclassicism 421
Balthasar Neumann 422
Le Nozze di Figaro 432
Orfeo ed Eurydice 438
Sebastiano Pombal 464
Jakob Prandtauer 469
public health 482
La Serva Padrona 551
Josef von Sonnenfels 562
Gerard van Swieten 580
Gottfried Bernhard Swieten
580
universities 607
Vigée Lebrun, Élisabeth-Louise
613–614
*Vindication of the Rights of
Woman, A* (Mary
Wollstonecraft) 494, **614**, 636,
637
viola 46, 409, 454, **614**
virtue 111, 188, 460, 511, 599,
607, **614–615**
vitalism x, **615–616**
animism 19
atheism 26
Paul-Joseph Barthez 41
Marie-François-Xavier Bichat
55
biology 57
Johann Friedrich Blumenbach
62

Charles Bonnet 65
Théophile de Bordeu 66
Ralph Cudworth 135
René Descartes 154
Luigi Galvani 223
Johann Wolfgang von Goethe 237
Albrecht von Haller 255
Friedrich Hoffmann 275
John Hunter 288
William Hunter 288
iatrochemistry 291
iatromechanics 291
intuition and imagination 300
Julien Offray de La Mettrie 330
Gottfried Wilhelm Leibniz 340
Carolus Linnaeus 345
Jean-Paul Marat 370
materialism 375
mechanical philosophy 380
medicine 380, 382
Alexander Monro 396
Montesquieu 398
nature 416
John Turberville Needham 419
John Pringle 473
psychology 481
romanticism 521
science 539
separation of powers 550
Georg Ernst Stahl 572
sympathy 582
universities 607
Robert Whytt 630
Vivaldi, Antonio 40, 130, 199–200, 293, 410, 583, 611, 616–617
Volney, Constantin-François Chasseboeuf, comte de 617
Volta, Alessandro Giuseppe Antonio Anastasio 223, 293, 617–618
Voltaire x, xv c, xvi c, 618–620, 619
absolutism 3
Jean Le Rond d'Alembert 11
Francesco Algarotti 12
anticlericalism 20
Jean-Baptiste de Boyer Argens 21
Marc-Pierre de Voyer Argenson 21
René-Lous Argenson 22
Aufklärung 27
Francis Bacon 36
Berlin Academy 52
Johann Jakob Bodmer 62
James Boswell 68
Henri de Boulainvilliers 70
Charles de Brosses 73
Jean Calas 83
Candide 89
Catherine II 97
Mme de Châtelet 102
China 108
Étienne-François Choiseul 110
Alexis-Claude Clairaut 112
Clement XIV 118

Marie Condorcet 124
Confessions 125
cosmopolitanism 130
Mme du Deffand 144
deism 148
demography 150
Dictionnaire philosophique 157–158
Denis Diderot 158
Jean-Baptiste Du Bos 165
Charles-Pinot Duclos 166
Encyclopédie 176
encyclopedists 177
England 178
enlightened despotism 155
enthusiasm 183
Louise d'Épinay 184
Leonhard Euler 191
France 201
Frederick II 207
freedom 209
Freemasons 211
French Revolution 216
Élie-Catherine Fréron 216
Ferdinando Galiani 219
Geneva 226
Antonio Genovesi 228
Marie-Thérèse Rodet Geoffrin 230
Edward Gibbon 231
Glorious Revolution 232
Friedrich Melchior Grimm 247
Johann Georg Hamann 257
Claude-Adrien Helvétius 267
Johann Gottfried Herder 268
Historical and Critical Dictionary 271
history 272
homosexuality 279
honor 280
Jean-Antoine Houdon 280
inoculation 299
Karl Wilhelm Ferdinand 321
Joseph de Lalande 328
Maurice-Quentin de La Tour 335
Gottfried Wilhelm Leibniz 340–341
Charlotte Ramsay Lennox 341
libertine 344
Lisbon earthquake 347
literature 348
Jean-Paul Marat 370
Jean-François Marmontel 373
René de Maupeou 378
Pierre-Louis Moreau de Maupertuis 379
Louis-Sébastien Mercier 388
Marin Mersenne 388
Elizabeth Montagu 396
Montesquieu 397
Isaac Newton 424
opera 436
optimism 438
orientalism 439
perfectibility 447
Philadelphia 451
philosopher-king 451
philosophes 452
Physiocrats 454

politeness 460
political theory 462
marquise de Pompadour 465
Principia mathematica 472
progress 476
Republic of Letters 505
revolution 506
Roman Catholicism 520
Jean-Jacques Rousseau 525
comte de Saint-Germain 530
Scientific Revolution 543
secret societies 545
separation of church and state 550
separation of powers 550
Siècle de Louis XIV 554
Adam Smith 557
Tobias George Smollett 558
social institutions 560
Benedict de Spinoza 569
superstition 577
theater 588
toleration 594
Abraham Trembley 599
Two Treatises of Government 603
United Provinces of Netherlands 604
Giovan Battista Vico 613
Christoph Martin Wieland 631
Mary Wortley 397
voyages of discovery 69, 91, 120, 131, 427, 491, 511, 565, 620–622, 621. See also Cook, James

W

Waldensians 88, 282, 355, 502, 520, 623
Walpole, Horace, fourth earl of Oxford 623–624
Catherine II 98
Mme du Deffand 145
Félicité de Genlis 228
Marie-Thérèse Rodet Geoffrin 230
Gothic revival 239
Gothic romance 239
Thomas Gray 243
Stephen Hales 255
William Hogarth 275
landscapes 331
Hannah More 403
picturesque 455–456
Republic of Letters 505
Joshua Reynolds 508
theater 589
women and the Enlightenment 637
Walpole, Robert 47, 196, 210, 250, 266, 564, 575, 581, 623, 624
War of the Austrian Succession xv c, 4, 21, 207, 298, 322, 356, 371, 422, 468, 552, 624
Washington, George 148, 211, 258, 280, 307, 308, 443, 514, 528, 545, 557, 624–626
water frame 23, 138, 198, 322, 422, 567, 626

Watt, James 71, 298, 358, 422, 471, 544, 574, 626, xvi c
Watteau, Jean-Antoine 99, 109, 201, 329, 330, 353, 384, 518, 626, 626–627
Wealth of Nations (Adam Smith) ix, 212, 328, 438, 454, 546, 557, 558, 627–628
Wedgwood, Josiah 100, 108, 139, 189, 358, 471, 628, 628, 639
Werner, Abraham Gottlob 289, 628–629
Wesley, Charles 390, 457, 629
Wesley, John 18, 172, 244, 364, 390, 629, 629–630
Whytt, Robert 57, 136, 170, 382, 616, 630
Wieland, Christoph Martin 126, 236, 257, 320, 364, 535, 631
Wilberforce, William 316, 403, 477, 493, 631–632
Wilhelm Tell (Friedrich Schiller) 348, 536, 632
Wilkes, John 70, 275, 276, 352, 596, 632–633
William III and Mary II xiv c, 17, 633–634
Aphra Behn 48
capitalism 93
Daniel Defoe 145
John Dryden 165
England 178
Glorious Revolution 232
David Hume 286
John Locke 350
political theory 462
revolution 506
separation of powers 550
Waldensians 623
Winckelmann, Johann Joachim xv c, 634
aesthetics 9
baroque style 38
Jacques-Louis David 141
Henry Fuseli 217
grand tour 241
Angelica Kauffman 321
Laokoon 333
Gotthold Ephraim Lessing 342
Anton Raphael Mengs 387
neoclassicism 421
Pompeii 466
witchcraft. See magic
Wolf, Friedrich August 546, 634–635
Wolff, Christian 635, 635–636
aesthetics 8
Aufklärung 27
Wilhelm Friedemann Bach 35
Alexander Gottlieb Baumgarten 43
Berlin Academy 52
Johann Jakob Bodmer 62
Candide 89
epigenesis 184
Leonhard Euler 191
August Hermann Francke 204
Germany 230
Johann Gottfried Herder 268
Immanuel Kant 317

Karl Wilhelm Ferdinand 321
Gottfried Wilhelm Leibniz 340
Lutheranism 359
Pierre-Louis Moreau de Maupertuis 379
Moses Mendelssohn 384
Johann David Michaelis 390
natural law 413, 414
psychology 481
Hermann Samuel Reimarus 501
Emanuel Swedenborg 579
Christian Thomasius 589
University of Halle 255
Emmerich de Vattel 610
Christoph Martin Wieland 631
Wollstonecraft, Mary xvii c, 636, 636
Joel Barlow 38
William Blake 60
Bluestocking 60
George Gordon Byron 81
Hannah Cowley 133
Maria Edgeworth 169
William Godwin 234
grand tour 241
prostitution 477
radical Enlightenment 494
rights 512, 513
John Horne Tooke 596
A Vindication of the Rights of Woman 614
women and the Enlightenment 637
women and the Enlightenment 636–638. See also specific women, e.g.: Aulnoy, Marie-Catherine d'
Bluestocking See Bluestocking
equality 186
grand tour 241
homosexuality 279
honor 280
Jews and Judaism 312
midwifery 89, 132, 391
John Millar 392–393
novel 429, 430
politeness 460
prostitution 476–477
radical Enlightenment 494
Samuel Richardson 509
rights 512–513
sensibility 548
social institutions 560
A Vindication of the Rights of Woman 614
Woolston, Thomas 158, 277, 638
Wren, Sir Christopher 352, 638
Wright, Joseph 638–639

Y

Young, Arthur 60, 597, 640

Z

Zimmermann, Johann Georg 641
Zinzendorf, Nicolaus Ludwig, count von xv c, 302, 403, 457, 642